Why Do You Need This New Edition?

If you're wondering why you should buy this new edition of *The New American Democracy*, here are 8 good reasons!

1. **New and expanded election-related coverage** includes a discussion of the 2010 congressional elections and gender differences in voter turnout (Chapter 6), a table on how various politically significant demographic groups have voted in recent presidential elections (Chapter 8), the political implications of the entertainment media and the change in the dominance of specific media (Chapter 9), the role of the invisible primary, the state of the economy as a performance issue, and what difference presidential campaigns make (Chapter 10).

2. **Learning Objectives** now appear at the beginning of each chapter; each is repeated as appropriate within the chapter and as a guide in the end-of-chapter summary. The Objectives are associated with important topics and subtopics on American politics.

3. **New Chapter Opener Vignettes** discuss the Tea Party movement (Chapter 7); the 2008 presidential contest (Chapter 8); media coverage of the 2008 primaries (Chapter 9); congressional elections and the fate of the Obama agenda (Chapter 11); the presidency as crisis management (Chapter 13); Sonia Sotomayor, the Supreme Court, and the meaning of experience (Chapter 15); healthcare reform (Chapter 18); and the impact of taxes on the American public and the economy (Chapter 19).

4. Four new **Election Voices** essays explore whether the government should enact a nationwide civic education program (Chapter 5), partisan polarization (Chapter 8), whether serving your constituency can go too far (Chapter 11), and entitlement reform (Chapter 18).

5. The book's already superior **graphs and charts** are now enhanced in four colors for easier understanding and visual attractiveness. All continue to have instructive captions and critical thinking questions.

6. **New and updated topics** include the impact of the stimulus bill on state and local governments (Chapter 3), immigration (Chapter 4); public opinion on terrorism (Chapter 5); new forms of voter mobilization (Chapter 6), the new and ever-changing media environment (Chapter 9), the modern caucus and primary system (Chapter 10), health care and entitlement policy (Chapter 18), governance in a time of fiscal constraint (Chapter 19) and counterinsurgency (Chapter 20).

7. **International Comparison** boxes compare elements of American Government with similar elements in other countries, putting the U.S. system in global context and giving students a better understanding of its strengths and limitations.

8. **MyPoliSciLab,** Pearson's interactive web site that contains an array of multimedia activities—videos, simulations, exercises, and online newsfeeds—has been completely integrated with this edition to make learning more effective.

PEARSON

ELECTORAL COLLEGE VOTES IN THE 2008 ELECTION

THE UNITED STATES
A political map showing the number of electoral votes per state

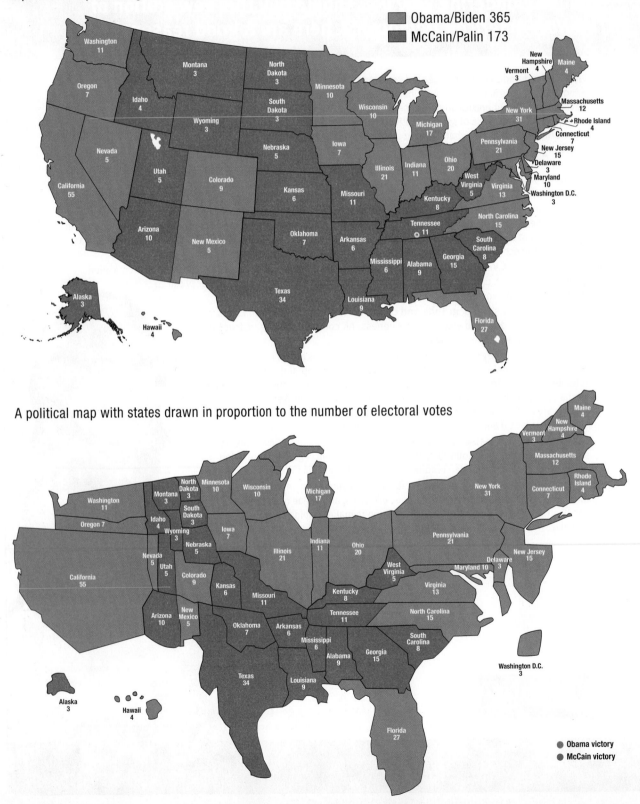

Obama/Biden 365
McCain/Palin 173

A political map with states drawn in proportion to the number of electoral votes

Obama victory
McCain victory

SEVENTH EDITION

The New American Democracy

Morris P. Fiorina
Stanford University

Paul E. Peterson
Harvard University

Bertram Johnson
Middlebury College

William G. Mayer
Northeastern University

Longman

Boston   Columbus   Indianapolis   New York   San Francisco   Upper Saddle River
Amsterdam   Cape Town   Dubai   London   Madrid   Milan   Munich   Paris   Montreal   Toronto
Delhi   Mexico City   Saõ Paulo   Sydney   Hong Kong   Seoul   Singapore   Taipei   Tokyo

Executive Editor: Reid Hester
Director of Development: Meg Botteon
Development Editor: Barbara Conover
Editorial Assistant: Elizabeth Alimena
Senior Marketing Manager: Lindsey Prudhomme
Supplements Editor: Donna Garnier
Senior Media Producer: Regina Vertiz
Production Manager: Stacey Kulig
Project Coordination, Text Design, and Electronic Page Makeup: Nesbitt Graphics, Inc.
Senior Cover Design Manager: Nancy Danahy
Cover Image: Nancy Danahy
Photo Researcher: Linda Sykes
Senior Manufacturing Buyer: Roy Pickering
Printer and Binder: R.R. Donnelley and Sons
Cover Printer: Lehigh-Phoenix Color Corporation

For permission to use copyrighted material, grateful acknowledgment is made to the copyright holders on pp. 679, which are hereby made part of this copyright page.

Library of Congress Cataloging-in-Publication Data

The new American democracy / Morris P. Fiorina ... [et al.]. -- 7th ed.
    p. cm.
  ISBN 0-205-78016-4
1. Democracy--United States--Textbooks. 2. United States--Politics
and government--Textbooks. I. Fiorina, Morris P.
  JK1726.N45 2011
  320.473--dc22

                        2010045576

Copyright © 2011, 2009, 2007 by Pearson Education, Inc.

1 2 3 4 5 6 7 8 9 10—DOW—13 12 11 10

The New American Democracy, Seventh Edition
ISBN-13: 978-0-205-78016-7
ISBN-10: 0-205-78016-4
The New American Democracy, Alternate Edition
ISBN-13: 978-0-205-79134-7
ISBN-10: 0-205-79134-4

Longman
is an imprint of

Visit us at www.pearsonhighered.com

Brief Contents

Detailed Contents

Chapter 15   The Courts   429

PART 5   CIVIL LIBERTIES AND CIVIL RIGHTS

Chapter 16   Civil Liberties   461

Appendices

Preface

Political scientists see U.S. politics differently today than they did just a generation or two ago. Journals used to overflow with articles describing the political process as a series of bargains between organized interests brokered by politicians who occupied positions well defined by formal rules. Today, the American political scene looks dramatically different—more fragmented and more plebiscitary than the old one, as Robert Dahl has argued. For better or worse, it has become something closer to a popular democracy.

In the pages that follow, we describe the forces that have brought about these changes. We examine their impact on contemporary politics, institutions, and policies. Chapter 1 establishes the context for this by exploring such issues as:

- The Permanent Campaign
- Separation of Elections
- Spread of Primaries
- Rise of Mass Communications
- Profusion of Interest Groups
- Proliferation of Polls

It is this very context, in fact, that we long ago established in our own courses and looked for in the available textbooks. We found, however, that the books published for the American Government course, while worthy in some respects, were unsatisfactory in other respects critical to our view of contemporary American politics. First, traditional texts gave less emphasis than we wished to topics that are essential parts of contemporary American politics—elections, most obviously, but also closely related topics such as public opinion, political participation, and the media. Second, many traditional texts implicitly assigned the role of prime mover to the courts, whereas we view electoral context as an important influence on judicial activity and judicial outcomes. Third, traditional textbooks typically separated the study of elections from other major headings: constitutional fundamentals, bureaucratic politics, the courts, and the formation of public policies. So, we wrote a book reflecting these views.

New to This Edition

This seventh edition includes substantive rewrites, extensively revised features, and the inclusion of the latest information and examples on key topics.

- The results of the 2010 congressional elections and coverage of key political events and issues of the first two years of the Obama administration have been added throughout the text.
- Election Voices essays, now appearing in each chapter, offer in-depth treatment of public policy issues. New essays have been added on whether the government should enact a nationwide civic education program (Chapter 5), on partisan polarization

(Chapter 8), and on whether serving your constituency can go too far (Chapter 11), and on entitlement reform (Chapter 18). Other essays have been heavily updated to reflect major changes taking place in the last two years: for example, the growing politics of immigration (Chapter 4) and energy policy (Chapter 13).

- Numbered Learning Objectives appear at the beginning of each chapter; each is repeated as appropriate within the chapter and as a guide in the end-of-chapter Summary. The Objectives are associated with important topics and subtopics on American politics. For example, Learning Objectives for Chapter 13 on the American presidency include "Understand the influence of the national and partisan constituencies of the president" and "Assess the importance of presidential reputation and popularity and understand arguments about why some presidents have been considered great."

- New chapter opener vignettes discuss the Tea Party movement (Chapter 7); the 2008 presidential contest (Chapter 8); media coverage of the 2008 primaries (Chapter 9); congressional elections and the fate of the Obama agenda (Chapter 11); the presidency as crisis management (Chapter 13); Sonia Sotomayor, the Supreme Court, and the meaning of experience (Chapter 15); healthcare reform (Chapter 18); and the impact of taxes on the American public and the economy (Chapter 19).

- The book's already superior graphs and charts are now enhanced in four colors for easier understanding and visual attractiveness. All continue to have instructive captions and critical thinking questions.

- The elections theme has been bolstered throughout the book. New and expanded coverage includes gender differences in voter turnout (Chapter 6), a table on how various politically significant demographic groups have voted in recent presidential elections (Chapter 8), the political implications of the entertainment media (Chapter 9), the role of the invisible primary (Chapter 10), the state of the economy as a performance issue (Chapter 10), and what difference presidential campaigns make (Chapter 10).

- New and updated topics include the impact of the stimulus bill on state and local governments (Chapter 3), immigration (Chapter 4); public opinion on terrorism (Chapter 5); new forms of voter mobilization (Chapter 6), the new and ever-changing media environment (Chapter 9), the modern caucus and primary system (Chapter 10), health care and entitlement policy (Chapter 18), governance in a time of fiscal constraint (Chapter 19) and counterinsurgency (Chapter 20).

Our Approach

This book gives added emphasis to topics underemphasized in traditional texts and breaks down the artificial and unfortunate separation of topics. Rather than discuss public opinion in one self-contained chapter, political participation in a second, and elections in a third, then move on to a series of institutional and policy chapters, we give public opinion and electioneering their due in individual chapters devoted to those topics, but we continue to trace their effects on other political and institutional processes, culminating in discussions of why American public policies have the shape they do. Thus, the chapters of this text bear the familiar titles, but they are linked by an extended discussion of the pervasiveness of electoral influences in the new American democracy.

Under recent presidents, the line between electioneering and governing all but disappeared, as the techniques of the campaign moved to the very pinnacle of government. Under George W. Bush, political adviser Karl Rove became a symbol of the permanent campaign, dividing his time between offering advice to the president and such tasks as selecting Republican precinct coordinators for the 2004 race and plotting strategy for the 2006 midterm elections. Barack Obama appeared to follow suit, appointing his chief campaign strategist, Robert Axelrod, to a top White House post. Upon assuming control of Congress in 2006, Rahm Emanuel (D-IL) declared, "It's time for the endless campaign to stop and the hard work of governing to begin." But campaigning for 2008 began immediately after the 2006 contests, and electioneering continued as Emanuel assumed the role of White House chief of staff in 2009. Our once controversial view that contemporary American politics is a "permanent campaign" is now commonly held.

On the one hand, the evolution of the permanent campaign is associated with a greater role for previously disadvantaged voices in the population. As the scramble to register new voters in recent campaigns illustrates, those who had been left out in the past can now exercise electoral power. On the other hand, the existence of the permanent campaign enhances the importance of special interests and limits opportunities for reflective consideration of the long-range consequences of policy choices. But there is no reason to rush to a critical judgment. Future generations of scholars can judge whether the new order does more or less to advance the welfare of the American people than the old one.

When we say that elections play a dominant role, we are thinking not only of their direct effects, but also of the indirect ways in which they affect the thinking of interest groups, parties, and public officials—both elected and appointed. It is not so much elections themselves as their anticipation that provides so much of the motive power in contemporary political life in the United States.

Save Time and Improve Results with

The most popular online teaching/learning solution for American government, MyPoliSciLab moves students from studying and applying concepts to participating in politics. Completely redesigned and now organized by the book's chapters and learning objectives, the new MyPoliSciLab is easier to integrate into any course.

✔ STUDY A flexible learning path in every chapter.

Pre-Tests. See the relevance of politics with these diagnostic assessments and get personalized study plans driven by learning objectives.

Pearson eText. Navigate by learning objective, take notes, print key passages, and more. From page numbers to photos, the eText is identical to the print book.

Flashcards. Learn key terms by word, definition, or learning objective.

Post-Tests. Featuring over 50% new questions, the pre-tests produce updated study plans with follow-up reading, video, and multimedia

Chapter Exams. Also featuring over 50% new questions, test mastery of each chapter using the chapter exams.

✔ APPLY Over 150 videos and multimedia activities.

Video. Analyze current events by watching streaming video from the AP and ABC News.

Simulations. Engage the political process by experiencing how political actors make decisions.

Comparative Exercises. Think critically about how American politics compares with the politics of other countries.

Timelines. Get historical context by following issues that have influenced the evolution of American democracy.

Visual Literacy Exercises. Learn how to interpret political data in figures and tables.

MyPoliSciLibrary. Read full-text primary source documents from the nation's founding to the present.

✔ PARTICIPATE   Join the political conversation.

PoliSci News Review. Read analysis of—and comment on—major new stories.

AP Newsfeeds. Follow political news in the United States and around the world.

Weekly Quiz. Master the headlines in this review of current events.

Weekly Poll. Take the poll and see how your politics compare.

Voter Registration. Voting is a right—and a responsibility.

Citizenship Test. See what it takes to become an American citizen.

✔ MANAGE Designed for online or traditional courses.

Grade Tracker. Assign and assess nearly everything in MyPoliSciLab.

Instructor Resources. Download supplements at the Instructor Resource Center.

Sample Syllabus. Get ideas for assigning the book and MyPoliSciLab.

MyClassPrep. Download many of the resources in MyPoliSciLab for lectures.

✓ 📖 👁 ✳ The icons in the book and eText point to resources in MyPoliSciLab.

With proven book-specific and course-specific content, MyPoliSciLab is part of a better teaching/learning system only available from Pearson Longman.

✔ To see demos, read case studies, and learn about training, visit **www.mypoliscilab.com.**

✔ To order this book with MyPoliSciLab at no extra charge, use **ISBN 0-205-07328-X.**

✔ Questions? Contact a local Pearson Longman representative: **www.pearsonhighered.com/replocator.**

🐦 Follow MyPoliSciLab on Twitter.

ELECTIONS THEME

This book offers a variety of special features and learning aids, many related to our elections theme, designed to stimulate critical thinking and help you understand the chapter material.

ELECTION VOICES For the seventh edition, we have further expanded to every chapter this selection of readings that appear in a debate-style format. Based on important current events, each of the twenty Election Voices presents analysis of a thought-provoking issue and then illustrates how that issue plays out in today's election-driven political environment. Every Election Voices includes a brief review of the issue at hand, consideration of opposing viewpoints, references to pertinent websites, and critical thinking questions. Topics include the growingly complex issue of immigration (Chapter 4), the impact of partisan polarization (Chapter 8), and an updated discussion of the politics of the Arab-Israeli conflict (Chapter 20).

ELECTION VOICES!

Can Serving Your Constituency Go Too Far?

Background

Members of the U.S. Congress are elected from 50 states and 435 congressional districts within those states. When senators and representatives talk about "my constituents" they are referring to the people who are eligible to vote for them. Naturally enough, members consider it their duty (not to mention a political imperative) to serve their constituents. But senators and representatives are members of the *United States Congress*, and presumably their duty includes not just serving the particular constituencies that elect them, but also serving the country as a whole. This dual responsibility gives rise to representational tensions.

If the national interest were simply the sum of the interests of individual states and districts, no tensions would arise. But often what is in the general interest harms particular interests. For example, every local industry and agricultural producer would like to be protected against foreign competition. But if Congress adopted a trade policy of universal protective tariffs and import quotas, the result would likely be foreign retaliation against American exports and even trade wars, which would lead to slower economic growth. Indeed, the U.S. Congress has done just that with the predictable negative consequences in the past.[1] Thus, most economists advocate a policy of free trade even though some domestic interests would be harmed.

One way to diminish negative impacts on individual states and localities and lessen political opposition to general legislation is to give *side-payments* to members whose districts or states are hurt by general legislation.[2] These special provisions, sometimes in completely unrelated legislation, help to offset the costs to particular interests or areas of the country. After all, if the country as a whole gains, the winners can give up some of their benefits to lessen the harm to the losers. Indeed, this practice is such a standard part of legislating that few commentators regard it as anything out of the ordinary. In the congressional battle over healthcare reform in 2009–2010, however, some members of Congress may have gone too far.

The Issue

After the House passed a healthcare reform bill in November, Senate Majority Leader, Harry Reid began the difficult process of constructing a 60 vote majority in the Senate—60 votes because that was the number necessary to cut off...

pick off a moderate Republican or two proved futile, and Reid eventually decided the only route to passage was to round up all 60 Democratic senators. But not all were in favor of the bill.[3] Senator Mary Landrieu of Louisiana was one of the holdouts. So Reid offered her $100 million in additional federal spending for Louisiana to help offset the rise in Medicaid costs that the healthcare bill would impose. Landrieu took the deal, claimed that she had actually gotten $300 million for Louisiana, and stated, "I am proud to have asked for it. I am proud to have fought for it."[4] Various pundits, not to mention Republicans, quickly pronounced the deal "The Louisiana Purchase."

A bit later Reid was one vote shy and Ben Nelson of Nebraska was the last Democratic holdout. Reid finally got Nelson's vote with the "Cornhusker Kickback," a special provision that would have the federal government pick up Nebraska's share of the increase in Medicaid expenditures, *forever*. In other words, taxpayers in 49 other states would pay for Nelson's vote. In response, thirteen state attorneys general threatened to sue, arguing that the deal was a violation of the Equal Protection clause of the Constitution, among other things.[5]

What Do Americans Believe?

The Louisiana Purchase and Cornhusker Kickback were widely publicized and roundly criticized. Some commentators believed that the only problem was that the legislative process had been so public. The deals that had been cut were nothing out of the ordinary, just unusually out in the open. Others believed that a line had been crossed—that there is a difference between giving a state a new water project or a community organization a new government grant and exempting the residents of an entire state from a law that applies to everyone else in the country. The public reaction to the Senate deals was so negative—even in Nebraska—that Nelson asked that the provision be removed, which President Obama did later when he laid out his own healthcare plan. And many observers felt that the deals played at least some role in the negative reaction to the Democratic plan and the election of Scott Brown in Massachusetts (see the opening vignette) shortly afterwards. By the time President Obama stepped in, approval of Congress had sunk to about 15 percent and disapproval had risen to nearly 75 percent. After the 2008 elections, declining evaluations of Congressional Democrats were credited with the change since Congressional Republicans had already been poorly evaluated (historic...

ELECTION CONNECTION

Primaries Versus Caucuses

When voters cast ballots in presidential primaries and caucuses, they are not voting directly for a candidate of their choice. Instead, they are voting for delegates who are pledged to support these candidates at party conventions. Since the reforms of the early 1970s, there have been three main ways to become a delegate to a party's national convention: via a primary election, via a caucus system, or as an automatic "superdelegate."

Primaries

Primaries work like other elections: Voters appear at the polls at some point on Election day, vote, and leave. After the votes are totaled, party officials use them to allocate national convention delegates. Democrats use a proportional representation system: If a candidate receives two-thirds of the vote, he or she receives two-thirds of the delegates and the other candidate or candidates receive the remaining one-third. Republicans use a winner-take-all system in most cases: 51 percent of the vote gets a candidate 100 percent of the delegates. The actual people who become delegates are drawn from lists of acceptable delegate candidates provided in advance by each campaign.

Caucuses

Some states (12...) ...select their

Superdelegates

The post-1968 party reforms sought to diminish the power of party leaders and increase the power of ordinary voters. But, by the 1980s, the Democratic Party reversed course somewhat, giving automatic delegate status to party leaders and elected officials such as senators, members of the House of Representatives, and governors. These "superdelegates" had 19 percent of the total Democratic Convention votes in 2008. Republicans have a smaller number of "automatic" delegates comprised of the top three party officials from each state and territory. They make up only 7 percent of the total Republican delegates.

Elected delegates may be chosen via caucuses or primaries, depending on the state. Party leaders and elected officials are known as "superdelegates" in the Democratic Party because they automatically get votes at the convention. Republicans give delegate status to each state's top three party leaders, but other Republican-elected officials do not automatically become delegates.

NATIONAL CONVENTION

State Conventions

ELECTION CONNECTION boxes describe the relationship between elections and institutions or policies, illustrating the book's focus on electoral forces. Topics include how amendments to the Constitution have extended liberties and tightened the election connection (Chapter 2), federalism and the Homeland Security Grant Program (Chapter 3), and a new discussion of primaries versus caucuses (Chapter 10).

CRITICAL THINKING

The Media: 800-Pound Gorilla or 98-Pound Weakling?

The national media had it all figured out. In the frenzied few days before the 2008 New Hampshire primary, an average voter following press coverage about the campaign would probably have said with a fair degree of certainty that the winners would be Barack Obama and Mitt Romney. Obama had just scored a triumphant victory in the Iowa caucuses and was making a triumphant tour of the state, drawing overflow crowds and adoring media coverage. ABC's Charlie Gibson pointed out what to most of the assembled TV anchors, radio hosts, bloggers, pundits, and newspaper writers seemed obvious: "There is talk and evidence of an Obama wave moving through this state on the eve of its primary."[1] A New York Post headline screamed that Obama rival Hillary Clinton's campaign was in a state of "PANIC," and even the more sedate Washington Post agreed that Obama had a "clear lead."[2]

Meanwhile, Romney was considered something of a favorite son, since he owned a summer home in New Hampshire and had served as governor of neighboring Massachusetts. He lost the Iowa caucuses to former Arkansas governor Mike Huckabee, but Huckabee had only a bare-bones operation in New Hampshire and was unlikely to do well there. Romney's other main opponent, John McCain, had been written off by the press months before. In mid-2007, the McCain campaign, suffering from staffing and money problems, seemed on the verge of collapse, and the press said so. "Left for dead" seemed to be the operative characterization of McCain: MSNBC's Chris Matthews, FOX News's Chris Wallace, the New York Daily News, the Washington Post, and others all used the phrase.[3] Finally, the wealthy Romney bought twice as much television advertising time as McCain.[4] If TV images had an effect on voters, Romney seemed to have the edge.

Considering the impressions the media conveyed, the actual primary results came as quite a surprise. McCain beat Romney and, even more surprisingly, Obama lost to Clinton by two percentage points. Voters appeared to have been indifferent to the tenor of the news coverage, and to the barrage of political advertising. Could it be that, despite all the hue and cry, the modern media have very little effect on voters?

No sooner had reporters and pundits been blindsided by the surprising outcome, however, than they came up with an explanation for it—on the Democratic side, at least— that made the media central again. The day before the primary, Hillary Clinton's eyes appeared to well with tears after a reporter asked her about how she held up under the stress of campaigning. Video of this event rocketed around the Internet and saturated news coverage for that day. In retrospect, argued many observers, this incident elicited sympathy for Clinton among voters—especially women—who had previously found it hard to identify with her. According to this explanation, rather than being ineffectual, the media were fundamental to the election outcome. "The Obama campaign calculated that they had the women's vote over the weekend," wrote columnist Maureen Dowd, "but watched it slip away in the track of her tears."[5]

Each chapter introduces you to the subject matter with an **OPENING VIGNETTE** on a high-interest issue or incident. Some vignettes are classics from American history, while others are based on current events. Examples include a discussion of the politics of Hurricane Katrina (Chapter 3), national reaction to "suspect" minorities in the wake of wars (Chapter 4), a discussion of the role of race and gender in the 2008 presidential campaign (Chapter 17), and a description of the difficulties in passing the healthcare reform bill (Chapter 18).

A **MAKING THE CONNECTION** passage follows each vignette, relating its themes to the chapter content and preparing students for the material to follow.

Making the Connection

How powerful are the media? Are they an overwhelming force that even presidents must fear, or a lot of sound and fury that ordinary Americans ignore? The answer is that, depending on the circumstances, the media can be either of these, and everything in between. Under some conditions, the media can have extremely powerful effects on public opinion, even to the extent of determining who wins elections and what governments do. But, under other conditions, media effects are sharply limited.

We begin our analysis of the role of the media by considering how the media have attained their present position as important political actors, and what kinds of media Americans rely on for political information. We then consider two other important issues: in what ways the media—including the latest methods of communication—affect public opinion today and what types of bias characterize media reports.

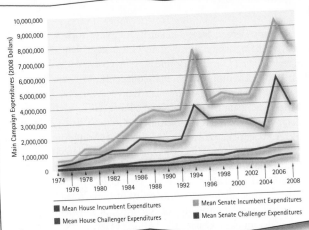

FIGURE 11.4

CONGRESSIONAL CAMPAIGN
SPENDING

Spending in House and Senate
campaigns has risen over the past
several decades.

• *Why do Senate candidates
spend so much more than House
candidates?*

Sources: Norman J. Ornstein, Thomas E.
Mann, and Michael J. Malbin, *Vital Statistics
on Congress, 2001–2002* (Washington, DC:
American Enterprise Institute, 2002),
pp. 81, 87; the Federal Election Commission;
and the Campaign Finance Institute.

**FOUR-COLOR INTERACTIVE
FIGURES** include informative captions
that highlight the most important
lessons to draw from the graphic, and
questions that inspire higher order
thinking and analysis of the data.

CRITICAL THINKING QUESTIONS accompany
the many thought-provoking photographs (now in four
colors), inspiring analysis and connecting the images
to the text discussion they amplify.

A **CHAPTER SUMMARY** concludes each chapter, as
a reminder of the key points covered.

ng money.
mits, presi-
campaigns
orters and
d, the can-
housands of
e has esti-
the invisi-

f the invisi-
number of
uses. Two
d a remark-
y and, con-
lds the first

the first primary.[12] Especially for a non-front-
nexpectedly strong showing in these two early
attribute known as "momentum," as the media,
take the candidate more seriously. In 2008, two
rty's Iowa Caucuses: Barack Obama, who ulti-
d Mike Huckabee, who went on to mount an
al Republican nominee, John McCain.
are usually followed by a large number of

**The New Hampshire
Primary, 2008**
Hillary Clinton greeting voters
on primary day in New
Hampshire. Clinton won the primary, but lost the nomination.
• *Why is the "invisible primary"
such an important precursor to
the primary season?*

INTERNATIONAL COMPARISON
boxes compare a feature of American
government with a similar feature in
other countries. These boxes will give you
a better understanding of the strengths
and limitations of American democracy
by encouraging you to think about real
alternatives, not just abstract ideals.
Updated subjects include citizenship
requirements in Europe compared with
those in the United States (Chapter 4),
campaign financing in other countries
(Chapter 10), and student learning and
school expenditures (Chapter 18). Many
of these features now include maps or
graphics, and all conclude with critical
thinking questions.

CHAPTER SUMMARY

11.1 Trace the development of the Congress as
a professional legislature.

The Congress is the world's foremost example of a professional legislature—a body of elected officials whose full-time
job is serving in Congress. The Constitution assigns each
state two senators and apportions representatives to the states
based on their populations.

11.2 Explain how congressional constituencies
are determined by means of reapportionment and
redistricting.

Reapportionment takes place after each census to reflect
population changes. Once the number of representatives
each state gets is known, state legislatures or commissions
draw the boundaries of the districts.

success does not violate the framers' intention of an electorally sensitive House. On the contrary, because representatives are so electorally sensitive, they work very hard at
serving their districts, try very hard to represent constituents'
policy concerns, and in general attempt to eliminate any
basis for a strong challenge against them. Contrary to the
charges of many critics, electoral success does not lead
members of the House to be lazy and unresponsive.
Rather, members are reelected *because* they are so hard-
working and responsive.

11.5 Determine why incumbency is less
important in Senate elections than in House
elections.

Senators, too, are hard-working and responsive (probably
more responsive than the framers intended) although they

ACKNOWLEDGMENTS

We want to thank the many people who helped us with the preparation of this book. Our deepest gratitude goes to the many undergraduate students whose questions forced us to refine our thinking about American government over the past ten years. We also thank numerous colleagues of teaching fellows for their perceptive comments, questions, and criticisms. We are also especially grateful to Bruce Nichols, who first argued with us the need for a new-century approach to the introductory text on American government. The Center for Advanced Study in the Behavioral and Social Sciences provided generous support for Paul E. Peterson's work on the first edition of the text during his academic year there.

Harding Noblitt of Concordia College read the entire first edition manuscript in search of errors of fact and interpretation, saving the authors much embarrassment. In addition, portions were read by Danny Adkison, Sue Davis, Richard Fenno, Gary Jacobson, Barry Rabe, and Chris Stamm, whose comments helped with fact checking. We especially appreciate John Ferejohn and the undergraduate students at Stanford University who took his course and tested an early draft of the entire manuscript, and Jay Greene and his students at the University of Texas at Austin who used subsequent page proofs. Larry Carlton supplied important factual material. Research assistance was provided by Ted Brader, Jay Girotto, Donald Lee, Jerome Maddox, Kenneth Scheve, Sean Theriault, and Robert Van Houweling—as well as William Howell who, in addition to making many other contributions, helped write the regulatory policy section in Chapter 18. Rebecca Contreras, Alison Kommer, Shelley Weiner, and Sarah Peterson provided staff assistance. Bert Johnson wishes to thank his American Politics students at Carleton College and Middlebury College, as well as Professors Sharon Navarro, Kanishkan Sathasivam, Steven Schier, and Kim Smith for their helpful suggestions. William Mayer would like to thank his wife, Amy Logan, for making sure he had time to do his share of the revisions.

We would like to extend our special thanks to Martin West of Harvard University and Jeremy Pope and Sam Abrams at Stanford University for the multitude of tasks they undertook to see this seventh edition into publication and improve upon the sixth.

In the course of writing this book, we benefited from the advice of many instructors across the country. We deeply thank all the following, but we are especially grateful for the expert advice of Stephen Ansolabehere, Richard Fenno, John Ferejohn, Bonnie Honig, and Diana Owen.

The following are reviewers who assisted in the preparation of the second, third, fourth, fifth, and sixth editions of the text: Danny M. Adkison, Oklahoma State University; Donald P. Aiesi, Furman University; Alan Arwine, University of Illinois; Michael Bailey, Georgetown University; Gordon Bennett, University of Texas; Brian A. Bearry, University of Texas at Dallas; Mark Berger, State University of New York at Stony Brook; William Bianco, Penn State University; Nancy Bond, Ranger College; Chris W. Bonneau, University of Pittsburgh; Mark Blitz, Claremont McKenna College; Brian Brox, Tulane University; Michael Caldwell, University of Illinois, Urbana–Champaign; Terrence Casey, Rose-Hulman Institute of Technology; Thomas A. Chambers, Golden West College; Mark A. Cichock, University of Texas at Arlington; Louis DeSipio, University of Illinois, Urbana–Champaign; Richard E. Dunn, College of Charleston; Michael C. Evans, University of Maryland; Christine Fastnow, University of Michigan; Charles J. Finocchiaro, State University of New York–Buffalo; Audrey Haynes, University of Georgia; Joe Gershtenson, Eastern Kentucky University; Anna Harvey, New York University; Eric Herzik, University of Nevada; M.V. Hood III, University of Georgia; Christopher Housenick, Pennsylvania State University; Jon Hurwitz, University of Pittsburgh; Robert Jacobs, Central Washington University; Carlos Juarez, Hawaii Pacific University; Kelechi Kalu, University of Northern Colorado; David Leal, State University of New York at Buffalo; Brad Lockerbie, University of Georgia; William Lyons, University of Tennessee; Cecilia Manrique, University of Wisconsin–La Crosse; Madhavi McCall, San Diego State University; Scott D. McClurg, Southern Illinois University; William P. McLauchlan, Purdue University; Michael E. Meagher, University of Missouri–Rolla; Charles Menifield, Murray State University; David S. Meyer, City College of New York; Sarah Miller, Lourdes University; Timothy Nokken, University of Houston; John H. Parham, Minnesota State University; Curt Reithel, University of Wisconsin–La Crosse; James A. Rhodes, Luther College; Beth Rosenson, University of Florida; Todd M. Schaefer, Central Washington University; Brett S. Sharp, University of Central Oklahoma; Fred Slocum, Minnesota State University-Mankato; Jeremy M. Teigen, Ramapo College; and Wilson O. Ugwu, Concordia University. Bruce Unger, Randolph-Macon College; Theodore M. Vestal, Oklahoma State University; Shirley Anne Warshaw, Gettysburg College; Linda Faye Williams, University of Maryland; and Jeremy Zilber, College of William and Mary.

The following are reviewers who assisted in the preparation of this seventh edition: Alexander Aguado, University of North Alabama; Prosper Bernard, College of Staten Island; Manar Elkhaldi, University of Central Florida; Sally Hansen, Daytona State College; Gary Malecha, University of Portland; James Rhodes, Luther College; Kevin Spiker, Ohio University -Eastern Campus and those who reviewed anonymously

M. P. F.
P. E. P.
B. J.
W. G. M.

Resources in Print and Online

NAME OF SUPPLEMENT	PRINT	ONLINE	AVAILABLE TO	DESCRIPTION
MyClassPrep		✓	Instructor	This new resource provides a rich database of figures, photos, videos, simulations, activities, and much more that instructors can use to create their own lecture presentation. For more information visit *www.mypoliscilab.com*.
Instructor's Manual 0205059619		✓	Instructor	Offers chapter overviews, lecture outlines, teaching ideas, discussion topics, and research activities. All resources hyperlinked for ease of navigation.
Test Bank 0205060366		✓	Instructor	Contains over 100 questions per chapter in multiple-choice, true-false, short answer, and essay format. Questions are tied to text Learning Objectives and have been reviewed for accuracy and effectiveness.
MyTest 0205059597		✓	Instructor	All questions from the Test Bank can be accessed in this flexible, online test generating software.
PowerPoint Presentation 0205059627		✓	Instructor	Slides include a lecture outline of the text, graphics from the book, animated figures to explain difficult processes, and quick check questions for immediate feedback on student comprehension.
Transparencies 0205005780		✓	Instructor	These PDF slides contain all maps, figures, and tables found in the text.
Pearson Political Science Video Program	✓		Instructor	Qualified adopters can peruse our list of videos for the American government classroom. Contact your local Pearson representative for more details.
Classroom Response System (CRS) 0205082289		✓	Instructor	A set of lecture questions, organized by American government topics, for use with "clickers" to garner student opinion and assess comprehension.
American Government Study Site		✓	Instructor/ Student	Online package of practice tests, flashcards and more organized by major course topics. Visit *www.pearsonamericangovernment.com*
You Decide! Current Debates in American Politics, 2011 Edition 020511489X	✓		Student	This debate-style reader by John Rourke of the University of Connecticut examines provocative issues in American politics today by presenting contrasting views of key political topics.
Voices of Dissent: Critical Readings in American Politics, Eighth Edition 0205697976	✓		Student	This collection of critical essays assembled by William Grover of St. Michael's College and Joseph Peschek of Hamline University goes beyond the debate between mainstream liberalism and conservatism to fundamentally challenge the status quo.
Diversity in Contemporary American Politics and Government 0205550363	✓		Student	Edited by David Dulio of Oakland University, Erin E. O'Brien of Kent State University, and John Klemanski of Oakland University, this reader examines the significant role that demographic diversity plays in our political outcomes and policy processes, using both academic and popular sources.
Writing in Political Science, Fourth Edition 0205617360	✓		Student	This guide, written by Diane Schmidt of California State University—Chico, takes students through all aspects of writing in political science step-by-step.
Choices: An American Government Database Reader		✓	Student	This customizable reader allows instructors to choose from a database of over 300 readings to create a reader that exactly matches their course needs. For more information go to *www.pearsoncustom.com/database/choices.html*.
Ten Things That Every American Government Student Should Read 020528969X	✓		Student	Edited by Karen O'Connor of American University. We asked American government instructors across the country to vote for the ten things beyond the text that they believe every student should read and put them in this brief and useful reader. Available at no additional charge when packaged with the text.
American Government: Readings and Cases, Eighteenth Edition 0205697984	✓		Student	Edited by Peter Woll of Brandeis University, this longtime best-selling reader provides a strong, balanced blend of classic readings and cases that illustrate and amplify important concepts in American government, alongside extremely current selections drawn from today's issues and literature. Available at a discount when ordered packaged with this text.
Penguin-Longman Value Bundles	✓		Student	Longman offers 25 Penguin Putnam titles at more than a 60 percent discount when packaged with any Longman text. Go to *www.pearsonhighered.com/penguin* for more information.
Longman State Politics Series	✓		Student	These primers on state and local government and political issues are available at no extra cost when shrink-wrapped with the text. Available for Texas, California, and Georgia.

*Visit the Instructor Resource Center to download supplements at www.pearsonhighered.com/educator

About the Authors

Morris P. Fiorina

Morris P. Fiorina is Wendt Professor of Political Science and Senior Fellow of the Hoover Institution at Stanford University. He received a B.A. from Allegheny College in Meadville, Pennsylvania, and a Ph.D. from the University of Rochester. Before moving to Stanford, he taught at the California Institute of Technology and Harvard University.

Fiorina has written widely on American government and politics, with special emphasis on representation and elections. He has published numerous articles and many books: *Representatives, Roll Calls, and Constituencies; Congress—Keystone of the Washington Establishment; Retrospective Voting in American National Elections; The Personal Vote: Constituency Service and Electoral Independence* (coauthored with Bruce Cain and John Ferejohn); *Divided Government; Culture War? The Myth of A Polarized America* (coauthored with Samuel Abrams and Jeremy Pope); and *Disconnect: The Breakdown of Representation in American Politics* (with Samuel Abrams). He has served on the editorial boards of a dozen journals in the fields of political science, economics, law, and public policy, and from 1986 to 1990, he served as chairman of the Board of Overseers of the American National Election Studies. He is a member of the National Academy of Sciences and is a Wendt Family Professor of Political Science.

In his leisure time, Fiorina favors physical activities, including hiking, fishing, and sports. Although his own athletic career never amounted to much, he was a successful youth baseball coach for 15 years. Among his most cherished honors is a plaque given by happy parents on the occasion of an undefeated Babe Ruth season.

Paul E. Peterson

Paul E. Peterson is the Henry Lee Shattuck Professor of Government and Director of the Center for American Political Studies at Harvard University. He received his B.A. from Concordia College in Moorhead, Minnesota, and his Ph.D. from the University of Chicago.

Peterson is an author or editor of 20 books and numerous articles on federalism, urban politics, race relations, and public policy, including studies of education, welfare, and fiscal and foreign policy. He received the Gladys Kammerer Award from the American Political Science Association for his book, *School Politics, Chicago Style* (1976), and the Woodrow Wilson Award for his book *City Limits* (Chicago, 1981). In 1996 his book, *The Price of Federalism* (Brookings, 1995), was given the Aaron Wildavsky Award for the best book on public policy. His most recent book is *Saving Schools: From Horace Mann to Virtual Learning* (Harvard University Press, 2010). He is a member of the American Academy of Arts and Sciences.

It is not only when writing a textbook that Peterson makes every effort to be as accurate as possible. On the tennis courts, he always makes correct line calls and has seldom been heard to hit a wrong note when tickling the ivories.

Bertram Johnson

Bert Johnson is Associate Professor of Political Science at Middlebury College in Middlebury, Vermont. He received his B.A. from Carleton College and his Ph.D. from Harvard University.

Johnson has written on federalism, intergovernmental relations, and campaign finance and has published articles in journals such as *Social Science History, Urban Affairs Quarterly,* and *American Politics Research*. His analysis of President George W. Bush's interactions with Congress appears in Steven Schier's edited volume, *Ambition and Division: Legacies of the George W. Bush Presidency* (Pittsburgh, 2009). When not investigating new ideas about American politics, he runs marathons and ultramarathons.

William G. Mayer

William G. Mayer is an associate professor of political science at Northeastern University in Boston, having received his B.A. and his Ph.D. from Harvard University. He is the author of six books and numerous articles on such topics as public opinion, political parties, voting and elections, media and politics, and the presidential nomination process. More importantly, he is married to Amy Logan and the father of two children, Natalie and Thomas. He also teaches Sunday School to kindergartners at St. Jude's Catholic Church in Waltham, Massachusetts.

1 Democracy in the United States

CHAPTER OUTLINE

LEARNING OBJECTIVES

1.1 Analyze the on-going role that free elections play in the governmental process and the power it gives those who participate.

1.2 Illustrate the reasons for the existence of government and identify its key functions.

1.3 Assess the strengths and weaknesses of the major types of government.

1.4 Compare and contrast the two types of ideal democracies.

1.5 Trace the evolution of the United States toward a more complex democracy that has necessitated a permanent campaign.

1.6 Characterize the factors that shift power from the majority of voters to specific groups.

1.7 Evaluate the strengths and weaknesses of the present political system in America and some of the requests for reform.

The Long, Long 2008 Election Campaign

The new American democracy is marked by a **permanent campaign.**[1] Literally, the phrase means that campaigning never ends: The next election campaign begins as soon as the last one has finished, if not before. The election of 2008 provides an illustration of this basic feature of American government.

Barack Obama's campaign for the presidency began years before his election on November 4, 2008. He became a viable presidential candidate after he gave the keynote address at the 2004 Democratic National Convention, months before Illinois voters elected him to the U.S. Senate. Democratic Party leaders chose Obama to give the address to recognize a talented, well-educated, youthful figure of both African American and white descent, a potential star able to reach across the racial divide and attract independent voters to the party's cause. His speech, in which he rejected the conventional wisdom that divided "red" (Republican) states from "blue" (Democratic) states, was so well received that pundits immediately began to consider him presidential timber. Upon his election to the Senate, Obama won key committee assignments that perfectly positioned him for a presidential run. By October 2006, he publicly admitted he was considering the option, an indication that he and his advisers had already given the matter considerable thought. The official announcement came on February 10, 2007, 25 months after he was sworn in as a senator, and

21 months before Election Day. After that, the Obama campaign went into high gear.

Obama's Republican opponent began his own campaign even earlier. Senator John McCain of Arizona had campaigned for the presidency 8 years before when he challenged George W. Bush for the nomination of their party in 2000. Although Bush defeated him that year, McCain kept himself in the news by showing independence from Republican orthodoxy. He broke with members of his party by urging tighter controls on campaign finance, stricter business regulation, greater concern for the environment, and friendlier policies toward illegal immigrants. Once Bush was re-elected in 2004, making it constitutionally impossible for him to run again for the nation's highest office, McCain began planning his 2008 run. He publicly announced his plans on a nightly entertainment program, *The Late Show with David Letterman*, just days after Obama had declared his candidacy.

No one should criticize either Obama or McCain for excess ambition. Both were forced to act quickly and decisively because each faced formidable rivals who began plotting their campaign strategies at much the same time. Obama first had to edge out former North Carolina Senator John Edwards and then win a vigorous, drawn-out battle with New York Senator Hillary Clinton, the early favorite for the Democratic nomination. McCain had to outpace an even larger set of Republican contenders—among

3

them former New York Mayor Rudolph Giuliani, former Massachusetts Governor Mitt Romney, and former Arkansas governor Mike Huckabee.

Meanwhile, in Washington, DC, a Republican president and a Democratic Congress battled over issue after issue in a drama that each side saw as positioning the two parties for advantage in the 2008 election. Congress criticized the president's management of the Iraq War, tax policy, and environmental policy. The president accused Democrats of obstructionism. Where partisans on one side saw an advantage, they pounced, as when Democrats attacked the profits of big oil companies when gas neared $4 per gallon in the summer of 2008, or when Republicans touted reports of reductions in violence in Iraq. Almost any issue could become fodder for partisan bickering. When baseball star Roger Clemens appeared on Capitol Hill to deny using performance-enhancing drugs, Democrats and Republicans wasted no time in lining up on opposite sides.

At times, the presidential candidates themselves took the lead in turning Washington politics into presidential campaign politics. A proposed free trade agreement with Colombia, scheduled to go before Congress for approval, became a critical issue in the Democratic primary race. The Obama and Clinton campaigns each accused the other of being insincere in their skepticism of free trade deals. Unions and working class voters in Ohio and Pennsylvania felt that unfair trade agreements had cost them their jobs, and many based their votes on the issue.

The Colombia trade deal, which the Bush administration had hoped Congress would approve without much fanfare, took center stage in the campaign, and soon fell victim to deadlock.

Not every issue met with partisan stalemate. On the contrary, when the parties saw no electoral advantage in opposing one another, quick action was possible. For example, in early 2008 after a collapse in the housing market threatened to tip the economy into recession, Congress and the White House took only weeks to agree on an economic stimulus package that, among other things, sent a one-time payment of $600 to most taxpayers. After the bill was signed into law, however, Democrats began to argue that more ought to be done, while Republicans and President Bush urged patience. Weblogs and talk radio erupted into charges and counter-charges. In the fall, Obama and McCain flooded the airwaves with advertisements touting their economic policies, while independent groups organized their own campaigns to put pressure on elected officials. All to select a president who would immediately have to begin planning for re-election in 2012.

To the dismay of many Americans, the election changed little. President Obama proposed an ambitious agenda and congressional Republicans lined up solidly in opposition. Republican Senator Jim DeMint of South Carolina rallied his partisans against the Democratic health insurance plan with the comment that "If we're able to stop Obama on this, it will be his Waterloo. It will break him."

It was the new American democracy in operation.

Making the Connection

Elections and the permanent campaign that accompanies them are key to understanding the new American democracy. Not only are elections more important in the United States than in other democracies, but they are more important today than they were in most earlier periods of our history.

Government is more than just elections, however. Government is the only organization in a society that has the power to use force legitimately to compel individuals to do what it decides. In this chapter we discuss the importance of government, compare the major types of governments, identify differences between direct and representative democracy, and show how elections have attained more importance in the United States than in other democracies. Finally, we consider whether elections produce a reasonably good government.

Elections and Government

Electoral influence on government is not limited to the day an election is held, or even just to the days when explicit political campaigns are taking place. That's part of the story, of course. But elections also play a critical role in the day-to-day governing of the United States. When they make public statements and enact laws, elected officials consider the likely effects of their actions on public support in future elections. Looking ahead to the next election affects the proposals presidents make, the issues special interest groups bring up, and the laws passed by Congress. Elections also shape how the news media choose to cover the people and topics involved in politics. Even nightly entertainment shows have become politicized, as indicated by President Obama's decision to appear on *The Tonight Show* with Jay Leno mere months after taking office.

Some government functions are more insulated from elections than others, of course. Courts make decisions that have large consequences, even though federal judges are appointed, not elected, officials. Laws enacted years ago remain in effect, despite changes in public opinion—in part because minorities can block any new legislation. Those who administer the bureaucracy are appointed by the president, but they can act with a good deal of independence, making key decisions of which the public may be quite unaware. Government is more than elections, and more than democracy in action.

Yet free elections are the hallmark of democracy. Dictators know this perfectly well. Joseph Stalin, the tyrant who ruled the Soviet Union for three decades, once commented, "The disadvantage of free elections is that you can never be sure who is going to win them."[2] As long as he lived, he made sure no Soviet elections were free.

When free elections are in play, they can affect government in many ways, simply because those in government constantly plan and prepare for the next election. We all know that football games are won and lost not just by the athletes' skills and toughness on the decisive day the game is played, but also by the training and strategizing that takes place in the months and years leading up to the opening kickoff. So it is with elections. Outcomes are shaped as much or more by events and policies that take place between elections as by last-minute appeals to the voters. Knowing that actions taken now can have future electoral consequences, political leaders strategize well in advance of the next election.

It is not that a **majority** (50 percent plus one) of the people always get their way, however. Elections give more power to some groups than to others. Those who vote exercise more influence than those who do not. Those who give money to candidates, work actively in campaigns, or have easy access to the news media have the most clout. The power of small, organized groups is especially great if they take a strong position on a policy about which a majority of the people have little knowledge or concern. During the 2008 financial crisis, banks succeeded in getting the government to bail them out—in part because they were well organized, very concerned about the situation, and had access to government decision makers, while the public as a whole was uncertain what should be done.

Still, majorities have the potential to be powerful even when the public is uninformed about or unaware of an issue. Elected officials realize that the media spotlight might suddenly shine into what seemed to be a dark corner. Additionally, challengers pore over the incumbent's record, searching for unpopular votes cast, positions taken, or statements made. If found, such matters become campaign issues.[3] Because leaders are never sure which issues will become central to election campaigns, they tend to be

1.1

Analyze the on-going role that free elections play in the governmental process and the power it gives those who participate.

permanent campaign
Condition that prevails in the new American democracy when the next election campaign begins as soon as the last has ended and the line between electioneering and governing has disappeared.

majority
Fifty percent plus one.

FIGURE 1.1

AMERICANS ARE MORE
SKEPTICAL OF THE
NATIONAL GOVERNMENT
THAN IN THE EARLY 1960s

Despite a few brief upswings,
trust in government, by several
measures, has decreased since
1964.

• *Why do you think trust in
government increased after the
events of 9/11, but then fell
thereafter?*

Note: The second item was not
surveyed in 1986.

Source: The American National Election
Studies, University of Michigan; 2006
figure reflects identical question asked by
CBS News/*New York Times* Poll, October,
2006.

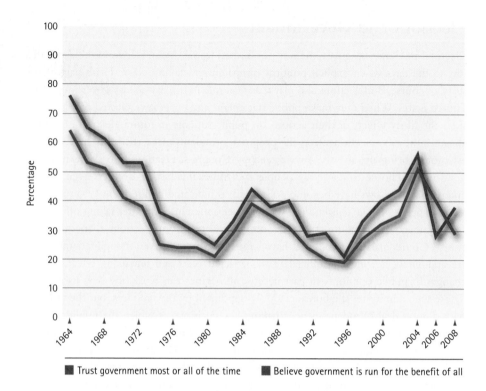

■ Trust government most or all of the time   ■ Believe government is run for the benefit of all

cautious in handling all of them. Hence, the power of minorities is limited by the potential threat that the majority will become activated.

Despite all the ways in which the public can shape the decisions politicians make, many Americans are frustrated by government. In fact, Americans do not trust government as much as they once did (see Figure 1.1). Citizens believe that government costs too much, delivers too little, and wastes their tax dollars. They think politics is needlessly contentious and often corrupt. Many Americans are suspicious of the established TV networks and major newspapers, and turn to alternative information providers such as talk show hosts, cable television comics, and Internet sites. Many are frustrated with existing political rules and support constitutional amendments to limit the number of terms elected officials may serve.[4] Ironically, the permanent campaign to win public support on election day has not endeared government to the people it is expected to serve.

1.2

**Illustrate the reasons
for the existence of
government and identify
its key functions.**

Governmental Power

To some extent, suspicion of government is healthy. By its very nature, governmental power threatens human liberty. The great German sociologist Max Weber defined the state as the institution in society holding a "monopoly of the legitimate use of physical force."[5] As the agent of the state, a government is the only institution that can *legally* appropriate people's property (by taxing them or by taking their private property for public use), restrict their movements (by imprisoning them or prohibiting certain kinds of behaviors), and even take their lives (by executing them). As George Washington put it a century before Weber, "Government is not reason, it is not eloquence—it is force."[6]

When campaigning for president, Jimmy Carter professed that "all I want is . . . to have a nation with a government that is as good and honest and decent and competent and compassionate and as filled with love as are the American people."[7] These are admirable sentiments, but with all due respect to the former president, government is necessary precisely because such qualities are often missing from human behavior. As another former president, James Madison, put it nearly 200 years earlier, "If men were angels, no government would be necessary."[8]

Governments are designed less for the times when people agree—when they are decent and compassionate and filled with love—than for the times when they disagree. No matter who you are, what you believe, what you want, or how you behave, it is an unfortunate fact of life that some of your fellow citizens dislike you for exactly those reasons. People can settle their disagreements and rise above enmity through peaceful political means, or they can kill each other, as Americans did in the Civil War and as so many peoples of the world have done before and since.

The political theorist Thomas Hobbes, writing in the seventeenth century, made the most basic case for government and politics. A world without government, he said, would be nothing less than "a war of all against all." Life would be "nasty, brutish and short."[9] The truth of that insight rings clear down to this very day, as shown by the conflict in Iraq, a nation so divided among ethnic and religious factions—Kurds, Shiites, and Sunnis—that no government has been able to assert its coercive authority over the entire country. As a result, the country has suffered the calamity that occurs when effective government is absent.

In addition to preserving the basic fabric of society, **government** performs four other key functions:

- *Protects citizens from unlawful activity.* If someone is mugged or burglarized, he or she immediately turns to the police for help. If minorities are mistreated, they ask the government to intervene.
- *Regulates social and economic relationships.* We can confidently eat in restaurants and buy food at grocery stores, because the government requires proprietors to follow appropriate sanitation procedures. Laws require that TV advertising not tell outright falsehoods and that drugs be tested before they are prescribed.
- *Provides services.* Government provides elementary and secondary schools for children, colleges for young adults, roads for commuters, medical care for the sick, food for the starving, housing for the homeless, and financial assistance to the elderly and impoverished.
- *Defends the country from foreign aggression.* In the name of national defense, the U.S. government fought World War I, World War II, the Korean War, and the Persian Gulf War.

None of these functions could be performed, however, if government did not have the legitimate authority to coerce individuals. Without a government, a modern society could not possibly exist. But if almost everyone agrees that government is necessary, that view still leaves an important question unanswered: What *kind* of government do we want?

Classic Types of Government

The English author Samuel Johnson once asserted that "I would not give half a guinea to live under one form of government rather than another. It is of no moment to the happiness of an individual."[10] Johnson may have been a brilliant conversationalist, and he

One Man's Good Government
When campaigning for president, Jimmy Carter said, "All I want is . . . to have a nation with a government that is as good . . . as are the American people."
- *How good would such a government be?*

government
The institution in society holding a monopoly on the legitimate use of physical force.

1.3

Assess the strengths and weaknesses of the major types of government.

TABLE 1.1		
ARISTOTLE'S CLASSIC DISTINCTIONS AMONG SIX TYPES OF GOVERNMENT		

For each of three general types, there is a legitimate and a perverse variety.

• *Do you believe it is easier to prevent a democracy from becoming a mobocracy than it is to prevent a monarchy from becoming a tyranny?*

Government by . . .	Legitimate	Perverse
One	Monarchy	Tyranny
Few	Aristocracy	Oligarchy
Many	Democracy	"Mobocracy"

deserves appreciation for fathering the modern dictionary, but this particular comment is silly. The type of government under which people live makes an enormous difference in the quality of their lives.

Twenty-three centuries ago, the Greek philosopher Aristotle classified governments into three general types: government by one person, government by the few, and government by the many (see Table 1.1). He said each type could have either a legitimate or a perverse form, making for six types of government altogether. Although others have proposed more complex classifications, Aristotle's simple scheme—good and bad forms of three types of government—remains a useful place to begin our examination of the different types of government.

Government by One Person

Historically, pharaohs, emperors, kings, tsars, and other monarchs ruled by hereditary right or religious appointment (although, like modern dictators, they usually needed the support of an army or a police force as well). The quality of government by a single ruler depends on who is in charge. The ruler can put the public interest first, last, or anywhere in between. But placing the coercive power of government in the hands of one person requires unlimited trust in that person, and few individuals, if any, are so deserving. As Lord Acton, another political theorist, observed in the nineteenth century, "Power tends to corrupt and absolute power corrupts absolutely." In the twentieth century alone, millions of people died at the hands of rulers who gained near-absolute power—tyrants such as Germany's Hitler, the Soviet Union's Stalin, China's Mao, and Cambodia's Pol Pot. For that reason, Aristotle distinguished between the good and legitimate ruler—perhaps best exemplified by Queen Elizabeth I, who was a single powerful English monarch at the time Shakespeare wrote his plays—and the tyrant, who seizes power by force and rules selfishly, without regard for the common good.

Government by the Few

aristocracy
A government by the few, in which the leaders are meritorious and chosen by virtue of their birth into noble families.

In Aristotle's scheme, government by the few may be called an **aristocracy** if most leaders are meritorious and chosen by virtue of their birth into noble families, a fact that he felt legitimated their rule and made them more likely to act in the common interest. The Roman Republic of the first century BCE is often considered the classic example of a good and legitimate aristocratic government because its senate (after which the U.S. Senate is in some ways modeled) consisted mainly of gentlemen of great wealth and noble lineage, who built public institutions (roads, aqueducts, and handsome buildings), provided popular entertainment (circuses and gladiators), and protected the country from its enemies. Aristocracies ruled many countries in the past, but in the modern world birthright no longer seems an acceptable justification for ruling over others. Instead, government by the few usually takes the form of an **oligarchy** in which the few are not titled nobility but individuals who have captured power either through military action or through a political party. The most important modern oligarchy governs China, where a small group of Communist Party leaders has remained in power since 1946.

oligarchy
A government by the few, in which the individuals in power are not titled nobility but capture power either through military action or through a political party.

Government by the few also may take a legitimate or a perverse form. The Roman Senate became corrupt and self-interested with the passage of time. Currently, observers debate whether government by the few in China is legitimate or perverse. Defenders say that the government, although bloodied by the crimes committed by Mao Zedong, has transformed itself into an effective, modern system capable of greatly improving the life of its citizens. If so, the Communist Party leadership has become a meritorious aristocracy. Skeptics say that the tension between tight political control and the dynamic of the open Chinese economy cannot be sustained. Either the government will become increasingly corrupt and perverse or it will give way to a democratic type of government.

Government by the Many

Government in which all citizens share power is called **democracy.** The word derives from the Greek word *demos*, which means "people." According to Aristotle, democracies, too, could be legitimate or perverse, public-spirited or selfish. In legitimate democracies the citizens gather together, discuss the problems at hand, and reach conclusions by majority vote after thinking the matter through from multiple perspectives. Through a process of careful deliberation, the common interest is most likely to be served. But Aristotle worried that democracy could turn perverse, if the *demos* became a selfish mob, which reacts without reflection and jumps to conclusions without due deliberation. At that point, one still has government by the many; however, it is no longer a democracy but is more accurately described as a "mobocracy."[11]

democracy
A government in which all citizens share power.

Ideal Types of Democracies

Aristotle's analysis about the benefits of democracy and the risks of its more perverse forms has influenced theorists and policymakers for over 2,000 years. In the modern era, democracies have taken several forms, depending upon whether the people rule directly or through a system of representation. For representative systems, theorists have debated whether representatives should mirror the voters' views exactly, or whether they should use their own judgment about the best interests of the citizens and of the country as a whole.

1.4

Compare and contrast the two types of ideal democracies.

Direct Democracy

In a **direct democracy,** all citizens participate personally in making government decisions. In ancient Athens, direct democracy meant that all free adult men with property were eligible to participate in the Assembly, which met at the center of the city on a hill called the Pnyx. There, citizens first heard speakers debate key issues and then voted on whether

direct democracy
A type of government in which all citizens participate personally in making government decisions.

Direct Democracy

Once a year, residents of hundreds of New England towns attend town meetings like this one in Brattleboro, Vermont, to deliberate and vote on local budgets and other policies.

• *How might direct democracy work in larger communities?*

to adopt certain policies. Direct democracy still exists today in many small New England towns, where community decisions are made at regular town meetings. Townspeople discuss and vote on spending, taxes, municipal rules, and other issues that may arise.

Direct democracy proponents say that citizens personally benefit by participating in democratic deliberation. Through participation and discussion, the public can reach consensus, better appreciate the differing perspectives of their fellow citizens, and become more public-spirited and community-minded. Thus, direct democracy is expected to produce both better citizens and better policies. The process of participation transforms "private into public," and "conflict into cooperation."[12]

In small towns, citizens may indeed have the opportunity to act with the reflection and deliberation that are crucial to public-spirited direct democracy, but most experts think such deliberation is impractical in large countries such as the United States. People would have to spend their entire lives attending meetings, debating, and voting in order to consider and decide all the questions that come up for their consideration.

One alternative might be to use modern technology to enact direct democracy. If tens of millions of Americans can cast their ballots for the current *American Idol* champion, why not allow them to use email, text messaging, and the Internet to deliberate and then cast their votes on pressing public policy issues? As attractive as the idea seems, the arrangement has considerable risks. Would individuals take the time needed to inform themselves and deliberate for the common good or would they just carelessly vote their "gut" reaction? Or worse, rather than deliberate, would they attack their fellow citizens by posting vicious comments such as those commonly found on political websites? Would they have enough information to make an intelligent decision, even if they wanted to reflect on the matter? Would questions be worded in such a way as to avoid skewing the answers the public gives to them (see Chapter 5)? Concerned about such issues, most political scientists feel that a direct democracy in which citizens decided policies by Internet voting would fail to encourage deliberation and would therefore be more likely to lead to a perverse democracy rather than a legitimate one.

Representative Democracy

Because of these concerns, most modern democracies are representative in nature. Citizens periodically choose **representatives** who have the authority to decide what governments do. A system of representation removes many of the practical problems of a direct democracy, but it gives rise to another concern. How can the people truly rule if they do not do so directly? In other words, how can voters maintain control over their elected representatives?

One possible answer to this question is fairly straightforward: During a campaign, candidates promise to take certain positions on key issues, and voters elect the candidate who most closely matches their preferences on those issues. While in office, the elected representative then faithfully abides by his or her campaign promises, and the process repeats itself at the next election. In order for elections to work this way, citizens must be well informed about public issues, and they must engage mostly in **prospective voting.** That is, they must look to the future while voting, taking into account each candidate's campaign promises. Each election becomes an occasion to decide the future direction of public policies. In addition, the representative must act as a **delegate,** one who reflects the opinions of those who elected him or her to office.

representatives

Individuals, periodically chosen by citizens, who have the authority to decide what governments do.

prospective voting

Voting pattern in which citizens look to the future while voting, taking into account each candidate's campaign promises; each election becomes an occasion to decide the future direction of public policies.

delegate

A representative who reflects the opinions of those who elected him or her to office.

The delegate model of representation has a long history in the United States, a nation that has always been suspicious of aloof leadership. At times, such suspicions led to suggestions that representatives should be subject to elections every year. "Where annual elections end, there slavery begins," said John Adams, who later became the second president of the United States.[13] American voters have a tradition of becoming passionately engaged in policy debates around election time. When the French scholar Alexis de Tocqueville visited the United States during the 1830s, he was astounded by the extent of popular participation. "It must be seen to be believed," he exclaimed. "No sooner do you set foot on American ground than you are stunned by a kind of tumult. . . . Almost the only pleasure an American knows is to take part in the government and discuss its measures."[14]

Critics of such a model of democracy argue that representatives who act as delegates have little opportunity to change their minds if they determine that the public good or the national interest require policies different from those that the voters endorsed in the most recent election. A state representative might have taken a "no new taxes" pledge, for example, but be faced with a budget crisis that requires new revenues. A member of Congress might have promised to slash defense spending, but a national emergency may require a larger military. According to this point of view, representatives do a disservice to the voters and their country if they hew to outdated campaign promises. Instead, they owe their **constituents,** those people legally entitled to vote for an officeholder, their informed judgment about what policies are best.

Under this model, a representative should not act as a delegate, but as a **trustee,** one who acts on behalf of the interests of the citizens rather than according to the citizens' past preferences. A representative acting as a trustee may find it necessary to explain his or her choices to constituents at the time of the next election. A voter should listen to these explanations and should engage in **retrospective voting,** looking at the results of past policies rather than guessing at which future policies are best. In essence, voters decide whether incumbents have done a good or a bad job. If the voters approve, voters reelect those who are in office; if they disapprove, they choose new leaders.

Which model of representative democracy—the delegate or the trusteeship—best approximates Aristotle's standard of a legitimate, rather than a perverse democracy? The answer to this question depends on whether you think voters or representatives are most competent to deliberate and decide on policies that are in the public interest. In a delegate model, most deliberation should occur during the campaign, where the pluses and minuses of various issue positions are debated and discussed. An informed public then chooses its representatives based on its considered judgment about which policies are best. For proponents of the delegate model, it would be foolish to allow elected politicians to decide these issues independently, because politicians left to their own devices are likely to be self-interested or even corrupt.

For proponents of the trustee model, it is the voters who are more likely to be self-interested. During the campaign, they may be distracted or uninformed, and then may vote on the basis of their own narrow interests rather than on considerations about the public good. Elected representatives, on the other hand, have the time and inclination to become well informed and to carefully consider the arguments for and against certain policies. Acting as trustees, they can legislate policies that benefit the nation as a whole, and then point out how these policies benefit voters when the next election rolls around. Proponents of the trustee model therefore argue that deliberation ought to occur mostly in the chambers of legislatures or on Capitol Hill, not during election campaigns.

constituents
Those people legally entitled to vote for an officeholder.

trustee
One who acts on behalf of the interests of the citizens rather than according to the citizens' past preferences.

retrospective voting
Voting on the basis of past policies rather than guessing at the results of future policies.

As useful as the distinction between the delegate and trustee models of representative democracy is, neither model provides an exact description of any particular system of representation. In the real world, every officeholder will in some way and on some occasions act as a delegate who abides by the views of his or her constituency. At the same time, only the most thoughtless of representatives would disregard the most urgent needs of his or her country. Similarly, the dangers of both models may be present in any system—the voters may be shortsighted and uninformed, and the elected representatives may be self-interested or corrupt.

The framers of the Constitution recognized the advantages and disadvantages of the two models, and tried to design a system that reduced the risks associated with both. To make it less likely that self-interested officeholders could do damage to the public good, the Constitution was created with a system of checks and balances that divided power among multiple officeholders chosen in different elections.[15] Power was split between the federal government and all the state governments. Within the federal government, power was further divided among the House of Representatives, the Senate, the president, and the courts. No single-minded, selfish group of "trustees" (the founders hoped) could ever gain control of all the levers of power.

To make it less likely that a large, self-interested group of voters would damage the public good, the Constitution assigned each office in the national government a separate constituency, and officeholders were to be chosen by these different constituencies at different times. The members of the House of Representatives were to be chosen by the people in elections held in districts within each state. The members of the Senate, two from each state, were to be chosen by state legislatures. The president was to be chosen by a complicated process in which each state would select electors who would vote for the president. The president would nominate the members of the Supreme Court, but the Senate would have to confirm his nominees. No single set of self-interested voters could ever elect delegates who could do swift and substantial damage to the public interest.

The framers tried to ensure that the division of power among separate constituencies and separate offices would encourage both voters and representatives to consider the public interest rather than their own selfish interests. Whether through a delegate or trustee model, or through a combination of both, the Constitution sought to devise a system of representation that would be likely to encourage a legitimate, rather than a perverse, form of democracy.

Today political commentators debate whether traditional concepts of representation still apply in the new American democracy.

1.5

Trace the evolution of the United States toward a more complex democracy that has necessitated a permanent campaign.

The New American Democracy

Both the delegate and trustee models of representation depend upon the assumption that elections and governance are separate and distinct. Although advocates of both models propose very different roles for elections and governance, in both cases an election occurs, followed by governance, followed by another election. But as political scientist Jane Mansbridge has pointed out, the modern political environment does not conform to this view of the world. Instead, elected officials remain in constant contact with their constituents, gauging their preferences, making arguments about the propriety of policies, receiving letters and emails, and taking the measure of potential challengers or interest groups that might affect the next election. In the modern era of "continuing communication and potentially changing voter preferences," argues Mansbridge, questions of representatives' accountability to voters have become more complicated.[16]

The move toward a broader and more complex democracy is partly the result of an electorate that has undergone dramatic expansions in the past century—women, minorities, and young people, all once excluded from the electorate, are now eligible to participate. But many other factors have also tightened the connection between representatives and the public.

Half-a-Million Elected Officials

Most importantly, the sheer number of elections has increased. The United States today has more elections that choose more officials for public offices than any other country on Earth. Unbelievable as it may seem, more than half-a-million people in the United States are elected officials, about 1 for every 500 Americans. If all these elected officials lived in one place, the population would exceed that of Cleveland.[17]

National elections, in which voters choose the officials of the federal government, are held every two years. These important elections determine the president, the vice president, 100 senators, and 435 members of the House of Representatives. Although national elections receive most of the media's attention, hundreds of thousands of elections occur at other levels of government.

In *state elections* the citizens of the 50 states choose their state public officials. Voters elect the governor and the state legislature in every state, and in nearly all states they elect a handful of other statewide offices such as the lieutenant governor, the treasurer, the state's attorney general, and the auditor. Finally, voters in some states elect state railroad and public utility commissioners.

The number of elections explodes when we move to *local elections*, in which officials for all governments below the state level are chosen. Voters in cities elect mayors and city councils. Voters in the more than 3,000 counties elect sheriffs, county treasurers, and county boards, among other officials. Voters select the membership of 90 percent of the nation's 16,000 school boards as well as numerous officials responsible for the governance of towns, villages, and special districts.

Even the judicial system, which is often viewed as insulated from political pressure, is permeated by elections. In 39 states, voters elect at least some judges.[18] Altogether, Americans elect more than 1,000 state judges and about 15,000 county, municipal, and other local judges and officers of the court.[19] Moreover, in recent years judges have been increasingly subject to **recall elections,** in which dissatisfied citizens try to remove incumbents from office before the completion of their terms.

recall elections
Attempts to remove incumbents from office before the completion of their terms.

Nominating Candidates and Deciding Issues

Although half-a-million elected officials sounds like a lot, there are far more elections than there are elected officials. For one thing, many officials must win not just one but two elections before they can take office. The **primary election** is a preliminary contest that narrows the number of the parties' candidates and determines who will be the nominees in the general election. Each party chooses a nominee who squares off against the nominees of other parties in the **general election.** Even in *nonpartisan elections*, where candidates do not run with party labels, primaries are sometimes used to narrow the field of candidates to just two candidates, who must then run again against each other.

primary election
A preliminary contest that narrows the number of the parties' candidates and determines who will be the nominees in the general election.

general election
Final election that selects an officeholder.

INTERNATIONAL COMPARISON

Elections in Other Democracies

In contrast to Americans, many of whom can vote more than a dozen times for scores of candidates and issues in any given four-year period, citizens of other democracies vote less frequently and for fewer offices. Consider Great Britain, which elected Tony Blair prime minister in 1997 and reelected him in 2001 and 2005. In each of these elections, Britons voted for only one person—a candidate for Parliament. These votes determined the party that had control of Parliament, and the winning party (Labour) picked the prime minister. In 2007, Gordon Brown succeeded Blair as prime minister without an election taking place—Blair simply stepped down as party leader, making way for Brown to ascend to the top post. Between the two national elections, Britons voted on only two other occasions, for only two offices—their local councilor and their representative to the European Community. Most of the other European democracies vote more often than Britain does but far less often than does the United States.

The U.S. system of elections even looks peculiar when compared to our North American neighbors. In Mexico, a presidential election is held every six years. Congressional elections are held every three years. Some Mexican states hold state and municipal elections at the same time as congressional elections, and others hold them at a different time. But at most, a Mexican citizen votes four times in a four-year period: in presidential, congressional, state, and municipal elections.

In Canada, too, provincial and municipal elections may or may not be coordinated with national elections. If the elections are not so coordinated, a Canadian votes at most three times (to elect national, provincial, and municipal officials) in a four-year period, except for an occasional referendum, such as Québec's vote on secession in 1995. Canadian officials are well aware of the contrast between the two systems. More than a decade ago former Prime Minister Jean Chrétien ruffled some American feathers when he commented that "In your system, you guys campaign for 24 hours [a day] every [day for] two years. You know, politics is one thing, but we have to run a government."[a] His observation is all the more valid today.

• *Do you believe, as Chrétien implies, that frequent elections interfere with governance? Why or why not?*

[a] David Shribman, "In Canada, the Lean Season," *Boston Globe* (May 23, 1997): A3.

---

initiative
Proposed law or state constitutional amendment placed on the ballot in response to a citizen petition.

referendum
A law or state constitutional amendment that is proposed by a legislature or other elected body but goes into effect only if approved by a specified majority of voters.

proposition
An initiative or a referendum that often provides a basis for political action.

In addition, many policy issues appear on the ballots of 27 states and the District of Columbia. There, citizens may express themselves by voting on initiatives or referenda, or both. An **initiative** is a proposed law or amendment to a state constitution placed on the ballot in response to a citizen petition. A **referendum** is a law or state constitutional amendment that is proposed by a legislature or other elected body but goes into effect only if approved by a specified majority of voters. Often lumped together as **propositions,** initiatives and referenda enable citizens to bypass or overrule elected officials and decide budgets, taxes, laws, and amendments to state constitutions directly (see the Election Voices feature on page 24).[20] Some states, such as California, frequently have more propositions on the ballot than elected offices to be filled.

Americans have become accustomed to the frequency and variety of elections, but observers from other countries are struck by Americans' repeated trips to the polls (see the *International Comparison*). Noted British analyst Anthony King argues that "American exceptionalism"—the distinctive shape of American democracy when seen from an international perspective—arises not from our culture or from our institutions, as others have argued (see Chapter 3), but rather from the multitude and frequency of our elections. King observes that

> Americans take the existence of their elections industry for granted. Some like it; others do not; most may be bored by it except in its most entertaining moments. But they are all conscious of it, in the same way that they are conscious of Mobil, McDonald's, *Larry King Live*, Oprah Winfrey, the Dallas Cowboys, Ford Motor Company, and all the other symbols and institutions that go to make up the rich tapestry of American life. In a meaningful sense, America is about the holding of elections.[21]

Permanent Campaigns

In announcing his retirement in 2010, Senator Evan Bayh (D-IN) lamented the changes that had taken place since his father was in Congress. "In my father's day," said Bayh, "you legislated for four years and campaigned for two; now it's full time. The politics never stops."[22] As elections have increased in number and frequency, campaigning for office has become virtually continuous. It is only a slight exaggeration to call the political situation in the United States a permanent campaign, because the line between running for office and governing when in office has all but disappeared. As officeholders have begun to take into account the public response to the decisions they make, representative democracy becomes more responsive than deliberative. Representatives act more as delegates than as trustees, and governing has become part of an overall campaign strategy.

In 2007 and 2008, nearly every action undertaken—or not undertaken—by Congress had the potential to become an issue in the upcoming presidential campaign. The Colombian trade agreement could not be passed because the issue had become campaign connected. And it was for election-connected reasons that Republicans and Democrats joined together to pass the tax cut expected to stimulate the economy.

As the last example suggests, the permanent campaign can at times facilitate the passage of needed policies. Yet on many other occasions it can be harmful. According to Professor Hugh Heclo, campaigns corrupt the governmental process more often than not: Public officials sacrifice the long-term good for short-term electoral advantage, they adopt adversarial rather than collaborative mindsets, and they abandon deliberation and education in favor of persuasion and selling.[23] While all that may be true, it must be admitted that officials who are constantly concerned with pleasing voters are relatively likely to be responsive representatives.

At least seven developments have contributed to permanent campaigning: the proliferation in the number of days on which elections are held, the decay of party organizations, the spread of primary elections, advances in mass communications, the explosion of interest groups, the use of scientific polling, and the increasing need for money (see Table 1.2). Together, these factors have shifted representative democracy in the United States away from deliberation and toward responsiveness.

TABLE 1.2

SEVEN KEY DEVELOPMENTS HAVE CONTRIBUTED TO THE PERMANENT CAMPAIGN

Development	Effect
Separate election days for federal, state, and local elections	Increased number of elections, shortened time between elections
Spread of primary elections	Increased number of elections, shortened time between elections
Decay of traditional party organizations	Candidates must build individualized, personal campaign organizations almost from scratch
Rise of mass communication	Candidates can communicate directly with voters, but their mistakes are easily publicized
Profusion of interest groups	Elected officials constantly being watched and their mistakes quickly publicized
Proliferation of polls	Provide constant feedback about potential election outcomes
Role of campaign money	Elected officials must spend more time fundraising

Separation of Elections   Imagine that all public officials were elected on the same day and served the same four-year term of office. There would be a long span of time between electoral contests during which no one had to think much about campaigning. Most other democracies are closer to this hypothetical scenario than to the electoral chaos that exists today in the United States.

A century ago, American officials usually *were* elected on the same day. A graduate student named Woodrow Wilson wrote in 1885 that "this is preeminently a country of frequent elections, and few states care to increase the frequency by separating elections of state from elections of national functionaries."[24] In Wilson's time, citizens of most states cast votes simultaneously for president, senator, representative, governor, mayor, state representative, state senator, city councillor, and so forth. In a few states today, voters still fill most offices on the same day, but the trend in the past half-century has been to separate election days.[25] In November of a given year, most Americans now turn out to vote for president at one general election, for governor at another, and for mayor at still another. Primary elections, as well as those for local offices, are held earlier in the election year. Initiatives and referenda may be scheduled on yet other occasions.

Thus, Americans today are called to the polls repeatedly. Rather than our imaginary Election Day that is held every four years, a conscientious citizen in California, for example, generally has to go to the polls on at least 16 separate occasions in each four-year presidential election cycle.[26] As election dates have proliferated, electioneering has become a pervasive feature of American politics. There is some campaign going on somewhere nearly all the time. There is very little "quiet time" during which there are no campaigns.

Decay of Party Organizations   Many political scientists think political parties are essential to the workings of a representative democracy. Although we cannot always detect clear differences between Republicans and Democrats, the two parties give voters a choice by offering different political philosophies. The Republican Party leans in a direction commonly called *conservative*, generally favoring smaller government, lower taxes, less regulation of business activity, and greater support for traditional family values. The Democratic Party leans in what is commonly called a *liberal* direction, usually favoring a strong federal government, more extensive social programs, more regulation, and legal accommodation for alternative lifestyles. Because party positions on issues shift only gradually, parties give continuity and familiarity to political life, making it easier for voters to make choices.

A century ago, many state and local party organizations were powerful, disciplined structures that could mobilize large numbers of voters on Election Day. Public officials relied on the parties to conduct their campaigns when election time rolled around. But governmental reforms and various social changes killed off these types of organizations (see Chapter 8). As a consequence, today's parties do not deliver the vote for all the candidates running under their label. Instead, elected officials must build individual organizations and develop *personal* constituencies to achieve election and reelection.[27]

Thus, John McCain captured the nomination of the Republican Party, despite the fact that he had been a long-term maverick disliked by key party leaders. Similarly, Barack Obama built his own grassroots organization that enabled him to win the Democratic nomination, even though the majority of party leaders felt a loyalty to Hillary Clinton, who, along with her husband, had done them many favors during the Clinton presidency. Winning from the outside would have been unthinkable a century ago when party organizations exercised a tight control over nominating conventions.

If such populist possibilities create a more exciting and dynamic electoral system, they nonetheless create a world in which public officials must constantly guard their flanks against new sources of political opposition.[28] Thus, those in office today must campaign constantly to forestall potential opposition and maintain their base of electoral support.

Spread of Primaries   In most countries, small groups of party leaders select candidates for office. A century ago, this was the standard procedure in the United States as well. Candidates were picked in "smoke-filled rooms" by party "bosses." To eliminate the corruption and unresponsiveness that often accompanied such deal making, reformers passed laws giving voters the right to select party nominees in primary elections.

Although they came into being about a century ago, primaries did not become a significant part of the presidential nominating process until after World War II. The first presidential candidate who owed his nomination in any significant degree to winning primaries was Dwight D. Eisenhower, elected in 1952. As late as 1968, the Democratic nominee, Hubert Humphrey, did not enter a single primary.

Primaries contribute substantially to today's permanent campaign. Whereas in 1968 fewer than 20 states held presidential primaries; in 2008 40 states did. Primaries shorten the time between one election and the next. As we have seen, behind-the-scenes planning for the presidential election of 2008 began the day the outcome of the 2004 election was known. Nor is the permanent campaign limited to the campaign for the White House. Some members of the House of Representatives face primaries more than six months before their two-year terms end. On May 11, 2010, for example, long-time Democratic Representative Alan Mollohan of West Virginia was defeated in a primary scarcely 16 months after his previous re-election.

Rise of Mass Communications   Techno-logical progress also has helped to make campaigns continuous. Today's candidates constantly work to get their names in the papers and their faces on television and popular websites. Moreover, cheap phone rates, email, video sharing sites, and other innovations give more opportunities for citizens and politicians to talk to each other. Dozens of cable television channels enable candidates to communicate with small, specialized audiences. C-SPAN provides continuous coverage of congressional debates, giving people outside Washington a chance to observe public officials directly. Radio talk shows have increased in popularity. Candidate and interest-group websites have proliferated. Sites such as YouTube are brim-

Dogged Coverage?
Members of the media surround the White House dog, Bo, in 2009.

• *Has constant public scrutiny made it tougher for elected officials to govern?*

ming with video snippets of politicians giving speeches, talking with voters, or making embarrassing mistakes. Conversation on the Internet, although often conspiratorial and inaccurate, is perhaps the fastest-growing mode of political communication.

The effects of technological change have been intensified by changes in the culture of the mass media. The demand for content has been greatly increased by 24-hour news services. Any move a politician makes might end up on television or online, and virtually every move a prominent politician makes is now evaluated for its political motivations and its electoral implications. Partly as a consequence of the media's insatiable appetite for news, the distinction between public and private life has eroded. The financial and medical histories of elected officials are treated as public knowledge, and reporters ask candidates almost any question imaginable, no matter how tasteless or unrelated to politics and government. For example, the *New York Times* publicized an alleged affair between John McCain and a female lobbyist, despite the fact that the two parties involved denied any relationship and no other source was able or willing to publicly provide any confirming evidence. Other media outlets gave widespread coverage to Chelsea Clinton's brusque response to a college student's question about her father's mid-1990s sexual relationship with White House intern Monica Lewinsky. All of this is justified as getting to know the candidate, or as one communications professor put it, "We like to know the character of a candidate."[29] But it is just as likely that the news organizations, free of many constraints that once limited inquiries into a candidate's personal life, are mainly seeking to titillate their audiences in order to sell more newspapers, attract more TV viewers, or get more hits on a website.

Profusion of Interest Groups   Continuous campaigning is also facilitated by an ever-growing number of interest groups, those who purport to represent their members and others with similar opinions and common interests that often provide a basis for political action. Interest groups range from business associations and trade unions to environmentalist groups and pro-choice and anti-abortion groups (see Chapter 7). Some of the old-style interest groups—business associations and trade unions, for example—have been around for a hundred years or more. But today those groups are supplemented by many newer groups that either are spin-offs of the social movements of the 1960s (the antiwar, civil rights, women's, and environmental movements) or reflect other contemporary concerns (privacy rights, homeschooling, renewable energy, immigration policy, and so forth). Computer technology has enabled many interest groups, old and new, to expand and mobilize their membership so they can have a greater impact on governmental policy. In the snail-mail era, it was far more difficult for those who shared the same interests or opinions even to locate each other, let alone to organize. Today, interest groups can monitor the actions of elected officials electronically and then post information on their websites or send blanket emails to their members and others with similar views.

Interest groups can pressure candidates running for office as well as those who have already been elected. As mentioned earlier, Clinton and Obama both had to worry about trade union opposition to foreign trade agreements that placed the jobs of some American workers into jeopardy. Days before a major series of primaries in February 2008, Numbers USA, a group opposed to amnesty for illegal immigrants, sent out an email to 1.5 million supporters that attacked McCain's sponsorship of congressional legislation allowing illegal immigrants to obtain citizenship if they satisfied certain conditions.[30]

Interest-Group Pressure

The National Abortion Rights Action League (NARAL) ran ads in an unsuccessful attempt to prevent the confirmation of John Roberts as chief justice of the U.S. Supreme Court.

• *How do you think such interest-group ads affect the way members of Congress negotiate over legislation?*

Figure shows the number of stories cited under "public opinion" in the *New York Times*. According to John Brehm, the cited public opinion stories "by and large report poll results, and are only rarely reflections on public opinion in the broader sense."

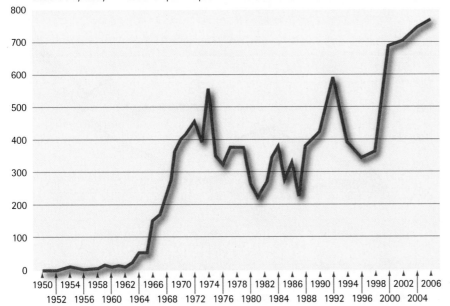

FIGURE 1.2

POLL COVERAGE HAS EXPLODED IN RECENT DECADES

Since at least 1970, news outlets have covered polls; news organizations also often conduct their own surveys and report on them.

• What do you think explains the dropoff in coverage of polls during the elections of 1984 (when Ronald Reagan won re-election) and 1996 (when Bill Clinton was re-elected)?

Proliferation of Polls   Polling contributes to the permanent campaign. When an issue or problem arises, politicians no longer wonder about the state of public opinion—the newspapers, TV channels, and political websites report it within days if not hours. Even if elected officials wanted to make decisions without thinking about their political implications, it would be difficult to do so: They are bombarded with information about political implications at every turn. As Figure 1.2 shows, the media have made public opinion a much more important part of their coverage both by sponsoring polls and by incessant reporting of polling results. As early as April 2008, one website was able to report results from no less than 106 separate national polls that had asked voters which candidate they preferred in a hypothetical race between McCain and Obama or, alternatively, a race between McCain and Clinton. That was only the tip of the iceberg, of course. In addition, polls reported opinions on the election races in each state for Republican and Democratic nominations, many campaign issues, and many congressional, state, and local races.

Leaders always have been concerned about public opinion, of course. In the closing days of the Constitutional Convention in 1787, George Washington proposed a major change in the representational scheme for the House of Representatives so that the new Constitution would stand a better chance of being ratified by the elected state conventions. During the Civil War, Abraham Lincoln waited for a military victory before he issued the Emancipation Proclamation abolishing slavery in the Confederate states, so that a happy northern public would be more inclined to support it. Politicians traditionally are portrayed as "watching which way the wind blows" and having their "ear to the ground." Until the introduction of modern polling in the 1930s, however, beliefs about the state of public opinion were only guesses. Polls have their limitations (see Chapter 5), but they undoubtedly *seem* more precise and scientific than old-fashioned guesses. It makes them all the more difficult to ignore.

FIGURE 1.3

AMERICAN ELECTIONS
HAVE BECOME MORE
EXPENSIVE IN THE PAST
FIVE DECADES

Even when controlling for inflation, the total amount spent by
political campaigns has gone up.

• *What role do you believe technological advances such as the
Internet have played in campaign
spending?*

Sources: Federal Election Commission,
"Congressional candidates raised $1.42 bil-
lion in 2007–2008," December 29, 2009,
www.fec.gov/press/press2009/
2009Dec29Cong/2009Dec29Cong.shtml,
accessed January 5, 2010; "House and
Senate Candidates Spend $936 million
During 2001–2002," June 18, 2003, www
.fec.gov/press/press2003/20030618canstat/
20030618canstat.html, accessed January 5,
2010; Herbert Alexander, *Financing the
1992 Election* (Armonk, NY: M.E. Sharpe,
1995), pp. 20, 178.

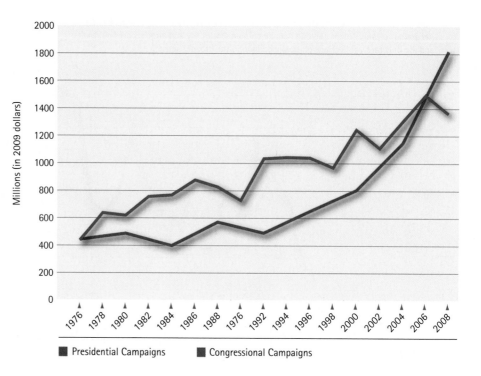

Rising Campaign Costs   Campaigning today is expensive. Polls, political consultants, and TV ads cost a great deal of money. As Figure 1.3 shows, the total costs of election campaigns have increased dramatically in the past three decades. Campaigns for the
House of Representatives, for example, were over three times more expensive in 2008
than in 1976, even after adjusting for inflation.

    Although elections may occur only every two, four, or six years, the quest for
money is continuous. One reason is that Senate races are expensive; on average, senators
must raise $27,000 every week of their six-year terms to run for reelection. United
States senators serve six-year terms, but most contemporary observers believe that the
Senate today is just as electorally sensitive as the House. One reason is that Senate races
are expensive; on average, senators must put into place a plan to raise the needed
money for the next election almost immediately after they have thanked the voters for
their election victory. Thus, the effect of the six-year term has been partially offset by
the constant quest for money.

1.6

Characterize the factors
that shift power from
the majority of voters
to specific groups.

The Power of the Few

All of these factors—more elections, weaker political parties, primary elections, relentless media coverage, intensifying group pressures, sophisticated polling, more campaign
money—have made American democracy more responsive to outside pressures. Yet
reactive democracy is not necessarily rule by the majority. Frequent elections and permanent campaigns do not guarantee that all citizens exert equal influence on their government. On the contrary, well-organized groups focused on particular issues can have
a good deal of influence, even when their views are not shared by the majority. A variety of factors—unequal participation, the way in which candidates are nominated by
their parties, the focus by voters on specific issues, inequality in campaign resources,

and poorly informed citizens—all shift power from majorities to specific groups that may be small in number but powerful in operation.

Voter Participation

In nearly all elections, most people do *not* vote (see Chapter 6). Even in the 2008 presidential election, only about 62 percent of the adult population voted. Only 37 percent voted in the 2006 congressional elections. Turnout rates in other elections are much lower—even under 10 percent in some local elections!

One vote does not count for much, but collectively the vote is an important political resource. The simple fact is that groups of people who vote at higher rates have more influence. For example, older people vote more frequently than the young or the poor.[31] Not surprisingly, programs for the elderly are therefore much better funded than programs that serve the young and the needy. Turnout is not the only explanation, of course, but elected officials naturally tend to pay greater heed to the demands of frequent voters than to those of people who do not vote.

Low Turnout

In 2006, a nonpresidential year, only 37 percent of the voting-age population made it to the polls to vote in the congressional elections.

• *Why don't more people vote?*

Nominating Candidates

Although primary elections were intended to enhance popular control, only party members can vote in these elections in many states, and the turnout for primaries everywhere is much lower than for general elections, often in single digits. Those who vote in primaries are usually more involved and more committed than citizens who do not vote. Republican primary voters tend to be more conservative than the typical American, and Democratic primary voters tend to be more liberal. To win primary elections, candidates have a strong incentive to take positions that appeal to the typical Democratic or Republican primary voter, even though these positions may seem extreme to the people who vote in general elections. As a result, elections may give middle-of-the-road Americans a choice between two unappealing candidates.

Single-Issue Voters

Suppose that there is a small group of voters—say 3 percent of the electorate—that is single-mindedly obsessed with one particular issue. The issue may be abortion or gun control or farm policy—whatever the precise subject, it is the only issue that these **single-issue voters** take into account when deciding how to vote. Suppose further that the rest of the electorate—the other 97 percent—don't care nearly as much about this issue—in particular, that it doesn't carry much weight in determining their votes.

In a situation such as this, candidates have a strong incentive to give in to the 3 percent and endorse their favored policy position—even if it conflicts with the opinion of the overwhelming majority. Such a strategy won't win the candidates a lot of votes, of course, but at least it won't cost any votes—and in a close election, 3 percent can spell the difference between victory and defeat.

single-issue voters

Voters who care so deeply about some particular issue that their votes are determined by a candidate's position on this one issue.

Local Politics

Candidates for local office can rarely afford expensive television advertising. Here, the father of a candidate volunteers his time.

• *Does a lack of media attention (and money to buy attention) mean that such races are unimportant?*

How many groups and issues resemble the circumstances just described is difficult to say. What is clear is that many interest groups try to convince candidates that their issue fits the profile: that they speak for thousands or millions of energized voters, who are just waiting to punish any candidate or officeholder who refuses to toe the line.

Campaign Resources

Modern campaigns increasingly rely on expensive hired help: consultants, pollsters, and other campaign professionals. Moreover, even in today's technologically advanced world, campaigns also require workers. Volunteers circulate petitions, stuff envelopes, knock on doors, make phone calls, stage rallies and other photo ops, and drive voters to the polls. Thus, paradoxically, a candidate who wants to win an election may, in order to acquire various kinds of essential campaign resources, take positions that are out of sync with those of the typical voter.

Other than voting, only small minorities engage in most kinds of political participation—giving money, attending campaign rallies, even displaying a campaign bumper sticker or yard sign. Those with a vested interest in a particular government program or a passion for a single issue or an extreme position on many issues are likely to be found in greater numbers among campaign donors and volunteers than they are to be found in the population as a whole. For this reason, political leaders, when responding to pressure, may pay more attention to the few than the many.

Uninformed Citizens

Most Americans pay only scant attention to debates in Congress, the details of particular issues, or even lively campaign debates (see Chapter 5). Politics often seems remote from people's everyday interests and concerns, and political controversies often are complicated and confusing. The situation is aggravated by the misleading arguments and information that are often part and parcel of the exchanges among candidates, groups, and news commentators. Influential participants in politics generally have a definite point of view, and they present the evidence consistent with what they want voters to believe. They are more like opposing lawyers trying to win a lawsuit than objective analysts of public policy issues. But, unlike lawyers in a courtroom, there is seldom a judge immediately available who can quickly correct obvious errors. Thus, there are frequent opportunities to manipulate public opinion and elections. As a result, a majority of voters may feel ill-equipped to have a strong opinion, one way or another.

1.7

Evaluate the strengths and weaknesses of the present political system in America and some of the requests for reform.

Should American Democracy Be Reformed?

Despite the power of the few over many specific issues, we should not exaggerate their control over American politics as a whole. As mentioned earlier, majorities, when they feel passionately about a question, can have a major impact. Their influence is the greatest when they feel those in power have done a bad job—failed to bring a war to a successful conclusion, left the economy in a weakened state, or behaved in a corrupt manner.

Even so, it is important to raise the question of whether the new American democracy works as well as it should. Does it result in real democratic discussion and consideration of policies? Are the outcomes that it produces likely to serve the public interest? Is the modern U.S. system an example of an effective, legitimate form of government, or does it risk becoming perverse? Continuous electioneering creates a governmental system that is unattractive in many respects. Scandals—real and trumped up—are common; inefficiency and stalemate are widespread; important problems are ignored; and actions are delayed or compromised into ineffectiveness.[32]

Most proposals for major reforms encourage further moves away from representation toward an even more direct democracy. The popular American theorist, John Dewey once said that "the cure for the ailments of democracy is more democracy," and most reformers seem to agree.[33] As the United States has moved in the direction of an inclusive, responsive democracy, there have been many indisputable improvements, not least among them the incorporation of women, minorities, and many other previously excluded groups into the mainstream of American politics. The election of a racially mixed American as president of the United States would have been inconceivable if there had not been a shift toward a new American democracy more sensitive than ever to multiple interests and concerns. But proposals to create a still more responsive democracy should be viewed cautiously. More primaries, initiatives, referenda, and recalls might only make officeholders even less reflective about the issues they are asked to consider. More open public meetings or electronic town halls might only make government by public opinion even more pervasive.

Some scholars have argued that popular influence on government may be part of the problem, not the solution.[34] For one thing, it can lead to a policy deadlock. Each public official answers to a somewhat different constituency. If all constituencies were similar, representatives would find it easier to reach agreement. But America is a diverse country, and the constituencies of elected officials reflect that diversity. People have conflicting interests and (even more important) conflicting values. Even if hundreds of officials were personally in agreement, which is unlikely, their views of governmental programs and policies often would conflict because they have an **electoral incentive**— the desire to be elected and re-elected to office—that compels them to represent the views of their different constituencies. It is impossible to reach decisions without resolving differences generated by these constituencies. Political leaders must either persuade their opponents or bargain for their support.

electoral incentive
Desire to be elected or re-elected to office.

Reforms that shift American politics in a still more reactive direction may make problems worse rather than solving them. Louder demands from an increasingly diverse public will only make problem solving more elusive. If reformers are to be effective, they must take into account the electoral incentives that public officials face, and either identify reforms that permit negotiation, bargaining, and compromise or actually change the political system so that agreement is easier to reach.

Evaluating Government

Ironically, the greater responsiveness of American government has been accompanied by a growing unease among citizens. However popular, few leaders have honeymoons that last much beyond their first few months in office. Popular evaluations soon turn sour as new problems arise, old ones resist solution, and the news media highlight failures more than successes. Certainly serious problems and unresolved conflicts exist,

Continued on page 25

Initiatives and Referenda

The Issue

Are initiatives and referenda good or bad for American democracy?

Background

As we point out in this chapter, American politics has become a "permanent campaign" in recent years. Advances in polling, interest group lobbying, and new media technology, among other factors, have ensured that elected officials are continually in the public eye. As one consultant put it, "Politicians have to assume they are on live TV all the time. You can't get away with making an offensive or dumb remark and assume it won't get out."[1]

But some activists argue that democracy works best when politicians are out of the picture altogether. They promote the institutions of direct democracy—the initiative, referendum, and recall—as a way to let the public make policies without the interference of flawed or corruptible elected officials.

In 27 states and in hundreds of local governments, citizens may alter the law through a direct popular vote. Rules vary, but measures can qualify for the ballot through a petition process (initiative) or through an act of the legislature (referendum), or through some combination of the two.[2] In 2008, California voters overturned a state court decision legalizing gay marriage, and Michigan voters legalized the use of medicinal marijuana.[3] One interpretation of direct democracy is that it takes the "delegate" model of representation to an extreme by removing the delegate from the equation altogether. "One big difference between initiatives and elected representatives," says one activist, "is that initiatives do not change their minds once you vote them in."[4]

Opposing Viewpoints on Initiatives and Referenda

Research shows that in certain cases, initiatives can educate voters, increase voter turnout, and force public officials to abide by the public's wishes.[5] Advocates of initiatives trumpet these findings, arguing that direct democracy can help produce a more informed and engaged citizenry.

> If the citizenry lacks civic virtue, that may be because it has been alienated from civic responsibility. Involving people in the process of making laws is a step in the direction of fostering public-spiritedness. By contrast, allowing people to vote only for representatives, who often duck hard choices and place their own ambitions ahead of public service, is a prescription for a selfish and apathetic citizenry.
>
> —Alan Hirsch, "Direct Democracy and Civic Maturation," *Hastings Constitutional Law Quarterly*, 29: 2 (April 2002), 185–246.

But critics argue that any pluses are swamped by minuses. Skeptics charge that policies resulting from initiatives and referenda are haphazard and contradictory, that majorities may use direct democracy to trample on minority rights, and that wealthy special interests can overwhelm opponents by spending outlandish sums of money.[6]

> Government by the initiative is not only a radical departure from the Constitution's system of checks and balances, it is also a big business, in which lawyers and campaign consultants, signature-gathering firms and other players sell their services to affluent interest groups or millionaire do-gooders with private policy and political agendas.
>
> —David Broder, *Democracy Derailed: Initiative Campaigns and the Power of Money*, (Orlando, FL: Harcourt, 2000), p. 5.

Despite these criticisms, some activists have proposed enacting a system of initiatives and referenda nationwide. If that were to take place, the move away from a deliberative model of democracy would surely accelerate.

What Do You Think?

1. Do initiatives and referenda enhance or detract from American democracy?

2. Are certain kinds of issues better decided by initiatives and referenda, and certain kinds of issues better decided by elected officials? Which types of issues fall into each category?

On the Web

For more on the debate over direct democracy, see the following websites:

PRO

The National Initiative for Democracy proposes a nationwide direct democracy system.

http://ni4d.us

The Initiative and Referendum Institute at the University of Southern California documents all aspects of direct democracy in the United States.

www.iandrinstitute.org

CON

The National Conference of State Legislators released a report in 2002 arguing that "representative democracy is more desirable than the initiative." The organization suggests reforms for states with existing direct democracy systems.

www.ncsl.org/programs/legman/irtaskfc/
IandR_report.pdf

[1]Howard Wolfson, senior adviser to Senator Hillary Rodham Clinton, quoted in Ryan Lizza, "The YouTube Election," *New York Times* (August 20, 2006), Section 4: 1.
[2]See "I & R Factsheet Number One," The Initiative and Referendum Institute, available at www.iandrinstitute.org, accessed August 22, 2006.

[3]Initiative and Referendum Institute, Ballotwatch, 2008 No. 3, November, available at www.iandrinstitute.org/BW%202008-3%20Results%20v4.pdf, accessed January 5, 2010.
[4]Grover Norquist, President, Americans for Tax Reform, quoted in "Statements Regarding the Initiative and Referendum Process," Initiative and Referendum Institute, available at www.iandrinstitute.org, accessed August 22, 2006.
[5]Elisabeth Gerber, "Legislative Response to the Threat of Popular Initiatives," *American Journal of Political Science*, 40: 1 (February 1996): 99–128; Mark A. Smith, "The Contingent Effects of Ballot Initiatives and Candidate Races on Turnout," *American Journal of Political Science*, 45: 3 (July 2001): 700–706; and Mark A. Smith, "Ballot Initiatives and the Democratic Citizen," *Journal of Politics*, 64: 3 (August 2002): 892–903.
[6]On this last point, see Barbara Gamble, "Putting Civil Rights to a Popular Vote," *American Journal of Political Science* 41: 1 (January 1997): 245–269.

Continued from page 23

but critics often apply unrealistic standards of evaluation. An old maxim states that "the best is the enemy of the good." Any policy or institution falls short when judged against some abstract ideal standard. Perfection does not exist in the real world.

Consider that, throughout history and continuing today, tens of millions of people left family and country behind to start over in the United States. Across the entire sweep of human history, most governments have been controlled by one or a few. Many were tyrannical: A government that did not murder and rob its subjects was about as good a government as people could hope for. Nor are tyrannical governments just a matter of ancient history. Today only a bare majority of the world's population lives under governments that can reasonably be considered democratic, and in the twentieth century alone, governments caused the deaths of 170 million people, *not including wars*.[35] In recent years, Americans have watched in horror as civil war or genocide has erupted in Iraq, Afghanistan, Sudan, Northern Ireland, Cambodia, Azerbaijan, Bosnia, Rwanda, Burundi, Chechnya, Albania, Zaire, Kosovo, East Timor, Sierra Leone, and Guinea. Official tyranny—and worse—remains a contemporary reality.

To be sure, Americans should not set too low a standard for their political life. No one would seriously argue that Americans should be satisfied just because their country has not dissolved into warring factions. But even compared to other advanced democracies the United States often fares better than many think. Critics cherry-pick their comparisons, selectively citing statistics that show that the United States is worse than Germany in one respect, worse than Japan in another regard, worse than Sweden in still some other ways, and so on. But is there persuasive evidence that any other government of a large country works better all around? We think not. This positive judgment certainly should not discourage us from continuing to strive for a better government, but it should remind us that we are striving for levels of achievement never yet attained by real governments responsible for large populations. Only when comparing the United States with other countries do we see that American democracy, for all its faults, has extraordinary strengths as well.

Defenders of democracy often cite Winston Churchill's remark that "democracy is the worst form of government except all those other forms that have been tried."[36] Churchill's observation applies with special force to the new American democracy, which carries this form of government toward its popular extreme. Citizens of the

United States enjoy rights and privileges that citizens in many other countries only dream of. Not only can American citizens vote more often, but they can also speak their minds more freely, find out more easily what their government is doing, and deal with a government less likely to discriminate against them on the basis of race, religion, gender, social status, sexual orientation, or anything else.

Citizens of the United States have enjoyed a government that has a better record than most at protecting them against foreign aggression while usually avoiding unwise involvement in foreign conflicts. On average, citizens of the United States are wealthier than citizens of any other comparably large country. They are better housed, better fed, and better clothed. Compared with residents of most other countries, they enjoy better communications, a better transcontinental highway system than Europe or Asia, more advanced medical services, and safer working conditions. Their physical environment is more protected against degradation. Even the large fiscal deficits that have caused political controversies since the 1980s compare favorably to the deficits of most other industrial countries. The United States, for all its problems, has as good a government as exists anywhere, and a better one than most.

Of course, the United States is not the best at everything. Economic inequality and poverty rates are higher in the United States than in countries with comparable living standards. More homeless people are visible in city streets in the United States than in other industrialized countries—a sign that the country's safety net has large holes.[37] More people lack access to adequate medical care than in other developed democracies (though for those who do have access, the quality of American medical care is superior to that in any other country). More people are murdered and more are imprisoned in the United States than in almost any other industrialized country. Just why the United States does poorly at some things and well at others will be among the topics considered in the chapters that follow.

CHAPTER SUMMARY

1.1 **Analyze the on-going role that free elections play in the governmental process and the power it gives those who participate.**

Elections have always been a prominent feature of American democracy, but the connections between elections and governance have been increasingly tightened. Elections affect government even when Election Day is far away because elected officials must continually anticipate how voters will react to their actions.

1.2 **Illustrate the reasons for the existence of government and identify its key functions.**

The fundamental feature of politics is that government is legitimate coercion. Because government can force citizens to act in specific ways, all citizens need to be skeptical of those who have the authority to compel others to behave in certain ways.

1.3 **Assess the strengths and weaknesses of the major types of government.**

Over the span of human history, governments have taken many forms. Some have been government by one (monarchies and tyrannies), others have been government by the few (aristocracies and oligarchies), and, finally, some have been government by the many (democracies and mobocracies).

1.4 **Compare and contrast the two types of ideal democracies.**

Democracies can be direct or representative. The United States is a representative democracy that originally blended two models of representation (delegate and trustee models) by arranging for elected officials to have different constituencies, and by allowing institutions to check one another.

1.5 Trace the evolution of the United States toward a more complex democracy that has necessitated a permanent campaign.

Candidates today, in order to hold and retain office, must win both primary elections held by their own political party and general elections in which candidates from all parties compete. Changing technologies in mass communications and public-opinion polling have helped bring this about. Institutional changes have also contributed, especially the weakening of political parties, the proliferation of primary elections, and the separation of election days. Social changes, such as the explosion of organized interests, have also played a role. And candidates' increased need for money has contributed to the permanent campaign, as well.

1.6 Characterize the factors that shift power from the majority of voters to specific groups.

The permanent campaign does not necessarily mean that majorities always rule. Unequal participation, the candidate selection process, single issue voters, and inequality in information and other resources can give minorities power disproportionate to their numbers.

1.7 Evaluate the strengths and weaknesses of the present political system in America and some of the requests for reform.

In weighing the costs and benefits of this shift away from a deliberative toward a responsive democracy, it is not easy to decide which way the balance tips. Pervasive elections and electioneering change the way the government does business: It is more difficult to plan for the long run, and it seems harder to find acceptable compromises. Yet the advantages of more widespread participation are clear as well. The needs of once-excluded groups now are given more consideration. Citizens' concerns quickly become public issues. Imperfect as they are, American political institutions are still the envy of much of the world.

---

mypoliscilab EXERCISES

Apply what you learned in this chapter on MyPoliSciLab.

Read on mypoliscilab.com
eText: Chapter 1

Study and Review on mypoliscilab.com
Pre-Test
Post-Test
Chapter Exam
Flashcards

Watch on mypoliscilab.com
Video: Mexico Border Security
Video: The Bailout Hearings
Video: Vaccines: Mandatory Protection

Explore on mypoliscilab.com
Timeline: Initiatives and Referendums
Timeline: Major Technological Innovations that Have Changed the Political Landscape

---

KEY TERMS

aristocracy, p. 8
constituents, p. 11
delegate, p. 10
democracy, p. 9
direct democracy, p. 9
electoral incentive, p. 23
general election, p. 13

government, p. 7
initiative, p. 14
majority, p. 5
oligarchy, p. 9
permanent campaign, p. 5
primary election, p. 13
proposition, p. 14

prospective voting, p. 10
recall elections, p. 13
referendum, p. 14
representatives, p. 10
retrospective voting, p. 11
single-issue voters, p. 21
trustee, p. 11

SUGGESTED READINGS

Of General Interest

Blumenthal, Sidney. *The Permanent Campaign*. New York: Simon & Schuster, 1982. A classic describing the electioneering side of the new American democracy.

Bok, Derek. *The Trouble with Government*. Cambridge, MA: Harvard University Press, 2001. Comprehensive analysis of the pros and cons of modern government in the United States.

Downs, Anthony. *An Economic Theory of Democracy*. New York: Harper, 1957. Seminal theoretical discussion of how elections shape the activities of voters, candidates, parties, and interest groups.

King, Anthony. *Running Scared: Why Politicians Spend More Time Campaigning Than Governing*. New York: Free Press, 1996. Provocative study by a British political scientist who shows how elections shape contemporary American politics.

Morone, James A. *The Democratic Wish*. Rev. ed. New Haven: Yale University Press, 1998. Brilliant historical analysis that shows how Americans have long tried to cure the ills of democracy by extending citizen participation.

Stanley, Harold, and Richard Niemi. *Vital Statistics on American Politics 2009–2010*. Washington, DC: CQ Press, 2010. Indispensable source of facts and figures about American government and politics.

Focused Studies

Chubb, John, and Paul Peterson, eds. *Can the Government Govern?* Washington, DC: The Brookings Institution, 1989. Hoary old collection of essays on the problems of governing a democracy that is moving in the popular direction.

Dahl, Robert. *Who Governs?* New Haven, CT: Yale University Press, 1961. Although it is a study of politics in New Haven, Connecticut, this classic shows more generally how elections shape power and influence.

Edwards, George C. III *Governing by Campaigning: The Politics of the Bush Presidency*. New York: Pearson Longman, 2007. Contemporary study of the Bush Presidency that argues that Bush chose the permanent campaign as his governing strategy.

Schier, Steven E. *By Invitation Only: The Rise of Exclusive Politics in the United States*. Pittsburgh: University of Pittsburgh Press, 2000. Argument that parties, interest groups, and candidates have switched in recent years from broad-based mobilization of voters to targeted "activation" of select portions of the public.

ON THE WEB

The Internet allows citizen activists, interest groups, and government agencies to disseminate more and more political information. Given that elections are the main focus of this textbook, here are four sites that can help citizens make sense of the vast amount of information in elections.

www.dnet.org

www.vote-smart.org

The Democracy Network and Project Votesmart are excellent, nonpartisan resources for learning about federal candidates' positions and records of public service. The Votesmart surveys of candidate positions (NPAT) are especially helpful for determining where your representatives stand on the issues.

www.fec.gov

The Federal Election Commission is responsible for monitoring federal elections. Its site links to candidate and interest-group financial filings, analysis of recent spending and fundraising in elections, and descriptions of current campaign finance law.

www.tray.com

Political Moneyline is a private watchdog organization that links to much the same information as the FEC, though in a somewhat more user-friendly—and opinionated—fashion. It is particularly useful for finding donors to campaigns and how much they donated.

2 Establishing a Constitutional Democracy

CHAPTER OUTLINE

LEARNING OBJECTIVES

2.1   Explain the reasons for the spread of democratic ideals before and during the Revolutionary War.

2.2   Identify the weaknesses of the Articles of Confederation and illustrate how they led to the drafting of a new Constitution.

2.3   Analyze the key proposals made by Constitutional Convention delegates and the major components of the final document.

2.4   Outline the process for amending the Constitution and identify the liberties that the amendments have strengthened.

2.5   Evaluate the strengths and the weaknesses of the U.S. Constitution in both historical and contemporary context.

The First National Election

Although the United States Constitution is revered today, many Americans were skeptical of the document when it emerged from the secretive Constitutional Convention in September 1787. The new plan's supporters were by no means assured of victory, and they succeeded only because they provided strong leadership, mobilized voters, sidestepped obstacles, and crafted powerful arguments in favor of ratifying (approving) the document.

In 1787 and 1788, in what might be called the first U.S. national election, voters chose delegates to ratification conventions in each of the 13 states. If nine of the 13 states approved the proposed constitution, its supporters asserted, it would become the law of the land.

In newspaper editorials, debates, and public rallies, the **Federalists** (page 32), those who wrote and campaigned for ratification of the Constitution, clashed with opponents, who called themselves **Anti-Federalists** (page 32). Each side argued that its position was in the best interests of the voters.

Anti-Federalists appealed to voters' suspicions about the structure of the new system. They claimed that a strong national government would lead to suppression of the rights of states and of individual citizens. In Virginia, the eminent American patriot Patrick Henry sounded the alarm. "I conceive the republic to be in extreme danger," he warned. "Here is a revolution as radical as that which separated us from Great Britain. . . . [O]ur rights and privileges are endangered, and the sovereignty of the States [shall] be relinquished. . . .The rights of conscience, trial by jury, liberty

of the press, all pretensions to human rights and privileges, are rendered insecure, if not lost."[1]

Like Henry, many opponents of ratification claimed to represent the interests of average people. Some wrote anonymous pamphlets and editorials under humble pseudonyms such as "A Federal Farmer," "A Son of Liberty," "A Citizen," and "A Countryman."[2] Federalists, while never conceding that the plan was bad for common farmers, appealed to different concerns of the voters, stressing that the new system and its strengthened central government would resolve costly economic conflicts among states and would enable the United States to negotiate more effectively with foreign countries.

Without a strong union, Alexander Hamilton of New York argued, even as minor an issue as payment of the nation's Revolutionary War debt could lead to disaster. States would disagree about who should bear the burden of repayment, while impatient foreign creditors might decide to make war on the young country: "The peace of the States would be hazarded to the double contingency of external invasion and internal contention."[3]

With energy and organization on their side, the Federalists easily won the first rounds in the ratification struggle. Conventions in four of the smaller states (Delaware, New Jersey, Georgia, and Connecticut) voted to ratify the document within just a few months.[4] Influenced by elder statesman Ben Franklin's prestige and some strong-arm tactics, Pennsylvania also quickly approved. Massachusetts signed on as well, after Federalists promised

TABLE 2.1
VOTING OF DELEGATES AT CONSTITUTIONAL RATIFYING CONVENTIONS

Article VII of the Constitution provided that "The Ratifications of the Conventions of nine States, shall be sufficient for the Establishment of this Constitution."

- *Why do you think the founders settled on nine states instead of all 13? Or just seven?*

State	Date	"Yes" Votes/"No" Votes
Delaware	Dec. 7, 1787	30/0
Pennsylvania	Dec. 11, 1787	46/23
New Jersey	Dec. 18, 1787	38/0
Georgia	Jan. 2, 1788	26/0
Connecticut	Jan. 9, 1788	128/40
Massachusetts	Feb. 6, 1788	187/168
Maryland	Apr. 26, 1788	63/11
South Carolina	May 23, 1788	149/73
New Hampshire	June 21, 1788	57/47
Virginia	June 25, 1788	89/79
New York	July 26, 1788	30/27
North Carolina	Nov. 21, 1789	194/77
Rhode Island	May 29, 1790	34/32

Source: Lauren Bahr and Bernard Johnson, eds., *Collier's Encyclopedia*, vol. 7 (New York: P. F. Collier, 1992), p. 239.

to add a Bill of Rights. By the end of 1788, Federalists had persuaded 11 of the 13 states to ratify the Constitution, and in February 1789 Revolutionary War hero George Washington was elected president. North Carolina ratified later that year. Rhode Island, which had refused even to send delegates to the Constitutional Convention, finally gave its grudging approval on May 29, 1790 (see Table 2.1).

At the time the Constitution was adopted, the United States was not a modern democracy. For example, only male property owners ("freeholders") could vote in the election of delegates to most ratifying conventions. Yet the provisions in the Constitution had to win the approval of a wide variety of these voters. Those who wrote the Constitution had to be sensitive to regional differences, immediate governmental needs, and inherited political traditions. In this sense, the Constitution was not the product of a secretive meeting of men in Philadelphia but was, rather, the work of all those who voted in the first national election. As James Madison, a key participant in the Constitutional Convention, said years later, "Whatever veneration might be entertained for the body of men who formed our Constitution, . . . it was nothing more than the draft of a plan, nothing but a dead letter, until life and validity were breathed into it by the voice of the people, speaking through the several State Conventions."[5]

Making the Connection

In this chapter, we consider the circumstances surrounding the drafting of the **Constitution,** the basic governing document of the United States. We also discuss its historical context, as well as several key problems and many significant successes associated with the document over the centuries since it went into effect.

Federalists

Those who wrote and campaigned for ratification of the Constitution.

Anti-Federalists

Those who opposed ratification of the Constitution.

Constitution

Basic governing document of the United States.

Although campaigning has become more pervasive in recent American politics, it is important to remember that elections have always played a key role in U.S. governance. The Constitution's authors drafted the document to win the support of the electorate in the late 1780s. Representatives at special state conventions were charged with accepting or rejecting the Constitution, and the voters who elected them were guided by their own practical interests, as well as by commonly accepted political theories and the colonial experience. In the pages that follow, you will learn about these interests, theories, and experiences in greater detail. Finally, you will learn about how well the Constitution has stood the test of time, and how it can be changed.

2.1

Explain the reasons for the spread of democratic ideals before and during the Revolutionary War.

The Colonial and Revolutionary Era

When delegates to the state conventions debated the Constitution in 1787, they drew on lessons from nearly two centuries of colonial history. Beginning in the 1600s, European settlers had brought with them political theories and methods of governance that later colonists adapted and extended on the basis of their own needs and experiences. In this section, we review the nature of early colonial political systems, discuss how democratic ideals spread before and during the Revolution, and describe the state of political thought at the dawn of U.S. independence.

The Colonial Experience with Democracy

Although the United States would become the modern world's first large, stable democracy, colonists first arrived as part of a failed business venture. In 1584, the British "Virgin Queen" Elizabeth granted Sir Walter Raleigh the right (a "charter") to explore and colonize a portion of the New World. Raleigh's attempts to establish a permanent colony came to nothing, although he succeeded in naming his territory "Virginia," after his benefactress. Years later, the Virginia Company, a group of investors who had inherited Raleigh's charter, made another attempt to found a profitable settlement. This colony, named Jamestown after King James, who had succeeded Elizabeth in 1603, was notable because it was there, in 1619, that settlers elected the first representative assembly in American colonial territory. Any semblance of self-government was short-lived, however, because in 1624 James reclaimed the territory from the now-bankrupt Virginia Company.[6] Like most monarchs at the time, James claimed to rule by **divine right,** a doctrine stating that God selects the sovereign for the people. Virginia became a **royal colony,** one governed by the king's representative with the assembly's advice.

divine right

Doctrine that says God selects the sovereign for the people.

royal colony

Colony governed by the king's representative with the advice of an elected assembly. See *proprietary colony*.

A small group of religious dissenters, now remembered as the Pilgrims, intended to sail to Virginia in 1620. After their ship, the *Mayflower*, was blown off course and arrived in what today is Provincetown, Massachusetts, the Pilgrims found that they lacked a clear governmental framework. Rejecting the divine right of kings, they believed that individuals should decide both religious and political matters for themselves. Their first political decision is still revered as the beginning of the democratic experiment in America. Before leaving the ship, the Pilgrims signed the **Mayflower Compact,** the first document in colonial America in which the people gave their express consent to be governed. The Pilgrims promised to "covenant and combine ourselves together into a civil Body Politick, for our better Ordering and Preservation."[7] The principle that

Mayflower Compact

First document in colonial America in which the people gave their express consent to be governed.

government resulted from the people's consent was thus established from the very beginning of colonial settlement.

Governance of the Colonies   As European settlement spread across the eastern shores of the North American continent, so did practical matters of politics and governance. Many colonies were initially organized as **proprietary colonies,** governed either by a prominent English noble (the proprietor) or by a company. Settlements organized by companies, such as the Jamestown colony, were founded almost exclusively for economic gain. But several of the most successful colonies, such as the Pilgrims' settlement in Massachusetts and the Maryland colony established for Catholics by Lord Baltimore, were founded as havens for the practice of particular religious beliefs. The more economically motivated of the proprietary colonies often ran into political difficulties and were eventually reorganized as royal colonies, such as Virginia. On the eve of the Revolution, nine of the 13 had become royal colonies.

In both proprietary and royal colonies, power was divided between the governor (appointed by either the proprietor or the king) and a two-chamber legislature. The **colonial assembly** was the lower legislative chamber elected by male property owners in the colony. The **colonial council** was the upper legislative chamber appointed by British officials upon the recommendation of the governor.

Governors could veto any measure passed by the legislature, but usually, instead of vetoing legislation, they maintained support in the assembly by means of their **patronage** power—the power to hand out jobs and benefits. Governors appointed their political supporters as sheriffs, judges, justices of the peace, militia officers, magistrates, and clerks. In Massachusetts, for example, 71 percent of the members of the 1763 assembly were simultaneously justices of the peace, giving "the Governors vast Influence."[8]

Although the governors' patronage influenced colonial assemblies, the assemblies held the power to levy taxes. They used this key authority to broaden their influence, often obtaining financial control of the salaries of the governor and his appointed officials.[9] The men elected to assemblies were usually esteemed members of the community. For example, Thomas Jefferson won both public respect and election to the Virginia assembly after persuading his fellow farmers to work together and clear the Rivanna River, making it navigable for their common benefit.[10] As the power of the elected colonial assemblies grew, the colonial councils appointed by the governors lost prestige and authority, gradually becoming little more than advisory bodies.

Voting Qualifications   Although the assemblies were gaining control over colonial affairs, they were not democratic in the modern sense of the word. Women, slaves, and indentured servants were excluded from the voting rolls. Even male white voters usually had to meet property qualifications: In Virginia, they had to own 25 acres and a house. In Maryland and Pennsylvania, voters needed to be worth 50 acres or 40 pounds. And in Connecticut, prospective voters not only had to own property, but also had to demonstrate that they were "civil in conversation."[11] By 1750, these and other restrictions denied the vote to as much as one-quarter to one-half of the male population.[12]

The Spread of Democratic Ideals During the Revolutionary War

The struggle for independence reinforced the democratic practices that had evolved in the colonial period.[13] Liberties that the colonists had taken for granted now had to be

proprietary colony
Colony governed either by a prominent English noble or by a company. See *royal colony*.

colonial assembly
Lower legislative chamber elected by male property owners in a colony.

colonial council
Upper legislative chamber whose members were appointed by British officials upon the recommendation of the governor.

patronage
Appointment of individuals to public office in exchange for their political support. Widely practiced in the eighteenth and nineteenth centuries and continues to present day.

defended against the fearsome power of the British king. The revolutionary struggle was set in motion with opposition to a tax, swelled into a question of rights and representation, and finally led to a Declaration of Independence cast in language that would shape American politics for centuries to come.

Taxation Without Representation   The revolutionary movement would eventually become a struggle for citizen rights and liberties, but it began as a tax revolt. Beset with rising military expenses, the British government decided to ask the colonists to pay the cost of keeping troops in the colonies—troops that were needed to defend against potential attacks by both American Indian tribes and French and Spanish soldiers. In 1765, the British Parliament imposed a **stamp tax,** which required that colonists purchase a small stamp to be affixed to pamphlets, playing cards, dice, newspapers, marriage licenses, and other legal documents. To the British, the stamp tax seemed reasonable—after all, colonial taxes were lower than those the British themselves paid. But to the colonists, who had never before paid a direct tax, it was an outrageous imposition by King George III on a free people.

Colonial leaders opposed what they called **taxation without representation,** the levying of taxes by a government in which the people are not represented by their own elected officials. To organize their protest, nine colonies sent delegates to a **Stamp Act Congress** in New York, which became the first political organization that brought together leaders from throughout the colonies for a common purpose.

The Stamp Act Congress gave clear expression to the American demand for representative government. One of its resolutions boldly proclaimed "that the only Representatives of the People of these Colonies are Persons chosen therein by themselves, and that no Taxes . . . can be Constitutionally imposed on them, but by their respective Legislature."[14] In Boston, a group of citizens calling themselves the Sons of Liberty decided to enforce the resolutions of the Stamp Act Congress. They hung in effigy the city's proposed tax collector and then looted his home—and that of the lieutenant governor for good measure. As violence spread throughout the colonies, some frightened tax collectors resigned their positions, others refused to take their places, and colonial assemblies banned the importation of English goods. Patrick Henry, one of the more outspoken members of the Virginia assembly, shouted, "Caesar had his Brutus; Charles the First his Cromwell; and George the Third [here the speaker of the assembly cried "Treason!"] may profit by their example. If this be treason, make the most of it."[15] In the face of a tax revolt inspired by rhetoric that compared King George with rulers who were overthrown and killed, the Stamp Act became unenforceable, and within a year the British Parliament repealed the legislation.

The British ignored the American demands for representation. They also unwisely replaced the stamp tax with a tax on tea, arousing passions even further. Colonists were urged on by leaders such as John Hancock and Samuel Adams, who began calling themselves **Patriots,** a political group defending American liberties against British infringements. In 1773, many Patriots organized the Boston Tea Party, a nighttime foray in which protesters disguised as American Indians dumped chests of tea into the city's harbor. Outraged at this lawlessness, Parliament punished the Bostonians by shutting down democratic institutions in the Massachusetts colony. It withdrew the colony's charter, closed its colonial assembly, banned town meetings, blockaded Boston's harbor, and strengthened the armed garrison stationed in the city.

stamp tax
Passed by Parliament in 1765, it required colonists to purchase a small stamp to be affixed to legal and other documents.

taxation without representation
Levying of taxes by a government in which the people are not represented by their own elected officials.

Stamp Act Congress
A meeting in 1765 of delegates from nine colonies to oppose the Stamp Act; the first political organization that brought leaders from several colonies together for a common purpose.

Patriots
Political group defending colonial American liberties against British infringements.

Patrick Henry Addresses the Virginia Assembly

Known for the famous 1775 speech in which he demanded liberty or death, Patrick Henry of Virginia later became a critic of the Constitution during the debate over ratification.

• *Considering his commitment to liberty, why was Henry suspicious of the Constitution?*

The Continental Congresses   The Patriots responded in 1774 by organizing the **First Continental Congress,** the first quasi-governmental institution that spoke for nearly all the colonies. Attended by delegates from 12 of the 13 colonies, the Continental Congress issued a statement of rights and called for a boycott of British goods, a measure the Patriots hoped would hurt the British economy. In Massachusetts, Patriots stockpiled guns and trained volunteers in military exercises.

First Continental Congress
Organized in 1774, the first quasi-governmental institution that spoke for nearly all the colonies.

To put down the rising insurrection, British soldiers marched from Boston Harbor on April 19, 1775, in search of weapons hidden in the nearby countryside. Warned by Boston silversmith Paul Revere that British Redcoats were approaching, 600 Patriots at Concord fired shots that poet Ralph Waldo Emerson would later write were "heard round the world." Certainly, word of the shots spread rapidly throughout the colonies, even to the Virginia assembly, where Patrick Henry cried, "Give me liberty, or give me death." Delegates from all 13 colonies soon journeyed to Philadelphia to participate in the **Second Continental Congress,** the political authority that, beginning in 1775, directed the struggle for independence. On July 4, 1776, the Continental Congress issued a **Declaration of Independence,** the document asserting the political independence of the United States of America from Great Britain. For seven long years the Patriots valiantly fought the British soldiers. Meanwhile, many **Tories,** colonists who opposed independence, lost their property and were imprisoned or chased from the colonies; some 80,000 fled to London, Nova Scotia, or the West Indies. In 1783, the British recognized American independence in the Treaty of Paris.

Second Continental Congress
Political authority that directed the struggle for independence beginning in 1775.

Declaration of Independence
Document signed in 1776 asserting the political independence of the United States from Great Britain.

Tories
Those colonists who opposed independence from Great Britain.

The Theory of Rights and Representation

The democratic experiment had officially begun, the new nation having committed itself to government by the people. Americans transformed colonial practice into a political doctrine stating that if governments are to be legitimate, they must be headed by leaders who have been chosen in elections.

No single document better expresses the democratic spirit that animates American politics than the Declaration of Independence. Written mainly by Thomas Jefferson, it both denounced King George III and expressed the country's commitment to certain

Leviathan

Thomas Hobbes (1588–1679) thought that humans are by nature warlike and selfish. His treatise *Leviathan* held that the only way to maintain human society was for individuals to consent to rule by a single, all-powerful leader or government.

• *Do you think that people are basically selfish? If so, does democracy function in spite of, or because of, this basic selfishness? How did Locke modify Hobbes's theory?*

separation of powers

A system of government in which different institutions exercise the different components of governmental power.

democratic principles. The Declaration asserts that God gave people the rights to "life, liberty, and the pursuit of happiness." People create governments so that these fundamental rights may be preserved and protected. If a government fails to safeguard these rights, however, the people may and should abolish the old government and create a new one. (See Appendix I for the full text of the Declaration of Independence.)

The Declaration of Independence "epitomizes and summarizes" a train of political thought that originated in England.[16] By the time of the Revolution, political thinkers who influenced the Patriots had long discarded the notion that kings had a God-given right to rule. In place of divine right stood three principles:

1. Government arises from the consent of the governed.
2. Power should be divided among separate institutions.
3. Citizen rights must be protected.

Each of these principles would shape the writing of the Constitution.

Consent of the Governed   As early as 1651, Thomas Hobbes, England's greatest political theorist, said that kings governed not by divine right but by the consent of the governed. People form a government because, without a government, they live in a chaotic state of nature in which there is a "war of all against all." Without a government, everyone must resort to violence simply to avoid being a victim. Life becomes "solitary, poor, nasty, brutish and short." Hobbes argued that only a sovereign king with absolute power can prevent the war of all against all. If power is divided among more than one person, conflict among them becomes inevitable.[17] People consent to be governed by one all-powerful ruler because the alternatives are too terrible to contemplate.

Separation of Powers   Accept Hobbes's premise that individuals are selfish and short-sighted, and his conclusion that the people readily consent to be ruled by an absolute sovereign seems almost inevitable. But the pragmatic English theorist John Locke shunned Hobbes's uncompromising defense of absolute kingly power. Writing in 1690, Locke agreed that government arises from the consent of the people, but he rejected Hobbes's conclusion that an all-powerful ruler was the only stable system.[18] Instead, Locke argued that governmental power took several different forms, each requiring a different institution. A country's founders should create a **separation of powers,** a system of government in which different institutions exercise the various components of governmental power. Locke thought each institution should be constituted as follows:

1. *Legislative power*, the making of law, to be exercised by an assembly with two chambers, the upper chamber consisting of the aristocracy and the lower chamber chosen by the people.
2. *Executive power*, the enforcement of law, to be exercised by a single person, often a king.

Nearly 60 years after Locke's writings, the French philosopher Charles de Secondat, Baron de Montesquieu, added a third institution:

3. *Judicial power*, the application of law to particular situations, exercised by independent judges.

Great political theorists often come to conclusions that differ very little from existing governmental practice. So it was with Locke, who set forth a theory that closely resembled English government. England had a legislature or parliament consisting of two chambers: the House of Lords (representing the aristocracy) and the House of Commons (representing the people). Executive power was exercised by the king. The House of Lords appointed the judges.

Cynics have said that the English discovered Locke's wisdom before he set it down on paper. More accurately, Locke's genius consisted of making theoretical sense of English practice, giving the English an enlightened way of thinking about a government that had evolved haphazardly over many centuries.

Citizen Rights and Representation   Not long after Locke wrote, British practice changed. Instead of being separated among the three branches, power became concentrated in a small group of ministers drawn from Parliament but appointed by the king. These ministers, who owed their livelihoods to the monarch, were naturally reluctant to criticize him.[19]

This system provoked intense opposition from a group known as **Whigs,** who attacked it as hopelessly corrupt and developed a counter-theory of citizen rights and representation. To the Whigs, a formal division of powers was not enough to ensure the security of the people. After all, in Great Britain powers were divided in principle, but concentrated in practice. Instead, Whigs argued, citizens themselves should be given increased power over the government. James Harrington, the Whigs' most influential thinker, argued that a centralized parliament should not exercise control over a large nation. Instead, Harrington favored small self-governing republics (cities governed by virtuous citizen leaders), each of which would protect the freedoms of its own people. In place of officeholders beholden to the king, he called for leaders to be elected for short periods of time. In place of an aristocracy of birth, he said ordinary citizens should choose to be governed by the most virtuous among them.[20]

> **Whigs**
> Political opposition in eighteenth-century England that developed a theory of citizen rights and representation.

Whig criticism of the British government made sense to many American colonists. The rough equality of colonial America stood in sharp contrast to the court intrigues in London. Colonial leaders thought of themselves as a natural aristocracy distinct from the inherited nobility in Britain. The more Parliament imposed taxes and interfered in colonial affairs, the more illegitimate and corrupt the English system appeared.

The Whig theory of rights and representation took its most forceful and popular form in *Common Sense*, written by Thomas Paine, a native Englishman who had immigrated to the colonies. Filled with heated rhetoric and widely read among Patriots in the months before the Declaration of Independence, the book declared kingship to be "the most bare-faced falsity ever imposed on mankind." Instead of contributing to peace, as Hobbes had claimed, a hereditary monarchy "makes against it." Peaceful government is better achieved by representatives "who . . . have the same concerns at stake" as the people. If elections were frequent, representatives would establish a "common interest with every part of the community."[21]

Still, the Whigs and their American followers were not modern-day democrats. Although they advanced a doctrine of rights and representation that was more participatory than that of previous theorists, they believed that only male property owners had the necessary virtues to be good citizens. Aside from philosopher and poet Alexander Pope, who blithely observed that "Most women have no characters at all," few theorists of the era bothered to explain why women could not be full citizens. But such views were so widespread that English author Mary Wollstonecraft, writing in 1787, the year the Constitution was drafted, lamented, "It would be an endless task to trace the variety of meannesses, cares, and sorrows into which women are plunged by the prevailing opinion that they were created rather to feel than reason."[22]

Only many years later would the theory of rights and representation come to include women, the propertyless, former slaves, and other previously excluded groups.

2.2

Identify the weaknesses of the Articles of Confederation and illustrate how they led to the drafting of a new Constitution.

Articles of Confederation
The first (1781–1789) basic governing document of the United States and forerunner to the Constitution.

Government After Independence

Independence had been won, but the hard work of governance lay ahead. The Revolution had united the colonies in one cause, but it remained to be seen whether there was cause enough to keep them united in the absence of the British threat. The new states were slow to reorganize their own governments during the war years, and the loose confederation plan established by the Second Continental Congress remained in place after the Treaty of Paris ended the conflict. But changes were afoot in two arenas. First, participation in government began to broaden. And second, the **Articles of Confederation,** the first basic governing document of the United States and forerunner of the Constitution, proved increasingly unworkable.

Broadening Participation

The Patriots gave voice to sweeping participatory ideals during the seven years they fought for independence from England. During the war, the colonies, now calling themselves "states," constructed governments of their own. For the most part, the 13 new states kept their colonial institutions much as they were, except "with Parliament and the King left out."[23] But the pace of democratization began to accelerate. Eight of the 13 states eased the property qualifications for voters, and five lowered them for candidates for the lower house of the state legislature.[24] Those of more modest means soon made up a greater proportion of state legislatures. Suspicious of executive power, ten states required that governors be elected annually, and six limited the number of terms they could serve.[25] In these states, voters increasingly expected their representatives to serve as delegates rather than trustees (see Chapter 1). "Where annual election ends," went an old Whig saying, "tyranny begins."[26]

Some leaders went as far as to argue that the Whig theory of the rights of man should apply to women. One such leader was Abigail Adams who, in a letter to her patriot husband, wrote, "In the new code of laws . . . I desire you would remember the ladies, and be more generous and favorable to them than your ancestors . . . . If . . . attention is not paid to the ladies we are determined to foment a rebellion, and will not hold ourselves bound by any laws in which we have no voice, or representation." But many of those who espoused Whig theory were unwilling to come to terms with all of its implications. Even Adams's husband, John, who became the nation's second president, argued against making changes in voting qualifications. "[T]here will be no end of it," he said. "Women will demand a vote; lads from twelve to twenty-one will think their rights not enough attended to; and every man, who has not a farthing, will demand an equal voice."[27]

The Articles of Confederation (1781–1789)

The new country needed, above all, a sense of national unity. In one of its more inspired decisions, the Second Continental Congress helped bring the nation together during the war by appointing George Washington, a Virginia plantation owner, as commander of a continental army—even though most soldiers initially came from northern colonies.

Washington's leadership was important, but tough constitutional decisions also needed to be made. The idea of creating a national government was so foreign to the colonial experience that it took the Continental Congress nearly five years after declaring independence to write and win ratification for the country's first system of government, the Articles of Confederation. In the meantime, the Continental Congress did its best to govern by means of its own cumbersome procedures.

Provisions of the Articles   Ratified in 1781, the Articles of Confederation amounted, in its own words, to little more than a "firm league of friendship" in which "each state retains its sovereignty, freedom and independence." There was no system of divided powers along the lines Locke had envisioned. Instead, the Articles granted all national powers to the Congress. But Congress was far from all-powerful: It had to rely on cooperation from the states if it hoped to accomplish anything. Congress could declare war, but it could raise an army only by requesting states to provide soldiers. Congress could raise revenues, but it had to rely on voluntary contributions from the states rather than on direct taxes on citizens. Congress could coin money, but it could not prevent states from also doing so. As a result, the country was flooded with many different currencies. Congress could negotiate tariffs with other countries, but so could each state. Most significant, Congress could not prevent states from interfering with interstate commerce. In fact, states imposed trade barriers on one another. New York, for example, taxed New Jersey cabbage and Connecticut firewood.[28]

Members of the Congress were elected annually by state legislatures. Each state, no matter how large or small, was equally represented. On all important issues, a supermajority of nine states (out of 13) had to agree before action could be taken. Even if this supermajority could agree on a policy, individual states frequently ignored Congress's wishes. Their behavior prompted a frustrated Alexander Hamilton to point out that national laws were "in practice . . . mere recommendations which the States observe or disregard at their option."[29]

There was no independent executive. A congressional Committee of the States could make decisions when Congress was not in session, but this was an unwieldy body because each state had representation. Again, nine of the 13 delegates had to agree before the committee could take action. States exercised most judicial functions, except that disputes between states were settled by ad hoc panels of judges selected by Congress. Congress could amend the Articles only with the approval of all the state legislatures.

Government Under the Articles   Members of Congress almost immediately recognized the problems with the Articles. Virginia delegate James Madison became convinced that a new constitution was necessary after he discovered that it was impossible for Congress to keep states from issuing their own money. National leaders watched helplessly as trade among the states was impeded by quarreling over the relative worth of the coins of New York, Pennsylvania, and Virginia.

Commercial problems were frustrating, but new threats to civil order made it clear that the Articles had difficulty even keeping the peace. **Shays's Rebellion,** an armed uprising in western Massachusetts in 1786 led by Revolutionary War captain Daniel Shays, was especially disruptive. A group of impoverished farmers, unable to pay their taxes or mortgages, rallied together to intimidate state courts into forgiving their debts. Because it took months to suppress the rebellion, many prominent leaders felt that this episode proved that state governments were too weak. Even more embarrassing was an

A League of Friendship

The Articles of Confederation, proposed in 1775, were finally ratified in 1781—eight years before the Constitution. Those eight years were marked by government instability.

• *How does the Constitution address the deficiencies of the Articles of Confederation?*

Shays's Rebellion

Armed uprising in western Massachusetts in 1786 led by Revolutionary War captain Daniel Shays.

Debtors Revolt

Scuffles broke out in western Massachusetts during Shays's Rebellion, when poor farmers and Revolutionary War veterans joined in an uprising.

• *How did this rebellion influence the writing of the Constitution?*

incident in which a group of ex-soldiers from the continental army descended on Congress in 1783, demanding their rightful back pay. Members of the Congress appealed to the state of Pennsylvania for help, but when none was forthcoming, they fled to Princeton College in New Jersey.

Threats from foreign countries were disturbing as well. Britain disputed the boundary between its Canadian colonies and the United States. The British navy routinely intercepted American ships and dragooned U.S. sailors into service, claiming that anyone who spoke English must be British unless he could prove otherwise. Spain, in possession of Florida and the lands west of the Mississippi River, claimed large segments of what are today the states of Mississippi and Alabama (see Figure 2.1).

FIGURE 2.1

MAP OF COMPETING CLAIMS

This map shows only some of the competing claims being made in North America in 1787. Because the British had a superior navy, the United States was, in a sense, surrounded by foreign powers.

• *How did this threat influence the debates over the Constitution?*

Source: Edgar B. Wesley, *Our United States: Its History in Maps* (Chicago: Denoyer-Geppert Co., 1965), p. 37.

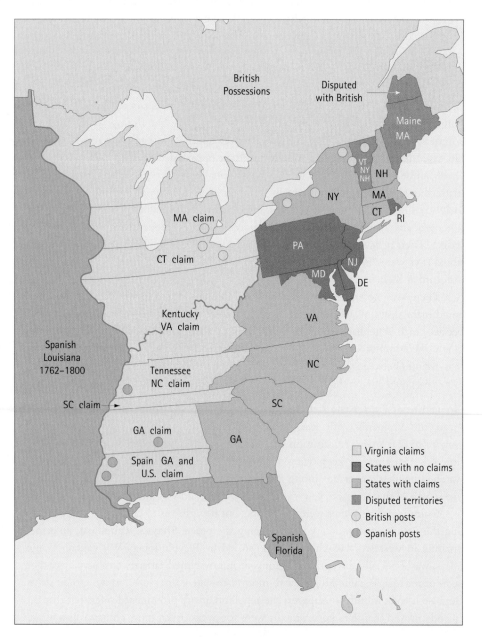

Even France, a Revolutionary War ally, blocked U.S. trade with its islands in the West Indies and demanded repayment of money advanced during the Revolution. Congress found it difficult to resolve these disputes, because it could not prevent individual states from undermining congressionally appointed diplomats by independently negotiating with foreign countries.

Drafting and Adopting a New Constitution

In light of the fragility of the American government in the 1780s, it is remarkable that the end of that decade produced a document that has, for the most part, remained intact for more than 200 years. James Madison pronounced it "a miracle" that agreement on a new constitution was reached at all.[30] In this section, we review the key events that led to this agreement and discuss the major components of the Constitution itself. We then turn to the important debates between Federalists and Anti-Federalists that set the stage for ratification.

The Constitutional Convention

Alexander Hamilton, James Madison, and ten other delegates met to discuss constitutional reforms in 1786 at what became known as the **Annapolis Convention,** but inasmuch as they represented only five states, they were unable to propose major constitutional changes. Later that year, however, in the aftermath of Shays's Rebellion, Madison persuaded Congress to ask each state legislature to elect delegates to a convention in Philadelphia for the "sole and express purpose of revising the Articles of Confederation."[31] Every state legislature but Rhode Island's agreed; Rhode Islanders feared that any revisions in the Articles would reduce the powers of their small state.

For the most part, states sent political leaders who favored major constitutional change; most of those opposed to changing the Articles stayed away. Patrick Henry, when asked to be a delegate, refused, saying he "smelt a rat."[32] True, ten delegates abandoned the convention before the Constitution was completed, and another three refused to sign the resulting document, but the great majority of those in Philadelphia agreed that the national government needed to be strengthened.

The delegates to the Constitutional Convention did not constitute a cross section of the population. They were bankers, merchants, plantation owners, and speculators in land west of the Appalachians.[33] Yet the delegates had not gone to Philadelphia just to protect the interests of their social class. They believed the country as a whole needed a stronger government that could provide political stability, mediate conflicts among the states, and defend the nation from foreign threats.[34]

Nor did delegates agree on all issues. Each owed allegiance to the state legislature that had elected him, and these local ties inevitably led to conflicts. Two divisions were paramount. Delegates from states with large populations often found themselves disagreeing with delegates from smaller states. And delegates from southern slave states opposed those from northern states, whose economies did not depend on slavery.

These differences were less apparent during the opening weeks of the convention, when a spirit of unity and reform filled the Philadelphia hall. But as the four-month

2.3

Analyze the key proposals made by Constitutional Convention delegates and the major components of the final document.

Annapolis Convention
Meeting in 1786 to discuss constitutional reform.

convention progressed, differences among the delegates emerged, and compromises had to be reached to produce a document that could be ratified.[35]

The Virginia Plan   Delegates made three important decisions at the very beginning of the convention:

- Hold discussions behind closed doors. If debates were held in public, disagreements could be exploited by Anti-Federalists.
- Write an entirely new constitution instead of simply following Congress's instruction to suggest amendments to the Articles of Confederation.
- Use the **Virginia Plan** as the basis for initial discussions.

Virginia Plan
Constitutional proposal supported by convention delegates from large states.

The Virginia Plan, which would win the support of most delegates from the larger states, had been prepared by Madison (with Washington's active involvement) prior to the gathering in Philadelphia. As Table 2.2 indicates, it proposed massive changes in the design and powers of the national government, creating a separation of powers along the lines that Locke had recommended. To win popular support for the new constitution, the Virginia Plan called for ratification by state convention delegates "expressly chosen by the people."[36]

Instead of a one-chamber Congress such as that of the Articles, Madison proposed two chambers. The lower chamber—the future House of Representatives—would be elected by the voters. The upper chamber—the future Senate—would be nominated by state legislatures and elected by the lower house.

The Virginia Plan changed representation in Congress dramatically from the pattern that prevailed under the Articles of Confederation. Instead of each state's having one vote, the number of both representatives and senators would depend on a state's population. Virginia, Pennsylvania, and other more populous states would have much more power under this plan than under the Articles.

The Virginia Plan also gave the national government vast powers far beyond those enjoyed by the old Congress. The new Congress could legislate on all matters that affected "the harmony of the United States" and could negate "all laws passed by the several states."[37] It could also use force to ensure that states fulfilled their duties.

TABLE 2.2
THE VIRGINIA AND NEW JERSEY PLANS

The differences between the Virginia Plan and the New Jersey Plan illustrate the disagreements between large and small states at the time of the convention.

- *Why were both large and small states willing to accept the Connecticut Compromise?*

Virginia Plan (favored by larger states)	New Jersey Plan (favored by smaller states)	Connecticut Compromise
Key Difference		
Each state is represented in proportion to its population.	Every state has the same number of representatives in Congress.	States represented equally in upper house; by population in lower house
Other Differences		
Congress has general power.	Congress has only limited, defined powers.	
Supreme Court settles disputes among individuals.	Supreme Court settles only certain disputes (for example, those involving foreigners).	

According to the Virginia Plan, the weak executive power under the Articles was to be replaced by a president chosen by Congress. A Supreme Court would have the authority to resolve disputes among individuals from different states, something that could not be done under the Articles of Confederation. The Virginia Plan received strong support from two of the most populous states, Virginia and Pennsylvania, as well as from states such as North Carolina, South Carolina, and Georgia that expected to grow rapidly in population in the next few years.

The New Jersey Plan   Delegates from smaller states, especially New Jersey and Delaware, were uneasy about the Virginia Plan. About two weeks into the convention, these states offered an alternative design prepared by New Jersey's William Paterson that became known as the **New Jersey Plan** (refer again to Table 2.2).

New Jersey Plan
Small-state proposal for constitutional reform.

The New Jersey Plan also separated powers into three branches, but, instead of creating a House and Senate, it kept a one-chamber Congress in which each state had a single vote. It also envisioned a more limited national government. Unlike the Virginia Plan, it did not grant Congress general legislative power. Instead, it gave Congress specific powers, including levying taxes on imported goods, compelling states to pay their share of taxes, and regulating "trade & commerce with foreign nations" and among the states. The judicial branch could hear only specific types of cases, such as those involving treaties or foreigners.[38]

Despite these limitations, the New Jersey Plan still granted the national government power far in excess of what existed under the Articles. The plan's supporters were not so much opposed to a stronger government as afraid that the big states would control such a government. As one delegate observed at the time, "Give New Jersey an equal vote, and she will dismiss her scruples, and concur in a National system."[39]

The Connecticut Compromise   The convention nearly collapsed when a majority of the delegates rejected the New Jersey Plan. Representatives from the small states considered walking out of the convention, which would have killed all hope of successful ratification. The large states flirted with the idea of forming their own union and then using economic pressure to force the small states to join.

To temper the debate, the convention turned the most divisive issues over to a committee controlled by moderates. This committee came back with a split-the-difference compromise offered by delegates from the medium-sized state of Connecticut. Proposing a Congress along the lines we know today, the **Connecticut Compromise** (sometimes called the "**Great Compromise**") called for a House proportionate to population and a Senate in which all states were represented equally (see Figure 2.2). Small states were placated by their strong representation in the Senate; large states took comfort in the requirement that representation in the House of Representatives be proportionate to a state's population.

Connecticut Compromise (also known as the "Great Compromise")
Constitutional Convention proposal that created a House proportionate to population and a Senate in which all states were represented equally.

Great Compromise
See *Connecticut Compromise*.

A Government of Separated Powers

Once the delegates accepted the Connecticut Compromise, they found it relatively easy to broker other differences between the Virginia and New Jersey plans. Following the Virginia Plan, they created a government with three branches—legislative, executive,

FIGURE 2.2

THE CONNECTICUT
COMPROMISE

These pie charts show the proportional representation accorded
to each state in the House and
Senate, according to the terms of
the Connecticut Compromise.

• *On the basis of the pie charts
shown here, why do you think
Connecticut was the state that
proposed the compromise?*

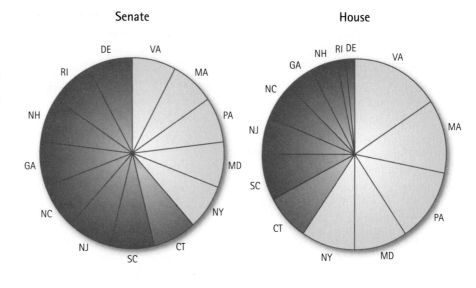

and judicial—and divided powers among them. But, in a step consistent with the New
Jersey Plan, they limited the powers of all three branches.

Congress   Echoing the New Jersey Plan, the convention delegates gave Congress a
number of specific powers, including the powers to tax, coin money, regulate
commerce, declare war, and maintain an army (see Table 2.3). But, to address the
concerns of the proponents of the Virginia Plan, they included the **necessary and
proper clause,** which says that Congress has the power to "make all laws which shall
be necessary and proper for carrying into Execution" its other powers. What is the

necessary and proper clause

Says Congress has the power to
"make all laws which shall be
necessary and proper for carrying
into Execution" its other powers.

TABLE 2.3	
THE CONSTITUTION AND THE ARTICLES OF CONFEDERATION COMPARED	
Many provisions of the Constitution directly address the failures of the Articles of Confederation.	
• *Are there problems with the previous system that were not addressed by the Constitution?*	
• *Why do you think these problems were not addressed?*	
Weaknesses of the Articles of Confederation	**How They Are Addressed in the Constitution**
Congress could not levy taxes.	Congress has the power to levy taxes (Article I, Section 8).
States could restrict commerce among states.	States cannot regulate commerce without the consent of Congress (Article I, Section 10).
States could issue their own currency.	States are prohibited from coining money (Article I, Section 10).
Executive was not independent of Congress.	An independently elected president holds the executive power (Article II).
There was no national judicial system.	The Supreme Court was created, and Congress was granted the power to establish lower federal courts (Article III, Section 1).
Amendments to the Articles had to have unanimous approval of states.	Large majorities are necessary to amend the Constitution, but there are several different ways to do so (Article V).

definition of *necessary and proper*? Some delegates thought it meant only what was absolutely essential. Others thought it meant anything convenient and useful. The phrasing was ambiguous enough that all delegates could interpret the language to their own liking.

The delegates were also influenced by the Whig theory on rights and representation that had proved so powerful during the Revolutionary War. Following Whig theory, the Constitution said that members of the House of Representatives were to be chosen by the voters and were to be subject to re-election every two years. Still, the convention created a system that allowed for at least some officials to serve as "trustees" rather than "delegates" (see Chapter 1). It departed from the Whig theory by not establishing a limit on the number of terms that a member could serve. The delegates modified Whig theory even further in regard to the Senate. Senators were to be elected not by voters but by state legislatures, and they would serve six-year terms of office instead of the very short terms recommended by Whig theorists.

The delegates settled on a delicate political solution to the question of voter qualifications. They said states could establish their own requirements, provided that anyone eligible to vote for the lower chamber of the state legislature must also be allowed to vote in elections for the House of Representatives. This arrangement avoided changing state voting requirements but still guaranteed the vote to everyone already eligible. The open-ended language also permitted a gradual, state-by-state extension of the right to vote to many who were excluded from the electorate in 1787.

The Executive   Some analysts have claimed that many convention delegates secretly harbored a desire to create an executive who had powers comparable to those of a British king.[40] The delegates, however, were too practical to treat such an idea seriously—except for Alexander Hamilton, who actually made a proposal along these lines. They knew that voters would reject out of hand a Constitution that threatened the return of anyone like King George.

Instead, the Constitution keeps presidential power under tight congressional control. The president is commander in chief of the armed forces, but only Congress can declare war. Presidents can call Congress into session and speak to Congress, but they cannot dissolve Congress or prevent it from meeting. Presidents are given the power to veto legislation, but Congress can override a presidential veto with a two-thirds vote of each chamber. (See Chapter 13 for a full discussion of how the constitutional system shapes the relationship between Congress and the president.)

Other presidential powers can be exercised only with senatorial **advice and consent**—support for a presidential action by a designated number of senators. For example, the president can sign treaties with foreign countries, but treaties can take effect only if two-thirds of the Senate approves. Also, the president can appoint both judges and executive branch officers, but appointees must be confirmed by a majority (50 percent plus one) of the Senate.

advice and consent
Support for a presidential action by a designated number of senators.

The impeachment clause makes clear the president's ultimate dependence on political support from Congress. The House of Representatives can impeach the president for "Treason, Bribery, or other high Crimes and Misdemeanors." If impeached, the president is tried in the Senate. If convicted by a two-thirds vote, the president is removed from office. Although no president has ever been removed in this way, in 1999 Bill Clinton was tried but not convicted, in 1974 Richard Nixon chose to resign in the face of almost certain impeachment and conviction, and in 1868 Andrew Johnson was impeached and avoided conviction by only one vote.

The Electoral College   Although the Constitution sharply checked presidential power, delegates to the Constitutional Convention still expected the president to be a powerful political figure. As a consequence, they debated at great length on the method of presidential selection. Once again, the dispute divided the big states from the small ones. If the president were chosen by popular vote, big states would prevail because most people lived in big states. If the choice were made by the House of Representatives, big states would once again dominate. If the choice resided in the Senate, the small states would have extra clout.

electoral college

Those chosen to cast a direct vote for president by a process determined by each state.

The delegates finally agreed on a compromise that created the **electoral college**—those electors chosen to cast a direct vote for president by a process determined by each state. The electoral college is part of a complicated two-stage procedure that remains in effect today. The first stage involves selection of the electoral college and gives an advantage to larger states. Each state chooses the same number of electors as it has senators and representatives in Congress. For example, in 2008 Texas had 34 electoral votes, because it elected two senators and 32 representatives. (In addition, as a result of the passage of the Twenty-Third Amendment, the District of Columbia now casts three electoral votes.) If a candidate receives a majority of the electoral votes, that person is elected president. If no candidate receives a majority in the electoral college, the action moves to the House of Representatives. In this stage, smaller states have an advantage, because each state delegation has a single vote.

The Constitution does not require that the members of the electoral college be chosen by the voters. Instead, the manner of selecting electors was left up to the states. Constitutional silence on this key matter was not an accident. Some delegates thought the president should be elected by the people; others felt a popular vote could lead to mob rule. The Constitutional Convention compromised on the question, as it did on so many, by leaving the issue up to the states. Although by the 1820s electors were chosen by the voters in the great majority of states, it was not until 1864 that the last state, South Carolina, gave voters the power to vote directly for its electors.[41]

Some critics think the electoral college compromise has proved to be less of a success than the Connecticut Compromise. In four elections (1824, 1876, 1888, and 2000), the candidate who won the most popular votes was not selected president. Some scholars favor eliminating the electoral college altogether, on the theory that the candidate receiving the most popular votes should win the election. Others think that the electoral college, for all its faults, helps to maintain the two-party system and provides representation for both the states and the people.

The Judicial Compromise   Most convention delegates thought the country needed a Supreme Court to adjudicate conflicts between the states. They also agreed that justices should be nominated for lifetime positions by the president and confirmed by a majority of the Senate.

The delegates differed over whether the Supreme Court needed lower federal courts to assist it. Advocates of the Virginia Plan wanted lower federal courts because state courts "cannot be trusted with the administration of the National Laws."[42] Advocates of the New Jersey Plan said the state courts were sufficient and protested that "the people will not bear such innovations" as a national court system.[43] The delegates compromised on the issue by leaving it to Congress to decide whether lower federal courts were needed. The first Congress created a system of lower federal courts whose essentials remain intact today, as we discuss in Chapter 15.

The delegates also seem to have disagreed on whether the Supreme Court should be given the power of **judicial review,** court authority to declare laws null and void on the grounds that they violate the Constitution. Although Madison's account of the debate over judicial review is sketchy, many delegates apparently favored judicial review as a check on the power of state legislatures. Yet there is no record of anyone's having risen to its defense when two delegates opposed judicial review. Although scholars have puzzled over the relative silence at the convention about an issue that would loom large in later years, this lack of debate is probably best explained by political expediency. Judicial review had provoked controversy in North Carolina and Rhode Island, and convention delegates avoided the issue because taking a clear position might have jeopardized ratification.

Instead of explicitly providing for judicial review, convention delegates inserted into the Constitution an ambiguous phrase that has become known as the **supremacy clause,** which says the Constitution is the "supreme Law of the Land," to which all judges are bound. To some, this phrase simply told state judges to be mindful of the Constitution when interpreting state laws. To others, it gave the Supreme Court the power to declare both state and federal laws unconstitutional. The issue was not settled until 20 years later, when, as we shall see in Chapter 15, the Supreme Court interpreted the supremacy clause as giving the Court the power of judicial review over both federal and state laws.

judicial review
Court authority to declare laws null and void on the grounds that they violate the Constitution.

supremacy clause
Part of the Constitution that says the Constitution is the "supreme Law of the Land," to which all judges are bound.

Compromising on the Issue of Slavery The delegates never seriously contemplated eliminating slavery under the Constitution. Many delegates owned slaves themselves, and the convention participants knew that southern states would not ratify the Constitution if it abolished slavery. The debate over slavery took other forms instead. Northerners wanted to end the international slave trade. Most southerners argued that the slave trade, however despicable, was necessary to fuel economic growth in unsettled parts of the South. The two sides compromised by agreeing not to abolish the slave trade for 20 years. Abiding by this provision, Congress waited until 1808 before taking that step.

Northern delegates did not want to count slaves when figuring state representation in the House of Representatives. Southerners thought they should be counted. The two sides came up with the expedient, if disreputable, **three-fifths compromise,** which counted each slave, for purposes of representation, as "three-fifths" of a person. One sign that this was a delicate arrangement is that the three-fifths clause identified slaves not as such but as "other persons." Not until after the Civil War did the Fourteenth Amendment repeal the three-fifths clause.

three-fifths compromise
Constitutional provision that counted each slave as three-fifths of a person when calculating representation in the House of Representatives; repealed by the Fourteenth Amendment.

North and South also split over tariffs. Northerners wanted to give Congress the right to impose tariffs on imports; southerners feared that Congress would use tariffs to protect northern manufacturing at southern expense. In exchange for the three-fifths compromise, southerners agreed to let Congress impose tariffs on foreign goods.

The Bill of Rights

The delegates to the Constitutional Convention made one mistake so serious that it nearly ruined their chances of securing ratification: They failed to include within the

Constitution clauses that clearly protected the liberties of the people. It is surprising that the delegates to the Philadelphia Convention, who otherwise showed excellent political judgment, made such a serious miscalculation. Ever since the Revolutionary War, the Whig concept of rights and representation had been central to American constitutional thinking. Quite apart from the Declaration of Independence, with its ringing endorsement of the "right to life, liberty, and the pursuit of happiness," the Virginia assembly—also in 1776—had passed a Bill of Rights protecting free speech, the right of the propertied to vote, the right to a trial by jury, the right not to be compelled to testify against oneself, and other civil liberties.[44] Many other states had similar provisions in their constitutions or statutes. Yet at the Constitutional Convention, when South Carolina's Charles Pinckney offered a motion to guarantee freedom of the press, a majority voted the proposal down on the grounds that regulation of speech and press was a state responsibility.[45]

The convention majority may have been technically correct, but they failed to appreciate how powerfully the demand for the protection of civil liberties would resonate with the voters. To win popular acceptance, the Constitution needed to contain an explicit expression of the Whig theory of rights and representation that the country had taken to heart during the Revolutionary War. When it failed to do so, Thomas Jefferson, author of the Declaration of Independence, wrote to Madison from his diplomatic post in Paris, arguing that a Bill of Rights was necessary and appropriate.

Eventually, the Federalists recognized their mistake. To win ratification in Massachusetts, Virginia, and New York, they promised to enact, as a series of amendments to the Constitution, a **Bill of Rights** that would guarantee civil liberties (see Table 2.4). North Carolina and Rhode Island even withheld their approval until after the first Congress added these amendments. The Bill of Rights, which comprises the

Bill of Rights

The first ten amendments to the Constitution, which guarantee civil liberties and protect states' rights.

TABLE 2.4
KEY CIVIL LIBERTIES PROTECTED BY THE BILL OF RIGHTS

Responding to criticism by Anti-Federalists, proponents of the Constitution agreed to add a Bill of Rights soon after ratification.

- *Why is a Bill of Rights important in a democracy?*
- *Do you think there are rights that are not in the Bill of Rights but should be?*

Freedom of speech, press, and assembly (Amendment I)

Free exercise of religion (Amendment I)

Right to bear arms (Amendment II)

Protection against soldiers being quartered in private homes (Amendment III)

Home security against unreasonable searches and seizures (Amendment IV)

Cannot be deprived of life, liberty, or property without due process of law (Amendment V)

Cannot be forced to testify against oneself (Amendment V)

Trial by jury (Amendments VI and VII)

No cruel or unusual punishment (Amendment VIII)

Assurance that people retain other rights not explicitly stated (Amendment IX)

Powers not delegated to national government are retained by states or people (Amendment X) first ten amendments to the Constitution, has played such a central role in the country's constitutional development that all of Chapter 16, on civil liberties, is devoted to it.

The Anti-Federalist–Federalist Debate

Although the absence of a Bill of Rights gave Anti-Federalists powerful ammunition for their assault on the Constitution during the ratification campaign, their critique of the document was more broadly based. Drawing on the Whig theory of rights and representation, which valued decentralized, popular government, they attacked the Constitution for laying the groundwork for a national tyranny. They said the shift in power from the states to the national government took power from the people. The number of representatives in Congress was too small to include a wide variety of citizens from all parts of the United States. In essence, presidents could become kings, because they could be reelected again and again for the rest of their lives. The reelection of senators and representatives would create a political aristocracy.[46] Again the debate over representation divided those who wished representatives to closely mirror the characteristics of the population from those who saw value in representatives being allowed, as James Madison put it, to "refine and enlarge the public views."[47]

Three Federalists—Alexander Hamilton, James Madison, and John Jay—wrote a series of newspaper columns to answer the Anti-Federalist arguments. Now known as **The Federalist Papers,** these essays are generally regarded as the finest essays on American political theory ever written.[48] The authors argued that tyranny could come from either outside or inside the country. The external danger came from European countries, which were eager to divide the new nation so that each section could be controlled. The Constitution would help prevent such divisions by creating a stronger national government that could defend the country.

Threats to liberty could also come from factions: self-interested groups that threatened individual rights or the common interest. The greatest threat to liberty came from a majority faction, because it could so easily impose its will on minorities. There were several ways of preventing majority factions from arising or, if they did arise, of preventing them from tyrannizing over the rights of others. The authors of *The Federalist Papers*

The Federalist Papers
Essays that were written in support of the Constitution's ratification and have become a classic argument for the American constitutional system.

James Madison (1751–1836), left, and Alexander Hamilton (1755–1804), Authors of *The Federalist Papers*
• *How did the Federalists respond to the Anti-Federalist claim that the new constitution would produce tyranny?*

said that the large size of the new nation was an important asset. It would not only ensure that there was a large pool of talented potential representatives, but it would also help to prevent majority factions from arising because of the "greater variety of parties and interests" that a bigger nation would necessarily include.[49]

The Constitution would provide "auxiliary precautions" against tyranny by creating a system of **checks and balances,** a division of governmental power among separate institutions, giving each institution the power to block the actions of the others. In the first place, power was split between the states and a national government. Then, at the national level, power was divided among three branches: legislative, executive, and judicial. Finally, the legislative branch was divided into two chambers, a Senate and a House of Representatives. Each was elected in a different way, which would make it more difficult for any momentary majority to seize total power.[50]

In retrospect, the Federalists seem to have had the better argument. They had a plan for the future; the Anti-Federalists had little to offer but the unsatisfactory status quo. When the Anti-Federalists claimed that the Constitution stripped the people of their rights and liberties, they relied on the not very convincing argument that the government of any large nation was likely to trample the liberties of the people. The writers of *The Federalist Papers* analyzed the situation more accurately; by creating a system of checks and balances that divided power into different branches and different levels, and by grounding each level in separate elections, they hoped to ensure that the ambitions of one group of politicians would restrain those of other groups. (See Appendix III and IV for two of *The Federalist Papers* that explain this argument in more detail: *The Federalist No. 10* and *The Federalist No. 51*.)

checks and balances
Constitutional division of power into separate institutions, giving each institution the power to block the actions of the others.

2.4

Outline the process for amending the Constitution and identify the liberties that the amendments have strengthened.

Amendments to the Constitution

The delegates to the Constitutional Convention, realizing that the document they were writing was not perfect and that future conditions might require alterations, considered ways in which the Constitution might be amended. Small states wanted to require the unanimous consent of state legislatures, but big states worried that a unanimity rule would lead to stagnation and protracted conflict. Southern states were afraid that slavery would be endangered if amendments could be made easily.

To reach agreement, Convention delegates designed a complicated formula that allowed amendment by any one of four different procedures, as shown in Figure 2.3. The simplest and most frequently used way to amend the Constitution requires a two-thirds vote in both houses of Congress and then ratification by three-quarters of the state legislatures. Of the 27 amendments to the Constitution, 26 have been enacted by this procedure. On one occasion, the amendment that repealed prohibition, the state legislatures were bypassed in favor of state-ratifying conventions attended by delegates chosen by the voters (the same procedure as that used to ratify the Constitution itself).

Amending the Constitution requires such overwhelming majorities that among the thousands of amendments proposed over the years, only 17 have been enacted since ratification of the Bill of Rights. Even popular amendments that have the endorsement of both political parties are not necessarily approved. For example, many people thought that the Equal Rights Amendment, which said that men and women had "equality of rights under the law," would win approval in the 1970s. The amendment

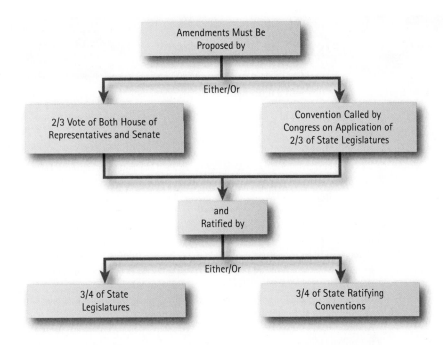

FIGURE 2.3

AMENDING THE CONSTITUTION: A TWO-STAGE PROCESS

The typical means of amending the Constitution is for proposed amendments to win approval by two-thirds of each house of Congress, and then by three-fourths of the state legislatures.

• *Why did the founders make the amendment process so complicated? Why do you think the founders provided several means by which the Constitution could be amended, rather than just one?*

received overwhelming support in both houses of Congress and was quickly ratified by 34 states. But, when the proposed amendment became intertwined with abortion and other disputed issues, it failed to win ratification by the final three state legislatures necessary to provide the required three-quarters approval.[51]

The one kind of amendment that seems capable of receiving the overwhelming support needed to achieve adoption is that which extends democratic electoral practices. Many amendments since the Bill of Rights have tightened the electoral connection well beyond what was originally envisioned by the Constitution—by broadening the electorate, by extending civil liberties, or by making the connections between leaders and voters more direct. Five amendments specifically extended the suffrage to citizens previously excluded from voting: African Americans, women, young people (ages 18–20), residents of the District of Columbia, and those unwilling or unable to pay a poll tax. Other amendments have corrected procedural deficiencies thought to be inconsistent with democratic practice. (See the *Election Connection* box on page 52.)

The Constitution: An Assessment

The debate over the Constitution did not end with its ratification in 1788. The influential historian Charles Beard wrote in 1913 that the Constitution represented a victory for the propertied classes against the masses of the people.[52] Beard pointed out that wealthy people wrote the document and that only people with property were allowed to vote in the ratification campaign. But modern-day historians Bernard Bailyn and Gordon Wood see it as moving the country toward the ideals of citizen rights and representation that motivated the revolutionary patriots.[53] In their view, the Whig ideals that spurred the war of independence were given practical expression in the Constitution.

2.5

Evaluate the strengths and the weaknesses of the U.S. Constitution in both historical and contemporary context.

ELECTION CONNECTION

Amendments to the Constitution Have Extended Liberties and Tightened the Election Connection

Amendment	Year Ratified	Provision
XIII	1865	Abolishes slavery.
XIV	1868	Defines "citizens" to include African Americans. Guarantees citizens the right of due process and equal protection before state law. Removes the three-fifths compromise from the Constitution.
XV	1870	Extends suffrage to African Americans.
XVII	1913	Institutes direct election of senators. Up to this point, senators had been selected by state legislatures.
XIX	1920	Extends suffrage to women.
XXII	1951	Imposes two-term limit on presidents, an idea discussed but not implemented by the founders.
XXIII	1961	Extends presidential suffrage to residents of the District of Columbia; grants the district three electoral votes in presidential elections.
XXIV	1964	Abolishes taxes on voting, which had barred many African Americans from the polls.
XXVI	1971	Extends suffrage to 18-year-olds.

A Step Backward?

Both sides of this debate probably overstated their cases. The adoption of the Constitution consolidated changes in citizen participation and representation that had already taken place in many states. The adoption of the Constitution did not broaden the right to vote, but neither did it further restrict it. The Constitution divided powers that had been lodged in a single representative body under the Articles of Confederation, but each of the new entities—the House, the Senate, the presidency, and the courts—was ultimately grounded in the people. Senators were elected by the legislatures of each state, but the members of each state legislature were chosen in popular elections. Presidents were chosen by electors, but the electors were chosen according to state rules, which since the 1830s have almost always called for direct elections by the voters. Judges were appointed for life, but they were selected by the president and confirmed by the Senate. If the U.S. government under the Constitution was a limited democracy in 1789, a more popular democracy evolved within the framework the Constitution set forth.

There remains much in the Constitution to criticize. The powers of the Supreme Court are poorly defined. While some scholars praise the electoral college for representing both the states and the people, others criticize it as a haphazard contraption that has more than once failed to work well. Many important issues are papered over with vague, ambiguous wording (see *Election Voices!* feature on page 56, for one example).

Certain clauses in the Constitution are especially disturbing to the modern eye. The Constitution explicitly permitted the slave trade to continue until 1808, even though many delegates thought it an evil practice. Nothing was done to extend voting rights to women, indentured servants, slaves, youths, or those without property. Until the Bill of Rights was added, the Constitution said nothing about basic freedoms of speech, religion, and assembly, which are now taken for granted.

But we cannot judge eighteenth-century decisions by twenty-first-century principles. Many of the flaws we see were written into the Constitution not to frustrate later generations but to get the votes needed to achieve ratification. Delegates compromised on the issue of slavery because that was the only way to win the support of voters in both northern and southern states. Even when slavery made its way into the Constitution, references to the practice were so oblique that reasonable people could disagree on the Constitution's aim. Famed abolitionist and escaped slave Frederick Douglass even argued that "If that Constitution had dropped down to us from the blue over-hanging sky, and we had read its contents, there [is] not a man who could reasonably suppose it was intended to sanction and support the slave system, but on the contrary . . . everything in it was intended to support justice and equality between man and man."[54]

The Constitution says nothing about the right to vote, because every state had its own voting rules. Had the Constitution proposed changes to them, the states would have complained that this violated their sovereignty. The procedures for electing the president were designed to reduce conflicts between large and small states. The one big mistake the convention could most certainly have avoided—neglecting to include a Bill of Rights—was corrected by the First Congress.

If we want to censure the Constitution for its undemocratic features, we must first criticize the limits on suffrage imposed by state voting laws inherited from the colonial period. Historians estimate that only 20 percent of the electorate representing 5 percent of the adult population voted.[55] The country was no longer ruled by King George III, but it was hardly a full-fledged democracy. The Constitution was written to win the support of the white, male, property-owning population. That it could do so—and still leave open the possibility for greater democratization in the centuries to come—is to the honor, not the discredit, of those who met in Philadelphia.

Achievements

The delegates to the Constitutional Convention wrote a document that contributed to the solution of two of the most immediate and pressing problems facing the United States under the Articles of Confederation. First, it created a unified nation capable of defending American sovereignty from foreign threats. True, the United States would fight a costly war against Britain in 1812. But the Constitution kept the country from disintegrating at a time when Britain, France, and Spain were all vying for territory in the New World. Instead of falling prey to European ambitions, the United States profited from European divisions by seizing the opportunity to make the Louisiana Purchase in 1803, which doubled the size of the country. This land was eventually incorporated into the Union as new member states.

Second, the new Constitution facilitated the country's economic development by outlawing the separate state currencies and state tariffs that had proliferated under the Articles. As a result, trade among states flourished, and the United States grew into an economic powerhouse more rapidly than any had expected.

The Constitution also created a presidency that was first filled by George Washington, the country's most beloved political leader. His great prestige gave the national government the additional strength it needed to overcome the many difficulties the new nation encountered.

The Constitution Today

In addition to solving immediate problems, the Constitution created a framework that facilitated an ever more popular democratic experiment. The document's durable but peaceful division of power, in which one branch can check another, would have surprised Thomas Hobbes, who said that a country could avoid chaos only by vesting power in a sovereign king. If a constitution separates powers into many parts and each part represents a different set of interests, then liberty can be preserved by giving minorities the opportunity to protect themselves from tyrannical majorities. The many compromises at the Constitutional Convention produced this kind of separation of powers that set competing interests against one another. The interests of big states, small states, northerners, southerners, commercial entrepreneurs, farmers, property owners, and debtors were all woven into the constitutional fabric.

In the more than two centuries that have followed, the main lines of conflict have changed. People no longer worry much about divisions between big and small states or differences between commerce and agriculture. The country today has quite different ethnic, gender, cultural, income, and generational issues to resolve. But the Constitution still gives the many different groups and interests clear opportunities to voice their concerns.

Constitutional Ambiguity: A Virtue The ambiguities embedded in the Constitution have also been a plus. Written as compromises among conflicting interests, such vague phrases as "necessary and proper" and "supreme Law of the Land" have had the elasticity necessary to accommodate powerful social and political forces that the founders could not have anticipated. Over the centuries, the Supreme Court has interpreted ambiguous constitutional phrases in ways that have allowed the Constitution to remain relevant to the issues of the day. In subsequent chapters, we shall discuss ways in which the compromises of 1787 have been redefined and given new meaning in response to changing political circumstances.

The Constitution's extraordinary adaptability over a prolonged period of time testifies to the framers' stunning accomplishment. Although the United States is often thought of as a relatively new country, its governing arrangements have remained intact for much longer than those in most other countries. Of all the great industrial democracies, only the British system comes close to enjoying basic governing arrangements that date back as far as those of the United States. And even the democratic features of British government are newer than those of the United States. Not until 1867 did most British men get the right to vote.

Most other countries have much newer constitutions. Iraq struggled to draft a new constitution in 2004 (see the accompanying *International Comparison* box). The latest Russian constitution was adopted in 1993. The current Spanish constitution was approved in 1978, the French constitution dates back only to 1958, the Danish to 1953, and the German, Italian, and Japanese constitutions to the late 1940s.

INTERNATIONAL COMPARISON

Constitution-Making in Iraq

After the U.S.-led overthrow of Saddam Hussein's government in 2003, Iraqis were faced with the daunting task of setting up a democratic system of government. After a brief period of rule by a U.S. administrator and an appointed "governing council," Iraqis set to work in spring 2004 to create a lasting constitution. They came up with a system that was similar in many respects to that of the United States. For example, it included protections of fundamental rights, as well as a federal system of government. As in the case of the U.S. Constitution, the Iraqi constitution had to secure the approval of voters, which it did in October 2005. Despite superficial similarities between the United States and Iraqi constitutions, however, the situation in Iraq is very different from that which faced the United States in its early days. Each of these differences may affect whether the constitution ultimately succeeds or fails.

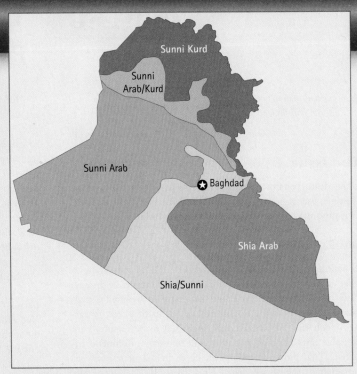

Regional divisions and sectarian strife have complicated Iraq's efforts to establish constitutional government.

Source: Data from CIA Atlas of the Middle East, Perry Castaneda Map Library, University of Texas.

1. The U.S. Constitution was written by revolutionary leaders who had won the country's independence. In Iraq, a dictatorship was overthrown by an outside power. Some Iraqis also questioned whether exiles who had not been in the country for years should be included in the process of rebuilding the nation.
2. George Washington was revered as a military hero. There is no such consensus choice for a leader in Iraq. Neither the country's first president under the new constitution, Jalal Talabani, nor its prime minister, Nouri al-Maliki, commanded universal respect and admiration.
3. In the United States, brief uprisings such as Shays's Rebellion, while alarming, were quickly quelled. In Iraq, an ongoing anti-U.S. insurgency has sought to disrupt the reconstruction efforts. In 2007, a suicide attacker even bombed the cafeteria of the Iraq Parliament building.
4. While there were religious and cultural differences in the early United States, the authors of the constitution were willing to compromise on them. In Iraq, religious differences between Sunni and Shiite Muslims, as well as cultural differences between Kurds and other Iraqis, were so intense as to threaten the stability of the new government. The 2010 Iraq election was nearly postponed indefinitely in a dispute over a new election law.
5. In the early United States, women were excluded from politics. In Iraq, the 2005 constitution prohibits gender discrimination, although many women worried that this guarantee would be weakened by traditional interpretations of religious law.

• *In light of the experience in Iraq, do you believe that the success of the United States Constitution was mostly due to careful planning or mostly due to favorable circumstances?*

Source: Ellen Knickmeyer, "Iraqi Women See Little But Darkness," *Washington Post* (October 15, 2005): A14.

The Stain of Slavery Despite everything positive that can be said for the Constitution, the stain of slavery remains indelible. In addition to validating the slave trade and stating that each slave could be counted as three-fifths of a person, the Constitution also explicitly required free states to return escaped slaves to the place from which they had fled.

Continued on page 59

The Politics of the Death Penalty

Excessive bail shall not be required, nor excessive fines imposed, nor cruel and unusual punishments inflicted.

—*Constitution, Amendment VIII*

The Issue

Is the death penalty a just and legitimate punishment for the most heinous of crimes? Or is it an unworkable violation of the Constitution's ban on "cruel and unusual punishment"?

Background

In drafting his proposed Bill of Rights in 1789, James Madison relied in many respects on previous such declarations. In the case of what would become the Eighth Amendment, he lifted text almost verbatim from the English Bill of Rights of a century earlier, which said, "[E]xcessive bail ought not to be required, nor excessive fines imposed; nor cruel and unusual punishments inflicted." That pronouncement had been drafted in response to the reign of the widely hated King James II, whose enemies were sometimes "hanged, cut down before death, disemboweled, beheaded, and hacked to pieces."[1] For those who wonder what the founders meant by "cruel and unusual," this gruesome punishment would surely fit the bill.

But what about the modern death penalty? Although the number of people executed in the United States is lower now than it was in the 1930s, it has increased since the 1970s, when several Supreme Court decisions made it clearer what kinds of capital-punishment statutes would survive legal scrutiny (see Figure 1). As of 2010, 35 states provide for a penalty of death for the most serious crimes, and criminals may be sentenced to death under federal law for crimes such as treason, grave drug offenses, terrorism, and, under extreme circumstances, murder.[2] In 2009, 52 convicted criminals were put to death, and 3,215 prisoners sat on "death row," awaiting execution.[3]

Proponents of the death penalty argue that capital punishment is the best way to deter heinous crimes, or that it can represent a just punishment for the most abhorrent conduct. As Barack Obama put it, "there are some crimes—mass murder, the rape and murder of a child—so heinous, so beyond the pale, that the community is justified in expressing the full measure of its outrage by meting out the ultimate punishment."[4] Proponents also claim that it offers closure to victims or their relatives. After John Allen Muhammad, the so-called "DC sniper" was put to death in 2009, a relative of one of his ten victims felt relieved: "I feel better. I think I can breathe better and I'm happy he's gone."[5]

FIGURE 1

Executions in the U.S. 1930–2010

• *Why do you think executions were more common in the 1930s than today?*

Sources: U.S. Department of Justice, Bureau of Justice Statistics, http://www.ojp.usdoj.gov/bjs/cp.htm, accessed January 12, 2008; www.deathpenaltyinfo.org, accessed February 23, 2010.

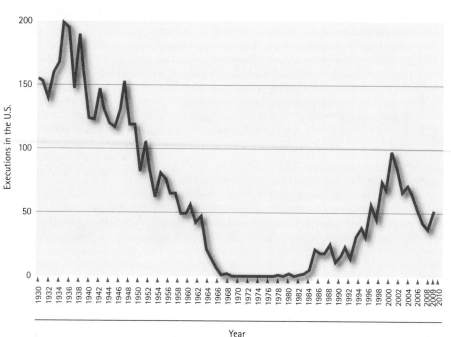

Year

Timothy McVeigh

• *Does the example of Oklahoma City bomber Timothy McVeigh demonstrate that the death penalty is justified?*

But opponents argue that although it is perhaps not so grotesque as the excesses of James II, the modern death penalty constitutes cruel and unusual punishment. One of the most eloquent critics of the death penalty, Supreme Court Justice William Brennan, argued that "the state, even as it punishes, must treat its citizens in a manner consistent with their intrinsic worth as human beings—a punishment must not be so severe as to be degrading to human dignity."[6]

In recent years, some anti-death-penalty groups have achieved success with a more practical approach, focusing on allegedly flawed state death penalty systems. Legislatures and governors in Maryland, Illinois, and New Jersey have halted the use of the death penalty, at least temporarily, in the face of evidence that poor and minority defendants are more likely to be wrongly convicted.[7] "The death penalty is typically about the poor, victims of child abuse, [and] people who had bad attorneys," said one expert.[8]

The Death Penalty and Elections

Sensing that a majority of the public supports capital punishment, most politicians adopt that perspective as well. The top presidential candidates in 2008 all favored the death penalty. Significant majorities of voters continue to be in favor of the death penalty for murder (see Figure 2).

Opposing Viewpoints on the Death Penalty

Against the Death Penalty

Opponents of capital punishment make two types of arguments. The first is that the death penalty in any form is fundamentally immoral:

> Each of us is called to respect the life and dignity of every human being. Even when people deny the dignity of others, we must still recognize that their dignity is a gift from God and is not something that is earned or lost through their behavior. Respect for life applies to all, even the perpetrators of terrible acts.
>
> —United States Conference of Catholic Bishops, "A Culture of Life and the Penalty of Death," December 2005, p. 11.

FIGURE 2

MOST AMERICANS FAVOR THE DEATH PENALTY, WITH RESERVATIONS

• *Should public opinion about the death penalty influence how the Supreme Court rules on the issue?*

Sources: Pew Research Center Poll, August 1-18, 2007; ABC News Poll, December 10-14, 2003; and Gallup Poll, May 6-9, 2002.

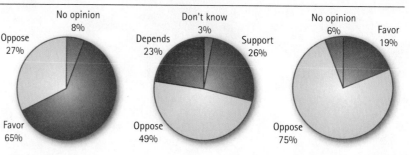

Are you in favor of the death penalty for a person convicted of murder?

- No opinion 8%
- Oppose 27%
- Favor 65%

Do you support or oppose the death penalty for people who are convicted of murder that they committed when they were juveniles—that is, when they were younger than 18?

- Don't know 3%
- Depends 23%
- Support 26%
- Oppose 49%

Do you favor or oppose the death penalty for the mentally ill?

- No opinion 6%
- Favor 19%
- Oppose 75%

A second argument is that the death penalty, as applied, violates civil rights and liberties by being levied against certain groups more than others:

> Minorities and the poor often cannot pay for adequate and competent [legal] representation. They cannot afford 'dream teams' who negotiate with prosecutors to eliminate the possibility of a death sentence before a trial begins. . . . Innocent people are often unable to adequately address their legal problems with definitive evidence of their innocence.
>
> —Rep. Jesse L. Jackson Jr. (D-IL), *CQ Researcher*, November 16, 2001

For the Death Penalty

Death penalty critics do not have a monopoly on moral argument. Defenders of capital punishment appeal to justice as well:

> If a man steals your bicycle and society allows him to keep and ride around on that bicycle, most of us would find that profoundly unjust. Why, then, is it just to allow everyone who steals a life to keep his own? . . . [A]llowing all murderers to keep their lives diminishes the worth of human life. The way society communicates what it thinks about a crime is by the punishment it metes out.
>
> —Dennis Prager, "Death Penalty Guards What Is Valued Most," *Milwaukee Journal-Sentinel*, June 9, 2001

They also argue that practical problems with state and federal systems are of minor significance and are being overcome:

> With the average time consumed by appeals between sentencing and execution now at about 10 years, and with the arrival of DNA testing . . . , the likelihood of wrongful executions is less than ever. . . . Compelled to administer justice in an imperfect world, we should not allow a utopian yearning for perfect certainty to render us moral eunuchs.
>
> —Eugene H. Methvin, "Death Penalty Is Fairer Than Ever," *Wall Street Journal*, May 10, 2000

What Do Americans Believe?

A majority of Americans appear to agree, more or less, with the voter who advised one pollster, "I'll tell you where I stand on the death penalty: right next to the switch!"[9] In 2009, 65 percent of Americans said that they favored the death penalty for those convicted of murder, and this number has remained high for many years.[10]

Nevertheless, when pollsters ask voters more complex questions, Americans' positions seem more conditional. Fully three-quarters of respondents oppose the death penalty for the mentally ill, and nearly half say they oppose the death penalty for minors.

Is the Death Penalty Constitutional?

In 1972, the Supreme Court ruled in *Furman v. Georgia* that the death penalty, as it was then being applied in the states, violated the Constitution's guarantee against cruel and unusual punishment. The majority of Justices felt that existing death penalty laws were too likely to be applied unfairly across racial and income groups.[11]

States struggled for several years to rewrite their laws, and in the meantime they refrained from executing criminals, as Figure 1 illustrates. Then, in 1976, the Court ruled that a new Georgia law, which included procedural safeguards against arbitrary executions, was constitutionally acceptable.[12] Since then, states have modeled their systems on this law, and the use of capital punishment has increased.

In the last decade, the Supreme Court has issued several important rulings on capital punishment that have altered the way states administer the death penalty, but it did not diverge from majority public opinion on the issue. First, in 2002 it ruled that juries—not judges—must be responsible for deciding whether to apply the death penalty in any given case. Second, that same year it declared that the execution of mentally retarded criminals constitutes cruel and unusual punishment. Third, in 2005 the Court banned the death penalty for those who committed crimes when they were under 18.[13] In keeping with public opinion, however, the Court ruled in 2008 that lethal injection is an acceptable form of capital punishment, despite detractors' claims that human error in its administration could cause pain and suffering to the condemned.

What Do You Think?

1. Should the constitutional guarantee of no cruel and unusual punishment protect criminals from being executed, or does it apply only to sadistic violence such as that practiced by James II?

2. Regardless of which position you take on the death penalty, which types of arguments are more convincing to you—moral arguments or practical arguments? Why?

3. Is the Supreme Court shaping public opinion on this question, or is public opinion affecting court decisions?

The death penalty is a subject of heated national debate. To conscientiously investigate this controversial issue and the arguments for and against, be sure to go to the websites of both those groups that are in favor of the death penalty and those groups that are opposed. In your opinion, which website(s) presents the most convincing argument?

On the Web

PRO

The Criminal Justice Legal Foundation is a pro-death-penalty organization that assists in a variety of legal cases.

www.cjlf.org

Justice for All, a victims'-rights organization, maintains an extensive website containing pro-capital-punishment articles and links, as well as a database of the victims of death row inmates.

www.prodeathpenalty.com

CON

The American Civil Liberties Union condemns capital punishment as "barbaric" and argues that it disproportionately affects poor minority defendants.

www.aclu.org

The National Coalition to Abolish the Death Penalty provides reports, informational materials, and links to other organizations that share its views.

www.ncadp.org

The Death Penalty Information Center provides a variety of in-depth statistical information on the death penalty and its administration, arguing that there are serious practical difficulties with capital punishment.

www.deathpenaltyinfo.org

[1] Barry Latzer, *Death Penalty Cases: Leading U.S. Supreme Court Cases on Capital Punishment* (Boston: Butterworth-Heinemann, 1998), p. 2.
[2] "Facts About the Death Penalty," Death Penalty Information Center, June 10, 2010, www.deathpenaltyinfo.org/FactSheet.pdf, accessed June 15, 2010.
[3] Death Penalty Information Center, www.deathpenaltyinfo.org/, accessed December 11, 2009.
[4] Barack Obama, *The Audacity of Hope: Thoughts on Reclaiming the American Dream* (New York: Vintage Books, 2006), p. 70.
[5] "Sniper's Death Brings Relief to Victim's Kin," *Harrisburg Patriot News* (November 11, 2009), p. A1.
[6] *Gregg v. Georgia*, 428 U.S. 153 (1976).
[7] Maryland halted executions from 2002 to 2003; Illinois from 2000 to the present (2006); New Jersey in 2006. See "Uncertain Justice: Efforts to Determine Whether a State Has Executed an Innocent Man Reflect the Country's Growing Unease with Capital Punishment," *Houston Chronicle* (January 24, 2006), p. B8.
[8] Michael Radelet, quoted in Michael Kranish, "McVeigh Case Defies Views on Death in General, Support for Executions Down," *Boston Globe* (June 11, 2001), p. A1.
[9] John Aloysius Farrell, "Lethal Dilemma: Five of the Prisoners Scheduled for Execution in Texas Early Next Year Will Highlight Gov. George W. Bush's Death Penalty Role," *Boston Globe*, December 19, 1999: p. A1.
[10] Gallup Poll, October 1-4, 2009.
[11] *Furman v. Georgia*, 408 U.S. 238 (1972).
[12] *Gregg v. Georgia.*
[13] The cases were: *Ring v. Arizona*, 536 U.S. 584 (2002) (juries, not judges must decide on death penalty); *Atkins v. Virginia*, 536 U.S. 304 (2002) (execution of mentally ill prohibited); *Roper v. Simmons*, 543 U.S. 551 (2005) (death penalty for minors prohibited); and *Baze v. Rees*, No. 07-5439 (2008) (lethal injection permitted).

Continued from page 55

Dividing and checking concentrations of power prevented the tyranny of the majority. But it also prevented a majority from undoing the tyranny of slavery. By denying the national government the capacity to bring slavery peacefully to an end, the separation of powers helped perpetuate the slave system at a time when the practice was disappearing throughout the rest of the world. Perhaps it is too much to ask of any constitution that it provide the tools for resolving what had become an intractable problem. Perhaps it was, as Abraham Lincoln once said, only providential that "every drop of blood drawn with the lash shall be paid by another drawn with the sword."[56] It is not easy to imagine how the delegates to the Constitutional Convention could have designed a constitution that would have both freed slaves and won ratification by the voters of 1788.

CHAPTER SUMMARY

2.1 Explain the reasons for the spread of democratic ideals before and during the Revolutionary War.

The new American democracy, in which elections and strategic calculations about elections have dominated the political landscape, has deep roots in the early history of the continent. The colonists who settled the eastern coast of North America established incomplete but meaningful rules of democracy through such institutions as the Mayflower Compact and elected colonial assemblies. These democratic institutions were reinforced by the spread of philosophical ideals during the Revolutionary War. Of critical importance was the concept that legitimate governments get their power from the consent of the governed. This principle formed the basis for the U.S. Constitution.

2.2 Identify the weaknesses of the Articles of Confederation and illustrate how they led to the drafting of a new Constitution.

The Constitution was written to rectify difficulties the country experienced under the Articles of Confederation. The national government could not raise its own army, levy its own taxes, or regulate commerce among the states. Many leaders believed the country was too weak to fend off potential threats from Britain, Spain, and France.

2.3 Analyze the key proposals made by Constitutional Convention delegates and the major components of the final document.

When drafting a new Constitution designed to address needs unmet by the Articles of Confederation, the delegates to the Constitutional Convention designed a new basic law acceptable to the voters who were asked to ratify it. As a result, they prepared a document built both on their own colonial experience and on political theories popular at the time. They also incorporated many of the ideals expressed during the revolutionary struggle against King George III.

The Constitution curbed the powers of state governments, gave Congress additional authority, created a presidency of limited powers, and established a Supreme Court as the head of the judicial system. By dividing power between the states and the national government, and by further dividing the power of the national government among the legislative, executive, and judicial branches, the Constitution provided an enduring system of limited government well designed to protect the liberties of the citizens.

To win ratification of the Constitution by voters in all parts of the country, the delegates to the Constitutional Convention had to reach many compromises. Congress was given not general power but a set of specific powers, along with the capacity to do anything "necessary and proper" to carry out these specific powers. Differences of opinion between delegates from big and small states were resolved by creating a Senate that gave equal representation to all states and a House of Representatives wherein states were represented in proportion to their population. Presidents were selected via a complicated two-stage system, which included a cumbersome electoral college arrangement. The Supreme Court was neither given nor denied the power of judicial review. Differences between the North and South were settled via a compromise: preserving the slave trade for 20 years and counting each slave as three-fifths of a person for purposes of representation.

2.4 Outline the process for amending the Constitution and identify the liberties that the amendments have strengthened.

The convention delegates erred in not including a Bill of Rights in the Constitution. But during the ratification campaign, Anti-Federalists insisted on, and the Federalists finally agreed to, 10 amendments to the Constitution that became known as the Bill of Rights. Although the procedures for amending the Constitution are complicated, 17 additional amendments have been approved since the Bill of Rights was drafted, and 13 of these have shifted American democracy in a popular direction.

2.5 Evaluate the strengths and the weaknesses of the U.S. Constitution in both historical and contemporary context.

The Constitution did not solve all the nation's problems—it would take a civil war to eliminate slavery, for example. But it has proved to be remarkably durable and adaptable.

mypoliscilab EXERCISES

Apply what you learned in this chapter on MyPoliSciLab.

Read on **mypoliscilab.com**

eText: Chapter 2

Study and **Review** on **mypoliscilab.com**

Pre-Test

Post-Test

Chapter Exam

Flashcards

Watch on **mypoliscilab.com**

Video: Animal Sacrifice and Free Exercise

Video: Polygamy and the U.S. Constitution

Explore on **mypoliscilab.com**

Simulation: You Are James Madison

Simulation: You Are Proposing a Constitutional Amendment

Comparative: Comparing Constitutions

Timeline: The History of Constitutional Amendments

Visual Literacy: The American System of Checks and Balances

KEY TERMS

advice and consent, p. 45

Annapolis Convention, p. 41

Anti-Federalists, p. 32

Articles of Confederation, p. 38

Bill of Rights, p. 48

checks and balances, p. 50

colonial assembly, p. 33

colonial council, p. 33

Connecticut Compromise
    ("Great Compromise"), p. 43

Constitution, p. 32

Declaration of Independence, p. 35

divine right, p. 32

electoral college, p. 46

The Federalist Papers, p. 49

Federalists, p. 32

First Continental Congress, p. 35

judicial review, p. 47

Mayflower Compact, p. 32

necessary and proper clause, p. 44

New Jersey Plan, p. 43

Patriots, p. 34

patronage, p. 33

proprietary colony, p. 33

royal colony, p. 32

Second Continental Congress, p. 35

separation of powers, p. 36

Shays's Rebellion, p. 39

Stamp Act Congress, p. 34

stamp tax, p. 34

supremacy clause, p. 47

taxation without representation, p. 34

three-fifths compromise, p. 47

Tories, p. 35

Virginia Plan, p. 42

Whigs, p. 37

SUGGESTED READINGS

Of General Interest

Dahl, Robert. *How Democratic Is the American Constitution?* New Haven: Yale University Press, 2003. A critical look at the Constitution from one of the country's most eminent political scientists.

The Federalist Papers. New York: Signet Classic (New American Library), 2003. Powerful defense of the proposed constitution by Alexander Hamilton, James Madison, and John Jay under the pseudonym Publius.

Johnson, Michael P. *Reading the American Past, Selected Historical Documents, Volume I* (to 1877) and *Volume II* (from 1865). New York: Bedford/St. Martin's, 2004 (Volume I) and 2002 (Volume II). Collection of key primary documents in American history.

McCullough, David. *1776.* New York: Simon & Schuster, 2005. Readable account of one key year of the Revolutionary War.

Rakove, Jack. *Original Meanings: Politics and Ideas in the Making of the Constitution.* New York: Random House, 1996. Pulitzer Prize-winning examination of the ideologies and political factors behind the drafting of the Constitution.

Storing, Herbert J., ed. *The Anti-Federalist*. Chicago: University of Chicago Press, 1986. Selection of Anti-Federalist writings.

Focused Studies

Bailyn, Bernard. *The Origins of American Politics*. New York: Knopf, 1968. Identifies the sources of the American Revolution in colonial thought and practice.

Beard, Charles A. *An Economic Interpretation of the Constitution of the United States*. New York: Free Press, 1913. Interprets the writing of the Constitution as an effort by the wealthy to protect their property rights.

Hartz, Louis. *The Liberal Tradition in America*. New York: Harcourt, 1955. A difficult but rewarding book that describes the distinctive quality of the American political tradition.

Roche, John P. "The Founding Fathers: A Reform Caucus in Action." *American Political Science Review 55* (December 1961): 799–816. Identifies the election connection at the Constitutional Convention.

Wood, Gordon S. *Empire of Liberty: A History of the Early Republic, 1789-1815*. New York: Oxford University Press, 2009. A historical account of the critical early years under the U.S. Constitution.

ON THE WEB

In this chapter, we examined the events that led to the drafting of the U.S. Constitution and the political struggles surrounding its ratification.

www.archives.gov/nae/index.html
The text of the Constitution and a high-resolution digital picture of the document itself is available at the National Archives and Records Administration website.

www.earlyamerica.com
The early American colonists brought with them traditional European ideas and forms of government. They also developed new ways of thinking by adapting these concepts to their own new world experiences. To learn more about the colonists, visit the website.

www.utm.edu/research/iep/l/locke.htm
www.iep.utm.edu/hobmoral
To learn more about one of the major political theories that influenced colonial thought, see the Internet Encyclopedia of Philosophy entries on John Locke and Thomas Hobbes.

www.pbs.org/ktca/liberty
For a comprehensive account of the Revolutionary War, including timelines, accounts of battles, and biographies of key figures, see the companion website to the PBS *Liberty!* series on the American Revolution.

http://avalon.law.yale.edu/subject_menus/fed.asp
The Avalon Project at Yale Law School provides a transcription of all 85 *Federalist Papers*, which can be searched by keyword.

www.usconstitution.net/constam.html
www.usconstitution.net/constamfail.html
As this chapter shows, the Constitution has been repeatedly amended, but this is a difficult and time-consuming process. These websites provide details on the amendment process, and on proposed amendments that have failed.

3 Federalism: Division of Power National, State, and Local Governments

CHAPTER OUTLINE

LEARNING OBJECTIVES

3.1   Differentiate between federalism and other forms of government.

3.2   Trace key developments in the historical debate over dual sovereignty and nullification.

3.3   Evaluate the impact of specific Supreme Court decisions on the relationship of national and state governments.

3.4   Compare and contrast the advantages and disadvantages of federal categorical and block grants distributed to state and local governments.

3.5   Outline the organization and responsibilities of local governments and identify the key challenges they face.

3.6   Outline the organization and responsibilities of state governments and identify the key challenges they face.

The Politics of Katrina

"I have no idea where my 2-year-old son is." Nicole Williams, a new arrival to Houston's Astrodome, was trying to enlist the help of the media. On her T-shirt she had written "Please help me find my family." Not long before, she explained, she and four relatives had gathered with thousands of other displaced New Orleans residents at the interchange of Interstate 10 and Causeway Boulevard for evacuation. After she boarded a bus bound for Texas, Williams realized to her dismay that her family would not be allowed to join her. Nor did state troopers allow her to disembark. Now, like countless other victims of Hurricane Katrina, she had to cope not only with the consequences of the winds and floods, but also with a haphazard and disorganized federal, state, and local government response.[1]

Hurricane Katrina roared ashore near New Orleans on August 29, 2005. The scale of the disaster that followed in Louisiana, Mississippi, and Alabama is difficult to comprehend. Over 1,300 people lost their lives,[2] 700,000 were displaced, hundreds of thousands were thrown out of work, and estimates of property damage approximated $100 billion.[3]

Experts had warned governments for years that the below-sea-level neighborhoods of New Orleans, protected by levees and canals, made the city vulnerable to such an event. Disappearing wetlands in the Mississippi delta had left the city even more exposed to the devasta-

tion that a major storm could bring.[4] Walter Maestri, a local emergency management official, said in 2001 that "Even though I have to plan for it, I don't even want to think about the loss of life a huge hurricane would cause."[5]

The 2005 storm was devastating, but what shocked most Americans was the seeming incapacity of all levels of government to respond to the calamity. For days, chaos and lawlessness gripped the city as thousands of increasingly desperate disaster victims waited for rescue in the Superdome, at the city Convention Center, at the I-10 cloverleaf, in hospitals and nursing homes, and on the roofs of their houses. Whatever plans each level of government had made seemed to be dependent on another level of government's bearing most of the burden. New Orleans Mayor Ray Nagin said that city had hoped to "Get people to higher ground and have the feds and the state airlift supplies to them—that was the plan, man."[6] Louisiana Governor Kathleen Blanco argued that the state lacked capacity to respond without significant federal assistance. As her chief of staff put it, "This was a bigger natural disaster than any state could handle by itself, let alone a small state and a relatively poor one."[7] Still, congressional investigators found that state and local governments were too slow to evacuate, had inadequate plans for sheltering evacuees, and suffered from poor coordination and communication.[8]

The federal government's own curiously flat-footed response compounded the problem. The Federal Emergency Management Agency (FEMA), which had recently made a difficult transition to the new Department of Homeland Security, was slow to realize how serious the disaster was, and its bureaucratic requirements held up the arrival of trailers, helicopters, and rescue personnel to the affected area.[9] President Bush himself appeared to have received poor advice in the disaster aftermath, and FEMA director Michael Brown had not even received the required training to act as a federal "incident management" coordinator.[10] For his part, Brown (who was fired in the wake of the disaster) blamed the delayed response on bickering between the state and the city. "I very strongly, personally regret," Brown told Congress, "that I was unable to persuade Governor Blanco and Mayor Nagin to sit down, get over their differences and work together."[11]

Five years later, complaints about the government response continued. Over $3 billion in appropriated intergovernmental aid had not been expended, the population of New Orleans was still nearly 25 percent smaller than it was before the hurricane, and the dikes protecting major parts of the city still were not designed to protect it from the largest hurricanes.[12] The Deepwater Horizon oil spill in the Gulf of Mexico in 2010 further devastated the local economy. "This place might come back one day," said Doloris Wells, a 69-year-old resident of one of the hardest hit areas, "but I'm afraid I will not live to see it."[13]

Disaster planning and response have always been a joint effort between all levels of government. States and cities serve as critical "first responders" in times of crisis, but their limited resources mean that they must work smoothly with the national government and rely on federal largesse when they are overwhelmed. Hurricane Katrina shook the faith of the public and of many policymakers that this process was working effectively. As Senator Susan Collins (R-ME) put it, "If our system did such a poor job when there was no enemy . . . how would the federal, state and local governments have coped with a terrorist attack that provided no advance warning and that was intent on causing as much death and destruction as possible?"[14]

Making the Connection

In this chapter, you will learn about the way in which authority is divided between states and the federal, or national, government in a system of government called *federalism*. You will also learn how responsibilities are divided between states and local governments, making for a three-tiered system of government. A disaster such as Hurricane Katrina highlights how difficult it can be to secure co-ordination between all three tiers of government when each has responsibilities that overlap with those of the other two tiers. Because different levels of government are led by elected officials, often from different political parties, who are constantly trying to satisfy their constituents, conflicts between levels of government are often difficult to reconcile. In the pages that follow, you will learn about how the contemporary system of federalism evolved from debates and conflicts that occurred over more than two centuries, beginning with the writing and ratification of the Constitution, up through the Civil War, down to the present day. Our federal system has been shaped not only by major Supreme Court rulings but by decisions made by the president and Congress as well as leaders at the state and local level. Opinions about federalism have often divided the political parties, and elections have played a critical role in determining how the shape of the federal system.

3.1

Differentiate between federalism and other forms of government.

sovereignty
Fundamental governmental authority.

federalism
Division of sovereignty between at least two different levels of government.

Dillon's rule
Legal doctrine that local governments are mere creatures of the state.

unitary government
System under which all authority is held by a single, national government.

The Federalism Debate: It's New but It's Old

Federalism is best understood as a question regarding which levels of government should exercise **sovereignty**—that is, fundamental governmental authority. **Federalism** divides sovereignty between at least two different levels. In the United States, the fundamental units are the national government and the state governments, and each has the power to act independently of the other. For a democratic government to be called a federal system, each fundamental level of government must have:

1. Its own set of elected officials.
2. Its own capacity to raise revenues by means of taxation.
3. Independent authority to pass laws regulating the lives of its citizens.

Local governments, such as cities, counties, towns, and school districts, are also important institutions of government in the United States, but they are not fundamental units in the U.S. federal system in the same way that the national and state governments are. According to a long-standing legal doctrine known as **Dillon's rule** (after the nineteenth-century Iowa judge John Dillon), local governments are, in legal terms, mere "creatures of the state." A state legislature can, at any time, alter the boundaries of any local government, expand or narrow its power, or abolish it altogether. Because local governments are by law secondary, we set them aside for the moment and begin by discussing the relationships between states and the federal government.

Federalism in Context

As a principle of government, federalism has had a dubious history. The vast majority of countries in the world reject federalism in favor of **unitary governments,** in which all authority is held by a single, national government. In unitary arrangements, regional and local governments are simply administrative outposts of the national government. In Britain, for example, Parliament has the power to abolish all local governments, a power it has often used to redesign the country's municipal and county governments. Even though Britain has granted some powers to local Scottish and Northern Irish parliaments, it could abolish or override these parliaments at any time (see the accompanying *International Comparison box*, page 67).

At the other extreme is *confederation*, a form of government in which subunits retain all of their sovereignty, delegating only a few specific tasks to the central government. One example of confederation is the national government formed by the states through the Articles of Confederation (see Chapter 2). Federalism lies in between the extremes of unitary governments and confederations. Because of this middle position, many political leaders have been skeptical that federalism would work in practice. Specifically, they feel that the powerful state and national governments will inevitably come into conflict with one another. Thomas Hobbes (see Chapter 2) thought that if local sub-governments were granted sovereign authority, they would eat away at the power of the national government "like worms in the entrails of a natural man."[15]

INTERNATIONAL COMPARISON

Great Britain and the United States: Unitary and Federal Governments

In Great Britain, which has a unitary government, the national government (Parliament) can reorganize regional and local governments whenever it wishes. In 1998, to put into effect a peace agreement reached between warring factions within the Catholic and Protestant communities in Northern Ireland, the British Parliament reorganized the government of Northern Ireland, granting it an autonomous assembly. Parliament has also created assemblies for Scotland and Wales. But Parliament, if it so desires, can at any time eliminate the regional governments of Wales, Scotland, and Northern Ireland, and it can pass legislation to override their policies. As it is, the new assemblies have power only over such "secondary" policy areas as health, agriculture, education, local government, and economic development. The National Assembly of Wales has endured particular ridicule for spending inordinate amounts of time on inconsequential matters such as the location of member seats in the chamber (an issue that occasioned a tumultuous floor debate in 2003) or whether drivers should be allowed to place the Welsh dragon emblem on their license plates (a controversy handled in 2008). As the presiding officer put it, "What is the point of getting up in the morning, cleaning my teeth, washing and shaving, if you go to work in an institution like this?"

• *In the United States, which has a federal system of government, Congress cannot change the constitutional powers of states, reorganize state government, or change state boundaries without the state's consent. In your view, what are the advantages and disadvantages of a federal system with regard to*

BRITAIN: A UNITARY GOVERNMENT

Regional and local boundaries can be changed by the British national government at any time.

(1) political accountability, (2) efficient administration, and (3) cultural identity?

Source: Alison Rowat, "Giving New Voice to the Valleys; The Welsh traditionally treat devolution with a kind of jokey contempt. Can the Assembly change that?" *The Herald* (Glasgow), (April 30, 2004): 13; WalesOnline, "Dragon Number Plate Move 'Waste of Time,'" October 2, 2008. http://www.walesonline.co.uk/news/wales-news/2008/10/02/dragon-number-plate-move-waste-of-time-91466-21946186/

Despite such skepticism, federalism proved to be essential to the founding and growth of the United States. The authors of the Constitution provided for a strong central government, but they preserved the sovereignty of the existing states to help win the ratification debate. As the United States added new territories in later decades, federalism allowed these territories to enter the union in an orderly way. Finally, because states are able to make their own policies, federalism has helped the United States adapt to different cultural and economic conditions. As early as the 1830s, the keen French observer of American politics Alexis de Tocqueville noted, "One can hardly imagine how much [the] division of sovereignty contributes to the well-being of each of the states that compose the Union. In these small communities . . . all public authority [is] turned toward internal improvements."[16]

Long before federalism had gained international respectability, Americans had reached almost universal agreement on its worth. But the skeptics were right on one point: The exact distribution of powers between the national and state governments has been a subject of great conflict over the course of the nation's history. Political parties and elected officials have infused these struggles with grand arguments based on fundamental principles of governance. But the political divisions over these issues have reflected the practical consequences of the distribution of power for policy and for elections. Those in control of the national government have frequently come to admire the centralization of power, while those in control of state governments stridently defend their autonomy.

Federalism and the Ratification of the Constitution

THE CONSTITUTION, TENTH AMENDMENT: *"The powers not delegated to the United States by the Constitution, nor prohibited by it to the States, are reserved to the States respectively, or to the people."*

The earliest debate over federalism divided the Federalists and the Anti-Federalists at the time the Constitution was being ratified. The Federalists were especially concerned with the military strength and economic vitality of the United States as a whole.[17] They favored a strong national government, arguing that only centralized power could overcome rivalries among the states and defend the nation against foreign powers. Many Anti-Federalists were suspicious of the potential threat of national power to the independence of states and localities.[18] They wanted to limit the authority of the central government, fearing that a powerful national government would trample the liberties of the people.

The Constitution represents a compromise between these competing groups. To appease those who wanted a weak national government, the Constitution denied Congress a general legislative power, giving it instead only specific, delegated powers, such as the right to levy taxes and to regulate interstate commerce. It also gave states independent authority, such as the responsibility for appointing officers in the militia (today known as the National Guard). In addition, it guaranteed existing state boundaries, saying that no state can be stripped of its territory or divided into parts without its consent. The Anti-Federalists also won (as part of the Bill of Rights) the Tenth Amendment, which reserved to the states and to the people all powers not delegated to the federal government.

To satisfy those who wanted a strong national government, the Constitution gave Congress, in addition to its delegated powers, the authority to undertake all activities "necessary and proper" to carry out its enumerated powers. It also enacted a **supremacy clause** stating that laws of the national government "shall be the supreme Law of the Land . . . any Thing in the . . . Laws of any State to the Contrary notwithstanding," a statement that comes close to saying (yet does not quite say) that only the national government is truly sovereign. Table 3.1 summarizes the allocation of powers between the national and state governments.

supremacy clause
Constitutional provision that says the laws of the national government "shall be the supreme Law of the Land."

TABLE 3.1
CONSTITUTIONAL DIVISION OF POWER BETWEEN NATIONAL AND STATE GOVERNMENTS

• *Why are both the national government and the state governments given vague grants of power (in the necessary and proper clause) and why are states given the right to exercise powers not granted to the national government?*

Powers Granted to the National Government	Powers Granted to the State Governments
Conduct foreign affairs	
Raise armies and declare war	Maintain state militias (the National Guard)
Regulate imports and exports	
Regulate interstate commerce	Regulate commerce within the state
Regulate immigration and naturalization	
Establish and operate federal court system	Establish and operate state court systems
Levy taxes	Levy taxes
Borrow money	Borrow money
Coin money	
Provide for the general welfare	
Make laws "necessary and proper" to accomplish the above tasks	Exercise powers not granted to the national government

Evolution of the Federalism Debate

3.2
Trace key developments in the historical debate over dual sovereignty and nullification.

Because the authors of the Constitution compromised on many of the differences between Federalists and Anti-Federalists, the issues raised at the time of the ratification campaign have never disappeared from American politics. Instead, the shape of American federalism has fluctuated over the course of American history, as the events in Figure 3.1 illustrate.

The driving force behind this fluctuation in the meaning of federalism has been political conflict between those who would benefit most from centralized power and those who would benefit most from local control. As the issues of the day changed, the coalitions favoring national power and local power shifted along with them. Changes in control of Congress and the presidency often have had direct and immediate effects on the federal system.

Political conflict over the meaning of federalism has also often found its way to the Supreme Court, as the federal government, states, and individuals have engaged in legal battles, hoping that the courts will validate friendly interpretations of the Constitution. Supreme Court decisions have had a fundamental impact because the Supreme Court has the power of **judicial review,** the authority to declare laws null and void on the grounds that they violate the Constitution (see Chapter 15). When the Supreme Court declares a law of Congress unconstitutional, it not only limits congressional power but also often expands the arena in which states are considered sovereign. When the Supreme Court declares state laws unconstitutional, its decisions often have the reverse effect—expanding national power at the expense of state sovereignty. In the pages that follow, we shall see how political conflict, elections, and the Supreme Court have altered the shape of federalism.

judicial review
Court authority to declare laws null and void on the grounds that they violate the Constitution.

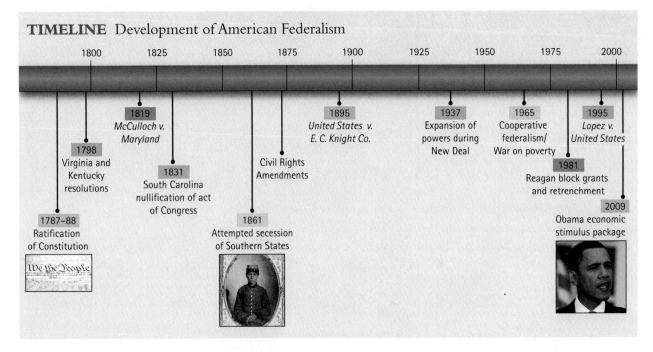

TIMELINE Development of American Federalism

1819
McCulloch v. Maryland

1798
Virginia and Kentucky resolutions

1831
South Carolina nullification of act of Congress

1895
United States v. E. C. Knight Co.

Civil Rights Amendments

1937
Expansion of powers during New Deal

1965
Cooperative federalism/ War on poverty

1995
Lopez v. United States

1981
Reagan block grants and retrenchment

1787–88
Ratification of Constitution

1861
Attempted secession of Southern States

2009
Obama economic stimulus package

We the People

FIGURE 3.1

DEVELOPMENT OF AMERICAN FEDERALISM

Nationally elected leaders, state legislators, and courts have all shaped the evolution of American federalism.

• *Which of these events has had the broadest impact on American politics?*

Dual Sovereignty and Nullification

dual sovereignty

A theory of federalism saying that both the national and state governments have final authority over their own policy domains.

Much of the legal debate over federalism, both historical and contemporary, concerns the doctrine of **dual sovereignty,** which says that both the national and state governments have final authority over their own policy domains. As a legal and political doctrine, dual sovereignty is an American invention that challenges Thomas Hobbes's argument that there could be only one sovereign (see Chapter 2).

The authors of *The Federalist Papers* defended dual sovereignty by turning Hobbes's argument on its head. Whereas Hobbes said that divided sovereignty would lead to war, they argued that ensuring the division of power was the best way of preserving liberty. If power is concentrated in any one place, it can be used to crush individual rights.

tyranny of the majority

Suppression of rights imposed by those voted into power by a majority.

Even in a democracy, a **tyranny of the majority** (a suppression of rights by those voted into power by a majority) may arise—and that is the worst kind of tyranny because it is stifling, complete, and seemingly legitimate. Dividing power between the national and state governments reduces the possibility that any single majority will be able to control all centers of governmental power.

nullification

A doctrine that says that states have the authority to declare acts of Congress unconstitutional.

Dual-sovereignty theory was an entrenched part of constitutional understanding during the first decades after the adoption of the Constitution. Some supporters of states' rights thought state sovereignty so complete that they propounded the doctrine of **nullification,** which says that state legislatures can invalidate acts of Congress that threaten state or individual liberties. States first used this doctrine in 1798 in response to the passage of the Alien and Sedition Acts, national laws that outlawed criticism of government officials. A Federalist-controlled Congress enacted the legislation to suppress the growing power of the Democratic–Republican Party, led by Thomas Jefferson. Opposition newspaper editors were imprisoned, and Vermont Congressman Matthew Lyon was even arrested and prosecuted under these laws. Invoking the doctrine of nullification, outraged Jeffersonian legislators in Virginia and Kentucky passed resolutions voiding the law within their states.

At first, the doctrine of nullification had no serious consequences for national unity. On the contrary, the idea that states could undermine or overrule national policy was firmly rejected in **McCulloch v. Maryland,** a sweeping 1819 Supreme Court decision that is among the most important the Court has ever made.[19] The issue involved a dispute over the Bank of the United States, an institution that national commercial interests thought was vital to economic prosperity but that many local farmers, small businesses, and debtors blamed for causing a recent financial crisis. Responding to popular opinion, the state of Maryland levied a tax on the bank. James McCulloch, an officer of the bank's Maryland branch, refused to pay this tax.

McCulloch v. Maryland
Decision of 1819 in which the Supreme Court declared unconstitutional the state's power to tax a federal government entity.

A unanimous Court found in favor of McCulloch and the national government. In his opinion, Chief Justice John Marshall dismissed Maryland's argument that the national government possessed only those powers delegated to it by the sovereign states. The nation's citizens, not the states', were the source of national power, he wrote. "The government of the Union . . . is, emphatically and truly, a government of the people. In form and in substance, it emanates from them." Because the people were the source of the central government's authority, a state could not override a national law. Although Marshall admitted that Maryland's tax was not a direct attempt to negate a law, as the Virginia and Kentucky resolutions had been, he said it was still unconstitutional because the "power to tax involves the power to destroy."[20] If a state government could tax a federal agency, then states could undermine the sovereignty of the federal government, just as if they had asserted that a national law was null and void. In declaring this state law unconstitutional, Marshall cast profound doubt on the power of the states to nullify acts of Congress.

Despite the *McCulloch* decision, the doctrine of nullification was not dead. The issue next arose shortly after the tumultuous 1828 election of Andrew Jackson as president. His vice president, John Calhoun of South Carolina, claimed that states had the power to nullify federal laws, such as a tariff law that harmed Southern interests. Northern manufacturers favored the law as a way of protecting the region's industries from foreign competition, but Southerners objected that it harmed their ability to export cotton and to import cheap European products.

After winning the 1832 South Carolina legislative elections, Calhoun's supporters called a special convention that declared the tariff null and void in the state. The state even threatened to secede from the Union if the federal government tried to collect the tariff by force. President Jackson prepared to use the U.S. Army and Navy to crush the dissidents, but cooler heads prevailed. Congress passed a lower tariff less objectionable to southern interests, and South Carolina agreed to pay it.

An even more important and less tractable issue was slavery. Afraid that Northerners would abolish slavery, southern leaders continued to espouse the doctrine of nullification as well as the right to secede peacefully from the Union. The issue came to a head with the election of Abraham Lincoln in 1860. Lincoln was the candidate of the new Republican Party, which opposed the extension of slavery into the western territories and favored its eventual abolition. Seeing the Republican victory as a direct threat to slavery, white Southerners invoked what they saw as their right of secession, and the United States experienced what Hobbes had most feared: a war between competing sovereigns. South Carolina, the state that had precipitated the tariff crisis, was the first to secede. Only after half a million soldiers had died and the southern countryside had been laid to waste was the doctrine of nullification finally repudiated. After the Civil War, it was clear that whatever dual sovereignty meant, it did not mean that state legislatures could declare null and void the decisions of the federal government.

3.3

Evaluate the impact of specific Supreme Court decisions on the relationship of national and state governments.

The Supreme Court and the Meaning of Dual Sovereignty

Once the doctrine of nullification had been laid to rest, it was up to the federal courts, not state legislatures, to decide the constitutional meaning of dual sovereignty. For more than 60 years following the Civil War, the Supreme Court generally defended the sovereignty of the states against national power. Although the war had settled the issue of whether states could secede, the Court preserved state autonomy in such areas as economic regulation and, distressingly, racial segregation (see Chapter 17). In the 1930s, after a political battle that threatened to change the structure of the Supreme Court (see below), the Court began to side most often with those who argued for broader national authority. The Court soon interpreted the Constitution's commerce clause and necessary and proper clause, which define the boundaries of national power, as allowing much more federal intervention into areas that were previously the domains of the states. Since the mid-1990s, however, a more conservative Court has used a series of key decisions that reassert states' rights under these clauses. The Court has also invoked the doctrine of state sovereign immunity, found in the Eleventh Amendment, to expand state authority in the federal system.

The Commerce Clause and the Court-Packing Episode

CONSTITUTION, ARTICLE I: *"Congress shall have power . . . to regulate commerce . . . among the several states."*

In 1932, Democrat Franklin D. Roosevelt defeated Republican incumbent Herbert Hoover in a bitter presidential election that foreshadowed a period of expansion of federal power. Campaigning in the midst of the Great Depression, Roosevelt promised to use the power of the federal government to make the country prosperous again. He and his Democratic Party allies in Congress enacted a series of governmental policies known as the **New Deal,** a wide array of programs that expanded the power of the federal government for the purposes of stimulating economic recovery and creating a national safety net for those in need. Many Republicans opposed these New Deal policies, arguing that they violated long-standing principles of federalism.

Roosevelt's critics challenged many New Deal programs in court, presenting the Supreme Court with the difficult problem of deciding whether the new laws abided by the Constitution. The critical issue was often whether the programs violated the **commerce clause,** which gives Congress the power to regulate commerce among the states. For example, the National Industrial Recovery Act (NIRA) of 1933 allowed

New Deal

Programs created by the Franklin Roosevelt administration that expanded the power of the federal government for the purpose of stimulating economic recovery and establishing a national safety net for those in need.

commerce clause

Constitutional provision that gives Congress power to regulate commerce "among the states."

the president to regulate most businesses in an effort to restrict "unfair competition." Regulated businesses could be local, regional, or national in scope. Under the law, President Roosevelt approved a "Live Poultry Code" in 1934 that regulated hours, wages, and other labor standards in the New York state poultry industry. The commerce clause says that the national government may regulate commerce "among the states"; did this mean that the poultry code was illegal because it concerned poultry operations within a single state?

The courts have generally distinguished interstate (between-state) commerce, which Congress may regulate, from intrastate (within-state) commerce, which only the states can regulate. In the nineteenth century, intrastate commerce was defined as including all commerce that did not overtly cross state lines. Thus, for example, the Supreme Court in 1895 said, in *United States v. E. C. Knight Co.*, that Congress could not break up a monopoly that had a nationwide impact on the price of sugar, because the company that enjoyed the monopoly refined its sugar solely within the state of Pennsylvania.[21] The fact that the sugar was to be sold nationwide was said to be only "incidental" to its production.

Roosevelt and his allies argued that commercial markets had become so intertwined by the 1930s that seemingly local activity affected the national economy. But the Supreme Court disagreed, and it ruled in the critical case of *Schechter Poultry Corp. v. United States* that the regulation of economic activity inside individual states under the NIRA was unconstitutional (see page 000 in Chapter 15). In authorizing codes that prescribed the manner in which animals were slaughtered and sold within states, said the Court, Congress had gone beyond its authority to regulate interstate commerce.[22]

Democrats were furious at this decision and others that restricted their ability to enact programs that they saw as necessary to combat the Depression. Roosevelt mocked the Court for using an outdated "horse-and-buggy definition of interstate commerce."[23] Never before had federalism placed the Supreme Court in such direct conflict with the president and Congress.

An unusual lack of retirements by Supreme Court justices had prevented Roosevelt from appointing any new members to the Court following his 1932 election. But, after his landslide reelection victory in 1936, Roosevelt believed he had the public mandate he needed to move against the Court politically. Early the following year, he surprised Congress with a proposal to add up to six new justices, one for each sitting justice older than 70. The resulting larger Court would be more efficient and more effective, argued the president. And—of course—it would be dominated by Roosevelt appointees. "The people are with me," FDR confidently told visitors to the White House.[24]

Many politicians and members of the public were uneasy with the president's proposal. They worried that the sudden increase in the size of the Court would upset the separation of powers between the branches of government. Roosevelt's "court-packing scheme" met stern opposition in Congress and was killed in the Senate Judiciary Committee.

Although Roosevelt lost the battle, he won the war. Less than two months after he announced his court-packing plan, Chief Justice Charles Evans Hughes and Justice

Packing the Court

This 1937 editorial cartoon shows the public's ambivalence about President Roosevelt's plan to add justices to the Supreme Court.

• *Did the "switch in time" really "save nine"?*

Owen Roberts, who had previously voted to restrict federal power, changed their views. This time the issue involved the recently passed Wagner Act, a New Deal law that protected union organizers. Despite the fact that the new law regulated activities within a state, a Court majority, in a 5 to 4 vote, declared it constitutional. Chief Justice Hughes explained: "When industries organize themselves on a national scale, . . . how can it be maintained that their industrial labor relations constitute a forbidden field into which Congress may not enter?"[25] Relations between employers and their workers, once said to be local, were now found to be part of interstate commerce.

The change of heart by Hughes and Roberts has been called "the switch in time that saved nine." In fact, the court-packing episode both illustrates the Court's susceptibility to political pressure and represents a critical shift in the dominant conception of federalism. With new appointments to the Court by President Roosevelt, the definition of interstate commerce continued to expand. In 1942, a farmer violated crop quotas imposed under New Deal legislation by sowing 23 acres of wheat. The Court ruled the quota law a constitutional regulation of interstate commerce, even though the farmer was feeding all the wheat to his own livestock. The Court reasoned that the farmer, by not buying wheat and instead producing his own, was depressing the worldwide price of grain.[26] With such an expansive definition of interstate commerce, hardly anything could be characterized as simply local or beyond the scope of Congress to regulate.

This broad interpretation of the commerce clause remained unquestioned until 1995. That year, the Supreme Court considered the constitutionality of the Gun Free School Zones Act. Enacted in response to public concerns about high crime rates, this law made it a federal crime to carry firearms near a public school.

In *United States v. Lopez*, a case involving a young man with no criminal record who brought a .38 caliber handgun (and five bullets) to school, the Court said that Congress did not have the power to enact this law. Rejecting the argument that education affects interstate commerce and is therefore fair game for congressional regulation, the Court said that states alone had the authority to govern this type of activity. "We do not doubt," wrote Chief Justice Rehnquist, "that Congress has authority . . . to regulate numerous commercial activities that . . . affect the educational process. That authority, though broad, does not include the authority to regulate each and every aspect of local schools."[27]

Since *Lopez,* the Supreme Court has been more willing to place limits on Congress's ability to intervene in state and local affairs. In 2000, for example, the Court invalidated a law that gave victims of domestic violence the power to sue their attackers in federal courts. Gender-motivated violence, the Court ruled, had little or nothing to do with interstate commerce.[28] The Court still has allowed Congress to regulate broadly when the activities at issue are more closely related to commerce, however. For example, in 2005 the Supreme Court allowed Congress to override state laws allowing the use of medicinal marijuana, on the grounds that marijuana cultivation, similar to wheat cultivation, has "a substantial effect on supply and demand in the national market."[29]

The medicinal marijuana issue illustrates that politics often regulates the interaction between states and the national government just as much—or more—than constitutional boundaries do. Despite the Supreme Court's endorsement of federal drug laws that prohibit the possession and distribution of cannabis, the Drug Enforcement Administration (DEA) has been reluctant to interfere with state policies in the 14 states that allow medicinal marijuana use. In 2009, Attorney General Eric Holder announced that the Justice Department would not seek to prosecute cases involving marijuana that was being grown

Marijuana—A Medical Necessity or an Illegal Drug?

This 67-year-old former paratrooper smokes medical marijuana at his home, in order to ease the pain of spinal cancer. He says that smoking the drug helps him sleep at night, has restored his appetite, and has reduced his need for expensive prescription drugs.

• *Should states or the federal government regulate drugs like marijuana?*

and used in compliance with state laws. Although officials stressed that "no state can authorize violations of federal law," they explained the change in policy as a way for the federal government to make "efficient and rational use of its limited . . . resources."[30]

Necessary and Proper Clause

CONSTITUTION, ARTICLE I: *"Congress shall have power . . . to make all laws which shall be necessary and proper for carrying into Execution the . . . Powers vested by this Constitution in the government of the United States."*

The delegated powers of Congress include those items specifically mentioned in the Constitution, such as the power to tax, borrow money, and establish a currency. The **necessary and proper clause** gives Congress the authority to "make all laws which shall be necessary and proper for carrying to execution" its delegated powers. Justice John Marshall first analyzed the words *necessary and proper* in the same decision that challenged the doctrine of nullification, *McCulloch v. Maryland*. Maryland argued that Congress had no authority to establish a national bank, because a bank was not *necessary* for Congress to carry out its delegated powers to borrow and hold money; it was only a *convenient* way of doing so. But Justice Marshall rejected such an interpretation as annihilating Congress's ability to select an appropriate means to carry out a task.

"Let the end be legitimate," Marshall said. "Let it be within the scope of the Constitution, and all means which are appropriate, which are plainly adapted to that end, which are not prohibited, but consistent with the letter and spirit of the Constitution, are constitutional."[31] Since this decision, the courts have found that almost any means selected by Congress is "necessary and proper." As a result, the necessary and proper clause has come to be known as the *elastic clause*: Over the centuries it has been stretched to fit almost any circumstance.

Even though an elastic interpretation of the necessary and proper clause has given Congress broad powers, the Supreme Court said in 1992 that these powers are not without limit. The case involved the disposal of low-level radioactive waste—waste from medical research, radiation detection equipment, and cleaning materials in power plants. The difficulty, as with other radioactive waste, is that choosing a site for waste disposal is complicated by a **NIMBY problem:** Everyone wants the problem solved, but "Not in My Back Yard."

In the 1980s, Congress settled on what seemed like a politically painless solution: require the states to figure it out. A federal law passed in 1985 told states either to dispose of the waste themselves or to face legal consequences for any damage the waste might cause.

When New York State sued to prevent enforcement of this law, the Supreme Court ruled in the state's favor, saying that constitutional principles prevent Congress from using "outright coercion" to solve the waste disposal problem.[32] Although the national government may use powerful incentives to encourage states to comply with its wishes (as we will see later in the chapter), it cannot simply issue a direct order. One New York official called the ruling a "terrific affirmation of states' rights."[33]

With the radioactive waste case, the old doctrine of dual sovereignty was clearly revived. All doubts seemed to vanish in 1997 when the Supreme Court invalidated a portion of a national gun control law (the Brady Law) that required local police to check the backgrounds of gun buyers. If such a law were allowed to stand, said the Court, it would "compromise the structural framework of dual sovereignty."[34]

---

necessary and proper clause
Constitutional clause that gives Congress the power to take all actions that are "necessary and proper" to the carrying out of its delegated powers. Also known as the *elastic clause*.

NIMBY problem
Problem in which everyone wants the problem solved, but "Not In My Back Yard."

State Sovereign Immunity

CONSTITUTION, ELEVENTH AMENDMENT: *"The Judicial power of the United States shall not be construed to extend to any suit in law or equity, commenced or prosecuted against one of the United States. . . . "*

The necessary and proper clause and the commerce clause gives power to the national government, but the Eleventh Amendment, ratified in 1795, explicitly restricts it. Since the mid-1990s, the Supreme Court has used the Eleventh Amendment to reinforce, and in some cases expand, the concept of **state sovereign immunity,** a legal doctrine that says states cannot be sued under federal law by private parties.

For example, the Americans With Disabilities Act of 1990 allowed disabled employees to sue their employers if they were mistreated because of their disabilities. But, when breast cancer sufferer Patricia Garrett sued her employer—the state of Alabama—charging discrimination, the Supreme Court ruled that her lawsuit was invalid. Because of their immunity, "[s]tates are not required . . . to make special accommodations for the disabled," wrote Chief Justice Rehnquist in his 2001 opinion.[35]

The doctrine of state sovereign immunity does not immunize states against all federal laws, however. In 2003, the Court found that the Eleventh Amendment did not exempt states from being sued under the Family and Medical Leave Act, a law that requires employers to grant up to 12 weeks of unpaid leave to employees caring for a new child or seriously ill relative. Because the law was designed to ensure the civil rights of women (see Chapter 17), the Court found that Congress was within its constitutional authority to enact the law. It seems clear that the Court is sympathetic to claims of state sovereign immunity, but not in cases where important constitutional rights may have been violated.

state sovereign immunity
Legal doctrine, based on the Eleventh Amendment, that says states cannot be sued under federal law by private parties.

3.4

Compare and contrast the advantages and disadvantages of federal categorical and block grants distributed to state and local governments.

marble-cake federalism
The theory that all levels of government can work together to solve common problems. Also known as *cooperative federalism.*

Cooperative Federalism

The commerce clause, the necessary and proper clause, and the doctrine of state sovereign immunity work to define the boundaries between the domains of the states and of the federal government. These provisions therefore establish a constitutional basis for dual sovereignty. The congressional power to tax and spend, on the other hand, provides the constitutional basis for what has become known as the theory of **marble-cake federalism,** or *cooperative federalism.* According to this theory, first propounded by political scientist Morton Grodzins, all levels of government should—and in fact do—perform all governmental functions together. Because the Supreme Court has established a broad interpretation of Congress's spending power, the most serious political conflicts over national powers to tax and spend have occurred not in courtrooms, but in Congress and the state legislatures. These battles have often revolved around the nature of federal grants to state and local governments.

Spending Clause

CONSTITUTION, ARTICLE I: *"Congress shall have power . . . to lay and collect taxes, duties, imposts and excises, to pay the debts and provide for the . . . general welfare of the United States."*

The **spending clause** grants Congress the power to collect taxes to provide for the general welfare. The New Deal Supreme Court considered the meaning of this clause

spending clause
Constitutional provision that gives Congress the power to collect taxes to provide for the general welfare.

when it ruled on the constitutionality of the social security program for senior citizens, which was enacted in 1935. A taxpayer challenged the program on the grounds that tax dollars were being spent for the *specific* welfare of the elderly, not for the *general* welfare. But the Supreme Court, now in tune with Roosevelt's enlarged conception of federal power, said it was up to Congress, not the Court, to decide whether any particular program provided for the general welfare. "[T]he discretion belongs to Congress," said the Court, "unless the choice is clearly wrong."[36] So far, the Court has never found Congress "clearly wrong."

Not only did the Supreme Court refuse to restrict the purposes for which Congress could tax and spend money, but it also conceded to Congress the right to attach any reasonable regulation to the money it spends. In 1984, Congress provided a grant to state governments for highway maintenance but withheld some of the funding unless states raised the drinking age from 18 to 21. South Dakota challenged the constitutionality of this mandate on the grounds that teenage drunkenness had only a remote connection to road repair. The Supreme Court rejected this argument.[37] State sovereignty was not violated, the Court concluded, because any state could choose not to accept the money (see the Election Voices feature on page 91).

The congressional power to tax and spend has remained one of the broadest federal powers because it allows Congress to attach whatever regulations it deems appropriate to the money it gives to states. Nevertheless, it is not beyond the realm of possibility that the Supreme Court could restrict this authority in its future decisions. In the South Dakota case, Chief Justice Rehnquist pointed out that "the spending power is of course not unlimited," and several judges have argued that the Court should begin to narrow its interpretation of the spending clause to safeguard some "sovereign rights" of the states.[38]

A Government of Shared Functions   Political scientist Morton Grodzins criticized proponents of dual sovereignty for viewing government as a layer cake, each level independent of and separate from the others.[39] He pointed out that Congress has established many programs in which the agencies established to operate them must work together with other levels of government, combining and intertwining their functions to such an extent that the intergovernmental system resembles a marble cake (see the *Election Connection* box).

In all policy realms, Grodzins said, we find many levels of government working together on similar tasks. For example, in the area of disaster planning and response, the national Federal Emergency Management Agency (FEMA) must coordinate its efforts with state offices of emergency preparedness as well as with local first responders such as police departments and rescue squads. As the Katrina case shows, coordination can often be difficult, but according to Grodzins all levels of government should work together for three reasons:

1. Cooperative federalism is democratic. The involvement of all levels of government ensures that many different interests in society are represented.
2. Compromises are reached among officials elected by different constituencies. Federal officials listen to state and local officials, because the latter have influence with members of Congress. Similarly, state officials listen to community leaders, because to stay in office state legislators must pay attention to local needs.

ELECTION CONNECTION

Cooperative Federalism and the Homeland Security Grant Program

In the 2010 fiscal year, the Department of Homeland Security distributed a total of $1.8 billion in homeland security grant funds to states and local governments. The process of deciding which governments received which grants provides a window into how the intergovernmental process works.

1. *All states got some amount of grant money.* No member of Congress or state government official would have to explain to his or her constituents that no money was forthcoming. Regardless of any estimates of risk or effectiveness, every state got some minimum allocation.
2. *A portion of the decision-making process involved risk assessment.* Relying on estimates provided by intelligence analysts, Department of Homeland Security officials divvied up the pot of funds based on which jurisdictions were most likely to suffer terrorist attacks or other disasters.
3. *State and local officials were deeply involved in the process.* States and localities were required to submit proposals indicating how they would use any grant money. But their involvement in the process did not end there. State and local homeland security officials also participated in a review process that examined the quality of the proposals.

Local governments use Homeland Security Grants to fund projects such as the San Antonio police department's mobile command post.

• *Does this process seem fair to you? How do you think elected officials at all levels of government would react if the grants were distributed based on risk alone?*

Source: United States Department of Homeland Security, "FY 2010 Homeland Security Grant Program," www.fema.gov/government/grant/hsgp/index.shtm, accessed December 31, 2009.

---

3. Professional administrators have similar training and values, no matter what level of government they work for. Law enforcement officials have numerous things in common, whether they work for the FBI or the local police. Most educational administrators, whether federal, state, or local, were once schoolteachers. These common backgrounds enable administrators at all levels to identify with one another and to work together toward common goals.

The 1964 election of Lyndon Johnson, together with an overwhelming Democratic majority in Congress, provided an opportunity to test more fully Grodzins's theory of cooperative federalism. Over the next few years, Congress passed a broad range of legislation that greatly enlarged the number, size, and complexity of **intergovernmental grants,** programs funded in part by the federal government but administered by state and local governments. State and local governments are often required to provide matching funds for a program in order to receive the grant. The typical "match" is 50 percent of total costs, but it can be as much as 90 percent or as little as 10 percent. Intergovernmental grants have become a key feature of the federal system. In 1930, only $102.5 million was spent on intergovernmental grants to local governments.[40] As Figure 3.2 on page 82 indicates, by 1962 grants to state and local governments had grown to $56.3 billion, and by 1982 they had more than tripled to $190.2 billion. (Unless otherwise indicated, all amounts in this chapter are in 2009 dollars.)

intergovernmental grant

Grant from the national government to a state or local government.

Growth in the number and size of intergovernmental grants was facilitated by their popularity with most members of Congress. Many found they could profit handsomely from new projects begun in their home districts. As Senator Barry Goldwater said, "I don't care what the piece of equipment is—or how bad it is—if it's done in his state, the senator has to stand up and scream for it."[41] Such grants are often criticized as mere **pork barrel projects**—special legislative benefits targeted toward the constituents of particular members of Congress, but with little or no general value (see the discussion of earmarking in Chapter 12).

Most grants are, of course, well received by the city or town lucky enough to get the money, and this goodwill can improve the chances of reelection for the members of Congress responsible for the grants. "I make no excuses for the fact that, representing the district that I do, I can get dollars for specific programs," said Representative José Serrano, Democrat of New York City.[42] In 2005, public interest groups criticized thousands of grants targeted at individual states and districts that were included in a major transportation bill. Funding for several bridges in Alaska came under severe scrutiny, especially when media reports indicated that one of them would connect a tiny town to a small island at the cost of $223 million.[43] Alaska's congressional delegation fought hard for the bridges, despite the negative publicity. Finally, the state's senators and representative agreed to a sort of compromise: The money would still go to Alaska, but could be used for any purpose—not just the controversial bridges.[44]

Categorical Grants

In the 1960s and 1970s, the theory of cooperative federalism was particularly well suited to the Democratic Party. It fit well with the Democrats' philosophy, and it was not difficult to pursue as a policy, because Democrats usually controlled Congress. Many Democrats saw federal grants as vehicles that could help the country address needs that state and local governments had long ignored. But the very fact that states and localities had not addressed these problems made national lawmakers cautious of sending money to states and cities without attaching strings. To ensure that funds were properly used, Democrats generally favored **categorical grants**—grants that include regulations specifying how the money is to be spent. Although some of these categorical grants fund basic government services, such as the construction of transportation and sanitation infrastructure, most have had social welfare purposes. Categorical grants provide compensatory education for those coming from disadvantaged backgrounds, fund special educational programs for the disabled, and train the unemployed. They provide housing for low- and moderate-income groups, and food stamps for the poor. Such grants also subsidize rapid-transit systems to help reduce commuting costs.

Problems of Implementation

The national government enacted a variety of categorical grant programs as part of President Lyndon Johnson's **War on Poverty,** a wide-ranging set of programs enacted in the mid-1960s designed to enhance the economic opportunity of low-income citizens.

pork barrel projects
Special legislative benefits targeted toward the constituents of particular members of Congress.

categorical grants
Federal grants to a state and/or local government that impose programmatic restrictions on the use of funds.

War on Poverty
Series of categorical grant programs enacted in the 1960s, designed to enhance the economic opportunity of low-income citizens.

Head Start
More than four decades after the War on Poverty launched a variety of such initiatives, Head Start remains one of the most visible and successful early-intervention programs for disadvantaged preschoolers.

implementation
The way in which grant programs are administered at the local level.

Although these programs had some success at serving poor children, senior citizens, and other disadvantaged groups, they came under tough scrutiny from those who studied their **implementation**—the way in which grant programs are actually administered at the local level. These arguments are important because they continue to be made about grant programs today. Public-policy scholars gave three reasons for doubting that many intergovernmental grants were as effective as Grodzins had said:[45]

1. National and local officials, serving different constituencies, often block and check one another, making it impossible to get much done. In the debate over the economic stimulus package in 2009, for example, several Republican governors, including Louisiana's Bobby Jindal and South Carolina's Mark Sanford, vowed to reject some grant money from the federal government on the grounds that it interfered with state laws governing unemployment benefits.
2. When many participants are involved, delays and confusion are almost inevitable. One study of the Transit Security Grant Program found that only 3 percent of grants allocated between 2006 and 2008 had been spent as of February 2009.[46] As former Massachusetts Governor and 2008 presidential candidate Mitt Romney put it, "The standard grant process and purchasing procedures that exist in our country at all levels of government don't work terribly well if your objective is speed."[47]
3. Federal policymakers often raise unrealistic expectations by using exaggerated rhetoric, thereby guaranteeing disappointment. It was a mistake to equate the mid-1960s poverty programs with a "war" when only limited resources were available.

These criticisms may exaggerate the difficulty of getting different governments to cooperate. Most of the studies that chronicle these problems focus on the first two or three years of a federal grant program's life. Other research has shown that many administrative problems diminish with the passage of time. For example, the federal compensatory education program at first stigmatized disadvantaged students by separating them from their classmates in order to make sure that federal funds were concentrated on the neediest. But once administrators determined that this requirement was counterproductive to education, they eliminated it.[48] As the Hurricane Katrina episode shows, however, sometimes different levels of government do not have the luxury of time. Under such circumstances, it makes sense to pay attention to the criticisms lodged by the implementation theorists.

Block Grants

block grants
Intergovernmental grants with a broad set of objectives, a minimum of federal restrictions, and maximum discretion for local officials.

Some programs that were part of the original War on Poverty in the 1960s still exist today, such as the Head Start program that provides early childhood education to nearly 1 million children each year. But other programs suffered from the problems of implementation described above. After the War on Poverty proved less successful than its advocates had hoped, Congress sought to simplify federal policy by replacing many categorical grants with **block grants,** intergovernmental grants with a broad set of objectives, a minimum of federal restrictions, and maximum discretion for local officials. Table 3.2 illustrates the difference between categorical and block grants and gives some examples of each.

The surge toward block grants has had three distinct waves, each prompted by Republican victories in national elections. Republicans were naturally hostile to

TABLE 3.2
CATEGORICAL GRANTS AND BLOCK GRANTS: SOME EXAMPLES

Type of Grant	Restrictions on Use of Funds	Examples
Categorical grant	Significant	Food stamps (created 1971): Provide funds to states and localities to supply food to eligible low-income residents.
		Medicaid (created 1965): Provides health insurance to low-income and disadvantaged citizens.
Block grant	Minimal	Housing and Community Development Block Grant (created 1974): Provides funds to states and localities for general development purposes.
		Temporary Assistance to Needy Families (created 1996): Provides funds to states to design and implement their own welfare programs.

categorical grants because many of these grants funded programs that Republicans had opposed in the first place and believed were unnecessary or counterproductive. The first wave of block grants began after President Nixon won election to the White House in 1968. The most comprehensive, **general revenue sharing,** gave state and local governments a share of federal tax revenues to be used for any purpose whatsoever. During this first wave, block grants did not replace categorical grants so much as supplement them. To win support for general revenue sharing and other block grants, Nixon was forced to agree to continue many of the categorical programs that Democrats in Congress favored. As a consequence, the amount spent on intergovernmental grants continued to grow throughout the administrations of Nixon and Gerald Ford. By the late 1970s, as the top line in Figure 3.2 shows, they cost nearly $200 billion.

The second wave of block grants came after Ronald Reagan's 1980 defeat of Democrat Jimmy Carter. President Reagan's administration, unlike the Nixon administration, enjoyed a Republican majority in the Senate. Bolstered by this congressional support, Reagan succeeded in converting a broad range of categorical grants in education, social services, and community development to block grants. During this second wave, the new block grants not only had fewer restrictions than the older categoricals,[49] but their funding levels also were reduced to comply with the administration's overall policy of "shrinking government." As Reagan put it in a speech to state legislators, block grants would make it easier to diminish the scope of the national government and return power to the states: "The ultimate objective . . . is to use block grants . . . as a bridge, leading to the day when you'll have not only . . . the programs that properly belong at the state level, but . . . the tax sources now usurped by Washington."[50]

The third wave of block grants took place after the congressional election of 1994, when Republicans captured control of Congress. Earlier block grant initiatives had not touched large social programs, such as Medicaid and Aid to Families with Dependent Children (AFDC). But in 1996 Congress transformed the AFDC program, commonly called "welfare," into a block grant that gave states broad discretion over the way monies could be used. Congress also tried to transform the Medicaid low-income health insurance program into a block grant, but this change was forestalled by

general revenue sharing
The most comprehensive of block grants, which gives money to state and local governments to be used for any purpose whatsoever.

FIGURE 3.2

GROWTH AND CHANGE IN FEDERAL GRANTS TO STATES AND LOCALITIES

Expenditures for categorical grants continue to rise, whereas expenditures for block grants have remained stable in recent years.

• *Why do you think expenditures for block grants have not increased? Why did categorical grants increase when they did?*

Note: 2009 figures are estimates. Totals exclude defense expenditures. Deriving precise estimates of block and categorical grants is difficult. Here, we have employed grants used mainly for developmental purposes as a proxy for block grants, and grants used mainly for redistributive purposes as a proxy for categorical grants.

Sources: Paul E. Peterson, *The Price of Federalism* (Washington, DC: The Brookings Institution, 1995), p. 74; U.S. Bureau of the Census, *Federal Aid to the States for Fiscal Year 1998*; U.S. Bureau of the Census, *Federal Aid to the States for Fiscal Year 2002*; U.S. Bureau of the Census, *Federal Aid to the States for Fiscal Year 2003*; and *Statistical Abstract of the United States, 2010*, Table 420.

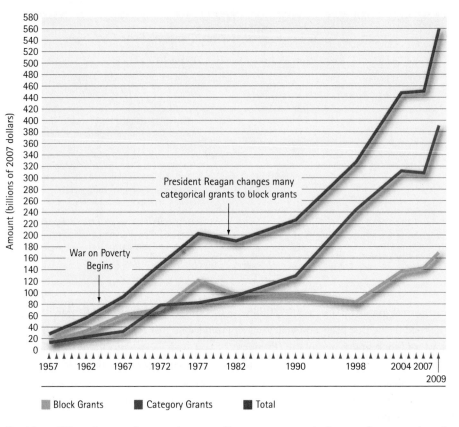

President Clinton's veto. As a result, expenditures on categorical grants have continued to rise (see Figure 3.2).

Since the 1994 election, the debate over categorical and block grants has become a matter of intense political conflict. Each side can make a compelling case for its point of view. Perhaps the best argument against both categorical and block grants is that even though they are often defended as a way of equalizing resources across the country, federal grants in fact do not have this effect.[51] Instead, wealthier states often receive more federal dollars than poorer states. Figure 3.3 shows that some of the wealthiest states get as much or more in block grants, per resident, as some of the poorest states.

Perhaps the best argument in favor of federal grants is that they are necessary to maintain properly funded social programs. Federal categorical grants, such as Medicaid, food stamps, and other social welfare programs are especially important, because states, when not subject to federal regulation, try to shift to other states the burden of serving the needy, the sick, and the poor. Fearful of migration from other places, many states feel pressured to offer fewer benefits than their neighbor states and thus create a vicious cycle of cuts that President Clinton called a "race to the bottom." From 1998 to 2009, in the wake of the reform of welfare that allowed states more flexibility, the number of people receiving welfare shrank by over 50 percent.[52] Whether a race to the bottom is responsible for these changes is unclear, but one study of state welfare programs found that "welfare policies are created in an extremely politicized environment," with state officials reacting strongly to constituent pressures and resource constraints.[53]

Although the debate over grants sometimes seems polarized between those in favor of a wide variety of intergovernmental grants and those opposed to all of them,

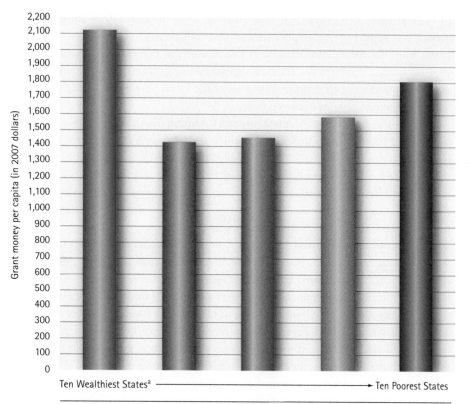

Grant money per capita (in 2007 dollars)

Ten Wealthiest States[a] ———————————————————→ Ten Poorest States

[a]Average for ten richest states. Graph groups states into quintiles.

FIGURE 3.3

STATES GET SIMILAR AMOUNTS OF GRANT MONEY

Richer states get as much or more grant money from the federal government than poorer states, controlling for population.

• *Is this unfair, or do rich states deserve more because they pay more to the federal government in taxes? Which quintile receives the least amount of grant money? Why do you think this might be?*

Note: State "wealth" defined as Gross State Product per capita.

Sources: Calculated by the authors from *Statistical Abstract of the United States,* 2010, Tables 12 and 421.

the most sensible solutions may lie somewhere in the middle. In areas where state and local governments have traditionally concentrated their efforts, including transportation, sanitation, and education, it may be appropriate to keep the federal role to a minimum, because states and localities can be expected to provide these services whether they receive federal aid or not. But in other areas, such as Medicaid and food stamps, it may be important to establish federal standards so that states do not "race to the bottom."

The Contemporary Debate

In recent years, each party has tended to favor categorical grant programs designed to advance preferred policies, and to oppose them when they go against party wishes. In 2001, for example, President George W. Bush enthusiastically signed into law a new education reform (the "No Child Left Behind" Act) that required all states, in exchange for federal dollars, to test students annually so that their educational progress could be monitored. Certain penalties are imposed on schools that fail to keep up. The intergovernmental grant program received a new stimulus in 2009 when Congress and President Barack Obama discovered it could be a powerful tool for distributing the funds appropriate as part of its economic stimulus package. Over one-third of the stimulus funds were to be spent by means of intergovernmental aid, making new use of well-established categorical grant programs for education, nutrition assistance, transportation, and public housing.[54]

The parties also have traded accusations involving **unfunded mandates,** the imposition of federal regulations on state and local governments without the appropriation

unfunded mandates
Federal regulations that impose burdens on state and local governments without appropriating enough money to cover costs.

of enough money to cover their cost. In most cases, these mandates are not "direct orders" that states must follow, but instead are stipulations that accompany categorical grants from the federal government. If a state wants to receive grant money, it must abide by certain standards and must also spend money of its own. These requirements are allowed under the Constitution because of the broad power that Congress has under the spending clause (see above).

Before the 1994 Republican takeover of Congress, mostly Democratic congresses had enacted countless mandates.[55] For example, state and local governments had to ensure equal access to public facilities by disabled persons but were given little money to cover the new construction costs. Clean-air legislation asked state and local governments to reduce air pollution but skimped on the funding necessary to do the job.[56] Medicaid required expanded services for low-income recipients, but for many states the law funded only half the cost of the program.[57]

devolution

Return of governmental responsibilities to state and local governments.

Critics of unfunded mandates had high hopes that after the 1994 elections, mandates would be a thing of the past. That year, Republican candidates campaigned in favor of governmental **devolution,** the return of governmental responsibilities to state and local governments. But Republican lawmakers soon proved that they were not immune to the practice. Bush's No Child Left Behind bill required states and school districts to set standards, but critics said it provided little money to help them do so. After 2001, new antiterrorism rules also placed severe strain on state and local governments, as law enforcement officials were required to step up their monitoring of potential terrorist targets around the country. With the shoe on the other foot, Democrats began complaining about unfunded mandates. "I find it ironic [that] . . . the party that talks about being opposed to unfunded mandates is giving us a very significant unfunded mandate," said West Virginia Governor Robert Wise, a Democrat, about the education program.[58]

The arrival of a Democratic president in 2009 signaled a swing of the pendulum back in the other direction. Republican governors complained that Medicaid provisions in the 2010 health care reform act amounted to unfunded mandates that would harm state budgets in the long term.

Whether they are Democrats or Republicans, members of Congress have strong incentives to impose mandates on state and local governments, and to leave them unfunded. When a mandate is imposed, members of Congress get the credit for helping constituents. When it is left unfunded, Congress, safe at a distance, evades the taxpayers' wrath.

3.5

Outline the organization and responsibilities of local governments and identify the key challenges they face.

Local Government

State and local governments now play a more prominent role in the federal system than they have for several decades. Even before the most recent devolution, a large proportion of all domestic government expenditure was paid for by taxes raised by state and local governments. This pattern, shown in Figure 3.4, is in keeping with long-standing American traditions. Nearly a century ago, the British scholar James Bryce identified the key role played by local governments in the American federal system:

> It is the business of a local authority to mend the roads, to clean out the village well or to provide a new pump, to see that there is a place where straying beasts may be kept till the owner reclaims them, to fix the number of cattle each villager may turn out on the common pasture, [and] to give each his share of timber cut in the common woodland.[59]

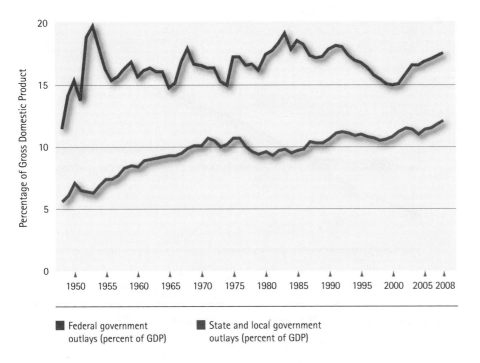

FIGURE 3.4

DOMESTIC EXPENDITURE OF GOVERNMENTS

State and local governments spend almost as much as the national government does.

• *Which trend is more stable, national government spending or state and local government spending? Why do you think this is the case?*

Note: Figures on national government spending do not include "off budget" items or defense expenditures; figures on state and local government expenditures do not include expenditures funded by federal grants.

Source: Office of Management and Budget, *United States Budget for Fiscal Year 2010*, Historical Tables, Table 15.3.

The nature of the work has been modernized since Bryce observed it, but the basic functions remain much the same. Local governments maintain roads; take care of parks; provide police, fire, and sanitation services; run the schools; and perform many other functions that affect the everyday lives of citizens.

The Numbers and Types of Local Governments

In sheer numbers, local governments constitute an overwhelming and growing presence; there were more than 76,000 in 2007, up from about 46,000 in 1942 (see Figure 3.5).[60] There are several different major types of local governments, each of which has responsibilities that vary from state to state. Although the basic unit in most states is the county, not all counties are alike. In some states they manage school systems, welfare programs, local roads, sanitation systems, a sheriff's office, and an array of other governmental activities. In other states they have hardly any duties. Many counties are divided into townships—there are 16,500 of them nationwide—whose duties generally include local road maintenance and other small-scale activities.

As the population has become concentrated in urban areas, the total number of municipalities—cities, suburbs, and towns—has increased to nearly 20,000. In most states, these municipal governments have assumed many of the responsibilities once performed by counties.

States, counties, and municipalities have also created an extraordinary array of special districts—more than 37,000 in all. Each special district has responsibility for only one or a few specific governmental functions. Such governments are unique in that they overlap the boundaries of other local governments, sometimes spanning many different municipal jurisdictions. As Figure 3.5 shows, special districts account for most of the increase in the number of local governments over the past 50 years. Some special districts run schools, others manage parks, and still others administer transportation systems

FIGURE 3.5

NUMBER OF LOCAL
GOVERNMENTS, 1942–2007

In 2007, there were over 76,000
local governments nationwide.

• *Which form of government
has increased the most over the
past 50 years? Why do you think
this is the case?*

Source: U.S. Bureau of the Census,
Statistical Abstract of the United States, 2008,
Table 415; United States Census of
Governments, 2007, www.census.gov/
govs/www/cog2007.html, accessed
May 21, 2008.

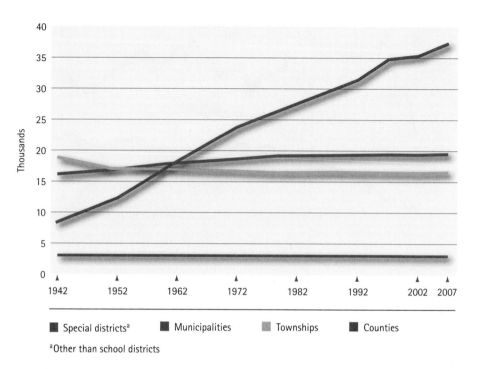

■ Special districts[a]   **■** Municipalities   **■** Townships   **■** Counties

[a]Other than school districts

or garbage collection.[61] Even as humble a task as mosquito abatement can be the responsibility of a special district.

Local Elections

Despite the large number of local elections, actual rates of citizen participation in them
are surprisingly low. When a particularly colorful candidate runs for mayor, or when ethnic or racial issues are raised, large numbers of voters can
show up at the polls, but much of the time the local
electorate is no more than half the size of the presidential electorate.[62] Like many features of local government,
local election dates and procedures are held according to
state-set rules, a fact underscored when Louisiana
Governor Kathleen Blanco postponed a New Orleans
election for more than two months after Hurricane
Katrina created a raft of logistical difficulties.[63]

Under ordinary circumstances, the near invisibility
of local elections helps to reduce local participation
rates.[64] The sheer number of elected officeholders often makes local government elections confusing to
many voters. Newspaper coverage is haphazard. Local
governments frequently hold elections at times that
coincide with neither state nor national elections, which further reduce turnout rates.[65]
When asked about the hotly contested 2001 Los Angeles mayoral race, one potential
voter gave a typical response: "I don't really care too much. All I know is that there is a
lot of bashing going on. One guy was like the D.A. or something like that and the
other guy worked for him . . . I don't know."[66]

Mr. Mayor

Los Angeles Mayor Antonio
Villaraigosa at a rally with
supporters.

• *Why are local governments
popular with voters?*

Surprisingly, local governments also oversee the administration of national elections. This local responsibility became a key issue in the close 2000 presidential election, when some voters in Palm Beach County, Florida, claimed that the county's confusing ballot design had led them to vote for the wrong candidate. The following summer, a nationwide commission of state and local election officials asked the federal government to provide procedural guidelines and standards—but not mandates—to prevent such confusion from occurring again.[67] The result, the 2002 "Help America Vote Act" (HAVA), provided $3.1 billion in grants to localities to update their voting machines.[68] As in the case of many grant programs, however, critics of HAVA complained of delays, intergovernmental conflicts, and unfunded mandates.

Popularity of Local Government

We might think that this diverse, complicated, and confusing system could not possibly succeed. Yet local government remains very popular. According to one survey, 69 percent of Americans express "a great deal" or "a fair amount" of "trust and confidence" in their local government, while the public is divided about 50-50 on a similar assessment of the national government.[69]

One explanation for the apparent popularity of local government, despite the low profile of its elections, is the ability of people to "vote with their feet"—that is, to move from one community to another—if they are unhappy with their local government. Americans are a mobile people: About 12 percent move each year.[70] Every local government has to remember that if it is inefficient or unresponsive, its city or town will suffer a decline in population and property values. As a result, most local governments have good reason to be mindful of their constituents' needs, despite low voting rates.

The wide variety of local governments also gives people a choice. Some people favor sex education programs and condom distribution in school; others do not. Some people think refuse collection should be publicly provided; others prefer to recycle their own garbage. Some people think police protection should be intensive; others think an intrusive police presence violates the civil liberties of citizens. By giving people a choice, the diversity of local governments reduces conflict and enhances citizen satisfaction.

Limits on Local Government

For all the strengths of local governments, they often do not have the resources to meet the needs of the poor, the sick, and the disabled. If a local government tries to provide substantial services to the needy, it runs the risk of attracting more poor people and driving away those who are better off. For example, in 2007 the city of Berkeley, California, long a bastion of generous social services and tolerance, took action in response to a ballooning homeless population. Although the city only makes up 7 percent of the county's population, one study found that 40 percent of the area's homeless live there. After a lengthy debate, the city council passed a new ordinance banning sleeping on the streets during the day and prohibiting smoking on many sidewalks. As a local business owner put it, "Instead of being so liberal and progressive here, as everyone wants to be in Berkeley, they have to address the problem. I don't think they're doing enough, but at least it's a big issue now."[71] Most other cities are also wary of attracting those who will not contribute to the tax base; local governments nationwide spend only about 11 percent of their budgets on social programs, compared to around 26 percent for the state governments and nearly 60 percent for the federal government.[72]

Local governments also compete with one another to attract businesses. Although such competition usually has positive benefits in that it keeps local governments sensitive to the community's economic needs, sometimes the competition can get out of hand. With state help, one county in Kentucky outbid its neighbors for a Canadian steel mill employing 400 people. It ended up costing the state $350,000 for every job created. Such bidding wars have spread across the country.

This competition became especially poignant in 2009 in the wake of the bankruptcy and restructuring of two of the three major U.S. automakers. Towns like Janesville, Wisconsin (that had hosted a General Motors factory for 89 years) saw their livelihoods disappear.[73] In other cases, cities and states competed to be chosen as the sites of new plants designed to build more fuel-efficient automobiles. General Motors agreed to keep its headquarters in Detroit after striking a deal for millions of dollars in state and local tax breaks. As Democratic Governor Jennifer Granholm put it, "It's a symbol. For [GM] to abandon Detroit would send a terrible message."[74]

In other cases, cities compete to secure or retain professional sports teams, often footing part of the bill for new state-of-the-art stadiums. Local governments paid at least part of the cost of Heinz Field in Pittsburgh (which opened in 2001), Qwest Field in Seattle (2002), and a new stadium for the Dallas Cowboys, which opened in 2009.

3.6

Outline the organization and responsibilities of state governments and identify the key challenges they face.

governor
A state's chief executive whose responsibilities roughly parallel those of the president.

laboratories of democracy
Doctrine that state and local governments contribute to democracy by providing places where experiments are tried and new theories about government are tested.

State Government

When the Constitution was written, the design of the federal government was adapted from that which existed in many states. Thus, it is not surprising that the basic organization of most state governments bears a strong resemblance to that of the national government. Just as Congress has the Senate and the House of Representatives, the legislatures in all states except Nebraska have an upper and a lower chamber (Nebraska has only one). All states have multi-tiered court systems roughly comparable to that of the federal system. And every state has an independently elected **governor,** the state's chief executive whose responsibilities roughly parallel those of the president.

State governments vary in many important ways, however. State legislatures vary greatly in size. Most lower houses have around 100 representatives, but in Alaska, Delaware, and Nevada they have as few as 40 members each, whereas in New Hampshire, with a similarly small population, the lower house includes 400 legislators. Some state governments hold their elections in even-numbered years, in conjunction with federal races; others do not. In some states, state administrative officers from the secretary of state to the attorney general are elected, whereas in other states, the governor appoints these officials.

State policies vary as well. State governments may serve as **laboratories of democracy**—places where experiments are tried and new theories about government are tested. If successful, an experiment may be copied by other states or by the national government. If it fails, the experiment is soon abandoned. For example, scholars have shown that states are more likely to establish state lotteries if their neighbors have their own lottery programs.[75] There is also significant state-by-state variation in the legality of assisted suicide, the rules governing a woman's access to an abortion, and social welfare policies.

Some scholars believe the reason for many of these differences lies in variations in state political cultures. Citizens from different backgrounds and historical traditions form governments and elect officials that reflect these traditions. Minnesota and Massachusetts voters, for example, hold more positive views toward active government than do voters in Texas or Florida.[76] It is no surprise, then, that Minnesota and Massachusetts have governments larger than those in other states, with more responsibilities.[77]

Variation in State Government Responsibilities

The size and range of state responsibilities have grown dramatically significantly in recent decades. As a percentage of gross domestic product (GDP), state expenditures increased by 20 percent between 1990 and 2006.[78] States bear heavy responsibilities for financing elementary and secondary education, as well as for funding state colleges and universities. They maintain state parks, highway systems, and prisons. They manage welfare and Medicaid programs that serve low-income populations. They give grants to local governments to help pay for police, fire, and other basic governmental services.

The amount spent on government services varies from state to state. For one thing, wealthier states spend much more than poorer states. In 2006, the state and local governments in the 10 richest states spent an average of $10,500 per person, whereas in the 10 poorest states they spent, on average, about $7,600.[79] Many liberals say that differences in spending for education, health, and other public services are inequitable and should be rectified by federal grants. Many conservatives say that it is only to be expected that wealthier people will spend more on public services, just as they spend more for clothes, houses, and cars. In any case, federal grants have done very little, if anything, to reduce interstate fiscal inequalities.

Expenditures are also affected by elections. Each party has its favorite type of public service. The more often Democrats are elected to the legislature, the higher the expenditure for social services. The more frequently Republicans win, the higher the expenditure for traditional government services.[80]

State Politics and Elections

Despite policy differences among states, state elections bear a strong resemblance to national elections. The same two political parties—Republican and Democratic—are the dominant competitors in nearly all state elections. For many decades following the Civil War, the party of Lincoln, the Republicans, dominated the North, whereas the South was solidly Democratic. These regional patterns of party dominance have broken down in recent years as a result of the civil rights movement and population shifts. Republicans now often win as many southern elections as Democrats do. A new trend toward competitive politics and divided government has developed in most states. Democrats have had the advantage in state legislative races; Republicans have more often elected governors. The voters may like it this way: Each party can act as a check on the other, and government does not drift to either political extreme.[81]

In recent years, state governments have evolved in several important ways. State political institutions have become professionalized, the role of governors has grown, and states have begun to develop their own economic policies.

Budget Battles   Because nearly all states are constitutionally required to have balanced budgets (unlike the national government), budget battles between governors and state legislatures can become dramatic and bruising affairs. These especially arise in periods of economic downturn, when state taxes may fail to take in enough money to keep services at previous levels. Because of the 2008 financial crisis and the recession that followed, for example, nearly all states suffered devastating declines in revenue. Legislators and governors were forced into the politically nauseating task of apportioning the pain to taxpayers, the beneficiaries of government programs, or some combination of the two. In New York City, subway lines were shuttered and some stops were curtailed to save money in the wake of state aid reductions. In California, declines in funding forced state universities to raise student fees by an astonishing 32 percent. As frustrated University of California President Mark Yudof put it, "The legislators have told us, essentially, 'The student is your A.T.M. They're how you should balance the budget.'"[82]

Reapportionment and Professionalization   When the state constitutions were written, many of them included provisions freezing the boundaries of their legislative districts. In many other states, legislatures did not bother to change district boundaries to reflect shifts in population. Because the country became more urbanized in the first half of the twentieth century, by the early 1960s these rigid district boundaries meant that rural areas were grossly over-represented in state legislatures. Soon, legal challenges brought these issues before the Supreme Court. In 1962 and 1964, the Court ruled that states must regularly redraw their districts so that all districts have similar numbers of residents,[83] a process known as **reapportionment.** In the wake of these decisions, turnover in state legislatures rose significantly as they became more representative. In the longer term, the reapportionment requirements have sparked regular partisan battles in many states, as Democrats and Republicans compete to draw district boundaries in ways most favorable to their party.[84]

reapportionment
Redrawing of electoral district lines to reflect population changes.

The reapportionment disputes following the 2000 census provide some insight into what may happen after the 2010 census. A Colorado state representative complained that his state's reapportionment process had been "submerged in a morass of partisan haranguing."[85] A local official in Louisiana protested that his constituents were "being shifted around like the red-headed stepchild."[86] In the most extreme case, 51 Democratic legislators in the state of Texas fled the state in 2003 in an effort to prevent Republicans from passing a redistricting plan that would deliver more U.S. House seats to the GOP. Without the 51 legislators present, the House did not have enough members to conduct business legally. As the Democrats huddled at the Holiday Inn in Ardmore, Oklahoma, just beyond the reach of Texas state troopers, the standoff drew national attention. A network news correspondent described the situation as "like an old Western: a band of outlaws headed for Oklahoma with the Texas Rangers hot in pursuit."[87] After a second walkout and three special sessions of the legislature, Texas lawmakers finally passed the Republican plan.

As state government has become more complicated, state legislatures have also become more professional. Scholars associate higher legislative "professionalization" with lower turnover rates, higher salaries, more staff, and longer sessions. In 2010, California's legislature was among the most modern. Its members remained in session throughout the year, receiving $95,000 in salary, retirement benefits, and handsome per diem expense pay, as well as the services of a full-time staff. By contrast, Wyoming paid its legislators

Continued on page 93

ELECTION VOICES!

The Drinking Age

The Issue

Should federal highway grants be linked to the stipulation that states set their legal drinking age at 21? Or should states be allowed to lower the drinking age without federal penalty?

Background

It only took Clarence William Busch two days out on bail from his hit-and-run drunken driving charge before he killed 13-year-old Cari Lightner on May 3, 1980. Busch already had two drunken-driving convictions, not counting the most recent charge. This tragic offense by a 47-year-old man set in motion a political process that eventually denied young adults across the nation the right to buy a beer.

Within a week of Cari's death, her mother, a Sacramento real estate agent, transformed her personal grief into a political crusade. Candy Lightner formed Mothers Against Drunk Driving (MADD) and within four years commanded a national organi-

zation claiming 258 chapters and 300,000 members.[1] In addition to sponsoring a wave of anti-drunk-driving publicity campaigns, the interest group threw its considerable muscle behind an effort to raise the legal drinking age to 21 nationwide, arguing that the 18 to 21 age group accounted for a disproportionate share of drunk-driving accidents.[2]

But there was a problem: The Constitution's Twenty-first Amendment clearly gives authority over liquor laws to the states. Supporters of a national drinking age needed a way for the U.S. government to wade into a policy area that appeared not to fall within its delegated powers. One New Jersey Democrat, U.S. Representative James Howard, came up with the answer: Rather than try to impose a drinking age directly, he proposed legislation yanking millions of dollars in federal highway funds from any state whose drinking age remained below 21. The bill passed both houses of Congress overwhelmingly, and President Reagan signed the National Minimum Drinking Age Act into law on July 17, 1984. States found the grant money impossible to give up, and within a decade the drinking age was 21 from "sea to shining sea."

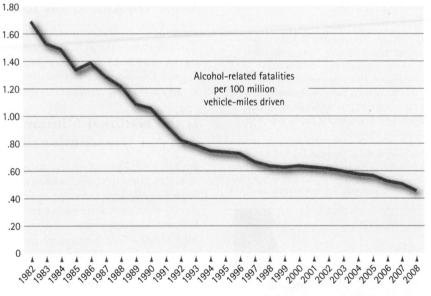

FIGURE 1

ALCOHOL-RELATED TRAFFIC FATALITIES, 1982–2008

Proponents of the national drinking age of 21 argue that the law, passed in 1984, reduces traffic fatalities.

- *What evidence does this graph offer for and against this point of view?*

Source: Calculated by the authors from data available at Alcohol Alert, www.alcoholalert.com/drunk-driving-statistics .html, accessed March 5, 2010, and the Federal Highway Administration, Traffic Volume Trends, http://www.fhwa.dot .gov/ohim/tvtw/08martvt/08martvt.pdf, accessed March 5, 2010.

Opposing Viewpoints on the National Drinking Age

In recent years, the national drinking age has become the subject of renewed debate, as several lawmakers and interest groups have questioned its wisdom. As with many issues involving federalism, proponents and opponents argue about the policy in two ways. First, they make claims about the pros and cons of the policy itself, and second, they argue about which level of government ought to be responsible for setting the policy.

Proponents of the 21 drinking age point out that alcohol-related driving fatalities have dropped since the law was put in place in 1984 (see Figure 1). They also cite studies that find that those who have their first alcoholic drink at younger ages are more likely to become dependent on alcohol, and less likely to exercise good judgment in deciding when they are sober enough to drive.

> Science speaks for itself. When the legal drinking age is 21, lives are saved and injuries are prevented. The 21 Law saves lives on the road and keeps countless youth from starting to drink at early ages.
>
> —Glynn Birch, president, Mothers Against Drunk Driving, "MADD, AMA, NTSB, and others Launch Support 21 Coalition," September 29, 2007, press release, www.madd.org, accessed January 30, 2008

Furthermore, they say, a national policy is preferable to a patchwork of state rules.

> We, at the Department of Transportation, were deeply troubled [in the mid-1980s] by the statistics of teens driving across state borders, "blood borders," into a neighbor state with a lower drinking age, and then driving back under the influence of alcohol. I was convinced that we needed to seriously eliminate the differences between state laws and was confident that raising the drinking age to 21 across our nation would save many, many lives and prevent disabling, crippling injuries.
>
> —Speech on the 21st Anniversary of the 21 Minimum Drinking Age Act— Senator Elizabeth Dole (R-NC), former Secretary of Transportation, April 13, 2005, www.womenspeecharchive.org/files/ d_1164640160078.pdf, accessed January 30, 2008

Pennsylvania teenagers drinking beer at Ozzfest.
• *Should the drinking age be a state or national issue?*

Opponents of the 21 drinking age argue that the law forces drinking out of the open and into dorm rooms and private apartments, where binge drinking and other forms of alcohol abuse are more likely.

> It would be better to allow drinkers 18 and up to drink in public spaces where they can be monitored by the police and other adults instead of forcing them underground where they take much higher risks in concealing their small infractions. Underage drinkers would be much more willing to take a taxi, or bus, instead of driving drunk if they knew they would not get in trouble. Likewise, they will be more likely to seek medical attention for someone who has overdosed instead of doing nothing out of fear of punishment.
>
> —John Tavares, "The Drinking Age Debate," *Oregon State University Daily Barometer*, October 15, 2007

They also argue that states' rights to have differing policies ought to be respected under principles of federalism.

> Federalism is untidy, but it's how we operate. We have 50 different tax laws. Fifty different lots of things. Is alcohol so exceptional as to require an abdication of the federal principle?
>
> —John McCardell, president, Choose Responsibility, quoted in Paula Routly, "All Stirred Up," *Seven Days in Vermont*, August 22, 2007

What Do Americans Believe?

Public opinion polls on this issue are scarce, but a 2009 survey shows that a majority of Americans oppose lowering the drinking age to 18 (see Figure 2). It is unclear how the public would respond to a question that asked whether responsibility for setting the drinking age should be returned to the states.

Is the National Minimum Drinking Age Act Constitutional?

In 1987, South Dakota took a constitutional challenge all the way to the U.S. Supreme Court—arguing that Congress could not use its authority under the spending clause to muscle its way into an area that the Constitution reserved for the states. But Chief Justice William Rehnquist, speaking for a seven-justice majority, wrote in *South Dakota v. Dole* that Congress can use the federal budget to expand its influence. His opinion dismissed the highway funds as "relatively mild encouragement." Although Congress "might lack the power to impose a national minimum drinking age directly," wrote Rehnquist, "we conclude that encouragement to state action . . . is a valid use of the spending power."[4]

What Do You Think?

1. Should Congress continue to use highway grant money as an incentive for states to keep the drinking age at 21?
2. According to the National Minimum Drinking Age Act, 10 percent of federal highway grants are withheld from

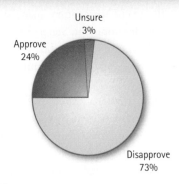

FIGURE 2

MOST AMERICANS OPPOSE LOWERING THE DRINKING
AGE TO 18 NATIONWIDE

Overall, voters oppose lowering the drinking age by a margin
of 73 percent to 24 percent.

• *As you may know, the legal drinking age is 21. Would you
approve or disapprove of states lowering the drinking age to 18,
if the states felt that would give police more time to enforce
other laws?*

• *How might an increase in voter turnout among young people
change the political debate over this issue?*

• *Would you favor or oppose a federal law that would lower
the drinking age in all states to 18?*

Source: CBS News Poll, March 12–16, 2009.

states that do not have a drinking age of 21. For a medium-
sized state, this can amount to $50 million.[5] Does this rep-
resent "mild encouragement," as the Supreme Court put it,
or is it unduly coercive?

3. In 2000, Congress passed a law requiring states to adopt a
.08 percent blood alcohol level standard for drunk drivers

or forfeit more highway grants. Should Congress use the
spending power to encourage states to enact seatbelt laws?
Helmet laws for motorcyclists? Laws banning texting while
driving?

On the Web

PRO

Supporters of the national drinking age of 21 include Mothers
Against Drunk Driving, the group that was pivotal in the law's
enactment in 1984. MADD has partnered with other groups to
set up Why21, a website that argues in favor of the law.

www.madd.org www.why21.org

CON

Choose Responsibility, a group headed by a former president of
Middlebury College in Vermont, argues for lowering the drinking age and instituting alcohol education programs and special
"drinking licenses" for 18–21-year-olds.

www.chooseresponsibility.org

---

[1]Candy Lightner's story comes from Jay Mathews, "One California
Mother's MADD Drive to Bar Highways to Drunken Killers,"
Washington Post (June 16, 1984): A2; and John J. O'Connor, "'MADD'
Drama Fights Drunken Driving," *New York Times* (March 14, 1983): C14.
[2]Jane Perlez, "Teen-Age Drinking Vote," *New York Times* (June 9, 1984): 5.
[3]Priscilla Painton, "Drinking Age Evokes Mixed Spirits," *Washington
Post* (July 7, 1984): B1.
[4]*South Dakota v. Dole* 483 U.S. 203 (1987).
[5]Missouri State Auditor's Office, Fiscal Note (07-07), June 11, 2007,
www.auditor.mo.gov/notes/07-07.pdf, accessed January 31, 2008.

Continued from page 90

only $150 a day (plus expenses) and limited its legislative sessions to a maximum of
40 working days in odd-numbered years and 20 days in even-numbered years.[88]

During the 1990s, voters reacted against the professionalization of state government, as many states limited the terms of legislators, cut their staffs, and reduced their
salaries and benefits. In the eyes of one expert, this trend has produced "a crumbling of
legislative power" in which "the legislature is becoming a less than equal branch of
government."[89] Term limit laws are now on the books in 16 states, including
California, Michigan, Florida, and Colorado, but the trend to limit legislative terms
has slowed recently.[90]

State Economic Action   In the nineteenth century, state governments played an
active role in their states' economies, granting charters to private corporations and
investing their resources to assist in the development of key industries. After the
New Deal, the federal government became predominant, and states relaxed their

economic roles. Then, toward the end of the twentieth century, many states again became more active players in their economic development. States especially hard-hit by a decline in manufacturing jobs and by economic recessions sought to reinvigorate their business climate through tax incentives and active recruitment of firms from out of state.

States with large economies and significant international exports, such as California and Texas, have arranged frequent trade missions to countries such as Mexico, Japan, and Canada. Even small and medium-sized states have begun to recognize the virtues of promoting their businesses in foreign countries. An enthusiastic Wisconsin governor Jim Doyle led a trade mission to Ireland and the United Kingdom in 2008, arguing that "These two markets offer great opportunities for Wisconsin firms."[91]

CHAPTER SUMMARY

3.1 Differentiate between federalism and other forms of government.

Federalism divides sovereignty between the states and the national government. Its existence in the United States is the result of a compromise between Constitutional Convention delegates who believed that a strong national government was necessary to preserve stability, and those who feared that centralized power would lead to tyranny.

3.2 Trace key developments in the historical debate over dual sovereignty and nullification.

Because the federal structure was a compromise, the Constitution does not clearly define the powers of the federal and state governments. The nature of American federalism has therefore changed in response to the wishes of the various electorates at the local, state, and federal level, and as a result of Supreme Court decisions that have defined what federalism requires in particular cases.

3.3 Evaluate the impact of specific Supreme Court decisions on the relationship of national and state governments.

Much of the debate over federalism has revolved around the meaning of dual sovereignty. The most extreme interpretation of dual sovereignty, the doctrine of nullification, was rejected with the end of the Civil War.

The power of the states was further eroded with the election of Franklin Roosevelt and the enactment of New Deal legislation that greatly enhanced the power of the federal government. Three provisions in the Constitution facilitated the expansion of federal power: the necessary and proper clause, the commerce clause, and the spending clause. The state sovereignty amendment has also been used recently to restrict its expansion.

3.4 Compare and contrast the advantages and disadvantages of federal categorical and block grants distributed to state and local governments.

With the election of strong Democratic majorities in the 1960s, there emerged a new theory of federalism known as *cooperative* or *marble-cake federalism*, which holds that all levels of government can and should work together. In accordance with this theory, many new federal grants were given to state and local governments. The majority of these grants were categorical in nature; they contained restrictions that specified how the money should be spent. In response to criticism of the implementation of categorical grants, Republican leaders called for their replacement with block grants that have few federal mandates or restrictions. The two parties remain divided over the merits of categorical and block grants, although disagreements over these topics have shifted when Republicans gained the upper hand in Congress and the presidency.

3.5 Outline the organization and responsibilities of local governments and identify the key challenges they face.

Despite the expansion of federal power, state and local governments remain vital components of the federal system. Nearly half the domestic expenditures of the government are paid for with state and local tax dollars. Even though few citizens participate in local elections, local governments are the most popular of all governmental levels, in part because people can "vote with their feet"—that is, they can choose to live in the local community they like best.

3.6 Outline the organization and responsibilities of state governments and identify the key challenges they face.

State governments can play key roles in economic development, and have been doing so with greater frequency in recent decades. Despite legal and structural variation, partisan battles on the state level can resemble those on the national level, as legislatures become more professional and voters increasingly choose "divided government" wherein neither party dominates all policy making.

FEARSON
mypoliscilab EXERCISES

Apply what you learned in this chapter on MyPoliSciLab.

📖—[●—[**Read** on **mypoliscilab.com**
    eText: Chapter 3

✔—[●—[**Study** and **Review** on **mypoliscilab.com**
    Pre-Test
    Post-Test
    Chapter Exam
    Flashcards

👁—[**Watch** on **mypoliscilab.com**
    Video: The Real ID
    Video: Water Wars
    Video: Battling City Corruption
    Video: Proposition 8

✳—[**Explore** on **mypoliscilab.com**
    Simulation: You Are a Federal Judge
    Simulation: You Are a Restaurant Owner
    Simulation: You Are the Mayor and Need to Get a Town Budget Passed
    Simulation: You Are a State Legislator
    Comparative: Comparing Federal and Unitary Systems
    Comparative: Comparing State and Local Governments
    Timeline: Federalism and Supreme Court
    Visual Literacy: Federalism and Regulations

KEY TERMS

block grants, p. 80
categorical grants, p. 79
commerce clause, p. 72
cooperative federalism, p. 76
devolution, p. 84
Dillon's rule, p. 66
dual sovereignty, p. 70
federalism, p. 66
general revenue sharing, p. 81
governor, p. 80

implementation, p. 80
intergovernmental grant, p. 78
judicial review, p. 69
laboratories of democracy, p. 88
marble-cake federalism, p. 76
McCulloch v. Maryland, p. 71
necessary and proper clause, p. 75
New Deal, p. 72
NIMBY problem, p. 75
nullification, p. 70

pork barrel projects, p. 75
reapportionment, p. 90
sovereignty, p. 66
spending clause, p. 76
state sovereign immunity, p. 76
supremacy clause, p. 68
tyranny of the majority, p. 70
unfunded mandates, p. 83
unitary government, p. 66
War on Poverty, p. 79

SUGGESTED READINGS

Of General Interest

Dahl, Robert. *Who Governs?* New Haven, CT: Yale University Press, 1961. Classic study of local politics in New Haven.

Nivola, Pietro S. *Tense Commandments: Federal Prescriptions and City Problems*. Washington, DC: The Brookings Institution, 2002. Argues that national prescriptions and mandates are restricting cities' ability to respond to local needs.

Peterson, Paul E. *The Price of Federalism*. Washington, DC: The Brookings Institution, 1995. Contrasts the responsibilities of national, state, and local governments.

Politics and Government of the American States Series. Lincoln: University of Nebraska Press. This multi-volume series studies the politics of each state—23 so far. Recent volumes include: Conant, James K. *Wisconsin Politics and Government: America's Laboratory of Democracy.* 2006; and Blair, Diane, and Jay Barth. *Arkansas Politics and Government*, 2nd ed., 2005.

Focused Studies

Berman, David R. *Local Government and the States: Autonomy, Politics, and Policy*. Armonk, NY: M.E. Sharpe, 2003. Interesting account of the relationships between cities and states.

Dreier, Peter, John Mollenkopf, and Todd Swanstrom. *Place Matters: Metropolitics for the Twenty-first Century*, 2nd ed., revised. Lawrence: University Press of Kansas, 2004. A detailed study of urban inequality and the public policies that have tried to address it.

Fiorina, Morris, *Divided Government*. New York: Macmillan, 1992. Explains why control of many state governments is divided between the Democratic and Republican parties.

Grodzins, Morton. *The American System: A New View of Government in the United States*. Chicago: Rand McNally, 1966. Classic study of cooperative federalism.

Miller, Lisa L. *The Perils of Federalism: Race, Poverty, and the Politics of Crime Control*. New York: Oxford University Press, 2008. A clever analysis of how law enforcement policies get made at different levels of government.

Smith, Jean E. *John Marshall: Definer of a Nation*. New York: Henry Holt, 1996. Excellent biography of the chief justice who helped define American federalism.

ON THE WEB

State and local governments have formed a variety of organizations to make their voices heard on the federal level.

www.nlc.org
www.ncsl.org
www.nga.org
The National League of Cities, the National Conference of State Legislatures, and the National Governor's Association provide information and policy priorities for state and local governments.

http://newfederalism.urban.org
The Urban Institute's "Assessing the New Federalism" project provides a variety of studies on the impact of recent devolutionary programs.

www.federalismproject.org
The American Enterprise Institute's Federalism Project advocates devolution of more rights and responsibilities to the states.

4 American Political Culture

CHAPTER OUTLINE

LEARNING OBJECTIVES

4.1   Characterize the American population as culturally diverse but similar in political beliefs.

4.2   Outline the evolution of social diversity in the United States and the debates over immigration.

4.3   Analyze American shared beliefs, their roots in classical liberalism, and their apparent contradictions.

4.4   Assess the various explanations for the persistence of American classical liberalism.

A Hard Test for American Diversity

On September 11, 2001, followers of Islamist fanatic Osama bin Laden hijacked four jetliners, crashing two into New York City's World Trade Center, another into the Pentagon, and a fourth into a remote Pennsylvania field. Almost 3,000 people died on this horrible day.[1]

All 19 of the terrorist hijackers came from Middle Eastern countries. In the aftermath of the attacks a few Americans chose to express their grief and anger by committing hostile acts against people of Middle Eastern background living in the United States. Some incidents were as minor as bullying at school recess. Others were fatal. A Sikh was gunned down in a deadly instance of mistaken identity. A Yemeni father of eight was shot and killed within sight of the U.S. flag hanging in the window of his shop. In all, Arab Americans suffered an estimated 270 violent assaults within a month of 9/11. Five resulted in death.[2] In 2001, California alone recorded 73 official hate crimes against people perceived to be Arabs (compared to three the year before). More than half of these were violent.[3]

These hostile acts, however, were carried out by a relatively small number of Americans acting on their own; none were official government actions. True, surveys reported that Americans overwhelmingly endorsed special airport security checks for those of Middle Eastern background, a majority favored requiring Arabs to carry special identification cards, and more than a third supported placing them under "special surveillance."[4] But the official response fell far short of such proposals.

Within two months of 9/11 the United States invaded Afghanistan and drove out the Taliban regime that had given refuge to Osama bin Laden. In the spring of 2003 the United States invaded Iraq and overthrew Saddam Hussein. At the time of this writing U.S. forces have been fighting in the Middle East for eight years.

Government policy has changed as a result of this ongoing conflict. Security in airports has become more intrusive.[5] States have tightened their screening of applicants for driver's licenses and other government documents.[6] Federal officials have slowed the rate at which foreigners receive permission to visit the United States, required the fingerprinting of applicants, and reversed years of lax enforcement by tracking down those who have overstayed their visas. Federal officials have asked colleges to ensure that international students have their paperwork in order. They have required more than 80,000 males from 25 mostly Middle Eastern countries to register at U.S. immigration offices. And law-enforcement officers have seized hundreds of foreigners, from U.S. Army privates to pizza deliverers, for minor legal violations that they previously had ignored.[7]

Although some critics believe that such government actions are discriminatory, the domestic response to the Middle Eastern conflicts pales in comparison to policies adopted during previous U.S. wars. Two generations ago, when the Japanese attacked Pearl Harbor, the government rounded up 120,000 Americans of Japanese ancestry—citizens and noncitizens alike—and held them for up to three years in internment camps. Detainees often lost their property and their jobs.[8] A generation earlier, during World War I, German Americans experienced a variety of official abuses—some jurisdictions passed laws prohibiting the use of the German language.[9] Social pressures were so great that some immigrants abandoned their family names to hide their ethnic origin.[10] Compared to historical experience, the reaction against Muslim Americans after 9/11 was relatively mild.

On November 5, 2009, Major Nidal Malik Hasan, a Muslim psychiatrist serving in the U.S. Army, killed 13 people and wounded 30 others in a shooting spree at Fort Hood, TX, where he was stationed. Investigations revealed that he had been in contact with radical Muslim clerics and had expressed jihadist beliefs in emails. A month later five American Muslims, all reportedly citizens, were arrested in Pakistan while attempting to join al-Qaeda to fight against the United States in Afghanistan. One had attended the same mosque as Major Hasan.

But once again, no outcry against American Muslims took place. Americans viewed Hasan's act of domestic terrorism as the product of one deranged individual. And the treasonous sentiments of the five young Americans in Pakistan were not seen as representative of the American Muslim community—after all, their own relatives reported them missing and the Council on American-Islamic Relations reported them to the FBI. No prominent politician or media commentator saw any advantage in questioning the loyalty of Muslim Americans generally.

It is easy to take this reaction for granted. "Why should the actions of a few Muslims make Americans doubt the loyalties of the larger community?" you might be thinking. "What does Americanism have to do with ethnicity or religion?" Such a distinction makes perfect sense in the United States, but it would be far from obvious in most other countries. Carl Friedrich, a professor who immigrated to the United States from Germany in the 1930s, once wrote that

Aftermath of 9/11
Border protections and all transportation security increased after the 9/11 attacks.

"To be an American is an ideal, while to be a Frenchman is a fact."[11] Friedrich was pointing out that in most of the world, **citizenship** (100), the status held by someone entitled to all the rights and privileges of a full-fledged member of a political community, is indeed defined by ethnicity. Either you are born a German or you are not (see the accompanying *International Comparison* box, page 100).

Making the Connection

The values held by a nation's people shape their political system. These core beliefs are more fundamental than the opinions citizens might hold about particular issues or public officials (see Chapter 5). They reflect a broad orientation toward how government should and should not operate, creating a set of expectations about how it should treat its citizens and how it should treat others. These assumptions define what leaders consider acceptable and what they rule out as unacceptable. Because such broad expectations are rather durable—a long-lasting tradition not unlike cultural preferences for certain foods or certain clothing—scholars often refer to them as a nation's **political culture.**

As you will see in this chapter, America's political culture stands out for the extent to which it defines the nation. It is unusually uniform, given the large land mass it covers and the diverse population it includes, and it distinguishes the United States from other advanced democracies. When you finish reading the chapter, therefore, you should understand why other U.S. citizens would accept that American Muslims could belong to the same nation as they do. More generally, you should be able to formulate an answer to the following questions:

citizenship
Status held by someone entitled to all the rights and privileges of a full-fledged member of a political community.

political culture
Collection of beliefs and values about the justification and operation of a country's government.

- What core beliefs set Americans apart from citizens elsewhere?
- What influences caused these values to develop and spread?
- How have these values stayed strong after more than 200 years?
- Do immigrants threaten America's political culture?

4.1

Characterize the American population as culturally diverse but similar in political beliefs.

Americans: A Contradictory People?

Americans are more ethnically and religiously diverse than the citizens of other democracies. Most long-lasting multicultural countries have been ruled by authoritarian regimes that suppressed cultural divisions, as in the nineteenth-century Austro-Hungarian and twentieth-century Soviet empires, and China today. By contrast, most of the world's multicultural democracies have not lasted long—Yugoslavia is one recent, particularly tragic, example. The United States is the exception, an unusual example of diverse people coexisting peacefully under a long-lasting democratic government.[12]

INTERNATIONAL COMPARISON

Citizenship in Europe and the United States

Any child born in the United States is a U.S. citizen. A child born outside the United States is a U.S. citizen if either parent is a U.S. citizen and that parent has lived in the United States for ten years—including two years after the age of 14. Legal immigrants can become "naturalized" citizens after five years of residence: They must learn English, demonstrate knowledge of U.S. history and government, renounce their previous citizenship, and swear allegiance to the Constitution and laws of the United States. Naturalized citizens may not serve as U.S. president because of a constitutional prohibition, but otherwise they have the same rights and privileges as native citizens.

Practices in other countries differ greatly. In Germany, for example, citizenship historically has been based on ethnicity. The constitution of the new German republic created after World War II carried over a 1913 law extending German citizenship to "a refugee or expellee of German stock or . . . the spouse or descendant of such a person." As a consequence, people from Eastern European and Russia whose ancestors left Germany centuries ago can emigrate to Germany and quickly assume the rights and privileges of citizenship (as can Americans of German descent if they can make a case for hardship). But the children of Turkish "guest workers," born in Germany and speaking German as their first language, typically face major bureaucratic obstacles to becoming citizens because they are not Germans by blood.

Political cultures that emphasize ethnicity struggle with the challenges of immigration. In Germany, the government attempted to liberalize immigration laws in 1999, but the proposals met strong resistance. A compromise reduced the residency requirement before an immigrant was eligible for citizenship from 15 years to eight years and granted citizenship to any child born in Germany whose parents had resided there for eight years or longer. Meanwhile, France contains the largest Muslim population of any European country. Ethnic tensions in 2004 led to a popular government crackdown on religious head coverings that obviously targeted the Islamic *hajib* or head scarf—a religion-based regulation similar to one that the U.S. Supreme Court declared unconstitutional in a 1993 case called *Hialeah v. Lukumi Babalu*. In the autumn of 2005, Muslim youths rioted for two weeks in nearly 300 cities and towns, throwing France into crisis. Although many of the rioters were citizens, by all accounts immigrants and their children were not treated as full members of the French polity, a situation that continues today.

Some critics of immigration today argue that the Constitution should be amended to abolish "birthright citizenship." That is, rather than grant citizenship to every child born in the United States, only if one or both parents are citizens should a child be given citizenship.

- *What consequences might follow from such a change in the Constitution?*

At the same time, many foreign observers point to a striking consistency in political beliefs across the United States, a consistency that seems at odds with its cultural diversity. More frequently than in other democracies, Americans agree on fundamentals and share basic assumptions about the nature of a good society. On first examination, this claim strikes many students as exaggerated, if not wrong. The United States certainly has its share of political conflict. Republicans and Democrats clash angrily in the halls of government. Liberals and conservatives argue noisily in the media. But the range of disagreement historically is narrower than that found in other democracies, which may contain political parties hoping to restore a royal family to the throne, establish an official church, or create a "dictatorship of the proletariat." Beliefs considered valid in other cultures fall outside the mainstream in the United States.

How might such a contradiction arise? How does an ethnically and religiously heterogeneous society develop a political culture more homogeneous than most? To answer this question, we must know more about both the makeup of the U.S. population and the core beliefs that Americans share. In the next section we consider the diversity produced by new immigrants continuously arriving in the United States. In the section that follows we will discuss the philosophy that unifies American beliefs and values.

Social Diversity

In "Federalist 2," John Jay described Americans as a "united people" who were "descended from the same ancestors, speaking the same language, professing the same religion, attached to the same principles of government, very similar in their manners and customs." Here, Jay was exaggerating American unity—a campaign tactic aimed at downplaying divisions that threatened ratification of the U.S. Constitution. In fact, no "united people" colonized the so-called New World.

The Dutch settled New York, and Swedes and Germans settled along the Delaware River. The French were present on the northern and western borders of the colonies, and a small Spanish population lived in the South. The British were most numerous, of course, but they were not all of a kind. Religious dissenters called Puritans settled in New England, but Virginia's colonists remained loyal to the Church of England. Maryland was a grant to Lord Baltimore, who welcomed his fellow Catholics, and Pennsylvania accepted Quakers, who were unwelcome almost everywhere else. Moreover, after 1700 British immigration came increasingly from Scotland, Wales, and Ireland, rather than from England.

Indentured servants—who made up half the population of Pennsylvania, New York, and New Jersey—included thousands of Germans, Scandinavians, Belgians, French, and Swiss. And these were only the voluntary immigrants; the involuntary immigrants—slaves—who made up about 20 percent of the population, were from Africa. (Native Americans, whose numbers had been decimated by wars and disease, were viewed as separate nations altogether.) Historians estimate that on the eve of the American Revolution only 50 percent of the population of the colonies was English.[13]

Students may react skeptically to this description of colonial diversity: A bunch of European Christians is your idea of diversity? Today, debates over **multiculturalism,** the idea that ethnic and cultural groups should maintain their identity within the larger society and respect one another's differences, do not revolve around whether Catholics

4.2

Outline the evolution of social diversity in the United States and the debates over immigration.

multiculturalism

The idea that ethnic and cultural groups should maintain their identity within the larger society and respect one another's differences.

and Calvinists should get along, or whether the British should tolerate the Dutch. Instead, we debate whether people with nontraditional lifestyles should enjoy the same rights and privileges as those who follow more traditional moral codes, or we struggle to formulate policies that will give people of color the same chances in life that the white majority has. But notions of diversity are relative to time and place. A few centuries ago, Protestants and Catholics looked upon each other with no more understanding (and possibly with less) than that with which a Christian might look upon a Muslim today—and the cultural distance between them often turned deadly.

Relative to other countries, and to the times, America has always been diverse. The national motto imprinted on the United States seal and on several coins, *E Pluribus Unum* ("out of many, one"), explicitly recognizes our diversity. It is a key ingredient of the nation's historical experience. In fact, the existence of distinct ethnic and religious groups and their desire to preserve some part of their distinctiveness underlie much of the history of political conflict in the United States. The contemporary debates over immigration, multiculturalism, and related issues show an unfortunate ignorance of U.S. history. For that reason we should take a brief look at our past.

A Nation of Immigrants Then

After the successful campaign for ratification of the Constitution, the new federal government maintained the status quo policy of unrestricted immigration—if you could get here, you could come. Of course, not everyone was happy about such open borders. One of the most cosmopolitan Americans of the time, Benjamin Franklin, expressed his resentment of Germans in various letters:

> Why should *Pennsylvania*, founded by the *English*, become a colony of Aliens, who will shortly be so numerous as to Germanize us instead of our Anglifying them, and will never adopt our Language or Customs any more than they can acquire our Complexion? [emphasis in original].[14]

Despite such misgivings, land was plentiful and labor scarce. The quicker the territory could be populated, the sooner economic development would follow. Immigration gradually increased, until by the mid-eighteenth century immigrants from England, Ireland, and Germany were arriving in numbers as high as 400,000 per year. Irish immigration became a major political issue. Many Protestants feared that Irish Catholics would put allegiance to the pope above loyalty to the United States and that they might even plot to overthrow the government. Cartoonists of the period depicted the Irish as dark, hairy, apelike people. In the 1854 elections, the anti-Catholic "Know-Nothing" party won 43 seats in the House of Representatives, almost a fifth of the chamber at the time. (The party's name came from its secret password, "I know nothing about it.")

Immigration increased considerably in the 1860s and continued at a high rate until World War I. In the 1860s and 1870s, the first of an eventual half-million French Canadians crossed the northeastern border of the United States, and several million Scandinavians joined a continuing stream of English, Irish, and Germans (see Figure 4.1 on page 105).

Political conflict in the late nineteenth century frequently was "ethno-cultural."[15] In the Midwest and much of the East, the Republican base lay in native Protestant communities, whereas the Democrats sank deep roots in the immigrant Catholic communities. Politics revolved around such issues as the prohibition or regulation of alcohol, public funding of parochial schools, bilingual schools (mostly German, but French in New

England), and Sunday "blue laws," which restricted commercial and recreational activities on Sundays. German Lutherans were an important "swing" group in some midwestern states; they generally voted Republican but cultural conflict sometimes swung them to the Democratic side. In Wisconsin, for example, the Republicans lost only two statewide elections between 1858 and 1890. One came after the party raised liquor license fees; the second, after it passed a measure requiring English language instruction in the schools.[16]

The Chinese were the first Asians to immigrate on a significant scale. More than 20,000 Chinese participated in the California Gold Rush, which began in 1849, and more than 100,000 Chinese laborers helped build the western links of the transcontinental railroads. At first these newcomers were viewed positively as peaceful, hard-working (and cheap) labor. Soon, however, a virulent backlash set in. During the congressional debate on the Chinese Exclusion Act of 1882, California Senator John Miller charged that:

> The experiment now being tried in California is to subject American free labor to competition with Chinese servile labor, and so far as it has gone, it has put in progress the displacement of American laborers, and the substitution of Chinese for white men. The process will continue if permitted until the white laborer is driven out into other fields, or until those who remain in the contest come down to the Chinese level.[17]

Bigotry on St. Patrick's Day c.1867
Thomas Nast portrays the Irish (celebrating a national holiday) as violent, apelike brutes that riot and attack the police.

• *Would you be likely to see such a cartoon today? How would racism be expressed today?*

Such charges were as common then as now: Cheap foreign labor will undercut the standard of living of "real" Americans—a charge that has repeatedly been leveled at immigrants through the decades.

Beginning in the 1880s, the character of immigration changed as millions of people from southern and eastern Europe followed their northern and western European predecessors. Once again, these new arrivals were viewed as threatening by many "real" Americans, who by now believed that pre-1880 immigrants "were drawn from the superior stocks of northern and western Europe, while those who came later were drawn from the inferior breeds of southern and eastern Europe."[18] In a best-selling book published in 1916, Madison Grant of the American Museum of Natural History described new immigrants as "the weak, the broken, and the mentally crippled of all races drawn from the lowest stratum of the Mediterranean basin and the Balkans, together with hordes of the wretched, submerged populations of the Polish ghettoes."[19]

Reflecting widespread popular concern, a government commission was established in 1907 to study the immigration situation. Three years later, the U.S. Immigration Commission issued an immense report. Here are a few generalizations, lifted from that report, which illustrate how Americans of the time period viewed outsiders, and also how quick they were to prejudge entire immigrant groups:

GREEKS: *"There is no doubt of their nimble intelligence. They compete with the Hebrew race as the best traders of the Orient."*

SOUTHERN ITALIAN: *". . . . excitable, impulsive, highly imaginative, impracticable . . . an individualist having little adaptability to high organized society."*

PERSIAN: ". . . . is rather brilliant and poetical than solid in temperament. Like the Hindu he is more eager to secure the semblance than the substance of modern civilization."

POLES: ". . . . are more high strung than are the most of their neighbors. In this respect they resemble the Hungarians farther south."

ROMANIANS: ". . . . more emotional than the Slav, less stolid and heavy than the Bulgarian."

SERBO-CROATIANS: "19th century 'savage manners' persist, illiteracy is prevalent and civilization at a low stage. . . ."[20]

Such ethnic stereotyping displays official insensitivity on a scale undreamed of today. No one should ever think that the American "melting pot" in any way resembled Mr. Rogers's neighborhood—a community of harmony and love.

Not all opposition to immigration reflected ethnic or religious bigotry. Some opposed further immigration for economic or political reasons. Trade union leaders feared that continued immigration would undercut the bargaining power of workers. And, in fact, U.S. business did encourage immigration as a source of cheap labor. The Progressives, a reformist political movement, opposed further immigration because they viewed immigrants as the foundation of corrupt urban political machines (see Chapter 8). The Progressives believed that shutting off immigration would shut off the supply of uninformed, ignorant voters whom the machines could manipulate.

For many reasons, then, anti-immigration sentiment grew. After two decades of agitation, a national literacy test was adopted in 1917. (As we shall see in Chapter 17, such a device had earlier been used to disfranchise African Americans and poor whites in the South.) Supporters of the test did not disguise their motives. The noted Massachusetts senator Henry Cabot Lodge observed that the test "will bear most heavily on the Italians, Russians, Poles, Hungarians, Greeks, and Asiatics, and very lightly, or not at all upon English-speaking emigrants or Germans, Scandinavians, and French."[21]

Contrary to what Senator Lodge believed, many would-be immigrants knew how to read—or learned to do so quickly—so stronger legislation was needed to close the door. A series of laws passed in the 1920s restricted immigration both quantitatively (the total was limited) and qualitatively (quotas gave northern and western Europeans preference over people from other areas).[22] The Japanese and other Asians were added to the Chinese as groups that were excluded altogether. By 1930 the era of the open door had ended, although Mexicans continued to enter the southwestern states to work in U.S. agriculture (joining those who had been incorporated when Mexico ceded a substantial part of its territory to the United States in 1848.). And, after World War II, Puerto Ricans emigrated to New York City in significant numbers. But, before the United States closed its doors to immigrants, more than 35 million people had left hearth and home to come to America. These immigrants and their children made a major contribution to the growth of the United States from a country of about 10 million inhabitants in 1820 to one of more than 100 million in 1920.

Restrictions on immigration were part of a general reactionary movement that broke out after World War I. During the "Red Scare," immigrants were persecuted as carriers of Bolshevik, anarchist, and other subversive foreign ideologies. In the 1920s, anti-Catholic and anti-Jewish sentiments energized the second Ku Klux Klan; it counted 25–30 percent of the adult male Protestant population in its membership.[23]

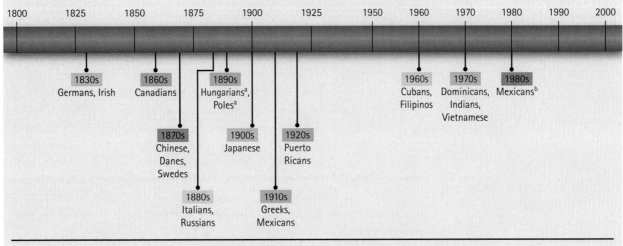

TIMELINE The Old Immigration to the United States—New Immigration to the United States (year immigration first reached 100,000)

^aEstimated because immigrants from the Austro-Hungarian Empire were not separately classified before World War I.

^bMexican immigration first reached 100,000 in the 1910s. However, in the post-1965 era of new immigration, Mexican immigration surged starting around 1980.

FIGURE 4.1

IMMIGRATION TO THE UNITED STATES

The quantity and origin of immigrants to the United States have changed sharply over time.

• *When was immigration from foreign countries NOT a common feature of U.S. history?*

• *Why might interest in emigrating to the United States rise and fall?*

Sources: Stephanie Bernado, *The Ethnic Almanac* (Garden City, NY: Doubleday, 1981), pp. 22–140; and the U.S. Immigration and Naturalization Service (www.ins.gov).

Not surprisingly, the 1928 Democratic presidential nomination of Catholic Al Smith caused a virulent reaction.[24]

In the 1930s, discrimination against Catholics and Jews was still widespread. Indeed, not until the 1960s did Ivy League universities eliminate informal quotas on admissions of Jewish students. Gradually, however, ethno-cultural tensions died down. The cumulative effects of economic depression, World War II, revulsion at the Holocaust, and the Cold War led to a general reduction in ethnic and racial tensions that lasted approximately a generation. However, this short period from the early 1930s to the mid-1960s, during which ethnic and religious issues were relatively dormant, was the exception, not the norm. From the founding through the 1930s, the kinds of issues now discussed under the heading of multiculturalism were an important part of U.S. politics.

A Nation of Immigrants Now

The Immigration Act of 1965 abandoned the national-quotas system favoring northern Europeans, opening the door to the largest surge of immigration since the 1900s. Immigration from Latin America and the West Indies increased rapidly. In addition, hundreds of thousands of new immigrants from Vietnam, Korea, Cambodia, India, Iran, the Philippines, and other countries became the first numerically significant Asian groups to arrive since the Japanese in the early years of the twentieth century (see Figure 4.1).

In the 1990s, the absolute number of immigrants was higher than in any previous decade, although it was lower as a proportion of the population than it had been at the turn of the century. Three million came from Mexico, Central America, and the Caribbean, and nearly as many from Asia. Nearly half a million came from South America and almost 200,000 from Africa. These figures include only legal immigrants; an estimated 11 million people now live in the United States illegally.

Figure 4.2 depicts the result of this newest wave of immigration. Euro-whites are now less than three-quarters of the population. And Hispanics, the largest newer immigrant group, now surpass African Americans as the nation's largest minority group. The Census Bureau projects that the population of European origin will fall to less than 60 percent by 2030. In some states (Texas, California) and large cities (Houston, Los Angeles) whites of European origin are already a minority. These dramatic changes underlie contemporary debates over issues such as bilingual education and the provision of social services to immigrants.

Immigration as a Contemporary Issue

In 1994, California voters overwhelmingly passed Proposition 187, an initiative that denied state services to illegal immigrants and their children. Although the proposition was struck down by the courts, the question of eligibility for governmental benefits such as food stamps and college scholarships has remained on the national agenda ever since. Most recently, illegal immigrant eligibility surfaced in the debate over health insurance reform in 2009. And the issue gained national attention again when Arizona passed a restrictive law in 2010 (see the *Election Voices* feature on page 121).

The Census Bureau projects a significant shift in the composition of the American population over the next two decades.

FIGURE 4.2

THE EVER-CHANGING U.S. POPULATION

The Census Bureau projects that the ethnic and racial composition of the U.S. population will undergo a significant shift over the next two decades.

• *Which ethnic or racial groups are growing the fastest in the United States? The slowest?*

Source: U.S. Census Bureau (www.census.gov).

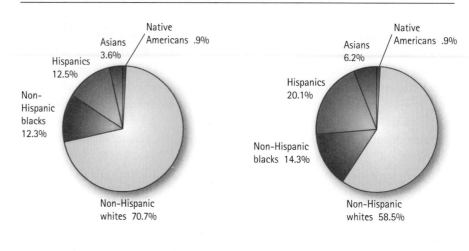

2005   2030

Much of the contemporary debate over immigration would sound familiar to Americans of earlier eras. In particular, does providing public services to immigrants impose a burden on native citizens? And do immigrants take jobs from native workers? As we have seen, such fears are not new, but historical analogies are never perfect. In some significant respects immigration today differs from that of the past.

One aspect of the contemporary immigration issue was almost completely absent in the past: the distinction between legal and illegal immigration. Before immigration was curtailed in the 1920s, immigration laws were minimal—except for bans on immigration from Asian countries. Generally, the law only barred "persons likely to become a public charge" (because of contagious illness or physical disability). Today, an estimated 11 million immigrants have entered the United States in violation of federal laws and regulations. Some commentators claim that the issue is not immigration, *per se*, but illegal immigration. Certainly, there is some validity to this argument. A law is a law, not an advisory opinion to be obeyed or not as one chooses. Other commentators believe that immigration would be almost as controversial today even if the 11 million undocumented immigrants had come to the United States through legal channels. As shown in Table 1 in the *Election Voices* feature on page 123, however, Americans clearly distinguish between legal and illegal immigration.

Whether legal or illegal, opposition to immigration has both economic and cultural sources. The economic benefit/cost ratio of immigration today is unclear. Most studies conclude that contemporary immigration makes a net positive contribution to the national economy, whereas some find a net negative contribution, but all agree that the net impact is small one way or the other.[25] In contrast, earlier waves of immigrants made a major contribution to the Industrial Revolution in the United States and were essential to the explosive growth of the U.S. economy in the nineteenth century. The Irish dug the canals. The Irish and Chinese laid track for the railroads. The Poles, Italians, and myriad other groups dug the coal and smelted the iron ore. But, for several decades now, the U.S. economy has been moving away from manufacturing to a globally integrated service and information economy. Many Americans, especially those who lack technical skills, are disadvantaged by the transition. Research indicates that competition from immigrants undercuts the wages of low-skilled Americans who already are struggling to make ends meet.[26]

The costs of immigration are higher today than in earlier eras. Then as now, immigration created increased demand for police and educational services, but there was no government-provided "safety net"—no disability payments or workman's compensation, no Medicaid, and no welfare or food stamps. Some scholars have pointed out that the costs of immigration could be lowered (and the benefits raised) by changing the criteria for legal immigration. About two-thirds of immigrants in

Illegal Immigrants: An Emerging Political Power?

In 2004, illegal immigrants held rallies throughout the country to demand increased access to government benefits and services routinely available to citizens and legal immigrants, such as driver's licenses. As the cartoon indicates, not everyone was delighted with this development.

recent decades have been admitted on the basis of family preferences—having relatives already in the United States—and only about one-eighth on the basis of essential skills.[27] This policy results in fewer productive workers and more dependents (especially older people) than would be the case if the law were changed to favor advanced education and valuable occupational skills. Thus, current U.S. immigration policy admits fewer taxpayers and more people in need of taxpayer-provided services than did earlier laws that gave first preference to productive workers. The immigration legislation that failed in 2007 would have moved immigration law closer to the kind of point system used in many other developed countries to select the most economically valuable immigrants.

Another economic difference between immigration today and in the past is the geographical and jurisdictional mismatch between the costs and benefits of immigration. In the past, the states and localities that received the most immigrants enjoyed the greatest economic growth, and the costs they incurred were relatively low—mainly schools and police services. For the past several decades, however, a large majority of contemporary immigrants have gone to a few states such as California, New York, Texas, Florida, New Jersey, and Illinois. Most of the taxes paid by immigrants are federal income and social security taxes that go to the national government rather than directly to the states where immigrants concentrate.[28] Although they do not directly receive the taxes immigrants pay, the localities within states are responsible for providing educational and social services to new immigrants. Disparities such as these focus the costs of immigration more narrowly than the benefits. Heavy immigration forces local and state governments to cut services, raise taxes, and plead for money from higher levels of government, options that elected officials naturally view as unpleasant.

It is easy to imagine changes in public policies that would alleviate such economic concerns. Restricting family preferences would raise the benefits and lower the costs of immigration. The costs of immigration could be spread more fairly across states and, within states, across the jurisdictions that provide services. Even if such changes in the law were implemented, however, some Americans would still oppose immigration because they regard it not just as an economic burden but as a cultural threat. They believe that immigrants who speak different languages, believe in different religions, and practice different customs threaten American unity. Harvard Professor Samuel Huntington, for example, claims that today's immigrants lack the Anglo-Protestant values that constitute the American identity.[29] Such critics urge the United States to close the door before too much *pluribus* destroys the *unum*.[30] To evaluate such concerns fairly, we need to understand the American identity that some opponents of immigration worry is at risk.

Philosophical Unity

4.3 Analyze American shared beliefs, their roots in classical liberalism, and their apparent contradictions.

liberalism
A philosophy that elevates and empowers the individual as opposed to religious, hereditary, governmental, or other forms of authority.

From the French visitor Alexis de Tocqueville in the 1830s to the Swede Gunnar Myrdal in the 1940s, foreign observers have claimed that Americans share basic values. These fundamental beliefs usually are described as *liberal*—but to political philosophers the term means something very different from its meaning in current politics.[31] Classical **liberalism** is a philosophy that emerged in Europe as medieval thought disintegrated in the religious wars of the seventeenth century. It sought to free individuals from a society structured by heredity and religious privilege and to empower them at the expense of the nobility and the clergy. Roughly speaking, liberal thinkers wanted people to make political and religious choices for themselves. Modern-day American conservatives, who champion keeping government out of economic decisions, and modern-day American liberals, who champion keeping government out of moral decisions, both have roots in a "liberal" political philosophy.

Focusing on individuals rather than groups gave liberal thinkers a unique perspective on society and government. They did not view people as a product of their society, a view that goes back to the Greeks. Rather, they considered society a product of the individuals who made it up. The writings of the "social contract" theorists, such as Thomas Hobbes, John Locke, and Jean-Jacques Rousseau, contain the purest expression of this perspective. These philosophers tried to imagine what human life would be like in a natural state, without society or government, so that they could deduce why people would create political institutions in the first place. That is, their approach started from an assumption that people can exist as isolated beings. They imagined government as nothing more than a creation of the individuals who chose to develop it, an agreement much like a contract in which both rulers and ruled accept certain rights, duties, and obligations.

Locke deduced a string of political principles from such assumptions. First, individuals have basic rights—life, liberty, and property—that precede the existence of government and that government therefore may not violate. Second, individuals are equal under the law; there are no distinctions based on heredity or religion. Third, to safeguard rights, government must be limited. Fourth, government is instrumental—not an end in itself but a means to the end of ensuring people's rights. Fifth, when a government threatens rights or fails to protect citizens, they may replace it with another.

The preceding principles should have a familiar ring. American colonists read social-contract theorists such as Locke in the years before rebelling against England. Thomas Jefferson encapsulated the spirit of classical liberalism in the Declaration of Independence:

> We hold these truths to be self-evident: That all men are created equal, that they are endowed by their Creator with certain inalienable Rights, that among these are Life, Liberty, and the Pursuit of Happiness.
>   That to secure these rights Governments are instituted among Men, deriving their just powers from the consent of the governed.
>   That whenever any Form of Government becomes destructive of these ends, it is the Right of the People to alter or to abolish it, and to institute new Government, laying its foundation on such principles and organizing its powers in such form, as to them shall seem most likely to effect their Safety and Happiness.

These eloquent sentences capture the five tenets of liberal philosophy: political equality, rights, instrumental government, limited government, and the right to rebel. The Constitution and its Bill of Rights followed on this liberal tradition by laying out in detail the rights of citizens, the limits on government, and rules for changing leaders that would make future rebellion unnecessary.

To some degree, philosophers and historians have exaggerated the extent to which all Americans share such a coherent political philosophy. Many writers refer to the American "creed" and the American "ethos," suggesting a more unified and well-defined set of beliefs than actually exists. In fact, at the time of the American Revolution, liberalism coexisted with a rival, civic republican tradition.[32] According to Gordon Wood, **civic republicanism** placed more emphasis on the obligation of

civic republicanism
A political philosophy that emphasizes the obligation of citizens to act virtuously in pursuit of the common good.

citizens to act virtuously in pursuit of the welfare of the community relative to the rights of the individual.[33] Called "communitarian" today, this tradition faded over time but certainly has not disappeared—as illustrated by President John F. Kennedy's famous exhortation: "Ask not what your country can do for you; ask what you can do for your country!"

Skeptics also point out that the rights and privileges exalted in the liberal tradition extended only so far. In particular, they did not extend to the Native American tribes that were destroyed by the American settlers, and they did not extend fully to African Americans until a century after the Civil War. Full rights and privileges did not extend to women until even later.[34] And the rights of other minority groups such as homosexuals remain matters of political disagreement today. But, even if the "liberal tradition" has been less than all-encompassing, there is plenty of evidence that Americans tend to agree on certain basic "liberal" principles and that Americans differ in systematic ways from the citizens of other democracies.

American Individualism

Perhaps the most striking way in which Americans differ from people elsewhere lies in the balance they strike between individual responsibility on the one hand and governmental responsibility on the other. International surveys consistently find that Americans lean more toward the side of individual responsibility than do citizens of other democracies. For example, Figure 4.3 compares the responses of citizens of 15 democracies to a question about individual versus government responsibility for the welfare of individuals. Although all countries display a mixture of viewpoints,

FIGURE 4.3

INDIVIDUAL RESPONSIBILITY

When surveyed, Americans emphasize individual responsibility more than people elsewhere.

• *Why might Americans place such heavy emphasis on individual responsibility compared to people in other countries?*

Source: The World Values Survey, 2005.

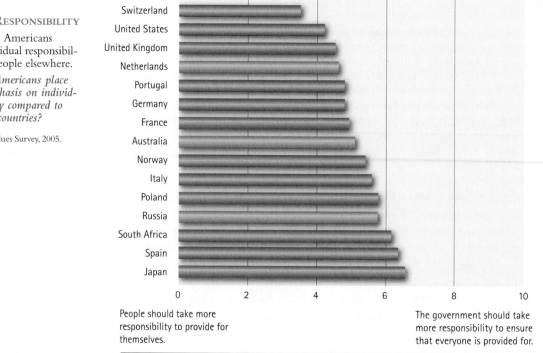

People should take more responsibility to provide for themselves.

The government should take more responsibility to ensure that everyone is provided for.

Nation's average score on the 10-point scale

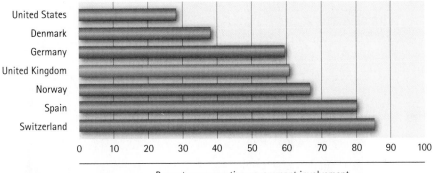

Note: Percentage who "Agree" and "Strongly Agree" that "The government should reduce differences in income levels."

FIGURE 4.4

REDUCE INEQUALITY?

Americans are less supportive of government actions to reduce economic inequality than are people elsewhere.

• *Why are Americans less enthusiastic about government action to reduce inequality compared to people in other economically advanced societies?*

Sources: The General Social Survey (2004) and the European Social Survey (2005).

on average Americans favor self-reliance more than do the citizens of 13 of the other democracies, exceeded only by the Swiss.

Other recent surveys show that Americans are much less supportive of government efforts to reduce inequality than are people elsewhere. As shown in Figure 4.4, just over a quarter of Americans support government policies to reduce income inequality, whereas majorities in Germany, Britain, and various other democracies support these policies. Americans are suspicious of governmental power and skeptical about governmental competence, attitudes that reinforce their emphasis on individual responsibility. As one scholar comments, "the distinctive aspect of the American creed is its antigovernment character. Opposition to power and suspicion of government as the most dangerous embodiment of power are the central themes of American political thought."[35] If people fundamentally doubt the motives and capabilities of government, they can hardly be expected to grant it expansive powers and responsibilities. Moreover, Americans believe that individual responsibility works, that hard work and perseverance pay off. People elsewhere are less likely to see personal effort as a sure means to better their lives, and therefore are less likely to be optimistic about getting ahead (see Figure 4.5).

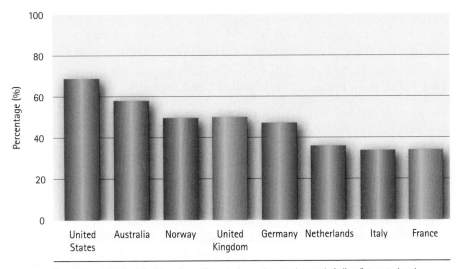

Percentage believing that they have "free choice and control over their lives" to get ahead.

FIGURE 4.5

AMERICAN OPTIMISM

Americans are more optimistic about their chances of getting ahead than people elsewhere.

• *Why might Australians be similar to Americans regarding their optimism about getting ahead?*

Note: On a 1–10 scale of "How much freedom of choice and control you feel you have over the way your life turns out," the reported percentages are a summation of the three most positive responses.

Source: The World Values Survey, 2005.

FIGURE 4.6

Dominant Values

Even racial minorities share the individualist values of the larger society.

• *Why might African Americans respond to such questions so much like white Americans?*

Source: The General Social Survey, 2004.

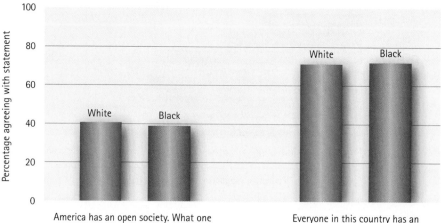

One of the most striking features of the American belief in individual responsibility is that it is not closely tied to the actual social and economic circumstances in which Americans find themselves. We might think those at the bottom of the economic ladder to be far less individualistic and optimistic than those at the top, but that expectation is wrong. Even the very poorest Americans reject a government-guaranteed income, and only the very poorest believe that the government should reduce income differences. There is little or no relationship between income and belief in the benefits of hard work: Majorities of the poorest Americans subscribe to this belief, just as do similar majorities of the most affluent.[36]

Other studies reveal that poor Americans are as likely as more affluent citizens to embrace the "work ethic," and are equally likely to take personal responsibility for their condition.[37] The poor dislike the progressive income tax almost as much as the rich (see Chapter 19).[38] Perhaps the most powerful illustration of American individualism lies in the attitudes of minorities. African Americans clearly share less in the American dream than do whites. On average, they earn less, work in less prestigious occupations, and suffer discrimination in many forms. It comes as a surprise, then, that they are almost as likely as whites to embrace the individualist ethic (see Figure 4.6). In sum, even those Americans who are faring poorly in an individualist social order still support its basic premises.[39]

The Tension Between Individualism and Equality

The findings on American individualism raise an important question: What about equality? Liberal philosophy places great importance on equality, and writers in the liberal tradition typically mention it just after liberty. Yet great inequalities exist in the United States. For example, the large gulf between the incomes of the poor and rich has actually increased since the early 1970s. Nevertheless, relatively few Americans demand that such income inequality be eliminated or even lessened.

At one time there was no incompatibility between liberty and equality. Indeed, de Tocqueville and other early-nineteenth-century visitors were struck by the extent of social and economic equality in the United States. Liberty and equality were thought to be complementary in the sense that free people would use their liberty to achieve economic success, and an economically secure middle class would use its resources to promote liberty. After the Civil War, however, economic development weakened the association between liberty and equality. The Industrial Revolution produced great concentrations of private wealth on the one hand and masses of low-wage workers on the other. Under such conditions, liberty and equality became detached.

Nevertheless, radical movements such as socialism have made little headway in the United States. American reform movements typically have focused on reducing economic inequality without attacking the foundations of the economic system that generates it. At first glance, this limited demand for change might suggest that Americans actually do not value equality very much, but the more likely explanation for this apparent inconsistency is that America's political culture supports only a limited kind of equality. Liberalism emphasized equality before the law, regardless of heredity or religious faith or personal connections; it did not demand economic equality. It guaranteed freedom to pursue happiness; it did not promise that everyone would achieve it. Most Americans regard economic inequality as not only inevitable but also generally fair—those who produce more deserve to receive more, even if they get rich. Majorities therefore reject aggressive government action to erase such inequalities.

Today, it is customary to talk about this distinction in terms of the difference between **equality of opportunity** and **equality of condition.** Americans strongly support equality of opportunity: Everyone should have a fair chance. After the competition starts, though, may the best person win! Americans just as strongly reject attempts to bring about equality of condition, because that may involve rewarding people who are undeserving at the expense of those who work harder. Survey data probing attitudes about affirmative action reflect this distinction. Americans favor affirmative action for women and minorities when the survey questions are clear that equal opportunity is the goal. For example, one study found that:

> Ninety-four percent agree that "Our society should do what is necessary to make sure that everyone has an equal opportunity to succeed."
> Seventy-nine percent agree that "After years of discrimination, it is only fair to set up special programs to make sure that women and minorities are given every chance to have equal opportunities in employment and education."

But Americans just as strongly oppose affirmative action when the survey questions indicate that equality of outcome is the goal:

> Eighty-six percent don't think "blacks and other minorities should receive preference in college admissions to make up for past inequalities."
> Eighty percent don't think "blacks and other minorities should receive preference in hiring to make up for past inequalities."[40]

As far as most Americans are concerned, equality of opportunity should be enough. The rest is up to the individual. This belief also shows up in government policy. As social critics have pointed out, the United States spends a smaller proportion of its national income on social welfare than most other democracies—and spends especially little on the young (see Chapter 18). But the United States historically has spent a larger proportion of its national income on education than other democracies. Education is not "welfare." It is a means to create equal opportunity, a way for individuals to improve their skills and become better economic competitors. That idea fits with American core values.[41]

equality of opportunity
The notion that individuals should have an equal chance to advance economically through their talent and hard work.

equality of condition
The notion that all individuals have a right to a more or less equal part of the material goods that society produces.

One Nation, Under God?

The American political culture stands out in one other notable way, one that is seemingly at odds with its emphasis on individualism: Americans are more religious than the citizens of most other democracies. Americans are more likely to believe in God, to attend religious services, and to report that religion plays an important role in their lives—far more so than citizens in the countries that originally settled the colonies (see Figure 4.7). And Americans do not separate their religious beliefs from their politics: A majority of Americans report that they will not vote for an atheist.[42]

FIGURE 4.7

A RELIGIOUS PEOPLE

Americans are more religious than people elsewhere.

• *In which countries do people seem to make a significant distinction between an inward sense of religion (thinking of themselves as religious people) and an outward display of religion (attending church)?*

Source: The World Values Survey, 2005.

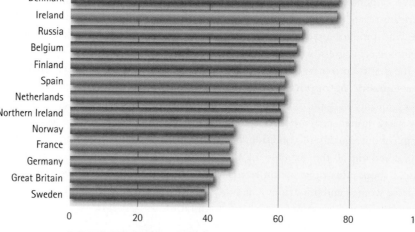

Percentage identifying themselves as "a religious person"

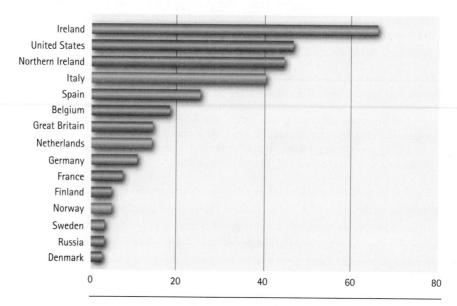

Percentage identifying themselves as attenders of religious services once a week or more

The prevalence of religious faith goes back to the nation's founding, of course. Many of the original settlers were people seeking the freedom to practice their religion. These deeply religious people sought to escape persecution by the established churches of Europe. Furthermore, the nation periodically has replenished its store of religious energy through great spiritual "awakenings" that wash over the country: the First Great Awakening in the 1730s and 1740s, the second around 1800 and into Jackson's presidency (1828–1836), and the third starting in the 1890s and lasting about two decades.

Although church and state institutions are separate in the United States (with early exceptions, such as the Congregational Church, which was the established church of Connecticut until 1818 and of Massachusetts until 1833), religion and politics have seldom been separate. Church leaders cannot impose laws on U.S. citizens and punish them for immoral behavior, as they can in some countries. Nevertheless, foreign observers agree that U.S. politics is highly moralistic. Throughout history, religiously motivated Americans have attempted to use government to improve the character of their fellow citizens—that is, "to legislate morality"—more so than people in other democracies. At various times and places, laws have restricted recreational activities on Sundays, prohibited people from drinking, and censored the books and magazines people can read or the movies they can watch.

The continued importance of religion in the United States puzzles many observers. The nation's historical origins alone cannot explain it. After all, numerous forces have changed U.S. society since the founding: westward expansion, the Industrial Revolution, immigration, and great wars, to name a few. Moreover, churches are not publicly supported in the United States. Some other democracies have an "established" church, an official religion that is subsidized by the state. The Anglican Church is the established church in Great Britain, the Catholic Church in Italy, the Lutheran Church in Norway, and the Eastern Orthodox Church in Greece. In the United States, no religious institution receives direct government support.

Furthermore, religiosity does not seem to fit well with American values. Christian faith, for example, may impose various burdens on members, in particular an obligation to help their fellow human beings. This orientation seems somewhat at odds with a political culture that emphasizes individualism. In addition, by calling Americans to reflect on spiritual matters, religion also seems to clash with the American reputation for practicality. Americans stereotypically focus on problem solving and on material success. They are supposed to show a trust in logic, in science, in technology, and in the evidence before their eyes (a way of thinking that philosophers call "positivism"). How can we explain the robustness of religious faith in a country with no established church, with a reputation for individualism, and with a people known for their hardheaded pragmatism?

The answer may be that religion and the liberal tradition are more compatible than it first appears. Some scholars argue that just as the liberal tradition encourages economic entrepreneurship, so it encourages religious entrepreneurship as well. Church leaders know that they do not have a captive audience, as in countries with established churches. They compete to retain the loyalty of their existing "customers" and adapt their "product" to the changing interests and values of potential new customers.

New Church, Traditional Faith

Members of the Lakewood Church worship at their megachurch in Houston. A new survey of Protestant megachurches shows that they are among the nation's fastest growing faith groups, using contemporary programming and conservative values to draw in younger people and families.

Thus, contemporary churches provide services and activities (youth clubs, sports clubs, and even singles clubs) that people value. Just as the free market in economics encourages economic enterprise, a free market in religion may encourage religious enterprise.

The result of all this religious enterprise is a greater *supply* of religion in the United States. Think of the wide assortment of religions, denominations, branches, and sects. This rich range of options makes it easier for a person to find a comfortable match with some religion in the United States than in other countries, where citizens typically have a much smaller range of choices. If an American does not like one religion, there are numerous others from which to choose, and exceptionally hard-to-please worshippers can always start their own churches, a solution that a fair number of people seek—just Google "house church" and look at what comes up. Thus, Americans may be more involved with religion than people in other countries because, stimulated by competition, American religion offers them more reasons to be.

Perhaps the most intriguing explanation for the persistence of religiosity in the United States has been proposed by Robert Booth Fowler, who argues that there is a greater *demand* for religion in the United States. Fowler argues that the liberal tradition and religiosity do not conflict. In fact, just the opposite is true—the liberal tradition creates a deep need for religion. People steeped in the liberal tradition jealously guard their rights and hold themselves personally responsible for their successes and failures. They create a society characterized by social and geographic mobility and by rapid social and economic change.

Fowler believes that many people find life in such a society precarious, or at least somewhat lonely. He sees religion as filling a gap in American life. Whereas citizens in communal cultures already feel part of something bigger than themselves, individualism leaves Americans with a greater need for a religious dimension in their lives:

> Religion has aided liberalism by being a *refuge* from liberalism. . . . [I]t provides an escape from liberal culture, a place of comfort where individualism, competition, this-worldly pragmatism, and relentless rationalism do not hold sway. In a liberal country with liberal citizens, religion is a place where one can come home . . . and *then* emerge refreshed for the battles of life in the liberal world.[43]

If true, this argument would explain the periodic occurrence of religious awakenings. They should result whenever the prosperity created by individualism draws Americans too far from the spiritual ideals that many of them hold.[44] People eventually begin to wonder whether there is something more to life than money and success. Others are troubled by the self-serving behavior of their fellow individualists. Thus, people turn to religion as an alternate avenue to personal satisfaction and as a means of correcting the destructive behavior of others.

Some observers believe that the United States is in the middle of its fourth great awakening, for reasons similar to those implied by Fowler's theory. They suggest that Evangelical Protestantism began a surge in the 1980s as a reaction to the excesses of the 1960s, a period of great economic growth during which the baby boomers—the individualistic "me generation"—came of age. Such sweeping historical claims are impossible to prove. Nevertheless, the last several decades only reinforce an indisputable feature of the American political culture: Along with individualism and belief in equality of opportunity, religiosity is a long-standing trait of the American public.

Why a Liberal Political Culture?

4.4

Assess the various explanations for the persistence of American classical liberalism.

The time has now come to answer the question posed at the start of this chapter: How can we explain the apparent inconsistency between a population that is strikingly heterogeneous in its ethnic, racial, and religious composition but surprisingly homogeneous in the beliefs and values that make up its political culture?

Traditional Explanations of American Liberalism

Early American colonists tended to come from the European "middle class." They usually were not poor peasants, but they also were not rich nobles. They were largely the very merchants, professionals, and artisans among whom liberal ideas had flourished, and they carried their political philosophy with them to North America, where they found little to contradict it. According to scholar Louis Hartz, the key to understanding America is that it lacked a feudal tradition. There was no hereditary aristocracy or established church to defend or to resist, nor was there an oppressed peasant class that might revolt.[45] In short, the United States took form among a white population for whom classical liberalism could be taken as "self-evident."

Others argue that perhaps as important as what the United States lacked is what it had: in particular, a great deal of land. North America was a sparsely populated continent over which the United States steadily expanded.[46] Some historians suggest that the frontier operated like a social safety valve: Rather than revolt against intolerable conditions, the only option in the settled countries of Europe, struggling Americans found it easier to pack up their belongings, move west, grab some land (often from Mexico or an indigenous tribe), and start again.

A plentiful supply of land and a scarcity of labor meant that ambitious individuals could and did succeed. Social conditions in the new country therefore reinforced the individualistic values that early settlers brought with them. And, with little competition from alternative value systems, a liberal political order and a market economy thrived. Generations of radical critics of American society have sadly asked, "Why no socialism in America?"[47] Many complex philosophical and historical answers have been offered, but the simplest answer is that Americans never saw much need for socialism. Under the conditions that prevailed, individual effort usually was enough to provide an acceptable life for most people; they did not require governmental solutions (let alone revolutionary ones).

Still, questions remain. The frontier was officially closed more than a century ago, and labor shortages have not been of much concern for more than half a century. So even if social conditions in the nineteenth century reinforced the beliefs and values of the early settlers, how relevant is that today? Slaves freed after the Civil War certainly had little experience with liberty or equality. Moreover, the millions of immigrants

Renewing the Tradition

Immigration is a difficult process that tends to attract people with a greater sense of individualism and independence than found among those who stay in their home countries.

political socialization

The set of psychological and sociological processes by which families, schools, religious organizations, communities, and other societal units inculcate beliefs and values in their members.

who arrived after the Civil War were not from liberal societies. Most of them came from authoritarian states with established churches and had lived their lives in communal peasant societies that *did* have feudal traditions. What is the basis for *their* adherence to the individualist values of the liberal tradition?

Perhaps the answer lies in a process of **political socialization.** This process continues to instill liberal values long after the initial basis for those values—social equality, an unsettled land, a frontier—eroded. Certainly, material conditions are not the only factor that determines how people think and view the world. Different cultures socialize their children into different ways of thinking and different ways of viewing the world, even under similar material circumstances. Beginning in the family and continuing through schools, religious institutions, and other organizations, societies instill certain values and patterns of thinking in their members. Thus, the explanation for the persistence of the liberal tradition could be simple: Socialization perpetuates a consensus established in the eighteenth century, a consensus that so dominated the schools and other social institutions that it was able to integrate the children of slaves as well as tens of millions of immigrants.

Many scholars find such an explanation insufficient. For one thing, one of the principal means by which immigrants were integrated into American society was through the efforts of political parties, particularly the urban machines discussed in Chapter 8. The machines were interested in controlling government; to do that they had to win elections, and immigrant votes counted just as much as those of the native-born. Thus, the machines organized each arriving group: In some eastern cities the Democrats gained an edge by organizing the Irish, the Republicans then countered by organizing the Italians, and so on. But the urban machines did not embody liberal, individualist values. On the contrary, the machines were something of an anomaly in the larger American political culture; they were collectivist and clannish—with an emphasis on obedience and loyalty, not on independence. Because machine politics and immigration are closely associated in U.S. history, we might expect political socialization to have pushed immigrants in a direction different from the liberal tradition.

Newer Explanations

Researchers skeptical of cultural explanations of how classical liberalism has survived over the centuries, despite the influx of millions of diverse people from different traditions, have proposed alternative explanations. In a provocative argument, Sven Steinmo suggests that the belief that liberal ideas shape U.S. government and politics is an oversimplification; rather, the reverse is also true—the government and politics of the United States recreate liberal ideas.[48] Specifically, Steinmo argues that U.S. government is so fragmented and decentralized that it rarely acts in a positive way to improve society. Often it is "gridlocked" or unable to act, and when it does act, its actions reflect deals among special interests. In consequence, successive generations of Americans learn the same basic lesson: Rely on yourself because you cannot rely on government, and best keep government limited because it will usually act in support of special interests. Given their institutions, Americans would have learned this lesson regardless of whether they were originally liberal individualists. Steinmo's key insight is that, once established, institutions that originally *reflected* particular values may come to *generate* those values.

More recently, scholars have begun to advance the argument that social diversity and the liberal tradition never contradicted each other in the first place. In fact, rather than posing a threat to American traditions, the flow of diverse peoples to America may have reinforced and strengthened American traditions. How could that be the case? The answer lies in what statistical analysts refer to as *self-selection*. With the notable exception of African Americans, immigrants came to the United States voluntarily. True, many came when crops failed, when they could not find work, or when they faced political persecution at home. Emigration under such circumstances might not seem to have occurred by choice, *but not everyone chose to emigrate*. Only a small fraction of the potential immigrants—less than 1 percent— actually left their own countries. Furthermore, not all of them chose to stay in the United States; about a third of immigrants eventually returned to their home countries.

What kind of person would have been most likely to travel to a new country, leaving family, friends, and village behind? Remember that immigration through most of history was not a matter of taking a train to Dublin, Frankfurt, or Rome and catching a flight to New York or Chicago. Before the Civil War, the journey usually took months, as immigrants walked to a port and then suffered through a long, miserable journey below decks on a sailing ship. Even after the Civil War, when the steamship shortened the ocean voyage and the railroad shortened the journey overland, it still took weeks. Many of the people who booked passage knew that they would never see their relatives or their homes again.[49] What kind of people made such a decision?

In all probability the people who immigrated already were—relative to their own societies—unusually individualistic. They were more motivated to break free from the traditions of their communities. They were more ambitious, more willing to run risks in the hope of bettering themselves—in Hartz's words, more likely to possess "the spirit which repudiated peasantry and tenantry."[50] Prejudiced as it was, even the Immigration Commission in 1911 conceded that "emigrating to a strange and distant country, although less of an undertaking than formerly, is still a serious and relatively difficult matter, requiring a degree of courage and resourcefulness not possessed by weaklings of any class."[51] In short, even if they had never heard of the liberal tradition, immigrants already embodied much of its spirit.

Given this independent spirit, immigration and the diversity it produced never were a threat to American values. On the contrary, successive waves of immigrants rejuvenated those values. People who were willing to endure hardships, eager to work hard, and convinced that they could have a better life were compatible with the American way of life. There is no reason to believe that today's immigrants are any different. They, too, have left homes and families. They have endured hardships to come to a new land with a different culture and language. In some extreme cases, they have risked life and limb to emigrate, as did the "boat people" of Vietnam who braved pirates, sharks, and storms—and the Cubans who swam from rafts to the Florida coast. Such people display a kind of individual initiative that can rightly be considered "American," regardless of their nationality.

Arguments similar to the preceding suggest that the fears of people such as Huntington are misplaced. Huntington worries that the processes of assimilation that imposed Anglo-Protestant values on earlier immigrants will not work on the new waves of Catholic—especially Latino—immigrants. The ideology of multiculturalism has made U.S. elites reluctant to encourage immigrants to adopt American values, and the contiguity of the United States to Mexico and Latin America make Spanish-speaking immigrants reluctant to cut their ties with their ancestral homes. But a person does not have to be Anglo or Protestant to have the kinds of values that Huntington believes define the American identity. Indeed, most non-Anglo, non-Protestants who emigrate to the United States probably have a greater commitment to such values than some Anglo-Protestants who have lived here for generations. One reason that scholars such as Huntington go astray is that they pay too much attention to the writing and rhetoric of unrepresentative ethnic activists and have too little contact with the great mass of immigrants. As we will note repeatedly in the chapters that follow, the leaders of interest groups generally have more extreme views than the people they claim to represent. For every activist demanding the preservation of a separate cultural identity (or even reuniting the U.S. Southwest with Mexico), there are thousands of ordinary immigrants working hard so that they and their children can enjoy the benefits of life in America.

In fact, systematic evidence strongly suggests that the Mexican laborers, Korean grocers, and Middle Eastern service-station operators are today's successors to the Irish laborers, Italian grocers, and Jewish shopkeepers of generations past. One widely noted study reports that on the basis of standard measures of assimilation (citizenship, home ownership, English acquisition, and intermarriage), today's immigrants "overwhelmingly do what immigrants have always done: slowly, often painfully, but quite assuredly, embrace the language, cultural norms and loyalties of America."[52] Other studies suggest that the use of English as a principal language is occurring *more* rapidly among the children of today's immigrants than in the past.[53] And educational and economic progress among Latinos is occurring faster than among earlier European immigrants.[54]

Similarly, in the less tangible realm of beliefs and values, Rodolfo de la Garza's surveys find that the children of Puerto Rican immigrants hold values almost indistinguishable from those of native English speakers in similar socioeconomic conditions.[55] His studies of Mexican immigrants reach very similar conclusions.[56] Earlier Gallup surveys found that immigrants, even those who have been in the country ten years or less, are virtually indistinguishable from native-born Americans—both in their beliefs about economic opportunity and in their general attitudes toward assimilation.[57]

The evidence is mounting that American society today is evolving along a path that it has followed in the past. Ethnic, racial, and religious diversity does not imply disagreement on basic values. Although the process has never been easy, Americans seem to be working their way through today's conflicts in much the same way that earlier generations did. All in all, the evidence suggests that today's diversity is more likely to reinforce than to undermine the American political culture.

The Politics of Immigration

Background

In the spring of 2006, political conflict over immigration once again boiled over. The central issue concerned "illegal," "undocumented," or "unauthorized" immigrants, in particular Mexicans, who account for the largest share of the currently estimated 11 million unauthorized immigrants. A few months earlier, House Republicans had passed an "enforcement-only" bill that would have made unauthorized entry into the country a felony (later amended to a criminal misdemeanor), provided for more than 700 miles of border fencing to keep people out, and imposed stiff penalties on employers who hire illegal immigrants. Some Republican hard-liners also tried to end "birthright citizenship"—automatic citizenship to children born in the United States—if their parents were not citizens or legal immigrants.

Most Democrats and some Republicans supported a plan closer to what former President George W. Bush had proposed, often called "enforcement-plus." Such a plan would provide stricter border controls, but also would allow undocumented immigrants to stay in the country and take advantage of a legal path to eventual citizenship. The Senate took up the subject of immigration in the spring with rival plans representing the enforcement-only and enforcement-plus points of view. Several months of negotiating proved fruitless and the legislation died in Congress. In the spring of 2007, Congress again took up the issue and once again it failed to act. The 2008 and 2010 elections came and went without President Obama or Congress tackling this difficult issue.

In the absence of federal legislation, Arizona, one of the states most impacted by illegal immigration, passed its own law, setting

Support for Immigration Rights: Demonstrators march through downtown Chicago in support of immigration reform and in opposition to legislation that would criminalize the actions of an estimated 11 million illegal immigrants.

121

off a political firestorm. The Arizona law allowed law enforcement officers to check the citizenship status of state residents who had been stopped for other reasons, such as traffic violations. Liberal groups in general and immigrant rights groups in particular charged that the law was racist, mean-spirited, unconstitutional, and unwise. But polls showed that a large majority of Americans, even a near majority among Democrats, supported the law. Failure of the national government to act left a political vacuum that people wanted filled.[1]

The Issues

The issues today are reminiscent of, but arguably more complex than, those of the past. On the economic side, some studies conclude that immigrants are a net benefit to the economy; others, that they are a net cost. Few studies, however, contend that the net benefits or costs are very large compared to major government programs such as Medicare and Social Security.[2] Of course, benefits and costs accrue to or fall on individuals, not on an abstract "national economy." Here the arguments become complex. Economists point out that not all immigrants are alike: Skilled immigrants are a significant net gain to the economy, but unskilled immigrants depress the wages of low-skilled native workers.[3] Those sympathetic to immigration retort that low-skilled immigrants only take jobs Americans would not take. As one poultry industry executive commented, "Reality speaks and it says that, absent Hispanic workers, we could not process chicken."[4] But that argument brings the objection that, without competition from low-skilled foreigners, wages might be high enough that Americans would take jobs in agriculture and service industries that they currently shun. Higher wages, however, would raise prices for consumers. Finally, other commentators point out that, whatever the national costs and benefits, these fall differently on government jurisdictions: State and local jurisdictions spend a lot more on social services for immigrants—education, police, medical care—than they receive in taxes.[5]

There is a cultural side to the debate as well, especially because today's immigrants include such a high proportion of Spanish speakers. Some immigration opponents contend that the greater homogeneity of today's immigrants has overwhelmed the processes of assimilation that worked in the past. Consequently, the new immigrants will become a large subpopulation of alienated "outsiders," and eventually the Southwest could become "Mexifornia."[6] In recent protest marches, some participants carried Mexican flags, stoking these fears. Other observers consider such fears to be exaggerated, pointing to evidence that today's immigrants want to be part of the United States, not separate from it. Under new laws, for example, Mexicans in the United States can register to vote in Mexico, but few do so.[7] Organizers in Los Angeles rented a 2000-seat auditorium for a rally attended by top Mexican officials and politicians; only 30 people showed up. Los Angeles mayor Antonio Villaraigosa, whose parents were immigrants, explained: "Most of us don't want to go back to Mexico and we don't want any

part of this country reverting to Mexico. We know we are a lot better off being Americans."[8]

A final complicating factor is security. Americans in the nineteenth century worried about Jesuit subversives and terrorists. Americans today worry about Al-Qaeda or other terrorists who might smuggle in chemical, biological, or nuclear weapons. Whereas the fear of Catholic conspiracies was indeed groundless, fear of Islamic terrorists has a basis in fact.

Immigration and Electoral Politics

The immigration issue splits both parties, although the political disagreement appears greater among Republicans.[9] Democrats are traditionally favorable to ethnic minorities, but low-skilled Americans who compete directly with low-skilled immigrants tend to be Democrats. Moreover, many local and state Democratic elected officials are on the firing line: Their constituents are exposed daily to new immigrants and are responsible for providing public services to people who pay relatively little in state and local taxes. In response, Democratic governors in Arizona and New Mexico had previously declared states of emergency.

Republicans are split into several factions. Many in the business wing of the party, such as the poultry industry executive quoted earlier, favor immigration as a source of plentiful and cheap labor. But other Republicans worry about the threats to national security and others about threats to American culture. Still others believe that people who enter the country without legal authorization should not be rewarded, especially ahead of those who patiently wait in line. All in all, the Republican Party includes every viewpoint on the issue, from most liberal to most conservative.

Many Republican politicos are concerned about the electoral danger immigration poses for their party.[10] On the one hand, there are votes to be won by responding to popular concerns. But, on the other hand, President Bush and some other Republicans made serious attempts to bring Hispanic voters into the Republican Party, arguing that Hispanics are an entrepreneurial, culturally conservative constituency that should look favorably on the Republican Party. Thus, short-term electoral gains risk alienating a large and growing bloc that eventually might become middle-class Americans.

What Do Americans Believe?

As they generally do on most issues, Americans occupy a middle ground on the immigration issue, agreeing neither with the most strident critics of immigration who dominate talk radio and some cable TV shows nor with its most ardent defenders among ethnic-group activists. Rather, showing their characteristic pragmatic streak, Americans agree with parts of the case made by each side and with parts of the solutions offered by each side. Table 1 shows a sampling of the numerous public opinion polls on this subject. Americans overwhelmingly agree that illegal immigration is out of control and that in principle it is unfair to grant rights to illegal immigrants while those who follow the law wait in line. As presidential candidate Hillary Clinton learned in a 2008 candidate

TABLE 1

PUBLIC OPINION ON IMMIGRATION

Is illegal immigration out of control? (*USA Today/Gallup, April 7–9, 2006*)	Yes: 81 %
Fair or unfair to grant rights to illegal immigrants while others wait in line for legal entry? (*Fox News/Opinion Dynamics, April 4–5, 2006*)	Unfair: 81%
States should or should not issue driver's licenses to illegal immigrants? (*CNN/Opinion Research Corporation, October 12–14, 2007*)	Should: 23% Should not: 76%
Illegal immigrants do more to help the country or do more to hurt the country?	Help: 34% Hurt: 54%
Legal immigrants do more to help the country or do more to hurt the country? (*CNN/Opinion Research Corporation, October 12–14, 2007*)	Help: 59% Hurt: 26%
Illegal immigrants mostly take jobs that American workers want, or mostly take low-paying jobs Americans don't want? (*Gallup, June5–July 6, 2008*)	Want: 15% Don't want: 79%
Build a fence along border with Mexico and hire and train more border patrol agents (*NBC News/Hart/McInturff, May 20–23, 2010*)	Favor: 71 Oppose: 26%
Deporting all illegal immigrants who are currently in the United States back to their native countries is a realistic and achievable goal or not? (*NBC/WSJ June 8–11, 2007*)	Is: 13% Is not: 85%
Allow illegal immigrants already in the country to pay a fine, learn English, and go to the back of the line for opportunity to become citizens? (*NBC News/Hart/Mcinturff, May 20–23, 2010*)	Support: 65% Oppose: 22%

Source: PollingReport.com (accessed February 15, 2010). (Question wordings are paraphrases, not exact).

debate when she waffled on a debate question about driver's licenses, citizens overwhelmingly oppose granting privileges enjoyed by citizens to illegal immigrants. Americans clearly differentiate between legal and illegal immigrants. They think the former help the country whereas the latter hurt it. On the other hand, a clear majority believe that illegal immigrants take jobs that nobody wants, rather than hurt the employment prospects of native-born Americans. Americans favor strengthening the border with Mexico, but they believe it is impractical to deport illegal immigrants and favor establishing a structured "path to citizenship" for illegal immigrants currently living in the country.

Thus, American public opinion seems generally supportive of the "enforcement-plus" plans that former President Bush and the Senate supported and immigration opponents vigorously fought. Americans agree that illegal immigration is a serious problem and that the country's borders must be secured, but that those already here should be offered the opportunity toward eventual status as legal residents or U.S. citizens.

What Do You Think?

1. Should the federal government take strong measures such as building fences and walls to secure the country's borders?
2. Should the principle of obeying the law be subordinated to the practical difficulties of doing anything about the illegal immigrants already here?
3. Should illegal immigrants be eligible for public services such as schools and medical care?
4. Should children born in the United States automatically be citizens, even if their parents are illegal immigrants?
5. Immigration has traditionally been considered a responsibility of the federal government, but some states have begun to

act on their own to curb illegal immigration.[11] Arizona was not the first. In 2007 Oklahoma made hiring illegal immigrants a felony and empowered police officers to check the immigration status of anyone arrested and hold noncitizens for deportation. Given the differential impact of illegal immigration on the country, should the states be free to deal with the problem as they see fit?

[1]"Broad Approval for New Arizona immigration Law," Pew Research Center for the People and the Press, May 12, 2010. http://people press.org/report/613/arizona-immigration-law.

[2]Studies by the Center for Immigration Reform often report costs: www.cis.org/topics/costs.html.

[3]Carolyn Lockhead, "Economists Support Entry of Educated Foreigners," *San Francisco Chronicle* (April 26, 2006): A4.

[4]Quoted in Peter Slevin, "Town's-Eye View of Immigration Debate," *Washington Post* (April 3, 2006): A01.

[5]Peter Brown, "Immigration Costs More than Thought," *Orlando Sentinel* (October 14, 2005).

[6]Victor Davis Hanson, *Mexifornia: A State of Becoming* (New York: Collier, 2004).

[7]Oscar Avila and Hugh Dellios, "Mexican Expatriate Voter Drive Comes up Far Short," *Chicago Tribune* (January 13, 2006).

[8]Thomas Elias, "Lack of Attendance at Forum Speaks Volumes," The Unon.com (December 9, 2005).

[9]Peter Brown, "Democrats Are Split on Immigration, Too," RealClearPolitics (April 3, 2006); and Mort Kondracke, "Bush Must Talk Sense to Republicans on Immigration," RealClearPolitics (January 10, 2006).

[10]Ruth Marcus, "The GOP Walks a Border Tightrope," *Washington Post* (March 29, 2006): A19.

[11]T. R. Reid, "Hill Impasse Spurs States to Tackle Illegal Immigration," *Washington Post* (May 3, 2006): A01.

CHAPTER SUMMARY

4.1 Characterize the American population as culturally diverse but similar in political beliefs.

Native born citizens have always feared that immigration was a threat to the distinctly U.S. political culture. But people in the United States agree on fundamental political principles more often than citizens of other democracies. Modern immigrants, similar to previous generations of immigrants, wish to maintain some part of their cultural distinctiveness. Ethnic diversity has not historically led to diverse political values, however.

4.2 Outline the evolution of social diversity in the United States and the debates over immigration.

Ever since the 1700s, "native citizens" have worried that new immigrants are too different to fit easily into American society. Today's debates about multiculturalism and immigration policy recapitulate these concerns. Yet the worst fears of previous generations of immigration critics failed to be realized.

4.3 Analyze American shared beliefs, their roots in classical liberalism, and their apparent contradictions.

The fundamental principles on which most Americans agree grew out of a classical liberal philosophy that stresses the rights and liberties of individuals. Those who prioritize individual liberty have at times come into conflict with those who wish to address inequalities. Still, most Americans are more comfortable with guarding equality of opportunity than they are with guaranteeing equality of result.

4.4 Assess the various explanations for the persistence of American classical liberalism.

Some argue that the liberal tradition survives because it is taught to children in families, schools, and places of worship. What is more, immigrants tend to reinforce rather than weaken the spirit of individualism in the United States. The very fact of their emigrating suggests that they possess the ambitious, individualistic outlook that is such a distinctive part of the American political culture.

PEARSON mypoliscilab EXERCISES

Apply what you learned in this chapter on MyPoliSciLab.

Read on mypoliscilab.com

eText: Chapter 4

Study and Review on mypoliscilab.com

Pre-Test

Post-Test

Chapter Exam

Flashcards

Watch on mypoliscilab.com

Video: Facebook Privacy Concerns

Video: The President Addresses School Children

Explore on mypoliscilab.com

Simulation: What Are American Civic Values?

Comparative: Comparing Political Landscapes

Timeline: Major Technological Innovations that Have Changed the Political Landscape

Visual Literacy: Using the Census to Understand Who Americans Are

Visual Literacy: Who Are Liberals and Conservatives? What's the Difference?

KEY TERMS

citizenship, p. 100
civic republicanism, p. 109
equality of condition, p. 113

equality of opportunity, p. 113
liberalism, p. 108
multiculturalism, p. 101

political culture, p. 100
political socialization, p. 118

SUGGESTED READINGS

Of General Interest

Hartz, Louis. *The Liberal Tradition in America*. New York: Harcourt, 1955. A classic, if impenetrable, discussion of the liberal tradition. Argues that the absence of feudalism allowed liberal ideas to spread without resistance in the United States.

Huntington, Samuel. *Who Are We? The Challenges to America's National Identity*. New York: Simon & Schuster, 2004. Controversial argument that Latino immigration threatens America's "Anglo-Protestant" values.

Lipset, Seymour Martin. *American Exceptionalism*. New York: Norton, 1996. An examination of the American political culture by an eminent senior scholar who spent much of his career studying it.

Focused Studies

Borjas, George. *Heaven's Door: Immigration Policy and the American Economy*. Princeton, NJ: Princeton University Press, 1999. Argues that immigration has hurt the poorest native-born workers, especially African Americans, and calls for restricting immigration and limiting it to better-educated and more highly skilled people.

Heclo, Hugh, and Wilfred McClay, eds. *Religion Returns to the Public Square*. Baltimore: Johns Hopkins University Press, 2003. Informative essays on various aspects of the relationship between religion and politics in the contemporary United States.

Kleppner, Paul. *The Cross of Culture*. New York: Free Press, 1970. This landmark example of the "ethno-cultural" school of political history provides a detailed account of political conflict in the Midwest from the rise of the Republican Party to the end of the nineteenth century.

Massey, Douglas S., ed. *New Faces in New Places*. New York: Russell Sage Foundation. 2008. Informative collection of up-to-date studies on the changing geography of contemporary immigration.

Smith, Christian, *Soul Searching: The Religious and Spiritual Lives of American Teenagers*. New York: Oxford University Press, 2005. Large national survey study that reveals a complex picture of religious beliefs among American youth.

ON THE WEB

Anyone with an interest in diversity can find websites addressing it on the Internet.

http://uscis.gov

The Department of Homeland Security's website on immigration and naturalization explains the naturalization process for aspiring citizens and provides statistical reports on the history of immigration to the United States.

www.cic.gc.ca
www.immi.gov.au
www.germany-info.org

Information on the immigration laws of some other countries (Canada, Australia, and Germany, respectively) can be found at these websites.

www.diversityinc.com

DiversityInc.com tries to take advantage of American diversity. Sponsored by several major corporations and public interest organizations, the site provides original content on many subgroups of the American population, with a particular focus on the advantages of diversity in the workplace.

www.academicinfo.net

Academia has responded to the call for more diversity by promoting new areas of study, including women's studies, African American studies, and gay and lesbian studies. The Academic Information Gateway contains bibliographies and guides for these subjects. Of course, these specific subpopulations—and any others you can think of—are represented by many interest groups or clubs, most of them with websites. A good search engine can find hundreds of pages, illustrating the diversity of the Internet.

www.public.iastate.edu/~savega/divweb2.htm

An online guide to sites relating to countless ethnic groups.

www.ellisislandrecords.org

American Family Immigration History Center helps people search for and tell stories about entrees to the United States through Ellis Island and the Port of New York.

www.umn.edu/ihrc

Immigration History Resource Center at University of Minnesota. Founded in 1965. International resource on American immigration and ethnic history. Collects, preserves, and provides archival and published resources documenting immigration and ethnicity on a national scope. Rich in history for 1880–1920 arrivals.

www.albany.edu/mumford/census

Lewis Mumford Center for Comparative Urban and Regional Research site located at SUNY Albany. Established in 1988, analyzes racial, ethnic and segregation composition of 331 metropolitan areas as shifts occur. Will be updated as 2010 Census data are released. Urban and suburban figures given. Asian population groups currently in progress.

5 Public Opinion

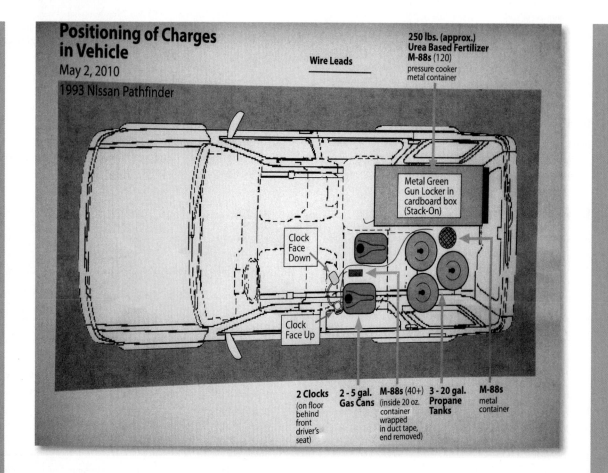

Positioning of Charges in Vehicle
May 2, 2010
1993 Nissan Pathfinder

Wire Leads

250 lbs. (approx.)
Urea Based Fertilizer
M-88s (120)
pressure cooker
metal container

Metal Green
Gun Locker in
cardboard box
(Stack-On)

Clock
Face
Down

Clock
Face Up

2 Clocks
(on floor
behind
front
driver's
seat)

2 - 5 gal.
Gas Cans

M-88s (40+)
(inside 20 oz.
container
wrapped
in duct tape,
end removed)

3 - 20 gal.
Propane
Tanks

M-88s
metal
container

CHAPTER OUTLINE

5.1 Define public opinion in the context of a democracy.

5.2 Identify the major sources of individuals' political attitudes.

5.3 Evaluate polling as a means of measuring public opinion.

5.4 Determine characteristics of public opinion that make it difficult to accurately measure.

5.5 Assess the extent to which public opinion influences policy makers.

Public Opinion and Terrorism

The chances that any given person will perish in a terrorist attack are indeed small. The statistics blogger Nate Silver calculates that the odds of dying on a hijacked flight over the last decade were 1 in 10,408,947.[1] Michael Rothschild, a professor at the University of Wisconsin, estimates that even if terrorists destroyed one shopping mall each week, the odds of being in the wrong place at the wrong time are at least one in a million.[2] By contrast, the lifetime chances of dying in an earthquake, from a dog bite, or from being struck by lightning, are all far greater.[3]

But when pollsters ask Americans what they consider to be the most important problem facing the nation, earthquakes, dog bites, and lighting strikes do not register a mention. Terrorism does. Since 9/11, terrorism has consistently ranked among the top three to five problems that Americans say are facing the nation. In 2010, with the unemployment rate at nearly 10 percent, the country engaged in two wars, and other controversial issues like immigration and the Deepwater Horizon oil spill dominating news coverage, terrorism still ranked as one of the first three issues that the public thought "should be the top priority for the federal government."[4] More than one third of Americans say they are "very" or "somewhat" worried that they or a member of their family will become a victim of terrorism.[5]

When a terrorist attack or an attempted attack occurs, public opinion reacts in ways that are sometimes surprising. In the immediate aftermath of 9/11, the public's approval of President George W. Bush soared to nearly 90 percent. This might seem natural, if we consider that Bush was leading the charge to respond to the attacks. But public approval also jumped for members of Congress, governors, mayors, and other public officials across the country who had little connection to or responsibility for the response to terrorism.[6] Even more surprisingly, when asked whether they were satisfied or dissatisfied with the direction of the country, Americans said they were significantly *more* satisfied after the 9/11 attacks than they had said they were beforehand.[7]

These facts may suggest that public opinion is irrational. Yet there are numerous instances in which public opinion has been "correct"—or at least in agreement with the best available knowledge on a subject. After the foiled 2009 Christmas bombing of a transatlantic flight, a solid majority of Americans saw a terrorist attack as more likely "within the next few months."[8] Indeed, another attempted attack occurred four months later in Times Square. Despite a media controversy, overwhelming majorities said in 2010 that they were unconcerned about any health risks posed by new "full body" scanners that were beginning to be used in more and more airports (an opinion in accord with expert judgments).[9] And, since 9/11, public opinion on many issues surrounding terrorism has been surprisingly stable and consistent: Two-thirds of the public think America is safer now than before 2001; slightly fewer than half think torture of terrorist suspects is (at least sometimes) justified; and a majority oppose the closing of the detention center in Guantanamo Bay, Cuba, where dozens of terror suspects have been held for nearly a decade. Most of these positions have changed little or not at all over the years, as Figure 5.1 shows. This stability is not what we might expect from an irrational, panicky public.

FIGURE 5.1

PUBLIC OPINION ON
TERRORISM-RELATED
ISSUES

Note: N = 1,001 adults nationwide. Margin of error ±3.

Source for first chart: CNN/USA
Today/Gallup Poll.

Sources for second chart: Gallup Polls ("satisfied"); *USA Today*/Gallup Polls (Obama
approval); CBS News Poll (Bush approval).

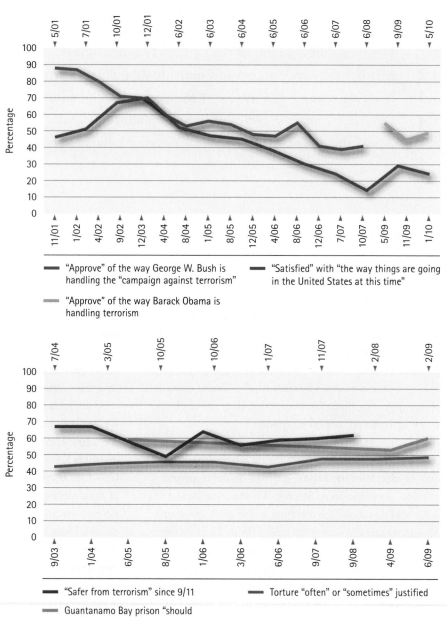

—— "Approve" of the way George W. Bush is
handling the "campaign against terrorism"

—— "Satisfied" with "the way things are going
in the United States at this time"

—— "Approve" of the way Barack Obama is
handling terrorism

—— "Safer from terrorism" since 9/11

—— Torture "often" or "sometimes" justified

—— Guantanamo Bay prison "should
not be closed"

Alexander Hamilton was an early critic of the people's ability to make reasonable judgments about public affairs. "The voice of the people has been said to be the voice of God," Hamilton observed in a speech at the Constitutional Convention in 1787, "and, however generally this maxim has been quoted and believed, it is not true in fact. The people are turbulent and changing; they seldom judge or determine right."[10] Hamilton's political rival, Thomas Jefferson, held the opposite view: "Whenever the people are well informed," he argued, "they can be trusted with their own government; . . . whenever things get so far wrong as to attract their notice, they may be relied upon to set them to rights."[11] The issue of terrorism seems to provide evidence on both sides. Is public opinion fickle, irrational, and dangerous, as Hamilton argued? Or can an informed public be trusted to make good decisions about important issues, as Jefferson claimed? This question lies at the heart of how we should evaluate the New American Democracy.

Making the Connection

In the era of the permanent campaign, public opinion probably is more important than it has ever been.[12] Certainly, modern politicians have more information about it than ever before—but the role that public opinion plays in determining what government does continues to be complicated and unpredictable. In this chapter, we define public opinion and explain how it is formed. We then explain how public opinion is measured—and often mismeasured. We discuss some important characteristics of public opinion. Finally, we consider the gap that sometimes exists between public opinion and public policy in our democracy.

What Is Public Opinion?

Public opinion is the aggregation of people's views about issues, situations, and public figures. Although conceptions of democracy differ (see Chapter 1), public opinion is an essential element of all of them—either determining policy outcomes directly or setting the bounds within which elected officials must operate when they choose public policies.

Political scientist V. O. Key, Jr., captures the importance of public opinion when he defines it as "those opinions held by private persons which governments find it prudent to heed."[13] Democratic governments find it "prudent" to heed the opinions of private persons, of course, because of elections. Note that, in Key's conception, public opinion need not be actively expressed. Even if public opinion is silent, or "latent," public officials may act or fail to act because they fear arousing it. This is the so-called "law of anticipated reactions," whereby public opinion influences government even though it does so indirectly and passively.[14] When we say "public opinion wouldn't stand for that," we are referring to this latent, constraining function of public opinion.

Sources of Public Opinion

If public opinion is nothing more than the aggregated opinions of individual people, the first step in understanding public opinion is to figure out where individuals get their political ideas. Most of the sources of political attitudes fall into several broad categories. These categories are not mutually exclusive; often they overlap.

Socialization

People learn political beliefs and values in their families, schools, communities, religious institutions, and workplaces—a process called **socialization.** And, although socialization can occur throughout a person's life, according to most studies the events and experiences of childhood and adolescence are particularly influential in shaping American public opinion. It has often been argued, for example, that people who came of age during World War II were, for the rest of their lives, relatively more supportive of American military interventions, since the principal lesson they took away from that event concerned the dangers of appeasement and the necessity of early and vigorous opposition to

5.1

Define public opinion in the context of a democracy.

public opinion
The aggregation of people's views about issues, situations, and public figures.

5.2

Identify the major sources of individuals' political attitudes.

socialization
The end result of all the processes by which social groups give individuals their beliefs and values.

foreign aggression. By contrast, Americans who grew up during the Vietnam War allegedly acquired a quite different worldview, one that emphasized the hazards and difficulties of sending U.S. troops into complicated foreign conflicts. Public opinion is thus often interpreted in generational terms, meaning that adults' political attitudes differ in regular and reliable ways based on the year in which they were born.[15]

Sometimes socialization occurs directly and explicitly, as when schools teach citizenship and patriotism. Catholic doctrine condemns abortion, and church-going Catholics are indeed less accepting of abortion than are mainline Protestants and Jews.[16] Most fundamentalist Protestant churches officially condemn homosexuality, and their rank-and-file members are indeed less tolerant of homosexuality than are mainline Protestants.[17] Labor unions typically endorse Democratic candidates, and union members are more Democratic in their voting than other blue-collar workers.[18] Sometimes socialization occurs indirectly, when someone observes or imitates others—a form of socialization that is no less powerful for being unplanned. Children begin to form political attitudes at an early age. Research carried out in the 1950s and 1960s usually concluded that the single most important socializing agent was the family (although a few scholars argued that schools carried more weight).[19] Within the family, studies generally found that the mother was most important because she spent more time with the children. Not surprisingly, then, studies have found that many children will identify themselves as Democrats or Republicans well before they have any idea what the parties stand for.[20] Older children are especially likely to share the party affiliation of their parents.[21]

Personal Experiences

Although people form many of their attitudes in childhood, political views continue to develop over the course of a lifetime. Childhood socialization can be modified or even reversed by adult experiences. The horrors of the Great Depression focused many Americans on the importance of economic issues and, after the depression lifted, cemented their loyalty to the Democratic Party. On the other hand, the severe economic problems of the 1970s left a generation of Americans disenchanted with the Democrats and later encouraged their identification with the Republican Party of Ronald Reagan. The economic turmoil that followed the 2008 financial crisis will undoubtedly shape voters' perceptions of the parties for years to come.

Not all experiences are historical ones that change entire generations. Some life experiences differ from person to person within a single generation, perhaps because of the place in which one lives or the groups one chooses to join. Life experiences may differ because of how a community treats different sorts of people: men vs. women, young people vs. the elderly, the poor vs. the affluent, or people of minority races, the disabled, overweight people, short people, and innumerable other categories. Varying life experiences can profoundly influence not only how we think about specific parties or policy proposals, but also how we feel about fundamental concepts such as fairness, authority, freedom, or justice. Hurricane Katrina, a disaster that disproportionately affected poor African American residents of New Orleans, prompted a much more critical response from blacks nationwide than from whites, for example.[22] It is likely that the wars in Afghanistan and Iraq had a different meaning for those in military families than it had for antiwar protestors.

Self-Interest

Public policies seldom affect everyone equally. Usually some people will benefit from a policy proposal and others will suffer. Some people profit from a political party's initiatives; others do not. Ordinary citizens show a rather impressive ability to determine which side their bread is buttered on, as the old saying puts it, when they approach public affairs.[23]

Voters do not always behave in a fashion that directly benefits them. People rarely abandon their party loyalties, for example, simply because one candidate or one policy position contradicts their personal tastes. Nevertheless, people's interests often determine where they stand in a political debate.[24] For example, blue-collar workers are more sensitive to a rise in unemployment that throws them out of work, and professionals and managers are more sensitive to a rise in inflation that drives up interest rates and depresses the overall business climate. Women working outside the home, who must balance the conflicting demands of home and workplace, are more supportive of gender equality than are stay-at-home mothers.[25]

Education

Although schools are socializing agents and an individual's training certainly affects self-interest, education belongs in something of a separate category—especially higher education. In general, education is associated with a somewhat more tolerant outlook; highly educated people are especially tolerant of minority groups and practices.[26] Apparently, values emphasized in higher education predispose college graduates to think about political issues differently; they are more likely to accept people different from themselves and practices different from their own (see Figure 5.2). They are also more likely to view political involvement as a duty to carry out rather than as a chore to be avoided. And higher education is associated with a greater sense of **political efficacy,** the belief that the citizen can make a difference by expressing an opinion or acting politically.

political efficacy
The belief that the citizen can make a difference in politics by expressing an opinion or acting politically.

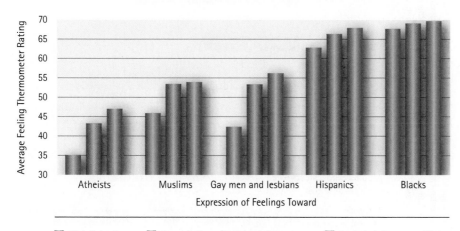

FIGURE 5.2

HIGHER EDUCATION IS ASSOCIATED WITH GREATER TOLERANCE OF DIVERSITY

Those with a college education are more likely to express positive feelings toward minority groups.

• *Why does education make only a small difference in attitudes toward blacks, but a larger difference in attitudes toward atheists?*

Note: Figures represent average "feeling thermometer" rating towards each group, on a scale of 0 to 100. Higher numbers equal more positive feelings.

Source: American National Election Studies, 2008.

Reference Groups

Members of various social groups often differ significantly in the opinions they hold (Figure 5.3). Weekly churchgoers show more hostility to homosexuality than those less religiously involved. African Americans endorse government involvement in healthcare at a higher level than whites customarily do. Women support banning pornography at much higher rates than men do. To a certain extent, such group differences likely result from the same sources of public opinion that we have already discussed: different interests, life experiences, forms of socialization, and levels of schooling. Many churches may socialize members to believe that homosexuality is wrong, for example. African Americans may be more likely to need improved healthcare, or they may be more likely to witness cases in which someone lacks adequate care. Women may be socialized against consuming pornography, leaving them little reason to support keeping it legal.

On the other hand, individuals may look to the groups of which they are a part to determine where they ought to stand in a political debate. Even if their experiences or their interests push them to oppose a proposed law, they may become friendlier toward it if they notice that people like them tend to be supporters. Individuals are especially likely to stick with their reference group when they identify closely with its fate, or if they tend to hear about public affairs through word of mouth, from the perspective of

FIGURE 5.3

EXAMPLES OF GROUP DIFFERENCES IN PUBLIC OPINION

People with different life experiences hold different views about politics.

• *What other kinds of major life experiences are likely to have an impact on important political issues?*

Source: Calculated from the National Election Studies and the Gallup Poll Cumulative Index.

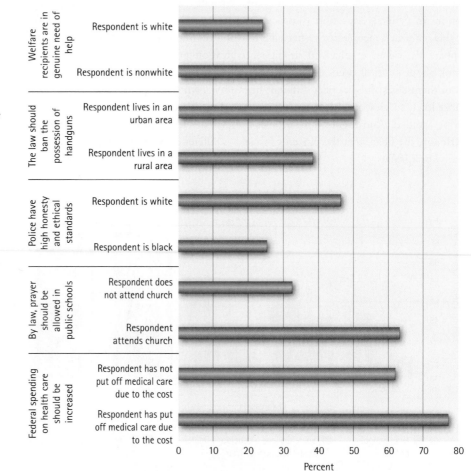

other group members. Some groups even attempt to enforce solidarity, as when union members disparage "scabs" who cross their picket lines or when African Americans dismiss those who break ranks as "Uncle Toms." The pushes and pulls of group identity can shape people's political attitudes beyond what one might expect given the other influences on their thinking.

The Media

In recent years, many people have expressed a fear that public opinion is increasingly shaped by the mass media. This substantial issue is steeped in controversy (which is examined more thoroughly in Chapter 9). For now, suffice it to say that under some circumstances the media can sway public opinion, while under other circumstances the media are surprisingly ineffectual. Overall, little evidence supports the worst fears of media critics. As the Internet has allowed news sources to proliferate, members of the public sometimes do rely on news sources that promote extreme and unrepresentative views. But the people who consume the most extremist news coverage are the ones who hold extreme views already, making it unclear whether the media is really changing any minds.[27]

Measuring Public Opinion

5.3

Evaluate polling as a means of measuring public opinion.

For most of the nation's history, figuring out what voters wanted was more art than science. Politicians attended public gatherings, scanned influential newspapers, or consulted with local party leaders and other notables to gauge the popular mood. Often they made mistakes and paid the price on Election Day.

Estimating public attitudes requires much less guesswork in modern times. A whole industry has sprung up dedicated to contacting individuals, asking them questions, and collecting the responses. Firms range from specialized campaign-consulting operations to highly reputable research and marketing companies such as Gallup, Roper, and Chilton. Sometimes these companies divulge their poll results to the media. So do various academic institutions and nonprofit foundations that conduct intensive surveys on particular public-affairs issues. Media corporations, meanwhile, have formed alliances to survey public opinion for their own news coverage; examples include CBS News/*New York Times* and ABC News/*Washington Post*.[28] Websites such as pollster.com and realclearpolitics.com gather these polls together and average them, producing composite measures of opinion that are updated constantly.

As a result, the United States is now awash in polling data. Almost every day brings the release of some new poll that reports on the president's approval ratings or what the public thinks about some hot policy issue or how the next election will turn out. For example, when pollsters are interested in learning what the public thinks about the president, the most frequently asked question is what is usually called the presidential approval question: "Do you approve or disapprove of the way [president's name] is handling his job as president?" The Gallup organization was the first to ask this question, and did so about 15 times a year during the 1950s and 1960s. About once every three and a half weeks, in other words, new data would be made public that claimed to show the latest ebbs and flows in Eisenhower's, Kennedy's, or Johnson's popularity. In 2009, in contrast, this question was asked in 396 separate polls—more than once a day—by two dozen different survey organizations.[29]

Sampling Error

sampling error
The chance variation that arises in public opinion surveys as a result of using a representative, but small, sample to estimate the characteristics of a larger population.

Americans sometimes express doubt about the reliability of all these opinion polls. They recognize that surveys rarely report the exact truth. Part of the problem with opinion polls is that even properly administered surveys contain **sampling error**—the chance variation that results from using a representative, but small, sample to estimate the characteristics of a larger population. People may not think about the problem in such technical terms, but they understand the idea intuitively. If you flip a coin, you expect that the chance of having it come up heads is the same as the chance of having it come up tails—which is why it is a fair method for deciding who gets to go first in a game or who gets the last piece of pie. If you flip a coin ten times, however, you would not be shocked by a result other than five heads and five tails. Coin tosses will vary by chance alone. Polling results also contain such sampling error. A survey of randomly selected people can tip this way or that through the luck of the draw.

For a good example of sampling error in practice, consider the data in Table 5.1, which shows the final results of 15 different polls of the 2008 presidential election, all of which were completed in the days just before Election Day. The results of all these polls were not, of course, precisely identical—and yet they were all "in the same ballpark." All 15 polls showed Barack Obama running ahead of John McCain. When all the poll results were averaged together, Obama was 7.6 percentage points ahead. In the actual voting, Obama beat McCain by 7.3 points.

TABLE 5.1				
Polling Organization	**Obama**	**McCain**	**Spread**	**N**
Marist	52	43	Obama +9	804
Battleground (Lake)	52	47	Obama +5	800
Battleground (Tarrance)	50	48	Obama +2	800
Rasmussen Reports	52	46	Obama +6	3000
Reuters/C-SPAN/Zogby	54	43	Obama +11	1201
IBD/TIPP	52	44	Obama +8	981
FOX News	50	43	Obama +7	971
NBC News/*Wall Street Journal*	51	43	Obama +8	1011
Gallup	55	44	Obama +11	2472
Diageo/Hotline	50	45	Obama +5	887
CBS News	51	42	Obama +9	714
ABC News/*Washington Post*	53	44	Obama +9	2470
Ipsos/McClatchy	53	46	Obama +7	760
CNN/Opinion Research	53	46	Obama +7	714
Pew Research	52	46	Obama +6	2587
Average	52.1	44.5	Obama +7.6	–
Actual Result	52.9	45.6	Obama +7.3	–

Source: All poll information from www.realclearpolitics.com, www.realclearpolitics.com/epolls/2008/president/us/general_election_mccain_vs_obama-225.html, accessed June 9, 2010.

The variability that results from sampling error makes people suspicious about polls. "I refuse to believe," they sometimes protest, "that the opinions of 1,500 people can speak for a nation of 230 million adults." This skepticism is unjustified, however. A properly administered survey of national opinion should not require more than about 1,500 people. A small sample of people *can* mirror a much larger population reasonably well.

Furthermore, statistical theory provides a means to determine how reliable a given survey should be, at least as regards sampling error. If every reader of this book flipped a penny 1,500 times, 95 percent of you would fall somewhere between 705 and 795 heads—that is, between 47 and 53 percent—within 3 points of the average. Bigger deviations are possible but they will occur rarely, about one time out of 20. Similarly, the answers provided by a random sample of 1,500 Americans on any political question would fall within 3 percentage points of national opinion 95 percent of the time. That is a statistical fact. It is what pollsters mean when they report that their survey has a "margin of error" of 3 percent. The natural variation caused by taking a random sample therefore does not explain most instances of misleading survey results. Two other sources of inaccuracy—selection bias and measurement error—usually account for misleading survey results.

Selection Bias

Survey researchers use a bewildering variety of techniques to ensure that their samples will mirror the larger population. However, the trait that unites most sampling methods is that they are devised to avoid **selection bias**—the distortion caused when a method systematically includes or excludes people with certain types of attitudes from the sample. Surveys that fail to guard against selection bias usually offer nothing of value; the results they report will not be *representative* of the larger population. For example, if we were to poll attendees at a hockey game, a heavy-metal concert, or even a political-science lecture, the results would say very little about public opinion in general, because these events attract audiences that differ from the American public at large in politically relevant ways.

Perhaps it seems obvious that the political attitudes held by heavy-metal fans would reveal little about national opinion. Yet real-life organizations regularly conduct polls just as likely to induce selection bias. Interest groups and magazines conduct mail surveys. Their samples are not representative, because their members and readers differ from the population at large. A survey about sexual attitudes and practices conducted among the subscribers to *Playboy* magazine, for example, might tell one something about the behavior of *Playboy* readers; it most certainly would *not* be a good guide to the sexual behavior of the American adult population as a whole. Moreover, those who bother to fill out and return the questionnaires are a biased sample of those who receive the survey—they are people who care more than others about the subject of the poll. Continuing with the example of sex, even if a magazine with a more representative readership did a mail-in survey of sexual practices, it is unlikely that the results would be very meaningful. The types of people who are willing to share information about the most intimate aspects of their lives are probably not representative of the general population, most of whose members are considerably more private about such matters. The same is true for call-in surveys conducted by radio and TV stations. These may be good ways of generating audience interest, but they have little or no scientific value.

selection bias
The distortion caused when a sampling method systematically includes or excludes people with certain attitudes from the sample.

The latest craze is online surveys, but few such polls take adequate care to ensure a proper sample. Most tap only the opinions of people with existing Internet connections who happen to find their way to the poll site and who have their own motivations for taking part in the exercise—hardly a representative group. For example, in 2006 an online poll sponsored by the liberal blog DailyKos found that Wisconsin Senator Russell Feingold was respondents' top choice for president in 2008, with 30 percent of the vote.[30] Other polls taken at the same time showed Feingold in the low single digits, and the senator later announced he would not run.

In a scientific poll, the investigator must control who is included in the sample and who is not. Pollsters typically select sampling methods that somehow choose participants *randomly,* with minimal differences from person to person in the chance of being picked. For example, telephone polls customarily rely on "random-digit dialing," in which a computer randomly selects some portion of the number being called. People with unlisted telephone numbers may be surprised and irritated when they answer their phone and hear a pollster, but no one has given out their personal information—the computer has found them by chance.

Not all selection bias results from flaws in the sampling method. Even if pollsters devise an approach that avoids favoring some types of people over others, potential respondents still control whether to participate in the survey. In a typical telephone poll, more than half the original sample either never answers the phone or refuses to be interviewed.[31] Research shows that, as a result, survey samples tend to contain too few men, whites, young adults, and wealthy people.[32] Although pollsters try to adjust their numbers to compensate for unequal rates of participation, they may not succeed in eliminating the bias. In 2008, for example, polls found that among those who watched the debates between Obama and McCain, Obama was the clear winner. But more Democrats than Republicans watched the debates in the first place.[33]

Some tools for exploring public opinion do not seek to eliminate selection bias. Researchers using these tools care less about getting a representative sample than they do about achieving a complex and detailed understanding of certain kinds of people. For example, political consultants increasingly rely on **focus groups,** small groups of people brought together to talk about issues or candidates at length and in depth. These groups are too small to provide good estimates of public opinion, but they are useful for testing the appeal of ads, terms, slogans, symbols, and so forth. For example, focus-group research led Republicans to advocate social security *personal* accounts rather than *private* accounts and Democrats to warn about *climate change* rather than *global warming.*

focus groups

Small groups of people brought together to talk about issues or candidates at length and in depth.

Measurement Error

Media accounts of poll results routinely report sampling error. They also often describe the method for gathering the sample, and may even report the rate of participation among the people contacted by interviewers. If sampling error and selection bias were the only two sources of inaccuracy in opinion polls, an attentive reader could judge their reliability fairly well. Unfortunately, sampling is a relatively unimportant source of error in most professional surveys. Various kinds of **measurement error,** the error that arises from attempting to measure something as subjective as opinion, are much more troublesome.

measurement error

The error that arises from attempting to measure something as subjective as opinion.

THE WIZARD OF ID   **parker and hart**

By permission of John L. Hart FLP and Creator's Syndicate.

Polling Wizardry

Surveys often provide inaccurate results because of errors in measurement, such as when the options available to respondents do a poor job of capturing the actual range of opinions. Pollsters who wish to avoid biased research must shape the wording of their questions carefully.

An individual's opinion is not an objective fact like the length of a stick. Ask ten people to measure a stick, and, if a ruler is handy, they will all do it about the same way. Unless they are careless, all ten will report approximately the same length. Opinions do not have such obvious physical properties; they are intangible. No obvious tool, such as a ruler, exists to measure them (although pollsters do sometimes settle on particular questions that they like to ask repeatedly).

Answers to survey questions can vary dramatically depending on how a question is asked. For example, poll responses vary according to the choices provided.[34] People tend to give more consistent answers to questions that allow graduated responses (agree strongly, agree somewhat, neither agree nor disagree, disagree somewhat, disagree strongly) than to either/or questions (agree/disagree). More people will choose a "don't know" or "not sure" answer when it is explicitly offered to them than will volunteer such an answer when it is not offered. Survey responses also depend on the larger context. People respond differently if earlier questions in a survey prompt them to think along certain lines, or if the interviewer lists arguments on each side of an issue before asking about it. People also respond differently when surveyed after significant social, economic, or political developments than when surveyed beforehand.[35]

Opinions are particularly hard to pin down when citizens are unfamiliar with an issue. To take just one example, a flurry of public opinion polls taken in the summer of 2010 probed whether citizens supported the financial reform bill being considered by Congress. Although Americans were angry about the 2008 financial crisis and recession, most had not given much thought to the particular details of the bill, nor did pollsters have an established way to ask about them. Not surprisingly, polls reported anywhere from 39 percent to 69 percent in favor of the legislation.[36] Sampling error certainly did not produce this much variability.

The wording of survey questions may be the most important source of measurement error. Even if people have fairly fixed opinions, the answers they provide pollsters will depend on exactly what they think a question is asking. Question wording may (1) confuse respondents, (2) prompt respondents to think about an issue in a certain way, or (3) oversimplify complex social issues. Let's consider examples of each of these problems.

Confusing Questions: The Holocaust Poll Fiasco Germany's Nazi leaders executed millions of innocent civilians during World War II. Although they targeted gypsies, homosexuals, and Poles—among others—Nazi officials put most of their genocidal efforts into exterminating European Jews. They shipped Jewish men, women, and children to concentration camps within Nazi-controlled territory, where victims either were worked to death or were executed outright. Careful research indicates that at least 5 million Jews died as a result of the Holocaust, including almost the entire Jewish populations of Czechoslovakia, Poland, and the Baltic states. Aside from a fringe group of conspiracy theorists who deny that such large-scale genocide really took place, scholars uniformly count the Holocaust as one of the worst horrors in a global war filled with tragedy.

Just before the opening of the Holocaust Memorial Museum in Washington, DC, a respected commercial polling organization called Roper Starch Worldwide tried to determine whether Holocaust deniers were making headway among the American public. Roper's survey, commissioned by the American Jewish Committee, produced some distressing results. It indicated that 22 percent of the American public believed it "possible the Nazi extermination of the Jews never happened," and that another 12 percent were unsure.

The news media jumped on the story. Editorialists pondered what might be wrong with the American public that it would give such shocking survey responses. Had anti-Semitism grown so strong that a third of Americans embraced the views of the lunatic fringe? Was the educational system failing so miserably that, just 50 years after World War II, the American public could have forgotten one of the best-documented tragedies of that global crisis? What did the Holocaust poll say about the American people?

Very little, it turned out. Social scientists knowledgeable about prejudice and public opinion were immediately suspicious of the poll findings, which contradicted other research on American attitudes. The Gallup organization—a Roper competitor—soon demonstrated that the Roper poll was seriously in error because it had asked a confusing question. The exact wording of Roper's question was:

> Does it seem possible, or does it seem impossible to you that the Nazi extermination of the Jews never happened?

One of the first rules of survey research is to keep questions clear and simple. The Roper question fails that test because it contains a double negative (*impossible . . . never happened*)—a grammatical construction long known to confuse people.

Gallup conducted a new poll in which half of the sample was asked the Roper question with the double negative and the other half an alternative question:

> Does it seem possible to you that the Nazi extermination of the Jews never happened, or do you feel certain that it happened?

This change in the question's wording may seem minor, but it made a great deal of difference. In the half of the sample that was asked the Roper question, one-third of the respondents again replied that it was possible the Holocaust never happened or that they were unsure, but in the half that were asked Gallup's alternative question, less than 10 percent of the sample were Holocaust doubters. The whole episode had been the product of a simple verbal mistake.[37] Nothing was wrong with the Roper sample, as verified by Gallup when it asked Roper's question. Rather, Roper asked a poorly constructed question that produced an inaccurate measurement.

Leading Questions: The Welfare Policy Mystery   What looks like a minor variation in question wording can elicit significantly different answers. Such an error is especially likely when questions use emotionally or politically "loaded" terms. A classic example comes from the policy area of government spending on the poor. Consider the following survey question:

> We are faced with many problems in this country, none of which can be solved easily or inexpensively. I'm going to name some of these problems and for each one I'd like you to tell me whether you think we're spending too much money, too little money, or about the right amount.[38]

When the public was asked in a recent poll about "welfare," the responses showed that a plurality of Americans believed that too much was being spent:

Too little: 26%
About right: 36%
Too much: 38%

Conservatives might interpret such a poll to mean that Americans oppose increasing aid to the poor. But when the *same people* in the *same poll* were asked about "assistance to the poor," a large majority responded that too little was being spent:

Too little: 70%
About right: 21%
Too much: 8%

Liberals could use the poll to argue that welfare spending should rise.

Although *welfare* and *assistance to the poor* may appear to mean the same thing—welfare is the policy used to provide assistance to poor families—the terms evidently tap into different attitudes. *Welfare* carries negative connotations; it seems to prompt people to think of lazy and undeserving recipients—the stereotypical welfare cheats. But *assistance to the poor* does not evoke these negative stereotypes. Careless (or clever) question wording can produce contradictory findings on a major public issue.

Reputable survey organizations work constantly to identify and eliminate loaded questions. Yet, in many cases, it is not clear that there is a single, "correct" way of asking about a particular issue. In the example just considered, a complete picture of American attitudes toward welfare policy would need to recognize at least two widely held opinions: that assistance should be provided to the truly needy, but also that current programs too often give money to those who do not need it. Any politician who does not take into account both of these attitudes is likely to be courting serious trouble.

Oversimplified Questions: Public Opinion on Abortion   In 1973, the Supreme Court handed down its *Roe v. Wade* decision, striking down any restrictions on a woman's right to terminate a pregnancy in the first trimester and limiting restrictions on that right in the second trimester. The *Webster v. Reproductive Health Services* decision in 1989 and the *Planned Parenthood v. Casey* decision in 1992 further refined the court's position. Most Americans long ago decided where they stood on the abortion issue. Indeed, when the *same* survey question is repeated over time, public opinion is strikingly constant. Yet support for abortion rights varies widely from one poll question to another—prompting both pro-choice and pro-life spokespersons to claim that a majority of Americans support their position. Unless the laws of arithmetic fail to hold in the case of this issue, one side or both must be wrong, but neither side makes up its figures. How can this be?

Does the Supreme Court Follow Public Opinion?

Pro-life and pro-choice supporters demonstrate outside the Supreme Court building in Washington. *Do you think the Supreme Court's ruling in* Roe v. Wade *more or less agrees with public opinion?*

As with welfare policy, part of the inconsistency comes from the use of leading questions.[39] One 2006 poll prompted

> Please tell me whether or not you think it should be possible for a pregnant woman to obtain a legal abortion if the woman wants it for any reason.

By a heavy margin (61 percent to 39 percent), Americans said no.[40] As pro-life spokespersons claimed, Americans were pro-life. Should Democratic campaign consultants have advised their clients to flip-flop to the pro-life side? Well, probably not. A few months later, a different survey asked,

> The 1973 Roe v. Wade decision established a woman's constitutional right to an abortion, at least in the first three months of pregnancy. Would you like to see the Supreme Court completely overturn its *Roe v. Wade* decision or not?

By a resounding margin (65 percent to 26 percent), Americans said that *Roe v. Wade* should not be overturned.[41] As the pro-choice spokespersons claimed, America had a pro-choice majority. Should Republican campaign consultants have advised their clients to flip-flop to the pro-choice side?

Which poll was right? Probably neither. Upon close examination, both survey questions are suspect. Each contains words and phrases that predispose people to answer in one direction. The first question uses the phrase "for any reason." If forced to choose yes or no unconditionally, some generally pro-choice people will say no, believing that some circumstances are not sufficiently serious to justify abortion. The second question leans in the opposite direction. The phrasing "completely overturn" suggests a comprehensive finality that makes many people uncomfortable. Some people who favor abortion restrictions might still be hesitant to "completely overturn" a major Supreme Court ruling.

In addition, Americans distinguish between the morality of behavior and the legality of behavior. A 2003 poll asked people whether they agreed or disagreed with the stark claim that "abortion is the same thing as murdering a child." Americans were evenly split (46 percent agreed, 46 percent disagreed).[42] Similarly, a plurality or majority of Americans think that "abortion is morally wrong."[43] On the other hand, majorities of Americans favor keeping abortion legal, and comfortable majorities say the *Roe. v. Wade* decision was generally "a good thing."[44] Thus, individualistic Americans favor freedom of choice, especially when it involves preventing government interference. Many Americans who are troubled—even deeply troubled—by abortion nonetheless will not support making it illegal.

The use of leading questions may be insufficient to explain the volatility in survey results on the abortion issue. More likely, opinions on abortion are too complex for pollsters to capture in a single, simple question. Evidence that pollsters often oversimplify the abortion issue appears in surveys taken by the National Opinion Research Center, which use a more complex question. The NORC question reads as follows:

> Please tell me whether or not you think it should be possible for a pregnant woman to obtain a legal abortion if

1. the woman's health is seriously endangered?
2. she became pregnant as a result of rape?
3. there is a strong chance of serious defect in the baby?
4. the family has low income and cannot afford any more children?
5. she is not married and does not want to marry the man?
6. she is married and does not want any more children?

As Figure 5.4 shows, after moving in a liberal direction in the late 1960s, opinion stabilized at the time of the 1973 *Roe v. Wade* decision, stayed remarkably constant for two decades, and then moved a bit in a conservative direction in the late 1990s. These trends across time vary much less than responses do across circumstances, showing that Americans are pragmatic, not ideological, when it comes to abortion. In particular, Americans appear to draw a sharp distinction between what are sometimes called the "traumatic" and "elective" circumstances for abortion. Large majorities of the American public support legal abortions in three circumstances: when the mother's life is in danger, when the woman becomes pregnant through rape or incest, and when serious birth defects are present. For all the publicity they receive, however, these three circumstances probably account for no more than about 5 percent of all U.S. abortions. In the far more typical circumstances—when the mother is unmarried, cannot afford additional children, or simply doesn't want any more—a narrow majority of Americans oppose making abortion legal.

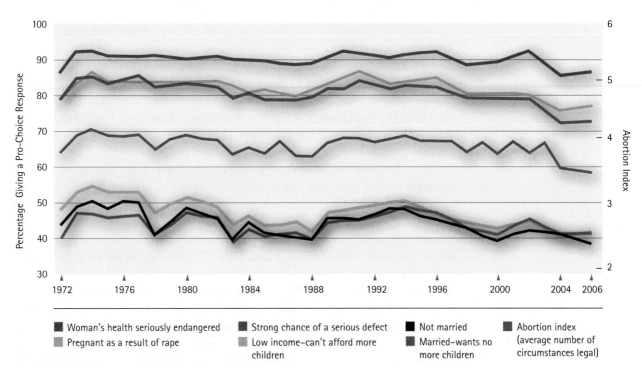

■ Woman's health seriously endangered?   ■ Strong chance of a serious defect   ■ Not married   ■ Abortion index
■ Pregnant as a result of rape   ■ Low income–can't afford more   ■ Married–wants no   (average number of
                                                 children   more children   circumstances legal)

FIGURE 5.4

POPULAR ATTITUDES TOWARD ABORTION HAVE BEEN REMARKABLY STABLE SINCE *ROE V. WADE* (1973)

• *Why does the American public appear to favor legal abortion in some circumstances but not in others? What values or distinctions lie behind the results in this figure?*

Note: Respondents who answered "don't know" are included in the calculation.

Source: Calculated by Sam Abrams from the General Social Survey 1972–2006 Cumulative Data File.

FIGURE 5.5

AMERICANS TEND TO
FAVOR ABORTION RIGHTS,
BUT WITH RESTRICTIONS

• *In political terms, do these results provide more support for
the pro-life or pro-choice side of
the abortion issue?*

Note: N = 1,001 adults nationwide. Margin of error ±3.

Source: CNN/*USA Today*/Gallup Poll.

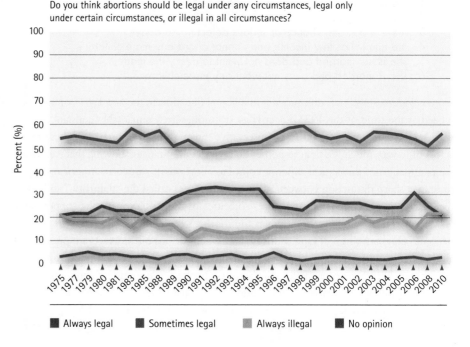

Do you think abortions should be legal under any circumstances, legal only
under certain circumstances, or illegal in all circumstances?

■ Always legal   ■ Sometimes legal   ▨ Always illegal   ■ No opinion

Figure 5.5 shows this complexity in a different way. It indicates that very few Americans hold absolute positions on abortion; only a fifth want abortion "always illegal" and only a quarter want to keep it "always legal." The majority of Americans hold a more complicated set of preferences that would make abortion legal in some circumstances and illegal in others. Thus, although opinion on abortion has been stable over time—indicating that it is not the result of haphazard poll responses—it does not accommodate the oversimplified questions that pollsters customarily ask about it.

One final point should be made about public opinion polls. Although it is easy to identify problems with polls and to provide examples of biased samples and loaded questions, one major thing needs to be said in their favor: As a way of measuring and monitoring public opinion, systematic sample surveys are far better than any of the alternatives. For all kinds of reasons, both practical and moral, elected officials and polit-ical activists need timely, reliable information about the state of public opinion: what issues the public cares about, how the public assesses officials' current performance, and the themes and policies the public favors or opposes. And although polls are not a fool-proof way of answering such questions, they do provide a considerably more accurate picture of the public mind than we might get by, for example, listening to talk radio or holding town meetings or reading letters sent in by constituents. The solution to bad or misleading surveys is not to abandon polls, but to learn how to use them carefully and how to interpret them correctly.

5.4

Determine characteristics
of public opinion that
make it difficult to
accurately measure.

Characteristics of Public Opinion

Why should the results of measuring public opinion be so sensitive to *how* it is mea-sured? The characteristics of public opinion often make it very hard to obtain reliable measurements.

Public Opinion Is Uninformed

On many issues, people have little or no information. The extent of popular ignorance is most apparent when surveys pose "factual" questions. As shown in Figure 5.6, fewer than half of 18- to 29-year-olds knew that there was more than one woman sitting on the Supreme Court in 2010. Less than one-third of those over 50 knew how many votes it takes to override a Senate filibuster.

Elections are not SAT tests, of course; it is not necessary to know the answers to all sorts of factual questions in order to vote intelligently. But widespread ignorance extends beyond such factual questions to important matters of government and public policy. At the height of the financial crisis in 2008 and 2009, only a bare majority of Americans were aware which auto company (Ford) did not receive public funds, and most Americans could not name the chairman of the Federal Reserve or provide a reasonable guess of the level of the Dow Jones Industrial Average.[45] Over 25 percent of Americans said they had not heard or read much of anything about the government's frantic efforts to provide money to failing financial institutions.[46]

Upon learning the full extent of popular ignorance, some politically involved students react critically, jumping to the conclusion that ordinary Americans are lazy and irresponsible people who fall far short of the democratic ideal. Such reactions are understandable, but unjustified. Many people fall short of the ideal, but it is the ideal that is unjustified. The simple fact is that most people have little time for politics. They work hard to take care of life's necessities, such as paying bills, caring for families, and nurturing

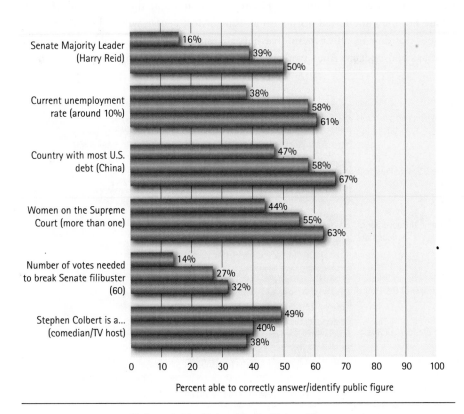

Percent able to correctly answer/identify public figure

■ Ages 18–29   ■ Ages 30–49   ■ Ages 50+

FIGURE 5.6

AMERICANS ARE NOT VERY KNOWLEDGEABLE ABOUT THE SPECIFICS OF AMERICAN GOVERNMENT

Young people know even less about government than relatively ill-informed older Americans.

• *Why do you think young people are better able to identify Stephen Colbert than older people? What do you think this fact says, if anything, about how people obtain political knowledge?*

Source: Pew Research Center for the People and the Press, "Public Knowledge: Senate Legislative Process a Mystery to Many," January 28, 2010, http://pew-research.org/pubs/1478/political-iq-quiz-knowledge-filibuster-debt-colbert-steele, accessed June 8, 2010.

personal relationships—leaving little time or energy to read the *New York Times* or watch C-SPAN. Nor do Americans stand out for their inattentiveness to public affairs. Citizens in other countries lack political and historical knowledge as well. A British Gallup poll, for example, found that only 40 percent of Britons knew that the United States once was part of their empire![47]

Those who criticize ordinary citizens for their lack of attention to public affairs often have jobs that enable them to stay informed with little effort. For example, political conversation is a common diversion on college campuses; professors and students find it easy to stay informed. Likewise, the jobs of many journalists involve following politics: If they are not informed, they are not doing their job. If everyone worked in a university or for the news media, we would all be much better informed. But most people do not—a fact that social critics tend to overlook.

The general point is that the act of gathering, digesting, and storing information is neither effortless nor free; it is costly. For most Americans, bearing such **information costs** brings them few immediate benefits.[48] Citizens doubt that they can make much difference when civil war rages in Somalia. When faced with a costly activity that has no clear benefit (i.e., learning enough about the conflict to have an informed opinion about it), many of them quite rationally decide to minimize their costs. Thus, from a logical standpoint, the puzzle is not that so many Americans are ill informed; rather, the puzzle is that as many are as well informed as they are.[49] Information costs do not fall equally heavily on all people. Education makes it easier to absorb and organize information; thus, it comes as no surprise that more-educated Americans are better informed than less-educated ones (see Figure 5.7). In addition, the benefits of information are not the same for all people on all issues. Most people will be better informed on issues that directly affect them. Teachers are especially knowledgeable about school operations and budgets. Auto workers have strong views on foreign imports. Farmers

information cost

The time and mental effort required to absorb and store information, whether from conversations, personal experiences, or the media.

FIGURE 5.7

HIGHER EDUCATION IS STRONGLY ASSOCIATED WITH GREATER KNOWLEDGE OF POLITICS AND GOVERNMENT

• *How much of the difference shown here is actually attributable to ideas or skills learned in college—and how much simply reflects that those entering college may, on average, be more curious and attentive to the news than their non-college bound peers?*

Source: *What Americans Know, 1989–2007,* Pew Research Center for The People and the Press, April 15, 2007.

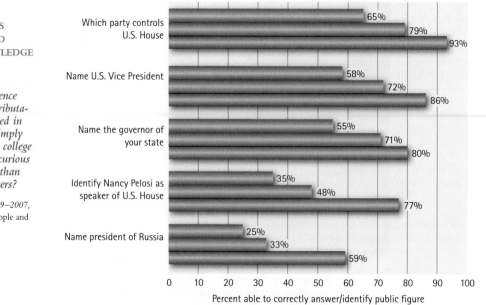

Percent able to correctly answer/identify public figure

■ High school or less   ■ Some college   ■ College grad

keep track of proposals to change agricultural subsidies. Such **issue publics,** groups of people who are particularly affected by, or concerned with, a specific issue, are different from the great majority of citizens in that they find relevant information particularly valuable and can gather it more cheaply.[50] Of course, some people will bear information costs even when they get little direct benefit from doing so. They may feel a duty as citizens to be informed, so they stay attuned to public affairs because they believe it is the "right thing" to do. Other people follow public affairs because they find it intrinsically interesting, just as some follow baseball or Hollywood gossip. For such people, following public affairs is a recreational activity. Probably most citizens know as much as they do because they enjoy staying informed, not because they derive any tangible benefit from doing so.[51]

issue public
A group of people particularly affected by, or concerned with, a specific issue.

Many of the Opinions Expressed in Polls Are Not Strongly Held

Elected officials and other political activists often use poll results as proof that the public approves of their actions and policies. Yet, even when survey data appear to support such claims, there is considerable evidence that many of the responses registered in public opinion surveys are not very strongly held: Respondents do give the answers recorded, but they are not firmly committed to them.

A group of researchers at the University of Cincinnati asked a sample of local residents the following question: "Some people say that the 1975 Public Affairs Act should be repealed. Do you agree or disagree with this idea?" Thirty-three percent of those interviewed took a position on this matter (16 percent agreed, 17 percent disagreed)—which is noteworthy because there was, in fact, no such act. In other words, 33 percent of the sample claimed to have an opinion on a completely fictitious issue.[52]

How do we explain such an anomalous finding? The answer says much about both the nature of public opinion and the peculiarities of the survey interview situation. Unlike most activists, most ordinary citizens do not have well-defined, clearly thought out opinions on numerous different policy issues. Nothing in their daily lives requires them to. Yet, when a survey interviewer calls them up on the phone or shows up at their door and asks them questions about such issues, they wish to be cooperative and are reluctant to admit ignorance. Hence, they invent opinions on the spot. Such responses are often called "nonattitudes" or "doorstep opinions."

A measure of the prevalence of such doorstep opinions comes from using screen or filter questions in public opinion surveys—phrases or sentences added on at the beginning or end of survey questions in order to exclude those who do not know about an issue or do not have a clear position. In a poll conducted by the University of Chicago, half of the sample was asked this question: "In general, do you think the courts in this area deal too harshly or not harshly enough with criminals?" The other half of the sample was asked a similar but slightly different question: "In general, do you think the courts in this area deal too harshly or not harshly enough with criminals, or don't you have enough information about the courts to say?" In the first case, 7 percent of those interviewed said they weren't sure or didn't have an opinion. For the second question, 29 percent chose the "no opinion" response. The number of "no opinion" responses jumped by 22 percentage points just because the question made it a little easier to take this position.[53]

Public Opinion Is Not Ideological

Another characteristic of public opinion that makes it easy to misinterpret is that even when people have reasonably firm views on issues, those views usually are not closely connected to one another. In short, most Americans are not ideological.

An **ideology** is a system of beliefs in which one or more organizing principles connect an individual's views on a wide range of particular issues. For example, if you are told that Representative Smith is a "liberal" Democrat, you can guess that Smith is pro-choice on abortion, favors gun control, and supports a strong government role in healthcare. Conversely, if you are told that Representative Jones is a "conservative" Republican, you might guess that she is pro-life, opposes gun control, and thinks that healthcare should be left to the private sector as much as possible. Such assumptions will usually be right. The reason is that **political elites**—people who are deeply involved in politics, whether as activists or as officeholders—tend to have well-structured ideologies that bind together their positions on different policy issues.

Ordinary citizens are another matter. People with little direct involvement in politics—a group traditionally called the **mass public**—usually are not ideological.[54] Their views on specific issues do not cluster together like those of elites, nor do their evaluations of party leaders or political groups.[55] Rather than believe consistently in either activist or minimal government, citizens favor government spending in some areas but oppose it in others. They like some Democratic politicians but dislike others. They favor toleration for some groups in some situations, but not for other groups in other situations.

Even when the standards for ideological thinking are rather low, the evidence indicates that few people follow conventional political ideologies. For example, *when given the option*, one-quarter to one-third of the population will not classify themselves on a liberal–conservative scale, and another one-quarter put themselves exactly in the middle: "moderate, middle of the road."[56] Furthermore, many Americans are unaware of the ideologies held by the people they elect. During the 2008 campaign, for example, only two-thirds of those polled considered the Republicans the more conservative of the two parties (more than 16 percent thought the Democrats were).[57]

Here again, there is a tendency to disparage regular citizens. Critics assume that ordinary Americans form their political attitudes haphazardly because their preferences do not follow conventional patterns. Although that certainly is true of some, it is not necessarily true of most, for ideologies are *social* constructions. Personal views aside, can anyone explain why a person who prefers lower taxes and a strong military necessarily should oppose abortion but not the death penalty and should support strip-club regulations but not gun control? Such issue positions may go together when people polarize across an ideological divide—that is, when they view the political world as a struggle between liberals and conservatives and adopt the many views that characterize their side—but no comprehensive political philosophy ties all these issue positions together. Indeed, ideologies change over time.[58] Rather than criticize normal nonideological citizens, maybe we should criticize political elites for slavishly conforming to a laundry list of policy preferences that have no logical connection to each other.

Whether you regard ideological thinking as good or bad, however, you should bear one point in mind. Because they presume that ideological thinking is the norm, party and

ideology
A system of beliefs in which one or more organizing principles connect the individual's views on a wide range of particular issues.

political elites
Activists and officeholders who have well-structured ideologies that bind together their positions on different policy issues.

mass public
Ordinary people for whom politics is a peripheral concern.

issue activists, media commentators, and many public officials will conclude too much on the basis of opinion polls and voting returns. Support for one variety of government action may indicate nothing about support for another, seemingly similar government action. Support for a candidate's position on one issue may suggest little or nothing about that candidate's "mandate" to act on seemingly related issues. The nonideological nature of public opinion means that elites often hear more than the voters are saying.

Public Opinion Is Inconsistent

Given that people often have not thought about issues, and given that most of them do not think ideologically, it is not surprising that the public sometimes sends contradictory messages. For example, in 1980, when Ronald Reagan defeated Jimmy Carter and the Republicans made striking gains in Congress, many observers interpreted the election results as a "resurgence of conservatism" or a "turn to the right" in American politics. In fact, the data were confusing: People were indeed more hostile toward government in general, but, on the other hand, most voters were wary of cuts in popular domestic programs. Often, they actually favored *higher* spending on these programs.[59]

Findings such as these are not unusual. In recent decades, the American people have never delivered a clear mandate either for the Republicans to cut and retrench or for the Democrats to tax and expand.[60] Early in his administration, President George W. Bush pushed a tax-cut plan that a plurality of voters supported at the same time that they endorsed increasing spending on social security and education.[61] Solid majorities supported the Obama administration's $787 billion economic stimulus bill, but nearly 60 percent also said that "the government should balance the budget even when the country is in a recession and at war."[62] Such contradictory views may be amusing—they recall the old maxim that "everybody wants to go to heaven but nobody wants to die"—but they confuse political debate. One consequence of inconsistent public preferences is that the political parties may have no incentive to compromise on major issues: Each party can cite public opinion polls supporting what it wishes to do.

Why is public opinion so inconsistent? Ignorance explains some of the contradictions. People think that the federal budget lavishes money on unpopular programs such as "welfare" and foreign aid, even though such policies account for relatively little federal spending. They also believe that government agencies waste so much money that elected leaders could slice funding without harming essential services. Citizens therefore unrealistically expect painless budget cuts.

Not all examples of inconsistency reflect inaccurate information, however. People oppose amending the Constitution in principle, but they endorse numerous specific amendment proposals. They support various fundamental rights, but not for groups they oppose.[63] As Figure 5.8 shows, nearly everyone says "people should be allowed to express unpopular opinions," but this support drops precipitously when people are presented with particular examples of unpopular expression. Citizens are so consistently inconsistent when applying general principles to specific cases that explanations other than ignorance must be at work.

Some social critics contend that Americans are hypocrites. Americans pay lip service to fine-sounding principles, but they do not really believe in these values and abandon them whenever it is convenient to do so. We have a more positive interpretation.

FIGURE 5.8

AMERICANS TEND TO
ENDORSE GENERAL
PRINCIPLES BUT MAKE
NUMEROUS EXCEPTIONS
TO THEM

• *Is it really inconsistent to
endorse general principles but
make exceptions for particular
groups? Or is there something
distinctive about song lyrics,
racial groups, or religious groups
that might make these exceptions
legitimate?*

The first three items show the percentage of people supporting the general principles indicated. The last four items show the percentage of people supporting specific civil liberties for the political or social group they dislike the most. The groups about which people were asked included members of the John Birch Society, the Ku Klux Klan, and the Black Panthers, as well as fascists, communists, socialists, atheists, anti-abortionists, and pro-abortionists.

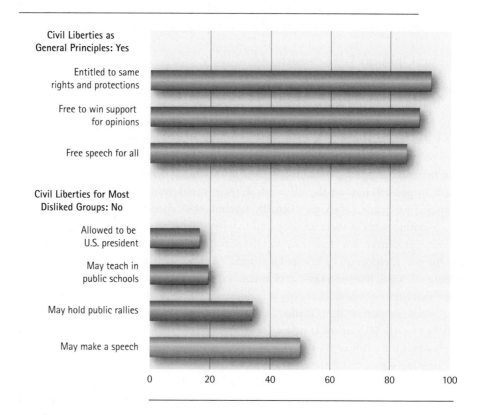

Percentage Expressing Tolerance

Law professors, newspaper editors, and political activists tend to view rights inflexibly—as rules that government officials must respect at all times. Once leaders start making exceptions, they can water down rights until they provide no protection whatsoever. Few Americans accept such an absolutist perspective, though. They tend to be more pragmatic. Rights are good things, but at times they conflict with other values.[64]

Most citizens are prepared to make trade-offs on a case-by-case basis,[65] relaxing rights when they threaten to produce "unreasonable" outcomes that violate "common sense." Yes, free speech is a good thing—but perhaps not enough to justify allowing Nazi rallies in a neighborhood where Holocaust survivors live. Yes, people should be treated equally—but perhaps historically disadvantaged groups should receive some special consideration when they apply for college as a way to erase social differences. Yes, police should follow proper procedures—but murderers should not necessarily go free just because police violated some technical point of law. To adults familiar with life's complexities, the realm of real-world politics has to be flexible. They may feel no contradiction in treating rights more as guidelines rather than as ironclad rules.[66]

Just What Is Permitted?
Americans are supportive of free speech in general, but many are willing to restrict hate groups.

• *If rights are considered as part of a trade-off, rather than as inalienable, what will the consequences be for the substance of those rights? What sorts of limits on extreme groups are permissible? For instance, is it fair to allow the individuals shown here to march, but not in a town filled with Holocaust survivors?*

Governing by Public Opinion?

Never before have American politicians had so much information about public opinion. Indeed, critics regularly complain that politics and government today are "poll-driven." As we have seen, however, given the characteristics of public opinion, trying to measure and interpret it is far from an exact science. At times it is more like reading tea leaves! Furthermore, even when public opinion is fairly clear, there is no guarantee that policymakers will follow it. Political scientists have tried to determine if public opinion influences policy, and if so, when it does or does not do so.

The Power of Public Opinion

Public opinion may be uninformed, nonideological, and inconsistent—but these flaws do not mean elected officials can ignore it. The public as a whole generally possesses enough information about the political system to understand the choices voters need to make. For example, the public at large understands that the Democrats are to the left of the Republicans on most issues.[67] Moreover, even within the same party, the public knew that Ronald Reagan was farther to the right than Richard Nixon and that George McGovern was farther to the left than Jimmy Carter. Political scientist James Stimson has shown that, when numerous survey questions are analyzed together, researchers can find distinct shifts in the general direction or "mood" of the public. For example, after analyzing hundreds of questions, he found that the electorate in fact did shift to the right in the years leading up to Ronald Reagan's election.[68] Similarly, the electorate shifted to the left in the years leading up to President Obama's victory in 2008.[69]

In the same vein, noted political scientists Benjamin Page and Robert Shapiro have argued that, viewed *collectively,* the public is reasonably "rational." Analysis of thousands of poll questions asked repeatedly over more than a 40-year period shows that in the aggregate, public opinion is far more stable than the opinions of individual members of

5.5

Assess the extent to which public opinion influences policy makers.

Continued on page 151

Should the Government Enact a Nationwide Civic Education Program?

As we have shown in this chapter, much of the public remains ignorant of important political events and institutions. Americans cannot be relied upon to know which party controls Congress, who serves as governor of their state, or who occupies the vice presidency. Is it safe for voters to know this little in a country in which elections are so central to public policy making? Some critics think not. As one puts it, "ignorance potentially opens the door for both elite manipulation of the public and gross policy errors caused by politicians' needs to appeal to an ignorant electorate in order to win office."[1]

Some scholars are so worried about the damage that might be done by uninformed voters that they have called for significant new civic education requirements at the local, state, and national levels. As many as 29 states currently mandate that high school students take a government or civics course, but requirements are varied and often lack specificity.[2] The 2006 National Assessment of Education Progress (NAEP) found that although two-thirds of American students have at least a "basic" knowledge of civics concepts, only about one in four is "proficient." Only 28 percent of eighth graders, for example, could explain the historical purpose of the Declaration of Independence. Minority and low-income students consistently have lower levels of civic knowledge than do others.[3] A renewed effort to bring clarity and focus to civic education programs might give elementary and secondary school students much more comprehensive exposure to the fundamentals of politics and government in the United States.

Students learning about Abraham Lincoln in a Virginia high school.

Because people acquire many lifelong habits in their early years, civics classes might socialize them to be better informed citizens as adults. As one interest group argues, "A free society must rely on the knowledge, skills, and virtue of its citizens and those they elect to public office. Civic education is the primary way our citizens acquire the knowledge and skills necessary for informed and engaged citizenship."[4]

Critics of such a program are uncomfortable with state and national governments controlling what local school districts teach. For example, conservative groups and home schooling advocates criticized the No Child Left Behind education bill because of its federal mandates. Furthermore, U.S. math, science, and writing instruction might suffer if an expanded civics curriculum suddenly became a requirement. Certainly less "fundamental" subjects such as music and the arts would seem poised to lose out. Finally, there is no guarantee that more civics instruction would increase voter knowledge in the long run. Can high school classes really compete with video games, Facebook, and iPhones—not to mention jobs and families—as a source of long-run habits?

What do you think?

1. Some scholars argue that in the aggregate, public opinion is rational, predictable, and knowledgeable (see p. 149). If "the sum is greater than the parts," does it matter if many individual voters lack political knowledge?

2. Do you favor a new national civic education program? Based on your own experience, would such a program be effective?

For more on civic education, see the following websites:

www.civiced.org

The National Center For Civic Education promotes state and local civic education programs.

www.civicyouth.org

The Center for Information and Research on Civic Learning & Engagement (CIRCLE) researches civic involvement by young Americans.

---

[1]Ilya Somin, "When Ignorance Isn't Bliss: How Political Ignorance Threatens Democracy," Cato Institute Policy Analysis No. 525, September 22, 2004, www.cato.org/pubs/pas/pa525.pdf, accessed June 10, 2010.
[2]National Alliance for Civic Education, "Civic Requirements and Guidelines," www.cived.net/req_guid.html, accessed June 10, 2010.
[3]National Center for Education Statistics, *The Nation's Report Card: Civics 2006*, May 2007, http://nces.ed.gov/nationsreportcard/pdf/main2006/2007476.pdf, accessed June 10, 2010.
[4]Center for Civic Education, "Campaign to Promote Civic Education: Overview," www.civiced.org/index.php?page=overview_of_campaign, accessed June 25, 2008.

Continued from page 149

the public. When it does shift, public opinion generally reacts to new events and conditions in natural ways. For example, when federal spending goes up, public preferences for continued increases go down, an effect that indicates some broad public recognition of the direction in which government policy has moved.[70]

Given the stability and sensibility of overall public opinion, elected officials usually feel compelled to give voters what they want. Page and Shapiro confirm that American policies follow public opinion. When trends in opinion are clearly moving in one direction, public policy generally follows. The more pronounced the trend in opinion, the more likely policy is to follow it.[71] Such findings show that an often uninformed, nonideological, and inconsistent public can still influence the direction of public policy.

Why can a limited public nonetheless guide the behavior of its government? The answer lies in the distinction between individuals and aggregates. Even if particular voters have little grasp of public affairs, as a group they may be much more capable—with the process of aggregation canceling out individual error and enabling the general public preference to emerge. Think of a grade school orchestra. Individually, the young musicians are so unsteady that it is difficult to identify the tune each is playing, but put them all together and the audience can make out "Twinkle, Twinkle Little Star." So it is with public opinion. On some issues and at some times, public opinion and public policy may not be closely aligned, but looking at the general direction of public policy over the long run reveals that it tends to follow public opinion.

Finally, it is important to note that, even if policymakers pay close attention to public opinion, the public as a whole may not get what it wants. The issue of gun

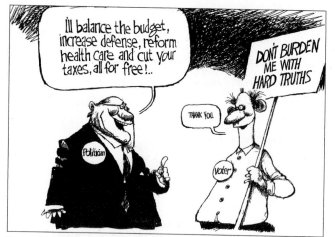

By permission of Mike Luckovich and Creator's Syndicate.

BY LUCKOVICH FOR THE ATLANTA CONSTUTUTION

The Irrational Public?

The inconsistencies in public opinion may suggest that voters are buffoons who think that government can provide anything they want. However, what seems like inconsistency may grow from the public's desire to avoid extremes and seek a practical balance between competing principles.

© Creators Syndicate.

control provides a stark illustration. In 1999, two deranged students at Columbine High School in Colorado killed 13 and wounded 20 others. In 2007, a mentally ill student went on a similar deadly rampage at Virginia Tech, killing 32. In the wake of both of these incidents, gun control advocates argued that new restrictions were needed, and interest groups lobbied Congress in support of new laws that would crack down on sales at gun shows, mandate trigger locks, and outlaw some kinds of ammunition. Momentum for such measures slowed rapidly, however, when it became clear that many members of Congress represented rural districts in which voters strongly opposed new gun laws. Although, as Figure 5.9 shows, public opinion in the *nation as a whole* may favor many gun control measures, public opinion in *key congressional districts* does not.

A second factor at work here is that many gun rights advocates feel very passionately about the issue, making their views heard through groups such as the NRA, and casting their votes in elections for those with whom they agree. Gun control supporters may be in the majority, but most don't feel as strongly about it and may not make the issue a top priority at the ballot box. As one former congressman remarked, "The 80 percent that are for gun safety just aren't for it very much. They're not intense."[72] As this example shows, aggregate public opinion is only imperfectly connected to national public policy.

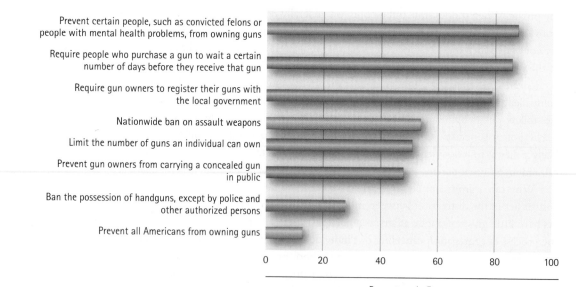

FIGURE 5.9

AMERICANS SUPPORT MANY—BUT NOT ALL—GUN CONTROL PROPOSALS
• *Why has Congress not passed laws on all measures that have majority support?*

Source: CNN/Opinion Research Corporation Poll, June 4-5, 2008 (all but "handguns" & "assault weapons"); CBS News/*New York Times* Poll April 22-26, 2009 ("assault weapons"); Gallup Poll, October 1-4, 2009 ("handguns").

CHAPTER SUMMARY

5.1   **Define public opinion in the context of a democracy.**

Public opinion is at the core of democratic politics. For the people to "rule," their opinions must translate into public laws and policies. Because opinions guide voting choices, politicians are keenly interested in the views their constituents hold—and the views that they may hold in the future.

5.2   **Identify the major sources of individuals' political attitudes.**

Public opinion is influenced by factors that include childhood socialization, personal experiences, group memberships, and education. The media may also influence opinions, although their level of influence is unclear.

5.3   **Evaluate polling as a means of measuring public opinion.**

Measuring public opinion is an inexact science at best. The design and question wording of surveys make interpreting opinion polls very tricky. And on many issues—among them abortion—the public truly does not have an answer

that is easily quantified. Even when public opinion seems relatively clear, therefore, governing by opinion poll may not be a good idea.

5.4   **Determine characteristics of public opinion that make it difficult to accurately measure.**

Citizens tend to be uninformed, so polling data may not represent firmly held opinions. Preferences can change with little notice, and the public may not connect two issues that elected officials consider clearly related.

5.5   **Assess the extent to which public opinion influences policy makers.**

Thus, leaders often misinterpret poll results. Politicians who respond too quickly to short-term fluctuations in the polls may get into political trouble. Rather, public opinion exerts its influence largely through the calculations of officials who try to anticipate what they must do to win re-election. Clearly, elected officials will hesitate to defy the will of an aroused public—but they pay more attention to the wishes of their own voters than they do to the wishes of the American public as a whole.

---

mypoliscilab EXERCISES

Apply what you learned in this chapter on MyPoliSciLab.

Read on mypoliscilab.com

  eText: Chapter 5

Study and Review on mypoliscilab.com

  Pre-Test

  Post-Test

  Chapter Exam

  Flashcards

Watch on mypoliscilab.com

  Video: Opinion Poll on the U.S. Economy

  Video: Obama Approval Rating

Explore on mypoliscilab.com

  Simulation: You Are a Polling Consultant

  Comparative: Comparing Governments and Public Opinion

  Timeline: War, Peace, and Public Opinion

KEY TERMS

focus groups, p. 136
ideology, p. 146
information cost, p. 144
issue public, p. 145

mass public, p. 146
measurement error, p. 136
political efficacy, p. 131
political elites, p. 146

public opinion, p. 129
sampling error, p. 134
selection bias, p. 135
socialization, p. 129

SUGGESTED READINGS

Of General Interest

Asher, Herbert. *Polling and the Public: What Every Citizen Should Know*, 7th ed. Washington, DC: CQ Press, 2007. Good introductory discussion of how polls are conducted and how to interpret them.

Mayer, William. *The Changing American Mind: How and Why American Public Opinion Changed Between 1960 and 1988*. Ann Arbor: University of Michigan Press, 1992. Masterful survey of the changing contours of public opinion over the past generation, with careful dissection of the sources of opinion change.

Page, Benjamin, and Robert Shapiro. *The Rational Public*. Chicago: University of Chicago Press, 1992. Prize-winning study of public opinion from the 1930s to the 1990s. The authors argue that, viewed as a collectivity, the public is rational, however imperfect the individual opinions that members of the public hold.

Stimson, James. *The Tides of Consent: How Public Opinion Shapes American Politics*. New York: Cambridge University Press, 2004. Readable argument that public opinion as a whole is greater because it is the sum of its parts.

Focused Studies

Cook, Elizabeth, Ted Jelen, and Clyde Wilcox. *Between Two Absolutes: Public Opinion and the Politics of Abortion*. Boulder, CO: Westview, 1992. Although more than a decade old, this careful, disinterested description and explanation of American attitudes toward abortion is still accurate today.

Geer, John. *From Tea Leaves to Opinion Polls*. New York: Columbia University Press, 1996. Thoughtful consideration of a democratic dilemma: Do politicians lead public opinion or follow it? Concludes that rational leaders always follow on salient issues but often lead on less salient ones.

Jacobs, Lawrence, and Robert Shapiro. *Politicians Don't Pander: Political Manipulation and the Loss of Democratic Responsiveness*. Chicago: University of Chicago Press, 2000. Provocative argument that today's politicians follow their own strongly held preferences and that polls are only a tool used to determine how best to frame the positions that the politicians personally favor.

Zaller, John. *The Nature and Origins of Mass Opinion*. New York: Cambridge University Press, 1992. An influential reinterpretation of public opinion findings that argues that people do not have fixed opinions on many subjects. Rather, their responses reflect variable considerations stimulated by the question and the context.

ON THE WEB

Academic organizations archive a great deal of public opinion data on political and social topics.

www.aapor.org

www.ropercenter.uconn.edu

www.norc.uchicago.edu

Some of the best sites are the American Association for Public Opinion Research, the Roper Center, and the National Opinion Research Center. The AAPOR site links to the best scholarly journal of public opinion, *Public Opinion Quarterly*. The world's largest collection of public opinion data can be found at the Roper Center for Public Opinion Research. This collection includes a huge amount of commercial and academic poll data. The Roper Center's service—iPoll—requires subscription, but your university may be able to help you gain access. The National Opinion Research Center site contains the 23 General Social Surveys (GSS) carried out since 1972.

www.pollingreport.com

The Polling Report summarizes recent media polls from major media outlets such as CNN/Gallup and the *New York Times*, among others. This site will have more current information than the academic sites, but because news organizations polling about trendy issues sometimes use inconsistent or inadequately tested question wordings, the findings are more subject to question and interpretation.

6 Individual Participation

CHAPTER OUTLINE

LEARNING OBJECTIVES

6.1   Trace the expansion of the franchise in the United States.

6.2   Identify the costs and benefits of voting.

6.3   Compare and contrast the United States and other democracies with regard to voter turnout and the costs and benefits of voting.

6.4   Explain the decline in American voter turnout.

6.5   Identify factors associated with higher and lower voter turnout.

6.6   Evaluate the arguments about why low turnout is or is not a problem.

6.7   Assess the role of forms of political participation other than voting.

Getting Out the Vote

"You can't always get them with the phone. You don't always get them with the mail. That's why we go to the door." That's how one party activist explained his role in a recent voter turnout operation.[1] A renewed focus on voter turnout is not just a product of the hard-fought Obama–McCain race of 2008. Over the last decade, the two major political parties have devoted an extraordinary amount of effort and resources to getting their voters to the polls, whereas in the past most efforts had been geared toward persuading independents.

Caught by surprise in 2000 by an unexpectedly successful Democratic Party turnout effort, Republicans responded with a "72-Hour Plan," a detailed get-out-the-vote plan implemented during the final three days of the campaign. By 2004, Republicans had painstakingly set up an extensive field organization in every major state that was expected to be competitive. In contrast with Democratic Party efforts, which relied on outside interest groups and labor unions for help, Republican state and national party organizations developed their own voter lists, precision targeting strategies, and grassroots organizing networks. The result was that, as the *New York Times* put it, the 2004 election saw "the most expensive and successful voter drive in history."[2]

But after 2008 those efforts seemed puny. The Internet had shown its potential in some earlier races (such as John McCain's 2000 presidential primary effort), but by the end of the decade, it truly came into its own. The 2008 McCain campaign used online videos to get free press for campaign ads that had aired only a few times on broadcast television, and more than 10 percent of McCain's contributors reported making a contribution over the Internet.[3] Barack Obama's campaign went even further, releasing YouTube videos, setting up an online social networking site so volunteers could connect with one another, and issuing frequent emails updating supporters and soliciting funds. Campaign workers urged the 84,000 supporters who gathered at Denver's Invesco Field to hear Obama accept the Democratic nomination to text message their friends and call unregistered voters while they waited.[4]

At the end of the decade, average people appeared more engaged with politics than they were at the beginning. In 2000, only about one-third of Americans said that a political party had contacted them about voting. In 2008, that figure was 43 percent. In 2000, only 9 percent said they contributed money; in 2008 the figure was 13 percent. Across the country people reported being more interested in the presidential campaign, more likely to follow campaign news, and more likely to care who won the election.[5] In 2008, 62.4 percent of the eligible electorate voted, the highest turnout in decades and several percentage points higher than turnout in 2004.

But it is unclear how much the party and campaign organizations had to do with this surge in interest and activity. In 2000, there were few gripping issues to captivate the electorate. By 2008, the United States was engaged in wars in Iraq and Afghanistan, terrorism seemed to be an ever-present threat, and a major economic crisis had just struck.

A significant portion of the increase no doubt reflected the emotion and energy generated by these and other controversial issues.

Moreover, whatever the contribution of the various factors, the simple fact remains that despite a close election, hotly contested issues, and a massive get-out-the-vote effort, 38 percent of eligible Americans sat out the election in 2008. In the 2010 midterm election, only 38.2 percent of adults turned out to vote. Even under highly favorable conditions, U.S. voter turnout still lagged well behind the levels routinely recorded in other democracies.

Making the Connection

Many Americans are concerned about turnout levels in the United States, because voting is widely regarded as the fundamental form of democratic participation. Indeed, in modern democracies, voting is the *only* form of participation for the bulk of the population. About one-third of Americans report having signed a petition, and a similar number claim to have contacted a government official at one time or another, but fewer make financial contributions to a party or candidate, and substantially fewer attend a political meeting or rally or work in a campaign.

For most people, then, failure to vote means failure to participate at all. And, if a bare majority—or even fewer people—vote, how representative are the public officials they elect, and how legitimate are the actions these officials take? Not very, some analysts answer. Democratic theorist Benjamin Barber charges that "In a country where voting is the primary expression of citizenship, the refusal to vote signals the bankruptcy of democracy."[6]

Should Americans worry about the dismal rate of voter participation in their country's elections? Answering that question requires a close look at the historical, personal, and institutional reasons why many Americans fail to vote and whether other forms of participation can substitute for voting. This chapter provides the background necessary to analyze the state of political participation in America. In the pages that follow first we recount how the **franchise**—or right to vote—spread in the United States. Then we address two general questions: Why is turnout lower in the United States than in other democracies, and why did turnout decline in the United States during the last third of the twentieth century? Then we consider whether Americans have developed alternate forms of participation that compensate for their failure to turn out on Election Day. With that background, we can reach a clearer understanding of whether low participation levels threaten the legitimacy of American government.

A Brief History of the Franchise in the United States

For a document that was proclaimed in the name of "we the people" and that guaranteed to every state "a republican form of government," the Constitution said remarkably little about who would be allowed to vote. The only clause in the original document that mentioned voting was in Article I, section 2. "Electors" for the House of Representatives were to have the "Qualifications requisite for Electors of the most numerous Branch of the State Legislature." Thus, voter eligibility was left up to the states, which could set pretty much any standards they wanted, as long as they applied those same standards to the lower houses of their own state legislatures.

6.1

Trace the expansion of the franchise in the United States.

franchise
The right to vote.

In the early days of the republic, most states limited the franchise to white male property holders. Although restrictions varied from state to state and were unevenly enforced, property qualifications were gradually eliminated, but most states restricted the franchise to taxpayers until the 1850s.[7] Not all voter qualifications were economic. Until the 1830s, a few states limited voting to those who professed belief in a Christian God. Not until the eve of the Civil War could it be said that the United States had universal white male **suffrage** (another term for the right to vote).[8]

suffrage
Another term for the right to vote.

Voting Rights in the Amendment Process

Between the Civil War and 1971 a series of constitutional amendments gradually expanded electoral access and today most Americans over 18 years of age hold the legal right to vote in all U.S. elections.

The Fifteenth Amendment to the Constitution, adopted in 1870, extended the franchise to black males. Within a few decades, though, violence, intimidation, and other discriminatory procedures disenfranchised African Americans in many states (see Chapter 17). Black men could not exercise their voting rights in many parts of the South until the 1960s, when the Voting Rights Act reestablished federal oversight of southern elections. The result was a sharp increase in voting among African Americans.

Women's suffrage also progressed slowly.[9] The first state that allowed women to vote in national elections, Wyoming, did not do so until 1890. Eleven other states had expanded the franchise to women by 1916. Most were western states, where frontier conditions often required women to be more independent than those living on or near the eastern seaboard. The suffrage movement won its crowning victory in 1920 when the Nineteenth Amendment granted women voting rights in every state.[10]

A small extension of the franchise occurred in 1961 when the Twenty-third Amendment to the Constitution was ratified. This amendment granted residents of the District of Columbia the right to vote for presidential electors. By law (if not in practice), all mentally competent, law-abiding Americans of voting age now had the right to vote for president. (The District of Columbia still lacks representation in the U.S. Senate, and its delegate to the House of Representatives may not vote on legislation.)

Demonstrating for Women's Suffrage

The suffragists put considerable pressure on President Woodrow Wilson to support the Nineteenth Amendment.

• *How did that increase the pressure on politicians to support an amendment to the Constitution?*

The next and, to date, the last constitutional extension of the franchise came in 1971 with the adoption of the Twenty-sixth Amendment, which lowered the official voting age to 18.[11] Prior to the amendment, the federal Constitution did not guarantee voting rights to those under 21 (although individual states could use a lower limit). During the Vietnam War, however, Americans began to ask why people old enough to die on a foreign battlefield were not old enough to vote for the officials who sent them to war.[12] As support for lowering the voting age grew, Republican president Richard Nixon announced his backing for a constitutional amendment, even though many Republicans feared it would help the Democrats.

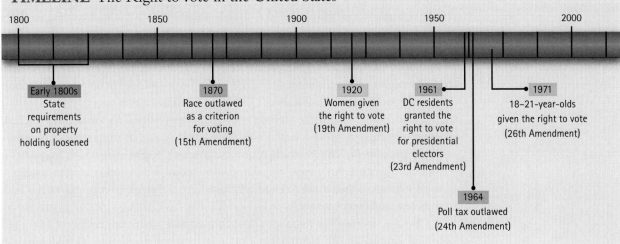

TIMELINE The Right to Vote in the United States

FIGURE 6.1

THE RIGHT TO VOTE IN THE UNITED STATES HAS BEEN STEADILY EXPANDED
The right to vote in the United States has been a story of continual, if uneven, expansion.
• *Can still more groups be enfranchised? Which ones?*

Today most adult U.S. citizens may vote if they wish. Convicted felons are not eligible in many states, but some critics argue that even this restriction ought to be abolished because it falls especially heavily on African Americans. One-eighth of the black male voting age population is ineligible to vote, and this proportion rises to one-third in states such as Alabama and Florida.[13] Exceptions aside, the trend over the course of American history has been a steady expansion of the franchise (see Figure 6.1).

How Voting Rights Spread

The separate states extended the suffrage in different ways at different times. During times of war, for example, a disenfranchised group usually could expect to receive the suffrage in at least some states as a reward for their military service—a process that opened the door for immigrants, for those who did not own property or pay taxes, and for young adults who were considered "old enough to fight, old enough to vote."[14] Once a group gained voting rights in one state, national candidates and political parties seeking their support had an incentive to back similar expansions in other states. Electoral pressures, therefore, often caused voting rights to spread quickly, a dynamic that was most apparent in the case of women's suffrage.

Woodrow Wilson won the three-way 1912 presidential election with only 42 percent of the popular vote. At that time, he had avoided taking a clear position on women's suffrage because many of his fellow Democrats feared that women would vote against key Democratic constituencies such as labor unions, liquor interests, and machine politicians. Southern Democrats also worried that granting voting rights to women would encourage African Americans to demand greater access to the ballot. Nevertheless, by 1916 when Wilson was running for reelection, women had gained the right to vote in 12 states, including California (1910) and Illinois (1913). The president signaled his support for women's suffrage by promising to vote for a related referendum in New Jersey, his home state.

Wilson's change of heart reflected the fact that his Republican opponent in 1916, Charles Evans Hughes, supported a constitutional amendment to let women vote. Had Hughes won every state with women's suffrage, their electors would constitute one-third of an Electoral College majority. Wilson could not afford to surrender the West to Hughes, so he adopted a moderate stance on women's suffrage. In the election, Wilson narrowly won, carrying 10 of the 12 states where women could vote.

World War I stalled the suffrage movement temporarily. As victory approached, however, suffragists pressed hard for congressional passage of the proposed constitutional amendment. The National American Women's Rights Association encouraged women to write letters, make campaign contributions, and use other conventional political strategies, while more militant suffragists engaged in confrontational tactics such as protests and demonstrations.

Because women's suffrage soon looked inevitable, politicians fearful of being left behind jumped on the bandwagon. Congress approved the suffrage amendment and sent it to the states, which ratified the provision within three years—in time for women in all 48 states to vote in the 1920 presidential election. Interestingly, the United States was far ahead of most of the world in granting full rights of citizenship to women. France and Japan did not allow women to vote until the mid-1940s, and the last Swiss canton did not enfranchise women until 1990![15]

Why People Participate: Costs and Benefits

6.2

Identify the costs and benefits of voting.

Voting rights have steadily expanded in the United States, but extending the franchise does not automatically lead to increased turnout. Even in presidential elections, as much as half the potential electorate stays home. After the election, some editorialists criticize the nonvoters for being lazy while others criticize the candidates for being uninspiring—but the question of why eligible voters abstain is more complicated than newspaper editorials usually imply.[16]

Voting is costly. If you are paid by the hour and you take time off in order to vote, you lose a portion of your wages. Even if you have flexible hours and can leave work early or arrive late, you may do less work on Election Day if you take the time to vote. You may have to wait in long lines to be able to vote before or after work. In 2008, people at some polling places were still waiting in line to vote hours after the polls were supposed to have closed. For some people with little information about politics, the entire voting situation can be uncomfortable; staying home enables them to avoid the discomfort. If you are surprised that such seemingly small considerations could lower turnout, consider that turnout generally falls when the weather is rainy or temperatures are extreme.[17]

There also are benefits to voting, of course. The most obvious is, however, logically the least important: the possibility that your vote might swing an election. Your vote determines an electoral outcome only if it creates or breaks a tie.[18] Otherwise, you could stay home and the election would come out the same way. The chance that a single voter will swing a state or national election in this way is infinitesimally small. In the 1996 presidential election, which attracted the lowest turnout rate of any presidential election in the twentieth century, almost 100 million Americans voted. In 2008, 131

Dilbert: © Scott Adams/reprinted by permission of United Features Syndicate, Inc.

Do Only Voters' Voices Deserve to Be Heard?

• *Are there principled reasons for not voting? If so, how much actual nonvoting occurs because of principled reasons?*

million people voted.[19] Given numbers such as these, a desire to determine who wins the election cannot realistically be an important motivation for turning out. From a purely individualistic standpoint, the puzzle is not that turnout is so low in the United States, but, rather, that turnout is as high as it is.

Late in the nineteenth century, when turnout levels were especially high (usually more than 75 percent outside the South), some voters had a compelling reason to show up at the polls: They were paid to do so, either by the political parties or the candidates. The typical price of a vote in some New York City elections was as much as $100 (as expressed in current dollars) and could soar even higher in particularly competitive circumstances.[20] Material rewards are a much rarer benefit of voting today, but direct payments for voting (sometimes called "walking-around money") still exist here and there, mainly in the poorer areas of eastern cities. Citizens also may be motivated to vote in elections because the outcome can directly affect their material interests. For example, government employees vote at higher rates than people employed in the private sector, other things being equal—especially in low-turnout local elections.[21]

Today, however, most of the individual motivations for voting are not material but psychological. Some people feel a civic duty to vote: They vote for the same reason that they give money to charity or pick up litter. Perhaps the most compelling benefit of voting is the pleasure it can bring. Some Americans take satisfaction in expressing their preference for a candidate or an issue position, much as they might enjoy cheering for an athletic team.[22] Psychological benefits are an important incentive for voting. Whereas your vote makes no difference unless it affects the outcome, you receive the psychological benefits regardless of the closeness of an election.

Another reason people vote goes beyond simple individual motivations. Sometimes people participate in elections because they have been encouraged to vote by others who have personal incentives to increase turnout. **Voter mobilization** consists of the efforts of parties, groups, and activists to turn out their potential supporters. Campaign workers provide babysitters and rides to the polls, thereby reducing the individual costs of voting. They apply social pressure by contacting citizens who haven't voted and reminding them to do so. Various groups and social networks to which individuals belong also exert social pressures, encouraging the feeling that a citizen has a responsibility to vote. Although pressures and benefits such as these may seem small, remember that although it costs more to vote than to stay home, these costs are relatively small.

Armed with some understanding of the general reasons why people vote or fail to vote, we can now address an important question raised in the introduction to this chapter: Why do Americans vote at lower levels than citizens in other countries?

voter mobilization
The efforts of parties, groups, and activists to encourage their supporters to turn out for elections.

6.3

Compare and contrast the United States and other democracies with regard to voter turnout and the costs and benefits of voting.

International Comparisons of Voter Turnout

Americans vote at much lower rates than people in most other countries, even countries such as Italy whose citizens are exceedingly cynical about politics (see Table 6.1). That being said, procedures for calculating turnout differ from country to country. These differences lower American turnout figures somewhat, relative to those in other democracies.

Turnout would seem to be simple enough to measure. For many years, the U.S. Census Bureau calculated official turnout in presidential elections as:

Number of people voting for president/Number of people in the voting-age population

This definition seems straightforward, but it lowers American turnout as much as 5 percent relative to other countries. Simply put, the numerator in this calculation is usually underestimated, whereas the denominator is overestimated.

Consider first the numerator. Most Americans who show up at the polls in a presidential general election will cast a vote for a presidential candidate. But every four years, a small percentage of the voters so thoroughly dislike all of the major presidential candidates that they leave that part of the ballot blank while casting a vote for a congressional or state legislative candidate whom they do like. In the formula reported above, these people are treated as nonvoters. Also left out of the count are write-in votes for frivolous candidates (actual examples from U.S. elections: Rambo, ZZ Top, Batman, and Mickey Mouse). For understandable reasons, election officials in many

TABLE 6.1					
AMERICANS ARE LESS LIKELY TO VOTE THAN THE CITIZENS OF OTHER DEMOCRACIES					
The following figures represent the average turnout (in percentages of the voting age population) in parliamentary or presidential (if applicable) elections in the year indicated.					
Malta (2008)	98.39	Norway (2005)	76.5	Bulgaria (2005)	62.4
Belgium (2007)	86	Venezuela (2006)	76.3	India (2004)	60.6
Iceland (2007)	84.6	Israel (2009)	76.3	United Kingdom (2005)	58.3
Brazil (2006)	83.5	Austria (2008)	75.6	United States (2008)★	58.2
Denmark (2007)	83.2	Germany (2005)	72.5	Luxembourg (2004)	56.5
Australia (2007)	82.7	Ireland (2007)	68.9	Poland (2007)	54.24
Sweden (2006)	80.6	Finland (2007)	68.2	Canada (2008)	53.5
Greece (2007)	79.6	Portugal (2006)	67	Estonia (2007)	53.4
Italy (2008)	79.1	Russia (2008)	67	Lithuania (2004)	50.3
New Zealand (2008)	77.8	Japan (2005)	66.6	Latvia (2006)	50.2
Netherlands (2006)	77.4	Czech Republic (2006)	65.1	Hungary (2006)	41.1
Spain (2008)	77.2	Costa Rica (2006)	63.9	Switzerland (2007)	39.79
France (2007)	76.8				

★As percent of the voting *eligible* population, U.S. turnout in 2008 was about 63 percent.

Source: Calculated from International Institute for Democracy and Electoral Assistance Data.

jurisdictions do not record such votes. In contrast, the French have a long tradition wherein alienated voters scribble an offensive suggestion across their ballots (the English translation has the initials "F.Y."). French election officials count such ballots, whereas most American officials would not.[23] Vote-counting machines, meanwhile, occasionally fail to register a person's vote. Technically speaking, these are all examples of **undervotes:** Although you cast your ballot, you are not counted. Alternatively, if you vote for more than one candidate, your ballot is classified as an **overvote** and, again, you are not included when officials compute the turnout rate. Procedures differ in other countries and U.S. procedures lower turnout figures by a couple of percentage points per election.[24]

Factors that affect the denominator of the ratio are even more significant. The **voting-age population,** or VAP, refers to the number of people over the age of 18, a number that includes some groups legally ineligible to vote: felons, people confined to mental or correctional institutions, and (most important) noncitizens. In 2008, according to a careful analysis by political scientist Michael McDonald, using the entire VAP rather than only the eligible VAP lowered U.S. turnout by almost 5 percentage points.[25] As a consequence, most sources that report turnout data have started using the **voting eligible population,** or VEP, as the denominator, a number that is calculated by taking the voting age population and subtracting out such groups as felons and noncitizens.

Personal Costs and Benefits: Registration

Traditionally, much of the gap in voter turnout between the United States and other countries has been explained by the type of voter registration system that this country uses. In most other countries, registering voters is the responsibility of the government. Shortly before each major election, the government sends out registrars who are supposed to visit each dwelling unit in the country and take down the names of all eligible voters. In the United States, by contrast, getting registered is the responsibility of the individual voter. Except in North Dakota, which does not have voter registration, any

undervotes

Ballots that indicate no choice for an office (e.g., for president in 2000), whether because the voter abstained or because the voter's intention could not be determined.

overvotes

Ballots that have more than one choice for an office (e.g., for president in 2000), whether because the voter cast a ballot for more than one candidate or wrote in a name as well as making a mark.

voting-age population

All people in the United States over the age of 18, including those who may not be legally eligible to vote.

voting eligible population

Voting-age population with groups such as felons and noncitizens subracted.

Compulsory Voting

Many countries force citizens to vote by imposing fines or other penalties on those who abstain. For example, voting is compulsory in the Philippines—the setting of this photograph.

American who wants to vote must make sure that he or she is registered. And though a handful of states permit people to register on Election Day, in most states the closing date—the final date on which a person can register and still vote at the next election—is between two weeks and 30 days before the election. This timeframe sets a major limit on how high American voter turnout can go. In 2008, according to a U.S. Census survey conducted shortly after the election, 90 percent of all **registered voters** actually voted—but only 71 percent of voting-age citizens were registered.

registered voters
Those legally eligible to vote who have registered in accordance with the requirements prevailing in their state and locality.

In response to statistics like these, for many decades those who wanted to increase voter turnout in the United States concentrated most of their efforts on reducing the costs of voting by making voter registration easier. And, at one level, these efforts were quite successful. By any reasonable measure, it is far easier to register today than it was 50 years ago. Poll taxes (taxes that some southern states once required all voters to pay) have been eliminated; the time between the closing date and Election Day has been dramatically shortened; literacy tests, which were once used by almost every southern state to keep blacks off the registration rolls, have been outlawed. With the passage of the so-called "Motor Voter" bill in 1993, most states now allow people to register while applying for a driver's license, a library card, or a welfare check. Yet there is remarkably little evidence to show that such changes have had a noticeable effect on American voter turnout levels. Indeed, between 1972 and 2000, U.S. voter turnout rates actually declined from the levels typically recorded during the 1950s and 1960s.

Of all the major proposals to make voter registration easier, almost the only one that has not been adopted is Election Day registration. According to its proponents, many Americans don't start getting interested in an upcoming election until the week or two just before Election Day—by which time it is usually too late to register. Hence, it is argued, voter turnout would increase if we permitted people to register at their local polling place on Election Day and then immediately cast a ballot. Opponents of Election Day registration, however, say that it would substantially increase the level of vote fraud in the United States. Whatever its effect on vote fraud, Election Day registration would probably have only a quite limited on voter turnout. In the nine states that had Election Day registration in 2008, the average turnout rate was 69.1 percent—but most of these states had higher than average turnout levels before they let their residents register on Election Day. As the figures in Table 6.1 show, even a 69 percent turnout rate would put the United States well behind most other contemporary democracies.

Personal Costs and Benefits: Compulsion

The personal registration system makes voting relatively costly in the United States. By contrast, some countries attach costs to *nonvoting* by making voting compulsory. In Australia and Belgium, for example, nonvoters are subject to fines. Greek electoral law provides for imprisonment of nonvoters for up to 12 months, although that penalty is never applied. Other democracies do penalize nonvoters, at least sometimes. Australian law allows for fines of up to 50 Australian dollars for not voting, and in one recent election, over 50,000 nonvoters paid fines.[26] In Italy, nonvoters are not fined, but "Did Not Vote" is stamped on their identification papers, threatening nonvoters with the prospect of unsympathetic treatment at the hands of public officials should they get into trouble or need help with a problem. Italian nonvoters also have their names posted on community bulletin boards. Turnout in democracies with compulsory voting is almost 15 percent higher than in democracies without it.[27]American turnout figures would undoubtedly increase greatly if people were compelled to vote, although such a policy shift might not solve the fundamental problem posed by low electoral interest.

Other Personal Costs and Benefits

Several additional institutional variations raise the costs of voting incurred by Americans. Elections in the United States traditionally are held on Tuesdays, an ordinary workday. In most of the rest of the world, either elections are held on Sundays or election days are proclaimed official holidays. Italian workers receive free train fare back to their place of registration, which is usually their hometown. In effect, the government subsidizes family reunions.

Some observers argue that turnout in the United States is low because Americans are called on to vote so often (see Chapter 1).[28] In most European countries, citizens vote only a few times in a four-year period: once for a member of parliament, once for a representative to the European Union, and perhaps once for a small number of local officials. In contrast, Americans vote for numerous national, state, and local officials—usually twice, once in a primary or caucus, and once in a general election. They also may vote for numerous ballot propositions or in a recall election. Moreover, these elections typically occur at different times. Some commentators have suggested, not completely tongue-in-cheek, that turnout in the United States should be calculated as the percentage who vote at least once during a four-year period. Some find it telling that the only European country where voters are called upon to vote frequently, Switzerland, has a turnout rate comparable to that in the United States.

Finally, some states use voter registration lists to select people for jury duty. The fear of losing a day's work or more if a trial is extended probably is sufficient to motivate some citizens to forfeit their right to vote. One study concluded that, in such jurisdictions, turnout could be as much as 5 to 10 percent lower than it otherwise would be.[29] Voters in other jurisdictions also sometimes avoid registering because they mistakenly believe that they might end up with jury duty as a result.

Mobilization and Turnout

Not only do Americans face higher costs for voting and lower costs for nonvoting relative to other countries, but they also have less help to meet these costs. The chief mobilizing agent in modern democracies is the political party. Parties have incentives to mobilize their supporters; indeed, they have often undertaken that task with excessive enthusiasm, as when urban political machines cast fraudulent votes on behalf of the dead or reported more votes for their candidates than there were residents in their cities. Political scientists Steven Rosenstone and Mark Hansen observe that

> [P]arty mobilization underwrites the costs of political participation. Party workers inform people about upcoming elections, tell them where and when they can register and vote, supply them with applications for absentee ballots, show them the locations of campaign headquarters, and remind them of imminent rallies and meetings. Campaigns drop by to pick up donations, telephone reminders to voters on the day of the election, and drive the lazy, the harried, the immobile, and the infirm to the polls.[30]

Certainly it is no accident that American turnout levels peaked in the late nineteenth century, when the power and resources of American parties were at a maximum and their ethics at a minimum. During this period the patronage system was in full bloom. With hundreds of thousands of government jobs at stake in elections, the parties had little trouble motivating government workers, not to mention their relatives and friends. And, unconstrained by conflict-of-interest or sunshine (open-government) laws, the parties were quite willing to do whatever it took to gain or keep control of government.

A Modern Tool of Voter Mobilization

A campaign volunteer texts on election night 2010.

• *How do you think new technologies will change voter mobilization?*

American parties have declined since the nineteenth century, at least as mobilizing agents (see Chapter 8). Voters are not as attached to them as in the past, and the parties have less in the way of inducements to turn out the faithful.[31] Progressive reforms instituted around a century ago undercut the mobilizing resources once enjoyed by political parties. The personal registration system discouraged voter fraud. Primary elections weakened the parties' control of nominations for office. Civil-service reforms took away much of the patronage that parties once used to buy loyalty. A significant part of the reason why turnout in the late twentieth century was lower in the United States than in other democracies is that parties generally were stronger and more active elsewhere than here.

Political parties are not the only mobilizing agent in democracies. Interest groups and associations also bring supporters to the polls (see Chapter 7). However, these organizations are not so deeply rooted in American politics as their counterparts elsewhere. Unions and churches form the very foundation of some political parties in Europe, but the same is not true in the United States. Thus, here too, Americans receive less support from collective political actors than do citizens in other democracies.

Several analysts have dissected statistically the difference in turnout levels between the United States and other countries.[32] All other things being equal, American turnout should actually be somewhat higher than turnout in Europe because of higher educational levels and American civic attitudes that encourage popular participation. But other things are far from equal. Bingham Powell, for example, estimates that differences in electoral institutions (especially registration systems) depress American turnout between 10 and 15 percent relative to Europe. Weaker mobilization efforts depress turnout by about 10 percent. In sum, it costs Americans more to vote, and they receive less support for voting than do citizens in most other countries.

6.4

Explain the decline in American voter turnout.

Why Has American Turnout Declined?

For many people the turnout problem is not only that voter turnout levels in the United States are lower than in other advanced democracies but also that turnout fell during the past generation. Figure 6.2 shows that turnout in presidential elections dropped between 1960 and 1988 and hit a half-century low in 1996, before rebounding

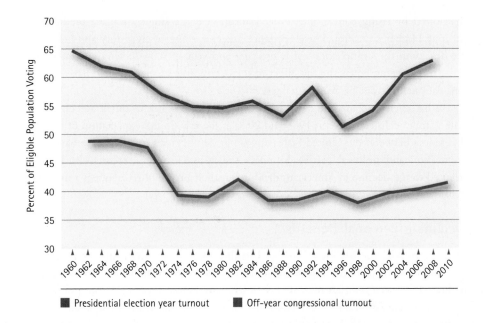

FIGURE 6.2

TURNOUT IN THE UNITED
STATES SELDOM REACHES
1960s LEVELS

• *What are the causes of declining turnout? Why is there a
difference between presidential
and off-year elections?*

Source: The Center for the Study of the
American Electorate.

in 2004 and 2008. In off-year elections, turnout declined more erratically, but it is significantly lower now than a generation ago.[33]

The decline in turnout was especially puzzling because developments late in the
twentieth century led to an expectation of *rising* turnout. First, as we have already
noted, court decisions, federal legislation such as the Voting Rights Act of 1965, and the
Twenty-fourth Amendment to the Constitution removed numerous institutional and
procedural impediments to voting and thus reduced the personal costs. Such reforms
were especially effective in the South, where they helped to overcome the terrible
legacy of racial discrimination. Figure 6.3 shows how turnout among African
Americans in the South increased sharply between 1960 and 1968.

Second, socioeconomic change should have raised turnout in the post-1964 period. True, the potential electorate was getting younger as the baby boom generation
came of age—a trend that should have lowered turnout—because young people traditionally vote at lower levels than older people. But that effect should have been more

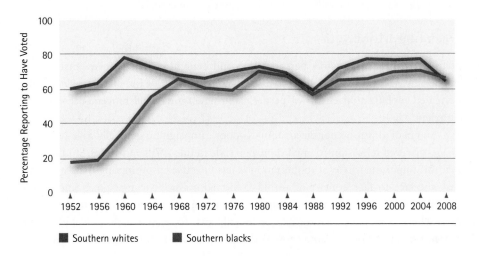

FIGURE 6.3

THE CIVIL RIGHTS
REVOLUTION OPENED
SOUTHERN POLITICS TO
AFRICAN AMERICANS

The turnout gap between
African American and white
voters narrowed as a result of
the civil rights movement of
the 1950s and 1960s.

• *Given that politicians respond
to voters, how did this narrowed
gap matter for public policy
changes?*

Source: National Election Studies: http://
electionstudies.org/nesguide/nesguide
.htm.

than offset by rising educational levels. Education is the single strongest predictor of turnout. Higher educational levels produce a keener sense of civic duty and help people deal with the complexities of registering and voting. Ruy Teixeira estimates that, other things being equal, the net effect of socioeconomic changes should have been to *raise* national turnout by about 4 percent.[34]

What, then, explains the decline in turnout? There is not so much agreement on why voting declined between 1968 and 2000 as there is on the explanation of turnout differences between the United States and other democracies (where, as we have seen, registration and political parties dominate the answer). Several factors clearly contributed to the decline in American turnout, but their precise importance is a matter of debate.

Declining Personal Benefits

One reason why the decline in voting costs did not increase voter turnout is that the benefits of voting may have declined at an even faster rate. Studies show that, despite higher educational levels, Americans are little, if any, better informed about politics today than a generation ago.[35] Generally, they are less interested in public affairs and in political campaigns and don't believe that government is as responsive as in times past.[36] Thus, they may not see as much riding on their decisions as in years past, and they may get less intrinsic satisfaction from supporting an admired candidate or party. On the other hand, these less interested and knowledgeable citizens report that they care more about who wins, so overall, their feelings are difficult to characterize.

One political factor that has lowered the benefits of voting is that elections have become less competitive. As we discuss in Chapter 11, the advantage of incumbency in congressional elections increased greatly after the mid-1960s. A similar process occurred more slowly in state legislative elections. A number of presidential elections in the 1970s and 1980s were landslides, and gubernatorial elections became less competitive as well. When candidates win by large margins, the notion that one's vote makes a difference must seem more outlandish than ever. Nor do blowout elections provide much incentive for campaign organizations to get out the vote. Rosenstone and Hansen find that in states with competitive gubernatorial campaigns turnout is 5 percent higher, other things being equal.[37] Notably, turnout increased in 2004 and 2008, when both the presidential elections and a handful of Senate elections were especially close.

Declining Mobilization

Statistical studies suggest that personal costs and benefits account for less than half of the decline in turnout from 1968 to 2000. The larger part of the decline reflected the decreased mobilization efforts of parties, campaigns, and social movements since the turbulent 1960s.

An era of grassroots, localized, door-to-door campaigning gradually gave way to an image-oriented television-focused campaign style in the 1970s and 1980s. Studies show that this impersonal style of mobilization is less effective in prompting people to vote than the face-to-face contact of an old-fashioned grassroots campaign.[38] Since 2000, political groups have taken this research to heart, focusing more on personal connections wherever possible. Mass emails are less effective, for example, than an appeal from a friend or neighbor, so campaigns work hard to build networks of voters who can contact each other. It remains to be seen, however, whether this new wave of mobilization can create sustained higher levels of turnout.

Declining Social Connectedness

You might interpret a turnout line trending downward to mean that any given citizen is less likely to vote today than a generation ago. Political scientist Warren Miller showed that such an interpretation is incorrect.[39] The decline in voter turnout is what social scientists call a **compositional effect**—a shift that results from a change in group composition rather than a change in the behavior of individuals already in the group. Older Americans learned to vote at high rates when they were young and they continue to do so. The turnout rates of middle-aged Americans (the baby boomers), by contrast, were lower when they entered the electorate and remain at that lower level. The turnout rates of succeeding generations are lower still. Thus, turnout is declining because of the simple fact that older Americans accustomed to voting at high rates are dying and being replaced by younger nonvoters.[40] Robert Putnam argues that the younger generation is less likely to participate in other ways as well.[41]

Why are younger adults less connected to the political world? Stephen Knack suggests that common thinking about voting is misconceived.[42] Rather than voting being the fundamental political act, voting may be a form of social behavior. People will vote when they are integrated into their communities through connections such as extended families, neighborhoods, religious organizations, and other social units. These forms of **social connectedness** are common among older Americans, who grew up in a simpler time when Americans were less mobile, more religious, and more trusting of their fellow citizens. Younger Americans have grown up in a highly mobile, worldly society where cynicism about their fellow citizens is widespread. They may not feel the social connections that prompt older individuals to participate in political life.

This argument can be taken too far, however. Arguments based on social connectedness often sound like nostalgia for the "good old days," which frequently were not so good to those who experienced them firsthand. After all, many social ties are built on exclusion, on a sense of being right while outsiders are wrong. Young people may stay out of politics because they have less desire to impose their will on others. As *Newsweek* columnist Fareed Zakaria writes, "Today's young . . . are less sure that they have the grand solutions for society's problems."[43] Younger adults also often experience their own forms of connectivity such as through Facebook, chat rooms, and other Internet-based forums. These "electronic communities" may not be as satisfying emotionally as real-life ties, but there is no reason they must be apolitical—especially because many of them link people with fairly similar personal interests, perhaps more similar than the interests of family or traditional organizations.

Nevertheless, a body of research does support looking to social explanations for the generational gap in voter participation. Voting is related to altruistic behavior such as giving blood, donating to charities, and doing volunteer work.[44] Turnout also is related to social connectedness. Even relying on such crude indicators as marriage rates, home ownership, church attendance, and length of residence in a community, studies find that decreased social connectedness accounts for as much as one-quarter of the decline in election turnout.[45] Along the same lines, although turnout is not related to trust in *government,* it is significantly related to trust in *people.*[46]

compositional effect
A shift in the behavior of a group that results from a change in the group's composition, rather than a change in the behavior of individuals already in the group.

social connectedness
The degree to which individuals are integrated into society—extended families, neighborhoods, religious organizations, and other social units.

6.5

Identify factors associated with higher and lower voter turnout.

Minority Voting

Signs in both Korean and English encourage Korean Americans to register to vote.

• *Why do you think Latino and Asian American turnout is lower than turnout among other groups?*

Who Votes and Who Doesn't?

Low voting rates probably would not stimulate as much discussion as they do if all social and economic groups in America voted at the same rate. But people differ in their ability to bear the costs of voting, in the strength of their feeling that voting is a duty, and in how often they are the targets of mobilization. Consequently, as Figure 6.4 indicates, turnout rates differ considerably across social and economic groups.[47]

Highly educated people are significantly more likely to vote than people with little formal education. Education instills a stronger sense of duty and gives people the knowledge, analytic skills, and self-confidence to meet the costs of registering and voting. Over and above education, income also matters. The wealthy are more likely to vote than the poor. Affluence, too, usually reflects a set of skills and personal characteristics that help people overcome barriers to voting.

Studies of turnout in the 1970s concluded that once disadvantages in education and income were factored out and their younger average age was considered, African Americans were at least as likely to vote as whites.[48] But more recent research finds that blacks are somewhat less likely to vote than whites, even taking into account differences in income and educational levels.[49] Other minorities, such as Latinos and Asians, still face language and citizenship barriers, although the situation is gradually improving.[50]

Turnout increases with age, until very old age when the trend reverses. People presumably gain experience as they age—experience that makes it easier for them to overcome any barriers to voting. They also become more socially connected, as well as more settled down in a life situation that clarifies their political preferences.

Another variable that once bore an important relationship to turnout is gender. For many decades after the passage of the Nineteenth Amendment, women voted at far

FIGURE 6.4

Do Social and Economic Differences Influence Public Policy?

• *What appears to be the strongest predictor that someone will vote? Do these differences have an effect on public policy?*

Source: U.S. Bureau of the Census, "Voting and Registration in the Election of November 2008," May 2010, Table 2, http://www.census.gov/prod/2010pubs/p20-562.pdf, accessed May 17, 2010.

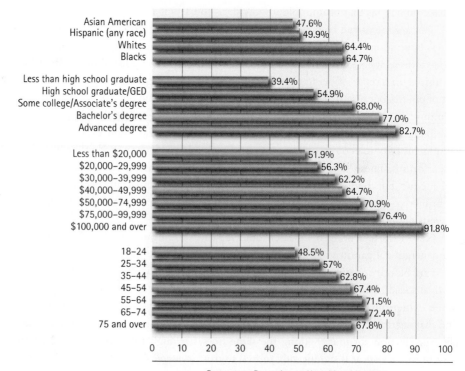

Percentage Reporting to Have Voted in 2008

lower rates than men. This pattern was particularly noticeable among older women, who were raised and socialized during an era when political participation was considered inappropriate for women. As these older individuals died, however, the gap between men's and women's participation rates narrowed until, beginning in 1980, women voted at a slightly higher rate than men. The increasing percentage of women in the workforce and the larger number of female candidates has also probably helped close the gender gap in participation.[51]

Importantly, these relationships between socioeconomic characteristics and turnout are consistently stronger in the United States than in other democracies. Indeed, in some countries there is almost no relationship between education and income on the one hand and voting on the other.[52] The explanation is that parties elsewhere are much more effective at mobilizing their supporters. In particular, European social democratic parties do a better job of getting their less advantaged potential voters to the polls than does the Democratic Party in the United States.

Is Low Turnout a Problem?

Given who votes and why, should the relatively low turnout rate in the United States be a cause for concern? Quite a few answers have been offered on both sides of this question. To a considerable degree, these differing views hinge on different beliefs about people's motives for voting. We will briefly sketch three arguments on each side of the debate.

Three Arguments Why Low Turnout Is Not a Problem

A Conservative (with a Small "C") Argument   Many people concerned about low turnout implicitly assume that high turnout indicates enthusiasm about politics and commitment to making the political order work. Maybe not. Some skeptics suggest that high turnout may indicate tension or conflict, even a belief that losing is unacceptable. They cite the experience of Austria and Germany as their democratic governments crumbled and the Fascist parties took power in the 1930s.[53] Turnout in those elections reached very high levels, but this mobilization probably reflected disillusionment and desperation more than commitment and enthusiasm. More recently, Anthony King observes that the highest turnouts in the United Kingdom occur in Northern Ireland, the home of centuries-old religious strife.[54] The 2010 U.S. Congressional elections are a less extreme case in point. Turnout rose among those groups of voters who were most upset about the economic downturn and about President Obama's policy initiatives, not among those who were content with the direction the country was heading. Generalizing from examples such as these, some commentators conclude that low turnout indicates contentment, not alienation. Therefore, low U.S. turnout levels are reassuring—a sign of political health, not disease.

An Elitist Argument   On average, nonvoters are less educated than voters. Studies also show them to be less informed, less interested in politics, and less concerned about it. Given these facts, some writers argue that the quality of electoral decisions is higher if no special effort is made to increase turnout. For example, David Reisman once remarked, "Bringing sleepwalkers to the polls simply to increase turnout is no service to democracy."[55] Columnist George Will provides a more succinct example of this elitist point of view: "Smaller is smarter."[56] According to this argument, high turnout

6.6

Evaluate the arguments about why low turnout is or is not a problem.

would bring lots of uninformed voters to the polls. Such individuals might be more likely to be swayed by demagogues or to vote on the basis of narrow self-interest. Of course, such arguments assume that nonvoters would remain ignorant, unconcerned, and subject to manipulation even after they decided to vote. If, instead, the process of turning people out to vote also informed them and raised their interest in politics, their preferences might well change.

A Cynical or Radical Argument   Some radicals contend that it is not the nonvoters but the voters who are a cause for concern. According to this viewpoint, elections in the United States do not matter—they are charades. The real decisions in America are made behind the scenes by power elites far from the popular arena.[57] The country actually is run by small cabals of bankers and financiers, the heads of large corporations, or a military-industrial complex. If so, voting is merely a symbolic act. It makes the masses feel as if they have a say in how they are governed when they really do not. From this perspective, high turnout rates may actually be harmful, since they only give greater legitimacy to a system that doesn't deserve it.

This is the one argument about the implications of low turnout that the evidence cannot support. Elections matter a great deal. They have an enormous impact on public policies that directly affect the quality of American life. The country is simply too large and diverse for any single interest to control the levers of power by itself.

Three Arguments Why Low Turnout Is a Problem

Voters Are Unrepresentative   The most obvious concern arising from low turnout is that the electorate is unrepresentative. The electorate is wealthier, whiter, older, and better educated than the population. Such an electorate is more Republican and more conservative than the population at large. Consequently, elections are biased, and public policies adopted by the winners are correspondingly biased. But as plausible as the argument seems, research suggests that it is overstated. Numerous studies have compared the policy views and the candidate preferences of voters and nonvoters. Typically, they differ little. Some studies have even found that contrary to the usual expectation, the conservative candidate at times was more popular among nonvoters (Ronald Reagan in 1984, for example).[58]

Given differences in voting rates across social groups, why do the preferences of nonvoters and voters differ so little? Minorities and the poor vote less often than whites and the affluent, but the differences are only matters of degree. Yes, blacks are less likely to vote than whites, but only about one-eighth of all the nonvoters are black. Similarly, the more highly educated are more likely to vote, but 25 percent of nonvoters have some college education. Nonvoters are not all poor, uneducated members of minority groups. Plenty of nonvoters are affluent, well educated, and white—especially those who do not vote because they have recently changed residences. (According to the U.S. Census Bureau, nearly one in five Americans moves during the two-year interval between national elections.)

Moreover, few groups are as one-sided in their political inclinations as African Americans, who vote about 8:1 Democratic. If turnout among most other groups were to increase, the Democrats would get somewhat more than half the additional votes, but the Republicans would get a fair proportion as well. Teixeira provides a striking illustration of these points. According to his calculations, if all the Hispanics and African

Americans in the country had voted in 1988 at levels 10 percent *higher* than whites, and all the white poor had voted at levels 10 percent *higher* than the white rich, the Democratic candidate, Michael Dukakis, would still have lost by two and a half million votes.[59] In sum, it is doubtful that plausible increases in turnout would produce a sea change in American politics—unless joining the political system produced a sharp change in the political outlook of former nonvoters.

One group that is seriously underrepresented in the electorate gets little attention: independents. Those who feel some form of allegiance to one of the major parties—either party—are substantially more likely to vote than those who lack party commitments. In 2008, for example, about 90 percent of Republicans and 84 percent of Democrats told pollsters they had voted (some were lying, of course), but only 67 percent of independents claimed to have voted.[60]

Low Turnout Reflects a "Phony" Politics   This argument emphasizes the character of political issues in contemporary politics. Social critics charge that low turnout among working-class Americans reflects a party system that fails to address "real" issues of concern to such people. What are real issues? Basically, they are economic issues: jobs, healthcare, housing, income distribution, and education. What the United States has is two upper middle-class parties obsessed with "phony" issues: flag burning, gun control, abortion, obscenity, prayer in school, capital punishment, gay rights, and evolution. (Political scientists refer to these issues that reflect personal values more than economic interests as **social issues** to distinguish them from pocketbook worries and concerns about foreign policy.)

Public opinion data support this criticism in some respects. A Gallup poll conducted in October 2008, just before the presidential election, found the American public concerned overwhelmingly with economic issues. Forty-two percent said that the economy was the "most important problem facing this country today"; 22 percent mentioned some other aspect of the economic crisis. By contrast, only 6 percent named a social issue. But the 2008 election was atypical in this respect. When Gallup asked a similar question in October 2000, only 6 percent of the sample cited the economy as the most important problem, with another 15 percent mentioning a particular economic ill such as unemployment, taxes, or poverty. In the same survey, 11 percent of the sample said the most important problem was "moral/religious decline," and 16 percent mentioned such issues as crime, drugs, gun control, abortion, and race relations.

Low Turnout Discourages Individual Development   The final claim is in some respects a counterargument to the elitist argument that low turnout is not a problem. Classical political theorists from Aristotle to John Stuart Mill emphasized that democracy has an important educational component. Participation in democratic politics stimulates individual development. Because participants become better citizens, they take politics to a higher level. Low turnout therefore signifies a lost opportunity to improve both the nonparticipants and politics itself.

Some analysts doubt that political participation is such an ennobling experience. Attending an intensive face-to-face political event such as a school board or city council meeting might improve a citizen. Pulling a few levers in a voting booth is unlikely to do so.[61] But the argument makes a valid point: Voting may affect not only who wins and what they do but also the voters themselves—what manner of people they are and what they want.

social issues
Issues (such as flag burning, gun control, abortion, obscenity, prayer in school, capital punishment, gay rights, and evolution) that reflect personal values more than economic interests.

Evaluating the Arguments

There is considerable disagreement about whether low turnout in the United States is a problem and, if so, how serious a problem it is. Well-intentioned and well-informed people disagree and offer persuasive arguments in support of their positions. Our view is that nonvoters and voters have diverse motives. Some nonvoters are content whereas others are alienated, and the same goes for voters. High turnout can indicate either high approval of the political order or serious dissatisfaction with it. Nonvoters don't have much political information, but neither do many voters—so raising turnout will not "dumb down" the electorate very much. Low turnout does make the actual electorate somewhat less representative than the potential electorate, but not nearly so much as critics often assume. Some potential voters undoubtedly are discouraged by a politics that discusses social issues of little relevance for them, but other citizens turn out to vote precisely because of their concern with such issues. And, although participation fosters citizen development, we doubt that the impersonal act of casting a vote will foster it very much. In short, we find some validity in each of the arguments presented above. We reject in its entirety only the argument that elections don't matter. Low turnout is a cause for concern, yes; a cause for despair, no.

6.7

Assess the role of forms of political participation other than voting.

Beyond the Voting Booth

As we noted earlier, voting is, for many people, their only form of political participation. Yet there are also a substantial number of Americans who participate in the political process in many other ways: by working in campaigns, contacting public officials, doing volunteer work in their local communities, or attending political meetings. All of these activities are performed by a considerably smaller proportion of the population than that which votes in presidential or midterm elections. Yet, as the data in Figure 6.5 show, Americans are more likely to take part in these more demanding types of political activities than are the citizens of Austria, Germany, the United Kingdom, and the Netherlands.

Similarly, a survey conducted by Sidney Verba and his associates estimated that one-quarter of Americans contribute money to political campaigns, and about 14 percent attend local school board meetings. Six percent of the survey respondents said they had engaged in some form of political protest.[62] All of these types of activities require much greater sacrifices from participants than the simple act of voting, yet Americans make such sacrifices at higher rates than citizens elsewhere.

Why would alternate forms of participation be more popular in the United States than in other democracies? Ironically, for many of the same reasons that voter turnout is so low.

- The frequency of elections in the United States opens up many opportunities for campaign involvement. Americans also have more opportunities to contact public officials and attend government board meetings, because the United States has so many elected officials and so many boards and commissions (see Chapter 1). Even if Americans are less likely to take advantage of any particular participatory opportunity, the sheer number of openings makes for a higher level of political participation than in other countries where opportunities are more limited. Indeed, as American elections have increased in frequency and as governmental bodies have

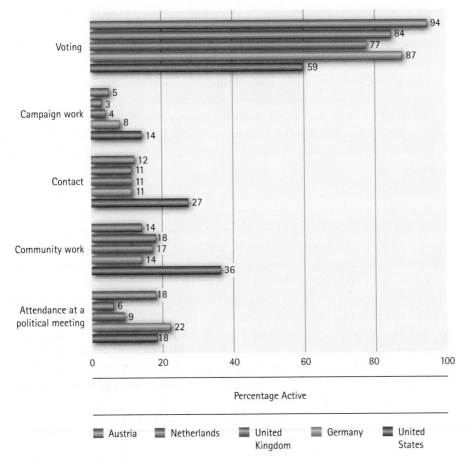

FIGURE 6.5

AMERICANS PARTICIPATE IN WAYS MORE DEMANDING THAN VOTING

• *Why might Americans not vote at rates as high as citizens of other democracies and yet participate at higher rates than others in relatively more demanding political activities?*

Source: Adapted from Sidney Verba, Kay Lehman Schlozman, and Henry Brady, *Voice and Equality* (Cambridge, MA: Harvard University Press, 1995), p. 70. Copyright © 1995 by the President and Fellows of Harvard College.

increased in number, some studies have found increases in some kinds of campaign participation.[63]

• Our individualistic political culture may suppress the sense of civic duty that promotes voter turnout. But the political culture's emphasis on rights and liberties encourages Americans to contact their public officials and to protest government actions. In contrast, the political cultures of most other democracies are more deferential to authority and discourage ordinary citizens from taking as active a role in politics as in the United States. Citizens elsewhere are less likely to protest government decisions—and when they do, their governments are more likely to ignore them.

• In the United States, candidates construct numerous personal organizations, many of whose members are temporary. In other countries, a small cadre of committed party workers shoulders most of the burden of campaigning year in and year out. "Occasional activists" drift in and out of political campaigns in America, depending on whether particular candidates or issues arouse their enthusiasm.[64] As a result, overall involvement in campaign activity brings in a wider variety of individuals.

• The United States gained independence through revolution, and protests have remained a regular feature of American politics ever since. In the 1850s, militant abolitionists fought slavery so aggressively that their actions resembled what we today call terrorism, as when John Brown and his abolitionist supporters seized a federal arsenal. Similarly, in the 1900s Carrie Nation waged her battle against "Demon Liquor" by invading taverns carrying an axe, which she used to bust open casks of beer and whiskey. In the 1960s, the civil rights movement fought for racial equality using marches, sit-ins, and boycotts. Direct action may not always be healthy for democracy. When a political movement resorts to taunting police and throwing rocks, one columnist suggests, "it is trying to achieve, through intimidation and scare tactics, what it has not been able to get through legislation."[65] Nevertheless, protests are as American as apple pie.

American participation outside the voting booth suggests a healthier political system than voter turnout rates alone might imply. Americans would not donate their money, their time, and their energy to a political system that only grappled with "phony" politics or that failed to include its citizens in the political community. At the same time, the population that works actively in campaigns, contacts their congressional representatives, or contributes money is even more unrepresentative of the general population than voters are. If the "messages" sent by voters slightly overamplify the concerns of better educated and wealthier Americans, the distortion is substantially greater if elected officials acquire their sense of the public mood and issue agenda by listening largely to their top campaign contributors. But most of the barriers to voting—such as registration laws, election scheduling, fear of jury duty, and disenfranchisement caused by a felony conviction—would not apply to these alternative avenues of participation. The availability of a wide variety of options, each with its own costs and benefits, provides some reassurance that most citizens who entirely abstain from political life do so because they prefer not to get involved.

Finally, many Americans who do not speak directly to their elected officials nevertheless communicate their needs and concerns by joining groups and organizations

Volunteering at a Local Food Bank

Americans are less likely to vote than citizens of other countries, but they are more likely to volunteer.

• Do you think most people see volunteering for a community group as more worthwhile than political activities? Why or why not?

Continued on page 179

Should Voting Be Compulsory?

The Issue

In reaction to America's chronically low electoral turnout, a number of analysts have concluded that the only sure remedy for this problem is to pass a law requiring all eligible Americans to vote in federal elections and imposing a small fine on those who do not. Others say that the right to vote also includes the right not to participate, and that compulsory voting laws would only compel many people who are not very interested in or informed about politics to cast ballots that they themselves do not regard as particularly meaningful.

Background

As we read in this chapter, the United States has the lowest voter turnout rate of any major democratic nation except Switzerland. In recent presidential elections, only slightly more than half of the eligible electorate has bothered to cast a ballot. Turnout rates at midterm elections have generally ranged between 35 and 40 percent. And, although turnout does occasionally increase above these levels—as it did in 2008, for example—there is no indication that America's low voter turnout is a temporary phenomenon, likely to be reversed in the next few years. If anything, studies of younger generations, who will constitute an increasingly large proportion of the U.S. electorate, indicate that they are less likely to follow news about government and politics, and therefore less likely to know or care much about these subjects, than were their parents and grandparents when they were at a similar age.[1] For many years, the standard "solution" to these problems was to liberalize American voter registration practices. Americans voted less, the argument went, because it was much more difficult to register in the United States than in other countries. Consequently, numerous legal changes have been made over the last four decades that have dramatically eased the process of voter registration. Yet all this activity has had almost no discernible effect on turnout. Although the number of registered voters has increased, most of the new registrants have not bothered to show up on Election Day. Over the last four decades, the average level of U.S. voter turnout has actually decreased.

Faced with this apparently intractable problem, many commentators have concluded that the only sure way to increase voter turnout is to make it mandatory: to pass a law (or possibly a constitutional amendment) that would require all eligible citizens to cast a ballot and would impose some kind of penalty—usually a small fine—on those who do not. Although such an arrangement is usually referred to as "compulsory voting," strictly speaking no one is actually compelled to *vote*. Rather, the law would require all citizens to show up at the polls on Election Day and receive an official ballot (or request an absentee ballot). Most people would then vote—but anyone who was repulsed by all of the available candidates or had some other principled reason for not voting could simply deposit a blank ballot into the ballot box. Exemptions presumably would be given to people who were sick on Election Day or had some other legitimate reason for being unable to get to the polls.

Although compulsory voting has never been tried in the United States, it is currently in use in a number of other democracies, including Australia, Belgium, and Luxembourg. And, as we can verify by examining the data in Table 6.1, all of these countries generally rank near the top in international comparisons of voter participation rates. More generally, as one political scientist has noted:

> On the basis of studies from the 1930s to the 1980s and 1990s, we know a great deal about the institutional mechanisms that can increase turnout . . . . And all of these studies . . . have found that compulsory voting is a particularly effective method to achieve high turnout—in spite of generally low penalties (comparable to a fine for parking violations), lax enforcement (more lenient than the enforcement of parking rules), and the secrecy of the ballot—which means that an actual vote cannot be compelled in the first place.[2]

Political Dilemmas

The case for compulsory voting is founded on the premise that one essential element of democracy is the fundamental equality of all citizens. But this equality is violated when some citizens vote and others do not. Not only might this inequality have an effect on who gets elected, it also means that the elected officials will almost certainly pay more attention to the needs and concerns of groups with higher participation rates than to those of groups that generally stay at home. And the lower that voter turnout falls, the greater the likelihood that differential participation rates may have a major impact on policy outcomes. As Sidney Verba, Norman Nie, and Jae-On Kim argued some years ago, to equalize political participation, governments need to establish both a "ceiling," a prescribed maximum, and a "floor," a prescribed minimum.[3] In the case of voter participation, the ceiling is, of course, the requirement that all citizens can cast only one vote, no matter how wealthy or well educated they are, and no matter how zealously they support their candidate. Compulsory voting would make sure that a floor is also in place.

Would compulsory voting have a noticeable impact on who gets elected? As we have already noted earlier in this chapter, the general consensus of most academic work on this subject is that the policy views of voters and nonvoters are not very different. Yet, it is wrong to say that there are *no* differences between these two groups. Even 100 percent turnout rates would not have altered the results of presidential elections in landslide years such as 1972 and 1984—but they might have made a difference in close elections such as those in 2000 or 2004.[4]

Opponents of compulsory voting make several arguments against it. Voting, they contend, is a right—and inherent in every right is a person's capacity to decide not to exercise it. The right to free speech also entails the right to keep silent if one chooses. The right to an attorney means that one can also waive that right. Forcing people to go to the polls every two or four years—even if they leave the ballot blank—is thus a violation of each person's right not to participate in an election.

On a more pragmatic level, opponents of compulsory voting question the desirability of pushing people to vote when they themselves appear to place little value on that act. There is, in this respect, a very important difference between the predicament of the contemporary nonvoter and the situation that confronted women before 1920 or African Americans in the South prior to the mid-1960s. Many women and blacks clearly *did* want to vote, but they were legally prohibited from doing so. Most nonvoters today, by contrast, almost certainly could vote if they wanted to. They just don't seem to think that it is worth the effort. If people place such a limited value on their candidate preference, what exactly do we gain by pushing them into the voting booths?

What Does the Public Believe?

Because it is such an unfamiliar idea, and because it runs against the traditional American concept of rights, at present there is remarkably little popular support for compulsory voting proposals. In June 2004, in the only recent survey question we know of that deals specifically with this issue, ABC News asked a national sample, "In a few countries every eligible citizen is required by law to vote in national elections. Those who don't have a good excuse for not voting are subject to a small fine. Do you think this would be a good law or a poor law to have in this country?" Only 21 percent of respondents said it was a good law (i.e., favored compulsory voting), versus 72 percent who thought it a poor law.

There is little chance that compulsory voting will be adopted in the United States over the next few years, but as advocates of compulsory voting have noted, many other intrusions into what were once believed to be private decisions are now sanctioned by law and widely endorsed by public opinion, because supporters worked hard to point out the advantages of such laws and thus changed public attitudes. (Two examples cited by one proponent of compulsory voting are the laws that ban smoking in restaurants and those that require automobile passengers to wear seat belts.)[5] Were a significant number of political scientists and civic groups to decide that compulsory voting is the only way to deal with the country's chronic turnout problem, perhaps, in time, a majority of Americans might come to share this belief.

How Have the Courts Ruled?

Any law that attempted to establish compulsory voting would almost certainly be challenged in the courts—but, because nothing like compulsory voting currently exists, it is difficult to say how the courts would decide such a case. The most basic challenge would concern whether the right to vote—which the U.S. Supreme Court has repeatedly recognized as enjoying substantial constitutional protection—also includes the right not to vote, and whether the latter right is violated by a law that compels every eligible voter to go to the polls.

Were compulsory voting to be instituted by federal statute, the law might also be challenged on federalism grounds: Does the Constitution give the federal government the right to regulate voting practices in the states? Through most of American history, it was assumed that all matters having to do with voter qualifications were under the control of state governments, save for the specific restrictions established in the Fifteenth and Nineteenth Amendments. More recently, however, the courts have argued that the clause in Article I, Section 4, which grants Congress the power to make regulations concerning the "times, places, and manner of holding [congressional] elections," in conjunction with the Fourteenth Amendment, gives the federal government substantial authority to pass laws that deal with voter eligibility and registration. Reasoning in this way, the Supreme Court upheld the National Voter Registration Act of 1993 (the so-called "Motor Voter" bill) and an earlier federal statute that had granted the right to vote to 18-, 19-, and 20-year-olds in all federal elections.

What Do You Think?

1. Is voting best thought of as a right or as a duty?

2. If a person favors one candidate but does not feel strongly enough about this preference to go to the polls, is society better off if the government encourages or requires such a person to vote?

3. Would compulsory voting have much effect on the outcomes of American elections? If so, which party would benefit most?

4. If voting is not made compulsory, is there any other way to ensure that such groups as young people and the poor vote in greater percentages?

[1]Martin P. Wattenberg, *Is Voting for Young People?* (New York: Pearson Longman, 2007), chaps. 1–3.
[2]Arend Lijphart, "Unequal Participation: Democracy's Unresolved Dilemma," *American Political Science Review* 91 (March 1997): 2.
[3]Sidney Verba, Norman H. Nie, and Jae-On Kim, *Participation and Political Equality* (New York: Cambridge University Press, 1978).
[4]For an argument that increased voter participation would have changed the results in 2000 and in the 1994 midterm elections, see Martin P. Wattenberg, *Where Have All the Voters Gone?* (Cambridge, MA: Harvard University Press, 2002), chap. 5.
[5]See Wattenberg, *Is Voting for Young People?* 172–174.

Continued from page 176

with like-minded fellow citizens. These interest groups mobilize their members to participate: soliciting their signatures for petitions, making contributions for fundraising drives, attending group meetings, and so forth. Organized groups also can encourage unconventional (or contentious) forms of participation: protests, demonstrations, and civil disobedience. Far more groups and associations are active in American politics than are found in other countries. We treat interest groups at length in the next chapter.

CHAPTER SUMMARY

6.1 Trace the expansion of the franchise in the United States.

Popular participation in democratic elections is the essence of democracy. Over the course of U.S. history, the franchise has expanded to include African Americans, women, and those between the ages of 18 and 21—all groups that were denied the vote in the first years after the Constitution's ratification.

6.2 Identify the costs and benefits of voting.

In most elections, a majority of the American electorate stay away from the polls. Only in presidential elections does a majority usually turn out—and often a bare majority at that. When it comes to participation in more demanding ways, far fewer people get involved. It takes time and effort to vote, and many citizens see other aspects of their lives as more important.

6.3 Compare and contrast the United States and other democracies with regard to voter turnout and the costs and benefits of voting.

American turnout levels are significantly lower than in other modern democracies, and they are lower than they have been in the recent past. The international difference is not hard to explain. In many ways the United States makes voting more costly than it is in other countries: Registration is left to the individual, voting is less convenient, and citizens are called on to vote much more often. In addition, mobilizing agents such as parties and unions are weaker in the United States than in other modern democracies, so Americans get less encouragement to vote from larger organizations.

6.4 Explain the decline in American voter turnout.

Voter turnout declined in the last third of the twentieth century, in part because people saw fewer benefits to voting and in part because political parties and interest groups devoted less attention to voter mobilization. People are also less trusting of one another than in the past, a factor that affects turnout because many view voting as a social obligation.

6.5 Identify factors associated with higher and lower voter turnout.

Education, income, and age all increase the likelihood that someone will vote.

6.6 Evaluate the arguments about why low turnout is or is not a problem.

Some argue that voter turnout should be as high as possible because only then would elections represent the true will of the people. Evidence on this point is mixed: Polls show that in many respects, nonvoters and voters have similar preferences. Others say that regardless of its policy impact, voting is an important part of citizenship.

6.7 Assess the role of forms of political participation other than voting.

The 2004 and 2008 elections saw an increase in voter turnout, to levels not seen since the late 1960s. Nonetheless, American elections have typically experienced lower levels of voting than other counties. Americans are more likely than citizens of other countries to participate in other kinds of activities, however, such as contributing money or volunteering.

mypoliscilab EXERCISES

Apply what you learned in this chapter on MyPoliSciLab.

Read on mypoliscilab.com

eText: Chapter 6

Study and Review on mypoliscilab.com

Pre-Test

Post-Test

Chapter Exam

Flashcards

Watch on mypoliscilab.com

Video: Candidates Court College Students

Video: Chicago Worker Protest

Video: L.A. Riots: 15 Years Later

Video: Teen Sues for Equal Protection

Explore on mypoliscilab.com

Simulation: You Are an Informed Voter Helping Your Classmates Decide How to Vote

Simulation: You Are the Leader of Concerned Citizens for World Justice

Visual Literacy: Voting Turnout: Who Votes in the United States?

KEY TERMS

compositional effect, p. 169
franchise, p. 157
overvotes, p. 163
registered voters, p. 164

social connectedness, p. 169
social issues, p. 173
suffrage, p. 158
undervotes, p. 163

voter mobilization, p. 161
voting-age population, p. 163
voting eligible population, p. 163

SUGGESTED READINGS

Of General Interest

Dalton, Russell, *The Good Citizen*. Washington, DC: CQ Press, 2008. Argues that when participation is defined broadly today's young people are significantly more engaged than conventional wisdom suggests.

Keyssar, Alexander. *The Right to Vote*. Revised Edition. New York: Basic Books, 2009. A comprehensive history of the evolution of the suffrage in America.

Putnam, Robert. *Bowling Alone*. New York: Simon & Schuster, 2000. Monumental study of the decline of participation in social and political life. Argues that American life is less healthy because of the decline in civic engagement.

Verba, Sidney, Kay Schlozman, and Henry Brady. *Voice and Equality: Civic Volunteerism in American Politics*. Cambridge, MA: Harvard University Press, 1995. Fascinating discussion of the development of political skills in nonpolitical contexts such as churches. Strong on attention to differences involving race, ethnicity, and gender.

Wattenberg, Martin. *Is Voting for Young People?* New York: Longman, 2007. Documents the decline in voting and general political engagement among young people, not only in the United States but in other developed democracies. Calls for compulsory voting.

Focused Studies

Piven, Francis, and Richard Cloward. *Why Americans Still Don't Vote*. Boston: Beacon Press, 2000. This example of critical commentary on nonvoting in the United States contends that "have-nots" are systematically discouraged from voting.

Rosenstone, Steven, and John Mark Hansen. *Mobilization, Participation, and Democracy in America*. New York: Longman Classics ed., 2003. Statistical study of electoral and governmental participation from the 1950s to the 1980s, with particular emphasis on the decline in turnout.

Norris, Pippa. *Democratic Phoenix*. New York: Cambridge University Press, 2002. Comparative study of political and civic activism that questions the common belief that these types of activism are in decline.

ON THE WEB

Significant numbers of temporary organizations are designed to increase voter turnout (usually for a specific candidate). These organizations are usually closely tied to or run by a specific campaign. Organizations committed to a broader vision of democracy are not nearly so common.

www.lwv.org

Perhaps the oldest and most respected of permanent organizations is the League of Women Voters, born out of the suffrage movement around the turn of the century. This nonpartisan group works to encourage informed and active participation.

www.rochester.edu/SBA

A useful summary of the suffrage movement, including its history and important documents, can be found via the University of Rochester.

www.vote-smart.org

One of the most useful sites for citizens interested in how to participate, and in information on candidates, is Project Vote Smart. It is also a nonpartisan site with a wealth of information on candidate backgrounds, positions, and records.

7 Interest-Group Participation in American Democracy

CHAPTER OUTLINE

Interest Groups in the United States
Growth and Development of Groups • The Nature and Variety of "Interest Groups"

Forming and Maintaining Interest Groups
The Free-Rider Problem • Overcoming the Free-Rider Problem

How Interest Groups Influence Government
Government Lobbying • Grassroots Lobbying • Electioneering and PACs • Persuading the Public • Direct Action • Litigation • Why Groups Use Particular Tactics

How Influential Are Interest Groups?
Subgovernments • Issue Networks

Interest Groups and Democratic Politics

7.1   Trace the development of U.S. interest groups and characterize interest groups today.

7.2   Analyze the free-rider problem and how interest groups overcome the problem.

7.3   Outline strategies interest groups use to directly and indirectly influence government.

7.4   Assess the influence of interest groups on American politics.

7.5   Evaluate the pluralist account of the role of interest groups in American politics.

The Tea Party Movement

The British author James Bryce once observed that "Associations are created, extended, and worked in the United States more quickly and effectively than in any other country. . . . Such associations," he continued, "have great importance in the development of opinion, for they rouse attention, excite discussion, formulate principles, submit plans, embolden and stimulate their members, produce that impression of a spreading movement which goes so far towards success with a sympathetic and sensitive people."[1] Bryce wrote over a century ago, but he might have been describing the Tea Party movement that sprang into existence in twenty-first-century America.

The "Tea Party" name, of course, is even older than Bryce's writings: It harks back to the Boston Tea Party of December 16, 1773, when a band of colonists dumped three shiploads of tea into Boston harbor to protest the British tea tax. Since at least the 1980s, anti-tax protestors have identified with this seminal event, which led to the closing of Boston harbor and, two years later, to the outbreak of military hostilities in Lexington and Concord. Republican presidential candidate Ron Paul, who trumpeted his opposition to government spending, regulation, and taxes, raised $6 million on the 234th anniversary of the original Tea Party, December 16, 2007.[2]

Shortly after Barack Obama had been sworn into office in 2009 and led Congress to pass a $787 billion economic stimulus package, people throughout the country began to organize rallies to protest what they saw as an unprecedented expansion of the size and power of the federal government. By some accounts, the "original Tea Party advocate" is Keli Carender, a 30-year-old Seattle teacher who organized an early protest against the Democratic stimulus bill.[3] CNBC reporter Rick Santelli appears to have been the first to use the term "Tea Party" in conjunction with such protests. In a live report on February 19, 2009, an irate Santelli attacked an Obama-sponsored plan designed to help pay off delinquent mortgages, calling for a "Chicago Tea Party" in which "all you capitalists" should dump "some derivative securities" into Lake Michigan. Soon, newspapers began running articles about the modern "Tea Party movement."[4]

Whatever its origins, the Tea Party movement grew rapidly. Keli Carender's first rally drew only 120 people. But a second event the following week attracted 300 people, and a third, held on April 15, 2009 (the day income tax returns must be filed with the IRS), drew a crowd four times that size. Aided by the Internet, organizers held similar rallies and protests all over the country. Tea partiers helped produce a show of opposition to the Democratic healthcare initiative in townhall meetings in August 2009; a September "Taxpayers March on Washington" drew "many tens of thousands" of participants.[5] By January 2010, *The Economist*, a British magazine, would call the Tea Party movement "America's most vibrant political force."[6] That fall, dozens of Tea Party-backed candidates won election to Congress with calls to "rein in spending and reduce the size of government."

The Tea Party is not a single organization, but is instead a decentralized association of many locally based groups. No single group or individual leader can claim to speak for the Tea Party movement as a whole. One national Tea Party group, the Tea Party Patriots, makes this point clear in its statement of purpose: "We understand that we do not set the course for our member groups, as they have developed their own vision and plan for how to address the local and national challenges that they are facing."[7] A group called Tea Party Nation organized a national Tea Party convention in 2010—but many Tea Party members criticized the effort for charging participants a $549 admission fee, for paying a $100,000 speaking fee to Sarah Palin, and for trying to impose a leader on a movement that didn't want one.[8] Yet another group, called Tea Party Express, organizes national tours of conservative speakers and celebrities to rally support for the movement.

The Tea Party movement's critics argue that these groups do not really represent the views of most Americans. As liberal economist Paul Krugman puts it, "the tea parties don't represent a spontaneous outpouring of public sentiment. They're Astro Turf [fake grass roots] events, manufactured by the usual suspects. In particular, a key role is being played by Freedom Works, an organization run by Richard Armey, the former House majority leader, and supported by the usual group of right-wing billionaires."[9] Others disagree. Law professor and commentator Glenn Reynolds has argued, "These aren't the usual semiprofessional protesters who attend antiwar and pro-union marches. These are people with real jobs; most have never attended a protest march before."[10]

Making the Connection

The Tea Party movement illustrates the ambivalent role that interest groups have long played in American democracy. On the one hand, organized groups play a critical role in helping people engage with politics—rarely do disorganized individuals play a pivotal role in policy debates. When lots of Americans discovered that they shared common convictions about the direction of American government, they formed local groups and then tried, in various ways, to link those groups into state and national organizations and alliances. It is this kind of activity that led founding father James Madison to assert that group activity was "sown in the nature of man."[11] Yet, as Krugman's criticism suggests, many Americans are troubled by such organizations. Do organized groups present a distorted picture of what the public really thinks? Do they give more advantages to the wealthy than to moderate or low income people? Is it legitimate for the government to pay more attention to those who are organized and passionate than to those who are less engaged with politics?

In this chapter, we examine interest groups and how they influence government. First, we discuss how interest groups organize to communicate their views. Then, we consider the problems that interest groups face in mobilizing their members and how they overcome these obstacles. How interest groups try to influence government and whether they are successful in their attempts are our next concern. In the concluding section, we discuss whether interest groups contribute to or detract from democratic government.

7.1

Trace the development of U.S. interest groups and characterize interest groups today.

interest group

Organization or association of people with common interests that engages in politics on behalf of its members.

Interest Groups in the United States

Americans are joiners, more so than the citizens of most other democracies (see Table 7.1). More than three-quarters of Americans belong to at least one group; on average they belong to two and they make financial contributions to four.[12] Many of these associations allow citizens to participate indirectly in politics because they are **interest groups**—organizations or associations of people with common interests that participate in politics on behalf of their members.

Of course, not all the groups with which people associate are political groups—many are social clubs, charities, service organizations, religious groups, and so forth—but

TABLE 7.1

AMERICANS TEND TO BE JOINERS

Of nine democracies surveyed to assess their level of group membership, only the Netherlands rivaled the United States as a nation of joiners. The Dutch, like the Americans, are particularly likely to participate in religious groups.

	Percent Belonging to No Groups	Percent Belonging to Four or More Groups
Netherlands	7.6	37.3
United States	10.3	39.1
Canada	26.3	16.7
Germany (West)	28.9	11.6
Mexico	53.6	7.0
Italy	58.0	4.6
France	60.6	2.4
Britain	66.4	2.6
Spain	69.1	3.0

Source: Figures drawn from the World Values Surveys, 2000, and the ESS, 2002, for West Germany.

literally thousands of groups do engage in politics. Moreover, even seemingly nonpolitical groups can engage in political activity. For example, parent-teacher organizations are active in school politics. Neighborhood associations lobby city governments about traffic, crime, and zoning policies. Hobby or recreation groups mobilize when they perceive threats to their favored activities—witness the National Rifle Association.

Growth and Development of Groups

Americans have a long-standing reputation for forming groups. In his classic book *Democracy in America,* Alexis de Tocqueville noted that Americans

> . . . are forever forming associations. . . . [A]t the head of any new undertaking, where in France you would find the government or in England some territorial magnate, in the United States you are sure to find an association.[13]

Perhaps Americans form groups because of some tendency in our culture that stems from our historical experiences, but several features of the American political system also have encouraged the formation of groups.[14] In particular, federalism and the separation of powers mean that there are lots of "points of access" or "pressure points" that groups can use to influence policy. In many countries, a teachers' group that opposes some major change in educational policy would have to defeat the policy in the national legislature. In the United States, a teachers' group might seek support within either

A Recreational Group Turns Political

The NRA was founded shortly after the Civil War to promote marksmanship among hunters, target shooters, and gun collectors. By the mid-twentieth century, the NRA operated safety programs and trained law enforcement officers. It is now known, however, as the chief opponent of gun-control legislation.

• *Under what circumstances do you think a recreational group would choose to enter politics?*

chamber of Congress, from the president, or from state and local governments. And, even if the new policy were written into law, its implementation could still be fought in the courts or the bureaucracy.

Whatever the reasons, the American tendency to form groups continues today. But group formation in the United States has not been a steady process; it has occurred in waves.[15] Before the Civil War, there were few national organizations. Life in general was local. The social organization of the United States was one of "island communities" with few social and economic links between them.[16] As the railroads connected the country after the Civil War, however, a national economy developed—and national associations were not far behind. The first two decades after the war saw the birth of national agricultural associations such as the Grange and of trade unions such as the Knights of Labor and the American Federation of Labor.

Another major wave of group organization occurred during the Progressive Era, roughly 1890 to 1917. Many of today's most broadly based economic associations date from that era: the U.S. Chamber of Commerce, the National Association of Manufacturers, and the American Farm Bureau Federation, for example. Other sorts of associations sprang up as well. For example, intellectuals and activists founded the National Association for the Advancement of Colored People (NAACP) to promote equality for black Americans; conservationists founded the National Audubon Society.

The post-1960 wave of group formation was by far the largest and the most diverse. Thousands of additional economic groups formed, but these tended to be more narrowly based than earlier ones. The American Soybean Association, the National Corn Growers Association, the Rocky Mountain Llama and Alpaca Association, and numerous other specialized organizations joined the more general agricultural associations. Similarly, in the commercial and manufacturing sectors, numerous specialized groups joined the older, more broad-based groups.

What are sometimes called "government interest groups" proliferated as older national associations of mayors, governors, teachers, and social workers were joined by newer, more specialized associations such as the National Association of State and Provincial Lotteries, the Association of State Drinking Water Administrators, and the U.S. Police Canine Association. Similarly, nonprofit groups now include all kinds of specialized occupational associations. Examples of particular relevance to likely readers of this book include the National Association of Student Financial Aid Administrators and the National Association of Graduate Admissions Professionals.

Innumerable other shared-interest groups have formed in recent decades. Some groups advocate a particular political ideology. Liberal groups such as the National Organization for Women (NOW, a feminist group) and People for the American Way (a civil-liberties group) are deeply involved in politics, as are such conservative groups as the Christian Coalition (a group promoting traditional morality) and the Club for Growth (a group that advocates minimal government taxation and regulation). Self-proclaimed "citizens'" groups purport to promote the interests of everyone by seeking the public good—even though their policy goals sometimes are just as controversial as those of more openly ideological groups. Examples include Common Cause (a political "reform" group), Greenpeace (an environmental group), the National Taxpayers' Union (an anti-tax and anti-spending group), and numerous other "watchdog" organizations, most of which are less than a generation old. Some groups are so narrowly focused that they are known as **single-issue groups.** Well-known examples are pro-choice groups

single-issue group
An interest group narrowly focused to influence policy on a single issue.

such as NARAL and pro-life groups such as Operation Rescue, which play prominent roles in debates over abortion.

Nearly every significant interest or activity in American society has groups that represent it—and under the right circumstances almost any group may become involved in politics. Associations representing hunters and fishers monitor regulations affecting natural resources. Associations representing snowmobilers and mountain bikers mobilize when government threatens to restrict their use of public lands. The American Association of Retired Persons (AARP), established in 1958, has become the largest voluntary association ever. It boasts upward of 40 million members—and is still growing. AARP is a major player whenever social security or Medicare is on the political agenda, as the latter was during the debate over healthcare reform in 2009 and 2010.

Interest groups proliferated during the past generation because of changes in both politics and technology. Increased government activity gave people more reasons to form groups. Businesses, for instance, organized to protect themselves from new taxes and regulations or to seek new government grants and contracts. Advances in communications technology, meanwhile, made groups easier to form. Computer databases permit the generation of all kinds of specialized mailing lists—and, once they have located each other, people with common interests can communicate easily and cheaply via the Internet. Furthermore, once new groups organize, they may stimulate the formation of other groups opposed to them. The pro-life movement formed at least in part because of the activities of the pro-choice movement.[17] Similarly, in reaction to the successes of the environmental movement, ranching, mining, lumber, and sporting interests in western states organized a "sagebrush rebellion" that tried to give more control over federally owned land to state and local authorities, who were thought to be more concerned with commercial and economic development issues and less sympathetic to environmental interests.

The Nature and Variety of "Interest Groups"

Interest group scholar Robert Salisbury has called attention to the variety of groups, associations, and organizations included under the term *interest groups*.[18] Some have elaborate formal organizations with membership dues, journals, meetings, conventions, and so forth; the American Medical Association is a well-known example. Others are little more than an address where sympathizers send contributions. One recent study found that of 14,000 interest groups with offices in Washington, DC, only 12.5 percent were associations of individuals.[19]

Some associations, such as Common Cause, are "membership groups" composed of numerous private individuals who make voluntary contributions. Others are associations consisting of corporate or institutional representatives who pay regular dues; trade groups provide one example. Some large corporations maintain their own Washington, DC, offices for political reasons, as do hundreds of state, city, and county governments and even universities.

About two-thirds of the interest groups with a presence in Washington, DC, represent corporations, professional groups, governments, or unions.[20] For most of these groups, economic matters are of crucial concern—but, because these groups are divided between those representing profit-seeking constituencies and those representing public and nonprofit constituencies, they do not exert a uniform influence on government taxing and spending policies. The other American interest groups reflect the activities of citizens with shared political goals, including those spawned by what are called social movements: broad-based reform or protest movements that bring new issues to the agenda. The civil rights movement, the environmental movement, the women's movement, and the religious right are important contemporary examples. We shall have more to say about these later in the chapter.

7.2

Analyze the free-rider problem and how interest groups overcome the problem.

Forming and Maintaining Interest Groups

Because so many Americans belong to so many groups and associations, people often overlook the difficulties many groups face.[21] But consider these facts:

- There are more than 230 million adult consumers in the United States, but Consumers' Union, a venerable consumer watchdog group, has only 8 million subscribers to its newsletters.
- There are approximately 39 million African Americans in the United States, but the NAACP has only about 600,000 members—including whites.
- More than 42 million American households have at least one gun, but membership in the NRA is only about 4 million.
- Majorities of the more than 230 million American adult population consistently support spending more on the environment, but the largest U.S. environmental group, the Sierra Club, has only 1.3 million members.[22]

As these examples indicate, millions of people do *not* join or support associations whose interests they share. In many cases, groups and associations include 1 percent or less of their potential membership. Thus, common interest may be a necessary condition for joining a group, but it is far from a sufficient one.

Why, then, do people join or decline to join groups? The question is important, because the answer bears on how well or how poorly interest groups represent the American citizenry. If some kinds of interests are not fairly represented, politics may be biased, despite the existence of thousands of groups with millions of members.

Like voting, joining or supporting a group requires some investment of *resources*. It is a costly activity. Contributing money or paying dues is the most obvious example, but the time required for group activities can also be a significant cost. People who have more resources will find participation easier. Thus, it is no surprise that the affluent contribute more than the poor and that two-worker families with small children participate less than people with more free time.[23] Regardless of the personal resources available, however, an individual will surrender them only if the *incentive* to do so—the expected benefit—justifies the investment.

Incentives take many forms and different groups rely on different kinds of incentives. Noted interest-group scholar James Q. Wilson divides incentives into three categories.[24] The first he calls *solidary*. Some people join a group for social reasons: They simply wish to associate with particular kinds of people. Religious groups and campus Greek organizations are examples. Where solidary incentives are dominant, membership in the group is an end in itself. Most such groups are nonpolitical, however—people who wish to socialize with each other usually do not need politics as an excuse. Conversely, it is unlikely that people join the National Taxpayers' Union to enjoy the company of other taxpayers, and people certainly do not send checks to such associations for social purposes!

A second category of incentives is *material*. Such incentives are economic rather than social: Some people join a group because membership confers tangible benefits. These are obviously the dominant incentive for economic groups and associations. Microsoft does not belong to various trade associations because its executives like to socialize with other computer executives—they have plenty of other opportunities to do that. Microsoft belongs because the executives see trade associations as a way of protecting and advancing their corporate interests. Material incentives also play a role in some political groups. Those who join taxpayers' associations hope to reduce their taxes. Those who join groups that support government subsidies or services for people like themselves (realtors, the handicapped, senior citizens, farmers) similarly hope to gain material benefits.

Finally, some people join groups for *purposive* reasons: People are committed to and wish to advance the group's political goals. They want to save the whales, to end abortion or to preserve freedom of choice, to bring about a liberal or a conservative Congress. Given that politically active groups usually publicize their purposive goals, such incentives would appear to be the dominant factor underlying the formation and persistence of most of the groups that are active in politics. Things are not so simple as they appear, however.

The Free-Rider Problem

Most groups, but especially groups that rely on purposive incentives, face what is known as the **free-rider problem:** People can enjoy the benefits of group activity without bearing any of the costs. Thus, they have an incentive to "free-ride" on the efforts of others.[25] This problem arises when individuals perceive that attainment of the group goal has little relationship to their personal contribution. If you donate $20 to the environmental group 350.org, does your contribution noticeably affect the rate of climate change? If you donate several hours of your time to march for the end of hunger, does your contribution measurably reduce the amount of malnutrition in the world? Although most well-meaning people are reluctant to admit it, the truthful answer is no.

free-rider problem

Problem that arises when people can enjoy the benefits of group activity without bearing any of the costs.

Solidary Benefits

Some people form groups for social reasons, as in the case of this "flash mob" pillow fight on Wall Street in New York City.

• *Do you think social networking software has increased the potential for "solidary" groups, or has it not made much difference?*

These examples have two common elements. First, on reflection, people realize that their personal impact on a particular problem or issue is so small as to be unnoticeable. If you don't contribute, just as much climate change will occur, just as many children will starve. So, if your contribution makes no difference, why contribute? The second element makes matters worse: Individuals receive the benefit regardless of whether they contribute. If *other* people manage to stabilize the climate or reduce world hunger, you enjoy those outcomes even if you did nothing to help out. So, if you get the same benefit regardless of your actions, why contribute? These two conditions are major obstacles to group formation and survival. They encourage individuals to free-ride on the contributions of others, a dynamic that prevents some interests from organizing and almost always hinders the efforts of those groups that do form.

Two considerations affect the severity of the free-rider problem. First, other things being equal, the larger the group, the greater the problem. A few neighbors can pool their efforts to clean up a vacant lot that borders their properties. It is easy to identify those who don't show up and subject them to social pressure. It is a much more difficult matter, however, for a large city to rely on volunteer effort to maintain city parks. Social pressure is less effective where people do not know each other. Thus, cities usually pay municipal employees or private contractors to maintain their parks.

Second, other things being equal, the free-rider problem is more serious the greater the distance and abstractness of the benefit the group seeks to achieve. It is much easier to see one's personal impact on cleaning up a vacant lot than on cleaning up the atmosphere. It is much easier to see one's personal impact on feeding the poor in a specific locale than on reducing world hunger.

public goods
Goods enjoyed simultaneously by a group, as opposed to a private good that must be divided up to be shared.

At issue here are what economists call **public goods,** which are enjoyed simultaneously by all members of a category of people, as distinct from private goods, which must be divided up to be shared. An apple is a private good. If you consume it, others cannot. Clean air is a public good. If the air is clean, everyone benefits from breathing it. Similarly, a law or policy is a public good for you, if you favor such a law or policy. If gun rights are preserved, everyone gets them—not just members of the NRA. Economists believe that because free-riders can enjoy or consume public goods even if they make no contribution to their provision, such goods typically are provided at lower than optimal levels.[26]

Economic goods can be public goods, too, so interest groups with an economic orientation also face free-rider problems. If General Motors lobbies successfully for a tariff or quota on Korean cars, Ford will enjoy the benefits (lower competition, higher prices) even if it did not aid GM in the lobbying effort. If members of the Corn Growers Association pool their efforts to get a higher corn subsidy, even growers who are not members reap the benefit of the higher subsidy. The free-rider problem is widespread.

The most important implication of the free-rider problem for democratic politics lies in the kinds of groups best able to overcome it. Our discussion suggests that—again, other things being equal—small groups organized for narrow purposes have an organizational advantage over large groups organized for broad purposes. For example, a small number of corporations will find it relatively easy to organize an association to lobby for regulations that raise prices; the millions of consumers who buy the products the corporations sell will find it much more difficult to organize an association to lobby against such anticompetitive regulations. The free-rider problem implies that democratic politics will favor narrow "special" interests at the expense of the broader "public" interest.

www.caglecartoons.com 04/07/06 Mike Keefe THE DENVER POST

A Swing and a Miss

The free-rider and other problems notwithstanding, attempts to limit the power of interest groups have not been very successful. In 2007, for example, Congress enacted lobbying reforms that, at least in the view of this cartoonist, did little to achieve their purported goal.

Overcoming the Free-Rider Problem

On first learning about the free-rider problem, some idealists protest, "What if everyone felt that way?" Well, a great many people do; that is why so many groups mobilize such a small proportion of their potential constituencies. Still, there are groups that represent broad purposive interests. How do these groups manage to overcome the free-rider problem? History reveals a number of useful strategies.

Coercion   If members of a labor union strike for higher wages, how can they prevent nonunion workers from enjoying the results? Historically, the answer has been coercion. Social pressure and even violence have been used to compel reluctant workers to join unions or prevent them from crossing union picket lines. Because violence is costly to inflict and often brings violence in return, unions preferred to rely on a strategy of negotiating "closed shops" with management. Such agreements require workers to join the union as a condition of employment.

Milder forms of coercion are still widespread, although they are often unrecognized. For example, professional and occupational associations lobby governmental jurisdictions to hire or certify only their members, thus making membership a condition of working or practicing in that jurisdiction. Practicing law usually requires membership in the state bar. Engaging in specialized trades such as plumbing or professions such as teaching may require a state license or other official recognition. Such requirements reward the members of professional and occupational associations, while denying benefits to potential free-riders.

Although it has been very effective historically, coercion appears to be a declining means of overcoming the free-rider problem. Society no longer tolerates the informal violence once associated with strikes, and state governments no longer regulate many of the occupations and professions they once did. As a result, occupational interest groups have lost members and influence. The union movement in particular has fallen on hard times, its membership declining from more than one-third of the workforce to less than one-eighth.[27]

social movement
Broad-based demand for government action on some problem or issue, such as civil rights for blacks, equal rights for women, or environmental protection.

Social Movements   At times, people do not think individualistically, as they do when they free-ride. In these instances, large numbers of people get swept up in a social cause. Such **social movements**—broad-based demands for government action on a problem or issue—have a long history in American politics. The abolitionist movement is one of the best known. Dedicated to ending slavery, the abolitionists forced the issue onto the national agenda. Their activism played a role in the political upheaval of the 1850s and, ultimately, in the outbreak of the Civil War. Other nineteenth-century social movements included the Populist and labor movements in the 1880s and 1890s and the women's suffrage movement, which culminated in passage of the Nineteenth Amendment in 1920.

The civil rights movement is probably the best-known example of a social movement in modern times. As we will discuss in Chapter 17, the massive demonstrations of the 1960s evolved from a few sit-ins and boycotts in the 1950s. The movement culminated with the adoption of landmark federal legislation: the Civil Rights Act of 1964 and the Voting Rights Act of 1965.

Other movements soon followed. On April 22, 1970, Earth Day marked the sudden eruption of an environmental movement. Within the year, the United States had an Environmental Protection Agency and a Clean Air Act. The women's movement took off at about the same time, flexing its muscle in the 1972–1982 campaign for ratification of the Equal Rights Amendment (ERA). The amendment was approved in 35 states, three short of the three-fourths majority needed to adopt a constitutional amendment (see Chapter 17).[28] On the other side of the political spectrum, the ranks of the religious right swelled in the late 1970s and contributed to Ronald Reagan's presidential victories in the 1980s and to the Republican congressional resurgence in the 1990s.[29] The movement supports constitutional amendments to outlaw abortion and ban same-sex marriage, but, similar to the feminists, the religious right has been unable as yet to achieve constitutional change.[30]

Social movements build on emotional or moral fervor. Many of those active within such movements dedicate themselves to what they see as a higher cause. When individuals think more collectively than individually, they may ignore the considerations that normally would lead them to free-ride. Yet, even in these cases, social movements typically mobilize only small proportions of the population. Some people can be induced to think in moral or collective terms, but not many. Moreover, most people cannot sustain political passions for long, especially once demands for reform get bogged down in the tedious details of legislation and bureaucratic regulations. Thus, a social movement has a tendency to "run down" as its emotional basis subsides. For a social movement to exert long-term influence, it must find a way to "institutionalize" itself—to spin off organized groups and formal associations that will continue to work for its political goals. At that point, it faces the same free-rider problem as any other organized interest.

Increasing the Perceived Impact   As we discussed earlier, the free-rider problem occurs because most people do not believe that their own contribution of time or money will have any noticeable impact on a particular issue or problem area. In an attempt to overcome this obstacle, groups may reformulate their appeals in order to suggest that even small contributions will have a measurable, concrete impact. For example, Kiva is an organization founded in 2005 that links particular contributors to particular "microfinance" projects in countries around the world. A student in Texas might lend $25 through Kiva to a family in Mongolia that wishes to purchase an energy-efficient stove. Kiva accepts the loan through its website and updates the donor on the progress of the family and its stove purchase. More than 720,000 people have used Kiva since it started operations.[31] In reality, the relationship between donor and recipient is more indirect than it seems, however: Kiva pools contributions and sends them to lending institutions abroad, which in turn make loans to needy individuals. As one researcher put it, "the person-to-person donor-to-borrower connections created by Kiva are partly fictional. I suspect that most Kiva users do not realize this."[32] Regardless of whether users realize it, however, the "personal connections" are an effective way of solving the free-rider problem by making the donor's impact seem significant.

Selective Benefits   Many groups that work to achieve collective goods also provide their members with valuable private goods. Professional associations publish journals and magazines that contain occupationally useful information but restrict subscriptions to members. Trade associations inform their members—and only their members—about important technological advances. Agricultural associations provide their members—and only their members—with the latest information about new varieties of crops and new growing methods. In short, people, corporations, and institutions may join associations less to support the collective goods that the association supports than to take advantage of the specific private goods that the association provides—selectively—to members: its **selective benefits.**

The American Association of Retired Persons (AARP) offers the most notable example of this strategy for overcoming the free-rider problem. For a mere $16 per year, members gain access to the world's largest mail-order pharmacy (where volume buying keeps prices low); low-cost auto, health, and life insurance; discounts on hotels, airfares, and car rentals; and numerous other benefits. Even a senior citizen who disagrees with the political positions of AARP finds it hard to forgo membership!

Selective benefits are not limited to direct economic benefits or to information that indirectly produces economic benefits. Anything that people like and that can be selectively provided may be a selective benefit. Some environmental groups produce magazines full of beautiful pictures, organize outings and activities, rate outdoor clothing and equipment, and so forth. These and other benefits of membership often are sufficient to induce people to pay the modest amounts that membership requires. In short, what seems to be the principal reason for a group's existence may not be the principal reason why many people belong.

And this anomaly, in turn, often creates significant questions about how well interest groups represent the political views of their members. The American Association of Retired Persons, for example, regularly issues statements and lobbies Congress on issues that affect the elderly. But, if most people join the AARP not because of its political stances but because of the various insurance, healthcare, and travel benefits, there is no guarantee that the members will agree with the association's positions. In particular, the AARP is often accused of having a staff and leadership that are considerably more liberal

selective benefits
Specific private goods that an organization provides only to its contributing members.

Perceived Impact
Kiva and other organizations encourage contributions by stressing the impact of each donation on individual cases, such as Ana Helena Domingos, who used a small loan to expand her wholesale business in Angola.

• *Why are such strategies likely to diminish the free-rider problem?*

than its membership. In 2009 and 2010, the AARP strongly supported the Obama administration's attempt to restructure the American healthcare system, and Democrats often pointed to that support as an indication that the Democratic plans would not hurt senior citizens. Yet, many polls showed that seniors as a whole were opposed to Obama's efforts. In August 2009, the organization admitted that between 50,000 and 60,000 AARP members had left the group in protest over its healthcare position.[33] Other critics claimed that the AARP supported Obama's efforts because the organization stood to gain substantial new revenues for itself by endorsing various private insurance policies targeted at the elderly.[34]

Patrons and Political Entrepreneurs   Discussions of the free-rider problem typically reflect a bottom-up notion of how groups form. The implicit assumption is that individual people, corporations, or institutions band together and form associations. Recent research, however, indicates that the process of group formation often is more top-down than bottom-up. Many groups owe their existence to a **political entrepreneur,** an individual or a small number of individuals who are willing to assume the costs of forming and maintaining an organization even when others may free-ride on them.[35]

In the first place, some individuals, institutions, or corporations are so influential that they do not face the free-rider problem. Their contributions to a group effort are not futile; they make a measurable difference. Microsoft founder Bill Gates stands at the head of a charitable foundation with a $35 billion endowment, for example.[36] This foundation has prevented 4 million premature deaths through its child immunization efforts alone, according to the World Health Organization.[37] Large corporations also can have a significant stake in the health of their industries. Their share of any group benefit is so great that they are not likely to consider political gains to be a public good. Google, for example, has its own Washington, DC, office staffed by paid employees. When the interests of Internet firms are at risk, Google may be willing to mobilize its team of lobbyists to protect the industry even if smaller firms free-ride, as in 2010 when Google organized a coalition of groups to lobby on electronic privacy issues.[38] Sometimes a large firm will bear most of the costs to support an industry association, which gives the appearance of a broad base of support.

Similarly, a wealthy individual with a deep commitment to the group goal may be able to make a difference. Your $20 contribution to Greenpeace may have no measurable impact, but if you are in a position to give a million dollars you can probably save some whales. Foundations also support interest groups with grants and contracts. In 2009, for example, the Ford Foundation gave grants to 50 different environmental and development groups, totaling $11.8 million.[39] Similarly, conservative foundations help to fund the Wise Use Movement, which opposes traditional environmental groups.

In the second place, political entrepreneurs often set up and maintain a group for their own reasons. Their motives are varied. Some feel so strongly about a goal that they are willing to let others free-ride on them. Others hope that the group may provide a platform for launching a candidacy for elective office. We call such people either fanatical or dedicated, depending on whether we sympathize with their goals. An ascetic lawyer, Ralph Nader, did more than anyone else to organize the consumer movement and has devoted his life to it. Candy Lightner formed Mothers Against Drunk Driving after a man on bail from his third drunken-driving charge killed her daughter (see the *Election Voices!* feature in Chapter 3). During the 1990s, Ross Perot founded and subsidized his own political party.

political entrepreneurs
People willing to assume the costs of forming and maintaining an organization even when others may free-ride on them.

Of course, some political entrepreneurs do have ulterior motives. They may be aspiring politicians who see an opportunity to use new groups as the basis of future constituencies. Candidates for city and state offices often emerge from neighborhood associations and local protest groups. They may enjoy the celebrity or power that comes from leadership positions. They may be able to convert their fame into board appointments, consulting contracts, or book royalties. In short, self-seeking political entrepreneurs may invest their resources in interest-group organization the same way that profit-seeking business entrepreneurs invest their resources in founding companies— taking on greater personal risk than others in the hope of reaping disproportionate personal gains if they succeed.

The government itself did much to organize the new groups of the 1960s and 1970s. As the role of government expanded, federal bureaucracies needed new ways to implement programs through a decentralized federal system. One strategy was to stimulate and subsidize organizations that they could use to help develop standards and regulations, and to publicize them and carry them out. (Examples include the American Public Transit Association and the American Council on Education.) These groups were politically useful as well because they often promoted generous funding of government programs. Not surprisingly, groups and associations that receive federal funds are more than twice as likely to support expanded government activity—and, by implication, the elected officials who expand it—as groups that do not.[40]

The available evidence suggests that the top-down activities of patrons and political entrepreneurs are a more important means of overcoming the free-rider problem than the provision of selective benefits, AARP notwithstanding.[41] Wealthy individuals, government agencies, corporations, and private foundations have been important sources of support for nonprofit-sector groups, especially citizens groups. About 90 percent of the latter have received such subsidies.

How Interest Groups Influence Government

The variety of groups, associations, and institutions that make up the interest-group universe engage in a wide array of political activities. We first discuss these political activities, which include government lobbying, grassroots lobbying, electioneering and political action committees, persuading the public, direct action, and litigation. We then focus on why groups choose certain tactics over others.

Government Lobbying

Many interest groups attempt to influence government the old-fashioned way: by lobbying public officials. **Lobbying** consists of interest-group activities intended to influence directly the decisions that public officials make. Groups and associations draft bills for friendly legislators to introduce, testify before congressional committees and in agency proceedings, meet with elected officials to present their cases, and provide public officials with information. In these and other ways, group representatives try to influence those who make governmental decisions.

People who engage in lobbying are called **lobbyists,** although the term is usually reserved for those who do it as their primary job. Some lobbyists are so-called "hired guns," people who will use their contacts and expertise in the service of just about anyone willing to pay their price, but some of the best known are closely associated with

7.3

Outline strategies interest groups use to directly and indirectly influence government.

lobbying
Interest-group activities intended to influence directly the decisions that public officials make.

lobbyist
One who engages in lobbying, especially as his or her primary job.

one political party or the other. Many large groups and associations have their own staff lobbyists. Others hire lobbyists on a part-time basis or share a lobbyist with other groups. Some groups simply have their own leaders engage in lobbying, although these individuals typically are not called lobbyists.

Lobbying to ensure favorable national policies and to prevent unfavorable ones has become a massive American industry. Spending on lobbying activities reached $3.47 billion in 2009; even with the recession in progress, lobbying expenditures increased 5 percent over the previous year. Corporations account for the lion's share of lobbying expenditures. The biggest spending business sector in 2009, not surprisingly, was the pharmaceutical and health products industry, which spent $266 million on lobbying. The largest lobbying firm, Patton Boggs, earned nearly $40 million from its lobbying work.[42]

There are federal and state laws that require lobbyists to register; however, because of disagreement about what lobbying is and who a lobbyist is, as well as lack of enforcement, those who register are only a fraction of those engaged in lobbying.[43] For example, the Center for Responsive Politics counts approximately 20,000 registered lobbyists in Washington, but it reports that the true numbers are many times higher than that.[44]

The term *lobbyist* has negative connotations; few parents dream that their child will grow up to be one. Movies, novels, and newspapers often portray lobbyists as unsavory characters who operate on the borders of what is ethical or legal—prompting critics to call for reform (see the *Election Voices!* feature on page 208). Although the media plays up every lobbying scandal, most scholars believe that the popular image of widespread illegality is an exaggeration. Numerous conflict-of-interest laws and regulations, along with an investigative media ever on the lookout for a hint of scandal, make outright corruption in today's politics rarer than in earlier eras of American history. Still, there is just enough truth behind the stereotype to make it credible. In 2006, for example, the well-connected lobbyist Jack Abramoff pled guilty to three felony counts in return for testimony that led to the conviction of two White House officials and a congressman. Among other things, Abramoff devised an imaginative scam in which he would take money from an Indian tribe seeking legislation to be passed that would close down a rival casino. Then, after the legislation was passed, he would go to the tribe that owned the closed casino and collect a lobbying fee to have its casino reopened.[45]

Scholars believe that lobbyists spend much more time providing sympathetic public officials with information and supporting arguments than they do trying to persuade skeptical officials to change their minds.[46] Lobbyists have little incentive to lie; to do so would destroy their credibility and undermine their future effectiveness. Of course, lobbyists are strategic actors who emphasize arguments and information favorable to their viewpoints, but they do not want to hurt their political allies by lying, concealing information, or otherwise exposing them to an embarrassing counterattack.[47] Many political scientists think that lobbyists serve a useful purpose, injecting valuable information into the legislative process. As former Senator and President John F. Kennedy observed,

> Competent lobbyists can present the most persuasive arguments in support of their positions. Indeed, there is no more effective manner of learning all important arguments and facts on a controversial issue than to have the opposing lobbyists present their case.[48]

With the explosive growth of interest groups during the past generation, there is undoubtedly more old-fashioned lobbying than ever before. Spending on lobbying increased by 85 percent between 1998 and 2009, even after accounting for inflation.[49] The number of active registered lobbyists increased by one-third during the same period, and some experts estimate that increases have been far higher depending upon how lobbying activity is defined.[50] Changes in the structure and organization of Congress (see Chapter 12) and the expansion of government helped stimulate such developments. In 1950, a group might have to lobby only one powerful committee chair or a key staffer, but in 2010 it had to lobby numerous subcommittee chairs as well as the rank and file and many of their staff.

Grassroots Lobbying

Whereas lobbying consists of attempts to influence government officials *directly*, **grassroots lobbying** consists of attempts to influence elected officials *indirectly* through their constituents. A Washington association communicates with its grassroots supporters, who in turn put pressure on their elected representatives. In recent years, specialized firms have cropped up that help companies and groups target local constituents—for a hefty fee. DDC Advocacy, for example, promises its clients "advocacy strategies that engage and empower the most credible constituent voices in support of your goals." Through targeted online communications, and engagement with local sympathizers, DDC Advocacy boasts that in one case it "generated more than 30,000 communications to Congress in less than two weeks on a single issue."[51]

grassroots lobbying
Attempts by groups and associations to influence elected officials indirectly through their constituents.

Some scholars believe that grassroots lobbying has grown in importance and the effectiveness of traditional lobbying has faded. As one healthcare lobbyist put it,

> One of the perceptions about lobbying is that you go out drinking, and the guy's your buddy so he does you favors. . . . Those days are long gone. That sort of thing may work on tiny things like a technical amendment to a bill, but on big, important issues personal friendships don't mean a thing.[52]

One reason that friendships may not sway policy is that Congress is more decentralized than it once was. When only a few leaders need to be persuaded, a personal approach may suffice. When dozens need to be persuaded, reaching out and touching their constituents through grassroots lobbying may be more effective—especially given the advent of modern communications technology. Also, government in general is more open than in the past. It is not so easy for Washington insiders to make private deals. It is more important than ever to show that there is popular support for a group's position. Grassroots mobilization can create an image of popularity.

One of the newest innovations in grassroots lobbying is "grass-tops" lobbying.[53] In this variation, an interest group makes an ad featuring a prominent local personality— especially one who is an important supporter of a member of Congress—and then plays the ad in the member's district. Such ads signal members in no uncertain terms that influential people back home stand behind the group's goals.

By no means should anyone think that grassroots lobbying is a new tactic, however; it has been around for a long time. In a classic study of the Anti-Saloon League (a prohibition group), Peter Odegard noted that this group had more than 500,000 names on its mailing list nearly a century ago—long before dependable long-distance telephone service, let alone email, Facebook, and Twitter![54] Influencing government officials' views by reaching out to their constituents is nothing new, but decentralized political institutions and rapid advances in communications technology have made such a strategy more attractive than ever.

Electioneering and PACs

Personal and grassroots lobbying try to influence the views of public officials on particular issues. One way to affect the views of public officials more generally is by influencing who gets elected in the first place. Groups have always been involved in the electoral process, supporting some candidates and opposing others—but, as the role of party organizations in campaigns and elections has eroded, and as campaigns have become more expensive, groups have become more active than ever before. A principal vehicle of this tactic is the political action committee.

political action committee (PAC)
Specialized organization for raising and spending campaign funds; often affiliated with an interest group or association.

Political action committees (PACs) are specialized organizations for raising and spending campaign funds. Many are affiliated with an interest group or association. They come in as many varieties as the interests they represent.[55] Some, such as the realtors' RPAC and the doctors' AMPAC, represent big economic interests. Others represent thousands of smaller interests—the beer wholesalers, for example, have SixPAC. Not all PACs represent economic interests. Supporters of Israel donate to AIPAC and NATPAC. Supporters of abortion rights send money to NARAL-PAC, while their pro-life adversaries send money to National Right to Life PAC. Pro-choice Republicans uncomfortable with the liberal positions of NARAL can give money to WISH LIST. Scores of individual politicians have established their own personal PACs.[56]

Like interest groups in general, PACs enjoyed explosive growth in the 1970s and 1980s, as Figure 7.1 shows. Reflecting the overall contours of the interest-group system, far more PACs represent business and commercial interests than represent labor or citizen interests.

FIGURE 7.1

PACS FORMED RAPIDLY AFTER THE 1974 FEDERAL ELECTION CAMPAIGN ACT (FECA) REFORMS

Whereas most PACs were once affiliated with labor unions, corporate PACs now dominate the field.

• *What groups in the American population are under- or over-represented?*

Source: "Number of Federal PACs Increases," Federal Election Commission press release, March 9, 2009, www.fec.gov/press/press2009/20090309PACcount.shtml, accessed June 6, 2010.

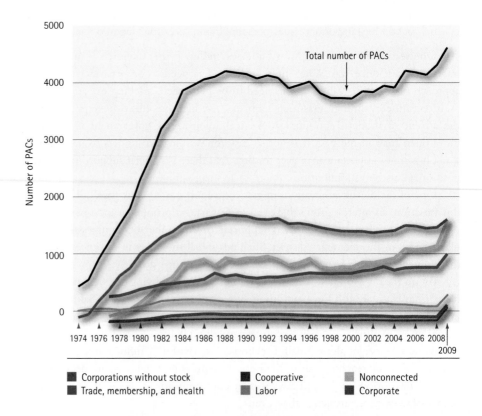

As their numbers have proliferated, PACs have played an increasingly prominent role in congressional campaign finance. (Most PACs do not get involved in presidential campaigns.) During the 2008 election cycle, 18 percent of the money contributed to Senate candidates and 31 percent of the money contributed to candidates for the House of Representatives came from political action committees.[57] Most PACs tend to give to candidates who are likely to win, in order to establish good relations with and access to the people who will occupy key positions in Congress after the election. Thus, most PACs contribute to incumbents, especially to incumbent members of key committees, regardless of party. When the Republicans are in the majority in Congress, as they were in 2005, PACs tend to give a very large proportion of their contributions to Republicans (see Table 7.2). By contrast, when Democrats are in the majority, as they were after the 2006 elections, business PACs give a lot more of their money to Democrats.

There is widespread public dissatisfaction with the role of PACs in campaign finance. The popular perception of campaign contributions is that they buy elections or buy support from elected officials. The PAC problem is exaggerated by the popular media, however. Most research has failed to establish a significant relationship between contributions and legislative votes.[58] PAC contributions tend to be small and are intended as a way of gaining access to public officials. Moreover, there is evidence that politicians extort PACs, pressuring them to buy tickets to fund-raisers and otherwise to make contributions as a condition of continued access. For example, a former congressional staffer told one of us the following story:

> In our office we loved the FEC [Federal Election Commission] reports. We'd comb through them and list all the business groups who had contributed to our opponent. Then we'd call them up and say, "Hey, we noticed that you contributed to our opponent's campaign. The Congressman just wants you to know that there are no hard feelings. In fact, we're holding a fund-raiser in a few weeks; we hope you'll attend and tell us your concerns."

TABLE 7.2		
BUSINESS PAC CONTRIBUTIONS TEND TO FOLLOW POLITICAL POWER—WHEN CONTROL OF CONGRESS CHANGED, SO DID THE PATTERN OF BUSINESS CONTRIBUTIONS		
	Percentage of Contributions to Republicans Jan.–Mar. 2005 (Republican majority)	Percentage of Contributions to Republicans Jan.–Mar. 2007 (Democratic majority)
Commercial Banks	69	55
Defense Aerospace	60	48
Electric Utilities	73	50
Health Professionals	66	43
Insurance	71	50
Securities and Investment	69	48
Lawyers and Law Firms	52	32

Source: Washington Post database on quarterly PAC giving, www.washingtonpost.com/wp-srv/special/politics/corporate_pac/index.html, accessed June 6, 2010.

Thus, influence runs in both directions; elected officials are not just pawns to be moved around by interest groups. Furthermore, at the risk of sounding too complacent, we suggest that reformers have not identified a clear means to keep money out of politics. In fact, the proliferation of PACs is partly an unintended consequence of a previous attempt to reform campaign finance.[59]

Persuading the Public

issue advocacy
Advertising campaigns that attempt to influence public opinion in regard to a specific policy proposal.

In recent years, what has come to be called **issue advocacy** has grown in prominence: Groups conduct advertising campaigns designed to move public opinion in regard to some policy proposal. This interest-group strategy overlaps somewhat with grassroots lobbying. There is no way to quantify all the issue advocacy spending that occurs in American politics: television and newspaper ads purchased by organized or ad hoc groups; company or union newsletters; groups leaders who appear as guests on television and radio programs; group-initiated letters to the editor; books written by group leaders or group-sponsored scholars. One of the few categories of issue advocacy spending that is monitored is the spending by so-called "527 committees," named after the provision in the federal tax code that governs their activities. These committees are organizations set up for the purpose of influencing the nomination and election of candidates for public office, although since they cannot directly advocate voting for or against a specific candidate, they generally do so by discussing the candidates' positions on the issues. In the 2008 election cycle, 527 groups spent $489 million.[60]

Many groups communicate with citizens even when no specific legislation or regulation is at issue. Their goal is to build general support for the group and its interests so that it will be more successful in the long run. Thus, in 2010, the U.S. Chamber of Commerce sponsored a nationwide "I Am Free Enterprise" video contest, in which entrepreneurs were encouraged to tell their stories in creative YouTube clips.[61] Such efforts are not specifically directed at a government activity or proposed law, but are simply attempts to publicize information and arguments favorable to business in general.

Interest-group advocacy has become increasingly aggressive. Elected officials today rarely have the luxury of "down time" between campaigns. They never know when a group might launch an issue advocacy campaign against them even if an election is far away. For example, in 2009 New York public employee unions ran a series of ads attacking Democratic Governor David Paterson for proposing layoffs as part of a budget deal. Although the election was 18 months away, union leaders defended the effort as a way to bring more leverage to bear on the negotiations. "We're trying to just say it a little more loudly and a little more aggressively, just to get someone's attention."[62]

direct mail
Computer-generated letters, faxes, and other communications by interest groups to people who might be sympathetic to an appeal for money or support.

One communications technique that is a product of modern electronic communications is **direct mail**.[63] Groups compile computerized mailing lists of people who might be favorably disposed toward their leader or cause and then send out computer-generated letters, emails, and other communications soliciting financial contributions. Often, in an attempt to scare or provoke the recipient into contributing, the mailing exaggerates the threat the group faces. Some groups depend almost completely on direct-mail fundraising for their budgets. The citizens' group Common Cause, for example, prides itself on its dependence on small contributions.[64] Once again, the rise of the Internet makes the direct-mail strategy both easier and cheaper. Tabulating who visits various websites makes it possible to compile email lists and contact prospective supporters for a much lower cost than that of traditional "snail mail" campaigns.[65]

Finally, any group likes to have favorable media coverage for its activities and points of view. Thus, groups are always on the lookout for opportunities to get such coverage—to plant stories, to associate themselves with popular issues and candidates, and to position themselves as opponents of unpopular issues and candidates. In sum, whether we call it public relations or education, communication with a wider audience is a significant concern for many interest groups.

Direct Action

As we noted in Chapter 2, protests, boycotts, and violence were an endemic feature of politics during the lead-up to the American Revolution and the first years under the Constitution. But these early conflicts were by no means the end of **direct action,** a term that includes everything from peaceful sit-ins and demonstrations to riots and even rebellion by citizens opposed to government policies. Urban workers rioted against the Civil War draft in 1863. In the 1880s and 1890s, state or federal troops battled strikers from West Virginia to Idaho and from Michigan to Texas. In 1932, more than 20,000 veterans marched on Washington and were dispersed by federal troops.[66]

direct action
Everything from peaceful sit-ins and demonstrations to riots and even rebellion.

Usually, tactics such as boycotts, sit-ins, marches, and demonstrations appeal to the members of social movements. These groups may be too disorganized to use established means of influencing government, or they may lack access to the resources needed to exploit other political strategies. Whereas boycotts and demonstrations are sometimes designed to disrupt the normal activities of governments or corporations and thereby compel them to accede to a group's demands, direct action is often organized for the purpose of gaining sympathetic coverage in the news media and thereby influencing public opinion. In one particularly famous episode in the civil rights movement, in March 1965 Dr. Martin Luther King Jr. attempted to lead a march from Selma, Alabama, to the state capitol in Montgomery to protest African Americans' inability to register to vote in many southern states. Shortly after setting out, the marchers were brutally beaten by state troopers. The attacks on the nonviolent demonstrators were widely shown on television and recounted in newspapers, where they horrified many Americans and, by all accounts, dramatically increased public support for the civil rights movement. Just eight days later, President Lyndon Johnson presented a voting rights bill to a joint session of Congress—a bill that ultimately became the landmark Voting Rights Act of 1965.

Litigation

As we shall see in detail in Chapter 17, the modern civil rights movement followed a careful legal strategy, selecting cases to litigate that eventually led to the landmark 1954 ruling *Brown v. Board of Education of Topeka, Kansas.* Drawing lessons from the success of the civil rights movement, environmentalists, feminists, advocates for the disabled, poor people, and other groups followed suit.[67]

Litigation strategies are by no means limited to groups ordinarily thought of as liberal. In the 1970s, the Pacific Legal Foundation was set up to oppose environmental protection groups. The U.S. Chamber of Commerce established a National Chamber Litigation Center to support business interests in the courts. And the religious right founded the Christian Legal Society, which focuses on issues of church and state.[68] Liberal groups continue to be more active in the courts, perhaps because they tend to find a friendlier audience among the members of the legal profession, but conservatives sometimes win important courtroom victories.

In addition to actually litigating cases, which is an expensive activity, interest groups engage in other activities intended to influence the course of litigation. Although it is improper to lobby judges directly, groups stage demonstrations in front of courthouses, generate letters and telegrams to judges, and file *amicus curiae* (a Latin term meaning "friend of the court") briefs in cases in which they are not otherwise directly involved.

Why Groups Use Particular Tactics

Different groups use different strategies or mixes of strategies. How they decide to allocate their resources depends both on their own characteristics and on the characteristics of the political situation in which they are operating.

Group Characteristics   How a group decides to deploy its resources depends on what kind of group it is, what kind of resources it has, and how much it has in the way of resources. A trade association representing profitable corporations has a Washington office with a full-time staff of experts. This gives such associations the wherewithal to maintain close personal contact with government decision makers. A mass-membership group may find grassroots lobbying a more effective use of its resources. A public-interest law firm with no citizen membership will naturally follow a litigation strategy; indeed, the group may have been formed by lawyers precisely because they wished to engage in such activities. A social movement representing a disadvantaged constituency such as the poor may find that direct action is the only means of calling attention to its cause. Wealthy groups of any size or type may find campaign contributions and media campaigns to be useful investments.

Some observers suggest that groups with a federal structure—local chapters under a national leadership—have a fundraising advantage because contributions are solicited by people personally known to members rather than by an impersonal mailing. In addition, such groups have chapters in many communities and therefore are constituents of a large number of representatives, which may give them an advantage in grassroots lobbying. Interest groups representing realtors, doctors, and banks are good examples.

Situational Characteristics   One of the reasons why the civil rights movement adopted a litigation strategy was that more traditional strategies were unavailable. African Americans were disenfranchised in much of the South (where most of them then lived) and were politically discriminated against elsewhere. In the Congresses of the 1940s and 1950s, the path of civil rights legislation was blocked by senior committee chairmen from the South. African Americans as a group were not wealthy, and they were a small minority of the population. As the movement won legal backing for its political activities and gained support, it was able to engage in direct action and later in electioneering to advance its goals further.

In contrast, an industry or corporation interested in the fine details of a bill or regulation may find it better to send an expert representative to discuss the matter with members of Congress and their staff or with regulators. Studies show that corporations spend much more on lobbying than they do on campaign contributions, probably reflecting their interest in legislative detail as opposed to their interest in the general ideological position of the legislator.[69]

Direct mail and other modern advertising and persuasion techniques were developed largely by conservative groups, probably because for 40 years Congress was controlled by Democrats who had little sympathy for their demands. Between 2001 and 2006, Republicans controlled the presidency, the House, and, for all but a year and a half, the Senate. Hence, conservative groups frequently engaged in direct lobbying during these years, while liberal groups were more likely to resort to protests and demonstrations, particularly against the Iraq war. By contrast, in 2009 and 2010, when Democrats occupied the White House and had majorities in both houses of Congress, it was Republicans who seem to have relied more on direct action of various kinds, as the description of the Tea Party at the beginning of this chapter indicates.

In sum, various situational characteristics—party control of Congress and the presidency, the economic situation, the mood in the country, what the interest group seeks to achieve and the resources it has to meet its goals—interact with the characteristics of interest groups to determine what mix of strategies the groups adopt.

How Influential Are Interest Groups?

7.4

Assess the influence of interest groups on American politics.

The answer to this question is a matter of enormous disagreement. On the one hand, some critics believe that interest groups dominate American politics. One critic charges that the United States suffers from "demosclerosis," a condition in which interest groups clog the veins and arteries of the body politic and thereby prevent action of any kind on many important problems.[70] Another claims that Americans have the "best Congress money can buy."[71] Certainly, the number of groups, the volume of their activities, and their massive expenditure of resources amount to strong circumstantial evidence that groups and associations are very influential in politics.

On the other hand, academic research yields conclusions that are less clear. Indeed, some of the most expert students of interest-group politics contend that a great deal of what groups do is canceled out.[72] There are so many groups, and so many *opposed* groups, that the efforts of one association's high-priced lobbyist only offset the efforts of another's, one group's media campaign only counteracts the effects of another's, one group's direct-mail barrage only neutralizes the effects of another's, and so on.

Even if the overall picture is ambiguous, it seems clear that changes in American politics have diminished the influence of interest groups in at least some areas. In particular, various changes have undermined the classic "subgovernments" that were described by an earlier generation of political scientists.

Subgovernments

Observers of American politics in the 1940s and 1950s often concluded that "subgovernments" dominated important areas of public policy.[73] In the idealized **subgovernment** three collective actors worked hand in hand to dominate policy making in some specific policy area:

subgovernment

Alliance of a congressional committee, an executive agency, and a small number of allied interest groups that combine to dominate policy making in some specified policy area.

- A *congressional committee* provided an executive agency with program authorization and budgetary support.
- The *executive agency* produced outcomes favored by an interest-group constituency.
- The *interest groups* provided the members of the congressional committee with campaign contributions and votes.

Subgovernments allegedly dominated critical policy areas such as agriculture, public works, and business regulation. In the most extreme cases, subgovernments were called "iron triangles" (see Chapter 14) in recognition of the difficulty faced by outsiders who wished to break into the cozy relationship uniting legislative committees, executive agencies, and interest groups.

Interest groups played a central role in this story because they were the outside actors who worked with executive and legislative officials to achieve favorable policy. Whatever their importance in the past, however, subgovernments are less important today. First, as we shall see in Chapter 12, Congress has changed. The party caucuses and leadership are stronger and the committees weaker; particular committees no longer have strangleholds on their jurisdictions.

Second, now there are many more groups, including many who oppose other groups. In particular, citizens' groups representing consumers, environmentalists, and taxpayers are much more active now than they were a half-century ago. They oppose the excesses of special-interest politics and publicize their opposition.

Third, as we discuss in Chapter 9, the focus of the media has changed with time. In particular, contemporary journalists are very much on the lookout for stories of what they consider to be special-interest profiteering at the expense of general interests. Changes in congressional and executive branch procedures, along with changes in technology, have also increased the transparency of governmental decision making, and thereby made it easier for the media and opposition groups to monitor back-room deals. During the extended debate over healthcare reform, for example, each successive draft of the healthcare bill was soon made available through the Internet, where reporters and conservative activists could scrutinize every line-item and publicize its more sordid aspects.

Issue Networks

issue network

A loose collection of interest groups, politicians, bureaucrats, and policy experts who have a particular interest in or responsibility for a policy area.

In the view of many scholars, subgovernments have been superseded by **issue networks**—bigger, broader, and much looser connections of interest groups, politicians, bureaucrats, and policy experts who have a particular interest in or responsibility for a policy area.[74] Given the enormous number and variety of interest groups today, the proliferation of legislative staff and other policy experts, and the interactions between policies in one area and those in another, issue networks are much more open than subgovernments and much less stable in their composition. Interest groups do not play such a central role in this new policy environment. They must compete with public officials and technical experts, as well as with each other, in an effort to influence public policy.

The academic community today clearly leans toward thinking of policy environments as networks rather than as iron triangles, but not everyone agrees with this conclusion. On the one hand, some scholars suggest that even the term *network* may exaggerate the degree of organization that characterizes interest-group activity in Washington, DC, today.[75] On the other hand, some scholars emphasize that organized interests directly shape laws and regulations in new policy areas such as energy and social regulation.[76] In short, judgments about the general importance of interest groups remain as divided as ever.

Probably the safest conclusion about the power of interest groups is that influence is conditional: It ranges from weak to strong, depending on the conditions under which groups try to influence politics. Professors Kay Schlozman and John Tierney conclude that groups are most influential when they act on low-profile issues, when they attempt to block action rather than originate it, when they are unopposed by other groups or politicians, and when they have plentiful resources.[77] Once again, the real world of American democracy is more complicated than many popular commentators suggest.

Interest Groups and Democratic Politics

The generic term *interest group* has a negative connotation, and terms such as *pressure group, vested interest,* and *special interest* have even more negative connotations.[78] Why do contemporary Americans hold interest groups in such low regard? After all, the Constitution protects the rights of citizens to work together to try to influence government. The First Amendment guarantees freedom of religion, speech, and the press, but it also prohibits any law abridging the "right of the people peaceably to assemble and to petition the government for a redress of grievances." Interest groups are the mechanism for exercising that right.

Political scientists generally have not held interest groups in as low regard as ordinary citizens have. In fact, one mid-century school of thought, **pluralism,** celebrated the role of groups in American politics.[79] The pluralists believed that American politics should consist of an interplay of numerous interests. In this view, virtually everyone is represented in a dense network of groups, no single interest is dominant, and all groups are required to bargain and compromise. Moreover, groups exercise countervailing power; if one interest or set of interests becomes too powerful, others mobilize to counteract it. As a consequence, public policies tend to be moderate and to change incrementally. That is, the system tends to do a good job representing the broad range of interests in the country.

Pluralism is out of fashion today. Critics cite several problems with the pluralist account. We have already discussed the first, the unrepresentativeness of the interest-group universe. As political scientist E. E. Schattschneider memorably put it, "The flaw in the pluralist heaven is that the heavenly chorus sings with a strong upper-class accent."[80] Because of the free-rider problem, small special interests have an advantage over large general interests. In particular, economic groups procure narrow economic benefits at the expense of the broader population of consumers and taxpayers. This is probably one reason why the term *interest group* has negative connotations in the popular mind; people see that most groups do not represent the general interests of Americans.

A second objection to the pluralist account would still apply even if interest groups were more representative: The interest of the whole nation is not equal to the sum of the interests of the parts. In our discussion of public opinion, we pointed out that majorities of Americans want to cut government spending and reduce government regulation, but majorities oppose specific cuts and reductions. Thus, if Congress heeds all the wishes of individual constituencies, it will displease the country as a whole by maintaining a bigger budget and more intrusive government than a majority desires.

Trade is another example. If the government erected a system of trade barriers to protect every American industry from foreign competition, the result would be retaliation against American exports, higher prices for consumers, and slower economic growth (if not worse). As Schattschneider long ago pointed out, a Congress operating according to pluralist principles enacted just such a trade policy in 1930—the Smoot-Hawley tariff, a policy that deepened and lengthened the Great Depression.[81] Simply adding up group interests is not enough. Ideally, politics harmonizes and synthesizes particular interests and incorporates them into the general interest of the nation.

7.5

Evaluate the pluralist account of the role of interest groups in American politics.

pluralism
A school of thought holding that politics is the clash of groups that represent all important interests in society and that check and balance each other.

A third criticism of pluralism is that a politics dominated by interest groups distorts political discussion and (ultimately) the political process. The reason is that groups reinforce extremism and undercut moderation. Ordinary citizens have multiple attachments and affiliations, which generally serve to moderate their outlooks. A retired couple, for example, might naturally favor higher social security and Medicare expenditures. But, if they also are parents and grandparents, they might accept more modest benefits for themselves to avoid higher taxes on their children or lower government expenditures on their grandchildren's schools. Leaders of interest groups, by contrast, act in someone else's interest. Typically, they see their job as maximizing group benefits. Thus, the leadership of a senior citizens group will be more supportive of higher benefits for the elderly than will many of its members. For example, AARP has been attacked as an organization composed of "tax-loving former teachers and government employees" who favor an "age-based welfare state."[82] This sharply worded attack was used by the National Taxpayers Union, an opposing interest group concerned with lowering taxes.

This crowding out of moderate demands by more extreme ones is reinforced by the tendency of group activists and leaders to be more extreme in their views than are nonmembers or even rank-and-file members. Thus, they push their demands beyond the point where ordinary members and sympathizers would stop. As we showed in Chapter 5, public opinion surveys on abortion, for example, generally show the public to have moderate and ambivalent attitudes on this issue. Yet the debate on this issue generally features two sharply polarized positions, one of which wants to legalize abortion without limitation, while the other seeks an almost equally complete ban on abortions of all kinds.[83] On many other issues, differences between Democratic and Republican party activists are also greater than differences between Democrats and Republicans in the electorate at large (see Table 7.3).

In the end, the general interests of a moderate population can get lost amid the bitter fighting of intense and extreme special interests. No one can deny that groups have a useful and legitimate role to play in articulating the interests of all components

Mobilizing Activists

An AARP volunteer hands out signs, buttons, and t-shirts before a rally in 2009.

• *What techniques does the AARP use to attract and retain members?*

TABLE 7.3
GROUP ACTIVISTS AND LEADERS HOLD MORE EXTREME VIEWS

Political activists are generally more extreme in their views than the people they purport to represent. For example, this table contrasts the issue disagreement between Republican and Democratic delegates to the 2008 national conventions with that between self-categorized Republicans and Democrats in the population at large. The activists differ far more than typical partisans do.

	Delegate Difference	Identifier Difference
Illegal Immigration Is a Very Important Problem	43%	28%
Very/Fairly Good National Economy	55	33
More Important to Provide Healthcare than to Hold Down Taxes	87	50
2001 Tax Cuts Should Be Made Permanent	84	13
Abortion Should Be Generally Available	61	23
Right Thing for the US to Have Taken Military Action Against Iraq	78	56
More Important to Protect Environment than to Meet Energy Needs	27	21
Personal Religious Beliefs Should Be Discussed in Presidential Campaigns	24	17
More Strict Gun Control	54	38
No Legal Recognition of Gay Relationships	41	28

Source: CBS News/*New York Times* Polls, 2008.

of American society, but many feel that groups somehow must be constrained. One of the first pluralists, James Madison, thought restraining the excesses of interest groups (which he called factions) was the greatest problem facing popular government. Indeed, as he explained in his classic essay *Federalist No. 10* (reprinted in Appendix III of this book), one of the strongest arguments in favor of an "extended republic," which included a large population and a wide geographical area, was its ability to cure "the mischiefs of faction." Yet, it can be argued that, as American politics has developed, several problems with Madison's "solution" have emerged.

First, Madison never anticipated the extent to which logrolling—the trading of favors—would become a common practice in Congress. Rather than check and balance each other, interest groups often cooperate, forming coalitions to exploit the general interests of consumers and taxpayers. Had Madison applied his argument to the issue of agricultural subsidies, for example, presumably he would have said that, since American climate and soil conditions were so diverse, lots of different crops would be grown and few legislators would therefore see much benefit in subsidizing any particular crop such as cotton, tobacco, or corn. In fact, what typically happens is that congressmen who represent cotton-growing districts agree to support subsidies for tobacco and corn if congressmen from tobacco- and corn-growing areas will support subsidies for cotton. These sorts of deals have been made throughout American history. Tariffs, public works, and tax policy are prominent examples of issues where special benefits were extended to so many interests as to make the resulting policy almost indefensible from any kind of plausible economic analysis.[84] Logrolling among interests is facilitated by a second development,

Continued on page 209

ELECTION VOICES!

Should Lobbying Be Restricted?

The Issue

Does lobbying need to be more closely regulated and the activities of lobbyists more tightly restricted? Or is lobbying a legitimate activity that, whatever its popular image, allows diverse groups to make their opinions and grievances known to national policymakers?

Background

Some 35,000 lobbyists are registered to do business in Washington, DC. As we discuss in this chapter, they spend much of their time tracking public policy issues, monitoring Congress, and meeting with representatives and senators. When the public hears about lobbyists, the news usually isn't good. In 2006, for example, a lobbyist and former aide to Congressman William Jefferson (D-LA), pleaded guilty to bribing the congressman in exchange for favorable treatment of a client. An FBI raid discovered a suspicious $90,000 in cash wrapped in tinfoil in Jefferson's freezer.[1]

Such incidents stoke outrage among public interest groups, and evidence does suggest that some policies designed to keep track of lobbying need improvement. One study, for example, found that almost 14,000 disclosure files were missing from the Senate Office of Public Records. Nearly every major lobbying firm has failed to file at least some of the required documentation in recent years.[2] Other practices are legal, but may seem fishy. Retired members of Congress often embark on second careers on K Street, the Washington corridor known for its heavy concentration of lobbying firms.

The Issues

In 2007, Congress enacted a new law to tighten the rules governing lobbying. Lobbyists must now disclose their fundraising activities, and members of Congress are prohibited from receiving gifts from them. Former government officials must also wait a certain interval before taking a job as a lobbyist—former senators and executive branch officials must wait two years; former House members must wait one year. Even as the law went into effect in 2008, some reformers called for more extensive measures, including an independent agency to enforce congressional ethics rules, a ban on all campaign contributions from lobbyists, prohibitions on lobbying by convicted felons, and prohibitions on lobbyists from also serving official roles in political action committees.

Proponents of such proposals argue that they would reduce corruption and place ordinary citizens back on a more level playing field with organized interests. Michael Kinsley argues that the system as it stands "is all corrupt bribery. People and companies hire lobbyists because it works. Lobbyists get the big bucks because their efforts earn or save clients even bigger bucks in their dealings with the government."[3] As a result, argues Kinsley, constituent interests are ignored.

But critics worry that these policy changes—especially the more stringent ones—would deprive lobbyists of their First Amendment right to "petition the government for a redress of grievances." Former Senator (and current Secretary of State) Hillary Clinton argued that "a lot of these lobbyists, whether you like it or not, represent real Americans. They represent nurses, they represent social workers, yes, they represent corporations that employ a lot of people."[4] As journalist Charles Krauthammer put it, "Lobbyists are people hired to [petition] for you, so that you can actually stay at home with the kids and remain gainfully employed rather than spend your life in the corridors of Washington."[5] Furthermore, critics argue, tight regulations on lobbying would reduce the amount of information available to lawmakers and detract from the quality of legislative debate.

What Do Americans Believe?

Americans are, as a whole, suspicious of lobbyists. When asked whether lobbyists have too much influence in Washington, 80 percent say "yes."[6] But any enthusiasm for putting a tighter rein on lobbying fades when lobby reform is weighed against other issues. A 2007 poll, for example, found that, out of six major bills expected to be taken up by Congress that year, the public ranked lobby reform sixth in importance.[7] The public clearly distrusts the lobbying industry, but it cares more about healthcare, education, the economy, and other major bread-and-butter issues.

What Do You Think?

1. Do lobbyists pose a threat to effective democracy, or do they help Congress make better decisions by adding information to the legislative process?

2. Do lobbyist disclosure rules deprive lobbyists of their First Amendment rights? How about bans on lobbying by former members of Congress or bans on campaign contributions from lobbyists?

For more on lobbying and lobbyists, see the following websites:

Checking email messages in the halls of the Rayburn House Office Building.

On the Web

The Center for Responsive Politics advocates lobbying reform and offers a comprehensive database of lobbyist expenditure information.

www.opensecrets.org

The Center for Public Integrity has investigated existing lobbyist disclosure rules and found them wanting.

www.publicintegrity.org

The American League of Lobbyists, a professional association for registered lobbyists, maintains a lobbying code of ethics and insists that lobbying is part of the First Amendment tradition.

www.allcd.org

[1]Shailagh Murray and Allan Lengel, "The Legal Woes of Rep. Jefferson," *Washington Post,* (February 16, 2006): A1.
[2]"Lobbying FAQ: What Is Permissible? Out of Bounds? Punishable?" Center for Public Integrity, www.publicintegrity.org/lobby/report.aspx?aid=775, accessed October 28, 2006.
[3]Michael Kinsley, "Business as Usual: Corrupt," *Washington Post,* (December 2, 2005): A23.
[4]Ben Smith, "Hillary Defends Lobbyists, Opens Doors for Rivals," *The Politico,* August 4, 2007, www.politico.com/news/stories/0807/5251.html.
[5]Charles Krauthammer, "In Defense of Lobbying," *Washington Post,* (February 29, 2008): A19.
[6]Harris Poll, February 5–11, 2008.
[7]Democracy Corps poll, June 10–14, 2007.

Continued from page 207

the rise of professional politicians who, in seeking reelection, broker the group deals in return for the electoral support that interest groups provide. Finally, developments in communications and transportation technology have made it vastly easier to organize and mobilize interests even if their members are spread all over the country.

But what can—or should—be done to reduce the influence of interest groups? As the critics look over the experience of democratic governments, they see only one means of controlling group demands that is both democratic and effective. Ironically, it is an institution that George Washington warned the country about—political parties, the subject of the next chapter.

CHAPTER SUMMARY

7.1 Trace the development of U.S. interest groups and characterize interest groups today.

Only half of the American citizenry votes in presidential elections, and only small minorities engage in other forms of political participation. But most Americans participate indirectly in politics by joining interest groups that attempt to influence government. In fact, Americans are more likely to participate indirectly through these groups than are citizens of other democracies who vote at higher levels. In the past generation or two, there has been a major increase in the number of interest groups.

7.2 Analyze the free-rider problem and how interest groups overcome the problem.

Successful groups have found ways to overcome the free-rider problem, the tendency of people to benefit from group activity without contributing to its costs. Some of the groups rely on selective benefits that are available only to group members, whereas others depend on the efforts of dedicated or wealthy members who will bear more than a proportionate share of the costs of group maintenance.

7.3 Outline strategies interest groups use to directly and indirectly influence government.

Group characteristics and their situations lead them to adopt a variety of political strategies. Traditional government lobbying involves attempts to influence elected officials directly by speaking personally to them; grassroots lobbying tries to influence elected officials indirectly by mobilizing constituents. Increasingly, groups engage in electioneering—contributing money to candidates and spending money independently to elect officials sympathetic to their interests and views. Groups also attempt to persuade or educate the public, and some resort to direct action—demonstrations, protests, and the like—to call attention to their positions. Finally, some groups end-run the political process and attempt to influence government through the courts.

7.4 Assess the influence of interest groups on American politics.

Despite extensive study of interest groups, there is wide disagreement about how influential they are. Popular commentators view them as more powerful than do most academic researchers. There is no doubt that groups engage in a vast amount of political activity and invest a great deal of money and other resources, but it is difficult to say how effective they are. For every issue that interest groups appear to dominate, skeptics can cite another issue on which interest groups seem to be ineffectual or to offset each other's efforts.

7.5 Evaluate the pluralist account of the role of interest groups in American politics.

Many social critics worry about the overall effect of interest-group activity, though. First, special interests are better represented than general interests. Second, even if that were not so, the interest of the nation as a whole is not merely the sum of the interests of the particular parts. Third, interest groups support extreme positions in political debate and thus polarize political discussion, injecting excessive conflict into the political process.

---

mypⓞliscilab EXERCISES

Apply what you learned in this chapter on MyPoliSciLab.

📖—Read on mypoliscilab.con
    eText: Chapter 7

✔—Study and Review on mypoliscilab.com
    Pre-Test
    Post-Test
    Chapter Exam
    Flashcards

👁—Watch on mypoliscilab.com
    Video: American Cancer Society Recommendation
    Video: California Teachers Stage Sit-Ins
    Video: Murtha and the PMA Lobbyists

✳—Explore on mypoliscilab.com
    Simulation: You Are a Lobbyist
    Comparative: Comparing Interest Groups
    Timeline: Interest Groups and Campaign Finance

KEY TERMS

direct action, p. 201
direct mail, p. 200
free-rider problem, p. 189
grassroots lobbying, p. 197
interest group, p. 184
issue advocacy, p. 200

issue network, p. 204
lobbying, p. 195
lobbyist, p. 195
pluralism, p. 205
political action committee (PAC),
    p. 198

political entrepreneurs, p. 194
public goods, p. 190
selective benefits, p. 193
single-issue group, p. 186
social movement, p. 192
subgovernment, p. 203

SUGGESTED READINGS

Of General Interest

Baumgartner, Frank R., Jeffrey Berry, Marie Hojnacki, David C. Kimball, and Beth L. Leech. *Lobbying and Policy Change: Who Wins, Who Loses, and Why*. Chicago: University of Chicago Press, 2009. A study of nearly 100 different policy areas that finds that lobbyists are not as influential as many Americans think they are.

Schattschneider, E. E. *The Semisovereign People*. New York: Holt, 1960. A delightful essay that remains timely. Argues that the pressure system of interest groups is biased and that the result is an artificially constricted range of political conflict in the United States.

Skocpol, Theda. *Diminished Democracy*. Norman: University of Oklahoma Press, 2003. Describes the evolution of interest groups from mass membership associations to top-heavy organizations managed by professionals, and considers the consequences of this transformation for American democracy.

Walker, Jack. *Mobilizing Interest Groups in America*. Ann Arbor: University of Michigan Press, 1991. Explores the Washington interest-group universe. Notable for discussion of outside support for establishment of groups.

Focused Studies

Freeman, Jo, and Victoria Johnson. *Waves of Protest*. Lanham, MD: Rowman and Littlefield, 1999. Useful collection describing the social movements active since the 1960s.

Mansbridge, Jane. *Why We Lost the ERA*. Chicago: University of Chicago Press, 1986. Thoughtful discussion of the narrow failure of the women's movement to win passage of the ERA. Argues that the movement overcame the free-rider problem by emphasizing the symbolism of the ERA, a strategy that precluded compromises that would have led to passage of the amendment.

Smith, Mark. *American Business and Political Power*. Chicago: University of Chicago Press, 2000. Argues that when business interests are united they are less influential, because the issues that unite business divide the political parties and arouse public opinion.

Wright, John. *Interest Groups and Congress*. New York: Longman, 2009. Discussion of interest-group politics in the contemporary Congress that puts special emphasis on the political and institutional context in which groups organize and act.

ON THE WEB

As we have noted, the Internet has been a valuable tool for interest groups. It has reduced organization and communication costs tremendously. It is no exaggeration to say that an interest group is probably not much of an interest group until it has its own Web page. (The reverse is not true, however; it is so easy to have a Web page these days that merely possessing one does not qualify a group as an interest group.) It would take too much space to list all of the interest groups with a presence on the Web.

www.aarp.org
www.aflcio.org
www.ama-assn.org
www.sierraclub.org
www.uschamber.org
www.now.org
www.cc.org

A sample of the most important interest groups with a presence on the Web are the American Association of Retired Persons, the AFL-CIO, the American Medical Association, the Sierra Club, the U.S. Chamber of Commerce, the National Organization for Women, and the Christian Coalition of America.

www.vegan.org
www.deathwithdignity.org
www.anarchy.no
www.atheists.org

A few less prominent groups, the very existence of which testifies to the power of the Internet to reduce organizational costs, are Vegan Action, Death With Dignity National Center (pro-assisted suicide), Anarchy.org, and American Atheists.

8 Political Parties

CHAPTER OUTLINE

LEARNING OBJECTIVES

8.1 Evaluate how parties both contribute to and detract from democratic politics.

8.2 Trace the history of political parties in the United States and assess the contemporary party system.

8.3 Compare and contrast the American two-party system with the more prevalent multi-party system.

8.4 Assess whether American political parties are experiencing a decline or a revival.

8.5 Evaluate the relationship between political parties and interest groups.

A Tale of Two Conventions

The Democrats and the Republicans held spectacular national conventions in the summer of 2008 to pick their presidential nominees. Each party spent over $70 million to kick off the general election in style—filling convention halls with red, white, and blue banners, with thousands of balloons, and with shouting delegates wearing colorful jackets and funny hats.[1] Political celebrities marched to each convention podium and gave fiery speeches to stir up the party faithful and attract uncommitted voters. Barack Obama delivered his acceptance speech before an unprecedented crowd at Invesco Field in Denver. On the Republican side Sarah Palin, the vice presidential nominee and a rising star within the party, gave a barnburner of an address that electrified conservative activists around the country. It was as close as political parties get to throwing the nation a real party.

The 2008 conventions drew the most public attention of any such events in decades. Over 30 million people, on average, watched each night's convention coverage on network TV or a cable channel.[2] But while this number might seem large, it represents only 13 percent of the voting age population. The Nielsen ratings company estimates that only about 20 percent of households had a TV tuned to the conventions.[3] The three major television networks gave the conventions just one hour per night over a four-day span.

Voters cannot be blamed for skipping the national conventions. All the spectacle aside, the conventions offered minimal political drama. Barack Obama and John McCain both had clinched their party's nominations much earlier, after primary and caucus wins that gave each candidate

enough delegates to claim victory. The vice presidential candidates, Joe Biden and Sarah Palin, were engaging personalities but both had been named prior to the conventions, eliminating any element of suspense. Nor did the events feature enough conflict to make up for the lack of surprise. Both campaigns had defused potential rivals much earlier—Hillary Clinton on the Democratic side, Mike Huckabee and Mitt Romney on the Republican side. There were no floor fights over policy planks in the platform. The conventions were basically long, expensive infomercials showcasing the party and its candidates.

Contrast these media events with the 1952 political conventions. That year, the three networks averaged 60 hours of convention coverage, essentially televising them from the opening gavel to the closing gavel (something only C-SPAN does now). Ratings showed that 80 percent of households watched.[4] Why were earlier conventions deemed so newsworthy? Because they actually made important decisions.

At the Democratic convention of 1952, four serious rivals vied for the nomination. Senator Estes Kefauver of Tennessee, who had achieved prominence investigating organized crime and campaigned in a coonskin cap, led on the first two ballots, but he could not secure a victory. Some minor candidates then withdrew and delegates flowed to President Truman's choice for the nomination, Governor Adlai Stevenson of Illinois. Stevenson, a northern liberal, won a narrow majority on the third ballot. Only then did Americans learn Stevenson's choice for the vice presidential nomination: Senator John Sparkman of Alabama, whose conservatism could balance the ticket.

The Republicans had a simpler choice. Senator Robert Taft of Ohio—known as "Mr. Republican" for his long service—faced a challenge from a man who had declared his GOP affiliation less than a year earlier: General Dwight Eisenhower, a popular World War II hero. Party insiders backed Taft, but the Republicans also wished to regain the White House after a 20-year absence. When Eisenhower's supporters challenged the seating of delegates from three pro-Taft states, they won the battle. Eisenhower still failed to attain a majority on the initial vote, but minor candidates threw him enough support that he won before a second official balloting became necessary. Eisenhower then named his running mate: a young anticommunist senator from California, Richard Nixon.

Why did no one know in advance who the nominees would be? In those days, there was no permanent campaign. Few states held primaries and the existing primaries selected few convention delegates. The great majority of delegates were party officials, loyalists, contributors, and influential politicians appointed by state and local party leaders. They were free to wheel and deal at the conventions, exchanging their support for promises of future political payoffs. Thus, campaigns took shape more slowly. In contrast to today's candidates, who begin organizing in the early primary states 18 months before the election, Stevenson never entered a single primary. Eisenhower was still serving as Supreme Allied Commander of NATO six weeks before winning the nomination!

Today the labels are the same as they were in 1952: "Democrats" and "Republicans." In fact, they have not changed since the nineteenth century. But the Democratic and Republican parties of 1952 looked more like those of 1852 than the parties navigating today's permanent campaign. This chapter tells the story of how and why American parties changed so radically over such a short span of time.

Making the Connection

All modern democracies have parties. Traditionally defined as groups of like-minded people who band together in an attempt to win control of government, political parties serve as the primary connection between ordinary citizens and the public officials they elect. They nominate candidates for office, defining the choices that face voters in elections. They mobilize voters, helping their allies to turn out at the polls. And, after the votes have been counted, parties coordinate the actions of elected officials in the government, working to lay the political terrain for the next election. Political scientists have long praised parties for providing these links between citizens and government, but recent critics have argued that parties have become too extreme in their views, leading citizens to feel poorly represented in important political debates. In this chapter, we evaluate this concern, addressing the following questions about political parties:

- Are parties essential to democratic politics?
- How have parties shaped the political history of the United States?
- Why does the United States have only two major parties?
- How do today's parties differ from those of earlier eras?
- How influential are parties today in American politics?

What Parties Do

To political commentators in most self-governed societies, democracy is unimaginable without **political parties.** The European University Institute, a research arm of the European Community, published a four-volume study on political parties that called them "the central institutions of democratic governments," the "working mechanism" of liberal democracy.[5]

Many American professors hold similar views. Political scientist E. E. Schattschneider devoted much of his life to making the case for the vital role played by political parties. In introducing his classic work *Party Government,* he wrote, "This volume is devoted to the thesis that political parties created democracy and that modern democracy is unthinkable save in terms of the parties."[6]

For contemporary Americans, though, life without political parties is not so unthinkable. When asked directly about parties, most Americans do not sing their praises. Indeed, surveys have shown that many Americans think government would be better without parties.[7] Could they be right, and the scholars and commentators wrong? To answer that question, this section describes both the positive and negative functions performed by parties within the political system.

How Parties Contribute to Democratic Politics

What do parties offer to make most Europeans and some Americans think they are essential for democratic government? The general answer is that, except at the local level, a democracy that relied on the activities of individuals and interest groups would be too disorganized to operate effectively. Politicians create parties to *organize* political life, and parties do so by carrying on a series of activities.[8]

Organizing and Operating the Government Parties coordinate the actions of thousands of public officials. This role is particularly noticeable in legislatures: With the exception of Nebraska, which is formally nonpartisan, every American legislature is organized on an explicitly partisan basis. The presiding officer, who generally determines the agenda (what issues get considered and when), is almost always the leader of the majority party (the party that won a majority of the seats in the most recent election). The committee chairs, who control committee agendas and hire most committee staff, are also all members of the majority party. To a great extent, the American political system also counts on parties to help make sure that the different branches of government work together at some reasonable level of effectiveness. At each level of government, executives count on the support of their fellow partisans in the legislature, and legislators trust the information they get from their fellow partisans in the executive branch. Parties also coordinate activities across levels of government. In 2010, for example, many Republican governors reinforced congressional Republicans' concerns about the Obama administration's healthcare bill by arguing that it would impose costly mandates on states. Similarly, local officials appeal to their partisan allies in the state governments, and the latter appeal to their partisan allies in Congress. American government often appears disorderly, but many political scientists believe it would be absolutely chaotic without parties.

Focusing Responsibility for Governmental Action Party labels operate much like brand names. Just as consumers might favor a reputable brand or avoid buying a brand that has sold poor merchandise in the past, voters judge Democrats and

8.1

Evaluate how parties both contribute to and detract from democratic politics.

political parties
Groups of like-minded people who band together in an attempt to take control of government. Parties represent the primary connection between ordinary citizens and the public officials they elect.

Republicans collectively.[9] The actions or performance of one leader influences the reputation of fellow party members seeking office. Parties therefore strive to fashion a record they can defend at the polls, which requires members to maintain a degree of unity. To paraphrase Ben Franklin, either party members hang together or they hang separately. President Barack Obama was able to rely on congressional support for his economic stimulus and healthcare proposals in part because other Democrats recognized the need for his administration to create a record of accomplishment.

Developing Issues and Educating the Public   Parties engage in a continual battle for control of public offices, and they sharpen their issue positions as weapons in this struggle. They identify problems, publicize them, and advance possible solutions. Much of their motivation is adversarial, somewhat like a court proceeding in which the opposing lawyers present their cases, but the outcome of the competition can be beneficial. It generates information, educates the public, and shapes the policy agenda. Where parties are weak, as in the American South during the first half of the twentieth century, politics degenerates into a battle over personalities and private benefits rather than public issues.[10]

Synthesizing Interests   Good public policy must be more than the sum of various groups' demands (see Chapter 7). Satisfying every specific interest can detract from the general interest. Also, some conflicting interests cannot be satisfied simultaneously; they require compromise. Translating societal demands into public policy therefore must go beyond simple addition to a more difficult and subtle kind of synthesizing or harmonizing. The major parties sometimes perform this critical role while trying to construct successful national coalitions. They develop platforms that offer a mix of benefits and burdens to all. When their platforms appear too focused on pleasing identifiable special interests, parties suffer electorally—as the Democrats did in 1984 and the Republicans did in 1996.

Recruiting and Developing Governmental Talent   There is an old adage in politics: "You can't beat somebody with nobody." Even if an elected official appears vulnerable, voters may continue to return that incumbent to office unless they are offered a plausible alternative—someone with the background and qualifications to hold the post.[11] Thus, parties are always on the lookout for promising candidates. They may make a special effort to recruit candidates who will improve the party's image, as the Democrats did in 2006 by trying to increase the number of veterans who ran for Congress.[12] The parties keep track of the weak members in the opposition and bring along potential replacements from their own ranks. Like predators in the natural environment, parties help strengthen public service by weeding out the weak.

Simplifying the Electoral System   Imagine that there were no parties to winnow the field of candidates. Rather than choosing between two options for most offices, voters might be faced with a multitude of choices, each supported by a tiny slice of the electorate. Furthermore, the candidates would lack party labels, which otherwise help voters anticipate each candidate's beliefs. Neither major party is homogeneous, of course, but the labels *Democrat* and *Republican* do convey a good bit of information. As we write this book in 2010, we have no idea whom the Democrats and Republicans will select as their presidential candidates in 2016. But we can predict, with a considerable

Presidential Primary Candidates
The 2008 Democratic presidential contenders.

• *Although the 2008 Democratic candidates presented a clear variety of styles and demographic traits, did they really disagree about any of the major issues? Were all of the major candidates, as critics sometimes charged, drawn from the far left end of the Democratic Party?*

measure of confidence, that the Democratic candidate will take the pro-choice position on abortion while the Republican candidate will be pro-life, that the Republican candidate will be more opposed to tax increases, that the Democratic nominee will be more supportive of national health insurance, and so on across a considerable range of issues. In the absence of parties, therefore, Americans would have to work much harder before knowing how to vote.

How Parties Detract from Democratic Politics

Despite the valuable organizational functions that political parties can perform, Americans are traditionally suspicious of parties and, since the end of the nineteenth century, have held them in relatively low esteem. Part of this scorn results from the fact that parties do not always perform the valuable functions of which they are capable. After all, politicians do not organize parties because they want to simplify the electoral system, recruit talent, or synthesize interests. They give structure to political life only insofar as such activities help them gain power.[13]

Thomas Jefferson nurtured the Democratic-Republican Party as a way to wrest power from the Federalists. Abraham Lincoln used the new Republican Party to overthrow a Democratic majority. Theodore Roosevelt established the Bull Moose Party because he could not win the GOP nomination. Once in office, public officials work to maintain their parties because parties help them govern. Andrew Jackson used the spoils of victory to consolidate his party's majority. Franklin Roosevelt used New Deal policies to strengthen the Democratic Party in electorally critical locales.[14]

Although party leaders may view their partisan activities as furthering the public interest, their opponents seldom agree. But even voters on the winning side may be critical of parties, because party influence is a double-edged sword. Parties strong enough to perform beneficial functions are also strong enough to abuse their power. Each of the positive functions that parties perform can be corrupted and, unfortunately, American history provides numerous such examples.

Capturing Governments and Dictating What They Do   At a certain point, coordination becomes control. A strong party that controls its members can force elected officials to stick with the desires of the leadership and ignore the wishes of voters back home (especially when candidates of the other party are equally unresponsive). At its extreme, party dominance becomes the equivalent of an elected dictatorship. In the contemporary House of Representatives, for example, both Democrats and Republicans, when they have been in the minority, have charged that the majority party was using its control of the agenda to prevent certain issues and bills from being considered and to prevent a fair vote on the minority's preferred amendments. In the early 1900s, Progressives leveled a similar charge against the urban machines that ruled many American cities. Despite facing periodic elections, the machines kept a stranglehold on elected offices through the calculated distribution of jobs, contracts, and other patronage. When private payoffs failed, they often exploited illegal methods for maintaining power—including vote fraud and police intimidation.

Confusing Responsibility   Because credit for good times and blame for bad times are valuable political currencies, the parties attempt to "manufacture" responsibility. Opposition members may blame the incumbent administration for events over which it had no control. Incumbents, in turn, may take credit for positive outcomes not of their making. Worse, rather than helping to solve a public problem, opposition parties may concentrate on undercutting the governing party's proposed solutions. The Democrats used this tactic with President George W. Bush's attempt to reform social security in 2005, and Republicans used it against the Obama administration's healthcare proposals in 2010. The temptation to torpedo the other party's initiatives is especially strong when **divided government** exists—when one party holds the presidency but does not control Congress—as was the case in 2007 and 2008. Under such conditions, voters are unsure how to assign responsibility for government inaction.[15]

divided government
Government in which one party holds the presidency but does not control both houses of Congress.

Suppressing the Issues   For various reasons, parties may prevent the political system from addressing new issues. The leadership of both parties may fail to appreciate new developments in society because they have grown out of touch, or they may ignore issues that threaten the internal harmony of both parties. For example, the two major parties avoided the slavery issue during the first half of the nineteenth century, when they both contained members from the North as well as the South. Today, Democratic and Republican candidates almost uniformly resist reforming programs for the elderly, promising instead to "protect social security and expand Medicare," because neither party wishes to risk antagonizing senior citizens. It often takes outsiders to force an issue onto the public agenda.[16]

Dividing Society   Rather than synthesize disparate interests into some larger whole, parties may do just the opposite. They may create or exacerbate social divisions as a means for gaining electoral advantage. President George Washington suggested as much two centuries ago in his farewell address: "The spirit of party agitates the community with ill-founded jealousies and false alarms, kindles the animosity of one part against another, [and] foments occasional riot and insurrection."[17] It is easy to identify such agitation in modern politics: Democrats accused President George W. Bush of lying about Iraq to build the case for war and of callousness and incompetence after Hurricane Katrina struck New Orleans. For their part, Republicans charged that President Obama's legislative agenda amounted to socialism.

Recruiting Candidates for the Wrong Reasons
Parties usually seek candidates who can win. In competitive environments, therefore, the desire for success may prompt parties to nominate seasoned leaders or to recruit accomplished political newcomers known for their intelligence, integrity, and good judgment. On the other hand, neither experience nor ability guarantees popularity—and sometimes potential candidates are popular for reasons that have nothing to do with their aptitude at governing. Celebrities, such as entertainers and former athletes, enjoy a distinct advantage in an electoral politics driven by media and money. Former California Governor Arnold Schwarzenegger may be the most obvious example, but Congress has seated movie actors (Sen. Fred Thompson), TV stars (Sen. Al Franken, Rep. Sonny Bono), and astronauts (Sen. John Glenn, Sen. Harrison Schmitt), as well as former stars of the NBA (Rep. Tom McMillan, Sen. Bill Bradley), the NFL (Rep. Heath Shuler), and major-league baseball (Sen. Jim Bunning). Well known? Yes. Qualified? Sometimes. In less competitive environments, meanwhile, parties may promote mediocre people characterized more by their unwavering partisanship than by their skills.

Oversimplifying the Electoral System   The voter who must choose between two candidates, one labeled Democrat and one labeled Republican, has a clearer and apparently easier choice than the voter who can choose among many candidates with no labels. But what if she doesn't like that clear but restricted choice? What if she is a pro-choice Republican or a pro-life Democrat? That's just tough. If there are only two major parties, she has only two serious alternatives. Her choice may be simple, but it also may be unsatisfactory.

The Balance Sheet

Given the conflict, who is correct—the scholars who champion political parties or the critics who think parties hinder democracy? Probably the safest answer is "both."

When evaluating political parties, most scholars have usually asked whether having parties is better than not having them at all. Overwhelmingly, they have concluded that it is better to have them. The functions performed by political parties are necessary for the successful operation of the political system, and scholars see no alternative institution prepared to perform those functions. They also are more likely to realize that parties inevitably act according to their political interests. They do not assume, naively, that a few legal changes suddenly will compel parties to promote the public good. Indeed, they recognize the danger of misconceived reforms, which may fail or even produce nasty

Polarized Perceptions
As George Washington warned, political parties often have a vested interest in fomenting disagreement. The same facts—in this case the budget deficit—can lead to quite different conclusions.

• *Do party differences on such issues help clarify issues for voters, or do they just confuse matters?*

unintended consequences.[18] Certainly scholars can risk becoming too complacent, confusing the way things are (which they may have devoted a lifetime to studying) with the way things ought to be. Nevertheless, they are right to value the important organizing role carried out by political parties.

Reformers focus on the ways in which existing parties detract from democratic government. Reformers run little risk of becoming complacent. Indeed, for many social critics, their fame and fortune depend on an ability to identify social problems. As part of this effort, reformers have publicized many real imperfections in how parties operate within the political system: abuses of power, gridlock that keeps problems unsolved, partisanship that makes political life unsavory, scandals and inefficiencies that alienate the public from its government. Certainly reformers can be too quick to demand radical change. They may not anticipate or care about the full consequences of the reforms they embrace. In particular, they do not bear the burden of identifying alternative institutions that could replace parties. Nevertheless, they are right to worry about the extent to which existing political parties undermine representation rather than promote it. As a result, the debate over party reform will continue.

8.2

Trace the history of political parties in the United States and assess the contemporary party system.

Political Parties in American History

The contemporary American lack of enthusiasm for parties is ironic, given that the United States pioneered the mass parties that are an essential component of politics in modern Europe. Indeed, parties have organized American elections since the time of George Washington. At first, the parties were composed of political notables who supported leaders such as Jefferson and Hamilton and had little or no local, grassroots organization. Such personal followings were the democratic counterparts of the "court" parties of monarchical governments—the groups of nobles who engaged in "palace intrigues" (and sometimes paid with their lives for their "treasonous" plotting).

American parties did not stay limited to national big shots for very long. During the administration of Andrew Jackson (1829–1837), the Democratic Party spread outward from Washington and downward into the grassroots, a movement soon imitated by its adversaries, the Whigs. By 1889 Lord Bryce, the famous English political commentator, could observe that, "In America the great moving forces are the parties. The government counts for less than in Europe, the parties count for more."[19] Today, of course, the first part of the statement remains true: The government counts for less than it does in most European countries in the sense that the public sector in the United States is smaller. But the second part of Bryce's statement can be turned around: The parties also count for less than in Europe. American parties now are weaker than most of their European counterparts, and they are weaker than those of other economically developed democracies such as Japan and South Korea.

Still, above the local level, nearly all American public officials are elected as Democrats or Republicans. Unlike Europeans, Americans may not *believe* that parties are essential to democracy—but in practice parties seem to be as pervasive as in Europe. Indeed, political historians of the past generation have developed general accounts of American history organized around the concept of "party systems."[20] These accounts describe the important role the political parties, appreciated or not, have played in American history.

The Party-Systems Interpretation of American History

Political change occurs constantly. Individuals float in and out of the electorate, or from one party to another—actions that cause election results to vary—but the system as a whole usually remains fairly stable. The same people tend to vote for the same parties, and the same parties tend to win in the same places. Occasionally, however, the political system undergoes sudden and sweeping changes. Large groups may swing their support from one party to another. Republican areas can become Democratic, and vice versa.

"Realignment" scholars have tried to formalize the study of political change by dividing American political history into a series of distinct electoral eras, or "party systems."[21] They argue that each of these party systems is a time of general stability. In particular, a party system is generally defined by four stable characteristics.

realignment
Shift occurring when the pattern of group support for political parties changes in a significant and lasting way.

1. *The identities of the major parties.* Although minor parties may come and go, the two major contestants for national power stay the same.
2. *The parties' relative balance of strength.* In most party systems, one party is the majority party; that is, it wins most elections. The other party comes to power only when it can capitalize on errors by or divisions within the dominant party. The years between 1876 and 1892 are, as we will see, a partial exception to this statement, when the Democrats and Republicans competed on remarkably even terms. Yet, even then, the balance was stable: Neither party was able to gain a large, lasting advantage over the other.
3. *The major issues.* Parties are organized around issue disagreements. And, while some issues are significant only for a very brief period of time (this is especially true in foreign policy), each party system has generally centered on one or two core concerns that are debated, in one form or another, in election after election. During the so-called New Deal party system, for example, Democrats and Republicans regularly disagreed about the role the federal government should play in regulating and controlling the national economy, with the Democrats always favoring a more extensive role for government and the Republicans invariably urging a greater reliance on private enterprise and individual initiative.
4. *The party coalitions.* Because the parties take the same relative positions on the major issues, they also tend to attract or repel the same kinds of voters. Within each party system, certain kinds of voters are reliable supporters of one party or the other, while others split their votes more evenly. This pattern means that there is considerable geographic stability from election to election: Each party has its core areas of support, while other areas are seen as contested or "battleground" regions.

These stable electoral eras or party systems theoretically could dissolve rather gradually. In fact, however, most party systems have ended suddenly. One or a very small number of **critical elections** takes place, decisively marking the end of one party system and the beginning of another. According to some scholars, these major changes in the party system, called realignments, take place with a surprising degree of regularity—about once every 30 years or so. According to most analysts the realignment is anticipated by underlying social changes that gradually make the old alignment less relevant and is usually triggered by a crisis, such as a major depression, that divides the existing parties and increases popular interest and participation in politics. Although defining "critical elections" or "electoral eras" is a tricky business, and some scholars doubt that it is

critical election
Election that marks the emergence of a new, lasting alignment of partisan support within the electorate.

TABLE 8.1

THE PARTY-SYSTEMS INTERPRETATION OF AMERICAN ELECTORAL HISTORY: 1796 TO 2011

	Number of Presidential Elections Won by Each Party		Number of Times Each Party Won a Majority of Seats in the House of Representatives		Number of Times Each Party Won a Majority of Seats in the Senate	
First Party System 1796–1824	Democratic-Republicans	7	Democratic-Republicans	13	Democratic-Republicans	13
	Federalists	1	Federalists	2	Federalists	2
Second Party System 1826–1858	Democrats	6	Democrats	13	Democrats	15
	Whigs	2	Whigs	2	Whigs	2
			Republicans	2		
Third Party System 1860–1894						
1860–1872	Republicans	4	Republicans	7	Republicans	7
	Democrats	0	Democrats	0	Democrats	0
1874–1894	Republicans	3	Democrats	8	Republicans	9
	Democrats	2	Republicans	3	Democrats	2
Fourth Party System 1896–1930	Republicans	7	Republicans	13	Republicans	15
	Democrats	2	Democrats	5	Democrats	3
Fifth Party System 1932–1966	Democrats	7	Democrats	16	Democrats	16
	Republicans	2	Republicans	2	Republicans	2
Contemporary Party System 1968	Republicans	7	Democrats	14	Democrats	11
	Democrats	4	Republicans	6	Republicans	9

Source: Compiled by the authors based on data in *Guide to U.S. Elections,* 5th ed. (Washington, D.C.: CQ Press, 2005); election results.

possible to do so without oversimplifying political history,[22] the party-systems interpretation nevertheless provides a useful way to remember how party competition has changed over time (see Table 8.1).

The First Party System (Jeffersonian)   Most historians believe that the first party system began in the early 1790s and lasted until about 1824.[23] George Washington hoped to govern without parties, but early in his first term a series of controversies began to divide both Congress and Washington's own cabinet. One group of officials, loyal to Treasury Secretary Alexander Hamilton, hoped to use the power of the new federal government to encourage commercial and manufacturing interests. They supported such policies as the creation of a national bank, the assumption of state war debts, and a high protective tariff. Known as the Federalists, Hamilton and his supporters favored a broad reading of the Constitution and a foreign policy that sought closer ties with Great Britain, then the world's dominant economic power. (These "Federalists" should not be confused with the proponents of the ratification of the Constitution, who were also called Federalists, as we explain in Chapter 2. The two groups overlapped but were not the same.) In reaction to Hamilton's early successes, a second group of officials coalesced around Secretary of State Thomas Jefferson. Usually referred to today as the Democratic-Republicans, the Jeffersonians hoped to keep the United States a predominantly agricultural country; adopted a much narrower, "strict" reading of the Constitution; and wanted a foreign policy that was more favorable toward France than toward Great Britain.

In some ways, partisan competition has never been as bare-knuckled as it was early in the first party system. In 1798, when it seemed that the United States might go to war against France, the Federalists passed the Sedition Act, which imposed criminal penalties on anyone who wrote, spoke, or published "any false, scandalous, and malicious writing" against any member or branch of the federal government. As one historian has summed up the intent of this law, it equated "Republican criticism of [Federalist] policies with a traitorous loyalty to the nation's enemy."[24] The act set the stage for the presidential election of 1800, perhaps the most bitter and divisive in all of American history, in which the Federalists accused Thomas Jefferson, the Democratic-Republican candidate, of being an atheist who would import the French Revolutionary terror to American soil. In return, Jefferson's partisans accused Federalist President John Adams of trying to establish an American monarchy. After a tie in the Electoral College, and 35 ballots in the House of Representatives, Jefferson was finally declared the victor.

The 1800 election marked the end of the Federalist Party as a significant force in American national government. The Federalists never won another presidential election and soon dwindled to a small minority in both houses of Congress. In part, the Federalists declined because they were simply on the wrong side of the issues, supporting commercial and manufacturing interests at a time when most voters identified with rural agriculture. The Federalists also suffered from weak leadership, particularly after Alexander Hamilton, their dominant personality and leading policy spokesman, was killed by Democratic-Republican Aaron Burr, vice president of the United States, in a duel in 1804. By 1816, the United States had become, in effect, a one-party nation, in which virtually every important politician and officeholder considered himself a Democratic-Republican. As a result, the years between 1816 and 1824 are often called the "Era of Good Feeling."

The Second Party System (Jacksonian Democracy)   Parties are held together, to a large extent, by fear of the opposition. Thus, with the Federalist Party no longer a serious contender for national power, the Democratic-Republicans also began to come apart. In the presidential election of 1824, the congressional caucus, the official nominating body of the Democratic-Republican Party, endorsed Treasury Secretary William Crawford. But, with no worry that partisan disunity might elect a Federalist, three other candidates also ran for president, each of whom claimed to be a member of the party of Jefferson and Madison.

Andrew Jackson, the only great military hero from the War of 1812, won the most popular and electoral votes, but his electoral vote total fell well short of the required majority. As specified in the Constitution, the choice was then made by the House of Representatives, which gave the nod to John Quincy Adams. Believing that they had been deprived of the presidency by a "corrupt bargain" between Adams and Speaker of the House Henry Clay, who was later named secretary of state, Jackson and his supporters almost immediately began organizing for the 1828 election. Buoyed by a huge increase in turnout, Jackson won a decisive victory.

Jackson proved to be a strong but controversial president, and out of the support for and opposition to his policies came the second party system. Jackson and his supporters called themselves the Democrats; his critics eventually settled on the name Whigs. The principal dividing line between the Democrats and the Whigs was the use of the federal government to promote national economic development, by financing such "internal improvements" as roads, bridges, and canals; using tariffs to protect infant industries from foreign competition; and rechartering a national bank. The Whigs favored such policies; the Democrats believed that these matters were better left to the states.

The two parties also disagreed about the extent of presidential power, with the Democrats supporting a more vigorous and active role for the nation's chief executive. One issue that did not separate the parties was slavery. Both parties contained active opponents and strong supporters of slavery. Hence, both did their best to straddle the issue, trying to keep it off the congressional agenda. Those wishing to express opposition to slavery in a presidential election thus turned to third parties: the Liberty Party in 1840 and 1844, and the Free Soil Party in 1848 and 1852.

Unlike the Federalists and Democratic-Republicans, the Democrats and Whigs were parties built on mass participation. Both had extensive grassroots organizations in every state. To coordinate their presidential campaigns, both parties developed **national nominating conventions,** quadrennial gatherings of party officials and delegates that select presidential and vice presidential nominees and adopt party platforms. They also established national committees to direct and coordinate the presidential campaigns, institutions that are still used today. As the figures in Table 8.1 show, however, the competition was not an even one. The Democrats were the dominant party of the second party system. The only times the Whigs won the presidency were when they nominated war heroes: William Henry Harrison in 1840 and Zachary Taylor in 1848. The Democrats also won regular majorities in both the House and the Senate.

national nominating convention

Quadrennial gathering of party officials and delegates that selects presidential and vice presidential nominees and adopts party platforms. Extension of the direct primary to the presidential level after 1968 has greatly reduced the importance of the conventions.

The Third Party System (Civil War and Reconstruction) Try as they might, the Democrats and Whigs could not keep slavery out of national politics forever. The key sticking point was the question of how to deal with slavery in the territories that were being added to the United States throughout the first half of the nineteenth century. Although the Constitution did not give the federal government any obvious way of regulating or outlawing slavery in the states, it did give Congress (in Article IV) the power "to dispose of and make all needful Rules and Regulations respecting the Territory . . . belonging to the United States." Pursuant to this clause, the Missouri Compromise of 1820 forbade slavery everywhere in the Louisiana Purchase territory north of Missouri. In 1854, however, Democrats in Congress and the White House upended this policy by enacting the Kansas-Nebraska Act, which allowed settlers to bring slaves into both of those territories. The turmoil that followed shattered what was left of the Whig Party. Meetings and conventions, held all over the North, sought to bring together Whigs, disaffected Democrats, and Free Soil party members—everyone who was opposed to the Kansas-Nebraska policy. Over the next several years, these groups gradually coalesced into the Republican Party.

Unlike the Whigs and Democrats, the Republicans were a highly regional party. Both of their first two presidential nominees did not win a single electoral vote in ten different southern states. They were, however, very strong throughout the North. In 1860, Abraham Lincoln won only 40 percent of the national popular vote—but he won enough northern states to gain a majority in the Electoral College.[25]

As the figures in Table 8.1 indicate, the third party system is perhaps best thought of as comprising two distinct subperiods. Between 1860 and 1872, the Republicans dominated both Congress and the presidency—but much of their success was attributable to the fact that the most Democratic region of the country, the South, had seceded from the Union. Once Reconstruction was over and federal troops were withdrawn from the former Confederate states, however, the two parties competed on remarkably even terms.[26] Of the next five presidential elections, the Republicans won three and the Democrats two—but all of these elections were very close and two of the Democratic losers actually won a plurality of the popular vote. In Congress, Democrats won regular majorities in the House of Representatives while the Republicans exercised a similar dominance in the Senate.

Between 1860 and 1876, the dominant issue in American politics was the Civil War and then the Reconstruction of the South, but after 1876 economic issues took center stage. The rise of large business organizations, industrialization and its associated dislocations, and a long agricultural depression inevitably raised questions about how the national government should relate to the U.S. economy. The third party system was also the time when party organizations reached their high point. Bitter memories of the Civil War left many people committed to the party of the Union (Republicans) or the party of the rebels (Democrats), and intense electoral competition encouraged these committed citizens to vote a straight party line. Indeed, independents often were viewed contemptuously as "traitors." With feelings so strong, the parties exerted tremendous effort in campaigns, with most of that effort devoted to the mobilization of the faithful, rather than to the conversion or persuasion of the undecided.[27] Parties reached such a high level of organization in many cities that they were referred to as **machines.**

machine
A highly organized party under the control of a boss and based on patronage and control of government activities. Machines were common in many cities in the late nineteenth and early twentieth centuries.

The Fourth Party System (Industrial Republican)

Partisan divisions rooted in the Civil War seemed increasingly outmoded as the United States emerged as an industrialized nation. The excesses and corruption of the urban machines spawned reform movements aimed at destroying their influence. Agricultural protest, common throughout the period, gave rise to the Populist Party that seriously challenged the major parties in the South and West.

The event that finally brought an end to the third party system was the severe depression that hit the country in the early 1890s—to that point, the worst depression in American history. Voters blamed the Democrats, as the party that then controlled the presidency and both houses of Congress, for the country's economic crisis. Their 1896 presidential candidate, William Jennings Bryan, although a hero to many farmers and evangelical Protestants, had a style that repulsed many Catholics and urban workers. As a result, a small but critical segment of the nonsouthern electorate jumped from the Democratic to the Republican Party—and the Democratic Party ceased to be competitive in most areas of the North. The Democrats retained their monopoly control over southern politics and had pockets of strength in many large cities, but most elections between 1896 and 1928 resulted in Republican presidents and Republican majorities in both houses of Congress. The Democrats won the presidency only twice during the fourth party system: in 1912, when Woodrow Wilson emerged the victor in a three-way race with President William Howard Taft and former president Theodore Roosevelt, which split the Republican Party; and again in 1916, when Wilson was narrowly reelected on a platform of keeping the United States out of World War I.

One of the most significant political forces during this period was a loose aggregation of politicians, political activists, and intellectuals known as the **Progressives.** There were prominent Progressives in both parties; other Progressives were nonpartisan and even anti-partisan. The Progressive movement drew most of its supporters from the urban middle class, and it tried to solve a host of problems connected with the industrialization and urbanization of America that occurred in the second half of the

Progressives
Loose aggregation of politicians, political activists, and intellectuals of the late nineteenth and early twentieth centuries who promoted political reforms in an effort to clean up elections and government.

THE MILLENNIUM. THE TIGER AND THE LAMB LIE TOGETHER

The Tammany Tiger

Urban political machines often appeared to threaten the nation's democratic institutions. Here, a cartoonist depicts New York City's Tammany Hall machine as a tiger.

• *Political parties may be effective at organization, but at what point does the political system become too organized?*

direct primary

A method of choosing party candidates that allows voters instead of party leaders to choose nominees for office; it weakened party control of nominations and the influence that parties could exercise over officeholders. This method of nominating candidates is virtually unknown outside the United States.

nineteenth century. The Progressives' most important legacy is the long list of political reforms they championed in an effort to "clean up" elections and government administration—initiatives and referendums, direct primaries, nonpartisan elections, voter registration systems, city managers, and the commission form of city government. Although contemporary historians and political scientists portrayed the Progressives in very positive terms, more recent commentators have often noted a dark side to these "reforms," which often served to push ordinary citizens out of politics and make it more difficult for poor and working-class ethnic neighborhoods to secure adequate representation.[28]

The Progressives undermined two principal resources used by political parties to maintain power: control of public employment and control of nominations. Civil service reforms begun at the national level with the Pendleton Civil Service Act of 1883 (see Chapter 14) were extended wherever possible, diminishing the spoils the parties had available to distribute to their members. The **direct primary** system, which allowed voters instead of party leaders to choose nominees for office, weakened party control of nominations and hence the influence that parties could exercise over officeholders. The reforms targeted real corruption, but they also weakened the parties, which were the principal mobilizing agents that brought many low-income and low-status people into politics.

The Fifth Party System (New Deal)   Like its predecessor, the fourth party system was brought to an end by an economic depression—the Great Depression of the 1930s, the worst in the nation's history. In November 1930, with the Depression barely a year old, the Republicans lost 53 seats in and control of the House of Representatives. The elections of 1932 swept in a Democratic Senate and, more importantly, made Franklin D. Roosevelt president, a man who was determined to fight the Depression with a much more active use of the federal government.

The New Deal period instituted a class-based party system that resembled electoral alignments in modern European democracies. Foreign policy was a key issue on the agenda during this period, as the U.S. fought in World War II and later led democracies against Communist nations in the Cold War, but these issues did not divide the parties as much as economic issues did. After Roosevelt's first term, the Democratic Party became the party of the "common" people (blue-collar workers, farmers, and minorities), whereas the Republican Party became, more than ever, the party of business and the affluent. The former accounted for a lot more voters than the latter, leading to a period of Democratic dominance not seen since before the Civil War. Only Republican war hero Dwight Eisenhower was able to crack the Democratic monopoly, which he did in 1952 and 1956. Republicans controlled Congress for only two terms, from 1947 to 1948 and from 1953 to 1954.

But racial divisions slowly eroded the Democratic Party's electoral coalition. The New Deal coalition that Roosevelt put together in the 1930s included a remarkable diversity of groups that had little in common except a proclivity for liberal economic policies. In particular, the Democrats struggled to balance the demands of both the white South (where blacks were almost completely excluded from voting) and of the increasing number of northern blacks who had migrated to American cities in search of greater opportunity. In 1948, Democrats finally included in their national platform a plank calling for "full and equal political participation" and "the right to equal opportunity of employment" for all Americans. Many southern delegates walked out of the convention and later nominated Governor J. Strom Thurmond of South Carolina as the States' Rights or "Dixiecrat" candidate for president. From that point forward, the South was, at best, an uneasy partner in the Democratic electoral coalition. Although southern voters continued to elect Democrats to the House and the Senate, Republican presidential candidates were, for the first time, able to break the Democratic monopoly on the once-solid South.

The Contemporary Party System

And what of the contemporary era? As is often the case in political science, it is easier to pronounce judgment on the past than on the present. Most commentators believe that the New Deal party system is gone, but they are in less agreement about what sort of party system has replaced it—or even if one has. The electoral alignments that began to develop in the late 1960s have puzzled scholars for much of the past generation because, in a number of important respects, they do not resemble realignments of the past.

Of the four characteristics listed earlier that are generally used to define a party system, the clearest change has occurred in the parties' electoral coalitions. Table 8.2

TABLE 8.2
GROUP VOTING IN PRESIDENTIAL ELECTIONS, 2000–2008

	2000	2004	2008
	Percent Democratic	Percent Democratic	Percent Democratic
Men	42	44	50
Women	53	52	56
White	43	40	43
Black	90	88	99
Hispanic	51	55	76
Attend church . . .			
Every week	38	40	38
Almost every week	45	50	48
Once or twice a month	56	44	64
Few times a year	53	58	63
Never	54	51	61
Union household	58	63	59
Nonunion household	47	45	53
Married	42	42	45
Unmarried	57	56	65
Protestant	46	45	37
Catholic	47	50	57
Income			
Bottom quintile	60	61	62
Second quintile	49	51	56
Third quintile	48	56	63
Fourth quintile	48	39	51
Top quintile	40	43	39
White South	29	32	30

Source: American National Election Studies.

shows how a large number of politically significant demographic groups voted in the 2000, 2004, and 2008 presidential elections. Although the candidates and final results of these elections were different, there is a striking consistency in the relative amount of support these groups gave to the Democrats and Republicans. In election after election, Democrats run well among women, blacks, Hispanics, union members, the unmarried, the less religious, and those with below-average incomes. Republicans draw consistent support from men, whites, nonunion households, the married, regular church attendees, the white South, and those with above-average incomes.

Some of the patterns in Table 8.2 were also present in elections of the 1930s and 1940s, but others are plainly new. The quintessential example of how the present-day party coalitions differ from those of the New Deal party system is the South. During the New Deal—indeed, well before it—Democratic presidential candidates, no matter what their problems, could almost always count on a solid vote from the South. In Franklin Roosevelt's four presidential elections, his *worst* showing in the 11 former Confederate states was in Tennessee in 1944—and he still won more than 60 percent of the vote. Through 1964 every Democratic presidential candidate in the twentieth century carried a majority of the southern states. Since 1968, by contrast, only one Democratic candidate—Jimmy Carter in 1976—has won a majority of southern states. Five different Democratic candidates did not carry a single southern state. At the other end of the spectrum, New England, once the most Republican region in the country, has now become reliably Democratic. In both 2004 and 2008, the Democratic presidential candidate carried all six New England states.

Other important changes have also occurred in the party electoral coalitions. Whereas Republican candidates once won about a third of the black vote, now they barely win 10 percent of it. During the New Deal, the major religious divide in American electoral politics was between northern Protestants, who disproportionately sided with the Republican Party, and northern Catholics, who generally supported the Democratic Party. Today, by contrast, there is remarkably little difference between Protestant and Catholic voting behavior. As Table 8.2 shows, the most significant religious fault line separates regular church attendees from those who rarely or never attend.

The issue agenda has also changed. The New Deal, as we have already noted, dealt almost exclusively with economic issues. Today, economic issues remain an important subject of debate between the parties, as can be seen in the debates over healthcare and the Obama administration's economic stimulus plan, but they have been joined by a set of social or cultural issues—crime, abortion, gay rights, pornography, school prayer, affirmative action—that were largely absent from national politics until the mid-1960s. In addition, foreign policy has lost its consensual, nonpartisan character. Since the early 1970s, Republicans have generally advocated larger defense budgets and a more aggressive use of American military strength, while the Democrats have shown a greater preference for negotiations and the use of multilateral organizations such as the United Nations.

platform
A statement of a party's positions on the major issues of the day.

Every four years, in conjunction with their national presidential nominating conventions, the two major parties each put together a party **platform,** a statement of the party's positions on the major issues of the day. Although commentators often dismiss these documents as nothing more than sound and fury, signifying nothing, historians and political scientists have found them to be good summaries of the issue positions the parties emphasized in their campaigns—and what they actually did after the election.[29] Table 8.3 provides a set of excerpts from the 2008 Democratic and Republican platforms.

TABLE 8.3

EXCERPTS FROM THE 2008 DEMOCRATIC AND REPUBLICAN PLATFORMS

Abortion

Democrats: "The Democratic Party strongly and unequivocally supports *Roe* v. *Wade* and a woman's right to choose a safe and legal abortion, regardless of ability to pay, and we oppose any and all efforts to weaken or undermine that right."

Republicans: "We support a human life amendment to the Constitution, and we endorse legislation to make clear that the Fourteenth Amendment's protections apply to unborn children."

Social Security

Democrats: "We will fulfill our obligation to strengthen Social Security and to make sure that it provides guaranteed benefits Americans can count on, now and in future generations. We will not privatize it."

Republicans: "Comprehensive reform should include the opportunity to freely choose to create your own personal investment accounts which are distinct from and supplemental to the overall Social Security system."

Iraq and Afghanistan

Democrats: "The central front in the war on terror is not Iraq, and it never was. We will defeat Al Qaeda in Afghanistan and Pakistan, where those who actually attacked us on 9-11 reside and are resurgent."

Republicans: "As the people of Iraq assume their rightful place in the ranks of free and open societies, we offer them a continuing partnership. . . . Additional forces are . . . necessary [in Afghanistan], both from NATO countries and through a doubling in size of the Afghan army."

Labor Unions

Democrats: "We will strengthen the ability of workers to organize unions. . . . [E]nsure that federal employees, including public safety officers who put their lives on the line every day, have the right to bargain collectively, and . . . . We will fight to ban the permanent replacement of striking workers."

Republicans: "We affirm both the right of individuals to voluntarily participate in labor organizations, and the right of states to enact

Right-to-Work laws. . . . To protect workers from misuse of their funds, we will conscientiously enforce federal law requiring financial reporting and transparency by labor unions."

Same-Sex Marriage

Democrats: "We support the inclusion of all families, including same-sex couples, in the life of our nation, and support equal responsibility, benefits, and protections. . . . We oppose the Defense of Marriage Act and all attempts to use this issue to divide us."

Republicans: "[W]e call for a constitutional amendment that fully protects marriage as a union of a man and a woman. . . . In the absence of a national amendment, we support the right of the people of the various states to affirm traditional marriage through state initiatives."

Affirmative Action

Democrats: "We support affirmative action, including in federal contracting and higher education."

Republicans: "Precisely because we oppose discrimination, we reject preferences, quotas, and set-asides, whether in education or in corporate boardrooms."

Environmental Protection

Democrats: "Global climate change is the planet's greatest threat, and our response will determine the very future of life on this earth. . . . We will implement a market-based cap and trade system to reduce carbon emissions by the amount scientists say is necessary to avoid catastrophic change."

Republicans: "By increasing our American energy supply and decreasing long-term demand for oil, we will be well positioned to address the challenge of climate change and continue our longstanding responsibility for stewardship over the environment. . . . Empowering Washington will only lead to unintended consequences and unimagined economic and environmental pain; instead, we must unleash the power of scientific know-how and competitive markets."

Sources: "The 2008 Democratic National Platform: Renewing America's Promise," www.democrats.org/a/party/platform.html, accessed June 13, 2010; "2008 Republican Platform," www.gop.com/2008platform/, accessed June 13, 2010.

The platforms provide a good guide to the issues—such as abortion—on which the parties assume directly opposite positions, versus the issues, such as labor unions, where the differences are matters of nuance.

Another important feature of the contemporary party system, which is only hinted at in Table 8.3, is that both parties have become increasingly unified along ideological lines. Although the New Deal plainly established the Democrats as the more liberal of the two American parties, there were, throughout the fifth party system, many exceptions. Many of the most conservative members of Congress were southern Democrats; many of the Republicans elected from the Northeast were moderate or even liberal. Over the last several decades, however, conservative Democrats and liberal Republicans have become increasingly rare. In 1960, political scientist and historian Clinton Rossiter famously noted that one of the most striking characteristics of American parties was "their lack of ideological or programmatic commitment. [Both major parties] are creatures of compromise, coalitions of interest in which principle is muted and often even silenced. They are vast, gaudy, friendly umbrellas under which all Americans, whoever and whatever and however-minded they may be, are invited to stand for the sake of being counted in the next election."[30] Today, scarcely anyone would apply such a description to either the Democrats or the Republicans. More than at any time in the twentieth century, party labels mean something: The party under which a person comes to office says a lot about the kinds of policies he or she supports (see *Election Voices!* feature on page 238).

Perhaps the most difficult question to answer is whether and how the balance of strength between the parties has changed. Between 1968 and 1988, Republicans won five of six presidential elections, several by landslide margins, suggesting that Democratic dominance of presidential elections had come to an end and leading some commentators to predict, rather rashly, that the Republicans now had a "lock" on the Electoral College. Yet, since that time, Democrats have done better, winning three of the five presidential contests from 1992 to 2008. Most races have also been closely contested during this more recent period: No winning presidential candidate since 1988 has received more than 53 percent of the popular vote.

Any argument that the late 1960s had ushered in a new Republican era was further undercut by the results of congressional elections. From 1968 through 1992, the Democrats retained a pretty firm hold on Congress. The 1980 elections did bring in a Republican majority in the Senate, but it lasted only six years. That aside, Democrats seemed to have a stranglehold on Congress, particularly the House of Representatives. Many political scientists accordingly labeled the new party system as the era of "divided government," when voters would regularly elect Republican presidents and Democratic Congresses. This result occurred because of a sharp increase in **ticket-splitting,** as many Americans voted for a Republican presidential candidate and a Democratic candidate for the House and/or Senate. Yet this verdict also proved to be temporary. In 1994, the Republicans unexpectedly won majorities in both the House and the Senate and President George W. Bush enjoyed a period of unified Republican government from 2001 to 2006. Democrats controlled both Congress and the presidency during the first two years of the Obama administration.

What should we make of the electoral era that has held sway since 1968? As late as the mid-1980s, there were some political scientists who argued that nothing very fundamental had changed—that we were still living in the New Deal party system, albeit in an extended, "decay phase" of it.[31] But, as electoral changes have accumulated, and particularly after the Republicans won control of both houses of Congress, it has been more and more difficult to defend such a claim. Instead, most contemporary analysts adhere to one of two schools of thought.

On the one hand, many scholars believe that a realignment did occur in the late 1960s and early 1970s, with 1968 being the best candidate for a true "critical" election. The major problem with this diagnosis concerns the timing of the key changes in electoral behavior and how extensive they were. Although the late 1960s clearly did usher in a series of major changes in the general pattern of presidential voting, similar changes, as we have seen, did not occur—at least at that time—in elections for the House, Senate, state legislatures, or any other set of "sub-presidential elections." Republicans did not start to show sustained strength below the presidency until 1994; the substantial Democratic advantage in mass partisanship, as we will see in Chapter 10, did not begin to change until 1984.

ticket-splitting
Voter selection of candidates from different parties at the same election—for example, a Republican presidential candidate but a Democratic candidate for the House of Representatives.

There are a number of plausible ways that we can explain why the presidential-level changes took so long to trickle down through the rest of the party system.[32] But one core component of the original theory of realignment was precisely the notion that change occurred very suddenly. In the early 1930s, for example, the Democrats went from being an apparently hopeless minority to having unified control of the federal and most state governments in the span of about three years. If change occurs gradually, over a period of two or three decades, does it make sense to keep using the term "realignment" to describe it?

Faced with this sort of problem, a different group of political scientists has argued that the whole theory of realignments is now outdated (indeed, it may never have been valid). Electoral change undoubtedly does occur, but not in the kind of regular, thorough-going way that the proponents of realignment envision. Yet many of the scholars who pronounce realignment dead nevertheless continue to use terms such as "party system" and "electoral era" to characterize both the broad sweep of American electoral history and the changes that have occurred since the 1960s.[33] That history, in the eyes of most observers, is not merely a succession of small, unconnected changes. Some changes are more important and more lasting than others, and thus make it difficult to resist the idea that it is possible to speak of distinct periods or eras in the history of American political parties.

Two-Party and Multi-Party Systems: American Parties in Comparative Perspective

Americans understandably regard a **two-party system,** in which only two significant parties compete for office, as a natural state of affairs. As the description of party systems showed, for most of the nation's history, two major parties have dominated elections for national office, although third parties regularly arise (see Table 8.4). Several third parties, such as the Progressive Party and the Green Party, have influenced the outcomes of some American elections, but nearly all third parties disappear.[34] Only once has a third party replaced a major party: The Republicans displaced the Whigs in the 1850s. Often, third parties are a reaction to a particular problem, and they fade when the problem does. If the problem persists, the third party usually is absorbed or "co-opted" by a major party, as were the Populists, who joined with the Democrats in the 1890s.

However "natural" this state of affairs may appear to Americans, most democracies have multi-party systems. Canadians, for example, spread their votes across a number of significant alternatives—including conservative, liberal, and social democratic parties as well as a reform party and a strong regional party centered in the province of Québec. When the political system offers so many options, often no single party can win control of government; rather, two or more minority parties must ally themselves and form a coalition government based on their combined parliamentary majority. This happened in Great Britain in 2010, when the Conservative Party formed a coalition with the smaller Liberal Democrats after an election in which the Conservatives fell 17 seats short of a majority in the House of Commons.

Why do some countries have two-party systems while others have a half dozen or more significant parties? Most scholars believe that the electoral system strongly affects how many parties a country can sustain. An **electoral system** is the way in which a

8.3

Compare and contrast the American two-party system with the more prevalent multi-party system.

two-party system
System in which only two significant parties compete for office. Such systems are in the minority among world democracies.

electoral system
The way in which a country's constitution or laws translate popular votes into control of public offices.

TABLE 8.4
THIRD PARTIES BY POPULAR SUPPORT

Year	Candidate	Party	Popular Votes (%)	Electoral Vote	Subsequent Events
1912	T. Roosevelt	Progressive	27.4	88	Supported GOP nominee in 1916.
1992	R. Perot	Independent	18.7	0	Created Reform Party, which failed.
1924	R. LaFollette	Progressive	16.6	13	Robert LaFollette died in 1925.
1968	G. Wallace	American	13.5	46	Dropped from 1972 election after being maimed in assassination attempt.
1848	M. Van Buren	Free Soul	10.1	0	Supporters eventually merged with Republican Party.
1892	J. B. Weaver	Populist	8.5	22	Party supported Democratic ticket in 1896.
1996	R. Perot	Reform	8.5	0	Party collapsed in 2000 elections.
1980	J. Anderson	National Unity	6.6	0	Candidate withdrew from politics.
2000	R. Nader	Green	3.0	0	Failed to qualify for 2004 federal funding.
1948	S. Thurmond	States' Rights	2.4	38	Democrats picked slate acceptable to South in 1952.
1948	H. A. Wallace	Progressive	2.4	6	Party disappeared.

Note: Candidates sorted by popular vote percentage.

single-member, simple-plurality (SMSP) system

Electoral system in which the country is divided into geographic districts, and the candidates who win the most votes within their districts are elected.

proportional representation (PR)

Electoral system in which parties receive a share of seats in parliament that is proportional to the popular vote they receive.

country's constitution or laws translate popular votes into control of public offices.[35] The United States relies almost exclusively on the **single-member, simple-plurality (SMSP) system.** Elections for office take place within geographic units (states, congressional districts, cities, and so on), and the candidate who wins the most votes wins the election. When only two candidates run, one candidate will win a majority; when more than two run, a simple plurality determines the winner. This electoral system is characteristic of the "Anglo-American democracies" (England and its former colonies). It is often called the "first past the post" system: Just as in a horse race, the winner is the one who crosses the finish line first, no matter how many others are in the race or how close the finish.

In most of the world's democracies, however, the electoral system is some version (there are many variations) of **proportional representation (PR).** In such systems, elections may (Germany) or may not (Israel) take place within smaller geographic units; but, even if they do, each unit elects a number of officials, with each party winning seats in proportion to the vote it receives.

To illustrate the operation of these differing electoral systems, consider an example. In the 1992 election, the state of Minnesota had 10 electoral votes. Its popular vote was divided as follows:

Bill Clinton: 52%
George H. W. Bush: 36%
Ross Perot: 12%

Had Minnesota divided its electoral votes on a proportional basis, Clinton would have won 5 votes, Bush 4, and Perot 1. Had the same sort of system been used everywhere in the country, Clinton would have been the leading candidate in the Electoral College—but he would have fallen far short of the majority required by the Constitution. Perot, meanwhile, would have had about 100 electoral votes—giving him and his supporters the balance of power between the two major parties and perhaps allowing them to extract policy concessions or major positions in the new administration from one of the other candidates as the price of their support.

In fact, however, the election laws in Minnesota—and in almost every other state—effectively treat the entire state as a single electoral unit, with all electoral votes going to whichever candidate wins the most votes, regardless of whether it is a majority. Thus, the actual electoral vote cast by the Minnesota electors in 1992 was Clinton 10, Bush 0, Perot 0. Aggregated across 50 states and the District of Columbia, Clinton won a comfortable majority in the Electoral College even though he received just 43 percent of the popular vote. As for Perot, who won 19 percent of the popular vote, he received not a single electoral vote.

As this example illustrates, in an SMSP electoral system, winning is everything—finishing in any position but first achieves nothing. Thus, if small parties have more in common with each other than with the largest party, they have an incentive to join together in a single opposing party to challenge the plurality winner, because dividing the opposition among more than one candidate plays into the hands of the enemy. Ordinary citizens, in turn, realize that voting for a small party is tantamount to "wasting" their vote, because such a party has no chance of coming in first.[36] Thus, they tend to support one of the two larger parties. In presidential election polls, for example, the standard pattern for third-party and independent candidates is that their share of the popular vote declines steadily the closer one gets to Election Day, as more and more voters begin to appreciate that the third-party aspirants have no real chance to win and that their votes are therefore better expended on one of the major-party candidates. In 1980, for example, third-party presidential candidate John Anderson had 24 percent of the vote in mid-June, 14 percent in September, 9 percent in late October, and 7 percent in the actual election.

In PR systems, by contrast, a party wins seats in proportion to its votes (as long as it finishes above some legally defined threshold). Because it is not necessary to finish first in order to win something, party leaders have more incentive to maintain their separate organizations. And, because only votes for tiny parties fail to count, voters are not motivated to abandon smaller parties. Thus, a multi-party system persists.

One other factor that affects the survival of third parties in SMSP systems is whether their votes are geographically concentrated. If they receive, say, 20 percent of the nationwide vote but it is distributed evenly across the country, they win nothing. On the other hand, if their votes are regionally concentrated so that they are the first or second party in some constituencies, they may persist indefinitely. The Liberal Democrats have survived in the United Kingdom, for example, by remaining dominant in several dozen key electoral districts. Nevertheless, because their share of the vote (23 percent in 2010) is far greater than their share of the seats in Parliament (less than 9 percent), Liberal Democrats have long advocated a switch to a proportional representation system.

The almost exclusive use of SMSP electoral systems throughout the United States is, then, an important part of the explanation for the American two-party system. And, as long as these rules persist, it is unlikely that a lasting third party will ever be established in this country. Yet a number of other factors also work to the disadvantage of third-party and independent candidates and may spell the difference between victory and defeat—or a strong showing and a weak showing—in a particular contest. The election laws in most states, for example, grant automatic ballot access to every party that won some minimum percentage of the vote in the last election.[37] In practice, this means that all candidates nominated by the Democratic and Republican parties automatically get their names listed on the general election ballot. Independent and third-party candidates must file a petition to get on the ballot—which often requires them to collect thousands of signatures, sometimes under complex, arcane regulations.

Major-party candidates also get far more coverage on television and in the newspapers than independents and minor-party contenders. Reporters and editors defend this practice by saying that they base their coverage on the polls and other indicators of how well the candidates are expected to do on Election Day—and because most third-party candidates lag well behind in the polls, they receive less coverage. Although the media's characterization of third-party support is generally accurate, it may also be self-fulfilling. At least some third-party candidates might do quite well if they received enough coverage to make the voters aware of their candidacies—but, not being affiliated with one of the major parties, they never receive that coverage. Similarly, televised debates, which have played an important role in many recent campaigns, are usually restricted to the major-party candidates.

8.4

Assess whether American political parties are experiencing a decline or a revival.

How Strong Are American Parties Today?

Scholars disagree about the strength of modern political parties, in part because people have different conceptions of what a party is.[38] In most of the world, parties are well-defined organizations. People join them in the same way they join clubs in the United States: They pay dues, receive official membership cards, go to regularly scheduled meetings, and have a right to participate in various party-sponsored activities (such as nominating candidates). In the United States, however, parties have a more nebulous existence. When Americans refer to parties, they may have in mind three distinct notions (or some combination of the three):

1. The party in the electorate: those voters who feel some kind of psychological loyalty or affiliation with the party and who will, as a result, vote for the party's candidates.
2. The party in government: those who have captured office under the label of the party and those who seek to do so; the party's candidates for public office and its state, local, and national officeholders.
3. The party organization: the formal machinery of the party—its leaders, committees, headquarters staff, and ward and precinct workers.

The party in the electorate is discussed more fully in Chapter 10. For now, it is enough to say that the percentage of the American adult population who have a party identification—who express a psychological tie with either the Democrats or the Republicans—declined between about 1964 and 1974. But the significance of this decline is uncertain because many people began to identify themselves as independents who "lean" toward a party. Some political scientists think these leaners are "closet partisans," while others think they are in fact independents. There is also some evidence, in recent years, that parties have recouped some of their earlier losses, and that the once-substantial rate of ticket-splitting and party defection has gone down. Unfortunately, there are not reliable survey measures of mass partisanship from the years prior to 1952, but for the years since then perhaps the safest conclusion is that the party in the elec-torate has declined somewhat, but not dramatically.

As we will see in Chapter 12, there is good reason to think that the U.S. parties in government, particularly in Congress, are stronger today than they have been at any time since the early 1900s. An increasing proportion of roll calls, across a growing set of issues, pit a majority of Democrats against a majority of Republicans.

The Decline of Party Organizations

It is more difficult to provide a clear conclusion about the growth or decline of party organizations. Historically, the United States did not have true national party organiza-tions. Rather, what passed for national organizations were temporary alliances of state parties and local machines that joined together every four years to work for the elec-tion of a president.

State and local party organizations were at their strongest about the time the Progressive movement began around 1900. The decline of American party organizations was largely a consequence of deliberate public policies instituted by the Progressives. As noted earlier, the two principal resources that party organizations depend on were control of patronage and control of nominations for office. The first was gradually eliminated by regular expansions of civil service protection and, after World War II, by unionization of the public sector, which gave government workers an additional layer of insulation from partisan politics. (Currently, the largest union in the AFL-CIO is the American Federation of State, County and Municipal Employees.) The final nail in the coffin came when the U.S. Supreme Court ruled that most forms of patronage are unconstitutional, because they penalize public employees for their beliefs and associations.[39] Today, the president personally controls fewer than 4,000 appointments.[40] At the height of the spoils system—and with a much smaller federal government—presidents controlled well over 100,000 appointments.[41] Similarly, governors and big-city mayors who once con-trolled tens of thousands of jobs now control, at most, only a few thousand—and usually far less.

Party control over nominations was greatly weakened by the spread of the direct primary, one of the most important Progressive reforms. As described in Chapter 10, the United States is the only world democracy that relies on open, popular elections to decide nominations. In all other democracies, much smaller groups of party activists and officials choose party nominees. In 2010, California's voters chose to weaken the parties' role in that state's nominating process even further by passing Proposition 14, which forces all candidates—of any party—to run in a single primary. The top two candidates in this election then compete in the general election—even if they share the same party affiliation. These and other reforms have diminished parties' control over who represents them in elections.

Deprived of their principal resources, modern American parties had few sticks and carrots to sway the behavior of members. Electoral defeat did not mean that tens of thousands of people would lose their jobs; hence, they were less inclined to work for

parties and support them through thick and thin. Similarly, outsiders could seek a party's nomination; if they won, the party had no choice but to live with the fact. Controlling neither the livelihoods of ordinary voters nor the electoral fates of public officials, the party organizations atrophied.

However, political reforms do not entirely explain the weakening of American parties. Other independent developments indirectly weakened them. For one thing, the communications revolution lessened the need for traditional parties. Candidates can raise funds through direct-mail and Internet appeals and then use these funds to reach voters directly through television ads, email messages, and social networking software. Technological developments have diminished the need for party workers and party support. Further, the parties do not control their own TV networks, as the major parties in Italy traditionally do. Elections now rely instead on information technology and money.[42]

A second development that undercut U.S. parties was the increase in mobility—social, economic, and residential—that followed World War II. Better-educated voters had less need of parties to make sense of politics and guide their behavior. In a booming economy, voters had less need of parties to help them get jobs. And, as the suburbs grew, the traditional, urban-based parties came to represent an ever-smaller proportion of the population, while the new, decentralized suburbs went largely unorganized.

The Revival of Party Organizations?

Through most of their 150-year history, the national committees were the weakest level of party organization. They became active only during presidential election years, when they coordinated the efforts of independent state and city organizations. Similarly, although powerful state organizations existed in some states, in many others the state organization was only a loose confederation of local organizations. That has changed greatly in the past quarter century. By the 1980s creative politicians began to find new ways for party organizations to help them obtain and keep political power.

Most observers credit Republicans such as William Brock, chairman of the Republican National Committee (RNC) from 1976 to 1982, for leading the way to modern-day party politics. These Republican strategists raised large sums of money, passing them on to friendly candidates as well as local party organizations. They hired full-time political operatives and experts on polling, fund-raising, campaigning, and the media. They retained lawyers versed in election law and specialists skilled in computers and other technologies. Such resources were made available at low cost to Republican campaigns nationwide. For their part, the Democrats eventually imitated the Republicans. By 2010, national party organizations were deeply involved in candidate recruitment, database management, media consulting, and other important elements of campaigning.

In sum, the national committees are active and well financed. They have been joined by senatorial and congressional campaign committees. Together, these national committees have helped rejuvenate party organization at lower levels. Party increasingly matters for public officials. Republicans are increasingly conservative and Democrats increasingly liberal, both in Congress and on the stump (see *Election Voices!* feature on page 238). Competition has become less civil, with both parties "increasingly waging the political equivalent of total war" through the use of devices such as recall elections, legislative redistricting, the blocking of judicial and bureaucratic nominees favored by the other party and even impeachment. The partisan ceasefire that followed the terrorist attacks in 2001 lasted only 43 days.[43]

The debate, however, is far from over. Some knowledgeable observers remain skeptical of the party-resurgence thesis. John Coleman asks whether the parties are resurgent or "just busy."[44] Others grant that the parties are more active now than in earlier decades but argue that the newer activities do not make them stronger "parties" in any traditional sense. According to these critics, the party organizations essentially have become large campaign-consulting firms, taking advantage of economies of scale to provide electioneering services to their associates.

Today's parties still do not have the control over the candidates that they had in the United States a century ago or that they have in most other democracies today. They cannot deny candidates a nomination or demand their loyalty once they are elected. Only rarely are "rebels" in office threatened with loss of party support, and, if a party recruited candidate is defeated in a primary, the party normally supports the victor. In 2010, for example, Pennsylvania Senator Arlen Specter (newly a Democrat after abandoning the Republican Party a year before) was challenged in his primary race by Representative Joe Sestak. Party leaders from the Pennsylvania Democratic State Committee to the White House supported Specter and urged Sestak to withdraw. But, when Sestak beat Specter, Democrats swiftly changed their tune, endorsing him and helping him in his (ultimately unsuccessful) campaign against Republican Pat Toomey.

Party Chair
Republican National Committee Chairman Michael Steele holds a news conference to argue against the Obama administration's healthcare bill.

• *How has the role of the national parties changed since the 1950s?*

There are obvious reasons why the parties are so reluctant to punish party members who fail to toe the line. Independence is highly valued in the United States. If a party tried to discipline a member, it might be more likely to help him or her than to hurt. Moreover, despite the impressive efforts of the modern parties, they contribute only a fraction of the resources devoted to electioneering. Candidates create personal organizations and raise their own war chests. Contributions by the parties to members of Congress, for example, make up less than 10 percent of all congressional campaign expenditures, although the amount spent "independently" is growing.

Continued on page 240

Partisan Polarization

When political scientists examined American political parties in the 1950s and 1960s, one question dominated their research: Why are the two political parties so much alike? In contrast to parties in Europe, the Democrats and Republicans had similar platforms, nominated similar-seeming candidates, and took pains to appear moderate on most relevant issues. Third-party presidential candidate George Wallace famously expressed this sentiment in 1968, saying voters could take the Democrats and Republicans, "Put 'em all in the same sack, shake 'em up. I don't care which one comes out, you stick him back in—because there isn't a dime's worth of difference in them."[1]

Scholars settled on a simple explanation for why parties were so similar. The American electorate was arranged roughly like a "bell curve," with many moderates in the center, and a few extremists on the far right and left of the spectrum (Figure 1). In a two-party system in which everyone votes for the party that is "closest" to them, the natural place for each party to position its platform is right in the middle—where the middle (median) voter is. The same logic explains why gas stations and grocery stores open up right next to each other in the middle of population centers: They want to be closest to the most people.[2]

This explanation is so clever and elegant that it seems a shame to have to point out that today's parties do not appear to conform to the theory. As we point out in Chapter 12, parties in Congress have become more unified, powerful, and distinct since the 1970s. Party activists hold views that are much more extreme than those of voters, as Table 7.3 shows. In a less tangible sense, the bitterness of partisan conflict seems to have increased over time. And, even though there is little evidence that American voters have become more polarized on the issues,[3] they are more likely than in the past to see the parties as having important differences (see Figure 2). In the early years of the Obama administration, major healthcare and economic legislation passed with solid Democratic Party backing and virtually no Republican support. As one former representative lamented, "Health care was too important, and too personal to all Americans, to allow a meaningful policy debate to be replaced by the partisan food fight voters were treated to."[4]

There are probably many reasons for the increasing party polarization. Opportunities for patronage have declined, so today's party activists tend to be more ideologically motivated than in the past.[5] Increasing economic inequality and immigration may have

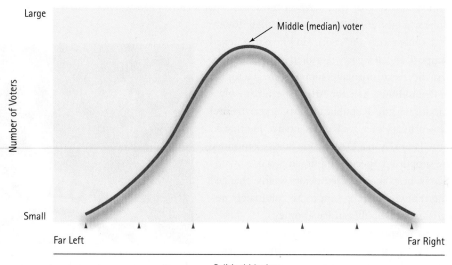

FIGURE 1

A SPATIAL EXPLANATION FOR PARTY SIMILARITY

If most voters are moderate, and if they vote for the party whose views most closely match their own, wise parties will design platforms that match the positions of the voter in the middle (the median).

• *Why do you think this model explained party politics better in the 1950s than today?*

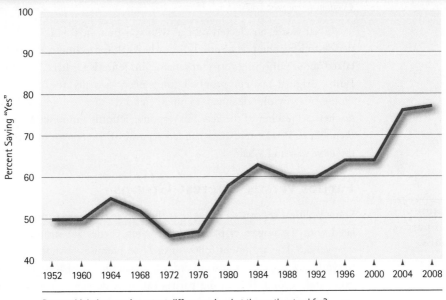

Do you think there are important differences in what the parties stand for?

FIGURE 2

AMERICANS INCREASINGLY SEE IMPORTANT DIFFERENCES BETWEEN THE PARTIES

In the 1960s, large numbers of voters saw little difference between the parties, but this number has dropped in recent years.

• *Some people say that increasing distinctions between the parties give voters clearer choices. Do you agree?*

Source: American National Election Studies.

contributed to growing differences between the parties' electoral bases.[6] Low voter turnout in party primaries may have increasingly ceded the field to the most unrepresentative voters.

Reformers sometimes argue for reforming the way congressional districts are drawn, making them less homogenous, but this change may not do much to diminish partisanship. The U.S. Senate has grown more partisan in tandem with the House, and the Senate obviously has large and varied "districts." Other possibilities might include mandatory voting (see *Election Voices!* feature in Chapter 6), which might dilute the power of extremist voters by drawing more Americans to the polls. In 2010, California voters sought to diminish partisanship by changing that state's rules so that candidates from all parties will now run in the same primary, with the top two vote-getters (regardless of party) advancing to the general election. The *Los Angeles Times* endorsed the change, predicting that "When voters are no longer restricted to candidates of their own party, candidates will be compelled to seek consensus positions rather than play to the extremes."[7]

Others say attempts to reduce partisanship are misguided. Tom Delay, upon his 2006 retirement as Republican majority leader, delivered an impassioned defense of partisanship. "You show me a nation without partisanship," he said, "and I'll show you a tyranny. For all its faults, it is partisanship, based on core principles, that clarifies our debates, that prevents one party from straying too far from the mainstream, and that constantly refreshes our politics with new ideas and new leaders."[8]

What Do You Think?

1. Is partisanship a problem, or is it a helpful way to clarify voters' choices?
2. Do you favor any of the proposed reform proposals aimed at decreasing partisanship? Why or why not?

[1]Stephan Lesher, *George Wallace: American Populist* (Cambridge, MA: Perseus Publishing, 1994), p. 367.

[2]Anthony Downs, *An Economic Theory of Democracy* (New York: Harper, 1957).

[3]Morris Fiorina with Sam Abrams and Jeremy Pope, *Culture War? The Myth of a Polarized America,* 3rd Edition (New York: Longman, 2010).

[4]Amo Houghton, "Voters Are Right to be Angry at Partisanship," *Roll Call,* June 8, 2010, http://www.rollcall.com/issues/55_143/ma_congressional_relations/47079-1.html, accessed June 14, 2010.

[5]Fiorina, et al.

[6]Nolan McCarty, Keith T. Poole, and Howard Rosenthal, *Polarized America: The Dance of Inequality and Unequal Riches* (Cambridge, MA: MIT Press, 2008).

[7]Dan Balz, "California's Possible Solution to Partisan Politics," *Washington Post,* June 6, 2010, http://www.washingtonpost.com/wp-dyn/content/article/2010/06/05/AR2010060502312.html, accessed June 14, 2010.

[8]"Rep. Tom Delay Delivers His Farewell Address," *Washington Post,* June 8, 2006, http://www.washingtonpost.com/wp-dyn/content/article/2006/06/08/AR2006060801376.html, accessed June 14, 2010.

Continued from page 237

Even worse, an elected official who was punished by his or her own party might decide to leave the party entirely. In early 2001, for example, Republicans in the Senate talked about punishing Vermont senator Jim Jeffords for his failure to vote for President Bush's original tax cut proposal (they never actually took any action). The White House, meanwhile, declined to invite Jeffords to a ceremony honoring a Vermont teacher as "Teacher of the Year." In response, Jeffords announced that he was leaving the Republican Party—and thus handed control of the Senate over to the Democrats for the next year and a half.

8.5

Evaluate the relationship between political parties and interest groups.

Parties Versus Interest Groups

Some political theorists believe that the power of interest groups is negatively corre-lated with the power of parties—that when parties are strong, groups are weak, and vice versa.[45] The argument follows from two premises: first, that parties have incentives to synthesize narrow interests in order to make the broad appeals necessary to win elec-tions; and, second, that strong parties can provide electoral resources and deliver the vote, thus freeing their candidates from dependence on interest-group resources and insulating them from interest-group reprisals.

This argument implicitly assumes two-party politics rather than multi-party poli-tics, because in the latter parties often make very narrow appeals. Indeed, in multi-party systems, there may be little difference between parties and large interest groups such as labor unions. But within the two-party context the argument has considerable plausibility.

As we saw in Chapter 7, interest groups proliferated in the Progressive Era, when the parties were systematically attacked by reformers, and again in the 1960s and 1970s, when American parties reached their nadir, before their recent recovery. Just as nature is said to abhor a physical vacuum, so it may be that political vacuums cannot persist. When parties do not fill them, groups or some other source of influence will.

If this argument is valid, then the real alternative to party domination of the elec-toral process is not popular influence but interest-group influence. Rather than reflect-ing the broad appeals of parties, elections will reflect the narrow views of special inter-ests. Of course, interest groups are not the only competitors of parties in modern societies. As we will see in Chapter 9, another potential competitor is the media. Debates about the relative merits of parties, interest groups, and the media all center around which type of organization is best equipped to help convey voter preferences to elected officials.

CHAPTER SUMMARY

8.1 **Evaluate how parties both contribute to and detract from democratic politics.**

Although the Constitution makes no mention of them, political parties have been part of American politics since the colonial period. Parties perform organizing and coordinating

functions that are essential in large-scale representative democracies. Parties coordinate the actions of numerous officeholders and focus responsibility for their actions. Parties develop issues, educate the public, and synthesize disparate interests. Parties recruit and develop governmental talent and simplify the choices of voters who would otherwise be overwhelmed by the task of choosing among numerous candidates for office.

But there are also disadvantages. Parties constantly struggle for political supremacy. Thus, they act in accordance with partisan self-interest and historically have behaved dictatorially, corruptly, and divisively. The question reformers must face, however, is whether they can identify an alternative to party influence and activity.

8.2 **Trace the history of political parties in the United States and assess the contemporary party system.**

American political history is often told in terms of "party systems," wherein each party has dependable support among particular social groups, so that elections tend to be similar within each system. At present, the United States has a party system that is less stable and more confusing than most of those systems that have preceded it.

8.3 **Compare and contrast the American two-party system with the more prevalent multi-party system.**

The United States has the world's longest lived two-party system, due in part to its single-member, simple plurality

(SMSP) electoral system. Election laws and patterns of media coverage also reinforce the advantages that the two main parties enjoy.

8.4 **Assess whether American political parties are experiencing a decline or a revival.**

Parties in the United States are not as strong today as they were in earlier periods. Similar to other American institutions and processes, the parties have been democratized. Few "bosses" remain, party processes are open to all who register, and those elected under the party flag go their own way when it suits them or their constituents. In short, political life is especially disorganized in modern America. Despite much discussion of party decline, though, the Democratic and Republican parties continue to dominate American elections and structure governance.

8.5 **Evaluate the relationship between political parties and interest groups.**

Some scholars see important competition for parties coming from interest groups, and from the mass media. Despite these challenges—and any challenges from third parties—parties are likely to endure and adapt to the New American Democracy.

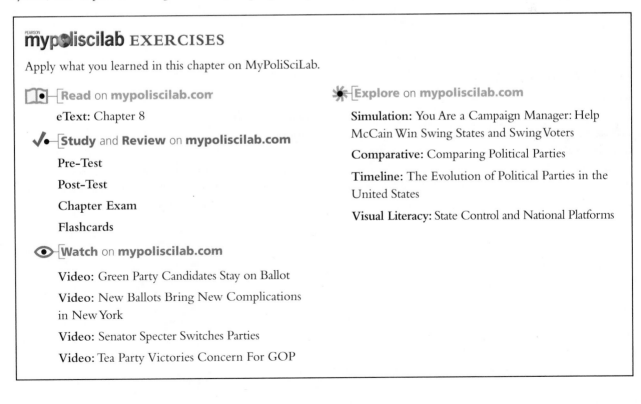

mypoliscilab EXERCISES

Apply what you learned in this chapter on MyPoliSciLab.

Read on mypoliscilab.com

eText: Chapter 8

Study and Review on mypoliscilab.com

Pre-Test

Post-Test

Chapter Exam

Flashcards

Watch on mypoliscilab.com

Video: Green Party Candidates Stay on Ballot

Video: New Ballots Bring New Complications in New York

Video: Senator Specter Switches Parties

Video: Tea Party Victories Concern For GOP

Explore on mypoliscilab.com

Simulation: You Are a Campaign Manager: Help McCain Win Swing States and Swing Voters

Comparative: Comparing Political Parties

Timeline: The Evolution of Political Parties in the United States

Visual Literacy: State Control and National Platforms

KEY TERMS

SUGGESTED READINGS

Of General Interest

Green, John C., and Paul Herrnson, eds. *Responsible Partisanship? The Evolution of American Political Parties Since 1950.* Lawrence: University Press of Kansas, 2003. Comprehensive analysis of how well the political parties have served the American electorate, spread out over essays by some of the most influential researchers on the topic.

Hershey, Marjorie Randon. *Party Politics in America,* 14th ed. New York: Longman, 2011. Probably the best current textbook on American parties and the party system.

Jewell, Malcolm E., and Sarah M. Morehouse. *State Politics, Parties, and Policy,* 2nd ed. Lanham, MD: Rowman & Littlefield, 2003. This textbook covers party politics at the state level.

Key, V. O. Jr. *Politics, Parties and Pressure Groups,* 5th ed. New York: Crowell, 1964. A classic text. Although dated, it can still be read both for historical interest and for theoretical observations about party politics in a democracy.

Focused Studies

Layman, Geoffrey. *The Great Divide: Religious and Cultural Conflict in American Party Politics.* New York: Columbia University Press, 2001. Thorough look at the continuing importance of cultural differences in defining the major political parties.

Mayhew, David. R. *Electoral Realignments: A Critique of an American Genre.* New Haven, CT: Yale University Press, 2002. Recent critique of the abstract theory of electoral realignment.

Sundquist, James. L. *Dynamics of the Party System,* Rev. ed. Washington, DC: The Brookings Institution, 1983. History of national politics since the 1840s told from a party-systems perspective.

ON THE WEB

www.rnc.org

www.dnc.org

Both national party committees also maintain websites that solicit contributions, attack their opponents, and generally promote party-advocated policies.

www.greenparty.org

www.reformparty.org

www.natural-law.org

www.lp.org

Third parties make tremendous use of the Web. The Green Party USA, the Reform Party, the Natural Law Party, and the Libertarian Party have the most prominent minor-party sites.

The Media

CHAPTER OUTLINE

LEARNING OBJECTIVES

9.1 Trace the development of the mass media from colonial times to the present day.

9.2 Identify the primary media through which Americans get their news.

9.3 Characterize the effects the media have on the public's political attitudes.

9.4 Outline the major kinds of media bias and assess criticisms of the media.

9.5 Illustrate the influence of entertainment media on American political attitudes.

9.6 Assess media coverage of the election process.

9.7 Assess media coverage of the government.

The Media: 800-Pound Gorilla or 98-Pound Weakling?

The national media had it all figured out. In the frenzied few days before the 2008 New Hampshire primary, an average voter following press coverage about the campaign would probably have said with a fair degree of certainty that the winners would be Barack Obama and Mitt Romney. Obama had just scored a triumphant victory in the Iowa caucuses and was making a triumphant tour of the state, drawing overflow crowds and adoring media coverage. ABC's Charlie Gibson pointed out what to most of the assembled TV anchors, radio hosts, bloggers, pundits, and newspaper writers seemed obvious: "There is talk and evidence of an Obama wave moving through this state on the eve of its primary."[1] A *New York Post* headline screamed that Obama rival Hillary Clinton's campaign was in a state of "PANIC," and even the more sedate *Washington Post* agreed that Obama had a "clear lead."[2]

Meanwhile, Romney was considered something of a favorite son, since he owned a summer home in New Hampshire and had served as governor of neighboring Massachusetts. He lost the Iowa caucuses to former Arkansas governor Mike Huckabee, but Huckabee had only a bare-bones operation in New Hampshire and was unlikely to do well there. Romney's other main opponent, John McCain, had been written off by the press months before. In mid-2007, the McCain campaign, suffering from staffing and money problems, seemed on the verge of collapse, and the press said so. "Left for dead" seemed to be the operative characterization of McCain: MSNBC's Chris Matthews, FOX News's Chris Wallace, the *New York*

Daily News, the *Washington Post*, and others all used the phrase.[3] Finally, the wealthy Romney bought twice as much television advertising time as McCain.[4] If TV images had an effect on voters, Romney seemed to have the edge.

Considering the impressions the media conveyed, the actual primary results came as quite a surprise. McCain beat Romney and, even more surprisingly, Obama lost to Clinton by two percentage points. Voters appeared to have been indifferent to the tenor of the news coverage, and to the barrage of political advertising. Could it be that, despite all the hue and cry, the modern media have very little effect on voters?

No sooner had reporters and pundits been blindsided by the surprising outcome, however, than they came up with an explanation for it—on the Democratic side, at least—that made the media central again. The day before the primary, Hillary Clinton's eyes appeared to well with tears after a reporter asked her about how she held up under the stress of campaigning. Video of this event rocketed around the Internet and saturated news coverage for that day. In retrospect, argued many observers, this incident elicited sympathy for Clinton among voters—especially women—who had previously found it hard to identify with her. According to this explanation, rather than being ineffectual, the media were fundamental to the election outcome. "The Obama campaign calculated that they had the women's vote over the weekend," wrote columnist Maureen Dowd, "but watched it slip away in the track of her tears."[5]

244

So which was it? Was the three-ring media circus central to the election outcome, or did the media represent a mere sideshow? The wiser media personalities called for humility in the face of such questions. As former NBC anchor Tom Brokaw put it, "the pirouettes are amazing.

The utter confidence with which everyone had been wrong 20 minutes earlier, they have the same utter confidence about what produced this surprise. It's intellectually dishonest."[6]

Making the Connection

How powerful are the media? Are they an overwhelming force that even presidents must fear, or a lot of sound and fury that ordinary Americans ignore? The answer is that, depending on the circumstances, the media can be either of these, and everything in between. Under some conditions, the media can have extremely powerful effects on public opinion, even to the extent of determining who wins elections and what governments do. But, under other conditions, media effects are sharply limited.

We begin our analysis of the role of the media by considering how the media have attained their present position as important political actors, and what kinds of media Americans rely on for political information. We then consider two other important issues: in what ways the media—including the latest methods of communication—affect public opinion today and what types of bias characterize media reports.

Development of the Mass Media

The term **mass media** refers to forms of communication that are widely affordable and technologically capable of reaching a broad audience. Such resources have existed for less than two centuries. Their development since then has shaped American democracy because politicians engage in a never-ending struggle to control the information that reaches their constituents. Information is power, and politicians contend with media organizations for control of it. In this section, we trace the development of the major forms of mass media used to spread political information: print (newspapers and magazines) and broadcast (radio and television). We also look at the emergence of such new media as websites, blogs, and other Internet-based communications tools. In each case we focus on control of the message: Who is responsible for the information transmitted?

When Europeans first established colonies in North America, the only technology capable of reaching a mass audience was the printing press. The first newspaper in the colonies, the *Boston News-Letter,* started publication in 1704.[7] By 1730, there were seven colonial newspapers; by 1800, there were more than 180.[8]

But these early newspapers were different from the publications we know today. Their circulation was quite limited—according to one estimate, the average newspaper in 1800 reached about 700 people—and they came out weekly or semi-weekly. It was difficult to print a large number of newspapers in a short period of time on that era's hand-operated presses. Almost all papers were sold by subscription, and few people could afford them—about 5 percent of free households in 1765—although there is some evidence that papers were passed around, read aloud, or posted in public areas.[9]

9.1

Trace the development of the mass media from colonial times to the present day.

mass media

Means of communication that are widely affordable and technologically capable of reaching a broad audience.

There was no such thing as a professional reporter, so early papers printed virtually everything they could get their hands on: official proclamations, advertisements and commercial news, letters and essays from readers, correspondence from people in other cities, news from the ships that had just arrived in port. These papers did not pursue or "dig up" stories in the way modern-day media do—a characteristic that helps explain how the Constitutional Convention of 1787 could be held behind closed doors and have virtually nothing about its deliberations appear in contemporary newspapers.

The Partisan Press and the Penny Press

The emergence and growth of political parties after the adoption of the Constitution led to a very important development in the fledgling newspaper industry: From 1787 until the Civil War almost all newspapers were openly and explicitly partisan.

Today, of course, lots of major news organizations are accused of providing slanted, partisan news, an issue we consider in detail later in this chapter. But most of these news organizations vehemently deny such charges. By contrast, for the first 70 years or so after ratification of the Constitution, almost all American newspapers were openly affiliated with one political party or another: They announced it proudly, often at the top of their mastheads, and consciously tried to bring a partisan perspective to their writing. Most of these papers also received some kind of subsidy or patronage from the party's supporters in government.

The pattern was set very early. As soon as the division between Federalists and Democratic-Republicans started to emerge (see Chapter 8), Alexander Hamilton, the leader of the Federalists, established a newspaper to support himself and his policies. The paper was called the *Gazette of the United States,* and to make sure the paper stayed in business, Hamilton, as secretary of the Treasury, gave the paper most of the Treasury Department's printing business. In reaction, Thomas Jefferson and his followers set up their own newspaper, the *National Gazette.* Because the State Department did not have a great deal of official printing business to offer, Jefferson put the paper's editor, Philip Freneau, on the State Department payroll, assuring Freneau that his job "gives so little to do, as not to interfere with any other calling the person may choose."[10] As one political scientist has written about this period, "Any wall between journalistic and political enterprises was gone; editors were party leaders, served on party central committees, and gave speeches on behalf of the federal and state party slates."[11]

In the early 1830s, however, a new and different form of journalism emerged: the penny press. As this name implies, one major characteristic of the penny newspapers was that each day's paper cost only one penny, compared to about six cents per copy for the more traditional, partisan papers. Technological improvements made it possible to print papers far more quickly and cheaply, and the resulting low price made the papers accessible to a larger, less educated audience. American cities were growing, and American politics had become more participatory and less elitist (see Chapter 6), so the market for the penny press expanded quickly.[12]

The penny press was very different from the old partisan press. Its writing style was simpler and less flowery. Advertising paid the bills rather than government subsidies. Because these daily newspapers had more space to fill, they began to hire reporters, people who went to city hall or the national capital in Washington and sent back regular accounts of what was going on there. Finally, although most of the penny papers had a political point of view, they also claimed to be independent in the sense that they did not take orders from party leaders. During the Civil War, for example, Republican newspapers supported the general thrust of that party's policies, particularly its opposition to the spread of slavery. But many were quite critical of how President Lincoln was conducting the war.

Newspapers and Magazines, 1865–1920

As large cities grew, so did newspapers. By the turn of the twentieth century, every major city in the United States had multiple competing newspapers. This competition resulted in the era of so-called "yellow journalism," when newspapers eagerly exploited scandals and any story involving sex or violence in an effort to attract more readers. Two of the most notorious practitioners were Joseph Pulitzer, who owned and edited the *New York World,* and William Randolph Hearst, who owned the *New York Journal.* The worst single example of their operating style occurred in 1897 and 1898, when the *World* and *Journal* gave a great deal of highly inflammatory coverage to events in Cuba, particularly the claim that Spanish saboteurs had blown up the *Maine,* an American battleship, and thereby played a major role in getting the United States to declare war against Spain.[13]

Yellow Journalism

William Randolph Hearst's *New York Journal* went on the warpath after the explosion of the *Maine* in Cuba (ultimately leading to the Spanish-American War). Many people suspected that the Spanish were responsible, and Hearst's papers played on that fear.

• *Compare this newspaper's coverage to the coverage of the Iraq war. How is the coverage different? How is it similar?*

Although local newspapers were clearly the dominant medium of this era, national magazines were also influential. Beginning in the 1890s, entrepreneurs founded a series of new magazines aimed at the country's middle class, including *McClure's, Cosmopolitan,* and the *Saturday Evening Post.* After the turn of the century, magazines began publishing articles exposing political malfeasance and business abuses. This "muckraking" became a sensation, making writers such as Lincoln Steffens and Ida Tarbell famous and often prompting major reforms. The muckrakers played an important role in the Progressive movement and set an example for future journalists. Modern-day investigative reporters often model themselves after the original muckrakers.

Radio and Television

Like many modern inventions, radio has had a complex history. Although the first radio broadcast occurred in 1906, World War I delayed the use of radio for news, commercial, and entertainment purposes. After the war, radio began to flourish.[14]

The 1920s saw the development of three important characteristics of U.S. radio that would serve as important precedents for the future of broadcast media.

1. *The licensing system.* In the United States, government had never tried to regulate the newspaper industry: Anyone who wanted to establish a newspaper could do so, subject only to their ability to pay the bills. But radio was different. In order for radio to work, two stations could not broadcast on the same frequency: Conflicting and overlapping signals would make the medium useless. Some kind of basic order had to be imposed. But what role would government play?

   In many European countries radio became a government-run enterprise. Government agencies such as the British Broadcasting Corporation (BBC) in England organized the airwaves and produced radio content. But the United States decided to go a different route. By passing the Radio Act of 1927, Congress established a system that, with a few modifications, is basically still with us today—for both radio and television. The Radio Act created a Federal Radio Commission (which in 1934 became the Federal Communications Commission, or FCC) with the power to issue licenses that gave an individual or group the exclusive right to broadcast on a particular frequency. Originally, lots of licenses were granted to church groups, universities, and nonprofit organizations, but soon radio came to be dominated more and more by profit-oriented companies.

   These licenses carried conditions. The legislation creating the FCC established the **equal-time rule,** which said that if a station gave or sold time to a legally qualified candidate for public office, it had to make equal time available to all such candidates, on equal terms. This rule has been modified slightly over the years, but remains in effect today. Between 1949 and 1987, the FCC also enforced a **fairness doctrine,** which required stations to air contrasting viewpoints on matters of public importance and to give public figures who had been criticized on any of the station's programs a free opportunity to reply.

2. *The importance of advertising.* In England, the BBC was funded by a tax on radio receivers, but in the United States, broadcasters had to figure out how to make money on their own. They did so by selling commercial time to advertisers. Because audience size determined advertising rates, this system gave broadcasters an incentive to build as large an audience as possible, which led to the third development.

equal-time rule
Licensing condition promulgated by the FCC requiring any station that gave or sold time to a legally qualified candidate for public office to make equal time available to all such candidates on equal terms.

fairness doctrine
FCC regulation, enforced between 1949 and 1987, that required stations to air contrasting viewpoints on matters of public importance and to give public figures who had been criticized on any of the station's programs a free opportunity to reply.

3. *The emergence of national networks.* After the initial novelty had worn off, radio broadcasters were faced with a major problem: What exactly should they broadcast, particularly if they wanted to attract and retain a large audience? It was not easy to fill 24 hours of airtime, particularly in smaller towns and cities that could not afford to hire high-priced talent.

The most important solution was the creation of national networks. A corporation, usually with headquarters in New York, would develop a lineup of programs that would then be sent by telephone wire to "affiliated" stations all over the country. Because at the time FCC rules prohibited any one entity from owning more than five stations, the network did not actually own most of the stations that ran its programs. Instead, affiliates agreed to run the programs because of the larger audience that was likely to listen to them, and in return they would give the network a portion of their precious advertising time. The first major network was the National Broadcasting Corporation (NBC), created by three radio manufacturers in 1926. One year later, a group called the United Independent Broadcasters established a rival network, later named the Columbia Broadcasting System (CBS). The American Broadcasting Company (ABC) began operations in 1943.

With the advent of radio it became clear that in theory, at least, it was possible to send pictures as well as sounds over the airwaves. The first public demonstration of television took place at the New York World's Fair in 1939. World War II put plans for developing television as a commercial medium on hold, but once the war was over, television took off. In May 1949, according to a Gallup Poll, just 6 percent of Americans owned a television set—and less than half of the public had ever seen a television program. But the number of Americans who owned a TV jumped to 45 percent in 1952, and to 90 percent in 1959. In just ten years, television went from being a technological curiosity to a fixture in American homes.[15]

The Contemporary Scene

The contemporary American political system is served by a large and growing variety of media, each of which is used in distinctive ways and for somewhat different purposes.

Television   When Americans hear the word "media," they think first of television: Ninety-nine percent of all U.S. households have at least one television set, and the average household has three of them.[16] The radio networks migrated to television, and the three major networks—ABC, CBS, and NBC—quickly came to dominate television viewing. On any given evening in the 1960s, about 90 percent of those who were watching television were likely to be tuned in to a program on one of these networks.

Since then, however, this near-monopoly has collapsed. The Fox network went on the air in 1986 as the first new broadcast network in decades. More importantly, cable television soared in popularity as deregulation in the early 1980s prompted entrepreneurs to create dozens of new channels. Scarcely one in five households had cable in 1980, but by the end of the decade this number had nearly tripled.[17] Today about 9 out of 10 households has cable or satellite TV service, as Figure 9.1 shows.[18] The networks still have larger audiences than any single cable channel, but the proliferation of channels has eroded the networks' earlier position as the dominant force in the media environment.[19]

FIGURE 9.1

MEDIA ACCESS, 2009

Nearly all households have televisions and most have Internet access.

• How has the increasing variety of media affected political news coverage?

Source: Cell phones: Stephen J. Blumberg and Julian V. Luke, "Wireless Substitution: Early Release of Estimates from the National Health Interview Survey, July-September 2009," Centers for Disease Control and Prevention, May 12, 2010; other information: Television Bureau of Advertising, "Media Trends Track," www.tvb.org/rcentral/mediatrendstrack/tvbasics/05_Computer-DigitalTVSales.asp, accessed June 18, 2010.

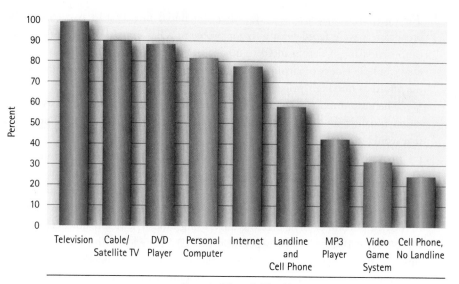

Percent of Households with . . .

Newspapers   The development of other media—first television, and later the Internet—has had a major impact on newspapers. In 1940, the United States had over 1,800 newspapers, but this figure has declined slowly but steadily: Today there are 1,400. Circulation has fallen from a peak of 63 million in 1984 to only 48 million today.[20] Fewer people say they rely on newspapers, as Figure 9.2 shows. Most newspapers have websites that attract many visitors, but papers have not been able to make much money off of Internet content—online ads generate less than 10 percent of what print ads do.[21] In light of these trends, it is not surprising that profits have plummeted: In 2009, total newspaper revenues were only half of what they were just nine years earlier.[22] In response to declining profits, papers have decreased the number of pages printed, laid off staff, and reined in more expensive aspects of news-gathering—such as international or investigative reporting.

Another effect of the economic trouble facing newspapers has been the spread of chain ownership. Increasingly, the nation's newspapers are owned by companies that also own a sizable number of newspapers in cities across the country. Chain ownership is not new: William Randolph Hearst, for example, at one point owned 26 daily newspapers. But where Hearst was once the exception, chain ownership is now becoming the predominant pattern. The largest single newspaper corporation is the Gannett Company, which owns *USA Today*, 83 other newspapers, and 23 TV stations. Many reporters and editors lament the new system. As one editor put it, "in corporate journalism . . . there are incessant demands on editors to be businessmen, to be community glad-handers, to be hand-holders at corporate [headquarters], and if you let the forces take their course with you, you won't be an editor and you won't be interviewing people, and you won't be doing stories."[23]

Radio   When MTV went on the air for the first time on August 1, 1981, the first video it aired was for the song "Video Killed the Radio Star." Yet that dire prophecy remains unfulfilled: Radio continues to be a popular medium from which many Americans get a good deal of their news.

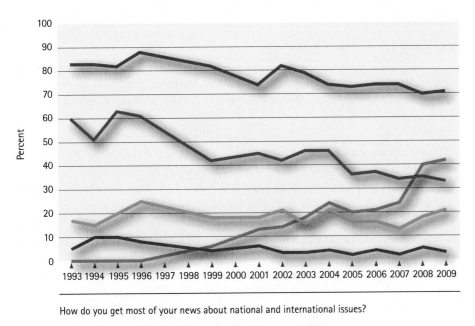

How do you get most of your news about national and international issues?

■ Television ■ Newspapers ■ Radio ■ Magazines ■ Internet

Note: Respondents allowed to give two answers.

FIGURE 9.2

CHANGING PATTERNS IN
NEWS SOURCES: 1993–2009

Newspaper use has dropped,
while Internet use has soared.

• *How would U.S. politics
change—if at all—if more
Americans read newspapers
and fewer relied on the Internet
for their news?*

Source: The Pew Center for the People
and the Press, July 2009 Political
Survey, http://people-press.org/reports/
questionnaires/543.pdf.

Note: Respondents allowed to
give two answers.

Indeed, one of the most noteworthy trends in American media over the last few decades has been the growth of talk radio. In 1980, only 75 stations in the United States were devoted exclusively to news and talk shows. But after the FCC's 1987 decision to repeal the fairness doctrine, radio stations no longer had to provide free airtime to anyone who had been attacked on a particular program. As a result, talk radio boomed. By 2009, the number of news and talk stations was over 1,500.[24] Of course, this figure includes many nonpolitical talk shows—sports, consumer affairs, advice to the lovelorn, "shock jocks" such as Howard Stern—but much talk radio is clearly and unabashedly political. The dominant figure in the industry is Rush Limbaugh, whose three-hour show attracts 15 million listeners every week. National Public Radio has also increased its audience since 2005.[25] As Figure 9.2 shows, the percentage of people who say they rely on radio has remained relatively constant over time.

Radio has held its own partly because it is well adapted to consumers' needs. The average person spends 14 hours per week in a car, where radio is an ideal medium.[26] Radio stations have also begun broadcasting streaming audio over the Internet, as well as packaging their programs into podcasts, a format used by 22 million Americans.[27]

Magazines   Although magazines were, as we have seen, quite important in the history of American journalism, as a news source they are increasingly marginal. *Time* and *Newsweek* used to be able to influence the political discussion in Washington, but in 2010, the Washington Post Company announced that it would sell *Newsweek* because "we don't see a sustained path to profitability."[28] When Americans are asked where they get most of their news, only a tiny minority mention magazines. Most magazines—and particularly the best-selling publications—are not news magazines, at least not news about government and politics. The magazine with the top circulation today is *AARP the Magazine,* which all AARP members receive automatically with their membership in the group. Also high on the list are *Reader's Digest* and *Better Homes and Gardens.*[29]

The New Media

new media
Cable and satellite TV, fax, email, and the Internet—the media that have grown out of the technological advances of the past few decades.

Beginning in the 1970s, a sizable number of new entrants were added to the menu of American media options. Often referred to collectively as the "**new media,**" these new forms of communication were made possible by the technological advances of the past few decades. Major examples include cable and satellite television and all aspects of the Internet.

Besides their reliance on new technologies, the new media tend to have a number of shared characteristics that may have important political consequences.[30] In particular, they dramatically expand the range of options available to media consumers in the United States. Traditional broadcast television might have made three or four stations available to the typical viewer, but cable allows viewers to choose among more than 100 if not 1,000 different channels. The Internet similarly allows users access to millions of different websites, including hundreds of newspapers and magazines and a wide array of specialized political sites.

One important question, however, is whether people will use their new menu of choices to seek out more political information—or to avoid it altogether. In the early days of television, some scholars argued that TV had created a large "inadvertent audience" for news. Many people watched the news, not because they were really interested in it, but because it was the only thing on.[31] Today, when there are so many more options available, it is likely that no one watches television news unless he or she wants to. One indication that younger generations may increasingly be shunning news is that the typical viewer of the main network news broadcasts is now over 62 years old.[32] Thus, the new media may lead to a system in which a small number of political activists are better informed than ever before—while Americans in general are actually less knowledgeable about politics.[33]

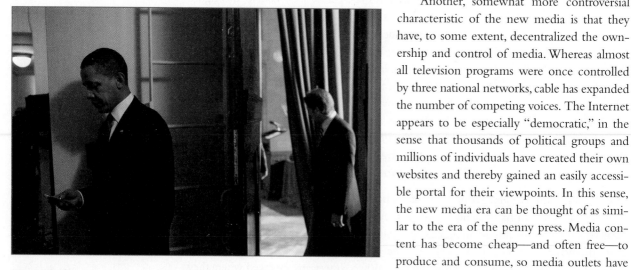

New Media
President Obama checks his BlackBerry before a speech.

• *How has the increased variety of media affected the way the public receives political news?*

Another, somewhat more controversial characteristic of the new media is that they have, to some extent, decentralized the ownership and control of media. Whereas almost all television programs were once controlled by three national networks, cable has expanded the number of competing voices. The Internet appears to be especially "democratic," in the sense that thousands of political groups and millions of individuals have created their own websites and thereby gained an easily accessible portal for their viewpoints. In this sense, the new media era can be thought of as similar to the era of the penny press. Media content has become cheap—and often free—to produce and consume, so media outlets have proliferated in number. Because competition is so fierce, media outlets sometimes resort to sensationalism and politicized perspectives to attract a larger number of consumers. Although the technology is different, this picture would be familiar to a reader of Joseph Pulitzer's *New York World* in the 1890s.

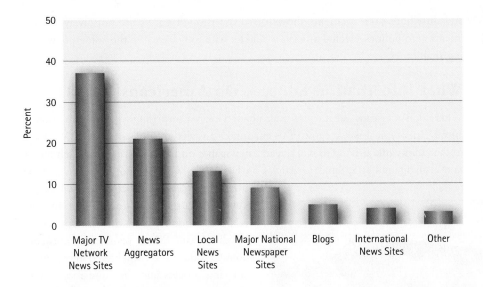

FIGURE 9.3

INTERNET USERS TEND TO RELY ON MAINSTREAM SITES

This graph shows the favorite sites among those who consume internet news.

• *Why do you think most people gravitate toward TV network news sites, considering the diverse array of available sources?*

Source: Pew Project for Excellence in Journalism, "The State of the News Media, 2010," www.stateofthemedia.org/2010/online_audience.php, accessed June 17, 2010.

We should not, however, overstate the diversity in new media ownership. Many of the most important cable stations are actually owned by older media corporations that have bought or created their own cable channels. Of the three largest cable news channels, CNN is now owned by Time Warner; Fox is owned by News Corp., which also owns numerous newspapers and magazines; and MSNBC is, as its name indicates, owned by NBC. Similarly, many heavily visited political websites such as nytimes.com or cbs.com are just the Internet version of a news organization that is primarily associated with a more traditional medium. When Americans seek out news on the Internet, they typically go to a site that is operated by a major network or newspaper, as Figure 9.3 shows.

For the minority of Americans who are highly attuned to politics, the capacity of any individual to be a producer as well as a consumer of media content has opened up new doors. Political campaigns have been quick to add the new media to their repertoire of mobilization techniques. In 2008, both presidential campaigns developed social media platforms in an effort to engage committed activists in their electioneering. Fundraising has hit new highs as Internet donations have continued to increase. Campaigns can now coordinate volunteer networks across states, or even across the country, with relative ease. The Internet, as one expert put it, has become a "vital aspect of campaign strategy."[34]

Beyond the campaigns themselves, individualized communications have also shown the potential to shake up politics in unexpected ways. Bloggers continually fact-check official statements and candidate pronouncements, sometimes uncovering embarrassing mistakes or misleading claims that can sink a candidacy or policy proposal. Gaffes delivered in unguarded moments can live on via YouTube or Twitter. In 2010, for example, when BP CEO Carl Henric-Svanberg awkwardly claimed to "care about the small people" in the wake of the Deepwater Horizon oil spill, video and commentary about the statement rocketed around the web, forcing a quick apology. That same summer, Rep. Bob Etheridge (D-NC) was filmed grabbing and briefly struggling with a student videographer; after the clip made the rounds online, Etheridge issued a statement saying he "deeply and profoundly" regretted his behavior.[35] The ability of activists to record and distribute such incidents shows that even though voters are not always paying attention to politics, elected officials would be wise to behave as if the voters are watching at all times.

9.2

Identify the primary media through which Americans get their news.

What Information Sources Do Americans Rely On?

Where do Americans get most of their news? This is a surprisingly difficult question to answer. In a typical week, most of us encounter a variety of different media. We listen to the radio while driving to work, read a newspaper on the bus or online, watch television at night, and swap links to articles on Facebook. We may also have conversations with family, friends, and co-workers, who tell us about what they have learned from the media, perhaps adding their own interpretations and distortions. Most people do not consciously monitor this complicated information-gathering process and therefore may not be able to say exactly what they have learned from any particular source.

When public opinion surveys ask Americans where they get most of their news, they usually say "television," as they have since the 1960s (see Figure 9.2, page 251). The Internet overtook newspapers as the second most commonly mentioned category in 2008; newspapers are on the decline, as we discussed above, and radio is holding steady as a news source.

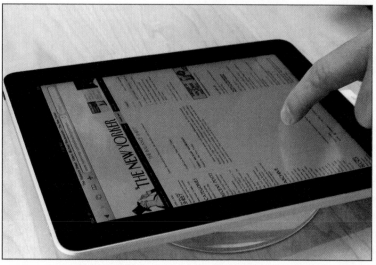

Web News
News agencies maintain Web pages that allow Americans to get world news immediately rather than waiting for a scheduled broadcast or for delivery of the daily paper.
• *How does this faster news cycle change the needs and expectations of consumers?*

But there is some reason to wonder about the validity of these results. While there is no doubt that the television is on a lot in the typical American household—about 8 hours a day, according to some estimates—in many cases, no one is paying much attention to it. People are cleaning or cooking or doing their homework—and the TV is little more than background noise. Striking testimony to how little attention people sometimes give to their television sets occurred on February 7, 1971, when a power failure on the East Side of Manhattan knocked out the transmitter on the Empire State Building, which at the time was used by all the TV stations in New York City. Electric power was still working in the city, however, which meant that television sets still worked, even though they all had blank, soundless screens. Nevertheless, according to the Nielsen rating service, about a half million New Yorkers continued to leave their television sets on.[36]

Whether because it is just background noise or because of inherent limitations in the medium itself, there is also a fair amount of evidence to indicate that even when people do watch television news, they do not retain or remember much of what they see. In one study conducted by researchers at the University of Michigan, interviewers located a random sample of respondents who said they had watched one of the network evening newscasts one to three hours earlier that day, and then asked them a series of questions about that newscast. When asked how many stories they remembered from it, the average respondent recalled fewer than two. Even when the interviewer provided a salient detail from each story, most people could remember the central point of that story only about a third of the time.[37]

As pollster Bud Roper has suggested, because television plays such an important role in many people's lives, there may be a kind of "halo effect" that causes people to overestimate its importance as a source of news.[38] This tendency may be reinforced by the fact that television clearly did play a major role in informing the public about certain landmark moments in American life—such as the assassination of John F. Kennedy or the terrorist attacks of September 11, 2001. Polls show that people paid significantly more attention to television news immediately after events such as 9/11, the start of the Iraq War, and Hurricane Katrina.[39]

One final problem with almost all of the studies on this topic is their failure to recognize that "news" is not a very well-defined concept. When most social scientists use the term, they are thinking of news about important matters of political and social concern: recent developments in the latest election campaign, the state of the economy, the progress of various bills being considered by Congress. But many members of the mass public, we suspect, have a less exalted notion in mind. To them, news includes things such as yesterday's sports scores, the weather forecast, and the latest reports about Hollywood's hottest stars. Because the public shows a lot of interest in such matters, the increasingly competitive media environment can lead media outlets to focus more on such "soft news" items and less on "hard news" like budget negotiations or international affairs.[40] A public that pays a lot of attention to soft news may be no better informed than a public that pays a little attention to hard news.

Media Effects

Scholarly assessments of the effects of media on public opinion have gone through several distinct stages or "schools." In the 1940s many observers viewed the potential of radio as a great danger to democratic politics, for the rapid spread of radio in the 1930s coincided with the rise of Fascism in Europe. Some commentators argued that one key source of power for both Hitler and Mussolini was their ability to speak directly to their audiences. Also influential was the remarkable reaction to Orson Welles's famous *War of the Worlds* broadcast on October 30, 1938, which convinced many Americans that the planet really was being invaded by Martians and set off panic throughout the country.[41] The label that has sometimes been given to this school of thought was the "hypodermic model," because the capacity of the media to put ideas into people's heads was seen as so direct and powerful, it was almost like injecting drugs into a person's bloodstream.

When social scientists first started conducting systematic tests of the media's impact on the public's attitudes, however, they found just the opposite. Particularly influential was a study called *The People's Choice,* which tracked reactions to the 1940 presidential campaign as it progressed in Erie County, Ohio. Contrary to their expectations, the study's authors found that most people wound up voting for the same candidate they had favored before the campaign began, that most of the voting decisions made by the initially "undecided" could be predicted in advance based on voters' social and demographic characteristics, and that the number of actual "conversions"—people who changed from Wilkie to Roosevelt or vice versa—was remarkably small.[42] For the next three decades, this became the dominant view of media effects.[43] Known as the "minimal effects school," we would almost certainly have endorsed it if we had written this textbook in the 1950s or early 1960s—if we had bothered to write about the media at all.[44] It was not until the 1970s that a younger generation of researchers started to question the view that the media had so little effect.

9.3

Characterize the effects the media have on the public's political attitudes.

Agenda Setting

agenda setting

The media affect the issues and problems people think about, even if the media do not determine what positions people adopt.

The first major crack in the "minimal effects" edifice concerned a function known as **agenda setting,** which occurs when the media affect the issues and problems people think about, even if the media do not determine what positions people adopt. As Bernard Cohen memorably put it, the press "may not be successful much of the time in telling people what to think, but it is stunningly successful in telling its readers what to think *about*."[45] Put another way, the media may not be able to change the *direction* of public attitudes, but it can change their relative *salience* (how important people think the issue is). The media can induce people to focus on an issue or problem by emphasizing it and whipping up their concern. The media set the agenda, even if they do not determine how issues are resolved.

Catastrophes in Third World countries, for example, largely go unnoticed unless the media—particularly television—turn their attention to such events. In the 1980s, a devastating Ethiopian famine failed to gain the attention of Americans until television beamed heartrending footage into the public's living rooms.[46] Once the public began paying attention, voters demanded a U.S. government response. Media analysts have even given government responses such as these a nickname, the **CNN effect,** after the tendency for a foreign tragedy to be raised to national prominence once the Cable News Network covers it. As the Internet has become more widely accessible, video sites and social media have made it even easier for vivid, disturbing images to reach a wide audience, as in the case of the crackdown on demonstrators in Iran in 2009, or the Haiti earthquake in 2010.[47]

Agenda setting is well documented, although much of the evidence is not conclusive.[48] When unemployment rose to near-double digits in the 2009 recession, the media focused heavily on unemployment, and polls showed that the public was concerned with the issue. Is this agenda setting, or are both the media and the people responding to the same real conditions? Some careful studies conclude that the independent impact of the media has been exaggerated; astute government officials use the media to place problems on the national and international agendas.[49] A study of healthcare reform efforts concluded that "peaks in the volume and substantive focus of media reporting coincided with upsurges in discussions of real-world developments and fierce political debate over policy reforms."[50] Nevertheless, experimental studies that raise viewer concern about subjects *not* high on the national agenda have been able to provide some evidence of agenda setting.[51]

The CNN Effect

News coverage of major disasters such as famine, war, and the 2010 Haiti earthquake has at times shaped the political agenda.

• *Why do the news media focus attention on some disasters and not others?*

CNN effect

Purported ability of TV to raise a foreign tragedy to national prominence by broadcasting vivid pictures.

Priming and Framing

In the spring of 1991, following an impressive American victory in the Gulf War, President George H. W. Bush's approval ratings soared, reaching unprecedented levels. With the war's end, however, journalists turned to other stories and gradually Bush's ratings became dependent on the nation's economic performance, which voters judged negatively.[52] He lost the 1992 election to Bill Clinton. Similarly, President George W. Bush enjoyed soaring popularity ratings after the 9/11 terrorist attacks. During the war in Iraq, though, media coverage dwelt on the administration's failings—including an inability to find "weapons of mass destruction" supposedly possessed by Iraq's government. Bush's ratings dropped steadily until the 2004 presidential campaign heated up, although he survived his reelection bid, and then plummeted further thereafter. These large shifts in public opinion are striking reflections of **priming**—changing the standards that citizens use to evaluate their leaders.

By what they choose to cover, the media can prime citizens to use some standards rather than others.[53] Obviously, the media do not have full control over which criteria Americans use to evaluate their presidents. War or an economic downturn pushes everything else off the agenda of public opinion: All other concerns seem minor when lives are in danger or family members are having trouble putting food on the table. Thus, both the media and the public react to the reality of war and recession. Similarly, after the crisis ends, both turn to other concerns.

Framing and priming are related notions.[54] **Framing** has been defined as "the way in which opinions about an issue can be altered by emphasizing or deemphasizing particular facets of that issue."[55] In Chapter 5 we explained that Americans tend to shift their opinions on abortion depending on how pollsters frame the question. How issues are framed shapes more than just survey results, however; framing also molds how the public thinks about issues more generally. For example, the 2010 Deepwater Horizon oil spill might be framed in a number of different ways. It could be thought of as a failure of government to respond adequately to a disaster; the failure of a company to act responsibly in guarding against mistakes; an illustration of the need to move away from oil as a source of energy; or an illustration that more accessible land-based oil reserves are a better bet than deep sea reserves. Which frame you accept will have a significant impact on your evaluation of President Obama, of BP, and of energy policy in the United States. Inducing people to think along certain lines rather than others can affect their positions on issues and their evaluations of public officials.

priming
The media affect the standards people use to evaluate political figures or the severity of a problem.

framing
The way in which opinions about an issue can be altered by emphasizing or de-emphasizing particular facets of that issue.

How Strong Are Media Effects?

Effects such as agenda setting, priming, and framing depend on both the characteristics of the audience and the nature of the information. People who are uninterested in and uninformed about politics are most susceptible to agenda setting. For example, political independents differ from partisans. Their concerns shift from one issue to another with the intensity of media coverage. Partisans, on the other hand, are inclined to think in terms of issues at the core of their party's concerns.[56]

The characteristics of the information being communicated are at least as important as the characteristics of the people receiving it. When the problem or event is far away—well beyond personal experience—the mass media provide the only information available. Their influence diminishes when information is closer to home and people have some personal basis for arriving at opinions.[57] When reporters were predicting an Obama victory in the 2008 New Hampshire primary, they may have convinced viewers watching from out of state, but they were less likely to sway New Hampshire voters, most of whom had thought more about the race and had made up their minds before the early January Obama "wave." Thus, the media *can* have a major impact on public opinion, but *whether* they do so depends on both whom they are reaching and what they are covering.

We also live in a world in which there are many different media sources telling many different stories. A voter may therefore receive a variety of "frames" that may cancel each other out or change over time, or may diminish as people talk with their friends and neighbors about the news.[58] These complex effects are difficult to sort out and are not yet well understood.

9.4

Outline the major kinds
of media bias and assess
criticisms of the media.

Media Biases

Most modern journalists purport to be objective. They are supposed to report events and describe conflicts accurately so that voters can make informed judgments. If reporters and editors lived up to this ideal, then media effects would not be much cause for concern. But news organizations and other media corporations represent important players in the political system, an institution with its own interests, values, and operating procedures. The result, almost all observers agree, is that the news we get through television, newspapers, and magazines is far from being a full, faithful, and undistorted reflection of what is going on in the world around us. In all sorts of major and minor ways, the media fall short of providing a "mirror" of reality.

Selection Bias

Periodically, frustrated citizens write to newspaper editors to complain that all their newspaper ever publishes is bad news. Why not more good news? The answer is that to a considerable extent, the media *define* news as bad news.[59] A government program that works well is not news; one that is mismanaged or a failure *is* news. An elected official who is doing a good job is not newsworthy; one who is incompetent or corrupt is. People working hard and contributing to their communities are not news; one sociopath who runs amok is. An emphasis on the negative is a kind of **selection principle,** a guideline according to which stories with certain characteristics are chosen over stories without those characteristics; reporters and editors give a skewed perception of reality based on the way they make decisions about what stories to cover.

selection principle
Guideline according to which stories with certain characteristics are chosen over stories without those characteristics.

Media critic Larry Sabato argues that the negative tone of the media has become much more prominent in recent decades. He contends that presidents from Franklin Roosevelt to John F. Kennedy enjoyed the support of a press with a "lapdog" mentality. Johnson and Nixon were subjected to far greater scrutiny by a press with a "watchdog" mentality. Succeeding presidents, he maintains, suffer mean treatment from a press with a "junkyard dog" mentality.[60] Some observers believe that the negative tone of press coverage has contributed to the increased cynicism of the American public about politics and government.[61] They suggest that politics today is no worse than in previous eras—it might even be better—but that media treatment makes things *seem* worse.

Another important selection principle is that "news" must be new, exciting, and unusual. Gradual developments and persistent conditions do not lend themselves to the kind of hit-and-run coverage favored by the contemporary media. A crisis does. President Obama did his best to keep news about ongoing economic stimulus programs on front pages in 2010, but coverage of the Deepwater Horizon oil spill saturated most media outlets.

The media look for heroes and villains, not for abstract social developments. This bias is particularly characteristic of TV, which is even more fast-paced than print. A frequently heard maxim to describe local TV news is "If it bleeds, it leads." TV needs dramatic events, colorful personalities, bitter conflicts, short and snappy comments, and above all, compelling pictures. The result can be insufficient treatment of stories that do not fit the needs of the media and distorted treatment of stories that are covered to make them fit those needs.[62] In 2010, an unprecedented flood struck Nashville, Tennessee, killing more than 30 people and destroying countless homes. But the national media largely ignored the story because it was focused on the other big

Calvin and Hobbes

As the public gets more reports of scandal and problems, some worry that the electorate grows more cynical.

• *Does excessive coverage of scandal "packaged as a soap opera and horse race" lead the public to distrust government and politicians?*

story that same week: an attempted car bombing in Times Square, New York. Terrorism was just too hot a story to resist. As one Tennessee journalist lamented, "if this had happened in another week, it would have been the flavor du jour."[63]

Selection biases probably colored the media's coverage of the 2008 financial crisis, an economic panic caused in part by risky and complex securities such as derivatives and credit default swaps that few members of the public understood. As a result, coverage mostly focused on more understandable topics, such as instances of actual fraud, high CEO salaries, and the shocking volatility of the Dow Jones Industrial Average. When automakers faced bankruptcy, media outlets played up a minor scandal in which executives took private jets to Washington for a Congressional hearing, rather than flying commercial. None of this had much to do with the causes of the crisis or with the major proposals for propping up the economy or for reforming the financial system. But it did make for a better story than an explanation of how ratings agencies judge the level of risk in particular collateralized debt obligations.

Some critics charge that the media desire for heroism and action—along with their desire for popularity—especially distorts the coverage of war and foreign affairs. Such criticism is not new. As early as 1966, one detractor wrote:

> Our remaining correspondents fly from earthquake to famine, from insurrection to massacre. They land running, as we were all taught to do, and they provide surprisingly good coverage of whatever is immediately going on . . . [But] we miss anticipation, thought, and meaning. Our global coverage has become a comic book: ZAP! POW! BANG-BANG.[64]

During the war in Iraq, both the pro- and antiwar sides complained about the slant of war reporting. In the early stages of the war, such complaints were most frequently voiced by those on the left. Many critics argued that the media were "shirking their duty" to keep an eye on government and instead had become boosters of military aggression. "Regardless of their own views on the war," according to Mark Weisbrot, co-director of the liberal Center for Economic and Policy Research, "American journalists became the Bush administration's major means of promoting it." The director-general of the British Broadcasting Corporation, meanwhile, expressed his shock at "gung-ho" war coverage, charging that reporters had "wrapped themselves in the American flag and swapped impartiality for patriotism." Beginning in about 2003, however, the tenor of most American war reporting became sharply more critical, leading to complaints from Republicans that the media were devoting too much attention to casualties and setbacks in Iraq and not enough to the many positive developments. As with public opinion, media coverage may be very supportive of an administration early in a foreign policy crisis, and less so as time passes.

Professional Bias

A second kind of media bias arises from the demands of the journalism profession today. A few journalists are experts who work specific "beats"—the business reporter, education reporter, health reporter, Supreme Court reporter, and so on. But most reporters and journalists are generalists who lack specific substantive expertise. They operate on tight deadlines and start from scratch on many stories. Thus, on subjects more complex than scandals and conflicts, they are dependent on experts and other outside sources for information and interpretation. Ironically, despite the familiar image of the investigative reporter, studies find that reporters uncover only a small fraction of the scandals they report—probably less than one-quarter.[65] Government agencies reveal the lion's share, and they generally do so officially, not through surreptitious "leaks." Reliance on government sources can make a big difference in news coverage and helps explain why U.S. news often differs sharply from the information available in other countries.

Moreover, as journalists themselves recognize, the news media have increased their emphasis on entertainment.[66] Especially in the case of TV, looks and personalities are more important today than they were a generation ago. With the growth of the new media, competitive pressures are greater than ever and have resulted in a race to the bottom, as network news becomes more like infotainment (a mixture of news and entertainment) and major newspapers become more like tabloids. Each time a tabloid website beats a major news outlet to a story, as the site TMZ.com did when it scooped major news outlets by being the first to report the death of pop star Michael Jackson, this competitive pressure intensifies.

The lack of internal expertise and the competitive pressure for ratings and sales contribute to an unattractive feature of modern political coverage: "pack journalism," in which reporters unanimously decide something is the big story and attack it like wolves tearing apart wounded prey or sharks engaging in a feeding frenzy.[67] Comedian Jon Stewart prefers a different image: small children playing soccer, all clumped together and thoughtlessly chasing a ball.[68] Normal people, observing such behavior, are puzzled by the media's pack behavior—but to journalists under great competitive pressure, there is safety in numbers. One can hardly be faulted for working on the same story as are other prominent journalists. Far better to focus on what turns out to be an overblown, inconsequential story than to "run the risk of going down in history as 'the reporter who missed the next Watergate.'"[69] Indeed, there is every indication that the "pack" mentality extends to editorial offices, where each news show or newspaper fears missing the "next big thing." The "pack" phenomenon is not unique to professional journalists either: Social networking sites like Twitter explode with repostings of similar stories, eyewitness accounts, and flat-out rumors when a crisis strikes. The accuracy of this information is often suspect, but there is significant pressure to post information immediately and sort out the facts later.

Ideological Bias

The first two kinds of media bias described here are, by most accounts, nonideological. The media report scandals, disasters, and stories with good pictures pretty much regardless of whether such stories benefit liberals or conservatives. The media showed great enthusiasm for reporting the Watergate scandals that brought down a Republican president—but they also salivated over every juicy detail of the Clinton sex scandals, when a Democrat was in the White House. Liberals often charge that public support for domestic programs is weakened because the media report program failures but not successes. But business people often make the same sort of complaint: Corporate corruption and mistakes get covered, but not the many products and services that work or the millions of people who are productively employed. Accusations of media bias are not unique to U.S. media outlets, as the International Comparison illustrates.

Yet many thoughtful media critics think the American media also have important ideological biases that systematically favor politicians and causes from one end of the ideological spectrum. What the critics do not agree about, however, is who benefits from this media malfeasance. Conservatives have long charged that the media have a liberal bias; liberals insist (although a bit less vociferously) that the media favor conservatives. For a variety of reasons, academic research has been equally divided about this question. Some books and articles by reputable scholars claim to find evidence documenting that the media do, indeed, have a liberal bias.[70] Others argue that the media are especially deferential to established interests in both government and business.[71] Still others insist that both sides are wrong and that while the media undoubtedly have their problems and shortcomings, the major political parties and ideologies are generally treated about the same.[72]

The clearest evidence supporting the case of critics who charge the media with having a liberal bias is the attitudes and opinions of professional journalists. Since the early 1960s, a number of scholars and polling organizations have conducted surveys of the reporters, editors, and producers at major news organizations. Without exception, these studies have found that those who report and edit the news are substantially more liberal than the American public, particularly on social and cultural issues such as abortion, affirmative action, and gay rights.[73] The liberal tilt of American journalists shows up particularly strongly in their voting habits. In a study conducted by the University of Connecticut, 68 percent of a sample of newspaper and television journalists reported voting for John Kerry in 2004; just 25 percent reported voting for George W. Bush.[74] In 2007, a report on MSNBC used Federal Election Commission records to find 143 journalists who had made political contributions to federal candidates or political action committees between 2004 and the start of the 2008 campaign: whereas 125 gave to Democrats and liberal causes, just 16 gave to Republicans and conservatives.[75]

An exception to this pattern is talk radio, which is dominated by people who are clearly and unabashedly conservative. Every year, *Talkers* magazine, a trade publication that serves the talk radio industry, compiles a list of the top talk radio programs in the United States and their cumulative weekly audience. As of 2009, all but one of the top 10 talk radio hosts were conservative or libertarian. The tenth was nonpolitical financial commentator Dave Ramsey. The most significant reason for this result is that conservatives feel they need an alternative to the so-called mainstream media. Public opinion surveys have shown quite consistently over the past few decades that a lot more Americans believe that the media have a liberal bias than believe that they are biased in the other direction.[76]

Liberals retort that what matters is not the political views of the journalists, but the kinds of organizations they work for. In the contemporary United States, news is produced by large, for-profit corporations engaged in a relentless struggle to improve their profit margins. As a result, liberals claim, the news tends to be especially docile and deferential towards business interests, especially those that are major advertisers.[77]

In addition, the news gathering process is structured around official government sources. A news organization is more likely to assign a reporter to cover the White House, the Congress, and the Pentagon on a regular basis than it is to cover labor unions, antiwar protestors, or consumer groups. Thus, most news comes from so-called "official sources," while the more severe critics of official policy rarely, if ever, get their views into print or on the airwaves.

It would seem that this controversy could be settled by examining the content of news reports and determining what biases, if any, they actually possess. But this is easier said than done. Part of the problem is that most allegations of media bias claim that some person or policy is getting more favorable or unfavorable coverage *than it deserves*—media coverage, in other words, is compared to reality—and often there is considerable disagreement as to how bad a problem is or how well or poorly some official has performed. From 2004 through 2006, for example, American policy and performance in Iraq received a good deal of negative coverage. Conservative critics charged that the media were giving a misleading picture of the state of affairs in Iraq; journalists replied that

INTERNATIONAL COMPARISON

Al Jazeera—Questionable Sources?

As Americans tuned in during the fall of 2001 to follow the war on terrorism, they were introduced to the "The CNN of the Arab World": Al Jazeera.[1] In early 2001, Thomas Friedman of the *New York Times* had described Al Jazeera as the "freest" cable network in the Arab world even though it received significant support from the government of Qatar. Aggressive marketing, lively debate and—according to Friedman— "uncensored" news stories attracted large blocs of viewers. Al Jazeera not only styled itself after Western news organizations, but actually was allied with CNN to provide content (the two networks have since severed their relationship).[2]

After 9/11, Al Jazeera provided CNN with video footage of al Qaeda training camps. The network's most controversial contribution, however, was a broadcast of Osama Bin Laden speaking in a very threatening manner about the decadent West. Secretary of State Colin Powell denounced Al Jazeera's "vitriolic, irresponsible" statements. Then–national security adviser Condoleezza Rice asked U.S. networks not to broadcast Bin Laden's speeches.[3] Originally heralded for its unprecedented access to news sources unavailable to American media outlets, the station increasingly faced criticism because of the perception that it had become too closely tied to those same sources. U.S. officials viewed Al Jazeera's coverage of the Iraq War, for example, as overly sympathetic to the Iraqi government.

Al Jazeera launched an English language channel in 2006 and attempted to break into the U.S. cable market. But U.S. cable providers shunned the network as too controversial, even as the network expanded to reach over 200 million people in Europe, Africa, and elsewhere. Meanwhile, Al Jazeera continued to provide unmatched coverage of events in the Middle East, such as the 2009 war between Israel and Gaza and the 2010 interception of a Gaza-bound flotilla by Israeli troops.[4] Accusations of bias continued: Egypt accused Al Jazeera of being overly sympathetic to that country's antigovernment Muslim Brotherhood; Israel and its allies argue that the network is too cozy with the radical Islamist group Hamas.[5]

• *Was Al Jazeera wrong to broadcast tapes of Osama Bin Laden's threats? Should American stations have rebroadcast these speeches?*

• *Does the reluctance of U.S. cable providers to carry Al Jazeera English suggest that corporate control is a key source of bias, as liberals claim? Or does it simply reflect market forces?*

[1]T. Straus, "The CNN of the Arab World," *Alternet*.org, October 26, 2001.
[2]Thomas L. Friedman, "The Fast Eat the Slow," *New York Times,* February 2, 2001, Associated Press, "Arab Network Cuts Ties with CNN," February 1, 2002.
[3]Straus, "The CNN of the Arab World."
[4]Aaron Barnhart, "Al-Jazeera English Relocates to the U.S. Border, Ready to Invade," *Kansas City Star,* June 9, 2010, http://www.kansascity.com/2010/06/09/2003811/al-jazeera-english-relocates-to.html, accessed June 22, 2010.
[5]"Al Jazeera: More Powerful than Ever," *The Economist,* May 27, 2010, http://www.economist.com/node/16222710?story_id=16222710&source=hptextfeature, accessed June 22, 2010.

things were, in fact, just as bad as they were being portrayed. It is difficult to imagine an "objective measure of conditions" that would definitively settle this kind of dispute.

Media biases, moreover, can manifest themselves in a variety of more subtle ways. Political scientist Martin Gilens has found, for example, that when news organizations need to choose a photograph of a "poor person," they disproportionately select photos of African Americans, despite the fact that most poor people in the United States are white.[78] There may be many such subtle biases in media coverage, but media studies have not done as thorough a job of studying such biases in objective ways.

Prospects for Change

However justified, criticisms of the media's coverage of politics and government miss an important point. The news media in the United States are not part of the public education system. As one journalist commented, "What few people recognize is that the purpose of the media is not to educate, it is to impress—to make an impression. There isn't the time or space to educate."[79]

As for complaints that their coverage falls short of what many would like to see, defenders of the media respond that they try to provide the kind of coverage people want, to the point of using focus groups and other measures of reader interest to serve the audience better.[80] A survey in April 2010, for example, found that the top four topics of interest to the public were the economy, the ash plume from an Icelandic volcano that was disrupting air travel, the oil rig explosion in the Gulf of Mexico, and financial reform. Analysis of news coverage showed that these were exactly the topics to which the media were devoting the most attention at the time.[81] Nonetheless, Americans are not happy with media behavior today. As Table 9.1 shows, popular evaluations of the media have declined sharply since the mid-1980s.

Furthermore, media representatives have always claimed that they are more than profit-making businesses. They claim to provide an essential public service. When they publish sensitive or private information, they justify their behavior with more than a sprinkling of righteousness—using weighty terms such as "the public's right to know" or "the free flow of information in the marketplace of ideas." Such an exalted self-image may carry with it the responsibility to give the public what it needs as well as what it wants.

TABLE 9.1
EVALUATIONS OF THE MEDIA HAVE WORSENED

Percent of those polled saying news organizations generally . . .	1985	1999	2009
Get the facts straight	55	37	29
Deal fairly with all sides	34	27	18
Are pretty independent	37	23	20
Are unbiased	36	31	26

Source: Pew Research Center for the People and the Press, "July 2009 Political Survey/Media Update," http://people-press.org/reports/questionnaires/543.pdf, accessed June 17, 2010.

9.5

Illustrate the influence of entertainment media on American political attitudes.

A Word About Entertainment Media

The principal subject of this chapter has been the *news* media: those forms of media that claim to provide reports or commentary about real-world events and conditions. Yet much of what are thought of as entertainment media—movies, situation comedies, detective shows, soap operas—may also contain material that has significant political implications. Over the last 20 years, for example, American attitudes toward homosexuality have become significantly more tolerant and even approving, in ways that have important consequences for such issues as gay rights and same-sex marriage (see Chapter 17). And, while this change has probably taken place for a number of reasons, one major source has almost certainly been the way that gay and lesbian characters are portrayed in movies and on television. Not only are such characters a good deal more visible than they once were; gay and lesbian characters are usually portrayed quite positively, while those who are critical of or opposed to homosexuality are condemned or ridiculed.

To take another example, during and after World War II, Hollywood produced a significant number of war movies, almost all of which made clear, implicitly or explicitly, that the United States was the good guy while the Germans and Japanese were the enemy. Although individual American soldiers or generals might have their faults, there was no doubting the justice of the American cause. By contrast, recent movies and documentaries about the war in Iraq and U.S. policies in the Middle East have been strikingly critical of the United States. Now the American side may commit atrocities or have corrupt motives, while Iraqis or Arabs can be portrayed as reasonable and peaceful. *Redacted,* for example, is about the rape and murder of an Iraqi girl by U.S. troops. *Lions for Lambs* is about how a cynical Republican senator devises a new war strategy that ultimately sends two idealistic young soldiers to their senseless deaths. Given the limited attention that many Americans give to news programming, entertainment media may be an important, additional source of influence on American political attitudes.

9.6

Assess media coverage of the election process.

The Media and Electoral Politics

The mass media play an important role in democratic politics. Ideally, they transmit information about problems and issues, helping voters make intelligent choices among the candidates who compete for their votes. But many critics feel that the biases and shortcomings discussed earlier cause media coverage of elections to fall far short of the ideal.

Campaign Coverage

Nowhere do critics of the mass media find more to criticize than in the coverage of political campaigns. Numerous studies report that the various media biases combine to produce campaign coverage that is characterized by sins of both omission and commission (see Chapter 10).

The media provide little coverage of policy issues: the nature of social and economic problems, the contrasts among the programs that candidates advocate, and so forth. Instead, critics charge, the media devote too much attention to "character" issues that have little to do with the ability of the candidates to govern. Thus the press dwells on whether Barack Obama is too aloof or whether John McCain is too hot-tempered. Such matters have some relevance, to be sure, and they may provide some indication of how a candidate would govern, but reporting on such matters should not crowd out more substantive election coverage.

Not only do the media concentrate on candidates' characters at the expense of genuine policy and performance issues, but their interest primarily stems from a wish to handicap each race. Campaign coverage usually focuses on an election as though it were a horse race, reporting which candidate is leading, which candidate is dropping back, which one is coming up on the rail, what the latest polls say, who got what endorsement, and how a change in campaign personnel will affect public perceptions of the candidate. Even when a candidate announces a proposal or issue position, it is evaluated as a tactical move that can affect the candidate's standing in the larger horse race. This tendency toward "horse-race coverage" has become much more pronounced over the past generation, as the attention devoted to substance has declined.[82]

Another important characteristic of television election coverage, which is actually a recent development, is the extent to which it centers around the reporter rather than the candidates. According to a study conducted by sociologist Kiku Adatto, in 1968 the media allowed candidates to present their views in their own words. The average **sound bite**—a piece of film or video that shows the candidate speaking in his or her own words—lasted for 42 seconds. By 1988, the average sound bite was just 10 seconds.[83] In other words, rather than allowing the candidates to speak for themselves, journalists increasingly assumed that it was their responsibility to summarize, edit, and interpret the candidates' words. Knowing this, the candidates began to deliver speeches that reduced complex ideas and issues to one or two pithy, oversimplified sentences. And, although the networks vowed to change this aspect of their coverage, subsequent studies have shown that television sound bites have actually grown shorter—down to an average of 7.8 seconds in 2004.[84]

sound bite
A piece of film or video that shows a candidate speaking in his or her own words.

Observers of contemporary political campaigns are not the only ones who are critical of media coverage. The candidates themselves are critical—so much so that they are finding ways to get around the contemporary media. As noted earlier, they have started appearing on popular television programs. They also make themselves available more frequently to state and local journalists. Reporters of national stature complain that the candidates are insulating themselves from the hard questioning of seasoned journalists, but the candidates seem to enjoy the opportunity to talk about issues rather than the trivia that often dominates national news coverage. Candidates have also increasingly used video sites like YouTube to share speeches and statements that exceed the average TV sound bite length by multiple orders of magnitude. This strategy became so popular that in 2010, Google and YouTube introduced a specialized suite of online tools for use by political campaigns.[85]

The Conventions

Before presidential candidates were chosen in the primaries, national conventions were important political events. Party leaders came together, made deals, hammered out a platform, nominated candidates, and (if successful) left with a unified party prepared to battle the opposition. In recognition of the importance of the conventions, CBS and NBC provided gavel-to-gavel coverage from 1956 to 1976 and regularly assigned their top anchors and reporters to the events.

The process for nominating presidential candidates was changed in 1972, in ways that removed the element of surprise from national party conventions (see Chapter 10). Since then, the conventions have not been nearly so important as in earlier eras, and media coverage has dropped accordingly (see Figure 9.4). As magazine writer Hendrik Hertzberg dryly put it, the "conventions are no longer troubled by the problem of being excessively

FIGURE 9.4

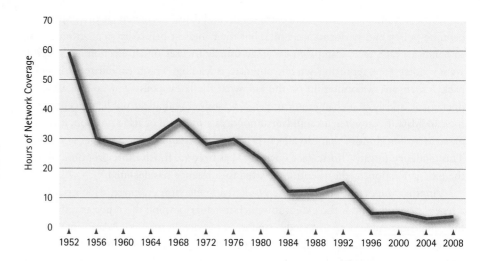

THE NETWORKS
INCREASINGLY IGNORE THE
NATIONAL POLITICAL
CONVENTIONS

This graph shows the average
coverage of each party's
convention.

• *Do the major broadcast television networks have some kind of civic obligation to televise at least some parts of the national political conventions?*

Source: Adapted by Sam Abrams from Harold W. Stanley and Richard G. Niemi, *Vital Statistics of American Politics, 2005–2006* (Washington, DC: QC Press), 195.

interesting."[86] The parties now treat the conventions as huge infomercials in an attempt to take advantage of their diminishing time on the screen. Attractive speakers are slotted for prime time, and the entire convention schedule is arranged with the media in mind.

The parties showcase their candidates in hopes of producing a post-convention "bounce" upward in the polls. Recent conventions that produced large bounces for the candidates were the 2004 Republican convention (for President Bush) and the 2000 Democratic convention (for Vice President Gore).[87] John McCain received a significant bounce from the 2008 Republican convention, but this advantage dissipated quickly. Media coverage is a double-edged sword, however. If coverage emphasizes a divided party or unpopular elements of the party, it will cause the candidate to drop in the polls. In 1992 Pat Buchanan gave an aggressive speech to the Republican convention that reportedly turned off many moderates.

The conventions probably will be even less important in the future. As one commentator observed after the 1996 events, "The more the party managers tried to package their message to please television, the less the major networks were interested."[88] About 38 million Americans watched convention speeches by Barack Obama and John McCain in 2008, a figure that is about comparable to an American Idol finale, smaller than the number of viewers who watched Michael Phelps set the record for gold medal wins at the 2008 Olympics (40 million), and far short of the number of people who watched the 2010 Superbowl (106 million).[89] This is probably a high-water mark for modern convention viewership because of the unusually interesting race and the lack of an incumbent candidate.

The Presidential Debates

One of the high points of modern presidential campaigns is the series of debates between the two—and in one case, three—major candidates. No other campaign events earn such high ratings. In fact, more people watch the debates than vote.

The first televised debates were held during the 1960 campaign between candidates Richard M. Nixon and John F. Kennedy. One of the surprising findings in studies of the debates was that people who listened to them on the radio evaluated Nixon's performance more favorably than people who watched them on TV, an indication that visual images could have impacts different from the words with which they were associated.[90] No debates were held in 1964, 1968, or 1972, but they have been held in every election since then. Although the format and arrangements usually are matters of some controversy, debates now appear to be an institutionalized part of presidential campaigns.

Studies show that performance in the debates has the potential to sway the undecided voter. For example, in 1984 President Reagan appeared tired and confused in his first debate with Walter Mondale. His unexpectedly poor performance raised the issue of his age (then 73) and resulted in a slight drop in the polls. Knowing how important the next encounter was, Reagan came in alert, prepared, and full of good humor. He dispelled the concerns raised in the first debate and gained 4 points in the polls.[91]

As in campaign coverage generally, the first question the media raise about debates is "Who won?" In many cases this can lead to exaggerated claims about the importance of small details, as the media focus on personality, strategy, and sound bites again comes into play. Pundits criticized John McCain's debate performances in 2008 in part because he avoided making eye contact with Obama and on one occasion referred to him as "that one." Such considerations may take up airtime on talk shows but likely mean no more to voters than other "horse-race" or personality-based coverage.

Media Coverage of Government

9.7

Assess media coverage of the government.

Media coverage of government exhibits problems and biases analogous to those evident in media coverage of campaigns. From the standpoint of the mass media, much of the routine work of government is dull—hence the media focus on what they consider more exciting.

Emphasis on the President (and Other Personalities)

The president is a single individual with personality and character. Naturally, then, he (and, one day, she) is inherently more interesting than a collectivity such as Congress or an abstraction such as the bureaucracy. The president receives the lion's share of the evening news coverage.[92] And not only does Congress play second fiddle in terms of media coverage, but coverage of Congress has declined in recent decades.[93] The problem, of course, is that the president is only one part of the government, and one with fairly limited powers (see Chapter 13). Thus, the media prime citizens to focus on presidents to a degree that is out of proportion to their real powers and responsibilities.

The exception to this generalization is one that proves the rule. For six months after the 1994 elections, the media virtually forgot about President Clinton as pack journalists turned their attention to Speaker of the House Newt Gingrich and the new Republican majority in Congress. For once, the media could represent Congress via a single personality. Now that the Democratic and Republican leaderships in Congress lack such colorful personalities, the media's former neglect of the institution has returned.

This focus of the media on personalities seems to be a universal tendency. It is similar to building military coverage around sympathetic war heroes or building sports coverage around a few outstanding superstars. An effective governmental team, similar to a winning sports team or a successful military unit, requires teamwork—but the media find individual heroics and failures to be more compelling stories. Unfortunately, in framing coverage in terms of individuals, the media probably discourage political entrepreneurs from building coalitions—and instead encourage them to promote themselves, to grandstand, to "hog the ball." Moreover, such media coverage primes citizens to think about government in terms of the heroic exploits and tragic failures of individuals rather than in terms of institutions and processes that are operating effectively or poorly.[94]

Emphasis on Conflict

Every time politicians make a controversial comment, they are assured of media coverage. Indeed, politicians who make the kind of inflammatory remarks the media love, and offer them up in convenient sound bites, can expect constant media attention. When issues are discussed in detail in a civil manner, the media can lose interest. In early 2010, for example, President Obama met with over three dozen lawmakers from both parties at a televised seven-hour summit on the healthcare bill then under consideration. The media largely did not know what to make of this mostly civil discussion; cable channels cut away after a few hours. One newspaper summed up the mood: "watching American politicians argue about health care can be seriously damaging to your health. Symptoms include migraines, extreme fatigue, and sudden violent urges."[95]

Ironically, the journalistic preference for conflict can discourage politicians from doing anything really interesting. When reporters learn of an innovative proposal, the necessity to portray conflict leads them to search out the idea's likely enemies and trumpet their hostile reaction. As a result, journalists "often lead the chorus of criticism of anyone who tries to upset the apple cart. In so doing, they implicitly side with the interest groups and old-line politicians whose prerogatives are being challenged." The clamor of opposition not only immediately threatens public perception of the proposal, but also threatens the person who floated it. The would-be reformer is likely to be portrayed "as naïve and politically unsophisticated" for taking the chance.[96]

Journalists especially like conflict when it revolves around some kind of scandal. The same study that found coverage of Congress to be declining also found that the focus of coverage had changed. Policy stories outnumbered scandal stories by 13 to 1 from 1972 to the mid-1980s, but since then the ratio has plunged to 3 to 1.[97] The Clinton administration faced repeated scandals, some sexual and some financial— culminating in incessant reports of Clinton's intimate relationship with White House intern Monica Lewinsky. George W. Bush faced a number of controversies that approached scandal-like proportions, including charges that his administration falsely manufactured reasons for going to war in Iraq and that his political advisers leaked the name of a CIA operative because her husband had criticized the war effort.[98] Given the media's obsession with scandal and conflict, it is no wonder that politicians often try to tell journalists as little as possible. As one former White House spokesman put it, "It's not easy getting up here and saying nothing. It takes a lot of preparation."[99]

Emphasis on the Negative

Media on the lookout for conflicts, scandals, and mistakes naturally emphasize the negative. What government does well is less newsworthy than what government does badly. Quiet compromises that improve public policies are less newsworthy than noisy arguments that accomplish nothing. Thus, according to one study, television coverage of Congress has become increasingly negative since 1972.[100] Newspapers also cover Congress less, and more negatively, than the presidency.[101] Has Congress become that much worse, or has the change been inside the media? Even entertainment shows now portray government officials more negatively than they did a generation ago.[102]

Continued on page 271

Should Freedom of the Press Be Limited to Protect National Security?

The Issue

Even though the First Amendment guarantees "freedom of the press," are there limits on what the media should be able to print or broadcast if a story might compromise American national security?

Background

The First Amendment to the Constitution clearly states that "Congress shall make no law . . . abridging the freedom of speech, or of the press. . . ." On its face, this seems to be a straightforward declaration. As one Supreme Court justice was fond of saying, "No law means no law." In practice, however, there is a long tradition in which courts, legislatures, and academic commentators try to carve out exceptions and qualifications to this general principle. Consult a typical textbook on constitutional law, and you will find literally hundreds of pages attempting to explain all the details and complexities of the law concerning freedom of speech and freedom of the press.[1]

One particular area of controversy concerns the duties and responsibilities of the press when it covers issues directly connected to American national security. As almost everybody concedes, secrecy is a useful, often essential attribute of decision making in foreign policy, particularly in a time of war. But, if citizens are to pass judgment on the government's performance in conducting foreign policy and prevent the abuse of governmental powers, the public must be kept informed about their country's international actions and policies. There is, in short, an unavoidable tension between secrecy and accountability when democracies conduct foreign policy, a tension that surfaces in a variety of ways.

Censorship in the Interests of National Security

Suppose that the federal government knows in advance that a newspaper will print a story that top officials in the executive branch believe will be harmful to U.S. national security. Should they be able to prevent the paper from printing the story? Should the federal government, in other words, be allowed to censor the American news media in the interests of national security?

The kind of case just described is, we should make clear, exceptional. Although top federal officials are often annoyed or outraged by what the media choose to print or broadcast, very rarely have they resorted to what is called *prior restraint*. But it has happened.

The most celebrated case of this kind was the publishing of the Pentagon Papers. In 1968, then–Secretary of Defense Robert McNamara commissioned the writing of a detailed, secret history of how the United States had become involved in the Vietnam War. In 1971, a former Defense Department employee named Daniel Ellsberg leaked a copy of this still-classified history to several newspapers. In mid-June, the *New York Times* and then the *Washington Post* began publishing portions of that history, now generally known as the Pentagon Papers. Top officials in the Nixon administration—Secretary of State Henry Kissinger, in particular—believed that this publication could "result in great harm to the nation," including "the death of soldiers, the destruction of alliances, the greatly increased difficulty of negotiation with our enemies, [and] the inability of our diplomats to negotiate." Hence, they sought an injunction to prevent these newspapers from publishing any more of the Pentagon Papers. Several courts did issue a temporary injunction, which prevented the newspapers from publishing further material from the history as the case was being decided. (All newspapers complied with the court orders.)

In a 6 to 3 decision, however, the U.S. Supreme Court rejected the government's claim and allowed the publication to continue. A majority of the justices did not contend that prior restraint could never be justified, but the Court did say that "any system of prior restraints . . . comes to this Court bearing a heavy presumption against its constitutional validity," and that the government therefore had a "heavy burden of showing justification for such a restraint." And the Nixon administration, in the Court's view, did not meet that burden.[2]

A closer call, for many commentators, occurred in 1979, when a left-wing magazine called *The Progressive* decided to print an article that explained how to build a hydrogen bomb. Saying that the article only synthesized information from publicly available documents, the author and the publisher claimed that the article would benefit the nation "by demonstrating that open debate [about nuclear weaponry] was preferable to an oppressive and ineffective system of secrecy and classification." The federal government replied that information in the article would present an "immediate, direct, and irreparable harm" to the interests of the United States, and it submitted affidavits from various cabinet members claiming that publication of the article would increase the risk of thermonuclear proliferation. In this case, a district court ruled in favor of the government, although the case was ultimately abandoned when a lengthy letter detailing the same information was published in two newspapers.[3]

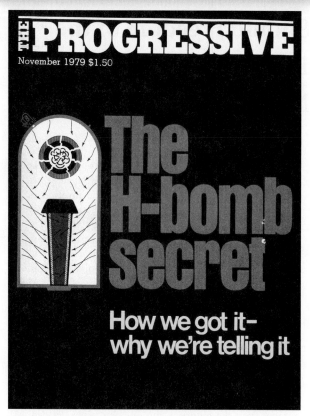

Should the media be allowed to publish stories disclosing information that may endanger the country?

Self-Policing by the Media

The cases just described are, as we have already noted, clearly exceptional. In the more typical case, the government does not find out about the story in advance—or if it does, it simply tries to persuade the news agency not to print or broadcast it. In other words, the decision about what might harm the nation's security, and whether that harm justifies suppressing the story, is left to the media.

An interesting case of this kind occurred in late June 2006, when the *New York Times* published a front-page story about a secret program, begun shortly after the terrorist attacks of September 11, 2001, in which counterterrorism officials had gained access to "financial records from a vast international database and examined banking transactions involving thousands of Americans and others in the United States." As the article noted, the Bush administration viewed the program as a "vital tool" in the war against terrorism, saying that it had played "a hidden role in domestic and foreign terrorism investigations . . . and helped in the capture of the most wanted [Al] Qaeda figure in Southeast Asia."

Indeed, after finding out about the investigation, administration officials made extensive efforts to persuade the paper not to publish the article, saying that "disclosure of the . . . program

could jeopardize its effectiveness." But the *Times* refused to halt publication. As Bill Keller, the newspaper's executive editor, summed up his conclusion, "We remain convinced that the administration's extraordinary access to this vast repository of international financial data, however carefully targeted use of it may be, is a matter of public interest."[4]

Over the next few days, there were numerous calls for an investigation of how the *New York Times* got the story and prosecution of the executive branch officials who had leaked it to the press, but no one in the administration seriously urged that the *Times* or its reporters be punished.

Protecting Confidential Sources

Many of the stories just described—and many non-foreign-policy stories as well—are obtained from reporters by so-called "confidential sources": sources who ask the reporter not to disclose their identity. This is a common practice among American reporters, and although it often annoys top decision makers (when they themselves are not the anonymous source), in most cases it does not present any particular legal dilemmas.

But suppose that the confidential source is breaking the law—as was almost certainly the case in both the Pentagon Papers and the more recent *New York Times* story. In order to prosecute the law-breaker, authorities need to find out who leaked the story—and the only way to do that, in most cases, is to ask the reporter. Should the reporter be compelled to disclose his or her sources to the police or prosecutors? Or does the First Amendment protect the reporter from such questioning?

The seminal Supreme Court case on this subject is *Branzburg v. Hayes,* decided in 1972. Branzburg was a reporter who wrote an article about a variety of illegal drug activities he had witnessed. Shortly thereafter, a prosecutor asked him to appear before a grand jury and identify the drug users. Branzburg refused—and was imprisoned as a result. His attorneys argued that the use of confidential sources was often essential to news gathering, and that if reporters were required to reveal their sources, they would be "measurably deterred from furnishing publishable information, all to the detriment of the free flow of information protected by the First Amendment." But the Court ruled against Branzburg: Reporters, similar to all other citizens, are not exempt from grand jury subpoenas.[5]

The Branzburg case, it is worth adding, only establishes that reporters do not enjoy a *constitutional* right to keep their sources secret. Partly in reaction to the Branzburg decision, more than half of the states have passed "shield" laws that provide at least a qualified privilege of confidentiality.[6]

How Have the Courts Ruled?

We should note here that the courts were a major player in almost all of the cases described above. This should come as no surprise. Whether one takes a broad or narrow view of freedom of the press, it is clear that the Constitution does pose a substantial hurdle to any legal attempts to command or regulate the press.

No matter how much legislatures or executives may resent it, the final say in most such cases will inevitably be pronounced by the courts.

What Do You Think?

1. Which should be a greater concern for contemporary Americans—the threat from terrorism or the threat from secret government programs that investigate or monitor the activities of ordinary citizens?
2. Of the three court cases described in this section, in which case(s)—if any—do you agree with the final decision? On the whole, do you feel that the courts have done a good or poor job of balancing freedom of the press against the needs of national security?
3. If you were a state legislator, would you vote for a shield law that provided full or partial immunity to reporters from having to reveal their confidential sources?
4. Did the *New York Times* make the right decision in publishing its story on the administration's use of financial data to track the activities of terrorists?

On the Web

For ongoing commentary about these and other issues in journalism ethics, see the following websites:

The Poynter Institute is a journalism school noted for its research about and discussion of ethical issues.

www.poynter.org

The Columbia Journalism Review is probably the best-known journal on media issues, although with a generally left-wing perspective.

www.cjrdaily.org

The Media Research Center monitors media coverage, from a conservative perspective.

www.mediaresearch.org

[1] See, for example, Kathleen M. Sullivan and Gerald Gunther, *Constitutional Law,* 14th ed. (New York: Foundation Press, 2001), 956–1433.
[2] All quotations are taken from *New York Times Co. v. United States* 403 US 713 (1971).
[3] All quotations are taken from *United States v. Progressive, Inc.* 467 F. Supp. 990 (W.D. Wis. 1979).
[4] The original article, which also discusses the decision to publish, is Eric Lichtblau and James Risen, "Bank Data Sifted in Secret by U.S. to Block Terrorism," *New York Times,* June 23, 2006: A1.
[5] *Branzburg v. Hayes* 408 U.S. 665 (1972).
[6] Sullivan and Gunther, *Constitutional Law,* p. 1410.

Continued from page 268

The Response: Exaggerated Concern with the Media

Because the media have become the principal link between citizens and their government, elected officials often lose sight of the people. American politicians have long known about the political importance of the press: Witness the efforts of the early parties to establish their own newspapers. As the media became more independent and nonpartisan, politicians gradually came to understand that special efforts were needed to cultivate favorable coverage. At the presidential level, Theodore Roosevelt was perhaps the first president to have an aggressive press strategy of this type. Nearly all of his successors added new weapons to the presidential arsenal or institutionalized older ones. National security concerns complicated the relationship between politicians and the press (see the *Election Voices*). By the 1980s, media strategy had become a constant, almost obsessive concern of U.S. politicians, particularly those in Washington. Three weeks before the 1980 election, then-vice president Walter Mondale actually said, "If I had to give up . . . the opportunity to get on the evening news or the veto power, . . . I'd throw away the veto power."[103] The importance of swift and conscientious attention to the media has only increased since then. Historian Michael Bechloss put it this way: "When the Berlin Wall went up in 1961, President Kennedy was on vacation. For six days, no one pressed him hard for a reaction. If that happened now, President Obama would have three seconds."[104]

CHAPTER SUMMARY

9.1 Trace the development of the mass media from colonial times to the present day.

The mass media have been important players in American politics almost from the beginning, setting the context for elections by informing voters about politics and policy. Their character has changed, however, from partisan allies of political elites in the early 1800s to the more fragmented and diverse outlets of today.

9.2 Identify the primary media through which Americans get their news.

Initially small-scale and elitist, the media have grown progressively more accessible to the average citizen. By most measures, television is now the most important form of mass communication—but recent technological developments have produced new media, such as cable and satellite TV and the Internet, that are weakening the traditional print and broadcast systems.

9.3 Characterize the effects the media have on the public's political attitudes.

Media effects on public opinion fall into several categories. Agenda setting occurs when media coverage affects what issues or problems people think about. Priming occurs when the media encourage people to evaluate political figures in terms of one set of considerations rather than another. Framing occurs when the media present problems or issues in such a way that people are stimulated to think about them in terms of one frame of reference rather than another. The media also may change attitudes more slowly through their role in political socialization.

9.4 Outline the major kinds of media bias and assess criticisms of the media.

Frequently, critics charge the media with one or another form of bias. Surveys show that reporters and editors are more liberal and more supportive of Democrats than is the public at large, but it is less clear whether the values and opinions of journalists have a significant effect on their political coverage. Moreover, other critics charge that professional and economic considerations lead the media in a conservative direction.

9.5 Illustrate the influence of entertainment media on American political attitudes.

More important than ideological biases are biases that arise from the definition of what is news, and especially what is considered good TV news. The media reflect an emphasis on the negative and an emphasis on conflict. They focus on dramatic incidents and colorful personalities rather than on more abstract forces and developments, even where the latter are far more important. Thus, "soft news" often crowds out "hard news."

9.6 Assess media coverage of the election process.

The media oversimplify complex situations and reduce complicated arguments and positions to ten-second sound bites. Campaign coverage focuses on competition rather than on detailed policy positions and arguments. Such biases are understandable in terms of media outlets' constant competition to reach a broader audience.

9.7 Assess media coverage of the government.

Unlike the media in many other countries, the U.S. media are organized and operated from the private sector. This has its benefits—the government cannot easily control the messages the media send to members of the public. But there are also costs. The role of the mass media in serving the public interest exists in constant tension with their role as profit-making enterprises serving their stockholders.

PEARSON
mypoliscilab EXERCISES

Apply what you learned in this chapter on MyPoliSciLab.

Read on mypoliscilab.com

eText: Chapter 9

Study and Review on mypoliscilab.com

Pre-Test

Post-Test

Chapter Exam

Flashcards

Watch on mypoliscilab.com

Video: YouTube Politics

Video: The Pentagon's Media Message

Explore on mypoliscilab.com

Simulation: You Are the News Editor

Comparative: Comparing News Media

Timeline: Three Hundred Years of American Mass Media

Visual Literacy: Use of the Media by the American Public

KEY TERMS

agenda setting, p. 256
CNN effect, p. 256
equal-time rule, p. 248
fairness doctrine, p. 248

framing, p. 257
mass media, p. 245
new media, p. 252
priming, p. 257

selection principle, p. 258
sound bite, p. 265

SUGGESTED READINGS

Of General Interest

Farnsworth, Stephen J., and S. Robert Lichter. *The Nightly News Nightmare,* 3rd ed. Lanham, MD: Rowman & Littlefield, 2010. Excellent summary of how television covered presidential campaigns between 1988 and 2008, with particularly good data on media content.

Lippmann, Walter. *Public Opinion.* New Brunswick, NJ: Transaction Publishers, 1991. Originally published in 1922, it is still the best book ever written about the mass media.

Neumann, W. Russell. *The Future of the Mass Audience.* Cambridge, England: Cambridge University Press, 1991. Thoughtful examination of the effects of technological change on mass communications. Concludes that new media will not fragment the audience as much as many think.

Norris, Pippa. *A Virtuous Circle.* Cambridge, England: Cambridge University Press. 2000. Hugely informative survey of politics and media in advanced industrial democracies. In general, Norris takes a more sanguine view of modern developments than many critics do.

Panagopoulos, Costas, ed. *Politicking Online: The Transformation of Election Campaign Communications.* Piscataway, NJ: Rutgers University Press, 2009. A set of essays dissecting the impact of the Internet on modern campaigns.

Focused Studies

Hewitt, Hugh. *Blog: Understanding the Information Reformation That's Changing Your World.* Nashville, TN: Thomas Nelson, 2005. Provocative argument about the importance of blogs, written by the author of one of the most important conservative blogs.

Iyengar, Shanto, and Donald Kinder. *News That Matters.* Chicago: University of Chicago Press, 1987. An exemplary experimental study that demonstrates the existence of agenda setting and priming.

Lavrakas, Paul, and Michael Traugott, eds. *Election Polls, the News Media, and Democracy.* New York: Seven Bridges Press, 2000. Comprehensive collection of essays on election polls. Suggests that the media make a significant contribution to American democracy through election polls, when properly done.

West, Darrell. *Air Wars,* 5th ed. Washington, DC: Congressional Quarterly, 2009. Readable study of the evolution and consequences of television advertising in campaigns since 1952.

ON THE WEB

Virtually every news organization these days has a website.

abcnews.go.com/politics

www.cnn.com/POLITICS

www.nytimes.com/pages/politics

www.latimes.com/news/politics

www.foxnews.com/politics

www.washingtonpost.com

This list consists of some of the most prominent news organizations' politics websites. In addition to these news sites, commentary has become extremely important, particularly with respect to framing and priming issues. The editorial sections of these websites are also good sources for learning about elite debate and dialogue.

www.tnr.com

www.theweeklystandard.com

Magazines such as the left-of-center *The New Republic* and the conservative *The Weekly Standard* have become important outlets for policy ideas.

www.people-press.org

The Pew Research Center for the People and the Press conducts survey research on how the media conduct themselves. Its website is invaluable for understanding how the public reacts to the media.

10 Electing the President

CHAPTER OUTLINE

LEARNING OBJECTIVES

10.1 Evaluate the strengths and weaknesses of the presidential and vice presidential nomination process.

10.2 Identify the sources used to fund presidential campaigns and explain how the electoral college system works.

10.3 Analyze factors that impact voting behavior in presidential elections.

10.4 Outline the changes in the presidential election scene that have occurred in the last 40 years.

The Meaning of Presidential Elections

The 2008 election was a presidential contest like no other. Barack Obama was the first African American presidential nominee of a major party. Sarah Palin, the governor of Alaska, was the first woman to appear on a Republican ticket. The Democratic Party primary season had been unusually hard fought, with Hillary Clinton contesting the nomination until the very last delegate was chosen. Republicans nominated John McCain as their standard bearer, an independent-minded Arizona senator whose positions on issues such as immigration, campaign reform, and the federal budget had often riled party leaders. Even before the fall campaign got under way, there was much about the race that defied expectations.

The events of the final two months of the campaign were even more extraordinary. The precipitous decline of the housing market and the consequent crisis on Wall Street pushed the U.S. economy to a precipice. As Congress considered a colossal rescue package, McCain briefly suspended his campaign so he could return to Washington to address the crisis. A surreal White House event gathered congressional leaders, President George W. Bush, both presidential candidates, and Treasury Secretary Hank Paulson around the same table to discuss the situation. Not surprisingly, this summit meeting failed to accomplish much: It took a House vote against the rescue bill and a subsequent 700-point stock market plunge to shock Congress into finally approving the legislation.

And then there were the less tangible issues. Would white voters really cast their ballots for a black candidate? Would McCain's reputation as short-tempered scare away voters? Did the candidates' debate performances—or those of their vice presidential nominees—make a difference? The McCain campaign cast Obama as a "celebrity" in the mold of heiress Paris Hilton and claimed that he couldn't connect with average Americans like "Joe the plumber," a voter who had encountered Obama at a campaign stop. For their part, Obama staffers did their best to link McCain to the unpopular outgoing president George W. Bush, running ads that called him a "maverick no more." Would these attacks stick? As one editorial put it, "Election '08, with its plot twists and vivid characters, topped any reality show the networks could cook up."[1]

Political scientists were watching the "reality show" with interest in the final days of the campaign just like everybody else, but most had long since placed their bets on how it would turn out. Using statistical models refined over many presidential elections, scholars committed themselves to predictions long before most of the remarkable campaign events took place. Some of the most sophisticated attempts at forecasting the election came out in July and August, before the time of the national party conventions and long before the first presidential debate. Out of nine published forecasts, only one predicted a Republican victory. On average, they predicted the Democratic candidate would receive 52.5 percent of the popular vote. Obama won with 53 percent.

What might seem even more remarkable is that these political science models were based on such factors as economic growth rates, the unemployment rate, overall presidential approval, and the amount of time that the incumbent party (the Republicans) had been in power. They incorporated no information on attack ads, personalities, or historic "firsts." No bailout bills, no campaign suspensions, no "Joe the Plumber." Overall, the political scientists gave much clearer and much earlier predictions than all of the pundits, and they basically got it right.

Making the Connection

News coverage of presidential elections typically focuses on the short-term events of election campaigns: the strategies, the personalities, the mistakes. Someone who judges American elections simply on the discussion found in newspapers, in magazines, and on the airwaves would conclude that voters make snap decisions based on short-term (if not trivial) considerations. It is hard to reconcile this story of last-minute decision making with the ability of political scientists to accurately forecast the presidential results long in advance, before all of the fluctuations in the polls and before all the campaign events that supposedly drive the outcome.

We begin the chapter with a discussion of the nomination process, considering how presidential candidates are nominated in the United States and how our unusual nominating process came to be. After a discussion of the pros and cons of the American nominating process, we turn to the general election, reflecting on how the Electoral College affects the nature of the campaign and how Americans vote in presidential elections. We then consider why the importance of the media and the campaign is often exaggerated and close with a discussion of what issues and other factors have influenced the most recent presidential elections.

Nominating a Presidential Candidate

One of the major functions played by political parties, as we have seen in Chapter 8, is to simplify and clarify elections. They do this mainly by nominating candidates for public office—designating one person as the official party candidate for each office on the ballot. Although parties do this for offices of all types and at all levels of government, the most important and visible nomination that the major parties make is their choice of a presidential candidate every four years.

Evolution of the Nomination Process

The Constitution does not explicitly say anything about how candidates for president (or for any other office) are to be nominated, but the dominant understanding at the Constitutional Convention was that this function would be filled primarily by the Electoral College.[2] The electors, meeting in their respective states, would scatter their votes among a large number of candidates, no one of whom would have a majority. The top five finishers in this initial balloting would thus, in effect, be "nominated," with the final choice then made by the House of Representatives. In fact, however, nothing like this scenario ever took place. In the first two presidential elections held under the Constitution, George Washington was the obvious consensus choice. In 1796, when Washington announced he would not seek a third term, both the Federalists and the Democratic-Republicans decided to nominate a presidential candidate *before* the members of the Electoral College were selected. The mechanism they devised for this purpose was the congressional caucus: a meeting of each party's members in the U.S. Senate and House of Representatives. The congressional caucus was the major, although not exclusive, means for nominating presidential candidates between 1796 and 1824.

10.1

Evaluate the strengths and weaknesses of the presidential and vice presidential nomination process.

Almost from the beginning, however, the congressional caucus came under attack. Some critics felt that involving Congress in the selection of presidential candidates implicitly violated the constitutionally prescribed separation of powers. Others felt that the procedure was undemocratic, especially as it meant that any district that elected a congressman from the other party was unrepresented in the caucus deliberations. After experimenting with a number of other nominating mechanisms, by the 1840s both the Democrats and Whigs were nominating their presidential and vice presidential candidates by national conventions. Each state party selected a number of delegates, usually at a state convention, who then met together at a central location in order to nominate the party's national ticket. It was a convention of this type that nominated, among others, Abraham Lincoln as the Republican Party presidential candidate in 1860.

In the early twentieth century, one important innovation was added to this system.[3] Spurred by the Progressive movement and its attack on corrupt party machines, a number of state legislatures required that the state parties select their national convention delegates through primary elections, rather than at state conventions. Sometimes called the "mixed system," this set of procedures was used by both the Democrats and Republicans to nominate presidential candidates between 1912 and 1968. As the name indicates, the principal virtue of this system was that it seemed to give both ordinary party voters and formal party organizations a voice in presidential nominations. Candidates who wanted to demonstrate their electoral appeal could do so by running in the primaries, but the number of primaries was sufficiently limited that party leaders still had the capacity to accept or reject the primary verdict. In 1960, for example, John Kennedy entered only seven primaries. After winning them all, he then used this showing to convince state party leaders of his electability.

The Contemporary Nomination Process

Similar to its predecessors, however, the mixed system came under attack for being unrepresentative and undemocratic. Particularly controversial was the Democratic nomination race of 1968. With many Democratic activists outraged about President Lyndon B. Johnson's conduct of the Vietnam War, two antiwar candidates, Eugene McCarthy and Robert Kennedy, won almost all of the primaries—yet the Democratic convention nevertheless gave its presidential nomination to vice president and Johnson-supporter Hubert Humphrey, who had not entered a single primary (Kennedy was assassinated just after winning the California primary). On the second night of a remarkably bitter and divisive convention, the Democrats adopted a vaguely worded resolution that, as eventually interpreted, authorized a special commission to rewrite the rules the party used for selecting delegates and nominating presidents. By 1972, the rules had been so completely transformed that most political scientists treat the nomination races since then as an entirely different era in nomination politics.[4] The changes, moreover, affected both parties—partly because the Republicans were anxious to show that they, too, were an open and responsive party, and partly because when state legislatures rewrote their primary laws they tended to make the changes applicable to both parties.

The central thrust of the new rules was to take a process that had been dominated by party leaders and formal party organizations and turn it into one in which almost all delegates were chosen to reflect the presidential preferences of ordinary party voters. Specifically, delegates to contemporary national conventions are chosen in three major ways:

1. *By primary election.* The most visible sign of the new system was a sharp increase in the number of **presidential primaries** from about 17 per year in the elections of 1952–1968 to 23 in 1972, 33 in 1980, and 41 in 2008. Moreover, unlike pre-1972 primaries, the new rules generally required that delegate selection be directly tied to the presidential preference vote cast in the primaries. Much like members of the Electoral College, national convention delegates were no longer elected as relatively free agents, who could go to a national convention and deliberate or bargain with other party leaders. Delegates were almost always elected in ways that made them little more than messengers, pledged to vote for a specific candidate unless that candidate withdrew and "freed" his delegates.

presidential primaries
Elections held for the purpose of selecting or instructing national convention delegates.

2. *By caucuses.* A small number of states continue to select their delegates through party-run **caucuses:** meetings of candidate supporters who choose delegates to a state or national convention. This complicated procedure generally begins with party meetings held in each town or precinct in the state. These precinct caucuses, as they are usually called, select delegates to county, congressional district, or state conventions, and it is only at these latter meetings that national convention delegates are chosen (see the *Election Connection* box on the next page).[5]

caucus
Meeting of candidate supporters who choose delegates to a state or national convention.

Caucuses differ from primaries in a number of ways: They take longer, their rules are more complicated, and they generally require participants to make a public expression of their candidate preferences (rather than casting a secret ballot). Hence, they tend to have a considerably smaller turnout than primaries: Whereas the typical primary brings about 20–30 percent of the party faithful to the polls, caucuses are rarely attended by more than 1 or 2 percent of the eligible electorate. For this reason, caucuses are sometimes more susceptible to domination by extremist candidates and issue zealots.

Yet in most respects caucuses are, as one presidential candidate described them, "the functional equivalent of a primary."[6] Similar to primaries, voters show up at caucuses, express their presidential preferences, and expect that national convention

The Caucuses
Iowa caucusers receive instructions on how to register their candidate preferences and then select delegates to the next round of meetings.

ELECTION CONNECTION

Primaries Versus Caucuses

When voters cast ballots in presidential primaries and caucuses, they are not voting directly for a candidate of their choice. Instead, they are voting for delegates who are pledged to support these candidates at party conventions. Since the reforms of the early 1970s, there have been three main ways to become a delegate to a party's national convention: via a primary election, via a caucus system, or as an automatic "superdelegate."

Primaries

Primaries work like other elections: Voters appear at the polls at some point on Election day, vote, and leave. After the votes are totaled, party officials use them to allocate national convention delegates. Democrats use a proportional representation system: If a candidate receives two-thirds of the vote, he or she receives two-thirds of the delegates and the other candidate or candidates receive the remaining one-third. Republicans use a winner-take-all system in most cases: 51 percent of the vote gets a candidate 100 percent of the delegates. The actual people who become delegates are drawn from lists of acceptable delegate candidates provided in advance by each campaign.

Caucuses

Some states (13 in 2008) choose to select their delegates via a caucus system. In this case, voters must show up at a designated location at a specific time. The Iowa caucuses began at 7 PM on January 3, 2008, for example. After some preliminaries, the assembled voters must break into smaller groups. Depending on the size of each group, these "subcaucuses" then elect from their number a set of delegates. Because larger groups can elect more delegates, often a fair amount of arguing and persuading takes place, as each group tries to win over undecided voters. This process can take hours, but eventually the caucus produces a final list of delegates. These delegates do not automatically get to go to the national convention, however: They must repeat the process at the county level, and again at a state convention. Only if a delegate wins election at three levels—the precinct, the county, and the state—does he or she advance to the national convention.

Superdelegates

The post-1968 party reforms sought to diminish the power of party leaders and increase the power of ordinary voters. But, by the 1980s, the Democratic Party reversed course somewhat, giving automatic delegate status to party leaders and elected officials such as senators, members of the House of Representatives, and governors. These "superdelegates" had 19 percent of the total Democratic Convention votes in 2008. Republicans have a smaller number of "automatic" delegates comprised of the top three party officials from each state and territory. They make up only 7 percent of the total Republican delegates.

Elected delegates may be chosen via caucuses or primaries, depending on the state. Party leaders and elected officials are known as "superdelegates" in the Democratic Party because they automatically get votes at the convention. Republicans give delegate status to each state's top three party leaders, but other Republican-elected officials do not automatically become delegates.

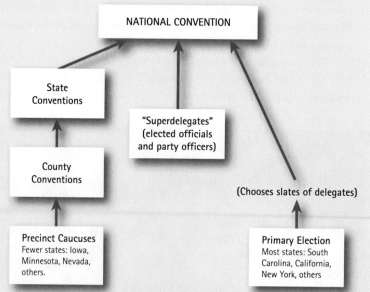

Three Routes to the National Convention

Source: "Delegate Selection Rules for the 2008 Democratic National Convention," as adopted by the Democratic National Committee, August 19, 2006, http://s3.amazonaws.com/apache.3cdn.net/de68e7b6dfa0743217_hwm6bhyc4.pdf, accessed June 16, 2010; "The Rules of the Republican Party," as adopted by the 2008 Republican National Convention, September 1, 2008, www.gop.com/images/legal/2008_RULES_Adopted.pdf, accessed June 16, 2010.

delegates will directly reflect those preferences. Also similar to primaries, caucuses are not restricted to formal party members, nor do they require participants to demonstrate that they have supported the party in the past. Virtually any voter who walks in off the street and is willing to sign a statement claiming that he or she is committed to the party or its principles can take part, with the same rights and privileges as the state party chairman or a long time member of the state legislature.

3. *Superdelegates.* In the first several nomination contests held under the new rules, there was a severe decline in the number of Democratic elected officials and party leaders who became delegates to that party's national conventions. Hence, in 1982 the Democratic Party adopted a new set of rules under which certain kinds of party leaders—members of the U.S. House and Senate, governors, members of the national committee—became automatic or ex-officio delegates. These **superdelegates,** as they are generally known, have accounted for about one-sixth of the votes at most recent Democratic conventions. Beginning with the 2004 election cycle, the Republicans conferred automatic delegate status on the Republican national committeeman and committeewoman from each state, in addition to the state party chair. In a closely fought nomination race, the superdelegates can hold the crucial balance of power. In 2008, for example, Obama did not technically possess a majority of delegates without taking superdelegates into account. But the superdelegates ultimately shifted their support to Obama because he had won the largest number of delegates during the primary season.

superdelegate
Certain party leaders—members of the U.S. House and Senate, governors, members of the national committee—who became automatic or ex-officio delegates.

Financing Nomination Campaigns

The new delegate selection rules were not the only source of change in the presidential nomination process. In 1974, in reaction to the Watergate scandals, Congress rewrote the laws governing how money could be raised and spent in federal election campaigns. Prior to the passage of the Federal Election Campaign Act amendments (FECA) of 1974, the financing of presidential campaigns was almost completely unregulated. Contributors could give as much money as they wanted and candidates spent everything they could raise; the law required candidates to disclose basic campaign finance information, but this requirement was rarely, if ever, enforced.

The new regime established by FECA had five major features:

1. *Contribution limits.* In the original law, no one could contribute more than $1,000 to any presidential candidate. And, even though the late 1970s were a time of rapid inflation, this limit remained unchanged. Finally, in 2002, the contribution limit was doubled and indexed to inflation—that is, it will be increased every two years at the same rate that the consumer price index has increased during the same period. The limit for the 2008 election cycle was $2,300.

2. *Matching funds.* To help make up for some of the money candidates lost because of the contribution limits, FECA also set up a system of federal subsidies to presidential nomination contenders. A candidate first had to demonstrate some minimum level of support, by raising $5,000 in contributions of $250 or less in 20 states. After that, every contribution of $250 or less would receive an equal amount of money in **matching funds,** public moneys (from $3 check-offs on income tax returns) paid out of the federal treasury.

matching funds
Public moneys (from $3 check-offs on income tax returns) that the Federal Election Commission distributes to primary candidates according to a prespecified formula.

3. *Spending limits.* The federal money came with strings attached, however. Candidates who accepted matching funds were also required to limit their spending. In 2008, the overall limit was $42.05 million. In the first five elections held under the FECA, almost every major candidate accepted the matching funds and, thus, the spending limits. But, over the last several election cycles, an increasing number of candidates have decided that the spending limits are too constraining and have thus opted to forgo federal funding. In 2008, the only major presidential candidate in either party who accepted federal matching funds was John Edwards. John McCain spent $219 million in the primary season—over five times what the limit would have been if he had accepted matching funds. Obama spent close to $350 million.[7] Because of the growing disparity between the spending limit and the amount that major candidates are spending, it is unlikely that competitive candidates will choose to accept matching funds in future presidential primaries.

4. *Self-financing.* For some candidates, there was one additional incentive to reject matching funds. When candidates accepted matching funds, they also had to agree that they would put no more than $50,000 of their own money into their campaigns. As a result of an important Supreme Court decision rendered in early 1976, however, candidates who did not take federal money could spend as much of their own money as they wanted *on their own campaign*. Historically, most presidential candidates have not been rich enough for this provision to matter.

5. *Disclosure requirements.* The one part of FECA that everyone seems to feel is a success is the disclosure requirements. All presidential candidates are required to file periodic reports (quarterly reports during the year before the election, monthly reports during the election year) indicating how much money they have raised and spent and, most importantly, the source of every contribution of $200 or more. Especially in the year before the election, these results are carefully monitored by the media—some pundits refer to it as "the money primary"—as an early indicator of the candidates' progress.

The Presidential Nomination Process in Action

How do these rules work in practice? One of the most conspicuous characteristics of contemporary presidential nomination campaigns is how long they are. In the old "mixed system," presidential candidates generally did not begin active campaigning until early in the election year itself or in the final months of the preceding year. Today, a presidential nomination race begins just a few weeks after the preceding midterm election.[8] By March of the year before the election—20 months before the general election—each party will likely have a half-dozen active presidential candidates, with a number of others seriously thinking about joining the fray. (The only exception is a party that has an incumbent president seeking reelection. Since 1980, incumbents have never faced serious opposition in their quest for renomination.)

This extended period of campaigning that goes on before a single primary or caucus takes place is called "the invisible primary."[9] During this period, candidates test out the issues and themes they hope to use to attract the voters, hone their messages, and try to get a handle on the "mood" of the electorate. Even though most voters are not paying attention to these efforts, evidence suggests that these early attempts to build popularity among the party faithful can be a good predictor of later success.[10]

Candidates also spend a lot of time raising money. As a result of the FECA contribution limits, presidential aspirants can no longer fund their campaigns by calling up a handful of wealthy supporters and soliciting a few large contributions. Instead, the candidates must obtain contributions from thousands of individual donors. One former candidate has estimated that 70 percent of his time during the invisible primary was devoted to fundraising.[11]

Finally, candidates spend a good deal of the invisible primary campaigning in a very small number of states that will hold early primaries and caucuses. Two states, in particular, have traditionally received a remarkably large share of candidate time and money and, consequently, of media attention: Iowa, which holds the first caucus, and New Hampshire, which holds the first primary.[12] Especially for a non-front-running candidate, a victory or even an unexpectedly strong showing in these two early events can endow the candidate with a key attribute known as "momentum," as the media, campaign contributors, and voters suddenly take the candidate more seriously. In 2008, two non-front-running candidates won their party's Iowa Caucuses: Barack Obama, who ultimately won the Democratic nomination, and Mike Huckabee, who went on to mount an unexpectedly strong challenge to the eventual Republican nominee, John McCain.

Iowa and New Hampshire primaries are usually followed by a large number of major primaries and caucuses, coming in quick succession. Knowing how important the early phases of the nomination race are, more and more states have moved their primaries and caucuses forward in the calendar, generating a process that is often described as "front-loading."[13] The contest may be hotly fought for a number of weeks, but rather quickly the combination of delegate numbers, monetary pressures, and the media's incessant desire to declare a "winner" brings the nomination race to an effective conclusion. Sometimes, as in the 2008 Democratic nomination race between Hillary Clinton and Barack Obama, a contest is so evenly matched that it remains undecided and hotly contested until the end of the primary season in early June. But the 2008 Democratic race was an exception: Most recent nomination races have been settled in March. In 2004, Democrat John Kerry clinched a first ballot nomination victory on March 13; John McCain clinched the 2008 Republican contest on March 4.

Technically, a presidential aspirant does not become the official party candidate until he or she is nominated by the party's national convention, which is usually not held until July or August. But, as we have already noted (see the introduction to Chapter 8), national conventions are no longer decision-making bodies. The real decision is rendered by the voters participating in the primaries and caucuses; the conventions simply count up the delegates won by each candidate months earlier.

The New Hampshire Primary, 2008
Hillary Clinton greeting voters on primary day in New Hampshire. Clinton won the primary, but lost the nomination.

• *Why is the "invisible primary" such an important precursor to the primary season?*

Strengths and Weaknesses of the Nomination Process

The contemporary presidential nomination process is now almost 40 years old. How well has it performed its basic function of narrowing the large field of presidential hopefuls down to two principal alternatives?

Perhaps the dominant goal of those who wrote the rules in the early 1970s was to increase the amount of popular participation in the presidential nomination process, and at one level they clearly succeeded. Total turnout in presidential primaries has increased dramatically as compared to the 1950s and 1960s. Few other democracies in the world give millions of ordinary party voters such an important role in selecting their party leaders and nominating the person who, if elected, will be the most important official in the national government.[14]

Yet, as the Democrats' decision to create "superdelegates" testifies, not everyone is delighted with this development. Although the final choice of president or prime minister should be made by the voters, some have argued, party nominations should be decided by those who have a demonstrated, long-term commitment to the party and a greater familiarity with its principles and candidates. Ordinary voters have no more business making party nominations than baseball fans have making the key personnel decisions for their favorite team. As E. E. Schattschneider, the most important defender of this position in American political science, has put it, "Democracy is not to be found in the parties but *between* the parties."[15]

Other critics have questioned just how open and egalitarian the contemporary nomination process really is. Clearly, the current system does not treat all voters equally. The voters in Iowa and New Hampshire have much more influence, and accordingly see much more of the candidates, than the voters in other states. In most recent contests (the 2008 Democratic nomination race is again an exception), about a third of all states held their primaries after both candidates had already clinched their party's nomination.

Even in the early states, there is reason to wonder whether the contemporary nomination process really has given "power to the people" in quite the way its designers intended. As we noted in the chapters on political parties and interests groups, taking power away from one group of elites seldom empowers ordinary citizens. Other elites are more often the beneficiaries. In the case of the nomination process, many commentators fear that stripping power from party leaders and government officials may only have empowered two groups that are less representative and less accountable: political activists and the media.

political activists
People who regularly participate in politics; they are more interested in and committed to particular issues and candidates than are ordinary citizens.

Because participation in primaries and (especially) caucuses is so low, small groups of dedicated **political activists,** those who regularly participate in politics and are more interested in and committed to particular issues and candidates than are ordinary citizens, can exert more influence in the nomination contests than they can in general elections, where turnout is much higher. In addition, it is activists who work in campaigns, donate money to candidates, and help mobilize other voters. As a result, some analysts worry that the nomination process confers an advantage on candidates who appeal to activists by taking positions far from the center of the political spectrum where the mass of Americans are located. Democratic candidates generally are more liberal, and Republican candidates generally are more conservative, than the average voter. In the general election, many voters consequently feel that they are offered a choice between two relatively extreme, polarized candidates, with no one speaking up for the broad middle of the electorate.

The media are the second group that has gained influence from the nomination process. Americans must look to broadcast, newspaper, and Internet reporters—as well as to commentators and editors—to interpret confusing primary and caucus developments for them. Critics complain that the press focuses too much on the "horse race":

who is ahead and by how far, who is coming up on the rail, and who is fading from contention. A database search of March 2008 newspaper articles about the presidential campaign finds few stories that focus on issue details and many stories that frame the race as a "game": "Presidential Campaigns Shifting into Overdrive," "Hurdles Line Path for Dem, GOP Candidates," "Back on Attack, Candidates Hit the Airwaves," and so on.[16] One study finds that such "game" themed stories have a 4 to 1 edge over substantive policy stories in the media.[17] Scandals and campaign blunders also receive prominent play. The media's defenders point out that this type of coverage is market driven: Excitement and gossip sells; policy minutia usually does not.

Another major criticism of the current system is simply that it takes too long. Presidential candidates must count on devoting about two full years to the endeavor. Many plausible candidates either cannot spare the time from their work in government or find the whole ordeal too exhausting and demeaning and therefore decide not to run. The candidates who do make the race are often compelled to ignore or give short shrift to their governing responsibilities. In 2007, for example, senators Hillary Clinton, Barack Obama, and John McCain, all of whom were running for president, missed, respectively, 23 percent, 38 percent, and 56 percent of the roll call votes held in the Senate that year (the average senator missed 5 percent of votes).[18]

Perhaps the most important question that we can ask about the presidential nomination process is: What kind of candidates does it finally nominate? Are they sufficiently representative? (Answering this question, of course, requires our deciding who the candidates are supposed to represent—all voters, party voters, or party leaders.) Are they qualified to hold the job and perform its manifold responsibilities? Unfortunately, it is very difficult to answer such questions with much assurance. Voters, pundits, and political scientists often lament the quality of recent presidents and presidential candidates. Whereas once the presidency was filled by giants such as Lincoln, Washington, and the Roosevelts, now it is occupied by men of considerably smaller stature.

These sorts of judgments, however, may tell us more about the current mood of the country and its high level of cynicism than about the reality of presidential performance. Contemporary observations and reactions are not always a good guide as to

The 2008 Vice Presidential Candidates
John McCain may have chosen Sarah Palin to bolster his reputation as a "maverick," while Barack Obama's choice of Joe Biden added foreign policy experience to the ticket.

• *How have vice presidential choices changed since the 1960s?*

how history will regard a president. During his years in the White House, Harry Truman had very low ratings in public opinion polls and was widely regarded by commentators and congressmen as a man who was "out of his league": a decent, well-meaning man who had been elevated to the White House by accident and simply could not fill the ample shoes of his predecessor. Today, historians generally rate Truman to be a "near great" president. And, if the old mixed system nominated Roosevelt and Truman, it also produced Warren Harding and Herbert Hoover—presidents that most historians place low on their lists.

One final point is worth making here. Although the designers of the contemporary presidential nomination process clearly intended to take power away from the established party leaders and increase the level of popular participation, many of the most noteworthy features of the current system were not the products of deliberate choice. Rather, they were the "unintended consequences of reform." For example, no one who wrote or approved the new delegate selection rules hoped to make the process so much longer. If anything, one of their complaints about the mixed system was that the delegate selection process in some states started too early. Yet the evidence unmistakably shows that, when the new rules were implemented, presidential nomination campaigns became dramatically longer.

The general lesson, which should be committed to memory by all future reformers, is that political systems and institutions are complex creatures, and that, whenever the rules are changed in a major way, the full consequences can rarely be predicted in advance. This observation does not mean that change should never be made, but it does suggest that change ought to be undertaken cautiously.

Who Nominates the Vice President?

Before the establishment of the contemporary nomination process, the conventions chose the vice presidential candidates as well as the presidential candidates. The choice usually was an effort to provide geographical or ideological "balance" to the ticket. Today, the choice of vice presidential candidates is in the hands of the presidential nominees, although they still attempt to choose a nominee who will improve the ticket's chances.[19] Presidential candidates usually announce the decision a week or so before the start of the national convention, as Obama and McCain did in 2008, and conventions vote to approve the nominations without controversy.

10.2

Identify the sources used to fund presidential campaigns and explain how the electoral college system works.

The General Election for President

Labor Day traditionally marks the start of the fall campaign, although today's nominees do not take so much of a break after the summer conventions as they did in the past. From the start of the campaign until Election day—the first Tuesday after the first Monday in November—the candidates maintain an exhausting pace, and the campaign dominates the news.[20]

Financing the General-Election Campaign

The 1974 FECA provided for a system of public funding in the general election for the two major-party candidates. As soon as the nominees are chosen, each candidate is eligible for a lump-sum payment from the federal government that is intended to pay for the entire fall campaign. The amount of the check was set at $20 million in the 1974 law but was, again, indexed to inflation; by 2008, the amount was $84.1 million. As with the funding in the primaries, however, this money comes with a condition: Candidates must raise or spend no other money. The $84.1 million represents a maximum.

From 1976 until 2004, every major party candidate took the money. Democrats such as Jimmy Carter and Bill Clinton as well as Republicans such as Ronald Reagan and George W. Bush all saw this bargain as worthwhile. But in 2008, awash in cash after raising hundreds of millions of dollars in the primary season, Barack Obama opted to decline the public funds. As he put it, his unprecedented online fundraising operation made the grant unnecessary. "We have created a parallel public financing system where the American people decide if they want to support a campaign, they can get on the Internet and finance it."[21] Accusing the Obama campaign of taking steps to "undermine the public financing system," the McCain campaign pledged to take the funds.[22] Obama raised and spent about $300 million in the fall campaign; McCain was able to spend only his $84.1 million lump-sum payment.

The disparity between these figures was not as great as it seems, however, because presidential campaigns are assisted and complemented by political party spending. In the 1990s, party fundraisers thrived by exploiting a category of donations called **soft money,** which was largely unregulated by federal law. Soft-money donors contributed to party committees established under relaxed fundraising guidelines, and these committees then channeled spending back into the presidential contests. Controversy erupted over this spending, a common occurrence in U.S. campaign finance policy (see the *International Comparison* box on page 289). As a result, in 2002, Congress passed and President George W. Bush signed the Bipartisan Campaign Reform Act of 2002 (sometimes called the "McCain–Feingold Act"), which has put a stop to the use of party soft money. Parties still raise and spend significant amounts of "hard" (that is, more closely regulated) money, however. The Democratic National Committee raised $260 million in conjunction with the 2008 election; the Republican National Committee raised almost $430 million.[23] This money bought television ads, "get-out-the-vote" efforts, and other campaign activity that benefited the presidential candidates.

Presidential campaigns can also be affected by spending from outside groups. These groups may include political action committees (PACs), groups known as **527s** (that are formed primarily to influence elections and are therefore exempt from most federal taxes), or even wealthy individuals with a bone to pick about an issue. The Supreme Court has ruled that such groups may be required to disclose information about their finances, but they cannot be limited in their spending (as long as they are not coordinating their activity with a campaign).[24] Because spending is akin to free speech, the Court has held, the government cannot restrict it. In the Court's 2010 *Citizens United v. FEC* decision, the Court extended this logic to apply to corporate and union independent expenditures. "The government may regulate corporate political speech through disclaimer and disclosure requirements," wrote Justice Anthony Kennedy in his majority opinion, "but it may not suppress that speech altogether."[25] Spending by outside groups is unpredictable: In 2004, such groups spent nearly $440 million, but in 2008 they spent only $245 million, as Figure 10.1 shows.[26]

Finally, we should say a few words about how third-party and independent candidates finance their presidential campaigns. In a sense, they get the worst of both worlds. They are required to abide by the contribution limits: $2,300 per donor in 2008. Yet the

soft money
Money contributed by interest groups, labor unions, and individual donors that is not subject to federal regulation.

527s
Political organizations formed primarily to influence elections and therefore exempt from most federal taxes.

FIGURE 10.1

CAMPAIGN SPENDING IN
FEDERAL ELECTIONS,
2007–2008

Do you believe the total amount
of money being spent on federal
elections is a reason for concern?
Are the levels of outside group
spending and party spending,
relative to candidate spending,
appropriate?

Note: Figures for the parties
include the DNC, the RNC,
and the congressional campaign
committees.

Sources: "2007–2008 Financial Activity of
All Senate and House Campaigns," Federal
Election Commission, http://fec.gov/
press/press2009/2009Dec29Cong/
1all2008final.pdf, accessed June 16, 2010;
"Party Financial Activity Summarized for
the 2008 Election Cycle, Federal Election
Commission, August 5, 2009, http://fec
.gov/press/press2009/05282009Party/
20090528Party.shtml, accessed June 16,
2010; "2008 Presidential Campaign
Financial Activity Summarized," Federal
Election Commission, June 8, 2009;
"Advocacy Group Spending," www
.opensecrets.org/527s/index.php,
accessed June 15, 2010.

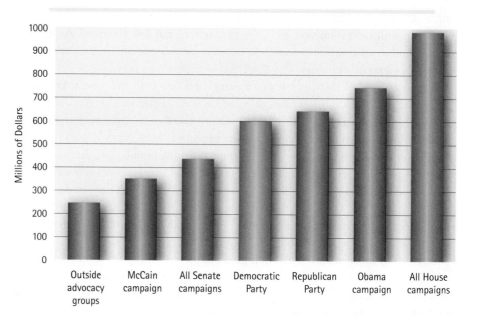

vast majority of such candidates are not eligible for a dime in federal funding. Federal law does provide some money to any third-party or independent candidate who receives 5 percent or more of the popular vote—but not having the money in advance, few third-parties have the resources to get anywhere near that figure. (Since the inauguration of public financing in 1976, third parties have qualified only three times: in 1980, when John Anderson ran, and in 1992 and 1996, when Ross Perot ran.) The only way around this dilemma is to nominate a candidate who is wealthy enough to finance his or her campaign almost entirely out of his or her own pocket. In 1992, Perot spent $65 million of his own money on his presidential campaign—and, not coincidentally, achieved the best popular-vote showing by a third-party or independent candidate in eighty years.

Spending in the General-Election Campaign

Campaign consultants oversee the expenditure of the large sums of money available to the campaigns—and they profit personally from such spending. These specialists in modern candidate-based campaigns have replaced the party leaders who supervised campaigns of earlier eras. Media consultants design the campaign ads or "spots," stage "media events" (appearances designed so that reporters get a story, not so that candidates meet voters), develop targeted online appeals, and schedule a candidate's time so as to maximize coverage. Derided by critics as "handlers" and "hired guns," some campaign consultants have become celebrities in recent decades. Modern campaigns also retain pollsters capable of measuring surges and slumps in candidate support.

The most important category of general-election spending is expenditures for broadcast media—TV and radio advertising, with the lion's share going to television. Although campaign advertising is widely criticized, studies have consistently found that it is informative, in that those exposed to ads know more about the candidates and where they stand than those not exposed to ads.[27] Indeed, contrary to popular percep-

INTERNATIONAL COMPARISON

Campaign Financing in Other Democracies

Campaign finance is rarely a major issue in democracies other than the United States. There are a number of reasons for this difference.

In the first place, much more money is spent in American elections—even relative to the size of the electorate—than in elections in other countries. For example, nationwide, the total amount spent in the 2008 U.S. elections was about $4.5 billion. Only Japan comes close to spending as much (relative to the size of its electorate).

One reason American campaigns are so expensive is the sheer number of candidates we elect in the United States. Whereas the citizens in most countries vote for no more than one or two candidates, in an election year such as 2008 Americans must select not only a president, but a member of the U.S. House of Representatives, possibly a governor, probably a senator, state legislators, and possibly a number of other state or local office holders. To make matters worse, American election campaigns are generally candidate-centered. Most other democracies, by contrast, have party-centered elections. The national party and its leaders conduct a single campaign on behalf of all the party candidates. Rather than having hundreds of individual candidates running duplicate campaigns, the parties take advantage of what economists call "economies of scale."

A second reason for the high cost of American campaigns is that they are increasingly fought over the airwaves, and TV time is expensive—as are the services of the consultants, ad people, and so forth.[1] In most other democracies, candidates still rely more on the campaign work of party members than on attempting to reach voters directly through broadcasting.

One reason why campaign finance is a lesser concern in other democracies is that spending is heavily regulated. In Britain individual candidates are not permitted to buy television or radio time! Even the parties cannot make media buys.

They are limited to a small number of publicly financed addresses by national party leaders. In Germany the law requires TV networks to give the parties free airtime during campaigns, but it is illegal for candidates to buy any additional radio or TV ads.[2] If strict limits such as these were adopted in the United States, the courts would strike them down on First Amendment grounds.

All of the post-Communist countries give the parties and/or candidates free radio and TV broadcasting.[3] Many of the more established democracies also provide at least some degree of public election financing.[4] For example, in Austria, Belgium, Denmark, Finland, Germany, Mexico, Sweden, and Turkey, the parties receive public subsidies in proportion to the number of votes they received in the last election or the number of seats they hold in parliament. In-kind subsidies, especially free media time, also are common. In the United States public financing has progressed only as far as presidential elections; attempts to extend it to Congress have failed.

In sum, candidate-centered media campaigns, the Constitution, and popular attitudes all interact to make campaign finance a more serious issue in the United States than elsewhere. Contrasts with other democracies raise a number of questions.

- *Should all legitimate candidates receive free TV time?*

- *Should all campaigns be publicly financed?*

- *Should the United States adopt a constitutional amendment that permits regulation of how much candidates can spend and what they can spend it on?*

---

[1]"Money and Politics," *The Economist*, February 8, 1997: 23.
[2]Charles Lane, "Kohl Train," *The New Republic*, February 14, 2000: 17.
[3]Charles W. Bryant, "How Campaign Finance Works." http://money.howstuffworks.com/campaign-finance7.htm. Accessed June 16, 2010.
[4]Richard Katz, "Party Organizations and Finance," in *Comparing Democracies*, eds. Lawrence LeDuc, Richard Niemi, and Pippa Norris (Thousand Oaks, CA: Sage, 1996), pp. 129–132.

---

tions that ads have been getting less substantive, research suggests that the issue content of ads actually has increased in recent years.[28]

Another less positive recent trend is the tone of campaign advertising: It has grown increasingly negative.[29] Rather than make a positive case for themselves, candidates make a negative case against their opponents. However, not all negative ads are bad; pointing out the failures and flaws of an opponent is a legitimate part of the campaign.[30] But too often the campaign debate is filled with exaggerations, distortions, and, on occasion, outright lies.

Negative advertising seems to work, though, in the sense that people remember more of what they have seen from negative than from positive spots.[31] Candidates often succeed when they "go negative." What is good for individual candidates, of course, may have harmful consequences for the larger political process. Much of what people remember may be inaccurate, and attack ads might reduce turnout (especially among the independent, more moderate segment of the population). Candidates, then, are playing to the more committed and more extreme voters, making campaigns even more polarized.[32]

Campaigns are becoming more sophisticated in their use of the Internet in all its forms, but these efforts are much less expensive than old-fashioned TV and radio. The 2008 presidential campaigns spent $43 million on Internet media. This was about the same amount as they spent on polling, and a fraction of what the campaigns spent on television, rent, or travel expenses.[33]

The Electoral College

electoral vote

Cast by electors, with each state receiving one vote for each of its members in the House of Representatives and one vote for each of its members in the Senate.

popular vote

The total vote cast across the nation for a candidate.

The Constitution stipulates that the president and vice president must be chosen by the Electoral College. Under this system, each state selects a number of electors equal to the sum of its House and Senate seats. After adding the District of Columbia's three votes under the terms of the Twenty-third Amendment, the nationwide total is 538 votes. These electors constitute the Electoral College and their **electoral vote** determines who will become the nation's chief executive. Thus, the candidate who wins the most votes—the so-called **popular vote,** or the total votes cast across the nation for a candidate—does not necessarily become president. Rutherford Hayes in 1876, Benjamin Harrison in 1888, and George W. Bush in 2000 all became president despite coming in second in the popular vote. Depending on how one tabulates the popular votes cast in Alabama, a strong case can also be made that in 1960 John Kennedy won a majority of electoral votes even though Richard Nixon actually received more popular votes.[34] If no one receives a majority of the electoral votes, then the election is decided by the House of Representatives, as it was when John Quincy Adams defeated Andrew Jackson in 1824.

Because every state has two senators, whereas the number of House seats depends on the state's population, the Electoral College gives a theoretical advantage to small states. For example, with two senators but only one seat in the House, Wyoming has three electoral votes—approximately 1 per 165,000 residents. With two senators but 53 seats in the House, California has 55 electoral votes, approximately 1 per 617,000 residents. In the 2008 election, if a candidate had won a plurality in each of the 40 least populated states, which together included only 43 percent of the U.S. population, he would have won a majority of the Electoral College and become president. (We must add, however, that such an outcome is highly unlikely: Small and large states are spread out all over the country and have such varied interests and ideologies that there is little likelihood that a candidate will ever win all of the 40 least-populated states and no others.)

winner-take-all voting

Any voting procedure in which the candidate with the most votes gets all of the seats or delegates at stake.

Other observers, however, believe that in practice the Electoral College has a bias in favor of large states. The reason is that almost all states assign electoral votes on a **winner-take-all voting** basis. Under state laws, the candidate who receives a plurality of a state's popular votes wins *all* of the state's electoral votes (except in Maine and Nebraska, which give the winner of each congressional district one electoral vote and the statewide winner the two remaining votes). Thus, a candidate who carries a large state by a tiny margin receives a windfall of electoral votes, whereas a candidate who wins small states by a landslide gets only a few. In 2008, for example, Obama won 53 percent of the popular vote but 68 percent of the electoral vote because of the winner-take-all system.

The Electoral College system has been controversial for a long time. Dozens of attempts have been made to amend the Constitution to do away with this provision. The leading alternative to the Electoral College is a pure popular vote system, although proposals have also been made that would retain the Electoral College but assign state electoral votes on a non-winner-take-all basis. The bottom line is that none of these attempts has succeeded; few have even come close.

The Electoral College survives for a number of reasons. First, it is difficult to amend the Constitution, as this requires two-thirds support in both houses of Congress and then ratification by three-fourths of the state legislatures. Second, small states (and sometimes big states as well) are convinced that they derive a significant advantage from the Electoral College, which makes their senators and representatives reluctant to vote for change. Finally, it is rare for the popular vote winner to lose in the Electoral College. The last time that happened, in 2000, Electoral College reformers drew some renewed interest, but other concerns—such as the 9/11 terrorist attacks—quickly focused the nation's attention elsewhere.

Voting Behavior in Presidential Elections

10.3

Analyze factors that impact voting behavior in presidential elections.

The Electoral College clearly impacts how presidential candidates allocate their personal campaign time and advertising money among the states. Candidates concentrate on the so-called "battleground states": the states that are sufficiently close that they might plausibly be won by either candidate. By contrast, the campaigns pay much less attention to states that they cannot win and those that they are almost guaranteed to win. If you live in a state such as Iowa, Ohio, or Pennsylvania, you probably saw a *lot* of the presidential candidates in 2008—if not in person, then in an endless succession of television ads. By contrast, if you spent the fall of 2008 in Massachusetts, New York, or California, you may not have seen a single ad for the major-party candidates.

Why do some states consistently support one party or the other for long periods of time? The reason is that there is considerable continuity in how citizens vote. This continuity, or "electoral inertia," not only explains why candidates know ahead of time how they will do in many states, but it also explains why campaign organizations and the media generally have a limited impact on general election outcomes.

When Americans Decide

Many people decide how they will vote before the campaign begins. Typically, one-third to one-half of the electorate reports deciding how to vote *before the primaries*. This decision is easy enough for people who always vote the party line. It is also rather easy for voters who know the identity of at least one of the nominees—usually an incumbent president who seeks reelection. Another portion of the electorate reports deciding how to vote between the start of the primaries and the end of the conventions. All told, between 50 and 80 percent of the electorate report that they decided how to vote by the end of the conventions—before the fall campaign gets under way. The figure was 79 percent in 2004, when Bush was seeking reelection, and 60 percent in 2008, when no incumbent ran.[35]

How Americans Decide

How can people make up their minds before policies, programs, and personal qualifications are debated in the fall campaign? The answer is that Americans decide how to vote not only on the basis of the short-term considerations that dominate campaign coverage (the candidates and the positions they advocate) but also on the basis of longer-term considerations that arise months or years before the campaign gets under way. The considerations that determine how Americans vote fall into four general categories: party loyalties, public policies, government performance, and the qualities of the candidates.

party identification
A person's subjective feeling of affiliation with a party.

Party Loyalties   Although pundits sometimes describe the contemporary American electorate as "disgusted with" or "turned off by" both major parties, the fact is that most Americans—about two-thirds, in fact—do feel some sort of basic psychological allegiance to either the Democrats or the Republicans. The name that is usually given to this attachment is **party identification,** or party ID for short.[36] It is measured by a question that asks the survey respondent, in straightforward fashion, "Generally speaking, do you usually think of yourself as a Republican, Democrat, independent, or what?"[37] This simple question is probably the most analyzed in all of political science—for it is also the best single predictor of voting behavior and many other important political attitudes.

Party ID is a long-term force that provides continuity from election to election. For example, the Civil War and Reconstruction created many "yellow dog" Democrats in the South—people who would not vote for a Republican even if the Democratic nominee were a yellow dog. Similarly, the Great Depression left many northerners intensely committed to the New Deal Democratic Party of Franklin Roosevelt. Such deeply held allegiances underlie the "party systems" discussed in Chapter 8.

At one time, party ID was considered to be much like a religious affiliation. Not only was it resistant to change, but it was also learned early in childhood and had little policy or ideological content. Just as children learn to call themselves Catholics, Jews, or Muslims before they know the doctrines of their religion, so children learned to call themselves Democrats or Republicans before they knew what the party stood for. The traumatic events of the 1960s severely tested party loyalties, though, lessening the proportion of voters holding strong party identifications and increasing the number of independents. Thus, scholars generally recognize that party ID responds to political events and conditions, although slowly and gradually in most cases.[38]

As shown in Figure 10.2, between the 1952 and 1984 elections, more Americans consistently considered themselves Democrats than Republicans. Republican candidates such as Eisenhower and Nixon were able to win by capturing a majority of the independents and by convincing a sizable share of Democratic identifiers to defect from their party. After Reagan's reelection in 1984, however, the gap between the parties began to close. For the strongest partisans, the campaign is largely irrelevant—come hell or high water, they will vote their party ID.

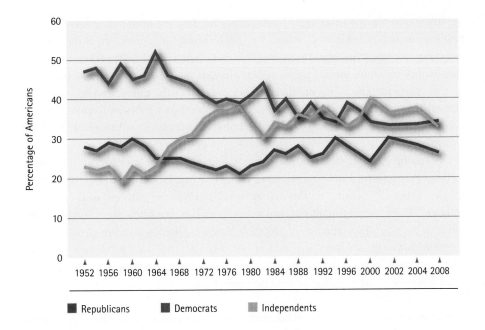

FIGURE 10.2

THE DEMOCRATIC
ADVANTAGE IN PARTY
IDENTIFICATION HAS
ERODED

• *Perhaps the most important change in this figure is the sharp increase in independents that occurred between 1964 and 1974. What occurred during this period that might be responsible for this change?*

Source: American National Election Studies.

Public Policies   For the most politically interested voters, policies and programs are the essence of politics. There are problems and conflicts in the United States and in the world. Problems cry out for solutions and conflicts for resolution. Elections decide these solutions and resolutions. For people with this view of politics, the campaign is a long-running debate—a chance to educate the electorate about alternative paths the country might choose and to persuade voters to follow one of them.

Surprisingly, research has found that, although policy concerns are important, in most elections they are not the dominant influence on voting.[39] One reason is that public policy debates often are complex, and people have limited information. To cite one extreme example, the final version of the 2010 healthcare reform act was 2,409 printed pages long. How could voters possibly be expected to have detailed views about such complex issues? Voters therefore seldom use elections as a means of giving public officials specific policy mandates. They select parties or party leaders, not policies.

Moreover, voters often are unsure where the candidates stand, because candidates equivocate and otherwise confuse voters about their positions. Research on the 1968 election, for example, found that views on U.S. policy in Vietnam (whether to escalate the war, maintain the status quo, or withdraw) were only minimally related to the presidential vote. How could that be true when intense disagreement about the war was tearing the country apart? The answer is that both candidates equivocated on the issue, and neither offered a specific set of policy changes on the issue.[40] Again, voters uncertain about what candidates believe cannot use their vote to mandate specific policies.

There are some important exceptions to the finding that public policies are not the dominant factor in most elections. Social or cultural issues, for example, occasionally do play a significant role. Candidates announce that they favor prayer in schools or that they oppose allowing same-sex unions. Such issues are "easy" for voters to process because the policy proposals and the desired outcome are one and the same: Start pray-

party image
The associations voters make between the parties and particular issues and values.

ing in schools, ban gay marriages.[41] Such issues are different from policy issues such as health insurance or education, where a chain of actions is required to bring about a particular outcome.[42] Social issues are as much about values held by different groups in society as they are about specific public policies. Indeed, such values often are incorporated into the party identifications of citizens. They are part of the **party images,** the associations that voters make between the parties and particular issues and values.[43] Voters concerned with moral issues gave overwhelming support to Republicans in 2004, for example.

A second example of issues mattering is when voters are upset about a problem and eager for government to do *something* about it. Thus, candidates talk about "getting tough on crime," "cleaning up the welfare mess," and "getting guns out of the hands of children." These are important political issues, to be sure, but often they do not involve much in the way of specific policy proposals. Voters are merely asked to choose among different priorities or between general approaches such as "soft" and "tough." Moreover, such issues at least implicitly reflect voters' unhappiness with the government *performance* that has allowed such problems to fester.

Government Performance   Real elections are a mix of considerations, but a great deal of research confirms the influence of past government performance.[44] Performance voting demands less of voters than policy voting. To make judgments about performance, voters do not have to watch C-SPAN or read the *New York Times*. Voters can judge economic conditions from their own experiences and those of their friends and neighbors. They can evaluate other social conditions by observing daily life in their communities, schools, and workplaces.

retrospective voting
Voting on the basis of the past performance of the incumbent administration.

prospective voting
Voting on the basis of the candidates' policy promises.

Voting by looking backward at performance (often called **retrospective voting**) may outweigh voting by looking forward at policy promises (often called **prospective voting**). The 1984 campaign provided a classic illustration. Public opinion surveys showed that on many issues, voters were closer to the Democratic nominee, Walter Mondale, than to President Reagan. A majority believed that tax increases were inevitable (Mondale's position), expressed skepticism about "Star Wars" (the missile defense system dear to Reagan's heart), rejected Reagan's call for further increases in defense spending, and doubted Reagan's Central America policy.[45] Nevertheless, Reagan carried 49 states. Was this overwhelming support just an expression of his winning personality? Probably not. Analysis of the election returns showed that a majority of voters approved of Reagan's performance as president, regardless of many of the specific policies he followed. Conversely, when most voters disapprove of the incumbent party's performance, as in 2008, the opposition party has a natural advantage.

The quintessential example of a performance issue is the state of the economy. Most voters do not have the time, interest, or sophistication to make a detailed analysis of each candidate's economic policy proposals and then decide which set of proposals is more likely to produce national prosperity over the next four years. Instead, they follow a far simpler decision rule. They assume that the party currently occupying the White House is primarily responsible for the economy's recent performance. If they are satisfied with that recent performance—if they think the economy is doing reasonably well—they will usually vote to keep the incumbent party in power. If recent economic performance is judged to be unsatisfactory, they vote for the presidential candidate of the other party. Evidence from elections over the last 60 years shows that, in order to get reelected, the incumbent party generally needs to have the U.S. economy growing at a real rate of about 2 percent during the first half of the election year.[46]

Voters hardly can be blamed for adopting shortcuts such as performance voting. The future is uncertain, the experts disagree, and time is limited, so how can one make an intelligent decision about complex policy alternatives? Moreover, candidates are not always clear about their intentions. At least good performance by government suggests competent leadership, so voters quite reasonably choose to stick with those in power when they are content.[47]

The important point to remember is that government performance is neither a long-term consideration nor a short one, but something in between. It refers to an assessment of leadership that reflects four years of activity, not something that suddenly arises when the campaign begins. Election-year campaign activity can attempt to put some "spin" on government performance, but it is difficult to make a bad economy or an unpopular war into a positive accomplishment for the incumbent administration, no matter how good the media experts and campaign consultants.

The Political Burdens of War

Most American military engagements are popular when they are first launched—but become steadily more unpopular the longer they last and the more American casualties mount. In 2006, increasing public opposition to the war in Iraq was a major reason that the Republicans lost their majorities in both houses of Congress.

• *Do you think the war in Afghanistan affected the 2010 elections?*

The Qualities of the Candidates   Not surprisingly, the individual candidates are the major source of change in how people vote from election to election.[48] Not since 1956, when Adlai Stevenson fought a rematch with Dwight Eisenhower, have Americans had the same choice of candidates in two presidential elections. In a country that exhorts voters to "support the person not the party," candidate quality is an important influence on how people vote. Note, however, that *quality* is not the same thing as *personality*. Personality is overrated, especially by the losers. It is comforting for candidates or parties to blame failure on the foolishness of voters duped by an opponent's sparkling personality or pleasing appearance; they would rather not admit that voters rejected their beliefs or doubted their competence.

Even the importance of candidate quality can be exaggerated, though, because after an election there is a tendency to downgrade the loser's personal qualities and to upgrade the winner's. For example, after their defeat in 2004, many Democrats concluded that John Kerry was a bad candidate who had run an uninspired campaign. Although there is sometimes truth to such charges, these critics seemed to forget that Kerry had been viewed much differently in the primary season, where most Democrats viewed his military record and experience in government as great assets. Did Kerry change in less than a year? No, he was the same Kerry, but losing had hurt his political reputation even though he had taken on an incumbent, President George W. Bush, who most voters trusted to handle the threat of terrorism, and who was running in stable economic times.

There are some striking contrasts between what voters actually thought of the candidates in a given campaign and how popular history now views the candidates.

The 1960 contest between John F. Kennedy and Richard Nixon is the most vivid example. Although historians have debunked much of the Kennedy mystique, you are probably familiar with the Kennedy legend—the charismatic leader of a new "Camelot." In fact, however, 1960 survey data show that Nixon was more favorably regarded as a candidate than Kennedy.[49] Kennedy owed his narrow victory primarily to the fact that he was a Democrat, at a time when there were more Democrats than Republicans.[50] Did the data indicate that Nixon had a more attractive personality than Kennedy? No. Nixon was viewed as more experienced and better qualified for the job. But what lives on in political folklore about the candidates may bear little resemblance to the reality of citizens' opinions when they voted.

Ronald Reagan is another example. When the former president died in 2004, commentators across the political spectrum praised his winning personality and admirable character and hailed his accomplishments as president. Thousands of Americans stood in lines for hours to pass by his coffin and the spectacle of the state funeral dominated the airwaves for days. Yet, before Reagan's election in 1980, voters evaluated Jimmy Carter's personal characteristics higher than Reagan's.[51] And average presidential approval ratings during his administration were not impressive—they were slightly below the average of the ten U.S. presidents between Truman and Clinton.[52] Memories of Reagan began to grow more positive after he left office, even before he became a victim of Alzheimer's disease. By the time he died, evaluations were considerably more positive than the views Americans had expressed at the time of his presidency.

Finally, we should remember that what people think about the candidates is partly based on the other influences shaping their voting behavior. Most citizens with a strong Democratic Party ID are going to like the Democratic candidate—any Democratic candidate. People with strong positions on certain policies probably are going to like any candidate who shares those policy commitments and to dislike any candidate who does not. People who think the president has performed very well probably are going to like him personally, although that affection is not guaranteed.

What Difference Do Presidential Campaigns Make?

When the effects of party identification, performance judgments, and long-standing issue divisions between the parties are taken into account, what role is left for the presidential campaigns that are waged so frenetically every fourth fall? The answer, according to most political scientists, is not much. Presidential campaigns may generate a lot of excitement and publicity, but they don't change many votes. And many of the changes that do occur can actually be predicted in advance. In one of the first great empirical studies of voting behavior, which tracked opinion formation in an Ohio county during the 1940 presidential election, its authors discovered that, of those voters who claimed to be undecided when the campaign began, they could predict how three-quarters would vote just by knowing such basic demographic facts as their religion, social class, and place of residence.[53] Much of what campaigns do, in other words, is not to remake a person's ideology or give them a fresh perspective on American politics, but simply to make people more aware of the loyalties, values, and interests they already possess, and remind them which party is more compatible with them.

Campaigns are constrained by history—in particular, by what goes on *between* elections. A card game provides a good analogy. Who wins a hand partly depends on the deal of the cards. No matter how skillfully you play, it may not be sufficient to overcome a bad draw. In politics, some cards are dealt years, even decades, before the election. The Democrats drew the Great Depression card in 1932 and played it successfully against Republicans until the 1960s. The Republicans drew the "frustration with big government" card in the 1970s and were still playing it against Democrats in 2010. Good economic conditions are aces dealt to the incumbent party; poor conditions are aces dealt to the opposition. The same is true for international embarrassments and costly wars.

The luck of the draw strongly affects the campaign. We praise and criticize campaigns, often forgetting that the candidates were limited in what they could do by social and economic realities. Did the fact that Michael Dukakis lost to Vice President Bush in 1988, whereas Clinton beat President Bush in 1992, indicate that Dukakis ran a poor campaign and Clinton a brilliant one? In retrospect, Dukakis surely could have done some things better, and Clinton did recruit some crack advisers.[54] But Clinton's brilliant campaign probably also reflects the fact that an economic recession made the Bush administration a much wider target in 1992 than the Reagan-Bush administration had been in 1988.

Of course, in a very close election, changing even a small number of votes may spell the difference between victory and defeat. Political scientist James Campbell has estimated that of the 36 presidential elections held between 1868 and 2008, unusually good or bad campaign strategies by one or both of the candidates, unexpected gaffes, and simple luck may have decided from five to seven of them. Put another way, whenever one candidate wins by more than 53 percent of the two-party vote, the odds are very strong that the campaign had nothing to do with the final outcome—that the winning candidate had the election "in the bag" before the fall campaign began.[55]

As one reflection of this reality, candidates, consultants, and reporters have recently begun to acknowledge that most votes are not "up for grabs" during the general election. Instead, campaigns and those who write about them have started to focus on that small number of voters who are still winnable by either side—a group known as *swing* or *persuadable voters*. Depending on the specific election and the particular survey questions that are used to identify them, swing voters typically constitute about 20 percent of all voters. As shown in Table 10.1, swing voters differ from "nonswing" voters in a number of ways. They are less partisan, and more moderate. They are also less informed and less interested in the election than those who are already firmly committed to one of the candidates.

It is this last fact that helps explain some of the most criticized features of contemporary campaigns. Why, for example, do candidates rely on 30-second television ads to get their message out, when it seems obvious that most of the critical issues in contemporary America cannot be adequately addressed in just 30 seconds? Why not use 5-minute or 30-minute ads or detailed position papers accessible via the candidates' websites? Part of the answer, of course, is that 5-minute ads cost a lot more than 30-second ones. But the more important reason is that most of the persuadable voters are not sufficiently interested in the campaign to sit through a 30-minute television program or to read a lengthy position paper. About a quarter of the population visited a major can-

TABLE 10.1
CHARACTERISTICS OF SWING VOTERS

	Swing Voters	Nonswing Voters
Party Identification		
Strong partisans	18%	41%
Weak partisans	42	31
Independents leaners	28	22
Pure independents	13	6
Ideology		
Extremely liberal	1	2
Liberal	4	10
Slightly liberal	11	10
Moderate	31	22
Slightly conservative	18	15
Conservative	10	18
Extremely conservative	1	3
Don't know	24	20
Interest in current campaign		
Very much interested	29	45
Somewhat interested	53	44
Not much interested	18	11
General level of information about politics		
Very or fairly high	42	52
Average	36	35
Very or fairly low	21	13

Source: Figures represent the average percentage for the nine American National Election Studies conducted between 1972 and 2004.

didate's website in 2008, but the vast majority of these people had already decided to vote for that candidate.[56] The decisive advantage of a 30-second ad, from the campaigns' perspective, is that you can reach people who are not all that interested in politics.

10.4

Outline the changes in the presidential election scene that have occurred in the last 40 years.

The Contemporary Presidential Election Scene

The New Deal party system splintered in the 1960s. The racial and social turmoil created by the civil rights revolution and the war in Vietnam forced President Lyndon Johnson to withdraw from the race in 1968 and enabled Republican Richard Nixon to win two terms. It was the beginning of a Republican streak that saw them win five of the six presidential elections between 1968 and 1988. Not until the 1990s were the Democrats able to overcome the problems that first arose in the 1960s. In this section, we survey these ups and downs in party fortunes in light of our discussion of American voting behavior in the previous section.

The 1970s and 1980s: The Republican "Lock"

The so-called Republican lock on the presidency during the 1970s and 1980s reflected developments that gave Republicans a clear advantage in two of the four major factors that determine how Americans vote: performance and issues. This advantage forced Democratic candidates to defend unpopular policies and eventually eroded the long-standing Democratic advantage in party ID. Although the Democrats enjoyed a brief recovery after the Watergate scandal, the extremely narrow margin of Jimmy Carter's victory suggested the severity of the Democrats' problems. The Carter administration retained the White House only for four years, after which Republicans won three consecutive elections: 1980, 1984, and 1988. During this period, Republican performance and policies beat the Democrats on each of the major fronts in contemporary politics: economic, foreign and defense, racial, and social.

For almost half a century, Americans viewed Democrats as the party of prosperity. But in the late 1960s an inflationary era began that economists blamed on President Johnson's attempt to wage war in Vietnam while also implementing major new domestic programs. The rising tide of inflation reached frightening levels (13 percent) under Democratic President Carter. As the party in power when economic conditions hit bottom, the Democrats took the blame.

Americans of the time also viewed Republicans as more capable in the international arena. The anti-Vietnam War movement pushed the Democratic Party toward a more dovish stance on foreign policy. But during the 1970s the United States faced a series of foreign challenges that voters were not confident that the Democratic Party could deal with. The final humiliation came in 1979 when Iranian militants seized 90 hostages from the American embassy in Tehran and held them for more than a year. This hostage crisis destroyed any remaining hope for President Carter's reelection and reinforced the popular perception that the Democrats were unable to keep America strong internationally.

Racial politics also hurt the Democrats. The exact role that racial issues played is not clear. Some analysts believe that white support of Republican candidates grew from lingering racism.[57] Others disagree, arguing that many policies currently proposed to help minorities—such as affirmative action—are inconsistent with traditional American values.[58] Regardless, political attitudes are sharply polarized by race (see Figure 10.3). Democrats were caught in the middle of such disagreements between the white majority and the party's most loyal constituency.

Finally, social issues hurt the Democrats during this period. Starting in the 1960s, liberalism became associated in some voters' minds with controversial changes in American life—for example, sexual permissiveness, declining religious faith, family breakdown, and violent crime. A popular reaction arose in the late 1970s in the form of the "new right," a socially conservative movement connected to evangelical religious groups. These voters swelled the Republican ranks in many elections.

The 1990s: Democratic Resurgence

In 1992 Bill Clinton was elected with 43 percent of the vote in a three-way election. Even without Ross Perot in the contest, Clinton would have won.[59] How did the Democratic Party revive? First, a recession rejuvenated the Democrats' image as the

FIGURE 10.3

BLACKS AND WHITES DIFFER IN THEIR VIEWS ABOUT RACE RELATIONS AND RACIAL POLICY, EVEN IN THE AGE OF OBAMA

• *If these questions were posed to a sample of college students, would the differences between black and white students be just as large?*

Source: Pew Research Center, "A Year After Obama's Election: Blacks Upbeat about Black Progress, Prospects," January 10, 2010, http://pewsocialtrends.org/, accessed June 16, 2010.

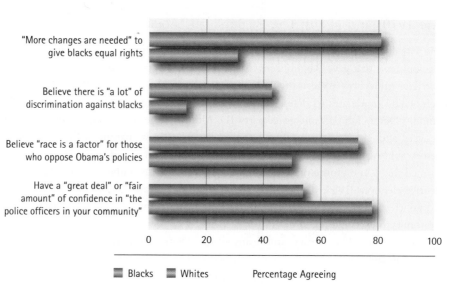

party of prosperity. The struggling economy was the foundation of Clinton's campaign. He promised to get the economy moving again, and he appealed to middle-class concerns with his support of universal healthcare. The end of the cold war, meanwhile, meant that foreign threats did not distract voters from their preoccupation with the economy. Clinton also distanced himself from prominent black leaders, such as Jesse Jackson, and criticized the lyrics found in some rap music. He prayed, talked about family values, promised "to end welfare as we know it," supported capital punishment, and in other ways tried to dispel the cultural liberal image that had dogged the Democrats for a generation.

The economy grew steadily throughout Clinton's first term, and by the 1996 elections most Americans were economically optimistic—indeed, as optimistic as they had been in 1984 when they overwhelmingly reelected Republican Ronald Reagan.[60] Incumbents who run during times of economic prosperity tend to be successful, and Clinton was no exception. Clinton also increased his support among moderates through a strategy of "triangulation"—positioning himself between liberal congressional Democrats and conservative Republicans.[61] A growing gender gap also helped Clinton. Some polls reported that if only men had voted in 1996, Robert Dole would have won the election; this was the first time that majorities of men and of women had voted for different candidates.

The gender gap is widely misunderstood. Many pundits understandably attributed the emergence of the gender gap to different male and female positions on "women's issues." On the contrary, men and women differ little in their views of abortion and issues related to equality of opportunity for women.[62] Rather, differences in voting appear to stem more from long-standing gender differences on issues of military force, the death penalty, and government activities in support of the disadvantaged (see Table 10.2).[63] There is considerable disagreement about why women and men differ on issues. Some experts argue that women's values are different from men's.[64] From an electoral standpoint, though, the origins of gender differences are less important than the fact that they exist.

	TABLE 10.2		
	WOMEN'S AND MEN'S ATTITUDES DIFFER		
		Women	Men
Consider self conservative		47%	50%
Role of Government Issues			
Government should provide more services than it does now		45	31
Increase federal spending on aid to the poor		52	49
Increase federal spending on childcare		53	51
Force and Violence Issues			
Favor torture for suspected terrorists		21	28
Federal government should make it more difficult to buy a gun		57	35
Favor the death penalty		65	76

Source: American National Election Studies, 2008.

2000 and 2004: The Bush Years

Prophets of doom predicted that the U.S. economy would melt down when the calendar changed from 1999 to 2000 (called Y2K at the time). The economy did just fine, but no one anticipated that the polity might melt down later in the year. It took five weeks to determine that Republican George W. Bush had won the presidential election, in a battle that led all the way to the U.S. Supreme Court. President Bush headed the first unified Republican government since 1954 (although his party temporarily lost control of the Senate when James Jeffords of Vermont left the party in May 2001).

The 2000 election underscored the difference between primary and general-election campaigns. In the primaries, hot-button issues such as abortion and gun control were prominent, but exit polls showed that such issues were of lesser importance in the general election. Democrat Al Gore had to back away from his primary position on guns because it was unpopular in many of the battleground states. Similarly, Bush downplayed his opposition to abortion. Instead, broad issues of concern to the great body of Americans—the economy, healthcare, and education—took center stage. The candidates talked long and in some detail about issues of concern to the American middle class: restructuring social security, reforming public schools, and determining what mix of taxing and spending is appropriate.

To many political scientists the 2000 election was puzzling. Given the long-standing importance of government performance to voters, most political scientists expected Gore to win. During the Clinton administration the country enjoyed unprecedented prosperity and relative peace. As the election approached, President Clinton's approval ratings were exceptionally high by historical standards, consumers felt optimistic about the economy, and people thought that the country was on the right track. Supposedly, incumbent administrations do not lose during times of peace and prosperity. So why did Gore lose?

Detailed statistical analysis indicates that the vote for Gore was less closely tied to the administration's record than were the votes for incumbent-party candidates in the previous seven elections.[65] Some analysts argue that Gore did not receive credit because he ran the wrong campaign. Although the effects of campaigns often are exaggerated, in this case Gore's critics may be right. Gore did not emphasize the administration's record. As one critic sarcastically observed, Gore's theme was "You've never had it so good, and I'm mad as hell about it."[66] In trying to distance himself from a scandal-plagued president, Gore may have thrown away his trump card. On the other hand, statistical evidence indicates that voter disapproval of Clinton's personal transgressions helped drag Gore down.

Gore also paid a penalty for being seen as farther from the average voter than Bush. Although polls showed that Gore was closer to the voting public than Bush was on specific issues such as education and social security, more people felt that Gore was too liberal than felt that Bush was too conservative.

Polls that showed a captivatingly close race in the final days of the 2004 campaign led many media commentators to speculate that the race would again be decided in the courts or in state-level recounts. Nevertheless, the result, although not an overwhelming victory for Bush, was at least a decisive one: for the first time since 1988, the winner of the presidency amassed a clear majority (51 percent) of the popular vote. Bush's victories in key states such as Florida and Ohio, as well as Republican gains in Congress, frustrated Democrats who were convinced that economic stagnation and the Iraq War would swing undecided voters their way. In the days after the election, pundits made much of an apparent finding (based on exit polls) that significant numbers of voters based their decisions on "moral values." Some argued that Democratic candidate John Kerry ought to have placed greater emphasis on morality in his campaign speeches.

In reality, the 2004 election was not much different from past elections. Any "moral values" voters probably decided on a candidate long before Election day. The economy, although not in great shape, was in better condition than it had been in past years when voters had thrown out incumbent presidents. And analysis of survey data shows that voter concern about terrorism and the Iraq War was more important in voters' choices than were "moral values" issues.[67]

2008: A Mandate for Change?

By 2006, it had become apparent that the next few years would be rocky ones for the Republican Party. There were increasing casualties and little sign of progress in Iraq, economic growth was uneven, and polls regularly showed that only about 30 percent of the American public approved of George Bush's performance as president. The Democrats tried to make the 2006 midterm elections a referendum on the Bush presidency and largely succeeded—with the result that the Democrats won a majority of seats in both the House and the Senate for the first time in fourteen years. Soon after the election, Bush announced a change of policy in Iraq, increasing the number of troops there and changing tactics in an effort to bring greater peace and stability to the country. By 2008, the surge, as it was called, had started to show positive results, but the economy deteriorated even further.

Continued on page 305

Is a National Primary the Best Way to Nominate Presidential Candidates?

"I don't care who does the electing as long as I do the nominating."
—*William M. "Boss" Tweed, leader of Tammany Hall, c. 1870*

The Issue

Should the current presidential nomination process, in which 50 state primaries and caucuses are used to select delegates to a national convention, be replaced by a national presidential primary?

Background

Of all the major institutions and processes in contemporary American government, few have been as widely criticized as the presidential nomination process. As described earlier in the chapter, the rules of the process were substantially rewritten in the early 1970s—and from the moment the new rules took effect they generated a firestorm of controversy. For decades, many political scientists, party leaders, and media pundits have declared that it is time to "reform the reforms."

Of all the proposals for restructuring the presidential nomination process, the national primary is both the simplest and the most radical. It is also the oldest of the reform proposals: A national presidential primary was endorsed by the Progressive Party in its 1912 national platform and was then recommended by Woodrow Wilson in his first annual message to Congress in 1913.

As its name implies, a national primary would scrap the current system of individual state primaries and caucuses followed by a national convention. Instead, a primary election would take place in all 50 states on the same day. According to one version of the plan, the winner of that election would then become his or her party's presidential candidate. In another variant, the winner would become the nominee only if he or she won at least 40 percent of the total vote. If no candidate achieved that threshold, a second, runoff election would be held between the top two finishers.

Political Dilemmas

According to its proponents, a national primary has several major advantages. First, it is much simpler than the current system.

John McCain and his wife Cindy celebrate at a rally in Texas on March 4, 2008—the night McCain officially amassed the 1191 delegates needed to win the Republican presidential nomination.

Instead of the complexity of 50 different state contests spread over three or four months, each with its own set of voting laws and delegate selection rules, the national primary would substitute one or at most two clear, decisive elections.

Second, a national primary would treat all states equally. The current process, as we have seen, gives a much greater voice to states that happen to come early in the delegate selection calendar. Two states in particular, Iowa and New Hampshire, have an outsized role in selecting presidential candidates. Meanwhile, at the other end of the calendar, between a third and a half of the states typically hold their primaries after one candidate has already clinched the nomination and all of the major rivals have withdrawn. (The 2008 Democratic primary season was a rare exception.) Both Iowa and New Hampshire are unrepresentative of the country as a whole in important ways. Neither state, for example, has a significant number of African Americans or a large city. In contrast, a national primary would put all states—and thus all voters—on an equal footing.

Third, as one consequence of eliminating these interstate inequalities, a national primary would almost certainly increase the number of people who participate in the presidential nomination process. Under the present system, voter participation rates vary widely according to when a state holds its primary. In the 2008 race, for example, 53 percent of the eligible electorate turned out for the New Hampshire primary on January 8. But, for the remaining primaries, the average turnout was only 30 percent—even though there was a tough battle for the nomination being fought in the Democratic Party.[1] By ensuring that all people would go to the polls while the race was still undecided, a national primary would almost certainly increase participation.

But the national primary also has a large number of opponents. The worst aspect of a national primary, according to these critics, is that it would limit the presidential nomination process to candidates who are already well known or well financed. Only someone who was famous before the race began or who had an enormous amount of money to spend could run a full-scale, national campaign. Talented senators and governors from small states, who had not managed to attract the favor of the national media, would never have a realistic chance.

For all its messiness and inequality, opponents of the national primary argue, the current system allows lesser-known candidates a better chance to compete, precisely because it does start in the two relatively small states of Iowa and New Hampshire. In these venues, lesser-known and underfinanced candidates can make their case before a smaller and more manageable audience. If they are successful there, they will then receive the additional press coverage and funding that gives them a better prospect of running a viable national campaign. John McCain worked hard and won the New Hampshire primary in 2000, propelling him into the national spotlight. Barack Obama won over Iowa caucus-goers in 2008, upending the hopes of front-runner Hillary Clinton. Such surprises would be impossible, according to most observers, under a national primary system.

Yet, supporters of the national primary might reply, is it really so bad to limit the presidential nomination process to a party's established national leaders? Critics of the current system have long deplored the fact that contemporary nomination races include so many candidates, many of whom have strikingly little previous experience in government, and that one of these little-known entities may suddenly get catapulted into the lead simply because he or she managed to gain the support of a comparative handful of voters in Iowa or New Hampshire.

For those who hold this view, the preeminent example is the candidacy of Jimmy Carter in 1976. By running a smart campaign, Carter won both the Iowa caucuses and the New Hampshire primary; on that basis, he achieved a burst of momentum that none of his rivals was able to stop. By early June, Carter had locked up the Democratic presidential nomination and then went on to win the general election against Gerald Ford—even though he had served just four years as the governor of Georgia and was, as even many in his own party came to concede, largely unprepared for the demands of being the nation's chief executive. There is much to be said in defense of a system that makes this type of candidacy less likely.

The Problem of the Zealous Minority

Depending on which specific plan is adopted, a national primary can also lead to another type of result that the current system avoids: the nomination of a candidate who is supported by a small but very zealous minority but is considered unacceptable by a large segment—perhaps even a majority—of the party. The kind of situation that could easily lead to such a result is aptly illustrated by the Democratic nomination race of 1988. Through the second half of 1987, the Democratic field consisted of Jesse Jackson and six other candidates, none of whom was particularly well known outside his own state or region. Because Jackson was well known, and because he attracted strong support from blacks and a very narrow slice of white liberals, national polls that asked Democratic identifiers whom they wanted to be their party's next presidential candidate consistently showed Jackson in the lead. Had a national primary been conducted at this point, it seems quite likely that Jackson would have won it, even though he probably would have received just 25 or 30 percent of the vote—and even though his presence at the head of the ticket would clearly have caused major problems for his party.

The sequential nature of the current primary system, by comparison, makes this sort of problem much less likely. A fringe candidate who has the support of only 25 or 30 percent of his or her party's voters may win some early primaries when the rest of the vote is divided among a large number of other candidates. But, as some of these candidates reveal their lack of support and begin to fade or drop out, the mainstream of the party usually coalesces around a more acceptable alternative. In 1988, for example, Jesse Jackson did just fine as long as the field stayed divided. As of March 15, 1988, Jackson was actually his party's leading vote-getter in the primaries, having won 27 percent of the total vote to 25 percent for Massachusetts governor Michael Dukakis. Once the other candidates dropped out, however, the limits on Jackson's vote became obvious. In the final 14 primaries, Jackson won only once (in the District of Columbia), and lost the preference vote to Dukakis by a two-to-one margin.

It is precisely to avoid this problem that most recent national primary proposals have been structured so as to require the winner to receive some minimum percentage of the total vote (usually 40 percent) and call for a runoff election if no candidate crosses that threshold. Yet runoff elections carry problems of their own. In those states that already use runoff elections, the evidence is clear that interest and participation in the second election are usually lower than they are in the first election.[2] And, because most recent national primary proposals call for the first-round primary to be held in the last half of August or the first week in September, Americans might face the routine prospect of holding three national elections over a period of just 70 days.[3]

What Does the Public Believe?

Reforms of the presidential nomination process are not, to say the least, a high-priority concern for most Americans. But, when they do think about such matters, Americans have consistently expressed strong support for the national primary. A 2007 *New York Times*/CBS News poll found that 72 percent of Americans would prefer it if there were "one single national primary day." Previous polls from Gallup find similar results.

What Do You Think?

1. Proponents of the national primary praise its simplicity. Is simplicity really an advantage in the design of political institutions? Given that they created the Electoral College, how might the founders have answered this question?

2. Is there an advantage to having one or two small states lead off the delegate selection process, or would we be better off if all 50 states voted at the same time?

3. Would a national primary with a runoff or without a runoff be preferable? Is it problematic if a candidate wins the presidential nomination with only 30 or 35 percent of the vote?

4. How much weight should be given to the public support for a national primary?

On the Web

www.nationalcaucus.com

The National Presidential Caucus is dedicated to pursuing presidential primary reform and favors a national primary.

www.nass.org

The National Association of Secretaries of State advocates a system of rotating regional presidential primaries.

---

[1]United States Elections Project, George Mason University, http://elections.gmu.edu, accessed June 16, 2010.
[2]See Stephen G. Wright, "Voter Turnout in Runoff Elections," *Journal of Politics* 51 (May 1989): 385–96; and Charles S. Bullock III and Loch K. Johnson, *Runoff Elections in the United States* (Chapel Hill: University of North Carolina Press, 1992), chap. 6.
[3]On this point, see James W. Davis, *U.S. Presidential Primaries and the Caucus-Convention System: A Sourcebook* (Westport, CN: Greenwood, 1977), 202–203.

Continued from page 302

Against that background, it should come as no surprise that the odds strongly favored the Democrats in 2008. That the Republicans stood any chance at all was due to their nomination of a candidate, John McCain, who, in addition to being a celebrated war hero, could credibly claim to have been a party maverick rather than a loyal supporter of George W. Bush's policies. To reinforce his independent image and energize the Republican base, McCain made a controversial vice presidential choice: first-term Alaska Governor Sarah Palin. The Democrats, meanwhile, had nominated Illinois Senator Barack Obama, a candidate with great appeal to many minority and young voters but relatively little previous governmental experience, especially in foreign policy. He chose Delaware Senator Joseph Biden as his running mate.

Obama led in the polls all summer, but for a brief period after the Republican convention polls showed McCain and Palin in the lead. Then, in the third week of September, the slow deterioration in financial markets turned into a panic, as the investment bank Lehman Brothers went bankrupt and the government had to step in to rescue a growing number of other firms (see Chapter 19). This series of events clearly benefited the Democrats—by playing up economic issues, widely seen as a major Bush

failing and a traditional Democratic strength, and making McCain's experience and military credentials seem less relevant. Many voters also reacted negatively to McCain's response to the crisis, which was to suspend his campaign temporarily and threaten not to participate in any presidential debate until a bailout bill was passed. By late September, Obama had surged into a comfortable lead that he never lost. On Election day, the Illinois Senator received 53 percent of the popular vote to McCain's 46 percent and won a comfortable victory in the Electoral College.

For all the emphasis on Obama's personal characteristics, the 2008 elections are best seen as a referendum on the Bush presidency—a referendum in which Bush was seen as sorely lacking. In exit polls taken on Election Day, 75 percent of voters said the country was on the wrong track, only 7 percent said the economy was in good or excellent shape, and just 27 percent approved of Bush. Voters in the 2010 midterm elections voiced similar frustration with economic conditions, this time taking it out on Democratic incumbents. Obama had until 2012 to win back voters' confidence.

Obama on the Hustings

Running on a theme of change at a time when most Americans felt the country was in serious trouble, Barack Obama was elected the 44th president of the United States, the first African American to hold that position.

CHAPTER SUMMARY

10.1 Evaluate the strengths and weaknesses of the presidential and vice presidential nomination process.

The American nomination process is far more open than the nomination processes of other democracies. It gives rank-and-file voters more influence than in other countries where party leaders and elected officials dominate the process, and it gives "outsider" candidates a chance by enabling them to contest the early, smaller primaries and caucuses. The process begins long before the election itself and sometimes lasts months before a nominee is determined. It also heightens the influence of party issue activists and the media.

10.2 Identify the sources used to fund presidential campaigns and explain how the electoral college system works.

Between 1976 and 2004, each major party nominee accepted a lump-sum public financing payment from the government to finance his campaign. In 2008, Barack Obama broke from this tradition, raising and spending far more than he could have, had he accepted the subsidy.

These funds are used largely for media expenditures in states in which the election is likely to be close. The Electoral College theoretically grants disproportionate impact to small states, but in practice may make large states more important because almost all states allocate their votes in a winner-take-all fashion.

10.3 Analyze factors that impact voting behavior in presidential elections.

Campaigns are limited in their impact because most voters do not make up their minds on the basis of the campaign. Many of them decide for whom they will vote for well before the campaign ever begins. They do so on the basis of long-standing party identifications, evaluations of government performance, and the associations between the parties and particular values and positions. Only a minority decide how to vote late in the campaign and on the basis of the particular candidates and the particular things they say. In a case such as the 2004 election, when neither campaign made a serious blunder, party identification, government performance, and deeper issues will determine which candidate ends up the winner.

10.4 Outline the changes in the presidential election scene that have occurred in the last 40 years.

A Republican Electoral College "lock" that gave that party an advantage in the 1970s and 1980s has given way to a period of more even balance and intense competition in presidential races in the 2000s. Barack Obama's 2008 election victory was aided by public disapproval of Bush administration policies; the 2012 race will likely hinge on the public's view of the Obama administration's record.

---

mypoliscilab EXERCISES

Apply what you learned in this chapter on MyPoliSciLab.

Read on mypoliscilab.com

eText: Chapter 10

Study and Review on mypoliscilab.com

Pre-Test

Post-Test

Chapter Exam

Flashcards

Watch on mypoliscilab.com

Video: Dissecting Party Primaries

Video: Oprah Fires Up Obama Campaign

Video: State Primary Race

Video: Who Are the Superdelegates?

Video: Money in the 2008 Presidential Race

Explore on mypoliscilab.com

Simulation: You Are a Campaign Manager: McCain Navigates Campaign Financing

Simulation: You Are a Campaign Manager: Countdown to 270!

Simulation: You Are a Campaign Manager: Lead Obama to Battleground State Victory

Comparative: Comparing Political Campaigns

Timeline: Nominating Process

Timeline: Close Calls in Presidential Elections

Timeline: Television and Presidential Campaigns

Visual Literacy: Iowa Caucuses

Visual Literacy: The Electoral College: Campaign Consequences and Mapping the Results

---

KEY TERMS

caucus, p. 279

electoral vote, p. 290

527s, p. 287

matching funds, p. 281

party identification, p. 292

party image, p. 294

political activists, p. 284

popular vote, p. 290

presidential primaries, p. 279

prospective voting, p. 294

retrospective voting, p. 294

soft money, p. 287

superdelegate, p. 281

winner-take-all voting, p. 290

SUGGESTED READINGS

Of General Interest

Abramson, Paul, John Aldrich, and David Rohde. *Change and Continuity in the 2008 Elections*. Washington, DC: CQ Press, 2009. This quadrennial publication provides a comprehensive overview of voting behavior in national elections.

Mayer, William, ed. *The Making of the Presidential Candidates 2008*. Lanham, MD: Rowman & Listtlefield, 2008. An informative collection of essays covering all facets of the contemporary nominating process.

Nelson, Michael, ed. *The Elections of 2008*. Washington, DC: Congressional Quarterly, 2010. This quadrennial publication by a group of knowledgeable authors complements Abramson, Aldrich, and Rohde, offering less detail about voting behavior but a broader view of the campaigns and the activities of elites.

Focused Studies

Campbell, James. *The American Campaign*. 2nd ed. College Station, TX: Texas A&M University Press, 2008. The most comprehensive scholarly study of presidential campaigns.

Carmines, Edward, and James Stimson. *Issue Evolution: Race and the Transformation of American Politics*. Princeton, NJ: Princeton University Press, 1989. An important argument about the significance of race in realigning American politics in the 1960s.

Judis, John B., and Ruy Teixeira. *The Emerging Democratic Majority*. New York: Scribner, 2002. Interesting—and controversial—argument about various trends that the authors believe will help Democrats win most elections in the future.

Mayer, William G., ed. *The Swing Voter in American Politics*. Washington, DC: The Brookings Institution Press, 2008. What swing voters are, how they are identified in survey data, and what we know about them.

ON THE WEB

www.multied.com/elections

A graphical history of presidential elections can be found through MultiEducator Incorporated.

www.archives.gov/federal_register/electoral_college

The official National Archive website on the Electoral College answers all basic questions about procedure, and even includes an Electoral College calculator.

www.electionstudies.org

Perhaps the most comprehensive source of political science data is the National Election Study Archive at the University of Michigan. The site contains a wealth of data as well as many charts and figures showing changes in American politics from election to election.

www.c-span.org

Some of the best websites for learning about a presidential campaign are the ones set up by the candidates themselves. Of course, the official 2004 campaign websites are mostly down now, but you can still see the major events of that election at C-SPAN's election archives.

11 Choosing the Congress

CHAPTER OUTLINE

11.1 Trace the development of the Congress as a professional legislature.

11.2 Explain how congressional constituencies are determined by means of reapportionment and redistricting.

11.3 Describe the congressional nomination process.

11.4 Analyze factors contributing to the incumbency advantage in contemporary House elections.

11.5 Determine why incumbency is less important in Senate elections than in House elections.

11.6 Explain the increased influence of national forces in recent congressional elections.

11.7 Assess the extent to which the gender, racial, and ethnic makeup of the Congress is representative and prospects for change.

Congressional Elections and the Fate of the Obama Agenda

When members of Congress returned to Washington in early 2010, the Democrats appeared headed for a historic legislative victory. After months of tortuous negotiations, passage of a major health insurance reform bill seemed imminent. The House had passed its bill in early November, with only five votes to spare. The Senate had taken much longer because Majority Leader Reid (D-NV) needed to corral the votes of all 60 Democrats in order to prevent a Republican filibuster that would prevent a vote on the bill. (As explained in Chapter 12, 60 voters are necessary to halt a filibuster.) There were important differences between the House and Senate bills, but the consensus among knowledgeable commentators was that these differences would be compromised and a bill passed in time for President Obama's State of the Union Address on January 27. Then a Massachusetts special election shook the Congressional world.

Democrat Edward Kennedy, the senior senator from Massachusetts and longtime advocate of national health insurance, died in August 2009. A temporary replacement was appointed and a special election was set for January 2010. The seat was universally viewed as safely Democratic—Massachusetts had not elected a Republican senator since 1972 and Obama had won the state by a 26 point margin in 2008. In consequence, the Democratic Primary was viewed as the real election. Attorney General Martha

Coakley won handily with 47 percent of the vote in a four-way race. Four times as many people voted in the Democratic primary as in the Republican primary, which had only one serious candidate, State Senator Scott Brown. Despite being viewed as a sure loser, Brown began to campaign vigorously, driving an old pickup truck around the state. Early polls showed him as much as 30 points behind Coakley. Coakley was so confident that she would be the next senator from Massachusetts that she took a Caribbean vacation during the campaign.

Meanwhile, at the same time that health insurance legislation was progressing through the Senate, popular support as measured in public opinion polls was falling and opposition gradually overtook support (see Chapter 5). The legislation was extremely complex, and many people who had insurance were concerned that they would see their coverage decline or their costs increase if the bill passed. Others worried about the huge costs of the bill, especially at a time when deficits were soaring. In addition, many citizens found the legislative process itself offensive. Much of it took place behind closed doors and special deals were cut with drug companies, unions, and the residents of Nebraska and Louisiana (the "Cornhusker Kickback" and the "Second Louisiana Purchase"—see the *Election Voices!* feature in Chapter 12). In Massachusetts Brown campaigned against government spending and deficits in general and against the health insurance legislation in particular, even writing "41" after signing his name to indicate that he would be the 41st vote that would prevent the legislation from passing in the Senate.

In early January a poll showed Brown closing to within single digits of Coakley. Sensing the possibility of a major upset, Brown's supporters redoubled their efforts and outside groups and volunteers joined the campaign. By mid-January Brown had closed the gap and soon pulled ahead.[1] During the last week of the campaign he was raising a million dollars a day over the Internet.[2] The Coakley campaign and national Democrats realized their peril too late. Despite the frenzied opposition of the state's largest newspaper, the *Boston Globe*, and last-minute visits by Bill Clinton and President Obama, the unthinkable occurred. On January 19, Brown defeated Coakley by a margin of 52–47.

No election is determined by a single factor. By all accounts Coakley ran a poor campaign. Her first attack ad misspelled Massachusetts. Her remarks in a radio interview indicated that she was unfamiliar with Red Sox World Series hero Curt Schilling. She appeared condescending when she commented that standing outside Fenway Park in the cold, shaking hands with voters was not a good use of her time. And she committed a serious gaffe during a debate with Brown, appearing to state (her comments were somewhat ambiguous) that the troops should come home from Afghanistan because the terrorists were gone—two days after funeral services for a Massachusetts resident killed in a terrorist bombing in Afghanistan. In addition to the poor campaign, the Massachusetts Democratic Party was out of favor—the governor was unpopular and the last three Speakers of the Massachusetts House had been indicted.

But national factors as well as personal and local factors clearly contributed to Coakley's defeat.[3] Turnout on a wintry January day normally would be quite low, but the turnout was as high as in the previous gubernatorial election. Brown was elected with heavy support from independents, who constitute a majority of the registered voters in Massachusetts. Although exit polls were not conducted, post-election polls reported that independents went for Brown by something between 2-1 and 3-1 and indicated that Brown voters were more concerned with the economy than with healthcare and disproportionately came from the ranks of those who disapproved of the healthcare legislation in particular and government spending and deficits in general.

In Washington, the Massachusetts outcome hit like a major earthquake. If Massachusetts could elect a Republican, no Democrat anywhere was safe in 2010. Suggestions that the Democratic Congress should rush the health legislation through using various parliamentary maneuvers were quickly rejected as likely public relations disasters. And, despite the desire of some Democrats to stay the course, others believed that the Massachusetts result had changed the political landscape. Liberal Anthony Weiner of New York became a YouTube sensation with his scatological comments about the need for his fellow Democrats to recognize a new political reality and revise their agenda. As observers digested the full scope of the Democratic debacle in Massachusetts, a new consensus quickly emerged: Health insurance reform was on life support. The future of cap and trade, the Administration's climate change proposal, was now in doubt. Other important pieces of the agenda would be put on the back burner. The Democratic emphasis in 2010 must be on "job, jobs, jobs," and serious efforts to address spending and deficits. The ambitious agenda the president had laid out in early 2009 was drastically altered by a single congressional election.

Making the Connection

Elections are never far from the minds of members of Congress, and electoral shocks like that in Massachusetts capture their immediate and full attention. All members of the House of Representatives are elected every two years, and some face primary challenges as early as the spring of election years, a little more than a year after they have taken the oath of office. In response to such realities, representatives campaign for reelection more or less continuously. They are Exhibit A of the permanent campaign.

Surprisingly, the situation isn't much different for senators. Although senators are elected for six-year terms, a third of them are elected every two years, so that at any given time one-third of the Senate is operating with the same short time horizon as members of the House. Moreover, Senate campaigns are so expensive that on average an incumbent running for reelection raises over $20,000 every week for six years—a time-consuming, psychologically draining activity that keeps all of them aware of their need to cultivate constituents and contributors, even if their actual reelection campaign is years away.

The great majority of congressional incumbents win reelection, but victory is rarely guaranteed. A politically damaging position, a personal impropriety, a past association with a corrupt lobbyist, a party affiliation with an unpopular president, a bad economy—these and other factors can lead to the end of a political career. That simple fact strongly affects what members of Congress do, and what they are unwilling to do.

This chapter focuses on elections for the United States Congress. In the pages that follow, you will learn how House and Senate elections differ from each other and from the presidential elections we discussed in Chapter 10, what members of Congress do to get elected and reelected, and why House incumbents have a much larger incumbency advantage than Senate incumbents. You will also learn how today's congressional elections differ from those held in the last third of the twentieth century. Finally, you will grapple with the long-standing question of whether 535 separate elections can select a representative Congress.

11.1

Trace the development of the Congress as a professional legislature.

The Electoral Evolution of the Congress

The framers of the Constitution did not expect Congress to operate the way today's Congress does. On the one hand, they thought that frequent elections would make the House of Representatives an unstable body whose members would come and go quickly. Madison wrote that the House should have "an immediate dependence on, and an intimate sympathy with, the people."[4] On the other hand, the framers expected the Senate, with members elected by state legislatures for six-year terms, to be stable and electorally insulated. According to Madison, the Senate would proceed "with more coolness, with more system, and with more wisdom, than the popular branch."[5] (Remember that not until after adoption of the Seventeenth Amendment to the Constitution in 1913 were all senators popularly elected.)

Neither chamber developed as the framers had anticipated. At first, the House was indeed unstable in its membership and disorderly in its operation. Turnover levels often were as high as 50 percent until after the Civil War.[6] But, contrary to Madison's argument, frequent elections were not the cause of high turnover. Before the Civil War, more representatives quit than were defeated. Living conditions were unattractive after the national government moved to the uninhabited, swampy lands that became Washington, DC. Moreover, the national government was not particularly important in the early years of the republic.[7] Many members found that they had less power in Washington than they would have in the capital cities of their home states.[8] Even those members willing to serve multiple terms sometimes were prevented from doing so by *rotation* practices, whereby a congressional district's political factions "took turns" holding the congressional seat. Abraham Lincoln, for example, was elected to the House in 1846 but stepped down after one term in accordance with local rotation agreements.[9] As a result of these various considerations, average service in the House of Representatives did not reach three terms until after 1900.

The early Senate, too, was far from being the stable, experienced body of statesmen that Madison had anticipated. In the first ten years of the republic, more than one-third of the senators failed to serve out their terms, and until 1820 more senators resigned during their terms than were denied reelection by their state legislatures. Although they had the opportunity to stay longer than members of the House, many senators chose to pass it up for the same reasons that House members went home.[10]

Today, things are much different. Congress is the world's foremost example of what political scientists call a **professional legislature.** Its members are full-time legislators who serve for long periods, as shown in Figure 11.1. Relatively few members quit voluntarily, and many intend to remain in Congress indefinitely. In fact, many people in the United States think that the membership of Congress is *too* stable. They support institutional changes such as term limits in order to shake up what they see as an unresponsive institution.

Claims of congressional unresponsiveness appear to clash with the general theme of this book—that American political institutions are electorally sensitive (if not hypersensitive). The explanation for this apparent contradiction is simple: Contemporary members of Congress win so often precisely *because* they are so electorally aware—they anticipate threats to their reelection and act to avoid them. Before reviewing the evidence for this claim, we will consider some background information on congressional elections.

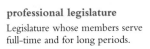

professional legislature
Legislature whose members serve full-time and for long periods.

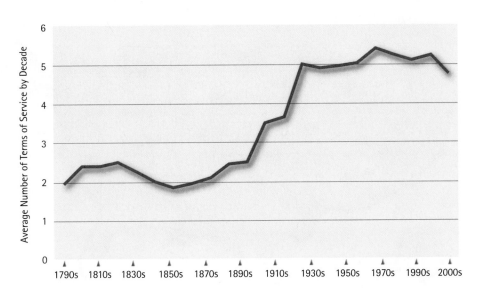

FIGURE 11.1

Tenure in the House

Congress became a career in the twentieth century.

• *During which decades did House tenure rise dramatically?*

• *What factors contributed to the doubling of House tenure between the 1890s and the 1920s?*

Sources: Nelson W. Polsby, "The Institutionalization of the U.S. House of Representatives," *American Political Science Review,* March 1968: 146; Norman J. Ornstein et al., eds., *Vital Statistics on Congress, 2001–2002* (Washington, DC: AB Press, 2002); and the Clerk of U.S. House of Representatives, http://clerk.house.gov.

11.2

Explain how congressional constituencies are determined by means of reapportionment and redistricting.

reapportionment
The allocation of House seats to the states after each decennial census.

redistricting
Drawing new boundaries of congressional districts, usually after the decennial census.

Reapportionment and Redistricting

How are the constituencies represented in Congress determined? In the Senate, representation is simple and unchanging. The Constitution gives every state two senators, regardless of population, and Article V states that no state can be deprived of equal representation without its consent. Because less populous states will not give up their political advantage in the Senate, equal representation in the Senate is essentially an amendment-proof feature of American democracy.

Representation is considerably more complicated in the House. The Constitution requires that a census be held every decade. After the census, the 435 seats in the House of Representatives are apportioned among the states according to their populations—a process called **reapportionment.** As Figure 11.2 illustrates, in the past half-century, northeastern and upper midwestern states have lost more than 60 House seats to southern and southwestern states as population has shifted from the Frostbelt to the Sunbelt.[11] Given the different political leanings of these regions, the net effect has been to strengthen Republican representation in the House.

Currently, seven states have such small populations that they receive only one congressional seat, a minimum guaranteed by Article I. After the other states learn how many House seats they have received, they set to work **redistricting**—drawing the boundaries of the new districts. Congressional districts within individual states once varied widely in population, but now they must be of virtually equal population, the result of Supreme Court decisions beginning with *Wesberry v. Sanders* in 1964. Subsequent decisions have refined the standard to one of precise numerical equality (at least as indicated by census figures, which are only approximate, of course). This principle has come to be known as "one person, one vote."

FIGURE 11.2

POWER SHIFT

House seats moved south and west between 1950 and 2000.

• *What factors have affected population movements in the United States during the past half-century?*

It is important to recognize that equal population refers to residents, not voters. Some districts contain people who turn out at very high rates, whereas others contain people who vote at very low rates. In 2008, for example, less than half as many people voted in some New York City districts as voted in some suburban districts. Thus, although theoretically equal, the constituencies that elect members of the House are not equal in practice. In addition, turnout in off-year congressional elections is only about two-thirds as high as turnout in presidential election years. Thus, the voting constituencies of members of the House vary greatly across both space and time. (Because states differ even more in population, Senate elections show even greater variation in the size of voter constituencies. In 2010, for example, more than 7.5 million people voted in the California Senate election, compared to a little more than 230,000 in the North Dakota election.)

In most states the legislature draws electoral maps, but in six states bipartisan commissions do the job, and in several others the lines are drawn by some combination of legislators and outside appointees. The redistricting process is often highly contentious, because political careers depend on which voters get placed in which districts. Charges of **gerrymandering**—drawing the boundary lines of congressional districts for partisan or other political advantage—fly back and forth. Some observers believe that partisan gerrymandering, in particular, has become so outrageous that the Supreme Court should impose some limits, although this matter remains unsettled at present. Here is another example of American exceptionalism (see Chapter 1). In most other democracies, the redistricting process is far more politically insulated than in the United States. The official bodies that draw parliamentary districts are much less influenced by partisan and incumbency considerations (see the *International Comparison* box on page 316).

gerrymandering
Drawing boundary lines of congressional districts in order to confer an advantage on some partisan or political interest.

Fair Weather for Republicans
Population growth in the heavily Republican Sunbelt has outpaced that in the North, causing congressional districts to migrate southward. The Detroit area of Michigan, where this cartoon was first published, has been especially hard hit.

• *Do you think it is harder for a region to recover if it loses political power after the area has gone into decline?*

© Thompson–Detroit Free Press 2000.

INTERNATIONAL COMPARISON

Redistricting Around the World[1]

Critics of American redistricting practices contend that representative democracy consists of voters choosing their representatives in free elections but that the United States is fundamentally corrupt in allowing representatives to choose their voters. This is literally true in the great majority of states where legislators draw the boundaries of the districts they represent and only slightly less true where congressional districts are drawn by partisan and personal allies in the state legislatures.

Some democracies with proportional representation (PR) electoral systems (see Chapter 8) do not have districts. Citizens vote for parties, and candidates are elected from party lists in proportion to the national party vote. Other countries with PR systems have multi-member districts but their boundaries seldom change—population change is accommodated by varying the number of representatives allocated to the districts. Most democracies do elect members of parliament from districts that change periodically; but, except for France, no other democracy allows legislators to determine their own constituencies. Rather, these democracies rely on expert, nonpolitical bodies to draw the lines. Variously called boundary authorities or commissions, or electoral authorities or commissions, these bodies generally are small—Canada's has only three members and Germany's has seven. Further, the members are experts in statistics, geography, and other relevant subjects. In some countries such as New Zealand, a small number of political appointees serve on the commission, but only to point out decisions that have disparate political impacts. Other countries such as Australia and India specifically prohibit anyone with political connections from serving on their commissions.

In some countries, the redistricting plan produced by the expert body is final—there is no amendment or appeal. In other countries such as the United Kingdom, the parliament has an up or down vote on the plan, but such votes generally are not controversial. In contrast to the United States, where the courts almost automatically review redistricting plans, the courts play no role in a majority of other democracies, and a very limited role in others.

Similar to the United States, in many democracies the most common interval between redistricting is ten years, but some nations require more frequent redistricting, such as Turkey's five years, and some allow longer intervals, such as France's 12–14 years. India has not redistricted since 1973, in violation of its own law. The laws of some countries do not specify an interval, but rather a "trigger." In the Czech Republic, redistricting occurs when malapportionment (unequal constituency populations) reaches 15 percent.

Although population equality is probably the most important criterion in redistricting in all democracies, none carries it to the extreme lengths that the United States does. (Given that census enumerators make mistakes and people are constantly moving, dying, and being born every day, the degree of equality required by American courts is beyond the accuracy of the census to count.)[2] In contrast to the virtually zero tolerance of population disparities in the United States, Italy allows a 5 percent population disparity, Germany 15 percent, Canada 25 percent (under unusual circumstances), and Singapore 30 percent. Such large population disparities typically occur when considerations of geography or natural community are present. For example, in Scotland some islands traditionally get a parliamentary representative even though their populations are much smaller than the mainland norm.[3] Boundary commissions in other countries balance population equality with other considerations rather than ignore all other considerations in pursuit of precisely equal numbers as is done in the United States.

• *Given that redistricting by state legislatures is almost universally criticized, can you think of any argument in favor of letting legislators draw their own districts?*

• *In the drawing of district boundaries, should equal population trump all other considerations such as compactness of a district, respect for jurisdictional boundaries, and preservation of natural communities?*

---

[1] This discussion is drawn from an exceptionally informative essay by Lisa Handley, "A Comparative Study of Structures and Criteria for Boundary Delimitation," in Bernard Grofman and Lisa Handley, *Redistricting in Comparative Perspective* (New York: Oxford, 2008), pp. 265–283.

[2] A federal appeals court rejected a Pennsylvania plan in 2002 because the most and least populous districts differed by 19 people.

[3] David Butler and Bruce Cain, *Congressional Redistricting: Comparative and Theoretical Perspectives* (New York: Macmillan 1992), pp. 120–21.

The Congressional Nomination Process

The congressional nomination process is much simpler than the presidential one: Nominees for the House or Senate must win at most one primary election in their state, not a sequence across many states. In a few states, party conventions can nominate candidates, but in most states the candidates are chosen in primaries. Some states hold their Senate and House primaries on the same day, and under the same rules, as their presidential primaries. Other states hold them at different times and/or under different rules.[12]

The dates of **filing deadlines** and primary elections also vary widely across states.[13] The filing deadline is the latest date on which a candidate who wishes to be on the primary ballot must file official documents with and/or pay required fees to state election officials. For the 2010 elections, Illinois had the earliest filing deadline, November 2, 2009, and Delaware had the latest, July 30, 2010. The earliest primaries were held in Illinois on February 2, 2010, and the latest were in Hawaii on September 18, 2010. Thus, some candidates knew the identity of their opponent more than seven months earlier than others did.

The hardest fought primaries occur when there is an **open seat,** a House or Senate race with no incumbent (because of death or retirement) running for reelection. If both parties have strength in the area, both will usually have competitive primaries. If one party is much stronger than the other, its primary will be hotly contested because the winner is expected to be the next member of Congress (as in the Massachusetts case discussed in the opening of this chapter). When incumbents run, however, they seldom lose in the primary: Indeed, they rarely face tough challenges from other members of their party. This fact does not necessarily show that primaries are unimportant; rather, it may indicate that incumbents usually are very good about keeping members of their own party satisfied, thus discouraging a strong primary challenge. In 2006, for example, only one incumbent senator—Democrat Joseph Lieberman of Connecticut—was defeated in a party primary. Although Lieberman ran as an independent and won the general election, his loss in the Democratic primary sent a clear signal to every other senator in his party (and many representatives as well): Any Democrat who supported the war in Iraq did so at his or her own peril.

Contemporary House Elections

House elections differ from the presidential elections described in the previous chapter in a number of significant ways. One reason is that members of Congress are only *collectively* responsible for the state of the nation, whereas the president is considered *individually* responsible. For example, presidents regularly take the blame for a poor economy, but it is unlikely (and hardly reasonable) that voters will hold their representative—who is only one of 435—responsible for the condition of the national economy.

Another reason why House and presidential elections differ is that in presidential elections the candidates compete on a roughly equal footing. By the time the fall campaign begins, both are well known to the electorate, have tens of millions of dollars to spend, and have scores of supportive groups and organizations campaigning for them. In contrast, in most House elections an incumbent faces a poorly known and underfunded challenger. Because most House races are foregone conclusions, challengers cannot raise enough money to mount serious campaigns against incumbents and outside groups do not lend their support because they do not wish to waste their resources in a lost cause.

11.3

Describe the congressional nomination process.

filing deadline

The latest date on which a candidate who wishes to be on a primary ballot may file official documents with and/or pay required fees to state election officials.

open seat

A House or Senate race with no incumbent (because of death or retirement).

11.4

Analyze factors contributing to the incumbency advantage in contemporary House elections.

The first problem most challengers face is low visibility. Surveys show that barely a third of the citizenry can recall the name of their representative, and even fewer can remember anything he or she has done for the district. Only about one in ten people can remember how their representative voted on a particular bill. But people know even less about challengers. Having little information on which to base their vote, many people simply go by the "brand name," voting for the candidate of the party with which they generally sympathize. In House elections, three-fourths of all voters who identify with a party typically support the House candidate with the same affiliation.[14] Given that the great majority of House districts are drawn to favor one party or the other, party-line voting largely determines the winners in such **"safe seats."**

The next problem challengers face is overcoming the advantages of incumbency. In presidential elections incumbency is a double-edged sword. A first term widely seen as successful may give the incumbent an insuperable advantage when he seeks reelection, as it did for Ronald Reagan in 1984. In contrast, a first term widely seen as unsuccessful may put an incumbent president at a great disadvantage, as when Jimmy Carter was soundly defeated for reelection in 1980. In House elections incumbency generally works in a positive direction because, as we discuss below, it is based on considerations other than the state of the country.

Incumbency has grown in importance over the past half-century. Statistical studies of House elections show that, other things being equal, the **incumbency advantage**—the electoral benefit a candidate enjoys by being an incumbent, over and above his or her other personal and political characteristics—grew from about 2 percentage points before 1960 to as high as 12 points in some late-twentieth-century elections.[15] The increase was not smooth. Rather, as shown in Figure 11.3, the incumbency advantage surged in the late 1960s, leveled off for a time, peaked in 1986, and then declined in the 1990s before creeping upward again in the most recent elections. At least five factors contributed to these trends: the decline of political parties in the mid-twentieth century, the expanding resources available to incumbents, change in the importance of "representative" activities, campaign funding disparities, and more responsive incumbents.

Party Decline

Although three-fourths of all party identifiers vote for the candidate of their party, that figure dropped somewhat in the 1960s and 1970s before recovering in recent years. In addition, more voters had a party allegiance in the 1950s than they did by the 1980s. When party affiliations weakened, more voters became "available," willing to vote on other less partisan bases such as the incumbent's personal characteristics and activities. Realizing that more voters now were "up for grabs," incumbents adjusted their behavior. Although their own partisan constituencies had become less secure, incumbents could provide voters with other, more personal reasons to support them. At the same time, as voters who normally might have supported the other party became more receptive to such personal appeals, incumbents began to court them. Not only did party affiliations among the voters weaken, but party organizations declined as well. Traditionally, congressional campaigns were conducted by local party organizations. As we discussed in Chapter 8, however, party organizations declined after World War II. Again, incumbents adjusted their behavior to take account of the new environment. They voted themselves resources (often called perks for "perquisites of office") that could make up for those no longer provided by party organizations.

safe seat
A congressional district certain to vote for the candidate of one party.

incumbency advantage
The electoral advantage a candidate enjoys by virtue of being an incumbent, over and above his or her other personal and political characteristics.

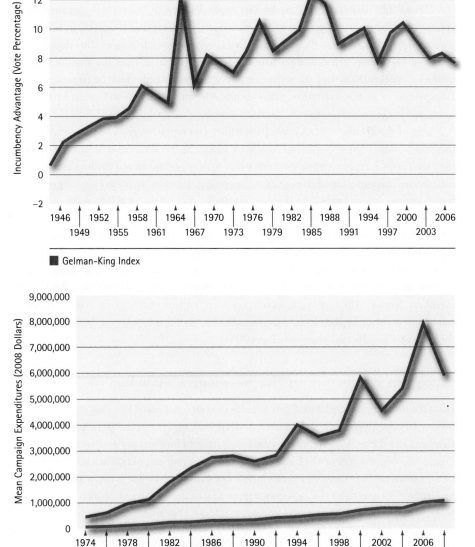

FIGURE 11.3

THE INCUMBENCY
ADVANTAGE

The advantage of incumbency
surged in the mid-1960s and
peaked in the mid-1980s.

• *How large was the incumbency
advantage in the 1950s?*

• *Why did the advantage of
incumbency surge in the 1960s?*

Note: The second election of
each decade is not plotted
because in those years decennial
redistricting altered the districts
of some incumbents, making
incumbency advantage impossible to calculate.

Source: Calculated by Sam Abrams and
Gary Jacobson using the Gelman-King
method.

Expanding Member Resources

In 1950 the average representative had three staff employees. And, as late as 1960, nearly
a third of the representatives lacked a district office that was open when the representative was in Washington. In contrast, by 1980 some observers compared members of
Congress to CEOs (chief executive officers) of small businesses.[16] Today, each member
has a Washington office and one or more district offices. The typical House member
employs 18 personal staff assistants, more than 40 percent of whom are assigned to district offices.[17] Senators have even bigger staffs, although office sizes depend on each
state's population. These offices have many responsibilities, but no one doubts that

much of their effort is directed toward the member's reelection. Indeed, it has been said that Capitol Hill is the headquarters of 535 political machines.

Travel subsidies and other perks also expanded greatly.[18] In 1960 members were reimbursed for only three trips to their districts per year. By 1976 the number had increased to 26, and today there is no limit except the overall budget allocated to each member. Of course, before the jet plane, it was not practical for many members to go home on weekends, as they do today—many went home only once or twice a session. Improvements in transportation made it possible for members of Congress to commute, so Congress authorized the funds to support that change.[19]

Use of the **frank**—the free use by senators and representatives of the U.S. mail for official business—has also grown. Although Congress has long subsidized communication with constituents, technological advances such as computerized mailing lists allowed members to take greater advantage of the privilege. Increase in congressional use of the frank occurred much faster than the rate of population increase or the increase in incoming mail that required a response. Not surprisingly, congressional mailings to constituents are much higher in even-numbered (election) years than in odd-numbered years.

Representatives naturally take political advantage of other new technologies as well. Today, offices have websites and members have Facebook pages. TV cameras have caught some members texting during prime-time presidential addresses. And some members Twitter. Although new technologies have great potential for communicating information about legislation to constituents, thus far House offices appear to be using them mostly to advertise their members.[20]

Change in Importance of "Representative" Activities

How did incumbents appeal to voters as partisan voting declined? You may think of members of Congress primarily as *lawmakers*. Indeed, making laws is the principal business of Congress and the major responsibility that the Constitution bestows on that body. But the official title of members of the House is *Representative,* and, as political scientists have long recognized, members view their job much more broadly than just writing and voting on legislation.[21] One activity that occupies a great deal of their time and effort is district service—making sure that their congressional districts get a fair share (or more) of federal programs, projects, and expenditures.[22] Although critics of Congress often deride such benefits as "pork barrel spending," constituents generally approve when their representatives and senators "bring home the bacon"—and reward them at the ballot box for their successes.

Another activity to which modern representatives devote a great deal of attention is constituent assistance, usually called **casework.** Citizens, groups, and businesses frequently encounter difficulties in qualifying for government benefits or subsidies or in complying with federal regulations. When their problems are not solved through normal channels, they appeal to members of Congress for assistance. About one in six voters reports having contacted a representative for information or help with a problem. In overwhelming numbers, these constituents report satisfactory resolution of their problems and, again, show their gratitude at the polls.[23]

District service and constituent assistance often are included together under the general rubric of **constituency service.** They share an important characteristic that sheds light on the advantage of incumbency: Such activities please voters back home regardless of their party identification or ideology. Most voters are happy when federal projects and grants come to the district—roads, buildings, and grants to

frank
Name given to representatives' and senators' free use of the U.S. mail for sending communications to constituents.

casework
Efforts by members of Congress to help individuals and groups when they have difficulties with federal agencies.

constituency service
Efforts by members of Congress to secure federal funding for their districts and to help constituents when they have difficulties with federal agencies.

community organizations are neither Republican nor Democratic. Similarly, Democratic incumbents willingly help Republican businesses deal with federal regulators, and Republican incumbents willingly help Democratic constituents qualify for federal benefits. Because these activities antagonize few if any constituents—in contrast to what happens when members of Congress take positions on controversial issues—they carry significant electoral benefits and little if any electoral cost.

Campaign Funds

Similar to presidential elections, congressional elections have become increasingly expensive: According to Federal Election Commission (FEC) reports, the average spending by a House candidate was almost $600,000 in 2008. (The average spending by a Senate candidate was about $2 million.) But congressional elections differ from presidential elections in an important respect: As Figure 11.4 shows, the gap between incumbents' spending and that of their challengers is wide and has grown wider since 1980. For many of today's reformers, the advantage of incumbency is simple and self-evident: money.

Money certainly affects candidate visibility, and congressional challengers are seriously underfunded. Nevertheless, research on the influence of money in congressional elections paints a surprisingly complex picture. Although money contributes significantly to the incumbency advantage, its contribution probably is exaggerated.

First, campaign spending has what economists call *diminishing returns:* The more a candidate spends, the less impact an additional dollar of spending has. In particular, for an incumbent who already controls perks valued at more than $1,000,000 per year, an extra $100,000 in campaign spending has less impact than it would for a challenger who lacks such taxpayer-provided resources. Sophisticated advocates of campaign finance reform therefore oppose low limits on campaign spending. Such limits would hurt challengers, who have little name recognition, much more than incumbents, who already enjoy high visibility.[24]

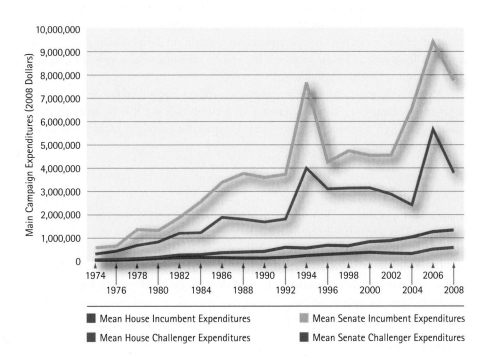

■ Mean House Incumbent Expenditures   ■ Mean Senate Incumbent Expenditures
■ Mean House Challenger Expenditures   ■ Mean Senate Challenger Expenditures

FIGURE 11.4

CONGRESSIONAL CAMPAIGN SPENDING

Spending in House and Senate campaigns has risen over the past several decades.

• *Why do Senate candidates spend so much more than House candidates?*

Sources: Norman J. Ornstein, Thomas E. Mann, and Michael J. Malbin, *Vital Statistics on Congress, 2001–2002* (Washington, DC: American Enterprise Institute, 2002), pp. 81, 87; the Federal Election Commission; and the Campaign Finance Institute.

Second, the surge in the incumbency advantage (in the mid-1960s) did not occur at the same time as the explosion of spending in congressional campaigns. House elections in the late 1960s and early 1970s were not nearly as expensive as they are today. Moreover, the explosive growth in political action committees (or PACs—see Chapter 7) took place *after* the adoption of campaign finance reform laws in 1974, when incumbents had already developed a significant advantage.

Finally, consider that heavy spending by an incumbent can be a sign of electoral weakness, not strength—a signal that an incumbent is in trouble.[25] For example, in 2008, the highest spending House candidate was Mark Kirk, a Republican from Illinois, who won reelection with only 52.5 percent of the vote. Sometimes big spenders do not win because they spend a lot; rather, they spend a lot because they were in danger of losing.

Some analysts believe that an important effect of an incumbent's advantage in campaign funds is one that is difficult to observe, let alone measure. Because it takes so much money for a challenger to mount a serious campaign, potentially strong challengers may decide not to enter the race.[26] If the incumbent has a widely publicized million-dollar "war chest," the prospect of mounting a challenge is daunting and may scare potential opponents out of the race, at least the majority of them who are not independently wealthy.[27] A challenger may have to take time off from a job, tap into personal savings, and go deeply in debt to construct a campaign organization. Well-funded incumbents make taking these risks seem like a poor investment.

In recent years the topic of campaign finance reform has received considerable attention, and members of Congress have grappled with a wide variety of reform proposals. Citizens are disgusted with the present system of campaign finance and, as a result, are cynical about government in general and the Congress in particular. The problem is that the reforms likely to do the most good are the least likely to be adopted. Public financing of congressional elections, for example, would relieve candidates of the burden of fund-raising, giving them time to spend on more productive activities. It also would partly insulate them from the influence of special interests. But setting subsidies high enough to make challengers credible—perhaps a half-million dollars in House races, not counting primaries—would no doubt require expenditures too large for a cynical public to accept (even if incumbents were ever willing to give their opposition that much funding).[28]

All in all, the great advantage in campaign spending that incumbent representatives enjoy surely contributes to the advantage of incumbency, but it is far from the only explanation. Even if spending disparities were wiped out overnight, incumbents would still do exceptionally well.

More Responsive Incumbents

Many critics of Congress believe that there is something wrong with its high rates of reelection. This is true if members' electoral success reflects the operation of some illegitimate factor—selling out to special interest groups, for example. But, as we have noted, one reason for members' success is that they work hard at helping their constituents and serving their districts. Another source of their success is that these legislators are extremely sensitive to the wishes of their constituents, perhaps even more so than members of Congress from earlier eras.

One explanation for this increased sensitivity is that members of Congress today have more and better information about their constituents than ever before, and vice versa.[29] Not only do their offices have fax machines, email, Web pages, and other new technologies undreamt of a few decades ago, but the members also physically return to their districts 30 to 50 times a year. Only a generation ago, a derisive name, "the Tuesday-to-Thursday Club" referred to a minority of East Coast members who lived close enough to Washington to go home to their districts on Friday and return to the Capitol on Monday. Today, jet transportation enables most of the Congress to belong to the Tuesday-to-Thursday club. Important legislative business is rarely scheduled for Mondays or Fridays, because so many members are traveling on those days. With members spending so much time in their districts, is it any surprise that they are highly attuned to the sentiments of constituents?

Moreover, polling is much more widespread today. Again, a generation ago only a few major interest groups ever conducted polls in congressional districts, and then usually only to gauge a candidate's chances. Today, with the growth of the survey research industry and the arrival of computer-assisted telephone interviewing, more members can afford to conduct surveys to learn the views of constituents. Today's members probably make fewer political mistakes than their predecessors did.

Contemporary members of Congress also may have greater incentive to act in accordance with the information they have. In the modern Congress, every vote is closely watched by interest groups who rate members. Moreover, years after a vote, opponents engaged in opposition research may bring it up in a campaign. In the House, more votes are public now than a generation ago. Until 1971, many votes were cast by standing up, by voice (aye–nay), or by "tellers" (depositing colored cards in boxes)—procedures that concealed the members' individual positions. But rule changes that year made it easy to demand a roll-call vote, and the number of roll calls in an average session more than doubled. Numerous interest groups tally up the votes and score members as friends or foes of legislation of particular concern to the groups' supporters.

End of the Electoral Road
Senator Blanche Lincoln (D-AR) far outspent her opponent, but lost her race for reelection in 2010.

• *Why do the highest-spending incumbents often lose?*

Challengers hire opposition researchers to pore over an incumbent's record to find obscure votes than can be linked to a policy that proved to be a failure or had negative consequences. In short, more recorded votes mean more electoral danger.

Thus, members of Congress take care not to cast votes that will damage them in their districts. When party and constituency collide, party leaders generally allow constituency to trump party—except under the most dire of circumstances. Today, members of Congress have enough information to know when their actions are electorally dangerous.

11.5

Determine why incumbency is less important in Senate elections than in House elections.

Contemporary Senate Elections

Incumbency is less important in Senate elections than in House elections. As Figure 11.5 shows, incumbent senators win more often than not, but they lose much more frequently than do representatives, and in a few elections (such as in 1980) barely more than half survive. In fact, despite their six-year terms, the average length of time a senator serves is the same as the average tenure of a representative: about 11 years.[30] The more precarious position of incumbents in Senate elections reflects differences in party competition, the information voters possess, the quality of challengers, and the higher ambitions of senators. Each of these differences, which we discuss below, makes the position of Senate incumbents less secure than that of House incumbents.

Party Competition

The two parties compete more evenly in Senate races than in House races.[31] Each senator has a state for a constituency and, in general, states are more heterogeneous than the smaller congressional districts included in them. This difference is significant because social and economic diversity provides a basis for party competition.[32] For example, an urban, heavily minority House district will be dominated by the Democrats, and a rural, white district usually will be dominated by the Republicans. If a state includes both kinds of districts, however, each party has a natural base on which to compete for the Senate seats. Only a minority of states are reliably "safe" for either party, whereas a large

FIGURE 11.5

REELECTION RATES

Representatives are reelected more often than senators.

• *Why do Senate incumbents lose so much more frequently than House incumbents?*

Source: Harold W. Stanley and Richard G. Nemi, *Vital Statistics on American Politics, 2005–2006* (Washington, DC: CQ Press, 2006), and the Federal Election Commission. Figures for 2010 are estimates based on available election results as of November 6, 2010.

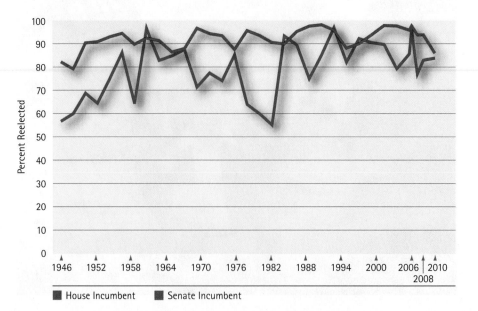

House Incumbent   Senate Incumbent

majority of the smaller, more homogeneous House districts are "safe" seats even without gerrymandering. Thus, part of the reason why senators lead less secure electoral lives than representatives is simply that they have larger, more diverse constituencies that are more difficult to represent.

Uncontrolled Information

Senators receive much more media coverage than do representatives.[33] Given the popular image of politicians as publicity seekers, greater media exposure might appear to benefit senators, but the source of the information is an important consideration. Nearly all the information that constituents receive about House incumbents comes *from* House incumbents—newsletters, press releases, and so forth.[34] Naturally, such information has an entirely positive slant: Representatives are not going to spread negative information about themselves! Senators also would like their constituents to receive nothing but positive information about them, but the media are not under Senate control. The media publicize controversial statements, personal embarrassments, and fights with the president and other politicians. Such coverage inevitably puts senators in a negative light in the eyes of at least some constituents.

Better Challengers

The office of senator enjoys a higher status than the office of representative. After all, the Senate is commonly referred to as the "upper" chamber, whereas the House is referred to as the "lower" chamber (in deference to sensitive House feelings, members of Congress refer to the "other" chamber). Naturally, high-quality challengers are more willing to risk a race for prestigious Senate seats than they are for House seats. Moreover, Senate seats are much scarcer. Every two years, all 435 House seats are available, compared to 33 or 34 Senate seats; a state with 20 House seats has 60 House elections in a six-year period, but only two Senate elections. Thus, far fewer credible challengers are needed to make Senate races competitive.

The combination of greater prestige and greater scarcity means that most Senate incumbents face serious challengers.[35] Senate challengers have more political experience, in terms of both campaigning and government service. They are better known and better liked than House challengers, and the funding gap between incumbents and challengers is smaller (review Figure 11.4). The combined effect of challengers who are more highly regarded and incumbents who are less highly regarded results in a smaller incumbency advantage for those who sit in the Senate.

High Ambitions

Another reason why senators are associated with more controversial matters than representatives is that many of them have higher ambitions. Pundits have joked that every senator looks in the mirror and sees a president looking back. The political system relies, of course, on ambitious office seekers putting themselves on the line.[36] But higher ambition has its risks. Senators cannot seek a presidential nomination solely on the basis of pork barrel projects. Jockeying for national exposure requires senators to take leadership positions on controversial issues, positions that are bound to offend some constituents. Moreover, involvement with broader national and international issues leaves senators vulnerable to the charge that they are neglecting their states.[37]

11.6

Explain the increased influence of national forces in recent congressional elections.

National Forces in Congressional Elections

Former Speaker of the House Thomas P. "Tip" O'Neill (D-MA) liked to say that "all politics is local." Although O'Neill's maxim in part reflected the parochial politics of Massachusetts, it reminds us that, even though members of Congress are national lawmakers, they are elected and reelected by people in hundreds of localities.

The relative importance of local and national considerations in congressional elections has varied over the course of history. National forces help or hurt a party's candidates across the board. Such forces—chiefly, popular reaction to wars, economic conditions, and the performance of the president—were powerful influences on congressional elections for most of U.S. history. For example, when a party won the presidency, many of its congressional candidates would ride into office on the president's **coattails.** But coattails declined in strength in the mid-twentieth century as more voters split their tickets, voting for presidential and congressional candidates of different parties. Moreover, as parties weakened and incumbency strengthened, fewer voters seemed to treat off-year elections as a means to express disappointment in the president they had elected two years before. In the 1970s and 1980s members of the House appeared to have learned how to insulate themselves from the kinds of national forces that had operated in earlier eras.[38]

The times were changing, however. In the historic 1994 election, a 52-seat loss cost the Democrats control of the House of Representatives for the first time in 40 years. Coupled with an eight-seat loss in the Senate, the election results suggested that a strong national tide had overcome the advantage of incumbency and destroyed the insulation of the Democratic Congress. But, to confuse matters, the 1998 election suggested that incumbency was still alive and well. In the year of the Monica Lewinsky scandal and the impeachment of a president, the Democrats actually gained five seats, the first time since 1934 that the president's party had gained seats in a mid-term election. Only one Democratic incumbent lost, as did four Republican incumbents, for an all-time record incumbent reelection rate of 98.5 percent. Not even a major presidential scandal disrupted congressional stability.

coattails

Positive electoral effect of a popular presidential candidate on congressional candidates of the president's party.

Congressional Elections in the 2000s: The Resurgence of National Forces

The congressional elections of 2002–2010 indicated that more voters than in the past were approaching these elections with national issues in mind. Republicans gained seats in both the House and the Senate in 2002, despite a Democrat in the White House; for the second consecutive midterm election voters flouted the historical norm of losses for the president's party. Studies found that Republican candidates got a boost from sharing a party affiliation with President Bush, who enjoyed unusually high approval ratings after the 9/11 terrorist attacks and who campaigned vigorously in the last weeks before the elections.[39] In 2004, President Bush's reelection was accompanied by additional Republican gains in both chambers, again largely attributable to voter concern with homeland security issues.

In 2006, a national tide appeared to have run almost as strongly as it did in 1994, but in the opposite direction. Although the economy was in reasonable shape by historical standards, the conflict in Iraq worsened in the late summer. President Bush's approval ratings were stuck in the 35–40 percent range, and by the time Congress adjourned and the campaign began in earnest, majorities of Americans had come to believe that the war had been a mistake and had not made America safer. In the November voting, the Democrats defeated six incumbent Republican senators to take control of the Senate with a 51–49 majority. The Democrats also gained 30 seats in the House of Representatives to take control of that chamber by a more comfortable margin.

By the time the 2008 congressional campaigns were under way, President Bush's approval ratings had slipped below 30 percent. Moreover, the economy began to deteriorate in 2007, a financial panic occurred in the fall of 2008, and as the election approached, many economists warned that a serious world wide recession was on the horizon, if it were not already here. More than three-quarters of Americans believed that the country was on the wrong track, and majorities gave the edge to Barack Obama and the Democrats on nearly every issue but terrorism and national defense, issues that declined in importance as economic conditions worsened. Democrats had a huge edge in money and enthusiasm and easily outspent the Republicans. Democrats gained about 20 seats in the House, holding all their open seats and defeating more than a dozen Republican incumbents while losing only a handful of theirs. Combined with the 2006 seat losses, Republican losses in 2008 reduced the party's share of the House to pre-1994 levels. In the Senate the Democrats won three open seats and defeated three Republican incumbents, giving incoming President Barack Obama solid majorities in both chambers.

The 2010 Congressional Elections

Just as political fortunes reversed in 1994 and 2006, so they reversed again in 2010, much sooner than many would have believed when Barack Obama was inaugurated in January 2009.

The reversal between 2008 and 2010 was even more dramatic than 2004–2006. Barack Obama took office amid rising optimism that the country was now on the right track. But the president's support began to erode very quickly. In his State of the Union Address Obama set out an ambitious agenda that included education, energy and the environment, health care, and the economy. Parts of the agenda—especially health care— quickly became very contentious, and as the recession proved deeper and more stubborn than expected, critics charged that the administration should have focused more heavily on jobs and the economy. By summer the Tea Party movement (pp. 183–84) had erupted, and the mounting national debt and the size and scope of the federal government had become major issues.

In the face of declining support, especially among political independents who had swung heavily to the Democrats in 2006 and 2008, Obama and the Democratic congressional leadership elected to push on, believing that legislative success eventually would lead to a resurgence in popular support. After a long hard battle health care was adopted (pp. 310–11). Later a financial reform bill also passed, but other parts of the president's agenda, including cap and trade, died. The president found himself attacked from both the right—as a liberal ideologue, and the left—for conceding liberal priorities too easily and following foreign policies that differed little from those of President Bush. By early 2010 it was clear that barring some unforeseen positive developments, it would be a bad year for Democratic candidates.

The political atmosphere grew steadily worse during the campaign season. Although academic economists pronounced the recession over, voters saw little improvement.

Republican enthusiasm rose, Democratic enthusiasm fell and independents moved toward the Republicans—a complete reversal of the previous two elections. Even seemingly weak Tea Party candidates found themselves leading in the polls. In the end the damage was far greater than most observers could have imagined in 2008. The Democrats suffered the biggest mid-term loss in the House since 1938, losing more than 60 seats and giving Republicans a majority of approximately 50 seats. In the Senate Republicans gained a net of six seats, but fell short of a majority. In the short span of six years the electorate had moved the country from unified Republican government to divided government (p. 218) to unified Democratic government and back to divided government.

In sum, national forces in congressional elections clearly have grown in importance in the past several decades (Figure 11.6). Still, incumbents continue to do well by conforming to the preferences of their own constituents. Congressional elections today illustrate both the strength of incumbency typical of elections in the 1970s and 1980s and the renewed importance of national forces that emerged in 1994.

Why Have National Forces Grown Stronger?

Although the changes represented by the 1994 elections may have been exaggerated, the evidence that has piled up since then confirms that congressional elections are more nationalized now than in Tip O'Neill's day when all politics was local. Two related developments contributed to this change. The first is the existence of more unified, and more distinct, political parties. The congressional parties are more unified today than they were a generation ago, and more polarized.[40] Thus, voters usually have a clear choice between two candidates who take distinct positions on national issues. Such clear differences are less likely to be overwhelmed by local factors or by a candidate's personal characteristics, both of which were more important in the preceding three decades.

The second reason lies in recent developments in campaign finance. Today parties and interest groups spend hundreds of millions of dollars on "issue advocacy," primarily TV commercials praising their own candidates or attacking the other

FIGURE 11.6

National Versus Local Forces in House Elections

• *Why did national forces resurge in the later decades of the twentieth century?*

Source: Matthew J. Dickinson, "The President and Congress," in Michael Nelson (ed.), *The Presidency and the Political System* (9th ed.) (Washington, DC: CQ Press, 2010), pp. 401–434.

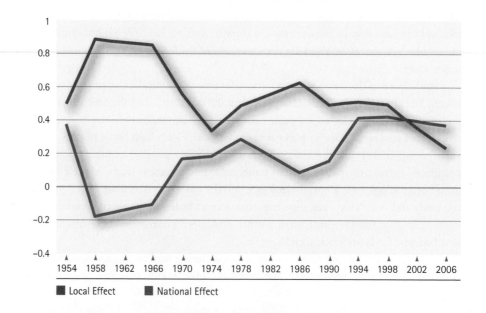

Local Effect   National Effect

party's candidates. Although issue advocacy by the parties was curtailed by provisions of the 2002 Bipartisan Campaign Reform Act (McCain-Feingold) discussed in Chapter 10, issue advocacy by groups has filled much of the void. Numerous "527 committees" sprang up to fund independent campaign ads in the 2004 and 2008 elections. Most of these committees were clearly identified as either pro-Democratic or pro-Republican, although their temporary nature allowed them to fund nasty attack ads without undermining their party's reputation. The *Citizens United* Supreme Court decision in early 2010 struck down many of the restrictions on issue advocacy and opened the door to direct corporate and union issue advocacy, so there is good reason to believe that issue advocacy will grow in importance.

The long-term implications of truly independent spending are significant. Candidates naturally prefer to control the campaign agenda as much as possible. Both candidates for a House seat may prefer that an issue not come up, either because their district is so split that neither candidate feels he or she can profit from the issue or, more innocently, because the issue is not important in their district and unnecessarily muddies the political waters. Groups can force candidates—and voters—to address these issues.

Although many people are troubled by these developments, two things can be said in their favor. First, they help to redress the imbalance between incumbents and challengers. Parties and interest groups can inject large sums into campaigns where credible challengers are running, thus helping to offset the incumbency advantage. Second, campaigns in which the parties and national interest groups actively participate will be more issue-oriented than those in which they are absent. Many people believe this is the way elections should be.

Do Congressional Elections Produce a Representative Body?

Members of Congress generally are well qualified. In contrast to earlier eras, today's Congress contains few political "hacks"—people lacking relevant qualifications but connected to some political influential in their home state. Of course, members today want to get reelected every bit as much as members did in the past, but current members are generally hard-working, well educated, bright, and personally interested in public policy. Moreover, despite periodic heavily publicized sex and corruption scandals, today's members are less corrupt than in most previous periods of American history. Scandals might seem to be more frequent now than in the past, but this impression probably reflects changing perspectives in the media—the rise of the "junkyard dog" mentality—rather than increased corruption in the Congress.

Still, some people look at the membership of Congress and are troubled. They see a supposedly representative body that does not mirror the diversity of the United States. The Congress consists overwhelmingly of white male professionals. The 112th House, elected in 2010, has between 70 and 72 women (depending on the outcomes of races still undecided.) It is the first time in 30 years that the number of women elected declined. The number of women Senators stayed constant at 17. The figures for racial and ethnic minorities are lower. In total the 112th Congress will have 41 African Americans (all in the House), 27 Latinos (two in the Senate, both Cuban-Americans), and 13 Asian-Americans (two in the Senate, from Hawaii). Of some significance, a record 8 Latino Republicans were elected, and 2 African-American Republicans will serve for the first time in a decade.[41] Minnesota elected the first Muslim to Congress

11.7

Assess the extent to which the gender, racial, and ethnic makeup of the Congress is representative and prospects for change.

FIGURE 11.7

WOMEN AND MINORITIES IN CONGRESS

Women and minority membership in the House of Representatives rose sharply after 1990.

• *Why are there more women in Congress than African Americans, and why are there more African Americans than Hispanics?*

Source: Library of Congress—Election Archive.

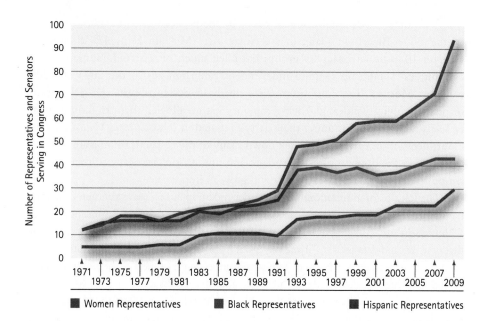

in 2006. He was joined by another in a 2008 special election. As shown in Figure 11.7, the numbers of women and minority members have been rising in recent decades, but the rate of increase, except for the 1992 surge, has been slow. Only slight changes resulted from the 2010 election.

The gender, racial, and ethnic diversity of the Congress has been a subject of considerable discussion in recent years. The concept of representation means different things to different people. For some, personal characteristics such as the gender or race of a representative are unimportant: As long as he or she is responsive to the interests of constituents, they feel well represented.[42] Others disagree. They contend that, almost by definition, a male representative cannot be responsive to the needs and aspirations of women, and that white representatives cannot truly understand the needs and aspirations of African Americans and other minorities. Those who hold such views believe that Congress must be *descriptively* similar to the country in order to be a successful representative body. Still others concede that white male representatives might be able to represent women and minorities but believe nonetheless that women and minority representatives have important symbolic value. A diverse presence in the councils of government will enhance the legitimacy of government actions and provide valuable role models for women and minorities in the population.[43]

Those who believe in either the actual or the symbolic importance of diversifying the Congress are not likely to see their goal achieved soon. Although the demography of the country is changing, as noted in Chapter 4, the composition of Congress is likely to lag behind the changes in the country. The Congress is not like a business that hires employees or a university that admits students. Its members are chosen by millions of citizens voting independently (and secretly) in hundreds of elections.

Electoral Prospects for Women

The United States ranks near the bottom among world democracies in the proportion of women in the lower chamber of its national legislature. Indeed, politics is the major arena in which American women trail women in other countries. In terms of female membership, the U.S. House ranks above France and about the same as Belgium, Britain, and Australia, but trails other advanced democracies.[44]

Undoubtedly there are many reasons for the low proportion of women representatives in the United States, but gender prejudice does not seem to be among the major ones. Societal prejudice against women serving in public office is low and has been diminishing.[45] Probably, though, a legacy of gender discrimination continues to operate. Winning a congressional seat is usually the result of a series of successful efforts, beginning with local office or leadership in a community organization and working up the political career ladder. Along the way, the member-to-be of Congress learns the art of politics, makes valuable political allies, becomes acquainted with those who bankroll campaigns, and generally acquires the experiences, characteristics, and resources that constitute the "qualifications" that someday will make her a "credible" challenger. Women have only recently gained admission to the networks that move politicians upward to higher office; men have had a long head start. As the pool of women in state legislatures and other lower offices grows, their representation in Congress should follow.

The electoral system functioning in the United States probably contributes to the slow rate of progress. The countries with the highest proportions of women tend to have some version or another of proportional representation (PR). In such systems, party leaders submit lists of candidates who will be elected in proportion to the party's vote. Judging by the results, these lists have significant numbers of highly ranked women. Women appear less successful where they have to contend with powerful men for the same geographically defined seat.

Overall, the underrepresentation of women in Congress naturally will lessen as women's career patterns become more like those of men. Some feminist thinkers may reject this analysis, believing that women should strive to be elected as *women,* politicians with a "different voice," not because they have learned to play the electoral game in the same way men do. Because American women have a complex combination of identities, though, they are unlikely to vote as a bloc. The traditional pattern of political advancement is likely the best and fastest method available.

Electoral Prospects for Minorities

The prospects for further increasing minority representation in Congress appear to be less favorable than they are for women, especially the prospects for African Americans. The critical difference is that in ethnically diverse constituencies, **bloc voting**—in which nearly all members of an ethnic or racial group vote for the same candidate or party—often occurs. When voting is racially polarized, for example, a black candidate is unlikely to win unless African Americans are a majority of the electorate. In the 103rd Congress, the first Congress after the 1990s redistricting, 32 of the 39 black members came from districts in which African Americans were in the majority, and in 5 of the remaining 7 districts African Americans plus Latinos made up a majority. Similarly, 15 of the 17 Latino members of the 103rd Congress came from majority Latino districts; none came from districts with a white majority. The 108th Congress, elected after the 2000 census, was not much different: In the 108th, 30 of 36 African American members came from majority black districts, and all 17 Hispanic members came from majority Hispanic districts.

bloc voting
Voting in which nearly all members of an ethnic or racial group vote for the same candidate or party.

majority-minority district

District in which a minority group is the numerical majority of the population.

affirmative action redistricting

The process of drawing district lines to maximize the number of majority-minority districts.

Given the historical tendency toward racially polarized voting, efforts to increase minority representation in Congress have been made largely through the redistricting process. The 1982 amendments to the Voting Rights Act and subsequent court decisions required the creation of **majority-minority districts** wherever possible. In such districts, a racial or ethnic minority constitutes a numerical majority of the population so they are able to elect a member of their group if they wish. Given the lower turnout rates that prevail among minority groups, the general guideline often has been to create districts with at least a 65 percent minority population (a figure that political science research suggests is unnecessarily high).[46]

Efforts to maximize the number of majority-minority districts—sometimes called **affirmative action redistricting**—have generated considerable controversy. Some of the districts that have been created have unusual shapes, uniting areas of different cities connected only by a highway. Such districts have provoked charges that they violate the constitutional guarantee that people will be treated equally regardless of race. In 1993, the Supreme Court ruled in *Shaw v. Reno* that majority-minority districting had limits: A district created on no basis other than to include a majority of minorities might raise constitutional questions. Since then, the Court has declared redistricting plans in various states to be unconstitutional racial gerrymanders.

Even racial liberals do not always support majority-minority districting. While they value the increased presence of African American and Latino representatives, research suggests that increasing descriptive representation for minorities undercuts the electoral position of the Democratic Party in surrounding districts, which are left whiter than they otherwise would be.[47] Thus, increasing the number of minorities can hurt the party that minority voters tend to support—and therefore decrease the likelihood of legislation that advances minority interests. Recognizing the partisan implications, Republican leaders often favor packing voters into majority-minority districts while Democratic leaders often oppose it. During the post-1990 redistricting, in particular, the Republican Justice Department aggressively pushed the creation of minority districts.

Whatever your view of such trade-offs, there is an upper limit on the number of majority-minority districts that can possibly be created: Racial minorities by definition consist of *minorities* of people, and electoral mapmakers cannot cross state boundaries to concentrate them. Indeed, given the recent court decisions, the United States may already be near that limit. If the maximum number of majority-minority districts that can be created is little more than the number that currently exist, then the upper limit for minority representatives will be correspondingly low unless minorities can break through and win in districts where they are not numerically dominant. Thus, many people are encouraged when minority incumbents win in districts that have been redrawn so that they are no longer majority minority.[48]

Another potentially negative effect of affirmative action redistricting is less obvious: It may work to marginalize minority members of Congress, particularly black representatives. The homogeneity of African American views should not be overstated.[49] Nevertheless, blacks are overwhelmingly Democratic in their allegiance, more liberal in general, and far more supportive of federal social programs in specific.[50] Representatives of such a group are correspondingly liberal. Indeed, members of the Congressional Black Caucus (CBC) are among the most liberal members of Congress, as measured by

Members of the Congressional Black Caucus

Nearly all minority Representatives in Congress represent majority-minority districts.

• *What factors affect whether majority-minority districts make it more or less likely that legislation which advances minority interests will pass?*

numerous interest-group ratings. But liberal records compiled as U.S. representatives may prevent African Americans from being credible challengers in gubernatorial, senatorial, and ultimately presidential elections.[51] Extremely liberal candidates (as well as extremely conservative candidates) rarely win elections in a diverse constituency, regardless of race.

In sum, the subject of minority representation in Congress is a difficult one, and existing court-imposed methods of encouraging more minority representation are controversial and limited in their effect. Each person must decide whether the gains that accrue from ensuring some level of minority representation exceed the costs. Unfortunately, those costs are uncertain and, to a considerable extent, subjective. Thus, people of good faith may disagree.

Elections, Parties, and Group Representation

Some of the difficulty in increasing minority representation reflects the basic fact that the single-member, simple-plurality (SMSP) electoral system (see Chapter 8) is not designed to produce a descriptively representative legislative body. The SMSP system puts all minorities, racial and otherwise, at a disadvantage. If you receive fewer votes than the leading candidate—even if you get 49 percent of the vote—you win nothing. Republicans in Democratic districts and vice versa, liberals in conservative districts and vice versa, pro-lifers in pro-choice districts and vice versa—all are unrepresented when their side loses. In one sense, U.S. courts have been trying to coax a more proportional result, in terms of minority representation, from an electoral system not designed to be proportional. Not surprisingly, they have had only limited success. Recognizing these realities, some academic critics have raised questions about the electoral system itself. But academic proposals to change the typical American electoral system are unlikely to have much practical impact.

Continued on page 335

Can Serving Your Constituency Go Too Far?

Background

Members of the U.S. Congress are elected from 50 states and 435 congressional districts within those states. When senators and representatives talk about "my constituents" they are referring to the people who are eligible to vote for them. Naturally enough, members consider it their duty (not to mention a political imperative) to serve their constituents. But senators and representatives are members of the *United States Congress,* and presumably their duty includes not just serving the particular constituencies that elect them, but also serving the country as a whole. This dual responsibility gives rise to representational tensions.

If the national interest were simply the sum of the interests of individual states and districts, no tensions would arise. But often what is in the general interest harms particular interests. For example, every local industry and agricultural producer would like to be protected against foreign competition. But if Congress adopted a trade policy of universal protective tariffs and import quotas, the result would likely be foreign retaliation against American exports and even trade wars, which would lead to slower economic growth. Indeed, the U.S. Congress has done just that with the predictable negative consequences in the past.[1] Thus, most economists advocate a policy of free trade even though some domestic interests would be harmed.

One way to diminish negative impacts on individual states and localities and lessen political opposition to general legislation is to give *side-payments* to members whose districts or states are hurt by general legislation.[2] These special provisions, sometimes in completely unrelated legislation, help to offset the costs to particular interests or areas of the country. After all, if the country as a whole gains, the winners can give up some of their benefits to lessen the harm to the losers. Indeed, this practice is such a standard part of legislating that few commentators regard it as anything out of the ordinary. In the congressional battle over healthcare reform in 2009–2010, however, some members of Congress may have gone too far.

The Issue

After the House passed a healthcare reform bill in November, Senate Majority Leader, Harry Reid began the difficult process of constructing a 60 vote majority in the Senate—60 votes because that was the number necessary to cut off an anticipated Republican filibuster. Procuring the last few necessary commitments turned out to be a slow and demanding task.

Attempts to pick off a moderate Republican or two proved futile, and Reid eventually decided the only route to passage was to round up all 60 Democratic senators. But not all were in favor of the bill.[3]

Senator Mary Landrieu of Louisiana was one of the holdouts. So Reid offered her $100 million in additional federal spending for Louisiana to help offset the rise in Medicaid costs that the healthcare bill would impose. Landrieu took the deal, claimed that she had actually gotten $300 million for Louisiana, and stated, "I am proud to have asked for it. I am proud to have fought for it."[4] Various pundits, not to mention Republicans, quickly pronounced the deal "The Louisiana Purchase."

A bit later Reid was one vote shy and Ben Nelson of Nebraska was the last Democrat holdout. Reid finally got Nelson's vote with the "Cornhusker Kickback," a special provision that would have the federal government pick up Nebraska's share of the increase in Medicaid expenditures, *forever.* In other words, taxpayers in 49 other states would pay for Nelson's vote. In response, thirteen state attorneys general threatened to sue, arguing that the deal was a violation of the Equal Protection clause of the Constitution, among other things.[5]

What Do Americans Believe?

The Louisiana Purchase and Cornhusker Kickback were widely publicized and roundly criticized. Some commentators believed that the only problem was that the legislative process had been so public. The deals that had been cut were nothing out of the ordinary, just unusually out in the open. Others believed that a line had been crossed—that there is a difference between giving a state a new water project or a community organization a new government grant and exempting the residents of an entire state from a law that applies to everyone else in the country. The public reaction to the Senate deals was so negative—even in Nebraska—that Nelson asked that the provision be removed, which President Obama did later when he laid out his own healthcare plan. And many observers felt that the deals played at least some role in the negative reaction to the Democratic plan and the election of Scott Brown in Massachusetts (see the opening vignette) shortly afterwards. By the time President Obama stepped in, approval of Congress had sunk to about 15 percent and disapproval had risen to nearly 75 percent. After the 2008 elections, declining evaluations of Congressional Democrats were credited with the change since Congressional Republicans had already been poorly evaluated.

What Do You Believe?

1. Were the Louisiana Purchase and Cornhusker Kickback acceptable examples of democratic politics?

2. If yes, are there any lines that should not be crossed? Should members of Congress go to any length, including voting for legislation they think is bad for the country, if they are able to make people in their own districts and states better off by doing so?

3. If no, why? Where do you draw the line?

[1]E.E. Schattschneider argued that in the 1930s just such a process resulted in the Smoot-Hawley tariff, which some economists believe deepened and lengthened the Great Depression. See his *Politics, Pressures, and the Tariff* (Englewood Cliffs, NJ: Prentice-Hall, 1935).

[2]Diana Evans, *Greasing the Wheels: Using Pork Barrel Projects to Build Majority Coalitions in Congress* (New York: Cambridge University Press, 2004).
[3]For overviews of the process, see Josh Gerstein, "Pork Greased Reform's Passage," *Politico,* December 22, 2009. www.politico.com/news/stories/1209/30877.html (accessed February 23, 2010). J. Taylor Rushing, "Sen. Landrieu Defends 'Louisiana Purchase,' Says Jindal Asked for It," *The Hill,* February 4, 2010. http://thehill.com/homenews/senate/79823-sen-landrieu-hits-back-over-louisiana-purchase (accessed February 23, 2010).
[4]Jonathan Tilove, "Landrieu Yea Vote Moves Health Bill; but It Doesn't Foretell Her Final Decision," *The Times-Picayune.* http://landrieu.senate.gov/mediacenter/inthenews/11-22-2009-1.cfm# (accessed February 23, 2010).
[5]Fred Lucas, "States Warn Congress of Possible Lawsuit over Nebraska's Cornhusker Kickback," CNSNews.com. http://cnsnews.com/news/article/59268. (accessed February 23, 2010).

Continued from page 333

CHAPTER SUMMARY

11.1 Trace the development of the Congress as a professional legislature.

The Congress is the world's foremost example of a professional legislature—a body of elected officials whose full-time job is serving in Congress. The Constitution assigns each state two senators and apportions representatives to the states based on their populations.

11.2 Explain how congressional constituencies are determined by means of reapportionment and redistricting.

Reapportionment takes place after each census to reflect population changes. Once the number of representatives each state gets is known, state legislatures or commissions draw the boundaries of the districts.

11.3 Describe the congressional nomination process.

Candidates for the House generally are nominated in primaries.

11.4 Analyze factors contributing to the incumbency advantage in contemporary House elections.

Once elected, members of the House of Representatives are reelected at very high rates—more than 90 percent in all recent elections, including the Republican landslide of 1994. Upon close examination, this high level of incumbent success does not violate the framers' intention of an electorally sensitive House. On the contrary, because representatives are so electorally sensitive, they work very hard at serving their districts, try very hard to represent constituents' policy concerns, and in general attempt to eliminate any basis for a strong challenge against them. Contrary to the charges of many critics, electoral success does not lead members of the House to be lazy and unresponsive. Rather, members are reelected *because* they are so hardworking and responsive.

11.5 Determine why incumbency is less important in Senate elections than in House elections.

Senators, too, are hard-working and responsive (probably more responsive than the framers intended), although they do not enjoy the same electoral success as members of the House. On average, their constituencies—states—are more competitive than House districts; they face stronger challengers; and their ambitions and prominence make them the object of media coverage that they do not control and that exposes them to expectations and ambitions that carry risks as well as rewards.

11.6 Explain the increased influence of national forces in recent congressional elections.

During the mid-twentieth century, the impact of national forces on congressional elections reached a historical low point. Incumbents managed to distance themselves from national leaders, deemphasize potentially damaging issues, and emphasize their personal records. In recent elections, however, national forces have grown stronger, reflecting the greater distinctiveness of today's parties and the increased emphasis on national issues by parties and interest groups engaging in issue advocacy.

11.7 Assess the extent to which the gender, racial, and ethnic makeup of the Congress is representative and prospects for change.

The single-member, simple plurality electoral system provides strong incentives for representatives to be *responsive* to the wishes of majorities in their districts. But the system in no way ensures that the composition of Congress will be *descriptively representative* of the country's population. On the contrary, if people vote as ethnic or racial blocs, the system will not elect a proportional number of ethnic and racial minorities. The courts have encouraged redistricting

arrangements that would produce more proportional outcomes, but these efforts have met with limited success; they typically require the creation of majority-minority districts that are politically divisive. In the long run, such procedures might even work against minority representation by encouraging bloc voting and promoting the election of minority representatives who have limited experience or ability attracting white votes.

For women, the problems are different, and the most promising solution—though not one that many activists want to hear—is time: As women increasingly win lower offices, the pool of qualified women candidates will inevitably expand. As the pool expands, the proportion of women candidates for Congress will increase. Otherwise, the solutions available to increase minority representation are not available for women: They are not segregated from men, so districts dominated by female voters are not feasible to draw, and women do not vote cohesively for female candidates.

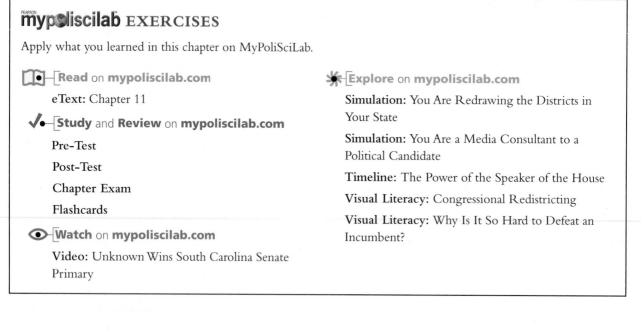

mypoliscilab EXERCISES

Apply what you learned in this chapter on MyPoliSciLab.

Read on mypoliscilab.com

eText: Chapter 11

Study and Review on mypoliscilab.com

Pre-Test

Post-Test

Chapter Exam

Flashcards

Watch on mypoliscilab.com

Video: Unknown Wins South Carolina Senate Primary

Explore on mypoliscilab.com

Simulation: You Are Redrawing the Districts in Your State

Simulation: You Are a Media Consultant to a Political Candidate

Timeline: The Power of the Speaker of the House

Visual Literacy: Congressional Redistricting

Visual Literacy: Why Is It So Hard to Defeat an Incumbent?

KEY TERMS

affirmative action redistricting, p. 332
bloc voting, p. 331
casework, p. 320
coattails, p. 326
constituency service, p. 320

filing deadline, p. 317
frank, p. 320
gerrymandering, p. 315
incumbency advantage, p. 318
majority-minority district, p. 332

open seat, p. 317
professional legislature, p. 313
reapportionment, p. 314
redistricting, p. 314
safe seat, p. 318

SUGGESTED READINGS

Of General Interest

Herrnson, Paul. *Congressional Elections: Campaigning at Home and in Washington.* 5th ed. Washington, DC: CQ Press, 2007. The most up-to-date study of congressional campaigns.

Jacobson, Gary. *The Politics of Congressional Elections.* 7th ed. New York: Longman, 2009. The definitive text on modern congressional elections.

Mayhew, David. *Congress—The Electoral Connection.* New Haven, CT: Yale University Press, 1974. Classic argument that much of congressional structure and behavior can be explained by the assumption that reelection is the most important goal of members.

Focused Studies

Ansolabehere, Stephen, and James M. Snyder, Jr. *The End of Inequality.* New York: Norton, 2008. Revisionist study of the "reapportionment revolution" of the 1960s and its consequences.

Brady, David. *Critical Elections and Congressional Policy Making.* Stanford, CA: Stanford University Press, 1988. Prize-winning account that ties together congressional elections, internal processes, and policy making.

Grofman, Bernard, and Lisa Handley, eds. *Redistricting in Comparative Perspective.* New York: Oxford, 2008. A highly informative collection of essays on redistricting practices in world democracies.

Tate, Katherine. *Black Faces in the Mirror.* Princeton, NJ: Princeton University Press, 2003. Comprehensive discussion of racial representation in Congress, including the value of majority-minority districts.

ON THE WEB

www.cookpolitical.com

One of the most famous handicappers of congressional races is Charlie Cook. To get all of his information, you have to subscribe, but a significant portion of his analysis is available free.

http://www.realclearpolitics.com/index.html

This website maintains comprehensive lists of congressional election polls.

www.vis.org

If you are looking for a more comprehensive discussion of election politics, Voter Information Services has a host of congressional report cards and records on voting.

12 The Congress and Its Work

CHAPTER OUTLINE

12.1 Describe the basic powers and structure of Congress.

12.2 Outline how the House of Representatives and Senate are organized by the committee system and the party leadership structure.

12.3 Trace the steps by which a bill becomes a law.

12.4 Evaluate how well Congress meets its responsibilities to the American public.

Homeland Security Pork

The 9/11 terrorist attacks showed that America was both poorly protected from acts of terrorism and poorly prepared to deal with the aftermath of such attacks. As a result, support for federal assistance to state and local law enforcement and emergency "first responders" soared. In the first year after 9/11, federal spending on such assistance increased tenfold to $20 billion, but many Americans felt that even that amount was grossly insufficient. In 2004 the Democratic presidential candidate John Kerry warned that the Bush administration was not doing enough to close the "preparedness gap," and a Council on Foreign Relations study issued under the title "Drastically Underfunded, Dangerously Unprepared" called for spending $100 billion more.[1] Congress responded enthusiastically to such recommendations for more spending. Since 9/11, homeland security spending has been the fastest growing federal budget function. In Fiscal Year 2009 total spending was over $50 billion.[2]

Many expert observers are highly critical of how taxpayer dollars have been spent, however, and doubt that the billions spent have purchased much security. We would expect spending to be heavily concentrated in large population centers because the potential loss of life and the amount of property damage are much greater there than in more sparsely inhabited areas. Similarly, we would expect that funds would be heavily concentrated on activities such as inspecting airline and shipping cargoes and protecting nuclear power plants and critical infrastructure such as bridges and tunnels. The reality is indeed different.

Rural Wyoming, for example, gets five times as many federal dollars per capita as do California and New York.[3] In fact, of the ten cities classified by the Department of Homeland Security (DHS) as most at-risk, only Washington, DC (where members of Congress spend much of their time), is among the top ten in federal assistance.

Moreover, wherever the money is spent—in rural or in urban areas—homeland security expenditures strike many observers as questionable, if not silly. Critics have pointed to scores of examples such as these:

- Santa Clara County, CA, purchased Segway scooters for its bomb squad.
- The Princeton, NJ, fire department purchased Nautilus equipment and a Bowflex machine.
- Columbus, OH, purchased Kevlar vests for its police dogs.
- Washington, DC, spent money on a computerized car-towing system and a summer jobs program.
- Newark, NJ, bought air-conditioned garbage trucks.
- Converse, TX, uses a newly purchased emergency disaster trailer to haul lawnmowers.

Additionally, federal funds went to other more worthwhile requests that were not obviously related to terrorism, such as forest fire claims in New Mexico and a federal child pornography tip line.[4] Even purchases more directly related to terrorist threats, such as chemical weapons suits for North Pole, Alaska (population about 1,600), seem to be rather low priority expenditures. What is going on?

After 9/11, Congress adopted a funding formula for homeland security spending that provided that each of the 50 states would get at least 0.75 percent of the funds. That guaranteed minimum largely explains why Wyoming, with 0.17 percent of the U.S. population receives 0.85 percent of federal grants—five times more money than would be expected from population alone. As we discussed in the preceding chapter, each state has two senators, and it is too much for us to expect politicians to stand idly by while money is being handed out to other states when their electoral survival depends on the voters in their states.

But the guarantees to each state still leave 60 percent of the funding available for allocation on the basis of risk assessment. As the preceding examples indicate, however, something other than rational analysis seems to be at work. Much of the explanation lies in the structure of Congress. When Congress created DHS, it rolled 22 separate federal agencies into the new department. These

agencies are under the jurisdiction of nearly 90 different congressional committees and subcommittees.[5] The members of these various panels authorize the programs administered by the agencies, appropriate the funds for the programs, and oversee their operation. These activities provide numerous pressure points for members to influence where the money goes, and members take full advantage of their opportunities. Even representatives whose districts contain no plausible terrorist target demand a share of homeland security funds.

Making the Connection

Homeland security is not an isolated example of a process gone awry. A look at agriculture policy, transportation policy, trade policy, and numerous other issue areas shows a similar picture. The electoral incentives of members of Congress lead them to organize their chambers and to use the congressional process to satisfy their electoral goals. But doing so often detracts from the capacity of the institution to act in the national interest. Although individual representatives and senators may care deeply about serving the nation, they can do nothing to address societal problems if they do not remain in office. The politics of lawmaking therefore always reflects electoral considerations. Members tend to perceive political issues in terms of the needs of their own constituencies. The deals that members make can distort the purpose of legislation or undercut efforts to reform a public policy. In this chapter, we will examine the workings of our most powerful, most complicated, most democratic, most electorally sensitive, but—ironically—our least respected political institution. Specifically, we will examine the party and committee organization that Congress has developed and the complex process of lawmaking. Then we will consider how the organization and operation of Congress explain the ambivalent feelings that Americans have about the institution, and why so many believe it needs reform.

12.1

Describe the basic powers and structure of Congress.

bicameral
Containing two chambers, as does a legislature such as the U.S. Congress.

Congress: The First Branch

Congress is called the first branch of government because the Constitution establishes the basic structure of Congress and sets out its powers in Article I. Table 12.1 lists the powers that the Constitution gives to Congress. Historically, the most important have been the "power of the purse"—the power to tax and spend—and the "power of the sword"—the power to declare war. Additionally, through the "necessary and proper" clause, Congress has asserted broad powers over many different aspects of American life.

Similar to many of the world's parliaments, Congress is **bicameral,** consisting of two chambers: an upper chamber called the Senate and a lower chamber called the House of Representatives. In other countries, the upper chamber of parliament typically has largely ceremonial duties or, at most, powers that are much weaker than those

TABLE 12.1
THE PRINCIPAL POWERS OF CONGRESS
To levy taxes
To borrow money
To regulate commerce
To decide requirements for citizenship
To make monetary policy
To establish a postal system
To establish federal courts below the Supreme Court
To declare war
To raise an army and a navy
To call up the state militias
To make all laws that shall be necessary and proper for executing the other powers of Congress

Source: U.S. Constitution, Article I.

of the lower chamber. The House and the Senate possess roughly equal powers, however, which can create a certain amount of interchamber rivalry. A Speaker of the House once called the Senate "a nice quiet place where good Representatives go when they die."[6] The Senate has a quick response to such jibes: In all of American history, only one senator (Henry Clay) has given up a Senate seat to run for the House, and that was in 1811.

The legislative branch includes tens of thousands of people in addition to the 435 members of the House and 100 members of the Senate. The members have personal staffs that total more than 7,000 in the House and 4,000 in the Senate, and each chamber hires about a thousand staff personnel to support its committees. Many of these staffers are clerical workers; others are policy experts who play an important role in the shaping of legislation, especially long time staff who speak for important members. Additional staff employees support the party leaders who coordinate the flow of bills through the legislative process. All in all, about 14,000 people are employed as congressional staff.

In addition to staff employed by members and committees, thousands of other people work in various support agencies of Congress. The General Accounting Office (GAO), the watchdog agency of Congress that oversees the operation of the executive branch, employs more than 3,000 people. A smaller number of people work for the Congressional Budget Office (CBO). This agency provides Congress with expert economic projections and budgetary information. In total, a broad definition of the legislative branch of government includes more than 20,000 people.

The Organization of Congress

Similar to other large decision-making bodies, the House and Senate have evolved an extensive division of labor—the committee system—as well as a means of organizing large numbers of people to make decisions—the party leadership structure. The Constitution says nothing about either committees or parties; they have developed to meet the needs of elected officials.[7] Both are more important in the House than in the Senate.

12.2

Outline how the House of Representatives and Senate are organized by the committee system and the party leadership structure.

Because the House is much larger, it needs to be better organized. It operates in more of a follow-the-rules fashion than the Senate, which is small enough to operate by informal coordination and negotiation.[8]

The Congressional Parties

Although parties do not dominate Congress as much as they dominate the parliaments of other democracies, they are still the principal organizing force in Congress. (See the *International Comparison*.)

INTERNATIONAL COMPARISON

Congress in a Presidential System

Most world democracies are "parliamentary" in form. Voters rarely choose the chief executive directly under such a system. Instead, voters choose representatives to the national assembly, who in turn choose ministers to govern the nation. Having executives elected by the legislative branch might seem to give special influence to legislators, but in fact it makes them more dependent. They cannot afford to defect from the governing party coalition because doing so might cause the government to fall, resulting in new elections—which they might lose. Members of a parliament therefore usually do little more than rubber-stamp the executive's policy program. Indeed, in parliamentary systems, elected assemblies generally are not called legislatures, because they do little law making. They are called parliaments, because they do a lot of talking.

The United States is one of the exceptions, a democracy with a "presidential" form of government—a government in which the chief executive is elected directly by the people. Ironically, legislators can be more independent and therefore more influential in a presidential system. Their electoral fates are not tied as closely to the performance of the chief executive; unhappy voters can withdraw their support from a president without disrupting the membership of the legislative branch.

To highlight the legislative independence allowed by a presidential system of government, consider the $286 billion Farm Bill passed by the Democratic Congress in 2008 over President Bush's veto. First, divided government (Chapter 8) cannot exist in a parliamentary system. The chief executive has a majority of his or her party or coalition in the parliament or else he or she would not be the chief executive. But, second, the Republican minority in Congress has more than enough seats in both the House and the Senate to sustain the president's veto. However, election year pressures fractured the party. Minority Leader John Boehner of Ohio voted against the bill but did not pressure his troops to follow him. Instead he advised them to "vote their districts." Minority Whip Roy

Blunt of Missouri supported the bill and the Conference Chairman Adam Putnam actively worked for it. In the Senate Minority Leader Mitch McConnell of Kentucky supported the bill. Republicans in the House voted 100-91 for the bill and then by a similar margin voted to override the president's veto. Almost three-quarters of the Republican senators voted for the bill and then voted to override the veto.

These actions of congressional Republicans would be unthinkable in a parliamentary system such as Britain's. Once the prime minister and cabinet decide on an important party policy, they expect virtually unanimous support from the rank and file in Parliament. High-ranking party members who oppose a key policy would either resign or be removed from their posts. In 2009, for example, James Purnell, a British cabinet minister and possible future Prime Minister, resigned rather than support the current prime minister's domestic spending plans.

As we noted, a major reason why the executive can impose such discipline is that, in most parliamentary systems, elections do not occur at fixed time intervals. Rather, new parliamentary elections often follow the legislative failure of a government's program, either because the opposition calls for a "vote of no confidence" or because the government itself chooses to dissolve Parliament and seek additional support from the nation's voters. Even if no new elections are called, the party's ministers may choose to step down if they cannot command sufficient legislative support. These various possibilities are all so dire to an executive's political allies that extreme party unity becomes the norm.

- *Do you think that members of Congress, rather than voters, should choose the president, as is common in many other democracies, such as Great Britain?*

- *Do you think that the president should have the constitutional power to order new elections if Congress doesn't do what he or she wants, as prime ministers can in many parliamentary systems?*

Speaker of the House   The Constitution stipulates that the House shall elect a **Speaker** to be its presiding officer. In practice, members vote the party line in leadership elections, so the Speaker is always the leader of the majority party. Despite being a partisan leader, the Speaker ordinarily does not vote on legislation. Only in close contests involving matters vital to the party does the Speaker vote. In 2009, for example, Speaker Nancy Pelosi participated in only 5 percent of the recorded votes.[9] Until the late nineteenth century, the Speaker was the only formal party leader in the House. Indeed, from the end of Reconstruction to the turn of the twentieth century, the Speaker often rivaled the president as the most powerful public official in the United States. Powerful Speakers awarded the chairmanships of important committees to their close allies, made all committee assignments, and punished disloyal members by removing them from committees on which they had previously served.[10] Joseph "Boss" Cannon was the last of the powerful nineteenth-century Speakers. In 1910, a coalition of Democrats and Republicans in the House revolted against "Boss" Cannon, taking away the Speaker's power to make committee assignments and removing him from the Rules Committee.

In the months immediately following the 1994 elections, which brought the Republican Party to power in the House after 40 years in the minority, Speaker Newt Gingrich moved boldly and decisively in a manner reminiscent of late-nineteenth-century Speakers. He elevated a few representatives to committee chairmanships even though other members had seniority over them, and in concert with other leaders he imposed more discipline on the House than it had seen since the days of Boss Cannon. When the Democrats regained control in 2006 Speaker Pelosi continued the tradition of strong leadership, reestablished by the Republicans.

Party Leadership: House   The Speaker's chief lieutenant is the **majority leader.** Chosen by the majority party caucus, majority leaders are responsible for the day-to-day work necessary to build political coalitions and enact laws: scheduling legislation, coordinating committee activity, and negotiating with the president, the Senate, and the minority party. Unlike the Speaker, the majority leader votes on legislation. The minority party caucus elects a **minority leader** who coordinates the minority's attempts to improve or defeat majority legislation. Professor Barbara Sinclair stresses that one important job of the leaders is to maintain "peace in the family." Different points of view flourish within parties, and it falls to the leadership to prevent minor spats and quarrels from developing into destructive feuds.[11]

The majority and minority leaders are assisted by **whips,** who link the leadership to the party's rank-and-file. The whips communicate leadership positions and strategies to the troops, count votes, and report rank-and-file opinions back to the leadership. The whip offices are rather large, with deputy, assistant, regional, and zone whips (upward of 25 in the Democratic Party, about 20 in the Republican Party). Although some whips, like former Republican whip Tom DeLay, have a reputation for threats and coercion, persuasion and appeals to party loyalty probably are more important day-to-day tools of the whips.

Many party members participate in the leadership via the whip organizations. Others participate via membership in party committees such as the Democratic Steering

Speaker
The presiding officer of the House of Representatives; normally, the Speaker is the leader of the majority party.

New Leadership
Republican House leaders Eric Cantor and John Boehner hold a press conference the day after the 2010 elections.
• *Why do House leaders have more formal authority than Senate leaders?*

majority leader
Title used for the Speaker's chief lieutenant in the House and for the most important officer in the Senate. Chosen by the majority party membership, majority leaders are responsible for the day-to-day work necessary to build political coalitions and enact laws.

minority leader
Leader of the minority party who coordinates the minority's attempts to improve or defeat majority legislation.

whips
Members of Congress who serve as informational channels linking the leadership and the rank and file, communicating the leadership's views and intentions to the members and vice versa.

and Policy Committee, the Republican Policy Committee, and the Republican Steering Committee. These party committees provide a forum for discussing issues and developing a party program. Occasionally they endorse legislation. When the Democrats are in the majority, the Speaker chairs the Democratic Steering and Policy Committee and appoints many of its members. Thus, this committee serves as an important lever for influencing the behavior of members in the various committees to which they are assigned. In contrast, the Republicans elect a chair of their Policy Committee and also a chair of their Steering Committee, which makes committee assignments.

Finally, Democratic members belong to their **party caucus** and Republican members belong to their **party conference**—meetings of the full party membership. These groups elect the party leadership and approve the slates of committees nominated by the Steering Committees. Sometimes they debate policies and attempt to develop party positions on policies. During President Woodrow Wilson's administration, they even adopted resolutions requiring party members to support particular policy proposals, a power that lies dormant today.

Party Leadership: Senate   Given that the Senate consists of two members from each state—an even number—the Constitution provides for a tie-breaking mechanism by giving vice presidents the authority to preside over the Senate and to cast a tie-breaking vote *when necessary*. The Constitution also provides for a **president pro tempore,** who serves as the Senate's presiding officer in the vice president's absence (which is nearly all the time). This office is mainly honorific and ordinarily goes to the most senior member of the majority party. The Senate's majority and minority leaders are the true leadership of the chamber.

Although the Senate leadership also has a structure of whips and expert staffs to assist them, Senate leaders are not as strong as those in the House. They spend much of their time negotiating compromises. Indeed, one of the main jobs of Senate leaders is to hammer out **unanimous-consent agreements** that set forth the terms and conditions according to which the Senate will consider a bill; these are individually negotiated by the leadership for each bill and are acceptable to all senators with any interest in a given proposal. These agreements specify the terms of debate—the amendments that will be in order, how long they will be debated, when votes will be taken, and so forth.[12] Such agreements are necessary because—unbelievable as it may sound—any senator can delay consideration of a bill or resolution.

The Senate has a tradition of unlimited debate: the **filibuster,** a delaying tactic by which one or more senators refuse to allow a bill or resolution to be considered, either by speaking indefinitely or by offering dilatory motions and amendments. The only way to silence a filibuster is for the Senate to adopt a **cloture** motion ending debate, which requires the support of 60 senators. The existence of the filibuster means that a simple majority of senators is not a winning coalition. A minority of 41 can prevent the Senate from acting on a measure, which is why Massachusetts Republican Scott Brown signed his name with a "41" after it during his campaign (Chapter 11). Unanimous-consent agreements represent one means of avoiding time-consuming filibusters; senators agree in advance to the terms under which they will consider legislation. These agreements require true unanimity, however, so a single senator may place a hold on debate or legislation by refusing to sign on, as Tennessee Republican Senator Jim Bunning did with a jobs bill in 2010. These practices allow minorities to obstruct legislation more easily in the Senate than in the House.

party caucus
All Democratic members of the House or Senate. Members in caucus elect the party leaders, ratify the choice of committee leaders, and debate party positions on issues.

party conference
What Republicans call their party caucus.

president pro tempore
The president of the Senate, who presides in the absence of the vice president.

unanimous-consent agreement
An agreement that sets forth the terms and conditions according to which the Senate will consider a bill; these agreements are individually negotiated by the leadership for each bill.

filibuster
Delaying tactic by which one or more senators refuse to allow a bill or resolution to be considered, either by speaking indefinitely or by offering dilatory motions and amendments.

cloture
Motion to end debate in the Senate; requires 60 votes to pass.

Ups and Downs of the Congressional Parties   In practice, it is difficult to measure party influence precisely because it often coincides with constituency sentiments and members' own views.[13] The power of congressional leadership clearly has varied over time, though, and appears to be greater now than it was for more than half a century after the revolt against "Boss" Cannon in 1910.

One likely reason for the growth of party power in recent decades is that the congressional parties have become more polarized. The members of each party are more similar than they used to be, and, collectively, they are more distinct from the other party than they used to be.[14] When party members are in agreement, leaders are likely to hold views consistent with those of the overall membership and members are willing to defer to their leaders. When party members are more diverse in their views, however, as in the mid-twentieth century, they are reluctant to give power to party leaders—who may act in ways objectionable, or even politically dangerous, to many of the rank-and-file.[15] As a result, institutional changes usually have followed changes in party unity (see Figure 12.1). The parties of the late nineteenth century represented distinct social groups, so Republican leaders in Congress were given great power; but they lost influence when the party divided into progressive and regular wings. When Democrats swept into power during the Great Depression, they included both northern liberals and southern conservatives, so leaders remained relatively weak.[16] The social changes of the 1960s and 1970s, though, produced more polarized parties.[17] As a result, members today are more willing to follow strong leaders committed to the party's platform rather than do anything that might help the opposition. President Obama promised to be more bipartisan during his campaign, but in today's Congress bipartisanship has become very difficult to achieve.

Of course, just because a member of Congress usually agrees with the leadership does not mean that leaders will always do what the member wants. Being a leader

FIGURE 12.1

MORE UNIFIED CONGRESSIONAL PARTIES

The graph shows the percentage of all recorded votes on which a majority of voting Democrats opposed a majority of voting Republicans. Numbers for each year have been averaged over each Congress.

• *Why did the parties become so much more unified during the past generation?*

• *Why was this unity not the case in the 1970s?*

Sources: Norman Ornstein, Thomas Mann, and Michael Malbin, *Vital Statistics on Congress,* 2001–2002 (Washington, DC: CQ Press, 2002), p. 172; *CQ Weekly* vote studies, various years.

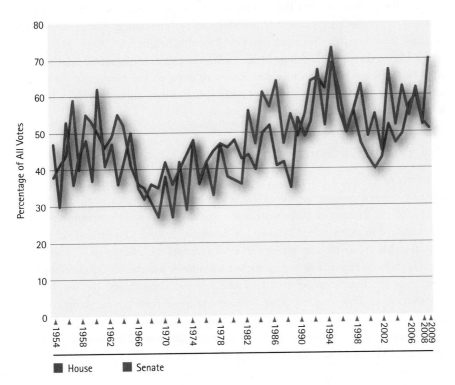

House   Senate

means making tough choices. Presumably some of those choices will be objectionable to some of the party membership. Why would a member of Congress voluntarily pass decision-making authority over to leaders rather than retain the right to "second guess" any decision?

Part of the answer is that an effective congressional party contributes to members' electoral prospects. Uninformed voters often choose among candidates on the basis of party image and performance. Members of Congress want to be part of an effective team, not part of a team that voters consider too divided to accomplish anything. As a result, they are willing to tolerate constraints imposed by their leadership—indeed, to pass rules formalizing and strengthening such limits—because they do not want to undermine the party's effectiveness.[18] The pressure for conformity can be especially strong when the president shares the member's party label. A successful president can help members running for reelection, as President Bush did in 2002. Conversely, as the Republicans found in 2006 and 2008, an unsuccessful president can hurt the party. Members of the president's party thus have an incentive to work together to help him succeed.

Another part of the answer is that members who opposed some of the party's positions may be compensated in other ways. The congressional parties are increasingly active in campaign funding. The House and Senate campaign committees are controlled by the leadership and most members of the leadership have established their own PACs.[19] Thus, members who cast tough votes with the party may receive additional campaign help. In addition, a recent study finds that moderate party members who go along with the core positions of their parties are compensated with greater pork barrel spending for their districts.[20]

Finally, members of Congress willingly accept some party discipline because they see it as necessary for attaining important policy goals. Every representative could imagine the perfect bill, one that would both please the voters back home and bring national policy into perfect alignment with his or her preferences. But could the representative then turn that dream bill into law? Probably not, because every other member would like to do the same thing. Sticking with the party's leaders increases the odds of real change. Representatives may not like every detail of legislation that party leaders negotiate, but they can put together something better than current law—and powerful leaders actually have the ability to get it passed.

The Committee System

Members of Congress introduce thousands of bills and resolutions every year. Since 1990, for example, on average about 9,000 bills have been introduced in each two-year session of the House of Representatives. Rather than expect everyone to master the details of so many bills, Congress has developed a screening process. Members of each chamber are divided up into different committees specializing in particular policy areas. Each bill is referred to one or more committees, and the whole chamber usually votes only on legislation approved by the relevant committees. (In the House of Representatives, floor majorities can remove a proposal from a recalcitrant committee via a discharge petition, but this process requires 218 signatures and is seldom used.) Of the thousands of bills introduced each year, on average about 5 percent eventually pass and most of the failed bills die at the committee stage.

Standing committees have fixed memberships and jurisdictions, and they continue from one Congress to another. The Appropriations, Commerce, and Foreign Relations Committees are examples. **Select committees,** by contrast, are temporary committees created to deal with specific issues. Both houses of Congress had standing committee systems in place by 1825.[21] The number of committees tends to expand until, at some point, the system is reorganized when majorities come to believe it has grown unwieldy and out of alignment with contemporary problems. The Legislative Reorganization Act of 1946 gave the committee system the shape it largely retains today, more than half a century later. In the 111th Congress (2009–2010), there were 20 standing committees in the House and 16 in the Senate (see Table 12.2). These "full" committees are subdivided into about 170 subcommittees. There also are four "joint" committees, with membership from both houses, and a small number of select committees on special topics such as national intelligence.

House Committees   House committees fall into three levels of importance. The top committees are Rules, Appropriations, Ways and Means, and Commerce. The Rules Committee is the right arm of the Speaker. It controls the flow of legislation to the floor and the conditions of debate. Appropriations and Ways and Means deal with spending and taxing, broad powers that enable them to affect nearly everything government does. Commerce has extensive jurisdiction over a wide variety of policy areas. A member who serves on one of these committees ordinarily is allowed no other assignment, except that he or she is eligible to serve on the Budget Committee. Committees at the second level of importance deal with nationally significant policy areas: armed services, civil rights, agriculture, and so forth. A member ordinarily serves only on one such major policy committee and on a third-level committee of lesser importance. These less important committees include "housekeeping" committees, such as Government Reform and Oversight, and committees with narrow policy jurisdictions, such as Veterans' Affairs. The Budget Committee has a special status. Members can serve for only four years in any ten-year period, and its membership is drawn from other committees and from the leadership.

Senate Committees   The Senate committee system is simpler than that of the House; it has just major and minor committees. Similar to their House equivalents, Appropriations and Finance are major committees, but the Senate Rules Committee is a minor committee with nothing like the power of its House counterpart (the Senate leadership itself handles the tasks performed by the House Rules Committee). Budget is also a major committee, as is Foreign Relations, reflecting the constitutional responsibilities of the chamber in that area (advise and consent to treaties, confirm ambassadors).

Committee power in the Senate is widely distributed: Chairs of major committees cannot chair any other committee or subcommittee, and chairs of minor committees can chair only one other panel. Each senator can serve on one minor and two major committees, and every senator gets to serve on one of the four major committees. On average, senators sit on more committees than do representatives—in part, a reflection of the simple fact that the Senate has nearly as many committees as the House with less than one-fourth as many members to staff them. But, in addition, senators represent entire states, which are typically more diverse than congressional districts; thus, they

standing committee
Committee with fixed membership and jurisdiction, continuing from Congress to Congress.

select committee
Temporary committee created to deal with a specific issue or problem.

TABLE 12.2

STANDING COMMITTEES OF THE 111TH CONGRESS

House			Senate		
Committee	Size (Party Ratio)	Number of Subcommittees	Committee	Size (Party Ratio)	Number of Subcommittees
Committee on Agriculture	46 (28D/18R)	6	Agriculture, Nutrition, and Forestry	17 (12D/9R)	5
Committee on Appropriations	60 (37D/23R)	12	Appropriations	30 (18D/12R)	12
Committee on Armed Services	62 (37D/25R)	7	Armed Services	28 (16D/12R)	6
Committee on the Budget	39 (24D/15R)	0	Banking, Housing, and Urban Affairs	23 (13D/10R)	5
Committee on Education and Labor	49 (30D/19R)	5	Budget	23 (13D/10R)	0
Committee on Energy and Commerce	59 (36D/23R)	5	Commerce, Science, and Transportation	25 (D14/11R)	7
Committee on Financial Services	71 (42D/29R)	6	Energy and Natural Resources	23 (13D/10R)	4
Committee on Foreign Affairs	47 (28D/19R)	7	Environment and Public Works	19 (12D/7R)	7
Committee on Homeland Security	34 (21D/13R)	6	Finance	23 (13D/10R)	5
Committee on House Administration	9 (6D/3R)	2	Foreign Relations	19 (11D/8R)	7
Committee on the Judiciary	40 (24D/16R)	5	Health, Education, Labor, and Pensions	23 (13D/10R)	3
Committee on Natural Resources	49 (29D/20R)	4	Homeland Security and Governmental Affairs	17 (10D/7R)	6
Committee on Oversight and Government Reform	41 (25D/16R)	5	Judiciary	19 (12D/7R)	7
Committee on Rules	13 (9D/4R)	2	Rules and Administration	19 (11D/8R)	0
Committee on Science and Technology	44 (27D/17R)	5	Small Business and Entrepreneurship	19 (11D/8R)	0
Committee on Small Business	29 (17D/12R)	5	Veterans' Affairs	16 (9D/I1/R5)	0
Committee on Standards of Official Conduct	10 (5D/5R)	0			
Committee on Transportation and Infrastructure	75 (45D/30R)	6			
Committee on Veterans' Affairs	29 (18D/11R)	4			
Committee on Ways and Means	41 (26D/15R)	6			
Select Committee on Intelligence	22 (13D/9R)	4			

Source: Office of the Clerk—U.S. Capitol.

cannot afford to limit their attention to one or two subjects, as many representatives can. Holding more committee assignments creates conflicting loyalties and makes it difficult for senators to specialize in a few subjects, as many House members do. As a result, the legislative lives of senators are not so closely tied to a particular committee as are the lives of representatives.[22]

How Committees Are Formed   The committee system is formally under the control of the majority party in the chamber. Party committees nominate members for assignment and party caucuses approve those assignments. As a result, each committee has a ratio of majority to minority members at least as favorable to the majority as is the overall division of the chamber. The more important committees are stacked in favor of the majority. In the 111th Congress, for example, the Democrats had a 9 to 4 advantage over the Republicans on the House Rules Committee, a ratio far greater than their 257 to 178 edge in the chamber as a whole. In contrast, the party ratio on the less important Small Business Committee was 17 to 12.

In practice, committees sometimes show considerable independence. Part of the reason is the traditional use of **seniority** to choose committee chairs. Under seniority, the majority-party member with the longest continuous service on the committee becomes the chair. Often called a "norm" because the use of seniority never was a formal rule, seniority became the mode of selecting Senate committee chairs in the 1880s and House chairs after the 1910 revolt, and was closely followed until 1995. The practice of seniority includes the right to continued reappointment to a committee. Thus, once a member initially joins a committee, he or she automatically rises on its seniority ladder. Members who are failing physically or mentally are sometimes moved aside and, on occasion, the leadership or caucus rejects a nomination for chair, but the system gives committee chairs specifically, and committee members in general, a degree of independence or autonomy.

The practice of seniority began to weaken in the 1970s when Democrats removed some senior chairs who were out of step with the caucus (including one who had addressed newly elected members as "boys and girls"). After the 1994 elections gave Republicans control of Congress for the first time in 40 years, Speaker Gingrich passed up the most senior committee member when he named the Republican chairs of Appropriations, Commerce, and Judiciary.[23] The Republican conference then adopted a three-term limit on committee chairs, which constituted a major revision of the seniority system. Senate Republicans adopted an analogous rule in 1996. When the Democrats regained control of Congress in the 2006 elections, they chose to keep the new rules rather than go back to the pre-1994 rules.

Purpose of Committees   Why does the standing committee system exist at all? Members of Congress are elected as equals. Why would a large majority give to a small minority exceptional influence in a policy area—the power to decide whether legislation should be considered, the power to shape the legislation if it is considered, and the power to review its implementation? Why not consider everything on the chamber floor (the so-called *Committee of the Whole*), where all members participate on an equal basis?

This distributive theory of committees holds that members defer to their colleagues on policies they care little about in exchange for greater influence on issues that deeply matter to them.[24] For example, members from urban districts seek membership on committees that deal with banking, housing, or labor, whereas members from rural districts have little interest in such issues and opt instead for committees that deal with agriculture and natural resources. Members of committees that directly distribute government benefits are in a position to please the voters back home. Indeed, party leaders often place their electorally vulnerable members on committees such as these so that the vulnerable members can deliver for their districts. Studies have documented how districts and states whose members serve on particular committees receive a disproportionate share of the projects and grants that fall within the jurisdictions of those committees.[25]

seniority
Practice by which the majority-party member with the longest continuous service on a committee becomes the chair.

Although it might seem right to give greater influence to members with greater interest, such a system can result in spending bills larded with expensive projects.

An alternative interpretation is that committees primarily serve a knowledge function.[26] Members frequently are uncertain about the outcomes that policies will produce, and bad policies can be electorally costly. Hence, they want some members to become experts in each subject area and share their knowledge with the broader membership. One way to encourage their hard work is to give committees disproportionate influence in shaping legislation, providing that they do their job conscientiously and not abuse their position. Committee members can exploit their position to gain a bit extra for their districts, but only to the extent that they specialize and give the chamber useful, reliable information.

Still another theory holds that committees are the tools of the congressional parties.[27] Proponents of this partisan theory of committees argue that the party is so concerned with controlling public policy that it stacks committees with loyal members and shapes the jurisdictions of committees so that only reliable committees write and revise important legislation. Proponents of the partisan theory point out that the average ratio of majority to minority party members typically favors the majority party—sometimes by a lot.[28] And committee jurisdictions are influenced by party leaders. But there are exceptions to these patterns, of course. Some committees behave in a more bipartisan fashion and the process of defining committee jurisdictions is extremely complicated, not clearly under the direct control of the leadership.[29]

Studies of committees are not conclusive about which of these three perspectives—distributive, informational, or partisan—is the best explanation for the committee system. Committees likely promote all three of these purposes as members try to balance their competing needs: to serve their local constituencies, to gain reliable information about public policy, and to accomplish partisan goals. It may also be that the type of committee matters. For instance, committees that hand out money for public projects or fund important programs seem to behave in distributive fashion. Other committees that deal with complex public policies such as environmental or telecommunications regulation may serve an informational function. Finally, some committees—such as the Rules Committee that controls the agenda and floor debate—seem dominated by the party leadership. The committee system probably reflects a mixture of the three theoretical purposes for committees, a mixture that varies over time and across committees.

Caucuses

caucus
A voluntary group within Congress, formed by members to pursue shared interests; a caucus can cross party, committee, and even chamber lines.

In recent years, voluntary groupings of members with shared interests have become increasingly common in the House of Representatives, adding a third level of congressional organization. Usually called **caucuses,** these groupings can cross party, committee, and even chamber lines. There were more than 250 such groups in the 111th House, ranging from important long-standing ones such as the Congressional Black Caucus and the Northeast-Midwest Congressional Coalition, to newer more fanciful ones such as the Small Brewers Caucus, the Caucus on Unmanned Aerial Vehicles, and the Congressional Soccer Caucus.[30]

Caucuses are extremely varied in their concerns, their activities, and their effects.[31] They can support the efforts of party or committee leaders, but they also can pressure party or committee leaders on particular issues. Similarly, they can be a vehicle for cooperation across chambers, across parties, or across committees—or they can obstruct the proposals of chambers, parties, or committees because of some special interest they feel is being slighted or dealt with unfairly (such as wine or potatoes). Some caucuses are lavishly financed by outside interests whereas others subsist with modest contributions of office space, money, and staff from their members.

There are few studies of caucuses and their activities as yet, but some observers regard them as increasingly important actors in the congressional process, another example of how congressional organization evolves to meet the needs of members in a changing political world.[32]

How a Bill Becomes a Law

12.3

Trace the steps by which a bill becomes a law.

Congress makes the laws that govern the United States. In addition to the specific legislative powers set out in Article I, the "necessary and proper" clause authorizes Congress "to make all laws which shall be necessary and proper for carrying into execution the foregoing powers, and all other powers vested by this Constitution. . . ." How do two parties in two chambers organized into over 200 committees and subcommittees get together and pass laws? We will describe the legislative process in idealized form, but no flowchart can accurately describe the process of getting a major bill through Congress today. Congressional scholar Barbara Sinclair concludes that so little important legislation goes through the "orthodox" process now that it is fair to say that "unorthodox" lawmaking has become the norm.[33] In particular, the House leadership may intervene, occasionally bypassing committees altogether, but more often negotiating compromises outside committee and directing committees to shape the legislation in particular ways (see the *Election Connection* feature on page 352).

As a first step, a bill or resolution is introduced by a congressional **sponsor** and one or more co-sponsors. The House Speaker or Senate presiding officer, advised by the chamber's parliamentarian (an expert on rules and procedures), refers the proposal to an appropriate committee. In some cases, sponsors are not serious but are acting only to please some constituency or interest group. If they *are* serious, they may draft their bill in such a way as to increase its chances of being referred to a friendly committee—often theirs. Sometimes the leadership decides on a **multiple referral,** sending the bill simultaneously to more than one committee or dividing it among several committees for consideration. Complex legislation and overlapping committee jurisdictions increase the likelihood of multiple referrals.

Once the bill goes to a committee, the chair gives it to an appropriate subcommittee. Here the real work begins. If the subcommittee takes the bill seriously, the staff schedules hearings at which witnesses speak in favor of or in opposition to the bill. Witnesses can be other members of Congress, members of the executive branch, representatives of relevant interest groups, or ordinary citizens. Sometimes hearings are genuine attempts to gather information. More often, hearings are carefully choreographed: The subcommittee staff stacks the witness list in favor of the subcommittee chair's position.[34]

After hearings, the subcommittee begins **markup** of the bill—revising it, adding and deleting sections, and (assuming the bill enjoys majority support) preparing it for report to the full committee. The full committee may repeat the process, holding its own hearings

sponsor
Representative or senator who introduces a bill or resolution.

multiple referrals
Process occurring when party leaders give more than one committee responsibility for considering a bill.

markup
Process in which a committee or subcommittee considers and revises a bill that has been introduced.

ELECTION CONNECTION

Unorthodox Lawmaking: The Congressional Politics of Healthcare Reform

High school civics textbooks often contain a chart entitled "How a Bill Becomes a Law" depicting the steps in the legislative process. But as Professor Barbara Sinclair has pointed out, in the contemporary Congress, the process of legislating often does not follow this "regular order." Especially with important and controversial legislation, Congress often resorts to "unorthodox" procedures. Congressional consideration of healthcare reform in 2009–2010 is a current example.

The House bill was formally introduced on July 14, 2009, by the chairs of the Energy and Commerce, Education and Labor, and Ways and Means Committees. The bill was multiply referred, not only to their three committees, but also to the Budget and Oversight Committees. The committees adopted somewhat differing versions that then went to the Rules Committee, where the Democratic leadership took the lead in merging the three bills.

Pro-life Democrats forced Speaker Pelosi to allow a vote on the Stupak amendment, which prohibited using federal funds "to pay for any abortion or to cover the costs of any health plan that includes coverage of abortion" except in the extreme cases of rape, incest, or danger to the mother's life. Pro-life Democrats joined Republicans to adopt the amendment by a vote of 240-194 over the bitter opposition of pro-choice Democrats. The amended bill then passed by a vote of 220–215 on December 7, with only one Republican voting yea.

Meanwhile in the Senate, the Health, Education, Labor and Pensions Committee had reported a bill on July 15, but the Finance Committee labored on for additional months attempting to craft a more bipartisan proposal or at least to satisfy moderate Democrats so that a filibuster could be prevented. On October 13 the committee adopted its bill

with the support of one Republican, Olympia Snowe of Maine. After much wheeling and dealing (see the *Election Voices!* feature in Chapter 11) the Senate passed the bill 60–39 on a solid party-line vote. Majority Leader Reid then began the difficult process of reconciling the House and Senate versions. But on January 19, 2010, a special election in Massachusetts drastically altered the legislative landscape (see the opening vignette in Chapter 11).

With 41 Republicans in the Senate, the Democrats no longer had the votes to shut off a filibuster, so Reid could not allow another floor vote on healthcare reform. Thus, the traditional route of a conference committee to synthesize the House and Senate bills was closed (because the product of the committee must be voted on by both chambers). The only hope for passage appeared to be for the House to accept the more moderate Senate bill (although it had more liberal language on abortion), then for both chambers to pass a package of fixes (mostly House amendments) under a special budget procedure, reconciliation, that required only a majority vote in the Senate. But because the House would have to accept the Senate bill first, many House Democrats did not trust that the Senate would keep their end of the bargain.

While these confusing maneuverings went on for months, the bill steadily lost support among the public. But the Administration decided that losing was unacceptable. President Obama, Speaker Pelosi, Majority Leader Reid, and other Democratic leaders negotiated, threatened, promised and pleaded, and finally the House passed the Senate version of Health Care Reform by a vote of 219-212, with every House Republican voting nay. Then the Senate passed the fixes package 56-43 and the House passed it 220-207. Any attempt to diagram this instance of unorthodox lawmaking would be extremely messy, with myriad loops and dead ends.

and conducting its own markup, or it may largely accept the work of the subcommittee.[35] If a committee majority supports the bill after committee markup, the bill is nearly ready to be reported to the floor—but not quite.

Let's first consider what happens in the House. Bills that are not controversial, either because they are trivial or they have extremely narrow impact, can be called up at specified times and passed unanimously with little debate. Somewhat more important bills are considered under a fast-track procedure called **suspension of the rules.** If a two-thirds majority of those voting agrees, the bill will be considered on the floor.

suspension of the rules
Fast-track procedure for considering bills and resolutions in the House; debate is limited to 40 minutes, no amendments are in order, and a two-thirds majority is required for passage.

Debate is limited to 40 minutes, no amendments are in order, and a two-thirds majority is required for passage. There is some risk in considering a bill under suspension: Even if a majority approves of it, the bill could fail to achieve two-thirds support. Indeed, a bill's opponents sometimes support the motion to suspend the rules precisely in order to raise the threshold for passage.

Legislation that is especially important, and therefore usually controversial, goes to the Rules Committee before going to the floor. The Rules Committee, too, may hold hearings, this time on the type of **rule** it should grant. In these hearings, only members of Congress may testify. The rule specifies the terms and conditions of debate, such as how long supporters and opponents will be allowed to speak. It may prohibit any amendments (a *closed rule*), allow any amendments (an *open rule*), or specify the amendments that are in order (a *restrictive rule*). In recent years, with the rise of stronger party leadership, three-quarters of all bills that have come from the Rules Committee have been granted restrictive rules.

Some rules are unusual. For example, so-called *king of the mountain rules* allow a number of (frequently conflicting) amendments to be offered, but they specify that only the last amendment that receives a majority is adopted. Naturally, the committee orders the amendments so that the one it favors goes last. This kind of rule allows committee members to vote for several conflicting amendments, thereby satisfying each of their supporters, all the while knowing that the last vote is the only one that matters.

If the Rules Committee recommends a rule, the floor then chooses to accept or reject it. In shaping the rule, the committee anticipates the limits of what the floor will accept. Thus, most rules receive approval—at which point the bill itself finally comes under consideration by the full chamber. The floor decides whether to adopt the "perfected" bill after any debate or amendment votes permitted by the rule.

The process in the Senate is simpler to describe. For uncontroversial legislation, a motion to pass a bill by unanimous consent is sometimes all that is necessary. More important and controversial legislation requires the committee and party leaders to negotiate unanimous-consent agreements, which are complicated bargains analogous to the rules granted by the House Rules Committee. Assuming that such an agreement is successfully crafted and thereby avoids a filibuster, the bill eventually comes to a floor vote.

If a majority votes to adopt the bill, are we at the end of the process? Not at all. Before the bill can be sent for the president's signature, it must pass both chambers in identical form. A bill may have started in one chamber before going to the other, or it may have proceeded simultaneously through both. In either case, the House and Senate seldom pass exactly the same legislation. In fact, their versions may be in serious conflict. Unless one chamber is willing to defer to the other chamber, the two must iron out their differences. Sometimes they do so informally, but for major legislation the traditional method has been that each chamber appoints representatives to a joint **conference committee** that can produce a compromise version.

In principle, each chamber's conferees are committed to the legislation approved by their colleagues, but in practice this allegiance is not likely. Conferences for some complex bills involve hundreds of members who support some parts of the bill, oppose other parts, and care little about still other parts. This complexity makes the situation

rule

The terms and conditions under which a bill or resolution will be considered on the floor of the House—in particular, how long debate will last, how time will be allocated, and the number and type of amendments that will be in order.

Star Power

Actress Ashley Judd, who is a global ambassador for YouthAIDS, an organization dedicated to educating and protecting young people from HIV/AIDS, testifies before the Senate Foreign Relations Committee. Judd has traveled extensively in Africa and Asia, where she has raised awareness of HIV prevention.

conference committee

A group of representatives from both the House and the Senate who iron out the differences between the two chambers' versions of a bill or resolution.

ideal for bargaining. When a majority of each chamber's conferees agree to the final compromise, the bill is reported back to the parent chambers, where another floor vote in each chamber is required for passage.[36]

You may think that we have finally reached the end of the process. The bill will be sent to the president and, assuming the president does not veto it, the bill will become a formal law. But there is no guarantee that the new law will have any effect. So far, we have been considering only the **authorization process.** All government action authorized by Congress—paying subsidies, issuing regulations, buying bombers, inspecting workplaces, whatever—also needs funding for it to be carried out.

authorization process
Term applied to the entire process of providing statutory authority for a government program or activity.

The Constitution grants Congress the power of the purse and makes the House the lead actor: All tax bills must originate in the House, and, by custom and tradition, all appropriations bills do, too. The **appropriations process** parallels the authorization process. Thirteen appropriations subcommittees in each chamber hold hearings and mark up the bill (the subcommittee chairs are commonly referred to as "the Cardinals of Capitol Hill").[37] The full committees may also do so, but they usually defer to their subcommittees. In the House, appropriations bills are privileged; they take precedence over other legislation, and a motion to take up an appropriations bill can be offered at any time. But, in practice, appropriations bills, too, usually pass through the Rules Committee. Thus, appropriations subcommittees in both chambers must report spending bills, the rank and file in both chambers must pass them, and a conference committee must agree on every dollar before the government actually has any money to spend on the actions it has authorized.

appropriations process
Process of providing funding for governmental activities and programs that have been authorized.

12.4

Evaluate how well Congress meets its responsibilities to the American public.

Evaluating Congress

It is easy to get so wrapped up in the details of Congress and its operations that we lose sight of the reason for our interest in the institution. The reason, of course, is that Congress is the first branch, arguably the most powerful and most important, of our three branches of government. It is the branch that bears primary responsibility for representing the needs and values of the American public and for developing legislation to improve its well-being. How well does Congress meet its responsibilities?

Criticisms of Congress

The most common criticism of the congressional process should be obvious: *It is slow and inefficient.* Legislation may take months or even years to wend its way through the process, and there is much duplication of effort—both within and between the chambers. Moreover, after all is said and done, Congress often produces a compromise that leaves no one satisfied. To those who want quick, decisive action, Congress-watching is enough to put their teeth on edge. And, of course, that is what the framers intended. They wanted to ensure that laws would pass only after they had been thoroughly considered and majorities were convinced that they were needed.

But the procedural hurdles in the congressional process raise a second criticism: *The congressional process works to the advantage of policy minorities, especially those content with the status quo.* Proponents of legislation must build many winning coalitions—in sub-committee, in full committee, in appropriations committee, and on the floor, in both chambers, and perhaps in conference committee. Opponents have it much easier. A minority that controls only a single stage of the process may be able to block action. Of course, a determined majority cannot be stopped indefinitely, except by a Senate fili-buster, but it can be held at bay for a long time or it can be forced to make undesirable compromises. Moreover, potential majorities sometimes decide not to act, calculating that the costs of overcoming all the obstacles are not worth the effort. Thus, the process hinders majorities who support change and helps minorities who are content to pre-vent change.

Two other criticisms focus on what Congress does when it acts, rather than on its failure to act. Given that members are trying to please their electoral constituen-cies, *they are constantly tempted to use their positions to extract constituency benefits,* even when important national legislation is at stake. Democratic President Jimmy Carter got so upset trying to deal with Congress on national energy policy that he wrote in his diary, "Congress is disgusting on this particular subject."[38] In both his first and second terms Republican President George W. Bush attempted to reform agricul-tural policy. Congress went the opposite direction both times, adding more farm welfare to the bills, even passing the 2008 legislation over Bush's veto. Numerous examples like these demonstrate that Congress defeats, distorts, and otherwise dam-ages national interests in pursuit of its members' parochial interests. The best that can be said about such behavior is that without such trading of favors no general inter-est legislation might pass.[39]

Finally, the nature of the congressional process is such that *sometimes the very process of passing legislation ensures that it will not work.* This paradox is especially true of propos-als that, in order to correct a social problem, would need to concentrate resources on a small portion of the population. As we discussed in the opening vignette of this chap-ter, members of Congress are reluctant to pass up any opportunity to deliver local benefits, even if their district or state does not have the problem a program addresses or does not need federal money to address it. Therefore, they often pass bills that sim-ply distribute money, rather than carefully target the problem the program is intended to solve. Consider, for example, the Economic Development Administration, created in the 1960s to subsidize the construction of infrastructure such as roads, utilities, and industrial parks in depressed areas. By the time the program was killed by the Reagan administration, *more than 80 percent of all the counties in the United States* had been clas-sified as "economically depressed" so that they would be eligible for the federal sub-

Shoe on the Other Foot
Members of Congress usually view legislation in terms of the needs and interests of their own districts. They expect other dis-tricts to bear the brunt of any sacrifices.

sidies.[40] Homeland security funds are only a more current and potentially far more serious example, as shown by the questionable expenditures noted at the beginning of this chapter.

Bashing the federal bureaucracy is a popular sport. Sometimes it is warranted—government programs may be poorly implemented or incompetently administered. But federal programs often fail because they were born to fail: Their enactment did not focus benefits where they would do the most good and did not concentrate resources sufficiently to have a major impact. Consequently, money is taken from some citizens and passed along to others but the nation has little to show for it. The failure does not result because government ignored the demands of voters. Quite the contrary: It results because members of Congress aggressively worked to promote the interests of the people who elect them.

Why Americans Like Their Members of Congress So Much More Than Congress Itself

A Congressional Debate
Disrespect for Congress is nothing new, as this 1798 print of the congressional floor shows.

More than people in other democracies, Americans are proud of their political institutions. They revere the Constitution, honor the law, and respect the presidency and the courts. But there is an exception to this generalization, and it is Congress. Congress is the butt of jokes. It has been defined as "a creature with 535 bellies, and no brain." Humorist Mark Twain once observed that "it could probably be shown with facts and figures that there is no distinctly native American criminal class except Congress."[41]

Disparaging quips such as these reflect popular sentiments. As Figure 12.2 shows, Americans view their popularly elected representatives as having ethical standards well below those of most occupations. Congress as a whole also suffers from a particularly negative public image, even though it is the national government's most electorally sensitive institution.[42] Majorities of Americans doubt the competence and integrity of the legislative branch.[43]

Why, then, do members of Congress win reelection at a high rate (see Chapter 11)? Why do American voters not "throw the rascals out" and substitute better people? The answer is simple: Americans judge their own representatives by standards different from those by which they judge the collective Congress.[44] Voters like their own elected representatives. Citizens invariably rate their members of Congress far more favorably than they rate Congress as a whole, an observation that has become known as "Fenno's paradox" (after political scientist Richard Fenno, who popularized the observation).[45]

Polls show that Americans generally take a dim view of how well Congress solves national problems and meets national challenges. Congress, they believe, rarely meets its collective responsibilities. Citizens take an equally dim view of how they think Congress operates—sluggishly, conflictually, inefficiently, and sometimes corruptly. They therefore have little good to say about the institution or its membership. But citizens judge their own representatives and senators positively for doing the very things that make the collective Congress so ineffective. Members fight for what

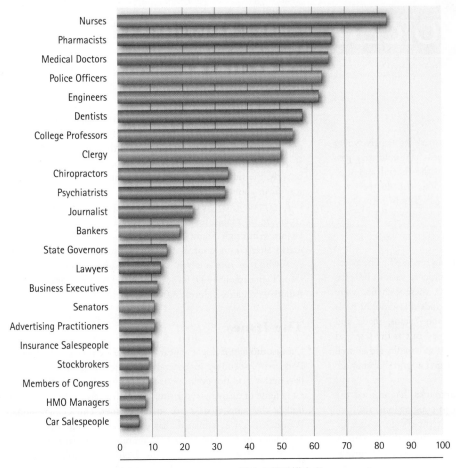

Nurses
Pharmacists
Medical Doctors
Police Officers
Engineers
Dentists
College Professors
Clergy
Chiropractors
Psychiatrists
Journalist
Bankers
State Governors
Lawyers
Business Executives
Senators
Advertising Practitioners
Insurance Salespeople
Stockbrokers
Members of Congress
HMO Managers
Car Salespeople

0   10   20   30   40   50   60   70   80   90   100

High or Very High, %

FIGURE 12.2

CONGRESSIONAL ETHICS

The public rates the honesty and ethics of members of Congress lower than those of other occupations.

• Why are members of Congress judged only a little more positively than car salesmen?

Source: The Gallup Organization.

their constituents want, even if it means blocking legislation, grabbing resources needed more by others, or demanding unreasonable alterations in a government program.

Voters may resent such behavior when conducted on behalf of others, but they shower electoral rewards on the public officials who do it for them. That is, they would prefer other people's representatives to be **trustees**—legislators who use their own judgment to decide what is best for the country—but demand that their own representatives serve as **delegates**—legislators who cater to the needs and views of their constituents back home regardless of what they personally believe good public policy ought to be. However, because voters everywhere demand roughly the same sort of responsiveness, members of Congress typically work as delegates to the federal government charged with getting constituents the resources they want. An old saying goes "if you want to make an omelet, you've got to break some eggs." Voters want omelets and reward legislators who deliver them to the table, but they complain if their members sacrifice any local eggs to make the national omelet.

trustee

Role a representative plays when acting in accordance with his or her own best judgment to decide what is best for the country.

delegate

Role a representative plays when following the wishes of those who have elected him or her regardless of what he or she believes good public policy ought to be.

earmarks

In a budget, designation of funds for a specific use.

Continued on page 361

An Explosion of Earmarks

The Issue

Should members of Congress specify ("earmark") precisely where and on what federal money is to be spent? Or should they pass general legislation and permit experts in the federal and state bureaucracies to decide where the spending will do the most good?

Background

Pork barrel politics is almost as old as Congress itself.[1] The pejorative term refers to members' efforts to procure various benefits for their districts and states. Originally, these benefits were mostly construction projects of various kinds that brought government money and jobs to constituents—dams, roads and bridges, public buildings, and military bases. But as the size and scope of government expanded, the kinds of benefits did as well until today, when all manner of projects, grants, and subsidies are considered part of the pork barrel.

In recent years the explosion of **earmarks,** has aroused the ire of critics. The term generally refers to congressional instructions that direct government activity or money to a specific project or activity in a particular location. Most such instructions are not actually included in the legislation that passes Congress, but are contained in the committee reports or the floor managers' explanatory statements that executive agencies rely on to implement the legislation.[2] Although such provisions do not have the force of law, government agencies ignore them at their peril, because they must request authorization from Congress periodically and appropriations annually.

Earmarking has exploded in the past decade or so. For example, in 2005 Congress passed a transportation bill that included more than 6,300 earmarks, including nearly half a billion dollars for the notorious Alaskan "bridges to nowhere." One bridge would have linked Ketchikan to a remote island with a population of 50 people. Another would have linked Anchorage to Port MacKenzie, a rural area with one resident.[3] Not coincidentally, Alaska representative Don Young is chair of the House Committee on Transportation and Infrastructure, and Alaska senator Ted Stevens was chair of the Senate Appropriations Committee. After a torrent of national ridicule from sources as diverse as Washington think tanks to comedian Jay Leno, the earmarks were withdrawn, but the money for Alaska was left in the bill.

Ironically, the practice of earmarking exploded after Republicans took control of Congress in 1995, defying the popular image of Democrats as the party of big spenders. In 1991, when the Highway Program was reauthorized by a Democratic Congress, the bill contained only 538 earmarks, less than a third as many as when the Republican Congress reauthorized the program seven years later, and one-twelfth as many as when the Republican Congress reauthorized the program in 2005.[4] More broadly, the number of earmarks in annual appropriations bills rose from about 1,400 in 1995 to about 14,000 in 2005, a tenfold increase in ten years.[5] Apparently fiscally conservative principles are no match for electoral incentives to bring home the bacon. Although Democrats held down the number of earmarks after taking control in 2006, the practice soon resurged. According to one analysis the 2010 Appropriations bills for three Departments—Defense, Homeland Security, and Veterans Affairs—contained almost 8,000 earmarks.[6]

The Issues

On first thought it might appear that there are no issues to discuss. Pork barrel spending in general and earmarking in particular is bad, period. But not everyone sees it that way. Probably the weakest defense of earmarks is the simple fact that relative to the federal budget the sums at stake are small potatoes. The Congressional Research Service estimated that earmarks accounted for about $67 billion in the 2006 budget.[7] (Demonstrating that earmarking is a nonpartisan activity, after the Democrats took control of Congress in 2006 they ordered the Congressional Research Service to quit keeping track of earmarks!) To any single person, that sounds like a lot of money, but given a federal budget that was more than $2.5 trillion, earmarks were about 2.5 percent of the total. In that light, trying to reform or eliminate earmarks hardly seems worth the effort. Critics retort that wasting any amount of taxpayers' hard-earned dollars is wrong. Money could always be spent on more worthwhile programs or simply applied to the deficit to lower the burden on future generations.

A second defense of earmarking is that earmarks pave the way for legislation to pass. Even a public policy change that is highly desirable from a national standpoint generally creates losers as well as winners, and one way to induce losers to go along with the change is to compensate their constituents for losses by giving them side payments from the pork barrel.[8] Without pork barrel spending Congress would be even more gridlocked than it often is! While examples of this legislative strategy clearly exist, skeptics retort that there is no evidence that earmarks in general are used to compensate constituencies for losses from other legislation. Rather, political influence, along with party and member electoral concerns, appears to be a more important factor. At any rate, some critics believe that the process is so out of control that rather than a means of passing legislation, earmarks have become the whole purpose of legislation.

An Earmark or Two?

Earmark requests sit in a file drawer at the House Transportation and Infrastructure Committee offices. Recent transportation bills have included thousands of earmarks for lawmakers' pet projects in their home districts.

Finally, members of Congress often defend their earmarking by pointing out that if they refrain from making spending decisions, those decisions will not be made by philosopher kings and queens. Rather, they will be made by federal bureaucrats, state governors and legislators, state and local bureaucrats, and city mayors and councils. All of these officials are subject to political pressures as well, and the incentives they face might well lead to poorer decisions than those made by members of Congress.[9] You can't take the politics out of politics, members say. Critics concede the point in part, but reply that the process of allocating federal money can be insulated from political pressure more than it is. Just because merit criteria can sometimes be difficult to apply doesn't mean that they should be abandoned altogether. Instead, we must work hard to design procedures to minimize political influence in the process of allocating federal funds.

What Do Americans Believe?

In recent years popular approval of Congress has plummeted (see Figure 1). Only one in five Americans approves of the job Congress is doing. (After discussing some of the earmarks in a 2006 "emergency" supplemental act columnist George Will wondered why even that many Americans approved.)[10] But, while approval of Congress flirts with modern lows, approval of individual members remains much higher. Fenno's paradox still lives: We like our members of Congress much more than we like Congress itself. As discussed earlier in this chapter, the reason is that we reward our members for much the same activities that we condemn the Congress. To viewers of Jay Leno, the Alaskan bridges to nowhere were a congressional travesty, but to many of the constituents of Representative Young and Senator Stevens the bridges and associated jobs and spending were benefits stemming from the hard work of their representatives in Washington, illustrating once again the old adage that one person's waste, fraud, or abuse is another person's income. As long as constituents reward their members for activities such as earmarking, such activities will continue.

What Do You Think?

1. Should the U.S. representative from your congressional district and the senators from your state earmark legislation to benefit your district and state?

2. In January 2008, former President Bush issued an executive order instructing executive agencies to ignore any earmarks that are not actually written into legislation (more than 90 percent of all earmarks). Is this proposal tantamount to an unconstitutional line item veto?

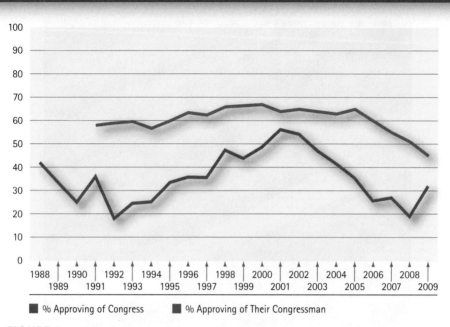

FIGURE 1

In recent years, popular approval of Congress has plummeted.

Source: The Gallup Organization. The figures for those who approve of their congresspersons are derived from the percent of respondents who believe that their individual congressperson should be reelected.

On the Web

Porkbusters

http://truthlaidbear.com/porkbusters/index.php
www.porkbusters.org

Citizens Against Government Waste

www.cagw.org

Taxpayers for Common Sense

www.taxpayer.net

---

[1] Pork Barrel—the state or national treasury, into which politicians and government officials dip for "pork," or funds for local projects. The phrase probably is derived from the pre-Civil War practice of periodically distributing salt pork to the slaves from huge barrels. From William Safire, *Safire's New Political Dictionary* (Random House, New York, 1993).

[2] Sandy Streeter, "Earmarks and Limitations in Appropriations Bills," *CRS Report for Congress* (December 7, 2004): 98–518.

[3] Rebecca Clarren, "A Bridge to Nowhere," http://dir.salon.com/story/news/feature/2005/08/09/bridges/index.html.

[4] Ronald Utt, "A Primer on Lobbyists, Earmarks, and Congressional Reform," The Heritage Foundation, Backgrounder #1924 (April 27, 2006): 3.

[5] Ibid., 2.

[6] Andrew Taylor, "Obama Beats Early Retreat on Promise to Fight Pork," www.realclearpolitics.com/news/ap/politics/2009/Mar/02/obama_beats_early_retreat_on_promise_to_fight_pork.html. Accessed March 22, 2010.

[7] Congressional Research Service, "Memorandum: Earmarks in FY2006 Appropriations Acts," March 6, 2006. http://demint.senate.gov/news/EarmarksFY2006.pdf.

[8] Diana Evans, *Greasing the Wheels* (New York: Cambridge University Press, 2004).

[9] Robert Shrum, "In Praise of Earmarks," http://mobile.theweek.com/bullpen/column/94082/In_praise_of_earmarks (accessed March 22, 2010).

[10] George Will, "Many Strange 'Emergencies,'" *Newsweek* (May 8, 2006).

Continued from page 357

CHAPTER SUMMARY

12.1 Describe the basic powers and structure of Congress.

The United States Congress is the world's most powerful legislature. It is also the most professionalized. Its members are full-time, career legislators. Congress has an extensive division of labor—the committee system—supported by an extensive party organization focused on getting bills through the difficult lawmaking process.

12.2 Outline how the House of Representatives and Senate are organized by the committee system and the party leadership structure.

Citizens hold Congress in much lower esteem than they hold their individual representatives and senators, whom they reelect regularly. This discrepancy arises because members of Congress depend for their election on specific constituencies. They act to satisfy those constituencies, even if doing so requires behavior that may not serve the larger interest of the nation. The result is that Congress is slow and inefficient, and what emerges from the complex legislative process may not be very effective. The structure of Congress is an uneasy compromise between what it takes to get the job done and what it takes to get reelected.

12.3 Trace the steps by which a bill becomes a law.

The process by which a bill becomes a law is complex. Numerous committees and subcommittees and the two chambers shape the content, and a variety of formal and informal rules determine the procedures. In recent years unorthodox lawmaking has made the process even more complex and difficult to describe in general.

12.4 Evaluate how well Congress meets its responsibilities to the American public.

Frustrated voters fail to see that members of Congress have powerful electoral incentives to behave as they do. The problems voters see with Congress result not from a lack of electoral responsiveness, but from an excess of it.

---

mypoliscilab EXERCISES

Apply what you learned in this chapter on MyPoliSciLab.

Read on **mypoliscilab.com**
eText: Chapter 12

Study and **Review** on **mypoliscilab.com**
Pre-Test
Post-Test
Chapter Exam
Flashcards

Watch on **mypoliscilab.com**
Video: Kagan Hearing

Explore on **mypoliscilab.com**
Simulation: How a Bill Becomes a Law
Simulation: You Are a Member of Congress
Comparative: Comparing Legislatures

KEY TERMS

appropriations process, p. 354
authorization process, p. 354

bicameral, p. 340
caucus, p. 350

cloture, p. 344
conference committee, p. 353

SUGGESTED READINGS

Of General Interest

Arnold, R. Douglas. *The Logic of Congressional Action*. New Haven, CT: Yale University Press, 1990. An excellent discussion of how the incentives that motivate members interact with the characteristics of public-policy problems to shape legislation.

Malbin, Michael, Norman J. Ornstein, and Thomas E. Mann. *Vital Statistics on Congress, 2008*. Washington, DC: Brookings Institution Press, rev. ed., 2008. Indispensable compendium of facts and figures about Congress.

Oleszek, Walter, and Roger Davidson. *Congress and Its Members*. 11th ed. Washington, DC: CQ Press, 2007. A readable text that relates the electoral and institutional arenas.

Sinclair, Barbara. *Unorthodox Lawmaking: New Legislative Processes in the U.S. Congress*. 3rd ed. Washington, DC: CQ Press, 2007. An up-to-date work that contrasts the idealized process of passing laws with the contemporary realities.

Smith, Steven, Jason Roberts, and Ryan Vander Wielen. *The American Congress*. 5th ed. New York: Cambridge University Press, 2007. A leading text that covers all aspects of the congressional process.

Focused Studies

Adler, E. Scott. *Why Congressional Reforms Fail*. Chicago: University of Chicago Press, 2002. Historical study arguing that members' desire for reelection consistently hampers efforts to reform the committee system.

Cox, Gary, and Mathew McCubbins. *Setting the Agenda*. New York: Cambridge University Press, 2005. Important work that shows how the majority party in Congress operates through its control of the agenda.

David R. Jones and Monika L. McDermott, *Americans, Congress, and Democratic Responsiveness* (Ann Arbor, MI: University of Michigan Press, 2012).

David W. Brady and Craig Volden, *Revolving Gridlock*. 2nd ed. Boulder, CO: Westview Press, 2006. Important work that melds theory and evidence about how congressional institutions and legislative-executive relations interact to determine policy outcome.

Krutz, Glen. *Hitching a Ride: Omnibus Legislating in the U.S. Congress*. Columbus: Ohio State University Press, 2001. Detailed study of another form of unorthodox lawmaking—congressional packaging of numerous bills into one big "must pass" omnibus.

Oleszek, Walter. *Congressional Procedures and the Policy Process*. 7th ed. Washington, DC: CQ Press, 2007. An accessible treatment of the rules and procedures governing the congressional process.

Schickler, Eric. *Disjointed Pluralism*. Princeton, NJ: Princeton University Press, 2001. Analyzes the historical development of congressional rules and procedures.

ON THE WEB

www.rollcall.com

Roll Call, the newspaper of Capitol Hill, is a definitive source of news on congressional affairs.

www.democrats.senate.gov

www.democrats.house.gov

www.gop.gov

These websites offer very current information on the partisan activities going on in Congress at any given time.

http://thomas.loc.gov

This website is the official source of information on Congress and has links to member offices, committee websites, historical documents, and (most important) the congressional record and index. The information is not always easily organized, but it is comprehensive.

www.congress.org

This website by Capitol Advantage is an alternative, private source of congressional information. It chronicles the daily activities of Congress in committee and on the floor and makes it easy to contact the members who represent your state or district. You can even send a hand-delivered letter.

13 The Presidency: Powers and Practice

CHAPTER OUTLINE

13.1 Analyze how the president's national and partisan constituencies shape presidential decision making.

13.2 Outline the major powers of the president and Congress's checks on presidential powers.

13.3 Assess why presidential reputation and popularity are important to presidential performance and what factors contribute to presidential greatness.

The Presidency as Crisis Management

If you had to pick a month to illustrate the nature of the modern presidency, it would be difficult to do better than December 2009. On December 1, President Barack Obama issued his controversial plan to send 30,000 more troops to Afghanistan to, as he put it, "disrupt, dismantle, and defeat al Qaeda in Afghanistan and Pakistan."[1] Liberals criticized the move as an escalation; conservatives panned Obama's promise to begin withdrawing troops in 18 months, claiming it was a concession to America's enemies. Ten days after the announcement, Obama flew to Oslo, Norway, to accept a Nobel Peace Prize, an honor that had been bestowed unexpectedly the previous fall amid, as the president acknowledged, "considerable controversy."[2]

Meanwhile, diplomats and activists from around the world were gathering in Copenhagen to discuss climate change, an issue that, during the campaign, both Obama and his Republican rival, John McCain, had highlighted as crucial to America's security (see the *Election Voices!* feature on page 387). But support for an agreement to curb greenhouse gas emissions was lacking, both in the U.S. Congress and among crucial world leaders like Chinese premier Wen Jiabao and Indian Prime Minister Manmohan Singh. Obama flew to Copenhagen to secure some kind of international accord, even bursting unannounced into a meeting with Wen, Singh, and leaders of Brazil and South Africa.[3] An obviously exhausted Obama declared victory the following day, but critics scoffed at the informal, non-binding agreement, which simply affirmed previously announced goals. Ironically, the president left the global warming conference early in order to beat a snowstorm that could have prevented Air Force One from landing.

The snowstorm did not deter the Senate, however, from remaining in session during the holiday season in a desperate effort to reach agreement on healthcare reform, another top administration priority. On December 24, upon urgent requests by President Obama, Democrats finally prevailed over a Republican filibuster to move the bill to the next stage. On Christmas Eve, the Senate adjourned for the holiday, and the Obama family flew to Hawaii for a welcome vacation.

But no sooner had Obama arrived in his home state than another crisis demanded his attention. A Nigerian youth had managed to smuggle a bomb onboard a flight from Amsterdam to Detroit and nearly downed the plane on its approach to landing. A faulty detonator and some quick-thinking passengers and crew prevented the worst from happening. The Christmas-day attempt renewed terrorist fears and prompted additional security measures at U.S. and international airports. It did not help that Obama's Homeland Security Secretary claimed the "system had worked," a phrase that referred to the government's response after the fact but that was interpreted by the press and the political opposition as a claim that all was well when it was clearly not. As a consequence, Obama spent much of Christmas in briefings, holding a press conference days later to decry "human and systemic failures" in intelligence gathering and to jump-start an investigation.[4] Again the administration's critics called Obama's leadership into question. Former Vice President Dick Cheney accused Obama of "trying to pretend we are not at war" with terrorists.[5] Administration officials and congressional Democrats took to the airwaves in the president's defense. The controversy died down only when the president released a particularly frank and open assessment of the intelligence failure.

This frenetic White House schedule is more the norm than the exception. As a former official in the George W. Bush administration put it, "There's the pace. There's the hours. There's the intensity. There's the anxiety. There's the pressure for results. I used to get up at 4 a.m. every day. It was like being shot out of a cannon."[6]

Making the Connection

The presidency occupies a unique position in the U.S. system of government. As President Obama's exhausting travails demonstrate, its formal powers and position in the constitutional system put presidents at the very center of national and international politics. Their capacity to accomplish big things varies, however. At times, presidents seem to have an easy time getting what they want, but at other times their agendas get derailed unexpectedly. This inconsistency is due both to the political pressures they face and to the nature of their powers.

In this chapter, you will learn not only about the formal, constitutional powers of the office, but also about the way they shape the relationship between presidents and their various constituencies. Success can depend not only on the presidents' personality but also on the historical circumstances that brought them into office.

Presidential Constituencies

Similar to other elected officials, presidents of the United States must take care to estimate and address the concerns of their constituencies. Presidents often find it challenging to strike the right balance between their national constituencies, which are created by the general election, and their partisan constituencies, which are shaped by presidential primaries. Both national and partisan constituencies play a role in presidential decision making.

National Constituency

Presidents have one unique political asset: They fill a position elected by a national constituency. Only presidents can persuasively claim to speak for the country as a whole, and they can use this national constituency to powerful effect. In late 1995, after budget negotiations between the Democratic president and the Republican Congress deadlocked, much of the government was shut down for nearly a month. National parks were closed and government bills went unpaid. In the midst of the crisis, President Bill Clinton asked Congress to place the national interest above partisan objectives. Republican Speaker of the House Newt Gingrich replied by saying it was the president who should put the country's future ahead of his own. Each appealed to a national constituency, but the president, in part because he was the president, proved to be more persuasive. According to polls, most Americans sided with Clinton and blamed Congress for the deadlock. One Republican strategist acknowledged the president's advantages: "We've learned that it's nearly impossible to frame the national debate from the lower chamber of the legislative branch."[7]

13.1

Analyze how the president's national and partisan constituencies shape presidential decision making.

In early 2003, President George W. Bush proposed a "jobs and growth" plan that had as its centerpiece a cut in the taxes that investors paid on corporate dividends. "Lower taxes and greater investment will help the economy expand," reasoned Bush in that year's State of the Union address.[8] Democrats argued that it would increase the country's fiscal deficit, with some pronouncing the bill "dead on arrival."[9] Nevertheless, after a series of high-profile public appearances in states with wavering senators, Bush carried the day. Although smaller than what the president initially asked for, the $350 billion tax cut was still one of the largest in history. Once again, the president's ability to mobilize his national constituency gave him key advantages over his opponents in Congress. President Obama was equally successful in early 2009 when he won quick Congressional support for his $787 billion stimulus package, despite united opposition from Republicans who complained that it would only increase the country's fiscal deficit.

Although the president's national constituency is a great political asset, it creates problems as well. Voters hold presidents responsible for many events and conditions over which they have little control. Presidents are expected to conduct foreign policy, manage the economy, administer a complex bureaucracy, promote desired legislation, respond to disasters, and address an endless variety of real and imagined social problems.[10]

Presidents are sometimes given credit for prosperity and success, but they are more often blamed when things go wrong. President George H. W. Bush, for example, enjoyed foreign policy triumphs equaled by only a few of his predecessors. Most notably, he achieved a spectacular victory in the 1991 Persian Gulf War. Yet when the economy faltered, Bush was drummed from office. Similarly, President Obama's popularity suffered a steep decline in approval ratings during his first year in office as unemployment rates rose to 10 percent.

Partisan Constituencies

In addition to a national constituency, presidents have a party constituency to which they must be responsive. They need to keep the support of those who work in and help finance their campaigns. If they do not satisfy their party constituency, they may encounter difficulties with the party faithful in presidential primaries.

A party constituency usually takes more extreme issue positions than does the national constituency. Presidents therefore have to find some way to balance the demands of their most ardent supporters with the more moderate concerns of the general-election voters who determine the outcome of national elections. At times, this balancing act proves unsuccessful. President Obama favored a tax on what were called "Cadillac" healthcare plans that he thought were driving up the cost of medical services, but trade unions, who had won such plans for their workers, insisted that their plans be exempted from the bill, complicating the president's ability to get his healthcare plan approved. The final bill included a smaller "Cadillac" tax than Obama had initially favored.

Partisan Support in Congress

Even if presidents can balance their national and party constituencies, they usually cannot take action on their pledges without considering their level of support in Congress. On most issues, presidents gain more support from members of their own party than

Partisan Support in Congress

Democratic Senators Chuck Schumer (NY), Dianne Feinstein (CA), Harry Reid (NV) and Dick Durbin (IL) hold a press conference.

• *Do you think divided government leads to inefficient gridlock, or is it a valuable check?*

from the opposition. As a consequence, when presidents have larger majorities in Congress, they are more likely to get their proposed legislation approved.[11]

The events surrounding the first Bush tax-cut bill provide a clear illustration of the importance to presidents of a party majority in Congress. When Bush entered office in 2001, his party had comfortable majority in the House of Representatives, but only a tiny majority in the Senate. Not surprisingly, Bush got almost all of the tax cuts he wanted from the House, but in the Senate he was forced to accept a bill that cut taxes by 25 percent less than what he had proposed. Similarly, President Obama's healthcare reform proposals won fairly quick backing in the House, where he had a clear majority, but ran into prolonged delays in the Senate, where it was tougher to get the super-majority he needed to move the legislation forward.

Partisanship is not as pervasive in the United States as it is in many European countries. Still, political scientists have debated whether it is good or bad to have **divided government**—control of the presidency by one party and control of one or both houses of Congress by the other (see Chapter 8). With the kind of unified government that President Obama enjoyed in his first two years—clear majorities of his own political party in both the Senate and the House of Representatives, it proved to be easier to enact a high-cost stimulus package and even to pass a major transformation of the healthcare system. But if unified government allows for major policy changes, it also can place the government at risk of moving forward without paying sufficient attention to the needs of minorities or even public opinion as a whole. One year into the Obama presidency, pundits were beginning to wonder whether the president's problems were, ironically, due to the very fact that he did not need to make the compromises that are usually made when control of the executive and legislative branches are divided between the two parties. As the 2010 elections neared, Republicans argued that if they

divided government
The control of the presidency by one party and the control of one or both houses of Congress by the other.

won control over Congress, they would act as a necessary check on the president. As Republican Texas Senator John Cornyn put it, in the election "Republicans have a big opportunity to help restore checks and balances . . . to Washington, DC."[12] But some pundits said the president might also benefit from divided government in the same way that Clinton did after 1994, when a short period of unified Democratic government was replaced by a division of power between the two parties.

13.2

Outline the major powers of the president and Congress's checks on presidential powers.

Separate Institutions Sharing Power

Although presidential power is limited in part by conflicts between the two political parties, the more important limitations on what presidents can do are written into the Constitution itself. Presidents can seldom force members of Congress to support them; they usually have to coax, beg, plead, and compromise to gain the necessary votes. Even when the same party controls both the presidency and Congress, presidents do not find it easy to get their proposals approved. For instance, Bill Clinton was unable to persuade a Democratic Congress to enact his healthcare reform proposals, and ten years later, President Obama fought for every last vote to enact a healthcare reform law that was finally adopted after a prolonged, politically costly debate. George W. Bush was unable to pass a Social Security reform measure through a Republican Congress.[13] More than 80 percent of the time, presidents either fail to secure passage of their major legislative agendas or must make important compromises to win congressional approval.[14] As presidential scholar Charles Jones has observed, "Presidents don't pass laws; they work with, alongside of, or against the House and Senate."[15]

When President Bush watched his proposals for Social Security reform wither in 2005, he was not the first president to be frustrated by Congress. Theodore Roosevelt sighed, "Oh, if I could only be president and Congress, too, for just ten minutes."[16] Presidents find their position particularly exasperating because they feel they have a duty to take decisive action. Facing a Republican Congress in 1995, President Clinton angrily charged congressional leaders with trying "to destroy the ability of the federal government to address the problems facing America—to move the country forward, to move the country together."[17]

Those who wrote the Constitution ensured that presidents would govern only with the help of Congress. Most delegates to the Constitutional Convention wanted to strengthen the executive branch beyond what was provided for by the Articles of Confederation. But the founders realized that voters would never ratify a constitution that created a strong executive who might become another King George. The result is a government of "separated institutions sharing powers."[18] We now turn to the many ways in which the Constitution has shaped presidential power and practice.

The Power to Inform and Persuade

PRESIDENTIAL POWER: *The President "shall from time to time give to the Congress Information of the State of the Union."*

CONGRESSIONAL CHECK: *None*

The Constitution requires presidents to give Congress information about the state of the union. Presidents have interpreted this requirement as authority to persuade Congress and the public at large to support their policies. Modern presidents rely on hundreds of

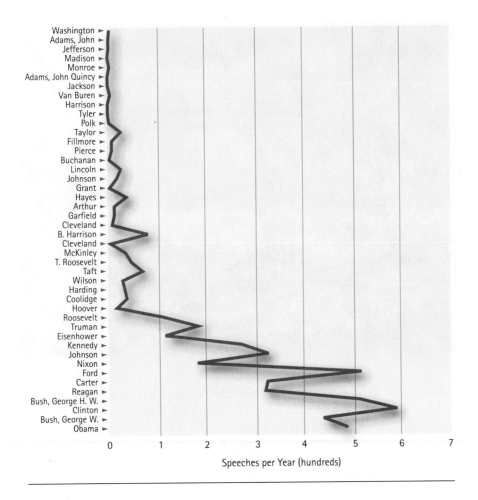

Speeches per Year (hundreds)

FIGURE 13.1

GROWTH IN PRESIDENTIAL
SPEECH MAKING

Presidents give far more speeches
than they used to.

• *Why have presidents made
more public speeches in the last
50 years?*

Note: Figures for Harding and
Franklin Roosevelt were unavail-
able. Estimates for Taft and
Coolidge are based on their first
year in office only. Figures on
Barack Obama are for 2009 only.

Sources: Data on Washington through
McKinley are taken from Jeffrey Tulis,
The Rhetorical Presidency (Princeton, NJ:
Princeton University Press, 1987), 64.
For Theodore Roosevelt, see Robert V.
Friedenberg, *Theodore Roosevelt and the
Rhetoric of Militant Decency* (New York:
Greenwood Press, 1990). For Taft, see
*Presidential Addresses and State Papers of
William Howard Taft,* Vol. 1, 1910 (New
York: Doubleday). For Wilson, see Albert
Shaw, ed., *Messages and Papers of Woodrow
Wilson,* Vols. 1 and 2 (New York: Review
of Reviews Corporation, 1924). For
Coolidge, see Claude M. Feuss, *Calvin
Coolidge: The Man from Vermont* (Hamden,
CT: Archon Books, 1965). For Presidents
Truman through Reagan, see Roderick
Hart, *The Sound of Leadership* (Chicago:
The University of Chicago Press, 1987).
For Hoover and presidents from George
H.W. Bush on, information is taken from
The Public Papers of the President, various
years, the *Weekly Compilation of Presidential
Documents,* various years, and the *Daily
Compilation of Presidential Documents*
(from 2009 to the present) available at
http://www.gpoaccess.gov/presdocs/
index.html.

speeches each year to set forth their vision of the country's future, but the most prestigious and formalized address is the **State of the Union address,** which is given
annually, in late January or early February. In this speech, the president usually outlines
his legislative and foreign-policy priorities for the coming year.

Early Use of Persuasion Power   Presidents use the power to persuade much more
publicly today than in times past, as Figure 13.1 illustrates. Early presidents seldom
spoke in public, and when they did, they made only vague and general remarks. To
fulfill their obligation to report on the state of the union, Thomas Jefferson and his
nineteenth-century successors sent written messages to Congress. Early presidents
found other ways of persuading Congress. Instead of using public rhetoric, Jefferson, a
master politician, invited members of Congress to the Executive Mansion (later called
the White House) for dinners at which he would persuade them to support his political agenda.[19] Not until Woodrow Wilson addressed a joint session of both houses of
Congress in 1913 did it become a regular practice for presidents to report in person on
the state of the union.[20]

Modern Persuasion Power   More than any other president, Theodore ("Teddy")
Roosevelt changed the definition of what was permissible in presidential rhetoric.

State of the Union address
Annual speech delivered by the
president in late January or early
February in fulfillment of the
constitutional obligation of reporting
to Congress the state of the union.

Establishing a Modern Tradition

In 1916 Woodrow Wilson (right of center) became the first president to address joint sessions of both houses of Congress regularly.

• *Why do you think Wilson began the practice of personally delivering the State of the Union speech to Congress? Why have all presidents since Wilson followed this practice?*

bully pulpit

The nature of presidential status as an ideal vehicle for persuading the public to support the president's policies.

Popular President

Although President Theodore Roosevelt was an avid hunter, it was his decision to spare the life of a bear cub in 1902 that led to the emergence of the term "Teddy Bear."

• *How can symbolic actions such as this one increase the power of the presidential "bully pulpit"?*

Roosevelt made frequent use of what he called the **"bully pulpit"** available to presidents. (*Bully* was nineteenth-century slang for "excellent.") He believed the nature of presidential status was an ideal vehicle for persuading the public to support the president's policies. Roosevelt suggested that, like a preacher, the president could use his position to move his "congregation"—the public—to action. He mobilized support through bold gestures, forceful speeches, presidential trips, and dramatic turns of phrase. Although, as one historian has noted, "The number of laws [Roosevelt] inspired was certainly not in proportion to the amount of noise he emitted," the president did generate critical public support for conservation measures, anti-trust suits, and the Panama Canal project.[21] Roosevelt's popular appeal was such that a cartoon depicting the president sparing the life of a bear cub while hunting resulted in the emergence of the term "Teddy Bear."

Presidents since Teddy Roosevelt have increasingly used the bully pulpit to persuade Congress and the public, as Figure 13.1 shows.[22] Franklin Delano Roosevelt's "fireside chats" over the radio enabled him to sidestep the print media, which he accused of being controlled by Republican publishers. John Kennedy had a compelling rhetorical style that both inspired and challenged his audience. To take advantage of the president's public speaking skills, the Kennedy administration began to televise his press conferences, a step that one newspaper reporter grumbled was "the goofiest idea since the hula hoop."[23] Unlike the hula hoop, the televised press conference, a vital part of the permanent campaign, remains with us today.

President Reagan, the first president with experience as a professional actor, used television more effectively than any of his predecessors. He understood that there is but "a thin line between politics and theatricals."[24] As Reagan once said, "I've wondered how people in positions of this kind . . . manage without having had any acting experience."[25] Learning from Reagan's example, Barack Obama frequently paired policy initiatives with symbolic and photogenic gestures meant to reinforce the president's message. Obama traveled to a Wisconsin middle school in November 2009 to announce education initiatives, for example. President Obama also pioneered the use of the Internet to distribute weekly addresses, as Roosevelt had pioneered the use of radio.

The Veto Power

PRESIDENTIAL VETO POWER: *Before any law "shall take effect," it must be "approved by" the president.*

CONGRESSIONAL CHECK: *Unless "repassed by two-thirds of the Senate and House of Representatives."*

The president's **veto power** is more concrete than is the power to inform: It gives presidents the capacity to prevent bills passed by Congress from becoming law. Before the Civil War, presidents seldom used the veto. President Washington cast only two vetoes. The average number cast by presidents between Madison and Lincoln was only a little more than four. As Figure 13.2 shows, presidents from Franklin Roosevelt on have been much more willing to use the veto power.

This presidential power to say "No" can be checked. But Congress usually fails to muster the necessary two-thirds vote in each chamber to pass an **override,** which makes the bill a law despite the president's veto. Since the Kennedy administration, Congress has overridden approximately only one out of every ten vetoes.[26] Only two of President Clinton's 37 vetoes and four of President Bush's twelve vetoes were overridden.[27]

veto power

Power giving presidents the capacity to prevent bills passed by Congress from becoming law. It may be overridden by a two-thirds vote in each congressional chamber. Most state governors also have veto power over their legislatures.

override

Congressional passage of a bill by a two-thirds vote despite the president's veto.

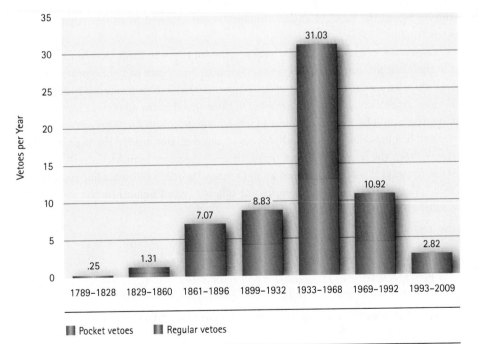

Pocket vetoes   Regular vetoes

FIGURE 13.2

TRENDS IN PRESIDENTIAL USE OF THE VETO POWER

Currently, presidents use the veto less than at mid-century, but more than in the early 1800s.

• *Why did presidents become more assertive in the early twentieth century? Why have recent presidents vetoed fewer bills?*

Note: Vetoes for the two administrations of Grover Cleveland (1885–1889, 1893–1897) have been excluded from these averages because of the unusual circumstances surrounding President Cleveland's use of the veto. See Theda Skocpol, *Protecting Soldiers and Mothers* (Cambridge, MA: Harvard University Press, 1992).

Sources: Michael A. Sollenberger, "Presidential Vetoes, 1789–Present: A Summary Overview," Congressional Research Service Report for Congress, 98–148 GOV, April 7, 2004; and United States Senate, "Summary of Bills Vetoed, 1789-present," available at http://www.senate.gov/reference/Legislation/Vetoes/vetoCounts.htm, accessed January 17, 2010.

Although the veto can seldom be used to initiate policy, it can be successfully employed as a weapon in negotiations with Congress. When Congress was controlled by their own party, neither George W. Bush nor Barack Obama vetoed many bills. But Bush used the threat of the veto in negotiations with Congress over such issues as homeland security legislation and reconstruction funds for Iraq, and Obama vowed to veto healthcare legislation if it added to the deficit.[28] These threats forced members of Congress to reconsider their plans.

pocket veto

Presidential veto after congressional adjournment, executed merely by not signing a bill into law.

If Congress enacts a law ten days before it adjourns, a president may exercise a **pocket veto** by simply not signing the bill into law. Congress has no opportunity to override a pocket veto, so congressional leaders view pocket vetoes as particularly irritating. Even Barack Obama's 2009 pocket veto of a minor appropriations measure prompted substantial grumbling from members of Congress.[29] The pocket veto strategy works only at the very end of a congressional session, however; if Congress remains in session for more than ten days after passing a bill, the president must explicitly cast a veto to prevent the bill from becoming law. As the distinction between campaigning and governing has disappeared, Congress has remained in session virtually throughout the entire year, giving more recent presidents fewer opportunities to cast pocket vetoes.

Although Congress sometimes manages to override vetoes, it more often counters the president's veto power indirectly, by incorporating policies that presidents oppose into large bills that contain items presidents feel they must approve. When faced with such a package, the president finds it difficult to cast a veto. For example, in 2005 George W. Bush opposed a congressional ban on "cruel and inhumane treatment of prisoners," arguing that the law would unduly tie the hands of the military. But he signed the measure anyway because it was attached to an important military spending bill.[30]

line item veto

Presidential authority to negate particular provisions of a law while letting the remainder stand; granted by Congress in 1996 but struck down by the Supreme Court in 1998.

Because Congress can artfully package laws in this way, many people favor giving the president the **line item veto**—the authority to negate particular provisions of a law while letting the remainder stand. The presidential line item veto has been a popular idea among congressional Republicans since the Reagan administration. In 1996, Congress passed legislation enacting a form of line item veto for the president, a measure that had President Clinton's wholehearted approval. But in 1998 the Supreme Court struck down the law as unconstitutional. In 2009, Senators John McCain (R–AZ) and Russ Feingold (D–WI) introduced a bill to grant President Obama a line item veto to reduce pork barrel spending. White House officials voiced support for the measure, but it failed to win congressional approval.[31]

The Appointment Power

PRESIDENTIAL POWER: *The president "shall appoint Ambassadors, other public Ministers and Consuls . . . and all other Officers of the United States."*

CONGRESSIONAL CHECK: *Appointments are subject to the "Advice and Consent of the Senate," which is taken to mean that a majority must approve the nomination.*

administration

The president and his political appointees, who are responsible for directing the executive branch of government.

The appointment power enables presidents to appoint thousands of public officials to positions of high responsibility within their **administration,** which consists of those responsible for directing the executive branch of government.

The Cabinet   The president's **cabinet** consists of the key members of the administration. Most are heads of government departments and carry the title **secretary.** Originally, the president's cabinet had but four departments, and the secretaries met regularly with the president, giving him confidential political guidance on a broad range of policies. It was in cabinet meetings, for example, that Abraham Lincoln developed his strategy for fighting the Civil War.

Over the years, government began to perform a much broader range of functions. As the number of departments grew from four to 15 (see Table 14.1, page 409), the cabinet lost its ability to assist presidents with the decision-making process on a regular basis. As the heads of large, complex departments, cabinet secretaries spend most of their time on management and less time giving advice to the commander in chief. In President Nixon's words, "Cabinet government is a myth and won't work. . . . No [president] in his right mind submits anything to his cabinet."[32] Today the cabinet meets only occasionally, primarily for ceremonial purposes or to help the president make some kind of political statement. Presidents rely on individual cabinet members for counsel when policy questions arise that fall within the purview of the department involved. But the cabinet as a whole makes few, if any, joint decisions. For more on the role of cabinet secretaries and executive branch agencies, see Chapter 14.

The White House Staff   Many of a modern president's closest advisers are not cabinet secretaries but White House aides who deal with presidential matters with utmost confidentiality. At one time, the president's personal staff was small and informal. Abraham Lincoln had just two young assistants. Even President Franklin Roosevelt originally had only a handful of personal aides. To address organizational problems caused by the growing size of the federal government, Roosevelt in 1936 asked a committee of specialists in public administration headed by Louis Brownlow to study the issue. Saying "the President needs help," the Brownlow Committee recommended sweeping changes, including additional appointments to the president's personal staff. Brownlow said presidential staff members "should be possessed of high competence, great physical vigor, and a passion for anonymity." Although Congress rejected most of the other Brownlow recommendations, it agreed to enlarge the White House staff.[33]

Brownlow envisioned only a "small number of executive assistants," but the president's staff has steadily increased in size and complexity.[34] The number of aides has grown from 48 in 1944 to over 400 today.[35] Its organization is now complex enough to confuse even well-informed citizens. One basic distinction to remember is the difference between the **White House Office,** the main subject under discussion here, which includes political appointees who work directly for the president, many of whom occupy offices in the White House, and the much larger **Executive Office of the President (EOP).** Although the names make it seem as though they are much the same thing, the White House Office is just one component of the EOP, which also includes other important coordinating bodies as well as operating agencies (see Table 13.1).

In Franklin Roosevelt's day, no single person—other than the president—headed the White House staff. Even as late as the Carter administration, White House aides worked together as "spokes in a wheel," each having direct access to the president. But today presidents usually place one person in charge.[36] This person, the **chief of staff,** meets with the president several times a day and communicates decisions to other staff, cabinet officers, and members of Congress.

cabinet
Top administration officials, most of whom are heads of departments in the executive branch.

secretary
The title of the head of a department within the executive branch.

White House Office
Political appointees who work directly for the president, many of whom occupy offices in the White House.

Executive Office of the President (EOP)
Agency that houses both top coordinating offices and other operating agencies.

chief of staff
Head of the White House staff, who has continuous, direct contact with the president.

TABLE 13.1
EXECUTIVE OFFICE OF THE PRESIDENT, BUDGET AND STAFF LEVELS

• *Why do you think the Office of Management and Budget is the largest component of the EOP after the White House (see Chapter 14)?*

	Budget (Millions)	Staff[a]
White House	$203	924
Office of Management and Budget	93	529
Office of National Drug Control Policy	30	118
Office of the U.S. Trade Representative	49	229
Office of Science and Technology Policy	7	40
Office of the Vice President	5	25
Council on Environmental Quality	3	24

Note: "The White House" includes the National Security Council and Homeland Security Council staff, the Office of Administration, and the Council of Economic Advisers, in addition to the White House Office and the Executive Residence.

[a]As of 2010.

Source: Executive Office of the President, *Budget of the United States Government, Fiscal Year 2011,* Appendix, 1145–1156.

The best chiefs are usually Washington insiders. Though little acclaimed, Ronald Reagan's 1987–1988 chief, Howard Baker, was one of the most powerful and effective. A former Senate majority leader, Baker helped boost Reagan's popularity, despite the fact that the aging president himself had lost much of his former vitality. Barack Obama's chief of staff, Rahm Emanuel, spent six years in the Clinton White House and served three terms on Capitol Hill as a Representative from Illinois before beginning work at the White House in 2009.

Newcomers to Washington are usually less successful. Typically, they become lightning rods—people to be blamed when things go wrong. John Sununu, former governor of New Hampshire, was forced to leave the job of chief of staff when he was blamed for urging President George H. W. Bush to sign an unpopular tax increase.[37] Thomas McLarty from Arkansas resigned after early Clinton administration missteps.[38]

Although Brownlow expected White House aides to have "no power to make decisions," modern presidents have regularly used their staffs to shape their public policy proposals.[39] Within the White House staff, more than anywhere else, presidents can count on the loyalty of those around them simply because, unlike the careers of department secretaries, those of staff members are closely intertwined with that of the president.

The White House staff is more potent than ever, in part because presidents have more need than ever for political help. Presidents today need pollsters who can keep them in touch with changes in public opinion.[40] They also need assistants who can help them communicate with the media, interest groups, and members of Congress. Once a major piece of legislation arrives for consideration on the chamber floor, White House aides are in regular contact with many legislators.[41] So intense is the work inside the White House that most staff jobs demand seven-day, 100-hour work weeks.

As a result, many positions go to young energetic people, and even they get tired after years on the job. In the later years of the George W. Bush administration, one long time White House staffer admitted, "We're all burned out."[42]

Quite apart from the president's genuine need for lots of political help, appointment to the White House staff is an excellent way to reward loyal campaign workers. After the presidency has been won, those who worked on the campaign often expect something in return. For example, when Barack Obama became president, he appointed his chief campaign strategist David Axelrod and his campaign spokesman Robert Gibbs to key White House posts. The White House Office is also a convenient place for the president to put campaign workers, because the president has exclusive control over appointments to his personal staff. Not even the chief of staff must be confirmed by the Senate.

The Power to Recommend

PRESIDENTIAL POWER: *The president may recommend to Congress for "their consideration such Measures as he shall judge necessary and expedient."*

CONGRESSIONAL CHECK: *Only Congress may enact measures into law.*

The power to recommend gives the president the power of initiation—the power to set the political agenda.[43] Presidents can shut down old policy options, create new possibilities, and change the political dialogue. George W. Bush placed tax cuts, education initiatives, and Medicare reform on the agenda; Barack Obama proposed an economic stimulus package, climate change measures, and healthcare reform.

However, this power does not go unchecked. Congress can—and often does—ignore or greatly modify a presidential recommendation. Congress rejected Clinton's healthcare proposals and greatly modified his proposals on welfare reform. Nor is the power to initiate limited to the president. In 2010, Congressional Republicans campaigned on a platform called the "Pledge to America" that they sought to implement upon winning control of the House of Representatives.

Early Use of the Power to Recommend   Presidents used the power to recommend with great restraint in the decades preceding the Civil War.[44] Because the president was the symbol of the nation as a whole, and because the nation was divided into free and slave states, presidents dared not talk about slavery, the most important political question of the period. This principle of silence was extended to other issues as well; in general, presidents were expected to remain publicly mute on an issue once deliberations about it had begun on Capitol Hill.[45]

Modern Use of the Power to Recommend   Use of the presidential power to recommend expanded rapidly after the end of the Civil War. The country was growing swiftly, and many social and economic problems were becoming national in scope. The nation's strongest presidents have had their greatest impact not so much by making decisions as by opening up new possibilities. For example, Franklin Roosevelt called for a New Deal that would protect Americans from economic downturns and persuaded Congress to pass dozens of important bills within 100 days of his inauguration. Lyndon Johnson proposed so-called "Great Society" programs to address the issues of poverty and health care for senior citizens.

Presidential Transitions

A White House staffer removes a portrait of outgoing president George W. Bush.

• *What advice would you give a president who wants to have a successful transition and honeymoon period?*

transition

The period after a presidential candidate has won the November election, but before the candidate assumes office as president on January 20.

honeymoon

The first several months of a presidency, when reporters are more forgiving than usual, Congress is more inclined to be cooperative, and the public is more receptive to new approaches.

Timing Presidential Initiatives Presidents make most new proposals at the very beginning of their first term. This is the time when presidential popularity is at a peak, and both Congress and the country are eager to hear what solutions the new president is bringing to the country's problems. Later in a presidency, unexpected events, the legacy of past policies, and rebellions within a president's own constituencies may make it difficult for presidents to get their message across. As one of Lyndon Johnson's top aides noted, "You've got to give it all you can that first year. . . . You've got just one year when they treat you right. . . . You can't put anything through when half of the Congress is thinking about how to beat you."[46] Thus, the Obama administration made a strong effort to get Congress to approve its healthcare legislation before the president's first year in office was up.

Because the beginning of a presidential term is so important, the **transition** period between the previous presidency and the new one is critical. The transition period consists of the approximately 75 days between Election Day and January 20, Inauguration Day. Incoming presidents do not yet have the burdens of office, but they have the time and resources to set the stage for a vigorous start. If the transition is well organized, this is the best of all times for building public support.

The transition period is typically followed by the presidential **honeymoon**—the first several months of a presidency, when reporters are kinder than usual, Congress is more inclined to be cooperative, and the public is receptive to new approaches.[47] Franklin Roosevelt's successful first 100 days set the standard by which all presidential honeymoons have been judged.

Some analysts have wondered whether presidential honeymoons have gone the way of rotary-dial telephones and wooden tennis rackets. As public expectations have risen and presidents have become ever more exposed to media scrutiny, chief executives can no longer count on a period of goodwill before facing determined opposition.[48] Certainly, the example of Bill Clinton's honeymoon seems to support this point of view—it hardly lasted the time it took him to traverse the Inauguration Day parade route from the Capitol to the White House. Embarrassing gaffes and delays in acting on core policy issues led to what one columnist called "the most politically troubled young presidency of the post–World War II period."[49]

Presidents George W. Bush and Barack Obama had more successful honeymoons, however. Both presidents swiftly named cabinet members, avoided controversies, and passed major economic legislation (tax cuts in Bush's case, an economic stimulus in Obama's). The contrast between Clinton's difficult honeymoon and these recent smooth transitions has quieted those who argued that modern honeymoon periods are doomed to failure. Planning, unity of purpose, and learning from previous mistakes may increase the chances of presidential success.

The President as Commander in Chief

PRESIDENTIAL POWER: *"The President shall be Commander in Chief of the Army, and Navy of the United States. . . ."*

CONGRESSIONAL CHECK: *"The Congress shall have power. . .To declare war. . . To raise and support armies. . .To provide and maintain a navy . . . [and] To make Rules for the government and regulation of the land and naval forces."*

Anyone who hears the president's official tune, "Hail to the Chief," is reminded that the president is the **commander in chief,** the constitutional head of the U.S. armed forces. (The Marine Band began routinely playing this piece for presidents in the 1830s.) Although Congress has the power to declare war, presidents have claimed the authority to send the military into combat without congressional authorization at least since Thomas Jefferson sent frigates to challenge the Barbary pirates off the coast of Tripoli in 1801.

commander in chief
The president in his constitutional role as head of the U.S. armed forces.

Often, presidents have justified their independent actions as necessary under the circumstances. As Alexander Hamilton wrote, "Decision, activity, secrecy, and dispatch" are characteristics most often found in a single person, and not in a legislature.[50] Nearly two centuries after Jefferson's action against the Barbary pirates, for example, President Ronald Reagan sent planes to bomb Libya in retaliation for the country's support of international terrorism. The president notified key members of Congress at the last minute, but did not seek their approval, so as not to warn the Libyan government that an attack was imminent.

Congress has not officially declared war since World War II, even though U.S. armed forces were repeatedly mobilized by the president to fight enemy forces in Korea, Vietnam, the Persian Gulf, Iraq, Afghanistan, and many other parts of the world. After the Vietnam conflict, Congress passed a resolution saying its authorization was required if a military conflict lasted for more than 60 days, and such authorizations were obtained before troops were placed in Iraq and Afghanistan. President Obama also secured explicit congressional support for the 2009 military buildup in Afghanistan. Congress affects presidential decisions in more subtle ways as well. For example, presidents are less likely to use force when the opposition party controls Congress, probably because of the increased potential for opposition to the conflict once it begins.[51] (See Chapter 20 for a more detailed discussion of foreign policy.)

The President as Chief of State

PRESIDENTIAL POWER: The President *"shall receive Ambassadors and other public Ministers . . . and shall Commission all the Officers of the United States."*

CONGRESSIONAL CHECK: *None.*

In bestowing one of the very few unchecked powers granted to the president, this constitutional clause seems to say little more than that presidents may welcome visitors and administer oaths of office. Yet the words endow presidents with an invaluable political resource, the capacity to act with all the dignity countries accord their heads of state. In many countries, the political leader and the head of state are institutionally separated (see the accompanying *International Comparison*). In the United States, the president plays both roles.

INTERNATIONAL COMPARISON

The Chief of State in Other Countries

In the 2006 film *The Queen,* starring Helen Mirren, there is a key scene that seems strangely alien to American eyes. Tony Blair, the newly elected prime minister of Great Britain, makes a ceremonial visit to Buckingham Palace in 1997 to seek Queen Elizabeth's blessing. He kneels before her and reverently kisses her hands. Such a ceremonial occasion would be impossible in the United States, where the president is both the political leader and the chief of state.[1]

In many countries, these two offices are institutionally separated. In Great Britain, the dignified chief of state is the queen. She symbolizes the unity of the nation, represents her country on formal international occasions, and presides over national holidays. The efficient aspect of British government is headed by the country's prime minister. Though powerful, prime ministers lack royal dignity. Their residence is a modest home tucked away on a small London side street.

The division of political responsibilities in Japan is much the same. The emperor of Japan is the dignified chief of state; the elected prime minister is—in ceremonial terms—nothing more than the emperor's efficient minister. Of course, the dignified queen and emperor have very little real power, but their presence as a symbol of the unity of the nation reminds people that the ministers can be ejected by the voters at any time.

In the United States, presidents are expected to combine both the efficient and the dignified aspects of government. In addition to their political and policy tasks, presidents are expected to be the symbol of national unity. When queens and emperors assemble, the United States is represented by its president. On days of national celebration, such as Independence Day and Thanksgiving, it is the president who is called upon to express national hopes and dreams. Presidents live in the White House, which, though modest by the standards of European and Japanese castles, has become an increasingly grand focal point of Washington society.

- *Do you think the dignified aspect of national leadership is necessary? What needs does it fill?*

- *What are the advantages and disadvantages of combining the efficient and dignified aspects of leadership in one person?*

[1] Alan Cowell, "Not Quite 'Liz' and 'Gordie,' but Palace Protocol Is Looser," *New York Times* (June 28, 2007), 12.

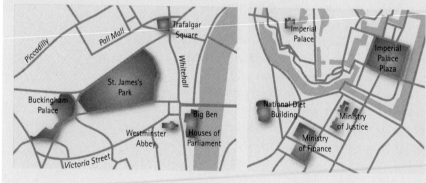

EFFICIENT AND DIGNIFIED ASPECTS

These maps of central London (left) and central Tokyo (right) illustrate that the dignified aspect, embodied in the monarch, remains integral to but distinct from, the rest of government. In London, Buckingham Palace is a short walk from the Houses of Parliament and in Tokyo, the Imperial Palace stands near the National Diet (legislature).

efficient aspect

According to Walter Bagehot, the aspect of government that involves making policy, administering the laws, and settling disputes.

dignified aspect

According to Walter Bagehot, the aspect of government, including royalty and ceremony, that generates citizen respect and loyalty.

According to Walter Bagehot, a nineteenth-century analyst of British politics, governments have both efficient and dignified aspects.[52] The **efficient aspect** of government involves the making of policy, administration of the laws, and the settling of political disputes. This is the nuts and bolts of day-to-day policymaking, the kind of activity enjoyed by the Washington insider, often derisively called a "policy wonk." It is also hard work that frequently generates conflict. But government also has a **dignified aspect** that Bagehot thought equally important to its long-term effectiveness. Governments must express the unity of the people, their high moral purposes, their hopes for the future, and their capacity to defend themselves against foreign aggressors. Ceremonial occasions provide opportunities for expression of the dignified aspect of government that helps sustain public trust and loyalty.

Early American presidents were expected to play only a limited role in the efficient aspect of government so that they could enhance the dignity of the national government and serve as a unifying symbol for a far-flung country. By remaining aloof from day-to-day legislative politics, presidents tried to retain the respect and admiration of citizens throughout the nation. As presidents have become increasingly engaged in the efficient aspect of government, they have sometimes found it more difficult to maintain their dignity.

Presidents Richard Nixon and Ronald Reagan chose to accentuate the dignified aspect of the presidency, with markedly different results. Nixon enjoyed the pomp and circumstance of office, but as the Watergate scandal developed, many Americans began to feel that the president's vaguely royal pretensions were endangering democratic practices. Seven years after Nixon left office, Reagan worked assiduously to restore grandeur to the presidency. White House social events once again became formal affairs. The unveiling of a restored Statue of Liberty was carefully designed to celebrate the country's past and future. At the same time, Reagan withdrew from day-to-day legislative politics. By emphasizing the dignity of the office, Reagan acquired the nickname "the Teflon president," because bad news never seemed to stick to him.

Presidents Gerald Ford, Jimmy Carter, and Bill Clinton de-emphasized the splendor of the office. Ford adopted a folksy, informal manner that provided a noted contrast with his predecessor, Nixon. Carter wore a sweater, carried his own suitcases, and remained on a first-name basis with ordinary voters. At the same time, Carter became deeply involved in the efficient aspects of government, working late into the night on policy issues and foreign policy crises. Clinton likewise became known as a "policy wonk" who was engaged with specifics, sometimes at the expense of broader themes. After advisers warned him that this style left the public without a broad sense of what the president was fighting for, Clinton began to stress larger themes in his speeches.[53]

George W. Bush faced an agonizing conflict between the efficient and dignified aspects of the presidency on September 11, 2001. After the attacks on the World Trade Center and the Pentagon, security officials whisked Bush onto Air Force One from a Florida elementary school where he had been speaking, keeping his location secret for hours. Secret Service and military aides insisted that the president be kept safe to ensure a clear chain of command. But the nation clearly needed a dignified president to reassure the public and provide a sense of unified national response to the terrorism. Accordingly, Bush returned to the White House at 7 p.m. and delivered a televised address 90 minutes later. The symbolism of the White House address was as important as its substance. "It cannot look as if the president has been run off," said former White House official William Bennett, "or it will look like we can't defend our most important institutions."[54]

The First Lady   The historical role of the president's wife, traditionally called the **first lady,** was to reinforce the dignified aspect of the presidency. In keeping with the traditional role women have played in American society, first ladies typically hosted social events, visited the sick, promoted children's issues, and loyally stood by their husbands in times of trouble. Yet some were able to use this dignified role to make contributions that will long be remembered. Jacqueline Kennedy invigorated interest in the arts and cultural activities in Washington, and restored the White House. Nancy Reagan's "Just Say No" educational program may have done more to reduce drug use than billions of dollars spent in antidrug enforcement efforts.[55] When Michelle Obama

An Informal President
President Jimmy Carter was uncomfortable with the formal trappings of the dignified aspect of the presidency, adopting a casual style even when meeting with chiefs of state. He donned his trademark sweater for negotiations with Egyptian president Anwar Sadat.

• *Does informality detract from the president's power?*

first lady
Traditional title of the president's wife.

An Aide Informs George W. Bush of the 9/11 Attacks

President Bush insisted on returning to the White House on September 11, 2001, to fulfill his role as national leader. But security officials worried about threats to the president's person and kept his location secret for much of the day.

• In such a crisis, how should we weigh the president's safety against the need for visible national leadership?

became first lady in 2009, she emphasized the dignified aspects of the role by visiting local schools and embarking on a campaign to reduce childhood obesity.

Not all first ladies have been content to confine themselves to the dignified aspect of the presidency, however. Eleanor Roosevelt promoted civil rights and other social causes supported only off-handedly by her husband.[56] But Hillary Rodham Clinton gave the role a dramatically new definition by participating in policy formation to a greater degree than any previous first lady. She parlayed this substantive policy role into a Senate seat, a presidential run of her own in 2008, and a position as Secretary of State in the Obama administration.

The Vice President   Traditionally, the vice president's impact on policy has been so limited that the dignity of the office suffered as well. The nation's first vice president, John Adams, wrote to his wife, "My country has in its wisdom contrived for me the most insignificant office that ever the invention of man contrived. . . . I can do neither good nor evil." Harry Truman, when he was vice president, allowed that the job was "about as useful as a cow's fifth teat."[57]

Jokes about the vice presidency have a basis in reality. The only formal responsibility of the office is to preside over the United States Senate and cast a vote there in case of a tie. Otherwise, the vice president's duties and influence depend entirely on the will of the president. As Vice President Hubert Humphrey put it, "He who giveth can taketh away and often does."[58]

Presidents have traditionally been reluctant to delegate responsibility to vice presidents, because they constitute a potential political problem. Presidents cannot fire their vice presidents, as they can other aides. If a vice president decides to criticize the president or pursue an independent policy line, the president can do little about it. When Vice President Nelson Rockefeller pushed more liberal policies than those favored by Gerald Ford, he proved an embarrassment to the president and was not chosen to be Ford's running mate in 1976. Some analysts claim the Rockefeller controversy cost Ford his reelection.

The vice presidential selection process accentuates the potential for conflict, because vice presidents often come from a wing of the party different from that of the president.[59] An aide to John Kennedy admitted that Lyndon Johnson was picked for vice president because "he was the leader of that segment of the party where Kennedy had very little strength—the South."[60] Later feuds between Kennedy's aides and Johnson could be traced in part to that basic fact. John McCain's choice of Sarah Palin as his running mate reinforced his image as a "maverick," willing to make unorthodox choices, but infighting between McCain's staff and Palin's proved to be distracting.

Even if presidents have powerful incentives to limit the vice presidential role, we can no longer dismiss vice presidents as political lightweights. For one thing, no person is more likely to become president of the United States than the vice president, who can succeed to the office through the death or resignation of the president, or by winning the next election. Twelve of the 44 presidents of the United States held the office of vice president, and no fewer than four of the last nine presidents were vice presidents.

Perhaps because of the greater awareness that the vice president may one day gain the highest office, the role of the vice president has steadily become more powerful. George W. Bush's vice president, experienced Washington insider Richard Cheney, was among the most powerful vice presidents in history. His lack of political ambition (he professed no desire for the presidency) ensured that he would not become the president's rival. Still, Cheney's advocacy of the Iraq War and his outspoken conservatism on other subjects often made him the target of administration critics. Before becoming vice president, Joe Biden chaired the Senate foreign relations committee. Inasmuch as he had bolstered Obama's foreign policy credentials during the 2008 campaign, it was only natural that he played a significant foreign policy role in the Obama Administration. However, he was known to be skeptical of the military buildup in Afghanistan that the president ordered.

Inherent Executive Power

PRESIDENTIAL INHERENT EXECUTIVE POWER: *"The executive power shall be vested in a President."*

Some scholars claim that this statement adds nothing to presidential power beyond the specific powers granted to the president. But many presidents have found in this clause the basis for a claim to additional rights and privileges. As we will see in Chapter 20, presidential claims to inherent executive power have been invoked most frequently in making foreign policy. But presidents have asserted **inherent executive power** on other occasions as well. Teddy Roosevelt placed 46 million acres of public land into the National Forest system just before signing a bill denying presidents the power to place any more land in the National Forest system.[61] After leaving office, Roosevelt admitted, "My belief was that it was not only the [president's] right but his duty to do anything that the needs of the Nation demanded unless such action was forbidden by the Constitution or by its laws."[62]

inherent executive power
Presidential authority inherent in the executive branch of government, although not specifically mentioned in the Constitution.

Executive Orders   One way in which presidents use their inherent executive powers is by issuing **executive orders**—directives that carry the weight of law even though they are not enacted by Congress. The Supreme Court ruled in 1936 that executive orders are constitutional, and since then they have increased in frequency and importance.[63]

executive order
A presidential directive that has the force of law, although it is not enacted by Congress.

Executive Order

President Obama signs an executive order to begin the process of closing the detention center at Guantanamo Bay, Cuba.

• *Why do you think recent presidents have issued more executive orders than presidents 50 or 100 years ago?*

Executive orders were used by Harry Truman to desegregate the armed forces, by Lyndon Johnson to institute the first affirmative action program, and by George W. Bush to authorize military trials for suspected Al Qaeda terrorists. Executive orders may not run counter to congressional legislation, and they may be overturned by Congress. The use of executive orders among modern presidents has increased sharply, from about five major orders a year in the 1950s, to more than a dozen in recent years.[64] President Obama used executive orders to begin the process of closing detention facilities at Guantanamo Bay, Cuba, and to relax restrictions on government-funded stem cell research.[65]

Executive Privilege   The most controversial invocation of inherent executive powers has been the doctrine of **executive privilege**—the right of the president to deny Congress information it requests on the grounds that the activities of the executive branch must be kept confidential. George Washington was the first to invoke executive privilege when he refused to provide Congress information about an ill-fated military expedition on the grounds that its "disclosure . . . would injure the public."[66] Ever since, presidents have claimed authority to withhold from Congress information on executive decision making. The Watergate scandal brought the question before the Supreme Court, which sanctioned the doctrine of executive privilege, saying that private communication among aides to the president was "fundamental to the operation of government and inextricably rooted in the separation of powers under the Constitution."[67]

The Supreme Court went on to say that, although Congress could not simply demand access to any and all conversations taking place among the president's advisers, executive privilege could not be invoked to cover up criminal conduct. Communication that might be privileged under other circumstances loses that status when wrongdoing occurs. Nor can it be left to the executive branch to decide whether the communication is part of a coverup. The disputed documents must be submitted to a court for its examination behind closed doors. When the Supreme Court examined the Watergate documents, they found sufficient evidence of criminal conduct such that President Nixon was forced to release the documents.

The Supreme Court's Watergate ruling did not halt presidents' invocation of inherent executive power, however. The George W. Bush administration successfully resisted Congressional attempts to obtain records of a controversial White House energy task force.[68] In 2009, the Obama administration declined to make staff available for congressional testimony when a couple in fashionable evening clothes, breaching security, crashed a White House dinner party in honor of the prime minister of India.[69]

The Power to Pardon   The constitution grants the president the "Power to Grant Reprieves and Pardons for Offenses against the United States." The president may use this power at his or her discretion, with the obvious exception of cases of impeachment. Pardons have stirred major controversies throughout American history. During and after the Civil War, Presidents Lincoln and Johnson pardoned many Confederate soldiers, to the consternation of radicals in Congress. President Ford pardoned former President Nixon for any crimes he committed in connection with the Watergate affair, and President Carter granted a blanket amnesty to draft resisters after the Vietnam War.

More recently, President Clinton was accused of abusing his pardon power when he pardoned an alleged tax evader whose ex-wife had donated hundreds of thousands of dollars to the Democratic Party and to Clinton's presidential library in Arkansas. When George W. Bush commuted the sentence of a Cheney aide convicted of perjury

executive privilege
The right of the president to deny Congress information it requests on the grounds that the activities of the executive branch must be kept confidential.

in the case of an administration leak, critics charged that the president was employing a double standard for administration officials.

The Impeachment Power

CONGRESSIONAL IMPEACHMENT POWER: *Presidents may be impeached by a majority of the House of Representatives for "high crimes and misdemeanors." The president is removed from office if the Senate convicts by a two-thirds vote.*

Nothing makes clearer the subordination of presidents to Congress than the fact that the House of Representatives can impeach and the Senate can convict and remove presidents from office. Though seldom used, the constitutional power of **impeachment** is no dead letter. Andrew Johnson was impeached in 1868, although the Senate, by one vote, failed to convict him.[70] Richard Nixon resigned in the face of almost certain impeachment in 1974. And President Clinton's affair with Monica Lewinsky, a White House intern, led to the first impeachment and trial of a president in more than a century.

In 1994, a three-judge panel appointed Kenneth Starr as **independent counsel** with the authority to investigate charges related to the questionable Whitewater land deal in which Clinton had been involved while governor of Arkansas. After a wide-ranging investigation, Starr concluded that Clinton had obstructed justice and committed perjury when, in a separate case, he denied under oath having sexual relations with Lewinsky.

The president argued that his carefully worded denial did not constitute perjury, and the electorate seemed to take his side: Republicans lost ground in the 1998 congressional elections. But, on December 19, 1998, the House voted (along mostly partisan lines) to impeach the president, making him only the second U.S. chief executive to be threatened with removal from office by Congress.

In early 1999, the Senate held its trial, with Chief Justice William Rehnquist presiding. In considering their votes, most senators believed that if they were to overturn a national election by removing Clinton from office, they needed a more serious cause. After all, polls showed that two-thirds of the public still thought the president should stay.[71] On February 12, the Senate voted for acquittal.

Some scholars have argued that the partisan nature of Clinton's impeachment is a sign that the practice is more likely to be used in the future as a political weapon. Others disagree, however, noting that the circumstances of the scandal were unique. "If Watergate was a 'long national nightmare,'" suggests one presidential scholar, the Lewinsky scandal "seems more like a drug-induced hallucination."[72] Clinton's continued popularity as the impeachment controversy progressed suggests that impeachment can be politically costly when employed against a popular president.

Presidential Expectations and Presidential Performance

Presidents are expected to be strong, yet presidential powers are limited. As a result, presidents seldom satisfy the hopes and aspirations of the voting public. To sustain their reputation and effectiveness, presidents can sometimes act with Machiavellian cleverness. When Abraham Lincoln took office, seven southern states had already seceded from the Union and were threatening a Union outpost at South Carolina's Fort Sumter.

impeachment
Recommendation by a majority of the House of Representatives that a president, another official in the executive branch, or a judge of the federal courts be removed from office; removal depends on a two-thirds vote of the Senate.

independent counsel
Legal officer (originally called special prosecutor) appointed by a court to investigate allegations of criminal activity on the part of high-ranking members of the executive branch.

13.3
Assess why presidential reputation and popularity are important to presidential performance and what factors contribute to presidential greatness.

Moving while Congress was out of session, Lincoln announced that he would order the U.S. Navy to send new supplies to the fort. After Confederates fired on Sumter as supply ships neared, Lincoln blamed the South for starting the war and received overwhelming support in the North. By forcing the South's hand, Lincoln created a situation that advantaged the Union cause.[73]

Presidents in the past were frequently able to cover ruthless actions with a cloak of dignity that the role of chief of state allowed them to wear. But, as the life of the president becomes more open to the media, it gets harder to keep the cloak of dignity firmly in place. As Bill Clinton put it, "It is difficult for people to function in an environment in which they feel that their character, their values, and their motives are always suspect, and where the presumption here is against them."[74]

Presidential Reputations

beltway insider
The politically influential people who work inside the highway that surrounds Washington, DC.

To meet public expectations despite their limited power, presidents need to protect their professional reputation among members of Congress and other **beltway insiders,** the politically influential people who live inside the highway that surrounds Washington, DC.[75] Presidential reputations inside Washington are shaped by the quality of the people who serve the presidents and the frequency with which presidents win political contests. President Obama initially won plaudits for his skill getting his stimulus package through Congress, but then suffered a series of setbacks, such as the failure to secure a global warming agreement in Copenhagen and passage of his healthcare reform bill within the first year of his administration. Some experts thought Obama's reputation would turn on his ability to focus public attention on other issues where his chances of succeeding were greater. Sometimes a reputation is best saved by a president's success at letting go of issues that cannot be won. As Lincoln put it, "When you have got an elephant by the hind legs and he is trying to run away, it is best to let him run."[76]

Presidential Popularity

presidential popularity
Evaluation of a president by voters, usually as measured by a survey question asking the adult population how well they think the president is doing the job.

In addition to guarding their professional reputation, presidents need to maintain their popularity with the general public. As Lincoln also shrewdly observed, "With public sentiment, nothing can fail; without it, nothing can succeed."[77] **Presidential popularity** is measured by asking the adult population how well they think the president is doing his job. Pollsters now ask the same question almost every week, so it provides a decent barometer of the public's current assessment of the president's performance.

All presidents experience fluctuations in their popularity over the course of their terms. But as a general rule, presidential popularity tends to decline over time as public expectations go unfulfilled.[78] A study of the first term of eight recent presidents indicates that apart from any specific economic or foreign policy events, their popularity fell by nearly 8 points in their first year in office and by 15 points by the middle of their third year. Their popularity recovered in their fourth year, when a presidential campaign was under way, probably because at that time, presidents make special efforts to communicate positive news about their administrations. Presidents regained popularity when reelected, but once again it trailed off.[79]

Barack Obama's approval ratings began high—around 75 percent—but sank below 50 percent by 2010 (see Figure 13.3). Presidential popularity and professional reputation were at one time regarded as two quite separate phenomena. Unpopular presidents

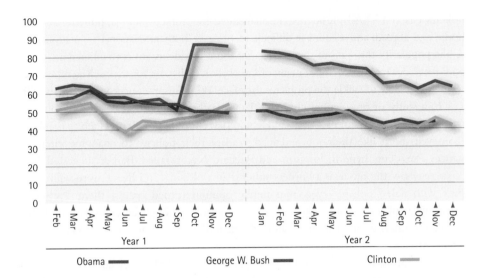

FIGURE 13.3

Presidential Approval Ratings in the First Two Years in Office

Presidential approval often falls after an initial "honeymoon" period.

• *Why do you think George W. Bush's approval ratings look different from Obama's or Clinton's?*

Source: Gallup Polls, various years.

could still have the respect of beltway insiders if they husbanded their political resources carefully. But the distinction between popularity and reputation has become clouded.[80] Presidents are the focus of seemingly inexhaustible television, newspaper, and Internet coverage. As soon as they have addressed one problem, they are urged to solve the next. As one commentator put it, "Getting the public's attention, particularly on a subject that the polls show is already gnawing at people, is no trick for a President. . . . The trick is holding that attention."[81]

The one kind of attention that presidents are likely to hold is the kind they don't want. When George H. W. Bush became nauseated at a state dinner in Tokyo, the embarrassing consequences were graphically reported by the media. President Clinton voiced exasperation over a "totally bogus story" that claimed he held up flights on a runway while getting a $200 haircut.[82] President Obama wandered into a racial controversy when asked about an altercation that occurred at Harvard University. A white police officer, responding to reports of a break-in, arrested a well-known African American professor after the scholar, using profane language, objected vociferously to having been asked in his own house to provide proof of his identity. Obama provoked an uproar when he said the police officer had "acted stupidly."[83] The president put the issue to rest by inviting both the officer and the professor to the White House for a conciliatory beer.

When these kinds of incidents cause a president's popularity to slip, weekly polling results transmit this information to beltway insiders. If the president's reputation is slipping in Washington, the news media just as quickly communicate insider opinions to the wider public. As a result, the president now has to work both the inside and the outside of the beltway at the same time.[84] This blurred line between Washington politics and national popularity is one of the key features of the new American democracy.

Great Presidents

"The best presidents," argued one perceptive observer, "are like magnets below a piece of paper, invisibly aligning iron filings into a new pattern of their making. Anyone can get experts to produce policy papers. The trick is to forge consensus to get those policies enacted."[85] All presidents are challenged by problems and opponents both at home and abroad, and all find it difficult to preserve both professional reputation and public popularity throughout their terms. Yet some presidents are remembered as "great presidents" because they achieve many of the objectives they set for themselves; others are seemingly unable to tackle the problems they face. Why do some succeed and others fail?

In a study of presidential character, James Barber argued that certain personality traits make for successful presidents.[86] He said that effective presidents (such as Franklin Roosevelt) both like their job and readily adapt their policies to changing circumstances. Presidents Lyndon Johnson and Richard Nixon failed, Barber suggested, because they saw the office as a burden rather than a blessing, and hence were willing to stick with failed policies even after public opinion turned against them. President Eisenhower missed the list of top presidents because, although he enjoyed his job, he waited for others to propose solutions to the nation's problems and so was too passive as a policymaker.

As tempting as explanations based on personality might be, they fail to account for the extent to which presidential performance depends on the conditions under which the officeholder must act.[87] Presidential scholar Stephen Skowronek says that most presidents are so hemmed in by the checks placed upon them that they simply cannot accomplish the job the public expects. As a result, presidents become "great" only when political circumstances allow them to repudiate the past and move in a sharply different direction. By rejecting the old way of doing things, they are able to discard political baggage that would limit presidential action.

Franklin Roosevelt was one such president. Running for office in 1932 in the midst of the Great Depression, he declared, "these unhappy times call for . . . plans . . . that build from the bottom up and not from the top down, that put their faith once more in the forgotten man." After an election that realigned the American party system (see Chapter 8), Roosevelt pushed through a huge volume of important legislation in his first 100 days in office.

A President's Resignation
Grimly determined to do his duty until the end, Richard Nixon doggedly repeats his "V for victory" sign upon leaving office on August 9, 1974.

• *Were Nixon's difficulties due to his personality?*

Continued on page 390

The Politics of U.S. Energy Policy

The Issue

What action should the president take to reduce dependency on foreign oil and to address the environmental damage that results from the use of oil, gas, and other fossil fuels?

Background

During the 2008 presidential race, candidates in both parties promised to reduce the country's dependence on foreign oil and to address the threat of global climate change. Democrat Barack Obama called climate change "one of the top priorities that the next president has to pursue."[1] Republican John McCain put it another way: "Suppose we do nothing, and we don't eliminate this $400 billion dependence we have on foreign oil. Some of that money goes to terrorist organizations and also contributes to greenhouse gas emissions. Then what kind of a world have we given our children?"[2]

Scientists have drawn attention to the climate change problem with increasing urgency. Average global temperatures have now reached levels higher than at any time within the last 400 years.[3] Although it remains uncertain as to exactly how much of the increase is due to the burning of fossil fuels, most of the increase in temperatures appears to have occurred since industrialization (which began around 1850), a timeframe suggesting that the

24 billion tons of carbon dioxide (CO_2) and related pollutants produced annually by automobiles, factories, and other industrial sources around the world have caused the atmosphere to trap more solar heat than in previous eras.[4] If warming continues at its current pace, most scientists predict that within a century habitats will undergo major changes, ice masses at the two poles will melt, and the resulting rise in sea levels will flood coastal areas worldwide. In 2007, former vice president Al Gore and the United Nations Intergovernmental Panel on Climate Change shared a Nobel Peace Prize for their work on the issue. "We have the ability to solve this crisis," argued Gore in his acceptance speech, "and avoid the worst—though not all—of its consequences, if we act boldly, decisively, and quickly."[5]

Most observers agree that it will take presidential leadership both to address the vulnerability of the country's energy supply and to rally the nation and the world around a plan to stem rising global temperatures. The government has not ignored these problems altogether. In 1975, Congress created a strategic petroleum reserve (oil purchased on a regular basis by the government to be held for potential use in times of national crisis). It also passed three pieces of energy legislation, the first in 1992, the second in 2005, and the third in 2007, but few believe the changes enacted were sweeping enough to be truly effective. The provisions of the 1992 act, for example, were found by a government auditing agency to be too weak to meet the law's

An Energy Policy Crisis
President Obama meets with local officials after the 2010 Deepwater Horizon oil spill in the Gulf of Mexico.

own energy conservation goals.[6] The 2005 and 2007 acts offered tax credits for purchasers of hybrid cars and increased fuel economy standards for the first time in decades, but did little to encourage widespread energy conservation or develop non-fossil fuel energy sources.[7]

The United Nations has sponsored several efforts to address climate change. The first, the Kyoto Protocol of 1997, was signed by more than 140 countries but failed to win U.S. backing, and left out developing countries like China and India altogether. Disagreements between developed and developing nations plagued the Copenhagen talks on climate change, which itself resulted in a minor nonbinding agreement in 2009 (see chapter opening). Negotiators held out hope for later negotiations in Mexico.

Energy Policy and Elections

Both global warming and the vulnerability of the nation's energy supply have been major issues in recent elections, but energy is by far the more volatile of the two. If oil supplies are disrupted and energy prices spike, the cost of transportation, heating, air conditioning, and other energy use could have a serious impact on the family budget. According to one study, the average family was paying over $1,300 more per year for gasoline in 2008 than it was in 2000.[8]

When an energy-related crisis occurs, political leaders are tempted to look for quick fixes that seem to ameliorate the situation. When BP's Deepwater Horizon oil rig exploded and spewed millions of barrels of oil into the ocean in 2010, for example, members of Congress berated oil executives and called for the company to compensate those affected. But enactment of legislation that could help address the long-term energy crunch—heavy taxes on energy usage, encouragement of nuclear energy, or comprehensive regulation of the transportation industry, for example—has been as rare as a $1.00 gallon of gas. "Congress is never at its best when it is trying to solve a long-term problem in the short term," said Representative Ellen Tauscher (D-CA).[9] When it comes to long-term vision and forceful leadership, the president is the person best positioned to succeed.

On the global warming question, neither Congress nor presidents have done much. Political pressures to address climate change are less intense. Furthermore, any actions to halt global warming will be extremely costly, requiring major societal changes, and will pay off only after many years. Even then, it may be impossible to avoid significant increases in temperature levels. Finally, because climate change is a global problem, policies will be effective only if the president and other leaders around the world engage in difficult international negotiations.

Opposing Viewpoints on United States Energy Policy

Most people agree that something needs to be done about the vulnerability of U.S. energy supplies. But there are significant disagreements about where the president and Congress ought to focus their efforts. Some policymakers say the main thing to do is to increase the sources of supply, whereas others would like to do more to limit energy demand, not only because it would reduce vulnerability but also because it could mitigate the rate of global warming.

Reducing Vulnerability to Supply Interruptions

Some experts argue that U.S. policy efforts ought to focus on increasing the supply of domestic energy resources. This might include allowing oil rigs and refineries in previously protected areas, such as the Alaska National Wildlife Refuge (ANWR). The Obama administration took a step in this direction by opening up some previously restricted areas to oil exploration in 2010, but this initiative was derailed by the Deepwater Horizon oil spill. Alternatively, the U.S. could focus on other domestic energy sources such as coal, ethanol (derived from corn), or, perhaps most importantly, nuclear energy. Advocates of a "domestic supply" approach point out that the demand for energy is steadily increasing and any efforts to thwart increasing demand will have serious economic repercussions for the economy as a whole.

> We need a policy that emphasizes energy in America and recognizes that the problem is government. It's not that we don't have energy sources. The Bakken Field in North Dakota, for example, in the last three years the estimate has gone up by 25 fold—2500 percent—the amount of oil available. Natural gas discoveries in the last six years . . . have produced over 100 years supply of natural gas. . . . We have bio-fuels and ethanol in growing abundance. . . . America today—in energy—is artificially weakened by bad government policies which favor imports over American energy. And let me assert clearly and simply, bowing to the Saudi king is not an energy policy.
>
> —Newt Gingrich, "Speech to the 2009 House/ Senate GOP Fundraising Dinner," available at newt.org, accessed January 16, 2010.

> American demand for oil is outpacing our nation's refining capacity, adding to the increases we're all seeing at the pump. . . . We can help reverse this trend by taking common sense, responsible steps . . . to improve our nation's ability to refine crude oil . . . recognizing environmental needs and continuing to develop alternative sources of energy.
>
> —Representative Greg Waldren (R-OR), House Committee on Energy and Commerce.
>
> Source: http://energycommerce.house.gov/108/News/ 06072996_1932.htm, accessed June 23, 2006.

Cutting the Demand for Energy

Others argue that the president should propose policies that reduce the demand for energy by encouraging conservation. Many experts believe the best way to cut demand is by placing a higher tax on oil, gas, and other fossil fuels. But because higher taxes are very unpopular, the United States has, up until now, tried to reduce the demand for energy through regulatory action instead. In 2009, the Obama Administration announced new efficiency standards that require automobile companies to make their cars and trucks almost 40 percent more efficient by 2016.[10] Similarly, home energy appliances—furnaces, hot water heaters, and refrigerators—must now meet certain efficiency standards. But these regulatory actions have not been as effective as originally anticipated.

Most Democratic political leaders place more emphasis on energy conservation and are less supportive of efforts to encourage growth in the supply of energy. They support international agreements to limit greenhouse gas emissions, favor tighter regulation of energy use, and oppose drilling in the ANWR. Meanwhile, most Republicans favor a greater emphasis on energy growth by lessening restrictions on oil drilling, coal mining, and the construction of nuclear plants. But the differences between the two parties may be receding, as both sides have come to realize that long-term growth will require both greater conservation and greater focus on energy supplies. This has given rise to bipartisan support for further research into alternative energy sources (wind, solar, and nuclear as well as ethanol and other biomass products). Over $30 billion for such projects—as well as for energy efficiency measures—was included in the 2009 economic stimulus bill.[11] But few leaders in either political party have been willing to bite the biggest energy bullet of all—a major tax increase on all gas, oil, and other fossil fuels.

> We are convinced . . . that changing the way we produce and use energy is essential to America's economic future—that it will create millions of new jobs, power new industries, keep us competitive, and spark new innovation. We're convinced, for our own self interest, that the way we use energy, changing it to a more efficient fashion, is essential to our national security, because it helps to reduce our dependence on foreign oil, and helps us deal with some of the dangers posed by climate change.
>
> —President Barack Obama, "Remarks at the Morning Plenary Session of the United Nations Climate Change Conference," Copenhagen, Denmark, December 18, 2009.

> We . . . need to take serious action to limit the extent of climate change by reducing our emissions. More than anything else, that will require a global technology revolution—and we need policies to make that revolution happen.
>
> . . . [W]e plainly do not have time to wait. The challenge before us requires a much more deliberate, enunciated effort to develop policies that will help push and pull climate-friendly technologies to the market. We need a guiding vision on the order of putting a person on the moon or developing a cure for cancer.
>
> —Eileen Claussen, President, Pew Center on Global Climate Change, "Climate Change: Beyond a Sideways Approach" speech at the Donald Bren School of Environmental Science and Management, January 14, 2005.
>
> Source: www.pewclimate.org/press_room/speech_transcripts/ speech.cfm, accessed June 23, 2006.

What Do Americans Believe?

Most Americans consider themselves to be environmentalists. But this consensus breaks down when they are asked whether global climate change is a serious problem, and what steps they would be willing to take to address this and other energy policy issues. As Figure 1 shows, most Americans favor regulations to address global warming, but they are less certain about these if they mean that their monthly bills would increase.

What Do You Think?

1. What is more important, increasing the energy supply or limiting energy demands?

2. Are energy demands better curbed by tighter regulations or higher taxes on gas, oil, and other fossil fuels?

3. Would you be willing to pay higher prices for energy if it reduced dependence on foreign energy sources? If it would slow global warming?

4. Should the president give higher priority to this issue than to other pressing issues such as healthcare or the fight against terrorism?

On the Web

The conservative Heritage Foundation recommends increasing domestic energy supplies.

www.heritage.org/Research/EnergyandEnvironment/

The environmental group The Sierra Club argues for less reliance on oil and more international engagement on climate change.

www.sierraclub.org/

A site created by working climate scientists, commenting on news related to climate-science.

www.realclimate.org/

The House Committee on Energy and Commerce and the Senate Committee on Energy and Natural Resources handle most energy-related legislation that passes through Congress.

http://energycommerce.house.gov/
http://energy.senate.gov/public/

[1]"Complete Debate Transcript," *Las Vegas Sun,* (transcript of Democratic debate of January 15, 2008), http://www.lasvegassun.com/news/2008/jan/15/debate-transcript/, accessed February 20, 2008.
[2]"Transcript of GOP Debate at Reagan Library" (debate of January 30, 2008), http://www.cnn.com/2008/POLITICS/01/30/GOPdebate .transcript/, accessed February 20, 2008.
[3]Committee on Surface Temperature Reconstructions for the Last 2000 Years, National Research Council, *Surface Temperature Reconstructions for the Last 2000 Years* (Washington, DC: National Academy of Sciences, 2006), Figure S-1.

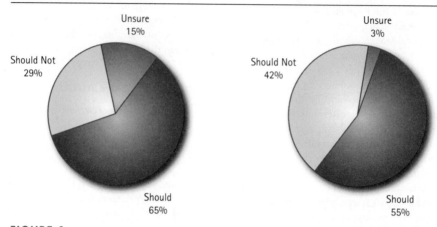

Do you think the federal government should or should not regulate the release of greenhouse gases from sources like power plants, cars, and factories in an effort to reduce global warming?

What if that significantly lowered greenhouse gases but raised your monthly energy expenses by 25 dollars a month? In that case, do you think the government should or should not regulate the release of greenhouse gases?

Unsure 15%
Should Not 29%
Should 65%

Unsure 3%
Should Not 42%
Should 55%

FIGURE 1

AMERICANS BELIEVE CLIMATE CHANGE IS IMPORTANT BUT ARE SKEPTICAL OF REGULATIONS THAT WOULD RAISE THEIR ENERGY COSTS

• *Do you think the federal government should or should not regulate the release of greenhouse gases from sources like power plants, cars, and factories in an effort to reduce global warming?*

Source: ABC News/*Washington Post* Poll, December 10–13, 2009.

[4]John R. Justus and Susan Fletcher, *Global Climate Change* (Washington, DC: Congressional Research Service), CRS Report for Congress IB89005, updated May 12, 2006, 2.

[5]Albert Gore, "Nobel Lecture," December 10, 2007, http://nobelprize .org/nobel_prizes/peace/laureates/2007/gore-lecture_en.html, accessed February 20, 2008.

[6]Energy Policy Act of 1992: Limited Progress in Acquiring Alternative Fuel Vehicles and Reaching Fuel Goals, GAO/RCED-00-59 (Washington, DC: United States General Accounting Office, 2000).

[7]Michael Grunwald and Juliet Eilperin, "Energy Bill Raises Fears About Pollution, Fraud," *Washington Post* (July 30, 2005): A1.

[8]Mark Cooper, "Ending America's Oil Addiction: A Quarterly Report on Consumption, Prices, and Imports, First Quarter 2008," Consumer Federation of America, April 2008, p. 7. Available at http://www .consumerfed.org/elements/www.consumerfed.org/file/energy/ First_Quarterly_Gas_Report_2008.pdf, accessed January 16, 2010.

[9]Mark Sandalow, "Congress Full of Sound and Fury on Energy Policy as Time Runs Out," *San Francisco Chronicle* (May 6, 2006): A4.

[10]John M. Broder, "Obama Proposes Rules for Automakers on Greenhouse Gas Emissions and Mileage," *New York Times* (September 16, 2009): p. B4.

[11]Committee on Appropriations, David Obey (D-WI), Chairman, "Summary: American Recovery and Reinvestment Conference Agreement," http://appropriations.house.gov/pdf/PressSummary02-13-09.pdf, accessed January 16, 2010.

Continued from page 386

Roosevelt was not the first effective president who profited by breaking with the past (see Table 13.2). Thomas Jefferson discarded the program of John Adams and the Federalist Party. Republican Abraham Lincoln attacked slavery. Ronald Reagan halted the growth in government that had occurred under his predecessors, saying, "Government is not the solution to our problem. Government is the problem."[88] Whether a president is able to repudiate the past successfully is somewhat beyond the president's control, however. Congress and the public must also agree that a new direction is needed. Some pundits think Obama has an opportunity of becoming one of the country's "great presidents," because he succeeded an unpopular president in the midst of a financial crisis. But only time will tell whether Obama's efforts to break will prove to be as successful as Roosevelt's.

	TABLE 13.2		
	DO FAILED POLICIES AND PRESIDENTS LEAD TO THE ELECTION OF PRESIDENTS WHO SUCCEED BY REPUDIATING THE PAST?		

According to political scientist Stephen Skowronek, the most successful presidents are the ones who follow ineffective presidents.

Year	Ineffective President	Leads to . . .	Very Successful President
1789	Articles of Confederation		George Washington
1800	John Adams		Thomas Jefferson
1828	John Q. Adams		Andrew Jackson
1860	James Buchanan		Abraham Lincoln
1932	Herbert Hoover		Franklin Roosevelt
1980	Jimmy Carter		Ronald Reagan

Source: Based on Stephen Skowronek, *The Politics Presidents Make* (Cambridge, MA: Harvard University Press, 1993).

Skowronek's model is not perfect. Many people think Theodore Roosevelt was one of the country's most successful presidents, but he did not become president through a pivotal election or at a time of crisis. And some people think other presidents—Eisenhower (for managing the Cold War) and Johnson (for initiating the Great Society)—deserve inclusion at the top of the list of presidents. But Skowronek does show that presidents are often most effective when they exercise their power to initiate new approaches. It is often left to other, less effective presidents to try to follow this lead.

CHAPTER SUMMARY

13.1 Analyze how the president's national and partisan constituencies shape presidential decision making.

Presidents must meet the high expectations of their national and partisan constituencies, despite the fact that Congress checks many of their most important powers. Presidents are responsible to a national electorate, but must also be sure to keep the support of those who work in and finance their campaigns.

13.2 Outline the major powers of the president and Congress's checks on presidential powers.

Congressional checks on presidential power include the following:

- Presidents can initiate legislation, but Congress often rejects or substantially modifies their proposals.
- Presidents can appoint executive and judicial officers, but the Senate must approve them.
- Presidents may invoke inherent executive power, including the right of executive privilege, but Congress can impeach them.

- Although the president can veto congressional bills, Congress may override the veto by a two-thirds vote.
- Presidential leadership depends most heavily on the power of the chief executive to initiate and persuade—capacities that derive as much from the dignity of the office as from any specific clauses in the Constitution.

13.3 Assess why presidential reputation and popularity are important to presidential performance and what factors contribute to presidential greatness.

To achieve their goals, presidents must preserve their professional reputation and their political popularity. Because their popularity tends to slip over time, it is at the beginning of their presidency—during the transition and honeymoon periods—that they have the most capacity to initiate change. Great presidents emerge not so much because they have the right personal qualities but because they come to office when the country thinks it is time for a change. Presidents who make big changes are capable of doing so because they have the public on their side.

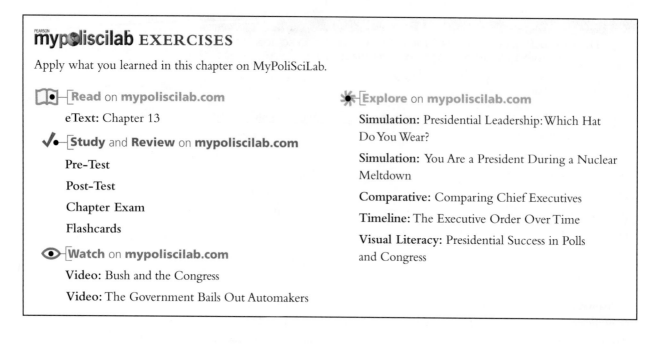

KEY TERMS

SUGGESTED READINGS

Of General Interest

Jones, Charles. *The Presidency in a Separated System.* 2nd ed. Washington, DC: The Brookings Institution, 2005. Examination of the role of the president under divided government.

Kernell, Samuel. *Going Public: New Strategies of Presidential Leadership.* 4th ed. Washington, DC: CQ Press, 2006. An account of the increasing tendency of presidents to use popular appeals to influence legislative processes.

Nelson, Michael, ed. *The Presidency and the Political System.* 9th ed. Washington, DC: CQ Press, 2009. Important contemporary essays on the presidency.

Neustadt, Richard E. *Presidential Power and the Modern Presidents.* New York: Free Press, 1990. Modern classic on the limits to presidential power.

Skowronek, Stephen. *Presidential Leadership In Political Time.* Lawrence: University Press of Kansas, 2008. Provocative analysis of what accounts for success or failure in a presidency.

Focused Studies

Howell, William G., and Jon C. Pevehouse, *While Dangers Gather: Congressional Checks on Presidential War Powers*. Princeton, NJ: Princeton University Press, 2007. Examination of the effect of domestic politics on the presidential use of the war power.

Mayer, Kenneth. *With the Stroke of a Pen: Executive Orders and Presidential Power*. Princeton, NJ: Princeton University Press, 2001. Study of how presidents use executive orders to make policy.

Rudalevige, Andrew. *The New Imperial Presidency: Renewing Presidential Power after Watergate*. Ann Arbor: University of Michigan Press, 2005. Argument that congressional checks on presidential power have eroded in recent decades.

ON THE WEB

www.whitehouse.gov
The official website of the White House offers current and historical information about U.S. presidents, as well as press releases and other policy statements.

www.thepresidency.org
Many political scientists study the factors that contribute to presidential success and failure. The Center for the Study of the Presidency publishes *Presidential Studies Quarterly* and showcases academic information and links.

www.archives.gov
Presidential libraries have been created for every president since Franklin Roosevelt. The National Archives and Records Administration (NARA) provides information about and links to these presidential libraries. NARA also provides a guide to presidential documents available online. These include executive orders, proclamations, speeches, and other materials.

www.vicepresidents.com
When Daniel Webster was offered the vice presidency, he famously demurred, saying "I do not propose to be buried until I am really dead." This website provides an online clearinghouse for information about this much maligned post and its occupants.

14 The Bureaucracy

SURGEON GENERAL'S WARNING: Quitting Smoking Now Greatly Reduces Serious Risks to Your Health.

CHAPTER OUTLINE

LEARNING OBJECTIVES

14.1 Describe the organization and role of the bureaucracy.

14.2 Identify the factors that create the bureaucracy problem.

14.3 Trace the history of governmental bureaucracy in the United States and evaluate the impact of political appointees today.

14.4 Outline the organization and functions of the cabinet, the independent regulatory agencies, and the Office of Management and Budget, and their relationship with the president.

14.5 Analyze the sources of Congress's power over the bureaucracy and the influence of the iron triangles and issues networks.

14.6 Assess the impact of elections and of public perception on the bureaucracy.

Regulating Tobacco as a Drug

His image was everywhere in the 1960s and 1970s. Cool and confident atop his horse, staring off into the sunset, one hand on the reins and another holding his cigarette: The Marlboro Man. For years his iconic portrait represented the American character, for people in the United States and around the world. As Philip Morris CEO George Weissman put it, "He's the man who doesn't punch a clock. He's not computerized. He's a free spirit."[1] But by the early 1990s two actors who played the Marlboro Man had been diagnosed with lung cancer and spoke out against their former employer. Wayne McClaren and David McClean, both "Marlboro Men" from the 1970s, attended stockholder meetings, testified before legislative committees, and spoke out publicly against cigarette smoke before their deaths in 1992 and 1995.[2] But they and their fellow activists had the greatest impact in an unlikely place: state and federal bureaucratic agencies.

After lobbying by the American Cancer Society, the American Heart Association, and other groups in the early 1960s, the office of the Surgeon General, a division of the U.S. Department of Health Education and Welfare (now Health and Human Services), conducted a wide-ranging study of the health effects of smoking.[3] The resulting report, issued in 1964, linked cigarette smoke to an array of health problems and recommended that smokers quit. The Federal Trade Commission (an independent government agency charged with ensuring fair business practices) immediately called for warning labels on tobacco products.[4]

Responding to swiftly changing public opinion on the issue, Congress soon passed a law requiring such labels and granting the FTC new enforcement powers.[5] Over the next few decades, as the Surgeon General published report after report on the hazards of smoking, national regulations became tighter and tighter, and state and local governments began banning cigarette smoking in public places and prohibiting sales to minors. Many smokers grew frustrated. After a county health department in Ohio announced new restrictions, one restaurant owner put it bluntly: "We don't like rules which affect our businesses being set forth by people who are unelected officials."[6]

In the mid-1990s, a group of attorneys general representing states across the country sued the tobacco companies for costing state-run health insurance programs billions of dollars. The final settlement, in the amount of $240 billion, supplemented state budgets for the next decade.[7]

By the 2000s, the Food and Drug Administration (FDA), charged by Congress with guaranteeing the safety of pharmaceuticals and the food supply, claimed that tobacco products should technically fall within their regulatory purview. In 2009, Congress formally gave the FDA that authority, and the FDA took action, banning flavored cigarettes and placing tobacco companies on notice that they were due for tighter scrutiny.[8] As Commissioner Margaret Hamburg put it, "The FDA will utilize regulatory authority to reduce the burden of illness and death caused by tobacco products to enhance our nation's public health."[9]

The change in government policy toward tobacco smoking since 1960 has been dramatic and comprehensive. Federal officials have gone from shrugging their shoulders at tobacco use to implementing an increasingly stringent series of restrictions and regulations. And these restrictions have been effective: In 1965, 42 percent of Americans smoked cigarettes. Today, that figure is less than 20 percent.[10] What may seem even more remarkable is that this change took place largely as a result of regulatory rule-making—not detailed management of the issue by elected office holders. To be sure, Congress and state elected officials have authorized the regulations in general terms. But the Surgeon General's Office, the state attorneys general, the FTC, and the FDA have all been free to design their own specific policies. By 2010, Marlboro cigarettes had gone from defining the national character to being an expensive and heavily regulated drug.

Making the Connection

The Surgeon General's Office, the FDA, the FTC, and the state attorneys general offices are all bureaucracies. Bureaucracies are hierarchical organizations of officials with responsibility for specific tasks. They have important roles to play in federal and state policymaking, but critics often worry about whether they are efficient enough or accountable enough to voters. In this chapter, we discuss how bureaucracies have developed and describe how they fit into modern American politics. In particular, we address the role that bureaucracies play in satisfying the demands of voters and consider the problems that impede bureaucratic performance. We review the history of the federal bureaucracy, with an eye to how historic reforms and reorganizations have changed it. Finally, we consider how Congress and the president influence the bureaucracy, and how the bureaucracy itself is organized.

14.1

Describe the organization and role of the bureaucracy.

bureaucracy
Hierarchical organization of officials with responsibility for specific tasks.

agency
The basic organizational unit of federal government. Also known as *office* or *bureau*.

department
A collection of federal agencies that reports to a secretary who serves in the president's cabinet.

The Role of the Bureaucracy

Bureaucracies are essential if government is going to provide the programs and services the public expects. Laws become effective only when a government agency enforces them. Without some kind of organization, governments cannot build roads, operate schools, put out fires, fight wars, distribute social security checks, or do the thousands of other things Americans demand from their government.

As the range of governmental responsibilities has grown, the number of bureaucrats in the United States has also increased. The most growth has occurred at state and local levels, where the vast majority of civilian government workers are employed, including school teachers, police officers, and sanitation workers (see Figure 14.1). In addition, many private contractors perform tasks paid for by government agencies. Although the number of employees who work directly for the federal government is smaller, we shall focus most of our attention on federal bureaucracies, because their policies and regulations are far-reaching and their impact is felt throughout the country.

The **agency,** also known as the office or bureau, is the basic organizational unit of the federal government. It is the entity specifically assigned by Congress to carry out a task. There are hundreds of agencies within the federal government, but most are grouped under one of 15 **departments**—collections of federal agencies that report to a secretary who serves in the president's cabinet. However, there are nearly 90 independent

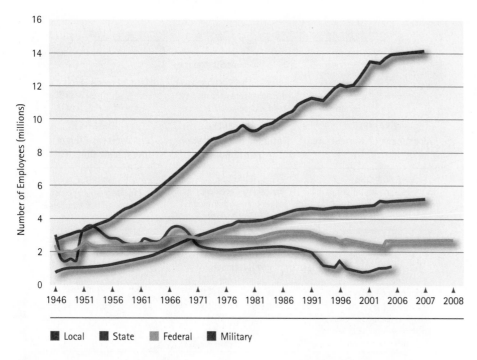

FIGURE 14.1

GOVERNMENT
EMPLOYMENT, 1946–2008

The number of state and local
employees has increased, but the
number of federal employees has
remained about the same.

• *Why do you think employment at the federal level has
remained stable, despite budget
increases and new government
programs? Which has increased
at a faster rate, state employment
or local employment?*

Note: Federal government employment figures include civilians
only. Military employment figures include only active-duty
personnel.

Sources: U.S. Bureau of the Census,
*Historical Statistics of the United States:
Colonial Times to 1970* (Washington, DC:
GPO, 1975), pp. 1100, 1141; *Statistical
Abstract of the United States, 1999,* Tables
534, 578; *Statistical Abstract of the United
States, 2008,* Tables 447, 482, 493; *Statistical
Abstract of the United States, 2010,* Tables
449, 484.

agencies or government corporations that are free standing entities reporting either to the president or to a supervisory board.[11] Independent agencies include the Central Intelligence Agency and the Environmental Protection Agency, as well as smaller and lesser known organizations such as the American Battle Monuments Commission and the National Council on Disability. **Government corporations** are particular types of independent organizations created by Congress to fulfill functions related to business.[12] Examples of government corporations include the Federal Deposit Insurance Corporation, which insures bank deposits, and the National Railroad Passenger Corporation, which runs Amtrak. Figure 14.2 illustrates how the federal bureaucracy is organized.

government corporation

Independent organization created by
Congress to fulfill functions related
to business.

Bureaucracies can have great influence over policy because of their **administrative discretion,** the power to interpret their legislative mandates. Congress can enact general rules, but it cannot anticipate every circumstance, nor can it apply these rules to every individual case. Congress may decide to provide benefits to the disabled, but it is up to a bureaucrat (in this case, an official within the Social Security Administration) to apply the rules that decide whether a particular disability precludes employment, thereby making a person eligible for special benefits.[13] Congress may decide to give loans to college students from families of moderate income, but it is up to a bureaucrat (in this case, an officer within the Department of Education) to interpret and apply the rules that determine what family resources count as income.

administrative discretion

The power of a bureaucracy to
interpret a legislative mandate.

The Bureaucracy Problem

If bureaucracies exist to address public demands for programs and services, we might think it should be easy to design effective government agencies. An ideal bureaucracy would be organized so that it could achieve the public's wishes most efficiently. The selection of people hired to work in the bureaucracy would be based on their ability to

14.2

Identify the factors that
create the bureaucracy
problem.

FIGURE 14.2

THE FEDERAL
BUREAUCRACY CONSISTS
OF DEPARTMENTS,
INDEPENDENT AGENCIES,
AND GOVERNMENT

*Top managers include an executive direc-
tor, managing director, chief financial officer, chief administrative law judge, and
general counsel.

**As a government corporation, OPIC
is self-funded rather than government-
funded.

Sources: United States Government Manual
2005–2006 (Washington, DC: GPO, 2005),
structure of Department of Agriculture and
NTSB; www.opic.gov, structure and
budget of OPIC; Office of Personnel
Management, Federal Civilian
Employment and Payroll by Branch,
Selected Agency, and Area, November
2008, http://main.opm.gov/feddata/html/
2008/november/index.asp, accessed
February 10, 2010, employment figures for
all agencies; and the Office of Management
and Budget, Budget of the United States
Government, Fiscal 2011, budget figures
for the Department of Agriculture and
NTSB.

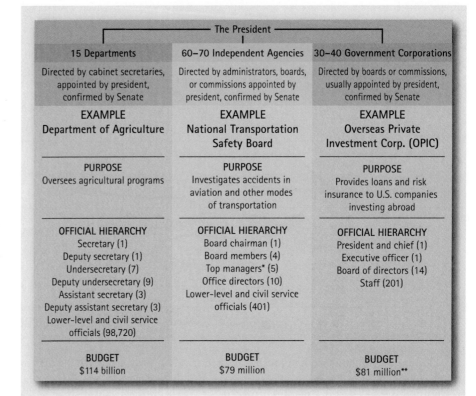

do the job. Each would report to his or her superior via a clear chain of command, and
ultimate authority would be exercised by the head of the bureau. Agency staff would
supply each worker with the materials necessary to get the job done. The ideal is best
exemplified by soldiers on parade, marching together in synchronized formation. When
all works perfectly, bureaucracies exhibit unity, focus, and power.[14]

Although the ideal bureaucracy has tremendous potential, many forces inhibit perfection. Some of the most significant flaws reflect the demands imposed on government bureaucrats by democratic elections: They often face impossible expectations or
debilitating limits. Other flaws are inherent in all bureaucracies: They are slow to
change, they tend to expand, and the quality of their performance is difficult to measure. Taken together, these factors create what is known as the bureaucracy problem.[15]

Impossible Tasks

Most governmental tasks are difficult to accomplish. Not only can agency objectives
be complicated, but goals themselves often remain vague and indefinite.[16] Americans
expect schools to teach their children—but many people disagree about what exactly
should be taught. Commuters expect transportation agencies to achieve smoothly
flowing traffic—but to avoid all bottlenecks in most large cities, construction crews
would have to turn to pavement much that citizens now value for other purposes.
The Environmental Protection Agency is charged with protecting the environment
from pollutants—but nearly all human activity increases pollution in some way. Because
their responsibilities are complicated and the limits of their objectives are seldom

well defined, bureaucracies are often blamed for problems even if they do the best possible job.

Difficulty Measuring Performance

It is often difficult to measure the performance of government bureaucracies.[17] In 2010, for example, consumer activists criticized the Food and Drug Administration (FDA) for failing to ban Bisphenol A, a chemical used in plastic containers that some researchers said posed a health hazard. But FDA officials argued that they had a responsibility to study the matter further before acting.[18] Because it is hard to measure the performance of most government bureaucracies, it is difficult for supervisors, elected officials, and the public to tell whether work is being performed carefully and promptly. If officials are unsure how to gauge a bureaucracy's performance, they will have trouble trying to improve it. As a result, bureaucracies often have a reputation for inefficiency.

Expansionary Tendencies

Once they are created to address a problem, bureaucracies generally try to expand so they can address it better. Government agencies almost always feel they need more money, more personnel, and more time to perform their tasks effectively.[19] Bureaucrats experience policy problems up close, are experts on these problems, and are under a lot of pressure to solve them, so they often sincerely believe that they need more resources. But, because they focus on specific issues, they can lose sight of the big picture. Congress cannot grant unlimited funds to every bureaucracy that wants them; trade-offs and choices have to be made.

There is nothing new about this debate between bureaucrats and Congress. "You may blame the War Department for a great many things," General Douglas MacArthur said back in 1935, "but you cannot blame us for not asking for money. That is one fault to which we plead not guilty."[20]

Slow to Change

Any large governmental organization has standard procedures through which it makes its decisions. And most standard procedures are essential if large numbers of people are to coordinate their work toward some common end. If rules were not clearly defined, those working within the bureaucracy would be so confused that they would soon be unable to do anything.

Standard procedures nonetheless make bureaucracies slow to adjust to new circumstances.[21] Schools still provide long summer holidays that were originally allowed so that children could help harvest crops on family farms. Despite massive increases in the use of energy in the United States, the Federal Energy Regulatory Commission has changed its approach to regulation of the electricity grid very little over the course of four decades.[22] New energy-saving technologies, such as "smart grid" initiatives that reduce waste in electricity allocation, can be hampered by a regulatory structure designed when such technologies were a distant dream. As the owner of a renewable energy business put it, "We are all entrenched in this broken system, and there is no agreement on how to fix it. It's a vicious circle."[23] As one humorist observed, "Bureaucracy defends the status quo long past the time when the quo has lost its status."[24]

Red Tape

The procedural hurdles that make bureaucracies slow and methodical have been collectively given the pejorative name "red tape," after the colored ribbons that traditionally bound packets of official papers in Great Britain. Nineteenth-century British essayist Thomas Carlyle complained that government offices made up "a worldwide jungle of red tape, inhabited by doleful creatures, deaf, or nearly so to human reason or entreaty."[25] As did Carlyle, modern Americans complain about governmental red tape; but, as one analyst has observed, "One person's red tape may be another's treasured procedural safeguard."[26]

People often complain, for example, that it takes forever to get a bridge repaired. But bridge repair can be complicated. Consider the repair of the interstate 35W bridge that collapsed in Minneapolis on August 1, 2007. Weeks after the disaster (which killed 13 people), the Minnesota government called for contractors to submit proposals for a new bridge. At the same time, the state department of transportation began holding a series of open houses and town hall meetings to gather public input on the proposed repairs. Citizens offered suggestions about everything from design aesthetics to public transit needs. In mid-September, contractors submitted their proposals, and administrators vetted each application based on a series of criteria, including safety, "visual enhancements," and, of course, cost. In October, the Minneapolis city council and mayor approved the state's construction plan. Construction finally began that winter, under the watchful eyes of state and federal inspectors.[27] The new bridge, which opened just over a year after the collapse of the old one, was delayed not by malice or ignorance, but by important considerations of politics and safety. Indeed, bureaucrats in this case won plaudits for their speed.

In extreme cases, bureaucratic agencies can make exceptions. During the 2008 financial crisis, for example, federal regulators waived key financial restrictions to smooth the way for healthier banks to acquire distressed ones.[28] But red tape was eliminated in this case only because most policymakers agreed that the urgency of the crisis should override procedural formalities.

Standard Operating Procedures

One of the drawbacks of standard operating procedures is that they may not work well in unprecedented circumstances such as the 2001 terrorist attacks.

• *What are the benefits of standard operating procedures?*

American Bureaucracies: Particularly Political

Trace the history of governmental bureaucracy in the United States and evaluate the impact of political appointees today.

The bureaucracy problem exists in all countries, but American bureaucracies have special problems that are rooted in the country's unusual political history. As we discuss in this section, U.S. bureaucracies had a difficult beginning, grew as elected officials gave government jobs to their supporters, and were only slowly modernized by a "bottom-up" civil-service reform. Government workers today fall into two categories: career civil servants who are hired according to educational qualifications and who have job security and political appointees at the highest level who can be dismissed at any time. Although the policy of reserving the top spots for political appointees makes the government more responsive to elections, it makes civil service jobs less attractive to bright young people.

Difficult Beginnings

American bureaucrats lack the noble heritage of their counterparts in Europe and Japan, where government departments evolved out of the household of the king, queen, or emperor. In the late 1600s, King Louis XIV constructed a great French administration within the Palace of Versailles. The extraordinarily efficient German administration, which became a model for the world, descended from the household of the King of Prussia. Japan's powerful bureaucracy owes its prestige to a time-honored relationship with the emperor. The lineage of federal bureaucrats in the United States is less distinguished. As one scholar has pointed out, "In England, France and Germany, . . . it is considered an honor simply to serve the state. . . . In the United States civil servants, instead of being regarded with honor, are often considered tax eaters, drones, grafters, and bureaucrats."[29]

The Patriots fought the American Revolution against King George's bureaucrats, who had been appointed to oversee the governments of the colonies. The resulting suspicion of appointed officials carried over to the time during which the Constitution was written, when the framers could not even agree on a site to locate the people who were to run the new national government. Finally, as part of a compromise, they agreed to create the District of Columbia, the new home of the federal government, on the Maryland-Virginia border near the small city of Georgetown.

Thomas Jefferson believed that the location would attract virtuous Virginians to federal jobs, leading to "a favourable bias in the Executive officers."[30] In fact, the land Congress had chosen was swampy and miserable. Visitors complained that it was thick with "contaminated vapour" and that its mud-spattered, ramshackle buildings gave it "the appearance of a considerable town, which had been destroyed by some unusual calamity."[31] If the government were to attract quality workers, its location would not be its main selling point.

Mountains of Patronage

The undistinguished living conditions in the District of Columbia may have made federal jobs less attractive to some, but after 1828 the bureaucracy began to swell with new workers who attained their posts by being political party loyalists. That year, Andrew Jackson won the presidency and, upon assuming office, promptly handed out political **patronage**—government jobs, contracts, and other favors—to his supporters. Jackson reasoned that this practice made government more democratic, because it ensured that

patronage
Jobs, contracts, or favors given by politicians to their friends and allies.

those who won elections were fully in control of the government. Furthermore, the quality of work by political appointees would not suffer, said Jackson, because "[t]he duties of all public officers are . . . so plain and simple that men of intelligence may readily qualify themselves for their performance."[32] The practice of hiring workers on the basis of party loyalty became known as the **spoils system** when New York Senator William Marcy attacked President Jackson for seeing "nothing wrong in the rule that to the victor belong the spoils."[33]

spoils system
A system of government employment in which workers are hired on the basis of party loyalty.

Politicians in both political parties quickly discovered that the spoils system suited their needs.[34] As barriers to voter participation fell in the mid-1800s, more and more Americans went to the polls to cast ballots (see Chapter 6). Because local, state, and national elections occurred frequently, mobilizing this growing electorate became a complicated and time-consuming task. Party politicians could use promises of government posts to enlist campaign workers to take on such thankless jobs as passing out pamphlets, organizing rallies, and transporting voters to the polls. The New York machine-politician George Washington Plunkitt explained the simple logic of patronage this way: "You can't keep an organization together without patronage. Men ain't in politics for nothin'. They want to get somethin' out of it."[35]

Patronage also made it easier for parties to raise large amounts of cash to fund their frequent campaigns. Every Pennsylvania state employee during this period received the following letter from the Republican State Committee: "Two percent of your salary is—. Please remit promptly. At the close of the campaign we shall place a list of those who have not paid in the hands of the head of the department you are in."[36] Politicians felt no need to be secretive about these practices, which they saw as natural and legitimate.

Plunkitt defended patronage, or graft, by making the fine distinction between its dishonest and honest varieties. Dishonest graft wasted the taxpayers' money or engaged in "blackmailin' gamblers, saloonkeepers, [and] disorderly people."[37] Honest graft simply paid a friend to build a bridge or roadway that needed to be constructed anyway. Or, as the patronage-prone Chicago mayor Richard J. Daley once said when asked to explain why he had given the city's insurance business to one of his sons, "If a man can't put his arms around his sons, then what kind of a world are we living in? . . . I make no apologies to anyone."[38] Mayor Daley's sons did well for themselves. Richard M. Daley was elected to a sixth term as Chicago mayor in 2007, and William M. Daley served as Secretary of Commerce under President Clinton.

Family Ties
The Mayors Richard Daley, father and son, in a moment of family resemblance.

• *When it comes to getting elected, what advantages do children of politicians have over other candidates?*

Advantages of the Spoils System

Looking back on American political history, many scholars have found much to praise in the old spoils system.[39] For one thing, it helped immigrants adjust to the realities of urban life in the United States by providing them jobs in city government. Irish immigrants

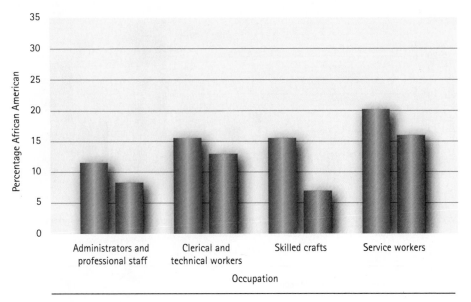

FIGURE 14.3

BLACK REPRESENTATION IN GOVERNMENT AND THE PRIVATE SECTOR

This graph illustrates the different employment levels of African American workers for similar positions in state and local government and the private sector workforce.

• Compare this figure with Figure 14.4. *What differences do you see in patterns of African American and Hispanic employment?*

Note: Government figures are from 2005; private-sector figures are from 2008.

Source: Statistical Abstract of the United States 2010, Table 452 (government workers), Table 603 (private sector).

were particularly good at using politics as a way of getting ahead. In Chicago, the percentage of public school principals of Irish background rose from 3 percent in the 1860s to 25 percent in 1914. In San Francisco, it climbed from 4 percent to 34 percent over a similar period.[40]

Some scholars have argued that contemporary affirmative action programs have many of the same pluses and minuses as the old-fashioned spoils system. When African Americans became part of urban governing coalitions, they gained better access to government jobs by invoking the principle of affirmative action.[41] Nationwide, African Americans are more likely to get a job in government than in the private sector (see Figure 14.3), a sign that politics still seems to help some disadvantaged groups get a toehold on the ladder to success. However, government employment for Hispanics still lags behind their positions in the private sector (see Figure 14.4), probably because the percentage of Hispanics who vote and otherwise participate in politics remains comparatively low.

Disadvantages of the Spoils System

Even though the spoils system helped incorporate immigrants into American politics and society, it nonetheless contributed to the negative image of American bureaucracies. Education, training, and experience counted for little, and jobholders changed each time a new party came to power. As one Democratic leader joked after his party had been in power for years, a bureaucrat was "a Democrat who holds some office that a Republican wants."[42]

The many decades of patronage politics produced an anti-bureaucratic sentiment among members of the public that continues to the present day. More than 60 percent of Americans think "people in the government waste a lot of money we pay in taxes."[43] Most Americans (51 percent) also think that "government workers" are paid too much, and 71 percent say that those in the government do not work as hard as private sector workers.[44]

FIGURE 14.4

HISPANIC REPRESENTATION IN GOVERNMENT AND THE PRIVATE SECTOR

This graph illustrates the different employment levels of Hispanic workers for similar positions in state and local government and the private sector workforce.

Note: Government figures are from 2005; private-sector figures are from 2008.

Source: Statistical Abstract of the United States 2010, Table 452 (government workers), Table 603 (private sector).

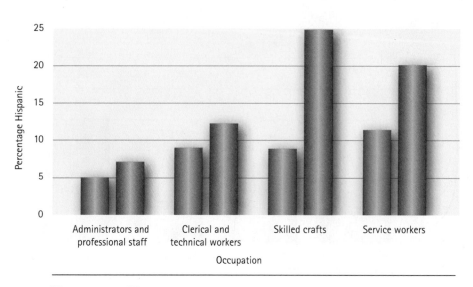

Erosion of the Spoils System

civil service

A system in which government employees are chosen according to their educational qualifications, performance on examinations, and work experience.

mugwumps

Organized in the 1880s, a group of civil-service reformers, including professors, journalists, clerics, and business leaders, who maintained that government officials should be chosen on a merit basis, not for their political connections.

Pendleton Act

Legislation passed in 1883 creating the Civil Service Commission.

Hatch Act

A 1939 law prohibiting federal employees from engaging in political campaigning and solicitation.

The mountains of patronage created by the spoils system gradually eroded as they were attacked by reformers who advocated a **civil service,** a system in which government employees were chosen according to their educational qualifications, performance on examinations, and work experience. In the 1880s, these reformers were called **mugwumps.** They were a stubbornly nonpartisan group of professors, journalists, clerics, and business leaders who insisted that government officials should be chosen on the basis of merit, not for their political connections. Originally a sarcastic term of abuse, the name is a modification of a Native American word meaning "great man" or "chief."

Even though the mountains of patronage did not erode easily, mugwumps won a succession of victories that gradually changed the system. Their first major breakthrough came in 1881 when President James Garfield was assassinated by a mentally disturbed man said to be a disappointed office seeker. Public scrutiny focused on the new president, Chester A. Arthur, who had once served as the New York customs collector and seemed the very personification of the spoils system. In 1883, as the demand for reform swept the country, Congress passed—and Arthur signed—the **Pendleton Act,** which created a Civil Service Commission to set up qualifications, examinations, and procedures for filling many government jobs.

Civil service reform occurred from the bottom up. In the first few years after the Pendleton Act, civil service requirements applied mainly to the lower-level, less skilled jobs performed by workers who swept the floors and typed government forms. Gradually, higher-level positions were included in the civil service; such additions were especially plentiful when the party in power expected defeat in the next election. By making a job part of the civil service, soon-to-be-ousted presidents "blanketed in" their supporters, making it impossible for their successors to replace them with patronage workers from the other party. Civil service reform became nearly complete when, in 1939, Congress passed the **Hatch Act,** which barred federal employees from political campaigning and solicitation. The mountains of patronage were all but worn away.

Political Appointees Today

In the arid expanses of Arizona and New Mexico stand mesas—often called islands in the desert—that tower over the surrounding flatlands. All that remain of ancient plateaus, long eroded by wind and water, mesas are ecologically distinct from the surrounding desert.

Just as we can find geological mesas in the deserts of the West, we can identify patronage mesas that have survived decades of civil service reform. One of the most heavily populated patronage mesas is also the most prestigious, for it includes thousands of policymakers at the top levels of the federal government. It consists of most members of the White House staff, the heads of most departments and agencies, and the members of most government boards and commissions. Political appointees also predominate in the upper levels of individual agencies and departments, inhabiting offices that bear such titles as deputy secretary, undersecretary, deputy undersecretary, assistant secretary, deputy assistant secretary, and special assistant.

This prestigious patronage mesa is becoming increasingly crowded. The estimated number of top-level agency appointees grew from fewer than 500 in 1960 to nearly 2,600 by the Barack Obama administration.[45] No other industrialized democracy gives its leader as much patronage power (see *International Comparison,* page 406).

The president's ability to recruit political allies for the top echelon of government has both advantages and disadvantages. On the positive side, it allows newly elected presidents to enlist many new people with innovative ideas. For example, Barack Obama drew on think-tank experts, academics, and leaders from interest groups to help shape economic stimulus and healthcare reform proposals after he took office in 2009. The wholesale changeover in personnel also helps presidents introduce their political agendas with minimal resistance from an entrenched executive branch. President George W. Bush's tax-cut plan and education policies were developed without the aid or obstruction of leftover Clinton advisers. Indeed, it is the power of appointment that makes presidents the most dynamic element in the American political system.

Yet the prevalence of political appointees at the highest levels may result in administrators who have little knowledge of their own organizations and do not manage those organizations as effectively as career appointees would.[46] European and Japanese governments are marked by close, informal, long time associations among leading administrators. In the United States, the average presidential appointee leaves office after about three and one half years; almost a quarter leave in less than 12 months.[47] By contrast, nearly 60 percent of career bureaucrats surveyed had worked for the same agency for 11 years or more.[48] These experienced bureaucrats may have the detailed knowledge that political appointees do not, but they often lack the political authority to make policy changes. In 2003, a bipartisan commission on reforming the government workforce found that, as a result, "Leadership responsibilities often fall into the awkward gap between inexperienced political appointees and unsupported career managers."[49]

The rapid turnover in high-level governmental personnel is so pervasive that it has been called a government of **in-and-outers**—political appointees who come in, go out, and come back in again with each change in administration.[50] Because they cannot count on long-term employment with the government, most political appointees begin planning a way of making a satisfactory departure shortly after they arrive. For some people, this will mean returning to their old positions in the business, legal, or academic world.

in-and-outers

Political appointees who come in, go out, and come back in again with each change in administration.

406 Chapter 14 ★ The Bureaucracy

INTERNATIONAL COMPARISON

Political Versus Professional Bureaucrats

Most high-level administrative positions in Europe and Japan are occupied by well-educated, highly experienced, professional civil servants who refrain from participating actively in politics. Most achieve their positions by studying in prestigious training programs. In France, for example, bureaucracies recruit new employees from the distinguished and highly selective École Nationale D'Administration, which graduates only 150 students per year; in Japan, about 80 percent of the nation's high-level bureaucrats attended Tokyo University. In these countries, upper-echelon administrators have spent years—even decades—in dedicated government service.

In the United States, high government officials often get their jobs only after gaining prominence outside government in business, law, medicine, education, or in a policy institute. Usually, they have worked in a presidential campaign, made financial contributions, or given other evidence of party loyalty. For example, President George W. Bush, when selecting his first secretary of energy, turned not to a long time government servant who had worked on nuclear power or energy efficiency but to Spencer Abraham, a political supporter and former Michigan senator who had co-sponsored legislation to eliminate the department outright. Similarly, Barack Obama awarded cabinet positions to key campaign allies such as former Kansas Governor Kathleen Sebelius (Health and Human Services) and Shaun Donovan (Housing and Urban Development).

More professionalized bureaucracies are not necessarily more popular with the general public. In 2007, for example, French President Nicolas Sarkozy won applause for his proposals to reduce the size of the French bureaucracy. But there is evidence that bureaucrats in other countries are less frustrated by political interference than are bureaucrats in the United States. According to one study, U.S. civil servants have more negative views of political parties and are more likely to resent the interference of politicians than are Japanese civil servants.

This difference in attitude probably occurs because in the United States the bureaucracy must respond to both the president and Congress. In most other industrial democracies, the legislative branch has less direct influence over the bureaucracy. Where the bureaucracy has only one master, bureaucrats can be professionals instead of politicians.

• *Should the bureaucracy be reformed so that it has only one boss?*

• *What are the advantages and disadvantages of the tug of war between Congress and the president over the bureaucracy?*

Sources: "Toward the Multiversity," *The Economist,* July 11, 1987; Joel D. Aberbach, Ellis S. Krauss, Michio Muramatsu, and Bert A. Rockman, "Comparing Japanese and American Administrative Elites," *British Journal of Political Science,* 20: 4 (October 1990), 461–488; Harry Eckstein, "The British Political System," in *Patterns of Government: The Major Political Systems of Europe,* ed. Samuel Beer and Adam Ulam (New York: Random House, 1962), 158–168; Hugh Heclo, *Modern Social Politics in Britain and Sweden: From Relief to Income Maintenance* (New Haven, CT: Yale University Press, 1974); Paul Pierson, *Dismantling the Welfare State* (New York: Cambridge University Press, 1994).

For others, it will be a matter of using connections inside the beltway to win new financial opportunities in the private or nonprofit sectors. After Bush adviser Karl Rove left the White House in 2007, for example, he took a job at Fox News as a political commentator. This can be a risky strategy, however, because someone's career as an "outer" may create a perceived conflict of interest when he or she tries to get back "in." Former Senator Tom Daschle had to withdraw his name from nomination as Secretary of Health and Human Services in 2009 after a controversy involving nonpayment of taxes during his work as a consultant.

These rapid changes in personnel create a government that lacks the continuity necessary for sustained policy focus. The newcomers bring energy and ideas, but by the time their ideas are turned into plans that can be brought to fruition, they are gone, succeeded by another energetic group with an altogether different set of priorities. The newcomers also run the risk of trying to make too many changes at once. When Barack Obama took office, his advisers hoped they could swiftly pass healthcare reform, curbs on greenhouse gases, and even immigration reform. But by the 2010 elections, only one of these measures—healthcare reform—had become law.

Worst of all, the denial of most top-level positions to nonpolitical civil servants makes the civil service a less attractive career for intelligent, ambitious young people. In Japan, many of the top students graduating from the country's most prestigious law schools go directly into government service, and the most gifted reach the highest levels of government. But the peak of the U.S. government is not part of a large mountain that employees can gradually ascend over a lifetime career. Instead, the top-level mesa positions are ordinarily cut off from the surrounding civil service desert, at elevations scaled only by a patronage-filled presidential helicopter. It should not come as much of a surprise, then, that when asked what kinds of careers they are contemplating, less than a quarter of young people say they are "very" or "fairly" likely to consider working for the federal government.[51]

The President and the Bureaucracy

CONSTITUTION, ARTICLE II, SECTION 3: *The President "shall take Care that the Laws be faithfully executed."*

The Constitution charges the president with enforcement of the laws. Presidents fulfill this obligation by overseeing the federal bureaucracy, which is formally responsible to the chief executive. The president's cabinet is the most visible and long-standing connection between the president and the bureaucracy. However, the president also exercises power through appointments to independent agencies and through the powerful Office of Management and Budget.

Despite these means of control, even presidents can be frustrated by the bureaucracy problem. As an exasperated President Harry Truman once said, "I thought I was the president, but when it comes to these bureaucrats I can't do a d—ed thing."[52]

The Cabinet

Most federal agencies are located in one of the major departments. The president appoints secretaries (subject to approval by the Senate) to head these departments. The secretaries, along with a few other top-ranking officials, form the president's cabinet (see also Chapter 13). The four original departments are known as the **inner cabinet,** because their secretaries typically have ready access to the president.[53] Even the locations of their offices are close to the White House, as you can see from Figure 14.5. These departments are the following:

- State, responsible for foreign policy.
- Defense, originally called War, responsible for the military.
- Treasury, responsible for tax collections, payments, and debt service.
- Justice, headed by the attorney general, who is responsible for law enforcement.

The remaining departments of the cabinet, which are known as the **outer cabinet,** have less access to the president but have evolved in such a way as to provide interest-group access to the executive branch of government.[54] The Interior Department's job was originally to regulate the use of federal land, particularly in the West. Today, it maintains close ties to ranchers, timber companies, mining interests, and others who depend on federal lands for their livelihood. The Agriculture Department serves farmers; the Commerce Department helps business and industry, especially firms with overseas contracts; Labor works closely with unions; Health and Human Services heeds the

14.4

Outline the organization and functions of the cabinet, the independent regulatory agencies, and the Office of Management and Budget, and their relationship with the president.

inner cabinet
The four original departments (State, Defense, Treasury, and Justice) whose secretaries typically have the closest ties to the president.

outer cabinet
Newer departments that have less access to the president but have evolved in such a way as to provide interest-group access to the executive branch of government.

FIGURE 14.5

WHERE ARE THE KEY BUILDINGS IN WASHINGTON?

The physical location of the headquarters of the inner cabinet suggests the comparatively close ties these departments have to the president. Treasury is located next door to the White House. The walks from State and Justice to the White House are also shorter than to Capitol Hill. Defense, almost a world unto itself, is headquartered in the Pentagon in nearby Virginia. Many of the departments of the outer cabinet, such as Transportation, Education, Agriculture, Labor, and Housing and Urban Development, are located at the foot of Capitol Hill. There they hunker, almost on bended knee, faceless and humorless, in the shadow of the magnificent Capitol building. The Office of Management and Budget (OMB), the nerve center of the executive branch, stands at the president's side, physically as well as metaphorically.

• *When purchasing a home, buyers are advised to think first about location. Why might the importance of location also be true in politics?*

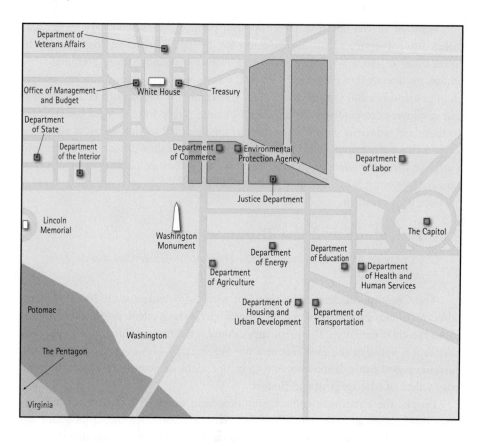

AARP (formerly the American Association for Retired Persons); and Education pays attention to teacher organizations (see Table 14.1).

The warm relationships between departments and interest groups can change overnight, however, if an event activates the public spotlight. Nowhere was this more evident than in the case of the financial crisis that arose in 2008. Companies such as Lehman Brothers and Bear Stearns, whose executives had socialized at the highest levels with Treasury Department and White House officials, saw their government allies disappear and their businesses collapse as a crash in the housing market rippled through the securities sector. After the government extended billions of dollars in aid to other troubled firms such as insurance giant AIG in an effort to stanch the crisis, administration officials lambasted corporate executives for their high salaries and bonuses. Such measures were not enough to appease an outraged public, however. In announcing a new effort to rein in big banks, President Obama acknowledged in 2010 that voters had "a sense that their voices aren't being heard and that institutions are betraying them."[55]

Presidents exercise their control over the cabinet departments primarily by appointing political allies to top positions in them. But once they become agency heads, these appointees often identify more closely with their turf than with the president's program. As FDR's top budget adviser put it, "Cabinet members are vice presidents in charge of spending, and as such they are the natural enemies of the President."[56] The bureaucracy problem, which tends to encourage sluggishness, red tape, and budgetary expansion, can be particularly frustrating for presidents, who are often interested in speed and efficiency.

TABLE 14.1
ESTABLISHMENT YEAR AND INTEREST-GROUP ALLIES OF EACH CABINET DEPARTMENT

• *Why have outer-cabinet departments formed alliances with outside groups?*

Department	Year	Interest-Group Allies
Inner Cabinet		
State	1789	
Treasury	1789	
Justice (attorney general)	1789	
Defense (as War)	1789	
Outer Cabinet		
Interior	1849	Timber, miners, ranchers
Agriculture	1889	Farm bureau, other farm groups
Commerce	1913	U.S. Chamber of Commerce, other business groups
Labor	1913	Labor unions
Health and Human Services	1953	American Association of Retired Persons
Housing and Urban Development	1965	National League of Cities, Urban League
Transportation	1966	Auto manufacturers, truckers, airlines
Energy	1977	Gas, oil, nuclear power interests
Education	1979	Teachers' unions
Veterans Affairs	1987	American Legion, Veterans of Foreign Wars
Department of Homeland Security	2003	Airlines, state and local governments
Environmental Protection Agency	Not an official department	Sierra Club, other environmental groups

Independent Regulatory Agencies

Not all agencies are members of cabinet departments. Some of the most important of these, the **independent regulatory agencies,** have quasi-judicial regulatory responsibilities, which are meant to be carried out in a manner free of presidential interference. These agencies are generally headed by a several-member board or commission appointed by the president and confirmed by the Senate. Independence from the president, which is considered desirable to insulate such agencies from partisan politics, is achieved by giving board members appointments that last for a specified number of years (see Table 14.2). In many cases, presidents may not be able to appoint a majority of these board members until well into their second term in office.

Congress created most independent regulatory agencies in response to widespread public pressure to protect workers and consumers from negligent or abusive business practices. For example, Congress established the Federal Trade Commission (FTC) in 1914 in response to the discovery of misbranding and adulteration in the meatpacking industry. The FTC was given the power to prevent price discrimination, unfair competition, false advertising, and other unfair business practices. Congress also created the

independent regulatory agencies

Agencies with quasi-judicial responsibilities that are meant to be carried out in a manner free of presidential interference.

TABLE 14.2

INDEPENDENT AGENCIES AND THEIR INTEREST-GROUP ALLIES

• Do the alliances many agencies form with interest groups undermine their initial goals?

Independent Agency	Board Size	Length of Term (years)	Interest-Group Allies
National Credit Union Administration	3	6	Credit unions
Federal Reserve Board	7	14	Banks
Consumer Product Safety Commission	5	5	Consumers Union
Equal Employment Opportunity Commission	5	5	Civil rights groups
Federal Deposit Insurance Corporation	5	3[a]	Banks
Federal Energy Regulatory Commission	4	4	Oil/gas interests
Federal Maritime Commission	5	5	Fisheries
Federal Trade Commission	5	7	Business groups
National Labor Relations Board	5	5	Unions
Securities and Exchange Commission	5	5	Wall Street
Tennessee Valley Authority	3	9	Regional farmers and utilities

[a]One member, the comptroller of the currency, serves a five-year term.

Mine Safety and Health Review Commission in 1977 to preside over disputes about mine safety, and it formed the Chemical Safety and Hazard Investigation Board in 1990 to investigate industrial chemical accidents.

When originally formed, most regulatory agencies aggressively pursued their reform mandates. But, as the public's enthusiasm for reform fades, many agencies find that their most interested constituents are members of the very community they are expected to regulate. Thus, the independent commissions, too, have tended to become connected to organized interest groups.[57] To protect against misleading business practices, the Securities and Exchange Commission (SEC) is responsible for ensuring that publicly traded companies provide stockholders with continually updated information about their true financial condition. Yet SEC officials missed a massive fraud after investment magnate Bernard Madoff and his lawyers repeatedly convinced regulators that nothing was amiss at his firm. By the time Madoff's unprecedented pyramid scheme unraveled in 2008, he had cheated investors out of a staggering $65 billion. The close connection between SEC officials and those who lobby them, an all too common phenomenon, can have serious consequences for investors.[58]

The Office of Management and Budget

Before 1921, each federal agency sent its own budget to Congress to be examined by an appropriations subcommittee. Without a single overseer to review all the requests at once, no one—not even the president—knew whether agency requests exceeded government revenues. When President Woodrow Wilson asked for an executive branch bureau to coordinate these requests, Congress at first refused to create one, saying such a bureau would encroach on congressional authority. However, when federal deficits ballooned during World War I, Congress, under pressure to make government more efficient, relented and gave the president the needed help.

Originally known as the Bureau of the Budget, the agency is now called the **Office of Management and Budget (OMB),** a name that reflects its enlarged set of responsibilities. Although development of the president's budget is still its most important job, OMB also sets personnel policy and reviews every piece of proposed legislation that the executive branch submits to Congress to ensure that it is consistent with the president's agenda. Agency regulations, too, must now get OMB approval. Even preliminary drafts have to be reviewed by OMB before they are unveiled to the public. One bureau chief claimed that OMB has "more control over individual agencies than . . . [the departmental] secretary or any of his assistants [do]."[59]

OMB was once a professional group of technicians whose only goals concerned efficiency and frugality in budgeting. But OMB became more political during the 1980s and 1990s, when budgetary priorities starkly defined the differences between Democrats and Republicans.[60] George W. Bush's OMB director, Josh Bolten, helped to negotiate congressional approval of a controversial $87 billion reconstruction aid package for Iraq.[61] Barack Obama's first OMB director, Peter Orszag, pressed for the enactment of the Obama economic stimulus package in 2009.

Although OMB has given presidents greater control over agencies, agency officials can still make **end runs** around OMB by appealing to their allies on Capitol Hill. For seven straight years, for example, the George W. Bush administration proposed cuts in funding to the Corporation for Public Broadcasting (CPB), a government corporation that produces public radio and television programs. But each year, CPB officials and their affiliated public broadcasting stations successfully lobbied Congress to restore most or all of the funding.[62]

To check OMB's growing power, Congress in 1974 created the **Congressional Budget Office (CBO),** an organization under the control of Congress that evaluates the president's budget as well as the budgetary implications of all other legislation. CBO's sophisticated analyses of budget and economic trends have enhanced its influence in Washington to the point where it now stands as a strong rival to OMB. In 2009 and 2010, for example, CBO estimates of the cost of President Barack Obama's health-care reform legislation were critical to negotiations with key members of Congress over whether to vote for the measure.

Congress and the Bureaucracy

It is a truism that no one should have more than one "boss." When two or more people can tell someone what to do, signals get crossed, delays ensue, and accountability is undermined. Government bureaucrats in Japan and in most European countries generally abide by this rule. Members of the civil service report to the heads of their departments, who report to the head of the government. Members of parliament have little to say about administrative matters.

Officially, federal bureaucrats in the United States have only one boss—the president, who according to the Constitution is the head of the executive branch. But they also have many bosses in Congress. One House subcommittee chair declared, "I've been running the Medicare system, or our committee has, for the past nine years. We're its board of directors."[63] With Congress divided into the House and Senate, and with

Office of Management and Budget (OMB)
Agency responsible for developing the president's budget, setting personnel policy in the executive branch, and reviewing all proposed legislation sent by the executive branch to Congress to ensure it is consistent with the president's agenda.

end run
An agency's effort to avoid OMB controls by appealing to its allies in Congress.

Congressional Budget Office (CBO)
Congressional agency that evaluates the president's budget as well as the budgetary implications of all other legislation.

14.5

Analyze the sources of Congress's power over the bureaucracy and the influence of the iron triangles and issues networks.

each chamber divided into many committees, bureaucrats often find themselves reporting to multiple committees, each of which considers itself a "board of directors." Further, the pressures on bureaucracies have intensified in an era of high exposure and perpetual campaigns. As Martha Derthick has observed, "[Although] the U.S. Constitution has not changed . . . the presidency ha[s] become much more vigilant and intrusive . . . [while] Congress has become more critical."[64]

Senate Confirmations

Congressional influence begins with the very selection of executive department officers. The Senate's confirmation power has long given senators a voice in administrative matters, traditionally via the practice of **senatorial courtesy.** This custom consists of an informal rule that the Senate will not confirm nominees for positions within a state unless they have the approval of the state's senior senator from the president's party. For example, there are 93 U.S. attorneys in the Department of Justice, appointed by the president to positions throughout the United States. A senator could block the approval of a U.S. attorney in his or her home state if for some reason the senator found the nominee unsatisfactory. Through the practice of senatorial courtesy, senators can protect their political bases by controlling patronage and shaping administrative practices within their states.

> **senatorial courtesy**
> An informal rule that the Senate will not confirm nominees for positions within a state unless it has the approval of the state's senior senator from the president's party.

The modern mass media have linked senatorial confirmations and election strategies even more closely. In an age when strong visual images are needed for the television screen, confirmation processes make for good political theater. Nominees have private lives to be examined. They can be asked embarrassing questions during their confirmation hearings. Conflicts between nominees and senators can elevate a little-known senator to the national stage.

Because the confirmation process has greater potential to affect elections than ever before, senators want more than just the usual "courtesy" traditionally extended to them from the nominee's home state. They now want to be assured that presidential nominees take acceptable policy positions, do not have private investments that conflict with their public duties, have not violated any laws, and have not acted contrary to conventional moral norms. In 2009, for example, Barack Obama's initial nominee for Commerce Secretary, New Mexico Governor Bill Richardson, had to withdraw because of an investigation into a state contracting deal. Richardson was never charged with any wrongdoing, but his nomination had become a political liability. As Richardson put it, "the ongoing investigation would have forced an untenable delay in the confirmation process."[65]

Senate rejections of presidential nominees are still the exception, not the rule. Yet, because presidents know that nomination fights damage their standing with Congress and the public, the confirmation process has become more complicated and time-consuming. To decrease the likelihood that the Senate will reject a nominee, the prospective appointee must first survive ethics inquiries by the FBI, the IRS, the Office of Government Ethics (an independent agency), and the ethics official from the agency to which the nominee will be appointed.[66] The White House must then defend the nominee against exhaustive senatorial scrutiny. Whereas Ronald Reagan had nearly 90 percent of his nominees in place after his first year in office, fewer than two-thirds of Barack Obama's appointees had been confirmed by early 2010 (see Figure 14.6).

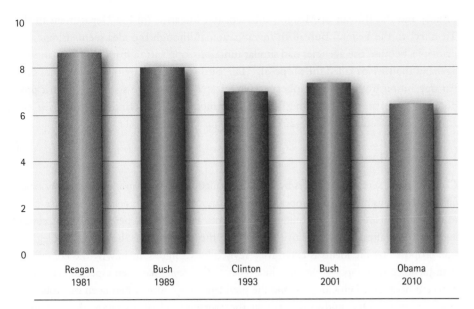

Percent Confirmed in First Year

FIGURE 14.6

PERCENT OF SENATE-
CONFIRMED
PRESIDENTIALLY APPOINTED
OFFICIALS CONFIRMED
IN FIRST YEAR OF
ADMINISTRATION

• *Why has it taken longer in
recent years for presidential
appointees to be confirmed? What
role might elections have played
in this trend?*

Source: Anne Joseph O'Connell, "Waiting
for Leadership: President Obama's Record
in Staffing Key Agency Positions and How
to Improve the Appointment Process,"
Washington, DC: Center for American
Progress, April 2010, Figure 2, p. 8.

Prolonging the confirmation process strengthens congressional control over administrative matters. As long as agency heads await confirmation, they hesitate before taking actions that might offend members of Congress.

Under Article II of the Constitution, presidents may make **recess appointments** without Senate confirmation "during the Recess of the Senate." Recess appointees may serve until the end of the next session of Congress, at which point they must resign if they have not been confirmed. Nothing in the Constitution precludes presidents from using the recess appointment repeatedly for the same person, even if that person is never confirmed. When Theodore Roosevelt could not secure confirmation of an African American as a customs collector in Charleston, South Carolina, the president reappointed him to the office during a Senate recess. Congress has since placed a check on the recess appointment power by passing legislation prohibiting payment of salary to appointees who serve more than a year without Senate confirmation. As a result, presidents today seldom exercise this power over congressional objections.[67] One exception occurred in 2010 when Barack Obama used a recess appointment to install Donald Berwick as the head of the federal Medicare and Medicaid programs. Republican senators had blocked the nomination, arguing that Berwick was too liberal; the White House countered by saying "there's no time to waste with Washington game-playing."[68]

recess appointment
A presidential appointment made without Senate confirmation while the Senate is in recess.

Agency Reorganization

Not only do presidents and Congress struggle over the appointment of agency officials, but Congress often opposes presidential proposals to reorganize executive agencies. Congress resists change because each agency reports to a specific congressional committee, and these committees are frequently protective of their power—no matter how duplicative or antiquated existing organizational structures might be.[69] For example, in the first Clinton administration, Vice President Gore proposed shifting the law enforcement functions of the Drug Enforcement Administration (in the Department of

Justice) and the Bureau of Alcohol, Tobacco, and Firearms (in the Department of the Treasury) to the Federal Bureau of Investigation. Although the idea seemed logical in principle, because the agencies had similar functions, opposition from Congress and the agencies themselves killed the proposal.[70] The Bush administration had to navigate similar opposition from some members of Congress and executive agencies when it proposed the creation of a cabinet-level Department of Homeland Security (see the *Election Voices!* feature on page 422).

Legislative Detail

Congress also exercises its powers by writing detailed legislation outlining an agency's specific legal responsibilities. In European countries, most legislation is enacted in a form close to the draft prepared by the executive departments.[71] In Japan, 90 percent of all successful legislation is drafted by an executive agency.[72] In the United States, however, most legislation proposed by presidents is extensively revised by Congress, mainly by the committee with jurisdictional responsibility for the agency.[73] This route has been especially common in recent decades, when Congress and the presidency have more often been controlled by different parties. One study suggests that the average level of discretion that Congress grants the agencies fell by as much as 25 percent in the last half of the twentieth century.[74]

Sometimes detailed but conflicting laws can have nonsensical results. For more than a decade, critics have ridiculed laws that give the Agriculture Department the authority to regulate sausage pizzas but give the Food and Drug Administration the authority to regulate cheese pizzas. The FDA operates under legislation authored by the House Commerce Committee and the Senate Human Resources Committee, whereas the Agriculture Department receives its mandates from the House and Senate Agriculture committees. Neither set of committees wishes to relax its control over its

ELECTION CONNECTION

Congressional Legislation: A Matter of Detail

To help themselves get reelected, members of Congress try to get what they want out of bureaucracies through the practice of *earmarking*. For example, the Tarleton State University Rural Law Enforcement Project in Texas received $1.5 million as part of the 2010 Commerce, Justice, and Science appropriations bill. Some members of Congress deride such projects as unnecessary "pork barrel" spending, while others see it as a fundamental part of the job of representing their constituents.

• *If you were an agency official, would you prefer more or less earmarking? What kinds of agencies might prefer more or less earmarking?*

Wind power projects in many states have received federal earmarks.

Source: Taxpayers for Common Sense, "Database of FY2010 Earmarks," www.taxpayer.net, accessed February 7, 2010.

agency, so the peculiar division of responsibilities persists. The result, according to one report, "hinders the government's efforts to efficiently and effectively protect consumers from unsafe food."[75]

Even if a statute itself does not dwell on administrative issues, agency operations can be influenced by committee reports accompanying the proposed legislation. Courts consider these reports to be evidence of congressional intent and frequently grant them the force of law. Even in the absence of court action, agencies pay attention to committee reports. In the words of one observer, "That language [in the reports] isn't legally binding, but the agencies understand very well what happens if they ignore it."[76]

The issue of legislative detail can be seen as a balancing act between administrative discretion, on the one hand, and congressional control, on the other. If the agency is mindful of congressional intent, Congress may allow it more freedom to act on its own. If an agency neglects a committee's wishes, Congress may enact legal restrictions or even use more forceful methods, such as its control over the agency's budget, to get its way.

Budgetary Control

Every year, each agency prepares a budget for the president to submit to Congress. Each agency must defend its budget before an appropriations subcommittee in both the House and the Senate, and those who offend committee members jeopardize their agency's funding.

To ensure that agencies spend monies in ways consistent with congressional preferences, significant portions of many agency budgets are subject to an **earmark,** a very specific designation of the way money is to be spent, sometimes even specifying particular congressional districts (see the *Election Voices!* feature in Chapter 12, on page 358).

Earmarking seems to be on the increase, and it became an issue in the 2008 election campaign. Republican candidate John McCain touted his opposition to all earmarks and promised to veto any bill containing them. Barack Obama argued that all earmarks should be well publicized, so that voters can make up their own minds about whether they are good or bad. In 2010, President Obama proposed that Congress create a website where all earmarks would be disclosed prior to any congressional vote.[77]

earmark
In an agency's budget, a specific congressional designation of the way money is to be spent.

Legislative Oversight

In addition to earmarking, committees hold hearings to ensure that agencies are not straying from their congressional mandates. The increase in such oversight hearings in recent decades has expanded committee control over administrative practice. The number of days each year that committees hold oversight hearings nearly quadrupled between the 1960s and the 1990s.[78] Although the number of oversight hearings has fallen as a result of reforms instituted in 1995, they still far outnumber hearings called to consider specific legislation.[79]

At oversight hearings, members of the administration are often asked to testify about agency experiences and problems. Witnesses representing outside groups are given opportunities to praise or criticize the bureaucrats. Through the oversight process, committees obtain information that can be used to revise existing legislation or modify agency budgets, sometimes to the consternation of bureaucrats. Even when committees do not hold hearings, the threat of doing so is sometimes enough to cow agency officials into following congressional wishes.[80] According to one survey, nearly half of high-level agency officials complain of "a great deal" of congressional "micromanagement" of their jobs.[81]

Iron Triangles and Issue Networks

Congress has such power over bureaucracies that many agencies seek to build coalitions of allies among congressional committees and interest groups in order to survive. These connections have become so intimate that some political scientists have said that most federal government programs are run by **iron triangles,** the close, stable connections among agencies, interest groups, and congressional committees.[82] Interest groups form the base of the triangle, because they have the membership and money that can influence the outcome of congressional elections, and agencies listen to interest-group demands to obtain committee backing (see Figure 14.7).

iron triangle
A close, stable connection among agencies, interest groups, and congressional committees.

The relationship is said to be an iron triangle because the connections among the threesome are strong and stable. Each of the three parties can deliver something the other needs. Compromises are readily arranged because interests are similar. Most oversight hearings are, in fact, three-way love fests. Interest-group representatives offer gracious testimony about agency work, and members of Congress chime in with words of endearment. When a congressional scholar asked congressional committee staff whether they considered their committee to be agency advocates, nearly two-thirds said "yes." One staff person admitted "we get in bed with agency people in some respects. We're hoping that they'll distribute good projects in our state . . . and it's a kind of a working with them so that, you know, there'll be more, more and better of everything for everybody."[83]

These relationships often transcend partisan divisions. When Republicans won control of Congress in 1995, the House leadership initially placed tight restrictions on committees in order to weaken the committee–agency relationship. But within a year the Republican leadership found it necessary to loosen its controls, and the natural tendency for committees to support "their" agencies reasserted itself.

Some iron triangles are no longer as rigid as they once were. As the number of interest groups and policy experts has expanded, congressional committees and government agencies have been bombarded with competing demands from multiple sides, which together form issue networks (see section (b) in Figure 14.7).[84] For example, nuclear energy policy was, at one time, of interest mainly to just four companies that built nuclear reactors and to the utility companies that used the electricity. After an accident in 1979 at the Three Mile Island reactor in Pennsylvania, however, the subject attracted the attention of environmental, safety, and antinuclear groups, all of whom pressed for tighter regulation of nuclear reactors. With the interests of the groups divided, the media took greater notice of the issue, and conflict between congressional committees and the Department of Energy intensified.[85] By 2010, when President Obama announced federal loan guarantees to build new nuclear power plants in Georgia, a wider variety of interest groups, companies, and even several U.S. states had become involved in the policy debate. As this example illustrates, issue networks include more conflict, more players, and more publicity than iron triangles.

Many scholars argue that the concept of *issue networks* presents a more realistic picture of the way Washington works today than does the older concept of iron triangles (see Chapter 7).

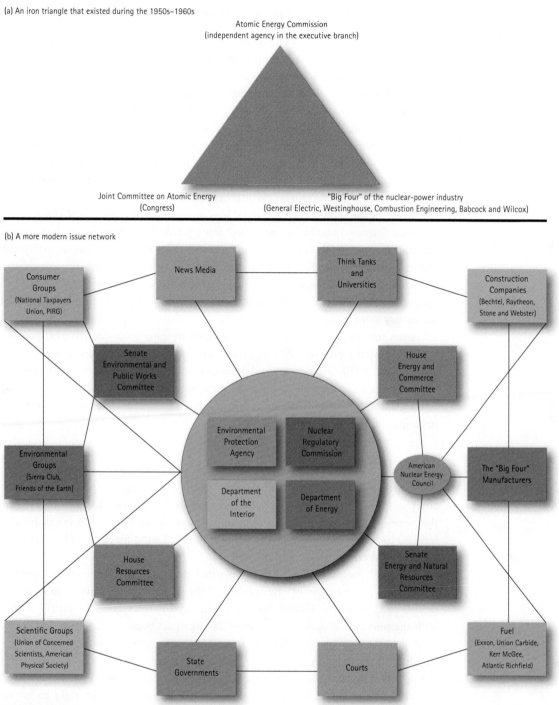

(a) An iron triangle that existed during the 1950s–1960s

Atomic Energy Commission
(independent agency in the executive branch)

Joint Committee on Atomic Energy
(Congress)

"Big Four" of the nuclear-power industry
(General Electric, Westinghouse, Combustion Engineering, Babcock and Wilcox)

(b) A more modern issue network

Consumer Groups
(National Taxpayers Union, PIRG)

News Media

Think Tanks and Universities

Construction Companies
(Bechtel, Raytheon, Stone and Webster)

Senate Environmental and Public Works Committee

House Energy and Commerce Committee

Environmental Protection Agency

Nuclear Regulatory Commission

American Nuclear Energy Council

The "Big Four" Manufacturers

Environmental Groups
(Sierra Club, Friends of the Earth)

Department of the Interior

Department of Energy

House Resources Committee

Senate Energy and Natural Resources Committee

Scientific Groups
(Union of Concerned Scientists, American Physical Society)

State Governments

Courts

Fuel
(Exxon, Union Carbide, Kerr McGee, Atlantic Richfield)

FIGURE 14.7

CHANGE OF NUCLEAR ENERGY POLICY ARENA FROM IRON TRIANGLE TO ISSUE NETWORK

In the 1950s and 1960s, the players in the nuclear policy arena were few and well connected, as the top illustration shows. But since that time, more interest groups, government officials, and private businesses have become involved, as the bottom illustration shows.

- *Why has the policymaking environment changed from a triangle to a web?*

Sources: Based on information in Seong-Ho Lim, "Changing Jurisdictional Boundaries in Congressional Oversight of Nuclear Energy Regulation: Impact of Public Salience," paper presented before the Annual Meeting of the American Political Science Association, 1992; and Frank R. Baumgartner and Bryan D. Jones, "Agency Dynamics and Policy Subsystems," *Journal of Politics* 53 (November 1991): 1044–1074.

14.6

Assess the impact of
elections and of public
perception on the
bureaucracy.

Elections and the Bureaucracy

For more than a century, reformers have tried to separate politics from administration. Government should serve the people, they argue, not the special interests. Departments should make decisions according to laws and regulations, not in response to political pressure. Agencies should treat every applicant alike, not favor those who contribute to political parties.

These reform principles are worthy of respect. When politics interferes, bureaucracies can be inefficient and ineffective. The Customs Service, its name once synonymous with political spoils, is still slow to report international economic transactions. The Department of Housing and Urban Development, always a political thicket, has at times so badly mismanaged its property that it has had to blow up buildings it constructed.[86]

Many of the more effective federal bureaucracies are less politically charged. The National Science Foundation, protected from political pressures by an independent board, is known for the integrity with which it allocates dollars among competing scientific projects. The Federal Bureau of Prisons does a better job than many state prisons of maintaining security without depriving prisoners of their rights; it has succeeded in part because members of Congress, respectful of prison leadership, have left the agency alone.[87]

Even though agency autonomy has worked in some instances, electoral pressures have also played a positive role and in any case are an essential feature of modern bureaucracies.[88] Public pressure exerted through elections has affected the way bureaucracies keep secrets, enforce the law, manage their budgets, and make decisions. In the end, elections create pressures that force many agencies to balance competing interests by striking compromises.

Bureaucratic Secrecy

Bureaucracies like to protect their secrets. "Inside knowledge" is power. Secrecy can cover mistakes. In Europe, where administrators are less exposed to electoral pressure, they work hard to guard their private information. In Britain, it is a crime for civil servants to divulge official information, and political appointees swear themselves to secrecy upon taking office.

Electoral pressures have sharply curtailed the amount of secrecy in American government. In the view of one specialist, "Secrecy has less legitimacy as a governmental practice in the United States than in any other advanced industrial society with the possible exception of Sweden," in large part because "Congress has done a great deal to open up the affairs of bureaucracy to greater outside scrutiny."[89] The **sunshine law,** passed in 1976, required that federal government meetings be held in public, unless military plans, trade secrets, or personnel questions are being discussed. Under the Freedom of Information Act of 1967, citizens have the right to inspect unprotected government documents. If the government believes the requested information needs to be kept secret, it must bear the burden of proof when arguing its case before a judge.

Even in the absence of new laws, the legislative and judicial branches can limit the degree to which executive agencies operate in secret. In 2007, for example, congressional investigators uncovered a concerted effort within the Justice Department to fire nine U.S.

sunshine law
A 1976 law requiring that federal government meetings be held in public.

attorneys for reasons that appeared to have more to do with politics than with job performance. That same year, Congress also pressed the Defense Department to be more open with information about the Iraq War. As House Armed Services Committee Chairman Ike Skelton (D-MO) put it, "Congress must have this information in order to carry out its constitutional oversight responsibilities."[90]

Secrecy can sometimes be essential in pursuing national security objectives, however. The Department of Homeland Security has often had to walk a delicate line between publicity, to keep the public adequately informed of threats, and secrecy, to more effectively detect or disrupt specific terrorist plotting. As of 2010, for example, the color-coded terrorism alert status had been steady at "yellow" (and at "orange" for airlines) since 2006, despite the ebb and flow of terrorist threat information. One reason is that the agency has come to the conclusion that frequent changes in the alert status are confusing and counterproductive. "When you raise the color-coded system," said one expert, "it's a blunt instrument."[91]

Despite the acknowledged benefits of some kinds of secrecy, many elected officials feel public pressure to force executive agencies to disclose as much information as possible. One survey found that government openness is "one of the most important priorities" for nearly 40 percent of Americans.[92] Voters apparently believe that, as one observer put it, "In order for people to direct their own government, they must have information about governance and be able to examine the performance of elected leaders and bureaucrats."[93]

Bureaucratic Coercion

Bureaucracies are often accused of using their coercive powers harshly and unfairly. Police officers stop young drivers for traffic violations that they often ignore when committed by older drivers. Bureaucratic zealots trap sales clerks into selling cigarettes to heavily bearded 17-year-olds. Disabled people are refused benefits because they do not fill out their applications correctly.

Although such abuses occur, they happen less frequently because agencies are held accountable to the electorate. In 1998, for example, Republican senators sensed popular discontent with the Internal Revenue Service (IRS), the government's tax collection agency. The agency's approval rating was an embarrassingly low 38 percent.[94] The Senate Finance Committee held a series of hearings that brought to light a litany of agency failings. The IRS had lost $150 billion in 1995 because of mistakes, unreported income, or improper deductions. Taxpayers were overbilled an average of $5 billion per year.[95] The technology the agency used was so outdated that IRS commissioner Charles Rossotti himself admitted, "I have never seen a worse situation in a large organization."[96] As a result of the hearings, Congress enacted a law restructuring the agency, making it harder for the IRS to accuse taxpayers of wrongdoing and bringing its tax collection systems up to date.[97] In the succeeding years, the IRS focused so much on customer service that some members of Congress ironically began to fear that the agency was not being tough enough in its enforcement actions.[98]

The example of the IRS illustrates a broader pattern in U.S. politics: If bureaucratic agencies make life difficult for the voting public, these agencies are more likely to be taken to task by elected officials.[99] Most agencies would prefer to avoid this painful scrutiny.

Curbing Agency Expansion

Agencies generally try to increase their budgets, but elections apply the brakes to such tendencies, if only because politicians get blamed for raising taxes. As analyst Martha Derthick puts it, "Congress likes to keep bureaucracy lean and cheap."[100] The number of people working for the federal government, as a percentage of the workforce, has declined since the 1980s, in large part because elected officials are under public pressure to cut bureaucracy. The overall size of the government grew during the George W. Bush administration for the first time in years, as agencies added half a million new anti-terrorism jobs.[101] But President Bush also worked to shrink the bureaucracy by forcing some bureaucrats to compete with private companies for their jobs. This "competitive sourcing" initiative rankled some federal employees, who staged a protest outside the White House and called upon their allies in Congress to defend them.[102] "The long-term [government] employee is feeling devalued," said an anonymous U.S. Park Service worker.[103] In one survey, 59 percent of federal workers said their agencies only "sometimes" or "rarely" have "enough employees to do their jobs well."[104]

Costly Contracting

Blackwater USA, whose guards are shown here securing the site of a bombing in Baghdad, was criticized in 2007 for its employees' behavior in a firefight that killed 17 civilians.

• *When the government contracts with private firms, is the public less able to hold officials accountable?*

Bush's competitive sourcing initiative is one example of a trend toward privatization, a practice in which governments hire private companies to perform government tasks. For decades, cities and counties have contracted with private companies to perform such tasks as garbage pickup and parking violations enforcement. In recent years, the national government has relied on private firms for everything from tax collection to writing and editing new regulations.[105] Although privatization may save money, critics worry that it makes government less accountable by placing key tasks out of the public view. For example, in 2007 Congress held hearings to investigate whether a military contractor, Blackwater USA, had abused its power after it was hired to guard state department officials and others in Iraq. That fall, company guards killed 17 Iraqi civilians in a bloody Baghdad firefight, and an FBI investigation later found that most of these deaths occurred "without cause."[106] Because private companies often operate out of the public eye, privatization may require more vigilance from Congress. As Congressman Henry T. Waxman (D-CA) put it, "if we are going to contract out, we have to have better oversight."

Administrator Caution

Federal agencies are sometimes accused of going beyond their legislative mandates. But most federal agencies are more likely to err on the side of caution. The worst thing any agency can do is make a major mistake that captures national attention. As one official explained, "The public servant soon learns that successes rarely rate a headline, but government blunders are front-page news. This recognition encourages the development of procedures designed less to achieve successes than to avoid blunders."[107]

In 1962, it was discovered to widespread horror that thalidomide, a sedative available in Europe, increased the probability that babies would be born with serious physical deformities. Congress immediately passed a law toughening the procedures the FDA was to follow before approving prescription drugs for distribution.[108] Decades later, in keeping with this policy, the FDA refused to approve the sale of several experimental drugs to terminally ill people suffering from AIDS. Patients desperate to try anything that might help them did not share the FDA's concern for ascertaining proven effectiveness. When the FDA's refusal to allow experimentation became a public issue, the agency began to allow AIDS patients to try the untested drugs, once again responding to pressure from the voting public.

Compromised Capacity

Agency effectiveness is often undermined by the very terms of the legislation that created it. For legislation to pass Congress, a broad coalition of support is necessary. To build this support, proponents must strike deals with those who are at best lukewarm to a proposed bill. Such compromise can cripple a program at birth.[109]

The politics of charter schools illustrates the restraint that compromises can place on organizational effectiveness. In the 1990s, school reform advocates began to establish charter schools—new schools free of most state regulations. Reformers expect charter schools to provide alternatives to, and competition for, traditional public schools. School boards and teacher organizations oppose the establishment of these schools, claiming they will attract students away from their local schools. Many state legislatures, under pressure from both sides, have compromised on the issue by passing legislation allowing charter schools but restricting their number, funding, and autonomy. Evidence on the effects of charter schools on student education has been mixed so far, and it remains to be seen whether charter schools can prosper within the constraints imposed by these legislative compromises.[110]

Muddling Through

American bureaucracies do not perform as badly as most Americans think. One study finds, for example, that those who interact with the national government rate it as being roughly as satisfying as wireless telephone providers or newspapers—and more satisfying than the airline industry or cable TV companies.[111]

The advent of the Internet has provided an opportunity for bureaucracies to communicate more effectively with citizens. According to one study, more than two-thirds of visitors to government websites found them to be useful and easy to navigate.[112]

When we add up all the pluses and minuses, the average government bureaucracy probably deserves something like a B-minus grade. A few agencies, such as NASA during the race to the moon, merited an A-plus, although its reputation has since slipped. A few others, such as the U.S. Customs and Border Protection Service, which is charged with preventing the entry of undocumented immigrants, probably don't deserve a passing grade. But the general tendency is toward a bland, risk-free mediocrity. Too much imagination generates too much controversy, which invites political retribution. One bureaucrat offered the following guidelines for his colleagues: "1) When in charge, ponder; 2) When in trouble, delegate; 3) When in doubt, mumble."[113] The best way to survive politically is to try to muddle through, making only gradual changes in policy and striving to satisfy everyone.[114]

Continued on page 426

The Politics of the New Department of Homeland Security

The Issue

Is government reorganization an effective way to tackle policy problems? Or do bureaucratic battles, congressional turf wars, and other disruptions make such efforts more trouble than they are worth?

Background

After nine months of struggling to manage a coordinated homeland security effort in the wake of the 9/11 attacks, President George W. Bush and other administration officials concluded that a new cabinet department had to be created. The administration realized that creating the department would be a challenge. The last time the United States had undergone significant national security reorganization was in the late 1940s, after what President Truman called a "long hard battle" that lasted at least four years.[1]

Some present-day political scientists believe that in the United States this kind of major governmental change is prohibitively difficult. Entrenched bureaucracies, allied with interest groups and key congressional committee members, have made it all but impossible to enact beneficial changes.[2]

The successful creation of a new department of homeland security in 2002 provides proof that major change in the structure of government can occur, at least under certain circumstances. But the department's mixed successes in the years since its inception have led some experts to question whether the reorganization changed things for the better. The reasons for this ambivalence are closely related to political considerations the department's creators had to manage back in 2002.

A Reorganization That Recognized Political Reality

When President Bush and his aides designed their original plan for a Department of Homeland Security (DHS), they chose a modest and realistic path to reorganization. This may seem an odd statement, considering the fact that the Bush plan led to the creation of a huge new agency, with 178,000 employees and a budget of $52 billion (as of 2010, see Figure 1). But Bush's team selected the agencies to incorporate into the department very carefully. Those that were easier to shift became part of the final proposal; others were left alone.

The administration chose to place in the new department the Federal Emergency Management Agency (FEMA), the Coast Guard, and the Transportation Security Administration—in part because these bureaucracies had less clout than some other governmental agencies. FEMA, an independent entity, had only 2,500 employees, many of whom were assigned to the agency's ten regional offices, far from Washington power centers. The Coast Guard was bigger, with 35,000 active duty personnel, but it had been moved among cabinet departments before. The Transportation Security Administration, although large, was brand new—it had been created in November 2001 to restructure airport security systems—and it had had little time to sink deep roots within the Department of Transportation.

Contrast these agencies with one other organization that many critics thought should have been included in the Bush proposal but was not: the Federal Bureau of Investigation (FBI). With a workforce of 27,000, a distinctive agency culture, and a history in the Justice Department that stretches back to 1908, the FBI would have been hard to change. According to one presidential aide, if they were threatened, Bureau officials would "throw a major fit and their friends in Congress would run us out of town for even proposing it."[3] Accordingly, despite its key role in investigating terrorists in the United States, the Bush team decided that "the organizational integrity of the FBI needs to be maintained."[4]

Decisions like this one made it easier to create the Department of Homeland Security, but they made it tougher to coordinate policy among multiple security and intelligence agencies after its creation. In 2008, an internal government report found that "the authorities of different agencies overlap or are thought to overlap, creating 'lanes in the road' disputes, many of which continue to be unresolved."[5] After the narrowly averted Christmas day airplane bombing in December 2009, complaints and recriminations about coordination and information sharing cropped up again.

Reorganization and the Congressional Committee System

Once the plan was announced, the entrenched congressional committee system threatened to derail the proposal. The prospect of a brand new department raised the possibility that Congress would have to restructure its oversight committees—and the Bush administration urged legislators to do just that.[6] But existing committees resisted any organizational changes that would lessen their power. "Hell hath no fury like a committee chairman whose jurisdiction has been taken away," warned Republican senator Robert Bennett.[7]

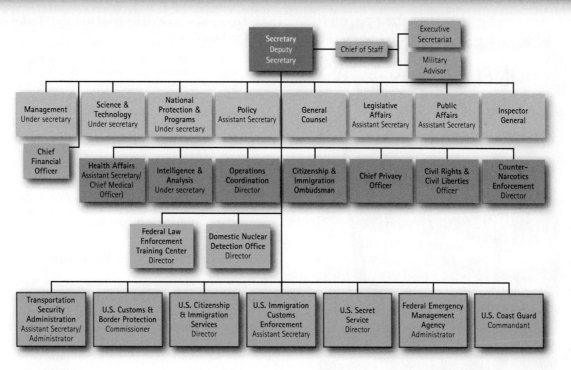

FIGURE 1

THE DEPARTMENT OF HOMELAND SECURITY

This organizational chart depicts the Department of Homeland Security.

- *Why isn't the FBI part of the new department?*

To avoid facing such fury, the new department's proponents postponed questions of committee jurisdiction until after Congress passed legislation creating the new department. The Senate chose to debate the Bush proposal on the chamber floor rather than letting committees get their hooks into the plan, and House leaders created a temporary special committee, composed of House leaders, to consider the matter.

After the creation of the new department, the House gave jurisdiction over most homeland security matters to a select committee on homeland security, while the Senate chose to divide jurisdiction among existing committees. Still, over 80 committees and subcommittees continue to have some kind of jurisdiction over homeland security matters—a situation that one analyst criticizes as "impractical, constitutionally deficient, and simply poor management."[8]

The Department of Homeland Security and Elections

At the time of its creation, the Department of Homeland Security received a critical boost from the high public regard for the proposal's sponsor. At the time, President Bush was enjoying a nearly unprecedented period of lofty approval ratings that outlasted the initial boost after September 11. But in the years that followed critics charged that the new department had little to show for itself, and public opinion began to become more negative. Complaints about the agency's color-coded terror warning system prompted an internal review.[9] The department's isolation from the FBI and other intelligence agencies led one former homeland security official to admit that DHS had too often "been on the outside of the intelligence community with its nose pressed against the glass."[10] Worst of all, after the disastrous intergovernmental response to Hurricane Katrina in 2005, many experts argued that FEMA should never have been absorbed into a department that was primarily concerned with terrorist threats. "As long as you require the FEMA director to go through two and three layers of bureaucracy to get a decision from the president, you're going to have a major problem," argued one former FEMA director.[11] By 2009, as Figure 2 shows, fewer Americans had a high opinion of the Homeland Security Department than of the FBI, the Centers for Disease Control, or the Department of Agriculture.

Optimistic Views on the Department of Homeland Security

Optimists argue that the case of the Homeland Security Department shows that government can adapt to changing circumstances and, in so doing, act in the public interest.

The color-coded terror alert system has been used more cautiously in recent years.

Problems exist, but they are the growing pains of a new organization, not fundamental weaknesses:

> The diverse capacities of our components, far from being a weakness, are in fact one of our biggest strengths . . . . Now in one sense, we will always be a department made up of agencies with their own unique histories. But what connects us all, what makes us look beyond the letters TSA [Transportation Security Administration], USCIS [U.S. Customs and Immigration Service], or I&A [Office of Intelligence and Analysis] or S&T [Science and Technology Directorate] is our common mission and the responsibilities that go with it.
>
> —Janet Napolitano, Secretary of Homeland Security,
> Remarks Highlighting DHS's Major Accomplishments in 2009,
> Washington, DC, December 16, 2009

Pessimistic Views on the Department of Homeland Security

Others argue that the new department represents more of the same: Bureaucratic squabbling has limited the department's initial scope; the agency has been slow to improve communications with state and local governments, and even has had trouble

coordinating its message on terrorism with that of other departments and agencies.[12]

> Although reorganizing federal bureaucracy is a typical governmental response to a disaster such as 9/11, in this case, growing evidence suggests that placing so many disparate agencies and departments under one roof has created more problems than it has solved. . . . Such a veritable smorgasbord of bureaucracy has led to continual inter- and intra-agency conflict. . . . The response to Hurricane Katrina illustrated the interagency rift vividly, as DHS and FBI officials fought over which would play a lead role in safety and law enforcement.
>
> — Laura H. Kahn, "The Problems with the Department of Homeland Security," *Bulletin of the Atomic Scientists,*
> June 9, 2009, available at www.thebulletin.org

What Do Americans Believe?

As Figure 2 shows, Americans supported President Bush's plan to create the Department of Homeland Security but had doubts about its performance years later. These doubts seem closely related to the department's botched response to Hurricane Katrina, as well as to more recent incidents such as the attempted Christmas day bombing of a Detroit-bound flight in 2009.

What Do You Think?

1. Was the creation of the new Homeland Security Department a substantive change or just a superficial one?

2. Does this case study show that the politics of elections does not interfere with effective government? Or does it illustrate the reverse?

On the Web

The Department of Homeland Security operates an official website with information about its current programs and activities, as well as Ready.gov, a practical Web guide that informs citizens about how to prepare for possible terrorist attacks.

> www.dhs.gov
> www.ready.gov

The House of Representatives created a new committee to handle most homeland security matters, while the Senate divided oversight responsibilities among existing committees. These two links lead to the House Select Committee on Homeland Security and to the Senate Homeland Security and Government Affairs Committee, respectively, the latter of which has jurisdiction over many—but by no means all—homeland security programs.

> http://hsc.house.gov
> http://hsgac.senate.gov

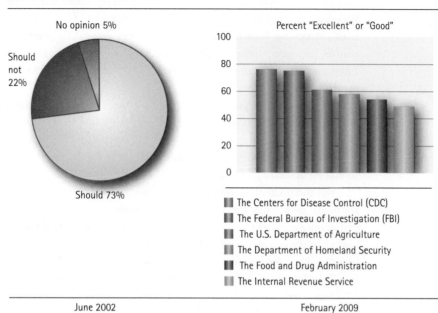

Do you think Congress should—or should not—pass legislation to create a new cabinet-level Department of Homeland Security?

No opinion 5%

Should not 22%

Should 73%

June 2002

Overall, how would you rate the job each of these federal government agencies does?

Percent "Excellent" or "Good"

- ■ The Centers for Disease Control (CDC)
- ■ The Federal Bureau of Investigation (FBI)
- ■ The U.S. Department of Agriculture
- ■ The Department of Homeland Security
- ■ The Food and Drug Administration
- ■ The Internal Revenue Service

February 2009

FIGURE 2

AMERICANS SUPPORTED THE BUSH PLAN, BUT LATER HAD DOUBTS

- *Overall, how would you rate the job each of these federal government agencies does?*
- *Did voters' opinions about the effectiveness of the Department of Homeland Security affect the 2010 congressional elections, in your view?*

Sources: Gallup Poll, June 21–23, 2002; Harris Poll, February 10, 2009.

[1]Harry Truman, *Memoirs, Vol. 2: Years of Trial and Hope* (Garden City, NY: Doubleday, 1956), p. 51.

[2]See, for example, Theodore Lowi, *The End of Liberalism: Ideology, Policy and the Crisis of Public Authority* (New York: Norton, 1969); Mancur Olson, *The Rise and Decline of Nations: Economic Growth, Stagflation, and Social Rigidities* (New Haven: Yale University Press, 1982); Jonathan Rauch, *Demosclerosis: The Silent Killer of American Government* (New York: Times Books, 1994); and Haynes Johnson and David Broder, *The System: The American Way of Politics at the Breaking Point* (Boston: Little, Brown, 1996).

[3]Michael Kramer, "No Place Like Homeland for FBI, CIA," *New York Daily News* (June 14, 2002): 26.

[4]Bill Miller and Mike Allen, "Homeland Security Dept. Could Receive Raw FBI, CIA Data; Bush Still Opposes Merging FBI," *Washington Post* (June 19, 2002): A8.

[5]Office of the Director of National Intelligence, Office of the Inspector General, "Critical Intelligence Community Management Challenges," November 12, 2008, http://www.fas.org/irp/news/2009/04/odni-ig-1108.pdf, accessed February 8, 2010, p. 2

[6]Bettelheim and Barshay.

[7]Ibid.

[8]Jena Baker McNeill, "Congressional Oversight of Homeland Security in Dire Need of Overhaul," Heritage Foundation Backgrounder, July 14, 2008, http://www.heritage.org/Research/HomelandDefense/upload/ bg_2161.pdf, accessed February 8, 2010.

[9]Jennifer A. Dlouhy, "U.S. Terror Alert System to Be Revamped," *Houston Chronicle,* May 15, 2005:A8.

[10]Clark Kent Ervin, "Homeland Security's Intelligence Gap," *New York Times* (July 17, 2005): Section 4, 12.

[11]Seth Borenstein, "Disaster Response Fixes Pushed; Homeland Security Chief Set to Face Critics," *Pittsburgh Post-Gazette* (February 14, 2006): A8.

[12]Thomas Frank, "Terror Warnings not Coordinated," *Newsday,* May 28, 2004, A4.

Continued from page 421

The Forest Service, which is responsible for managing most of the millions of acres owned by the federal government, does a pretty good job of muddling through. Although its rangers are professionally trained, talented individuals, its political problems are vexing. Ranchers, miners, and timber companies want to exploit the land's natural resources. Others want to use the land for hiking, camping, and fishing. Environmentalists want to convert as much of the land as they can into wilderness areas for the benefit of future generations.

To balance these pressures, the Forest Service came up with the doctrine of multiple use. It proposed to manage the land in such a way that its multiple uses could be blended together and harmonized. Timber harvests should be accompanied by reforestation. Especially scenic areas should be preserved for recreational activities. Mining should be as inconspicuous as possible.

But the doctrine of multiple use did not so much resolve conflicts as institutionalize them. As a result, the Forest Service is under constant pressure. Ranching, timber, and mining interests have clout at the local level, where political leaders make the potent claim that the economy will suffer unless these interests are protected. Environmentalists, however, have the greatest influence on those chosen in elections affected by the national media, which dramatically depict the desecration of the American landscape.

Any attempt to balance these interests antagonizes one or more sides of the dispute. Only by muddling through can the Forest Service survive politically and manage the federal lands as well as it does.[115]

CHAPTER SUMMARY

14.1   Describe the organization and role of the bureaucracy.

Government bureaucracies are essential, and bureaucratic problems are inevitable. But American bureaucracies have specific troubles that can be attributed to the electoral climate in which they have evolved. The federal bureaucracy consists of 15 departments, as well as many independent agencies and a few government corporations. The discretion these agencies have allows them significant influence over policy.

14.2   Identify the factors that create the bureaucracy problem.

Complaints about the bureaucracy usually focus on inefficiency, red tape, expanding budgets, or slow responses to changing conditions. But these problems occur for understandable reasons, such as the difficulty of defining bureaucratic goals and performance measures, and the need for standard operating procedures.

14.3   Trace the history of governmental bureaucracy in the United States and evaluate the impact of political appointees today.

With the creation of the spoils system in the 1800s, bureaucrats were often regarded as slow, inefficient, and corrupt political hacks. Gradually, civil-service reforms eliminated the worst of the abuses. But the reforms occurred in a bottom-up, not top-down, fashion. The highest levels of government continue to be filled with political appointees—generally capable but not always experienced government administrators.

14.4   Outline the organization and functions of the cabinet, the independent regulatory agencies, and the Office of Management and Budget, and their relationship with the president.

As chief executive, the president is nominally in charge of the bureaucracy, appointing key officials and exerting control through the Office of Management and Budget.

OMB has far-reaching authority over personnel policy and budgetary decisions, giving it significant leverage over federal departments and agencies.

14.5 Analyze the sources of Congress's power over the bureaucracy and the influence of the iron triangles and issues networks.

But Congress also influences federal agencies via its confirmation of presidential nominees, detailed legislative enactments, the budget process, and legislative oversight. To survive, agencies build ties to key interest groups, who form the base of what are known as iron triangles. Today, some of these iron triangles are being transformed into more complex, unstable, and conflictual issue networks.

14.6 Assess the impact of elections and of public perception on the bureaucracy.

Elections influence agencies in diverse ways. On the one hand, they keep agencies from becoming too secretive and coercive. On the other hand, they can also make agencies too cautious or force them to operate under compromise-crafted laws that undermine their effectiveness. Most of the time, agencies respond to politics by muddling through, for which they deserve more credit than they usually get.

---

mypoliscilab EXERCISES

Apply what you learned in this chapter on MyPoliSciLab.

Read on mypoliscilab.com

eText: Chapter 14

Study and Review on mypoliscilab.com

Pre-Test

Post-Test

Chapter Exam

Flashcards

Watch on mypoliscilab.com

Video: The CDC and the Swine Flu

Video: Internal Problems at the FDA

Explore on mypoliscilab.com

Simulation: You Are a Deputy Director of the Census Bureau

Simulation: You Are a Federal Administrator

Simulation: You Are the Head of FEMA

Simulation: You Are the President of MEDICORP

Comparative: Comparing Bureaucracies

Timeline: The Evolution of the Federal Bureaucracy

Visual Literacy: The Changing Face of the Federal Bureaucracy

---

KEY TERMS

administrative discretion, p. 397

agency, p. 396

bureaucracy, p. 396

civil service, p. 404

Congressional Budget Office (CBO), p. 411

department, p. 396

earmark, p. 415

end run, p. 411

government corporation, p. 397

Hatch Act, p. 404

in-and-outers, p. 405

independent regulatory agencies, p. 409

inner cabinet, p. 407

iron triangle, p. 416

mugwumps, p. 404

Office of Management and Budget (OMB), p. 411

outer cabinet, p. 407

patronage, p. 401

Pendleton Act, p. 404

recess appointment, p. 413

senatorial courtesy, p. 412

spoils system, p. 402

sunshine law, p. 418

SUGGESTED READINGS

Of General Interest

Aberbach, Joel D., and Bert A. Rockman. *In the Web of Politics: Three Decades of the U.S. Federal Executive.* Washington, DC: The Brookings Institution, 2000. Traces controversies over the federal bureaucracy since the 1970s, including recent attempts to "reinvent" government.

Light, Paul. *A Government Ill-Executed: The Decline of the Federal Service and How to Reverse It.* Cambridge, MA: Harvard University Press, 2009. Criticizes bureaucratic problems and proposes some solutions.

Meier, Kenneth J., and Laurence J. O'Toole, Jr. *Bureaucracy in a Democratic State: A Governance Perspective.* Baltimore, MD: The Johns Hopkins University Press, 2006. Argues that bureaucracies help governments respond to the wishes of voters.

Niskanan, William A. *Bureaucracy and Representative Government.* Chicago: Aldine-Atherton, 1971. Develops the argument that government bureaucracies seek to maximize their budgets.

Wilson, James Q. *Bureaucracy: What Government Agencies Do and Why They Do It.* New York: Basic Books, 1989. Comprehensive treatment of public bureaucracies.

Focused Studies

Chubb, John, and Terry Moe. *Politics, Markets and America's Schools.* Washington, DC: The Brookings Institution, 1990. Brilliant, controversial account of the way in which politics interferes with effective management of public schools.

Kettl, Donald F. *System Under Stress: Homeland Security and American Politics,* 2nd ed. Washington, DC: CQ Press, 2007. Chronicles how government agencies have reacted to terrorist threats since 2001.

Stanton, Thomas H., and Benjamin Ginsberg. *Making Government Manageable: Executive Organization and Management in the Twenty-First Century.* Baltimore, MD: Johns Hopkins University Press, 2004. A series of scholarly essays on various aspects of executive branch organization.

ON THE WEB

www.usa.gov

Most U.S. government agencies and departments have informative websites that can be reached through the federal government's central site, USA.gov.

www.whitehouse.gov/omb

The Office of Management and Budget, the president's main resource in controlling and organizing the federal bureaucracy, offers Web-accessible copies of budget documentation, testimony before Congress, and regulatory information.

www.opm.gov

The Office of Personnel Management calls itself "the federal government's human resources agency." It organizes the federal civil service system, and its website provides information on federal pay scales, worker performance, and job opportunities.

www.gsa.gov

The General Services Administration sets acquisitions and management policies for much of the federal bureaucracy.

www.cbo.gov

The Congressional Budget Office, created in 1974 as Congress's counterpart to the Office of Management and Budget, produces reports on the economy, the budget, and the impact of current proposed legislation.

www.gao.gov

The General Accounting Office is the investigative arm of Congress and assists Congress in its oversight of the executive branch. It produces reports that evaluate the effectiveness of various federal agencies.

www.gpo.gov

The Government Printing Office provides the text of the Federal Register, where all new and proposed regulations are published.

15 The Courts

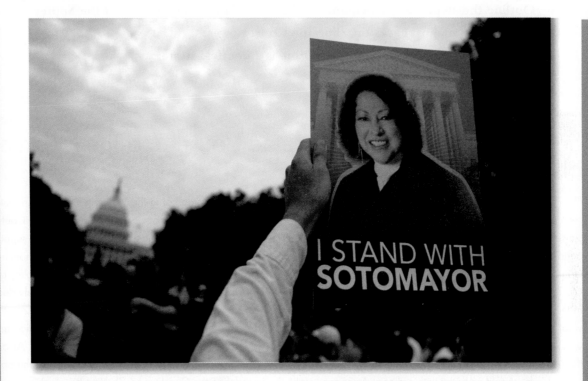

I STAND WITH SOTOMAYOR

CHAPTER OUTLINE

15.1   Describe the state court system and its politics.

15.2   Analyze sources and consequences of the power of the federal judiciary and compare and contrast approaches to constitutional interpretation.

15.3   Describe the federal court system and the relationship between state and federal courts.

15.4   Outline the steps and participants in the decision-making process of the Supreme Court.

15.5   Identify the major checks on Supreme Court power.

15.6   Explain interest groups' use of litigation as a political strategy.

Sonia Sotomayor, the Supreme Court, and the Meaning of Experience

"I will look for judges who have an outstanding judicial record, who have the intellect, and who hopefully have a sense of what real world folks are going through."[1] Thus Senator Barack Obama outlined his criteria for Supreme Court appointments in a debate with Republican John McCain in 2008. This statement might seem uncontroversial in the context of a modern presidential campaign, but it would have been surprising to Chief Justice John Marshall, who argued in 1803 that judges should do nothing more than say "what the law is."[2] If a judge is simply a legal analyst, why should empathy with ordinary Americans make a difference? In the New American Democracy, the courts have increasingly become another venue for representation of conservative or liberal views.

Not long after his inauguration, President Obama got a chance to put his philosophy of judicial nominations into practice upon the retirement of Justice David Souter, a quiet and unassuming New Hampshire judge who had turned out to be much more liberal on the Supreme Court than his Republican supporters had anticipated back in 1990. Souter's nomination had become a cautionary example for conservative activists, who now insisted that any nominee by a Republican president must have unassailable conservative credentials in order to win their support. Two of George W. Bush's nominees—John Roberts and Samuel Alito—had passed the test; nominee Harriet Miers did not have a clear paper trail and had to withdraw.

With a Democrat in the White House, conservative activists stood ready to oppose any new Supreme Court nominee, while liberal groups began to mobilize in support of Obama's choice for the Court even before the nomination had been announced. Each side saw crucial policy questions in the balance. The Supreme Court routinely decides cases involving the size and scope of government—to say nothing of the major social issues such as abortion and gay rights that so often polarize activist groups. As one Senator put it, "We're choosing someone with the power to redefine the Constitution. That's a big deal."[3]

On May 26, 2009, Barack Obama introduced his choice, Sonia Sotomayor, in a triumphant ceremony in the East Room of the White House. As a judge on a federal appeals court in New York, Sotomayor's rulings had been meticulous and workmanlike. But it was her background, her character, and her identification with "real-world folks" that made her popular among liberals and unpopular with many conservatives. Raised in New York after her parents moved to the Bronx from Puerto Rico during World War II, Sotomayor had studied hard, worked incessantly, and excelled at Princeton, at Yale Law School, and as an assistant district attorney in Manhattan. Her background, as President Obama put it, gave her "a common touch and a sense of compassion, an understanding of how the world works and how ordinary people live."[4] As the first Latina justice on the U.S. Supreme Court, she also had the potential to bring Hispanic voters—one of the fastest growing voting blocks in the country—to the Democratic Party.

Sotomayor's nomination was not without controversy, however. In 2002 she expressed the view that a "wise Latina woman with the richness of her experiences would more often than not reach a better conclusion than a white male who hasn't lived that life."[5] Conservatives saw the speech as an admission of bias—former Republican House Speaker Newt Gingrich even called her a "racist."[6]

Sotomayor replied that a "wealth of experiences, personal and professional . . . have helped me appreciate the variety of perspectives that present themselves in every case that I hear."[7] After a spirited debate, the Senate confirmed Sotomayor by a vote of 68 to 31. Although the vote passed by a wide margin, the battle showed once again that in the American democracy of the twenty-first century, each Supreme Court vacancy presents an occasion for political wrangling.

Making the Connection

In recent years, the courts have been increasingly influenced by electoral politics, even though the founders meant the courts to be more isolated from public pressures than other institutions of government. This chapter describes the U.S. judicial system, which is headed by the Supreme Court and includes other federal and state courts. Later in this chapter, we look in detail at the way in which the justices of the Supreme Court are selected and how, once appointed and confirmed, they make their decisions. But first we place the Supreme Court in a larger context that discusses the role the courts play in affecting public policy.

State Courts

The first American courts were state courts. Under the Articles of Confederation, there was no national judiciary, and virtually all disputes were handled by the various state legal systems. The Constitution created a national judicial branch, but most legal cases continued to be handled in the states, a practice that remains true today. The vast majority of judicial activity takes place within state trial courts under the control of state and local governments. In fact, 99 percent of all legal cases in the United States originate in these courts.[8]

Every state has its own way of organizing its court system, but in most states the basic structure has three tiers: trial courts, courts of appeals, and a court of last resort, usually called the state supreme court. Parties to a case may appeal from a trial court to a higher court if they believe the trial court has made an error in judgment. Decisions of state supreme courts may be appealed to the federal Supreme Court if the case involves a federal statute or an interpretation of the federal Constitution. For example, the famous *Bush v. Gore* case that grew out of the 2000 presidential election was first decided in favor of Bush in a state trial court, then decided in favor of Gore by the state supreme court (after bypassing the state court of appeals), and finally decided in favor of Bush by the U.S. Supreme Court. But in very few instances does a case travel all this distance through the legal system.

State Trial Courts: The Judicial Workhorses

Most cases are decided at the very first tier, the trial court, where, as the name suggests, all trials in the state courts are held. In trials, there are two sides: the **plaintiff,** the party

15.1

Describe the state court system and its politics.

plaintiff
One who brings a complaint or suit against another.

TABLE 15.1

DIFFERENCES BETWEEN CIVIL AND CRIMINAL TRIALS

Different jurisdictions may have slightly different rules, but these are the major differences between civil and criminal cases.

- *Why can a defendant be forced to testify in a civil case, but not in a criminal case?*

	Criminal Trial	Civil Trial
Plaintiff	The federal or state government	Private person or group
At issue	Duty of citizens to obey the law	Legal rights and obligations of citizens to one another
Type of wrongdoing	Transgression against society	Harm to private person or group
Remedy	Punishment (fine, imprisonment, etc.)	Compensation for damages or order to cease committing an act
Standard of proof	Beyond a reasonable doubt	Preponderance of the evidence
Can defendant be forced to testify?	No	Yes

defendant

One accused of violating the civil or criminal code.

civil code

Laws that regulate the legal rights and obligations of citizens with regard to one another. Alleged violators are sued by presumed victims, who ask courts to award damages and otherwise offer relief for injuries they claim to have suffered.

criminal code

Laws regulating relations between individuals and society. Alleged violators are prosecuted by the government.

bringing the complaint, or suit, and the **defendant,** the party accused of violating the civil or criminal code, against whom the complaint is made.

Trials settle alleged violations of the civil and criminal codes. The **civil code** regulates the legal rights and obligations of citizens with regard to one another. Alleged violations of the civil code are stated by individuals, who ask the court to award damages and otherwise offer relief for injuries they claim to have suffered. For example, if your landlord violates your lease by failing to heat your apartment, you can act as plaintiff and sue, asking for monetary damages and a guarantee that this will not happen in the future. People cannot be imprisoned for violating the civil code (although they can be jailed if they ignore a court order issued in conjunction with a civil suit).

Violations of the **criminal code,** the laws regulating relations between individuals and society, are offenses against society as a whole and are enforced by the government itself, which acts as plaintiff and initiates charges against those suspected of a crime. If convicted, the criminal owes a debt to society, not just to the injured party. The debt may be paid by fine, imprisonment, or (in the case of capital crimes) execution. Table 15.1 summarizes the differences between civil and criminal cases.

The same action can simultaneously be a violation of both the criminal and the civil code. After a jury found former football star O. J. Simpson not guilty of criminal charges in conjunction with the murders of his ex-wife, Nicole Brown Simpson, and her friend Ron Goldman, their relatives filed civil charges, alleging that the families should be compensated for pain and suffering caused by their wrongful deaths. The plaintiffs were able to secure a guilty verdict in the civil suit and a monetary award, despite the finding of not guilty in the criminal prosecution, because in civil suits the accused can be forced to testify and the standards of proof are less stringent.

The Politics of Selecting State Judges

State courts are in a position to be significantly influenced by politics because of the way judges are selected. In 39 of the 50 states, at least some judges are elected (see the

Election Voices! feature on page 456). Exactly which judges are elected varies from state to state. In New York, trial court judges are elected but appellate judges are appointed.[9] In Georgia the process is reversed.[10] In Texas, municipal judges are appointed by city governments, but all other judges are elected in partisan races.[11] Studies show that, at least on a few key issues, elected state judges are more likely to follow closely the opinions of their constituents.[12]

Because the public knows very little about most judges, most judicial campaigns "are sedate and cordial," and voter turnout is low.[13] Still, interest groups have had a growing influence on judicial elections, especially as the cost of running campaigns for judgeships has increased. In the 2007–2008 cycle, candidates for state supreme court seats raised and spent nearly $45 million nationwide. In Pennsylvania alone, candidates spent over $9 million.[14] Much of the money to fund judicial races is donated by single-issue groups—pro- or anti-abortion groups, for example—that may be especially concerned about the way certain cases are decided. According to one observer, "The involvement of such groups has . . . intensified the battles . . . and the viciousness of judicial campaigns has clearly increased."[15]

Prosecuting State Cases

After they receive information from the police about criminal wrongdoing, prosecutors in the office of the local **district attorney** determine whether the evidence is strong enough to justify asking a grand jury (usually consisting of about two dozen citizens) to indict, or bring charges against, the suspect. Because accused people cannot defend themselves before a grand jury, the prosecutor's advice usually determines the outcome. As one skeptic observed, "Under the right prosecutor, a grand jury would indict a ham sandwich."[16] However, after the indictment, government prosecutors may find it more difficult to convince the trial jury to convict the defendant.

district attorney
Person responsible for prosecuting criminal cases.

In large cities the district attorney has enormous responsibilities. In Los Angeles, for example, the district attorney's office prosecutes over 300,000 cases a year.[17] Because they are responsible for the prosecution of all criminal cases, some of which have high visibility in local news media, many prosecutors earn recognition that wins them election or appointment to the judiciary. About one-third of state supreme court judges were once prosecutors.[18]

At times prosecutors, similar to other public figures, can allow their ambitions to get the better of their judgment. In 2006, the district attorney in Durham, North Carolina, Mike Nifong (who was engaged in a tough reelection race) began a rape investigation against three Duke University lacrosse players that continued for over a year, even after evidence emerged that appeared to demonstrate the players' innocence. In the end, the players were exonerated, Nifong was stripped of his law license, and the city of Durham had to defend itself against three civil lawsuits.[19]

An Independent and Powerful Federal Judiciary

As the case of the Sonia Sotomayor nomination to the Supreme Court shows, interest groups and politicians place great weight on each new appointee to the nation's highest court. They do this because of two fundamental characteristics of the federal judiciary: its independence from other political institutions and its singular and long-established

15.2

Analyze sources and consequences of the power of the federal judiciary and compare and contrast approaches to constitutional interpretation.

power to say what the Constitution means. The federal courts are independent from Congress and the presidency because of constitutional guarantees of life tenure and stable salaries. This independence does not set the courts apart from politics, however. On the contrary, the power to interpret the Constitution and laws passed by Congress has placed the judicial branch at the center of key political controversies throughout the country's history.

Tenure and Salary

> CONSTITUTION, ARTICLE III: *"The Judges . . . shall hold their Offices during good behaviour and shall . . . receive for their Services a Compensation, which shall not be diminished during their Continuance in Office."*

The framers of the Constitution believed the appointment of federal judges for life tenure (or "good behaviour") was essential to the system of separation of powers. As Alexander Hamilton expressed it, life tenure was an "excellent barrier to the encroachments and oppressions of the representative body."[20] The only way Congress may remove federal judges is through the impeachment process (a process that is analogous to the presidential impeachment process described in Chapter 13). Standards for impeachment are so high, however, that only 14 federal judges have been impeached in U.S. history, and of these only seven were removed from office.[21] The offenses in which these seven judges were found to have engaged included accepting bribes, committing perjury, and, in one case, applying for a job as a Confederate judge during the Civil War. In 2009, Judge Samuel Kent of the Southern District of Texas was impeached for sexual assault, making false statements, and related offenses.[22] If judges avoid such extreme transgressions, they are virtually assured of holding their positions for as long as they want them.

The Constitution further protects judicial independence by fixing judicial salaries. Although Congress may increase the salaries of judges, it may not lower them for any judge, once that judge has taken office. Some legal scholars have argued that Congress has been less than diligent in raising judges' salaries to keep pace with inflation as well as with private sector salaries, and that the quality of the judiciary has suffered as a result. Chief Justice John Roberts argues that this salary gap "has now reached the level of a constitutional crisis that threatens to undermine the strength and independence of the federal judiciary."[23] Others point out, however, that, although pay is lower for judges than for many lawyers, the shorter work hours and job security are adequate incentives to lure well-qualified people to the bench.[24]

Judicial Review

> CONSTITUTION, ARTICLE VI: *"This Constitution, and the Laws of the United States which shall be made in Pursuance thereof . . . shall be the supreme Law of the Land."*

judicial review
Power of the courts to declare null and void laws of Congress and of state legislatures that they find unconstitutional.

The federal courts often find themselves at the center of major political controversies because their great political authority includes the power of **judicial review**—the power of the courts to declare null and void laws of Congress and state legislatures that they find unconstitutional. This power can be exercised by any court, federal or state, but all lower-court decisions are subject to review by the Supreme Court, if it chooses to do so. The significance of the courts' power of judicial review can hardly be overestimated.

Judicial review gives judges who are appointed for life the power to negate laws passed by the elected representatives of the people. As Senator George W. Norris (R-NE) complained decades ago, "The people can change Congress but only God can change the Supreme Court."[25]

Although the Constitution affirms that it is the "supreme law of the land," it says nothing explicit about judicial review. The founders provided for the Supreme Court but offered few details about its powers (see Chapter 2, page 47). As political scientist Robert McCloskey observed, "The United States began its history . . . with a Supreme Court whose birthright was most uncertain."[26]

Despite its uncertain status during the first years of the new republic, in 1803 the Supreme Court successfully asserted the power of judicial review for the first time in the most important of all its decisions, *Marbury v. Madison.* In this complex case, Supreme Court Chief Justice John Marshall used a dispute over patronage as an occasion to assert the Court's power to declare the acts of Congress null and void.

In 1801, before John Adams and the Federalists relinquished control of the White House and Congress to Thomas Jefferson's Democratic-Republicans, they appointed and confirmed 42 new justices of the peace for Washington, DC. The appointments had been so hastily arranged, however, that no one in the outgoing administration had time to deliver the official commissions to the appointees. Upon their arrival, Jefferson and his secretary of state, James Madison, declined to do so, making it impossible for the appointees to take office.

According to the Judiciary Act of 1789, the jilted appointees could request a court order to force the Jeffersonians to grant the appointments. Furthermore, said the act, the Supreme Court would have original jurisdiction in such cases—that is, it would be the first and only court to which such cases would be brought. On the basis of this law, one appointee, William Marbury, filed suit with the Supreme Court, demanding that they order Madison to grant him the job.

The case offered the Court no easy solution. The justices were sure that if they issued the order, the Jefferson administration would ignore it, making the Court seem weak and ineffectual. On the other hand, if they declined to issue the order, the Court would appear to be caving in to pressure from the Jeffersonians.

Marshall solved this problem by asking an unexpected question: Was the Supreme Court the proper place to address Marbury's complaint? His stunning conclusion was that it was not—because the Constitution granted the Supreme Court original jurisdiction only in "all Cases affecting Ambassadors, other public Ministers and Consuls, and those in which a State shall be Party."[27] By giving the Court original jurisdiction in the case of the secretary of state (who did not qualify as a "public minister" in the accepted sense of the term), Section 13 of the Judiciary Act of 1789 had violated the Constitution and was therefore void.

Marshall's brilliant decision had transformed a situation that looked sure to sap the power of the federal courts into one that strengthened this power tremendously. By denying the Supreme Court's jurisdiction in the case, he invoked the power of judicial review for the first time. This authority has been acknowledged and accepted ever since.

In asserting the power of judicial review, Marshall's reasoning was simple and straightforward. Any new law overrides older laws on the same subject, except when the older law has been issued by a higher governmental entity. If a city passes a law declaring

Marbury v. Madison
Supreme Court decision (1803) in which the court first exercised the power of judicial review.

John Marshall
Appointed by John Adams to serve as chief justice (1801–1835), John Marshall was also a Revolutionary War soldier, a supporter of the Constitution at the Virginia ratifying convention, a Federalist member of Congress, and secretary of state.

• *Aside from* Marbury v. Madison, *can you name another key court decision that Marshall wrote?*

its speed limit to be 30 miles an hour, an older law that sets a speed limit of 40 miles an hour is automatically void, unless the old law was passed by a higher level of government, such as the state. In that case the state law, even if it is from an earlier date, takes precedence. The highest law of the land, according to Marshall, is the Constitution. It was established by the people, and no entity subject to the Constitution—not even Congress itself—can enact legislation that contravenes the will of the people, as expressed in the Constitution.

Approaches to Constitutional Interpretation

The reasoning behind judicial review is impeccable as long as one assumes that judges only examine a law of Congress, compare it to the Constitution, and determine whether the law runs counter to clear constitutional language. The simplest case might be a law that changed the president's term in office to six years. Since the Constitution sets the president's term at four years, such a law would be invalid. But very few issues of constitutionality are that simple. The Constitution bans laws "abridging the freedom of speech," but does that mean that people cannot be punished for inciting others to violence? It bans "cruel and unusual punishments," but does the death penalty count as "cruel and unusual"? And what weapons must Americans be allowed to possess if there are to be no laws abridging the right "to keep and bear arms"? It is these kinds of cases—in which the Constitution is vague—that have prompted judges and legal scholars to develop alternative theories that guide their interpretations as to whether or not laws are constitutional.

original-intent theory
A theory of constitutional interpretation that determines the constitutionality of a law by ascertaining the intentions of those who wrote and ratified the Constitution.

Original-intent theory determines whether a law is constitutional by ascertaining the intentions of those who wrote and ratified the Constitution. To establish the intentions of the founders, judges examine such documents as James Madison's notes from the Constitutional Convention, the *Federalist Papers,* and the speeches made during the ratifying campaign in 1787 and 1788. Among today's sitting Supreme Court justices, Clarence Thomas relies most frequently on the theory of original intent. For example, he favors overturning the 1973 *Roe v. Wade* decision legalizing abortion because he finds nothing in the Constitution that gives women the right to choose an abortion. On the contrary, he points out that at the time the Constitution was ratified, many states outlawed abortion, a suggestion that the framers had no intention of denying the states this authority.

plain-meaning-of-the-text theory
A theory of constitutional interpretation that determines the constitutionality of a law in light of what the words of the Constitution obviously seem to say.

If the founders' intentions are unclear, or if there are competing interpretations of the founders' intent, some jurists argue that the courts should rely on the **plain-meaning-of-the-text theory.** According to this theory, the constitutionality of a law ought to be determined by what the words of the Constitution obviously seem to say. Justice William O. Douglas pointed out that the First Amendment requires that, "Congress shall make no law . . . abridging freedom of speech," adding, "The First Amendment is couched in absolute terms—freedom of speech shall not be abridged. . . . No leeway is granted."[28]

Plain meaning has several clear advantages. Similar to original-intent theory, it suggests that the courts should be cautious in the scope of their decisions and should not go beyond the printed word of the Constitution. But, unlike original-intent theory, it does not require extensive inquiry into debates undertaken in the distant past. The constitutional text itself is taken as a guide to action.

But plain-meaning theory has its own limitations. The Constitution is a short document that left many issues undecided and contains ambiguous language that its drafters added in order to win ratification. Words that appear plain do not always have a clear meaning, and they may have been the result of compromises between those who held contradictory beliefs. Even if the founders were united in their opinions, should the perspectives of 55 men gathered together in Philadelphia in the summer of 1787 constrain the actions of the U.S. government more than 200 years later?

Critics of the original intent and plain-meaning-of-the-text theories offer instead a **living-constitution theory** of constitutional interpretation, which says that a law's constitutionality ought to be judged in the context of the entire history of the United States as a nation. The determining factors should include not only the opinions expressed at the time the Constitution was written but also ideas and judgments shaped by American experience since then.

living-constitution theory
A theory of constitutional interpretation that places the meaning of the Constitution in the context of the total history of the United States.

Those who support living-constitution theory see a broader role for the courts to play in contemporary political controversies, especially when fundamental principles are at stake. "Our constitution," argued Justice William Brennan, "was not intended to preserve a preexisting society, but to make a new one, to put in place principles that the prior community had not sufficiently recognized."[29] Consequently, there may be public policy issues on which the other branches of government and the public feel one way, but on which justices are "bound, by a larger constitutional duty to the community . . . to point toward a different path."[30] For example, Brennan believed that the death penalty violates the Eighth Amendment's prohibition of "cruel and unusual punishment," despite evidence that the founders did not oppose capital punishment.

Justice Stephen Breyer advocates a version of this theory, arguing that the Constitution ought to be interpreted in light of a principle he calls "active liberty." According to this view, judges should interpret the Constitution in such a way as to promote "the people's constitutional right to an active and constant participation in collective power."[31] Breyer believes, for example, that certain campaign finance regulations ought to be allowed because they promote equal participation in campaigns by all voters, even though some critics argue that they infringe on the First Amendment's free speech guarantees.

Opponents charge that the living constitution theory reduces constitutional interpretation to the judge's personal understanding of the meaning of American history. And, because no two judges' interpretations of the country's history are likely to be the same, constitutional interpretation may become highly subjective. Justice Antonin Scalia (who advocates the original-intent and plain-meaning approaches) argues, "The Constitution does not change. It means today what it meant when it first was written. . . . It does not morph." Accordingly, he says, "My constitution is not living, it is dead."[32]

Judicial Review in Practice

The manner in which the courts interpret the Constitution can have serious consequences for the nation. In three celebrated instances, the Supreme Court created constitutional crises by declaring laws unconstitutional, thereby defying the declared will of Congress and the president. Because of its experience in cases such as these, the Supreme Court tends to be very cautious in exercising judicial review, using this power only when it feels that it is absolutely necessary.

FIGURE 15.1

THE MISSOURI COMPROMISE

The Dred Scott decision invalidated the Missouri Compromise, an 1820 agreement that averted a sectional crisis by fixing a line (pictured) south of which slavery would be permitted. Areas north of the line would be free.

• *Why was the Supreme Court's invalidation of the Compromise so destructive?*

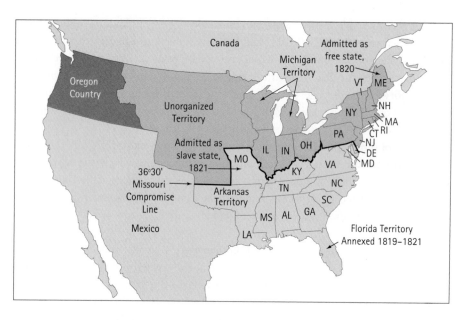

Dred Scott

This painting depicts Dred Scott, a slave whose master had brought him outside slave-owning states. Scott sued for his freedom, arguing that when he set foot in a free state, he became free. In an infamous decision, the Supreme Court ruled that Scott had no right to sue and that Congress had no right to prohibit slavery in the territories.

• *How has the Dred Scott decision contributed to contemporary arguments against judicial review?*

The first case, *Dred Scott v. Sandford* (1857), declared unconstitutional the Missouri Compromise law passed in 1820.[33] The law drew a line coinciding with the Arkansas–Missouri border, north of which there could never be slavery (see Figure 15.1). Missouri, the exception, was allowed to legalize slavery. The Missouri Compromise had been so successful at preventing a breakup of the Union that few politicians of the day even considered the possibility that the Supreme Court would dare to call it unconstitutional. But, instead of respecting Congress's capacity to find satisfactory compromises, the Supreme Court denied the power of Congress to prohibit slavery in the territories, claiming it was an unconstitutional restriction on property rights. Few, if any, court decisions have been more disastrous. The Dred Scott decision alarmed many northerners, who feared that slavery would, in practice, be extended throughout the Union.[34] And, for southerners, the Court's arguments helped justify armed resistance.

In the early twentieth century, the Supreme Court once again unwisely used its power of judicial review to declare a law unconstitutional, this time to block legislation designed to curb the abuses of industrial capitalism. In *Lochner v. New York* (1905), the Court said the state of New York could not regulate the number of hours that bakers worked, because to do so deprived them of the "right" to work as long and as hard as they pleased. The New York legislature had passed the law at issue, limiting the work week to 60 hours, to protect workers from unscrupulous employers. In his dissent from the Court's decision, Justice Oliver Wendell Holmes insisted that the Constitution be interpreted as a living document:

> This case is decided upon an economic theory which a large part of the country does not entertain. A Constitution is not intended to embody a particular economic theory. It is made for people of fundamentally differing views.[35]

Holmes's dissent in *Lochner* eventually became the view of the Supreme Court. Today, it is accepted that government can regulate working conditions.

A third unfortunate use of the power of judicial review occurred after Franklin Delano Roosevelt became president in 1933. Coming to power in the midst of a depression, Roosevelt and his Democratic Party allies in Congress passed a host of new legislation, known as the New Deal, designed to stimulate economic recovery. The Supreme Court, which included a majority of justices appointed by Republican presidents, declared many of the New Deal laws unconstitutional (see Chapter 3, page 72). These decisions placed the Supreme Court at odds with the president and Congress, creating a constitutional crisis that was not resolved until several justices switched their votes on such cases in the wake of Roosevelt's overwhelming reelection.

Cases such as these have led some legal theorists to argue that judicial review should be abandoned because it is anti-democratic. "If judicial review is a means to check encroachments," asks political scientist John Agresto, "what means exist to check the encroachments of the judiciary[?]"[36] But others see judicial review as a valuable protection against majority infringement on minority civil rights and civil liberties. Despite the controversy, judicial review has become a well-established practice in American government. It survives in part because justices use this power sparingly, seldom defying the strongly held views of the president and Congress. On only 162 occasions, between 1803 and 2008, did the Supreme Court decide that a federal law was unconstitutional.[37] Most of these decisions affected old laws no longer supported either by a majority of Congress or by the president.

Political scientist Robert Dahl has gone so far as to claim that, because elected officials nominate and approve its members, "the Supreme Court is inevitably a part of the dominant political leadership."[38] Although some scholars think the Court is less sensitive to political pressure than Dahl claims, a recent study has identified changes in Supreme Court policy that parallel swings in public opinion. These policy shifts are not as pronounced as those in Congress, the study finds, but justices still seem to pay "attention to what the public wants."[39] Indeed, some have argued that political leaders might prefer an active Supreme Court because court decisions tend to add force to the majority's policy priorities.[40] The *Dred Scott* and *Schechter Poultry* cases are the exception, not the rule. Irish bartender Mr. Dooley, the creation of columnist Finley Peter Dunne, was not wide of the mark when he observed in 1901 that "th' supreme court follows th' illiction returns."[41]

Statutory Interpretation

Judicial review is only the most sweeping and controversial of judicial powers. The courts also engage in **statutory interpretation,** the application of the laws of Congress and of the states to particular cases. American courts have great discretion in exercising this power, much more than their counterparts in Great Britain (see the accompanying *International Comparison*). For example, in 1970 Congress passed the Clean Air Act, which gave the Environmental Protection Agency the power to regulate automobile emissions that "may reasonably be anticipated to endanger public health or welfare."[42] In 2007 the Supreme Court interpreted that law as granting the agency the authority to regulate carbon dioxide emissions because of their harmful effect on the global climate, even though the immediate aim of the law had been to restrict more localized air pollution.

statutory interpretation
The judicial act of interpreting and applying the laws of Congress and the states, rather than the Constitution, to particular cases.

INTERNATIONAL COMPARISON

Statutory Interpretation in the United States and Britain

When interpreting statutes, British judges have less leeway than American judges because they operate within a less fragmented governmental system. In Britain, the party of the prime minister exerts effective control over Parliament. Every piece of legislation passed by the party in power is carefully examined by specialists, who ensure that new legislation is internally coherent and consistent with existing laws. If a judge says government administrators have misinterpreted the law, the party in power can also, if it chooses, quickly pass new legislation. Political scientist Shep Melnick points out that as a result, "it is not surprising that British judges seldom question the interpretive authority of administrators."[1]

American judges work within a more decentralized governmental context. To obtain a majority of votes when writing legislation, members of Congress are tempted to use ambiguous language that may include phrases that come close to contradicting one another. In Melnick's words, "The openness and messiness of the legislative process in the United States ensures that when judges scrutinize a statute and its history, they will seldom discover a single, coherent purpose or intent."[2] In the voting-rights legislation of 1982, for example, Congress forbade electoral arrangements that gave minorities "less opportunity than other members of the electorate to elect representatives of their choice" but, a few sentences later, said that nothing in the legislation required minorities to be elected "in numbers equal to their proportion in the population." The "less opportunity" forbidden in the first phrase seemed permitted by the second phrase, which indicated that "equal numbers" need not be elected.[3]

When federal courts are asked to sort out the meaning of this kind of vague and potentially contradictory language, the office of the solicitor general may express the opinion of the presidential administration. But, if the courts ignore the solicitor general, the administration must try to persuade Congress to enact a new law—a far more difficult task for

A Less Powerful Judiciary
British judges walk to Parliament to mark the beginning of the new judicial year.

• *Why do courts in the United Kingdom defer more often to administrators than do courts in the United States?*

U.S. presidents than for British prime ministers. Knowing this, U.S. courts feel free to interpret laws in any way that is not plainly contrary to the intent of Congress. As Supreme Court Justice William Brennan once said, "the Court can virtually remake congressional enactments."[4]

• *Is it better to allow the courts wide latitude for interpretation, or to restrict their authority through the use of precise legislative language? Why?*

[1] R. Shep Melnick, *Between the Lines: Interpreting Welfare Rights* (Washington, DC: The Brookings Institution, 1994), p. 13.
[2] Ibid.
[3] As quoted in Bernard Grofman, Lisa Handley, and Richard G. Niemi, *Minority Representation and the Quest for Voting Equality* (New York: Cambridge University Press, 1992), p. 39.
[4] Melnick, *Between the Lines*, p. 13.

15.3

Describe the federal court system and the relationship between state and federal courts.

The Federal Court System

CONSTITUTION, ARTICLE III, SECTION 1: *"The judicial power . . . shall be vested in one supreme Court, and in such inferior Courts as the Congress may from time to time ordain and establish."*

Although the Supreme Court provides the linchpin for the nation's system of courts, resolving difficult questions of constitutional or statutory interpretation, most of the day-to-day work of the federal judicial branch is carried out at lower tiers. These lower courts are less visible institutions, but they are no less affected by political and electoral forces. In this section we describe the federal court system.

District Courts

The Constitution established the Supreme Court, leaving it to Congress to decide what lower federal courts were needed. The first Congress enacted the Judiciary Act of 1789, which, although it has been updated in many ways, still provides the basic framework for the modern federal court system.

Most federal cases are initially filed in one of the 94 **federal district courts,** the lowest tier of the federal court system. These courts are the trial courts of the federal system, and they are similar to the trial courts that exist in each state. As a consequence, many high-profile cases pass through the federal district courts. In 2010, for example, former Illinois governor Rod Blagojevich appeared in federal district court to face charges that he had abused the powers of his office by using a vacant Senate seat as a political bargaining chip. As Figure 15.2 shows, the vast majority of federal legal proceedings begin and end in these district courts.

Appeals Courts

The federal district courts are organized into 13 circuits (including 11 numbered regional circuits, a DC circuit, and a federal circuit), each of which has a **circuit court of appeals,** the court to which all federal district court decisions may be appealed (see Figure 15.3). The name circuit, which means "a regularly traveled route around a given territory," recalls the early years of the courts, when, to hear cases, judges journeyed by stagecoach from district to district.

Nearly all appeals court cases today are heard by three of the six to 28 judges who serve on each court of appeals. The senior appeals-court judge assigns the three judges to each case. In most courts of appeals, the judges are chosen by lot. In exceptionally important cases, a session may be held in which all of the appeals judges in the circuit participate. Courts of appeals confine their review to points of law under dispute; they ordinarily take as given the facts of the case, as stated in the trial record and decided by district judges. They do not accept new evidence or hear additional witnesses. Although decisions by an appeals court may be taken up by the Supreme Court, most appeals-court decisions are final.

Specialized Courts

Two trial courts have nationwide jurisdiction over specialized issues that do not fall within the purview of the federal district courts. The Court of International Trade handles cases concerning trade and customs, and the U.S. Court of Federal Claims hears suits concerning federal contracts, money damages against the United States, and other issues that involve the federal government. Cases originating in either of these courts may be appealed to the court of appeals for the federal circuit.

A Federal District Court's Responsibility

In 2010, former Illinois governor Rod Blagojevich appeared in federal district court to respond to corruption charges.

• *How do federal district court responsibilities differ from those of a circuit court of appeals?*

federal district courts

The lowest tier of the federal court system and similar to the trial courts that exist in each state.

circuit court of appeals

Court to which decisions by federal district courts are appealed.

FIGURE 15.2

FEDERAL AND STATE COURT SYSTEMS

State and federal trial courts hear the bulk of cases; only a few make it to the U.S. Supreme Court.

• *Why does the Supreme Court handle so few cases each year?*

Sources: Federal statistics: Administrative Office of the U.S. Courts, "Judicial Business of the United States Courts: Caseload Highlights: 2008," www.uscourts.gov/judbus2008/JudicialBus2008.pdf, accessed February 22, 2010; state statistics: National Center for State Courts, "Examining the Work of State Courts: An Analysis of 2007 State Court Caseloads" (2009), www.ncsonline.org/D_Research/csp/2007B_files/EWSC-2007-v21-online.pdf, accessed February 22, 2010.

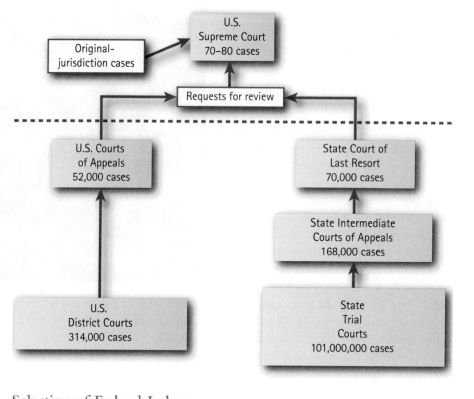

Selection of Federal Judges

All federal judges hold lifetime positions after their nomination by the president and confirmation by the Senate. Because of long-standing agreements among senators, known as *senatorial courtesy,* any presidential nominee must be acceptable to the senior senator of the court's state who is of the same political party as the president (see Chapter 14).

FIGURE 15.3

COURTS OF APPEALS CIRCUIT BOUNDARIES

• *What is the role of the federal appeals court?*

Source: Robert A. Carp and Ronald Stidham, *The Federal Courts,* 2nd ed. (Washington, DC: CQ Press, 1991), p. 18.

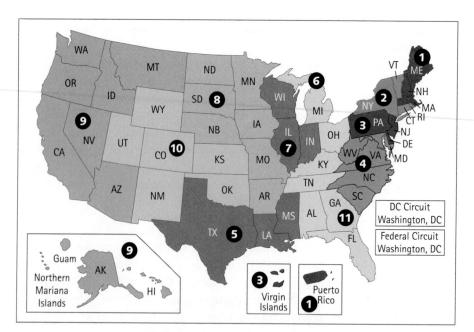

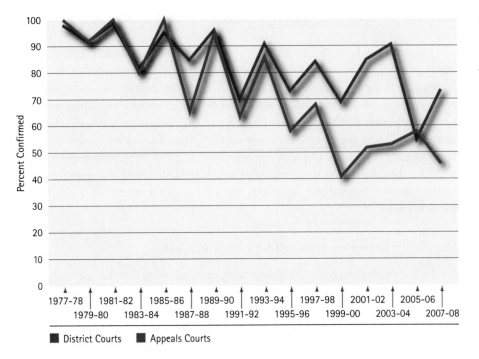

■ District Courts   ■ Appeals Courts

FIGURE 15.4

THE SENATE HAS BECOME LESS LIKELY TO CONFIRM JUDICIAL NOMINATIONS IN RECENT YEARS

In the 1970s, the Senate confirmed nearly all of the president's judicial nominees, but confirmation today is much less certain.

• *Why do you think the Senate confirms a greater percentage of district court appointees than appeals court appointees?*

Note: Nonconfirmation may be either the result of rejection or of the failure of a nomination to come to a vote.

Source: Sheldon Goldman, "Obama and the Federal Judiciary: Great Expectations but Will He Have a Dickens of a Time Living Up to Them?" *The Forum,* Vol. 7, Issue 1, Article 9 (2009).

Political influence plays a major role in the selection of federal judges. Most judges share the same partisan identification as the president who nominates them; 87 percent of Bill Clinton's nominees were Democrats, and 90 percent of George W. Bush's nominees were Republicans.[43]

Although most lower-court nominees are confirmed, rejections do occur and they have become more frequent in recent years, as Figure 15.4 shows. Rejection is at times a result of some financial or personal problem uncovered during the confirmation process, but ideological battles have also become more common. When George W. Bush was president, Democrats used the filibuster (see Chapter 12) to block floor votes on a handful of judicial nominees that they argued were "extreme conservatives."[44] After Barack Obama became president, Republicans attempted filibusters on some of his nominees, although in 2009 and 2010 they rarely had the votes to block them for long. One reason why parties are willing to do battle over nominations is that there are important ideological differences between potential judicial appointees. Overall, district judges' decisions reflect the political orientation of the president who nominated the particular judge; for example, judges appointed by Democratic presidents are more likely than those appointed by Republican presidents to hand down liberal decisions.[45]

Deciding to Prosecute

Suspected violations of the federal criminal code are usually investigated by the Federal Bureau of Investigation, although other federal agencies, such as the Secret Service and the Bureau of Alcohol, Tobacco, and Firearms, also exercise investigative powers. The evidence collected is given to prosecutors in the office of a **U.S. attorney,** who is responsible for prosecuting violations of the federal criminal code. Appointed by the president and confirmed by the Senate, the 93 U.S. attorneys act as the government's

U.S. attorney

Person responsible for prosecuting violations of the federal criminal code.

chief litigators. If persuaded that a prosecution is warranted, a U.S. attorney asks a grand jury to indict the suspect.

U.S. attorneys have a particularly high political profile. They usually share the president's party affiliation and, although they are expected to be incorruptible, they often are sensitive to the political needs of their superiors in Washington. Because routine law enforcement is left in the hands of state officials, U.S. attorneys concentrate on high-visibility, attention-grabbing federal crimes. If they are particularly successful, they may become candidates for higher office. For example, Republican New Jersey Governor Chris Christie served as a U.S. attorney from 2002 to 2008 before winning the governor's race the following year. Supreme Court Justice Samuel Alito also served as a U.S. attorney in New Jersey in the late 1980s, where he earned a reputation as a confident, if low-key, leader.[46]

Relations Between State and Federal Courts

For the first few decades under the Constitution, the relationship between state and federal legal and judicial systems remained vague. Then, in an important early decision, *Martin v. Hunter's Lessee* (1816), the Supreme Court ruled that it had the power to review and, if necessary, to overturn the decisions of state courts. In that case, a Virginia court had argued that the decisions of state courts were final and could not be appealed to the national level. The Supreme Court disagreed, saying that "the importance, and even necessity of uniformity of decisions throughout the whole United States" made the Virginia court's argument untenable.[47] Three years later, in **McCulloch v. Maryland** (1819), the Supreme Court made it clear that the power of judicial review applied to state as well as federal laws (see Chapter 3, page 69).

McCulloch v. Maryland
Decision (1819) in which the Supreme Court first used judicial review to declare a state law unconstitutional.

The Supreme Court's power to review state laws and the decisions of state courts is essential for maintaining basic uniformity in the laws of the United States. Over the decades, the Supreme Court has found over 1,100 state and local statutes and constitutional provisions contrary to the federal Constitution.[48] The judicial power to declare state laws unconstitutional is much less controversial than the power to declare laws of Congress unconstitutional. As Justice Holmes once said,

> I do not think the United States would come to an end if we lost our power to declare an act of Congress void. I do think the Union would be imperilled if we could not make that declaration as to the laws of the several states. For one in my place sees how often a local policy prevails with those who are not trained to national views.[49]

Most cases are heard in state courts, but a case can be shifted to a federal court if a federal law or constitutional principle is involved. The federal courts have higher prestige than state courts; to become a federal judge is to hold a position of great honor. But as Justice Sandra Day O'Connor, a former state judge, acutely observed, "When the state court judge puts on his or her federal court robe, he or she does not become immediately better equipped intellectually to do the job."[50]

double jeopardy
Placing someone on trial for the same crime twice.

The same act can simultaneously be a violation of both state and federal laws. Although the Fifth Amendment to the Constitution forbids **double jeopardy**—placing someone on trial twice for the same crime—something very close to double jeopardy can occur if a person is tried in both federal and state courts. In such cases, multiple trials are allowed if the same actions gave rise to distinct crimes. In 1897, the

Supreme Court permitted dual prosecutions, saying that "an act denounced as a crime by both national and state sovereignties is an offense against the peace and dignity of both."[51]

Dual state and federal prosecutions remain unusual, however. Usually, federal and state officials reach an agreement that allows one or the other to take responsibility for a case. Generally speaking, the federal government takes over the prosecution only when the case has national implications. For example, the 1995 bombing of a federal building in Oklahoma, in which 168 people lost their lives, constituted a violation of both state laws against murder and federal laws against conspiracy and manslaughter. Although state officials began the investigation, federal investigators quickly took charge and the accused, Timothy McVeigh and Terry Nichols, were convicted in a federal courtroom. Later, when Nichols failed to receive the federal death penalty for his role in the crime, state prosecutors brought state murder charges against him. (The jury in the state case also declined to give him the death penalty, however.)

A State Supreme Court
The Supreme Court of California caused controversy in early 2008 when it ruled that the California constitution protected the right of gays and lesbians to marry. That fall, the state's voters passed an initiative that reversed the court's decision.

• *California high court justices are appointed by the governor and reappointed by voters in judicial retention elections. Do you think the ruling would have been different in this case if the justices had been appointed by some other method?*

The Supreme Court

The Supreme Court sits atop a massive pyramid of judicial activity. Each year prosecutors and private citizens bring more than 27 million criminal trials and civil suits before the state and federal courts.[52] Yet, in the 2009–2010 term, the nation's high court decided only 77 cases.[53] In this section, we explain how the Court exerts its substantial influence through such a small number of cases and we describe the practical process of how justices make decisions and write each opinion. First, we discuss Supreme Court appointments. Next, we consider two important rules of court procedure as well as the important players involved in the Court's activity. Finally, we consider the process of Supreme Court decision making itself.

15.4

Outline the steps and participants in the decision-making process of the Supreme Court.

The Politics of Supreme Court Appointments

CONSTITUTION, ARTICLE II: *"The President shall nominate . . . and by and with the Advice and Consent of the Senate, shall appoint . . . Judges of the Supreme Court."*

The judicial system is supposed to be politically blind. Justice is expected to fall equally, like the rain, on rich and poor, male and female, Democrat and Republican, black, white, Latino, Asian, and Native American. Judges are appointed for life because they are expected to decide each case without any concern for its political consequences. Chief Justice Warren E. Burger went so far as to claim that "Judges . . . rule on the basis of law, not public opinion, and they should be totally indifferent to pressures of the times."[54]

Despite this ideal, however, the process by which justices are selected is a political one, and it has become more so in recent decades. Justices are nominated by the president, evaluated by the Senate Judiciary Committee, and confirmed by a vote of the full Senate. The Court's chief justice must also be nominated and confirmed in this

The Supreme Court

Originally conceived by President and Chief Justice William Howard Taft to instill public respect for the judicial branch, the Supreme Court building resembles a Greek temple built to house ancient gods.

• Do you think the Supreme Court building succeeds in elevating public respect for the Court? Why or why not?

manner, even if he or she is already a member of the Court. Because of this procedure, elected officials, as well as interest groups and the media, have a voice in choosing members of the Court. These players pay close attention to the electoral consequences of their actions, so elections inevitably affect nominations to the Court, and confirmation battles affect elections.

William Howard Taft, the only person ever to serve both as president (1909–1913) and as chief justice of the Supreme Court (1921–1930), worked hard during his tenure in each office to separate political disputes (which had roiled many nineteenth-century nominations) from Supreme Court confirmations. Because of his efforts, nominees became better qualified, confirmation procedures were simplified, and the Court's prestige was enhanced. Taft also made sure that the new Supreme Court building, completed in 1935, was designed to resemble a Greek temple, so that Americans would respect their laws with the same reverence with which the ancient Greeks venerated their gods.

Taft was so successful that in the four decades after his time on the Court, the Senate confirmed every nominee but one, most without significant dissent. But in recent years the Senate has been more willing to exert its power to review nominations. Since 1955 every Supreme Court nominee has appeared before the judiciary committee, and since 1968 the Senate's propensity to reject presidential nominees has increased, as Table 15.2 indicates. One of the most celebrated cases involved Robert Bork, a Reagan nominee rejected by the Senate in 1987. A staunch conservative, Bork had produced a long record of journal articles and speeches, which interest groups and Senate opponents used to attack him in a concerted national campaign.

borking

Politicizing the nomination process through an organized public campaign that portrays the nominee as a dangerous extremist.

Bork's rejection, in fact, gave American politics a new word, **borking,** which means politicizing the nomination process through an organized public campaign that portrays the nominee as a dangerous extremist. Both Congress and the media now subject each nomination to intense scrutiny. Borking is less likely when the president's party also controls the Senate, as in the case of George W. Bush nominee Samuel Alito, or Barack Obama nominees Sotomayor and Elena Kagan.

TABLE 15.2

PRESIDENTIAL NOMINEES TO THE SUPREME COURT NOT CONFIRMED BY THE SENATE, 1900–PRESENT

Some nominees are not confirmed due to scandals or questions about their qualifications, but others fall victim to political disputes.

• *Why have nominees faced more difficulties in the Senate in recent years?*

Nominee	Year	President	Main Reason for Rejection/Withdrawal
John Parker	1930	Hoover	Anti-labor
Abraham Fortas (sitting justice nominated to be chief justice)	1968	Johnson	Too liberal; resigned from Court in 1969 over alleged financial abuses
Homer Thornberry	1968	Johnson	No vacancy when Fortas not confirmed for chief justice
Clement Haynesworth	1970	Nixon	Alleged financial abuses
G. Harrold Carswell	1970	Nixon	Racially conservative
Robert Bork	1987	Reagan	Controversial conservative record
Douglas Ginsburg	1987	Reagan	Smoked marijuana with students
Harriet Miers	2005	Bush	Controversy over qualifications

Even if the Senate is controlled by the opposition, presidents may avoid borking by choosing a nominee whose views are unknown, a "stealth" strategy named after the bomber that cannot easily be detected by radar.[55] In 1990, President George H. W. Bush nominated stealth candidate David Souter, a New Hampshire state supreme court justice who had never written an opinion or treatise on any major constitutional question. Stealth candidates, however easy to appoint, can backfire upon taking office. Bush thought Souter would strengthen the conservative side of the Supreme Court, but the justice proved to be one of the Court's most articulate liberals.

Most Supreme Court nominees now tell senators that they feel it would be improper to comment on specific issues that might come before the Court. Legal scholars lament such conflict avoidance. As a law professor, Elena Kagan criticized Senate hearings for not being substantive enough, and urged future nominees to be more forthcoming with their views "on prior case law, on hypothetical cases, [and] on general issues like affirmative action or abortion."[56] As a Supreme Court nominee herself, however, Kagan proved to be just as reticent in discussing specifics as other prospective justices. Her earlier views, she admitted, had been "a little bit off."[57]

Although many critics think the politicization of judicial appointments destroys "the public's belief in the fairness of those on the bench and . . . undermine[s] confidence in the Court,"[58] future trends seem clear. The United States is unlikely to go back to the older way of selecting Supreme Court justices. Modern technology and the media ensure that presidents will choose justices with an eye to avoiding potential public controversies.

Stare Decisis

A small number of Supreme Court decisions can have a far-ranging impact because lower federal and state courts are expected to follow the principle of ***stare decisis.*** The phrase is Latin for "let the decision stand." This is to say that, in deciding cases,

stare decisis
In court rulings, reliance on consistency with precedents. See also "precedent."

precedent
Previous court decision or ruling applicable to a particular case.

legal distinction
The legal difference between a case at hand and previous court decisions.

appeal
The procedure whereby the losing side asks a higher court to overturn a lower-court decision.

reversal
The overturning of a lower-court decision by an appeals court or the Supreme Court.

cert
See "writ of *certiorari*."

writ of *certiorari* (cert)
A document issued by the Supreme Court indicating that the Court will review a decision made by a lower court.

judges should adhere to **precedents,** or prior decisions, as well as to the logic of their written opinions. *Stare decisis* is a powerful judicial principle that can be ignored only at risk to the stability of the legal system. Only if court decisions are consistent with one another over time can a country live under a rule of law, where citizens know what rules they are expected to obey. In the words of one judge, "We cannot meddle with a prior decision [unless it] strikes us as wrong with the force of a five-week-old unrefrigerated dead fish."[59]

When reaching a decision that seems contrary to prior decisions, courts try to find a **legal distinction** between the case at hand and the earlier court decisions, usually by emphasizing that the facts of the current case differ. The process of drawing a legal distinction can sometimes become the refined art of perceiving a distinction when others can see no difference. As an attorney once bragged, "Law school taught me one thing: how to take two situations that are exactly the same and show how they are different."[60] If the legal distinctions drawn by a lower court seem unconvincing to the losing side, it may **appeal** the decision to the next-higher court. If the higher court thinks the lower court has strayed too far from legal precedents, it may decide on a **reversal,** or overturning, of the lower court's decision.

Certs

At one time, the Supreme Court was required by law to review many appeals, but the workload became so excessive that in 1925 Congress gave the Court the power to refuse to review almost any case it did not want to consider. Today, nearly all cases argued before the Court arrive upon the Court's grant of what is known by court insiders as a **cert.** Cert is an abbreviation of the Latin term in **writ of *certiorari*,** which means "to be informed of." The granting of a cert means the Court has agreed to consider the case.[61] The Court rejects most cert petitions because it is only practical to consider a fraction of the 8,000 to 10,000 cases appealed to it each year.[62]

The number of certs granted by the Supreme Court has fallen markedly in recent decades. In the 1970s, the Supreme Court decided as many as 400 cases annually.[63] But, as we have noted, only 77 cases were decided in the 2009–2010 term. Certs are granted only for those cases that raise the most important legal or constitutional issues. In the words of one chief justice, "To remain effective the Supreme Court must continue to decide only those cases which present questions whose resolution will have immediate importance far beyond the particular facts and parties involved."[64]

To issue a cert requires the vote of four justices. The mere fact that an issue is controversial does not necessarily mean the Court will grant a cert. The justices may decide to let the issue remain in the lower courts for a few years until the matter is ripe for decision.

The case for cert is strongest if two lower courts have reached opposite conclusions on important cases in which the facts seem virtually identical. In such cases, the Supreme Court may wish to clarify the law so that its effect is uniform throughout the United States. In 1998, for example, the Wisconsin Supreme Court upheld a state law establishing a school voucher program in Milwaukee. Low-income families could receive state money and use it to attend a private school of their choice. Although many religious schools participated in the program, the Wisconsin court ruled that the law did not violate the constitutional clause prohibiting the establishment of religion (see Chapter 16). When a similar law was passed by the Ohio legislature for low-income families in Cleveland, a federal appeals court ruled that it unconstitutionally established religion. Because two lower courts had decided the same issue in contrary ways, the Supreme Court granted a cert and heard the Ohio case in early 2002. That summer, the Court finally decided the issue. In a landmark ruling, a slim majority found that vouchers did not violate the establishment clause because parents could decide whether the money went to religious institutions. Such a program of "true private choice," said Chief Justice Rehnquist, passed the constitutional test.[65]

The Role of the Chief Justice

The Supreme Court consists of eight **associate justices** and the **chief justice,** who heads the Court and is responsible for organizing its work. Although the chief justice has only one vote and many of the chief's tasks are of a ceremonial or housekeeping nature, certain responsibilities give the office added influence. For one thing, the chief justice, if voting with the majority, assigns the responsibility for writing the majority opinion. Because the content of the Court's opinion is often as important as the actual decision, this assignment power can have far-reaching consequences; some cases are "destined for the history books, whereas others are, in [former Justice Lewis] Powell's term, 'dogs.'" Powell's biographer tells us that Warren Burger, not the most popular of chief justices, was suspected by his colleagues of voting with the majority, even when privately opposed, simply in order to exercise his assignment power.[66]

> **associate justice**
> One of the eight justices of the Supreme Court who are not the chief justice.
>
> **chief justice**
> Head of the Supreme Court.

Some chief justices have used their position to facilitate compromise and achieve consensus. In the case of *Brown v. Board of Education of Topeka, Kansas* (1954), the landmark decision desegregating schools, Chief Justice Earl Warren was able to win the support of two judges who were initially inclined to dissent (see Chapter 17). To achieve the unanimity he thought crucial, Warren agreed to write a less-than-sweeping opinion. *Brown* banned segregation in schools but not in other public places, and it specified delay in the implementation of the ruling. Warren was willing to make these compromises because he thought that only a unanimous Court could order such a major social change—which at the time ran contrary to strongly held opinions of many southern whites.[67]

The Role of the Solicitor General

A powerful figure who regularly appears before the Supreme Court is the **solicitor general,** the government official responsible for presenting before the Court the position of the presidential administration. Involvement of the solicitor general is a signal that the president and the attorney general have strong views on the subject, which enhances its visibility and political significance. Because the Court pays close attention to the position of the solicitor general, the person who holds this office is sometimes referred to as "the tenth justice." About 60 percent of the solicitor general's cert petitions are accepted by the Court.[68]

> **solicitor general**
> Government official responsible for presenting before the courts the position of the presidential administration.

Solicitors general are employees of the Justice Department and as such report to the attorney general. However, they are always carefully selected by the president for their legal skills and are "in fact what the Attorney General is in name—the chief legal officer of the United States government as far as the courts are concerned."[69] The solicitor general presents the case for the government whenever it is party to a suit. In other important cases, the solicitor general may submit an *amicus curiae* brief—literally, a brief submitted by a "friend of the court." (*Amicus curiae* briefs can also be submitted by others who wish to inform the court of a legal issue presented by a particular case.) When the office of the solicitor general files an *amicus curiae* brief, it finds itself on the winning side approximately three-quarters of the time, a batting average envied by even the most successful private attorneys.[70] Several solicitors general, including William Howard Taft, Thurgood Marshall, and Elena Kagan, have gone on to become Supreme Court justices themselves.[71]

The Role of Clerks

law clerk
Young, influential aide to a Supreme Court justice.

Much of the day-to-day work within the Supreme Court building is performed by **law clerks**—young, influential aides hired by each of the justices. Recently out of law school, most will have spent a year as a clerk with a lower court before being asked to assist a Supreme Court justice. Each justice has between two and four law clerks.[72] Not only do clerks initially review certs, but they also draft many opinions. After one year of service to the Court at comparatively low salaries, Supreme Court law clerks move on to illustrious careers in the private sector, in legal academia, or perhaps on the bench. Three current justices (Roberts, Stevens, and Breyer) once served as Supreme Court clerks.

Law clerks have become so important to the Court's routine that some observers claim that a junior Supreme Court of bright but unseasoned attorneys, unconfirmed by the Senate or anybody else, is the true "Supreme Court" of today. Others reply that well-trained graduates of the country's most prestigious law schools may be better judges than aging titans who refuse to leave office well beyond the age of normal retirement. The truth probably lies between these two extremes: The brilliance of the young clerks and the political and legal experience of the justices are probably better in combination than either would be without the other.[73] As Chief Justice Rehnquist once said of the clerk system, "The Justice may retain for himself control not merely of the outcome of the case, but the explanation for the outcome, and I do not believe this practice sacrifices either."[74]

Supreme Court Decision Making

brief
Written legal arguments presented to a court by lawyers on behalf of clients.

plenary session
Activities of a court in which all judges participate; in the case of the Supreme Court, the chief justice presides.

Before reaching its decisions, the Supreme Court considers **briefs,** written legal arguments presented to a court by lawyers on behalf of clients. (Unfortunately for judges, briefs are often anything but brief.) The justices then listen to oral arguments from attorneys on both sides in a **plenary session**—one attended by all justices—the chief justice presiding. During the half-hour allotted to each side to present its case, attorneys often find themselves interrupted by searching questions from the bench. Former law professor Antonin Scalia is especially well known for his willingness to turn the plenary session into a classroom seminar. Yet it is not always clear how closely the justices attend to the responses. As Chief Justice John Marshall said many years ago, "The acme of judicial distinction means the ability to look a lawyer straight in the eye for two hours and not hear a damned word he says."[75]

After hearing oral arguments, the justices usually reach a preliminary decision during the same week in a private conference presided over by the chief justice. No outsiders, not even a secretary, are permitted to attend. The only record consists of handwritten notes taken by individual justices. From the outside, it may appear that the private conferences are opportunities for great minds to gather and discuss fundamental legal questions. But in most instances the justices have already discussed the case with their clerks and enter the conference room with their intentions fixed. The justices express their views and cast preliminary votes in order of seniority, beginning with the chief justice.[76] If the chief justice is in the minority, the writing of the opinion is assigned by the senior associate justice in the majority.[77]

The justice assigned the responsibility for preparing the Court's **opinion** circulates a draft version among the other eight. The author may then revise the opinion in light of comments and criticisms from the other justices. On rare occasions, the justice writing the opinion has "lost a court"—that is, one or more justices who voted with the majority at the first conference have changed their minds. To keep a majority, the justice writing the opinion may produce a bland opinion that gives little guidance to lower-court judges. In the 1993 sexual harassment case *Harris v. Forklift Systems*, for example, the majority hardly created any precedent at all, saying only that courts should look at the "totality of the circumstances" in order to decide whether harassment in the workplace had occurred.[78]

Justices who vote against the majority may prepare a **dissenting opinion** that explains their disagreement. **Concurring opinions** may be written by those members of the majority who agree with the basic decision but disagree with some aspect of the reasoning included in the majority opinion or who wish to elaborate by raising further considerations. Two hundred years ago, when John Marshall was chief justice, the court was nearly always unanimous, and the chief justice wrote most opinions. Today, the Court is unanimous in its judgments in only about half its cases,[79] and, quite apart from the dissenting opinions, concurring opinions are filed often enough that it is sometimes difficult to ascertain exactly what the majority has decided.

Although the proliferation of dissenting and concurring opinions has caused considerable confusion about some Supreme Court rulings, these opinions themselves often have a clearer and more convincing style than majority opinions—in part because they are signed by only one or two justices, making compromise language unnecessary. In *Harris v. Forklift Systems,* the sexual harassment case mentioned above, Justice Ginsburg, although agreeing with the decision, wrote a crisp concurring opinion that proposed a simple, straightforward standard for ascertaining whether harassment had occurred: Harassment, she wrote, exists whenever discriminatory conduct makes it more difficult for a person to perform well at a job. Convincingly written concurring and dissenting opinions such as Ginsburg's sometimes become even more influential than majority opinions.

Once the Court reaches a decision, it usually sends, or **remands,** the case to a lower court for implementation. Because the Supreme Court regards itself as responsible for establishing general principles and an overall framework, it seldom becomes involved in the detailed resolution of particular cases. This practice leaves a great deal of legal responsibility in the hands of lower courts.

Voting on the Supreme Court

It is important to remember that despite the amount of media coverage granted to cases in which the Court splits almost evenly, many cases are decided by near—if not total—unanimity. Chief Justice John Roberts lamented in an interview that during his first term on the Court "we had more unanimous opinions announced in a row than ever before in the modern era, but in the first 5-4 decision, people [in the media] are writing 'So much for unanimity.'"[80]

opinion
In legal parlance, a court's written explanation of its decision.

dissenting opinion
A written opinion presenting the reasoning of judges who vote against the majority.

concurring opinion
A written opinion prepared by judges who vote with the majority but who wish either to disagree with some aspect of the majority opinion or to elaborate on the decision.

remand
To send a case to a lower court to determine the best way of implementing the higher court's decision.

The Roberts Court

In this composite, the justices of the Supreme Court as of 2010 are pictured from left to right according to their judicial philosophies. On the left are Ruth Bader Ginsburg, Stephen Breyer, Elena Kagan, and Sonia Sotomayor. In the middle is moderate Justice Anthony Kennedy. On the right are Chief Justice John Roberts, Samuel Alito, Antonin Scalia, and Clarence Thomas.

• *When the next justice is appointed, where do you think the new justice's picture will be positioned?*

Still, justices often fall into predictable voting blocs. On some of the most controversial cases involving Constitutional interpretation, certain justices vote together fairly often. The liberal justices, consisting of the two Clinton appointees Ruth Bader Ginsburg and Stephen Breyer and Obama appointees Sonia Sotomayor and Elena Kagan, are more likely to read the Constitution broadly, in light of modern circumstances. They are more likely to favor expansive interpretations of individual rights, such as to privacy and to free expression, and are more sympathetic to the rights of criminal suspects. Finally, they are often sympathetic to government programs that are designed to ensure equality, even if some critics might see these programs as infringing on some rights and freedoms. For example, these justices tend to favor affirmative action programs (see Chapter 17), as well as campaign finance reform programs that seek to limit the impact of money on politics.

Three Republican appointees, conservative justices Clarence Thomas, Antonin Scalia, and Samuel Alito, usually take the opposite view from Sotomayor, Ginsburg, Breyer, and Kagan, narrowly interpreting the Constitution and rejecting readings of the document that rely on the modern context or on evolving moral doctrines. For example, they favor reversing *Roe v. Wade,* the decision that enunciated a (qualified) right to abortion, on the grounds that the Constitution makes no mention of abortion. They oppose programs such as affirmative action on the grounds that the Constitution forbids taking race into account in government decision making. Chief Justice John Roberts often votes with this conservative group.

Finally, Justice Anthony Kennedy occupies a moderate position on the court that often makes him the swing vote. Kennedy's position in between the liberal and conservative voting blocs has meant that he has written some of the Court's most controversial and important opinions in recent years, including the *Lawrence v. Texas* opinion striking down anti-sodomy laws (see Chapter 17) and the *Citizens United v. Federal Election Commission* decision, striking down a ban on corporate and union expenditures in political campaigns. A strong supporter of *stare decisis,* Justice Kennedy has at times been willing to uphold prior decisions even when he does not necessarily agree with them. Although he may not agree that *Roe v. Wade* was a correct decision, he has expressed a reluctance to reverse it.

In the 1970s and 1980s, conservative critics of the liberal justices' approach decried such justices as practitioners of **judicial activism**—a doctrine that says that the principle of *stare decisis* should sometimes be sacrificed in order to adapt the Constitution to changing conditions. The term found its way into campaigns, in which Republican presidential candidates vowed not to appoint such "activist judges." After presidents Ronald Reagan and George H. W. Bush appointed more conservative justices to the Court, liberals began criticizing these justices for judicial activism in the opposite direction, arguing that their rulings would roll back legal progress that had already been made. With certain kinds of activism being criticized by all sides, one law professor concluded that "in practice 'activist' turns out to be little more than a rhetorically charged shorthand for decisions the speaker disagrees with."[81]

> **judicial activism**
> Doctrine that says the principle of *stare decisis* should sometimes be sacrificed in order to adapt the Constitution to changing conditions.

Critics of judicial activism (from whatever quarter) often argue in favor of **judicial restraint,** a doctrine that says that courts should, if at all possible, rule narrowly and avoid overturning prior court decisions. Chief Justice Roberts, for one, argues that the Court should rule on "the narrowest possible grounds" to better achieve consensus and to avoid overreaching.[82] For example, in a 2008 case that challenged the constitutionality of execution by lethal injection, the Court ruled that the specific procedure at issue appeared not to violate the Constitution, but left open the possibility that evidence in later cases might show otherwise.

> **judicial restraint**
> Doctrine that says courts should, if at all possible, rule narrowly and avoid overturning a prior court decision.

Most of the time, justices vote along lines anticipated by those who nominated and confirmed them. According to one study, information about the political views of Supreme Court justices at the time they were being confirmed by the Senate allows one to predict correctly the justices' decisions in civil liberties cases more than 60 percent of the time.[83] That the future behavior of the typical justice is predictable may seem to suggest that the justices do not decide each case on its facts and merits. But this may simply reflect the fact that certain types of judges are likely to give greater weight to certain types of evidence and arguments in their decisions. Predictability allows elected officials—both presidents and senators—to influence the future direction of the Supreme Court, thereby maintaining some degree of popular control of the courts.

Not every prediction of future behavior is correct, however. The justice who most surprised those who favored his selection was Harry Blackmun, thought to be a judicial conservative when President Nixon appointed him in 1970. Yet just three years later Blackmun wrote the famous opinion in *Roe v. Wade* declaring state laws forbidding abortion unconstitutional. Blackmun himself once said, "Having been appointed by a Republican president and being accused now of being a flaming liberal on the court, the Republicans think I'm a traitor, I guess, and the Democrats don't trust me. And so I twist in the wind . . . beholden to no one, and that's just exactly where I want to be."[84]

Checks on Court Power

Although the judicial system is more independent and powerful in the United States than in many countries, the consequences of court decisions can be limited by other political actors. As political scientist Jack Peltason has put it, "Judicial decision making is

15.5

Identify the major checks on Supreme Court power.

one stage, not the only nor necessarily the final one."[85] Alexander Hamilton, writing in the *Federalist Papers,* explained why this was to be expected under the Constitution:

> The judiciary will always be the least dangerous to the political rights of the Constitution. The executive not only dispenses honors but holds the sword of the community. The legislature not only commands the purse, but prescribes the rules. The judiciary, on the contrary, has no influence over either the sword or the purse. It may truly be said to have neither force nor will, but merely judgment.[86]

Other branches of government can alter or circumscribe court decisions in three important ways: by constitutional amendment, by statutory revision, and by nonimplementation.

Constitutional Amendment

The power to amend the Constitution is the formal constitutional check on the Supreme Court's power of judicial review. But this constitutional check has been used on only a few occasions. The Eleventh Amendment overturned an early Court decision that gave citizens of one state the ability to sue another state. The Sixteenth Amendment, allowing an income tax, was prompted by a Court decision that seemed to prohibit one. Many amendments under consideration by Congress today have been generated by Court decisions, including proposed amendments to ban abortions, prohibit gay marriages, and allow greater restrictions on campaign spending. For amendments to pass, supporters must ordinarily win a two-thirds vote in Congress and the backing of three-quarters of the states. In practice, the complexities of the amendment process make it the weakest check on court power.

Statutory Revision

Congress can reverse court decisions without resorting to a constitutional amendment if the decision involves only statutory interpretation. In such cases, Congress can simply pass a clarifying law that reverses a court's interpretation of earlier legislation. In the case of *Wards Cove Packing Co. v. Atonio,* for example, the Supreme Court gave a narrow interpretation to a congressional law banning race and gender discrimination. The Court said that Congress intended that women and minorities bringing a discrimination complaint bear the burden of proof, a difficult assignment in these kinds of cases. Under pressure from women's groups and civil rights organizations, Congress responded in 1991 by passing a law that said the burden of proof had to be borne by the business, thereby reversing the Supreme Court decision.

Although passing new legislation is much easier than amending the Constitution, it may still be difficult and is ineffective if the Court decision involves constitutional interpretation.

Nonimplementation

Court decisions can also be checked simply by being ignored. When told of a Supreme Court decision he did not like, President Andrew Jackson reportedly replied, "Justice Marshall has made his decision, now let him enforce it."[87] Since Jackson's day, the prestige and authority of the Supreme Court have become deeply entrenched in American life. Outright refusal to obey a Supreme Court decision is now most unlikely. Even in the extraordinary *Bush v. Gore* controversy surrounding the 2000 election, the parties to the case readily obeyed the Court's decisions. When the Court ordered vote counters in Florida to stop counting ballots, it took less than an hour for ballot counting to come to a halt—despite the emotional intensity that had been aroused by the dispute over the recounts. By contrast, only days earlier ballot counting in one Democratic-controlled county had continued for several hours after a deadline had been imposed by Florida's Republican secretary of state, even though her authority to set deadlines was written into state law.

Still, the power of courts to implement their decisions is not unlimited. State and local governments may mount strong resistance to lower-court and even Supreme Court decisions. After the Supreme Court declared Bible reading in public schools unconstitutional, the practice in most Tennessee school districts continued unchanged. As one school board attorney explained, "My personal conviction is that the Supreme Court decisions are correct, and I so told the Board and Superintendent, but I saw no reason to create controversy. If the Board had made public a decision abolishing devotional exercises, there would have been public outcry."[88]

To ensure implementation of judicial orders, courts sometimes appoint a **receiver,** an official who has the authority to see that judicial orders are carried out. For example, in 2005 a federal district court judge in San Francisco ordered a receiver to take charge of the healthcare system in California state prisons. The judge described the conditions there as so "horrifying" and "abysmal" that they violated constitutional guarantees against cruel and unusual punishment.[89]

receiver
Court official who has the authority to see that judicial orders are carried out.

Litigation as a Political Strategy

Interest groups have increasingly used the courts to place issues on the political agenda, particularly when elected officials have not responded to group demands. This strategy was first used successfully by civil rights groups, a topic discussed in detail in Chapter 17. But the technique has since spread and become a common political phenomenon.[90] This development is fully consistent with Alexis de Tocqueville's observation more than a century and a half ago that "there is hardly a political question in the United States which does not sooner or later turn into a judicial one."[91]

Disabled Americans owe many of their current legal rights in the United States to an extraordinarily successful use of litigation as a political strategy. As late as 1970, school officials told many parents of disabled children that their sons and daughters were not qualified to attend public school. Challenging such denial of equal educational opportunity, advocacy groups won, in 1972, two federal court rulings that gave the disabled a right to an "appropriate education." Anticipating further litigation, many school officials felt that a federal law might clarify the situation. In response, Congress within two years passed a law said to be the "most significant child welfare legislation" of the decade.[92]

To advance an issue, advocacy groups often file a **class action suit** on behalf of all individuals in a particular category, regardless of whether they are actually participating in the suit. For example, in 2010 Toyota owners filed class action lawsuits against the company, claiming that the automaker was negligent in its handling of acceleration and braking problems in many of its vehicles.[93]

15.6

Explain interest groups' use of litigation as a political strategy.

class action suit
Suit brought on behalf of all individuals in a particular category, regardless of whether they are actually participating in the suit.

Continued on page 458

ELECTION VOICES!

Should Judges Be Elected?

The Issue

Would electing judges be beneficial because it would link them more closely to the electorate, or is an appointed judiciary best?

Background

Federal judges are appointed for life. Many state judges are appointed by governors and state legislatures without a ripple of public notice. But their rulings affect many of the most important and controversial issues in American politics, such as abortion, education policy, the rights of those accused of crimes, and even the conduct of antiterrorism efforts. In some states, all judges are appointed by the governor or the legislature; in others, special nonpartisan nominating commissions appoint judges on the basis of merit (see Figure 1). But, in 39 out of the 50 states, at least some judges face the voters in elections.

Most commonly, states have mixed systems for selecting judges. For example, in the state of Missouri the seven state

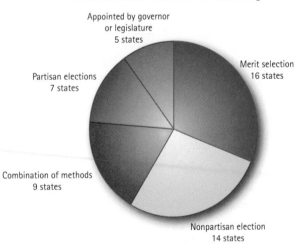

Initial Selection Methods for State Judges

- Appointed by governor or legislature — 5 states
- Merit selection — 16 states
- Partisan elections — 7 states
- Combination of methods — 9 states
- Nonpartisan election — 14 states

FIGURE 1

INITIAL SELECTION METHODS FOR STATE JUDGES

This graph depicts the method for the initial selection of state judges—that is, the method by which they are first appointed. (In some states, once a judge has been appointed, he or she must win reinstatement via a different method.)

Source: American Judicature Society, Judicial Selection in the States, "Summary of Initial Selection Methods," www.judicialselection.us/uploads/documents/Summary_Initial_Selection_1196092501390.pdf, accessed June 23, 2008.

supreme court judges and 32 appeals court judges are selected by the governor from lists of qualified candidates drawn up by nonpartisan nominating commissions. After their initial appointments, these judges must win retention elections in order to keep their jobs. This means that judges appear on a ballot without a designated party affiliation or an opponent, and if they win a majority of votes, they get to keep their seats. If not, the governor appoints a replacement based on a list from the relevant nominating commission.[1]

It would take a constitutional amendment to change the federal system of judicial selection, but a number of states have changed their systems over the years. In light of this, should voters be more involved in the selection of judges in states without judicial elections?

Opposing Viewpoints on Judicial Elections

Advocates of judicial elections say yes. They argue that elections increase the accountability of the judicial branch and make it less likely that judges will issue rulings that depart from common-sense interpretations of the law.[2] As evidence, they point to studies showing that, on at least several issues, elected state judges are more likely to mirror the opinions of their constituents.[3] Public outrage at state judicial rulings on issues such as same-sex marriage and education funding seem to support this perspective. The authors of one study that compared elected and appointed judges on key measures of effort, skill, and independence found little difference between elected and appointed judges. In fact, they conclude that "It may be that elected judges are indeed superior to appointed judges."[4]

But advocates of judicial appointment object to this analysis, arguing that most elections for judgeships fail to attract the attention of the public, and therefore cannot help the court system become more accountable. Most judicial campaigns "are sedate and cordial," and voter turnout is low.[5]

Finally, judicial elections present a special problem for candidates for the office. On the one hand, they must give the public some useful information with which to make a voting decision, but, on the other hand, it would be wrong to comment on future cases that might come before the courts. Even raising money from interest groups and private citizens risks the appearance of impropriety if these groups or citizens might one day become litigants. "It raises a lot of ethical questions

456

A Judge Reviews Her Notes

that are not there for the average person running for election," says one elected California judge.[6] In 2009, the U.S. Supreme Court ruled that a West Virginia judge was obligated to recuse himself in a case involving a businessman who had donated $3 million to his campaign.[7] Former Supreme Court Justice Sandra Day O'Connor—who founded the O'Connor Judicial Selection Initiative to oppose judicial elections—argues that such fundraising efforts "threaten the integrity of judicial selection and compromise public perception of judicial decisions."[8]

Defenders of elections respond that politics is always an issue in the selection of judges. When the president nominates a new justice to the Supreme Court, when a governor appoints a new judge to the state bench, and even when so-called "nonpartisan" commissions choose judges, political considerations are always present. At least if judges are elected, the public will have a say—not just interest groups and backroom deal makers.

What Do Americans Believe?

The federal court system is among the most respected institutions in America today, winning consistently higher approval than the president or the Congress. Pollsters seldom ask about elected judges, but when they do, the public appears ambivalent. A 2009 poll asked, "Do you think elected officials should have more control over federal judges and the decisions they make in court cases?" The results indicated that 68 percent

didn't think so.[9] On the other hand, another poll found that a plurality of 47 percent thought "more judges should be elected," while only 15 percent thought fewer should be elected.[10]

What Do You Think?

1. Should judges be appointed or elected?

2. All federal judges are appointed, but in 39 states some judges are elected. Are elections a better idea on the state level than they would be at the federal level?

3. Which types of rulings do you think would be the most affected by judicial elections, if any?

On the Web

The National Center for State Courts, an organization of state judicial officials, provides evaluations and reports on judicial selection.

www.ncsconline.org

The American Judicature Society promotes merit selection of judges.

www.ajs.org

[1]Missouri Courts website, www.courts.mo.gov/, accessed May 15, 2008.
[2]See "The Case for Partisan Judicial Elections," Federalist Society White Paper, www.fed-soc.org/Publications/White%20Papers/judicialelection .htm, accessed February 2, 2007.
[3]Melinda Gann Hall, "Justices as Representatives: Elections and Judicial Politics in the American States," *American Politics Quarterly* 23 (October 1995): 485–503.
[4]Stephen J. Choi, G. Mitu Gulati, and Eric A. Posner, "Professionals or Politicians: The Uncertain Empirical Case for an Elected Rather Than an Appointed Judiciary," John M. Olin Law and Economics Working Paper No. 357, University of Chicago Law School, August 2007, pp. 42–43.
[5]Henry R. Glick, "Courts: Politics and the Judicial Process," in Virginia Gray and Russell L. Hanson, eds., *Politics in the American States: A Comparative Analysis,* 8th ed. (Washington, DC: CQ Press, 2004), p. 240.
[6]Jessica Garrison, "Politics Creeps into Judge Races," *Los Angeles Times* (October 25, 2006): B3.
[7]*Caperton v. Massey,* 08-22 (2009).
[8]Sandra Day O'Connor, "Justice for Sale," *Wall Street Journal,* November 15, 2007, http://online.wsj.com/article/SB119509262956693711.html? mod=WSJBlog, accessed May 15, 2008.
[9]National Center for State Courts Poll, April 2009, available at www .ncsc.org/Web%20Document%20Library/Publications_Separate Branches.aspx, accessed February 21, 2010.
[10]"Judges and the American Public's View of Them: Results of the Maxwell Poll, Conducted in October 2005," www.maxwell.syr.edu/ news/MaxwellPoll.pdf, accessed May 15, 2008.

Continued from page 455

Attorneys have been accused of abusing their power to file class action suits by filing problematic claims and then reaching settlements that mainly benefit lawyers, not clients. A class action suit filed against the city of Chicago in 2001 on behalf of 5,000 homeless people who claimed to have been harmed by the city's anti-begging law resulted in an average payment of less than $20 per plaintiff, and a total of $375,000 for the lawyers.[94] But proponents justify class actions suits on the grounds that a legal issue often affects many people in essentially the same way, and it would be costly and complicated for each member of the class to bring a separate individual suit in order to secure relief.

CHAPTER SUMMARY

15.1 Describe the state court system and its politics.

The state court system predates the federal court system. Most cases begin and end in trial courts, the lowest rung of the judicial system, which consider alleged violations of state criminal or civil codes. One major difference between state and federal court systems is that in most states, at least some judges are elected.

15.2 Analyze sources and consequences of the power of the federal judiciary and compare and contrast approaches to constitutional interpretation.

The federal courts are the branch of government most removed from political influences. The courts often have a say in major political issues, however. They interpret laws as well as the Constitution and have the power to invalidate laws that violate the Constitution.

15.3 Describe the federal court system and the relationship between state and federal courts.

The president nominates federal judges to life terms on district courts, appeals courts, and the Supreme Court; the Senate must approve these appointments. The power of judicial review is broad enough to allow the federal courts to invalidate state laws that violate the United States Constitution.

15.4 Outline the steps and participants in the decision-making process of the Supreme Court.

Supreme Court nominations have increasingly been characterized by public political battles. When justices are selected for the Supreme Court, their political and judicial philosophies are closely evaluated by both the president and Congress. Once on the Court, justices rely on a small staff of clerks to select which cases to hear and to research and help write opinions.

15.5 Identify the major checks on Supreme Court power.

Constrained by the principle of *stare decisis*, judges are expected to rely on legal precedents when reaching their decisions. Most Supreme Court justices decide cases in ways that are consistent with views they were known to have at the time of their selection. The Court's decisions are usually responsive to contemporary political currents. If the decisions challenge deep-seated political views, they may be modified by new legislation, frustrated by nonimplementation, or even reversed by constitutional amendment.

15.6 Explain interest groups' use of litigation as a political strategy.

When elected officials are slow to respond to interest group demands, these groups often turn to the courts, especially when fundamental rights or constitutional principles are at stake.

mypoliscilab EXERCISES

Apply what you learned in this chapter on MyPoliSciLab.

Read on **mypoliscilab.com**

eText: Chapter 15

Study and **Review** on **mypoliscilab.com**

Pre-Test

Post-Test

Chapter Exam

Flashcards

Watch on **mypoliscilab.com**

Video: Most Significant Abortion Ruling in 30 Years

Video: Prosecuting Cyber Crime

Video: Court Rules on Hazelton's Immigration Laws

Video: Prosecuting Corruption

Explore on **mypoliscilab.com**

Simulation: You Are a Young Lawyer

Simulation: You Are a Clerk to Supreme Court Justice Judith Gray

Simulation: You Are the President and Need to Appoint a Supreme Court Justice

Comparative: Comparing Judiciaries

Timeline: Chief Justices of the Supreme Court

Visual Literacy: Case Overload

KEY TERMS

appeal, p. 448

associate justice, p. 449

borking, p. 446

brief, p. 450

cert, p. 448

chief justice, p. 449

circuit court of appeals, p. 441

civil code, p. 432

class action suit, p. 455

concurring opinion, p. 451

criminal code, p. 432

defendant, p. 432

dissenting opinion, p. 451

district attorney, p. 433

double jeopardy, p. 444

federal district courts, p. 441

judicial activism, p. 453

judicial restraint, p. 453

judicial review, p. 434

law clerk, p. 450

legal distinction, p. 448

living-constitution theory, p. 437

Marbury v. Madison, p. 435

McCulloch v. Maryland, p. 444

opinion, p. 451

original-intent theory, p. 436

plain-meaning-of-the-text theory, p. 436

plaintiff, p. 431

plenary session, p. 450

precedent, p. 448

receiver, p. 455

remand, p. 451

reversal, p. 448

solicitor general, p. 449

stare decisis, p. 447

statutory interpretation, p. 439

U.S. attorney, p. 443

writ of *certiorari* (cert), p. 448

SUGGESTED READINGS

Of General Interest

Breyer, Stephen. *Active Liberty: Interpreting Our Democratic Constitution.* New York: Knopf, 2005. Explanation by a sitting justice as to his approach to constitutional interpretation.

Friedman, Barry. *The Will of the People: How Public Opinion Has Influenced The Supreme Court and Shaped the Meaning of the Constitution.* New York: Farrar, Straus, and Giraux, 2009. Argument that the Supreme Court follows the election returns.

McCloskey, Robert G. *The American Supreme Court.* 4th ed. Revised by Sanford Levison. Chicago: University of Chicago Press, 2004. Excellent analysis that shows the close connection between public opinion and court decisions.

Scalia, Antonin. *A Matter of Interpretation: Federal Courts and the Law.* Princeton, NJ: Princeton University Press, 1997. A sitting justice explains his approach to constitutional interpretation.

Toobin, Jeffrey. *The Nine: Inside the Secret World of the Supreme Court.* New York: Doubleday, 2007. A captivating and readable account of the recent history of the Supreme Court and its justices.

Focused Studies

Epstein, Lee, and Jeffrey A. Segal. *Advice and Consent: The Politics of Judicial Appointments.* New York: Oxford University Press, 2005. Comprehensive study of federal judicial appointments.

Melnick, R. Shep. *Between the Lines: Interpreting Welfare Rights.* Washington, DC: The Brookings Institution, 1994. Insightful analysis of the Court's role in the interpretation and elaboration of statutory law.

O'Brien, David M., ed. *Judges on Judging: Views from the Bench.* 3rd ed. Washington, DC: CQ Press, 2008. A fine selection of writings from Supreme Court justices and other judges.

ON THE WEB

www.supremecourtus.gov

The official website of the U.S. Supreme Court contains information on the Court's docket, the text of recent opinions, the rules of the Court, and links to related websites. It also posts copies of Chief Justice Roberts's annual report on the federal judiciary.

www.fjc.gov

In 1967, Congress created the Federal Judicial Center to produce research aimed at improving the administration of the judicial branch. Its reports, which are available online, cover general legal topics, such as antitrust law, as well as practical and institutional questions, such as media in the courtroom, caseloads, and the relationship between state and federal courts.

www.law.cornell.edu

The Legal Information Institute at Cornell Law School archives information on federal and state laws, and rules of civil and criminal procedure, and also provides a searchable database of Supreme Court decisions.

www.uscourts.gov

There is more to the federal court system than the Supreme Court. The Federal Judiciary home page provides a concise guide to the federal court system, a regular newsletter, and annual reports on the state of the judiciary written by Chief Justice John Roberts.

16 Civil Liberties

CHAPTER OUTLINE

16.1   Trace the development of the Bill of Rights and its expansion to the states.

16.2   Outline the rights and limitations of freedom of speech, press, and assembly.

16.3   Distinguish the two clauses guaranteeing freedom of religion and illustrate how they can conflict.

16.4   Outline the procedural rights of the accused.

16.5   Assess the relationship of the right of privacy to sexual behavior, abortion, and information-age technologies.

Privacy in the Age of Terrorism

When most people think of government surveillance and spying, they think of the Central Intelligence Agency (CIA), based in Langley, Virginia, on the outskirts of Washington, DC. But the largest U.S. spy agency is actually a 45-minute drive northeast, in a boxy, obsidian building in Fort Meade, Maryland: the National Security Agency (NSA).

Created in 1952, the NSA is charged with breaking enemy codes and eavesdropping on suspicious communications around the world. Its 30,000 employees are more likely to be experts on mathematics and cryptography than they are to be adept at disguise or misdirection.[1] They use their skills to sift through a mind-boggling 650 million intercepted communications per day, searching for patterns, contacts with suspicious persons, and other "red flags" that would signal terrorist plotting, espionage, and other threats against the United States.[2]

Although Americans have always accepted the need to spy on those who might be threats to the country, they have also been reluctant to allow espionage agencies to operate unchecked. The zeal to catch foreign plotters can easily evolve into a determination to apprehend American criminals, and in turn lead to surveillance of innocent Americans. A cautionary tale on this note occurred in the 1960s and early 1970s, when the NSA and other agencies spied on such "subversives" as folksinger Joan Baez and civil rights activist Martin Luther King, Jr.[3] Since that time, spy agencies have been prohibited by law from monitoring Americans without obtaining a warrant from a secret federal court, established exclusively to handle such sensitive cases.

But in the age of terrorism, things may be changing. In 2005, the *New York Times* revealed that, pursuant to an executive order from the Bush White House (see the discussion of executive orders, Chapter 13), the NSA had been wiretapping many (perhaps millions of) communications between American citizens and foreigners abroad without obtaining a warrant.[4] Grounding his justifications on congressional enactments that authorized steps to be taken against al Qaeda terrorists, President Bush argued that the wiretaps were a crucial part of the war on terror, and said "there's no doubt in my mind it is legal."[5] Months later, more press reports claimed that, in a second program, the NSA had worked with major telephone companies such as Verizon, AT&T, and BellSouth to compile a massive database of billions of domestic telephone records. These records were then used in so-called "network analysis" that might reveal patterns that could lead to the uncovering of terrorist plots.[6] The spy agency did not listen to the content of phone conversations in this second program, but scanned only the numbers called and the times calls were made.

In 2007, Congress passed and the president signed an act temporarily allowing warrantless surveillance "directed at a person reasonably believed to be outside the United States." When the act came up for renewal in 2008, Democrats in Congress and President Bush fought over whether private companies that aided in the surveillance should be immune from lawsuits by people who had been monitored. For their part, Verizon and BellSouth denied that they had ever provided records to the NSA. The exact details of the calling database therefore remained unclear. The Obama administration appeared to continue Bush administration policies on this issue: Administration lawyers filed suit to block a federal court case on the matter, citing the congressional authorization as well as national security concerns. In 2010, the Court agreed, dismissing the case.[7]

Is this kind of monitoring acceptable? Some experts argued that it was essential in the new terror war and did not unduly intrude into Americans' lives.[8] "The architect of [the telephone records] program deserves our thanks and probably a medal," wrote one authority on terrorism, stressing that the phone records the NSA used were stripped of information that could easily identify individuals.[9] President Bush insisted that "the privacy of ordinary Americans is fiercely protected in all our activities."[10] Others argued that the White House and the NSA had gone too far. The telecommunications company Qwest said it had refused to hand over its records to the government because of privacy concerns.[11] ABC News aired reports that NSA eavesdroppers had monitored communications from overseas aid workers, journalists, and others, paying close attention to salacious or scandalous information. Senate Intelligence Committee Chairman Jay Rockefeller (D-WV) called such revelations "deeply disturbing."[12]

Surveys revealed cautious public support of the NSA intelligence gathering initiatives—a slim majority in several national polls voiced approval of such policies.[13] But many Americans—voters and government officials alike—seemed to need more time to absorb the news about the NSA programs and consider whether they violated privacy guarantees. As former Senator Arlen Specter (D-PA) put it, "We're really flying blind on the subject [right now] and that's not a good way to approach . . . the constitutional issues involving privacy."[14]

Making the Connection

For some, NSA eavesdropping is an essential and appropriate response to a significant threat. To others, such surveillance measures represent an infringement on the rights of individuals driven by a desire to respond to public demands for security. In this chapter, we place such debates in a larger constitutional context by describing the evolution of civil liberties under the U.S. Constitution. The concept of civil liberties, the fundamental freedoms that together preserve the rights of a free people, is never mentioned in the Constitution, nor has it ever been explicitly defined by the Supreme Court. But specific rights that together make up the civil liberties of U.S. citizens are to be found in the Bill of Rights—the first ten amendments to the Constitution—and again in amendments added to the Constitution after the Civil War. These rights include the right to free speech, free association, and free exercise of religion.

Civil liberties should be distinguished from civil rights (which we will consider in Chapter 17), which concern the rights of citizens to equal treatment under the law. This distinction may seem confusing, because at times both categories of protection may be referred to as "rights." But civil liberties are fundamental freedoms from government interference, whereas civil rights are fundamental guarantees of equal treatment by the government. In this chapter we focus on civil liberties.

First, we discuss the origins and evolution of civil liberties in the United States. Next, we consider the practical meaning of the freedoms of speech, press, and assembly. Then, we describe the two components of the Constitution's guarantee of freedom of religion and discuss how these two components may at times conflict with one another. Finally, we examine the rights that accused criminals have under the law and explain how conflicting views of citizens' right to privacy shape modern court decisions and policy disputes.

16.1

Trace the development of the Bill of Rights and its expansion to the states.

civil liberties
The fundamental freedoms that together preserve the rights of a free people.

Origins of Civil Liberties in the United States

The evolution of **civil liberties** in the United States has been shaped by Supreme Court rulings. But these liberties have also been affected by political debates, interest-group activism, and election outcomes. Civil liberties have not been created simply through the decisions of a small number of justices; rather, they reflect basic values shared by most citizens (see Chapter 4). In this section, we discuss the constitutional beginnings of civil liberties and how Americans' understanding of these liberties has evolved since then.

Origins of the Bill of Rights

America's revolutionary leaders rallied supporters to their side by invoking the liberties of Americans. Not only did the Declaration of Independence assert fundamental rights to "Life, Liberty, and the pursuit of Happiness," but many states incorporated similar principles into their constitutions and statutes. For example, the Virginia Assembly passed a bill of rights a month before the Continental Congress approved the Declaration of Independence. Among its provisions was the pronouncement that "freedom of the press" was "one of the great bulwarks of liberty."[15]

Despite their expressed commitment to basic freedoms, the colonial revolutionaries had little regard for the liberties of the Tories, who opposed the revolution. They closed Tory newspapers, threatened well-known Tory editors, confiscated their property, and so intimidated the royalists that some 80,000 to 100,000 people fled to Canada, England, and the West Indies.[16] Even future president John Adams vowed that "the [Tory] presses will produce no more seditious or traitorous speculations."[17]

Nor did those who drafted the Constitution include explicit protection for individual civil liberties. When anti-Federalist Charles Pinckney offered a motion at the Constitutional Convention to guarantee freedom of the press, the Federalist majority voted the measure down—on the grounds that states, not the central government, should be responsible for regulating speech and the press.[18] Only when ratification of the Constitution seemed in danger did Federalists agree to add a bill of rights in the form of a series of amendments to the Constitution (see Chapter 2). The first Congress approved the ten amendments that make up the Bill of Rights in 1790 only at James Madison's insistence. Madison, then a member of the House of Representatives, felt significant pressure from his Virginia constituents to press for the amendments. Most others in Congress voted for the amendments, it seems, because they thought the provisions would have little practical effect.

Few Liberties Before the Civil War

At first, the Bill of Rights applied only to the national government, not to the states. The First Amendment, for example, focused solely on the national legislature, saying that "Congress shall make no law" abridging speech or religious practice. As a result, for example, Massachusetts, Connecticut, and New Hampshire continued to support Congregationalist ministers with tax money for several decades.[19]

Other provisions in the Bill of Rights did not specifically mention either the national or the state governments, leaving open the possibility that they applied to both. For example, the Fifth Amendment said that "no person shall ... be deprived of life, liberty, or property, without due process of law." But, when the owner of Barron's Wharf

New Hampshire

Stamp Master in Effigy

Not Much Free Speech
Many a Tory editor was hanged
in effigy before and during the
American Revolution.

• *Why was free speech limited
at the time of the American
Revolution?*

complained that the City of Baltimore had deprived his company of property without "due process of law," the Supreme Court, in 1833, said the Fifth Amendment limited the powers of the federal government but not those of the states. The Bill of Rights, wrote Chief Justice John Marshall in *Barron v. Baltimore,* "contain[s] no expression indicating an intention to apply them to the state governments. This court cannot so apply them."[20]

It would have been difficult for Marshall to apply the Bill of Rights to the states prior to the Civil War, because doing so would have forced the country to confront the slavery issue head-on. Were slaves people who had liberties granted to them by the First Amendment, or were they property that belonged to their masters, according to the Fifth Amendment? For decades, this was a question too controversial to consider.

When the Supreme Court finally did consider the issue in 1857, coming down on the side of slave owners, the decision damaged the authority of the Court and helped accelerate a national crisis. In the extraordinary *Dred Scott v. Sandford* case, Chief Justice Roger Taney reached the conclusion that the Fifth Amendment precluded Congress from denying Dred Scott's master his right of property. As for Dred Scott, the slave, Taney ruled that he did not qualify as a "person" and therefore was not entitled to protections under the Fifth Amendment (see Chapter 15, p. 438). Abraham Lincoln and other Republicans vehemently criticized the Court in the 1858 and 1860 election campaigns, and the issue was not settled until the brutal war that followed reached an end in 1865.

Applying the Bill of Rights to State Governments

CONSTITUTION, FOURTEENTH AMENDMENT: *"No State shall . . . deprive any person of life, liberty, or property, without due process of law."*

The Civil War transformed the spirit, meaning, and application of the Bill of Rights. Once slavery had been abolished, the words in the first ten amendments could begin to be applied to all Americans. To give the Bill of Rights new meaning, Congress and the states enacted three **civil rights amendments,** the Thirteenth, Fourteenth, and

civil rights amendments
The Thirteenth, Fourteenth, and Fifteenth Amendments, which abolished slavery, redefined civil rights and liberties, and guaranteed the right to vote to all adult male citizens.

Fifteenth Amendments, which abolished slavery, redefined civil rights and liberties, and guaranteed the right to vote to all adult male citizens, respectively.

Of all the provisions in the civil rights amendments, the one that has had the greatest significance for civil liberty is the **due process clause** of the Fourteenth Amendment, which says that a person cannot be "deprive[d] . . . of life, liberty, or property without due process of law." As we have noted, a nearly identical phrase had already appeared in the Fifth Amendment, but the Fourteenth Amendment, by specifying that "no *state* shall" infringe upon these liberties, greatly expanded individual freedoms. Now neither the national government nor the states were permitted to arbitrarily interfere with personal freedoms.

due process clause
Clause found in the Fifth and Fourteenth Amendments to the Constitution; forbids deprivation of life, liberty, or property without due process of law.

This expansion did not occur all at once, however. Despite the language in the Fourteenth Amendment, the Supreme Court did not immediately conclude that the states must abide by the entire Bill of Rights. The Fourteenth Amendment does not refer to the Bill of Rights, and the Court appeared to believe that a sweeping decision applying the entire Bill of Rights to the states would be impractical, creating a "vast and perhaps unmanageable problem" of enforcement.[21] Instead, the Court has taken a gradual approach known as **selective incorporation,** a process by which it considers provisions of the Bill of Rights on a case-by-case basis, deciding over time whether the Fourteenth Amendment's due process clause applies sections of the Bill of Rights to the states.

selective incorporation
The case-by-case process through which the Supreme Court applies the Bill of Rights to the states by invoking the due process clause of the Fourteenth Amendment.

God-Given Rights?
A man with a pistol sits in a Kentucky church at an "open carry celebration," in honor of the Second Amendment right to bear arms.
• *What regulations on firearms, if any, do you believe are permissible under the Constitution?*

Over the course of many decades, nearly all of the provisions in the Bill of Rights have been incorporated. But a few exceptions remain, such as the Seventh Amendment's guarantee of the right to a jury trial in civil cases.

The most recent right in the Bill of Rights to be incorporated was the Second Amendment's "right of the people to keep and bear arms." For decades, legal scholars had argued that because this amendment qualified this right by referring to "a well regulated militia," the amendment was intended to preserve states' rights to maintain militias (such as the modern National Guard), rather than individuals' rights to own weapons. But in 2008, in a case involving a handgun ban in the District of Columbia, the Court ruled that the Second Amendment preserved an individual right.[22] In the 2010 case of *McDonald v. City of Chicago,* the Court found that this right applied to state governments as well. As Justice Alito, writing for the majority, put it, "it is clear that the Framers and the ratifiers of the Fourteenth Amendment counted the right to keep and bear arms among those fundamental rights necessary to our system of ordered liberty."[23]

16.2   Freedom of Speech, Press, and Assembly

Outline the rights and limitations of freedom of speech, press, and assembly.

CONSTITUTION, FIRST AMENDMENT: *"Congress shall make no law . . . abridging the freedom of speech, or of the press; or the right of the people peaceably to assemble, . . ."*

Of the liberties listed in the Bill of Rights, one trio is paramount: freedom of speech, press, and assembly. The three are closely intertwined. If free speech is to be effective, it must be communicated through a free press. Unless an audience can be assembled to listen, speakers might as well keep silent.

Even though the beginnings of these freedoms date back to the colonial period, the doctrine of free expression, as we know it today, is not so deeply entrenched in the American tradition as Fourth of July speakers often proclaim. Despite the First Amendment, the federal and state governments have passed many laws over the years that restrict expression in some way. As activists have challenged many of these laws, the Supreme Court has developed a set of standards for interpreting the First Amendment that has been as much a reaction to the climate of public sentiment as it has been a reading of clear legal precedents. We spend the bulk of this section considering free speech, and then illustrate how the Supreme Court has applied constitutional doctrines developed in free-speech cases to cases involving freedom of the press and free assembly. Finally, we point out key limitations of free expression in such areas as commercial speech, obscenity, and libel, areas that the public—and the courts—are more willing to regulate.

Free Speech and Majoritarian Democracy

Free speech is vital to the workings of a democratic society. Elections have little meaning when candidates cannot express their opinions without fear of punishment.

Even so, elections are won by candidates who are backed by a majority of the voters, and majorities can at times be as tyrannical as single-minded despots. The greatest threat to the rights of the people, said James Madison, is the **tyranny of the majority**—the suppression of minority opinions by those voted into power by a majority.[24] The larger a majority gets, the more confident it is that its views are correct, and the more capable it is of punishing dissenters.[25] As British historian Lord Acton said in 1878, "The one pervading evil of democracy is the tyranny of the majority, or rather of that party, not always the majority, that succeeds, by force or fraud, in carrying elections."[26]

tyranny of the majority
The suppression of minority opinions by those voted into power by the majority.

Because of such fears about unscrupulous political coalitions, Madison believed that free speech should be placed outside the reach of even very powerful majorities. Accordingly, the Constitution's First Amendment specifically protects speech from regulation by Congress. Enshrining free-speech rights in the Constitution meant that majorities would have to tolerate dissent—at least until they could muster the strength to change the Bill of Rights.

The classic defense of free speech was provided by the English civil libertarian John Stuart Mill, who insisted that in the free exchange of ideas truth would eventually triumph over error. This argument, said Mill, applied not just to politics, but to many aspects of life. Galileo's declaration that the Earth is not at the center of the universe eventually became accepted as true, although informed opinion initially regarded his claims as preposterous. Modern events seem to bear out Mill's argument. Seventy years ago, geologists laughed at Alfred Wegener's suggestion that the world's continents gradually drift over long distances. We now know that they do.

These examples illustrate the value of free speech in scientific debates, but must we tolerate even offensive and vicious error? It is not easy to accept the idea of people enjoying the freedom to spread doctrines of racial hatred, for example. Are their beliefs not founded on false premises that could never be shown to be true? To such contentions, Mill replied that "he who knows only his own side of the case, knows little of that."[27]

Mill argued further that error suppressed becomes more powerful by virtue of its suppression. Only if error is allowed to express itself can its proponents be denied the privilege of a false martyrdom.

From "Bad Tendency" to "Clear and Present Danger"

bad tendency test
A rule from English law saying that expression could be punished if it could ultimately lead to illegal behavior.

In colonial days, punishment for supposedly harmful speech was allowed under an English judicial standard known as the **bad tendency test,** a rule that held that expression could be punished if it could ultimately lead to illegal behavior. For example, if a merchant grumbled that the tax collector ought to be tarred and feathered for bleeding the local businesses dry, he could be punished because the comments could lead to something illegal: tarring and feathering. British courts developed the bad tendency standard to protect the monarchy from criticism and also used it broadly to punish speech that was harmful to public morals and to the official church.[28] After the ratification of the Constitution, many Americans disagreed about whether the First Amendment simply restated the bad tendency test or instead provided a much broader range of protection from government interference.

Unfortunately, an answer to this question would have to wait for many years. The courts did not enforce the Bill of Rights immediately, in part because until the ratification of the Fourteenth Amendment, it protected the right of free speech only against actions by Congress, not against those by state governments.

Even in more recent times, the Supreme Court has not been a leader in protecting those with unpopular opinions from the tyranny of the majority. Instead, the Supreme Court's view of what free speech entails has moved along at about the same speed as—or perhaps a little slower than—that of the rest of the country. In the words of one scholar, "the Court has seldom lagged far behind or forged far ahead of America."[29]

The first major Supreme Court decision affecting freedom of speech arose out of the conscription of young men into the army during World War I. The occasion for the ruling was the conviction of Charles Schenck, a socialist who had mailed anti-conscription materials to draft-age men during the war. A jury concluded that Schenck had violated the 1917 Espionage Act, which made it illegal to obstruct armed forces recruitment.

clear and present danger doctrine
The principle that people should have complete freedom of speech unless their language endangers the nation.

When asked to review Schenck's conviction, the Supreme Court, in *Schenck v. United States* (1919), enunciated the **clear and present danger doctrine**—the principle that people should have complete freedom of speech unless there is a "clear and present danger" that their language will provoke "evils that Congress has a right to prevent." The Supreme Court, which was no more sympathetic to socialists than Congress had been when it passed the Espionage Act, upheld Schenck's conviction and sent him to prison. The Schenck case nevertheless marked the first time the Court moved to limit the regulation of speech by proposing a definite standard. Justice Oliver Wendell Holmes, author of the Court's opinion in the case, made the common-sense observation that no person has the right falsely to cry "Fire" in a crowded theater: Such a cry creates a clear and present danger to the public safety because panicking theatergoers might trample one another as they bolt for the exits. In the same way, he argued, Congress could regulate speech only when there was a clear and present danger that the speech would provoke serious evils. His example seemed to capture succinctly the appropriate balance between the right of free speech and the need to maintain social order.

The meaning of clear and present danger, however, is open to different interpretations. A critical question is whether this standard simply restates the old bad tendency test (which allows limitations if speech *could* lead to illegal activities), or whether it instead defines a much narrower set of circumstances under which the government could legitimately limit speech (involving a determination about whether speech is *very likely* to lead to illegal activities).

For example, in recent decades, a majority of the nation's colleges and universities have attempted to adopt speech codes that would limit the use of so-called "hate speech." Critics of such regulations might argue that in no sense do offensive racist or sexist slurs pose the kind of immediate peril that crying "Fire" in a crowded theater does. Jason Shepard, an openly gay student at the University of Wisconsin, argues that "Racism, sexism, homophobia are all parts of our society, whether we like it or not. We can't erect a wall around our university and pretend those things don't exist."[30] Others might reply that if slurs came to be widely used, they would indeed constitute a clear and present danger to the safety of individuals, to the public order, and to the climate of intellectual growth. Take, for example, the true story of a farm-science professor who used a *Playboy* centerfold to illustrate different cuts of meat. This kind of speech might not only make women feel unwelcome and belittled in the classroom, but might also create a climate in which violence against women outside the classroom is more likely.[31] To keep that from happening, say advocates of speech codes, this kind of speech should be restricted before the danger becomes too present. Under this second interpretation, the clear and present danger standard seems to be closer to the bad tendency test.

Holmes himself took this second point of view in the Schenck case, appearing to argue that the clear and present danger test was the same as the bad tendency test. He said that Schenck's actions constituted a clear and present danger to the successful prosecution of the war because, if the mailing of anti-draft pamphlets to draft-age men achieved its ends, it could endanger the war effort.[32] In a very similar case, however, Holmes tried to separate his clear and present danger test from the bad tendency standard. In *Abrams v. United States* (1919), several activists were charged with violating the Espionage Act when they printed and distributed leaflets advocating socialism. Although the majority of the Court felt that the pamphlets had a tendency harmful enough for the government to jail the activists, Holmes dissented, arguing that the "publishing of a silly leaflet by an unknown man" posed no grave danger to the war effort.[33]

In cases after *Abrams,* Holmes continued to argue for a clear and present danger test that allowed for fewer restrictions on speech than the bad tendency test did. Although the rest of the Court was at first reluctant to follow him, the doctrine became the foundation upon which a free-speech tradition was gradually built. During the 1930s, when the public was more tolerant of dissenting opinion, the Supreme Court, reflecting the changing political climate, explicitly defended the civil liberties of minorities. A 1931 case, *Stromberg v. California,* was particularly important, because for the first time it gave First Amendment protection to extremely unpopular opinions. Yetta Stromberg had encouraged children attending a camp operated by the Young Communist League to pledge allegiance to the flag of the Soviet Union, a violation of California's "red-flag" law.[34] The Supreme Court overturned her conviction, saying that the California law limited "free political discussion." Because Stromberg did not constitute a clear and present danger, said the Court, her civil liberties should not be curtailed.

The Fighting Words Doctrine

The toleration that emerged during the 1930s did not survive the onset of World War II. In 1940, Congress responded to public outrage against fascism by enacting the Smith Act, which forbade advocating the overthrow of the government by force. Even some university administrators prohibited demonstrations against the draft, arguing that such demonstrations would reflect poorly on their schools. Columbia University president Nicholas Butler justified the ban in these words: "Before academic freedom comes university freedom to pursue its high ideals, unembarrassed by conduct which tends to damage its reputation."[35]

fighting words doctrine
The principle, endorsed by the Supreme Court in *Chaplinsky v. New Hampshire* (1942), that some words constitute violent acts and are therefore not protected under the First Amendment.

Instead of acting as a bulwark against majority tyranny during World War II, the Supreme Court endorsed limitations on free speech. In the 1942 case of *Chaplinsky v. New Hampshire,* the Court enunciated the **fighting words doctrine** that some words constitute violent acts and are therefore not protected under the First Amendment. Walter Chaplinsky, a member of the Jehovah's Witnesses religious group, had asked a policeman to guard him from a threatening crowd objecting to his pacifist address. When the policeman gave him no protection but instead cursed him and asked him to "come along," Chaplinsky called the policeman "a God damned racketeer" and "a damned Fascist." The Supreme Court upheld Chaplinsky's conviction on the grounds that he had used threatening words that "are no essential part of any exposition of ideas" and that "by their very utterance inflict injury or intend to incite an immediate breach of the peace."[36] This new fighting words doctrine seriously qualified the Court's earlier inclination to protect most speech under the clear and present danger doctrine.

The Balancing Doctrine

After World War II, those who were regarded as Communist sympathizers suffered harassment by government officials responding to public concern about the growing conflict between the United States and the Soviet Union. Republican Senator Joseph McCarthy of Wisconsin gained political popularity by accusing artists, teachers, and government officials of having ties to the Communist Party. As part of the anti-Communist crusade, Congress voted to require that all employees of the federal government take an oath swearing loyalty to the United States. Students also had to take this oath when applying for student loans. Many careers were damaged irreparably.

balancing doctrine
The principle enunciated by the Supreme Court that freedom of speech must be balanced against other competing public interests at stake in particular circumstances.

Once again, it was up to the courts to protect the free speech of minority dissidents. But, instead of taking special care to protect free speech, the Supreme Court enunciated the **balancing doctrine**—the principle that freedom of speech had to be balanced against other competing public interests at stake in particular circumstances. The Court developed this doctrine when considering a case in which 11 leaders of the Communist Party had been convicted under the Smith Act for espousing the revolutionary overthrow of the government. In *Dennis v. United States* (1951), the Court said the convictions had been constitutional, arguing that the "balance . . . must be struck in favor" of the governmental interest in resisting subversion.[37] The balancing doctrine was used to reinterpret and place limits on the clear and present danger doctrine.

It was elected political leaders, not judges, who resisted the threat that McCarthyism posed to the country's civil liberties. A disgusted President Eisenhower refused to act on McCarthy's most outrageous accusations, and McCarthy's Senate colleagues finally

Senator Joseph McCarthy

Senator Joseph McCarthy built a career in the 1950s on investigating alleged Communist sympathizers.

• *His methods outraged many, but should civil liberties be balanced against other important governmental interests, such as national security?*

inquired into the senator's methods of operation, later censuring him for his inappropriate conduct.

The Fundamental Freedoms Doctrine

After an elected president and Congress had exposed and discredited McCarthy, public opinion became increasingly supportive of protecting the free-speech rights of all Americans, even radicals and Communists.[38] Reflecting these changes in public opinion, the Supreme Court gradually became committed to the **fundamental freedoms doctrine**—the principle that some constitutional provisions, such as the freedoms of speech, press, and assembly, ought to be given special preference because they are basic to the functioning of a democratic society. The doctrine has its origins in a Supreme Court opinion written in 1938 by Justice Harlan Stone, who said that some freedoms, such as freedom of speech, have a "preferred position" in the Constitution; any law threatening these freedoms must be subject to strict scrutiny by the Supreme Court.[39]

Although no single court case specifically set forth the fundamental freedoms doctrine, it became the Supreme Court's governing principle during the 1960s in the midst of the Vietnam War. Under its guidance, the Court was more effective at defending dissenters against government repression than in any previous war. As one civil libertarian wrote in 1973, "The truly significant thing in recent years has not been the attempt of the current administration to suppress criticism, but rather the marked inability of the administration to do so effectively."[40] In virtually every case that came before it, the Court ruled against efforts to suppress free speech. For example, it overturned the expulsion from the University of Missouri of a student who had distributed a newspaper containing a picture of a policeman raping the Statue of Liberty. Said the Court, "The mere dissemination of ideas—no matter how offensive to good taste—on a state university campus may not be shut off" in the name of decency.[41]

fundamental freedoms doctrine

The judicial doctrine stating that laws impinging on the freedoms that are fundamental to the preservation of democratic practice—the freedoms of speech, press, assembly, and religion—are to be scrutinized by the courts more closely than other legislation. These are also termed the preferred freedoms.

In a 1989 case, *Texas v. Johnson*, the Supreme Court overturned Gregory Johnson's conviction for burning an American flag, saying the principal purpose of free speech is to invite dispute and the mere burning of the flag was "expressive conduct" that did not breach the peace.[42] Many thought it an indication that the commitment to free speech was now very broadly based when Antonin Scalia, one of the Court's most conservative justices, voted with the majority.

If anything, Supreme Court conservatives have become champions of free speech. In *R.A.V. v. City of St. Paul* (1990), Scalia wrote a majority opinion that gave protection to speech criticizing particular ethnic groups. The City of St. Paul had passed an ordinance forbidding the placement on public or private property of a symbol that "arouses anger, alarm or resentment in others on the basis of race, color, creed, religion or gender." When a group of teenagers was caught placing a "crudely made cross" made of "broken chair legs" inside the fence of the yard of a black neighbor and setting fire to it, the City of St. Paul charged them with violating the ordinance. The Supreme Court unanimously ruled that the ordinance infringed upon free speech, saying that ordinary trespassing laws were adequate to deal with the alleged intrusion on a person's property.[43]

Freedom of the Press

prior restraint doctrine
Legal doctrine that gives individuals the right to publish without prior restraint—that is, without first submitting material to a government censor.

Freedom of the press during the early colonial period was governed by the **prior restraint doctrine,** which said the government could not censor an article before it was published. However, the prior restraint doctrine did not prevent prosecution after the fact. Instead, the publisher could be convicted under the bad tendency test for bringing the government's "dignity into contempt," even if what he said were true. Thus, in 1734, when John Peter Zenger published an accurate critique of an incompetent, unprincipled New York governor, the governor put Zenger in jail for ten months while he was awaiting trial. In one of the great early victories for freedom of the press, the jury found Zenger innocent after his attorney argued that the issue at stake was "the Liberty—both of exposing and opposing arbitrary Power . . . by speaking and writing Truth."[44]

Although the Zenger case was an important event in the history of press freedom, it took nearly two more centuries for the Supreme Court to rule that a publisher could not be punished for promoting a particular point of view. In 1931 the Supreme Court, in *Near v. Minnesota,* overruled a Minnesota law that prohibited newspapers from publishing "malicious, scandalous and defamatory" material. Even though a publication banned under the law had printed vicious anti-Semitic and racist harangues, the Court regarded the law as "the essence of censorship."[45]

In one of its most significant decisions, *New York Times v. United States* (1971), the Supreme Court rejected an attempt by the Nixon administration to prevent, on grounds of national security, the *New York Times* from publishing the "Pentagon Papers," a lengthy Defense Department document detailing mistakes made by government officials in their conduct of the Vietnam War. Although the Court suggested that prior restraint might be permitted under particularly extreme circumstances if national security were endangered, it ruled in the newspaper's favor on the grounds that the "Pentagon Papers" did not, in fact, include highly sensitive material (see Chapter 9).

The Supreme Court has often treated freedom of the press as synonymous with freedom of speech. If speech is permitted in a certain case, a publication containing the same message is also permitted under the Constitution. On the one hand, newspapers, pamphlets, and the Internet enjoy the broadest First Amendment protections because they are, in theory, accessible to all. On the other, the Court has ruled that radio and television may be regulated by the government, since technically the airwaves are public property and comparatively few people have access to them (see Chapter 9). Although prior restraint of radio and television programs is not permitted, the Federal Communications Commission may levy fines or refuse to renew a station's broadcast license if it fails to meet particular standards. After Janet Jackson bared a breast during the 2004 Super Bowl halftime show, for example, Congress increased maximum fines for indecency from $32,500 per violation to $325,000.[46]

Freedom of Association

The freedom of association has long been considered inseparable from the freedoms of speech and of the press. Without the ability to assemble, the free exchange of ideas that John Stuart Mill advocated would be difficult if not impossible. Although the Court was willing to limit the activities of some fringe groups in the 1950s, as the *Dennis v. United States* case discussed above shows, the justices gradually broadened their interpretation of the rights of popular assembly in succeeding years. In the case of *NAACP v. Alabama* (1958), for example, the Court ruled that Alabama could not compel the National Association for the Advancement of Colored People to turn over its membership lists to the state. In this case, said Justice Harlan, a requirement of membership disclosure would be "as effective a restraint on freedom of association" as the direct governmental punishment in cases such as *Near v. Minnesota*.[47]

Some rulings on freedom of association have been controversial because they concern the ability of private organizations to exclude particular members. In *Boy Scouts of America v. Dale* (2000), the Court ruled that the Scouts could refuse to accept a prospective scoutmaster who was gay. Accepting gay scoutmasters, argued the Court, would infringe upon the Scouts' ability to convey their system of values to youth, one of the tenets of which is that "homosexual conduct is not morally straight."[48] In *Rumsfeld v. Forum for Academic and Institutional Rights* (2006), the Court ruled that Congress could force colleges and universities to accept military recruiters on campus. Some universities had claimed that they had a right not to associate with military organizations because of the military's discriminatory policy toward gays and lesbians. But the Court found that Congress was within its rights under the spending clause (see Chapter 3) to threaten to withdraw federal funding from academic institutions that excluded the recruiters.[49]

Limitations on Free Expression

Although free expression has now been firmly established as one of the country's fundamental freedoms, not all expression is free of government control. The Supreme Court has recognized that at particular times and places, certain types of speech may be circumscribed. A city is within its rights to restrict the use of bullhorns in residential neighborhoods in the early hours of the morning, for example. In addition, public school officials may punish students for speech they deem to be disruptive. In 2007, the Court ruled that a high school principal was justified in punishing a student who had unfurled a banner reading "BONG HiTS 4 JESUS." Although the student would have been allowed to propound this bizarre message in another context, doing so at a school-sponsored event made him subject to punishment.[50]

BONG HiTS 4 JESUS

This banner, unfurled at a school-sponsored event in Alaska, became the occasion for a 2007 Supreme Court case when the school's principal punished the student responsible.

• *The school's attorneys argued that the banner was disruptive because it advocated illegal drug use, and the Supreme Court agreed. The student claimed the message was nonsense designed to get media attention. What do you think?*

commercial speech

Advertising or other speech made for business purposes; may be regulated.

obscenity

Publicly offensive language or portrayals with no redeeming social value.

Three other types of speech are subject to regulation: commercial speech, obscenity, and libel. **Commercial speech**—advertising or other speech made for business purposes—may be regulated. According to the Court, regulation of commercial speech is needed so that companies will not take advantage of consumers by providing false or misleading information. Also, commercial speech can be controlled to discourage the consumption of substances the government regards as harmful. For example, cigarette advertising on television and radio is forbidden, despite the complaints by tobacco companies that this prohibition interferes with their right to free speech.

Obscenity—publicly offensive language or portrayals with no redeeming social value—is not protected under the First Amendment. Whether explicit sexual material is obscene depends on whether it has some social or cultural purpose. The Court, in *Redrup v. New York* (1967), came close to saying that it would not uphold any obscenity conviction unless the obscenity involved a juvenile, was forced upon unwilling adults, or "pandered" to the most disgusting of prurient interests. But just a few years later, in *Miller v. California* (1973), a more conservative Court said that obscenity is a matter to be settled according to local community standards.[51] Overall, the Court seems to have said that local communities may ban hard-core pornography if they wish to do so. Less explicit sexual material may not be outlawed, particularly if presented within an artistic or literary context.

With the growth of the Internet, the distinction between national and local standards is rapidly disappearing, and sexually explicit material has become generally available. In 1996 Congress passed the Communications Decency Act, which prohibited posting or sending on the Internet obscene material that might be viewed by minors. The following year the Supreme Court struck down this law as unconstitutional, arguing that its restrictions were too broad.[52] But Congress responded by writing a narrower law targeting commercial pornographers. A lower court later struck down this narrower law, and in 2009 the Supreme Court refused to hear an appeal, effectively killing the measure.[53]

Libel—a false statement defaming another—is not constitutionally protected if made by one private person about another. But what if press reports about public figures are erroneous? Can a newspaper then be successfully sued? This issue was raised by a fund-raising advertisement that a civil rights group placed in the *New York Times* on March 29, 1960. The advertisement reported on student demonstrations against segregation in Montgomery, Alabama. In addition to containing several relatively innocuous errors (student demonstrators sang the national anthem, not "My Country 'Tis of Thee," as claimed), the advertisement implied that the local police were part of a "wave of terror" directed at protesters. "When the entire student body protested to state authorities by refusing to reregister," read the advertisement, "their dining hall was padlocked in an attempt to starve them into submission."

Pointing out that the police had never padlocked the dining hall, the local official charged with supervising the police department, Montgomery County Commissioner J. L. Sullivan, sued for libel. An all-white Alabama jury found the *New York Times* and those who placed the ad guilty to the tune of half a million dollars per allegation.[54]

In *New York Times v. Sullivan* (1964), the Supreme Court reversed the libel conviction, holding that untruthful statements made about public figures were not actionable for libel unless the errors were made knowingly or with reckless disregard for the truth. In the Court's view, the errors in the advertisement were reasonable mistakes. The Court's decision in this case reflected national public opinion, which at the time was supportive of the civil rights movement.

Freedom of Religion

> CONSTITUTION, FIRST AMENDMENT: *"Congress shall make no law respecting an establishment of religion, or prohibiting the free exercise thereof."*

Freedom of religion is guaranteed by two clauses in the First Amendment. The **establishment of religion clause** denies the government the power to establish any single religious practice as superior. The **free exercise of religion clause** protects the right of individuals to practice their religion without government interference. As we shall see, when interpreting these clauses, the Supreme Court has often been influenced by the political and electoral context in which its decisions have been made.

The Establishment of Religion Clause

The constitutional prohibition against government establishment of religion may seem unequivocal, but we can find many gray areas and seeming contradictions in the way it has been enforced. The motto "In God We Trust" appears on U.S. currency, yet courts have ruled against nativity scenes in village squares. Each session of Congress opens with a prayer, but public schools cannot begin their day in a similar fashion.

Religious issues often arise in conjunction with the provision of public education, in large part because many parents and policymakers think schools need to teach not only reading and arithmetic but morals and values as well. The issue is one of the oldest in American politics. Massachusetts passed the nation's first compulsory-schooling law in 1852, because many Protestants felt something had to be done about the waves of Catholic immigrants arriving in Boston from Ireland and Germany.

---

libel
A false statement defaming another.

16.3

Distinguish the two clauses guaranteeing freedom of religion and illustrate how they can conflict.

establishment of religion clause
Clause denying the government the power to establish any single religious practice as superior.

free exercise of religion clause
Clause protecting the right of individuals to practice their religion without government interference.

The anti-Catholic forces were so strong nationwide that in 1875 they nearly succeeded in passing a constitutional amendment that explicitly forbade state aid to religious schools.[55]

Although the proposed amendment failed to pass, Supreme Court decisions interpreting the establishment of religion clause reflected the views of the Protestant majority, which opposed aid to religious schools. As a result, the Court has for the most part followed the **separation of church and state doctrine,** which says that a wall should separate the government from religious activity. (This metaphor comes from a letter President Thomas Jefferson wrote in 1802 to a group of Connecticut Baptists in which he argued that the establishment clause set up a "wall of separation between Church & State."[56]) For example, in *Meek v. Pittenger* (1975), the Court struck down most forms of aid that Pennsylvania provided to religious schools as part of its federally funded compensatory education program.[57] The Court said public monies cannot be used for payment to religious-school teachers, for curricular materials, or for any other expense at such schools, except for textbooks and the cost of transporting students to school.

separation of church and state doctrine
Principle that a wall should separate the government from religious activity.

Although it began hearing cases on the establishment clause beginning in the 1940s, the Supreme Court took nearly a quarter century to evolve a particular test for determining whether laws violate the First Amendment's establishment of religion clause. It is usually called the **Lemon test** after a 1971 case, *Lemon v. Kurtzman,* although the heart of the rule dates from earlier decisions. The Court (a) required all laws to have clear secular (that is, not religious) purposes, (b) did not permit laws to advance or inhibit either one religion or religion in general, and (c) considered it one sign of a religious establishment if the law entangled public officials with religious institutions or activities.

Lemon test
Supreme Court standard for determining whether the First Amendment's establishment of religion clause has been violated.

Few people openly endorse the Lemon test these days. Even those who prefer a strong division between church and state recognize that federal courts have not done a very good job of applying *Lemon*.[58] Yet no ruling has ever cast out *Lemon* entirely, because its detractors cannot agree on a replacement. Instead, the evolution of case law has forced repeated modifications to how and when federal courts use the test.

For example, during the 1960s and 1970s, as the Court was reinforcing its commitment to broad interpretations of other parts of the Bill of Rights, the separation doctrine was applied rigorously to most forms of state-supported religious activity. School prayer, a sacred moment of silence, reading from the Bible as a sacred text, and the celebration of religious holidays in schools—all once widely practiced—were banned on the grounds that they advanced religion.[59] After evangelical religious groups protested these decisions in the 1980s and 1990s, however, a more conservative Supreme Court relaxed the ban on prayer in school somewhat, saying students may form Bible-study or school prayer clubs as long as other clubs are allowed to use school property.[60]

Other recent decisions have also opened up windows in the wall of separation between church and state. In 2000 the Supreme Court ruled that states could provide private religious schools with computer equipment.[61] More important, in *Agostini v. Felton* (1997) the Supreme Court ruled that public school teachers can provide specialized remedial instruction in religious schools, so long as this instruction does not discriminate against students on the basis of religion, and any aid to religious institutions occurs "only as a result of the genuinely independent and private choices of individuals."[62] By justifying its decision in terms of the "private choices of individuals," the Court showed a concern for the right to the free exercise of religion, the subject to which we now turn.

The Free Exercise of Religion Clause

If the establishment of religion clause seems to bar state involvement in religion, this clause seems to instruct states not to interfere with religious practices. Once again, this issue frequently arises in the context of education policy. The Supreme Court has often protected private religious schools from hostile action by state legislatures. For example, during the 1920s, anti-immigrant sentiments were so strong in Nebraska that the legislature tried to close private religious schools that provided instruction in foreign languages. In 1923, the Supreme Court ruled that the law violated the free exercise clause of the First Amendment because it prevented parents from exercising "the right of the individual to . . . establish a

Free Exercise of Religion

The Supreme Court ruled in 1972 that Wisconsin's requirement that Amish children attend high school violated the First Amendment's free exercise clause.

• *Why do you think education is often at the center of controversies concerning the "separation of church and state"?*

home and bring up children [and] to worship God according to the dictates of his own conscience."[63] Extending this line of reasoning, the Court in *Wisconsin v. Yoder* (1972) disallowed the application of a compulsory public school attendance law to two Amish children, whose parents opposed their attendance on religious grounds.[64]

The guarantee of free exercise of religion has often forced the Court to draw fine distinctions about how the government can make its rules. In a 1993 case, the Court invalidated a Hialeah, Florida, city ordinance that banned animal sacrifices because it unduly infringed on the practices of the Santeria religion.[65] On the other hand, in *Oregon v. Smith* (1990) the Court ruled that peyote-smoking members of a Native American church could be denied unemployment compensation under Oregon law after getting fired from their jobs as drug rehabilitation counselors. Although the peyote was used as a sacrament, Justice Antonin Scalia wrote in his majority opinion that the state could enforce its ban on the drug in this case because the law was "not specifically directed at [Native American] religious practice."[66]

Establishment of Religion or Free Exercise?

The *Wisconsin v. Yoder* case involving the Amish children raises the issue of what the courts ought to do when the establishment clause and the free exercise clause come into conflict with one another. Some critics might argue that by allowing the Amish to be exempt from certain laws to ensure that they could exercise their religion freely, the Court was violating the establishment clause by giving the Amish preferential treatment. A similar quandary arises when we consider the case of overseas members of the armed services. Should the army hire chaplains to ensure soldiers' right of free religious exercise? Or does the army violate the establishment clause by employing religious leaders?[67] The debate over school choice also raises the question of whether the establishment clause is violated if families and students are given a choice of school, whether religious or secular (see the *Election Voices!* feature on page 488).

The Supreme Court's rulings in cases involving the establishment clause and the free exercise clause have occurred in the context of a heavily religious society in which religion has frequently played a pivotal political role. Nineteenth-century abolitionists argued, along with William Lloyd Garrison, that "freedom is of God and slavery is of the devil."[68] Temperance crusaders promoted teetotaling as a Christian virtue when they lobbied for prohibition. Civil rights pioneers, abortion opponents, and anti-poverty activists have all been guided by religious faith. In a nation in which 90 percent of people believe in God and nearly 70 percent believe that it is important for a president to have strong religious beliefs, it is not surprising that religion enters into political controversies.[69] On the other hand, nearly two-thirds of Americans believe that it is improper for churches to endorse candidates for office, and the public's views about religion's role in government are more complex than they might seem.[70] The balance that the Supreme Court has struck in establishment and free exercise cases is probably a good approximation of the public view.

16.4

Outline the procedural rights of the accused.

Law, Order, and the Rights of Suspects

The political context also affects court interpretations of the procedural rights of the accused. On the one hand, the government must ensure that procedural rights are followed; on the other hand, it must also maintain social order. Many public officials believe procedural obstacles protecting the rights of suspects unduly handicap the efforts of the police to find and prosecute criminals. They seem to share the view of the ancient jurist who said, "The judge is condemned when the criminal is absolved."[71] But others think that unless procedural safeguards are carefully observed, innocent people will be unjustly convicted. "I think it a less evil," said Justice Oliver Wendell Holmes, "that some criminals should escape than that the government should play an ignoble part."[72] In this section, we first summarize the role that elections play in this debate and then review the rights of the accused, including the rights of suspects against unreasonable police intrusion, as well as their rights at and after criminal trials.

Election Politics and Criminal Justice

Politics affects criminal justice procedures, because almost everyone worries about being a victim of a crime. According to the Department of Justice, around a quarter-million violent and property crimes occur each year.[73] Most of these crimes—thefts, burglaries, and robberies—take place at more or less the same rate in the United States as in other major industrial countries. But many people in the United States today are especially afraid of personal injury and violent death, and their fears are not unfounded (see *International Comparison*, p. 480).

In response to public demands to solve these problems, politicians often feel they must "do something." As one senator remarked, "There is a mood here that if someone came to the floor and said we should barbwire the ankles of anyone who jaywalks, I suspect it would pass."[74]

The ways in which the police and the courts treat suspects were severely scrutinized during the 1960s, when civil liberties and civil rights groups focused public attention on the rights of the disadvantaged. Influenced by political currents at the time, the Supreme Court, under the leadership of Chief Justice Earl Warren, issued a series of decisions (discussed below) that interpreted the Bill of Rights as providing significant protections of the rights of the accused. Warren was a former governor of California who one of his colleagues described as holding "a simple belief in the things we now laugh at: motherhood, marriage, family, flag, and the like."[75] He also believed that the Court had a duty to actively adapt constitutional principles to modern circumstances, as the living-constitution theory says (see Chapter 15). Warren guided the Court through what one historian calls one of the "great creative periods in American public law."[76]

As the Warren Court decisions extended the rights of the accused, many law-enforcement officials claimed that the courts had forgotten about the rights of victims. An increasing number of voters agreed, favoring rigorous enforcement of laws and harsh punishments for criminals, including the death penalty. Court procedures soon became a campaign issue, and many who sought office called for tougher law enforcement. Richard Nixon's successful 1968 presidential campaign was the first to become known as the "law and order" election. After that, the issue arose frequently in national and local campaigns.

After Warren's retirement in 1969, the Supreme Court, in conjunction with changing political circumstances, began to temper its decisions on the rights of those accused of a crime. Yet, as we shall see in the remainder of this section, the post–Warren Court did not reverse but only qualified the major Warren Court decisions (see Table 16.1). Most debate over the rights of those suspected of criminal activity has focused on five constitutional provisions: (1) search and seizure, (2) immunity against self-incrimination, (3) impartial jury, (4) legal counsel, and (5) double jeopardy. These are the topics of the remainder of this section.

TABLE 16.1
KEY CHANGES IN THE RIGHTS OF THE ACCUSED: THE WARREN COURT AND LATER LIMITATIONS

• *How did voter concerns affect court decisions from the 1960s to the 1980s on the rights of the accused?*

Constitutional Post-Provision	Amendment	Extensions by Warren Court	Limitations by Warren Court
Search and seizure	4	*Mapp v. Ohio*, 1961	*United States v. Leon*, 1984
		Improperly collected evidence cannot be introduced in court.	But such evidence can be used if officers collected it in "good faith" belief that search was legal.
No self-incrimination	5	*Miranda v. Arizona*, 1966	*Harris v. New York*, 1971
		Officers must inform suspects of their rights before questioning.	But if suspects testify, evidence obtained without their "rights" can be introduced.
		Dickerson v. U.S., 2000; *Miranda* reaffirmed.	
Impartial jury	6	*Sheppard v. Maxwell*, 1966	*Nebraska Press Association v. Stuart*, 1976
		Establishes guidelines to protect jurors from biased news coverage.	But pretrial publicity does not necessarily preclude a fair trial.
Legal counsel	6	*Gideon v. Wainwright*, 1963	No limitation
		Indigent defendants are guaranteed legal counsel.	
No double jeopardy	5	*Benton v. Maryland*, 1969	No limitation
		Applies to state as well as federal trials.	

INTERNATIONAL COMPARISON

United States Has Much Higher Murder, but Not Burglary, Rates Than Most Other Countries

Election campaigns in the United States often emphasize issues of "law and order." This focus may be the result of higher rates of violent crime in the United States than in many other countries. As one expert pointed out, "The assault rate in New York and London is not that much different. But if you look at the murder rate, particularly with firearms, it's much higher."[1] The graphs here, which depict murder and burglary rates in seven countries, illustrate a similar point.

• *Why do you think the murder rate is so much higher in the United States than in other countries, whereas the rate of burglaries is about average? Do you think the Second Amendment right to "keep and bear arms" has an effect one way or the other?*

Note: Comparisons among nations should be interpreted with caution because of different definitions of crimes and methods of calculation.

[1]Adam Liptak, "Inmate Count in U.S. Dwarfs Other Nations," *New York Times,* April 23, 2008: p. A1.

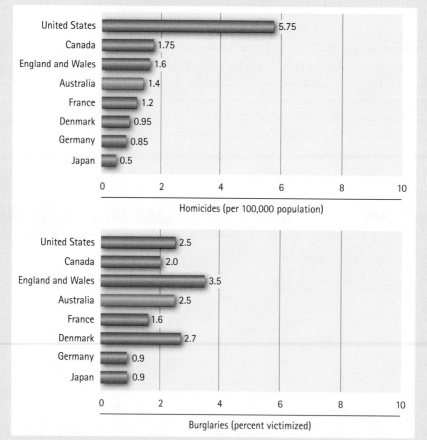

Sources: United Nations Office on Drugs and Crime, "International Homicide Statistics," May 2009, available at www.unodc.org/documents/data-and-analysis/IHS-rates-05012009.pdf, accessed March 24, 2010; United Nations Office on Drugs and Crime, "Criminal Victimisation in International Perspective," 2007, Table 8, available at http://rechten.uvt.nl/icvs/pdffiles/ICVS2004_05.pdf, accessed March 24, 2010.

Search and Seizure

CONSTITUTION, FOURTH AMENDMENT: *"The right of the people to be secure in their persons, houses, papers, and effects, against unreasonable searches and seizures, shall not be violated, and no Warrants shall issue, but upon probable cause."*

Your house cannot be searched without your permission unless a search warrant, based on evidence that a crime has probably been committed, is properly issued by a court. Prior to the Warren Court era, police officers could conduct thorough searches of a suspect's property based only on arrest warrants. In 1969, however, the Court ruled, in *Chimel v. California,* that arrest warrants only allowed officers to search a suspect's person and his or her close proximity (to prevent the suspect from retrieving a weapon, for example).[77]

If law enforcement officers illegally search a suspect's belongings and discover incriminating evidence, a legal standard known as the **exclusionary rule** prohibits that illegally obtained evidence from being admitted in a court of law. First enunciated for federal trial proceedings in 1914, the exclusionary rule was firmly established as constitutional law and applied to the states in the case of ***Mapp v. Ohio*** (1961). In that case, Cleveland police officers had searched Dollree Mapp's property without a proper warrant and had arrested her for possession of "certain lewd and lascivious books, pictures, and photographs" that they found there.[78] Saying that "[t]here is no war between the Constitution and common sense," the Court ruled that Mapp could not be convicted on the basis of such illegally obtained evidence.[79]

In the post–Warren Court years, there have been several significant conservative modifications of the principle enunciated in *Mapp*. In 1984 the Court heard a case in which a California police officer seized evidence based on a search warrant that was later discovered to be invalid. This evidence was admissible, said the Court majority, because the officer had acted in "good faith," believing the search was proper.[80] In 2000 a unanimous Court ruled that officers may sometimes stop and search people simply because they turn and run when they see police approaching. Running away, argued the Court, is cause for "reasonable suspicion," which can justify such a search.[81] Finally, in 2009, the Court ruled that evidence from unlawful searches may be admissible in court if it is not the result of "systemic error or reckless disregard of Constitutional requirements."[82]

Immunity Against Self-Incrimination

CONSTITUTION, FIFTH AMENDMENT: *"Nor shall [any person] be compelled in any criminal case to be a witness against himself."*

The Fifth Amendment protects individuals from torture and coerced confessions by saying that persons cannot be forced to testify against themselves. In ***Miranda v. Arizona*** (1966), the Warren Court gave teeth to this constitutional provision by requiring police officers to tell suspects, before questioning them, that they have the right to remain silent and that they may request the presence of an attorney. If suspects are not so "Mirandized," then any information obtained may not be presented in court. After Richard Nixon made the *Miranda* decision an issue in his 1968 presidential campaign, the Supreme Court softened the ruling somewhat. In *Harris v. New York* (1971), it found that information gathered in violation of the *Miranda* decision may be introduced in evidence if defendants testify in their own defense, and in *New York v. Quarles* (1984) the Court said that if questioning had been the result of a threat to public safety, this evidence, too, was admissible. In 2000 the Court affirmed the basic principle of the *Miranda* ruling, however, saying it has "become part of our national culture."

The *Miranda* requirements again became a source of controversy in the wake of several attempted terrorist attacks in the United States in 2009 and 2010. In these cases, FBI interrogators questioned suspects for hours before Mirandizing them. Civil libertarians argued that the suspects ought to have been advised of their rights

exclusionary rule
Legal standard that says illegally obtained evidence cannot be admitted in court.

Mapp v. Ohio
Supreme Court decision saying that any evidence obtained without a proper search warrant may not be introduced in a trial.

Miranda v. Arizona
Supreme Court decision stating that accused persons must be told by police that they need not testify against themselves.

Ernesto *Miranda*
Ernesto *Miranda*, the namesake of the "*Miranda* rights" that are read to all suspects before questioning. The Supreme Court ruled that *Miranda*'s confession was inadmissible in court because he had not been advised of his right not to answer questions.

• *The suspect in the attempted 2009 "Christmas bombing" of a Detroit-bound jet was not read his Miranda rights for nearly an hour after his arrest. FBI agents questioned him during that time, but the suspect became quiet after the Miranda warning. Did government officials act too quickly or too slowly in advising this terrorism suspect of his Miranda rights? Explain.*

immediately, while on the other side, some objected that terror suspects should not have to be Mirandized at all. The Obama administration proposed loosening the *Miranda* requirement on the grounds that security concerns may call for immediate and unrestrained questioning. As Attorney General Eric Holder put it, "if we are going to have a system that is capable of dealing in a public safety context with this threat, I think we have to give serious consideration to at least modifying that public safety exemption."[83]

Impartial Jury

> CONSTITUTION, SIXTH AMENDMENT: *"The accused shall enjoy the right to a speedy and public trial, by an impartial jury."*

The requirement that a jury be impartial is difficult to meet when a crime becomes newsworthy, because jurors may be biased by media accounts of the alleged crime both before and during the trial. The Warren Court considered these issues in *Sheppard v. Maxwell* (1966), a case that grew out of the trial of medical doctor Sam Sheppard, who was accused of murdering his wife. (The case became the basis for the television show and movie *The Fugitive.*) Sheppard complained about the excessive news coverage to which jurors were exposed, including the fact that the media were positioned in the courtroom in such a way that they could listen in on his conversations with his attorneys.[84] This complaint has been echoed in later years by such high-profile suspects as Oklahoma City bomber Timothy McVeigh and Washington, DC–area snipers John Muhammad and Lee Boyd Malvo. The Supreme Court overturned Sheppard's conviction and set forth the following guidelines in an effort to ensure impartial juries in the future:

1. Trials should be postponed until public attention has subsided.
2. Jurors should be questioned to screen out those with detailed knowledge or fixed opinions.
3. Judges should emphatically instruct jurors to consider only the evidence presented in the courtroom, not any evidence obtained from an external source.
4. A court may **sequester** jurors during a criminal trial—that is, keep them away from all sources of information about the crime other than information presented in the courtroom.
5. Courts should consider changing the **trial venue**—the place where the trial is held—in order for the case to be heard by a jury less exposed to pre-trial publicity.[85]

Although these constitutional safeguards designed to prevent the jury from becoming biased have never been reversed, the post-Warren Court, in *Nebraska Press Association v. Stuart* (1976), handed down a decision reflecting the country's more conservative political mood. It said that "pre-trial publicity—even pervasive, adverse publicity—does not inevitably lead to an unfair trial."[86]

Legal Counsel

> CONSTITUTION, SIXTH AMENDMENT: *". . . and to have Assistance of Counsel for his defense."*

The Warren Supreme Court ruled in **Gideon v. Wainwright** (1963) that all citizens accused of serious crimes, even the indigent, are constitutionally entitled to legal representation. If the accused is too poor to hire an attorney, then the court must assign one.

As a result, most states have created the office of **public defender,** an attorney whose full-time responsibility is to provide for the legal defense of indigent criminal

sequester
The housing of jurors privately during a criminal trial, keeping them away from any information about the crime other than that presented in the courtroom.

trial venue
The place where a trial is held.

Gideon v. Wainwright
Supreme Court decision in 1963 stating that all citizens accused of serious crimes, even the indigent, are constitutionally entitled to legal representation.

public defender
Attorney whose full-time responsibilities are to provide for the legal defense of indigent criminal suspects.

suspects. But this solution has had its problems. The job of a public defender is thankless, pay is low, and defenders are forced to deal with "rotten case after rotten case."[87] Furthermore, public defender systems and standards vary widely from state to state and, in some cases, from county to county.[88]

Double Jeopardy

> CONSTITUTION, FIFTH AMENDMENT: *"Nor shall any person be subject for the same offence to be twice put in jeopardy of life or limb."*

The Warren Court ruled in *Benton v. Maryland* (1969) that states cannot try a person twice for the same offense, thereby placing the defendant in **double jeopardy.** Despite this rule, the Supreme Court, in an old decision that has never been overturned, has said that a person can be tried in federal courts, even if acquitted in a state court. As noted in Chapter 15, the decision was made because the same conduct may constitute a violation of both state and federal criminal statutes, and both levels of government can prosecute without technically placing the defendant in double jeopardy.

double jeopardy
Fifth Amendment provision that prohibits prosecution for the same offense twice.

Rights in Practice

Habeas Corpus

> CONSTITUTION, ARTICLE ONE: *"The privilege of the Writ of Habeas Corpus shall not be suspended, unless when in Cases of Rebellion or Invasion the public Safety may require it."*

If a prisoner believes his or her constitutional rights have been violated, he or she may file for a **writ of habeas corpus,** a judicial order that a prisoner be brought before a judge to determine the legality of his or her imprisonment. A prisoner may petition for such a hearing for a variety of reasons, usually having to do with violation of procedural rights, and may do so before trial, during a trial, or after conviction.

writ of habeas corpus
A judicial order that a prisoner be brought before a judge to determine the legality of his or her imprisonment.

Legal scholars have called the writ of habeas corpus "the Great Writ" because it preserves the right of the accused to due process of law. Even after having been convicted of a crime and after having exhausted all normal appeals, a prisoner may still file for a writ of habeas corpus. Similarly, if a person is detained indefinitely without trial, he or she may file for a writ of habeas corpus, arguing that his or her right to a speedy trial has been violated.

Terrorism Suspects   After the 9/11 terrorist attacks, civil libertarians used writs of habeas corpus to challenge the Bush administration's indefinite detention of so-called "enemy combatants." These challenges occasioned a series of Supreme Court rulings affirming the writ of habeas corpus, both for U.S. citizens and for noncitizens imprisoned on U.S. territory. In 2004, the Supreme Court ruled that Yasser Hamdi, a U.S. citizen who had been imprisoned indefinitely as an accused al Qaeda affiliate, had the right to appear before a judge. In a similar case, the Court also said that noncitizens detained at the Guantanamo Bay naval base in Cuba must be granted an opportunity to legally contest their detention.[89] In the Military Commissions Act of 2006, Congress attempted to overrule this decision, denying habeas corpus for the Guantanamo Bay inmates. But in 2008 the Court again repudiated this approach in the case of *Boumediene v. Bush.* "The laws and Constitution are designed to survive, and remain in force, in extraordinary times," wrote Justice Kennedy in his majority opinion.[90]

The *Boumediene v. Bush* ruling did not end the debate over the rights that should be accorded to terrorism suspects, however. President Barack Obama reaffirmed the need to try some suspects via the military commission system, even as he vowed to close the Guantanamo Bay facility as quickly as possible. But Attorney General Eric Holder caused controversy by choosing to prosecute some of the most high-profile terrorist suspects in the civilian court system, including high ranking al Qaeda operative Khalid Sheikh Muhammad.

Holder's supporters pointed to the successes of the civilian court system, including the guilty plea in 2010 from Najibullah Zazi, who had been charged with plotting to set off a bomb on a New York City subway. They also pointed out that the Supreme Court has ruled since 1896 that foreign citizens charged with crimes on U.S. soil must be accorded the same legal rights as everyone else.[91] Holder's critics argued that the U.S. war against extremists necessitated wartime judicial measures. After all, Abraham Lincoln had suspended the writ of habeas corpus for some rebel agitators, and Franklin Roosevelt had set up a military tribunal to prosecute eight Nazi saboteurs who had crept ashore on Long Island in 1942. The question of what rights ought to be accorded to terrorism suspects continues to challenge the U.S. legal system.

The Plea Bargain If a case is newsworthy, constitutional procedures are generally observed: The public is looking on, and those participating in the trial must take political pressures into account. But the reality of justice in most criminal cases is very different from that in the most high-profile cases. Hardly anyone accused of a crime is actually tried by a jury, and nearly all those convicted of a crime testify against themselves. The accused have their rights, to be sure, but very few actually choose to exercise them. Most of the time, it is to their advantage not to do so.[92]

Trial court judges depend on the willingness of prosecutors and defenders to settle cases before going to trial. The number of people accused of crimes is high, the list of cases on the court docket is seemingly endless, court personnel resources are limited, and court time is precious. To speed the criminal justice process, defenders and prosecutors are usually expected to try to arrange a **plea bargain,** an agreement between prosecution and defense that the accused will admit to having committed a crime, provided that other charges are dropped and a reduced sentence is recommended. The Supreme Court has approved of this transformation of the rights of the accused into bargaining chips that can be used "to cop a plea." In the words of Justice Burger, plea bargaining is "an essential component of the administration of justice. Properly administered, it is to be encouraged."[93]

plea bargain
Agreement between prosecution and defense that the accused will admit to having committed a crime, provided that other charges are dropped and the recommended sentence is shortened.

16.5

Assess the relationship of the **right of privacy** to sexual behavior, abortion, and information-age technologies.

right of privacy
Right to be free of government interference in those aspects of one's personal life that do not affect others.

The Right of Privacy

CONSTITUTION, NINTH AMENDMENT: *"The enumeration in the Constitution, of certain rights, shall not be construed to deny or disparage others retained by the people."*

The civil liberties discussed thus far are explicitly mentioned in the Bill of Rights. In addition, the Supreme Court has enunciated another liberty, the **right of privacy,** the right to be free of government interference in those aspects of our personal lives that do not affect others. Although the right of privacy is not explicitly mentioned in the Constitution, the Ninth Amendment says that some rights may be retained by the people even though they are not enumerated. The Third Amendment, prohibiting the quartering of soldiers in homes, and the Fourth Amendment, protecting people from "unreasonable searches and seizures," also seem to be motivated by an underlying concern for personal privacy.

Some constitutional scholars believe that the judicial power to identify any right not explicitly mentioned in the Constitution should be exercised with great caution, because abuse of this power would give an unelected judiciary the authority to overrule the will of elected public officials. "Where constitutional materials do not clearly specify [a right]," judicial scholar Robert Bork has said, "the judge must stick close to the text and history, and their fair implications, and not construct any new rights."[94]

Nevertheless, in the 1960s and 1970s the Court went a long way toward recognizing a right to privacy. In this section, first, we consider the Court's rulings on this issue with regard to private sexual behavior and abortion. Finally, we consider the growing concerns about personal privacy in the information age.

Regulation of Sexual Behavior

The modern right to privacy owes its existence to the Supreme Court's ruling in *Griswold v. Connecticut* (1965).[95] Estelle Griswold, executive director of Planned Parenthood, was fined $100 for violating a Connecticut law prohibiting the use of contraceptives. Declaring the law unconstitutional, Justice William Douglas discerned "a right of privacy older than the Bill of Rights." "Would we allow the police to search the sacred precincts of marital bedrooms for telltale signs of the use of contraceptives?" asked Douglas. "The very idea is repulsive to the notions of privacy surrounding the marriage relationship." In a dissent, Justice Potter Stewart declared the Ninth Amendment "but a truism" that could hardly be used to "annul a law passed by the elected representatives of the people."[96]

Despite Stewart's objection, there is little doubt that a national majority agreed with the Supreme Court that a married couple should have the right to use contraceptives. But would the Supreme Court be equally protective of the right of privacy when the actions in question were not approved by a majority of the public? This question arose in 1986 in *Bowers v. Hardwick,* when the Court was asked to rule on a Georgia law prohibiting sodomy under which two homosexuals had been convicted. Noting that laws against sodomy existed at the time the Constitution was written, the Court majority found no reason to think that its authors intended to exempt homosexual behavior from state regulation. In the 2003 case of *Lawrence v. Texas,* however, the Court revisited this issue and made an almost complete reversal. In a very unusual repudiation of a case so recently decided, Justice Kennedy wrote in the majority opinion that "Bowers was not correct when it was decided, and it is not correct today. It ought not to remain binding precedent."[97]

Celebrating a Landmark Ruling

Activists celebrate the Supreme Court's 2003 ruling in *Lawrence v. Texas,* which declared antisodomy laws unconstitutional.

• *Which theory of Constitutional interpretation (see Chapter 15) do you think is most likely to lead to a broad understanding of privacy rights?*

Although these rulings are clearly at odds with one another, they are consistent with one measure: public opinion. In 1986, when *Bowers* was decided, a majority of those surveyed believed that homosexual relations should be outlawed. But, by 2001, polls found that Americans favored legalizing homosexual behavior by a margin of 54 to 42 percent. Similarly, 85 percent of people thought gays and lesbians should have equal rights in the workplace—a figure up more than 25 percentage points from the early 1980s. In deciding the *Lawrence* case in favor of privacy rights, the Supreme Court once again shifted with changing public sentiment.[98]

Abortion: Right to Life or Right to Choose?

Although the Court has left uncertain the range of sexual acts to which the right of privacy extends, it ruled in *Roe v. Wade* (1973) that the right of privacy was broad enough to include at least a partial right of abortion. The case arose out of a request from Norma McCorvey, using the pseudonym Jane Roe. Roe, seeking to terminate a pregnancy, asked for a judgment declaring unconstitutional the Texas law prohibiting abortion. Writing for the Court majority, Justice Harry Blackmun said that the woman's right of privacy was so fundamental that it could be abridged only when the state interest in doing so was compelling. Dissenting justices objected to judicial interference with a state legislature's right to balance a woman's rights against the welfare of her unborn child.

Roe v. Wade launched two powerful political movements that have helped to shape American politics in the three decades since the Court's decision. The "right-to-life" crusade was organized by Catholic and other religious groups opposed to abortion on the grounds that inasmuch as human life begins at conception, abortion cannot be distinguished from infanticide. These "right-to-life" supporters became actively engaged in state and national politics, lobbying legislatures to impose as many restraints on abortion as the courts would allow.

Opposition to "right-to-life" groups was at first weak and uncertain, mainly because many of those who supported a woman's constitutional "right of choice" thought it had been permanently protected by the Supreme Court decision. But as the "right-to-life" movement gained momentum and it appeared more likely that *Roe v. Wade* would be overturned, the "right-to-choose" movement gained in strength and aggressiveness. Abortion-rights activists became an important force in Democratic Party politics.

Both sides of the controversy waited anxiously for the 1992 court decision in *Planned Parenthood of Southeastern Pennsylvania v. Casey*.[99] The organization challenged a Pennsylvania law that placed a number of restrictions on the right to an abortion that went well beyond what seemed permissible under *Roe v. Wade*. The Court majority satisfied neither side entirely, crafting a compromise that upheld some of the Pennsylvania restrictions on abortion but—respecting the rule of *stare decisis* (see Chapter 15)—left intact the principle that states cannot simply outlaw all abortions.

In the words of Justice Sandra Day O'Connor, "Where . . . the Court decides a case in such a way as to resolve the sort of intensely divisive controversy reflected in Roe . . . the promise of constancy, once given, binds its maker for as long as . . . the understanding of the issue has not changed so fundamentally as to render the commitment obsolete."[100] In other words, the Court said it was not changing its mind.

In *Casey*, the Court majority once again adopted a position very close to that of the average American voter. It permitted restrictions (such as a requirement that teenagers obtain parental consent) endorsed by a majority of voters but rejected those most people think are not warranted (such as a requirement that a married woman obtain the consent of her husband). In the 2007 decision of *Gonzales* v. *Carhart*, the Supreme Court again sided with public opinion in upholding a ban on certain late-term abortions. In 2003 Congress had passed a law prohibiting so-called "partial birth abortions," and the Supreme Court concluded that this type of restriction did not place an "undue burden" on a woman's right to an abortion.[101] Even in matters as sensitive as the right of privacy, the Court seems to be influenced by majority opinion, as expressed in the outcome of recent elections.

Privacy in the Information Age

The Internet and related technologies have sparked an information revolution, but technology also reduces the privacy of individuals. A number of free or low-cost websites, for example, allow researchers to uncover all publicly available data about a person, from criminal records to property holdings to professional licensing information. Armed with such details, businesses can target consumers for nuisance appeals, or—much worse—unscrupulous outlaws can commit the growing crime of "identity theft." Credit-card records and other financial data are protected by 1970s-era laws that allow customers to review their files and demand corrections, but some lawmakers and experts have called for strict new laws that would guarantee consumer privacy. Companies like Facebook and Google have drawn criticism in recent years for failing to protect individual privacy in social networking and mapping applications.

Private firms are, of course, not the only ones in the information business. Whereas some advocates urge the government to protect personal privacy with new legislation, others fear that the government itself will be the biggest intruder into the private lives of average Americans. The case of the National Security Agency's surveillance programs, discussed at the beginning of this chapter, shows only one way that the government can monitor citizens. Passengers boarding planes at some airports now have their faces electronically scanned and checked against databases of known criminals.[102] In 2005 Congress enacted the "Real ID Law" that standardizes data requirements and security measures for driver's licenses—a first step toward what some would call a "national identity card system." And there are already more than 2 million video cameras stationed in public places in the United States, from street corners to subway tunnels, which may soon be used to search for and apprehend dangerous suspects.[103]

Many supporters of these efforts argue that they achieve the goal of protecting Americans from criminals and terrorists without compromising citizens' fundamental freedoms. As one expert put it, "We as a people are willing to trade a little less privacy for a little more security. . . . If using more intrusive technology is the only way to prevent horrible crimes, chances are that we'll decide to use the technology, then adjust our sense of what is private and what is not."[104] Public opinion confirms this claim. One poll, for example, found that a majority of Americans support increased security checks for travelers, monitoring of credit card transactions, camera surveillance on the streets, and a national I.D. system.[105] More intrusive government action wins less approval, however: The public opposes email and cell phone monitoring, and a majority rejects the suggestion that, to protect against terrorism "it will be necessary for the average person to give up some civil liberties."[106] Critics fear that even the technological innovations that appear innocuous will lead to increased government suppression of dissent. One authority cautioned that "law enforcement has a history of snooping on 'enemies' that are a far cry from terrorists, such as Martin Luther King, Jr. and John Lennon."[107]

Continued on page 491

School Choice: Vouchers and Charter Schools

The Issue

Should parents be given a choice of the school their child attends? Would competition among schools prompt them to improve their performance?

Background

Although per-pupil expenditures in constant dollars have more than tripled since the early 1970s, American students have only made modest—if any—academic advancements.[1] Math, reading, and science performances of 9-year-olds have improved, but these gains disappear by the time students reach the age of 17. At that age, students score at the same level as their peers did more than a generation ago.[2]

Some policy experts have proposed to improve schools by introducing competition. School choice programs allow parents to send their children to a school other than the one assigned to them by the local school district. The most controversial forms of school choice are vouchers and charter schools.

Vouchers are scholarships that allow students to attend a private school. Vouchers are typically offered to students from low-income families or to students attending chronically underperforming schools.[3] Participating private schools are usually asked to accept all eligible students who choose to attend them, regardless of academic aptitude, behavioral history, and religious background. When applicants surpass available seats, scholarships are awarded via lottery.

Charter schools are privately managed schools that operate under a performance contract. Although they are publicly funded and are generally open to all students within the district, charters operate free from most regulations to which traditional public schools must conform; for example, only a few find their policies subject to collective bargaining agreements with teachers' unions. Consequently, charters have more flexibility to innovate and provide alternative curricula. In exchange for this freedom, most charter schools must have their charter renewed every five years.

Since 1990, voucher programs have been implemented in Milwaukee, Cleveland, and the District of Columbia, among other places, although new students cannot be admitted to the DC program after 2010.[4] Nationwide, approximately 64,000 children received vouchers during the 2009-2010 academic year.[5]

Charter schools have spread more rapidly, however. Since 1991, 40 states and the District of Columbia have enacted charter school laws permitting the creation of this type of public school, with various degrees of flexibility. However, in spite of a steady increase in charter school enrollment (see Figure 1), the more than one million students attending one of the 4,200 charter schools in 2008 represent only 2.4 percent of all public school students.[6]

The Politics of School Choice

Most Republicans find school choice consistent with their political philosophy that supports free markets and small government. In 2004, for example, George W. Bush won congressional support for a pilot voucher program for the District of Columbia. Meanwhile, most Democrats, who have close ties to the union movement and a history of support for public institutions, are skeptical of many forms of choice, especially vouchers. The Democratic-controlled Congress forbade new entrants into the voucher program in 2010.

But positions do not always break out along partisan lines. President Barack Obama supports charter schools—and has pressed state governments to reduce restrictions on them—while some suburban Republicans think vouchers are just another form of charity for inner-city families. Indeed, some school choice initiatives, with their focus on helping inner-city, low-income children, have created unusual alliances between small government proponents and civil rights advocates. The bipartisan support of charter schools led even the teachers' unions to start some charters of their own.

Opposing Viewpoints on School Choice

For School Choice

> Proponents of school choice say that families should have the liberty to select the school of their choice, public or private, and still receive government help to cover the costs of their children's education. They also claim that competition among schools will improve school performance. In addition, they point out that higher income people already have a choice of school because they can afford to move into neighborhoods with good schools. School choice is widespread in America—unless you are poor. Affluent families have choice because they can move to different neighborhoods or communities, send their children to private schools, or supplement schooling with tutors and enrichment programs. Lower-income and working-class families, meanwhile, are typically trapped with one option—a school in need of improvement.
>
> —Black Alliance for Educational Options,
> www.baeo.org/programs?program_id=5, accessed June 29, 2008

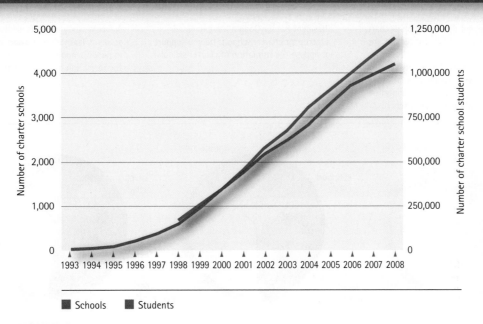

FIGURE 1

CHARTER SCHOOLS AND CHARTER ENROLLMENT

Charter schools are increasing in popularity, but the vast majority of students still attend conventional schools.

• *Based on this graph, do you think the number of charter schools depends on the party in power in the White House?*

Sources: U.S. Department of Education, Common Core of Data, http://nces.ed.gov/ccd, accessed June 29, 2008; and Center for Education Reform, www.edreform.com/charter_schools, accessed June 29, 2008.

Against School Choice

Opponents argue that school choice programs in general, and vouchers in particular, damage the education system by taking resources away from traditional public schools and reducing public control over an institution financed with public funds. They also contend that vouchers worsen the racial, ethnic, and economic injustices already present in our social fabric:

> A pure voucher system would only encourage economic, racial, ethnic, and religious stratification in our society. . . . Despite desperate efforts to make the voucher debate about "school choice" and improving opportunities for low-income students, vouchers remain an elitist strategy. . . . [P]rivatization strategies are about subsidizing tuition for students in private schools, not expanding opportunities for low-income children.

> —National Education Association, www.nea.org/vouchers/index.html, accessed June 29, 2008

What Do Americans Believe?

Support for charter schools is fairly evenly divided, but it changes depending on whether an individual is told that the president supports the idea or whether a research project has found that students learn more in charter schools (see Figure 2). Why do you think some Americans respond differently to questions when told about presidential support or the results of a study?

Is School Choice Constitutional?

In 2002 the Supreme Court ruled 5 to 4 in favor of the constitutionality of the Cleveland voucher program in *Zelman v. Simmons-Harris,* denying that parents' use of public funds to send their children to a religious school violated the Establishment Clause of the First Amendment. The Court deemed the program to be neutral with respect to religion because it simply permitted parents "to exercise genuine choice among options."[7]

The Supreme Court decision aside, challenges against voucher programs continue to be fought in state courts on the basis that they violate state constitutions. A pilot voucher program in Colorado was struck down by a state court, because it was found to violate the requirement that schools be locally controlled that is part of the Colorado state constitution. The program was determined to strip school districts of control over locally raised funds and of "any discretion over the character of instruction participating students will receive at district expense."[8] In early 2006, school choice opponents had another major victory when the Florida Supreme Court struck down the state's voucher program on the grounds that the state constitution requires all schools to be uniform."[9]

Many states permit the formation of charter schools, which are publicly funded but are not managed by the local school board. These schools are expected to meet promised objectives, but are exempt from many state regulations. Do you support or oppose the formation of charter schools?

President Barack Obama has expressed support for charter schools. Do you support or oppose the formation of charter schools?

A recent study presents evidence that students learn more in charter schools than in public schools. Do you support or oppose the formation of charter schools?

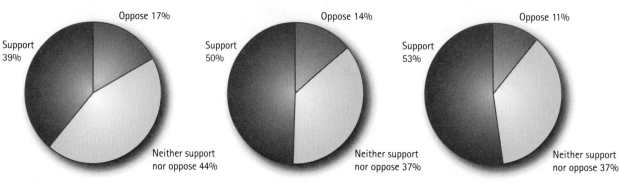

FIGURE 2

PUBLIC OPINION ON CHARTER SCHOOLS

The public differs on whether to support charter schools, depending on how the question is worded.

• *Which version of the question do you think does the best job of posing the issue to voters?*

Source: Education Next Poll, Fall 2009, http://educationnext.org/files/pepg2009.pdf, accessed May 2, 2010.

What Do You Think?

1. Are vouchers a good option for increasing the educational opportunities for low-income children? What other options are available, in your view?

2. Do you think that competition among schools would spur higher performance? Or do you think public schools would suffer needlessly?

On the Web

School choice is a subject of heated national debate. To conscientiously investigate this controversial issue and the arguments pro and con, be sure to go to the websites of both those groups that are in favor of voucher programs and charter schools and those groups that are opposed. In your opinion, which website(s) presents the most convincing argument?

PRO

The Center for Education Reform

www.edreform.com

Cato Institute

www.cato.org

The Heritage Foundation

www.heritage.org

Milton and Rose D. Friedman Foundation

www.friedmanfoundation.org

CON

American Federation of Teachers

www.aft.org

National Education Association

www.nea.org

Economic Policy Institute

www.epinet.org

---

[1]For the 1970–1971 school year, an average of $4,682 (in constant 2004–2005 dollars) was spent per pupil in public elementary and secondary schools. For the 2002–2003 school year, the average per-pupil expenditure had increased to $9,788 (also in constant 2004–2005 dollars). U.S. Department of Education, Institute of Education Sciences, National Center for Education Statistics, *Digest of Education Statistics,* 2005, Table 162: Total and current expenditure per pupil in public elementary and secondary schools: Selected years, 1919–1920 through 2002–2003.
[2]U.S. Department of Education, Institute of Education Sciences, National Center for Education Statistics, *NAEP 2004 Trends in Academic Progress: Three Decades of Student Performance in Reading and Mathematics,* July 2005; and U.S. Department of Education, Institute of Education Sciences, National Center for Education Statistics, *NAEP 1999 Trends in Academic Progress: Three Decades of Student Performance,* August 2000.

[3]Voucher programs only offered to students with disabilities are excluded from this discussion because they are not justified on the same grounds.
[4]In addition, Ohio enacted a pilot voucher program that began its operations in 2006–2007; and Vermont and Maine have voucher-like tuitioning programs, which provide scholarships to children residing in districts without public schools to attend either a secular private school or a public school in another district.
[5]Alliance for School Choice, *2009-2010 Yearbook*, www.alliance-forschoolchoice.org/UploadedFiles/ResearchResources/ASC_Yearbook_2010_FINAL.pdf, accessed May 2, 2010, p. 17.

[6]According to the Center for Education Reform, in 2007–2008 there were 4,200 charter schools serving 1.2 million students. The National Center for Education Statistics projected that in the fall of 2007 49.61 million students would enroll in one of the public elementary and secondary schools in the country. Sources: Center for Education Reform, "National Charter School Data At-a-Glance," and U.S. Department of Education, "Digest of Education Statistics, 2007," Table 2.
[7]*Zelman v. Simmons-Harris,* 536 U.S. 662 (2002).
[8]*Owens v. Colorado Congress of Parents,* No. 03–0364 (Colo. June 28, 2004).
[9]*Holmes v. Bush,* No. 04-2323 (Fla. Jan. 5, 2006).

Continued from page 487

Because technology has advanced so quickly, the Supreme Court has not yet had time to establish a clear set of rules with which it will interpret the Constitution in cases involving information-age privacy. But a 2001 ruling suggests that the Court remains concerned with protecting the privacy of individuals. In the case of *Kyllo v. United States,* the Court considered whether police departments could make use of thermal imaging equipment to examine a suspect's home without a search warrant. Officers suspected that the defendant, Danny Kyllo, was illegally growing marijuana in his home, and they used the thermal equipment to check for the hot halide lamps necessary to grow the plants indoors. Police argued that no violation of the Fourth Amendment's ban on "search and seizure" had occurred, because officers did not actually enter the suspect's home, but Kyllo argued that his home had for all practical purposes been unconstitutionally searched without a warrant. In a 5 to 4 opinion that surprised many observers, the Court sided with Kyllo. Justice Scalia, writing for the majority, argued that, although "It would be foolish to contend that the degree of privacy secured to citizens by the Fourth Amendment has been entirely unaffected by the advance of technology," nevertheless, "we must take the long view, from the original meaning of the Fourth Amendment forward."[108]

CHAPTER SUMMARY

16.1 Trace the development of the Bill of Rights and its expansion to the states.

The Bill of Rights remained pretty much a dead letter until the Civil War ended slavery. Only as key provisions of the Bill of Rights were gradually and selectively incorporated into the due process clause of the Fourteenth Amendment did they become effective components of the country's constitutional makeup.

16.2 Outline the rights and limitations of freedom of speech, press, and assembly.

Although the courts are expected to protect civil liberties against majority tyranny, most of the time the Supreme Court has followed, not led, public opinion. In 1919 the Supreme Court said speech could not be prohibited unless it created a clear and present danger to a peaceful society, but it initially applied the doctrine in a way consistent with the common-law bad tendency test, by convicting a socialist for his political speech. Although it protected minority dissent during the 1930s, it later elaborated the fighting words doctrine, which declared certain phrases to be the equivalent of violent acts. Not until McCarthyism had been rejected by elected officials did a Court majority say free speech was a fundamental freedom that required special protection.

16.3 Distinguish the two clauses guaranteeing freedom of religion and illustrate how they can conflict.

Freedom of religion is protected by two separate clauses in the First Amendment. The establishment of religion clause prohibits the propagation of religious beliefs by public institutions and direct aid to churches, religious schools, and other religious institutions. The free exercise of religion clause prevents the government from interfering with the religious activities of citizens. At times, the two clauses come into conflict, as the issue of school vouchers has shown.

16.4   **Outline the procedural rights of the accused.**

When balancing the rights of the accused against the need to maintain social order, Supreme Court decisions have fluctuated with changes in public opinion. During the 1960s, the Warren Court expanded the rights of the accused by tightening the rules under which police and prosecutors could obtain evidence, question suspects, and hold trials. After "law and order" became a campaign issue, the Supreme Court modified, although it did not reverse, many of these decisions.

16.5   **Assess the relationship of the right of privacy to sexual behavior, abortion, and information-age technologies.**

The Court has also discerned a right of privacy, despite the fact that no such right is mentioned explicitly in the Bill of Rights. This right of privacy is broad enough to cover private, consensual sexual behavior as well as to include a woman's right to terminate a pregnancy. But it is not absolute. As interpreted by the Court, the right of privacy does not preclude regulation of abortions, especially for minors and after the first trimester of pregnancy. The right of privacy discerned by the Court comes very close to the viewpoint held by most Americans. The country's definition of civil liberties seems to depend as much on the thinking of its citizens as on its judicial system.

---

mypoliscilab EXERCISES

Apply what you learned in this chapter on MyPoliSciLab.

Read on mypoliscilab.com

eText: Chapter 16

Study and Review on mypoliscilab.com

Pre-Test

Post-Test

Chapter Exam

Flashcards

Watch on mypoliscilab.com

Video: D.C.'s Right to Bear Arms

Video: Funeral Protestors Push the Limits of Free Speech

Explore on mypoliscilab.com

Simulation: You Are a Police Officer

Simulation: You Are a Supreme Court Justice Deciding a Free Speech Case

Simulation: Balancing Liberty and Security in a Time of War

Comparative: Comparing Civil Liberties

Timeline: Civil Liberties and National Security

KEY TERMS

bad tendency test, p. 468

balancing doctrine, p. 470

civil liberties, p. 464

civil rights amendments, p. 465

clear and present danger doctrine, p. 468

commercial speech, p. 474

double jeopardy, p. 483

due process clause, p. 466

establishment of religion clause, p. 475

exclusionary rule, p. 481

fighting words doctrine, p. 470

free exercise of religion clause, p. 475

fundamental freedoms doctrine, p. 471

Gideon v. Wainwright, p. 482

Lemon test, p. 476

libel, p. 475

Mapp v. Ohio, p. 481

Miranda v. Arizona, p. 481

SUGGESTED READINGS

Of General Interest

Abraham, Henry J. and Barbara A. Perry. *Freedom and the Court: Civil Rights and Liberties in the United States.* 8th ed. Lawrence: University Press of Kansas, 2003. Comprehensive discussion of the Constitution's protections of civil rights and civil liberties.

Bogira, Steve. *Courtroom 302: A Year Behind the Scenes in an American Criminal Courthouse.* New York: Alfred A. Knopf, 2005. A journalist chronicles the cases that come before one Chicago court.

Rehnquist, William H. *All the Laws but One: Civil Liberties in Wartime.* New York: Knopf, 1998. The late chief justice of the Supreme Court considers instances in which civil liberties have been sacrificed for the sake of security, focusing on cases from the Civil War and World War II.

Focused Studies

Ackerman, Bruce. *Before the Next Attack: Preserving Civil Liberties in an Age of Terrorism.* New Haven, CT: Yale University Press, 2007. Makes a controversial argument that the United States should have an "emergency constitution" that could grant broad, but temporary, powers to a government racing against time to prevent a terrorist strike.

Garrow, David J. *Liberty and Sexuality, Updated Edition.* New York: Macmillan, 1998. Comprehensive account of the legal debate over abortion before and after *Roe.*

Lewis, Anthony. *Make No Law: The Sullivan Case and the First Amendment.* New York: Random House, 1992. Excellent, readable case study of the politics of the *Sullivan* decision and the evolution of the free-speech doctrine.

Wice, Paul B. *Public Defenders and the American Justice System.* Westport, CT: Praeger, 2005. A detailed case study of public defenders in Newark, NJ, which shows the role that public defenders play in the modern justice system.

Zittrain, Jonathan. *The Future of the Internet and How to Stop It.* New Haven: Yale University Press, 2009. Argues that new information technology may place privacy at risk and stifle innovation.

ON THE WEB

www.aclu.org

The American Civil Liberties Union provides legal assistance to many who feel that their civil liberties have been violated. The sometimes-controversial organization has a detailed website outlining its agenda for promoting civil liberties, as well as describing the history and present status of civil liberties law.

www.freedomforum.org

The First Amendment freedoms of speech and of religion may seem clear-cut, but some First Amendment issues remain controversial, as we have seen in this chapter. The Freedom Forum is a nonpartisan foundation that publicizes and analyzes current issues involving First Amendment freedoms.

http://religiousfreedom.lib.virginia.edu

Thomas Jefferson, founder of the University of Virginia, argued for a "wall of separation" between government and religion. The University of Virginia's Religious Freedom Page carries on the Jeffersonian tradition by providing analysis of many key Supreme Court decisions concerning religious freedom and by including links to other key religious freedom organizations.

www.naral.org

www.nrlc.org

Does a constitutional right of privacy protect a woman's right to have an abortion? The National Abortion and Reproductive Rights Action League (NARAL) says yes, whereas the National Right to Life Committee (NRLC) disagrees.

www.eff.org

www.cdt.org

As we have seen in this chapter, a growing area of controversy regarding civil liberties concerns issues of information technology and privacy on the Internet. The Electronic Frontier Foundation (EFF) and the Center for Democracy and Technology (CDT) follow issues and provide information about free speech and privacy in the information age.

17 Civil Rights

CHAPTER OUTLINE

LEARNING OBJECTIVES

17.1 Establish the origins of the struggle for civil rights in developments from after the Civil War through the 1940s.

17.2 Trace the rise of the civil rights movement following *Brown* and its subsequent decline in strength and assess results so far.

17.3 Outline civil rights issues for, and efforts undertaken by, minorities other than African Americans.

17.4 Assess the civil rights objectives achieved by women and ongoing issues.

17.5 Describe judicial and legislative victories for Americans with disabilities.

Race and Gender in the 2008 Campaign

Barack Obama was in the middle of answering CNN anchor Wolf Blitzer's question about poverty during a Democratic primary debate in South Carolina in January 2008. To his left and right stood Hillary Clinton and John Edwards, his remaining competitors. Poverty was an issue that should unite people of all races, Obama argued. Unfortunately, the media focused instead on divisions between groups of people. "And, I mean, I'm not entirely faulting the media," Obama admitted, acknowledging that the diverse pool of candidates naturally drew attention to issues of race and gender. "There's no doubt that in a race where you've got an African American, a woman," he paused. "And John. . . ." The audience erupted in laughter.[1]

The fact that the white male on the stage that night seemed unusual was one sign that the 2008 presidential race was truly unprecedented. Hillary Clinton and Barack Obama were living symbols of how far the country had come over the last century. At her rallies, Clinton met women in their 90s who could remember when only men were allowed to vote. Obama was born in the summer of 1961 as hundreds of "freedom riders" rode integrated buses in southern states to test a Supreme Court ruling that desegregated interstate transportation.

When the Democratic campaign got under way in mid-2007, those who had fought for the equal rights of women and minorities seemed dazzled by the diverse candidate pool. Not only were Clinton and Obama running, but New Mexico Governor Bill Richardson sought to be the nation's first Hispanic president. "Isn't it a wonderful time we live in?" asked one interest-group leader. An Iowa

caucus-goer agreed that the campaign showed "the maturing of American society." Race and gender, he said, "are basically irrelevant."[2]

But no sooner had a crowd started chanting "race doesn't matter" at Obama's Iowa victory party than the campaign began to change in ways that deflated the early optimism. At a New Hampshire rally for Clinton, two men (later discovered to be radio show pranksters) leaped up waving signs and yelling "iron my shirt." Days later, responding to an Obama speech that lauded the accomplishments of Martin Luther King, Jr., Clinton pointed out that Lyndon Johnson—a seasoned veteran of Washington politics like herself—was instrumental in passing the civil rights legislation that King had dreamed of. Obama supporters took offense, seeing the remark as a slight of the slain civil rights leader.

Battle lines began to harden. In New Hampshire, women voters rallied to Clinton; in the South Carolina primary, African Americans flooded to Obama. Former President Bill Clinton compared Obama's South Carolina victory to the losing campaigns of Jesse Jackson in the 1980s—a comment that the Obama team saw as an attempt to marginalize him as "the black candidate." Clinton supporters took Obama's remark that Clinton was "likable enough" as a patronizing slight. A series of incidents built up that collectively brought the campaign down from its optimistic beginnings. Dismayed party officials began to worry that the battle might become toxic enough to damage the party's prospects in the fall. "If the Democrats are drawn into a victimization contest," wrote one columnist, "the winner will be John McCain."[3]

But Republicans were having their own problems. Crowds booed the party's candidate, John McCain, at a speech he made in Memphis to commemorate the fortieth anniversary of Martin Luther King's murder. Critics had pointed to his vote in 1983 against creating a holiday honoring King—a vote McCain said he regretted. Republican leaders had difficulty recruiting minority candidates for Congress and state offices, a discouraging problem for the party that counted among its number the first African American secretary of state and the first Hispanic attorney general.[4]

In the heat of the primary season, Barack Obama's campaign was thrown off balance by a series of video clips (posted on the media-sharing site YouTube) depicting Obama's former pastor, Jeremiah Wright, making divisive, racially motivated statements in his sermons. Wright condemned the United States for sponsoring what he called "state terrorism" around the world and advanced conspiratorial claims that the U.S. government invented the AIDS virus "as a means of genocide against people of color."[5] Obama repeatedly denounced these statements and, in a detailed speech on the subject of race, urged Americans to embark on an honest discussion that could help overcome their divisions. "If we walk away now, if we simply retreat into our respective corners," said Obama, "we will never be able to come together and solve challenges like health care, or education, or the need to find good jobs for every American."[6]

Making the Connection

The debate over race and gender in 2008 raises broader questions. What does it mean to say the Constitution is color-blind? When may people be legally classified by race, ethnicity, or gender? Do the courts define the issues, and then voters and elected officials follow? Or is it the other way around? In this chapter, we discuss the struggle for civil rights for African Americans, other minority groups, women, and the disabled. These struggles shaped—and continue to shape—the context in which modern debates over civil rights occur.

In most cases, we find that, in characterizing the legal meaning of civil rights, the Supreme Court followed trends initiated by the public debates and coalition building that make up electoral politics. As Justice Ruth Bader Ginsburg once observed, "the Court generally follows, it does not lead, changes taking place elsewhere in society."[7] Nonetheless, the Court has played a major role by codifying civil rights policy into constitutional doctrine. We explore these issues by first discussing the beginnings of the struggle for the civil rights of African Americans, moving on to examine how civil rights activists persuaded the Supreme Court to become involved. Next, we discuss how the Supreme Court's interpretation of the Fourteenth Amendment's equal protection clause shaped the development of civil rights. Finally, we detail the steps that other groups, such as women, gays and lesbians, and the disabled, have taken to ensure their civil rights, and we note how the courts and elected officials have responded.

17.1

Establish the origins of the struggle for civil rights in developments from after the Civil War through the 1940s.

The Origins of Civil Rights

CONSTITUTION, FOURTEENTH AMENDMENT: *"No state shall . . . deny to any person within its jurisdiction the equal protection of the laws."*

Although the terms "civil liberties" and "civil rights" are often used interchangeably, there is an important distinction between them. Civil liberties are the freedoms that together preserve the rights of a free people (see Chapter 16, p. 463). **Civil rights** embody the general right to equal treatment under the law. In Chapter 16, we emphasized how important the due process clause of the Fourteenth Amendment has been to the protection of civil liberties in the United States. The civil rights of Americans are guarded by a no less important provision in the Fourteenth Amendment, the **equal protection clause,** which says that no state can deny any of its people equal protection under the law.

Although the equal protection clause has been a part of the Constitution since 1868, its legal and cultural meanings have changed over the years. These changes have most often been the result of one of two phenomena. First, minority groups with grievances have mobilized in electoral politics and other venues such as protests or boycotts. By undertaking such activities, they unify their numbers to influence elections more effectively, and they win popular opinion to their side, broadening their impact on elected officials. "One of the difficult lessons we have learned," wrote Martin Luther King, Jr., "is that you cannot depend on American institutions to function without pressure. Any real change in the status quo depends on continued creative action to sharpen the conscience of the nation."[8]

Second, because minorities are seldom able to control the outcome of elections directly, and because at times in American history they have been prevented from freely exercising their right to vote, they have often pursued a legal strategy, bringing apparent violations of civil rights to the attention of the courts. But legal strategies do not always work. Judges, too, are concerned about preserving credibility with majorities. If judges defy public opinion regularly, they might undermine confidence in the courts. Also, if judges persist in deviating from the majority view, elected officials will eventually appoint judges willing to reverse direction. As a result, the Supreme Court has not provided steady leadership on civil rights questions. As one legal scholar has noted, "For every case destructive of racial segregation, other cases can be cited with greater force to support the view of judicial power as fundamentally unfriendly to civil rights."[9]

Because most people have personal experience with the relationships among races, genders, and ethnic groups, differing interpretations of the meaning of the equal protection clause have generated intense political controversy.[10] In this section, we first describe actions taken in the years following the Civil War that affected the civil rights of African Americans, then review the Supreme Court's early rulings on these efforts, and finally examine the changes in political power that led up to the Court's major rulings on civil rights in the mid-twentieth century.

Conflict over Civil Rights After the Civil War

At the end of the Civil War, some southern states passed **black codes,** restrictive laws that applied to newly freed slaves but not to whites. "Persons of color . . . must make annual written contracts for their labor," one of the codes read, adding that if blacks ran away from their employers they had to forgo a year's wages.[11] Other black codes denied African Americans access to the courts or the right to hold property, except under special circumstances. Northern abolitionists, who thought the fight against slavery had been won, urged Congress to override these black codes. Congress responded by passing the Civil Rights Act of 1866, which gave citizens "of every race and color . . . the same right . . . to full and equal benefit of all laws." Almost the same words were incorporated into the equal protection clause of the Fourteenth Amendment, which won final ratification two years later.

civil rights
Specific rights that embody the general right to equal treatment under the law.

equal protection clause
Fourteenth Amendment clause specifying that no state can deny any of its people equal protection under the law.

black codes
Restrictive laws, passed in some southern states after the Civil War, that applied to newly freed slaves but not to whites.

Reconstruction
A period after the Civil War when southern states were subject to a federal military presence.

poll tax
Fee that one must pay in order to be allowed to vote.

grandfather clause
Racially restrictive provision of certain southern laws after Reconstruction permitting a man to vote if his father or grandfather was eligible to vote before the Civil War.

white primary
A primary election, held by the Democratic Party after Reconstruction, that excluded nonwhites from participation in many southern states.

The federal government's civil rights stance was imposed on southern whites during **Reconstruction,** a period after the Civil War when southern states were subject to a federal military presence. During this period, blacks exercised their right to vote, although that right was denied to many whites who had served in the Confederate army. In addition, Congress (under the control of the Republican Party) established a Freedman's Bureau, which was designed to provide blacks with education, immediate food relief, and inexpensive land from former plantations.[12]

Many southern whites bitterly resented the federal Reconstruction policies and some took violent action to resist them. The Ku Klux Klan, a fraternal organization founded in Tennessee, terrorized blacks and Republicans throughout the South from 1866 to the early 1870s.[13] Whites became targets if they aided Republicans or blacks; blacks could fall under suspicion just by becoming educated. The Klan murdered one former slave in Georgia because "he can write and read and put it down himself."[14] In 1871 Congress passed the Force Act, which temporarily succeeded in disbanding the Klan, but similar organizations continued to terrorize African Americans for many years.

The close election of 1876 brought Reconstruction to an end. Republican presidential candidate Rutherford B. Hayes claimed victory, but the outcome depended on allegedly fraudulent vote counts reported by several southern states. Democrats contested Hayes's victory, and the compromise resolving the dispute gave each side what it most wanted. Republicans were given the presidency, but Democrats won removal of the federal army from the South and control of future southern elections.

With the end of Reconstruction, whites gradually restored many of the old racial patterns.[15] State legislatures enacted laws requiring voters to pass a literacy test, meet strict residency requirements, and pay a **poll tax,** a fee that allowed one to vote. The chair of the suffrage committee in Virginia, like many other southern officials, bluntly admitted that his state's literacy test would be directed at blacks: "I do not expect an impartial administration of this clause."[16] States also enacted what was to become known as a **grandfather clause,** a law that exempted men from voting restrictions if their fathers and grandfathers were eligible to vote before the Civil War. Of course, only whites benefited from this exemption.

The most successful restriction on the right to vote was the **white primary,** an election held by the Democratic Party that excluded nonwhites from participation. Southerners saw Republicans as the hated instigators of Reconstruction, so Democrats won

Jim Crow Laws
Men drink from segregated fountains in the U.S. South.
• *What was the purpose of such laws, and why were they enacted following the Civil War?*

nearly all southern elections at that time. As a result, the winner of the white primary nearly always won the general election.[17] Because blacks were denied a meaningful vote, in 1910 only 10 percent of adult African American males were registered to vote in most of the states of the old Confederacy.[18] African Americans were also subject to **Jim Crow laws,** state laws that segregated the races from each other. (The name comes from a stereotypical, belittling characterization of African Americans used in minstrel shows popular at the time.) Jim Crow laws required African Americans to attend segregated schools, sit in separate areas on public trains and buses, eat in separate restaurants, and use separate public facilities. The reason for these regulations was clear. As one (white-owned) New Orleans newspaper put it, "The quarter-century that has passed since the war has not diminished in the slightest degree the determination of the whites to prevent such dangerous doctrine as social equality, even in the mildest form."[19]

Jim Crow laws
Laws, passed by southern states after Reconstruction, enforcing segregation.

Early Court Interpretations of Civil Rights

With little public support for civil rights, the Supreme Court of the day adopted a narrow view of the Fourteenth Amendment's equal protection clause. In a decision that was given the ironic title of the *Civil Rights Cases* (1883), the Court declared the Civil Rights Act of 1875 unconstitutional.[20] This law, written just before Reconstruction came to an end, had abolished segregation in restaurants, train stations, and other public places. In striking down the law, the Supreme Court invoked the **state action doctrine**—the principle that only the practices of state and local governments, not those of private individuals, must conform to the equal protection clause. The Court said that Congress could prevent state and local governments from discriminating against blacks but that it had no constitutional authority to tell private business owners whom to serve in their restaurants and hotels, and on their railroads.[21]

state action doctrine
Rule stating that only the actions of state and local governments, not those of private individuals, must conform to the equal protection clause.

A second major decision by the Supreme Court, ***Plessy v. Ferguson*** (1896), had even more sweeping consequences. It developed the **separate but equal doctrine,** the principle that laws mandating segregated facilities were constitutional as long as the separate facilities were equivalent. Homer Plessy had challenged a Louisiana law that required "equal but separate accommodations" for white and black railroad passengers.[22] But by a majority of 8 to 1 the Supreme Court said the Louisiana statute was constitutional, because the mere fact that the racial groups were required to use separate rail cars did not stamp African Americans with a "badge of inferiority." In a famous dissent, Justice John Marshall Harlan protested that "Our Constitution is color-blind, and neither knows nor tolerates classes among citizens." Laws enforcing segregation, argued Harlan, violated this constitutional principle.[23]

Plessy v. Ferguson
Supreme Court decision declaring separate but equal public facilities constitutional.

separate but equal doctrine
Supreme Court rule stating that the equal protection clause was not violated by the fact of state mandated racial segregation alone, provided that the separated facilities were equal.

Blacks Get Electoral Power

Because of the court decisions in the *Civil Rights Cases* and *Plessy v. Ferguson,* legally sanctioned segregation remained intact until well into the middle of the twentieth century. Black civil rights activists were by no means quiescent during this period. Between 1900 and 1910, for example, African Americans in more than two dozen cities took part in organized boycotts of segregated streetcars.[24] But significant gains in dismantling the old system of segregation took place only after African Americans gained electoral clout by moving in large numbers from southern states, where they could not vote, to northern states, where they could. During World War I and World War II, industrial northern cities faced labor shortages, and many African Americans gave up sharecropping in Mississippi and Alabama for factory work in the sweatshops of New York, Chicago, and Detroit.

Northerners harbored many of the same racial prejudices as southerners did, but northern machine politicians who dominated urban politics were not fussy about the color or religion of the voters they organized. The tough, shrewd, urban political organizer knew that a black vote counted as much as the vote of any other resident of the city.[25] One Chicago newspaper assessed the situation in 1927: "Their solid vote is the Negroes' greatest weapon. They have a total vote in Chicago of about 40,000. This total vote is cast for the candidate who makes the best bargain with them."[26]

By the 1930s, African Americans used their votes to win a small place in the politics of a few big cities. African American politicians won election to city councils and became neighborhood leaders in party organizations, obtaining jobs and other benefits for their constituents.[27] Recognizing the power of black voters in key states such as Ohio, Illinois, and Michigan early in the 1948 presidential campaign, President Harry Truman called for the abolition of poll taxes, more effective protection of voting rights, the creation of a Fair Employment Practices Commission with authority to stop racial discrimination, and an end to racial segregation within the armed forces. Some scholars have argued that the president's slim margins of victory in several crucial states were due to his two-thirds support among African Americans.[28] This growing electoral clout, and the increasing rhetorical support President Truman gave to the cause of civil rights, lent added force to civil rights lawsuits that activists began to bring before the Supreme Court.

Awakening the Supreme Court to Civil Rights

National Association for the Advancement of Colored People (NAACP)

Civil rights organization, founded in 1909, that relied heavily on a legal strategy to pursue its objectives.

The legal case against segregation was gradually developed by the **National Association for the Advancement of Colored People (NAACP),** a civil rights organization, founded in 1909 by a multiracial group of intellectuals and activists, which relied heavily on a legal strategy to pursue its objectives. After several failed attempts to persuade Congress to pass a law against lynching, the NAACP chose the courtroom strategy because its leaders concluded that the electoral strength of African Americans was too small to effect dramatic change.

But a legal strategy carried out without the support of black votes was not very effective. Despite the care with which cases were prepared by the NAACP's lead attorney, Thurgood Marshall (who later became the first black Supreme Court justice), the organization initially had few successes in the courtroom. It was able to outlaw neither the poll tax nor the education requirements for voting. For all of the legal efforts of the NAACP, only 12 percent of the southern black adult population was registered to vote in 1947.[29]

The NAACP's legal strategy gained strength as northern blacks became more politically potent. President Roosevelt took minor symbolic steps to court the black vote in the 1940 presidential race, and in 1941 the threat of a summer march on Washington by up to 100,000 African Americans drew a promise from the president to eliminate discriminatory employment practices in the defense industry.[30] Around this time, FDR appointed to the Supreme Court five justices who were known to be friendly to the NAACP's point of view.[31] Finally, this substantially new Court outlawed the white primary in the 1944 case *Smith v. Allwright,* saying that political parties were not private organizations but integral parts of a state electoral system.[32] After this decision, black voting in the South gradually began to increase.

In 1948, the very year blacks helped elect Harry Truman, the Court outlawed **restrictive housing covenants,** legal promises by those buying houses that they would not resell to an African American. Under the state action doctrine enunciated by the Court in the *Civil Rights Cases,* the contract seemed a private matter, not subject to constitutional scrutiny. But, in its 1948 ruling in *Shelley v. Kraemer,* the Court held that, although the contracts themselves were indeed private, any state enforcement of such covenants was a public act that violated the equal protection clause.[33] By making this decision, the Court greatly narrowed the range of activities in which segregation could be legally practiced, laying the groundwork for a redefinition of the equal protection clause.

restrictive housing covenants
Legal promises by home buyers that they would not resell to an African American; enforcement declared unconstitutional by the Supreme Court.

Redefining the Equal Protection Clause

17.2

Trace the rise of the civil rights movement following *Brown* and its subsequent decline in strength and assess results so far.

Although Harry Truman's election and the Court's decisions in *Smith v. Allwright* and *Shelley v. Kraemer* offered some hope, the legal rights of African Americans in the United States had changed little from the 1890s to the 1940s. Most blacks lived in segregated neighborhoods, many could not vote, and violence and intimidation directed against blacks continued.

From the mid-1950s to the early 1970s, however, the status of African Americans changed dramatically, through both legal victories and popular mobilization. By no means were all problems solved in this period, but blacks made great advances in redefining and strengthening the constitutional guarantee of "equal protection of the laws." In this section, we review the history of the civil rights movement that began in the 1950s, consider the debate over affirmative action, and assess the current state of civil rights for African Americans.

Brown v. Board of Education of Topeka, Kansas

Civil rights groups tried hard to reverse the separate but equal doctrine set forth in *Plessy v. Ferguson,* but for decades the Supreme Court resisted.

The NAACP scored a key early victory in 1938 when it won a suit on behalf of a black law student denied access to Missouri's all-white law school.[34] Missouri had no black law school but offered to pay students' tuition to attend a law school in an adjacent state. When the Court ruled that this policy was unconstitutional, Missouri and other southern states responded by creating all-black law schools of inferior quality, leaving blacks worse off than they were before the decision.

After blacks demonstrated their electoral influence in 1948, the NAACP proved more effective in the courtroom, as the Supreme Court began to reconsider the separate but equal doctrine enunciated in *Plessy*. First, in 1950, the Court unanimously declared that requiring black law students to attend an all-black school was inherently unconstitutional because such a school could not be an effective "proving ground for legal learning and practice."[35] By focusing on law schools, the NAACP had shrewdly aimed at the weakest point in the separate but equal doctrine. Most Supreme Court justices were attorneys, and they knew from personal experience the importance of a law school's reputation to a lawyer's subsequent career.

Once the law school decision provided an opening wedge, the NAACP attacked the separate but equal doctrine directly by encouraging Oliver Brown to file suit saying his daughter, Linda, was being denied equal protection by the board of education of

Topeka, Kansas, by being forced to attend an all-black school. The fact that the black schools in Topeka seemed to be just as good as the white schools was irrelevant, argued the NAACP. This suit led to the Supreme Court's **Brown v. Board of Education of Topeka, Kansas,** decision in 1954 that finally declared racial segregation unconstitutional.[36]

Brown v. Board of Education of Topeka, Kansas
1954 Supreme Court decision declaring racial segregation in schools unconstitutional.

Newly appointed Chief Justice Earl Warren, a former California governor, was keenly aware of the political significance of the Brown case, so he worked hard to convince the rest of the Court to issue a unanimous decision. At first it seemed that Warren would fail, because two members of the Court thought a decision to reverse *Plessy v. Ferguson* would violate the principle of *stare decisis,* a rule that says courts should adhere to the doctrines set forth in prior decisions (see Chapter 15, page 448). But Warren argued that the *Brown* decision could be distinguished from *Plessy* because the *Plessy* case had involved trains, not schools.

To distinguish segregation in schools from segregation in transportation, Warren cited psychological studies provided by the NAACP to show that racial separation created a sense of inferiority among black children. One study showed, for example, that black children favored white dolls over black ones.[37] Focusing on the particularly harmful effects of segregation on children allowed Warren to limit his opinion to schools, thereby avoiding a direct reversal of *Plessy.* By so limiting the effect of the decision, Warren was able to obtain a unanimous vote from the justices, but in pursuing a legal doctrine Warren might have done better to have followed Justice Harlan's dissent in *Plessy* that simply said, "the Constitution is color-blind." Since the *Brown* decision, many critics have argued that the constitutionality of racial segregation should depend not on its psychological effects, which may vary from person to person, but on whether racial criteria are valid grounds for classifying individuals.

Years later, the Supreme Court did provide this very rationale for its finding that segregation was unconstitutional. In 1973 it said that any legal distinction based on race or on membership in any other ethnic group that had been discriminated against in the past was a **suspect classification,** which required "strict scrutiny" by the courts to make sure that its use did not violate the Fourteenth Amendment's equal protection clause. This concept, which is now the standard tool with which the courts adjudicate civil rights cases, soon became crucial for ensuring that racial and ethnic minorities received equal protection before the law.[38]

suspect classification
Categorization of a particular racial or ethnic group that will be closely scrutinized by the courts to see whether its use is unconstitutional.

In 1954, however, Chief Justice Warren realized he could not get a unanimous Court to back such a sweeping statement outlawing all forms of segregation. Thus, in *Brown,* he settled for less by focusing on segregation's psychological effects on young children. Also, to preserve court unanimity, Warren postponed consideration of the exact way in which school boards were to rectify their segregation practices. The following year, the Court handed down a separate ruling (*Brown v. Board of Education* II) on this enforcement issue, calling for school desegregation "with all deliberate speed," a phrase that appeared to have contradictory meanings. "Deliberate" implied a slow, methodical pace, whereas "speed" suggested a need for prompt compliance. Most southern school boards focused on deliberation, enacting as little desegregation as possible.

In spite of its defects, scholars believe *Brown* to be among the most important decisions the Supreme Court has ever made.[39] In this decision, the Supreme Court declared unconstitutional a system of racial segregation that from the earliest colonial settlements had organized social life in a large part of the United States. Within two years, the border states of Maryland, Kentucky, and Missouri, as well as Kansas and the District of Columbia, eliminated formal segregation in their schools.

Civil Rights After *Brown*

Brown also energized civil rights activists around the country. The impact on young people and religious leaders was particularly noticeable. Immediately after the decision, three new civil rights organizations—the Congress of Racial Equality (CORE), the Student Nonviolent Coordinating Committee (SNCC), and the Southern Christian Leadership Conference (SCLC)—rose to prominence. Consisting mainly of college students and ministers, these groups held demonstrations, led boycotts, undertook voter registration drives, and appealed to the federal government for intervention into southern racial practices.[40]

One year after *Brown,* a more activist phase of the civil rights movement erupted. In December 1955, Rosa Parks of Montgomery, Alabama, engaged in an extraordinarily successful act of **civil disobedience**—a peaceful, well-publicized violation of a law designed to dramatize that law's injustice. Her arrest for refusing to vacate her seat in the white section of a segregated bus prompted a bus boycott led by a 27-year-old Baptist minister, Martin Luther King, Jr., who had just earned his Ph.D. in theology. "If there is a victory [over segregation]," King wrote, "the victory will not be merely for the Negro citizens and a defeat of the white citizens, but it will be a victory for justice and a defeat of injustice. It will be a victory for goodness in its long struggle with the forces of evil."[41]

civil disobedience
A peaceful, well-publicized violation of a law designed to dramatize that law's injustice.

Rosa Parks
Parks marked the beginning of the modern civil rights movement when she refused to move to the back of a bus in Montgomery, Alabama.

• *Why did acts of civil disobedience prove so effective during the civil rights movement?*

Using boycotts, protests, and acts of civil disobedience, the southern civil rights movement gained strength by winning sympathetic coverage in the northern press.[42] But activists met intense opposition from government officials in the South. In March 1956, nearly every southern member of Congress signed the Southern Manifesto, committing themselves to resist the enforcement of the *Brown* decision by "all lawful means."[43] Southern resistance to court-ordered integration was so consistent and complete that in the states of the old Confederacy, hardly any school desegregation actually occurred. When school began in the fall of 1964, ten years after the *Brown* decision, only 2.3 percent of black students in the states of the old Confederacy attended integrated schools.[44]

Yet the protests and demonstrations gradually had their effect. For one thing, southern African Americans were registering to vote. The percentage that registered more than doubled from 12 percent in 1947 to 28 percent in 1960. At the same time, African Americans were becoming a more powerful political force in the large industrial states of the North. With civil rights demonstrators focusing national attention on racial issues, presidential candidates had to balance southern resistance against the need to get black votes in big northern states.

John F. Kennedy's victory over Richard M. Nixon in the close election of 1960 owed much to his success in attracting the black vote. To strengthen his support in the black community, Kennedy placed a well-publicized phone call to Coretta Scott King expressing sympathy for the plight of her husband, Martin Luther King, Jr., who had been jailed in Birmingham after participating in a student sit-in. That phone call took on great symbolic significance and helped generate support for Kennedy in the

Civil Rights Activist

Activists worked to pressure politicians and shape public opinion, while at the same time, civil rights lawyers brought cases before the courts challenging segregation.

• *Why did activists bring court challenges in addition to protesting Jim Crow laws?*

black community. Kennedy, who had begun the campaign with little support among African Americans,[45] captured enough black votes to win such crucial states as Ohio, Michigan, and Illinois.

Once in office, Kennedy proposed civil rights legislation that received vigorous support from civil rights demonstrators. In the largest of these demonstrations, more than 200,000 black and white demonstrators marched on the Washington Mall in the summer of 1963, calling for congressional passage of the proposed legislation and other reforms. From the steps of the Lincoln Memorial, King delivered his powerful and moving "I Have a Dream" oration, in which he firmly connected the struggle for civil rights to mainstream American values. The dream of African Americans, he said, was "deeply rooted in the American dream that one day this nation will rise up and live out the true meaning of its creed . . . that all men are created equal."[46] These appeals persuaded many ordinary voters. In the wake of the march, for the first time a plurality of Americans that were polled said they viewed civil rights as the country's most important problem.[47] Just a few months later, Kennedy's assassination generated an unprecedented outpouring of moral commitment to racial justice.

Elected political leaders responded quickly to this transformation in the public mood. The new president, Lyndon Johnson, though himself a southerner, called upon Congress to memorialize the dead president by enacting his civil rights legislation. After intense debate, majorities of both Republican and Democratic members of Congress voted in favor of the Civil Rights Act of 1964, the most sweeping civil rights legislation passed since Reconstruction. This act banned segregation in all places of public accommodation, prohibited federal money from being used to support segregated programs,

"I Have a Dream"
Martin Luther King, Jr., delivers his "I Have a Dream" speech at the March on Washington in August 1963.

• *Why did the civil rights movement lose support just a few years later?*

FIGURE 17.1

CHANGES IN BLACK AND
WHITE PARTICIPATION IN
PRESIDENTIAL ELECTIONS,
BY REGION

Although differences in electoral
participation have declined over
the years, they still exist.

• *Why do both southern and
northern blacks now vote at
similar rates as whites?*

• *Which group has remained
most consistent over time in
its participation? Why do you
think this group has been most
consistent?*

Source: U.S. Bureau of the Census, *Current
Population Survey Reports,* various years.
(South is defined as the states that formed
the Confederacy. North is defined as
Census categories "Northeast" and
"Midwest." Non-citizens excluded from
calculations.)

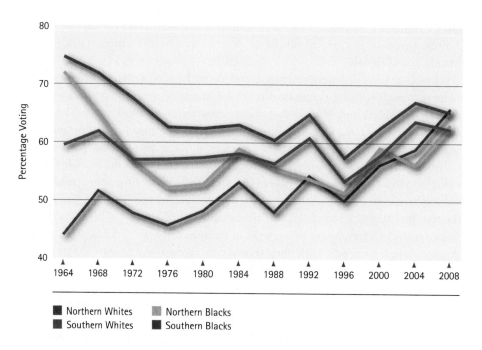

■ Northern Whites   ■ Northern Blacks
■ Southern Whites   ■ Southern Blacks

and created the Equal Employment Opportunity Commission (EEOC) to guard against
employment discrimination. The law brought about major changes in race relations
throughout the South. Enticed by new federal funds facilitating desegregation, and
intimidated by the new enforcement powers of federal officials, many southern schools
desegregated. The percentage of black students in southern schools that included
whites increased dramatically from 2.3 percent in 1964 to 91.3 percent in 1972.[48]

Buoyed by economic prosperity and his civil rights achievements, Lyndon Johnson
won a sweeping election victory in the fall of 1964. Not one to rest on his accomplishments, Johnson soon engineered congressional passage of the Voting Rights Act of
1965, which guaranteed black voting rights by stationing federal examiners in southern
registration halls and polling places.[49] As a result, the percentage of voters among southern black adults jumped upward after 1964, as shown in Figure 17.1.[50] The number of
elected officials of African American descent rose from fewer than 500 in 1965, to
6,056 in 1985, to more than 9,500 in 2007.[51] In 2006, Massachusetts elected Deval
Patrick governor—the second African American governor since Reconstruction. And,
in 2008, Barack Obama became the first African American elected to the presidency as
voter turnout among blacks reached historic highs.[52]

The Decline in Strength of the Civil Rights Movement

Segregation and discrimination were not limited to the South. Most northern blacks
lived in racially isolated neighborhoods, sent their children to predominantly black
schools, and found it hard to get good jobs. Even as Congress passed the Voting Rights
Act of 1965, Martin Luther King, Jr., shifted the focus of the civil rights movement to
the north by mounting a series of civil rights demonstrations in Chicago.[53] This shift
changed the way the public viewed the civil rights movement. As school busing and
job discrimination became a northern issue as well, support for civil rights protests
among many northern whites dwindled.[54] At the same time, new black leaders such as

black nationalist Malcolm X took a more militant position, affirming black culture, denying the value of integration, and suggesting that violent "self defense" might be needed. "If Negroes can get freedom nonviolently, good," said Malcolm X. "But that's a dream. Even King calls it a dream."[55]

Civil violence began to break out in black neighborhoods, beginning in Los Angeles in 1964 and spreading to other cities over the next three years. When King was assassinated by a white man in Memphis, Tennessee, in April 1968, violent racial disturbances broke out in dozens of cities across the country.

After these events, the white majority began to view the problem of civil rights as less important. As long as civil rights issues were being addressed by nonviolent demonstrations in the South, African Americans appealed successfully to the moral instincts of northern whites. But once those whites realized that the problem was national in scope, and that civil disobedience could turn violent, many had second thoughts. Opposition to busing, affirmative action, and other programs of racial integration split the biracial political coalition that had elected Harry Truman and John Kennedy.

Race issues then began to divide the two political parties further. When Senator Barry Goldwater voted against the Civil Rights Act of 1964, he was among a minority of Republicans to do so. But by 1968 Republicans were pursuing what was known as a "southern strategy," an appeal to those who thought the civil rights movement had gone too far. Meanwhile, blacks solidified their allegiance to the Democratic Party.[56] The percentage of black delegates attending the Democratic convention grew from 6.7 to 14.6 percent between 1968 and 1972.

The Supreme Court No Longer Forges Ahead

Encountering increasing popular resistance to further legislation, civil rights groups once again turned to the courts for assistance. But the courts, following the direction in which public opinion was moving, also adopted a more conservative attitude. For example, the Supreme Court drew a distinction between two types of segregation: **De jure segregation,** the legal separation of the races practiced in the South, was said by the Court to violate the equal protection clause of the Constitution. But segregation in the North was said to be **de facto segregation,** occurring as the result of private decisions made by individuals, such as their choice of residence.

de jure **segregation**
Racial segregation that is legally sanctioned.

de facto **segregation**
Segregation that occurs as the result of decisions by private individuals.

In *Milliken v. Bradley* (1974), the Supreme Court considered the constitutionality of the most pervasive form of *de facto* segregation.[57] Bradley argued that the state of Michigan (under Governor William Milliken) tolerated racial segregation by allowing virtually all-white suburban school districts to surround the city of Detroit, whose schools were predominantly black. In rejecting Bradley's argument that the whole metropolitan area ought to be desegregated, the Court ruled that suburban school districts in the North had never practiced *de jure* racial segregation. The segregation that had occurred was *de facto*—simply the result of private decisions to live in Detroit or in its suburbs. Dissenting from the Court's decision, Justice Thurgood Marshall, the former NAACP lawyer, warned that racial segregation would increase as "whites flee . . . to the suburbs to avoid integration."

After the *Milliken* decision, little additional school desegregation took place in either the North or the South. In recent years, school segregation among African Americans and Latinos has actually increased, as Figure 17.2 illustrates.

FIGURE 17.2

PERCENTAGE OF AFRICAN
AMERICAN AND LATINO
STUDENTS IN SEGREGATED
SCHOOLS, 1972–2007

Although segregation went down
in the 1960s, it has crept upward
since then.

• *In your opinion, why has segregation increased since the
1980s?*

Sources: Gary Orfield, *Schools More Separate:
Consequences of a Decade of Resegregation*
(Cambridge, MA: The Civil Rights
Project, Harvard University, July 2001),
Table 9; Gary Orfield, *Reviving the Goal of
An Integrated Society: A 21st Century
Challenge* (Los Angeles: The Civil Rights
Project, UCLA, 2009), Table 23.

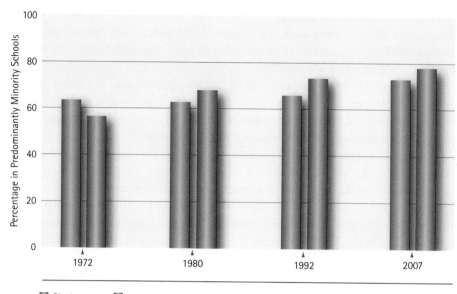

affirmative action

Programs designed to enhance
opportunities for race- or gender-
based groups that have suffered
discrimination in the past.

Affirmative Action

Civil rights groups also called upon government agencies, universities, and businesses to
rectify past discrimination by taking steps to provide increased educational and job opportunities for African Americans. In response to these demands, many organizations
have instituted policies of **affirmative action,** programs designed to enhance opportunities for race- or gender-based groups that have suffered discrimination in the past
(see the *Election Voices!* feature on page 519).

The Supreme Court first considered the constitutionality of affirmative action
programs in a 1978 case that involved Allen Bakke, a Norwegian American who sued
for admission to the medical school of the University of California at Davis.[58] Bakke
argued that he had been denied admission because of the school's affirmative action
policy, which set aside 16 spots in each entering class of 100 for minority applicants.
A divided Court found that strict quotas such as Davis's were unconstitutional, but it
suggested that affirmative action programs that used race as one among many factors
were permissible if the goal was to ensure a diverse community that would benefit all.

In 2003, the Supreme Court heard two affirmative action cases that prompted the
justices to reexamine the *Bakke* decision. Both cases began at the University of
Michigan. In the first, *Grutter v. Bollinger,* Barbara Grutter argued that she had been denied admission to the University of Michigan's law school because of an affirmative action system that considered race as one of a number of criteria in a process that placed
great importance on creating a diverse student body.[59] In the second, *Gratz v. Bollinger,*
Jennifer Gratz similarly argued that she had been refused a spot in Michigan's undergraduate program because of the school's affirmative action policy. Both Grutter and
Gratz alleged that that Michigan's affirmative action programs should be struck down
as a violation of the Fourteenth Amendment's equal protection guarantee.

The undergraduate admission system differed from the law school system, however.
Law school admissions officers considered race as one "plus" factor in a "highly individualized, holistic review" of each candidate.[60] The undergraduate process operated under

a "points" system, in which membership in an "underrepresented minority group" automatically secured an applicant a fixed number of additional points.[61] The Court invalidated this points system because it was too blunt an instrument. Even though the Court admitted that diversity was a valid goal, the undergraduate system was not "narrowly tailored" to avoid undue discrimination.

The law school system, on the other hand, was acceptable, wrote Justice Sandra Day O'Connor for the majority in *Grutter*. O'Connor argued that "diversity will, in fact, yield educational benefits," and that affirmative action would help educational institutions train "a set of leaders with legitimacy in the eyes of the citizenry."[62] In rejecting a rigid points system while allowing some forms of affirmative action, the Court again struck a compromise that placed it in the mainstream of public opinion.

Elections, Courts, and Civil Rights: An Appraisal

Significant problems still beset African Americans. Chief among them is the persistence of poverty in the black community. Poverty rates among blacks remain more than double those of whites.[63] Even at the height of the recession in 2009, black unemployment was 50 percent higher than that of whites.[64] African American children continue to score worse on tests than their white counterparts, while teen pregnancy and infant mortality rates are far higher among African Americans than among others.[65] And the proportion of African Americans in prison is more than five times that of whites.[66] Critics argue that although middle- and upper-class blacks have made progress, these successes have not translated into wide-reaching economic gains for all African Americans.[67]

But there is increasing reason for optimism about the status of African Americans. The victories of the civil rights movement have promoted advancement in almost every sector. The percentage of black men and women in professional and managerial positions increased markedly in the decades following the passage of the Civil Rights and Voting Rights Acts.[68] Blacks have also made political gains, winning an increasing number of mayoral elections, state legislative races, and seats in Congress, and they have made noticeable educational advances. Whereas in 1960, only 20 percent of African Americans said they had graduated from high school, by 2008, 83 percent reported having a high school diploma or its equivalent.[69] And during the 1970s and 1980s, black high school test scores in reading and math improved significantly, particularly in the southern states, the very region of the country where school desegregation was moving forward most rapidly.[70] African American poverty rates, while still high, shrank from more than 32 percent to 25 percent from 1980 to 2007.[71]

The Civil Rights of Other Minorities

Most of the civil rights issues and rulings discussed thus far apply as much to other racial and ethnic groups as they do to African Americans. Neither the 1964 nor the 1965 civil rights legislation identified any groups other than blacks as deserving affirmative action to redress historical grievances. But, after the civil rights movement defined many issues in terms of equal protection under the Constitution, groups representing other ethnic minorities began to make similar civil rights claims, and Congress has given them recognition.

The pace of this process and the degree to which each group receives recognition in law have in large part depended on how effectively each group has mobilized its

17.3

Outline civil rights issues for, and efforts undertaken by, minorities other than African Americans.

members in elections. Latinos, Asian Americans, and gays and lesbians have recently begun to exert their influence on national electoral politics. But, until very recently, Native Americans remained a small, politically inactive voting bloc.

Latinos

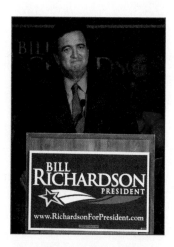

Candidato a la Presidencia
New Mexico Governor Bill Richardson announces his candidacy for president in 2007. Richardson, whose mother was born in Mexico, is fluent in Spanish.

• *Why are parties paying closer attention to Latino voters?*

Latinos are now the largest minority group in the United States. In 1980 they made up only 6.4 percent of the U.S. population, but by 2008 they had grown to 15.4 percent, surpassing the 13.5 percent that are African American.[72] In contrast to African Americans, who have been politically assertive for nearly 50 years, Latinos are only beginning to exercise their influence regularly in elections. There are several reasons for this difference. A sizable percentage of the Latino population lacks citizenship, and even among Latino citizens voting rates are lower than among African Americans, partly because most Latinos have not experienced a prolonged—and unifying—civil rights struggle.[73]

Building a broad-based political coalition is further complicated by the fact that Latinos come from many different countries and differ from one another in important cultural and political respects. For example, Mexican Americans in California and Texas who are concerned about job discrimination and working conditions may have a hard time identifying with Cuban Americans in Florida who are primarily concerned with the restoration of democracy in their home country. Latino voters are also less likely than African Americans to vote as a bloc. Whereas 72 percent of blacks consider themselves Democrats, only 65 percent of Latinos do.[74]

Similar to African Americans, Latinos have mobilized through both social protest and legal activism. In the late 1960s and early 1970s, Mexican Americans in the Southwest founded the Chicano movement, which argued for cultural and social separatism from white America. But it was the United Farm Workers Union, under the leadership of César Chavez, that drew mainstream public attention to Latino concerns. In the late 1960s, Chavez organized a five-year national boycott of grapes to protest working conditions for migrant farm workers. The boycott, along with marches, strikes, and other nonviolent protest tactics, led to California legislation that guaranteed farm workers rights. In addition, Chavez's principled appeals drew respect from large numbers of Americans, just as the African American civil rights movement had. Reflecting on his uncle's legacy, Federico Chavez said, "He taught us to persevere in a nonviolent way so when you won, it would be a moral victory as well as an organizing victory . . . . In that way, I think, he was able to gain the support of the American people."[75]

In 1968, while Chavez was organizing California farm workers, Latinos in Texas founded the Mexican American Legal Defense and Education Fund (MALDEF), a legal advocacy organization that has focused on voting, education, and immigration issues (see Chapter 4 for discussion of immigration). In 1974, in response to MALDEF complaints, the Supreme Court interpreted the 1964 Civil Rights Act to mean that schools must provide special educational programs for those not proficient in the English language.[76] MALDEF and other groups also argued that Latinos and other language minorities were discriminated against because ballots and other voter registration materials were published only in English. Congress responded to these concerns in 1982 by requiring that ballots be printed in the language of any protected minority that constitutes more than 5 percent of a county's population, thereby extending protection not only to Latinos but also to Asian Americans and American Indians.[77]

Latinos have also begun to make their influence felt in elections—first in state and local politics, later in national campaigns—although their voter turnout remains low relative to other groups.[78] In the 2000 and 2004 election campaigns, George W. Bush actively courted the Latino vote by promising, among other things, immigration reform. The Bush plan, which included a guest worker program and a method by which workers could eventually gain U.S. citizenship, failed amid disputes within the Republican Party. In 2010, immigration reform again became a key campaign issue after Arizona lawmakers passed a bill giving state and local law enforcement officers strict enforcement powers over undocumented immigrants (see discussion in Chapter 4). Although comprehensive reform proposals again went nowhere in Congress, Democratic candidates gained Latino votes because of the perceived harshness of the Republican position.

Asian Americans

Like Latinos, Asian Americans have only recently begun to make their voices heard in national electoral politics. They constitute 5 percent of the population, and more than 60 percent are foreign-born.[79] Similar to Latinos, they represent many different nationalities and have differing—even conflicting—policy concerns. Asian Americans are also less likely to support affirmative action programs and more likely to vote Republican than other ethnic minorities.[80]

In 1996 activists in the Asian American community flexed their political muscle by mounting a coordinated national fund-raising and voter-registration drive.[81] That year, Gary Locke of Washington state was elected the first Asian American governor of a state other than Hawaii. Since the 1990s, Asian Americans have become increasingly active at the state and local levels, organizing cultural celebrations, urging quick responses to anti-Asian slurs and ethnically motivated violence, and lobbying for official recognition of the Chinese New Year holiday.[82] Today over 2,000 elected and appointed officials claim Asian heritage.[83]

The major civil rights victory for Asian Americans in the past three decades has been the compensation paid to Japanese Americans for their internment in relocation camps during World War II. Responding to public concern that Japanese Americans on the West Coast might act as spies or saboteurs for Japan, President Franklin Roosevelt ordered 70,000 Japanese American citizens and another 40,000 resident Japanese— men, women, and children—to leave their homes and live in "relocation centers" for the duration of the war. Those adults who swore loyalty to the United States were released, but if they lived close to either coast they were told they could not return home. Earl Warren, the California attorney general and later chief justice of the Supreme Court, gave a race-based rationale for these actions: "When we are dealing with the Caucasian race we have methods that will test the loyalty of them . . . . But when we deal with the Japanese . . . we cannot form any opinion that we believe to be sound."[84]

In *Korematsu v. United States* (1944), the Supreme Court went along with ferociously anti-Japanese public opinion and found the relocation centers constitutional. But in his dissent from the Court's decision, Justice Frank Murphy condemned the relocation as "one of the most sweeping and complete deprivations of constitutional rights in the history of this nation."[85] At the instigation of Japanese American activists organized as the National Coalition for Redress and Reparations, Congress agreed in 1988 to apologize for the incident and pay each internee (or the internee's heirs) $20,000. [86]

Because of the diversity of the Asian American community, a unified political agenda for the future has yet to take shape. Some Asian American activists and political organizations are concerned with issues such as immigrant rights and expanding the Supreme Court's definition of a suspect classification to include Asian language speakers.[87] However, other Asian Americans favor the elimination of quotas and affirmative action programs from which they are excluded.

Gays and Lesbians

Some of the most contentious political debates in the early twenty-first century surround the rights of gays and lesbians. It is no accident that at the same time, gays, lesbians, bisexuals, and transgender people are more engaged in electoral politics than ever before. The origins of the gay rights movement date back to 1969, when an aggressive police raid on the Stonewall Inn in New York City sparked violent clashes with the Inn's gay patrons. Similar to many nascent groups, gay activists first sought to address ill treatment by local governments, winning key policy victories in some of the nation's larger cities after staging protests and electoral mobilization.[88] Although the first local law protecting individuals against discrimination on the basis of sexual orientation was passed in 1973, and the first such state law in 1982, it has only been since the early 1990s that the gay and lesbian community has exerted significant influence in national elections.[89] Congressional and media attention paid to gay and lesbian issues also rose around the same time, in part as a result of pressure from organized gay and lesbian interest groups.[90] Since the early 1990s, the number of openly gay government officials has jumped from 49 to more than 650.[91]

In the last decade a majority of the American public grew to believe that gays deserve equal job opportunities, as Figure 17.3 shows. Laws barring employment discrimination on the basis of sexual orientation have been passed in 20 states and have bipartisan support in Congress.[92] In 2010, Congress, with the support of many military leaders, passed a law allowing gays and lesbians to serve openly in the armed forces.[93] State supreme court decisions made gay marriages legal in Massachusetts, Connecticut,

FIGURE 17.3

PUBLIC OPINION ON GAY RIGHTS HAS CHANGED AS GAY AND LESBIAN POLITICAL ACTIVISM HAS INCREASED

Whereas fewer than 60 percent of Americans approved of equal rights for gays and lesbians in the late 1970s, today the figure is close to 90 percent.

• *Why do you think support for gay rights declined slightly in the late 1990s after rising steadily for so long?*

Source: The Gallup Poll, various years.

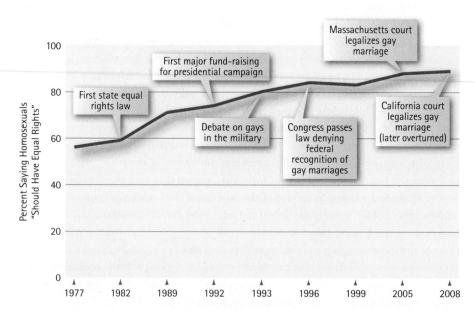

Iowa, and California, although California voters subsequently reversed that state's decision in an initiative. In 2009, Vermont became the first state to legalize same-sex marriage through the legislative process rather than via a court decision.

Public opinion remains conservative on some issues regarding gay rights. Large majorities disapprove of gay marriage, for example.[94] Forty-one states have passed laws or state constitutional amendments banning same-sex marriages, even as 21 states prohibit employment discrimination on the basis of sexual orientation.[95] At the national level, President Obama directed federally funded hospitals to extend visitation rights to gay and lesbian partners, and pressed to end the ban on gays and lesbians in the military, but he has stated his opposition to same-sex marriage. Republicans in Congress have at times voiced support for a Constitutional amendment that would ban same-sex marriage. Gay rights issues do not always follow party lines, however: Republican former vice president Dick Cheney went on record in 2009 as favoring gay marriage, for example. And former Bush Administration solicitor general Ted Olson argued the case for gay marriage in federal court in a closely watched legal case.

Native Americans

The rights and liberties of descendants of indigenous tribes are not protected by the Bill of Rights, because at the time of the writing of the Constitution these peoples were considered members of a foreign nation. As one authority on Indian rights has put it, "No constitutional protections exist for Indians in either a tribal or an individual sense."[96]

The relations between Native Americans and the government are instead governed by laws of Congress and by the many treaties that have been signed by the United States and American Indian tribes. Over the long course of American history, the United States government, under political pressure from those migrating westward, ignored or broke many of the treaties it made with indigenous tribes. Still, the Supreme Court today interprets some of these treaties as binding.[97] As a result, members of these tribes have certain rights and privileges not available to other groups. For example, Court interpretations of treaties have given tribes in the Pacific Northwest special rights to fish for salmon—rights that tribes view as vital in preserving their cultural and religious traditions. These exemptions can also be economically important for Native Americans, who suffer from the highest poverty rates of all U.S. racial and ethnic groups.[98]

Another economically significant tribal right recognized in recent years has been the authority to provide commercial gambling on tribal property. In several cases, tribes have used resources from these gambling operations to increase their political clout. For example, the Choctaw Native American tribe in Mississippi spends $300,000 annually on Washington, DC, lobbyists.[99] According to Choctaw chief Philip Martin, "If you don't have some political influence in this country, you don't have anything."[100]

Most of the rights contained in the Bill of Rights have been applied to members of tribes through congressional legislation. To protect tribal religious freedom, Congress in 1978 passed the American Indian Religious Freedom Resolution. Tribal leaders have argued that the resolution gives them special access to traditional religious sites in national parks and other government-owned lands. But the federal courts have interpreted the resolution narrowly, saying it does not make indigenous Americans "supercitizens." Rather, it gives them religious freedoms comparable to those granted to other citizens.[101]

17.4

Assess the civil rights objectives achieved by women and ongoing issues.

Women's Rights

Although gender is not mentioned in the equal protection clause of the Fourteenth Amendment, the meaning of the clause has been gradually redefined to refer to equal rights for women as well as for racial and ethnic groups. As one constitutional scholar has written, "It is in the very nature of ideas to grow in self-awareness, to work out all their implications over time . . . ."[102] Changes in the meaning of the equal protection clause were won as a result of a broad struggle for women's rights played out as much among the electorate as in the legal arena.

The first struggle for women's rights focused on the right to vote (see Chapter 6). Once the Nineteenth Amendment was passed in 1920, the women's movement became dormant for nearly 50 years, finally to be reawakened in the late sixties by the civil rights movement.[103] Since then, women's groups have achieved four civil rights objectives: the right to equal treatment before the law, tough enforcement of this right, the right not to be sexually harassed in the workplace, and access to state-funded educational institutions. Achievement of these objectives required both electoral involvement and courtroom presentations.

The Right to Equality Before the Law

As unlikely as it may seem, it was a conservative southerner, Representative Howard Smith of Virginia, who proposed an amendment to Title VII of the Civil Rights Act of 1964 that would prohibit discrimination on the basis of sex as well as race, religion, or national origin. Although the amendment passed overwhelmingly, activist women formed the National Organization for Women (NOW) in 1966 because they became concerned that the gender provision in Title VII would not be enforced. To guarantee enforcement of women's civil rights, NOW, together with other women's organizations, backed the **Equal Rights Amendment,** a proposed amendment to the Constitution that banned gender discrimination. Proponents expected this amendment to give the courts the tools necessary to strike down gender inequities.

Equal Rights Amendment (ERA)

Proposed amendment to the Constitution that banned gender discrimination.

Women's Rights Across the Century

(left) Women's rights issues in the United States at first focused on women's right to vote. (right) In August 1970, 50 years after women had won the franchise, 10,000 women's liberationists marched to a "Women's Strike for Equality" rally at New York City's Bryant Park.

• *Why did the women's rights movement begin in the 1970s, when women had voting rights as early as 1920?*

Women in the Military

Classifications by gender still exist in the military. Although women can serve as combat pilots, and will begin serving on navy submarines in 2012, they may not serve in frontline Army infantry units, for example.

• *Why do you think these gender distinctions still exist?*

At first, it seemed that women's groups would succeed in winning passage of this measure. Responding to polls that showed overwhelming public approval,[104] Congress passed the ERA by large majorities by the spring of 1972. Within a year most states had voted to ratify it.[105] But at the very moment when the ERA was about to become a part of the U.S. Constitution, it encountered increasing resistance led by groups of conservative women who were concerned, among other things, that the amendment would require government funding of abortions and the application of the military draft to women.[106] Upon hearing these arguments, the public began to have second thoughts. In the end, 35 states approved the ERA—three states short of the three-fourths majority necessary to enact a constitutional amendment (see Chapter 2).

As discouraging as the ERA defeat was for its supporters, in retrospect it seems that they won the war by losing the battle. Fifty years earlier, the women's movement had collapsed immediately following passage of the Nineteenth Amendment. This time, the women's movement continued to forge on, perhaps partly because the Equal Rights Amendment did not pass. In the 25 years after the ERA campaign began in earnest, women's place in politics changed more dramatically than in any previous quarter-century. More women were elected to public office in the 1990s than ever before.[107] In mid-2010, the House of Representatives included 79 women (including Speaker Nancy Pelosi), the Senate had 17, 3 of the 9 Supreme Court justices were female, and women held 4 of 15 positions in President Obama's cabinet.[108] Perhaps most importantly, in 2008 Hillary Clinton waged a far more successful campaign for president than any previous woman candidate, and later became the nation's third female secretary of state.

The Initial Court Response to Women's Rights

The ERA also had an impact on Supreme Court decisions. Before the ERA campaign, the Court had done little for women's rights. As late as 1961, in an opinion ironically signed by Earl Warren, the same chief justice who wrote the *Brown* decision, the Court unanimously upheld a Florida law that made a clear gender distinction. It said that men were required to serve on juries but that women could serve on a jury only if they volunteered for duty.[109]

Court opinions changed after the House of Representatives voted overwhelmingly in favor of the ERA. The Supreme Court, in *Craig v. Boren* (1976), declared unconstitutional an Oklahoma law that allowed women to drink at age 18 but denied that privilege to men until the age of 21. Oklahoma defended the law on the grounds that young men were more likely than young women to drive when drunk and were therefore more likely to have accidents. But the Supreme Court rejected this argument as irrelevant on the grounds that the law constituted "invidious gender-based discrimination" that constituted "a denial [to males] of equal protection of the laws in violation of the Fourteenth Amendment."[110]

Although the Supreme Court said that gender discrimination violates the equal protection clause, it has not placed gender discrimination in the same "strict scrutiny" category as race discrimination. Instead, the Court has used "intermediate scrutiny," saying only that it will rule against a law that includes gender distinctions unless those distinctions have "a substantial relationship to an important objective."[111]

National defense remains the most important arena in which classifications by gender remain intact. According to federal law, men must register for the draft but women need not, and men carry out combat assignments whereas women are not allowed to do so—although many "noncombat" positions now assigned to women may actually place women in danger of enemy fire. The Supreme Court ruled gender distinctions within the military constitutional in *Rostker v. Goldberg* (1981) on the grounds that on military matters, "Congress' constitutional power" is broad and "the lack of competence on the part of the courts is marked."[112] The ruling was consistent with the view of a majority of the voters, who favored—and continue to favor—certain restrictions on female participation in military combat.[113] These distinctions have not prevented many women from excelling in the military, of course. In 2008 the Army's Ann Dunwoody became the military's first four-star general.

Discrimination in the Workplace

Employers sometimes argue that they have legitimate reasons for not hiring representative numbers of women and members of disadvantaged groups. Certain jobs might be performed effectively only by people of a particular gender. (The position of prison guard could be one example.[114]) Qualified job applicants from disadvantaged groups may also be in short supply. In such cases of "business necessity," the Supreme Court has allowed employers to maintain unrepresentative workforces.[115] In the 1989 case of *Ward's Cove Packing Co. v. Atonio,* the Court also said that, under Title VII of the Civil Rights Act of 1964, workers who bring discrimination suits have a responsibility to prove that business necessity is not at issue in their cases.[116] This ruling prompted quick action from Congress, which overruled the Court by passing a new Civil Rights Act in 1991 to place the burden of proof back on businesses rather than on employees. As in past cases, elected officials, not the Court, took the lead on this gender discrimination issue.

Sexual Harassment

The Supreme Court did not rule on the meaning of sexual harassment in the workplace until *Meritor Savings Bank v. Vinson,* a case decided in 1986.[117] In this case,

Michelle Vinson said that she had been psychologically damaged as a result of sexually abusive language used in her presence. In deciding in Vinson's favor, Justice Rehnquist wrote a narrow opinion that strongly implied that sexual harassment would be considered illegal only if it caused psychological damage to the victim. In other words, the Court said sexual harassment had to be experienced as personally devastating before it constituted a violation of Title VII.

Sexual harassment became a major political issue in 1991, when Clarence Thomas was nominated to serve on the Supreme Court, and a former aide publicly accused him of sexual harassment. The issue so energized the women's movement that 1992, the election year that followed, became known as the "year of the woman" when nearly two dozen women were newly elected to Congress. Responding to the change in the political atmosphere, the Supreme Court, in the unanimous 1993 decision *Harris v. Forklift Systems,* expanded its definition of sexual harassment.[118] Teresa Harris resigned her position at Forklift Systems Inc., a heavy equipment rental firm, because her employer called her "a dumb-ass woman" and made other derogatory remarks. Lower courts denied her compensation, because no psychological damage could be shown. But Justice Sandra Day O'Connor wrote, in the majority opinion, that Title VII "comes into play before harassing conduct leads to a nervous breakdown." Once again, the Supreme Court moved forward in the wake of public pressure and political events. In the wake of the Harris decision, sexual harassment claims increased by over 40 percent, then declined again between 1997 and 2009, perhaps because such incidents were becoming less common or at least less severe.[119]

Single-Sex Schools and Colleges

Single-sex schools have long been a significant part of American education. As late as the 1950s, well-known private colleges such as Princeton and Yale limited their admissions to men. Although these colleges now admit approximately equal numbers of men and women, single-sex education survives at some private women's colleges. These colleges assert that women learn more in an environment where many can assume leadership roles. Hillary Clinton, who graduated from Wellesley, a Massachusetts women's college, said it "was very, very important to me and I am so grateful that I had the chance to go to college at a place where women were valued and nurtured and encouraged."[120]

Although policymakers continue to debate the pros and cons of single-sex education, the Supreme Court in 1996 cast doubt on its constitutionality. In *United States v. Virginia,* the Court ruled that women must be admitted to Virginia Military Institute (VMI), even though the state had recently established a separate military education program for women.[121] The Court said the newly established military training program for women did not match the history, reputation, and quality of VMI. It remains unclear, however, whether the Court will extend its decision to private schools or to state programs beyond those that prepare young people for military careers.

The Future of Women's Rights

Despite many gains, the women's movement has not yet realized its entire civil rights agenda. Sexual harassment remains a burning issue within the military and in many business firms. Women still earn less than what men earn, on average—a wage gap that has decreased over time (and may be related to the disproportionate number of women

glass ceiling
The invisible barrier that has limited women's opportunities for advancement to the highest ranks of politics, business, and the professions.

who enter and leave the labor force) but remains significant.[122] They still face difficulties breaking through what is known as the **glass ceiling**—the invisible barrier that has limited their opportunities for advancement to the highest ranks of politics, business, and the professions.[123] And no woman has yet been nominated for president by either major political party, although Hillary Clinton came close. These and other continuing concerns suggest that women's issues are likely to remain an important feature in American politics in the twenty-first century.

17.5

Describe judicial and legislative victories for Americans with disabilities.

Americans with Disabilities

According to the U.S. Census Bureau, disabled Americans constitute 18 percent of the population.[124] A number of factors make coordinated political efforts difficult, however: Disabilities differ in kind and severity, the disabled are more scattered geographically and less visible than ethnic minorities, and the more severely mentally disabled neither vote nor engage directly in politics. The cost of helping people with disabilities is another drawback. As of the 2010 fiscal year, the federal government budgets $123 billion on the relatively small Social Security Disability Insurance program (SSDI) alone.[125] When insurance costs, additional government programs, lost work hours, and other factors are taken into account, the total cost of disabilities is daunting. Although many people are, in principle, sympathetic to the needs of the disabled, they do not necessarily like to pay the taxes needed to fund appropriate services.

quota
Specific number of positions set aside for a specific group; said by the Supreme Court to be unconstitutional.

The needs of the disabled were first successfully cast in terms of civil rights not by an interest group but by one individual, Hugh Gallagher, a wheelchair-bound polio victim who in the mid-sixties served as a legislative aide to Alaska Senator E. L. Bartlett. Gallagher constantly faced great difficulty using public toilets and gaining access to such buildings as the Library of Congress. At his prodding, Congress in 1968—just four years after the 1964 Civil Rights Act—passed a law requiring that all future public buildings constructed with federal monies provide access for the disabled. Similar language was inserted into transportation legislation in 1970.[126]

Disability Rights Rally in Washington, DC
Some 300 wheelchair-bound people protest in front of the White House.

• *Are the rights of the disabled more effectively protected by the courts or by elected officials? Why?*

Continued on page 521

Affirmative Action

The Issue

Should colleges, universities, and employers consider race, ethnicity, and gender in admissions or hiring decisions? Or do such policies violate the principle of equal opportunity?

Background

This term "affirmative action" first appeared in an executive order issued by President John F. Kennedy that mandated equal opportunity in government contracting. Hobart Taylor, Jr., an African American lawyer who helped write the order, recalled that "I was torn between the words 'positive action' and 'affirmative action'. . . . And I took 'affirmative' because it was alliterative."[1]

From these beginnings, affirmative action programs designed to address historical imbalances in opportunities for ethnic and racial minorities, as well as for women, have grown in prominence. Today, federal contractors must possess written affirmative action policies and ensure that their employees have equal opportunities, without regard for their race, sex, national origin, or religion.[2] Many selective colleges and universities use affirmative action in their admissions programs as well, both to remedy past wrongs and to ensure that all students experience a more diverse environment.

Affirmative action programs rarely, if ever, take the form of **quotas**—set targets for numerical representation of particular groups. Instead, employers and universities say they make extra efforts to reach out to a diverse pool of applicants and may use a person's race, ethnicity, or gender as one of a number of factors in determining admissions or employment decisions. For example, the University of Colorado's policy states that "The University takes affirmative action to increase ethnic, cultural, and gender diversity; to employ qualified disabled individuals; and to provide equal opportunity to all students and employees."[3]

Opposing Views on Affirmative Action

Those in favor of affirmative action make two types of arguments. First, they say that affirmative action is necessary to level the playing field because of the enduring legacy of discrimination. As President Lyndon Johnson once said, "You do not take a man who has been hobbled by chains, liberate him, bring him to the starting line of a race, saying, 'you are free to compete with all the others,' and still justly believe you have been completely fair."[4]

Second, affirmative action advocates argue that education, in particular, is enriched by a diverse environment. The quality of education for all students, they say, improves when students from different backgrounds meet and interact. Without affirmative action, colleges and universities might have too little diversity to achieve this effect.

> I cannot imagine teaching constitutional law to an all white class. Most of this subject is about race. . . . I would not want to teach First Amendment [law], and discuss hate speech, without having some students from minority backgrounds in the class. . . . A diversity of views leads to a better discussion and better understanding among the students.
>
> —Paul Finkelman, law professor, Albany Law School, "Affirmative Action, Diversity, and College Admissions," *ABA Focus* 13:2 (Spring 1998)

Opponents of affirmative action charge that the practice undermines the constitutional principle that all people should be equal in the eyes of the government. Affirmative action, according to this view, sets a dangerous precedent.

> In public universities, preferences have broken down constitutional protections against classification by race—protections that form a still insecure bulwark against habits of racial abuse and oppression that have festered for centuries. Erosion of the legal doctrine of racial neutrality is a high price to pay for a system of preferences that moves only a few thousand students a year from one college to another.
>
> —Marie Gryphon, "The Affirmative Action Myth," Policy Analysis No. 540, Washington, DC: The Cato Institute, April 6, 2005

Opponents also say that affirmative action creates suspicions and racial and ethnic divisions that threaten to divide Americans.

> [Affirmative action] poisons the relationships between people based on their groups and based on the perception that some are being left behind because of it. I can't tell you the number of people who are white and male who say that 'I would've been here except for affirmative action.' There's no evidence of that, but there's that perception in their minds. And perception becomes reality. It poisons relationships and builds resentment, often needlessly.
>
> —Ward Connerly, "A Poison Divides Us," Salon.com interview with Alicia Montgomery, March 27, 2000, http://archive .salon.com/politics2000/feature/2000/03/27/connerly/ index.html?CP=SAL&DN=110, accessed May 23, 2008

Is Affirmative Action Constitutional?

The Supreme Court has struck a compromise on the issue of affirmative action, ruling in both the 1978 case of *Regents of the University of California v. Bakke* and the 2003 case of *Grutter v. Bollinger* that colleges and universities may use race as one factor

Pro Affirmative Action
Activists rally in support of affirmative action at the Supreme Court.

among many in their admissions decisions, but may not use out-right quotas (see p. 508). In 2007, the Court invalidated two public school desegregation plans because they used race as a tiebreaker whenever more students sought to attend a particular school than could be accommodated. The goal of the program was to achieve the same racial balance at the school as existed district-wide. In a 5-4 vote, the Court ruled that explicit use of race as a tiebreaker was unconstitutional. But Justice Anthony Kennedy, in a separate opinion, indicated that school boards could consider racial factors in making other decisions (e.g., neighborhood attendance boundaries) affecting the student composition at a school.[5]

What Do Americans Believe?

Americans as a whole seem divided over the policy of affirmative action. A poll taken in 2009, for example, found that 56 percent favored it.[6] This figure grows to 63 percent if affirmative action is linked to efforts to "counteract the effects of discrimination against minorities."[7] But Americans resist affirmative action when they consider the specific example of college and university admissions (see Figure 1). Over 50 percent of whites, African Americans, and Hispanics say that public schools "probably" or "definitely" should not be "allowed to take

FIGURE 1

PUBLIC SUPPORT FOR AFFIRMATIVE ACTION PROGRAMS

Depending on the context, views about affirmative action vary.

Sources: AP-GfK Poll, May 28-June 1, 2009 (favor or oppose); Pew Research Center poll, September 5–October 6, 2007 (overcome past discrimination); Quinnipiac University Poll, May 26-June 1, 2009 (hiring, promotions, admissions).

Do you generally favor or oppose affirmative action programs for racial minorities?

In order to overcome past discrimination, do you favor or oppose affirmative action programs designed to help blacks get better jobs and education?

Do you think affirmative action programs that give preferences to blacks and other minorities in hiring, promotions, and college admissions should be continued, or do you think these affirmative action programs should be abolished?

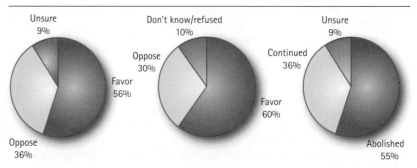

the racial background of students into account when assigning students to schools."[8] Misgivings about affirmative action have won out at the polls in recent years. Voters in three states have outlawed the practice in statewide referenda: California in 1996, Washington in 1998, and Michigan in 2006. More states may face such votes in the future as debates over the policy continue.

What Do You Think?

1. Should governments consider race as a factor in making decisions about university admissions, contracting, and other matters? What are the benefits and costs of such policies?

2. The Supreme Court has found that the government needs to show a "compelling interest" if race classifications are to stand up to constitutional scrutiny. Universities argue that maintaining a diverse student body constitutes such an interest. What is your view on which state interests are "compelling" enough to warrant classification by race?

On the Web

For more information on affirmative action, see the following websites:

The Leadership Council on Civil Rights promotes affirmative action and provides a number of reports and policy briefs.

www.civilrights.org

Founded by anti-affirmative action leader Ward Connerly, the American Civil Rights Institute presses for state-level bans on affirmative action policies.

www.acri.org

The Association of American Colleges and Universities maintains a Diversity website so that schools can share their strategies for ensuring diversity on campus.

www.diversityweb.org

[1]Terry H. Anderson, *The Pursuit of Fairness: A History of Affirmative Action,* New York: Oxford University Press, p. 61.
[2]Executive Order 11246, as amended, www.dol.gov/esa/regs/statutes/ofccp/eo11246.htm, accessed May 22, 2008.
[3]University of Colorado at Boulder, "Equal Opportunity/Affirmative Action Policy," www.colorado.edu/policies/aaeop.html, accessed May 23, 2008.
[4]Lyndon B. Johnson, "Commencement Address at Howard University: 'To Fulfill These Rights,'" June 4, 1965, Lyndon Baines Johnson Library and Museum, www.lbjlib.utexas.edu/johnson/archives.hom/speeches.hom/650604.asp, accessed May 23, 2008.
[5]*Parents Involved in Community Schools v. Seattle School District No. 1 et al* 551 U.S. ___ (2007).
[6]AP-GfK Poll, May 28–June 1, 2009.
[7]NBC News/*Wall Street Journal* Poll, June 12–15, 2009.
[8]EducationNext Poll, released August 2008.

Continued from page 518

Once elected officials had responded to the demands of the disabled, the courts, too, became more sensitive. Previously, many developmentally disabled children were denied access to public education on the grounds that they were not mentally competent. But, in the early seventies, federal courts required that states provide disabled children with equal educational opportunity.[127] These decisions generated a nationwide movement for disabled children, culminating in the passage in 1975 of the Education for All Handicapped Children Act. Reauthorized as the Individuals with Disabilities Education Act in 2004, this legislation guarantees children with special needs the right to an appropriate education.[128]

Encouraged by both judicial and legislative victories, disability rights groups became increasingly energetic and assertive. Legislative victories in education, transportation, and construction of public buildings finally culminated in the Americans with Disabilities Act of 1991, signed by President George H. W. Bush. This act made it illegal to deny employment to individuals on the grounds that they are disabled, unless the person's disability "pose[s] a direct threat to the health or safety of other individuals in the workplace."[129] In addition, workplaces and public accommodations must be adapted to the capacities of disabled persons, whenever feasible.

Because of these laws, opportunities for the disabled have greatly increased. Twenty years ago, public toilets for the disabled hardly existed; sidewalks and staircases had no ramps; buses and trains were inaccessible to those in wheelchairs; colleges and universities were designed in ways that all but precluded attendance by the physically challenged; and developmentally disabled children were denied a public education.

The courts themselves have shown considerable reluctance to interpret the rights of the disabled in sweeping terms. For example, in 2001 the Supreme Court ruled against an Alabama state employee who was punished for taking time off from her job to be treated for breast cancer. The employee, Patricia Garrett, argued that the Americans with Disabilities Act protected her from discrimination. But the Court said that state governments were not covered by the act because of their rights under federalism (see Chapter 3).[130] In 2002, a unanimous Court ruled that to qualify for protection under the ADA a person must have a condition that impairs activities "central to daily life"—not just workplace activities.[131] In these and other cases, the disabled have found that legislators have been friendlier to their cause than judges.

CHAPTER SUMMARY

17.1 Establish the origins of the struggle for civil rights in developments from after the Civil War through the 1940s.

Civil rights groups have achieved many of their advances by persuading majority populations of the justice of their causes through participation in political demonstrations and electoral politics.[134] When the country abandoned Reconstruction in the latter part of the nineteenth century, the Supreme Court, in the *Civil Rights Cases* and *Plessy v. Ferguson,* ruled against civil rights demands. When blacks moved north to jurisdictions in which they could vote more easily, public opinion began to change, elected officials became more sympathetic, and the Supreme Court began to reverse its earlier rulings.

17.2 Trace the rise of the civil rights movement following *Brown* and its subsequent decline in strength and assess results so far.

The 1954 Supreme Court ruling in *Brown* was the culmination of this reversal. Following the ruling, the civil rights movement made great strides in winning over the public and legislators. Bipartisan congressional majorities passed the Civil Rights Act of 1964 and the Voting Rights Act of 1965. In the 1970s and 1980s, public opinion became more cautious on civil rights issues, and policies such as affirmative action became controversial.

17.3 Outline civil rights issues for, and efforts undertaken by, minorities other than African Americans.

Latinos, Asian Americans, gays and lesbians, and American Indians have achieved varying degrees of legal rights, and the differences have largely reflected their electoral clout. In general, these groups have only begun to exert their strength in national elections, although they were influential in some states and localities much earlier.

17.4 Assess the civil rights objectives achieved by women and ongoing issues.

The modern women's rights movement grew out of the civil rights movement. Once women's groups became active, they achieved striking changes in legal doctrine, even though they did not succeed in securing passage of the ERA. The Supreme Court has outlawed most forms of gender discrimination, but women are not allowed in combat positions within the military. The Court has declared gender discrimination and sexual harassment in the workplace contrary to the Civil Rights Act of 1964 and has ruled state-funded, single-sex military training unconstitutional.

17.5 Describe judicial and legislative victories for Americans with disabilities.

The civil rights movement also helped focus attention on the rights of the disabled. Once again, the most important steps forward were taken not by the courts but by Congress, which acted in response to electoral-based political pressure.

mypoliscilab EXERCISES

Apply what you learned in this chapter on MyPoliSciLab.

Read on mypoliscilab.com

eText: Chapter 17

Study and Review on mypoliscilab.com

Pre-Test

Post-Test

Chapter Exam

Flashcards

Watch on mypoliscilab.com

Video: Supreme Court: No Race-Based Admissions

Video: Should Don't Ask Don't Tell Go Away?

Explore on mypoliscilab.com

Simulation: You are the Mayor and Need to Make Civil Rights Decisions

Comparative: Comparing Civil Rights

Timeline: The Civil Rights Movement

Timeline: The Mexican-American Civil Rights Movement

Timeline: The Struggle for Equal Protection

Timeline: Women's Struggle for Equality

Visual Literacy: Race and the Death Penalty

KEY TERMS

affirmative action, p. 508

black codes, p. 497

Brown v. Board of Education of Topeka, Kansas, p. 502

civil disobedience, p. 503

civil rights, p. 497

de facto segregation, p. 507

de jure segregation, p. 507

equal protection clause, p. 497

Equal Rights Amendment (ERA), p. 514

glass ceiling, p. 518

grandfather clause, p. 498

Jim Crow laws, p. 499

National Association for the Advancement of Colored People (NAACP), p. 500

Plessy v. Ferguson, p. 499

poll tax, p. 498

quota, p. 518

Reconstruction, p. 498

restrictive housing covenant, p. 501

separate but equal doctrine, p. 499

state action doctrine, p. 499

suspect classification, p. 502

white primary, p. 498

SUGGESTED READINGS

Of General Interest

Ifill, Gwen. *The Breakthrough: Politics and Race in the Age of Obama.* New York: Anchor, 2009. A journalist's perspective on a new generation of black leaders, including President Obama.

McClain, Paula D., and Joseph Stewart, Jr. *"Can We All Get Along?": Racial and Ethnic Minorities in American Politics,* 5th Edition. Boulder, CO: Westview Press, 2009. An in-depth political science analysis of the status of blacks, Latinos, Asian Americans, and Native Americans in U.S. politics.

Rosenberg, Gerald N. *The Hollow Hope: Can Courts Bring About Social Change?* Chicago: University of Chicago Press, 1991. Argues that courts are generally unable to act contrary to majority opinion.

Wolbrecht, Christina, and Rodney E. Hero, eds. *The Politics of Democratic Inclusion.* Philadelphia: Temple University Press, 2005. A series of essays describing how underrepresented groups have made themselves heard in the democratic process.

Focused Studies

Deloria, Vine, Jr., and David E. Wilkins. *Tribes, Treaties, and Constitutional Tribulations.* Austin: University of Texas Press, 1999. Discusses the constitutional status of the rights of indigenous peoples.

Garcia, F. Chris, and Gabriel Sanchez. *Hispanics and the U.S. Political System: Moving into the Mainstream.* New York: Prentice Hall, 2007. Focuses on the growing importance of Latinos in U.S. politics and elections.

Cushman, Clare, ed. *Supreme Court Decisions and Women's Rights*. Washington, DC: CQ Press and the Supreme Court Historical Society, 2000. With a foreword by Supreme Court Justice Ruth Bader Ginsburg, this volume provides a comprehensive resource on court decisions affecting women's rights.

Key, V. O., Jr. *Southern Politics*. New York: Random House, 1949. Classic study of the effects of racial conflict on southern politics.

Lien, Pei-te. *The Politics of Asian Americans: Diversity and Community*. New York: Routledge, 2004. An account detailing Asian Americans' engagement in U.S. politics.

Rimmerman, Craig A., and Clyde Wilcox, eds. *The Politics of Same-Sex Marriage*. Chicago: University of Chicago Press, 2007. Authors consider religious, legal, and political perspectives on the same-sex marriage issue.

Switzer, Jacqueline Vaughn. *Disabled Rights: American Disability Policy and the Fight for Equality*. Washington, DC: Georgetown University Press, 2003. A political scientist examines the evolution of disability policy and the disability rights movement.

ON THE WEB

www.usdoj.gov

In this chapter, we discussed several important pieces of civil rights legislation, such as the Voting Rights Act and the Americans with Disabilities Act. The U.S. Department of Justice's Civil Rights Division provides information on its enforcement of these and other civil rights laws.

www.usccr.gov

In 1957, one year after the Montgomery bus boycott, Congress created the U.S. Commission on Civil Rights. The commission remains active today, investigating complaints of discrimination in many sectors of American society.

http://mlk-kpp01.stanford.edu

Martin Luther King, Jr., effectively used nonviolent protest tactics to persuade the majority of Americans of the importance of civil rights. The Martin Luther King, Jr., Papers Project at Stanford University maintains a website with many of King's speeches and sermons, as well as several scholarly articles and book chapters.

www.naacp.org

The NAACP, the nation's oldest civil rights organization, successfully pursued the legal strategy that led to the *Brown v. Board of Education* decision.

www.now.org

Created to promote the Equal Rights Amendment, the National Organization for Women is the country's largest feminist organization, with more than 500,000 members.

www.nclr.org

In the 2000 census, Latinos surpassed African Americans in population for the first time. This and other factors have convinced Democrats and Republicans that future election victories may depend on the Latino vote. The National Council of La Raza monitors issues of concern to Hispanic Americans.

www.hrc.org

Gay and lesbian activists have achieved important goals, but public opinion on this group remains divided. Human Rights Campaign, a leading gay rights organization, monitors changes in public policy toward gays and lesbians at the local, state, and federal levels.

www.leap.org

Leadership Education for Asian Pacifics, Inc. (LEAP), houses the Asian Pacific American Public Policy Institute, which authors numerous reports on Asian Americans.

www.ncd.gov

The National Council on Disability is an independent federal agency that makes recommendations to the president and Congress regarding policy on Americans with disabilities. The agency's site provides links to other relevant federal agencies, press releases, and in-depth reports.

18 Domestic Policy

CHAPTER OUTLINE

Healthcare Reform

It was August 12, 2009. The ranking Republican on the Senate Finance Committee, Charles Grassley, stood in front of a town hall meeting in Afton, Iowa, taking notes on his constituents' concerns. A quiet, middle-aged woman wearing a t-shirt depicting an American flag stood near the back of the room and stated her case. "When 9/11 happened," she said, "I was very terrified, but I honestly am more terrified now. Then, I felt my government was going to protect me, and now I'm afraid of my government. We have the car industry, is taken over, the banks were taken over, and now I feel our healthcare, and I think we're leaning toward socialism, and that scares me to death." The crowd erupted in applause.[1]

It is difficult to say for certain when a bipartisan deal on healthcare reform became impossible, but this moment is as good a candidate as any.

Every Democratic president since Harry Truman—and some Republican ones—had tried to enact comprehensive reform of the nation's healthcare system. Unlike most other industrialized nations, however, at the time Barack Obama was inaugurated in 2009, the United States still had a largely private, although heavily regulated, system of health insurance and hospitals. To be sure, President Lyndon Johnson had pressed for, and won, health insurance programs for the aged (Medicare) and for low-income people (Medicaid) in 1965, but about two-thirds of Americans under the age of 65 still received health insurance from their employers or bought their own on the private market.[2] By contrast, in European countries such as the United Kingdom, Canada, and France, the government provided some system of nationalized healthcare. The United States spent more per person on healthcare than any other industrialized democratic nation, and 44 million Americans had no insurance at all.[3]

Democrats had long viewed healthcare as a critical issue for their party. Healthcare reform was Bill Clinton's top priority during the first few years of his presidency, but his plan died in Congress amid criticism by Republicans that its requirements that insurance be purchased through large cooperatives was too bureaucratic and heavy-handed. Fourteen years later, Obama ran for president promoting a slimmed-down reform proposal that would encourage people to purchase insurance and would subsidize those who might have trouble paying.

Once in office, Obama pressed Congress to get to work on a bill. Senator Max Baucus, the Democratic chairman of the Finance Committee, held talks with his Republican counterpart, Senator Grassley, in the spring of 2009, and a bipartisan deal looked possible. Even the health insurance industry appeared to be on board. As one industry lobbyist put it, "we're all in agreement that everyone should have health insurance, that we should control costs, and that the quality of health care should be improved."[4]

But hardening battle lines in late summer 2009 dispelled any illusions of consensus. The Democratic plan now included a mandate that all Americans purchase health insurance, new local health insurance "exchanges" that would channel the market for insurance, and a combination of subsidies for low-income people and new revenue from people who were better off. Conservative activists argued that the plan constituted a reckless and unprecedented "government takeover" of the healthcare system. Members of Congress who went home to their districts in August, Senator Grassley among them, got an earful from angry constituents, many of whom already had health insurance and saw no reason for a change. Soon, Republicans were almost united in opposition: Republican

Senator Olympia Snowe voted in October to advance a healthcare bill out of committee, but that would be the last time a Republican Senator joined Democrats on the issue. Even some moderate Democrats, like Nebraska's Ben Nelson and Arkansas's Blanche Lincoln, began to waver.

From October 2009 to March 2010, healthcare reform seemed to be continually on the brink of failure. The House—with only a single Republican "yes" vote—passed its healthcare bill in early November by a razor-thin margin. Over the next three weeks, Senate Majority Leader Harry Reid (D-NV) fought a Senate filibuster that threatened to prevent the measure from even reaching the floor. The bill finally moved ahead, but Republicans vowed to continue fighting. As Senator John Cornyn put it, "in the light of the unpopularity of what is being jammed down the throats of the American people, there will be a day of accounting."[5] As Cornyn pointed out, the healthcare bill had become less popular over time: Polls showed a majority of the public now opposed the plan.[6]

Still, the White House and Democratic congressional leadership pressed forward. Democrats argued that the bill was a moderate, market-driven reform proposal—certainly a far cry from the "single payer" government-run system that some left-wing activists wanted. Indeed, as part of the Senate negotiations, Democrats agreed to drop a provision for a "public option," an insurance plan operated by the government that would compete with private plans. On Christmas Eve, 2009, after a flurry of White House lobbying, a healthcare bill passed the Senate in a close vote, again with no Republican support. Again success appeared likely. But on January 19 Massachusetts voters elected a Republican—Scott Brown—to fill a senate seat left vacant by the late healthcare reform advocate Ted Kennedy. Healthcare's victory margins had been so narrow that Brown's election seemed poised to sink negotiations between the House and Senate over a final bill. And it was now 2010: an election year.

Two months of chaotic political battle followed. Some moderate Democrats in the House threatened to withdraw their support if the final bill allowed taxpayer funds to pay for abortion. Republicans cried foul when Democrats decided to use a rare parliamentary tactic called "reconciliation" to evade filibusters in the Senate. President Obama hosted an exhausting day-long meeting at the White House, where Democrats and Republicans explained their differences to each other—and to a nationwide television audience. Finally, on March 25, the House and Senate passed the final version of the healthcare bill and sent it to the president's desk. Obama heralded the new law—the most significant change in social policy since the 1960s—as a reform that "generations of Americans have fought for, marched for, and hungered to see."[7] House Republican leader John Boehner called the law "a sloppy mess that the majority of the American people believe should be repealed and replaced."[8] With such diverging views on the new policy, it is no wonder that, as Representative Sander Levin (D-MI) put it, "We are anxious to go home and stand up and talk to our constituents and explain this bill."[9]

Making the Connection

Does the battle over the healthcare bill show that the process of making domestic policy is broken, or does it instead prove that it works in the face of daunting odds? Why are some issues, like abortion funding, the subject of intense debate even though they represent only small components of an overall policy program? How can the two parties have such different views about what the American public wants? Why did the U.S. government have a host of programs that support some populations (such as older Americans), but many fewer programs that support other populations (such as the working poor)?

To provide a way of thinking about these questions, this chapter examines the electoral and political forces that shape domestic policy. We discuss the various stages through which all domestic policies proceed and then consider three major types of domestic policy: social policy, education policy, and regulatory policy. For each, we examine the political factors that help shape policy outcomes.

18.1

Identify the major types of public policy and the stages in its formation.

domestic policy
All government programs and regulations that directly affect those living within a country.

agenda setting
Making an issue so visible that important political leaders take it seriously.

policy deliberation
Debate and discussion by interest groups and political leaders over issues placed on the policy agenda.

policy enactment
Passage of a law by public officials.

Types of Public Policy

Public policy is a term applied to all government programs and regulations. Often policies are classified as foreign or domestic. Foreign policy involves relations with other nations (see Chapter 20). **Domestic policy** consists of all government programs and regulations that directly affect those living within a country. It includes everything from education and healthcare to transportation and garbage collection—hundreds of different kinds of governmental activity. However, the distinction between domestic and foreign policy is not always sharp and clear. Some domestic policies, such as immigration policy or homeland security, affect relations with other countries. Some foreign policies, such as foreign trade regulations, have major domestic consequences. Of all the domestic policies, economic ones are among the most complex and important, and Chapter 19 is devoted to a discussion of economic policy. In this chapter, we look at a variety of other domestic policies.

The Stages of Policymaking

The making of policy is a complex, never-ending series of events. It is by no means assured that any given policy will be enacted. On the contrary, scholars have found that enacted policies are often the result of unique combinations of problems, solutions, and opportunities for action.[10] To clarify what is often a very messy process, political scientists have described it in terms of six stages that are together known as the policymaking round, shown in Figure 18.1. At each stage, policymakers pay close attention to public opinion and try to estimate the consequences of their choices for the next election.

The first stage is **agenda setting,** making an issue visible enough that important political leaders take it seriously.[11] When elected officials think a problem is serious and might even affect an election, the issue has reached the agenda stage. The second stage consists of **policy deliberation,** the debate and discussion over issues placed on the policy agenda.[12] At this stage, interest groups and policy experts try to convince leaders not only that their proposals are a good way to deal with the problem, but also that these proposals are popular with the electorate. Next comes **policy enactment,** the

FIGURE 18.1

POLICYMAKING STAGES

The policymaking round is a rough approximation of the stages that proposed policies go through. Keep in mind that at each stage, a policy might suffer setbacks or even defeat.

• *Match each stage with events in the development of healthcare policy. What do you think the next healthcare policy round will look like?*

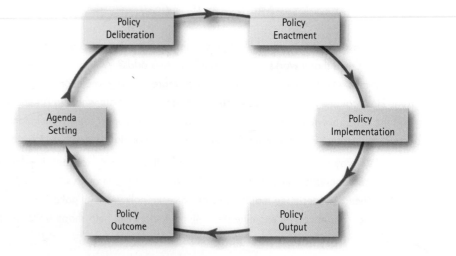

passage of a law by public officials. Enactment may involve passage by Congress, a state legislature, or a city council, and signing into law by a president, governor, or mayor. Elected officials who vote for the law usually expect that its passage will enhance their popularity, although there have been a few celebrated instances in which political leaders have sacrificed their careers for what they saw as the good of the country. The fourth stage is **policy implementation,** translation of the legislation into an actual set of government programs or regulations.[13] When fashioning the details, bureaucrats are expected to carry out the intentions of the legislative branch and not to stray too far from what is politically acceptable. At the fifth stage, government produces **policy outputs,** the provision of services to citizens or the regulation of their conduct. Beneficiaries usually think well of those who established the program; those who are hurt by the policy outputs probably feel otherwise. Finally, **policy outcomes** are the effects of policy outputs on individuals and businesses.[14] These outcomes often give rise to new issues, which are then placed on the policy agenda, completing the policymaking round.

The history of the 2010 healthcare legislation illustrates the way politics affects the various stages of the policy round. The first stage, placing the issue on the policy agenda, occurred when Barack Obama scored points in his 2008 campaign for president by promising to make healthcare reform one of his top three priorities. The second stage, policy deliberation, occurred when interest groups, policy experts, members of Congress, and the media debated many different ways of redesigning the healthcare system. Early in the debate, polls showed broad support for reform, but once the details of specific plans were released, public support for the Obama plan shrank to about 40 percent. The third stage, policy enactment, saw Congress enact a new law that created new health insurance "exchanges," mandated that all Americans have health insurance by 2014, and subsidized the purchase of insurance for low-income people. President Obama signed the bill into law despite the public's misgivings because he believed that once the results of the reform were clear, support for it would grow. The fourth stage, policy implementation, began in 2010. The fifth stage, policy outputs, will take place from 2010 to 2014. After that, policymakers, politicians, and activists will begin to take stock of policy outcomes.

The political forces that shape public policies differ from one policy to the next. In the remainder of this chapter we describe the political factors shaping three major types of public policy: social policy, education policy, and regulatory policy.

Social Policy

Social policy is a type of domestic policy that consists of programs designed to help those thought to be in need of government assistance. People may be regarded as needy because they are old, infirm, young, disabled, unemployed, poor, or some combination of these conditions. The Obama healthcare reform measure, for example, requires all Americans to purchase health insurance beginning in 2014, but will provide subsidies so that poorer people can afford to do this.

Elderly people have done particularly well in securing government help. As Figure 18.2 shows, poverty among senior citizens fell from 25 percent in 1970 to less than 10 percent in 2008, but the poverty rate of another seemingly needy population—children—did not decline over this period. The poverty rate among families with

policy implementation
Translation of legislation into a set of government programs or regulations.

policy output
Provision of services to citizens or regulation of their conduct.

policy outcome
Effect of policy outputs on individuals and businesses.

18.2

Trace the origins and development of public assistance programs.

social policy
Domestic policy programs designed to help those thought to be in need of government assistance.

FIGURE 18.2

U.S. Poverty Rates for Senior Citizens and Children, 1970–2008

In the past, poverty rates for senior citizens were higher than for other groups of Americans. Today, however, the poverty rate for seniors is lower than the poverty rate among children.

• *Why are poverty rates higher for children than for seniors? When did poverty rates for senior citizens drop below poverty rates for children? Why?*

Source: U.S. Census Bureau, *Historical Poverty Tables—People,* Table 3: Poverty Status by Age, Race, and Hispanic Origin, 1959–2008, www.census.gov/hhes/www/poverty/histpov/perindex.html, accessed May 9, 2010.

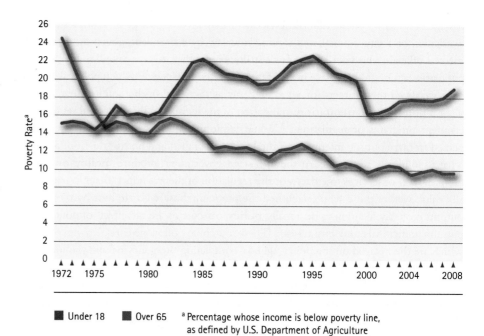

■ Under 18   ■ Over 65   ª Percentage whose income is below poverty line, as defined by U.S. Department of Agriculture

children in the United States is twice as high as in most other advanced industrial societies;[15] however, the poverty rate among senior citizens is about the same or only slightly higher in the United States as in these societies.[16]

Poverty is not just a matter of money; it pervades many aspects of life. For example, the chances of being in good health are different for senior citizens and children. Of the seven developed countries with the largest economies, the United States has the highest infant mortality rate.[17] But, if one reaches old age, one has a better chance of living longer in the United States than in any of the other six countries. As one analyst put it, the United States is perhaps the "healthiest place to grow old but the riskiest [in which] to be born."[18]

In the next two sections, we explain how this phenomenon came to be. First we describe the development of social programs for senior citizens and the powerful political support that sustains them. Then we examine the development of social programs for children and the more limited support they enjoy.

Social Insurance for Senior Citizens

As the population has aged, the government has expanded programs to meet the retirement income and medical needs of the elderly. Between 1960 and 2008, spending on those older than 65 more than doubled as a percentage of the federal budget.[19] In this section we describe the conditions that led to this dramatic increase in social insurance.

Origins and Development of Social Insurance Programs   Public demands for aid to senior citizens escalated during the Great Depression of the 1930s, when poverty among the elderly was particularly acute. Approximately five million senior citizens rallied behind the proposals of Dr. Francis E. Townsend, a 67-year-old Californian who promised to end the Depression by giving everyone over the age of 60 the equivalent in today's dollars of $3260 a month, provided that they spent it immediately (unless otherwise indicated, all dollar figures in this chapter are expressed in constant 2010 dollars so as to adjust for inflation).[20] Always quick to recognize potential electoral threats, President Franklin Roosevelt checked Townsend's soaring popularity by appointing an advisory committee to recommend better ways of meeting the needs of the elderly. The committee recommended a policy of **social insurance,** a program that provides benefits in return for contributions made by workers. In a response consistent with the committee's recommendations, in 1935 Congress enacted the landmark Social Security Act, which created a broad range of social programs, including a social insurance program for senior citizens generally known as **social security.**[21]

The social security program initially cost the government little. Most of those who first retired under the program received minimal benefits because they had paid into the program for only a brief time. Also, retirement costs were low because, in 1935, average life expectancy for those reaching the age of 65 was only an additional 13 to 15 years. In contrast, a worker retiring at 65 today is expected to live nearly 19 more years.[22]

Gradually, the program expanded. The number of people covered went up; so did the length of their retirement. Benefits increased in size and cost. Two major changes deserve particular attention. In 1965, the year after Democrats won an overwhelming election victory, Congress enacted **Medicare,** which provides a broad range of medical benefits to social security recipients. In 1972, an election year, Congress gave senior citizens a large increase in their monthly social security checks and linked, or indexed, this amount to the cost of living. If inflation goes up 10 percent, so does the paycheck.[23] Passed at a time when prices were rising, this new benefit soon became very popular.

The popularity of both social security and Medicare is due in part to the fact that they are based on the insurance principle—that is, the principle that people receive benefits in return for contributions they have made. In the case of social security, the insurance principle works in the following way: People become eligible for benefits by

social insurance
Program that provides benefits in return for contributions made by workers.

social security
Social insurance program for senior citizens.

Medicare
Program that provides social security recipients a broad range of medical benefits.

Johnson Signs Medicare Bill

President Lyndon B. Johnson signs the Medicare bill in 1965 as Vice President Hubert Humphrey and former president Truman look on.

• *Why did Congress and President Bush agree to expand Medicare benefits in 2003?*

• *Why does the insurance principle help make Medicare popular?*

paying a portion of their regular salary—a payroll tax—to social security during their working years. To get social security benefits, beneficiaries need only prove that they are over the age of 65. (This eligibility age gradually increases for those born after 1937; those born in 1960 and later are eligible for full benefits at age 67.) Because of the insurance principle, a retiree does not have to show a need. Even billionaire Microsoft founder Bill Gates will be eligible to receive a social security check when he reaches the eligibility age.

Although social security is called an insurance program, it differs from a true insurance program in one fundamental respect: It operates at a loss. In private insurance programs, most people pay more in initial payments and forgone interest than they receive in benefits; if this were not the case, the insurance company could not make a profit. From the beginning, however, social security has given most people more in benefits than they contributed in their social security tax. For example, a couple with a single average wage earner retiring in 2014 can expect to receive 4.4 percent more in benefits than the worker in the family paid in, even after taking inflation into account.[24]

How is this magic possible? How can benefits exceed contributions? Why have social security and Medicare not gone broke? Up until now, there have been three reasons:

1. Workers have grown in number, as women and "baby boomers" have entered the workforce and unemployment rates have fallen. Thus, more people are contributing to the social security program.

2. Workers today produce more and earn more than their predecessors did. As result, more money is available to distribute to retirees.

3. Workers today pay a higher percentage of their earnings in social security taxes than their predecessors did. Essentially, younger generations have been asked to pay more to cover the expenses of older ones. As economist Lester Thurow has pointed out, "the current generation of retirees . . . did not have to pay [much] into the system but gets benefits financed by those behind them."[25] The practice is not new. Jonathan Swift saw the same thing happening in England three centuries ago. "'Tis pleasant to observe," he said, "how free the present Age is in laying taxes on the next."[26]

Some of these circumstances may be changing:

1. Experts do not expect the number of workers to increase much in the next several decades. The massive baby boom generation will reach retirement age from 2010 to 2030. As they leave the workforce, the number of retirees will grow faster than the number of workers. As a result, the cost of retirement programs will increase, as Figure 18.3 shows.

2. Rates of growth in economic productivity may not always be as high as they have been in recent decades. After the 2008 financial crisis, experts were reminded that an economic recession could quickly change the picture. If the economy rebounds too slowly, workers in the future may not be produce enough to cover the higher cost of social security caused by the retirement of the baby boomers.

3. Workers may be less willing to pay higher taxes. It will be difficult to increase their taxes to cover the retirement costs of the baby boomers.

For these reasons, a presidential panel declared in December 2001 that "the system is not sustainable as currently structured."[27] Politicians agreed on the problems with the

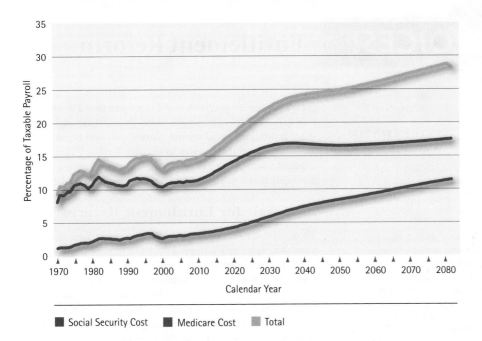

FIGURE 18.3

PROJECTED COST OF SOCIAL INSURANCE FOR SENIOR CITIZENS

This graph depicts the projected increase in costs of social security and Medicare under an "intermediate costs" scenario. Figures after 2007 are estimates.

• *Why will the costs of programs for senior citizens rise rapidly in the coming years? When do projected costs make the biggest leap upward? Why do you think they rise so much in this specific period?*

Source: U.S. Department of Health and Human Services, Social Security Administration, "Status of the Social Security and Medicare Programs," A Summary of the 2008 Annual Reports, www.ssa.gov/OACT/TRSUM/index .html, accessed May 27, 2008.

program but disagreed over the varied proposals for reform (see the *Election Voices!* feature on the next page). More than most other issues, changes in social security are politically excruciating to make, as we explain in the next section.

Politics of Social Insurance   Many subway systems use dangerous middle rails, or third rails, that provide the electricity that drives the trains. Social security and Medicare are said to be the "third rail" of American politics—"touch it and you die." Richard Morin put it another way: "The bottom line on the public's attitude is: Spend whatever is needed—particularly on me—just don't bill us for it."[28]

Proposed Changes to Social Security—Because most public officials know they will be punished by the voters if they are perceived as threatening social security programs, only rarely do they suggest changes. In 2005, however, President George W. Bush advocated major alterations to social security to address the factors outlined above. Bush proposed giving workers the choice of placing some of their social security taxes in market-based accounts, and slowing the expansion of benefits for most social security recipients. Although Bush and members of his cabinet traveled around the country promoting the plan, Democrats attacked it as an attempt to undermine the insurance principle. For their part, congressional Republicans offered what one analyst described as a "din of silence."[29] Bush's plan died a quiet death in Congress. Just a few years later, the stock market's plunge during the 2008 financial crisis made the idea of placing social security funds in the market even less politically palatable.

The Complexities of Medicare—The politics of Medicare are much the same, making it difficult to keep the program from growing rapidly. The cost of the program grew from about $40 billion in 1970 to over $520 billion by 2010.[30] Numerous factors contribute to the rapidly rising cost of Medicare. The number of elderly is growing rapidly, increasing the demand for medical services. Doctors can use better (and more expensive) technology to diagnose and treat more crippling injuries and life-threatening diseases.

Continued on page 536

Entitlement Reform

The Issue

What should be done, if anything, to slow or reverse the growth of entitlements in light of their burgeoning share of the federal budget?

Background

When Franklin Roosevelt signed the Social Security Act of 1935 he explained the measure this way:

> The civilization of the past hundred years, with its startling industrial changes, has tended more and more to make life insecure. . . . We can never ensure one hundred percent of the population against one hundred percent of the hazards and vicissitudes of life, but we have tried to frame a law which will give some measure of protection to the average citizen and to his family against the loss of a job and against poverty-stricken old age.[1]

In light of the economic turmoil that followed the financial crisis of 2008, many Americans understand well what Roosevelt meant by the "hazards and vicissitudes" of the modern economy. But another danger looms that complicates the picture: growing federal deficits that some economists warn will accelerate capital flight from the United States, add to inflation pressures, and crowd out savings and investment in the private sector.[2]

Social security, Medicare, and Medicaid are the three largest entitlements—programs that distribute benefits by law to people in eligible categories. Most of these benefits go to Americans over the age of 65, a group projected to grow from 13 percent of the population today to 21 percent by 2050.[3] Under current

policy, entitlement programs could cost more than 25 percent of taxable income two generations from now, as Figure 18.3 shows. What is more, the social security system will soon begin spending more money than it takes in via payroll taxes. Can the government afford to keep paying these benefits at current rates as the population ages and the economy continues to struggle?

Proposals for Entitlement Reform

Those who answer "no" to the question above suggest one or more of three possible changes. First, some propose to *increase taxes* to pay for these programs. The social security and Medicare programs are financed by payroll taxes that are deducted from workers' paychecks. In 1983 a modest increase in the payroll tax ensured social security's solvency for decades. Medicaid funds are culled from state and federal general revenues, but a tax increase of some kind could be used to shore up that program as well. Second, some analysts advocate *changing the eligibility criteria* for these entitlements. Raising the age at which Americans are eligible for full social security and Medicare benefits, for example, would create more room for spending on those who are eligible. Medicaid and Medicare benefits could also be made less generous. Another possibility might be to restrict the availability of social security and Medicaid, targeting benefits at the neediest populations and allowing wealthier retirees to make their own way.

Finally, some suggest partial or full *privatization* of these programs. In 2005, President George W. Bush proposed a system in which younger people could keep a portion of their social security contributions in private accounts. Conservatives have also

Trays of social security checks wait to be mailed at a U.S. Treasury facility in Philadelphia.

TABLE 1

TEN-YEAR BUDGET FIGURES ON ENTITLEMENT PROGRAMS, SOCIAL SECURITY SHORTFALL, AND SELECTED POLICY CHANGES

Costs	(over ten years)
Social security cost:	$9,220 billion
Medicare cost:	$7,729 billion
Medicaid cost:	$3,445 billion

Revenues	(over ten years)
Medicare premiums:	$1,126 billion
Payroll taxes:	$11,822 billion
Long-term social security shortfall, per decade:	$706 billion

Policy Changes	(amount of new revenue over ten years)
Increase payroll tax by 1 percent:	$592.2 billion
Increase cigarette tax by $1 per pack:	$94.9 billion
Raise the retirement age to 70:	$91.9 billion

suggested doing something similar with Medicare, encouraging so-called personal "health savings accounts" that retirees could tap into to buy insurance.

Table 1 illustrates the impact of some of these policy options relative to the projected social security shortfall, and relative to the overall budgets for the three major entitlements.

Opposing Views on Entitlement Reform

Conservative advocates for redirecting entitlement spending into private accounts argue that this will not only result in fiscal solvency, but also will provide a better deal for younger Americans.

> Social Security taxes are already so high, relative to benefits, that Social Security has simply become a bad deal for younger workers, providing a below-market rate of return. In fact, many young workers will end up paying more in taxes than they receive in benefits. And most important, workers have no ownership of their benefits. This means that they are left totally dependent on the goodwill of 535 politicians to determine what they'll receive in retirement.
>
> Benefits are not inheritable, and the program is a barrier to wealth accumulation. Lower-income families, African-Americans, and working women suffer disproportionately.
>
> —Michael D. Tanner, "Fixing Social Security," *National Review* (online), August 18, 2010.

Liberals, by contrast, argue for strengthening existing programs, either by raising the payroll tax, taking more from general revenues, or making slight changes to eligibility criteria.

> [O]ur longer-term goal should be . . . a new public-private partnership that builds upon and extends the basic underlying principle of the New Deal. That principle—even more true today than it was in the 1930s—is that security is not opposed to opportunity but essential to it. In a dynamic and flexible economy, well-designed policies of economic security are critical if workers are going to have the confidence they need to invest in and achieve the American dream.
>
> —Jacob Hacker, "A Strong Safety Net Encourages Healthy Risk Taking," *The American Prospect*, May 7, 2009.

What Do Americans Believe?

Americans are skeptical that entitlement programs will remain as they are. When asked whether they think full social security benefits will be available to them when they retire, 60 percent of working Americans—and 70 percent of those younger than 50—say they will not.[4] But unanimity disappears when pollsters suggest different reform proposals. A bit more than one third say increased contributions from the wealthy should be considered; about half would reject any attempt to curb benefits for existing retirees, and 59 percent disagree with the statement that "social security and Medicare should be privatized."[5] Proponents of policy change face serious obstacles in convincing the public to accept any particular reform.

What Do You Think?

Should entitlement reforms focus on reducing the size of government and returning funds to private accounts, or should they concentrate on shoring up the safety net to protect Americans from risk?

Whatever reforms you favor, how would you go about convincing policymakers and the public that your program should be adopted?

On the Web

www.cbo.gov

The Congressional Budget Office produces economic and budget forecasts projecting how much entitlement programs will cost in the long term.

http://www.socialsecurityreform.org/

The Heritage Foundation's social security reform center argues that entitlements should be reformed to direct some money to private individual accounts.

http://www.aflcio.org/issues/retirementsecurity/socialsecurity/

The AFL-CIO, the largest union in the United States, favors proposals that would "protect and strengthen" the existing entitlement system.

---

[1]Transcription by authors from video of speech by Franklin Roosevelt, available at http://www.archive.org/details/fdrbig, accessed September 10, 2010.

[2]Douglas Elmdorf, Director, Congressional Budget Office, "Aging and Health: The Challenges of Entitlement Growth," presentation to the Association for Public Policy Analysis and Management, November 2009, available at http://www.cbo.gov/doc.cfm?index=10707, accessed September 10, 2010.

[3]United States Bureau of the Census, "U.S. Interim Projections by Age, Sex, Race, and Hispanic Origin: 2000-2050," http://www.census.gov/population/www/projections/usinterimproj/, accessed September 10, 2010.

[4]CNN/Opinion Research Corporation Poll, August 6-10, 2010.

[5]Bloomberg Poll, March 19-22, 2010.

Continued from page 533

Finally, patients expect error-free medicine; when mistakes are made, lawsuits drive up doctors' insurance costs (and the fees doctors must charge to cover them).

Analysts expect Medicare costs to rise even faster when the baby boom generation retires and needs more medical services. The Obama administration argues that the new healthcare bill will generate over $400 billion in savings from Medicare over 10 years, but a prescription drug benefit added in 2003 and rising healthcare costs are still projected to grow the cost of Medicare substantially in the near term.[31]

The Influence of Senior Citizens—The electoral impact of the social security issue is likely to remain central to American politics. At a time when overall voter turnout has been declining, senior citizen turnout rates are high and have been climbing. Between 1972 and 2008, turnout among voters aged 18 to 24 dropped by 5 percent, while turnout among voters over 65 climbed by 5 percent.[32] Around 70 percent of eligible voters over the age of 65 said they voted in the 2008 presidential election, but only 48 percent of those between the ages of 18 and 24 reported voting.[33] Senior citizens are also much more likely than young people to back up their votes with other political actions, such as writing letters to elected officials and contributing money to political campaigns.[34]

More than 40 million people have joined the American Association of Retired Persons (AARP), the largest and one of the most influential interest groups in the United States.[35] Upon reaching the age of 50, any person can become a member of AARP for $16 per year. Members are eligible for a wide range of travel and other discounts worth much more than their annual dues. They also receive a magazine that keeps them up to date on policy proposals that might affect their social security and Medicare benefits. AARP employs more than 1,800 people, works with more than 4 million volunteers, and has an annual budget of $1.1 billion.[36] AARP was a strong supporter of the 2010 healthcare reform bill and promised to support those members of Congress who voted for it in the 2010 election.

Broad Support—AARP has the advantage of promoting a cause that few voters strongly oppose. In fact, young people are just about as likely to support benefits for senior citizens as those over the age of 65. When asked during the 2003 debate over expanding Medicare prescription drug benefits whether they would be willing to pay higher taxes to fund a prescription drug program for seniors, overwhelming majorities of both young voters and senior citizens said they would do so.

There are three main reasons for the broad support that social security and Medicare enjoy. First, most people hope to benefit from these programs someday themselves. In addition, many have parents who currently receive these benefits, relieving their children of financial responsibility. Finally, most people think that, because senior citizens contributed to social security, they now deserve the benefits they were promised, and few are aware that these benefits are usually in excess of the contributions.

Public Assistance to Poor Families

The interests of senior citizens may be well protected by AARP and both political parties, but the same cannot be said for the interests of poor families with children. Programs designed for poor families are neither as lavish nor as user-friendly as those designed for the elderly. Neither political party is strongly committed to expanding them, and no association comparable to AARP defends the interests of Americans with low incomes.

The Origins and Development of Public Assistance Programs   **Public assistance** consists of programs that provide low-income households with income subsidies and access to essential goods and services. Together, the programs make up what is often known as the "safety net" that catches those who fall into financial difficulty. The sheer number of major public assistance programs actually exceeds the number of major programs for the elderly. Public assistance programs include Temporary Assistance for Needy Families, food stamps (SNAP), the Earned Income Tax Credit, rent subsidies, Medicaid, and the State Children's Health Insurance Program.

Temporary Assistance for Needy Families (TANF)—The **Temporary Assistance for Needy Families (TANF)** program, enacted by Congress in 1996, gave the states the responsibility for designing income-maintenance programs for poor families. However, state programs are subject to certain limitations. For example, no family may receive more than two consecutive years of assistance, and no family may receive more than five years of assistance altogether.

TANF replaced the long-standing public assistance program known as Aid to Families with Dependent Children (AFDC), which was established in 1935 as part of the Social Security Act. AFDC was designed to serve widows, but as the number of unmarried women increased, the size of the program grew sharply. Conservatives claimed that it discouraged recipients from working.[37] Liberals believed that the benefits were too low and that program eligibility and administrative restrictions were too harsh.[38] TANF has proved to be a more popular program because welfare rolls have fallen and poverty rates have not increased dramatically, as some critics predicted.

Supplemental Nutrition Assistance Program (SNAP)/"Food Stamps"—This public assistance program provides recipients with vouchers (credited to a debit card) that can be used to purchase food. Enacted by Congress on an experimental basis in the early 1970s, it has been gradually expanded and today is larger than TANF. Benefits depend on the recipient's income and household size, but the average is about $125 per person per month.[39] The **food stamps** program has been more popular than has AFDC, because

public assistance
Programs that provide low-income households with a limited income and access to essential goods and services.

Temporary Assistance for Needy Families (TANF)
Welfare reform law passed by Congress in 1996.

food stamps
Public assistance program that provides recipients with stamps that can be used to purchase food. Formally named the Supplemental Nutrition Assistance Program (SNAP).

Food Stamps
All 50 states now use Electronic Benefit Transfer (EBT) cards to distribute food stamps. Here, a California man holds his EBT card.

• *Why do you think food stamps are more popular than other "welfare" programs?*

most Americans believe everyone should be provided with enough food to avoid going hungry—especially when agricultural surpluses exist.

Earned Income Tax Credit (EITC)—This program uses the tax structure to benefit those who have little income. Initially proposed by Republicans in the early 1970s as a way of simultaneously helping the poor and rewarding work, the **Earned Income Tax Credit (EITC)** program was greatly expanded in 1993. Only those in the labor force qualify for this benefit, a provision designed to make even low-paying jobs worthwhile. An eligible person who fills out a tax return can receive an EITC reimbursement even if he or she has paid no taxes. In 2009, an eligible family of four could receive a credit of as much as $5,028.[40]

Supplemental Security Income (SSI)—**Supplemental Security Income** provides income assistance to disabled people of low income. Created in 1972, SSI succeeds programs of aid to the blind and the deaf established by the Social Security Act of 1935. As of 2010, the average monthly benefit for SSI's 7.4 million recipients was $498.[41]

Rent Subsidies—This policy provides low-income families with government vouchers to help pay their rent, provided that they select designated housing. Congress created the **rent subsidies** program in the early 1970s to replace public housing programs, which had been criticized for encouraging racial segregation and creating large concentrations of poverty.[42]

Medicaid—This program pays for medical services for the poor. A person becomes eligible only if he or she has no more than a minimal income and few assets other than a home. Congress created **Medicaid** in 1965, at the same time as Medicare, in response to Republican objections to Medicare on the grounds that it was designed to serve the middle class but not the poor. The cost of Medicaid benefits has risen rapidly—from $15.3 billion in 1970 to $275 billion in 2010.[43] The 2010 healthcare reform bill creates a new subsidy with which poor people can buy health insurance. About 19 million Americans will likely qualify for this subsidy, but it will not be available until 2014.[44]

State Children's Health Insurance Program (SCHIP)—Created in 1997 after the Clinton administration tried and failed to create a new health insurance program for all Americans, SCHIP covers health insurance for children in low-income families not poor enough to be eligible for Medicaid. In 2009, the program covered nearly 8 million people.[45]

Limitations on Public Assistance Programs   This list of public assistance programs that help poor families with children seems impressive, but the government spends nearly twice as much on social security and Medicare as it spends on all these programs combined, as Figure 18.4 illustrates. In addition, programs for families with children are more restrictive than programs for senior citizens. Five factors make programs for families with children less user-friendly.[46]

Fewer Cash Benefits—The elderly receive about 64 percent of their benefits in cash,[47] whereas only 32 percent of the benefits received by poor families with children are cash benefits.[48] Because most people prefer cash income to benefits in the form of goods and services, senior citizens have the better arrangement. Cash income enables one to purchase what one wants and to purchase it when, where, and from whom one wishes.

Less Indexation—Nearly all benefits to the elderly, including social security and other retirement pensions, are indexed to changes in the cost of living. Although some programs for families with children are also indexed, the main welfare program, TANF,

Sidebar Definitions

Earned Income Tax Credit (EITC)
Program that gives back tax payments to those who have little income.

Supplemental Security Income (SSI)
Program that provides disabled people of low income with income assistance.

rent subsidies
Program that helps pay rent for low-income families, provided that they select designated housing.

Medicaid
Program that provides medical services to the poor.

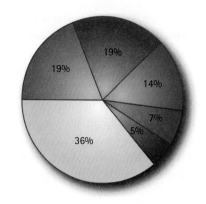

Defense
Social security
Medicare
Medicaid
Interest on national debt
All other spending

19%
19%
14%
7%
5%
36%

FIGURE 18.4

FEDERAL GOVERNMENT
SPENDING

Social security and Medicare
make up one-third of federal
spending.

• *Why is social security the
most costly social program?*

Note: Percentages based on 2009
federal spending.

Source: Office of Management and Budget,
*Budget of the United States Government, Fiscal
Year 2011,* Historical Tables.

is not. Instead of keeping pace with increases in the cost of living, average monthly benefits under this program fell nearly 23 percent between 1996 and 2008.[49]

Assistance, Not Insurance—Unlike social security, which distributes benefits automatically according to age and contributions made to an insurance fund, programs for families with children are paid out only after family income has been carefully scrutinized. To become eligible for benefits, a low-income family must demonstrate that it has virtually no other means of livelihood. To receive cash benefits, the potential recipient must document that the family does not own a home of any significant value, has virtually no savings, and has hardly any income. According to one survey, more than 20 percent of charity food bank users had not even applied for food stamps because it was "too much hassle."[50]

State, Not National, Programs—Families with children receive benefits that vary from one state to another. Only EITC benefits are uniform throughout the country. For the other major programs—TANF, food stamps, SSI, housing assistance, Medicaid, and SCHIP—eligibility rules and benefit levels vary from state to state. In the case of TANF, the benefits can be four times as much in one state as in another.[51]

Because public assistance programs are state-operated, families who have children and who move from one state to another must reconnect to public assistance programs. For example, tens of thousands of evacuees from New Orleans after Hurricane Katrina had to re-enroll in public assistance programs in Texas and other states. In this case, Congress enacted special legislation to make the transition easier, but in normal circumstances such help is not available.[52] As a result, poor families may not be able to respond quickly to job opportunities or changing family circumstances.[53]

These restrictions do not apply to senior citizens because social security is a national program. Senior citizens can move from New Jersey to Florida (or even overseas) without jeopardizing the amount or delivery of their social security check.

Benefits Cannot Supplement Income—The benefits that poor families with children receive are usually a substitute for other income; they do not supplement it. In many states, families are not eligible for income assistance if they have savings of more than $2,000, a car worth more than $5,000, or anything other than a very modest home (the exact value varies from state to state).[54] Under the old AFDC program, families lost a dollar in benefits for every dollar they earned. Under TANF, states have the flexibility to continue benefits for some working recipients,[55] but these benefits count toward a federal lifetime limit of five years of TANF participation.[56]

By comparison, senior citizen benefits supplement the recipient's own resources. Senior citizens may receive their Medicare and social security benefits even if they are working full-time, have savings, earn dividends and interest on their investments, and are homeowners. Before 2000, social security recipients between 65 and 69 years old lost $1 in benefits for every $3 they earned in wages above $17,000 per year. But Republicans and Democrats in Congress, eager to please elderly voters in an election year, repealed this "earnings penalty" unanimously.[57]

The Politics of Public Assistance   Programs for low-income families with children are poorly funded and restrictively designed because, unlike the elderly, children and the poor do not exercise direct political power. Instead, they are dependent on others who provide only limited help: policy analysts who offer competing explanations for the persistence of poverty, a weak network of interest groups that fight among themselves, a divided public, and opportunistic political parties.

Policy Debate—Before the government can design solutions, it has to decide what the problem is. But policy experts disagree about the causes of poverty among families with children. Three different theories have influenced the welfare debate.

Liberal theory argues that poverty rates among children have risen because the government has not maintained an adequate level of governmental assistance. Sociologist Theda Skocpol points out that lower poverty rates in European countries are due in part to government programs that aid low-income families.[58] She advocates the establishment of a similar family allowance program that would guarantee all families with children a basic stipend not unlike the social security checks that the elderly receive.

Conservative theory finds the explanation for rising poverty rates in what is identified as a "culture of poverty," in which young people are encouraged to place short-term pleasures ahead of long-term goals. Beliefs that opportunities for advancement do not exist become self-fulfilling prophecies as the poor do not seek the jobs they assume they cannot find. Public assistance programs can perpetuate this cycle. "Until recently," says policy analyst Lawrence Mead, "a defeatist culture was abetted by permissive public policies. Programs [such as AFDC] gave benefits to people . . . without expecting constructive behavior from them."[59]

Conservatives also point out that between 1970 and 2008, the percentage of women with children who were living without a spouse more than doubled—from 11 percent to 25 percent.[60] These female-headed families are particularly at risk of living in poverty. Many women find it difficult to both work and raise children. Mothers who do work find it hard to get full-time jobs at good wages. Poverty rates among single female-headed households are over five times greater than poverty rates among households headed by a married couple.[61] Liberals respond by noting that poverty rates among families with children are much lower in other countries such as Great Britain, France, and Sweden, despite the fact that the frequency of out-of-wedlock births is higher there than in the United States.[62]

Offering a third explanation, sociologist William J. Wilson attributes a growing culture of poverty to changes in the postindustrial economy. Physically demanding blue-collar jobs, which can be performed by unskilled workers with minimal education, are declining in number. These jobs have been lost to technology or have moved overseas.[63] As a result, from 1975 to 2005, annual salaries for men without a high school degree plunged from 92 percent to less than 55 percent of the national median income.[64]

According to Wilson, when young men cannot find work, they refuse to take on the responsibilities of marriage and child rearing. Young women do not want to marry men with few prospects.

Group Organization—No group speaking on behalf of children has a mass membership of a size remotely comparable to that of AARP. Instead, many small, competing groups take stances as varied as the alternative explanations for rising poverty rates. The most significant pro-welfare group, the Children's Defense Fund, headed by Marion Wright Edelman, has fought welfare reform to no avail. Although the group has an annual budget of $19 million and a staff of 178, it lacks a large membership that can effectively lobby Congress.[65] The group lobbied hard in 2007 for an expansion of SCHIP, but a bill that would have doubled the program's funding was vetoed by President Bush as too costly.

On the conservative side, Gary L. Bauer, a Republican candidate for president in 2000, built the Family Research Council into a 450,000-member organization committed to the protection of family values.[66] The group favored the welfare reform bill, a stance reflecting its conviction that welfare programs, by helping unwed mothers make ends meet, discourage family formation and allow fathers to neglect family responsibilities.

Other groups adopt positions on issues that affect children's welfare, but these groups typically have other objectives more central to their mission. For example, the Urban League has long emphasized the importance of youth programs, but its fundamental objective remains the protection of African Americans' civil rights. Major labor unions such as the AFL-CIO support most legislation intended to promote child welfare, but their main concern is the protection of workers' interests. Although many women's groups care about children's issues, they tend to remain focused on issues of gender discrimination and sexual harassment. In short, the interest-group chorus on children's issues sings separate songs in different keys. They are unable to focus on a common cause in the way AARP does.

Public Opinion—The general public wavers between liberal and conservative beliefs about rising poverty rates. In 2005, during a period of economic uncertainty, the population was evenly divided on the question of whether poverty was due mainly to circumstances beyond a person's control or to a lack of effort. But ten years earlier, when the economy was booming, twice as many people thought poverty was due to a lack of effort than to circumstances beyond a person's control.[67] This public variability makes it difficult for policymakers to generate enthusiasm for public-assistance programs.

Political Parties—Because public opinion on welfare policy fluctuates, so do the positions of the political parties. Most of the time, the Democratic Party takes a more liberal position and the Republican Party takes a more conservative one. Democratic Secretary of State Hillary Clinton, for example, was once a member of the board of directors of the liberal Children's Defense Fund. Tony Perkins, the current director of the Family Research Council, is a former Republican state legislator and candidate for the Senate.[68] As in the case of healthcare reform, partisan divisions can be stark and bitter, but the party that takes the initiative on innovative social policy has shifted back and forth, depending on the issue at hand.

When the country was building the Great Society in the 1960s and 1970s (see Chapter 3), Democrats took the lead, but Republicans were not far behind. Republican presidents signed into law several welfare programs for children. President Nixon proposed the food stamp and SSI programs. Republicans proposed, and President Ford

Spokeswoman for Children
Marian Wright Edelman, founder of the Children's Defense Fund.
• *Why does Edelman have less clout in Washington than the head of AARP?*

signed, the law creating the Earned Income Tax Credit. Republicans in Congress initiated the Medicaid program.

As the public mood shifted in a conservative direction, the positions of both parties changed accordingly. In 1995 it was the Republicans who took the lead, proposing cuts in many of the programs they had once sponsored.[69] Although some Democrats opposed the cuts, a majority voted in favor of welfare reform, and President Clinton signed the bill into law. Today, both parties take credit for the passage of TANF.

18.3

Compare and contrast the positions of the Republican and Democratic parties on U.S. education policy.

Education Policy

Although social policy has long been one of the domestic policies of great interest to voters, education policy has recently become almost as significant in the public debate. Historically, Americans have supported a large, well-financed education system. Equal opportunity meant equal access to good schools. But the commitment to public schools, although still strong, has been modified by increasing concern about the quality of education provided in traditional public schools. In this section we discuss the history of locally controlled public education in the United States, current policy on education, and the interest groups that shape this increasingly visible policy debate.

Local Control

Responsibility for education is divided among local school boards, state departments of education, and the federal Department of Education, but the bulk of control over education policy remains at the state and local levels. Keeping the control of public schools in the hands of local communities is an important issue for many parents and educators who do not want distant politicians making decisions about their children's lives.

Today, 89.5 percent of the cost of public education is paid for out of state and local budgets, each contributing approximately half the cost (although the exact percentage paid varies widely from one state to another).[70] The 10.5 percent contribution by the federal government is spent mainly on programs enhancing equal opportunity, such as special education for the disabled and compensatory programs for disadvantaged children.[71] Core education programs are generally paid for with state and local dollars.

Contemporary Issues in Education Policy

America has a strong tradition of providing public education, going back to 1785 when Congress set aside the revenue from the sale of one-sixteenth of the land west of the Appalachian Mountains to help pay for "the maintenance of public schools."[72] Discrimination against racial and ethnic minorities characterized many schools for a time, but in many cases public schools played a key role in reinforcing a distinctive American identity.

Despite this long historical commitment to education, Americans seem to be increasingly dissatisfied with traditional public schools. The per pupil cost of schooling has increased by 23 percent since 1990, even after adjusting for inflation.[73] But other nations, once far behind in school spending, have now nearly caught up. State and local governments in the United States spend 3.9 percent of the U.S. gross domestic product on primary and secondary education. Although Japan and Germany still spend less than the United States, countries such as the United Kingdom, France, and Sweden spend more (see the *International Comparison* feature on the next page).

INTERNATIONAL COMPARISON

Student Learning and School Expenditures

Policymakers often debate whether Americans are "getting their money's worth" from the education system. These bar graphs provide grist for such a debate. Student math literacy is lower in the United States than in other industrial countries, yet Americans pay more for schools than do the citizens of many other countries.

- *Do you believe that test scores would improve if the United States spent more on education? Why or why not?*

- *Which country has the most "math-literate" students? Does this success appear to be the result of high education spending?*

Source: U.S. Department of Education, National Center for Education Statistics, *Digest of Education Statistics, 2009*, Table 390 and Table 417. Math figures from 2006; expenditure figures from 2007, except for Canada's, which are for 2006.

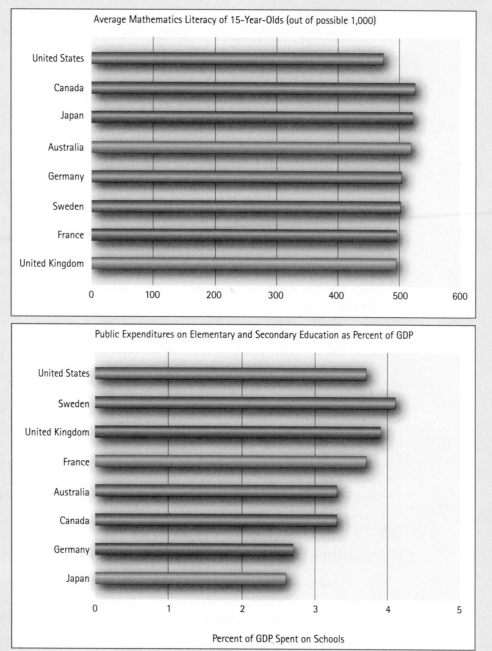

American schools also seem to be doing an inferior job at converting dollars into programs that help students learn.[74] Students in American schools learn less in reading, science, math, and geography than students in most other industrial countries (see the *International Comparison*). Not surprisingly, the public's assessment of the quality of its schools has slipped. The percentage of Americans who expressed "a good deal" or "quite a lot" of confidence in the public schools dropped from 58 percent in 1973 to 38 percent in 2009.[75]

As in other areas, different policymakers diagnose the problem differently and offer competing solutions. There are at least three major sets of proposals that seek to improve the system of education in the United States.

First, some policymakers recommend redesigning the educational system so that students and parents have their choice of schools, just as senior citizens, under Medicare, have their choice of doctors and hospitals.[76] Proponents say the resulting competition among schools would prompt poorly performing schools to improve. Opponents argue that giving parents a choice would increase disparities between schools, thereby broadening racial, religious, and ethnic divisions.[77] (For more on this conversation, see the *Election Voices!* feature in Chapter 16, on page 488.)

A second set of policymakers suggests that the problem with public schools is that their educational goals are seldom well defined and that they are often unable to tell whether students are really learning. Accordingly, these policymakers recommend a set of national standards, as well as a national curriculum.[78] Critics worry that rigid nationwide standards would rob states and school districts of flexibility and prevent adaptation to new conditions. In 2002, President George W. Bush signed the "No Child Left Behind Act," a law that compromised on the issue. Under the new system, states must establish clear goals in math and reading, testing students in grades 3 through 8 annually to make sure that they meet these expectations. However, states may set their own standards and design their own tests and procedures for meeting them. At the same time, new federal funds assist students at poorly performing schools.

Critics of the bill argued that, although it was well intentioned, it was underfunded and thus did not give schools the resources necessary to improve themselves. As part of its stimulus package, the Obama administration allocated approximately $50 billion in order to double the funding for No Child Left Behind and for federally funded special education programs. Although the package was promised as a one-time assistance package to the states, pressures for a permanent increase in the federal fiscal role continued. The Obama administration's Department of Education also allocated $4.35 billion in stimulus funds that were given to states that submitted "ambitious, yet achievable plans" for education reform.[79] In the first rounds of grants under the program, only two states—Delaware and Tennessee—submitted acceptable plans. More states hoped to win awards later, but the administration came under increasing criticism for unwarranted intrusion into state and local government affairs.

The Politics of Education

In the past, public schools were, similar to baseball and apple pie, beyond partisan dispute. But, in recent years, the two political parties have begun to disagree over a broad range of educational issues. Republicans have increasingly supported holding schools to

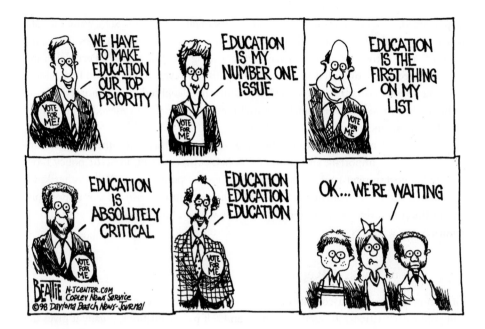

Campaigning on
Education
Education is a perennial issue
in political campaigns.
• *Can presidential decisions
have a significant effect on school
policies? Why or why not?*

high standards by testing students annually and giving parents greater choice through
vouchers and charter schools, whereas Democrats have won strong support from the
two largest teachers' groups, the National Education Association and the American
Federation of Teachers, by proposing higher levels of funding for traditional public
schools.

Despite the partisan controversy, both parties remain strongly committed to public
education. For all the current discontent, Americans still think schools are crucial for
achieving the American dream. As long as the electorate holds this belief, schools will
continue to have bipartisan support.

Regulatory Policy

On December 23, 2003, as many American families headed home for the holiday season, the United States Department of Agriculture (USDA) announced that a case of
bovine spongiform encephalopathy, otherwise known as "mad cow disease," had been
discovered in one Washington State cow. The fatal disease, which rapidly destroys brain
tissue, can spread from cattle to humans and is exceedingly difficult to eradicate from
the environment.

This was the first known case of the disorder in the United States, but it had not
come without warning. Dr. Stanley Prusiner, a Nobel Prize-winning biologist who had
studied the disorder, said he had recently warned Secretary of Agriculture Ann
Veneman that her department's animal inspection procedures were too lax to determine even the extent of the problem.[80] In fact, many so-called "downer cows," animals
that are too sick to walk, had been slaughtered and added to the country's meat supply.

The USDA acted swiftly to calm public fears and shore up the international market for American beef, banning the use of downer cows for food, stepping up inspections, and implementing several other safeguards.[81] "The downer decision is a huge

18.4

Evaluate the justifications
for regulation and the
public policy processes involved in regulation and
deregulation.

leap forward," said one consumer advocate "but it's really too bad USDA waited to take this step and others until after the first case was found. These are changes that many scientists and consumer advocates have been calling for for years."[82] Periodic scares about tainted beef continued to startle Americans, however. In 2008, YouTube videos showing downer cows being processed at a California slaughterhouse prompted schools to briefly eliminate beef from lunch menus. In response, the USDA moved to punish the slaughterhouse operators for breaking the rules.

The case of mad cow disease raises questions about the government's regulatory policymaking, an important and often overlooked component of domestic policy. Does the federal government have a responsibility to ensure public safety? What other kinds of activities should be regulated? How should the government exercise this responsibility? In the remainder of this chapter, we discuss why and how the federal government regulates many aspects of our lives.

The Rise of Federal Regulation

regulation
Rules and standards that control economic, social, and political activities.

Government **regulation** consists of rules and standards that control economic, social, and political activities. Although Congress can itself pass regulations, usually it gives the responsibility to agencies within the executive branch, which issue rules within general congressional guidelines. Such rules affect the lives of average Americans at nearly every turn. For example, the Food and Drug Administration sets safety standards for medical devices, agricultural products, and nutrition; the Securities and Exchange Commission protects small investors by requiring companies to disclose standardized financial information; and the Consumer Products Safety Commission organizes the recall of products deemed to be hazardous.

Regulation dates back to feudal times. For example, businesses in sixteenth-century England "were required to set prices and render service in a socially responsible manner."[83] In the United States, the basis for federal regulation is found in the Constitution, which gives Congress the power "to regulate Commerce." Regulations under the authority of the commerce clause were originally applied to the railroad industry, with the passage of the Interstate Commerce Act of 1887. They have since been applied by Congress to regulate everything from civil rights to national insurance standards. Since the New Deal, the Supreme Court has generally found regulatory policies constitutional (see Chapter 3).[84]

Government regulations increased in number and significance at three distinct periods in the country's history: the Progressive Era, the New Deal era, and the 1960s and 1970s. Each period is marked by a strong political movement that identified major abuses in certain sectors of society, and each period produced legislation that created a host of new government agencies with new regulatory powers.

During the Progressive Era of the 1890s and early 1900s, writers and journalists known as muckrakers exposed the worst abuses of industrialization (see Chapter 9). Initially, they focused attention on the power of large corporations such as Standard Oil Company, which exercised almost complete control over the oil industry. When the public demanded antitrust legislation, Congress enacted the Sherman Act (1890), which made it a crime to "restrain" or "monopolize" trade. This law still plays a major role in government-industry relations. Under this statute, for example, Microsoft, producer of computer operating systems and software, was found guilty of creating a monopoly and restraining trade. Although the company was not required to break itself into pieces, as some had hoped, Microsoft did have to abide by an agreement with the Justice Department aimed at halting its unfair business practices.[85]

The muckrakers also publicized other abuses, leading to the creation of additional regulatory agencies. For example, Upton Sinclair's best-selling novel *The Jungle* detailed horrible sanitation conditions in the meat-packing industry and resulted in the passage of the Meat Inspection Act of 1906.

The second regulatory wave occurred during the 1930s, when the government tried to prevent financial practices that were thought to have caused the Great Depression. The eight major regulatory agencies created at that time, including the Federal Deposit Insurance Corporation (FDIC), the Federal Communications Commission (FCC), and the Civil Aeronautics Board (predecessor to the modern Federal Aviation Administration), formed an important component of Franklin Roosevelt's New Deal.

A third wave of regulatory innovation took place in the 1960s and 1970s. During this period, the issues were consumer safety, occupational safety, and environmental protection. In 1965 Ralph Nader, an enterprising young lawyer, published a best-selling book, *Unsafe at Any Speed,* that revealed serious safety problems with a popular sports car, the Corvair. His efforts were so effective that General Motors halted production and new government regulations required manufacturers to install seat belts in all cars. Nader founded several consumer advocacy organizations, hiring young people who came to be known as "Nader's Raiders." In time, they found safety problems in many domains, including other consumer products, occupational environments, and industrial pollutants. In the ensuing years, Congress passed 61 significant pieces of new regulatory legislation and established or substantially enhanced the role of nine regulatory agencies. Nader has remained politically active, running for president in 2000, 2004, and 2008.

The most important of the new agencies formed in this period was the **Environmental Protection Agency (EPA),** which has the main responsibility for issuing regulations designed to protect the environment from pollutants. Its controls on air and water pollution have done much to improve air and water quality throughout the United States. Between 1970 and 2003, for example, total emissions of six major air pollutants "decreased by 51 percent, even while the nation's population grew by 39 percent, the gross domestic product (GDP) rose by 176 percent, vehicle miles traveled increased by 155 percent, and energy consumption grew by 45 percent."[86] Major environmental challenges remain, not least of which is the threat of climate change (see the *Election Voices!* feature in Chapter 13, on page 387), but this record suggests that regulations can be effective in addressing at least some key problems.

Environmental Protection Agency (EPA)
Agency responsible for issuing regulations designed to protect the environment from pollutants.

Justifications for Regulation

As a result of these waves of regulatory expansion, the government now regulates many business and social activities. As Murray Weidenbaum, a former chairman of the Council of Economic Advisers, put it, "No business, large or small, can operate without obeying a myriad of government rules and restrictions. Costs and profits can be affected as much by a directive written by a government official as by a management decision in the front office or a customer's decision at the checkout counter."[87]

Why have the regulatory responsibilities of government expanded so dramatically during the past century? Economists describe a variety of situations in which government regulation may be appropriate, most of which fall under the category of **market failures,** situations in which the free market does not lead to efficient outcomes or to outcomes that are good for society. Scholars have identified three broad types of market failures: natural monopoly, externalities, and incomplete information.

Natural Monopoly   In a **natural monopoly** a public service is best provided by a single company. To make sure that the company does not take advantage of its monopoly power and charge consumers unnecessarily high prices, natural monopolies are usually subject to regulation. For example, local governments may regulate the rates charged by cable television companies that face no effective competition from other vendors. In addition, these cable companies must offer most local broadcast stations as part of their "basic" packages.[88] Regulations also control the prices of gas, electricity, and other utilities that have exclusive rights in a particular state or locality. Otherwise, it is likely that these companies would charge excessively high rates.

Negative Externalities—An **externality** is any consequence of an activity that has an impact on those not responsible for the action. An externality may be positive or negative. If neighbors plant beautiful flowers in their front yard, then they provide those nearby with a positive externality. But, if the same neighbors pile unsightly, reeking garbage on their front lawn, then those nearby suffer a negative externality. Because neighbors—and corporations—may not care about the consequences of their actions for others, the government may regulate them to prevent or adjust for externalities.

One of the best examples of a negative externality is air pollution. A company may try to keep its costs low by using cheap fuel, even though burning that fuel emits black soot into the air. The black soot does not seriously affect the company, but it both threatens the health of those living nearby and creates a nuisance for them. To prevent companies from imposing this externality on others by polluting their environments, the EPA has imposed numerous regulations on industry to control the emission of pollutants.

A recent controversy about government regulation of externalities took place over the use of U.S. national park land. Until 2000, more than 180,000 snowmobile aficionados used the national parks each winter, sometimes racing through the woods at speeds in excess of 60 miles per hour. Environmentalists protested this use of public property, arguing that "the national parks should be places where the public can go to escape traffic. . . . And clearly these snow machines are loud, they're polluting, and they cause conflict with other visitors." In 2000, the National Park Service sided with the environmentalists, announcing a sweeping ban on snowmobile use in the national parks, with only minor exceptions. As in many other cases of regulation, those being regulated became very upset. Fumed one angry rider, "It's part of a planned campaign by this administration to

market failures

Situations in which the free market does not lead to efficient outcomes or to outcomes that are good for society.

natural monopoly

A situation in which a public service is best provided by a single company.

externalities

Any consequence of an activity that has an impact on those not responsible for the action.

Snowmobiling in Yellowstone

The debate over snowmobiles in Yellowstone pitted environmental groups against recreational snowmobilers.

• *Do snowmobilers in U.S. national parks represent an externality-producing nuisance that must be regulated?*

limit access to public lands."[89] The Bush administration reversed most of these restrictive rules in 2001, but a federal judge blocked this move in 2003, denouncing it as "completely politically driven."[90] The Park Service eventually issued a compromise set of rules that required snowmobilers to use less polluting vehicles and limited the number of snowmobile visits to 318 per day (as of 2010).[91]

Incomplete Information   Regulations are also used to protect those who cannot be expected to be well informed, most notably consumers. For example, many government rules forbid the marketing of unsafe products or the use of deceptive advertising and labeling. These rules can get very specific. For example, for a "meal" or "main dish" food product to be labeled "sugar-free," it has to contain less than 0.5 gram of sugar per labeled serving. A grain, fruit, or vegetable food product that is high in fiber may note on the package that a low-fat, high-fiber diet "may reduce the risk of some kinds of cancer." Manufacturers are prohibited from replacing "may reduce" with "reduces" or from specifying exactly which cancers the product might help prevent.[92]

The need for regulation is especially great in the case of medications. When citizens catch the flu, they cannot be expected to research the side effects of every cold medication on the market. Thus, government regulation is necessary to ensure that drugs sold over the counter meet specified safety standards.

The regulation of drugs began during the Progressive Era. In 1906 Congress created the Food and Drug Administration (FDA), granting it the power to regulate the production and labeling of goods sold in interstate commerce. The initial legislation gave the FDA only limited powers. To garner public support for stronger regulatory authority, in the 1920s the FDA established a museum known as the Chamber of Horrors that contained such atrocities as

> samples seized from goods on public sale—samples of patent medicines to cure every known disease, with testimonials from their users, accompanied by copies of their death certificates; and samples of cosmetics—eye-lash beautifiers containing poisonous aniline dyes, hair removers containing thallium acetate, and hair tonics, freckle removers, ointments, and salves containing mercury or other dangerous ingredients—together with photographs of women who had been blinded, paralyzed, or permanently disfigured by their use.[93]

The museum effectively aroused public concern. The FDA now monitors the production of everything from drugs to cosmetics to therapeutic devices such as muscle developers and sun lamps.

The Politics of Regulation

When and how regulations are imposed are political decisions. Broadly speaking, Republicans—valuing free markets—tend to favor fewer regulations, and Democrats—valuing consumer protections—tend to favor more. There are frequent exceptions to this rule of thumb, however. Regulations are continually shaped by election pressures on Congress, government agencies, and even the courts.

Congress   Members of Congress often create regulatory agencies in order to escape criticism when things go wrong. Laws frequently win passage in response to a well-publicized incident or disaster. Reacting to the 2008 financial crisis, for example, Congress passed a law in 2010 that (among other things) created a new consumer protection agency charged with policing unfair lending practices. With each disaster or scandal, congressional representatives demonstrate their responsiveness to public concerns by passing another regulatory act. The end result is that regulations often duplicate and overlap one another.

Although regulation may help reassure the public after a crisis has occurred, it is inherently unpopular with at least some voters. Regulations require certain people to follow restrictive procedures in order to avoid injuring others. For example, the regulations that restrict the use of snowmobiles in national parks may win the approval of environmentalists, but they almost certainly alienate devotees of the sport. Because compelling people to do something is likely to make them upset or angry, members of Congress usually employ a strategy known as **blame avoidance,** a set of political techniques designed to disguise their actions and shift the blame to others. In the case of regulatory policy, Congress avoids blame by not directly imposing the regulations but handing that job off to a regulatory agency.

When creating a regulatory agency, Congress often defines its task in general terms. As one group of policy analysts has said about the EPA, its "discretion [is] truly enormous. It produce[s] hundreds of pages of regulations, embodying dozens of significant policy choices, all on the basis of the most elliptical statutory language and the sparsest of legislative records."[94] Congress justifies leaving the terms of reference vague on the grounds that the authors of the legislation cannot anticipate every circumstance requiring regulatory action. Legislators can correctly claim that only those who know the facts in detail can come up with the appropriate regulation. But Congress has also discovered that it can avoid "unpleasant truths" by keeping regulatory legislation broad and general.[95] Different members of Congress may then interpret the law in contrasting ways. Some may claim they have satisfied the concerns of environmentalists and consumers; others will insist they have not imposed undue burdens on business and industry.

In rare cases where the public has become upset at the vagueness of congressional legislation, Congress has taken further (although still less than specific) steps. One such measure is to set specific goals and then to include a **hammer**—a harsh penalty to be imposed if a regulatory agency does not achieve a statutory objective. For example, the Clean Air Act of 1990 says that if certain goals are not met in particular metropolitan areas by a specific deadline, then the "sale of all gasoline in the designated area must cease."[96] Such draconian penalties make Congress appear tough, but they are typically so impractical that they would never be imposed, and the legislation still usually includes no guidelines regarding how the goals should be met.

Agency Discretion   Because of the very ambiguity of much congressional legislation, agencies often enjoy considerable freedom in deciding how to execute their mandates. When Congress charged the EPA with improving air quality in metropolitan areas, the agency had to decide the following kinds of questions: Should automobile manufacturers be required to build and sell some electric cars within ten years? Should every vehicle be checked at a state-run inspection station? Should inner-city highways be subject to a toll during rush hour? Should states be told they cannot build new roads? Although EPA officials have considered each of these difficult questions, nothing in the Clean Air Act of 1990 provides precise answers.

The autonomy afforded to regulatory agencies is not limitless. There exists a **zone of acceptance**—a range within which Congress will accept whatever an agency decides

---

blame avoidance
Set of political techniques employed by political leaders to disguise their actions and shift blame to others.

hammer
Harsh penalty set by Congress to be imposed if a regulatory agency does not achieve a statutory objective.

zone of acceptance
Range within which Congress allows agencies to interpret and apply statutes.

is the correct interpretation and application of the statutes.[97] When an agency goes beyond this informal and ambiguous zone, political opposition arises and the agency backtracks. For example, all of the clean-air options mentioned here provoked controversy and, as a result, the EPA has been slow to implement them.

Courts   Although regulatory policies are enacted by Congress and executed by agencies, courts interpret the meaning of congressional statutes and decide whether their application in specific cases conforms to congressional intent. Courts exercise considerable discretion when performing this role, because they are often asked to interpret vague, and even contradictory, laws passed by Congress.

Court interpretations of the 1973 Endangered Species Act illustrate how federal judges influence public policy. The law protects any species on federal lands that is found by the U.S. Fish and Wildlife Service to be threatened with extinction. Such a species' natural habitat is to be safeguarded from human activity that threatens it, no matter what the economic consequences of such protection. In voting for this legislation, most members of Congress probably thought they were protecting large mammals and birds such as wolves, whooping cranes, and eagles. And, indeed, the Endangered Species Act has been successful in protecting the American bald eagle. In 1963 there were only 417 nesting pairs; by 2006, the numbers had increased to 7,066, and the Department of Interior announced that it was prepared to remove the animal from the endangered species list.[98] However, the Fish and Wildlife Service greatly expanded the scope of the legislation when it found nearly 1,000 species to be in danger of extinction. And the federal courts have interpreted the law as applicable even to little-known species. Judges have halted the growth of suburbs in order to protect desert kangaroo rats, they have prevented the construction of a billion-dollar dam in order to save the tiny snail darter, and they have halted logging operations in order to safeguard the spotted owl.

Deregulation

Although regulation is an inevitable part of modern society, it can be carried to excess, and regulations intended to protect consumers may have the opposite effect. For example, regulating drugs may prevent some patients from receiving the treatment they need. Furthermore, regulation is expensive. Salaries for bureaucrats, lawyers, and investigators generate an annual price tag that runs to billions of dollars. Regulatory policies may also limit the ability of businesses to compete effectively. The additional paperwork, inspections, procedures, and mandates imposed by regulatory agencies can spell the difference between a business that thrives and provides good jobs to Americans and one that cannot remain solvent and has to reduce its workforce.

To address these concerns, Congress has introduced in many areas policies of **deregulation,** the removal of government rules that once controlled an industry. It has systematically authorized the partial deregulation of the trucking, banking, and communications industries.[99] Banks may now provide customers with insurance and handle the purchase and sale of stocks—freedoms that some critics claim contributed to the 2008 financial crisis (see Chapter 19). Regional telephone companies may now offer long-distance and cellular service.

Perhaps the most celebrated deregulation occurred within the airline industry. At one time, a government agency approved the airfare set for every route a plane flew. Although it was originally enacted to prevent price gouging by airlines that had

deregulation
Removal of government rules that once controlled an industry.

a monopoly in a particular city, many policy analysts claimed that the effect of the law was precisely the opposite of its intent: Regulators were letting airlines charge excessively high prices.

To address this and other problems, Congress enacted the Airline Deregulation Act of 1978. Most policy outcomes were favorable. Airline competition increased, companies became more efficient, service to remote areas increased, and airfares fell with the emergence of low-cost carriers such as JetBlue and Southwest.[100] Although some worried about the effect on safety,[101] the number of deaths per passenger mile also declined. Yet many experts argue that some regulation must remain in place to ensure that airline companies, in their eagerness for profit, did not cut corners too closely.[102] Furthermore, even the most committed deregulators backed government assistance to the airline industry after the 9/11 attacks.[103] In this industry, as in many industries, complete deregulation is unlikely, because the public will always expect government to act in the wake of disasters or to prevent costly externalities.

CHAPTER SUMMARY

18.1　**Identify the major types of public policy and the stages in its formation.**

Domestic policy involves government spending on social, education, and regulatory policies. Policymaking is a perpetual process that begins with agenda setting, progresses through deliberation and policy enactments, and continues through assessments of policy outputs and outcomes. These assessments in turn may form the basis for new agenda setting, and a new round of policymaking.

18.2　**Trace the origins and development of public assistance programs.**

Social security, enacted in 1935, and Medicare, enacted in 1965, are the largest federal social policies in the United States. Both these programs emerged to address poverty among the country's senior citizens and have succeeded in greatly reducing it. These social policies designed to aid the elderly are far more popular and more extensive than similar policies designed to aid poor children, which are more complicated to apply for and are more likely to be administered by state governments.

18.3　**Compare and contrast the positions of the Republican and Democratic parties on U.S. education policy.**

The two political parties are divided on many domestic policies. Democrats typically want to spend more on social and education policy, and they usually favor more regulation. Republicans usually favor less spending and less regulation. The public wants national candidates to address education policy but does not want to relinquish local control over public schools. Still, both Democratic and Republican administrations have recently moved in the direction of requiring schools to measure education outcomes.

18.4　**Evaluate the justifications for regulation and the public policy processes involved in regulation and deregulation.**

Policymakers justify regulations by arguing that free markets may produce negative consequences when left to their own devices. A natural monopoly may develop, for instance, or negative externalities such as pollution may result from industry. The politics of regulation introduce complications, however. Congress is quick to pass regulatory legislation in the wake of disasters, but otherwise tends to write vague legislation, leaving interpretation to the agencies and the courts. Only through a clear understanding of how elections affect the policy process can one understand these complex, even contradictory outcomes.

mypoliscilab EXERCISES

Apply what you learned in this chapter on MyPoliSciLab.

Read on **mypoliscilab.com**

eText: Chapter 18

Study and **Review** on **mypoliscilab.com**

Pre-Test

Post-Test

Chapter Exam

Flashcards

Watch on **mypoliscilab.com**

Video: Chicago Gun Laws

Video: Making Environmental Policy

Video: America's Aging Population

Video: Health Care Plan

Video: Raising the Minimum Wage

Video: Three Mile Island

Explore on **mypoliscilab.com**

Simulation: You Are an Environmental Activist

Comparative: Comparing Social Welfare Systems

Comparative: Comparing Health Systems

Timeline: The Evolution of Social Welfare Policy

KEY TERMS

agenda setting, p. 528

blame avoidance, p. 550

deregulation, p. 551

domestic policy, p. 528

Earned Income Tax Credit (EITC), p. 538

Environmental Protection Agency (EPA), p. 547

externalities, p. 548

food stamps, p. 537

hammer, p. 550

market failures, p. 548

Medicaid, p. 538

Medicare, p. 531

natural monopoly, p. 548

policy deliberation, p. 528

policy enactment, p. 528

policy implementation, p. 529

policy outcome, p. 529

policy output, p. 529

public assistance, p. 537

regulation, p. 546

rent subsidies, p. 538

social insurance, p. 531

social policy, p. 529

social security, p. 531

Supplemental Security Income (SSI), p. 538

Temporary Assistance for Needy Families (TANF), p. 537

zone of acceptance, p. 550

SUGGESTED READINGS

Of General Interest

Bane, Mary Jo, and Lawrence M. Mead. *Lifting Up the Poor: A Dialogue on Religion, Poverty, and Welfare Reform*. Washington, DC: Brookings Institution Press, 2003. A liberal and a conservative debate U.S. policy on poverty.

Hacker, Jacob S. *The Great Risk Shift: The New Economic Instability and the Decline of the American Dream*. Revised and expanded edition. New York: Oxford University Press, 2008. Argues that social programs are less effective than they once were at protecting Americans from risk.

Kingdon, John. *Agendas, Alternatives and Public Policies*. Boston: Little, Brown, 1984. Discusses the policymaking process, paying special attention to how problems become issues on the political agenda.

Skocpol, Theda. *Protecting Soldiers and Mothers: The Politics of Social Provision in the United States*. Cambridge, MA: Harvard University Press, 1993. Fascinating, comprehensive historical analysis of the evolution of the U.S. welfare state.

Staff of the *Washington Post. Landmark: The Inside Story of America's New Health-Care Law and What It Means for Us All*. New York: Public Affairs, 2010. An early journalistic account of the passage of the 2010 healthcare reform bill.

Focused Studies

Howell, William, and Paul E. Peterson, with Patrick Wolf and David Campbell. *The Education Gap: Vouchers and Urban Public Schools*. Washington, DC: The Brookings Institution, 2002. Analysis of school choice initiatives by scholars sympathetic to vouchers.

Vig, Norman J., and Michael E. Kraft, eds. *Environmental Policy: New Directions for the Twenty-First Century*. 7th ed. Washington, DC: CQ Press, 2009. Excellent essays on modern U.S. environmental policy.

ON THE WEB

In this chapter, we discussed a variety of government programs and regulations. Many programs and regulatory agencies have websites that provide information to the public. They include the following:

www.medicare.gov
The official government information site for Medicare, the health insurance program for the elderly.

www.ssa.gov
The Social Security Administration (SSA), which administers the social insurance program that makes up a quarter of the federal budget.

www.acf.dhhs.gov
The Administration for Children and Families, which runs the federal side of the Temporary Assistance for Needy Families (TANF) program.

www.ed.gov
The U.S. Department of Education, which provides statistical information on the state of education in the United States and describes national education programs.

www.fda.gov
www.epa.gov
www.sec.gov
www.osha.gov
www.cpsc.gov
The Food and Drug Administration, the Environmental Protection Agency, the Securities and Exchange Commission, the Occupational Safety and Health Administration, and the Consumer Product Safety Commission, five major regulatory agencies.

In this chapter we also discussed a number of interest groups and organizations that affect the design and implementation of domestic policy in the United States. They include:

www.aarp.org
The American Association of Retired Persons (AARP), the large and influential lobby for senior citizens.

www.childrensdefense.org
The Children's Defense Fund, which works to provide "a voice for all the children of America who cannot vote, lobby, or speak for themselves."

www.frc.org
The Family Research Council, a conservative foundation that "champions marriage and family."

www.hoover.org/publications/ednext
Education Next is a journal that discusses contemporary education policy issues.

19 Economic Policy

CHAPTER OUTLINE

19.1 Analyze the relationship between governments and markets.

19.2 Outline the business cycle and evaluate its impact on economic growth.

19.3 Assess the influence of economic conditions on the political fortunes of elected officials.

19.4 Define fiscal policy and explain its use and decline.

19.5 Define monetary policy and analyze the role of the Fed in the implementation of this policy.

19.6 Compare the tax burden, the national debt, and employment opportunities in the United States with similar economic aspects in other developed countries.

The Economic Crisis of 2008–2009

It seemed almost too good to be true. Julio Borrero, a 46-year-old part-time worker at a Lowell, Massachusetts, auto repair shop, moved with his family into a $295,000 home in January 2006. Borrero didn't have much money—his main source of income was an $800 monthly disability benefit check—but a local lender helped secure him two separate mortgage loans to cover the cost of the home by falsely claiming on the application that Borrero's monthly salary was $6,200.

Still, Borrero's poor credit rating meant that he qualified only for "sub-prime" loans—loans with higher interest rates and less favorable terms than most loans, offered to high-risk borrowers. Borrero's two mortgages charged interest rates that were twice what many other new homebuyers were paying, and after a short period of time the interest rate on the largest loan was slated to go up even further. Before long, the Borreros were paying $2,300 per month in mortgage bills, rather than the $1,000 they had expected to pay. In July—just seven months after moving in—Julio Borrero gave up. The bank foreclosed on his home, and Borrero, his wife, and his three children moved out. "We fell in love with this house," said Jeremias Borrero, 19. "When this all came out, it destroyed our family."[1]

What was not yet clear was that this family tragedy was an early warning sign of a national economic crisis of historic magnitude. During a ten-year housing boom that began in the mid-1990s, millions of Americans bought their first homes. Mortgage lenders, eager to sell as many loans as possible, became increasingly creative in crafting lending policies to appeal to people who might not otherwise be able to afford a house. Meanwhile, banks, to reduce their risks, "securitized" mortgages by chopping the value of the loans into parts, combining them with parts of other loans, and sold packages of these parts to investors and investment banks like Bear Stearns, Lehman Brothers, and Merrill Lynch.

The risks to this strategy were small as long as home prices nationwide were going up steadily. But in 2006 housing prices began a long, relentless decline. Foreclosures soared as homeowners fell behind on their mortgage payments. In parts of the country that had seen the biggest increases in homebuilding, such as Nevada, Florida, and California, whole neighborhoods were up for sale at bargain prices as ruined families packed up and moved away. Financial markets teetered as investors refused to buy those sophisticated packages except at bargain prices.

In 2008, the edifice finally collapsed. What had begun with a few highly risky products began to spread with lightning speed to ruin the credit of investment houses around the world. By September, the government was forced to bail out Fannie Mae and Freddie Mac, two government-chartered corporations that had made billions of dollars worth of loans to would-be homeowners whose credit rating was weak. Bear Stearns and Merrill Lynch were taken over by other companies, and Lehman Brothers went bankrupt.

When still more banks, investment firms, and insurance companies teetered on the edge of bankruptcy, three government officials, Secretary of the Treasury Henry Paulson, Chair of the Federal Reserve Board Ben Bernanke (whose job is described later in this chapter), and Timothy Geithner, president of the Federal Reserve Bank of New York, realized the banking system would need extraordinary assistance. The world's credit market was "freezing up." Banks and firms were beginning to refuse to extend credit to each other. If that happened, said Bernanke, "we may not have an economy on Monday."[2]

The trio recommended that the government restore order to credit markets by buying up to $700 billion worth of the most questionable financial products. Six weeks before the 2008 election, Congress was being asked to approve a new policy, the Troubled Asset Relief Program (TARP), that would permit the largest government intervention in the economy since the Great Depression. Almost immediately, phone calls and emails opposing the idea poured into congressional offices. Many members of Congress called the rescue plan a bailout of rich bankers, insurance companies, and Wall Street investment firms. Afraid of voter reprisals, neither presidential candidate endorsed the proposal. On September 29, the House defeated the bailout bill by a slim margin, and the stock market plunged by 7 percent, the largest decline in American history. The value of the pensions many Americans depended upon for their retirement was vanishing. An economic recession seemed certain.

Politics seemed to have triumphed over economic necessity. Seldom had government inaction posed such a serious threat to the health of the economy. Fortunately, cooler heads soon prevailed, as unnerved House and Senate leaders constructed a slightly revised plan that won bipartisan support and congressional passage later in the week. Both Barack Obama and John McCain voted in favor.

The economic crisis quickly became the dominant issue in the November elections, and the public clearly blamed the Republicans, the party in power. Democrats gained a sizable majority in the House of Representatives and gave the party a filibuster-proof majority in the Senate, while their presidential candidate, Barack Obama, swept to a lopsided victory. What began as a personal crisis for countless families like the Borreros had become a political scythe that cut a deep swath through the country's partisan landscape.

But this unusual political scythe had two edges. Not only did it cause havoc for the Republicans in the 2008 election, but it challenged the new Obama Administration to such an extent that it gave Republicans renewed hope as early as the 2010 congressional elections. President-elect Obama displayed his support for TARP by appointing one of its designers, Timothy Geithner, as his Secretary of the Treasury. The Geithner appointment seemed to make political sense when in 2009 the banks and other financial institutions paid in full with interest their TARP loans. The Treasury Secretary could claim that his policy had ameliorated the credit crisis of 2008—and the government had actually made money on its TARP bank loans.

Still, the financial crisis had left the economy in a serious recession. To get the economy going again, Obama proposed an $800 billion fiscal stimulus package. Although some dollars went for a small tax cut, the lion's share of the stimulus package funded an array of federal, state, and local government programs. Most Republicans voted against the stimulus on the grounds that it would increase the country's debt without actually helping the economy, but the Democratic majority in both the House and Senate ensured the bill's enactment.

The debate over the stimulus bill continued well beyond its passage into law, especially when unemployment rates rose to 10 percent by the end of 2009. Activists organized under the banner of the Tea Party (see Chapter 7) objected to TARP, the stimulus package, and to the passage of the president's healthcare reform bill. Much of the blame for the continuing high unemployment rate began to shift away from the Republicans to a Democratic president who had made TARP, a stimulus bill, and healthcare reform the bedrock of his economic policy. As economic recovery took longer than expected, a re-energized Republican party made a major comeback within two years of its smashing defeat in the 2008 presidential election. In short, a fiscal and economic crisis had cut in the most unpredictable of ways. Not only had it helped elect a unified, filibuster-proof Democratic government in 2008, but it also undermined that party's dominant position within a short two years.

Making the Connection

Elections are often decided on the basis of economic factors. But how much control do the president and Congress have over economic trends? What is the role of the Federal Reserve Board? Can the government stimulate the economy by cutting taxes and increasing expenditures? How big is the public debt of the United States? How does politics affect the decisions leaders take? In this chapter, we consider the policies that the government may use to affect the economy, and the effects these policies have on elections.

19.1

Analyze the relationship between governments and markets.

Governments and Markets

It may not be obvious that governments and markets should have anything to do with one another. When British economist Adam Smith wrote his famous treatise on commerce in the 1770s, he praised the capacity of the free market's "invisible hand" to promote prosperity for all with minimal government interference. Self-interested exchanges among countless people could naturally lead to greater prosperity. "It is not from the benevolence of the butcher, the brewer, or the baker, that we expect our dinner," Smith wrote, "but from their regard to their own interest."[3]

In large complex societies, even self-interested citizens need government protection if they are to engage in the simplest of economic transactions. Even when we buy fresh vegetables from a farmer, we presume that the food has not been contaminated, and only a government has the power to punish farmers who do not take all due precaution before selling their product.

The role of government in the economy has become more expansive (and politically controversial) over time, as we shall see. But it is important to understand that, at a basic level, government institutions are needed to provide a stable and supportive legal framework that makes market economies work effectively.

19.2

Outline the business cycle and evaluate its impact on economic growth.

Economic Growth and the Business Cycle

Economies grow as the result of technological innovations, investments in physical capital (factories, agricultural machinery, communication systems, and so on), and investments in human capital (education, worker training, and the like). The U.S. economy has grown enormously over the long term, and many of those who have invested in American industry have reaped huge rewards. For example, if you had purchased $25 worth of stock in a cross-section of American companies in the late 1920s, that stock would be worth about $1,040 today.[4]

In any given year, however, short-term fluctuations in the economy can adversely affect stock values. For example, that $25 investment would have lost more than two-thirds of its value from 1929 to 1933, the early years of the Great Depression, and would not have regained its original value until the mid-1950s.

Few economic downturns are as severe as was the Great Depression. But **recessions**—slowdowns in economic activity that are officially defined as a decline that persists for two quarters (six months)—occur periodically. Economists refer to these episodes of economic slowdown, followed by renewed expansion, as the **business cycle.** Figure 19.1

recession
A slowdown in economic activity, officially defined as a decline that persists for two quarters (six months).

business cycle
The alternation of periods of economic growth with periods of economic slowdown.

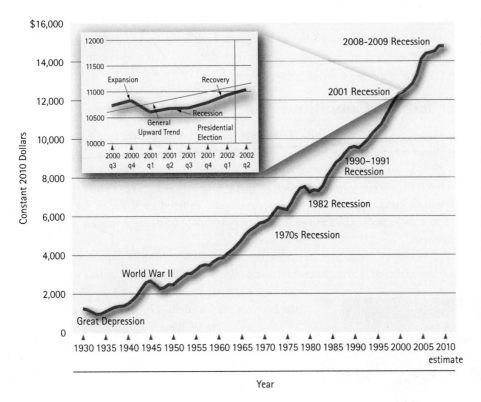

FIGURE 19.1

LONG-TERM GROWTH AND
THE BUSINESS CYCLE IN
THE UNITED STATES

Although the general economic
trend may be upward over the
long run, expansions and recessions that characterize the business
cycle can—in the short term—
harm both citizens and elected
officials. As this figure shows, over
the long run GDP in the United
States has grown. But there are
periodic downturns in which
GDP declines, as illustrated here
by the 2000–2002 period. These
periods are painful for voters, and
for elected officials.

• *Can you identify any political
consequences for the party in
power during each economic
downturn labeled in the figure?*

Source: Office of Management and Budget,
*Budget of the United States Government, Fiscal
Year 2009,* Historical Tables, Table 1.2.

provides an illustration of this phenomenon. In years past, experts believed that the
business cycle, similar to the weather, was unpredictable and impossible to control. In
the twentieth century, policymakers came to believe that government could play a role
in limiting the damage the business cycle can cause.

Governments try to set economic policies that minimize the disruptions caused by
the business cycle so that most people keep their jobs and prices remain stable. In other
words, they try to avoid two major problems: inflation and unemployment. **Inflation**—
a rise in price levels—makes consumers pay more money for an equal amount of goods
and services. For example, in 1995, the average ticket for a movie cost $4.35, a price that
seems a bargain by today's standards.[5] If inflation rates become too high, those who have
saved dollars discover they can purchase much less than when they earned those dollars.
Rising food and fuel prices in 2008, for example, prompted many Americans to cut
down on other spending, because they had to use more dollars to pay for these basics.
Inflation can occur so gradually it is hardly noticed, but increases in **unemployment**—
which occurs when people willing to work at prevailing wages cannot find jobs—
attract newspaper headlines and widespread anxieties. When unemployment rates
reached 10 percent of the workforce in 2009, and rates close to that level persisted into
2010, the public became increasingly uneasy, the president's popularity slipped, and the
Republicans made strong gains in the 2010 elections.

Government officials are often asked to strike a balance between inflation and unemployment. To keep inflation low may require higher levels of unemployment, and
efforts to keep unemployment low may drive inflation upward. When the economy becomes completely disjointed, both can happen at the same time, a circumstance that is

inflation

A sustained rise in price levels such
that people need more money to
purchase the same amount of goods
and services.

unemployment

The circumstance that exists when
people who are willing to work at
the prevailing wage cannot find jobs.

politically lethal to those in power. President Jimmy Carter had the misfortune to run for re-election at a time of "stagflation," when both inflation and unemployment were high. He suffered a humiliating defeat. For the next three elections, Republicans reminded the public of the economic chaos of the Carter years.

19.3

Assess the influence of economic conditions on the political fortunes of elected officials.

Economic Conditions and Political Fortunes

As Carter's experience and the 2008–2009 recession show, people tend to blame those in charge when times are hard. George W. Bush's approval rating sank below 30 percent in 2008 as gas prices hit record highs and housing values deteriorated. Republicans at all levels of government suffered defeats that year, partly as a result of voter dismay with economic conditions. The Obama administration suffered a setback in the 2010 congressional elections when the economic recovery did not occur as quickly as had been expected.

Bush and Obama have not been the only presidents to lose popularity when the economy faltered. Throughout the course of American history downturns in the economy have repeatedly caused serious election losses for the party of the president. The depression of the 1890s ushered in an era of Republican dominance, and the Great Depression of the 1930s did the same for the Democrats. Prosperity, in contrast, strengthens a president's position in a bid for re-election. With the help of booming economies, Lyndon Johnson trampled Barry Goldwater in 1964, Richard Nixon crushed George McGovern in 1972, Ronald Reagan trounced Walter Mondale in 1984, and Bill Clinton overwhelmed Bob Dole in 1996. Of course, a healthy economy does not guarantee presidential popularity. For example, prosperity did not keep Johnson's ratings in the opinion polls from falling sharply in response to the increasing casualties in Vietnam.[6] Nonetheless, presidents usually do better in elections when the economy is strong.

National economic conditions may influence congressional elections as well, as the 2010 elections demonstrated.[7] But the economy is most critical for presidential elections, so it is the president who pays the closest attention to economic policy. Presidents often try to shape overall economic conditions by using two major policy tools, fiscal policy and monetary policy. We discuss these policy tools in the next two sections.

Herbert Hoover

Herbert Hoover, a Republican, was president when the United States plunged into the Great Depression.

• *How did this event affect Republican Party fortunes? Why?*

19.4

Define fiscal policy and explain its use and decline.

fiscal policy

The sum total of government taxing and spending decisions, which determines the level of the deficit or surplus.

Fiscal Policy

A government's **fiscal policy,** the sum total of government taxation and spending, determines whether government revenues exceed expenditures. When yearly spending exceeds tax receipts, the government runs a **deficit.** When the amount collected in taxes exceeds spending, the government enjoys a **surplus.** When the two are exactly the same, the budget is said to be balanced. The nation's fiscal policy is formulated in a **budget,** the government's annual plan for taxing and spending. The government collects

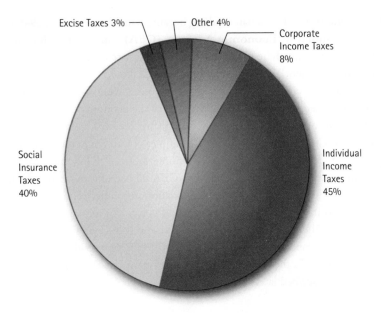

Excise Taxes 3%   Other 4%
Corporate
Income Taxes
8%
Social
Insurance
Taxes
40%
Individual
Income
Taxes
45%

FIGURE 19.2

FEDERAL REVENUES BY
SOURCE

Most revenues come from income taxes and social insurance
taxes, as this pie graph of 2007
revenue figures shows. Excise
taxes include taxes on alcohol,
cigarettes, and gasoline. (See
Chapter 18 for more details on
social insurance taxes.)

• *Do these revenue figures surprise you? Can you think of revenue sources that deserve less
taxation? More taxation?*

Source: Historical Budget Data,
Washington, DC: Congressional Budget
Office, May 2010.

taxes from a variety of sources, as Figure 19.2 indicates, and uses these funds, often
together with borrowed monies, to finance government programs. In 2010 the federal
budget amounted to about $3.7 trillion, or about 25 percent of the nation's gross
domestic product.[8] Since the 1970s, the president has proposed a budget to Congress
each year, but Congress usually makes major changes to the president's plan before
passing it. The largest portion of federal budget expenditures—about 21 percent—
goes to the social security program. National defense claims just over 20 percent and
Medicare and Medicaid account for another 20 percent of the nation's spending (for
more on social security, Medicare, and Medicaid, see Chapter 18). Interest paid on
the sizable national debt consumes an additional 8.3 percent. Everything else the government spends money on—from highway funds and education programs to child
nutrition, housing subsidies, and foreign aid—constitutes the remaining 31 percent of
the budget.[9]

deficit
The amount by which annual
spending exceeds revenue.

surplus
The amount by which annual
revenue exceeds spending.

budget
The government's annual plan for
taxing and spending.

The Use of the Budget Deficit

According to John Maynard Keynes, an influential English economist of the 1920s and
1930s, there is nothing sacred about a balanced government budget; on the contrary, he
said, budget deficits can lift an economy out of a recession. If government spends
money when no one else does, thus stimulating demand, it can jump-start the economy, which then can begin to grow on its own. Following this line of reasoning, which
came to be called **Keynesianism,** Franklin Roosevelt broke with the traditional belief
in a balanced budget (a belief held by his predecessor Herbert Hoover) and ran large
deficits during the 1930s in an attempt to get the country moving again.

Keynesianism
Economic policy based on the belief
that governments can control the
economy by running deficits to
expand it and surpluses to contract
it, and by manipulating demand.

John Maynard Keynes

John Maynard Keynes was the economic theorist responsible for the school of macroeconomics that came to be called "Keynesianism." Traditional economists argued that economic downturns would end without government help, in the long run. Keynes's tart response was, "In the long run, we're all dead."

• *Why is Keynesian thinking on fiscal policy less influential today than it was in past decades?*

Council of Economic Advisers (CEA)

Three economists who head up a professional staff that advises the president on economic policy.

---

monetarism

An economic school of thought that rejects Keynesianism, arguing that the money supply is the most important influence on the economy.

After World War II, Keynesian thinking became widely accepted. In 1946 Congress established a **Council of Economic Advisers (CEA)** composed of three prominent economists who would advise the president about the state of the national and international economy, present economic forecasts, and make recommendations about the budget. Because deficits were thought to create jobs, whereas surpluses held prices down, the CEA tried to help presidents "fine-tune" the economy to ensure steady prosperity. On the recommendation of the CEA to stimulate a sluggish economy, John F. Kennedy urged Congress to pass a deficit-creating tax cut. Some credit the cut, passed in 1964, with stimulating the mid-1960s economic boom.[10] Conversely, to slow down the inflation rate, Lyndon Johnson followed CEA advice and persuaded Congress to pass a tax increase in 1968. Despite the tax, inflation continued. Some said that the tax increase failed to have the desired effect because it was not big enough.[11] Others said that the failure of the tax increase to stop inflation proved Keynes's theory wrong. The CEA declined in importance in the 1980s and 1990s, as presidents relied more on White House staffers, the Secretary of the Treasury, and the chair of the Federal Reserve Board (described later in this chapter).

How Important Is Fiscal Policy?

The extent to which fiscal policy can moderate the business cycle has become a matter of intense political debate in recent years, especially in light of the growing budget deficits and the severe recession of 2008 and weak recovery thereafter. Presidents faced with recessions often resort to fiscal policy tools, but a number of factors—divided government, budget deficits, and internationalization, among them—make it difficult to use them effectively

Divided Government   Fiscal policy and divided government do not mix well. An economic policy must be implemented quickly if it is to improve the economic conditions it is designed to alleviate. But, when control of Congress and the presidency is divided between the two parties, it is difficult to enact fiscal policy quickly in response to changing economic conditions. When George W. Bush proposed a tax cut in 2001, he justified it according to Keynesian principles, arguing that it was needed to stimulate a slowing economy. Responding to the president's urgent request, Congress moved quickly to pass a long-term tax cut and an immediate tax rebate for Americans. However, the bulk of the tax cuts took effect only several years later, too late to jump-start the faltering economy, and experts differed on whether 2001's one-time tax rebate provided much stimulus. Even under unified government it is not easy to get programs quickly implemented. Much of the stimulus package that the Obama Administration persuaded Congress to pass in 2009 was expended only gradually over several years.

Monetarism   Those who oppose using fiscal policy as a tool to manage the economy are often adherents to a doctrine called **monetarism,** a school of economic thinking that rejects Keynesianism and says that the money supply, not the pattern of government taxing and spending, is the most important influence on the economy. Monetarists argue that the deficits that Keynesians favor in times of economic distress are paid for by borrowing money from investors. Thus, every dollar the government spends is one less dollar to be invested in other productive activities. According to this point of view, budget deficits do not add any extra stimulus—they just transfer available dollars from the private sector to the government. In the next section, we outline what steps monetarists favor in lieu of deficits.

Even Keynesians, who disagree with the monetarists, favor only temporary deficits; they do not believe that a government budget can be continuously in deficit. Over the long run, a nation's economy can grow only if people save money and invest it in productive enterprises. The problem is that when a government borrows money, it soaks up some of the country's savings, and with less savings to finance investment, economic growth slows. Thus, most economists today agree that persistent deficits result in lower long-term economic growth. The near bankruptcy of the Greek government in 2010 served as a warning to many other European nations, and even to the United States, of the risk that large annual deficits can pose to the long-term health of a nation.

Growing Budget Deficits   In the 1960s, when regulation of the economy by means of fiscal policy was a popular idea, the federal **debt**—the accumulation of annual deficits—was still declining from the peak to which it had climbed during World War II. Thus, modest adjustments in fiscal policy could be made from one year to the next without creating long-term problems. But, in the 1970s, large defense expenditures, coupled with growing spending on social programs, began to regularly produce unbalanced budgets in which total expenditures exceeded tax revenues by significant amounts (see Figure 19.3).

During the 1990s, sustained voter concern about the deficit, coupled with the independent presidential candidacy of Ross Perot, provoked action on the issue. Perot made deficit reduction the centerpiece of his campaign for the presidency in 1992, and the 19 percent of the vote that he received convinced Bill Clinton that budgetary reform had

debt
The accumulation of annual deficits.

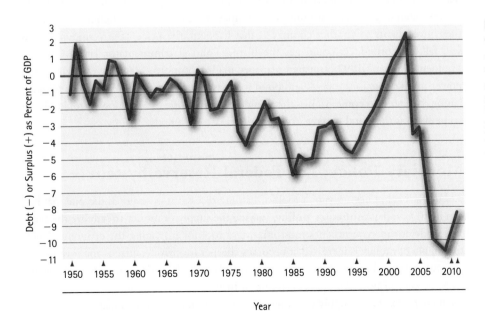

FIGURE 19.3

THE FEDERAL DEFICIT OR SURPLUS, 1950–2009

This graph shows the deficit or surplus as a percentage of GDP since 1950. When the line falls below zero, the federal government runs a deficit; when the line rises above zero, it indicates a surplus.

• *What accounts for the large deficits of the 1980s and the sudden surpluses of the late 1990s?*

Source: Office of Management and Budget, *The Budget of Fiscal Year 2011*, Historical Tables, Table 1.2.

Note: Figures for 2010–2011 are estimates.

popular backing. Still, elected officials struggled to find a way to satisfy public demands for a reduced deficit without angering voters by raising taxes or cutting spending.

In 1997, Clinton and a Republican Congress finally agreed on a balanced budget, an achievement aided by economic growth that by itself dramatically increased government revenue, as people, earning more, were paying more in taxes. Suddenly it became easy to balance the budget without making sharp cuts in government spending.

Predictably, when economic growth slowed, deficits moved back into the picture. Beginning in 2002, the federal government began running deficits again, and the budget shortfall in 2010 grew to 10 percent of GDP.[12] The Bush tax cuts, the Obama stimulus package, as well as the increased spending on the wars in Afghanistan and Iraq, homeland security, social security, Medicare, and the new health plan seemed likely to result in deficit spending for the foreseeable future. High deficits, coupled with public concern about their size, make it politically and economically more difficult for the president and Congress to lift the economy by means of deficit spending.

Internationalization   Fiscal policy has been further limited by the internationalization of the economy. Economic activity has become increasingly linked to overseas markets, so the reactions of economic actors to government policies are no longer limited to conditions in their own countries. If American investors think the government is spending too much, they can move billions of dollars to markets in Europe or Asia. Investors in other countries can do the same. Thus, advances in international finance and communication have enabled investors in stocks and bonds to quickly move their investments away from countries with governments that are running large deficits.

The impact on the United States is greater than ever, because many foreign investors in Japan, China, India, Europe, and the oil-producing countries of the Middle East have extremely large investments in U.S. bonds. In the past they have made these investments because they saw America's economic and political institutions as very strong and enduring. But, if these investors should come to believe that the United States is no longer a safe place to invest their monies, perhaps because the government's tax and spending policies are unwise, they may decide to move a significant share of their investments to another country. If that happens, the price of government bonds will fall, and presidents could get the blame. Political commentator James Carville, President Clinton's 1992 campaign manager, made a humorous remark recognizing the power of investors in the stock and bond markets: "I used to think if there was reincarnation, I wanted to come back as the president or the Pope . . . but now I would like to come back as the bond market. You can intimidate everybody."[13]

19.5

Define monetary policy and analyze the role of the Fed in the implementation of this policy.

monetary policy

The actions taken by government to vary the supply of money in an effort to stabilize the business cycle.

Monetary Policy: The Federal Reserve System

Although fiscal policy remains a tool for battling recessions as severe as the one that began in 2008, today **monetary policy,** varying the supply of money to stabilize the business cycle, is the government's most important tool for managing the economy. When the supply of money is increased, it becomes cheaper for private citizens and investors to borrow and spend more of it (interest rates—the cost of borrowing money—go down). This increase in borrowing and spending in turn leads to economic growth and lower unemployment. If the supply of money increases too fast, however, inflation may result. Conversely, when the supply of money goes down, it becomes more costly to borrow and spend (interest rates go up). With less to spend and invest, the economy slows and inflationary pressures ease. If the economy contracts, unemployment increases.

Many economists believe that monetary policy is an effective tool for managing the economy because, unlike fiscal policy, it can be altered quickly in response to changing economic circumstances. A rapid reaction is possible because decisions affecting the money supply are made not by Congress or even by the president, but by the **Federal Reserve Board,** the governing board of the country's banking system, which executes U. S. monetary policy through the Federal Reserve System by manipulating the supply of funds that member banks can lend.

Created in 1913, the Federal Reserve System (commonly known as the Fed) is headed by a board consisting of seven governors appointed by the president and confirmed by the Senate with each Fed governor holding office for 14 years. The Fed acts on the economy through the operations of its 12 regional banks, each of which oversees member banks in its part of the country. Figure 19.4 illustrates the structure of the Fed and its relationship to the federal government.

The most important decisions affecting the day-to-day workings of the economy are made by the Fed's Open Market Committee. This committee considers whether interest rates are too high or too low and what adjustments it should make. The committee consists of the seven governors, all of whom vote, and the 12 regional bank presidents, only five of whom have a vote (the New York bank president always has a vote; the remaining four votes rotate among the other 11 banks). The Open Market Committee has three primary tools with which to affect the supply of money: It may buy and sell federal securities (Treasury bills, notes, and bonds); it may change the interest rate it charges other banks; it may change the percentage of deposits that banks are required to hold in reserve; or it may choose to loan money directly to businesses. In practice, the Fed usually makes policy using the first two methods, but during the 2008 financial crisis it made extensive use of its power to loan money directly.

Federal Reserve Board

The governing board of the country's central bank, which executes monetary policy by manipulating the supply of funds that member banks can lend.

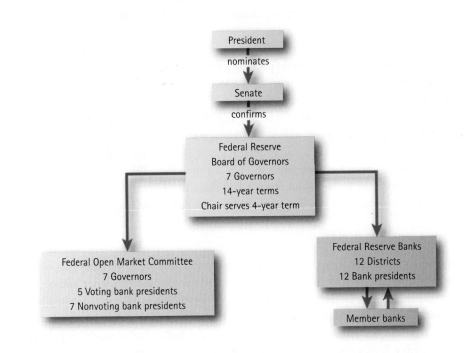

FIGURE 19.4

THE STRUCTURE OF THE FEDERAL RESERVE SYSTEM

The Federal Reserve System is headed by a board of governors nominated by the president and confirmed by the Senate. The board of governors and the 12 district banks communicate frequently with private banks and other financial institutions.

• *The leaders of many bureaucratic agencies are appointed by the president, confirmed by the Senate, and communicate with constituency groups (see Chapter 14). Do you think the Fed is similar in most respects to these other agencies, or does it have more autonomy and power than the typical bureaucracy?*

Ben Bernanke, Chairman of the Fed

Ben Bernanke, chairman of the Fed, testifies on the state of the U.S. economy.

• *Why is congressional influence over the Fed less than its influence over other agencies?*

A financial reform bill enacted in 2010 gave the Fed several additional powers. A new interagency oversight panel may recommend steps that the Fed should take to maintain the stability of the overall economy. Congress also created a Bureau of Consumer Financial Protection, housed within the Federal Reserve, to ensure fair credit card and mortgage practices.

Often the Fed is said to be the most powerful agency in the government after the Executive Office of the President. Its decisions affect interest rates, employment levels, and economic growth rates. The great American humorist Will Rogers once remarked that "two things can disrupt business in this country. One is a war and the other is a meeting of the Federal Reserve Board."[14] Surprisingly (given its importance), the Fed's activities are relatively unknown to many Americans.

The Fed Chair

If the Fed is the second most powerful agency in Washington, the chair of the Federal Reserve Board, currently Benjamin Bernanke, ranks among the most powerful persons in government. The chair's great power derives from close ties to the president, direct access to up-to-date economic information supplied by the Fed staff, and the power to approve the appointment of the 12 presidents of the Federal Reserve Banks (upon the recommendation of the member banks in each region). In addition, the chair inherits a job held in the past by powerful, prestigious people. Martin Eccles, head of the Fed during the 1930s, is acclaimed for taking actions to get the country out of the Great Depression, Paul Volcker is remembered for bringing the double-digit inflation of the late 1970s to an end, and Alan Greenspan added to this tradition by managing the sustained economic growth of the 1990s.

During the 2008 financial crisis, Bernanke took an unusually active role, huddling with lawmakers working on a rescue package for the financial industry and engaging in weekend crisis negotiations as key firms teetered on the brink of bankruptcy. Bernanke's intervention won praise from many quarters, but some cautioned, along with *The Economist,* that a larger role for the Fed "could make it a larger political target and distract it from monetary policy, and damage its reputation if it were to fail."[15] Indeed, after the financial crisis, the Federal Reserve Board came under greater public scrutiny than at any other time since the Great Depression. When President Obama nominated Bernanke for a second term as Fed chair, more senators (30) voted against his confirmation than had voted against any previous Fed chair.

Who Controls the Fed?

Surprisingly, in an elections-dominated political system, this key government agency is relatively insulated from electoral pressures. The Fed's power, independence, and objectivity are symbolized by its Washington home, a magnificent quasi-palace fronted by a remote—almost forbidding—facade and located two miles from Capitol Hill, adjacent to the National Academy of Sciences. Of course, the Fed is not immune to political pressure, but it is more insulated than are most government agencies.

Congressional Influence   Like all other government agencies, the Fed was created and its powers were defined by congressional statutes. Nominees to the Federal Reserve Board must be approved by the Senate, and the Fed must make quarterly reports to the banking committees of the House and Senate.

Despite these legal obligations to Congress, the Fed is remarkably free of congressional influence. For one thing, the Fed's budget is not congressionally determined. Instead, the Fed raises its own revenue by creating money (almost literally) and using this money to buy U.S. Treasury bonds, from which it earns interest. Creating money and buying Treasury bonds are a necessary part of the Fed's job—they are among the ways the Fed puts money into and takes money out of the economy. But Fed investments have a side benefit for the agency. Every year Fed investments earn billions of dollars (about $55 billion in 2009).[16] Most of this money is turned over to the federal treasury, but the Fed keeps about a tenth for its own operations.[17] As a result, the Fed does not need to ask Congress for an appropriation in the way most agencies must. The Fed owns squash courts in its building near the Washington Monument and recreational space on Wall Street, the most expensive real estate in the world—a reflection of the fact that it can almost literally manufacture its own money.

The Fed is also relatively free of congressionally determined salary schedules and personnel controls. Consequently, it is able to hire a better trained, more professional, and more prestigious staff than are other government agencies. In fact, the Fed is the one agency of the United States government that has a civil service that resembles the type found in Europe and Japan (see *International Comparison,* Chapter 14, page 406). Instead of political appointees who rotate in and out of office, the Fed staff consists of expert, career appointees.

In general, congressional influence on the Fed is exerted indirectly. Congress "jawbones" the Fed when it feels that monetary policy is not appropriate for prevailing conditions. Individual members make critical speeches and committees hold hearings at which the Fed chair is asked to testify. In these ways, some members make known their belief that monetary policy is too restrictive, and others announce their conviction that monetary policy is too loose. There is an implied warning in these pronouncements that if the Fed is not responsive, more serious attempts to influence it may be forthcoming. But members of Congress usually cannot agree on any specific course of action. Congress nearly forestalled the almost trillion dollar TARP legislation recommended by the chair of the Federal Reserve, as we saw at the beginning of this chapter. But even that vast expenditure was eventually approved, although by only a small margin.

Although observers usually agree that Congress usually does not exert significant control over the Fed, there is less consensus on the influence of other groups and institutions. Three distinct interpretations of the sources of influence over Fed operations have been offered: banker dominance, presidential control, and Fed independence.

Banker Dominance   The first interpretation, held by many liberal critics of the Fed, is that the banks control the Fed.[18] Just as interest groups underpin other iron triangles (see Chapter 14), so the banking industry, which has a huge stake in Fed decisions, forms the primary base of support for the Fed. Bankers influence the appointment of the board of governors, and they nominate the Federal Reserve Bank presidents, who cast five votes on the Open Market Committee.

As evidence of banker dominance, proponents point to the apparent policy bias of the Fed, which is thought to regulate banks with a lenient hand and is generally viewed as being less concerned about reducing unemployment than about lowering inflation rates. To put it another way, the Fed seems to be more worried about avoiding rising prices than about staving off recessions. The Fed "can't stand prosperity." When jobs are plentiful and people are spending freely, the Fed typically responds by raising interest rates and slowing down the economy: "Just when the party gets going, the Fed takes away the beer."[19] Proponents of the banker dominance theory also point out that, during the financial crisis, meetings at the New York Fed included representatives of the Department of the Treasury, Fed officials, and the CEOs of major investment banks like Goldman Sachs and Morgan Stanley.

The Fed defends itself against such accusations of policy bias by saying that unless inflation is checked quickly much stronger action will eventually have to be taken, creating more hardship in the long run. The Fed offers as evidence its policy in the late 1970s, when it mistakenly let inflation get out of control. Only after the deep and painful recession of 1981–1982 did it bring inflation and interest rates down to acceptable levels. As the economic recovery progressed in the years following the financial collapse of 2008, all eyes were watching the pace at which the Federal Reserve was raising interest rates to control any emerging inflationary signs.

Presidential Dominance   A second interpretation emphasizes not the bankers, but the president, as the main source of influence on the Fed. And, indeed, most observers believe that the president, who appoints its members and chairs, has a great deal more influence than Congress.[20] But how much influence do presidents have, and to what ends do they use it?

Some political scientists suggest that presidents try to manipulate Fed policy for their own political purposes. These scholars note that the chair of the Federal Reserve Board, in order to win reappointment, must be sensitive to signals from the White House. Even more important, the Fed's very desire to appear nonpolitical creates a dependence on the president. If the president publicly criticizes the Fed, it becomes the subject matter of news commentaries and talk shows because the Fed's actions have become matters of partisan controversy. The best way for the Fed to appear independent is that its chair listens carefully to suggestions coming from presidents and their advisers and avoids acting in such a way as to provoke controversy.

There are two versions of the presidential-control interpretation—the partisan and the election-cycle interpretations.[21] The **partisan interpretation** distinguishes between the constituencies of Republican and Democratic presidents.[22] The Republican constituency includes more upper-income business and professional people, who traditionally are less worried about unemployment (which strikes them less frequently) than about inflation. The Democratic constituency includes more lower-income, blue-collar workers, who traditionally are more concerned about rising unemployment (which usually hits them hardest). Indeed, studies show that inflation rates tend to rise under Democratic presidents and fall under Republican presidents, and that stocks and bonds earn higher returns under Republican administrations.[23]

But there are reasons to doubt the more extreme version of the partisan interpretation. Most citizens, regardless of income, occupation, or partisan affiliation, dislike both rising unemployment and rising prices; they do not want to lose their jobs, but neither do they want to see the purchasing power of their wages eroded by inflation. Similarly, investors dislike inflation, but if growth slows and unemployment rises, their investments will earn lower returns. Thus, whatever their party, presidents are better off striking a balance between the two goals rather than focusing on either one and neglecting the other. Nevertheless,

partisan interpretation
The argument that Republican administrations set economic policy to benefit higher-income, business, and professional groups, and that Democratic administrations set economic policy to benefit lower-income, blue-collar, wage-earning groups.

Democrats and Republicans strike different balances, reflecting their different constituencies. Republican administrations seem more willing to accept a little more unemployment in order to avoid inflation. Democrats strike the opposite balance. They appear more likely to accept somewhat higher inflation in order to avoid unemployment. To keep from provoking presidents, the Fed probably tends to slant its decisions in the direction of these well-known partisan preferences. But the effect is too small to call it presidential control.

The second version of the presidential dominance view, the **election-cycle interpretation,** says that presidents deliberately manipulate the economy to engineer their reelection. They tolerate slow growth, even a recession, early in their term of office so they can step on the gas and "rev up" the economic engine when the election payoff is greatest. Richard Nixon's first term is a clear example of presidential manipulation. The Nixon administration pulled out all the stops and achieved a huge increase in household income during the election year 1972.[24] Nixon was reelected overwhelmingly.

election-cycle interpretation
The argument that, whatever their party, presidents attempt to slow the economy early in their terms and then to expand it as their opportunity for re-election approaches.

If Nixon's first term fit the election-cycle interpretation, George H. W. Bush's single term directly contradicts it. In the beginning of his term the country enjoyed steady growth, but later the economy reversed, and Bush's fortunes shifted with it. Bush's son, George W. Bush, appears to fall somewhere in between. The slowdown of 2001 occurred very early in the younger Bush's presidency, allowing plenty of time for recovery in advance of the 2004 elections. But the 2008 mortgage crisis and the economic woes that followed did serious damage to the outgoing president's party in that year's elections, and the slow recovery, with continuing high unemployment rates, rendered President Obama's political situation increasingly precarious at the time of the 2010 congressional elections.

Combining information for all years since World War II yields some evidence, but not a lot, that presidents manipulate the economy to their political advantage. In years when presidents themselves are running for re-election, growth rates are, on average, somewhat higher, but not a lot higher, than in other years.[25]

An Independent Fed   Fed supporters say the agency is independent of both politics and external pressure groups.[26] The independence of the Fed is guaranteed by the fact that board members are appointed for 14-year terms. They can be removed only through the impeachment process. Because board members serve such long terms, presidents may not be able to appoint a majority of the board until they themselves have been in office six years.

There are other reasons for the Fed's independence. Business confidence in government economic policy is strengthened by the belief that Fed decisions are above politics. The board acts on the advice of a strong, independent staff. The chair is usually more knowledgeable about economic policy than any other presidential appointee. Monetary policy is too arcane to engage the general public; consequently, Fed-bashing is not a very effective campaign tactic.

Further, those who say the Fed is independent usually believe this is a good idea. They say that an independent Fed has improved the management of the economy. In particular, they emphasize that the country has had fewer and shorter recessions since the Fed was established than it had earlier in its history.

The Fed may be given a good deal of independence simply because presidents want it that way. Its goals are similar to those of presidents who want what nearly everyone desires: steady, stable economic growth.

A case in point is the relationship President Clinton had with Fed chair Alan Greenspan. Ronald Reagan first appointed Greenspan as Fed chair, and Clinton sought to reassure financial markets in the election year of 1996 by renominating him.[27] Because both Greenspan and Clinton were interested in stable growth, each felt it was in his interest to leave the other alone. Similarly, Obama, shortly after his election, reappointed Bernanke as Fed chair, despite the fact that Bernanke had originally been appointed by his predecessor George Bush, and some members of the president's party blamed Bernanke for allowing the financial credit crisis to occur. That Obama ignored such criticism and reappointed Bernanke showed once again that the consensus on monetary policy is often much greater than partisan debaters would have one believe.

19.6

Compare the tax burden, the national debt, and employment opportunities in the United States with similar economic aspects in other developed countries.

The U.S. Economy: An International Comparison

Even though we have focused on government and the economy, the truth is that the extent to which the economy can be controlled by government is limited—and has become much more so in recent years. When the Fed loosens or tightens the money supply, it is reacting to national and global economic forces that may overcome its best efforts. Indeed, all over the world, countries with very different political systems are struggling to meet economic challenges similar to those in the United States. Relative to other advanced democracies, the United States is dealing reasonably well with its economic difficulties, although concerns have grown noticeably in recent years. In this section we shall place U.S. taxes, national debt, and employment opportunities in comparative perspective.

Tax Burden

The tax burden in the United States compares very favorably with that in the world's other developed countries. As of 2008, the tax burden in the United States (including state and local government taxes) was among the lowest of 13 major industrialized countries: less than 34 percent of GDP. As can be seen in Figure 19.5, the public sector in Sweden taxes away 54 percent of the country's GDP. Taxes in Denmark, France, Greece, and Italy all exceed 40 percent of GDP. (See the *Election Voices!* feature for a discussion of tax issues in the United States.)

To be sure, other countries provide more services in exchange for the money they extract in taxes. The most important example is healthcare; about half of it is paid for by the private sector in the United States, whereas it is almost entirely government-provided in other countries.

If their tax rates and the overall tax burden are the lowest in the developed world and are continuing to fall, why have Americans traditionally been so unhappy with taxes? We doubt that there is any single explanation for the American aversion to taxes. Part of the answer may lie in the nature of the American tax system. The United States relies more heavily than most other countries on income and payroll taxes to raise revenues; nearly two-thirds of total tax revenues come from such sources, a figure exceeded only by Switzerland and Belgium. Other countries rely more heavily on consumption taxes, such as a sales tax known as the value-added tax (VAT), which is hidden in the prices of goods and services. Thus, their voters may not realize the full tax cost of the services they receive, despite the fact that the VAT affects low-income families the most. Ironically, Sweden, Germany, and Italy—with their large welfare states—rely heavily on the VAT, a tax that American liberals view as regressive. Only Japan, with its minimal provision of social services, relies less on sales taxes than the United States.

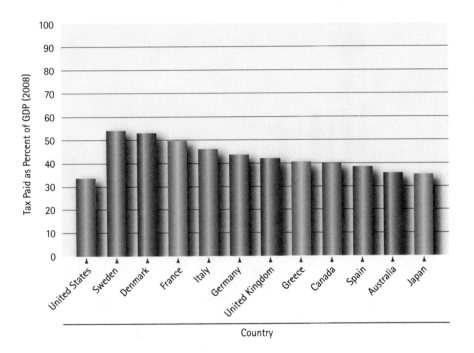

Tax Paid as Percent of GDP (2008)

Country

United States, Sweden, Denmark, France, Italy, Germany, United Kingdom, Greece, Canada, Spain, Australia, Japan

FIGURE 19.5

U.S. TAX BURDEN IS LESS THAN THAT IN MANY OTHER DEMOCRACIES

The total tax burden—the percent of taxes paid to the government as a percentage of GDP—includes taxes paid to the national government, as well as state and local taxes.

• *Why are U.S. taxes lower than taxes in other countries? Based on this graph, in which countries would you expect public opinion on taxes to be most similar to opinions on taxes in the United States?*

Source: U.S. Bureau of the Census, *Statistical Abstract of the United States, 2010,* Table 1324.

Historical experience in the United States is probably more important for explaining the views of Americans than the type of tax levied, however. In Chapter 4 we saw that, more than the citizens in other countries, Americans are economic individualists who wish to limit the role of government. They expect less from government, and prefer to keep more of their money for their own use.

The National Debt

Thirteen trillion dollars, the size of the national debt in 2010, is an almost unimaginable number. But such numbers are meaningful only relative to baselines, and the natural baseline—the size of the American economy—was more than $14 trillion. Relative to the size of the economy, the public debt in the United States reached 90 percent in 2010. Although that is considerably larger than it was only a few years before, France, Germany, and Great Britain have historically all had larger national debts than the United States (see Figure 19.6). By 2010, the Greek debt became so large, and had grown so rapidly, and had for years been so carefully disguised from international creditors by shady accounting practices, that when the reality of the situation was discovered, only a European rescue package was able to keep the Greek government from defaulting on its debt.

If the United States situation is utterly different from the Greek one, this is not to say that concern about the debt is unwarranted, especially since the United States was in 2010 running annual deficits at the rate of 10 percent of GDP and is expected to incur ever rising costs in many government programs, including social security, Medicare, Medicaid, and other health-related programs. The size of publicly held debt is expected to be a major political issue at all levels of government in coming years, although a very strong economic recovery could change that picture.

FIGURE 19.6

U.S. Debt Is Smaller
Than the Debt of Other
Countries

Here we graph the central government's debt in each country
as a percentage of that country's
GDP.

• *Note the countries that are
highest and lowest in central government debt. Compare them
with their tax burdens, as illustrated in Figure 19.5. Should
countries with high central government debt increase the tax
burden to pay down the debt?
Should countries with low debt
decrease the tax burden?*

Source: Public debt, *The World Factbook,*
United States Central Intelligence Agency,
2010.

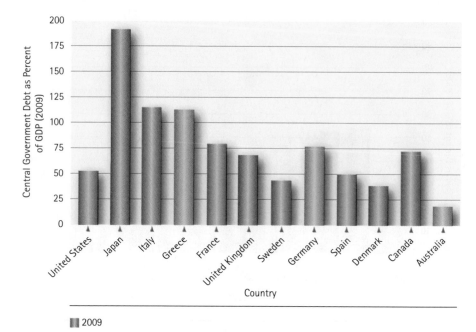

■ 2009

Employment Opportunities

A strong economic recovery is not impossible for the United States, because in the past
the country did a better job than most countries of incorporating new workers into the
economy. In 2007, for example, the unemployment rates in Germany and France were
around 8 percent—significantly higher than the 4.6 percent rate in the United States.[28]

That situation prevailing as recently as 2007 in the United States was the result of
changes that date back to the 1980s. At that time, the workforce in the Western world
expanded rapidly as the baby boom generation reached working age and as women
moved into the workforce in greater numbers. The American economy absorbed these
new workers far more successfully than did European economies, creating three times
more new jobs per 1,000 people than did France and Germany. Moreover, European
countries were able to keep their unemployment rates as low as they did only by introducing policies that would be unacceptable in the United States. For example, policies
in Germany and Switzerland induced so-called guest workers to return to their countries of origin. The United States, in contrast, allowed immigration to increase beginning in the 1980s (see Chapter 4). Some countries absorbed new workers by expanding
their public sectors. Sweden, for example, dealt with the surge of women into the labor
force by doubling public-sector employment.[29] In the United States, public-sector employment grew very slowly.

Since 2007, there has been a growing concern that the United States economy is
beginning to resemble the slow-growth economies of Europe, however. For one thing,
European and American unemployment rates converged in 2010. In April of that year
U.S. unemployment was 9.9 percent, slightly higher than the 9.8 percent rate in France
and the 7.5 percent rate in Germany.[30]

Quite apart from converging unemployment rates, the enlarged U.S. government
debt, the greater governmental regulation of the economy, the growth in public-sector
employment, and the creation of a new set of national health arrangements have all

shifted the United States in a policy direction closer to that prevailing in Europe. With the leaner economies of China, India, and other Asian countries growing at a much faster pace than the United States, the U.S. economy may not dominate the world economy in the 21st century in the same way that it did in the last half of the 20th century.

Still, the situation remains unclear. Although some analysts have expressed the concern that many of the jobs that have been created in the United States are low-skill, low-paying "McJobs," and that many good jobs have been exported abroad by U.S. companies, the evidence suggests that such claims are at least somewhat exaggerated. According to several studies, much of the job growth in recent years has been in higher-paying occupations and industries—again, a performance far superior to western European democracies.[31] The American economy remains less restricted by government policies and regulations than European, if not Asian, economies. This lack of restriction gives it a greater capacity to adapt to changing economic conditions. For example, changes in the world economy have had an adverse effect on workers in the manufacturing sector. In 1950 these industries accounted for 34 percent of U.S. jobs, but by 2009 this figure had shrunk to less than 10 percent.[32,33] Amazingly, the United States produces no more steel today than it did in the early 1960s, despite the great increase in the worldwide demand for steel.[34] But the decline in manufacturing has been offset by gains in the service, communications, and technology industries, so the U.S. economy could begin growing rapidly once again. The U.S. information technology sector grew at stunning rates beginning in the 1990s, and officials estimate that employment in data processing and related services will increase by over 50 percent between 2008 and 2018.[35] The United States is better equipped than most of its European peers to handle this rapid transition to a high-technology economy. For example, the number of secure Internet servers per capita is far higher in the United States than in Europe.[36]

Inequality

Compared to other advanced democracies, income inequality in the United States is higher (see Figure 19.7). After declining between 1930 and 1970, inequality has risen

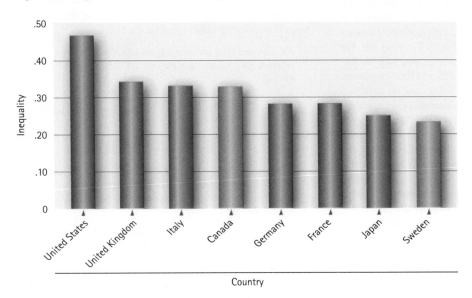

FIGURE 19.7

INCOME INEQUALITY IS GREATER IN THE UNITED STATES THAN IN MANY OTHER COUNTRIES

Here inequality is measured using the GINI coefficient. The coefficient varies between 0, representing complete equality (that is, a situation in which everyone has exactly equivalent wealth), and 1, representing complete inequality (one person has all the wealth and everyone else has nothing). The higher the GINI coefficient, the greater the degree of inequality.

• *Why is inequality greater in a wealthy country such as the United States?*

Source: *World Development Report 2006: Equity and Development* (Washington, DC: World Bank, 2005), Table A2, 279–280.

Continued on page 577

Taxes

The Issue

In 2010, the federal government deficit was estimated to have been over 10 percent of the country's Gross Domestic Product (GDP) (see Figure 1). Some economists believe the best way to reduce the size of that annual deficit is to cut spending, while others believe that taxes must be raised to cover the shortfall. With budget deficits of over 10 percent of GDP, a combination of these measures will likely be taken. If taxes are to be raised, how should the increased tax burden be distributed? Should it be concentrated on the well off, or distributed evenly across the nation? Further, what should be taxed? Should everything be taxed or should taxpayers be allowed to deduct their expenses for certain things, such as college tuition, home mortgages, and charitable contributions, even though it means everything else has to be taxed at a higher rate?

Background

Taxation is the oldest political question in the United States. It was a key issue that drove the independence movement of 1776. Even to this day, license plates in Washington, DC, read "Taxation without representation," echoing a slogan from the nation's revolutionary past. More recently, the debate over taxation has also focused on how progressive or regressive the tax system should be.

Taxes are said to be *progressive taxes* if people with higher income pay a higher tax rate. The most important progressive tax is the federal income tax. In 2008, individual taxable incomes up to $8,025 were taxed at a 10 percent rate, while additional income between $8,025 and $32,550 was taxed at a 15 percent rate. For example, if your annual income was $20,000, you paid 10 percent, or $802.50, in taxes on the first $8,025, and then 15 percent, or $1,796.25 on the remaining $11,975. Tax rates on additional income (called "marginal rates") increased up to a maximum rate of 35 percent for income more than about $358,000.

Taxes that require low-income people to pay a higher rate are called *regressive taxes*. The payroll or social security tax is a regressive tax, because as of 2008 it was levied only on the first $102,000 that a person earns. Because all earnings in excess of that figure are exempt from the tax, higher-income people pay a smaller share of their income for social security than do lower-income people.

For example, if you made $40,000 per year, you would pay 6.2 percent of your income, or $2,480, in social security taxes. If you made $1 million, you would pay 6.2 percent in taxes on the first $102,000 you made, or $6,324. In the second case, the amount paid is larger, but note that it makes up only a little

more than half a percent of total income, whereas in the first case, 6.2 percent of total income goes for the tax.

Numerous taxes are levied in the United States. The federal personal income tax and some state personal income taxes are progressive. Social security and state sales taxes are regressive. The impact of property taxes varies from place to place, but it generally falls in between. When all taxes levied by federal, state, and local governments are taken into account, it is difficult to say whether the tax structure in the United States is progressive.

Opposing Views on Taxation

Progressive taxes traditionally have been defended by liberals, who claim that progressive rates reduce income inequality in the society. Thus, Bill Clinton and congressional Democrats pushed through an increase in the taxes paid by high-income taxpayers over united Republican opposition in 1993. Progressive taxes traditionally have been opposed by conservatives, who claim that progressive rates discourage investment and hard work by the most productive members of society. Thus, the Bush tax cut of 2001 made the tax system less progressive because the largest cuts in tax rates went to those with the highest incomes. Tax progressivity became a flash point of the 2008 elections; Democrats argued that the tax system ought to be made more progressive again, and that Republican tax policy "mostly benefits the wealthy and Wall Street." During the 2008 election, Senator Obama made it clear that he favored a more progressive tax system by accusing his opponent of favoring a system of taxation that would benefit the wealthy.

> McCain and I are boh offering tax cuts. The difference is, he wants to give the average Fortune 500 CEO a $700,000 tax cut.
>
> —Then-Senator Obama giving a presidential campaign speech in Dayton Ohio, October 9, 2008

Consistent with that view, Obama, as president, has proposed ending the Bush era tax cuts for wealthier individuals.

> We extend middle-class tax cuts in this budget . . . but we will not continue costly tax cuts for oil companies, investment fund managers, and those making over $250,000 a year. We just can't afford it.
>
> —President Obama, commenting on the 2011 budget. *Wall Street Journal*, Marketwatch, February 1, 2010.

Republicans counter that most Americans benefited from the tax cuts and that a more progressive system of taxation would hurt small business owners, negatively affecting overall economic activity. Senator McCain, in the 2008 presidential election, suggested that the progressivity of a tax system must be viewed in light of broader economic activity.

> Sen. Obama's secret that you don't know is that his tax increases will increase taxes on 50% of small business revenue. Small businesses across America will have to cut jobs and will have their taxes increase and won't be able to hire because of Sen. Obama's tax policies.
>
> —Senator McCain debating Senator Obama during the presidential debate at Belmont University in Nashville, Tennessee, October 2008.

The most famous and powerful opponent of progressive taxation, Ronald Reagan, largely made a political career out of attacking what he perceived to be the opposition's sympathies toward taxing the most productive members of society.

Tax Reform

Even though the tax burden is the most frequently discussed tax-related topic, it is not necessarily the most important. At least as critical is the breadth of the *tax base,* the income, property, wealth, or economic activity that is taxed. Many economists argue that taxes are less intrusive if they are broad based—that is, imposed on all economic activity at the same rate. For example, the Tax Foundation, a nonpartisan organization based in Washington, argues that "The fewer economic decisions that are made for tax reasons, the better. The primary purpose of taxes is to raise needed revenue, not to micromanage the economy. The tax system should not favor certain industries, activities, or products." Thus, the amount you pay in taxes should depend only on the amount you make, not on how you make it. Whether you make your money growing crops, making movies, writing wills, or running a charity should not matter. Nor should the amount you pay in taxes depend on whether you spend money on groceries, cars, beer, or medical insurance. If everything is taxed alike, then tax policy will not distort the economy. That is, it will not influence the choices people make.

Broad-based taxes are more easily recommended than enacted into law, however. Frequently, good reasons can be given for not taxing some particular activity. For example, according to President Obama, "tax credits [for college tuition] . . . make sure any young person who works hard and desires a college education can access it." There are numerous organized groups that offer good (and often not-so-good) reasons to persuade elected officials to give favorable treatment to the activities of their members. In response to these pressures, national and state legislators have enacted thousands of *tax preferences* that exempt particular types of economic activity from taxation. Critics say these tax preferences distort economic activity and cost the government billions of dollars in forgone revenues.[1] Here are some major examples of tax preferences and the economic distortions that critics say they foster:

- *Tax credits for college tuition* ($11 billion).[2] In 1997 Congress allowed a tax credit for college tuition, a tax break popular with college students. Critics say colleges, realizing that students have more tuition dollars, will simply boost tuition.

- *Deductions for mortgage interest on owner-occupied homes* ($94 billion). Developers and brokers claim that this tax preference encourages home ownership, which is said to be good for families and to boost community stability. Critics say the preference primarily benefits higher-income people who can afford huge mortgages and subsidizes their overinvestment in big houses and vacation homes.

- *Deductions for charitable contributions* ($52 billion). Defenders of this tax preference claim that it encourages public support for the arts, education, and the needy. But critics say many charities are actually businesses that provide services to those who "give" them money.

Tax preferences are the classic "slippery slope." Once government grants them to any group, it abandons the principle of neutral taxation and encourages other groups to lobby for their own preferences. Tax preferences distort the economy by encouraging people to make economic decisions on the basis of tax considerations. Moreover, granting preferences to some activities requires that taxes be higher on other activities that lack defenders strong enough to get their own tax break. Some economists argue that the only solution to this dilemma is somehow to restrict the government's ability to grant tax breaks to any activity or group.[3] Yet it is unlikely that all tax preferences will be eliminated. Some activities—getting an education, owning a home, donating to charities—are so popular that most people think they should get a tax break.

Not all special treatment is favorable. The government also sometimes imposes *sin taxes,* taxes intended to discourage unwanted behavior. The most prominent examples of sin taxes are the taxes on the consumption of cigarettes and alcohol. Critics of such measures argue that they fall primarily on the poorest segments of the population and fail to have a significant impact on the consumption of addictive products.

The best known tax reform is the *flat tax,* a proposal that would eliminate progressive income tax rates and would tax all income groups above a certain minimum at the same rate. Advocates argue that it is unfair to require some people to pay a higher percentage of their income in taxes than others. Supporters of a flat tax also defend it on the grounds of efficiency—the more progressive taxes are, the greater the incentive for the wealthy to hire accountants, lawyers, and lobbyists to help them avoid taxes. Indeed, the wealthy are not the only ones who pay: As of 2008, 63 percent of Americans used professional tax preparers, and taxpayers spent more than $300 billion a year on record keeping, filling out forms, complying with audits, and paying for accountants and lawyers.[4]

The debate over tax reform is likely to remain fractious and many sided because people want to use the tax system to achieve different—often conflicting—goals. They want to raise revenue, to reduce income inequality, to discourage some kinds of behavior, and to give breaks so as to promote other kinds of activity, such as education and home ownership.

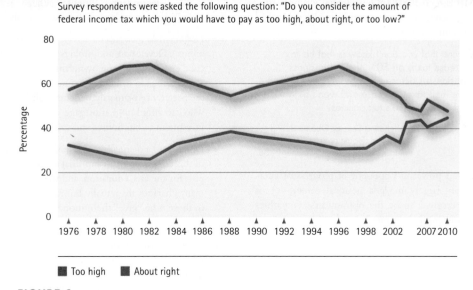

Survey respondents were asked the following question: "Do you consider the amount of federal income tax which you would have to pay as too high, about right, or too low?"

■ Too high   ■ About right

FIGURE 1

Public Opinion About Taxes

Americans are wary of higher taxes, as this graph indicates. Those who think taxes are "too low" make up too negligible a number to plot on a graph.

• *At which times have more Americans been more upset about the tax burden? Do you think taxes are too low or too high? Why?*

Source: National Opinion Research Center, *General Social Survey;* 2003–2007 figures from identical question asked by Gallup.

What Do Americans Believe?

Evidence from public opinion surveys seems to show that Americans are sensitive to their own individual tax burdens, but place less weight on the overall progressivity of the tax system when deciding on how to vote (Figure 1).

As of 2010, according to Gallup, 48 percent of Americans say that the amount of federal income taxes they pay is "about right," and 46 percent say it is "too high." But for those making above $75,000 a year, the proportion saying that taxes are too high increases to 52 percent. Views of taxation seem to vary significantly by party affiliation. In 2008, 45 percent of Democrats said their taxes were too high, compared to 58 percent of Republicans. Views of taxation also seem to depend on government uses of revenue: According to Gallup, during World War II, more than 85 percent of Americans said the taxes they paid were "fair." That number dropped to 62 percent by 1946, the year after the end of the war.

What Do You Think?

1. Should the tax system be used to create disincentives to those engaging in socially stigmatized behaviors, such as drinking and smoking? Would increased taxes on these activities be more acceptable if their revenue was used to pay for their broader economic costs, for example, to the healthcare system? Which other activities do you think should be subject to sin taxes? Should sin taxes extend to environmental issues, for example, sin taxes on driving unnecessarily large or polluting automobiles?

2. Why should students receive favorable treatment by the tax system, in the form of tax credits? How about homeowners? Should they get a tax break? Does the fact that everything and everyone is not taxed equally seem unfair? Why or why not?

On the Web

www.ctj.org
www.taxfoundation.org

The contentious debates over taxation in Washington have been enough to inspire a number of interest groups to people the barricades on both sides. Citizens for Tax Justice (CTJ) argues for progressive taxation, whereas the Tax Foundation promotes the idea of a flat tax.

[1]William C. Mitchell and Michael Munger, "Economic Models of Interest Groups: An Introductory Survey," *American Journal of Political Science* 35(2) (May 1991): 512–546.

[2]Figures for this and other tax preferences are drawn from the *Budget of the United States Government, Fiscal Year 2009* (Washington, DC: U.S. Government Printing Office, 2008), Analytical Perspectives, Table 19.1. College tuition tax credits include the Lifetime Learning Tax Credit, the HOPE Tax Credit, exclusion of scholarship and fellowship income, deductibility of student loan interest, deduction for higher education expenses, state prepaid tuition plans, and exclusion of interest on student loan bonds. Charitable contribution figures include charitable contributions to educational and health institutions. Figures are estimates for 2008.

[3]Howard Schuman, *Politics and the Budget,* 3rd ed. (Englewood Cliffs, NJ: Prentice-Hall, 1992), p. 121.

[4]Associated Press/AOL Poll, March 24–April 3, 2008; "Total Federal Income Tax Compliance Costs, 1990-2015," Tax Foundation, www.taxfoundation.org/taxdata/topic/96.html, accessed August 12, 2010.

Continued from page 573

in recent decades so that today it is higher than at any time since the 1930s.[37] Some social critics see in such trends a "class war" of the rich against the poor, while others fear a class war initiated by those of lower income will stunt future economic growth. But such extreme positions are seldom politically popular. The Obama administration has proposed an end to the tax cuts initiated during the Bush administration, and many Democrats in Congress have proposed a concentration of all future taxes on a fairly small segment of top earners. But, apart from widespread support for taxing banks and investment firms in the wake of the 2008 financial crisis, efforts to levy heavy taxes on high-income groups have not been particularly popular.[38] Candidates who advocate a greater role for government and a greater degree of income redistribution sometimes win election to the Senate and the House of Representatives, but the majorities necessary to change tax policy in a major way have generally fallen short. With Republican gains in the House of Representatives and Senate, a concentration of future tax increases on just the highest income groups, even if done in order to lower budget deficits, is unlikely in the near future.

CHAPTER SUMMARY

19.1 Analyze the relationship between governments and markets.

People care a lot about whether they can find a job and what they have to pay for the things they buy. When times are bad, the president takes the blame. When times are good, the president usually—but not always—gets the credit. The popular standing of presidents and their odds of reelection are significantly influenced by national economic conditions. To a somewhat lesser extent, these conditions also have an effect on members of Congress and even on state-level elected officials.

19.2 Outline the business cycle and evaluate its impact on economic growth.

Business cycles used to appear uncontrollable, with expansions in employment and national income followed by contractions in patterns that resembled regular but unpredictable waves. If the economy expands too rapidly, inflation may rob people of their savings; if it expands too slowly, unemployment may shrink personal incomes. In the last century, economists have found that governments can affect these cycles.

19.3 Assess the influence of economic conditions on the political fortunes of elected officials.

Given these political facts of life, presidents assign economic policy top priority. To achieve this objective, they grant the agency responsible for monetary policy, the Federal Reserve, a good deal of independence. Although they may try to shape policy on occasion, presidents generally realize that the Fed needs independence to do its job well. And when the Fed does a good job by keeping economic growth steady, the president usually gets the credit.

19.4   Define fiscal policy and explain its use and decline.

For half a century, presidents tried to use fiscal policy—the management of budget deficits and surpluses—to manage the economy. Even today, politicians often debate the impact of specific tax and spending proposals on U.S. economic indicators. But the importance of fiscal policy for managing the economy has been reduced by a combination of factors, including divided government, declining faith in Keynesian theory, a rising public debt, and the globalization of economic activity.

19.5   Define monetary policy and analyze the role of the Fed in the implementation of this policy.

Monetary policy, in contrast with fiscal policy, affects the economy by increasing or decreasing the money supply.

The Fed usually does this by raising or lowering interest rates, although it may provide more direct cash infusions to businesses, as in the case of the 2008 financial crisis.

19.6   Compare the tax burden, the national debt, and employment opportunities in the United States with similar economic aspects in other developed countries.

The United States has a lower tax burden, a smaller national debt, and lower unemployment rates than many other countries. But Americans also seem more willing than people in other nations to tolerate economic inequality.

mypoliscilab EXERCISES

Apply what you learned in this chapter on MyPoliSciLab.

Read on mypoliscilab.com

eText: Chapter 19

Study and Review on mypoliscilab.com

Pre-Test

Post-Test

Chapter Exam

Flashcards

Watch on mypoliscilab.com

Video: Recession Hits Indiana

Video: The Stimulus Breakdown

Video: Economic Policy Debate at the G20

Video: Fed Approves Mortgage Crackdown

Video: Who is in the Middle Class?

Explore on mypoliscilab.com

Simulation: You Are the President and Need to Get a Tax Cut Passed

Simulation: Making Economic Policy

Comparative: Comparing Economic Policy

Timeline: Growth of the Budget and Federal Spending

Visual Literacy: Evaluating Federal Spending and Economic Policy

Visual Literacy: Where the Money Goes

KEY TERMS

SUGGESTED READINGS

Of General Interest

Ferguson, Niall. *The Ascent of Money: A Financial History of the World*. The Penguin Press HC, 2009. A historian chronicles the development of the financial sector.

Sorkin, Andrew Ross. *Too Big To Fail: The Story of How Wall Street and Washington Fought to Save the Financial System—and Themselves*. New York: Penguin, 2009. An engaging account of the frantic attempts to rescue the economy in 2008.

Stiglitz, Joseph. *Making Globalization Work*. New York: W.W. Norton, 2006. A Nobel Prize–winning economist offers some ideas about how domestic and international institutions can adapt to the new globalized economy.

Yergin, Daniel, and Joseph Stanislaw. *The Commanding Heights: The Battle Between Government and the Marketplace That Is Remaking the Modern World*. Revised and updated ed. New York: Free Press, 2002. A Pulitzer Prize–winning writer and a business consultant examine the implications of globalization for the United States and other nations.

Focused Studies

Hibbs, Douglas A., Jr. *The American Political Economy*. Cambridge, MA: Harvard University Press, 1987. Provides detailed statistical evaluations of partisan and election-cycle interpretations of presidential management of the economy.

Kettl, Donald F. *Deficit Politics: The Search for Balance in American Politics*. 2nd ed. New York: Longman, 2002. Short, readable book on budget deficits.

Shull, Bernard. *The Fourth Branch: The Federal Reserve's Unlikely Rise to Power and Influence*. Westport, CT: Praeger Publishers, 2005. Chronicles the Fed's increasing influence from 1913 to the present.

ON THE WEB

www.fcic.gov

The Financial Crisis Inquiry Commission is a bipartisan commission that has been given a critical non-partisan mission—to examine the causes of the financial crisis that has gripped the country and to report its findings to the Congress, the President, and the American people.

www.federalreserve.gov

Some claim that the Federal Reserve holds power second only to the president of the United States. The Federal Reserve System maintains an informative website, complete with publications, congressional testimony, and economic data.

www.commerce.gov

The Department of Commerce houses the Economics and Statistics Administration and the Bureau of Economic Analysis, which provide regular data and analysis on the U.S. economy.

www.nber.org

The National Bureau of Economic Research is considered the unofficial arbiter of many economic issues, such as when recessions begin and end. It publishes an excellent series of working papers by eminent economists.

www.publicdebt.treas.gov

Debate over the budget deficit defined economic policy debates in the 1970s and 1980s, and continues to affect discussions of new taxing and spending. The Bureau of the Public Debt, located in the Department of the Treasury, provides precise daily updates of how much the government owes. While there, you may peruse information on how to buy federal securities, thus helping to finance the national debt.

20 Foreign and Defense Policy

CHAPTER OUTLINE

LEARNING OBJECTIVES

20.1 Identify the roles of the president, interest groups, and the Congress in the development of foreign policy.

20.2 Detail the foreign policy powers of the president and of the Congress.

20.3 Trace the development of foreign policy institutions from the Cold War to post-9/11.

20.4 Analyze the conflict between American philosophical ideals and a practical need to defend the country.

Foreign Policy: Critically Important Once Again

In 2000, the Council on Foreign Relations, a prestigious research and policy organization, decided to arrange a series of public debates between prominent government officials and experts on foreign policy topics. Timed to coincide with the presidential race that year between Vice President Al Gore and Texas Governor George W. Bush, these forums were to be held on university campuses and draw attention to some of the most important issues that the United States would have to confront in its role as a world power over the coming four years.

But organizers quickly discovered that they faced an almost complete lack of interest on the part of the public. After decades of global competition with the monolithic Communist Soviet Union, the United States was now enjoying what many voters saw as the fruits of victory. Since 1991, when the Soviet empire had finally collapsed, there had been few wars to speak of, little international conflict, and a booming economy. As one former policymaker put it, "The American public is not engaged in foreign affairs because they say 'Look, we're secure.' They're not making...demands on either candidate to spell out details in foreign affairs."[1] Another expert put it more bluntly. Americans, he said, are "fat and happy."[2] "I've been here [in Washington] for six presidents," said Senator Joe Biden (D-DE), "and I can't think of a time when foreign and defense policy was less of an issue in a presidential campaign."[3] Bowing to this lack of interest, the Council on Foreign Relations cancelled most of its planned debates.

It may have seemed natural at the time, but the 2000 campaign's lack of attention to foreign policy is remarkable in light of the dramatic changes in U.S. foreign policy that began to occur within a year. In September 2001, the United States suffered the most devastating terrorist attack in its history. Within a month, U.S. forces began a retaliatory invasion of Afghanistan. In 2002, President Bush signed into law an act creating the Department of Homeland Security, the largest reorganization of government in nearly a half-century. Amid concerns that Iraqi dictator Saddam Hussein posed a threat, U.S. forces invaded Iraq in 2003, deposing him. The prolonged occupation and guerrilla conflict that followed dragged on for years and cost the United States thousands of lives and hundreds of billions of dollars.

The next two presidential campaigns took place in an atmosphere that seemed worlds apart from the placid, inwardly focused environment of 2000. George W. Bush won reelection in 2004 in a campaign focused on the Iraq War and the threat of terrorism. In 2008, Democrat Barack Obama and Republican John McCain challenged each other directly on Iraq, on Afghanistan, and on foreign policy, with Obama calling for withdrawal from Iraq and a more conciliatory approach to diplomacy and McCain making the case for a continued Iraq presence. As president, Obama began withdrawing troops from Iraq, but boosted U.S. forces in Afghanistan by 30,000. International terrorism remained an ever present threat, with a botched car bombing in Times Square in May 2010, and attempted package bombings by Yemeni extremists in October that same year.

The changes in foreign policy that two expert observers called a "revolution" had made foreign affairs central to elections once again.[4]

Making the Connection

Democracies are slow to respond to problems in foreign policy until they become full-blown crises because the public pays little attention to these issues if outward appearances suggest no imminent danger. This is why, between the early 1990s and 9/11, most elected officials paid less attention to foreign affairs than they did thereafter. Although presidents are uniquely positioned to make a difference in world politics, even they may not be able to mobilize public support for strong action until a foreign policy problem becomes urgent. Still, once a major crisis develops, voters can make rapid adjustments in their priorities and rally behind presidents, generating momentum in favor of foreign policy changes even if elections are years away. Presidents and members of Congress may be rewarded or punished in the long run for successes and failures in foreign affairs, and therefore officials pay close attention to what the public thinks. In this chapter, we explore how America conducts its foreign policy and examine the connections between foreign policy and electoral politics. In doing so, we pay close attention to the transitions that the major foreign policymaking institutions have made in light of the campaign against terrorism and the wars in Iraq and Afghanistan.

20.1

Identify the roles of the president, interest groups, and the Congress in the development of foreign policy.

foreign policy
Conduct of relations among nation-states.

two-presidency theory
Theory that explains why presidents exercise greater power over foreign affairs than over domestic policy.

Elections, Presidents, and Foreign Policy

Foreign policy is the conduct of relations among nation-states. The most important foreign policy issues involve war and peace. Of all foreign policy objectives, the most critical is to prevent the country from being attacked or invaded by a foreign power. But foreign policy also involves economic trade among nations, as well as such mundane matters as issuing passports to citizens who wish to travel abroad.

Whereas many scholars see the domestic policymaking process as complex and messy, with numerous groups and elected officials competing for attention (see Chapter 18), in the foreign policy arena one person stands above all others: the president. In a classic essay, political scientist Aaron Wildavksy developed the **two-presidency theory,** which explains why presidents exercise greater power over foreign affairs than over domestic policy.[5] On domestic matters, presidents are usually subject to interest-group politics and congressional checks. On foreign policy questions, however, presidents have a degree of autonomy that enables them to manage the external relations of the country in relative freedom from short-term interference. In this section, we describe four reasons why foreign policy differs from domestic policy: (1) the need for fast action, (2) the voters' focus on presidents, (3) the limited role of interest groups, and (4) the comparatively minor role of Congress.

The Need for Fast Action

On domestic issues, the president may negotiate with Congress over the course of several years, but foreign policy questions often require rapid, decisive action. As Alexander Hamilton observed, governments require a single executive leader in order to achieve "decision, activity, secrecy, and dispatch."[6] Or, in the words of nineteenth-century humorist Artemus Ward, "Thrice is he armed that has his quarrel just—And four times he who gets his fist in first."[7] Following this principle, for example, President Bush sent

Patriotic Fervor

Three spectators on a rooftop watch as an American flag is carried in the "Maine Heroes Parade."

• *Why does the "rally 'round the flag" effect dissipate over time?*

marines to Haiti in 2004 to guard U.S. interests as the government of Haitian president Jean Bertrand Aristide crumbled. Secretary of State Colin Powell briefed Congress on the operation, but Bush did not seek lawmakers' approval for it.

The Voters' Focus on Presidents

On key domestic issues, members of Congress know that voters hold them to account, but on foreign affairs, Wildavksy points out, voters "expect the president to act."[8] In the early days of a crisis, voters often ignore those who criticize presidential actions. After the 9/11 terrorist attacks, for example, President George W. Bush's popularity, which had been hovering around the 50 percent level, skyrocketed to above 90 percent.

The tendency among the public to back presidents in the event of foreign crises, which is often called the **"rally 'round the flag" effect,** shows up in opinion polls in almost every instance in which the United States becomes involved in a foreign policy emergency.[9] Support for the president nearly always goes up in the first days of a conflict with another nation. Figure 20.1 shows the crises that presidents from Truman to Bush have faced and the changes in opinion polls that have occurred after those crises broke. Between 1950 and 2010, public support for presidents increased by an average of 7 percentage points in the month after a foreign policy crisis occurred.

Although voters support presidents initially, they nonetheless demand quick results. When Iranian radicals took dozens of American embassy workers hostage in 1979, President Jimmy Carter's approval rating initially rose by nearly 20 points. But as the Tehran hostage crisis dragged on—eventually lasting more than a year—Carter's support evaporated and he was defeated in the 1980 election.

The public seems especially ready to hold presidents accountable when war breaks out and American casualties mount. The public supported U.S. entry into both the Korean War and the Vietnam War. But, when the conflicts dragged on, both Harry Truman, in the case of the Korean War, and Lyndon Johnson, in the case of the Vietnam

"rally 'round the flag" effect
The tendency for the public to back presidents in the event of foreign crises.

FIGURE 20.1

"RALLY 'ROUND THE FLAG" EFFECT

Presidential gains in popularity average 7 percentage points in the months following a crisis.

• *Why do you think President Clinton did not experience as large a boost in public support after foreign policy crises as his predecessors?*

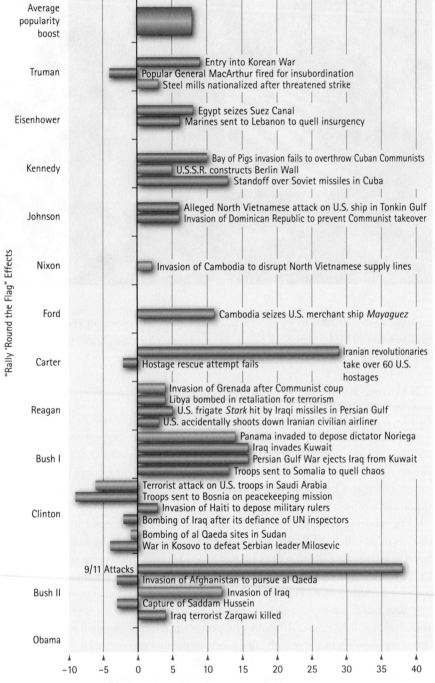

War, lost so much public support that they announced they would not run for reelection. The opposition party won the next election in each instance.[10] More than two-thirds of the public approved of President George W. Bush's presidency during the initial phase of the Iraq War in 2003, but, as more and more American troops were killed or wounded and occupation forces failed to prevent repeated attacks by insurgents, the president's popularity suffered. By the time he left office, Bush's approval rating had fallen to below 30 percent. As a result, Republican presidential candidate John McCain did his best to disassociate himself from Bush, and Republican congressional candidates did the same. Acknowledging his political liabilities, Bush jokingly said of McCain, "If he wants me to show up [at rallies] I will. If he wants me to say 'You know, I'm not for him,' I will."[11]

Not only do voters demand quick results, but they also soon forget foreign policy victories. If the economy steadily improves, presidents receive credit for the progress year after year. But, unless a foreign policy accomplishment immediately precedes an election, there are few electoral dividends. Before too long, voters forget and turn to domestic concerns. For example, during the first three years of the George H. W. Bush presidency, the Soviet Union collapsed and the United States won the Persian Gulf War. Yet, one year later, the voters, deciding that domestic issues were more important, voted Bush out of office.

As media coverage has become more intense and technologically more sophisticated, pressure on presidents has increased. During the initial stages of the Iraq War, many journalists traveled into combat zones with troops, and news networks aired live video and audio feeds of battles taking place at remote desert outposts. Although in the early phases of the conflict the effect of this unprecedented access was to improve the president's stature by highlighting the armed forces' rapid progress, later events made journalistic scrutiny more problematic. When media outlets published graphic photographs of prisoner abuse at Iraq's Abu Ghraib prison, President Bush was placed on the defensive, and he repeatedly denied that he or other top administration officials had condoned the abuse.[12]

Limited Role of Interest Groups

On domestic issues, many interest groups with large constituencies constantly mobilize voters and urge members of Congress to take action. But on foreign policy questions, "the interest group structure is weak, unstable, and thin."[13] The most important national membership organization influencing foreign affairs is the Council on Foreign Relations, a prestigious group that includes former secretaries of state, former ambassadors, foreign policy experts, and prominent business leaders. But the organization influences government action by the quality of its advice, not by its ability to mobilize votes, as the chapter's opening vignette shows.

On some occasions, organized groups capable of mobilizing large numbers of voters play a role in foreign policy issues. For example, the hundreds of thousands of people living in Florida whose families fled Cuba in the 1950s when Communist leader Fidel Castro came to power continue to pressure the U.S. government not to recognize the Castro regime, despite the fact that nearly every other country now does.

Middle East policies are also shaped by group pressures. Former Secretary of State James Baker has observed that the conflict between Israel and the Palestinians is "a perpetual fixture of domestic politics" as a result of "the political power of the American Jewish community."[14] Because a strong domestic constituency is vitally interested, Congress regularly becomes actively engaged (see the *Election Voices!* feature on page 606).

The examples of Cuba and Israel are "exceptions that prove the rule," however. Most nationality groups are not large enough, concentrated enough, or sufficiently attentive to events overseas to influence election outcomes and thereby affect U.S. foreign policy.

Congressional Role

Although Congress plays a central role in the formation of domestic policy, when it comes to foreign affairs, members of Congress restrain themselves more often, following a "self-denying ordinance."[15] This self-denial position was particularly true in the years immediately after World War II. During these years, Congress's prestige with respect to foreign policy was seriously damaged because it had left the country unprepared for the war. Just four months before the Japanese attacked Hawaii's Pearl Harbor, the incident that provoked U.S. involvement in the war, a bill requiring young men to register for service in the armed forces passed in the House of Representatives by only a single vote. In the period after World War II, Congress, embarrassed by its earlier mistakes, let the president make most major foreign policy decisions.

Later, after the Vietnam War prompted congressional distrust of the executive branch, Congress played a more assertive foreign policy role, and conflict between Congress and the president intensified.[16] But the victory in the Persian Gulf War in 1991 erased some of the bad memories from the Vietnam War and helped boost the prestige of the executive office. For example, after 9/11, Congress for the most part allowed the Bush administration to develop antiterrorist policies on its own and overwhelmingly approved military action in Afghanistan and Iraq. Nor did Congress seriously object to President Obama's troop increase in Afghanistan, despite grumbling by skeptics.

20.2

Detail the foreign policy powers of the president and of the Congress.

Foreign Policy Responsibilities of the President and Congress

CONSTITUTION, ARTICLE I, SECTION 8: *"The Congress shall have power to . . . declare war, . . . raise and support armies, . . . provide and maintain a navy, . . . [and] make rules for the government and regulation of the land and naval forces."*

CONSTITUTION, ARTICLE II, SECTION 2: *"The President shall be commander in chief of the army and navy."*

CONSTITUTION, ARTICLE II, SECTION 1: *"The executive power shall be vested in a President of the United States."*

Although the president plays the dominant role in the making of foreign policy, the Constitution gives clear responsibilities to Congress as well. As a consequence, a constitutional debate over the power of Congress and of the presidency has continued from the early years of the republic to the present day. In this section, we review how the power to wage war has evolved through American history, describe congressional attempts to limit presidential war powers, and consider the treaty-making power, which the Constitution divides between the president and the Senate.

War Power

The debate over which institution ought to control the nation's war power goes back at least as far as the debate over the ratification of the Constitution. As part of that debate, Alexander Hamilton argued that "of all the concerns of government, the direction of war most peculiarly demands the exercise of power by a single hand."[17] Yet the Constitution gives Congress the authority to declare war and to raise and maintain the armed forces. The president's constitutional powers are less clearly defined; the Constitution says only that the president is commander in chief and exercises executive power. Chief Justice John Marshall interpreted these powers broadly: "The President is the sole organ of the nation in its external relations, and its sole representative with foreign nations."[18] But nineteenth-century representative Thaddeus Stevens, a great defender of congressional prerogatives, proclaimed that "though the president is commander-in-chief, Congress is his commander, and God willing, he shall obey."[19] The issue has been debated ever since.

Prior to the Civil War, presidents seldom acted on their own on military matters. President James Madison, for example, refused to attack Great Britain in 1812 until Congress had declared war. Abraham Lincoln was the first president to take action based on an expanded interpretation of the role of commander in chief. When the southern states seceded from the Union, Lincoln proclaimed a blockade of southern ports and enlisted 300,000 volunteers before Congress had a chance to convene. Decades later, Theodore Roosevelt further broadened the role of commander in chief by exercising executive powers in a much less urgent situation. He sent naval ships to Japan even when Congress refused to appropriate enough money for the mission. He said that the president, in his role as commander in chief, would send the ships. Congress, if it wished, could appropriate enough funds to get them back. Congress did.

Following Lincoln and Roosevelt's lead, modern presidents have felt free to initiate military action even in the absence of congressional approval. Not since World War II has Congress officially declared war, and many presidential uses of force have never received even nonbinding resolutions of support from Congress. President Truman fought the Korean War without any congressional declaration whatsoever. More recently, President Obama oversaw a campaign of unmanned drone strikes against al Qaeda and Taliban forces in northwest Pakistan without seeking Congressional approval.

Two major Supreme Court decisions have set the boundaries within which presidents exercise their authority as commander in chief. In 1936 the Court was asked, in *United States v. Curtiss-Wright Export Corporation,* if Congress could delegate to the president the power to determine whether arms could be sold to Bolivia and Paraguay, countries engaged in a border dispute. In his decision in favor of presidential power, Justice George Sutherland wrote that the authority of presidents on foreign affairs was greater than their discretion over domestic policy. Echoing Justice Marshall's statement of many years before, Sutherland referred to "the very delicate, plenary and exclusive power of the president as the sole organ of the federal government in the field of international relations." He went on to say that the president had "a degree of discretion and freedom…which would not be admissible were domestic affairs alone involved."[20]

Curtiss-Wright was qualified by the 1952 *Youngstown Sheet & Tube Co. v. Sawyer* case, in which the Supreme Court placed limits on the president's power. At the height of the Korean War, trade unions in the steel industry announced that they would go on

United States v. Curtiss-Wright Export Corporation
Supreme Court decision in which Congress was given the authority to delegate foreign policy responsibilities to the president.

Youngstown Sheet & Tube Co. v. Sawyer
Case in which the Supreme Court placed limits on the executive power of the president.

strike. Claiming that the steel industry was crucial for national defense, President Truman ordered the federal government to seize control of the steel mills and commanded union members to continue to work. In doing so, Truman ignored alternative procedures for handling labor disputes that had recently been enacted by Congress. When the steel companies challenged Truman's claim of executive power in this case, the Supreme Court ruled against the president, saying he should have instead observed the congressionally defined procedures. Justice Robert Jackson wrote that when a president "takes measures incompatible with the expressed or implied will of Congress, his power is at its lowest ebb."[21]

When the *Curtiss-Wright* and *Youngstown* cases are considered together, the Court seems to have said that presidents have more constitutional discretion with respect to foreign than to domestic policy issues. However, presidents may not act contrary to the clearly expressed will of Congress.[22]

War Powers Resolution

The issue of executive authority arose again during the Vietnam War. Presidents Eisenhower and Kennedy had sent soldiers to Vietnam to serve as "advisers" to the South Vietnamese army, which was engaged in a war against Communist guerrillas trained in North Vietnam. Neither Eisenhower nor Kennedy had received congressional authorization to send these advisers and, as the war intensified, U.S. military personnel became ever more directly involved. Then, in the summer of 1964, North Vietnamese torpedo boats apparently fired on several U.S. destroyers stationed in Tonkin Bay off the coast of Haiphong, North Vietnam's second-largest city. President Lyndon Johnson denounced the action as an unlawful attack on U.S. ships that, he said, were sailing in international waters. He asked Congress for a resolution authorizing him to respond with armed force. By a nearly unanimous vote, Congress passed the **Tonkin Gulf Resolution,** which gave the president the authority to "take all necessary measures" to repel any attacks and to "prevent further aggression."[23] The resolution became the legal basis for a war that would last for eight more years. Only much later was it revealed that Johnson had misled Congress by inaccurately claiming that the United States had not invaded North Vietnam's territorial waters.

Tonkin Gulf Resolution
Congressional resolution that gave the president the authority to send troops to Vietnam.

The experience of a long and discouraging war in Vietnam prompted Congress to rethink its broad approval of the president's authority over military action. In 1970 it repealed the Tonkin Gulf Resolution. As a further precaution against presidential usurpation of congressional prerogatives, Congress in 1973 passed, over President Nixon's veto, the **War Powers Resolution,** which required that the president formally notify Congress anytime he orders U.S. troops into military action. The resolution further specifies that troops must be withdrawn unless Congress approves the presidential decision within 60 days after notice of the military action has been received.

War Powers Resolution
1973 congressional resolution requiring the president to notify Congress formally upon ordering U.S. troops into military action.

In many cases, presidents have simply ignored the War Powers Resolution. President Reagan invaded Grenada, bombed Libya, and placed military troops in Lebanon without notifying Congress. President Clinton bombed Iraq, deployed troops in Bosnia, bombarded Serb positions in Kosovo, and struck at terrorist sites in Sudan and Afghanistan without notifying Congress. On five separate occasions, individual

members of Congress sued in federal courts, attempting to force the president to abide by that resolution. In each case, however, judges dismissed the suit.[24]

Although they did not accept the validity of the War Powers Resolution, both presidents Bush sought Congressional approval for their military actions. In doing so, they turned a potential weakness into a strength by rallying congressional support around their policies. President George H. W. Bush asked for and received congressional authorization to use force against Iraq before the Persian Gulf War of 1991. George W. Bush went even further: After 9/11, at the administration's request, Congress passed, with but one dissenting vote in the House of Representatives, a sweeping resolution that authorized the president to "use all necessary and appropriate force against those nations, organizations, or persons he determines planned, authorized, committed, or aided the terrorist attacks that occurred on September 11, or harbored such organizations or persons, in order to prevent any future acts of international terrorism." No limit is placed on the time period in which the president may act.[25]

A second resolution, authorizing the use of force to "defend the national security of the United States against the continuing threat posed by Iraq" was passed by Congress overwhelmingly in late 2002. The resolution gave President Bush crucial backing for the subsequent Iraq War.[26]

Treaty Power

CONSTITUTION, ARTICLE II, SECTION 2: *"[The President] shall have power, by and with the advice and consent of the Senate, to make Treaties, provided two-thirds of the Senators present concur."*

The power of the president to negotiate **treaties**—official agreements with foreign countries that must be ratified by the Senate—is the most circumscribed of all presidential

treaties

Official agreements with foreign countries that must be ratified by the Senate.

powers. A treaty does not take effect until it wins approval by a two-thirds vote in the Senate. Because this supermajority can be difficult to achieve unless a treaty has overwhelming public support, presidents have often felt constrained by senatorial pressures when negotiating with foreign countries. In negotiating a nuclear weapons treaty with Russia, for example, President Obama demanded that the treaty not constrain the deployment of missile defense systems in Europe, knowing that key senators viewed the issue as nonnegotiable.[27] Although the Senate has approved about 90 percent of the treaties that presidents have submitted to it from the 1780s to the present, this fact may simply indicate that presidents decline to negotiate or submit treaties that they feel have no chance of passage.[28]

No president was more frustrated by this constitutional check on presidential power than Woodrow Wilson. When negotiating the Versailles Treaty that ended World War I, President Wilson pursued one objective above all others: the establishment of a **League of Nations,** an international organization created to settle disputes between nations, which became the precursor to the United Nations. Wilson felt that such an organization was essential if future world wars were to be avoided. The other nations at the Versailles conference and a considerable portion of the American public supported Wilson's ideas. But the Senate voted down the treaty, primarily because many members believed the League of Nations would undermine U.S. sovereignty.

Eighty years later, President Clinton faced similar difficulties with Congress. In October 1999, the Senate considered the Comprehensive Nuclear Test Ban Treaty, which had been negotiated in 1996. The multinational agreement would have prohibited the testing of nuclear weapons and enacted more stringent monitoring systems to ensure compliance. Proponents of the treaty argued that it was essential to slowing the spread of nuclear weapons around the world. But critics, including many Senate Republicans, were skeptical of its effectiveness and worried that it would hamper the nation's ability to modernize its armed forces. After negotiations broke down between Republican leaders and the Clinton administration, the Senate voted against ratification, 51 to 48.

Because one-third-plus-one of the Senate can block passage of a treaty, presidents often negotiate **executive agreements,** legal contracts with foreign countries that require only a presidential signature. Nothing in the Constitution explicitly gives the president the power to make executive agreements, but the practice has long been established. The first executive agreement—limiting the size of the U.S. and British naval forces on the Great Lakes—was signed by President James Monroe in 1817. In 1937, the Supreme Court affirmed the constitutionality of executive agreements.[29] Since that decision, presidents have increasingly relied on this method as a vehicle for negotiating with other nations. Most executive agreements either are extensions of treaties ratified by the Senate or involve routine presidential actions that have otherwise been authorized by Congress. But presidents sometimes use executive agreements to implement major foreign policy decisions. For example, the Obama administration has sought an executive agreement with the EU, Canada, Japan, and other nations to coordinate enforcement of intellectual property laws.[30] In recent years, about 20 executive agreements have been signed for every treaty submitted to the Senate for its approval (see Figure 20.2).

League of Nations

International organization created after World War I to settle disputes between nations; precursor of the United Nations.

executive agreements

Legal contracts with foreign countries that require only a presidential signature.

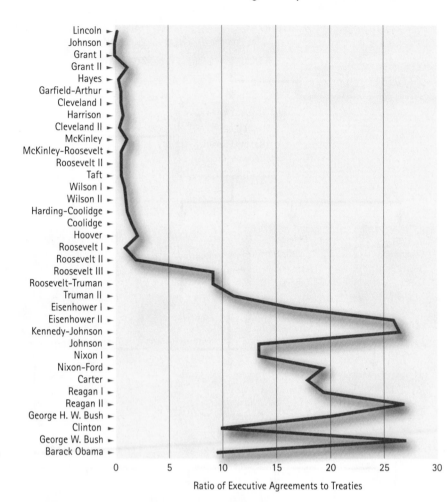

FIGURE 20.2

GROWING PRESIDENTIAL POWER: EXECUTIVE AGREEMENTS ARE REPLACING TREATIES

Presidents are increasingly likely to enter into agreements with foreign nations that do not require Senate approval.

• *When did the increase in executive agreements begin? Why do you think executive agreements increased in number at that time? Does this behavior deny the Senate its constitutional role in foreign policy?*

Note: Data for Barack Obama are for 2009.

Sources: Gary King and Lynn Ragsdale, *The Elusive Executive: Discovering Patterns in the Presidency* (Washington, DC: CQ Press, 1988), pp. 131–140; and Harold Stanley and Richard Niemi, *Vital Statistics on American Politics, 2001–2002* (Washington, DC: CQ Press, 2001), p. 334. Data for George W. Bush and Barack Obama calculated by authors from data on treaty actions available at Department of State, Office of the Legal Adviser, www.state.gov/s/l/index.htm, accessed May 26, 2010.

Foreign Policy Institutions: From Cold War to Homeland Defense

World politics has changed quickly in the last decade of the twentieth century and the first decade of the twenty-first, but most critical institutions that are responsible for U.S. foreign policy today were designed to address a far different global situation. These cabinet posts, agencies, and advisory structures took shape in the early years of the **cold war,** the 43-year period (1946–1989) during which the United States and the Soviet Union threatened one another with mutual destruction by nuclear warfare. The modern Department of State, the Department of Defense, the Central Intelligence Agency, and the office of the National Security Adviser were all designed to meet the cold war threat posed by the Soviet Union. The relationships of each of these foreign policy institutions to one another and to the president are shown in Figure 20.3. In the wake of 9/11, policymakers reevaluated their design and capacities in light of the new threat posed from terrorist organizations, in some cases making significant changes. In this section, we begin with a discussion of the cold war world, and move on to discuss the post–cold war era. We address the emergence of each of the foreign policy institutions, and consider their new role in an era of potential terrorist attacks.

20.3

Trace the development of foreign policy institutions from the Cold War to post-9/11.

cold war

The 43-year period (1946–1989) during which the United States and the Soviet Union threatened one another with mutual destruction by nuclear warfare.

FIGURE 20.3

THE FOREIGN POLICY
INSTITUTIONS

This figure depicts the organizational structure of the main U.S. institutions with responsibility for foreign policy. As we discuss in this chapter, this structure took its modern shape during the cold war.

• *Which institutions report to two different entities? Why is this the case?*

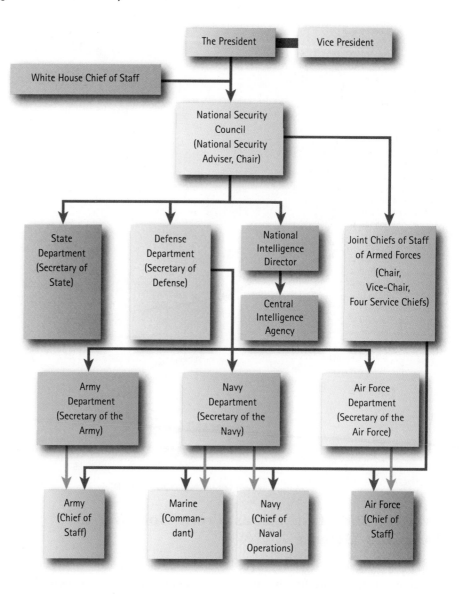

The Cold War

Prior to the cold war, U.S. engagement with world affairs was episodic and characterized by swift mobilization and equally rapid disengagement. After the Spanish-American War of 1898, Congress passed legislation designed to better integrate the National Guard into the country's fighting forces, so as to improve the nation's ability to respond to threats. President Theodore Roosevelt also extended U.S. influence throughout the Americas with his construction of the Panama Canal and his pledge to prevent European intervention in South America and the Caribbean. But after World War I, Congress resisted President Woodrow Wilson's efforts to build lasting international institutions that were intended to prevent future world conflicts. The Senate rejected the League of Nations treaty by a vote of 38 to 53, amid fears that the organization would undermine American sovereignty.

The Berlin Wall

Built during the presidency of John F. Kennedy, the Berlin Wall (left) symbolized what British Prime Minister Winston Churchill called the Iron Curtain. The wall, and the curtain, crumbled in 1989 (right).

• *How has American foreign policymaking changed since the end of the cold war?*

At the outset of the cold war, U.S. officials recognized that it represented the greatest foreign policy challenge the country had yet faced. In the months following World War II, Germany was divided into eastern and western parts, and Korea was split into a North and South; one-half of each country was under Western influence, while the other half was within the Communist domain. In short order, the Soviet Union consolidated its control over much of Eastern Europe, establishing Communist governments in Poland, Hungary, Bulgaria, Romania, and Czechoslovakia. In 1961, pursuant to Soviet directives, East Germany constructed a huge concrete wall through the middle of Berlin, dramatically symbolizing the division of the world into Communist and Western parts. Under such dire circumstances, most policymakers agreed that the United States faced a sustained period in which it had to be directly engaged in world affairs. The key questions involved how best to arrange foreign policymaking institutions to meet the threat of Communism, and how best to rally public opinion to the cause.

The cold war began at a time when the prestige of the executive branch had been greatly enhanced by its successful prosecution of World War II. As a result, President Truman was able to mobilize bipartisan support for his foreign policy and recruit to key positions the most talented group of foreign policy advisers the country had ever assembled. These advisers saw the world as **bipolar,** divided between two major centers of power: the United States and its allies, and the Soviet Union and its allies. "The assault on free institutions is worldwide now," they wrote in a 1950 memo to the president, "and in the context of the present polarization of power a defeat of free institutions anywhere is a defeat everywhere."[31] Accordingly, they decided that the United States should use its military might to deter a direct attack by the Soviet Union, while at the same time countering aggression by the Soviets in other countries, when it occurred.[32] This overall strategy was called **containment,** a policy that attempted to stop the spread of Communism in the expectation that this system of government would eventually collapse on its own. The policy, originally proposed by George Kennan, a brilliant State Department specialist, won bipartisan support.[33] Importantly, the public

bipolar
Cold war view of the world as divided into two centers of power, the United States and its allies, and the Soviet Union and its allies.

containment
U.S. policy that attempted to stop the spread of Communism in the expectation that this system of government would eventually collapse on its own.

was ready to commit to the effort. By 1950, polls found that nearly 70 percent of Americans thought it "would be best for the future of this country if we take an active part in world affairs."[34]

Although it took nearly 50 years, containment proved successful. Unrest began in the Communist-dominated countries of Eastern Europe during the 1980s and spread to the Soviet Union by the end of the decade. When East Germany allowed demonstrators to tear down the Berlin Wall in 1989, the cold war finally came to an end. Two years later, the Soviet Union officially dissolved itself.

The Post–Cold War World

At the end of the cold war, some observers predicted an era of peace and security. But more astute experts cautioned that new and unpredictable conflicts might surface, leading to dangerous instability in key areas of the world. During the 1990s, presidents George H. W. Bush and Bill Clinton sought to lessen regional instability by intervening in important local conflicts. The first President Bush, for example, fought the 1991 Persian Gulf War in response to an Iraqi invasion of Kuwait and sent troops to Somalia when it seemed that chaos in that country was creating a humanitarian and political crisis. Clinton led an international effort to defeat Serbian leader Slobodan Milosevic, who had engaged in years of brutal wars in the former Yugoslavia.

After 9/11, however, the George W. Bush administration reevaluated the nature of threats to the United States. Rather than the clear threat of a competing superpower, as in the cold war, or indirect political and economic threats resulting from regional instability, as in the 1990s, foreign policymaking officials now saw direct peril from secretive terrorist organizations that might not even be linked to specific countries. "Enemies in the past needed great armies and great industrial capabilities to endanger America," wrote the White House national security staff in 2002. "Now, shadowy networks of individuals can bring great chaos and suffering to our shores for less than it costs to purchase a single tank."[35]

Leaders in both political parties agreed that the United States should dedicate itself to addressing this new environment. Although Barack Obama campaigned against some Bush administration policies, and argued that the Iraq War had been unnecessary, as president he continued his predecessor's focus on terrorism as the preeminent threat to national security. Because the major foreign policymaking institutions in the United States were developed to address the cold war, however, the new threat required policymakers to critically examine the role that each of these institutions plays. Large organizations develop routines and standard operating procedures that are often difficult to alter, and they are not always suited for unexpected circumstances, as we discuss in Chapter 14. On 9/11, for example, the pilot of a military jet that was ordered to Washington to defend U.S. airspace later told investigators, "I reverted to the Russian threat . . . I'm thinking cruise missile threat from the sea."[36] In the sections that follow, we examine each of the major U.S. foreign policymaking institutions and discuss the challenges that each institution faces in the post–cold war world.

State Department

It was during the cold war that the modern, professional State Department emerged from the patronage-ridden entity that preceded it. However, the State Department itself—

the agency responsible for conducting diplomatic relations—dates back to the administration of George Washington and his secretary of state, Thomas Jefferson.

Ever since that time, the **secretary of state** has been the president's official foreign policy adviser. In most administrations, the secretary of state is also the nation's chief diplomat. The art of **diplomacy,** the conduct of negotiations between representatives of different nations, can include everything from formal treaty negotiations to informal communications about topics of shared interest to carefully worded public statements that signal the U.S. position on international issues. Hillary Clinton, Barack Obama's secretary of state, played a major role in crafting the administration's foreign policy, traveling to Afghanistan, China, Mexico, and many other countries to engage in top-level negotiations. The job of chief diplomat is extremely challenging. As former secretary of state George Marshall once commented, "In diplomacy, you never can tell what a man is thinking. He smiles at you and kicks you in the stomach at the same time."[37]

Reporting to the secretary of state are **ambassadors,** who head the diplomatic delegations to foreign countries. Ambassadors are responsible for the management of major U.S. **embassies** abroad, the structures that house diplomatic delegations in the capital cities of foreign countries. Consulates are maintained in important cities that are not foreign capitals. If you wish to travel abroad, you must first obtain a passport from the State Department. If you encounter difficulty while traveling in a foreign country, your first phone call might well be made to the closest embassy or consulate.

Although embassies and consulates help American tourists and businesses, their most important political responsibility is to provide the State Department with detailed information on the government and politics, as well as on the economic and social conditions, of the host country. The ambassador also conveys to the host country the views of the U.S. government, as he or she is instructed by the State Department. An ambassador must be able to listen to others carefully and communicate no more than what the president wants to convey.[38]

Before the cold war, U.S. ambassadorial appointments were as important for rewarding those who helped presidents win elections as for the diplomacy the ambassador carried out. The most prestigious ambassadorships were given to longtime political supporters who had raised large sums of money for the president's election. As one historian put it, "Most diplomats earned their appointments through party affiliation, personal wealth, or social position, seldom through training. Many lacked knowledge; some lacked dignity, although few were as tactless as John Randolph, who allegedly commented, when presented to the czar in 1830, 'Howaya Emperor? And how's the madam?'"[39] Even today, some ambassadorial positions remain frankly political. For example, when President Obama entered office, he nominated many of his top fundraisers as ambassadors, including those appointed to posts in the United Kingdom, Ireland, Argentina, and Denmark.[40] But patronage today is more the

secretary of state
Officially, the president's chief foreign policy adviser and head of the State Department, the agency responsible for conducting diplomatic relations.

diplomacy
The conduct of negotiations between representatives of different nations.

ambassador
The head of a diplomatic delegation to a foreign country.

embassy
The structure that houses ambassadors and their diplomatic aides in the capital cities of foreign countries.

Secretary of State Hillary Clinton

Clinton shakes hands with South Korean Foreign Minister Yu Myung-hwan on a 2010 trip to address tensions between North Korea and South Korea.

• *How does a modern secretary of state use the resources of the State Department to influence U.S. foreign policy?*

exception than the rule, as we discuss in Chapter 14. Those appointed to less prestigious diplomatic positions are nearly always trained career officers who are familiar with the language and customs of the host country.

foreign service
Diplomats who staff U.S. embassies and consulates.

Ever since the 1920s these officers have been organized into a **foreign service,** which consists of the diplomats who staff U.S. embassies and consulates. After World War II, the foreign service was strengthened as part of the effort to fight the cold war. In particular, Dean Acheson, President Truman's secretary of state, did much to improve the professional caliber of the foreign service. A reporter at the time declared, "For the first time in the memory of living man, the American foreign office comes somewhere near being adequate to the needs of the country."[41]

Today, the State Department is responsible for coordinating international antiterrorism efforts and for promoting U.S. policy goals regarding Iraq, Afghanistan, North Korea, and Iran. The power of precise language in diplomacy can be seen in the case of terrorism, where a clear definition of the term is often difficult. Does the concept include any explicit attack on civilians and civilian property, regardless of circumstance? Or are there conditions under which civilians are appropriately treated as military targets? These questions pose real problems for U.S. diplomats seeking to resolve the conflict between Israel and the Palestinians (see the *Election Voices!* feature on page 606).

Defense Department

Ever since the first decades of the country's independence, Americans have been concerned about the ill effects of a large military. The nation has sometimes looked to popular generals, such as George Washington, Andrew Jackson, Ulysses S. Grant, and Dwight Eisenhower, for political leadership. But generals must give up their military appointment when running for president. Congress and the president have always made certain that the military was controlled by civilian appointees. As one analyst puts it, freedom "demands that people without guns be able to tell people with guns what to do."[42] The cold war posed new challenges for this ideal of civilian control. To ensure the country's continued international leadership and to carry out its policy of containment, Congress provided for the largest military establishment in the nation's history. In an effort to better handle this large peacetime standing army, the military went through several major organizational changes.

Department of Defense
Cabinet department responsible for managing the U.S. armed forces.

secretary of defense
The president's chief civilian adviser on defense matters and overall head of the army, navy, and air force.

Organization of the Defense Department   At the close of World War II, the army and navy were two separate departments, each with its own air force and its own seat in the president's cabinet. With the onset of the cold war, to better coordinate civilian control of the armed forces, the 1947 National Security Act created a single **Department of Defense** that contained within it the departments of the Army, Navy, and Air Force, each with its own civilian secretary appointed by the president. The secretaries for the army and the air force are responsible for their respective branches of the armed services. The secretary of the navy is responsible for both the naval forces and the marines. All three secretaries report to the **secretary of defense,** the president's chief civilian adviser on defense matters and the overall head of the three departments.

Subordinate to the civilian leadership of the secretary of defense and the other three appointed secretaries, military professionals direct the armed forces. At one time, each armed force had its own military leadership, and they acted more or less independently of each other. To achieve better coordination, Congress formally created the **Joint Chiefs of Staff** in 1947. The Joint Chiefs consist of the heads of all the military services—the army, navy, air force, and Marine Corps—together with a chair and vice-chair nominated by the president and confirmed by the Senate. Omar Bradley, the first chairman of the Joint Chiefs of Staff, suggested that the organization was essential if the country were to achieve a unified, effective military force: "Our military forces are one team—in the game to win regardless of who carries the ball. This is no time for 'fancy dans' who won't hit the line with all they have on every play unless they can call the signals."[43] (See the accompanying *International Comparison*.)

Rivalries among the armed services have been so intense that it took decades to achieve what Bradley promised in 1949, but eventually a unified command structure was created in each of six regions of the world. Perhaps the most important of these unified commands today is the U.S. Central Command, known as CENTCOM. CENTCOM coordinates all branches of the armed forces throughout the Middle East, including Iraq, Iran, Afghanistan, and Pakistan.[44]

The Military After 9/11   The military was given the central role in responding to the 9/11 terrorist attacks in part because the Bush administration redefined U.S. counterterrorism policy in two important respects.[45] First, the president called upon government agencies to treat terrorist actions as acts of war that need to be anticipated and prevented, not criminal activities to be investigated and prosecuted. Second, the problem was defined not simply as consisting of private individuals or groups engaged in terrorist activities but, rather, as also including governments and states that allowed such activities within their borders. These governments and states had to be held accountable, just as much as the terrorists themselves.

The initial military actions in Afghanistan and Iraq were surprisingly effective—so effective that they surpassed the expectations of many commentators. The explanation for this fact illustrates some of the changes that have been under way in the armed forces since the end of the cold war. Newer lightweight, high-technology weapons make it possible for military campaigns to be executed with greater precision than ever before. In Iraq and Afghanistan (and later in the tribal areas of northwest Pakistan), unmanned drones dropped bombs without risking the lives of American pilots. Fewer troops were needed to defeat enemy armies and to move rapidly toward securing strategic objectives. All in all, technology had advanced far beyond that employed at the height of the Vietnam War.

But technology is only part of the story. Just as important are the new governance structures that have been created within the U.S. armed forces. In conflicts prior to the first Gulf War, presidents and secretaries of defense found that the chain of command from the White House to military field commanders was layered and cumbersome, and rivalries between different branches of the armed forces hampered the military's effectiveness. A reorganization in the late 1980s placed unified command over each particular conflict in the hands of one senior officer, who then reported directly to the secretary of defense and to the president.[46] This system worked smoothly in the first Gulf War, as well as the early stages of the Iraq and Afghanistan conflicts.

But the new methods of armed conflict looked less impressive after the swift and successful war to depose dictator Saddam Hussein gave way to a costly occupation in Iraq, during which congressional critics complained that technology and agility were no substitutes for the larger numbers of troops needed to keep the peace. Afghanistan,

Joint Chiefs of Staff
The heads of all the military services, together with a chair and vice-chair nominated by the president and confirmed by the Senate.

INTERNATIONAL COMPARISON

The United States—Historically Lucky in War

Isolationist sentiments have been fed by the country's historical wartime successes, which fostered the belief that the United States is invincible. After the War of 1812 and until the Vietnam War, the United States had an impressive military record. The Mexican War, the Spanish-American War, and World Wars I and II all ended in overwhelming victories. Few, if any, other world powers achieved such an unbroken string of successes. Japan and Germany can never forget their humiliating defeats in World War II. The French cannot forget the ease with which German troops captured Paris in both 1870 and 1940. The Russians cannot readily dislodge the memory of their defeat by Japan in 1905 or the collapse of their army in 1917. Only the British have nearly as enviable a historical record as the Americans, and even Britain suffered more than one defeat at the hands of the French.

Not only did the United States win its wars, but it did so quickly. The Mexican War, although spread over three years, consisted of three short and decisive campaigns. The Spanish-American War was over in eight months. Even U.S. involvement in the two world wars was of relatively short duration. Within six months of the arrival of U.S. troops in Europe, an armistice brought World War I to an end. The pattern was not altogether different in World War II. Little more than a year after U.S. troops landed in Normandy, Germany was defeated.

Japan struggled for an additional two months until nuclear bombs dropped by the United States over Hiroshima and Nagasaki forced its surrender. Before 9/11, American civilians rarely suffered significantly from foreign attack. Not since the British burning of Washington, DC, in 1814 has the mainland of the United States been invaded by foreign troops. Apart from the 9/11 attack and the bombing of Pearl Harbor, the United States has been free of aerial raids. During World War II, German tanks overran Europe and Russia, German airplanes bombed Britain, and U.S. airplanes all but destroyed German and Japanese cities. As the graph here shows, even U.S. troop casualties have been small.

• *Do you think that this history of success has made the U.S. public more likely or less likely to support wars? More likely or less likely to become impatient with lengthy conflicts?*

• *How do you think current military operations have been affected by the U.S. historical experience with wars?*

Sources: R. Ernest Dupuy and Trevor N. Dupuy, *The Harper Encyclopedia of Military History: From 3500 B.C. to the Present* (New York: HarperCollins, 1993); Y. Takenob, *The Japan Year Book: 1919–1920* (Tokyo: Japan Year Book Office, 1921); B. R. Mitchell, *International Historical Statistics: Europe 1750–1988* (New York: Stockton Press, 1992); B. R. Mitchell, *International Historical Statistics of the Americas: 1750–1988* (New York: Stockton Press, 1993); B. R. Mitchell, *International Historical Statistics: Africa and Asia* (New York: New York University Press, 1982); and Raymond E. Zickel, ed., *Soviet Union: A Country Study* (Washington, DC: U.S. Government Printing Office, 1991).

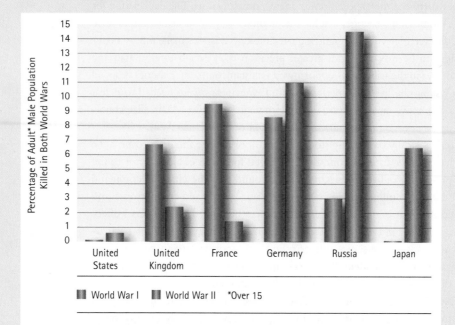

Note: Population figures are from the following years: France, 1911, 1936; Germany, 1910, 1939; United Kingdom (including Scotland), 1911, 1931; United States, 1910, 1940; Russia, 1930 (estimated), 1939; Japan, 1913, 1940.

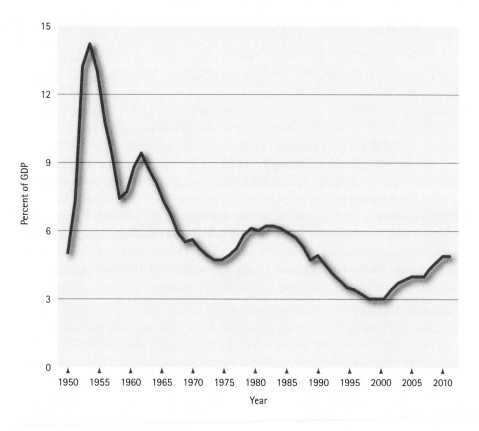

FIGURE 20.4

DEFENSE EXPENDITURES AS A PERCENTAGE OF GDP, 1950–2011

United States defense spending has declined over time as a percentage of GDP.

• *What accounts for the increases in defense expenditures in the early 1950s, the late 1960s, and the mid-1980s?*

• *How does the recent increase in defense spending compare with previous increases? Should we be spending more on defense?*

Note: Figures for 2010 and 2011 are estimates.

Sources: Office of Management and Budget, "Budget of the United States Government, Fiscal Year 2011," Historical Tables, Table 3.1, www.gpoaccess.gov/usbudget/fy11/hist.html, accessed May 26, 2010.

too, remained dangerous and unstable a decade after the 2001 U.S. invasion. Skeptics argued that the new approach to fighting wars had failed to take into account the need to maintain control of occupied territories. *Counterinsurgency*, the practice of battling a decentralized guerilla force, requires many troops and good relations with the local population if it is to be successful.[47] In recognition of this fact, President Bush sent tens of thousands of additional troops to Iraq in 2007, and President Obama similarly boosted forces in Afghanistan in 2009. These troops were aided by new technology, but they were mostly engaged in traditional security operations, in economic development efforts, and in ensuring stable governance.[48] New technologies are not much different from ancient bayonets. As one witticism has put it: "You can do almost anything but sit on them." And "sitting" is precisely the challenge that comes with occupying and holding territories one has invaded. Most U.S. troops had exited Iraq by 2011, but, as Figure 20.4 shows, the new defense challenges in Iraq, Afghanistan, and elsewhere continue to drive defense expenditures higher than they were prior to 2001.

The Central Intelligence Agency

"I only regret that I have but one life to lose for my country," said the Revolutionary War hero Nathan Hale, after he had been caught spying and was about to be hanged by the British. A statue erected in Hale's memory stands at the entrance to the main offices of the **Central Intelligence Agency (CIA),** the agency primarily responsible for gathering and analyzing information about the political and military activities of other nations. The subject of many a spy novel, it is lovingly referred to as "the Company" or "the Pickle Factory" by members of the intelligence community.[49]

Central Intelligence Agency (CIA)

Agency primarily responsible for gathering and analyzing information about the political and military activities of other nations.

Formation of the CIA   If spying is an ancient and honorable practice, its organization into an independent agency is of fairly recent vintage. The need for better-organized intelligence became clear during World War II, especially at Hawaii's Pearl Harbor on December 7, 1941, called a "day of infamy" by President Roosevelt. It was a day of particular disrepute for the intelligence community, inasmuch as naval officers at Pearl Harbor were completely unaware that Japan had both the capability and the intention of destroying half the U.S. naval force. (The chief naval official in Hawaii had an appointment with the Japanese envoy on that infamous day.)

The U.S. government made haphazard efforts to improve intelligence capabilities after Pearl Harbor, but it was not until the cold war began that Congress established a systematic, centralized system of intelligence gathering. The National Security Act of 1947 created the CIA as a separate agency independent of both the Department of State and the Department of Defense. Although State and Defense (as well as other departments) continue to have their own sources of intelligence, the 1947 law made the CIA the main intelligence collection agency. It also gave the CIA the authority to conduct secret operations abroad at the request of the president.

Covert Operations   It is the CIA's authority to conduct clandestine, or covert, operations that has been most controversial, because critics argue that only the armed forces ought to conduct secret military activities. The CIA's most notorious covert operation was the ill-fated attempt in 1961 to dislodge Communist leader Fidel Castro from Cuba.[50] In an effort to overthrow Castro, the CIA helped Cuban exiles plan an invasion on the shores of Cuba's **Bay of Pigs** that was expected to foment a popular insurrection. President Kennedy approved the invasion attempt but decided against giving it naval or air support. The effort failed, leaving in doubt the CIA's ability to conduct large-scale military operations. Although the Bay of Pigs has been the CIA's most visible covert operation, the agency drew criticism for covert activities in Chile in the early 1970s, in Nicaragua and Afghanistan in the 1980s, and in a number of other nations as well.

Bay of Pigs
Location of CIA-supported effort by Cuban exiles in 1961 to invade Cuba and overthrow Fidel Castro.

Response to Terrorism   To avoid such criticism, the CIA limited the scale of its covert operations and reduced its number of agents. In the period leading up to the 9/11 terrorist attacks, it actually had "fewer Arabic-speaking case officers than in the Cold War," making it difficult for the agency to interpret intercepted conversations. Agents who can penetrate terrorist groups have proved extremely difficult to recruit. One problem is that it is often hard for some Arabic speakers with foreign friends or relatives to obtain security clearances. "It is easier to get a security clearance if you don't have any interaction with foreigners," says one expert, "which is not what you want if you want better interaction with foreigners."[51]

After 9/11 the agency felt overwhelming pressure to move quickly against terrorist organizations, and it reacted by taking steps that civil liberties groups saw as illegal. CIA agents scooped up suspected terrorists, transported them to hidden prisons, and questioned them under duress, using techniques (such as "waterboarding") that international agreements defined as torture.[52] This activity, sanctioned at least in part by justice department lawyers, remained a potent political issue in the first year of the Obama presidency. Obama and his CIA director, Leon Panetta, condemned the "enhanced interrogation techniques," but they argued that any questionable activity had long since ceased, and that the country needed to deal with present and future threats rather than investigating past actions. "Judgments were made," said Panetta. "Some of them were wrong. But that should not taint those public servants who did their duty pursuant to the legal guidance provided."[53]

Another recurrent challenge has been that the CIA has not always found it easy to work closely with the Federal Bureau of Investigation (FBI). Cooperation between the two agencies was curtailed because both had been criticized for illegal spying on U.S. citizens during the Vietnam War. As a result, intelligence operations within the United States were left solely to the FBI, which lacked information on the presence of foreign terrorists within the United States and could wiretap suspects only after obtaining a court order. Although these procedures helped safeguard the civil liberties of American citizens, they also contributed to a major intelligence failure on September 11. As one analyst pointed out, "At least 19 people worked for as long as five years, mostly in the United States, on a complex operation to crash multiple airliners into several targets. And America's $30-billion-a-year intelligence services hardly got a whiff of them."[54]

In response to such failures, the special commission appointed to investigate the 9/11 attacks proposed creating the position of **national intelligence director** to coordinate intelligence gathering among the CIA, the FBI, and a dozen other intelligence agencies. Congress created this position in 2004. While some observers worried that the CIA would be discontented with the arrangement because of its loss in rank (the CIA director now reports to the national intelligence director rather than directly to the president), others argued that a discontented CIA was less of a concern than the need for better-coordinated intelligence. In fact, the office of the national intelligence director has struggled to assert its authority over the traditionally powerful CIA. President Obama's first national intelligence director, Dennis Blair, resigned in 2010 after months of (mostly losing) battles with CIA director Panetta.[55]

national intelligence director
An office that coordinates intelligence gathering among the CIA, the FBI, and other intelligence agencies.

The National Security Council

Because so many departments and agencies needed to work together to formulate U.S. cold war policy, Congress created the **National Security Council (NSC)** in 1947. This organization, located inside the White House Executive Office of the President, is responsible for coordinating U.S. foreign policy. Meetings of the NSC are generally attended by the president, the vice president, the secretary of state, the secretary of defense, the national intelligence director, the chair of the military Joint Chiefs of Staff, the president's chief of staff, and such other individuals as the president designates.[56] The council is assisted by a staff located in the White House under the direction of the national security adviser (NSA). The NSA has often played simply a coordinating role by reconciling interagency disagreements or, if that proved impossible, by reporting them to the president. Because it has no budget authority over other departments and agencies, its ability to control ongoing policy operations is limited. But inasmuch as the NSA has more access to the president than any other member of the foreign policy team, the adviser can wield great influence in crises. During the Nixon administration, National Security Adviser Henry Kissinger became the president's most influential aide, overshadowing the secretary of state. Under President Barack Obama, NSA Tom Donilon plays a key role in defining the administration's official security strategy.

National Security Council (NSC)
White House agency responsible for coordinating U.S. foreign policy.

National Security Adviser
National Security Adviser Tom Donilon (center) briefs President Obama.

• *What role does the NSA play in foreign policy formulation?*

Iran-Contra affair
An allegedly illegal diversion of funds, derived from the sale of arms to Iran, to anticommunist rebels in Nicaragua during the Reagan administration.

The office of the NSA has not escaped controversy. The most notorious event in which it played a major role has become known as the **Iran-Contra affair,** an allegedly illegal diversion of funds from an Iranian arms sale to anticommunist rebels in Nicaragua known as the Contras. In this case, President Ronald Reagan's NSA office, which was officially responsible only for policy coordination, actually attempted to conduct a covert operation of the type ordinarily conducted by the CIA. In a clear violation of U.S. antiterrorist policy, National Security Adviser Robert McFarlane helped orchestrate a secret arms sale to Iran in an effort to secure the release of several American hostages in the Middle East. Profits from this sale were then diverted to the Contras, to whom Congress had cut off U.S. aid several years before.

In the Iran-Contra episode, the NSC staff appeared to have ignored both administration antiterrorist policy and clear congressional directives. Congress held hearings on the scandal, and an independent prosecutor conducted a thorough investigation, although the most significant convictions were overturned in courts of appeals. A specially appointed presidential commission recommended that, in the future, the office of the NSA limit itself to a coordinating role and not involve itself in covert operations. By following these guidelines, the NSA has since avoided political controversy.

20.4   Ideals, Interests, and the Campaign Against Terrorism

Analyze the conflict between American philosophical ideals and a practical need to defend the country.

The way in which the president and his advisers resolve foreign policy questions is shaped by a long-standing tension between American philosophical ideals and the country's practical need to defend itself against foreign aggression. Alexander Hamilton, in the *Federalist Papers,* made the best case for placing the highest priority on the country's practical interests: "No Government [can] give us tranquility and happiness at home, which [does] not possess sufficient stability and strength to make us respectable abroad."[57] The idealist point of view was best expressed by Abraham Lincoln, who reminded his fellow citizens that one purpose of the American experiment was to spread liberty throughout the world. "The Declaration of Independence . . . [gave] liberty, not alone to the people of this country, but hope to the world for all future time."[58]

The tension between ideals and interests that has long been part of the American foreign policy tradition continues to shape policy debates today. On the one side, **idealists** say that U.S. foreign policy should be guided primarily by democratic principles—the spread of liberty, equality, human rights, and respect for international law throughout the world. On the other side, **realists** say that U.S. foreign policy best protects democracy when it guards its own economic and military strength.

One can find both idealists and realists in each political party and in all government agencies, and some people are idealistic on one issue yet realistic on another. In fact, many foreign policymakers use both idealist and realist arguments to make their points.

The events of 9/11 changed the nature of the debate between idealists and realists in many ways, including their consideration of strategies for nation building, the role of international organizations, and the role of human rights in relations with nations such as Russia and China.

Strategies for Nation Building

Interventions designed to enhance democratic practices in other countries—actions known as **nation building**—have long been a point of contention between idealists and realists. According to realists, the United States should avoid getting involved in nation building unless U.S. interests are directly at stake. If the United States continues to involve itself in the internal political life of foreign countries, they argue, it will eventually find itself unprepared or unable to defend its true interests when they are threatened.

Nation building can at times be fraught with peril. For one thing, actions taken can have unanticipated consequences. Unjustified intervention in the internal affairs of other countries, moreover, runs contrary to international law, which regards each legitimate government as sovereign over its own citizens. Idealists nonetheless suggest that Americans should intervene to enhance democratic practices and safeguard human rights, especially if governments seek to deport or eliminate entire ethnic groups, a practice known as **ethnic cleansing.**

Differences between idealists and realists were evident after the collapse of Yugoslavia in Eastern Europe at the end of the cold war. When the country split into pieces, armed struggle broke out among Bosnians, Serbs, and Croats. Idealists supported the Clinton administration's decision to send troops to separate the warring parties in Bosnia and to conduct aerial bombing to end the Serbian invasion of Kosovo, while realists were wary of these efforts.

The terrorist attacks on 9/11 changed the way many realists and idealists viewed foreign policy. If nation building had at one time seemed little other than dreamy-eyed idealism, it suddenly emerged as an important realist objective as well. Where foreign governments were weak and illegitimate, terrorists could roam unchecked. From George W. Bush's perspective, the clearest examples of such weak governments were Afghanistan and Iraq. In Afghanistan, the al Qaeda terrorist organization formed an alliance with the Taliban government and operated for years without hindrance. In Saddam Hussein's Iraq, the Bush administration argued, terrorists had also been granted

idealists
Those who say that U.S. foreign policy should be guided primarily by democratic principles—the spread of liberty, equality, human rights, and respect for international law throughout the world.

realists
Those who say that U.S. foreign policy best protects democracy when it safeguards its own economic and military strength.

nation building
Intervention designed to enhance democratic practices in another country.

ethnic cleansing
Seeking to deport or eliminate entire ethnic groups from a country or region.

safe haven and might have had access to dangerous weapons. The president stated the case for involvement in Iraq in both realist and idealist terms: "Our actions . . . are guided by a vision. We believe that freedom can advance and change lives in the greater Middle East, as it has advanced and changed lives in Asia, and Latin America, and Eastern Europe, and Africa. . . . And when that day comes, the bitterness and burning hatreds that feed terrorism will fade and die away. America and all the world will be safer when hope has returned to the Middle East."[59]

But Bush's critics, who had in many cases defended President Clinton's involvement in the former Yugoslavia, made the realist argument that the Iraq operation was contrary to our national interest. From this perspective, the war in Afghanistan was justifiable as retaliation for specific attacks on U.S. soil, but the war in Iraq was an unnecessary distraction. As former vice president Al Gore put it, "As the main body of our troops were deployed for the new invasion [in Iraq], those who had organized the attack against us escaped, and many are still at large."[60] As he accepted his Nobel Peace Prize in 2009, President Obama explained U.S. involvement in its wars as both an idealist and realist project: "The United States of America has helped underwrite global security for more than six decades with the blood of our citizens and the strength of our arms. . . . We have borne this burden not because we seek to impose our will. We have done so out of enlightened self-interest—because we seek a better future for our children and grandchildren, and we believe their lives will be better if others' children and grandchildren can live in freedom and prosperity."[61]

The Role of International Organizations

Regardless of whether cooperation occurs in any specific instance, two major types of international organizations are of abiding concern to policymakers: the United Nations and free trade agreements.

United Nations (UN)

Organization of all nation-states, whose purpose is to preserve world peace and foster economic and social development throughout the world.

The United Nations   At the end of World War II, the victorious nations agreed to establish the **United Nations (UN),** an international organization of all nation-states whose purpose is to preserve world peace and foster economic and social development throughout the world. Although the United Nations has been more successful than its predecessor, the ill-starred League of Nations, idealists and realists within the United States often find themselves at odds concerning the usefulness of the United Nations and other international organizations as vehicles for the conduct of U.S. foreign policy.

Idealists recommend that the United States work through the United Nations and other international organizations to achieve closer international cooperation. Idealists argue not only that these goals place American foreign policy on a high ethical plane, but also that they are an important tool for promoting peace and stability. If countries work together in international organizations, they are less likely to engage in warfare.[62]

Realists are reluctant to give the United Nations or other international organizations responsibility for the conduct of U.S. policy. They insist that decisions to intervene in world affairs must be predicated not on some vague ideal but on a calculation of the extent to which the United States has a substantial and visible interest at stake.[63] These decisions must be made on a case-by-case basis by the United States alone. Realists point out, for example, that the United Nations has condemned Israel, a U.S.

The United Nations
The United States has worked with countries around the world to combat terrorism, but it was criticized for going to war in Iraq without a broad coalition.

• *Are international coalitions more important or less important now than during the cold war?*

ally, for its treatment of Arab Palestinians. They also criticize U.N. officials for wasteful and inefficient administration of the organization.

Free Trade Agreements   When the cold war began, the Truman administration took the position that the growth of free markets would aid in the effort to contain Communism. International banks were created to lend money to needy countries, United Nations' organizations handled world health and refugee problems, and an international trade agreement reduced tariffs around the world. In late 1947, for example, 23 countries founded the General Agreement on Tariffs and Trade (GATT) in Geneva, Switzerland.

Believing that it might be difficult to persuade Congress to approve GATT, Truman signed on to the measure anyway, proclaiming that it was an executive agreement that did not need Senate approval. This action set the pattern for the conduct of trade policy ever since. The executive branch takes the lead in formulating trade policy, although Congress must approve the overall framework within which policies are determined.[64]

In recent years, trade policy has grown increasingly contentious, as labor and environmental groups have become concerned that firms in other countries need not follow the labor and environmental regulations to which U.S. firms are subject. First came the 1993 battle over the North American Free Trade Agreement (NAFTA), which eliminated trade barriers between the United States, Canada, and Mexico. Negotiated by President George H. W. Bush and promoted by President Clinton, NAFTA won only a narrow majority in Congress after fierce lobbying by all sides.

Opponents included not only labor unions but some business interests, environmental groups, consumer groups, and isolationist politicians. They worried that trade agreements would cost jobs, harm the environment, and lead to the nullification of U.S. laws and standards. Proponents included business groups and those who favored greater ties with other nations.

Continued on page 609

The U.S. Politics of the Arab-Israeli Conflict

I have about come to the conclusion that the Palestine problem is insoluble, but I suppose we will have to keep working on it.

—President Harry S. Truman, letter to
Senator Elbert Thomas, November 9, 1947[1]

The Issue

Israel and Palestinian Arabs are unable to resolve their differences over their competing territorial claims. Should the United States back Israel, back the Palestinians, back neither, or impose a settlement?

Background

When Israel became a nation in 1948, the United States was the first country to recognize it. Arab states in the region, however, were upset by the creation of a Jewish nation on land that until the twentieth century had been occupied mainly by Arabs. As Jewish immigrants fled the Nazis and moved to the area during the 1930s, guerrilla skirmishes between Jews and Arabs intensified. In 1947, a United Nations partition proposal called for the creation of separate Jewish and Arab states. But, when a provisional Israeli government declared itself to be a sovereign state, six Arab nations invaded Israel. Israel won that war, gained more territory than it lost, and then greatly expanded the territory under its control in successive wars with its Arab neighbors in 1956, 1967, and 1973. As a result, many Palestinians left Israel to live in refugee camps in neighboring countries.

Egypt and Jordan sought to make peace with Israel beginning in the late 1970s. But many Palestinian Arabs, especially those in refugee camps who longed to return to the land where they had once lived, resented their status and condemned the atrocities the Israelis were alleged to have committed. They especially resented the establishment of a large number of Jewish settlements within areas that had historically been settled by Arabs (such as the West Bank and Gaza Strip), but that Israeli armies occupied at the conclusion of the Arab-Israeli wars (see Figure 1). Control of the ancient, religiously significant city of Jerusalem was yet another point of great controversy between the two sides. Many Palestinians engaged in strikes, civil disorder, and even suicide bombings and other terrorist attacks to advance their cause.

In recent years, there have been brief periods in which peace has appeared to be within reach, but resurgent hostility has inevitably followed. After Palestinian leader Yasir Arafat's death in 2004, progress seemed possible, and Israel voluntarily vacated the occupied Gaza Strip region. But in 2006 the militant group Hamas, an organization that experts believe is responsible for at

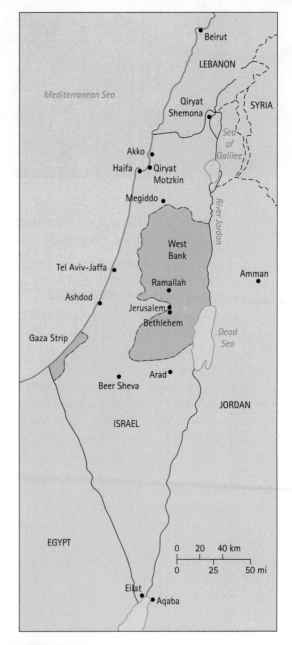

FIGURE 1

ISRAEL This map shows Israel, as well as the Palestinian regions of the West Bank and Gaza Strip.

• *Why is a permanent settlement so difficult to achieve?*

least 350 terrorist attacks, won parliamentary elections in the Palestinian Authority.[2] A three-week war between Israel and Hamas burst out in Gaza in early 2009. President Barack Obama appointed former senator George Mitchell as a special envoy to the region, and Secretary of State Clinton urged Israel to cease new construction in the West Bank. Israeli Prime Minister Benjamin Netanyahu resisted Clinton's demands, however, and negotiations stalled.

Options for U.S. policy include the following alternatives, each with its own drawbacks:

1. Support Israel's crackdowns on militant Palestinian groups. But would this position alienate Arab allies of the United States, such as Saudi Arabia, and complicate the war on terrorism?

2. Support the rapid creation of a Palestinian state. But would this position send the message that terrorist bombings are effective?

3. Force the two parties to the bargaining table, taking a hands-on role in negotiations and in the implementation of whatever peace plan might result. Perhaps the United States could even produce a peace plan of its own. But would such an effort waste U.S. diplomatic energy, taking attention away from the nation's other international responsibilities?

Elections and U.S. Policy Toward Israel

The United States has always been a key ally of Israel. In the aftermath of the Holocaust, Americans felt sympathy for the Zionists, advocates of a Jewish state in Palestine, many of whom had escaped from Europe and had endured great hardships under the Nazi regime. The case for a Jewish homeland, wrote one senator at the time, had been "written in blood and suffering."[3] In the aftermath of the September 11 terrorist attacks, many people in the United States felt renewed kinship with Israeli citizens, who had long lived their daily lives under the threat of terrorism. Since 1976, Israel has been the number-one recipient of U.S. foreign aid. American presidents have also often backed Israel in the United Nations, where it otherwise might have been outvoted by Arab states.

In recent decades, however, the U.S. alliance with Israel has become an uneasy one. Many critics in the United States and abroad have objected to the Israeli government's "aggressive behavior" in its responses to the suicide bombers. These responses have included such tactics as assassinating terrorist leaders, bulldozing the homes of terrorists' families, constructing a 450-mile "security fence" that would restrict travel between the West Bank and the rest of Israel, and engaging in retaliatory military incursions into Palestinian cities.[4] More than 1,000 Israeli citizens were killed in the spate of conflict from 2000 to 2008, but nearly five times as many Palestinians died during the same period.[5] Accordingly, the U.S. government has officially stated that, in George W. Bush's words, "a stable, peaceful [independent] Palestinian state is necessary to achieve the security that Israel longs for."[6]

It can be perilous for U.S. elected officials to appear to be anti-Israel. Although Jewish Americans make up only 2 percent of the population,[7] several key interest groups are extremely well-organized advocates for Israel. In particular, the American Israel Public Affairs Committee (AIPAC) has more than 100,000 members, meets with members of Congress more than 2,000 times a year, and is active on many college campuses.[8] In addition to lobbying, political fund-raising by pro-Jewish groups exceeds fund-raising by pro-Arab groups by a factor of about 140 to 1.[9] Two prominent foreign policy scholars have gone so far as to argue that "the overall thrust of U.S. policy in the region is due almost entirely to U.S. domestic politics, and especially to the activities of the 'Israel Lobby.'"[10] Other academics dismiss this perspective as "paranoid and conspiratorial."[11]

Opposing Viewpoints on a Palestinian State

For a Palestinian State

Advocates of a Palestinian state argue that the United States should act quickly to force Israel to accept a new nation of Palestine within the territories of the West Bank and Gaza Strip:

> There are no other people on earth who need freedom more than the Palestinians, who have lived under the longest military occupation of modern times. . . . The urgency of timely intervention cannot be overstated.
>
> —Ziad Asali, president, American Task Force on Palestine, "The Way Forward in the Middle East Peace Process," testimony before the House Committee on International Relations, February 10, 2005

Some who favor an independent Palestine also argue that to build a lasting solution, the United States should use its clout to prod both parties to the negotiating table:

> The Israelis and the Palestinians . . . have not—on their own—been able to reach agreement. After nearly two decades of negotiations, we believe bold American leadership can help Israelis and Palestinians make the difficult decisions necessary to achieve lasting peace and hold the parties to account, should they fail to honor their commitments.
>
> —Joint Statement of Ethnic and Religious Leaders in Support of Middle East Peace, The Arab American Institute, October 9, 2009, www.aaiusa.org/press-room/4277/ethnic-and-religious-coalition-join-together-to-support-middle-east-peace, accessed May 26, 2010.

Against a Palestinian State

Advocates of the Israeli position argue that the Palestinian Authority either has allowed terrorism to continue or even has encouraged it. According to this perspective, the Hamas victory in the 2006 elections makes it even more likely that a Palestinian state would constitute a terrorist state:

> A government dominated by a terrorist organization undermines the effort to establish a democratic, non-violent society and jeopardizes efforts to achieve a lasting

peace. . . . The United States must not recognize Hamas as a legitimate party in the democratic process until it agrees to renounce and end violence, dismantle the terrorist infrastructure, recognize Israel's right to exist, and agree to conduct direct negotiations with Israel.

—AIPAC, press release, January 26, 2006, www.aipac.org/PDFdocs/ Press_PLC_Elections012606.pdf, accessed June 15, 2006

Like America, Israel is a vibrant democracy, with a robust civil society, an independent judiciary, and a free press. While the United States should help find a solution that serves the interests of both Israelis and Palestinians, there is no moral equivalence between the two sides.

—Abraham Foxman, National Director of the Anti-Defamation League, "Beyond 'Evenhandedness,'" *The Forward*, February 4, 2009, www.adl.org/ADL_Opinions/Israel/20090205-Oped+-+Forward.htm, accessed May 26, 2010.

What Do Americans Believe?

Americans have consistently expressed support for Israel (see Figure 2). Nevertheless, they also feel that a Palestinian state is justified—especially if terrorist groups pledge to end the suicide bombings.[12]

Public sympathy for Israel, coupled with the active organization and fund-raising skills of pro-Israel organizations such as AIPAC, has convinced many elected officials that they oppose Israel at their peril. Members of Congress are reluctant to be seen as opposing the only democracy in the Middle East and, especially since 9/11, members who support the Palestinians risk appearing to be soft on terrorism. As one Arab American expert lamented, "You see more criticism of Israel in Israeli newspapers than you do in Congress. I guess the newspaper editors aren't trying to get reelected."[13]

What Do You Think?

1. Should Americans become deeply involved in bringing the two parties to agreement, or would this waste energy that could be better expended elsewhere?

2. Should the fact that Israel is a democracy affect our foreign policy decisions related to the country? Why or why not?

3. Should elected officials pay much attention to public opinion on this issue, or are Americans' views on foreign policy too vague and ill-informed to be meaningful?

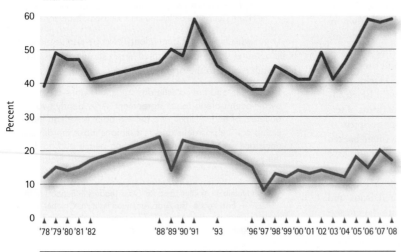

In the dispute between the Israelis and the Palestinians, which side do you sympathize with more?

■ Israel ■ Palestinians

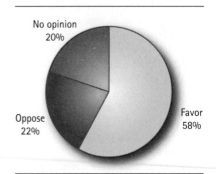

Do you favor or oppose the establishment of an independent Palestinian state on the West Bank and Gaza Strip?

No opinion 20%
Oppose 22%
Favor 58%

FIGURE 2

AMERICAN VIEWS ON THE CONFLICT

Americans express more sympathy with Israel in the Arab–Israeli Conflict but also support creation of a Palestinian state.

• *What has happened to American sympathy toward Israel in the last decade? Why do you think this is the case?*

• *Do you think Americans express support for Israel because of cultural affinities between the two countries, because Israel is a democracy, or for reasons of strategic national interest?*

Sources: Gallup, Harris, Pew Research Center polls, various years.

On the Web

Pro-Israel

The American Israel Public Affairs Committee (AIPAC) is the largest pro-Israel lobby in Washington and conducts many outreach activities in the rest of the country as well. Browse its issue papers for a detailed defense of the Israeli perspective.

>   www.aipac.org

The American Jewish Committee publishes a variety of briefings and issue papers on the Arab-Israeli conflict and other pertinent issues.

>   www.ajc.org

The Israeli government, through its ministry of foreign affairs, sponsors an official website with the latest details on Israel's policies and actions in the conflict.

>   www.israel.org

Pro-Palestinian

The Arab American Institute is a lobbying and outreach organization concerned with the Middle East conflict and with other issues of concern to Arab Americans.

>   www.aaiusa.org

The Palestine Solidarity Campaign is an activist organization dedicated to an independent Palestinian state.

>   www.palestinecampaign.org

---

[1] Available at the Truman Presidential Museum and Library, Recognition of Israel Study Collection, www.trumanlibrary.org, accessed July 18, 2002.

[2] Council on Foreign Relations, "Backgrounder: Hamas," updated June 14, 2006, www.cfr.org/publication/8968/, accessed June 15, 2006.
[3] Letter from Senator Robert F. Wagner (D-NY) to President Harry S. Truman, June 20, 1946, Truman Presidential Museum and Library, Recognition of Israel Study Collection, www.trumanlibrary.org, accessed July 19, 2002.
[4] Laura King and Fayed abu Shammalah, "Israel Kills New Leader of Hamas," Los Angeles Times (April 18, 2004): A1; Patrick McMahon, "Terrorism Stirs Jews in USA to Activism," USA Today (June 25, 2002): 13A.
[5] "Conflict Statistics," Middle East Policy Council, www.mepc.org/resources/mrates.asp, accessed June 14, 2006.
[6] Robin Wright, "A Palestinian State Requires New Leadership, Bush Says," Los Angeles Times (June 25, 2002): A1.
[7] U.S. Bureau of the Census, Statistical Abstract of the United States: 2006, Table 71.
[8] American Israel Public Affairs Committee, www.aipac.org, accessed June 14, 2006.
[9] David Lightman, "Arab Lobby Gains Clout; Fighting Image, History; Small Victories Add Up," Hartford Courant (May 26, 2002): A1.
[10] John J. Mearsheimer and Stephen M. Walt, "The Israel Lobby and U.S. Foreign Policy," Harvard University, John F. Kennedy School of Government, Faculty Working Paper RWP06-011, March 2006, 1.
[11] Harvard University Law Professor Alan Dershowitz, quoted in Michael Powell, "Academic Paper Stirs Debate," Washington Post (April 3, 2006): A3.
[12] This is especially true if the establishment of such a state would lead to an end to terrorism. Fully 74 percent say "favor" when asked the question "Do you favor or oppose the establishment of an independent Palestinian state on the West Bank if the Palestinian government demonstrates that it can end the suicide bombings in Israel?" Gallup Poll, June 21–23, 2002.
[13] Abraham Hooper, spokesman for the Council on American-Islamic Relations, quoted in Deirdre Shegreen, "Gephardt Says Bush's Proposal for Palestinian State is 'Problematic,'" St. Louis Post-Dispatch (June 21, 2002): A7.

Continued from page 605

The battle over NAFTA proved to be only the beginning of a very public debate over the status of world trade. In 1994, negotiators from 104 nations officially transformed GATT into the World Trade Organization (WTO), a trade body much more powerful than GATT, with enforcement and dispute resolution mechanisms. Opposition to the organization was significant and vocal and was led by the same groups that opposed NAFTA.

Despite the controversy, U.S. presidents have generally supported free trade, feeling that U.S. economic interests are served by the open flow of commerce. President George W. Bush sought—but did not win—congressional approval of a free trade agreement with Colombia. Although as a presidential candidate President Obama signaled his suspicion of NAFTA, he did not seek to significantly alter the agreement upon winning office.

CHAPTER SUMMARY

20.1 Identify the roles of the president, interest groups, and the Congress in the development of foreign policy.

Electoral considerations help to account for the fact that presidents dominate policymaking on foreign policy questions more than on domestic ones. Voters expect presidents to take the lead. In the short run, they tend to support presidents in crises no matter what action is taken. Only later, if things do not turn out well, do voters penalize presidents for choosing the wrong policy.

20.2 Detail the foreign policy powers of the president and of the Congress.

Other factors reinforce the president's dominant role in foreign policy. Fast action is often needed; interest-group pressures are less intense than on domestic issues; the Supreme Court has interpreted the powers of the president broadly; and Congress tends to defer to the executive. In the campaign against terrorism, Congress, acting under procedures set forth in the War Powers Resolution, authorized the president to take all military action necessary to find and punish those who aided or harbored the 9/11 terrorists, as well as to conduct military action against Iraq.

20.3 Trace the development of foreign policy institutions from the Cold War to post-9/11.

The Department of State, the Department of Defense, and the national intelligence director (who oversees the Central Intelligence Agency as well as other agencies), together with the head of the Joint Chiefs of Staff, all sit on the National Security Council, which is managed by a national security adviser responsible to the president for overall coordination of foreign policy. These institutions took their modern shape during the early years of the cold war, and are all seeking to adapt to the post–cold war world of terrorist threats.

20.4 Analyze the conflict between American philosophical ideals and a practical need to defend the country.

Both idealistic and realistic factors help shape American foreign policy. On the one hand, the United States feels responsible for promoting the democratic experiment abroad. On the other hand, the United States, similar to any other country, has its own interests to protect. Idealist and realist considerations both play a role in current debates over international organizations and nation building. But since 9/11, both realists and idealists believe it is important to help establish strong, legitimate governments throughout the world.

---

myp●liscilab EXERCISES

Apply what you learned in this chapter on MyPoliSciLab.

📖 Read on mypoliscilab.com

  eText: Chapter 20

✔ Study and **Review** on mypoliscilab.com

  Pre-Test

  Post-Test

  Chapter Exam

  Flashcards

👁 Watch on mypoliscilab.com

  Video: NYC's Subway Surveillance System

  Video: Sanctions on Iran

  Video: Three Vivid Years—But Progress?

✳ Explore on mypoliscilab.com

  Simulation: You Are the President of the United States

  Simulation: You Are the Newly Appointed Ambassador to the Country of Dalmatia

  Simulation: You Are President John F. Kennedy

  Comparative: Comparing Foreign and Security Policy

  Timeline: The Evolution of Foreign Policy

  Visual Literacy: Evaluating Defense Spending

KEY TERMS

ambassador, p. 595
Bay of Pigs, p. 600
bipolar, p. 593
Central Intelligence Agency
   (CIA), p. 599
cold war, p. 591
containment, p. 593
counterinsurgency, p. 599
Department of Defense, p. 596
diplomacy, p. 595
embassy, p. 595
ethnic cleansing, p. 603

executive agreements, p. 590
foreign policy, p. 582
foreign service, p. 596
idealists, p. 603
Iran-Contra affair, p. 602
Joint Chiefs of Staff, p. 597
League of Nations, p. 590
nation building, p. 603
national intelligence director, p. 601
National Security Council
   (NSC), p. 601
"rally 'round the flag" effect, p. 583

realists, p. 603
secretary of defense, p. 596
secretary of state, p. 595
Tonkin Gulf Resolution, p. 588
treaties, p. 589
two-presidency theory, p. 582
United Nations (UN), p. 604
*United States v. Curtiss-Wright Export
   Corporation,* p. 587
War Powers Resolution, p. 588
*Youngstown Sheet & Tube Co. v.
   Sawyer,* p. 587

SUGGESTED READINGS

Of General Interest

Daalder, Ivo, and James Lindsay. *America Unbound: The Bush Revolution in Foreign Policy*. Hoboken, NJ: Wiley, 2005. Two foreign policy scholars argue that George W. Bush made dramatic changes in U.S. foreign policy.

Jervis, Robert. *American Foreign Policy in a New Era*. New York: Routledge, 2005. A scholar of international relations examines the recent changes in U.S. foreign policy.

Wildavsky, Aaron. "The Two Presidencies." In Steven A. Shull, ed., *The Two Presidencies: A Quarter Century Assessment*. Chicago: Nelson-Hall, 1991, pp. 11–25. Explains how politics differs between foreign and domestic issues.

Zakaria, Fareed. *The Post-American World*. New York: W.W. Norton & Co., 2009. Discusses the consequences for U.S. policy of a world in which China, India, and other nations are on the rise.

Focused Studies

Allison, Graham, and Philip Zelikow. *Essence of Decision: Explaining the Cuban Missile Crisis.* 2nd ed. New York: Longman, 1999. Fascinating account of the Cuban missile crisis, the closest the United States and the Soviet Union ever came to nuclear confrontation.

Gordon, Michael R., and Bernard E. Trainor. *Cobra II: The Inside Story of the Invasion and Occupation of Iraq*. New York: Random House, 2006. A journalist and a general conduct a detailed study of the early stages of the Iraq War.

Huntington, Samuel. *The Clash of Civilizations*. New York: Simon & Schuster, 1996. Argues that future world conflicts will occur between clusters of nations that share a common cultural heritage.

Richardson, Louise. *What Terrorists Want: Understanding the Enemy, Containing the Threat*. New York: Random House, 2007. A leading scholar dissects the origins of terrorism and evaluates policies that seek to contain it.

United States Army/Marine Corps Counterinsurgency Field Manual. Chicago: University of Chicago Press, 2007. Written by military officers, scholars, and other experts, this guide to combating insurgents became the blueprint for the U.S. strategy in Iraq and Afghanistan after a change of direction in 2006.

ON THE WEB

www.state.gov
www.defenselink.mil

The Department of State and the Department of Defense are the oldest and most important cabinet agencies with responsibility for conducting American foreign policy.

www.odci.gov (Central Intelligence Agency)
www.whitehouse.gov/nsc/
www.jcs.mil
www.dni.gov

In this chapter we discussed the changes to the U.S. foreign policymaking agencies that occurred at the beginning of the cold war. The Central Intelligence Agency, the National Security Council, and the Joint Chiefs of Staff were all created after World War II to conduct foreign affairs more effectively. The director of national intelligence (DNI) is a new office, designed to address intelligence failings prior to 9/11.

www.ustr.gov

The U.S. trade representative, located in the Executive Office of the President, is the U.S. government's chief trade negotiator.

www.un.org

www.wto.org

The United Nations and the World Trade Organization are two key international organizations that have at times weathered criticism from both realists and idealists in the United States.

www.cfr.org

www.aipac.org

www.canf.org

One of the reasons why the president has more authority over foreign affairs than over domestic affairs is the comparative lack of interest groups with a foreign policy focus. Nevertheless, there are at least several interest groups that pay close attention to foreign policy, including the Council on Foreign Relations (CFR), the American Israel Public Affairs Committee (AIPAC), and the Cuban American National Foundation (CANF).

www.senate.gov/~foreign/

Although Congress plays a smaller role in foreign affairs than in domestic politics, the Senate has the constitutional responsibility to approve or reject foreign treaties and confirm nominees for key posts. Such issues are handled by the Senate's Committee on Foreign Relations.

Appendix I

The Declaration of Independence

In Congress, July 4, 1776

The Unanimous Declaration of the Thirteen United States of America

WHEN IN THE COURSE of human events it becomes necessary for one people to dissolve the political bands which have connected them with another, and to assume, among the powers of the earth, the separate and equal station to which the Laws of Nature and of Nature's God entitle them, a decent respect to the opinions of mankind requires that they should declare the causes which impel them to the separation.

We hold these truths to be self-evident, that all men are created equal, that they are endowed by their Creator with certain unalienable Rights, that among these are Life, Liberty and the pursuit of Happiness. That to secure these rights, Governments are instituted among Men, deriving their just powers from the consent of the governed. That whenever any Form of Government becomes destructive of these ends, it is the Right of the People to alter or to abolish it, and to institute new Government, laying its foundation on such principles and organizing its powers in such form, as to them shall seem most likely to effect their Safety and Happiness. Prudence, indeed, will dictate that Governments long established should not be changed for light and transient causes; and accordingly all experience hath shewn that mankind are more disposed to suffer, while evils are sufferable, than to right themselves by abolishing the forms to which they are accustomed. But when a long train of abuses and usurpations, pursuing invariably the same Object evinces a design to reduce them under absolute Despotism, it is their right, it is their duty, to throw off such Government, and to provide new Guards for their future security.—Such has been the patient sufferance of these Colonies; and such is now the necessity which constrains them to alter their former Systems of Government. The history of the present King of Great Britain is a history of repeated injuries and usurpations, all having in direct object the establishment of an absolute Tyranny over these States. To prove this, let Facts be submitted to a candid world.

He has refused his Assent to Laws, the most wholesome and necessary for the public good.

He has forbidden his Governors to pass Laws of immediate and pressing importance, unless suspended in their operation till his Assent should be obtained; and when so suspended, he has utterly neglected to attend to them.

He has refused to pass other Laws for the accommodation of large districts of people, unless those people would relinquish the right of Representation in the Legislature, a right inestimable to them and formidable to tyrants only.

He has called together legislative bodies at places unusual, uncomfortable, and distant from the depository of their Public Records, for the sole purpose of fatiguing them into compliance with his measures.

He has dissolved Representative Houses repeatedly, for opposing with manly firmness his invasions on the rights of the people.

He has refused for a long time, after such dissolutions, to cause others to be elected; whereby the Legislative Powers, incapable of Annihilation, have returned to the People at large for their exercise, the State remaining in the mean time exposed to all the dangers of invasion from without, and convulsions within.

He has endeavored to prevent the population of these States; for that purpose obstructing the Laws of Naturalization of Foreigners; refusing to pass others to encourage their migration hither, and raising the conditions of new Appropriations of Lands.

He has obstructed the Administration of Justice, by refusing his Assent to Laws for establishing Judiciary powers.

He has made Judges dependent on his Will alone, for the tenure of their offices, and the amount and payment of their salaries.

He has erected a multitude of New Offices, and sent hither swarms of Officers to harass our people, and eat out their substance.

He has kept among us, in times of peace, Standing Armies without the Consent of our legislatures.

He has affected to render the Military independent of and superior to the Civil power.

He has combined with others to subject us to a jurisdiction foreign to our constitution, and unacknowledged by our laws, giving his Assent to their Acts of pretended Legislation:

For quartering large bodies of armed troops among us:

For protecting them, by a mock Trial, from punishment for any Murders which they should commit on the Inhabitants of these States:

For cutting off our Trade with all parts of the world:

For imposing Taxes on us without our Consent:

For depriving us in many cases, of the benefits of Trial by Jury:

For transporting us beyond Seas to be tried for pretended offences:

For abolishing the free System of English Laws in a neighboring Province, establishing therein an Arbitrary government, and enlarging its Boundaries so as to render it at once an example and fit instrument for introducing the same absolute rule into these Colonies:

For taking away our Charters, abolishing our most valuable Laws, and altering fundamentally the Forms of our Governments:

For suspending our own Legislatures, and declaring themselves invested with power to legislate for us in all cases whatsoever.

He has abdicated Government here, by declaring us out of his Protection and waging War against us.

He has plundered our seas, ravaged our Coasts, burnt our towns, and destroyed the lives of our people.

He is at this time transporting large Armies of foreign Mercenaries to compleat the works of death, desolation and tyranny, already begun with circumstances of Cruelty and perfidy scarcely paralleled in the most barbarous ages, and totally unworthy the Head of a civilized nation.

He has constrained our fellow Citizens taken Captive on the high Seas to bear Arms against their Country, to become the executioners of their friends and Brethren, or to fall themselves by their Hands.

He has excited domestic insurrections amongst us, and has endeavored to bring on the inhabitants of our frontiers, the merciless Indian Savages, whose known rule of warfare, is an undistinguished destruction of all ages, sexes and conditions.

In every stage of these Oppressions We have Petitioned for Redress in the most humble terms: Our repeated Petitions have been answered only by repeated injury: A Prince, whose character is thus marked by every act which may define a Tyrant, is unfit to be the ruler of a free people.

Nor have We been wanting in attention to our British brethren. We have warned them from time to time of attempts by their legislature to extend an unwarrantable jurisdiction over us. We have reminded them of the circumstances of our emigration and settlement here. We have appealed to their native justice and magnanimity; and we have conjured them by the ties of our common kindred to disavow these usurpations, which would inevitably interrupt our connections and correspondence. They too have been deaf to the voice of justice and consanguinity. We must, therefore, acquiesce in the necessity, which denounces our Separation, and hold them, as we hold the rest of mankind, Enemies in War, in Peace Friends.

We, therefore, the Representatives of the United States of America, in General Congress, Assembled, appealing to the Supreme Judge of the world for the rectitude of our intentions, do, in the Name, and by Authority of the good People of these Colonies, solemnly publish and declare, That these United Colonies are, and of Right ought to be Free and Independent States; that they are Absolved from all Allegiance to the British Crown, and that all political connection between them and the State of Great Britain, is and ought to be totally dissolved: and that as Free and Independent States, they have full power to levy War, conclude Peace, contract Alliances, establish Commerce, and to do all other Acts and Things which Independent States may of right do. And for the support of this Declaration, with a firm reliance on the protection of divine Providence, we mutually pledge to each other our Lives, our Fortunes and our sacred Honor.

JOHN HANCOCK

NEW HAMPSHIRE
Josiah Bartlett,
Wm. Whipple,
Matthew Thornton.

MASSACHUSETTS BAY
Saml. Adams,
John Adams,
Robt. Treat Paine,
Elbridge Gerry.

RHODE ISLAND
Step. Hopkins,
William Ellery.

CONNECTICUT
Roger Sherman,
Samuel Huntington,
Wm. Williams,
Oliver Wolcott.

NEW YORK
Wm. Floyd,
Phil. Livingston,
Frans. Lewis,
Lewis Morris

NEW JERSEY
Richd. Stockton,
In. Witherspoon,
Fras. Hopkinson,
John Hart,
Abra. Clark.

PENNSYLVANIA
Robt. Morris,
Benjamin Rush,
Benjamin Franklin,
John Morton,
Geo. Clymer,
Jas. Smith,
Geo. Taylor,
James Wilson,
Geo. Ross.

DELAWARE
Caesar Rodney,
Geo. Read,
Tho. M'kean.

MARYLAND
Samuel Chase,
Wm. Paca,

Thos. Stone,
Charles Caroll of Carollton.

VIRGINIA
George Wythe,
Richard Henry Lee,
Th. Jefferson,
Benjamin Harrison,
Thos. Nelson, Jr.,
Francis Lightfoot Lee,
Carter Braxton.

NORTH CAROLINA
Wm. Hooper,
Joseph Hewes,
John Penn.

SOUTH CAROLINA
Edward Rutledge,
Thos. Heyward, Junr.,
Thomas Lynch, jnr.,
Arthur Middleton.

Appendix II

The Constitution of the United States of America

WE THE PEOPLE of the United States, in Order to form a more perfect Union, establish Justice, insure domestic Tranquility, provide for the common defence, promote the general Welfare, and secure the Blessings of Liberty to ourselves and our Posterity, do ordain and establish this Constitution for the United States of America.

ARTICLE I

SECTION 1. All legislative Powers herein granted shall be vested in a Congress of the United States, which shall consist of a Senate and House of Representatives.

SECTION 2. The House of Representatives shall be composed of Members chosen every second Year by the People of the several States, and the Electors in each State shall have the Qualifications requisite for Electors of the most numerous Branch of the State Legislature.

No person shall be a Representative who shall not have attained to the Age of twenty five Years, and been seven Years a Citizen of the United States, and who shall not, when elected, be an Inhabitant of that State in which he shall be chosen.

Representatives and direct Taxes shall be apportioned among the several States which may be included within this Union, according to their respective Numbers which shall be determined by adding to the whole Number of free Persons, including those bound to Service for a Term of Years, and excluding Indians not taxed, three fifths of all other Persons. The actual Enumeration shall be made within three Years after the first Meeting of the Congress of the United States, and within every subsequent Term ten Years, in such Manner as they shall by Law direct. The Number of Representatives shall not exceed one for every thirty Thousand, but each State shall have at Least one Representative; and until such enumeration shall be made, the State of New Hampshire shall be entitled to chuse three, Massachusetts eight, Rhode-Island and Providence Plantations one, Connecticut five, New-York six, New Jersey four, Pennsylvania eight, Delaware one, Maryland six, Virginia ten, North Carolina five, South Carolina five, and Georgia three.

When vacancies happen in the Representation from any State, the Executive Authority thereof shall issue Writs of Election to fill such Vacancies.

The House of Representatives shall chuse their speaker and other Officers; and shall have the sole Power of Impeachment.

SECTION 3. The Senate of the United States shall be composed of two Senators from each State chosen by the Legislature thereof, for six Years; and each Senator shall have one Vote.

Immediately after they shall be assembled in Consequence of the first Election, they shall be divided as equally as may be into three Classes. The Seats of the Senators of the first Class shall be vacated at the Expiration of the second year, of the second Class at the Expiration of the fourth Year, and of the third Class at the Expiration of the sixth Year, so that one third may be chosen every second Year and if Vacancies happen by Resignation, or otherwise, during the Recess of the Legislature of any State, the Executive thereof may make temporary Appointments until the next Meeting of the Legislature, which shall then fill such Vacancies.

No Person shall be a Senator who shall not have attained to the Age of thirty Years, and been nine Years a Citizen of the United States, and who shall not, when elected, be an Inhabitant of that State for which he shall be chosen.

The Vice President of the United States shall be President of the Senate, but shall have no Vote, unless they be equally divided.

The Senate shall chuse their other Officers, and also a President pro tempore, in the Absence of the Vice President, or when he shall exercise the Office of President of the United States.

The Senate shall have the sole Power to try all Impeachments. When sitting for that Purpose, they shall be on Oath or Affirmation. When the President of the United States is tried, the Chief Justice shall preside: And no Person shall be convicted without the Concurrence of two thirds of the Members present.

Judgment in Cases of Impeachment shall not extend further than to removal from Office, and disqualification to hold and enjoy any Office of honor, Trust or Profit under the United States; but the Party convicted shall nevertheless be liable and subject to Indictment, Trial, Judgment and Punishment, according to Law.

SECTION 4. The Times, Places and Manner of holding Elections for Senators and Representatives, shall be prescribed in each State by the Legislature thereof; but the Congress may at any time by law make or alter such Regulations, except as to the Places of chusing Senators.

The Congress shall assemble at least once in every Year, and such Meeting shall be on the first Monday in December, unless they shall by Law appoint a different Day.

SECTION 5. Each House shall be the Judge of the Elections, Returns and Qualifications of its own Members, and a Majority of each shall constitute a Quorum to do Business; but a smaller Number may adjourn from day to day, and may be authorized to compel the Attendance of absent Members, in such Manner, and under such Penalties as each House may provide.

Each House may determine the Rules of its Proceedings, punish its Members for disorderly Behaviour, and with the Concurrence of two thirds, expel a Member.

Each House shall keep a journal of its Proceedings, and from time to time publish the same, excepting such Parts as may in their judgment require Secrecy; and the Yeas and Nays of the Members of either House on any question shall, at the Desire of one fifth of those present, be entered on the Journal.

Neither House, during the Session of Congress, shall, without the Consent of the other, adjourn for more than three days, nor to any other Place than that in which the two Houses shall be sitting.

SECTION 6. The Senators and Representatives shall receive a Compensation for their Services, to be ascertained by Law, and paid out of the Treasury of the United States. They shall in all Cases, except Treason, Felony and Breach of the Peace, be privileged from Arrest during their Attendance at the Session of their respective Houses, and in going to and returning from the same; and for any Speech or Debate in either House, they shall not be questioned in any other Place.

No Senator or Representative shall, during the Time for which he was elected, be appointed to any civil Office under the Authority of the United States, which shall have been created, or the Emoluments whereof shall have been encreased during such time; and no Person holding any Office under the United States, shall be a Member of either House during his Continuance in Office.

SECTION 7. All Bills for raising Revenue shall originate in the House of Representatives; but the Senate may propose or concur with Amendments as on other Bills.

Every Bill which shall have passed the House of Representatives and the Senate, shall, before it become a Law, be presented to the President of the United States; If he approves he shall sign it, but if not he shall return it, with his Objections to that House in which it shall have originated, who shall enter the Objections at large on their journal, and proceed to reconsider it. If after such Reconsideration two thirds of that House shall agree to pass the Bill, it shall be sent, together with the Objections, to the other House, by which it shall likewise be reconsidered, and if approved by two thirds of that House, it shall become a Law. But in all such Cases the Votes of both Houses shall be determined by Yeas and Nays, and the Names of the Persons voting for and against the Bill shall be entered on the Journal of each House respectively. If any Bill shall not be returned by the President within ten Days (Sundays excepted) after it shall have been presented to him, the Same shall be a Law, in like Manner as if he had signed it, unless the Congress by their Adjournment prevent its Return, in which Case it shall not be a Law.

Every Order, Resolution, or Vote to which the Concurrence of the Senate and House of Representatives may be necessary (except on a question of Adjournment) shall be presented to the President of the United States; and before the Same shall take Effect, shall be approved by him, or being disapproved by him, shall be repassed by two thirds of the Senate and House of Representatives, according to the Rules and Limitations prescribed in the Case of a Bill.

SECTION 8. The Congress shall have Power To lay and collect Taxes, Duties, Imposts and Excises, to pay the Debts and provide for the common Defence and general Welfare of the United States; but all Duties, Imposts and Excises shall be uniform throughout the United States;

To borrow Money on the credit of the United States;

To regulate Commerce with foreign Nations, and among the several States, and with the Indian Tribes;

To establish a uniform Rule of Naturalization, and uniform Laws on the subject of Bankruptcies throughout the United States;

To coin Money, regulate the Value thereof, and of foreign Coin, and fix the Standard of Weights and Measures;

To provide for the Punishment of counterfeiting the Securities and current Coin of the United States;

To establish Post Offices and post Roads;

To promote the Progress of Science and useful Arts, by securing for limited Times to Authors and Inventors the exclusive Right to their respective Writings and Discoveries;

To constitute Tribunals inferior to the supreme Court;

To define and punish Piracies and Felonies committed on the high Seas, and Offences against the Law of Nations;

To declare War, grant Letters of Marque and Reprisal, and make Rules concerning Captures on Land and Water;

To raise and support Armies, but no Appropriation of Money to that Use shall be for a longer Term than two Years;

To provide and maintain a Navy;

To make Rules for the Government and Regulation of the land and naval Forces;

To provide for calling forth the Militia to execute the Laws of the Union, suppress Insurrections and repel Invasions;

To provide for organizing, arming, and disciplining, the Militia, and for governing such Part of them as may be employed in the Service of the United States, reserving to the States respectively, the Appointment of the Officers, and the Authority of training the Militia according to the discipline prescribed by Congress;

To exercise exclusive Legislation in all Cases whatsoever, over such District (not exceeding ten Miles square) as may, by Cession of particular States, and the Acceptance of Congress, become the Seat of the Government of the United States, and to exercise like Authority over all Places purchased by the Consent of the Legislature of the State in which the Same shall be for the Erection of Forts, Magazines, Arsenals, dock-Yards, and other needful Buildings;—And

To make all Laws which shall be necessary and proper for carrying into Execution the foregoing Powers, and all other Powers vested by this Constitution in the Government of the United States, or in any Department or Officer thereof.

SECTION 9. The Migration or Importation of such Persons as any of the States now existing shall think proper to admit, shall not be prohibited by the Congress prior to the Year one thousand eight hundred and eight, but a Tax or duty may be imposed on such Importation, not exceeding ten dollars for each Person.

The Privilege of the Writ of Habeas Corpus shall not be suspended, unless when in Cases of Rebellion or Invasion the public Safety may require it.

No Bill of Attainder or ex post facto Law shall be passed.

No Capitation, or other direct, Tax shall be laid, unless in Proportion to the Census or Enumeration herein before directed to be taken.

No Tax or Duty shall be laid on Articles exported from any State.

No Preference shall be given by any Regulation of Commerce or Revenue to the Ports of one State over those of another; nor shall Vessels bound to, or from, one State, be obliged to enter, clear, or pay Duties in another.

No Money shall be drawn from the Treasury, but in Consequence of Appropriations made by Law; and a regular Statement and Account of the Receipts and Expenditures of all public Money shall be published from time to time.

No Title of Nobility shall be granted by the United States: And no Person holding any Office of Profit or Trust under them, shall, without the Consent of the Congress, accept of any present, Emolument, Office, or Title, of any kind whatever, from any King, Prince, or foreign State.

SECTION 10. No state shall enter into any Treaty, Alliance, or Confederation; grant Letters of Marque and Reprisal; coin Money; emit Bills of Credit; make any Thing but gold and silver Coin a Tender in Payment of Debts; pass any Bill of Attainder, ex post facto Law, or Law impairing the Obligation of Contracts, or grant any Title of Nobility.

No State shall, without the Consent of the Congress, lay any Imposts or Duties on Imports or Exports, except what may be absolutely necessary for executing its inspection Laws: and the net Produce of all Duties and Imposts, laid by any State on Imports or Exports, shall be for the Use of the Treasury of the United States, and all such Laws shall be subject to the Revision and Controul of the Congress.

No State shall, without the Consent of Congress, lay any Duty of Tonnage, keep Troops, or Ships of War in time of Peace, enter into any Agreement or Compact with another State, or with a foreign Power, or engage in War, unless actually invaded, or in such imminent Danger as will not admit of delay.

ARTICLE II

SECTION 1. The executive Power shall be vested in a President of the United States of America. He shall hold his Office during the Term of four Years, and, together with the Vice President, chosen for the same Term, be elected as follows.

Each State shall appoint, in such Manner as the Legislature thereof may direct, a Number of Electors, equal to the whole Number of Senators and Representatives to which the State may be entitled in the Congress; but no Senator or Representative, or Person holding an Office of Trust of Profit under the United States, shall be appointed an Elector.

The Electors shall meet in their respective States, and vote by Ballot for two Persons, of whom one at least shall not be an Inhabitant of the same State with themselves. And they shall make a List of all the Persons voted for, and, of the Number of Votes for each; which List they shall sign and certify, and transmit sealed to the Seat of the Government of the United States, directed to the President of the Senate. The President of the Senate shall, in the Presence of the Senate and House of Representatives, open all the Certificates, and the Votes shall then be counted. The Person having the greatest Number of Votes shall be the President, if such Number be a Majority of the whole Number of Electors appointed; and if there be more than one who have such Majority, and have an equal Number of Votes, then the House of Representatives shall immediately chuse by Ballot one of them for President; and if no Person have a Majority, then from the five highest on the List the said House shall in like Manner chuse the President. But in chusing the President, the Votes shall be taken by States, the Representation from each State having one Vote; A quorum for this Purpose shall consist of a Member or Members from two thirds of the States, and a Majority of all the States shall be necessary to a Choice. In every Case, after the Choice of the President, the Person having the greatest Number of Votes of the Electors shall be the Vice President. But if there should remain two or more who have equal Votes, the Senate shall chuse from them by Ballot the Vice President.

The Congress may determine the Time of chusing the Electors, and the Day on which they shall give their Votes; which Day shall be the same throughout the United States.

No Person except a natural born Citizen, or a Citizen of the United States, at the time of the Adoption of this Constitution, shall be eligible to the Office of President; neither shall any Person be eligible to that Office who shall not have attained to the Age of thirty five Years, and been fourteen Years a Resident within the United States.

In Case of the Removal of the President from Office, or of his Death, Resignation, or Inability to discharge the Powers and Duties of the said Office, the Same shall devolve on the Vice President, and the Congress may by Law provide for the Case of Removal, Death, Resignation or Inability, both of the President and Vice President, declaring what Officer shall then act as President, and such Officer shall act accordingly, until the Disability be removed, or a President shall be elected.

The President shall, at stated Times, receive for his Services, a Compensation, which shall neither be encreased nor diminished during the Period for which he shall have been elected, and he shall not receive within that Period any other Emolument from the United States, or any of them.

Before he enter on the Execution of his Office, he shall take the following Oath or Affirmation—"I do solemnly swear (or affirm) that I will faithfully execute the Office of President of the United States, and will to the best of my Ability, preserve, protect and defend the Constitution of the United States."

SECTION 2. The President shall be Commander in Chief of the Army, and Navy of the United States, and of the Militia of the several States, when called into the actual Service of the United States; he may require the Opinion, in writing, of the principal Officer in each of the executive Departments, upon any Subject relating to the Duties of their respective Offices, and he shall have Power to grant Reprieves and Pardons for Offences against the United States, except in Cases of Impeachment.

He shall have Power, by and with the Advice and Consent of the Senate, to make Treaties, provided two thirds of the Senators present concur; and he shall nominate, and by and with the Advice and Consent of the Senate, shall appoint Ambassadors, other public Ministers and Consuls, Judges of the supreme Court, and all other Officers of the United States, whose Appointments are not herein otherwise provided for, and which shall be established by Law: but the Congress may by Law vest the Appointment of such inferior Officers, as they think proper, in the President alone, in the Courts of Law, or in the Heads of Departments.

The President shall have Power to fill up all Vacancies that may happen during the Recess of the Senate, by granting Commissions which shall expire at the end of their next Session.

SECTION 3. He shall from time to time give to the Congress Information of the State of the Union, and recommend to their Consideration such Measures as he shall judge necessary and expedient; he may, on extraordinary Occasions, convene both Houses, or either of them, and in Case of Disagreement between them, with Respect to the Time of Adjournment, he may adjourn them to such Time as he shall think proper; he shall receive Ambassadors and other public Ministers; he shall take Care that the Laws be faithfully executed, and shall Commission all the Officers of the United States.

SECTION 4. The President, Vice President and all civil Officers of the United States, shall be removed from Office on Impeachment for, and Conviction of, Treason, Bribery, or other high Crimes and Misdemeanors.

ARTICLE III

SECTION 1. The judicial Power of the United States, shall be vested in one supreme Court, and in such inferior Courts as the Congress may from time to time ordain and establish. The Judges, both of the supreme and inferior Courts, shall hold their Offices during good Behaviour, and shall, at stated Times, receive for their Services, a Compensation, which shall not be diminished during their Continuance in Office.

SECTION 2. The judicial Power shall extend to all Cases, in Law and Equity, arising under this Constitution, the Laws of the United States, and Treaties made, or which shall be made, under their Authority;—to all Cases affecting Ambassadors, other public Ministers and Consuls;—to all Cases of admiralty and maritime Jurisdiction;—to Controversies to which the United States shall be a Party;—to Controversies between two or more States;—between a State and Citizens of another State;—between Citizens of different States,—between Citizens of the same State claiming Lands under Grants of different States,—and between a State, or the Citizens thereof, and foreign States, Citizens of Subjects.

In all Cases affecting Ambassadors, other public Ministers and Consuls, and those in which a State shall be Party, the supreme Court shall have original Jurisdiction. In all the other Cases before mentioned, the supreme Court shall have appellate Jurisdiction, both as to Law and Fact, with such Exceptions, and under such Regulations as the Congress shall make.

The Trial of all Crimes, except in Cases of Impeachment, shall be by Jury; and such Trial shall be held in the State where the said Crimes shall have been committed; but when not committed within any State, the Trial shall be at such Place or Places as the Congress may by Law have directed.

SECTION 3. Treason against the United States, shall consist only in levying War against them, or in adhering to their Enemies, giving them Aid and Comfort. No Person shall be convicted of Treason unless on the Testimony of two Witnesses to the same overt Act, or on Confession in open Court.

The Congress shall have Power to declare the Punishment of Treason, but no Attainder of Treason shall work Corruption of Blood, or Forfeiture except during the Life of the Person attainted.

ARTICLE IV

SECTION 1. Full Faith and Credit shall be given in each State to the public Acts, Records, and judicial Proceedings of every other State. And the Congress may by general Laws prescribe the Manner in which such Acts, Records and Proceedings shall be proved, and the Effect thereof.

SECTION 2. The Citizens of each State shall be entitled to all Privileges and Immunities of Citizens in the several States.

A Person charged in any State with Treason, Felony, or other Crime, who shall flee from Justice, and be found in another State, shall on Demand of the executive Authority of the State from which he fled, be delivered up, to be removed to the State having Jurisdiction of the Crime.

No Person held to Service or Labour in one State under the Laws thereof, escaping into another, shall, in Consequence of any Law or Regulation therein, be discharged from such Service or Labour, but shall be delivered up on Claim of the Party to whom such Service or Labour may be due.

SECTION 3. New States may be admitted by the Congress into this Union; but no new State shall be formed or erected within the Jurisdiction of any other State; nor any State be formed by the Junction of two or more States, or Parts of States, without the Consent of the Legislatures of the States concerned as well as of the Congress.

The Congress shall have Power to dispose of and make all needful Rules and Regulations respecting the Territory or other Property belonging to the United States; and nothing in this Constitution shall be so construed as to Prejudice any Claims of the United States, or of any particular State.

SECTION 4. The United States shall guarantee to every State in this Union a Republican Form of Government, and shall protect each of them against Invasion, and on Application of the Legislature, or of the Executive (when the Legislature cannot be convened) against domestic Violence.

ARTICLE V

The Congress, whenever two thirds of both Houses shall deem it necessary, shall propose Amendments to this Constitution, or, on the Application of the Legislatures of two thirds of the several States, shall call a Convention for proposing Amendments, which, in either Case, shall be valid to all Intents and Purposes, as Part of this Constitution, when ratified by the Legislatures of three fourths of the several States, or by Conventions in three fourths thereof, as the one or the other Mode of Ratification may be proposed by the Congress; Provided that no Amendment which may be made prior to the Year One thousand eight hundred and eight shall in any Manner affect the first and fourth Clauses in the Ninth Section of the first Article; and that no State, without its Consent, shall be deprived of its equal Suffrage in the Senate.

ARTICLE VI

All Debts contracted and Engagements entered into, before the Adoption of this Constitution, shall be as valid against the United States under this Constitution, as under the Confederation.

This Constitution, and the laws of the United States which shall be made in Pursuance thereof; and all Treaties made, or which shall be made, under the Authority of the United States, shall be the supreme Law of the Land; and the Judges in every State shall be bound thereby, any Thing in the Constitution or Laws of any State to the Contrary notwithstanding.

The Senators and Representatives before mentioned, and the Members of the several State Legislatures, and all executive and judicial Officers, both of the United States and of the several States, shall be bound by Oath or Affirmation, to support this Constitution; but no religious Test shall ever be required as a Qualification to any Office or public Trust under the United States.

ARTICLE VII

The Ratification of the Conventions of nine States, shall be sufficient for the Establishment of this Constitution between the States so ratifying the Same.

Done in Convention by the Unanimous Consent of the States present the Seventeenth Day of September in the Year of our Lord one thousand seven hundred and Eighty seven and of the Independence of the United States of America the Twelfth. In witness whereof we have hereunto subscribed our Names,

GO. WASHINGTON
Presid't. and deputy from Virginia

Attest

WILLIAM JACKSON
Secretary

Articles in addition to, and amendment of the Constitution of the United States of America, proposed by Congress and ratified by the Legislatures of the several states, pursuant to the Fifth Article of the original Constitution.

(The first ten amendments were passed by Congress on September 25, 1789, and were ratified on December 15, 1791.)

AMENDMENT I

Congress shall make no law respecting an establishment of religion, or prohibiting the free exercise thereof; or abridging the freedom of speech, or of the press; or the right of the people peaceably to assemble, and to petition the Government for a redress of grievances.

AMENDMENT II

A well regulated Militia, being necessary to the security of a free State, the right of the people to keep and bear Arms, shall not be infringed.

AMENDMENT III

No Soldier shall, in time of peace be quartered in any house, without the consent of the Owner, nor in time of war, but in a manner to be prescribed by law.

AMENDMENT IV

The right of the people to be secure in their persons, houses, papers, and effects, against unreasonable searches and seizures, shall not be violated, and no warrants shall issue, but upon probable cause, supported by Oath or affirmation, and particularly describing the place to be searched, and the persons or things to be seized.

AMENDMENT V

No person shall be held to answer for a capital, or otherwise infamous crime, unless on a presentment or indictment of a Grand Jury, except in cases arising in the land or naval forces, or in the Militia, when in actual service in time of War or public danger; nor shall any person be subject for the same offence to be twice put in jeopardy of life or limb; nor shall be compelled in any criminal case to be a witness against himself, nor be deprived of life, liberty, or property, without due process of law; nor shall private property be taken for public use, without just compensation.

AMENDMENT VI

In all criminal prosecutions, the accused shall enjoy the right to a speedy and public trial, by an impartial jury of the State and district wherein the crime shall have been committed, which district shall have been previously ascertained by law, and to be informed of the nature and cause of the accusation; to be confronted with the witnesses against him; to have compulsory process for obtaining witnesses in his favor, and to have the assistance of counsel for his defence.

AMENDMENT VII

In Suits at common law, where the value in controversy shall exceed twenty dollars, the right of trial by jury shall be preserved, and no fact tried by a jury, shall be otherwise re-examined in any Court of the United States, than according to the rules of the common law.

AMENDMENT VIII

Excessive bail shall not be required, nor excessive fines imposed, nor cruel and unusual punishments inflicted.

AMENDMENT IX

The enumeration in the Constitution, of certain rights, shall not be construed to deny or disparage others retained by the people.

AMENDMENT X

The powers not delegated to the United States by the Constitution, nor prohibited by it to the States, are reserved to the States respectively, or to the people.

AMENDMENT XI
(Ratified on February 7, 1795)

The Judicial power of the United States shall not be construed to extend to any suit in law or equity, commenced or prosecuted against one of the United States by Citizens of another State, or by Citizens or Subjects of any Foreign State.

AMENDMENT XII
(Ratified on June 15, 1804)

The Electors shall meet in their respective states, and vote by ballot for President and Vice-President, one of whom, at least, shall not be an inhabitant of the same state with themselves; they shall name in their ballots the person voted for as President, and in distinct ballots the person voted for as Vice-President, and they shall make distinct lists of all persons voted for as President, and of all persons voted for as Vice-President, and of the number of votes for each, which lists they shall sign and certify, and transmit sealed to the seat of the government of the United States, directed to the President of the Senate;—The President of the Senate shall, in the presence of the Senate and House of Representatives, open all the certificates and the votes shall then be counted;—The person having the greatest number of votes for President, shall be the President, if such number be a majority of the whole number of Electors appointed; and if no person have such majority; then from the persons having the highest numbers not exceeding three on the list of those voted for as President, the House of Representatives shall choose immediately, by ballot, the President. But in choosing the President, the votes shall be taken by states, the representation from each state having one vote; a quorum for this purpose shall consist of a member or members from two-thirds of the states, and a majority of all the states shall be necessary to a choice. And if the House of Representatives shall not choose a President whenever the right of choice shall devolve upon them, before the fourth day of March next following, then the Vice-President shall act as President, as in the case of the death or other constitutional disability of the President.—The person having the greatest number of votes as Vice-President, shall be the Vice-President, if such number be a majority of the whole number of Electors appointed, and if no person have a majority, then from the two highest numbers on the list, the Senate shall choose the Vice-President; a quorum for the purpose shall consist of two-thirds of the whole number of Senators, and a majority of the whole number shall be necessary to a choice. But no person constitutionally ineligible to the office of President shall be eligible to that of Vice-President of the United States.

AMENDMENT XIII
(Ratified on December 6, 1865)

SECTION 1. Neither slavery nor involuntary servitude, except as a punishment for crime whereof the party shall have been duly convicted, shall exist within the United States, or any place subject to their jurisdiction.

SECTION 2. Congress shall have power to enforce this article by appropriate legislation.

AMENDMENT XIV
(Ratified on July 9, 1868)

SECTION 1. All persons born or naturalized in the United States, and subject to the jurisdiction thereof, are citizens of the United States and of the State wherein they reside. No State shall make or enforce any law which shall abridge the privileges or immunities of citizens of the United States; nor shall any State deprive any person of life, liberty, or property, without due process of law; nor deny to any person within its jurisdiction the equal protection of the laws.

SECTION 2. Representatives shall be apportioned among the several States according to their respective numbers, counting the whole number of persons in each State, excluding Indians not taxed. But when the right to vote at any election for the choice of electors for President and Vice President of the United States, Representatives in Congress, the Executive and Judicial officers of a State, or the members of the Legislature thereof, is denied to any of the male inhabitants of such State, being twenty-one years of age, and citizens of the United States, or in any way abridged, except for participation in rebellion, or other crime, the basis of representation therein shall be reduced in the proportion which the number of such male citizens shall bear to the whole number of male citizens twenty-one years of age in such State.

SECTION 3. No person shall be a Senator or Representative in Congress, or elector of President and Vice President, or hold any office, civil or military, under the United States, or under any State, who, having previously taken an oath, as a member of Congress, or as an officer of the United States, or as a member of any State legislature, or as an executive or judicial officer of any State, to support the Constitution of the United States, shall have engaged in insurrection or rebellion against the same, or given aid or comfort to the enemies thereof. But Congress may by a vote of two-thirds of each House, remove such disability.

SECTION 4. The validity of the public debt of the United States, authorized by law, including debts incurred for payment of pensions and bounties for services in suppressing insurrection or rebellion, shall not be questioned. But neither the United States nor any State shall assume or pay any debt or obligation incurred in aid of insurrection or rebellion against the United States, or any claim for the loss or emancipation of any slave, but all such debts, obligations and claims shall be held illegal and void.

SECTION 5. The Congress shall have power to enforce, by appropriate legislation, the provisions of this article.

AMENDMENT XV
(Ratified on February 3, 1870)

SECTION 1. The right of citizens of the United States to vote shall not be denied or abridged by the United States or by any State on account of race, color, or previous condition of servitude.

SECTION 2. The Congress shall have power to enforce this article by appropriate legislation.

AMENDMENT XVI
(Ratified on February 3, 1913)

The Congress shall have power to lay and collect taxes on incomes, from whatever source derived, without apportionment among the several States, and without regard to any census or enumeration.

AMENDMENT XVII
(Ratified on April 8, 1913)

The Senate of the United States shall be composed of two Senators from each State, elected by the people thereof, for six years; and each Senator shall have one vote. The electors in each State shall have the qualifications requisite for electors of the most numerous branch of the State legislatures.

When vacancies happen in the representation of any State in the Senate, the executive authority of such State shall issue writs of election to fill such vacancies: Provided, That the legislature of any State may empower the executive thereof to make temporary appointments until the people fill the vacancies by election as the legislature may direct.

This amendment shall not be so construed as to affect the election or term of any Senator chosen before it becomes valid as part of the Constitution.

AMENDMENT XVIII
(Ratified on January 16, 1919)

SECTION 1. After one year from the ratification of this article the manufacture, sale, or transportation of intoxicating liquors within, the importation thereof into, or the exportation thereof from the United States and all territory subject to the jurisdiction thereof for beverage purposes is hereby prohibited.

SECTION 2. The Congress and the several States shall have concurrent power to enforce this article by appropriate legislation.

SECTION 3. This article shall be inoperative unless it shall have been ratified as an amendment to the Constitution by the legislatures of the several States, as provided in the Constitution, within seven years from the date of the submission hereof to the States by the Congress.

AMENDMENT XIX
(Ratified on August 18, 1920)

The right of citizens of the United States to vote shall not be denied or abridged by the United States or by any State on account of sex.

Congress shall have power to enforce this article by appropriate legislation.

AMENDMENT XX
(Ratified on February 6, 1933)

SECTION 1. The terms of the President and Vice President shall end at noon on the 20th day of January, and the terms of Senators and Representatives at noon on the 3d day of January, of the years in which such terms would have ended if this article had not been ratified; and the terms of their successors shall then begin.

SECTION 2. The Congress shall assemble at least once in every year, and such meeting shall begin at noon on the 3d day of January, unless they shall by law appoint a different day.

SECTION 3. If, at the time fixed for the beginning of the term of the President, the President elect shall have died, the Vice President elect shall become President. If a President shall not have been chosen before the time fixed for the beginning of his term, or if the President elect shall have failed to qualify, then the Vice President elect shall act as President until a President shall have qualified; and the Congress may by law provide for the case wherein neither a President elect nor a Vice President elect shall have qualified, declaring who shall then act as President, or the manner in which one who is to act shall be selected, and such person shall act accordingly until a President or Vice President shall have qualified.

SECTION 4. The Congress may by law provide for the case of the death of any of the persons from whom the House of Representatives may choose a President whenever the rights of choice shall have devolved upon them, and for the case of the death of any of the persons from whom the Senate may choose a Vice President whenever the right of choice shall have devolved upon them.

SECTION 5. Sections 1 and 2 shall take effect on the 15th day of October following the ratification of this article.

SECTION 6. This article shall be inoperative unless it shall have been ratified as an amendment to the Constitution by the legislatures of three-fourths of the several States within seven years from the date of its submission.

AMENDMENT XXI
(Ratified on December 5, 1933)

SECTION 1. The eighteenth article of amendment to the Constitution of the United States is hereby repealed.

SECTION 2. The transportation or importation into any State, Territory, or possession of the United States for delivery or use therein of intoxicating liquors, in violation of the laws thereof, is hereby prohibited.

SECTION 3. This article shall be inoperative unless it shall have been ratified as an amendment to the Constitution by conventions in the several States, as provided in the Constitution, within seven years from the date of the submission hereof to the States by the Congress.

AMENDMENT XXII
(Ratified on February 27, 1951)

No person shall be elected to the office of the President more than twice, and no person who has held the office of President, or acted as President, for more than two years of a term to which some other person was elected President shall be elected to the office of the President more than once. But this Article shall not apply to any person holding the office of President when this Article was proposed by the Congress, and shall not prevent any person who may be holding the office of President, or acting as President, during the term within which this Article becomes operative from holding the office of President or acting as President during the remainder of such term.

AMENDMENT XXIII
(Ratified on March 29, 1961)

SECTION 1. The District constituting the seat of Government of the United States shall appoint in such manner as the Congress may direct:
A number of electors of President and Vice President equal to the whole number of Senators and Representatives in Congress to which the District would be entitled if it were a State, but in no event more than the least populous State; they shall be in addition to those appointed by the States, but they shall be considered, for the purposes of the election of President and Vice President, to be electors appointed by a State; and they shall meet in the District and perform such duties as provided by the twelfth article of amendment.

SECTION 2. The Congress shall have power to enforce this article by appropriate legislation.

AMENDMENT XXIV
(Ratified on January 23, 1964)

SECTION 1. The right of citizens of the United States to vote in any primary or other election for President or Vice President, for electors for President or Vice President, or for Senator or

Representative in Congress, shall not be denied or abridged by the United States or any State by reason of failure to pay any poll tax or other tax.

SECTION 2. The Congress shall have power to enforce this article by appropriate legislation.

AMENDMENT XXV
(Ratified on February 10, 1967)

SECTION 1. In case of the removal of the President from office or of his death or resignation, the Vice President shall become President.

SECTION 2. Whenever there is a vacancy in the office of the Vice President, the President shall nominate a Vice President who shall take office upon confirmation by a majority vote of both Houses of Congress.

SECTION 3. Whenever the President transmits to the President pro tempore of the Senate and the Speaker of the House of Representatives his written declaration that he is unable to discharge the powers and duties of his office, and until he transmits to them a written declaration to the contrary, such powers and duties shall be discharged by the Vice President as Acting President.

SECTION 4. Whenever the Vice President and a majority of either the principal officers of the executive departments or of such other body as Congress may by law provide, transmit to the President pro tempore of the Senate and the Speaker of the House of Representatives their written declaration that the President is unable to discharge the powers and duties of his office, the Vice President shall immediately assume the powers and duties of the office as Acting President.

Thereafter, when the President transmits to the President pro tempore of the Senate and the Speaker of the House of Representatives his written declaration that no inability exists, he shall resume the powers and duties of his office unless the Vice President and a majority of either the principal officers of the executive department or of such other body as Congress may by law provide, transmit within four days to the President pro tempore of the Senate and the Speaker of the House of Representatives their written declaration that the President is unable to discharge the powers and duties of his office. Thereupon Congress shall decide the issue, assembling within forty-eight hours for that purpose if not in session. If the Congress, within twenty-one days after receipt of the latter written declaration, or, if Congress is not in session, within twenty-one days after Congress is required to assemble, determines by two-thirds vote of both Houses that the President is unable to discharge the powers and duties of his office, the Vice President shall continue to discharge the same as Acting President; otherwise, the President shall resume the powers and duties of his office.

AMENDMENT XXVI
(Ratified on July 1, 1971)

SECTION 1. The right of citizens of the United States, who are eighteen years of age or older, to vote shall not be denied or abridged by the United States or by any State on account of age.

SECTION 2. The Congress shall have power to enforce this article by appropriate legislation.

AMENDMENT XXVII
(Ratified on May 7, 1992)

No law varying the compensation for the services of Senators and Representatives shall take effect until an election of Representatives shall have intervened.

Appendix III

The Federalist No. 10

November 22, 1787

James Madison

TO THE PEOPLE OF THE STATE OF NEW YORK.

Among the numerous advantages promised by a well constructed Union, none deserves to be more accurately developed than its tendency to break and control the violence of faction. The friend of popular governments, never finds himself so much alarmed for their character and fate, as when he contemplates their propensity to this dangerous vice. He will not fail therefore to set a due value on any plan which, without violating the principles to which he is attached, provides a proper cure for it. The instability, injustice and confusion introduced into the public councils, have in truth been the mortal diseases under which popular governments have every where perished; as they continue to be the favorite and fruitful topics from which the adversaries to liberty derive their most specious declamations. The valuable improvements made by the American Constitutions on the popular models, both ancient and modern, cannot certainly be too much admired; but it would be an unwarrantable partiality, to contend that they have as effectually obviated the danger on this side as was wished and expected. Complaints are every where heard from our most considerate and virtuous citizens, equally the friends of public and private faith, and of public and personal liberty; that our governments are too unstable; that the public good is disregarded in the conflicts of rival parties; and that measures are too often decided, not according to the rules of justice, and the rights of the minor party; but by the superior force of an interested and over-bearing majority. However anxiously we may wish that these complaints had no foundation, the evidence of known facts will not permit us to deny that they are in some degree true. It will be found indeed, on a candid review of our situation, that some of the distresses under which we labor, have been erroneously charged on the operation of our governments; but it will be found, at the same time, that other causes will not alone account for many of our heaviest misfortunes; and particularly, for that prevailing and increasing distrust of public engagements, and alarm for private rights, which are echoed from one end of the continent to the other. These must be chiefly, if not wholly, effects of the unsteadiness and injustice, with which a factious spirit has tainted our public administrations.

By a faction I understand a number of citizens, whether amounting to a majority or minority of the whole, who are united and actuated by some common impulse of passion, or of interest, adverse to the rights of other citizens, or to the permanent and aggregate interests of the community.

There are two methods of curing the mischiefs of faction: the one, by removing its causes; the other, by controlling its effects.

There are again two methods of removing the causes of faction: the one by destroying the liberty which is essential to its existence; the other, by giving to every citizen the same opinions, the same passions, and the same interests.

It could never be more truly said than of the first remedy, that it is worse than the disease. Liberty is to faction, what air is to fire, an aliment without which it instantly expires. But it could not be a less folly to abolish liberty, which is essential to political life, because it nourishes faction, than it would be to wish the annihilation of air, which is essential to animal life, because it imparts to fire its destructive agency.

The second expedient is as impracticable, as the first would be unwise. As long as the reason of man continues fallible, and he is at liberty to exercise it, different opinions will be formed. As long as the connection subsists between his reason and his self-love, his opinions and his passions will have a reciprocal influence on each other; and the former will be objects to which the latter will attach themselves. The diversity in the faculties of men from which the rights of property originate, is not less an insuperable obstacle to a uniformity of interests. The protection of these faculties is the first object of Government. From the protection of different and unequal faculties of acquiring property, the possession of different degrees and kinds of property immediately results: and from the influence of these on the sentiments and views of the respective proprietors, ensues a division of the society into different interests and parties.

The latent causes of faction are thus sown in the nature of man; and we see them every where brought into different degrees of activity, according to the different circumstances of civil society. A zeal for different opinions concerning religion, concerning Government and many other points, as well of speculation as of practice; an attachment to different leaders ambitiously contending for pre-eminence and power; or to persons of other descriptions whose fortunes have been interesting to the human passions, have in turn divided mankind into parties, inflamed them with mutual animosity, and rendered them much more disposed to vex and oppress each other, than to cooperate for their common good. So strong is this propensity of mankind to fall into mutual animosities, that where no substantial occasion presents itself, the most frivolous and fanciful distinctions have been sufficient to kindle their unfriendly passions, and excite their most violent conflicts. But the most common and durable source of factions, has been the various and unequal distribution of property. Those who hold, and those who are without property, have ever formed distinct interests in society. Those who are creditors, and those who are debtors, fall under a like discrimination. A landed interest, a manufacturing interest, a mercantile interest, a monied interest, with many lesser interests, grow up of necessity in civilized nations, and divide them into different classes, actuated by different sentiments and views. The regulation of these various and interfering interests forms the principal task of modern Legislation, and involves the spirit of party and faction in the necessary and ordinary operations of Government.

No man is allowed to be a judge in his own cause; because his interest would certainly bias his judgment, and, not improbably, corrupt his integrity. With equal, nay with greater reason, a body of men, are unfit to be both judges and parties, at the same time; yet, what are many of the most important acts of legislation, but so many judicial determinations, not indeed concerning the rights of single persons, but concerning the rights of large bodies of citizens, and what are the different classes of legislators, but advocates and parties to the causes which they determine? Is a law proposed concerning private debts? It is a question to which the creditors are parties on one side, and the debtors on the other. Justice ought to hold the balance between them. Yet the parties are and must be themselves the judges; and the most numerous party, or, in other words, the most powerful faction must be expected to prevail. Shall domestic manufactures be encouraged, and in what degree, by restrictions on foreign manufactures? are questions which would be differently decided by the landed and the manufacturing classes; and probably by neither, with a sole regard to justice and the public good. The apportionment of taxes on the various descriptions of property, is an act which seems to require the most exact impartiality; yet, there is perhaps no legislative act in which greater opportunity and temptation are given to a predominant party, to trample on the rules of justice. Every shilling with which they over-burden the inferior number, is a shilling saved to their own pockets.

It is in vain to say, that enlightened statesmen will be able to adjust these clashing interests, and render them all subservient to the public good. Enlightened statesmen will not always be at the helm: Nor, in many cases, can such an adjustment be made at all, without taking into view indirect and remote considerations, which will rarely prevail over the immediate interest which one party may find in disregarding the rights of another, or the good of the whole.

The inference to which we are brought, is, that the causes of faction cannot be removed; and that relief is only to be sought in the means of controlling its effects.

If a faction consists of less than a majority, relief is supplied by the republican principle, which enables the majority to defeat its sinister views by regular vote: It may clog the administration, it may convulse the society; but it will be unable to execute and mask its violence under the forms of the Constitution. When a majority is included in a faction, the form of popular government on the other hand enables it to sacrifice to its ruling passion or interest, both the public good and the rights of other citizens. To secure the public good, and private rights, against the danger of such a faction, and at the same time to preserve the spirit and the form of popular government, is then the great object to which our enquiries are directed: Let me add that it is the great desideratum, by which alone this form of government can be rescued from the opprobrium under which it has so long labored, and be recommended to the esteem and adoption of mankind.

By what means is this object attainable? Evidently by one of two only. Either the existence of the same passion or interest in a majority at the same time, must be prevented; or the majority, having such co-existent passion or interest, must be rendered, by their number and local situation, unable to concert and carry into effect schemes of oppression. If the impulse and the opportunity be suffered to coincide, we well know that neither moral nor religious motives can be relied on as an adequate control. They are not found to be such on the injustice and violence of individuals, and lose their efficacy in proportion to the number combined together; that is, in proportion as their efficacy becomes needful.

From this view of the subject, it may be concluded, that a pure Democracy, by which I mean, a Society, consisting of a small number of citizens, who assemble and administer the Government in person, can admit of no cure for the mischiefs of faction. A common passion or interest will, in almost every case, be felt by a majority of the whole; a communication and concert results from the form of Government itself; and there is nothing to check the inducements to sacrifice the weaker party, or an obnoxious individual. Hence it is, that such Democracies have ever been spectacles of turbulence and contention; have ever been found incompatible with personal security, or the rights of property; and have in general been as short in their lives, as they have been violent in their deaths. Theoretic politicians, who have patronized this species of Government, have erroneously supposed, that by reducing mankind to a perfect equality in their political rights, they would, at the same time, be perfectly equalized and assimilated in their possessions, their opinions, and their passions.

A republic, by which I mean a government in which the scheme of representation takes place, opens a different prospect, and promises the cure for which we are seeking. Let us examine the points in which it varies from pure democracy, and we shall comprehend both the nature of the cure and the efficacy which it must derive from the union.

The two great points of difference, between a democracy and a republic, are, first, the delegation of the government, in the latter, to a small number of citizens, elected by the rest; secondly, the greater number of citizens, and greater sphere of country, over which the latter may be extended.

The effect of the first difference is, on the one hand, to refine and enlarge the public views, by passing them through the medium of a chosen body of citizens, whose wisdom may best discern the true interest of their country, and whose patriotism and love of justice, will be least likely to sacrifice it to temporary or partial considerations. Under such a regulation, it may well happen, that the public voice, pronounced by the representatives of the people, will be more consonant to the public good, than if pronounced by the people themselves, convened for the purpose. On the other hand the effect may be inverted. Men of factious tempers, of local prejudices, or of sinister designs, may by intrigue, by corruption, or by other means, first obtain the suffrages, and then betray the interest of the people. The question resulting is, whether small or extensive republics are most favorable to the election of proper guardians of the public weal, and it is clearly decided in favor of the latter by two obvious considerations.

In the first place, it is to be remarked that, however small the republic may be, the representatives must be raised to a certain number, in order to guard against the cabals of a few; and that however large it may be, they must be limited to a certain number, in order to guard against the confusion of a multitude. Hence, the number of representatives in the two cases not being in proportion to that of the constituents, and being proportionally greatest in the small republic, it follows, that if the proportion of fit characters be not less in the large than in the small republic, the former will present a greater option, and consequently a greater probability of a fit choice.

In the next place, as each Representative will be chosen by a greater number of citizens in the large than in the small Republic, it will be more difficult for unworthy candidates to practise with success the vicious arts, by which elections are too often carried; and the suffrages of the people being more free, will be more likely to center on men who possess the most attractive merit, and the most diffusive and established characters.

It must be confessed, that in this, as in most other cases, there is a mean, on both sides of which inconveniences will be found to lie. By enlarging too much the number of electors, you render the representatives too little acquainted with all their local circumstances and lesser interests; as by reducing it too much, you render him unduly attached to these, and too little fit to comprehend and pursue great and national objects. The Federal Constitution forms a happy combination in this respect; the great and aggregate interests being referred to the national, the local and particular, to the state legislatures.

The other point of difference is, the greater number of citizens and extent of territory which may be brought within the compass of Republican, than of Democratic Government; and it is this circumstance principally which renders factious combinations less to be dreaded in the former, than in the latter. The smaller the society, the fewer probably will be the distinct parties and interests composing it; the fewer the distinct parties and interests, the more frequently will a majority be found of the same party; and the smaller the number of individuals composing a majority, and the smaller the compass within which they are placed, the more easily will they concert and execute their plans of oppression. Extend the sphere, and you take in a greater variety of parties and interests; you make it less probable that a majority of the whole will have a common motive to invade the rights of other citizens; or if such a common motive exists, it will be more difficult for all who feel it to discover their own strength, and to act in unison with each other. Besides other impediments, it may be remarked, that where there is a consciousness of unjust or dishonorable purposes, communication is always checked by distrust, in proportion to the number whose concurrence is necessary.

Hence it clearly appears, that the same advantage, which a Republic has over a Democracy, in controlling the effects of faction, is enjoyed by a large over a small Republic—is enjoyed by the Union over the States composing it. Does this advantage consist in the substitution of Representatives, whose enlightened views and virtuous sentiments render them superior to local prejudices, and to schemes of injustice? It will not be denied, that the Representation of the Union will be most likely to possess these requisite endowments. Does it consist in the greater security afforded by a greater variety of parties, against the event of any one party being able to outnumber and oppress the rest? In an equal degree does the increased variety of parties, comprised within the Union, increase this security? Does it, in fine, consist in the greater obstacles opposed to the concert and accomplishment of the secret wishes of an unjust and interested majority? Here, again, the extent of the Union gives it the most palpable advantage.

The influence of factious leaders may kindle a flame within their particular States, but will be unable to spread a general conflagration through the other States: a religious sect, may degenerate into a political faction in a part of the Confederacy but the variety of sects dispersed over the entire face of it, must secure the national Councils against any danger from that source: a rage for paper money, for an abolition of debts, for an equal division of property, or for any other improper or wicked project, will be less apt to pervade the whole body of the Union, than a particular member of it; in the same proportion as such a malady is more likely to taint a particular county or district, than an entire State.

In the extent and proper structure of the Union, therefore, we behold a Republican remedy for the diseases most incident to Republican Government. And according to the degree of pleasure and pride, we feel in being Republicans, ought to be our zeal in cherishing the spirit, and supporting the character of Federalists.

PUBLIUS

Appendix IV

The Federalist No. 51

February 6, 1788

James Madison

TO THE PEOPLE OF THE STATE OF NEW YORK.

To what expedient then shall we finally resort for maintaining in practice the necessary partition of power among the several departments, as laid down in the constitution? The only answer that can be given is, that as all these exterior provisions are found to be inadequate, the defect must be supplied, by so contriving the interior structure of the government, as that its several constituent parts may, by their mutual relations, be the means of keeping each other in their proper places. Without presuming to undertake a full development of this important idea, I will hazard a few general observations, which may perhaps place it in a clearer light, and enable us to form a more correct judgment of the principles and structure of the government planned by the convention.

In order to lay a due foundation for that separate and distinct exercise of the different powers of government, which to a certain extent, is admitted on all hands to be essential to the preservation of liberty, it is evident that each department should have a will of its own; and consequently should be so constituted, that the members of each should have as little agency as possible in the appointment of the members of the others. Were this principle rigorously adhered to, it would require that all the appointments for the supreme executive, legislative, and judiciary magistracies, should be drawn from the same fountain of authority, the people, through channels, having no communication whatever with one another. Perhaps such a plan of constructing the several departments would be less difficult in practice than it may in contemplation appear. Some difficulties however, and some additional expense, would attend the execution of it. Some deviations therefore from the principle must be admitted. In the constitution of the judiciary department in particular, it might be inexpedient to insist rigorously on the principle; first, because peculiar qualifications being essential in the members, the primary consideration ought to be to select that mode of choice, which best secures these qualifications; secondly, because the permanent tenure by which the appointments are held in that department, must soon destroy all sense of dependence on the authority conferring them.

It is equally evident that the members of each department should be as little dependent as possible on those of the others, for the emoluments annexed to their offices. Were the executive magistrate, or the judges, not independent of the legislature in this particular, their independence in every other would be merely nominal.

But the great security against a gradual concentration of the several powers in the same department, consists in giving to those who administer each department, the necessary constitutional means, and personal motives, to resist encroachments of the others. The provision for defense must in this, as in all other cases, be made commensurate to the danger of attack. Ambition must be made to counteract ambition. The interest of the man must be connected with the constitutional right of the place. It may be a reflection on human nature, that such devices should be necessary to control the abuses of government. But what is government itself but the greatest of all reflections on human nature? If men were angels, no government would be necessary. If angels were to govern men, neither external nor internal controls on government would be necessary. In framing a government which is to be administered by men over men, the great difficulty lies in this: You must first enable the government to control the governed; and in the next place, oblige it to control itself. A dependence on the people is no doubt the primary control on the government; but experience has taught mankind the necessity of auxiliary precautions.

This policy of supplying by opposite and rival interests, the defect of better motives, might be traced through the whole system of human affairs, private as well as public. We see it particularly displayed in all the subordinate distributions of power; where the constant aim is to divide and arrange the several offices in such a manner as that each may be a check on the other; that the private interest of every individual, may be a sentinel over the public rights. These inventions of prudence cannot be less requisite in the distribution of the supreme powers of the state.

But it is not possible to give to each department an equal power of self defense. In republican government the legislative authority, necessarily, predominates. The remedy for this inconveniency is, to divide the legislature into different branches; and to render them by different modes of election, and different principles of action, as little connected with each other, as the nature of their common functions, and their common dependence on the society, will admit. It may even be necessary to guard against dangerous encroachments by still further precautions. As the weight of the legislative authority requires that it should be thus divided, the weakness of the executive may require, on the other hand, that it should be fortified. An absolute negative, on the legislature, appears at first view to be the natural defense with which the executive magistrate should be armed. But perhaps it would be neither altogether safe, nor alone sufficient. On ordinary occasions, it might not be exerted with the requisite firmness; and on extraordinary occasions, it might be perfidiously abused. May not this defect of an absolute negative be supplied, by some qualified connection between this weaker department, and the weaker branch of the stronger department, by which the latter may be led to support the constitutional rights of the former, without being too much detached from the rights of its own department?

If the principles on which these observations are founded be just, as I persuade myself they are, and they be applied as a criterion, to the several state constitutions, and to the federal constitution, it will be found, that if the latter does not perfectly correspond with them, the former are infinitely less able to bear such a test.

There are moreover two considerations particularly applicable to the federal system of America, which place that system in a very interesting point of view.

First. In a single republic, all the power surrendered by the people, is submitted to the administration of a single government; and usurpations are guarded against by a division of the government into distinct and separate departments. In the compound republic of America, the power surrendered by the people, is first divided between two distinct governments, and then the portion allotted to each, subdivided among distinct and separate departments. Hence a double security arises to the rights of the people. The different governments will control each other; at the same time that each will be controlled by itself.

Second. It is of great importance in a republic, not only to guard the society against the oppression of its rulers; but to guard one part of the society against the injustice of the other part. Different interests necessarily exist in different classes of citizens. If a majority be united by a common interest, the rights of the minority will be insecure. There are but two methods of providing against this evil: The one by creating a will in the community independent of the majority, that is, of the society itself; the other by comprehending in the society so many separate descriptions of citizens, as will render an unjust combination of a majority of the whole, very improbable, if not impracticable. The first method prevails in all governments possessing an hereditary or self appointed authority. This at best is but a precarious security; because a power independent of the society may as well espouse the unjust views of the major, as the rightful interests, of the minor party, and may possibly be turned against both parties. The second method will be exemplified in the federal republic of the United States. While all authority in it will be derived from and dependent on the society, the society itself will be broken into so many parts, interests and classes of citizens, that the rights of individuals or of the minority, will be in little danger from interested combinations of the majority. In a free government, the security for civil rights must be the same as for religious rights. It consists in the one case in the multiplicity of interests, and in the other, in the multiplicity of sects. The degree of security in both cases will depend on the number of interests and sects; and this may be presumed to depend on the extent of country and number of people comprehended under the same government. This view of the subject must particularly recommend a proper federal system to all the sincere and considerate friends of republican government: Since it shows that in exact proportion as the territory of the union may be formed into more circumscribed confederacies or states, oppressive combinations of a majority will be facilitated, the best security under the republican form, for the rights of every class of citizens, will be diminished; and consequently, the stability and independence of some member of the government, the only other security, must be proportionally increased. Justice is the end of government. It is the end of civil society. It ever has been, and ever will be pursued, until it be obtained, or until liberty be lost in the pursuit. In a society under the forms of which the stronger faction can readily unite and oppress the weaker, anarchy may as truly be said to reign, as in a state of nature where the weaker individual is not secured against the violence of the stronger: And as in the latter state even the stronger individuals are prompted by the uncertainty of their condition, to submit to a government which may protect the weak as well as themselves: So in the former state, will the more powerful factions or parties be gradually induced by a like motive, to wish for a government which will protect all parties, the weaker as well as the more powerful. It can be little doubted, that if the state of Rhode Island was separated from the confederacy, and left to itself, the insecurity of rights under the popular form of government within such narrow limits, would be displayed by such reiterated oppressions of factious majorities, that some power altogether independent of the people would soon be called for by the voice of the very factions whose misrule had proved the necessity of it. In the extended republic of the United States, and among the great variety of interests, parties and sects which it embraces, a coalition of a majority of the whole society could seldom take place on any other principles than those of justice and the general good; and there being thus less danger to a minor from the will of the major party, there must be less pretext also, to provide for the security of the former, by introducing into the government a will not dependent on the latter; or in other words, a will independent of the society itself. It is no less certain than it is important, notwithstanding the contrary opinions which have been entertained, that the larger the society, provided it lie within a practicable sphere, the more duly capable it will be of self government. And happily for the republican cause, the practicable sphere may be carried to a very great extent, by a judicious modification and mixture of the federal principle.

PUBLIUS

Appendix V

Presidents of the United States

President	Year	Party	Most Noteworthy Event
George Washington	1789–1797	Federalist	Establishment of Federal Judiciary
John Adams	1797–1801	Federalist	Alien-Sedition Acts
Thomas Jefferson	1801–1809	Dem.-Republican	First President to Defeat Incumbent/Louisiana Purchase
James Madison	1809–1817	Dem.-Republican	War of 1812
James Monroe	1817–1825	Dem.-Republican	Monroe Doctrine/ Missouri Compromise
John Quincy Adams	1825–1829	Dem.-Republican	Elected by "King Caucus"
Andrew Jackson	1829–1837	Democratic	Set up Spoils System
Martin Van Buren	1837–1841	Democratic	Competitive Parties Established
William H. Harrison	1841	Whig	Universal White Male Suffrage
John Tyler	1841–1845	Whig	Texas Annexed
James K. Polk	1845–1849	Democratic	Mexican-American War
Zachary Taylor	1849–1850	Whig	California Gold Rush
Millard Fillmore	1850–1853	Whig	Compromise of 1850
Franklin Pierce	1853–1857	Democratic	Republican Party Formed
James Buchanan	1857–1861	Democratic	Dred Scott Decision
Abraham Lincoln	1861–1865	Republican	Civil War
Andrew Johnson	1865–1869	Republican	First Impeachment of President
Ulysses S. Grant	1869–1877	Republican	Reconstruction of South
Rutherford B. Hayes	1877–1881	Republican	End of Reconstruction
James A. Garfield	1881	Republican	Assassinated by Job-seeker
Chester A. Arthur	1881–1885	Republican	Civil Service Reform
Grover Cleveland	1885–1889	Democratic	Casts 102 Vetoes in One Year
Benjamin Harrison	1889–1893	Republican	McKinley Law Raises Tarrifs
Grover Cleveland	1893–1897	Democratic	Depression/Pullman Strike
William McKinley	1897–1901	Republican	Spanish-American War
Theodore Roosevelt	1901–1909	Republican	Conservation/Panama Canal
William H. Taft	1909–1913	Republican	Judicial Reform
Woodrow Wilson	1913–1921	Democratic	Progressive Reforms/ World War I
Warren G. Harding	1921–1923	Republican	Return to Normalcy
Calvin Coolidge	1923–1929	Republican	Cuts Taxes/Promotes Business
Herbert C. Hoover	1929–1933	Republican	Great Depression
Franklin D. Roosevelt	1933–1945	Democratic	New Deal/ World War II
Harry S Truman	1945–1953	Democratic	Beginning of Cold War
Dwight D. Eisenhower	1953–1961	Republican	End of Korean War
John F. Kennedy	1961–1963	Democratic	Cuban Missile Crisis
Lyndon B. Johnson	1963–1969	Democratic	Great Society/Vietnam War
Richard M. Nixon	1969–1974	Republican	Watergate Scandal
Gerald R. Ford	1974–1977	Republican	War Powers Resolution
James Earl Carter	1977–1981	Democratic	Iranian Hostage Crisis
Ronald Reagan	1981–1989	Republican	Tax Cut/ Expenditure Cuts
George Bush	1989–1993	Republican	End of Cold War/Persian Gulf War
William J. Clinton	1993–2001	Democratic	Deficit Reduction
George W. Bush	2001–2008	Republican	U.S. Response to Terrorism
Barack Obama	2008–	Democratic	First African American President

Refer to www.ablongman.com.fiorina

Glossary

administration The president and his political appointees, who are responsible for directing the executive branch of government.

administrative discretion The power of a bureaucracy to interpret a legislative mandate.

advice and consent Support for a presidential action by a designated number of senators.

affirmative action Programs designed to enhance opportunities for race- or gender-based groups that have suffered discrimination in the past.

affirmative action redistricting The process of drawing district lines to maximize the number of majority-minority districts.

agency The basic organizational unit of federal government. Also known as *office* or *bureau*.

agenda setting Making an issue so visible that important political leaders take it seriously.

ambassador The head of a diplomatic delegation to a foreign country.

Annapolis Convention Meeting in 1786 to discuss constitutional reform.

Anti-Federalists Those who opposed ratification of the Constitution.

appeal The procedure whereby the losing side asks a higher court to overturn a lower-court decision.

appropriations process Process of providing funding for governmental activities and programs that have been authorized.

aristocracy A government by the few, in which the leaders are meritorious and chosen by virtue of their birth into noble families.

Articles of Confederation The first (1781–1789) basic governing document of the United States and forerunner to the Constitution.

associate justice One of the eight justices of the Supreme Court who are not the chief justice.

authorization process Term applied to the entire process of providing statutory authority for a government program or activity.

bad tendency test A rule from English law saying that expression could be punished if it could ultimately lead to illegal behavior.

balancing doctrine The principle enunciated by the Supreme Court that freedom of speech must be balanced against other competing public interests at stake in particular circumstances.

Bay of Pigs Location of CIA-supported effort by Cuban exiles in 1961 to invade Cuba and overthrow Fidel Castro.

beltway insider The politically influential people who work inside the highway that surrounds Washington, DC.

bicameral Containing two chambers, as does a legislature such as the U.S. Congress.

Bill of Rights The first ten amendments to the Constitution, which guarantee civil liberties and protect states' rights.

bipolar Cold war view of the world as divided into two centers of power, the United States and its allies, and the Soviet Union and its allies.

black codes Restrictive laws, passed in some southern states after the Civil War, that applied to newly freed slaves but not to whites.

blame avoidance Set of political techniques employed by political leaders to disguise their actions and shift blame to others.

bloc voting Voting in which nearly all members of an ethnic or racial group vote for the same candidate or party.

block grants Intergovernmental grants with a broad set of objectives, a minimum of federal restrictions, and maximum discretion for local officials.

borking Politicizing the nomination process through an organized public campaign that portrays the nominee as a dangerous extremist.

brief Written legal arguments presented to a court by lawyers on behalf of clients.

Brown v. Board of Education of Topeka, Kansas 1954 Supreme Court decision declaring racial segregation in schools unconstitutional.

budget The government's annual plan for taxing and spending.

bully pulpit The nature of presidential status as an ideal vehicle for persuading the public to support the president's policies.

bureaucracy Hierarchical organization of officials with responsibility for specific tasks.

business cycle The alternation of periods of economic growth with periods of economic slowdown.

cabinet Top administration officials, most of whom are heads of departments in the executive branch.

casework Efforts by members of Congress to help individuals and groups when they have difficulties with federal agencies.

categorical grants Federal grants to a state and/or local government that impose programmatic restrictions on the use of funds.

caucus A voluntary group within Congress, formed by members to pursue shared interests; a caucus can cross party, committee, and even chamber lines. Also meeting of candidate supporters who choose delegates to a state or national convention.

Central Intelligence Agency (CIA) Agency primarily responsible for gathering and analyzing information about the political and military activities of other nations.

cert See "writ of *certiorari*."

checks and balances Constitutional division of power into separate institutions, giving each institution the power to block the actions of the others.

chief justice Head of the Supreme Court.

chief of staff Head of the White House staff, who has continuous, direct contact with the president.

circuit court of appeals Court to which decisions by federal district courts are appealed.

citizenship Status held by someone entitled to all the rights and privileges of a full-fledged member of a political community.

civic republicanism A political philosophy that emphasizes the obligation of citizens to act virtuously in pursuit of the common good.

civil code Laws that regulate the legal rights and obligations of citizens with regard to one another. Alleged violators are sued by presumed victims, who ask courts to award damages and otherwise offer relief for injuries they claim to have suffered.

civil disobedience A peaceful, well-publicized violation of a law designed to dramatize that law's injustice.

civil liberties The fundamental freedoms that together preserve the rights of a free people.

civil rights Specific rights that embody the general right to equal treatment under the law.

civil rights amendments The Thirteenth, Fourteenth, and Fifteenth Amendments, which abolished slavery, redefined civil rights and liberties, and guaranteed the right to vote to all adult male citizens.

civil service A system in which government employees are chosen according to their educational qualifications, performance on examinations, and work experience.

class action suit Suit brought on behalf of all individuals in a particular category, regardless of whether they are actually participating in the suit.

clear and present danger doctrine The principle that people should have complete freedom of speech unless their language endangers the nation.

cloture Motion to end debate in the Senate; requires 60 votes to pass.

CNN effect Purported ability of TV to raise a foreign tragedy to national prominence by broadcasting vivid pictures.

coattails Positive electoral effect of a popular presidential candidate on congressional candidates of the president's party.

cold war The 43-year period (1946–1989) during which the United States and the Soviet Union threatened one another with mutual destruction by nuclear warfare.

colonial assembly Lower legislative chamber elected by male property owners in a colony.

colonial council Upper legislative chamber whose members were appointed by British officials upon the recommendation of the governor.

commander in chief The president in his constitutional role as head of the U.S. armed forces.

commerce clause Constitutional provision that gives Congress power to regulate commerce "among the states."

commercial speech Advertising or other speech made for business purposes; may be regulated.

compositional effect A shift in the behavior of a group that results from a change in the group's composition, rather than a change in the behavior of individuals already in the group.

concurring opinion A written opinion prepared by judges who vote with the majority but who wish either to disagree with some aspect of the majority opinion or to elaborate on the decision.

conference committee A group of representatives from both the House and the Senate who iron out the differences between the two chambers' versions of a bill or resolution.

Congressional Budget Office (CBO) Congressional agency that evaluates the president's budget as well as the budgetary implications of all other legislation.

Connecticut Compromise (also known as the "Great Compromise") Constitutional Convention proposal that created a House proportionate to population and a Senate in which all states were represented equally.

constituency service Efforts by members of Congress to secure federal funding for their districts and to help constituents when they have difficulties with federal agencies.

constituents Those people legally entitled to vote for an officeholder.

Constitution Basic governing document of the United States.

containment U.S. policy that attempted to stop the spread of Communism in the expectation that this system of government would eventually collapse on its own.

Council of Economic Advisers (CEA) Three economists who head up a professional staff that advises the president on economic policy.

criminal code Laws regulating relations between individuals and society. Alleged violators are prosecuted by the government.

critical election Election that marks the emergence of a new, lasting alignment of partisan support within the electorate.

debt The accumulation of annual deficits.

Declaration of Independence Document signed in 1776 asserting the political independence of the United States from Great Britain.

de facto **segregation** Segregation that occurs as the result of decisions by private individuals.

defendant One accused of violating the civil or criminal code.

deficit The amount by which annual spending exceeds revenue.

de jure **segregation** Racial segregation that is legally sanctioned.

delegate A representative who reflects the opinions of those who elected him or her to office.

democracy A government in which all citizens share power.

department A collection of federal agencies that reports to a secretary who serves in the president's cabinet.

Department of Defense Cabinet department responsible for managing the U.S. armed forces.

deregulation Removal of government rules that once controlled an industry.

devolution Return of governmental responsibilities to state and local governments.

dignified aspect According to Walter Bagehot, the aspect of government, including royalty and ceremony, that generates citizen respect and loyalty.

Dillon's rule Legal doctrine that local governments are mere creatures of the state.

diplomacy The conduct of negotiations between representatives of different nations.

direct action Everything from peaceful sit-ins and demonstrations to riots and even rebellion.

direct democracy A type of government in which all citizens participate personally in making government decisions.

direct mail Computer-generated letters, faxes, and other communications by interest groups to people who might be sympathetic to an appeal for money or support.

direct primary A method of choosing party candidates that allows voters instead of party leaders to choose nominees for office; it weakened party control of nominations and the influence that parties could exercise over officeholders. This method of nominating candidates is virtually unknown outside the United States.

dissenting opinion A written opinion presenting the reasoning of judges who vote against the majority.

district attorney Person responsible for prosecuting criminal cases.

divided government Government in which one party holds the presidency but does not control both houses of Congress.

divine right Doctrine that says God selects the sovereign for the people.

domestic policy All government programs and regulations that directly affect those living within a country.

double jeopardy Fifth Amendment provision that prohibits prosecution for the same offense twice.

dual sovereignty A theory of federalism saying that both the national and state governments have final authority over their own policy domains.

due process clause Clause found in the Fifth and Fourteenth Amendments to the Constitution; forbids deprivation of life, liberty, or property without due process of law.

earmark In an agency's budget, a specific congressional designation of the way money is to be spent.

Earned Income Tax Credit (EITC) Program that gives back tax payments to those who have little income.

efficient aspect According to Walter Bagehot, the aspect of government that involves making policy, administering the laws, and settling disputes.

election-cycle interpretation The argument that, whatever their party, presidents attempt to slow the economy early in their terms and then to expand it as their opportunity for re-election approaches.

electoral college Those chosen to cast a direct vote for president by a process determined by each state.

electoral incentive Desire to be elected or re-elected to office.

electoral system The way in which a country's constitution or laws translate popular votes into control of public offices.

electoral vote Cast by electors, with each state receiving one vote for each of its members in the House of Representatives and one vote for each of its members in the Senate.

embassy The structure that houses ambassadors and their diplomatic aides in the capital cities of foreign countries.

end run An agency's effort to avoid OMB controls by appealing to its allies in Congress.

Environmental Protection Agency (EPA) Agency responsible for issuing regulations designed to protect the environment from pollutants.

equal protection clause Fourteenth Amendment clause specifying that no state can deny any of its people equal protection under the law.

Equal Rights Amendment (ERA) Proposed amendment to the Constitution that banned gender discrimination.

equal-time rule Licensing condition promulgated by the FCC requiring any station that gave or sold time to a legally qualified candidate for public office to make equal time available to all such candidates on equal terms.

equality of condition The notion that all individuals have a right to a more or less equal part of the material goods that society produces.

equality of opportunity The notion that individuals should have an equal chance to advance economically through their talent and hard work.

establishment of religion clause Clause denying the government the power to establish any single religious practice as superior.

ethnic cleansing Seeking to deport or eliminate entire ethnic groups from a country or region.

exclusionary rule Legal standard that says illegally obtained evidence cannot be admitted in court.

executive agreements Legal contracts with foreign countries that require only a presidential signature.

Executive Office of the President (EOP) Agency that houses both top coordinating offices and other operating agencies.

executive order A presidential directive that has the force of law, although it is not enacted by Congress.

executive privilege The right of the president to deny Congress information it requests on the grounds that the activities of the executive branch must be kept confidential.

externalities Any consequence of an activity that has an impact on those not responsible for the action.

527s Political organizations formed primarily to influence elections and therefore exempt from most federal taxes.

fairness doctrine FCC regulation, enforced between 1949 and 1987, that required stations to air contrasting viewpoints on matters of public importance and to give public figures who had been criticized on any of the station's programs a free opportunity to reply.

federal district courts The lowest tier of the federal court system and similar to the trial courts that exist in each state.

Federal Reserve Board The governing board of the country's central bank, which executes monetary policy by manipulating the supply of funds that member banks can lend.

federalism Division of sovereignty between at least two different levels of government.

Federalists Those who wrote and campaigned for ratification of the Constitution.

fighting words doctrine The principle, endorsed by the Supreme Court in *Chaplinsky v. New Hampshire* (1942), that some words constitute violent acts and are therefore not protected under the First Amendment.

filibuster Delaying tactic by which one or more senators refuse to allow a bill or resolution to be considered, either by speaking indefinitely or by offering dilatory motions and amendments.

filing deadline The latest date on which a candidate who wishes to be on a primary ballot may file official documents with and/or pay required fees to state election officials.

First Continental Congress Organized in 1774, the first quasi-governmental institution that spoke for nearly all the colonies.

first lady Traditional title of the president's wife.

fiscal policy The sum total of government taxing and spending decisions, which determines the level of the deficit or surplus.

focus groups Small groups of people brought together to talk about issues or candidates at length and in depth.

food stamps Public assistance program that provides recipients with stamps that can be used to purchase food. Formally named the Supplemental Nutrition Assistance Program (SNAP).

foreign policy Conduct of relations among nation-states.

foreign service Diplomats who staff U.S. embassies and consulates.

framing The way in which opinions about an issue can be altered by emphasizing or de-emphasizing particular facets of that issue.

franchise The right to vote.

frank Name given to representatives' and senators' free use of the U.S. mail for sending communications to constituents.

free exercise of religion clause Clause protecting the right of individuals to practice their religion without government interference.

free-rider problem Problem that arises when people can enjoy the benefits of group activity without bearing any of the costs.

fundamental freedoms doctrine The judicial doctrine stating that laws impinging on the freedoms that are fundamental to the preservation of democratic practice—the freedoms of speech, press, assembly, and religion—are to be scrutinized by the courts more closely than other legislation. These are also termed the preferred freedom.

general election Final election that selects an office-holder.

general revenue sharing The most comprehensive of block grants, which gives money to state and local governments to be used for any purpose whatsoever.

gerrymandering Drawing boundary lines of congressional districts in order to confer an advantage on some partisan or political interest.

Gideon v. Wainwright Supreme Court decision in 1963 stating that all citizens accused of serious crimes, even the indigent, are constitutionally entitled to legal representation.

glass ceiling The invisible barrier that has limited women's opportunities for advancement to the highest ranks of politics, business, and the professions.

government The institution in society holding a monopoly on the legitimate use of physical force.

government corporation Independent organization created by Congress to fulfill functions related to business.

governor A state's chief executive whose responsibilities roughly parallel those of the president.

grandfather clause Racially restrictive provision of certain southern laws after Reconstruction permitting a man to vote if his father or grandfather was eligible to vote before the Civil War.

grassroots lobbying Attempts by groups and associations to influence elected officials indirectly through their constituents.

Great Compromise See *Connecticut Compromise*.

hammer Harsh penalty set by Congress to be imposed if a regulatory agency does not achieve a statutory objective.

Hatch Act A 1939 law prohibiting federal employees from engaging in political campaigning and solicitation.

honeymoon The first several months of a presidency, when reporters are more forgiving than usual, Congress is more inclined to be cooperative, and the public is more receptive to new approaches.

idealists Those who say that U.S. foreign policy should be guided primarily by democratic principles—the spread of liberty, equality, human rights, and respect for international law throughout the world.

ideology A system of beliefs in which one or more organizing principles connect the individual's views on a wide range of particular issues.

impeachment Recommendation by a majority of the House of Representatives that a president, another official in the executive branch, or a judge of the federal courts be removed from office; removal depends on a two-thirds vote of the Senate.

implementation The way in which grant programs are administered at the local level.

in-and-outers Political appointees who come in, go out, and come back in again with each change in administration.

incumbency advantage The electoral advantage a candidate enjoys by virtue of being an incumbent, over and above his or her other personal and political characteristics.

independent counsel Legal officer (originally called special prosecutor) appointed by a court to investigate allegations of criminal activity on the part of high-ranking members of the executive branch.

independent regulatory agencies Agencies with quasi-judicial responsibilities that are meant to be carried out in a manner free of presidential interference.

inflation A sustained rise in price levels such that people need more money to purchase the same amount of goods and services.

information cost The time and mental effort required to absorb and store information, whether from conversations, personal experiences, or the media.

inherent executive power Presidential authority inherent in the executive branch of government, although not specifically mentioned in the Constitution.

initiative Proposed law or state constitutional amendment placed on the ballot in response to a citizen petition.

inner cabinet The four original departments (State, Defense, Treasury, and Justice) whose secretaries typically have the closest ties to the president.

interest group Organization or association of people with common interests that engages in politics on behalf of its members.

intergovernmental grant Grant from the national government to a state or local government.

Iran-Contra affair An allegedly illegal diversion of funds, derived from the sale of arms to Iran, to anticommunist rebels in Nicaragua during the Reagan administration.

iron triangle A close, stable connection among agencies, interest groups, and congressional committees.

issue advocacy Advertising campaigns that attempt to influence public opinion in regard to a specific policy proposal.

issue network A loose collection of interest groups, politicians, bureaucrats, and policy experts who have a particular interest in or responsibility for a policy area.

issue public A group of people particularly affected by, or concerned with, a specific issue.

Jim Crow laws Laws, passed by southern states after Reconstruction, enforcing segregation.

Joint Chiefs of Staff The heads of all the military services, together with a chair and vice-chair nominated by the president and confirmed by the Senate.

judicial activism Doctrine that says the principle of *stare decisis* should sometimes be sacrificed in order to adapt the Constitution to changing conditions.

judicial restraint Doctrine that says courts should, if at all possible, rule narrowly and avoid overturning a prior court decision.

judicial review Court authority to declare laws null and void on the grounds that they violate the Constitution.

Keynesianism Economic policy based on the belief that governments can control the economy by running deficits to expand it and surpluses to contract it, and by manipulating demand.

laboratories of democracy Doctrine that state and local governments contribute to democracy by providing places where experiments are tried and new theories about government are tested.

law clerk Young, influential aide to a Supreme Court justice.

League of Nations International organization created after World War I to settle disputes between nations; precursor of the United Nations.

legal distinction The legal difference between a case at hand and previous court decisions.

Lemon test Supreme Court standard for determining whether the First Amendment's establishment of religion clause has been violated.

libel A false statement defaming another.

liberalism A philosophy that elevates and empowers the individual as opposed to religious, hereditary, governmental, or other forms of authority.

line item veto Presidential authority to negate particular provisions of a law while letting the remainder stand; granted by Congress in 1996 but struck down by the Supreme Court in 1998.

living-constitution theory A theory of constitutional interpretation that places the meaning of the Constitution in the context of the total history of the United States.

lobbying Interest-group activities intended to influence directly the decisions that public officials make.

lobbyist One who engages in lobbying, especially as his or her primary job.

machine A highly organized party under the control of a boss and based on patronage and control of government activities. Machines were common in many cities in the late nineteenth and early twentieth centuries.

majority Fifty percent plus one.

majority leader Title used for the Speaker's chief lieutenant in the House and for the most important officer in the Senate. Chosen by the majority party membership, majority leaders are responsible for the day-to-day work necessary to build political coalitions and enact laws.

majority-minority district District in which a minority group is the numerical majority of the population.

Mapp v. Ohio Supreme Court decision saying that any evidence obtained without a proper search warrant may not be introduced in a trial.

marble-cake federalism The theory that all levels of government can work together to solve common problems. Also known as cooperative federalism.

Marbury v. Madison Supreme Court decision (1803) in which the court first exercised the power of judicial review.

market failures Situations in which the free market does not lead to efficient outcomes or to outcomes that are good for society.

markup Process in which a committee or subcommittee considers and revises a bill that has been introduced.

mass media Means of communication that are widely affordable and technologically capable of reaching a broad audience.

mass public Ordinary people for whom politics is a peripheral concern.

matching funds Public moneys (from $3 check-offs on income tax returns) that the Federal Election Commission distributes to primary candidates according to a prespecified formula.

Mayflower Compact First document in colonial America in which the people gave their express consent to be governed.

McCulloch v. Maryland Decision (1819) in which the Supreme Court first used judicial review to declare a state law unconstitutional.

measurement error The error that arises from attempting to measure something as subjective as opinion.

Medicaid Program that provides medical services to the poor.

Medicare Program that provides social security recipients a broad range of medical benefits.

minority leader Leader of the minority party who coordinates the minority's attempts to improve or defeat majority legislation.

Miranda v. Arizona Supreme Court decision stating that accused persons must be told by police that they need not testify against themselves.

monetarism An economic school of thought that rejects Keynesianism, arguing that the money supply is the most important influence on the economy.

monetary policy The actions taken by government to vary the supply of money in an effort to stabilize the business cycle.

mugwumps Organized in the 1880s, a group of civil-service reformers, including professors, journalists, clerics, and business leaders, who maintained that government officials should be chosen on a merit basis, not for their political connections.

multiculturalism The idea that ethnic and cultural groups should maintain their identity within the larger society and respect one another's differences.

multiple referrals Process occurring when party leaders give more than one committee responsibility for considering a bill.

nation building Intervention designed to enhance democratic practices in another country.

National Association for the Advancement of Colored People (NAACP) Civil rights organization, founded in 1909, that relied heavily on a legal strategy to pursue its objectives.

national intelligence director An office that coordinates intelligence gathering among the CIA, the FBI, and other intelligence agencies.

national nominating convention Quadrennial gathering of party officials and delegates that selects presidential and vice presidential nominees and adopts party platforms. Extension of the direct primary to the presidential level after 1968 has greatly reduced the importance of

National Security Council (NSC) White House agency responsible for coordinating U.S. foreign policy.

natural monopoly A situation in which a public service is best provided by a single company.

necessary and proper clause Constitutional clause that gives Congress the power to take all actions that are "necessary and proper" to the carrying out of its delegated powers. Also known as the *elastic clause*.

New Deal Programs created by the Franklin Roosevelt administration that expanded the power of the federal government for the purpose of stimulating economic recovery and establishing a national safety net for those in need.

New Jersey Plan Small-state proposal for constitutional reform.

new media Cable and satellite TV, fax, email, and the Internet—the media that have grown out of the technological advances of the past few decades.

NIMBY problem Problem in which everyone wants the problem solved, but "Not In My Back Yard."

nullification A doctrine that says that states have the authority to declare acts of Congress unconstitutional.

obscenity Publicly offensive language or portrayals with no redeeming social value.

Office of Management and Budget (OMB) Agency responsible for developing the president's budget, setting personnel policy in the executive branch, and reviewing all proposed legislation sent by the executive branch to Congress to ensure it is consistent with the president's agenda.

oligarchy A government by the few, in which the individuals in power are not titled nobility but capture power either through military action or through a political party.

open seat A House or Senate race with no incumbent (because of death or retirement).

opinion In legal parlance, a court's written explanation of its decision.

original-intent theory A theory of constitutional interpretation that determines the constitutionality of a law by ascertaining the intentions of those who wrote and ratified the Constitution.

outer cabinet Newer departments that have less access to the president but have evolved in such a way as to provide interest-group access to the executive branch of government.

override Congressional passage of a bill by a two-thirds vote despite the president's veto.

overvotes Ballots that have more than one choice for an office (e.g., for president in 2000), whether because the voter cast a ballot for more than one candidate or wrote in a name as well as making a mark.

partisan interpretation The argument that Republican administrations set economic policy to benefit higher-income, business, and professional groups, and that Democratic administrations set economic policy to benefit lower-income, blue-collar, wage-earning groups.

party caucus All Democratic members of the House or Senate. Members in caucus elect the party leaders, ratify the choice of committee leaders, and debate party positions on issues.

party conference What Republicans call their party caucus.

party identification A person's subjective feeling of affiliation with a party.

party image The associations voters make between the parties and particular issues and values.

Patriots Political group defending colonial American liberties against British infringements.

patronage Appointment of individuals to public office in exchange for their political support. Widely practiced in the eighteenth and nineteenth centuries and continues to present day.

Pendleton Act Legislation passed in 1883 creating the Civil Service Commission.

permanent campaign Condition that prevails in the new American democracy when the next election campaign begins as soon as the last has ended and the line between electioneering and governing has disappeared.

plain-meaning-of-the-text theory A theory of constitutional interpretation that determines the constitutionality of a law in light of what the words of the Constitution obviously seem to say.

plaintiff One who brings a complaint or suit against another.

platform A statement of a party's positions on the major issues of the day.

plea bargain Agreement between prosecution and defense that the accused will admit to having committed a crime, provided that other charges are dropped and the recommended sentence is shortened.

plenary session Activities of a court in which all judges participate; in the case of the Supreme Court, the chief justice presides.

Plessy v. Ferguson Supreme Court decision declaring separate but equal public facilities constitutional.

pluralism A school of thought holding that politics is the clash of groups that represent all important interests in society and that check and balance each other.

pocket veto Presidential veto after congressional adjournment, executed merely by not signing a bill into law.

policy deliberation Debate and discussion by interest groups and political leaders over issues placed on the policy agenda.

policy enactment Passage of a law by public officials.

policy implementation Translation of legislation into a set of government programs or regulations.

policy outcome Effect of policy outputs on individuals and businesses.

policy output Provision of services to citizens or regulation of their conduct.

political action committee (PAC) Specialized organization for raising and spending campaign funds; often affiliated with an interest group or association.

political activists People who regularly participate in politics; they are more interested in and committed to particular issues and candidates than are ordinary citizens.

political culture Collection of beliefs and values about the justification and operation of a country's government.

political efficacy The belief that the citizen can make a difference in politics by expressing an opinion or acting politically.

political elites Activists and officeholders who have well-structured ideologies that bind together their positions on different policy issues.

political entrepreneurs People willing to assume the costs of forming and maintaining an organization even when others may free-ride on them.

political parties Groups of like-minded people who band together in an attempt to take control of government. Parties represent the primary connection between ordinary citizens and the public officials they elect.

political socialization The set of psychological and sociological processes by which families, schools, religious organizations, communities, and other societal units inculcate beliefs and values in their members.

poll tax Fee that one must pay in order to be allowed to vote.

popular vote The total vote cast across the nation for a candidate.

pork barrel projects Special legislative benefits targeted toward the constituents of particular members of Congress.

precedent Previous court decision or ruling applicable to a particular case.

president pro tempore The president of the Senate, who presides in the absence of the vice president.

presidential popularity Evaluation of a president by voters, usually as measured by a survey question asking the adult population how well they think the president is doing the job.

presidential primaries Elections held for the purpose of selecting or instructing national convention delegates.

primary election A preliminary contest that narrows the number of the parties' candidates and determines who will be the nominees in the general election.

priming The media affect the standards people use to evaluate political figures or the severity of a problem.

prior restraint doctrine Legal doctrine that gives individuals the right to publish without prior restraint—that is, without first submitting material to a government censor.

professional legislature Legislature whose members serve full-time and for long periods.

Progressives Loose aggregation of politicians, political activists, and intellectuals of the late nineteenth and early twentieth centuries who promoted political reforms in an effort to clean up elections and government.

proportional representation (PR) Electoral system in which parties receive a share of seats in parliament that is proportional to the popular vote they receive.

proposition An initiative or a referendum that often provides a basis for political action.

proprietary colony Colony governed either by a prominent English noble or by a company. See royal colony.

prospective voting Voting pattern in which citizens look to the future while voting, taking into account each candidate's campaign promises; each election becomes an occasion to decide the future direction of public policies.

public assistance Programs that provide low-income households with a limited income and access to essential goods and services.

public defender Attorney whose full-time responsibilities are to provide for the legal defense of indigent criminal suspects.

public goods Goods enjoyed simultaneously by a group, as opposed to a private good that must be divided up to be shared.

public opinion The aggregation of people's views about issues, situations, and public figures.

quota Specific number of positions set aside for a specific group; said by the Supreme Court to be unconstitutional.

"rally 'round the flag" effect The tendency for the public to back presidents in the event of foreign crises.

realignment Shift occurring when the pattern of group support for political parties changes in a significant and lasting way.

realists Those who say that U.S. foreign policy best protects democracy when it safeguards its own economic and military strength.

reapportionment Redrawing of electoral district lines to reflect population changes.

recall elections Attempts to remove incumbents from office before the completion of their terms.

receiver Court official who has the authority to see that judicial orders are carried out.

recess appointment A presidential appointment made without Senate confirmation while the Senate is in recess.

recession A slowdown in economic activity, officially defined as a decline that persists for two quarters (six months).

Reconstruction A period after the Civil War when southern states were subject to a federal military presence.

redistricting Drawing new boundaries of congressional districts, usually after the decennial census.

referendum A law or state constitutional amendment that is proposed by a legislature or other elected body but goes into effect only if approved by a specified majority of voters.

registered voters Those legally eligible to vote who have registered in accordance with the requirements prevailing in their state and locality.

regulation Rules and standards that control economic, social, and political activities.

remand To send a case to a lower court to determine the best way of implementing the higher court's decision.

rent subsidies Program that helps pay rent for low-income families, provided that they select designated housing.

representatives Individuals, periodically chosen by citizens, who have the authority to decide what governments do.

restrictive housing covenants Legal promises by home buyers that they would not resell to an African American; enforcement declared unconstitutional by the Supreme Court.

retrospective voting Voting on the basis of past policies rather than guessing at the results of future policies.

reversal The overturning of a lower-court decision by an appeals court or the Supreme Court.

right of privacy Right to be free of government interference in those aspects of one's personal life that do not affect others.

royal colony Colony governed by the king's representative with the advice of an elected assembly. See *proprietary colony*.

rule The terms and conditions under which a bill or resolution will be considered on the floor of the House—in particular, how long debate will last, how time will be allocated, and the number and type of amendments that will be in order.

safe seat A congressional district certain to vote for the candidate of one party.

sampling error The chance variation that arises in public opinion surveys as a result of using a representative, but small, sample to estimate the characteristics of a larger population.

Second Continental Congress Political authority that directed the struggle for independence beginning in 1775.

secretary The title of the head of a department within the executive branch.

secretary of defense The president's chief civilian adviser on defense matters and overall head of the army, navy, and air force.

secretary of state Officially, the president's chief foreign policy adviser and head of the State Department, the agency responsible for conducting diplomatic relations.

select committee Temporary committee created to deal with a specific issue or problem.

selection bias The distortion caused when a sampling method systematically includes or excludes people with certain attitudes from the sample.

selection principle Guideline according to which stories with certain characteristics are chosen over stories without those characteristics.

selective benefits Specific private goods that an organization provides only to its contributing members.

selective incorporation The case-by-case process through which the Supreme Court applies the Bill of Rights to the states by invoking the due process clause of the Fourteenth Amendment.

senatorial courtesy An informal rule that the Senate will not confirm nominees for positions within a state unless it has the approval of the state's senior senator from the president's party.

seniority Practice by which the majority-party member with the longest continuous service on a committee becomes the chair.

separate but equal doctrine Supreme Court rule stating that the equal protection clause was not violated by the fact of state mandated racial segregation alone, provided that the separated facilities were equal.

separation of church and state doctrine Principle that a wall should separate the government from religious activity.

separation of powers A system of government in which different institutions exercise the different components of governmental power.

sequester The housing of jurors privately during a criminal trial, keeping them away from any information about the crime other than that presented in the courtroom.

Shays's Rebellion Armed uprising in western Massachusetts in 1786 led by Revolutionary War captain Daniel Shays.

single-issue group An interest group narrowly focused to influence policy on a single issue.

single-issue voters Voters who care so deeply about some particular issue that their votes are determined by a candidate's position on this one issue.

single-member, simple-plurality (SMSP) system Electoral system in which the country is divided into geographic districts, and the candidates who win the most votes within their districts are elected.

social connectedness The degree to which individuals are integrated into society—extended families, neighborhoods, religious organizations, and other social units.

social insurance Program that provides benefits in return for contributions made by workers.

social issues Issues (such as flag burning, gun control, abortion, obscenity, prayer in school, capital punishment, gay rights, and evolution) that reflect personal values more than economic interests.

social movement Broad-based demand for government action on some problem or issue, such as civil rights for blacks, equal rights for women, or environmental protection.

social policy Domestic policy programs designed to help those thought to be in need of government assistance.

social security Social insurance program for senior citizens.

socialization The end result of all the processes by which social groups give individuals their beliefs and values.

soft money Money contributed by interest groups, labor unions, and individual donors that is not subject to federal regulation.

solicitor general Government official responsible for presenting before the courts the position of the presidential administration.

sound bite A piece of film or video that shows a candidate speaking in his or her own words.

sovereignty Fundamental governmental authority.

Speaker The presiding officer of the House of Representatives; normally, the Speaker is the leader of the majority party.

spending clause Constitutional provision that gives Congress the power to collect taxes to provide for the general welfare.

spoils system A system of government employment in which workers are hired on the basis of party loyalty.

sponsor Representative or senator who introduces a bill or resolution.

Stamp Act Congress A meeting in 1765 of delegates from nine colonies to oppose the Stamp Act; the first political organization that brought leaders from several colonies together for a common purpose.

stamp tax Passed by Parliament in 1765, it required colonists to purchase a small stamp to be affixed to legal and other documents.

standing committee Committee with fixed membership and jurisdiction, continuing from Congress to Congress.

stare decisis In court rulings, reliance on consistency with precedents. See also "precedent."

state action doctrine Rule stating that only the actions of state and local governments, not those of private individuals, must conform to the equal protection clause.

State of the Union address Annual speech delivered by the president in late January or early February in fulfillment of the constitutional obligation of reporting to Congress the state of the union.

state sovereign immunity Legal doctrine, based on the Eleventh Amendment, that says states cannot be sued under federal law by private parties.

statutory interpretation The judicial act of interpreting and applying the laws of Congress and the states, rather than the Constitution, to particular cases.

subgovernment Alliance of a congressional committee, an executive agency, and a small number of allied interest groups that combine to dominate policy making in some specified policy area.

suffrage Another term for the right to vote.

sunshine law A 1976 law requiring that federal government meetings be held in public.

superdelegate Certain party leaders—members of the U.S. House and Senate, governors, members of the national committee—who became automatic or ex-officio delegates.

Supplemental Security Income (SSI) Program that provides disabled people of low income with income assistance.

supremacy clause Constitutional provision that says the laws of the national government "shall be the supreme Law of the Land."

supremacy clause Part of the Constitution that says the Constitution is the "supreme Law of the Land," to which all judges are bound.

surplus The amount by which annual revenue exceeds spending.

suspect classification Categorization of a particular racial or ethnic group that will be closely scrutinized by the courts to see whether its use is unconstitutional.

suspension of the rules Fast-track procedure for considering bills and resolutions in the House; debate is limited to 40 minutes, no amendments are in order, and a two-thirds majority is required for passage.

taxation without representation Levying of taxes by a government in which the people are not represented by their own elected officials.

Temporary Assistance for Needy Families (TANF) Welfare reform law passed by Congress in 1996.

The Federalist Papers Essays that were written in support of the Constitution's ratification and have become a classic argument for the American constitutional system.

three-fifths compromise Constitutional provision that counted each slave as three-fifths of a person when calculating representation in the House of Representatives; repealed by the Fourteenth Amendment.

ticket-splitting Voter selection of candidates from different parties at the same election—for example, a Republican presidential candidate but a Democratic candidate for the House of Representatives.

Tonkin Gulf Resolution Congressional resolution that gave the president the authority to send troops to Vietnam.

Tories Those colonists who opposed independence from Great Britain.

transition The period after a presidential candidate has won the November election, but before the candidate assumes office as president on January 20.

treaties Official agreements with foreign countries that must be ratified by the Senate.

trial venue The place where a trial is held.

trustee One who acts on behalf of the interests of the citizens rather than according to the citizens' past preferences.

trustee Role a representative plays when acting in accordance with his or her own best judgment to decide what is best for the country.

two-party system System in which only two significant parties compete for office. Such systems are in the minority among world democracies.

two-presidency theory Theory that explains why presidents exercise greater power over foreign affairs than over domestic policy.

tyranny of the majority Suppression of rights imposed by those voted into power by a majority.

unanimous-consent agreement An agreement that sets forth the terms and conditions according to which the Senate will consider a bill; these agreements are individually negotiated by the leadership for each bill.

undervotes Ballots that indicate no choice for an office (e.g., for president in 2000), whether because the voter abstained or because the voter's intention could not be determined.

unemployment The circumstance that exists when people who are willing to work at the prevailing wage cannot find jobs.

unfunded mandates Federal regulations that impose burdens on state and local governments without appropriating enough money to cover costs.

unitary government System under which all authority is held by a single, national government.

United Nations Organization of all nation-states, whose purpose is to preserve world peace and foster economic and social development throughout the world.

United States v. Curtiss-Wright Export Corporation Supreme Court decision in which Congress was given the authority to delegate foreign policy responsibilities to the president.

U.S. attorney Person responsible for prosecuting violations of the federal criminal code.

veto power Power giving presidents the capacity to prevent bills passed by Congress from becoming law. It may be overridden by a two-thirds vote in each congressional chamber. Most state governors also have veto power over their legislatures.

Virginia Plan Constitutional proposal supported by convention delegates from large states.

voter mobilization The efforts of parties, groups, and activists to encourage their supporters to turn out for elections.

voting eligible population Voting-age population with groups such as felons and noncitizens subtracted.

voting-age population All people in the United States over the age of 18, including those who may not be legally eligible to vote.

War on Poverty Series of categorical grant programs enacted in the 1960s, designed to enhance the economic opportunity of low-income citizens.

War Powers Resolution 1973 congressional resolution requiring the president to notify Congress formally upon ordering U.S. troops into military action.

Whigs Political opposition in eighteenth-century England that developed a theory of citizen rights and representation.

whips Members of Congress who serve as informational channels linking the leadership and the rank and file, communicating the leadership's views and intentions to the members and vice versa.

White House Office Political appointees who work directly for the president, many of whom occupy offices in the White House.

white primary A primary election, held by the Democratic Party after Reconstruction, that excluded nonwhites from participation in many southern states.

winner-take-all voting Any voting procedure in which the candidate with the most votes gets all of the seats or delegates at stake.

writ of *certiorari* (cert) A document issued by the Supreme Court indicating that the Court will review a decision made by a lower court.

writ of habeas corpus A judicial order that a prisoner be brought before a judge to determine the legality of his or her imprisonment.

Youngstown Sheet & Tube Co. v. Sawyer Case in which the Supreme Court placed limits on the executive power of the president.

zone of acceptance Range within which Congress allows agencies to interpret and apply statutes.

Endnotes

CHAPTER 1

1. Sidney Blumenthal, *The Permanent Campaign* (New York: Simon & Schuster, 1982).

2. Sidney Blumenthal, *The Permanent Campaign* (New York: Simon & Schuster, 1982).

3. R. Douglas Arnold, *The Logic of Congressional Action* (New Haven, CT: Yale University Press, 1990).

4. Joseph S. Nye, Jr., Philip D. Zelikow, and David C. King, eds., *Why People Don't Trust Government* (Cambridge, MA: Harvard University Press, 1997).

5. H. H. Gerth and C. W. Mills, trans., *From Max Weber* (New York: Oxford University Press, 1946), p. 78.

6. Chuck Henning, *The Wit and Wisdom of Politics: Expanded Edition* (Golden, CO: Fulcrum, 1992), p. 91.

7. Jimmy Carter, *A Government as Good as Its People* (New York: Simon & Schuster, 1977), p. 102.

8. "Federalist No. 51," in James Madison, Alexander Hamilton, and John Jay, *The Federalist Papers* (New York: Penguin Books, 1987 [1788]), p. 319.

9. Thomas Hobbes, *Leviathan* (New York: Dutton, 1973), p. 65.

10. Henning, *Wit and Wisdom*, p. 89.

11. James Morone, *Democratic Wish: Popular Participation and the Limits of American Government* (New York: Basic Books, 1990), p. 5. Morone is summarizing the claims of others; he himself is a critic of popular democracy.

12. John Adams, *The Political Writings of John Adams*, ed. George Peek, Jr. (New York: Macmillan, 1985), p. 89.

13. Alexis de Tocqueville, *Democracy in America*, 2nd ed., trans. Henry Reeve, 2 vols. (Cambridge, MA: Sever & Francis, 1863), I, pp. 318–319, as quoted in Morone, *Democratic Wish*, p. 86.

14. "Federalist No. 51."

15. Jane Mansbridge, "Rethinking Representation," *American Political Science Review*, 97:4 (December 2003): 515–528.

16. "Half-a-Million Voters' Choices," *Governing* (April 1995): 15.

17. *The Book of the States, 2002* (Lexington, KY: Council of State Governments, 2002), pp. 209–211.

18. The Brennan Center for Justice, www.brennancenter.org/content/section/category/state_judicial_elections, accessed February 17, 2010.

19. Thomas Cronin, *Direct Democracy* (Cambridge, MA: Harvard University Press, 1989); and David Magleby, *Direct Legislation* (Baltimore, MD: Johns Hopkins University Press, 1984).

20. Anthony King, *Running Scared: Why America's Politicians Campaign Too Much and Govern Too Little* (New York: Free Press, 1996), pp. 2–3.

21. Adam Nagourney, "Democrats Reel as Senator Says No to 3rd Term," *New York Times*, February 16, 2010, nytimes.com, accessed February 17, 2010.

22. Hugh Heclo, "The Permanent Campaign: A Conspectus," in *Campaigning to Govern or Governing to Campaign?*, Thomas Mann and Norman Ornstein, eds. (Washington, DC: The Brookings Institution, 2000).

23. Woodrow Wilson, *Congressional Government* (Cleveland, OH: Meridian Books, 1956), p. 39.

24. Richard Boyd, "Decline of U.S. Voter Turnout: Structural Explanations," *American Politics Quarterly* 9 (1981): 133–159.

25. One of the authors attempted to keep an accurate account during the 2004–2008 election cycle.

26. Frank Sorauf, *Political Parties in the American System* (Boston: Little, Brown, 1964); and Martin Wattenberg, *The Decline of American Political Parties, 1952–1984* (Cambridge, MA: Harvard University Press, 1986).

27. Gary Jacobson finds that national swings in House elections are much more heterogeneous than at mid-century. See "The Marginals Never Vanished: Incumbency and Competition in Elections to the U.S. House of Representatives, 1952–1982," *American Journal of Political Science* 31 (1987): 126–141.

28. Susan Baer, "Candidates' Spouses Revisit Traditional Role," *Baltimore Sun* (January 23, 2004): 1A. Julia Preston, "Issues Start Rush to Citizenship by Hispanics," *New York Times*, (February 5, 2008): A15.

29. Julia Preston, "Issues Start Rush to Citizenship by Hispanics," *New York Times* (February 5, 2008): A15.

30. Calculation based on $8.5 million average winning Senate campaign. See www.opensecrets.org.

31. John Alford and John Hibbing, "Electoral Convergence of the Two Houses of Congress," paper presented at the Norman Thomas Conference on Senate Exceptionalism, Vanderbilt University, Nashville, TN, October 21–23, 1999.

32. Susan A. Macmanus, *Young v. Old: Generational Combat in the 21st Century* (Boulder, CO: Westview Press, 1996), chap. 2.

33. Benjamin Ginsberg and Martin Shefter, *Politics by Other Means: The Declining Importance of Elections in America* (New York: Basic Books: 1990); and Terry Moe, "The Politics of Bureaucratic Structure," in *Can the Government Govern?*, John Chubb and Paul Peterson, eds. (Washington, DC: The Brookings Institution, 1989), pp. 267–329.

34. John Dewey, as quoted in Morone, *Democratic Wish*, p. 322.

35. Morone, *Democratic Wish*.

36. "A League of Evil," *The Economist* 352, issue 8136 (September 11, 1999), p. 7.

37. Henning, *Wit and Wisdom*, p. 58.

CHAPTER 2

1. Herbert Storing, ed., *The Complete Anti-Federalist: Maryland and Virginia and the South*, vol. 5 (Chicago: University of Chicago Press, 1981), pp. 210, 212; selections from two speeches.

2. Herbert Storing, ed., with the assistance of Murray Dry, *The Complete Anti-Federalist* (Chicago: University of Chicago Press, 1981).

3. Alexander Hamilton, "Federalist 7," *The Federalist Papers* (New York: Bantam Books, 1982), p. 31.

4. Owen S. Ireland, *Religion, Ethnicity and Politics: Ratifying the Constitution in Pennsylvania* (University Park: Pennsylvania State University Press, 1995).

5. Quoted in Jack Rakove, *Original Meanings: Politics and Ideas in the Making of the Constitution* (New York: Vintage, 1997), p. 17.

6. Alan Brinkley, *The Unfinished Nation: A Concise History of the American People, 2nd ed.* (New York: Alfred A. Knopf, 1997), pp. 23–32.

7. Thomas A. Bailey, *The American Pageant: A History of the Republic* (Boston: D.C. Heath, 1956).

8. Gordon S. Wood, *The Radicalism of the American Revolution* (New York: Knopf, 1992), p. 80.

9. Jack P. Greene, "The Role of the Lower Houses of Assembly in Eighteenth-Century Politics," in *The Reinterpretation of the American Revolution 1763–1789*, ed. Jack P. Greene (New York: Harper & Row, 1968), pp. 86–109.

10. Merrill D. Peterson, *Thomas Jefferson and the New Nation* (New York: Oxford University Press, 1970), pp. 22–23.

11. Robert J. Dinkin, *Voting in Revolutionary America: A Study of Elections in the Original Thirteen States, 1776–1789* (Westport, CT: Greenwood Press, 1982); and Robert J. Dinkin, *Voting in Provincial America: A Study of Elections in the Thirteen Colonies, 1689–1776* (Westport, CT: Greenwood Press, 1977).

12. Wood, *Radicalism*, p. 55.

13. J. Franklin Jameson, *The American Revolution Considered as a Social Movement* (Princeton, NJ: Princeton University Press, 1926).

14. Edmund S. Morgan and Helen M. Morgan, *The Stamp Act Crisis: Prologue to Revolution* (Chapel Hill: University of North Carolina Press, 1953), p. 106.

15. Ibid.

16. Bernard Bailyn, *The Origins of American Politics* (New York: Knopf, 1968), p. 12.

17. Thomas Hobbes, *Leviathan* (New York: Oxford University Press, 1996). Originally published in 1651.

18. John Locke, *Two Treatises on Civil Government* (London: Dent, 1924). Originally published in 1690.

19. J. H. Plumb, *The Origins of Political Stability* (Boston: Houghton Mifflin, 1967).

20. For a discussion of the influence of James Harrington on colonial thought, see Samuel H. Beer, *To Make a Nation: The Rediscovery of American Federalism* (Cambridge, MA: Harvard University Press, 1993).

21. Thomas Paine, *Common Sense* (New York: Penguin, 1986). Originally published in 1776.

22. John Bartlett, *Familiar Quotations*, 15th ed. (Boston: Little, Brown, 1980), pp. 334, 342, 414.

23. C. L. Becker, *Freedom and Responsibility in the American Way of Life* (New York: Knopf, 1945), p. 16, as quoted by Louis Hartz, *Liberal Tradition in America* (New York: Harcourt, 1955), p. 61.

24. Dinkin, *Voting in Revolutionary America*; and Dinkin, *Voting in Provincial America*.

25. Willi Paul Adams, *The First American Constitutions: Republican Ideology and the Making of the State Constitutions in the Revolutionary Era* (Chapel Hill: University of North Carolina Press, 1980), pp. 245, 308–311.

26. Gordon Wood, *The Creation of the American Republic, 1776–1787* (New York: W. W. Norton, 1972), p. 166.

27. Ibid, p. 207.

28. Bailey, *American Pageant*, p. 136.

29. Alexander Hamilton, James Madison, and John Jay, "Federalist 15," in *The Federalist Papers* (New York: Mentor Books, 1999 [1787]), p. 76.

30. James Madison, "Letter to Thomas Jefferson, October 24, 1787," in James Madison, *Letters and Other Writings of James Madison* (Philadelphia: Lippincott, 1865).

31. "Report of Proceedings in Congress, February 21, 1787," The Avalon Project at Yale Law School, www.yale.edu/lawweb/avalon/const/const04.htm, accessed January 22, 2004.

32. Henry Mayer, *A Son of Thunder: Patrick Henry and the American Republic* (New York: Grove Press, 2001), p. 370.

33. Charles A. Beard, *An Economic Interpretation of the Constitution of the United States* (New York: Free Press, 1913).

34. Robert E. Brown, *Charles Beard and the Constitution* (Princeton, NJ: Princeton University Press, 1956); and Forrest McDonald, *We the People* (Chicago: University of Chicago Press, 1958).

35. John P. Roche, "The Founding Fathers: A Reform Caucus in Action," *American Political Science Review* 55 (December 1961): 799–816.

36. Winton U. Solberg, ed., *The Federal Convention and the Formation of the Union of the American States* (New York: Bobbs-Merrill, 1958), p. 78.

37. Ibid.

38. Ibid., pp. 131–134.

39. Max Farrand, *The Framing of the Constitution of the United States* (New Haven: Yale University Press, 1913), p. 113.

40. Thornton Anderson, *Creating the Constitution: The Convention of 1787 and the First Congress* (University Park: Pennsylvania State University Press, 1993).

41. Arthur M. Schlesinger, Jr., ed., *History of American Presidential Elections, 1789–1968*, vol. 2 (New York: McGraw-Hill, 1971), p. 1244.

42. Anderson, *Creating the Constitution*, p. 148.

43. Ibid.

44. Henry Steele Commager, ed., *Documents of American History* (New York: Appleton-Century-Crofts, 1958), p. 104; and Willi Paul Adams, *The First American Constitutions: Republican Ideology and the Making of the State Constitutions in the Revolutionary Era* (Chapel Hill: University of North Carolina Press, 1980).

45. Arthur M. Schlesinger, *Prelude to Independence* (New York: Knopf, 1958), p. 299.

46. C. M. Kenyon, "Men of Little Faith: The Anti-Federalists on the Nature of Representative Government," in *The Reinterpretation of the American Revolution, 1763–1789*, ed. Jack P. Green (New York: Harper & Row, 1968), pp. 526–567; and Herbert J. Storing, ed., *The Anti-Federalist* (Chicago: University of Chicago Press, 1986).

47. James Madison, "Federalist 10," in John Jay, Alexander Hamilton, and James Madison, writing under the pseudonym Publius, *The Federalist Papers* (New York: New American Library, 1961).

48. John Jay, Alexander Hamilton, and James Madison, writing under the pseudonym Publius, *The Federalist Papers* (New York: New American Library, 1961).

49. James Madison, *Federalist 10*, in John Jay, Alexander Hamilton, and James Madison, writing under the pseudonym Publius, *The Federalist Papers* (New York: New American Library, 1961).

50. James Madison, *Federalist 51*, in John Jay, Alexander Hamilton, and James Madison, writing under the pseudonym Publius, *The Federalist Papers* (New York: New American Library, 1961).

51. Jane Mansbridge, *Why We Lost the ERA* (Chicago: University of Chicago Press, 1986).

52. Beard, *An Economic Interpretation of the Constitution of the United States*.

53. Bernard Bailyn, *The Ideological Origins of Revolution* (Cambridge, MA: Harvard University Press, 1967); and Gordon S. Wood, *The Creation of the American Republic, 1776–1787* (Chapel Hill: University of North Carolina Press, 1969).

54. Frederick Douglass, "Is the Plan of the American Union Under the Constitution Anti-Slavery or Not?" *The Frederick Douglass Papers*, ed. John W. Blassingame (New Haven: Yale University Press, 1979), vol. 3, p. 157.

55. Beard, *Economic Interpretation*, chap. 9.

56. Second Inaugural Address, 1865, as quoted in John Bartlett, *Familiar Quotations*, 16th ed. (Boston: Little, Brown, 1992), p. 450.

CHAPTER 3

1. Evan Thomas, "The Lost City; What Went Wrong: Devastating a Swath of South, Katrina Plunged New Orleans into Agony," *Newsweek* (September 12, 2005): 42.

2. National Weather Service, "Service Assessment: Hurricane Katrina, August 23–31, 2005," U.S. Department of Commerce, National Oceanic and Atmospheric Administration (NOAA) (Silver Spring, MD: July, 2006), p. 1.

3. Thomas Gabe, Gene Falk, Maggie McCarty, and Virginia Mason, "Hurricane Katrina: Social-Demographic Characteristics of Impacted Areas," Congressional Research

Service report RL33141 (Washington, DC: Congressional Research Service), p. 14.

4. Mark Fischetti, "Drowning New Orleans," *Scientific American* (October 2001): 76–85.

5. Ibid, p. 85.

6. Robert Block, Amy Schatz, Gary Fields, and Christopher Cooper, "Behind Poor Katrina Response, a Long Chain of Weak Links," *Wall Street Journal* (September 6, 2005): A1.

7. Eric Lipton, Christopher Drew, Scott Shane, and David Rohde, "Breakdowns Marked Path from Hurricane to Anarchy," *New York Times* (September 11, 2005): 1.

8. "A Failure of Initiative: Final Report of the Select Bipartisan Committee to Investigate the Preparation for and Response to Hurricane Katrina," United States House of Representatives, Washington, DC, February 15, 2006, pp. 3–5, 108.

9. See, for example: Office of Senator Trent Lott (R–MS), "Senator Lott Demands Help for Katrina Victims," press release, September 5, 2005, http://lott.senate.gov/index.cfm? FuseAction=PressReleases.Detail& PressRelease_id=187&Month=9&Year=2005, accessed September 6, 2005; Block, et al., "Behind Poor Katrina Response, a Long Chain of Weak Links"; Spencer S. Hsu and Susan B. Glasser, "FEMA Director Singled Out by Response Critics," *Washington Post* (September 6, 2005): A1.

10. "A Failure of Initiative: Final Report of the Select Bipartisan Committee to Investigate the Preparation for and Response to Hurricane Katrina," United States House of Representatives, Washington, DC, February 15, 2006, p. 135.

11. Spencer S. Hsu, "Brown Defends FEMA's Efforts," *Washington Post* (September 28, 2005): A1.

12. Greater New Orleans Community Data Center, "The New Orleans Index: Tracking the Recovery of New Orleans and the Metro Area," August 2009 (available at https://gnocdc.s3.amazonaws.com/NOLAIndex/ESNOLAIndex.pdf, accessed December 31, 2009), p. 8, 14.

13. Roman Deininger, "Lower Ninth Ward Struggles 4 years later," *The Philadelphia Inquirer* (August 29, 2009): A1.

14. Jere Longman and Sewell Chan, "Flooding Recedes in New Orleans; U.S. Inquiry is Set," *New York Times* (September 7, 2005): 1.

15. Thomas Hobbes, *Leviathan* (Indianapolis, IN: Hackett Publishing Co., 1994), Chapter 29.

16. Alexis de Tocqueville, *Democracy in America*, vol. I, ed. Philips Bradley (New York: Knopf, 1945), p. 169.

17. Gordon S. Wood, *The Creation of the American Republic, 1776–1787* (New York: Norton, 1972), pp. 483–499.

18. Ibid.

19. Jean E. Smith, *John Marshall: Definer of a Nation* (New York: Henry Holt, 1996), pp. 440–446.

20. *McCulloch v. Maryland* (1819), 4 Wheaton 316, as reprinted in Henry Steele Commager, ed., *Documents of American History*, 6th ed. (New York: Appleton-Century-Crofts, 1949), p. 217.

21. *United States v. E. C. Knight Co.*, 156 U.S. 1 (1895).

22. The Court also ruled that Congress had delegated too much power to the president in this case. *A. L. A. Schechter Poultry Corp. v. United States*, 295 U.S. 495 (1935).

23. James MacGregor Burns, *Roosevelt: The Lion and the Fox* (New York: Harcourt Brace, 1956), p. 223.

24. Ibid., p. 298.

25. *NLRB v. Jones & Laughlin Co.*, 301 U.S. 1 (1937).

26. *Wickard v. Filburn*, 317 U.S. 111 (1942).

27. *United States v. Lopez*, 514 U.S. 549 (1995).

28. *United States v. Morrison*, 99-5 (2000).

29. *Gonzales v. Raich*, 545 U.S. 1 (2005).

30. David W. Ogden, Deputy Attorney General, "Memorandum for Selected United States Attorneys," October 19, 2009, available at http://blogs.usdoj.gov/blog/archives/192, accessed December 31, 2009.

31. *McCulloch v. Maryland* (1819), as reprinted in Commager, p. 217.

32. *New York v. U.S.* 488 U.S. 1041 (1992).

33. Ruth Marcus and Thomas W. Lippman, "Court Rejects Key Parts of A-Waste Law," *Washington Post* (June 20, 1992): A1.

34. *Printz v. U.S.*, 521 U.S. 98 (1997).

35. *Board of Trustees of the University of Alabama v. Garrett*, 99-1240 (2001).

36. *Helvering v. Davis*, 301 U.S. 548, 599 (1937).

37. *South Dakota v. Dole*, 483 U.S. 203 (1987).

38. Simon Lazarus, "The Federalist Society; Their Judicial Ideology Would Dismantle Accepted Social Policy," *Milwaukee Journal Sentinel* (July 1, 2001): 1J.

39. Morton Grodzins, *The American System: A New View of Government in the United States*, ed. Daniel J. Elazar (Chicago: Rand McNally, 1966).

40. Calculated from data in Ester Fuchs, *Mayors and Money* (Chicago: University of Chicago Press, 1992), p. 210.

41. Chuck Henning, comp., *The Wit and Wisdom of Politics: Expanded Edition* (Golden, CO: Fulcrum, 1992), p. 208.

42. Carl Hulse, "Spending Bill Is Approved, with Its Storehouse of Pork," *New York Times* (February 14, 2003): A24.

43. Shailagh Murray, "For a Senate Foe of Pork Barrel Spending, Two Bridges Too Far," *Washington Post* (October 21, 2005): A8; Shailagh Murray, "Some in GOP Regretting Pork-Stuffed Highway Bill," *Washington Post* (November 5, 2005): A1.

44. Shailagh Murray, "Funding for Alaskan Bridges Eliminated; Republicans Make Largely Symbolic Move in Reaction to Criticism of Transportation Spending," *Washington Post* (November 17, 2005): A18.

45. Jeffrey L. Pressman and Aaron Wildavsky, *Implementation*, 3rd ed. (Berkeley: University of California Press, 1984); Martha Derthick, *New Towns in Town: Why a Federal Program Failed* (Washington, DC: Urban Institute, 1972); and Eugene Bardach, *The Implementation Game*, 4th ed. (Cambridge, MA: MIT Press, 1982).

46. Government Accountability Office, "Transit Security Grant Program," Report to the Chairman, Committee on Homeland Security, House of Representatives, GAO-09-491, June 2009, available at www.gao.gov/new.items/d09491.pdf, accessed December 31, 2009.

47. Ibid., p. 12.

48. Paul E. Peterson, Barry Rabe, and Kenneth Wong, *When Federalism Works* (Washington, DC: The Brookings Institution, 1986).

49. Timothy Conlan, *New Federalism: Intergovernmental Reform from Nixon to Reagan* (Washington, DC: The Brookings Institution, 1988).

50. Quoted in Timothy Conlan, *From New Federalism to Devolution: Twenty-Five Years of Intergovernmental Reform* (Washington, DC: The Brookings Institution, 1998), p. 152.

51. David McKay, *Domestic Policy and Ideology: Presidents and the American State, 1964–1987* (New York: Cambridge University Press, 1989), Chapter 4.

52. Calculated from caseload data available at U.S. Department of Health and Human Services, Administration for Children and Healthy Families, www.acf.hhs.gov/programs/ofa/data-reports/caseload/caseload_recent.html, accessed December 31, 2009.

53. Matthew C. Fellowes and Gretchen Rowe, "Politics and the New American Welfare States," *American Journal of Political Science* 48: 2 (April 2004): 362–373. Quote from p. 370.

54. Joseph Schatz and David Clarke, "Congress Clears Stimulus Package," *CQ Weekly*

(February 16, 2009), p. 352; Government Accountability Office, "Recovery Act: Status of States' and Localities' Use of Funds and Efforts to Ensure Accountability," December 2009, available at www.recovery.gov/Accountability/Documents/d10231.pdf, accessed January 21, 2010.

55. Timothy Conlan, "And the Beat Goes On: Intergovernmental Mandates and Preemption in an Era of Deregulation," *Publius* 21 (Summer 1991): 57.

56. On the costs of environmental mandates, see Richard C. Feiock, "Estimating Political, Fiscal and Economic Impacts of State Mandates: A Pooled Time Series Analysis of Local Planning and Growth Policy in Florida." Paper prepared for the annual meeting of the American Political Science Association, 1994.

57. Colleen M. Grogan, "The Influence of Federal Mandates on State Policy Decision-Making." Paper prepared for the annual meeting of the American Political Science Association, 1994; Teresa Coughlin, Leighton Ku, and John Holahan, *Medicaid Since 1980* (Washington, DC: Urban Institute, 1994); and John Holahan et al., "Explaining the Recent Growth in Medicaid Spending," *Health Affairs* 12 (Fall 1993): 177–193.

58. Jim VandeHei, "Education Law May Hurt Bush; No Child Left Behind's Funding Problems Could Be '04 Liability," *Washington Post* (October 13, 2003): A01.

59. James Bryce, *Modern Democracies* (New York: Macmillan, 1921), vol. I, p. 132.

60. This figure excludes school districts. School districts have dramatically decreased in number, from over 108,000 in 1942 to about 14,000 today. This is, for the most part, the result of consolidation of rural school districts in the 1940s and 1950s (see *Statistical Abstract of the United States, 2000*, Table 490).

61. For more data on special districts, see *Finances of Special District Governments, 1997* (Washington, DC: U.S. Census of Governments, 2000). For a study of how and why special districts form, see Nancy Burns, *The Formation of American Local Governments: Private Values in Public Institutions* (New York: Oxford University Press, 1994).

62. Robert R. Alford and Eugene C. Lee, "Voting Turnout in American Cities," *American Political Science Review* 62 (September 1968): 796–813; and Albert Karnig and B. Oliver Walter, "Decline in Municipal Voter Turnout: A Function of Changing Structure," *American Politics Quarterly*, 11: 4 (October, 1983): 491–505.

63. Adam Nossiter, "For New Orleans, Election Could Bring a New Order," *New York Times* (February 3, 2006): A1.

64. Village politics are well described in A. J. Vidich and J. Bensman, *Small Town in Mass Society* (New York: Harper & Row, 1972). For descriptions of courthouse gangs in the county politics of the South, see V. O. Key, *Southern Politics* (New York: Random House, 1949).

65. Paul E. Peterson, *City Limits* (Chicago: University of Chicago Press, 1981).

66. Soloman Moore, "A Heavy Turnout for Apathy," *Los Angeles Times* (May 25, 2001): 12.

67. Edward Walsh, "Report Urges Expanding Federal Role in Elections; Task Force Recommends Guidance, Not Mandates," *Washington Post* (August 10, 2001): A02.

68. United States Election Assistance Commission, "Appropriation and Distribution of Help America Vote Act (HAVA) Funds Administered by the U.S. Election Assistance Commission," September 2008, available at www.eac.gov/election/requirements-payments, accessed January 1, 2010.

69. Gallup Poll, August 31–September 2, 2009.

70. *Statistical Abstract of the United States, 2010*, Table 30.

71. Maura Dolan, "Berkeley No Longer a Haven for the Homeless; City OKs a Get-Tough Plan to Control Behavior on Its Streets," *Los Angeles Times* (November 29, 2007): B1.

72. Calculated from *Statistical Abstract of the United States, 2010*, Tables 424 and 461. "Social programs" are defined for state and local governments as the U.S. census of government categories "public welfare" and "health and hospitals." For the federal government, "social programs" include Office of Management and Budget categories "health," "Medicare," "income security," "social security," and "veterans benefits and services."

73. Jim Leute, "Janesville's GM Plant to Close," *Janesville Gazette* (June 3, 2008), available at http://gazettextra.com/news/2008/jun/03/janesvilles-gm-plant-close/, accessed January 1, 2010.

74. Robert Snell, Mark Hornbeck, and David Shepardson, "GM Offered $2.6 Million Tax Break to Stay at RenCen," *The Detroit News* (November 18, 2009, http://detnews.com/article/20091118/AUTO01/911180329/GM-offered-$2.6M-tax-break-to-stay-at-RenCen, accessed January 1, 2010.

75. Frances Stokes Berry and William D. Berry, "State Lottery Adoptions as Policy Innovations: An Event History Analysis," *American Political Science Review*, 84: 2 (June 1990): 395–415.

76. Daniel Elazar, *American Federalism: A View From the States* (New York: Harper & Row, 1984).

77. See, for example, John Kincaid, ed. *Political Culture, Public Policy, and the American States* (Philadelphia: Institute for the Study of Human Issues, 1982).

78. *Statistical Abstract of the United States, 2010,* Table 439.

79. Calculated from *Statistical Abstract of the United States, 2010*, Tables 12 and 431. Wealthy and poor states are defined in terms of gross state product per capita. Data are expressed in 2009 dollars and combine expenditures by state and local governments. Because the sharing of responsibilities by state and local governments varies widely from state to state, any interstate comparison that looks at state government expenditures alone can be quite misleading.

80. Peterson, *The Price of Federalism*, p. 105.

81. Morris Fiorina, *Divided Government* (New York: Macmillan, 1992).

82. Tad Friend, "Letter from California: Protest Studies," *The New Yorker* (January 4, 2010): 22.

83. *Baker v. Carr*, 369 U.S. 186 (1962); *Reynolds v. Sims*, 377 U.S. 533 (1964).

84. See Gordon E. Baker, *The Reapportionment Revolution* (New York: Random House, 1966); and Timothy G. O'Rourke, *The Impact of Reapportionment* (New Brunswick, NJ: Transaction Books, 1980).

85. John Sanko, "Boundary Map Favors Democrats," *Rocky Mountain News* (November 28, 2001): 23A.

86. Paul Bartels, "Plan to Redraw 11th District Opposed," *New Orleans Times-Picayune* (October 4, 2001): Metro 1.

87. Peggy Ficak, "Lights! Camera! Lawmakers!" *San Antonio Express News* (May 15, 2003): 9A.

88. "State Lawmakers, Others Get Pay Cut Today," L.A. Now, available at http://latimesblogs.latimes.com/lanow/2009/12/state-lawmakers-others-get-pay-cut-today.html, accessed January 2, 2010; The Council of State Governments, *The Book of the States: 2004 Edition* (Lexington, KY: Council of State Governments), Tables 3.2 and 3.9, pp. 78–80; 94–95; California Department of Personnel Administration, "Salaries of Elected Officials," www.dpa.ca.gov/salaries/elected.htm, accessed February 2, 2008; and State of Wyoming Legislature, "Legislative Handbook," http://legisweb.state.wy.us/LEGINFO/POLICIES/LHbook/L-HBOOK07.pdf, accessed February 2, 2008.

89. Thad Kousser, quoted in Alan Greenblatt, "The Truth About Term Limits," *Governing* (January 2006): 24–26.

90. U.S. Term Limits, "State Legislative Term Limits," www.ustl.org/Current_Info/

State_TL/index.html, accessed February 2, 2008.

91. Office of Governor Jim Doyle, "Governor Doyle to Lead Trade, Investment Mission to Ireland and United Kingdom," press release, Friday, February 1, 2008.

CHAPTER 4

1. For the official history of the terrorist attacks see http://www.gpoaccess.gov/911/index.html.

2. Karen Breslau, "Hate Crime: He Wasn't Afraid," *Newsweek* (October 15, 2001): 8.

3. "Rights and the New Reality," *Los Angeles Times* (September 21, 2002): part 2, 22.

4. Sam Howe Verhovek, "Americans Give in to Racial Profiling," *New York Times* (September 23, 2001): 1A; and Sandra Tan, "Change of Heart," *The Buffalo News* (October 22, 2001): A1.

5. American Arab Anti-Discrimination Committee, press release, September 21, 2001.

6. Mary Jordan, "It's Harder to Cross the Mexican Border," *Washington Post Weekly Edition* (June 3–9, 2002): 17; and Anne Hull, "A New Anxiety," *Washington Post Weekly Edition* (December 3–9, 2002): 9.

7. "Fewer Foreign Students," *Lexington (KY) Herald-Leader* (November 3, 2003): A3; and David J. Jefferson, "Stopped at the Border," *Newsweek* (October 14, 2002): 59.

8. For background, go to www.oz.net/~cyu/internment/main.html.

9. Elizabeth Becker, "All White, All Christian, and Divided by Diversity," *New York Times* (June 10, 2001).

10. Some German children pricked their fingers "to let the German blood out." Recollection of Louise Bauer Ritschard, mother-in-law of Morris Fiorina.

11. Carl J. Friedrich, *Problems of the American Public Service* (New York: McGraw-Hill, 1935), p. 12.

12. See Alvin Rabushka and Kenneth Shepsle, *Politics in Plural Societies* (Columbus, OH: Merrill, 1972).

13. John A. Garrity and Peter Gay, eds., *The Columbia History of the World* (New York: Harper & Row, 1972), p. 673.

14. Quoted in Marc Shell, "Babel in America; Or, The Politics of Language Diversity in the United States," *Critical Inquiry* 20 (1993): 109.

15. Richard McCormick, "Ethno-Cultural Interpretations of Nineteenth-Century American Voting Behavior," *Political Science Quarterly* 89 (1974): 351–377.

16. Richard Wayman, "Wisconsin Ethnic Groups and the Election of 1890," *Wisconsin Magazine of History* 51 (1968): 273. More

generally, see Paul Kleppner, *The Third Electoral System, 1853–1892: Parties, Voters, and Political Cultures* (Chapel Hill, NC: University of North Carolina Press, 1979).

17. John Miller, "Chinese Exclusion Act," *Congressional Record–Senate 1882* (13, Pt. 2): 1484–1485.

18. Ibid.

19. Madison Grant, *The Passing of the Great Race* (New York: Scribner's, 1916), pp. 80–81.

20. *Abstracts of Reports of the Immigration Commission* (Washington, DC: U.S. Government Printing Office, vol. 1, 1911). The quoted passages can be found on pp. 244, 251, 259, 261, 265, and 229. The characterization of southern Italians is based on work by an Italian (presumably a northern Italian) sociologist, but the commission clearly agrees with the description.

21. Henry Cabot Lodge, "Immigration Restriction," *Congressional Record–Senate 1896* (28, Pt. 3): 2817.

22. "Emergency" immigration restrictions passed in 1921 were fine-tuned and formalized in the National Origins Act of 1924 and the National Origins Quota Act of 1929.

23. Seymour Martin Lipset and Earl Raab, *The Politics of Unreason* (New York: Harper & Row, 1970), p. 111.

24. Alan Lichtman, *Prejudice and the Old Politics: The Presidential Election of 1928* (Chapel Hill, NC: University of North Carolina Press, 1979).

25. For a summary of research on the economic benefits and costs of immigration with citations to the relevant academic research, see Council of Economic Advisers, "Immigration's Economic Impact," June 20, 2007, www.whitehouse.gov/cea/cea_immigration_062007.html.

26. George Borhas, *Increasing the Supply of Labor Through Immigration* (Washington, DC: Center for Immigration Studies, May 2004).

27. McKay Ramah, *Family Reunification* (Washington DC: Migration Policy Institute, May 1, 2003).

28. For example, a recent study by a pro-immigration economist estimated that an average immigrant family in Florida consumes $1,800 per year more in state services than they pay in state and local taxes. David Denslow, "The Myth of No-Cost Immigrants," *Investor's Business Daily* (November 14, 2005).

29. Samuel Huntington, *Who Are We? The Challenges to America's National Identity* (New York: Simon & Schuster, 2004).

30. Arthur Schlesinger, Jr., *The Disuniting of America* (Knoxville, TN: Whittle, 1991).

31. Louis Hartz, *Liberal Tradition in America* (New York: Harcourt, 1955).

32. Bernard Bailyn, *The Ideological Origins of the American Revolution* (Cambridge, MA: Harvard University Press, 1967).

33. Gordon Wood. *The Creation of the American Republic* (New York: Norton, 1972); and J. G. A. Pocock, *The Machiavellian Moment* (Princeton, NJ: Princeton University Press, 1975).

34. Rogers Smith, "Beyond Tocqueville, Myrdal and Hartz: The Multiple Traditions in America," *American Political Science Review* 87 (1993): 549–566. These inconsistencies were not lost on earlier thinkers, to be sure. Recall Jefferson's pessimistic predictions in his *Notes on the State of Virginia 1781–1785*. Also see Alexis de Tocqueville, *Democracy in America*, ed. J. P. Mayer (New York: Harper, 1969), pp. 340–363.

35. Samuel Huntington, *American Politics: The Promise of Disharmony* (Cambridge, MA: Harvard University Press, 1981).

36. Everett Carll Ladd, *American Ideology* (Storrs, CT: The Roper Center, 1994), p. 76.

37. I. A. Lewis and William Schneider, "Hard Times: The Public on Poverty," *Public Opinion* (June/July 1985): 2–8, 59–60.

38. "Income Tax Irritation." *Public Perspective* (July/August, 1990): 86.

39. Stanley Feldman, "Structure and Consistency in Public Opinion: The Role of Core Beliefs and Values," *American Journal of Political Science* 32 (1988): 416–440.

40. Ladd, *American Ideology*, pp. 56–57.

41. Sidney Verba and Gary Orren, *Equality in America* (Cambridge, MA: Harvard University Press, 1985).

42. Mariana Servin-Gonzalez and Oscar Torres-Reyna, "Trends: Religion and Politics," *Public Opinion Quarterly* 63 (1999): 613–614.

43. Robert Booth Fowler, *Religion and Politics in America* (Metuchen, NJ: American Theological Library Association, 1985), p. 27.

44. Huntington, *American Politics*.

45. Hartz, *Liberal Tradition*.

46. Frederick Jackson Turner, *The Frontier in American History* (New York: Holt, 1920).

47. Ibid.

48. Sven Steinmo, "American Exceptionalism Reconsidered," in *The Dynamics of American Politics*, ed. Larry C. Dodd and Calvin Jillson (Boulder, CO: Westwood, 1994), pp. 106–131.

49. For a sympathetic description of the trials and ordeals of the immigrants, see Oscar Handlin, *The Uprooted*, 2nd ed. (Boston: Little, Brown, 1973).

50. Hartz, *Liberal Tradition*, p. 18.

51. *Abstracts of Reports of the Immigration Commission*, p. 170.

52. Gregory Rodriguez, quoted in Patrick McDonnell, "Immigrants Quickly

Becoming Assimilated, Report Concludes," *San Francisco Chronicle* (July 7, 1999): A4.

53. Philip Martin and Elizabeth Midgley, *Immigration to the United States* (Washington, DC: Population Reference Bureau, June 1999), p. 37.

54. James Smith, "Assimilation Across the Latino Generations," *American Economic Review* 93 (2003): 315–319.

55. Rodolfo de la Garza, "The Effects of Ethnicity on Political Culture," in *Classifying by Race*, ed. Paul Peterson (Princeton, NJ: Princeton University Press, 1995), pp. 351–352.

56. Rodolfo de la Garza, Angelo Falcon, and F. Chris Garcia, "Will the Real Americans Please Stand Up: Anglo and Mexican American Support of Core American Political Values," *American Journal of Political Science* 40 (1996): 335–351.

57. Lydia Saad, "Immigrants See United States as Land of Opportunity," *Gallup Poll Monthly* (July 1995): 19–33.

CHAPTER 5

1. "The Odds of Airborne Terror," Nate Silver, December 27, 2009, www.fivethirtyeight.com/2009/12/odds-of-airborne-terror.html, accessed June 7, 2010.

2. Ronald Bailey, "Don't Be Terrorized," Reason.com, August 11, 2006, http://reason.com/archives/2006/08/11/dont-be-terrorized, accessed June 7, 2010.

3. See National Safety Council, "The Odds of Dying From . . ." www.nsc.org/news_resources/Documents/nscInjuryFacts2011_037.pdf, accessed June 7, 2010.

4. NBC News/*Wall Street Journal* poll, May 6-10, 2010.

5. CNN/Opinion Research Poll, January 8-10, 2010.

6. James Stimson, *Tides of Consent: How Public Opinion Shapes American Politics* (New York: Cambridge University Press, 2004), Chapter 1.

7. Gallup Polls.

8. CBS News Poll, Jan. 6-10, 2010.

9. CBS News Poll, Jan. 6-10, 2010.

10. Alexander Hamilton, *The Works of Alexander Hamilton*, ed. Henry Cabot Lodge (New York: G.P. Putnam & Sons, 1904), Vol. 1, p. 401.

11. Thomas Jefferson, *The Political Writings of Thomas Jefferson*, ed. Merrill D. Peterson (Chapel Hill: University of North Carolina Press, 1993), p. 85.

12. Paul Quirk and Joseph Hinchliffe, "The Rising Hegemony of Mass Opinion," *Journal of Policy History* 10 (1998): 19–50.

13. V. O. Key, *Public Opinion and American Democracy* (New York: Knopf, 1961).

14. Carl Friedrich, *Man and His Government* (New York: McGraw-Hill, 1963), pp. 199–215.

15. The evidence to support these assertions is somewhat mixed. For a thorough look at the evidence, see William G. Mayer, *The Changing American Mind: How and Why American Public Opinion Changed Between 1960 and 1988* (Ann Arbor: University of Michigan Press, 1992), chap. 5.

16. Elizabeth Cook, Ted Jelen, and Clyde Wilcox, *Between Two Absolutes: Public Opinion and the Politics of Abortion* (Boulder, CO: Westview Press, 1992).

17. David Leege, Kenneth Wald, and Lyman Kellstedt, "The Public Dimension of Private Devotionalism," in *Rediscovering the Religious Factor in American Politics,* ed. David Leege and Lyman Kellstedt (Armonk, NY: Sharpe, 1993), pp. 139–156; and Alan Hertzke and John Rausch, "The Religious Vote in American Politics: Value Conflict, Continuity, and Change," in *Broken Contract,* ed. Stephen Craig (Boulder, CO: Westview Press, 1996), p. 188.

18. The ANES Guide to Public Opinion and Electoral Behavior: www.umich.edu/~nes/nesguide/nesguide.htm.

19. Robert Hess and Judith Horney, *The Development of Political Attitudes in Children* (Garden City, NY: Doubleday, 1967).

20. Fred Greenstein, *Children and Politics* (New Haven, CT: Yale University Press, 1969), chap. 4.

21. M. Kent Jennings and Richard G. Niemi, *Generations and Politics* (Princeton, NJ: Princeton University Press, 1981), p. 51.

22. Leonie Huddy and Stanley Feldman, "Worlds Apart: Blacks and Whites React to Hurricane Katrina," *Du Bois Review* 3:1 (2006), pp. 97–113.

23. Arthur Lupia, "Shortcuts versus Encyclopedias: Information and Voting Behavior in California Insurance Reform Elections," *American Political Science Review* 88 (1994): 63–76.

24. For a survey of positive and negative findings, see Jack Citrin and Donald Green, "The Self-Interest Motive in American Public Opinion," *Research in Micropolitics,* vol. 3 (Greenwich, CT: JAI Press, 1993), pp. 1–28.

25. David Sears and Leonie Huddy, "On the Origins of Political Disunity Among Women," in *Women, Politics, and Change,* ed. L. Tilly and P. Gurin (New York: Russell Sage, 1990), pp. 249–277.

26. Norman Nie, Jane Junn, and Kenneth Stehlik-Barry, *Education and Democratic Citizenship in America* (Chicago: University of Chicago Press, 1996).

27. Norman H. Nie, Darwin W. Miller III, Saar Golde, Daniel M. Butler, and Kenneth Winneg, "The World Wide Web and the U.S. Political News Market," *American Journal of Political Science* 54:2 (April 2010), pp. 428–439.

28. Details on how these polls are conducted appear in D. Stephen Voss, Andrew Gelman, and Gary King, "Preelection Survey Methodology: Details from Eight Polling Organizations, 1988 and 1992," *Public Opinion Quarterly* 59 (Spring 1995): 98–132.

29. The figure for the 1950s and 1960s is based on the complete collection of Gallup results reported in George C. Edwards III and Alec M. Gallup, *Presidential Approval: A Sourcebook* (Baltimore, MD: Johns Hopkins University Press, 1990). Results for 2009 are based on the polls listed at www.realclearpolitics.com.

30. Craig Gilbert, "Feingold Clicks with Blog Fans," *Milwaukee Journal Sentinel* (February 27, 2006): 1.

31. Don Van Natta, Jr., "Polling's 'Dirty Little Secret': No Response," *New York Times* (November 21, 1999): sect. 4, pp. 1, 16.

32. John Brehm, *The Phantom Respondents* (Ann Arbor, MI: University of Michigan Press, 1993), chap. 2.

33. Jeffrey Jones, "Obama Viewed as Winner of Third Debate," Gallup.com, October 17, 2008, www.gallup.com/poll/111256/obama-viewed-winner-third-debate.aspx, accessed June 10, 2010.

34. Jon Krosnick and Matthew Barent, "Comparisons of Party Identification and Policy Preferences: The Impact of Survey Question Format," *American Journal of Political Science* 37 (1993): 941–964.

35. On these topics, see Howard Schuman and Stanley Presser, *Questions and Answers in Attitude Surveys* (New York: Harcourt, Academic Press, 1981); and the essays in Thomas Mann and Gary Orren, eds., *Media Polls in American Politics* (Washington, DC: The Brookings Institution, 1992).

36. FOX News/Opinion Dynamics Poll, May 4-5, 2010; Pew Research/National Journal poll, June 3–6, 2010.

37. For a full discussion, see David Moore and Frank Newport, "Misreading the Public: The Case of the Holocaust Poll," *Public Perspective* (March/April 1994): 28–30; and Tom Smith, "Review: The Holocaust Denial Controversy," *Public Opinion Quarterly* 59 (1995): 269–295.

38. General Social Survey 2006, www.norc.org.

39. "Abortion: Overview of a Complex Opinion," *The Public Perspective* (November/December 1989), 19–20.

40. General Social Survey 2006, www.norc.org.

41. Pew Research Center survey, Nov. 3–6, 2005.

42. Morris Fiorina, Samuel Abrams, and Jeremy Pope, *Culture War? The Myth of a Polarized America* (New York: Longman, 2006), p. 81.

43. Gallup Poll, May 3-6, 2010.

44. CBS News/*New York Times* Poll, April 5–12, 2010.

45. "Public Knows Basic Facts about Financial Crisis," Pew Research Center, April 2, 2009, http://people-press.org/report/504/knowledge-update, accessed June 10, 2010.

46. CBS News/*New York Times* Poll, Feb. 18–22, 2009.

47. Anthony King, "Names and Places Lost in the Mists of Time," *Daily Telegraph* (August 26, 1997): 4.

48. Anthony Downs, *An Economic Theory of Democracy* (New York: Harper & Row, 1957), chaps. 11–13.

49. Morris P. Fiorina, "Information and Rationality in Elections," in *Information and Democratic Processes,* ed. John Ferejohn and James Kuklinski (Urbana: University of Illinois Press, 1990), pp. 329–342.

50. John Krosnick, "Government Policy and Citizen Passion: A Study of Issue Publics in Contemporary America," *Political Behavior* 12 (1990): 59–92. The seminal study is Peter Natchez and Irvin Bupp, "Candidates, Issues, and Voters," *Public Policy* 1 (1968): 409–437.

51. Fiorina, "Information and Rationality in Elections."

52. George F. Bishop, Robert W. Oldendick, Alfred J. Tuchfarber, and Stephen E. Bennett, "Pseudo-Opinions on Public Affairs," *Public Opinion Quarterly* 44 (1980): 198–209.

53. For this and many similar results, see the classic study by Howard Schuman and Stanley Presser, *Questions and Answers in Attitude Surveys* (New York: Academic Press, 1981), chap. 4.

54. Philip Converse, "The Nature of Belief Systems in Mass Publics," in *Ideology and Discontent,* ed. David Apter (New York: Free Press, 1964), pp. 206–261.

55. M. Kent Jennings, "Ideological Thinking Among Mass Publics and Political Elites," *Public Opinion Quarterly* (1992): 419–441.

56. The ANES Guide.

57. American National Election Studies, 2008.

58. Vernon Van Dyke, *Ideology and Political Choice* (Chatham, NJ: Chatham House, 1995), chaps. 3–5.

59. James A. Davis, "Changeable Weather in a Cooling Climate Atop the Liberal Plateau," *Public Opinion Quarterly* 56 (1992): 261–306; and Morris P. Fiorina, "The Reagan Years: Turning to the Right or Groping Toward the Middle?" in *The Resurgence of Conservatism in Anglo-American Democracies,* eds. Barry Cooper, Allan Kornberg, and William Mishler (Durham, NC: Duke University Press, 1988), pp. 430–459.

60. Morris P. Fiorina, *Divided Government,* 2nd ed. (Boston: Allyn & Bacon, 1995), pp. 173–177.

61. "Public Expects GOP Miracles," *Times-Mirror News Release* (December 8, 1994); CNN, "Gallup Poll: 50 Percent Americans Support, 33 Percent Oppose, Bush Tax Plan," February 27, 2001.

62. ABC News/*Washington Post* Poll, Feb. 19–22, 2009; NBC News/*Wall Street Journal* Poll, Feb. 26-March 1, 2009; CNN/Opinion Research Corporation poll, Nov. 13–15, 2009.

63. Classic studies include Samuel Stouffer, *Communism, Conformity, and Civil Liberties* (New York: Doubleday, 1955); and James Prothro and Charles Grigg, "Fundamental Principles of Democracy: Bases of Agreement and Disagreement," *Journal of Politics* 22 (1960): 176–194.

64. For evidence that people's opinions reflect a smaller number of "core beliefs" that may conflict with each other or situational characteristics, see Stanley Feldman, "Structure and Consistency in Public Opinion: The Role of Core Beliefs and Values," *American Journal of Public Opinion* 32 (1988): 416–440; and Stanley Feldman and John Zaller, "A Simple Theory of the Survey Response: Answering Questions Versus Revealing Preferences," *American Journal of Political Science* 36 (1992): 579–616.

65. R. Michael Alvarez and John Brehm, "American Ambivalence Toward Abortion Policy," *American Journal of Political Science* 39 (1995): 1055–1082.

66. On the effects of posing political conflicts as matters of conflicting rights, see Mary Anne Glendon, *Rights Talk: The Impoverishment of Political Discourse* (New York: Free Press, 1991).

67. "A Macro Theory of Information Flow," in *Information and Democratic Processes,* ed. John Ferejohn and James Kuklinski (Urbana: University of Illinois Press, 1990), pp. 345–368.

68. James Stimson, *Public Opinion in America: Moods, Cycles, and Swings* (Boulder, CO: Westview Press, 1991).

69. James Stimson, "Public Policy Mood, 1952–2009," www.unc.edu/~jstimson/, accessed June 10, 2010.

70. Christopher Wlezien, "The Public as Thermostat: Dynamics of Preferences for Spending," *American Journal of Political Science* 39 (1995): 981–1000.

71. Benjamin Page and Robert Shapiro, *The Rational Public* (Chicago: University of Chicago Press, 1992).

72. Kathy Keily, "After Failed Gun Legislation, Political Finger Pointing Begins," *USA Today,* June 21, 1999: 14A.

CHAPTER 6

1. Michael D. Shear, "Virginia Sizzling with Election Fever," *Washington Post* (October 24, 2004): C7.

2. Robert D. McFadden, "Record Turnout Forecast; Vote Drives Intensify," *New York Times* (November 2, 2004): A1.

3. David B. Magleby, Jay Goodliffe, Joseph Olsen, David Lassen, and Bradley Jones, "Small Donors in the 2008 Elections: Putting the Small Donor Surge in Context," Paper presented at the 2010 Meeting of the Midwest Political Science Association, Chicago, IL, April 22–25.

4. "Invesco Dems Text, Call En Masse," ABC News, August 28, 2008, http://abcnews.go.com/Technology/story?id=5692456, accessed May 14, 2010.

5. All figures based on the National Election Studies, University of Michigan, www.electionstudies.org.

6. Benjamin Barber, *Strong Democracy: Participatory Politics for a New Age* (Berkeley and Los Angeles: University of California Press, 1984), p. xiii.

7. Chilton Williamson, *American Suffrage from Property to Democracy: 1760–1860* (Princeton, NJ: Princeton University Press, 1960); and Alexander Keyssar, *The Right to Vote* (New York: Basic Books, 2000), p. 29.

8. Ibid., p. 277.

9. Eleanor Flexner, *Century of Struggle*, rev. ed. (Cambridge, MA: Harvard University Press, 1975); and Anne Scott and Andrew Scott, *One Half the People* (Philadelphia: Lippincott, 1975).

10. For a history of the drive to enfranchise women, see Keyssar, *The Right to Vote*, chap. 6. On the strategies used by the suffrage movement, see Anna Harvey, "The Political Consequences of Suffrage Exclusion," *Social Science History* 20 (1996): 97–132.

11. "18-Year-Old Vote: Constitutional Amendment Cleared," *Congressional Quarterly Almanac* (Washington, DC: Congressional Quarterly, 1972): 475–477.

12. Keyssar, *The Right to Vote*, pp. xxi, 14–15.

13. "Felons and the Right to Vote," *nytimes.com* (July 11, 2004); and "Can the Black Vote Hold Up?" *The Economist* (April 3, 1999): 24.

14. Keyssar, *The Right to Vote*.

15. For a comparative study of the American and Swiss suffrage movements, see Lee Ann Banaszak, *Why Movements Succeed or Fail* (Princeton, NJ: Princeton University Press, 1996).

16. Rosenstone and Hansen, *Mobilization, Participation, and Democracy*, chap. 2.

17. Jeffrey Jones, "Does Bringing Out the Candidate Bring Out the Votes?" *American Politics Quarterly* 26 (1998): 406.

18. John Ferejohn and Morris Fiorina, "The Paradox of Not Voting: A Decision Theoretic Analysis," *American Political Science Review* 68 (1974): 525–535.

19. United States Bureau of the Census, "Voting and Registration in the Election of November 2008," May 2010, www.census.gov/prod/2010pubs/p20-562.pdf, accessed May 14, 2010.

20. John Milholland, "The Danger Point in American Politics," *North American Review* 164 (1897), p. 95. In 1890s dollars, between $2 and $5.

21. Raymond Wolfinger and Steven Rosenstone, *Who Votes?* (New Haven, CT: Yale University Press, 1980), p. 101.

22. A more sophisticated variant of this argument appears in Alexander A. Schuessler, *The Logic of Expressive Choice* (Princeton, NJ: Princeton University Press).

23. Howard Rosenthal and Subrata Sen, "Electoral Participation in the French Fifth Republic," *American Political Science Review* 67 (1973): 29–54.

24. McDonald's results for 2008 and earlier elections are reported on his website: www.elections.gmu.edu.

25. Ruy Teixeira, *The Disappearing American Voter* (Washington, DC: The Brookings Institution, 1992), p. 10.

26. Parliament of Australia, Department of Parliamentary Services, "Compulsory Voting in Australian National Elections," No. 6, 2005-06, updated March 3, 2008, www.aph.gov.au/library/pubs/rb/2005-06/06rb06.pdf, accessed May 14, 2010.

27. Mark Franklin, "Electoral Engineering and Cross-National Turnout Differences: What Role for Compulsory Voting?" *British Journal of Political Science* 29 (1999): 205.

28. Richard Boyd, "Decline of U.S. Voter Turnout: Structural Explanations," *American Politics Quarterly* 9 (1981): 133–159.

29. Stephen Knack, "The Voter Participation Effects of Selecting Jurors from Registration Lists," Working Paper No. 91-10, University of Maryland, Department of Economics; and J. Eric Oliver and Raymond Wolfinger, "Jury Aversion and Voter Registration," paper presented at the 1997 Annual Meeting of the American Political Science Association, Washington, DC.

30. Rosenstone and Hansen, *Mobilization, Participation, and Democracy*, p. 175.

31. Martin Wattenberg, *The Decline of American Political Parties, 1952–1996* (Cambridge, MA: Harvard University Press, 1998). Interestingly, the percentage of voters who reported being contacted by a party rose from 1956 to 1982 but declined thereafter. Party efforts would appear to have met with very limited success, inasmuch as turnout was falling throughout the period. See Rosenstone and Hansen, *Mobilization, Participation, and Democracy*, p. 163.

32. G. Bingham Powell, "American Voter Turnout in Comparative Perspective," *American Political Science Review* 80 (1986): 17–43; and Robert Jackman, "Political Institutions and Voter Turnout in the Industrial Democracies," *American Political Science Review* 81 (1987): 405–423.

33. Rosenstone and Hansen, *Mobilization, Participation, and Democracy*, pp. 63–70. There is some conflict between their figures and those reported by Verba, Schlozman, and Brady in *Voice and Equality*, pp. 69–74. Part of the explanation may be that the survey items relied on by Rosenstone and Hansen generally have more specific referents (such as this year's elections), whereas the items relied on by Verba, Schlozman, and Brady ask more generally about activity in the last year or two. Thus, the Verba, Schlozman, and Brady figures may reflect the increasing number of opportunities.

34. Teixeira, *The Disappearing American Voter*, p. 49.

35. Michael Delli Carpini and Scott Keeter, *What Americans Know About Politics and Why It Matters* (New Haven, CT: Yale University Press, 1996).

36. See the National Election Studies data archived at http://electionstudies.org/nesguide/gd-index.htm#6.

37. Rosenstone and Hansen, *Mobilization, Participation, and Democracy*, p. 183.

38. Donald Green and Alan Gerber, *Get Out the Vote: How to Increase Voter Turnout* (Washington, DC: Brookings Institution Press, 2004).

39. Warren Miller, "The Puzzle Transformed: Explaining Declining Turnout," *Political Behavior* 14 (1992): 1–43.

40. Martin Wattenberg, *Is Voting for Young People?* (New York: Longman, 2007).

41. Robert Putnam, *Bowling Alone* (New York: Simon & Schuster, 2000), chap. 14.

42. Stephen Knack, "Civic Norms, Social Sanctions, and Voter Turnout," *Rationality and Society* 4 (1992): 133–156.

43. Fareed Zakaria, "The Character of Our Campuses," *Newsweek* (May 28, 2001): 31.

44. Knack, "Civic Norms."

45. Rosenstone and Hansen, *Mobilization, Participation, and Democracy*, chap. 7; and Teixeira, *The Disappearing American Voter*, chap. 2.

46. Eric Uslaner, "Faith, Hope, and Charity: Social Capital, Trust, and Collective Action" (College Park, MD: University of Maryland, unpublished manuscript).

47. For detailed analyses of the relationship between demographic characteristics and voting, see Wolfinger and Rosenstone, *Who Votes?* and Rosenstone and Hansen, *Mobilization, Participation, and Democracy*, chap. 5.

48. Sidney Verba and Norman H. Nie, *Participation in America: Political Democracy and Social Equality* (New York: Harper & Row, 1972), pp. 170–171; and Wolfinger and Rosenstone, *Who Votes?* p. 90.

49. See, for example, Rosenstone and Hansen, *Mobilization, Participation, and Democracy in America*, chap. 5.

50. On language and political participation, see Sidney Verba, Kay Schlozman, and Henry Brady, *Voice and Equality: Civic Volunteerism in American Politics* (Cambridge, MA: Harvard University Press, 1995); for turnout figures by race and ethnicity, see U.S. Bureau of the Census, Voting and Registration in the Election of November 2008, May 2010, www.census.gov/prod/2010pubs/p20-562.pdf, accessed May 14, 2010.

51. Nancy Burns, Kay Lehman Schlozman, and Sidney Verba, *The Private Roots of Public Action: Gender, Equality, and Political Participation* (Cambridge, MA: Harvard University Press, 2001), chaps. 3, 13.

52. Russell Dalton, *Citizen Politics in Western Democracies* (Chatham, NJ: Chatham House, 1988), pp. 51–52.

53. Herbert Tingsten, *Political Behavior: Studies in Election Statistics* (London: King & Son, 1937), pp. 225–226.

54. "Why Poor Turnout Points to a Healthy Democracy," *Gallup Poll Release* (May 23, 2001).

55. Quoted in Seymour Martin Lipset, *Political Man* (New York: Anchor, 1963), p. 228, note 90.

56. George Will, "In Defense of Nonvoting," in *The Morning After*, ed. George Will (New York: Free Press, 1986), p. 229.

57. A classic example is C. Wright Mills, *The Power Elite* (New York: Oxford University Press, 1956).

58. Stephen Bennett and David Resnick, "The Implications of Nonvoting for

Democracy in the United States," *American Journal of Political Science* 34 (1990): 771–802.

59. Teixeira, *The Disappearing American Voter*, p. 92.

60. Figures are based on the 2008 American National Election Study survey.

61. Political theorist Benjamin Barber refers to the face-to-face political event as an example of "strong democracy" and to pulling levers in the voting booth as an example of "thin democracy." See Barber, *Strong Democracy*.

62. Verba, Schlozman, and Brady, *Voice and Equality*, p. 50.

63. Ibid., p. 72.

64. David Nexon, "Asymmetry in the Political System: Occasional Activists in the Democratic and Republican Parties, 1956–1964," *American Political Science Review* 65 (1971): 716–730; and Warren Miller and M. Kent Jennings, *Parties in Transition* (New York: Russell Sage, 1986), chap. 2.

65. Fareed Zakaria, "The New Face of the Left," *Newsweek* (April 30, 2001): 32.

CHAPTER 7

1. James Bryce, *The American Commonwealth, Volume 2*, 3rd edition (New York: Macmillan, 1907), p. 278.

2. Julie Bosman, "More Hiring and Advertising Ahead for Paul Campaign as the Donations Pour In," *New York Times* (December 18, 2007): A28.

3. Kate Zernike, "A Young and Unlikely Activist Who Got to the Tea Party Early," *New York Times* (February 28, 2010): A1.

4. Brian Stelter, "CNBC Replays Its Reporter's Tirade," *New York Times* (February 23, 2009), B7; and Ben McGrath, "The Movement," *New Yorker* (February 1, 2010): 40–49.

5. Emma Brown, James Hohmann, and Perry Bacon, Jr., "Lashing Out at the Capitol: Tens of Thousands Protest Obama Initiatives and Government Spending," *Washington Post* (September 13, 2009): A1.

6. "Big Government: Hostility to the State," *The Economist* (January 21, 2010).

7. See www.teapartypatriots.org/AboutUs.aspx (accessed May 24, 2010).

8. See, for example, Kate Zernike, "Disputes Among Tea Party Groups Are Taking a Toll on February Convention," *New York Times* (January 26, 2010): A12.

9. Paul Krugman, "Tea Parties Forever," *New York Times* (April 13, 2009): A21.

10. Glenn Reynolds, "Tea Parties: Real Grassroots," *New York Post* (April 13, 2009).

11. James Madison, Alexander Hamilton, and John Jay, *The Federalist Papers* (New York:

Random House, 2000 [1788]), "Federalist No. 10," p. 55.

12. There is some controversy about how to measure group membership and consequently about its exact figures. For differing viewpoints, see Frank Baumgartner and Jack Walker, "Survey Research and Membership in Voluntary Associations," *American Journal of Political Science* 32 (1988): 908–928; Tom Smith, "Trends in Voluntary Group Membership: Comments on Baumgartner and Walker," *American Journal of Political Science* 34 (1990): 646–661; and Baumgartner and Walker, "Response to Smith's 'Trends in Voluntary Group Membership,'" *American Journal of Political Science* 34 (1990): 662–670.

13. Alexis de Tocqueville, *Democracy in America*, ed. J. P. Mayer (New York: HarperPerennial, 1969), p. 513.

14. Theda Skocpol, *Diminished Democracy* (Norman, OK: Oklahoma University Press, 2003), chap. 2.

15. Kay Schlozman and John Tierney, *Organized Interests and American Democracy* (New York: Harper & Row, 1981), p. 75.

16. Robert Wiebe, *The Search for Order, 1877–1920* (New York: Hill and Wang, 1967).

17. Kristen Luker, *Abortion and the Politics of Motherhood* (Berkeley: University of California Press, 1984), chaps. 5–6.

18. Robert H. Salsbury, "Interest Representation: The Dominance of Institutions," *American Political Science Review* 78 (1984): 64–76.

19. Kay L. Schlozman, "Who Sings in the Heavenly Chorus? The Shape of the Organized Interest System," in *The Oxford Handbook of American Political Parties and Interest Groups,* ed. L. Sandy Maisel and Jeffrey Berry (New York: Oxford University Press, 2010), p. 430.

20. Calculated by authors from data in Kay L. Schlozman, "Who Sings in the Heavenly Chorus? The Shape of the Organized Interest System," in *The Oxford Handbook of American Political Parties and Interest Groups,* ed. L. Sandy Maisel and Jeffrey Berry (New York: Oxford University Press, 2010), Table 22.1, p. 433.

21. An excellent source of basic information about groups and associations in the United States is the *Encyclopedia of Associations,* ed. Carol Schwartz and Rebecca Turner (Detroit, MI: Gale Research, annual).

22. Membership figures for the Consumers Union, the NRA, and the Sierra Club come from these organizations' websites: www.consumersunion.org/, http://www.nra .org, www.sierraclub.org/, accessed June 5, 2010. NAACP membership figures from James H. Burnett III, "NAACP Plans to Move in New Direction," *Miami Herald*, May 29, 2010,

www.miamiherald.com/2010/05/29/1655232/naacp-plans-to-move-in-new-direction.html, accessed June 5, 2010. Population figures come from the U.S. Census, http://quickfacts.census.gov, and are estimates as of 2009; number of households with guns taken from: L. Hepburn, M. Miller, D. Azrael, and D. Hemenway, "The U.S. Gun Stock: Results from the 2004 National Firearms Survey," *Injury Prevention,* 13 (2007): 15–19.

23. Henry Brady, Sidney Verba, and Kay Schlozman, "Beyond SES: A Resource Model of Political Participation," *American Political Science Review* 89 (1995): 271–294.

24. James Q. Wilson, *Political Organizations* (New York: Basic Books, 1973), chap. 3.

25. Mancur Olson, *The Logic of Collective Action* (Cambridge, MA: Harvard University Press, 1965).

26. R. Cornes and T. Sandler, *The Theory of Externalities, Public Goods and Club Goods* (Cambridge, England: Cambridge University Press, 1986), chap. 6.

27. See Bureau of Labor Statistics press release of January 22, 2010, available at www. bls.gov/news.release/union2.nr0.htm.

28. Jane Mansbridge, *Why We Lost the ERA* (Chicago: University of Chicago Press, 1986).

29. Kenneth Wald, *Religion and Politics in the United States,* 2nd ed. (Washington, DC: CQ Press, 1992), chap. 7.

30. Kenneth Wald, *Religion and Politics in the United States,* 2nd ed. (Washington, DC: CQ Press, 1992), chap. 7

31. Kiva Facts and History, www.kiva .org/about/facts, accessed June 5, 2010.

32. Stephanie Strom, "Confusion on Where Money Lent to Kiva Goes," *New York Times*, November 8, 2009, www.nytimes.com/2009/11/09/business/global/09kiva.html, accessed June 5, 2010.

33. See Katharine Q. Seelye, "AARP and Advocacy," *New York Times* (August 19, 2009): A16.

34. The controversy is discussed in Dan Eggen, "AARP: Reform Advocate and Insurance Salesman," *Washington Post* (October 27, 2009): A1.

35. The term is from Richard Wagner, "Pressure Groups and Political Entrepreneurs," *Papers in Nonmarket Decision Making* 1 (1966): 161–170. For extended discussions, see Norman Frolich, Joe Oppenheimer, and Oran Young, *Political Leadership and Collective Goods* (Princeton, NJ: Princeton University Press, 1971); and Terry Moe, *The Organization of Interests* (Chicago: University of Chicago Press, 1980), chaps. 3–4.

36. Bill and Melinda Gates Foundation, "Fact Sheet," www.gatesfoundation.org/about/

Pages/foundation-fact-sheet.aspx, accessed June 9, 2010.

37. Gavi Alliance, "Key Indicators," www .gavialliance.org/performance/global_results/ GAVI_Alliance___Results_2008___Vaccines. php, accessed June 9, 2010.

38. Google Public Policy Blog, "An Important Step Toward Updating ECPA," May 5, 2010, http://googlepublicpolicy.blogspot .com/2010/05/important-step-toward-updating-ecpa.html, accessed June 5, 2010.

39. Calculated by authors from Ford Foundation grants database, www.fordfound. org/grants, accessed June 5, 2010.

40. Walker, *Mobilizing Interest Groups in America,* pp. 98–99.

41. Jack Walker, "The Origins and Maintenance of Interest Groups in America," *American Political Science Review* 77 (1983): 390–406; Jack Walker, *Mobilizing Interest Groups in America: Patrons, Professions, and Social Movements,* (Ann Arbor: University of Michigan Press, 1991).

42. All statistics are taken from a report by the Center for Responsive Politics, available at 222.opensecrets.org/news/2010/02/ federal-lobbying-soars-in-2009.html.

43. Carl Weiser, "Enforcement of Law Almost Non-existent," *USA Today* (November 16, 1999): 11A.

44. Center for Responsive Politics, various issues of *Influence, Inc.,* available at www .opensecrets.org.

45. See Paul Alexander, *Machiavelli's Shadow: The Rise and Fall of Karl Rove* (New York: Modern Times, 2008), pp. 204–206.

46. Richard L. Hall and Alan V. Deardorff, "Lobbying as Legislative Subsidy," *American Political Science Review,* 100:1 (February 2006): 69–84.

47. Jack Wright, *Interest Groups and Congress* (New York: Longman, 2003).

48. Chuck Henning, *The Wit and Wisdom of Politics* (Golden, CO: Fulcrum Publishing, 1992), p. 137.

49. From $1.89 billion (in 2009 dollars) in 1998 to $3.49 billion in 2009. Data from www.opensecrets.org/lobbyists, accessed June 6, 2010.

50. Data on registered lobbyists from www.opensecrets.org/lobbyists, accessed June 6, 2010; on larger increases see Jeffrey H. Birnbaum, "The Road to Riches Is Called K Street," *Washington Post,* June 22, 2005, www. washingtonpost.com/wp-dyn/content/article/ 2005/06/21/AR2005062101632.html, accessed June 6, 2010.

51. www.ddcadvocacy.com/results/ manufacturing-industry-case-study/, accessed June 6, 2010.

52. Lobbyist Michael Bromberg, quoted in Eleanor Clift and Tom Brazaitis, *War Without Bloodshed: The Art of Politics* (New York: Scribner, 1996), p. 100.

53. Jackie Koszczuk, "Hitting Them Where They Live," *Congressional Quarterly Weekly Report* (October 2, 1999): 2283–2286.

54. Peter H. Odegard, *Pressure Politics: The Story of the Anti-Saloon League* (New York: Columbia University Press, 1928), p. 76.

55. Frank Sorauf, *Inside Campaign Finance* (New Haven, CT: Yale University Press, 1992), chap. 4. A basic reference on PACs is *The PAC Directory* (Cambridge, MA: Ballinger, various editions).

56. Ross Baker, *The New Fat Cats: Members of Congress as Political Benefactors* (New York: Priority Press, 1989); and Eliza Carney, "PAC Men," *National Journal* (October 1, 1994): 2268–2273.

57. Figures are taken from the Federal Election Commission press release of December 29, 2009, available at www.fec .gov/press/press2009/2009Dec29Cong/ 2009Dec29Cong.shtml.

58. For a discussion, see Richard Hall and Frank Wayman, "Buying Time: Moneyed Interests and the Mobilization of Bias in Congressional Committees," *American Political Science Review* 84 (1990): 797–820 and Stephen Ansolabehere, John Defiguerido, and James Snyder, "Why Is There So Little Money in U.S. Politics?" *Journal of Economic Perspectives,* 17 (2003): 105–130.

59. See Edward Epstein, "Business and Labor Under the Federal Election Campaign Act of 1971," in *Parties, Interest Groups, and Campaign Finance Laws,* ed. Michael Malbin (Washington, DC: American Enterprise Institute, 1980), pp. 107–151.

60. Figure is reported at www .opensecrets.org/527s/index.php.

61. See www.freeenterprise.com.

62. Jeremy W. Peters, "Unions Go On Attack Over Paterson's Layoff Threat," *New York Times* (April 14, 2009):. A17.

63. R. Kenneth Godwin, *One Billion Dollars of Influence* (Chatham, NJ: Chatham House, 1988).

64. Andrew McFarland, *Common Cause: Lobbying for the People* (Chatham, NJ: Chatham House, 1984), pp. 74–81.

65. Ed Henry, "It's the '90s: Old Dogs, New Tricks," *Roll Call Monthly* (November 1997): 13.

66. For details, see Hugh Graham and Ted Gurr, *The History of Violence in America* (New York: Bantam, 1969).

67. For an analysis of the expansion by the judiciary of federal programs for the handicapped and the poor, see R. Shep Melnick,

Between the Lines (Washington, DC: The Brookings Institution, 1994).

68. Karen O'Connor and Bryan McFall, "Conservative Interest Group Litigation in the Reagan Era and Beyond," in *The Politics of Interests,* ed. Mark Petracca (Boulder, CO: Westview Press, 1992), pp. 263–281.

69. Jeffrey Milyo, David Primo, and Timothy Groseclose, "Corporate PAC Campaign Contributions in Perspective," *Business and Politics* 2 (2000): 75–88.

70. Jonathan Rauch, *Demosclerosis* (New York: Random House, 1994).

71. Philip Stern, *The Best Congress Money Can Buy* (New York: Pantheon, 1988).

72. John Heinz, Edward Laumann, Robert Nelson, and Robert Salisbury, *The Hollow Core: Private Interests in National Policy Making* (Cambridge, MA: Harvard University Press, 1997).

73. J. Leiper Freeman, *The Political Process,* rev. ed. (New York: Random House, 1965); Grant McConnell, *Private Power and American Democracy* (New York: Knopf, 1966); and Theodore Lowi, *The End of Liberalism* (New York: Norton, 1969).

74. Hugh Heclo, "Issue Networks and the Executive Establishment, in *The New American Political System,* ed. Anthony King (Washington, DC: The Brookings Institution, 1978), pp. 87–124.

75. Robert Salisbury, John Heinz, Robert Nelson, and Edward Laumann, "Triangles, Networks, and Hollow Cores: The Complex Geometry of Washington Interest Representation," in *The Politics of Interests,* ed. Mark Petracca (Boulder, CO: Westview Press, 1992), pp. 130–149.

76. John Chubb, *Interest Groups and the Bureaucracy* (Stanford, CA: Stanford University Press, 1983), pp. 249–265; and Richard Harris, "Politicized Management: The Changing Face of Business in American Politics," in *Remaking American Politics,* ed. Richard Harris and Sidney Milkis (Boulder, CO: Westview Press, 1989), pp. 261–286.

77. Schlozman and Tierney, *Organized Interests and American Democracy,* pp. 314–317.

78. John Hibbing and Elizabeth Theiss-Morse, *Congress as Public Enemy* (New York: Cambridge University Press, 1995), pp. 63–65, 147.

79. Earl Latham, *The Group Basis of Politics* (New York: Cornell University Press, 1952); and David Truman, *The Governmental Process* (New York: Knopf, 1958).

80. E. E. Schattschneider, *The Semisovereign People* (New York: Holt, 1960), pp. 34–35.

81. ———. *Politics, Pressures, and the Tariff* (New York: Prentice-Hall, 1935).

82. ———. "The Gerontocrats," *The Economist* (May 13, 1995): 32.

83. See Morris P. Fiorina, Samuel J. Abrams, and Jeremy C. Pope, *Culture War? The Myth of a Polarized America,* 2nd ed. (New York: Pearson Longman, 2006), chap. 5.

84. Peter Aranson and Peter Ordeshook, "A Prolegomenon to a Theory of the Failure of Representative Democracy," in *American Re-evolution,* ed. Aranson and Ordeshooks (Tucson, AZ: University of Arizona, 1977), pp. 23–46.

CHAPTER 8

1. Figures include both the $16.8 million FEC grant and host committee spending as detailed at www.opensecrets.org/pres08/convcmtes.php?cycle=2008, accessed June 11, 2010.

2. David Bauder, "Republican National Convention Ratings," Associated Press, September 5, 2008, www.huffingtonpost.com/2008/09/05/republican-national-conve_n_124305.html, accessed June 11, 2010.

3. Jill A. Edy and Miglena Daradanova, "Conventional Wisdom: Putting National Party Convention Ratings in Context," *Journalism and Mass Communication Quarterly* 86:3 (Autumn 2009): 505.

4. Ibid, 499.

5. The first phrase comes from Richard Katz, "Party Government: A Rationalistic Conception," in *Visions and Realities of Party Government,* ed. F. Castles and R. Wildenmann (Berlin: deGruyter, 1986), p. 31. The second comes from Geoffrey Smith, "The Futures of Party Government," p. 206 of the same volume.

6. E. E. Schattschneider, *Party Government* (New York: Farrar and Rinehart, 1942), p. 1.

7. Martin Wattenberg, *The Decline of American Political Parties, 1952–1992* (Cambridge, MA: Harvard University Press, 1994).

8. John Aldrich, *Why Parties?* (Chicago: University of Chicago Press, 1995), chap. 2.

9. See, for example, James Campbell, *The Presidential Pulse of Congressional Elections* (Lexington: University Press of Kentucky, 1993); Eric McGhee, "National Tides and Local Results in U.S. House Elections," *British Journal of Political Science* 38 (2008): 719–738.

10. V. O. Key, Jr., *Southern Politics* (New York: Knopf, 1949).

11. Richard Fenno, *Home Style* (Boston: Little, Brown, 1978), chap. 3.

12. Juliet Eilperin, "GOP, Trying to Expand, Aids Black Candidates," *Washington Post* (July 16, 2000): A6.

13. Anthony Downs, *An Economic Theory of Democracy* (New York: Harper & Row, 1957).

14. Gavin Wright, "The Political Economy of New Deal Spending: An Econometric Analysis," *Review of Economics and Statistics* 56 (1974): 30–38.

15. Morris Fiorina, *Divided Government,* 2nd ed. (Boston: Allyn & Bacon, 1996), pp. 107–110.

16. R. Michael Alvarez and Jonathan Nagler, "Economics, Issues, and the Perot Candidacy: Voter Choice in the 1992 Presidential Election," *American Journal of Political Science* 39 (1995): 714–744.

17. Discussed in James MacGregor Burns, *The Deadlock of Democracy* (Englewood Cliffs, NJ: Prentice-Hall, 1964), chap. 2.

18. Austin Ranney, *Curing the Mischiefs of Faction* (Berkeley: University of California Press, 1975); and Nelson Polsby, *Consequences of Party Reform* (New York: Oxford University Press, 1983).

19. James Bryce, *The American Commonwealth,* 4th ed. (London: Macmillan, 1910), vol. 2, p. 5.

20. See, for example, William Chambers and Walter Dean Burnham, eds., *The American Party Systems: Stages of Political Development* (New York: Oxford University Press, 1975).

21. The seminal contribution was V. O. Key, Jr., "A Theory of Critical Elections," *Journal of Politics* 17 (1955): 3–18. The most influential elaborations and extensions of the idea are Walter Dean Burnham, *Critical Elections and the Mainsprings of American Politics* (New York: Norton, 1970) and James Sundquist, *Dynamics of the Party System,* rev. ed. (Washington, DC: The Brookings Institution, 1983).

22. David R. Mayhew, *Electoral Realignments: A Critique of an American Genre* (New Haven, CT: Yale, 2002).

23. For a good overview of the origin and development of America's first political parties, see William Nisbet Chambers, *Political Parties in a New Nation: The American Experience, 1776–1809* (New York: Oxford University Press, 1963).

24. Jack N. Rakove, *James Madison and the Creation of the American Republic,* 2nd ed. (New York: Longman, 2002), p. 149.

25. It is sometimes claimed that Lincoln was elected only because of a split in the Democratic Party. Actually, Lincoln won an absolute majority in enough northern states to achieve a majority in the Electoral College.

26. For a history of the period, see Paul Kleppner, *The Third Electoral System, 1853–1892: Parties, Voters, and Political Cultures* (Chapel Hill, NC: University of North Carolina Press, 1979).

27. Michael McGerr, *The Decline of Popular Politics* (New York: Oxford University Press, 1986).

28. Richard Hofstadter, *The Age of Reform* (New York: Vintage, 1955); and Gabriel Kolko, *The Triumph of Conservatism* (New York: Free Press, 1963).

29. See, in particular, Gerald M. Pomper and Susan S. Lederman, *Elections in America: Control and Influence in Democratic Politics,* 2nd ed. (New York: Longman, 1980), chap. 8.

30. Clinton Rossiter, *Parties and Politics in America* (Ithaca, NY: Cornell University Press, 1960), pp. 11–12.

31. See, for example, Jerome M. Clubb, William H. Flanigan, and Nancy H. Zingale, *Partisan Realignment: Voters, Parties, and Government in American History* (Beverly Hills, CA: Sage, 1980); and James Sundquist, *Dynamics of the Party System,* pp. 444–449.

32. For a good overview of the various theories about the electoral origins of divided government, see Gary W. Cox and Samuel Kernell, ed., *The Politics of Divided Government* (Boulder, CO: Westview Press, 1991).

33. See, for example, the essays by Everett Carll Ladd and Byron E. Shafer in *The End of Realignment? Interpreting American Electoral Eras,* ed. Byron E. Shafer (Madison, WI: University of Wisconsin Press, 1991).

34. Steven Rosenstone, Roy Behr, and Edward Lazarus, *Third Parties in America* (Princeton, NJ: Princeton University Press, 1981).

35. Maurice Duverger, *Political Parties: Their Organization and Activity in the Modern State* (New York: Wiley, 1963), book II, chap. 1.

36. Ibid. For elaboration, see Thomas Palfrey, "A Mathematical Proof of Duverger's Law," in *Models of Strategic Choice in Politics,* ed. Peter Ordeshook (Ann Arbor, MI: University of Michigan Press, 1989), pp. 69–91 and Gary Cox, *Making Votes Count: Strategic Coordination in the World's Electoral Systems* (New York: Cambridge University Press, 1997).

37. For a good introductory discussion of how ballot access laws work, see Emmet T. Flood and William G. Mayer, "Third-Party and Independent Candidates: How They Get on the Ballot, How They Get Nominated," in *In Pursuit of the White House: How We Choose Our Presidential Nominees,* ed. William G. Mayer (Chatham, NJ: Chatham House, 1996), pp. 285–306.

38. The idea that the word "party" can be used to refer to "many types of groups and near-groups" is generally credited to V. O. Key, Jr. See *Politics, Parties, and Pressure Groups,* 4th ed. (New York: Thomas Y. Crowell, 1958), pp. 180–182. Our own discussion draws heavily on Paul Allen Beck and Frank Sorauf,

Party Politics in America, 7th ed. (New York: HarperCollins, 1992), chap. 1.

39. The seminal case here is *Elrod v. Burns,* 427 U.S. 347 (1976).

40. Writing in the 1970s, Hugh Heclo put the number at 3,000. See his *A Government of Strangers* (Washington, DC: The Brookings Institution, 1977). By 1992, Thomas Weko put the number at about 3,700. See Thomas J. Weko, *The Politicizing Presidency* (Lawrence, KS: University of Kansas Press, 1995), p. 161.

41. Stephen Skowronek, *Building a New American State* (New York: Cambridge University Press, 1992), p. 69.

42. Stephen Frantzich, *Political Parties in the Technological Age* (New York: Longman, 1989).

43. Dick Polman, "American Politics Circa 2003: Neither Kind nor Gentle," Knight-Ridder News Service, August 17, 2003; and David S. Broder, "Fighting Over the Economy," *Washington Post Weekly Edition,* November 5–11, 2001: 4.

44. John Coleman, "Resurgent or Just Busy? Party Organizations in Contemporary America," in *The State of the Parties,* 2nd ed., ed. John Green and Daniel Shea (Lanham, MD: Rowman & Littlefield, 1996), pp. 312–326.

45. Robert Dahl, *Dilemmas of Pluralist Democracy* (New Haven, CT: Yale University Press, 1982).

CHAPTER 9

1. Howard Kurtz, "In Picking the Victors, Media Get Another Drubbing," *Washington Post* (January 10, 2008): C1.

2. Ibid..

3. Ibid..

4. Jessica Van Sack, "Mitt Toils to Erode McCain Lead," *Boston Herald* (January 8, 2008): 5.

5. Maureen Dowd, "Can Hillary Cry Her Way Back to the White House?" *New York Times,* January 9, 2008 www.nytimes.com/2008/01/09/opinion/08dowd.html, accessed June 26, 2008.

6. Kurtz.

7. Edwin Emery and Michael Emery, *The Press and America: An Interpretive of the Mass Media,* 5th ed. (Englewood Cliffs, NJ: Prentice-Hall, 1984), chap. 2.

8. Daniel J. Boorstin, *The Americans: The Colonial Experience* (New York: Vintage Books, 1958), chap. 50.

9. Jeffrey B. Abramson, F. Christopher Arterton, and Gary R. Orren, *The Electronic Commonwealth: The Impact of New Media Technologies on Democratic Politics* (New York: Basic Books, 1988), pp. 74–75.

10. Timothy E. Cook, *Governing with the News: The News Media as a Political Institution* (Chicago: University of Chicago Press, 1998), p. 26.

11. Ibid., p. 29.

12. Our discussion of the penny press draws especially on Michael Schudson, *Discovering the News: A Social History of American Newspapers* (New York: Basic Books), chap. 1.

13. For a more detailed discussion of these events, see Emery and Emery, *The Press and America,* chap. 17.

14. Our history of early radio draws especially on Emery and Emery, *The Press and America,* chap. 20.

15. For more data on the early spread of television, see William G. Mayer, "Trends in Media Usage," *Public Opinion Quarterly* 57 (Winter 1993): 593–611.

16. "More than Half the Homes in U.S. Have Three or More TVs," Nielson Wire, July 20, 2009, http://blog.nielsen.com/nielsenwire/media_entertainment/more-than-half-the-homes-in-us-have-three-or-more-tvs/, accessed June 18, 2010.

17. Media Info Center, www.mediainfocenter.org/television/cable/size.asp, accessed June 18, 2010.

18. Television Bureau of Advertising, www.tvb.org, accessed June 18, 2010.

19. In an average week, the four major networks reach over 70 percent of households, but no cable channel reaches 40 percent. Television Bureau of Advertising, www.tvb.org, accessed June 18, 2010.

20. Newspaper Association of America, "Total Paid Circulation," www.naa.org/TrendsandNumbers/Total-Paid-Circulation.aspx, accessed June 18, 2010.

21. Pew Project for Excellence in Journalism, "The State of the News Media, 2010," www.stateofthemedia.org/2010/, accessed June 18, 2010.

22. Ibid.

23. John Carroll, quoted in Leonard Downie, Jr. and Robert G. Kaiser, *The News About the News: American Journalism in Peril* (New York: Random House, 2002), p. 93.

24. "Number of Stations by Format," News Generation, Inc., www.newsgeneration.com/radio_resources/stats.htm, accessed June 18, 2010.

25. "Public Radio Today: 2009 Edition," Arbitron, www.arbitron.com/downloads/public_radio_today_2009.pdf, accessed June 18, 2010.

26. "The National In-Car Study: Fighting for the Front Seat," Arbitron/Edison Media Research Report, Spring 2003, www.arbitron.com/downloads/In-Car_Newstalk.pdf, accessed June 18, 2010.

27. "Podcasting: Into the Mainstream," eMarketer.com report, March 2009, www.emarketer.com/Report.aspx?code=emarketer_2000569, accessed June 18, 2010.

28. "With Newsweek for Sale, an Era Fades," *New York Times* DealBook Blog, May 6, 2010, http://dealbook.blogs.nytimes.com/2010/05/06/with-newsweek-for-sale-an-era-fades/, accessed June 18, 2010.

29. "Average Total Paid and Verified Circulation for Top 100 ABC Magazines, 2009," Magazine Publishers of America, www.magazine.org/CONSUMER_MARKETING/CIRC_TRENDS/ABC2009TOTALrank.aspx, accessed June 18, 2010.

30. For a good discussion of the differences between the old and new media, see Abramson, Arterton, and Orren, *The Electronic Commonwealth,* chap. 2.

31. See, for example, Michael J. Robinson, "Public Affairs Television and the Growth of Political Malaise: The Case of 'The Selling of the Pentagon,'" *American Political Science Review* 70 (June 1976): 426–27.

32. Louisa Ada Seltzer, "Nightly News Viewers Are Aging Faster," *Media Life Magazine,* April 30, 2010, www.medialifemagazine.com/artman2/publish/Dayparts_update_51/Nightly-news-viewers-are-aging-faster-.asp, accessed June 21, 2010.

33. Michael Delli Carpini and Scott Keeter, *What Americans Know About Politics and Why It Matters* (New Haven, CT: Yale University Press, 1996).

34. Costas Panagopoulos, *Politicking Online: The Transformation of Election Campaign Communications,* (Piscataway, NJ: Rutgers University Press, 2009), p. 3.

35. Bridget Johnson, "Media Winner of the Week: It Certainly Wasn't Golfing, Yachting, or Joe Barton," The Hill, June 20, 2010, http://thehill.com/homenews/news/104363-media-winner-of-the-week-it-wasnt-golfing-or-yachting, accessed June 21, 2010.

36. This incident is discussed in Edwin Diamond, *The Tin Kazoo* (Cambridge: MIT Press, 1975), p. 24.

37. For this and a number of related studies, see John P. Robinson and Mark Levy, *The Main Source: Learning from Television News* (Beverly Hills: Sage, 1986).

38. As quoted in Evans Witt, "Here, There, and Everywhere: Where Americans Get Their News," *Public Opinion* 6 (August/September 1983): 45–48.

39. Pew Center on the People and the Press, http://people-press.org/reports/questionnaires/543.pdf, accessed June 21, 2010.

40. Matthew A. Baum, *Soft News Goes to War: Public Opinion and American Foreign Policy in the New Media Age* (Princeton, NJ: Princeton University Press, 2005).

41. The best study of the broadcast is Hadley Cantril, *The Invasion from Mars: A Study in the Psychology of Panic* (Princeton: Princeton University Press, 1940).

42. Paul F. Lazarsfeld, Bernard Berelson, and Hazel Gaudet, *The People's Choice,* 2nd ed. (New York: Columbia University Press, 1948).

43. The single best summary of this literature is Joseph Klapper, *The Effects of Mass Communication* (New York: Free Press, 1960).

44. It is worth noting, for example, that V. O. Key, Jr.'s celebrated textbook, *Politics, Parties, and Pressure Groups,* 4th ed. (New York: Thomas Y. Crowell, 1958), devotes just four of its 764 pages to the mass media.

45. Bernard Cohen, *The Press and Foreign Policy* (Princeton, NJ: Princeton University Press, 1963), p. 13.

46. Robert Rotberg and Thomas Weiss, eds., *From Massacres to Genocide* (Washington, DC: The Brookings Institution, 1996).

47. See, for example, "Too Graphic?" *American Journalism Review,* 32:1 (Spring 2010), pp. 28–33.

48. M. McCombs and D. Shaw, "The Evolution of Agenda-Setting: Twenty-Five Years in the Marketplace of Ideas," *Journal of Communications* 43 (1993): 58–67.

49. Steven Livingston and Todd Eachus, "Humanitarian Crises and U.S. Foreign Policy: Somalia and the CNN Effect Reconsidered," *Political Communication* 12 (1995): 413–429.

50. Lawrence Jacobs and Robert Shapiro, *Politicians Don't Pander* (Chicago: University of Chicago Press, 2000).

51. Shanto Iyengar and Donald Kinder, *News That Matters: Television and American Opinion* (Chicago: University of Chicago Press, 1987).

52. Jon Krosnick and Laura Brannon, "The Impact of the Gulf War on the Ingredients of Presidential Evaluations," *American Political Science Review* 87 (1993): 963–975.

53. Marc Hetherington, "The Media's Role in Forming Voters' National Economic Evaluations in 1992," *American Journal of Political Science* 40 (1966): 372–395.

54. The most extensive study of framing is Shanto Iyengar's *Is Anyone Responsible?* (Chicago: University of Chicago Press, 1991).

55. This definition is from Shanto Iyengar and Jennifer A. McGrady, *Media Politics: A Citizen's Guide* (New York: Norton, 2007), p. 219.

56. Iyengar and Kinder, *News That Matters,* chaps. 6, 10.

57. Bernard Cohen, *Press and Foreign Policy.* See also Lutz Erbring, Edie Goldenberg, and Arthur Miller, "Front-Page News and Real-World Clues: A New Look at Agenda-Setting by the Media," *American Journal of Political Science* 24 (1980): 16–49.

58. James N. Druckman, Cari Lynn Hennessy, Kristi St. Charles, and Jonathan Webber, "Competing Rhetoric Over Time: Frames vs. Cues," *Journal of Politics* 72(1) (January 2010): 136–148.

59. G. C. Stone and E. Grusin, "Network TV as Bad News Bearer," *Journalism Quarterly* 61 (1984): 517–523; R. H. Bohle, "Negativism as News Selection Predictor," *Journalism Quarterly* 63 (1986): 789–796; and D. E. Harrington, "Economic News on Television: The Determinants of Coverage," *Public Opinion Quarterly* 53 (1989): 17–40.

60. Larry Sabato, *Feeding Frenzy* (New York: Simon & Schuster, 1991).

61. Michael Robinson, "Public Affairs Television and the Growth of Political Malaise," *American Political Science Review* 70 (1976): 409–432. On TV making people more negative about human nature generally, see George Comstock, *The Evolution of American Television* (Newbury Park, CA: Sage, 1989), pp. 265–269.

62. A widely cited study of what constitutes news is provided by Herbert Gans, *Deciding What's News: A Case Study of CBS Evening News, NBC Nightly News, Newsweek and Time* (New York: Vintage, 1979).

63. Howard Kurtz, "The Flood the Media's Radar Missed," *Washington Post,* May 17, 2010, www.washingtonpost.com/wp-dyn/content/article/2010/05/17/AR2010051700752.html, accessed June 21, 2010.

64. Quoted in James Fallows, *Breaking the News* (New York: Pantheon, 1966), p. 137.

65. John David Rausch, Jr., "The Pathology of Politics: Government, Press, and Scandal," *Extensions: A Publication of the Carl Albert Congressional Research and Studies Center* (Norman, OK: Carl Albert Congressional Research and Studies Center, Fall 1990), pp. 11–12.

66. A Gallup survey of former Nieman Journalism Fellows found that more than three-quarters believe that traditional journalism is being replaced by tabloid journalism. See "The State of the Public Media Today" (Cambridge, MA: Nieman Foundation, April 1995).

67. Sabato, *Feeding Frenzy.*

68. Marc Peyser, "Red, White, and Funny," *Newsweek* (December 29, 2003): 77.

69. Fallows, *Breaking the News,* p. 132.

70. The best book of this kind is S. Robert Lichter, Stanley Rothman, and Linda S. Lichter, *The Media Elite* (New York: Hastings House, 1986).

71. For example, Gans, *Deciding What's News.*

72. See Michael J. Robinson and Margaret A. Sheehan, *Over the Wire and on TV: CBS and UPI in Campaign '80* (New York: Russell Sage, 1983), esp. chap. 5.

73. The best single study of this kind is William Schneider and I. A. Lewis, "Views on the News," *Public Opinion* 8 (August/September 1985): 6–11.

74. The study is summarized in importance.corante.com/archives/UCONN_DPP_ress_Release.pdf.

75. See msnbc.msn.com/id/19113485.

76. For a review of the evidence, see William G. Mayer, "Why Talk Radio Is Conservative," *Public Interest,* 156 (Summer 2004): 99–100.

77. For a compendium of such charges, see Ben J. Bagdikian, *The Media Monopoly,* 6th ed. (Boston: Beacon Press, 2000).

78. Martin Gilens, Why Americans Hate Welfare: Race, Media, and the Politics of Anti-Poverty Policy (Chicago: University of Chicago Press, 2000).

79. John Kramer, vice president for communication, Institute of Justice, personal communication, September 9, 1999.

80. Alison Carper, "Paint-by-Numbers Journalism: How Reader Surveys and Focus Groups Subvert a Democratic Press" (Barone Center on the Press, Politics and Public Policy, Harvard University Kennedy School of Government, Discussion Paper D-19, April 1995).

81. Pew Research Center for the People and the Press, "Economy, Volcanic Ash Top News Interest," April 28, 2010, http://people-press.org/report/609/, accessed June 22, 2010.

82. Thomas Patterson, *Out of Order* (New York: Knopf, 1993), chap. 2.

83. Kiku Adatto, *Picture Perfect* (New York: Basic, 1993).

84. Stephen J. Farnsworth and S. Robert Lichter, *The Nightly News Nightmare: Network Television's Coverage of U.S. Presidential Elections, 1988–2000* (Lanham, MD: Rowman & Littlefield, 2003), p. 81.

85. Leena Rao, "YouTube Launches Campaign Toolkit for Politicians," TechCruch.com, June 3, 2010, accessed June 22, 2010.

86. Quoted in Craig Lambert, "Hertzberg of the *New Yorker,*" *Harvard Magazine* (January-February 2003): 36.

87. Ibid.

88. Pippa Norris, "Editorial," *Press/Politics* 2 (1997): 1.

89. Sara Murray, "McCain Scores with TV Viewers," WSJ Blogs: Washington Wire, September 5, 2008, http://blogs.wsj.com/washwire/2008/09/05/mccain-scores-with-tv-viewers/, accessed June 22, 2010.

90. Elihu Katz and Jacob Feldman, "The Debates in the Light of Research: A Survey of Surveys," in *The Great Debates*, ed. Sidney Kraus (Bloomington: University of Indiana Press, 1962), pp. 173–223.

91. Thomas Holbrook, "Campaigns, National Conditions, and U.S. Presidential Elections," *American Journal of Political Science* 38 (1994): 973–998.

92. John David Rausch, Jr., "The Pathology of Politics: Government, Press, and Scandal," *Extensions: A Publication of the Carl Albert Congressional Research and Studies Center* (Norman, OK: Carl Albert Congressional Research and Studies Center, Fall 1990), pp. 11–12.

93. A Gallup survey of former Nieman Journalism Fellows found that more than three-quarters believe that traditional journalism is being replaced by tabloid journalism. See "The State of the Public Media Today" (Cambridge, MA: Nieman Foundation, April 1995).

94. Sabato, *Feeding Frenzy*.

95. David Bauder, "News Channels Quickly Lose Interest in Summit," Associated Press, February 25, 2010.

96. Marc Peyser, "Red, White, and Funny," *Newsweek* (December 29, 2003): 77.

97. Fallows, *Breaking the News*, p. 132.

98. The best book of this kind is S. Robert Lichter, Stanley Rothman, and Linda S. Lichter, *The Media Elite* (New York: Hastings House, 1986).

99. For example, Gans, *Deciding What's News*.

100. See Michael J. Robinson and Margaret A. Sheehan, *Over the Wire and on TV: CBS and UPI in Campaign '80* (New York: Russell Sage, 1983), esp. chap. 5.

101. Stephen J. Farnsworth and S. Robert Lichter, "The Mediated Congress: Coverage of Capitol Hill in the *New York Times* and the *Washington Post*," Harvard International Journal of Press/Politics 10(2) (2005): 94–107.

102. The best single study of this kind is William Schneider and I. A. Lewis, "Views on the News," *Public Opinion* 8 (August/September 1985): 6–11.

103. Stanley Rothman and Amy E. Black, "Media and Business Elites: Still in Conflict?" *Public Interest* (Spring 2001): 80.

104. Quoted in Ken Auletta, "Non-Stop News: With Cable, the Web, and Tweets, Can the President—or the Press—Still Control the Story?" *The New Yorker* (January 25, 2010): 38.

CHAPTER 10

1. "Amazing Race of '08 Arrives at Finish Line," *USA Today* (November 2, 2008): 10A.

2. For a good history of the early presidential nomination process, on which the following account draws, see Richard P. McCormick, *The Presidential Game: The Origins of American Presidential Politics* (New York: Oxford University Press, 1982).

3. The best account of the origins of presidential primaries and their use during the "mixed system" period is James W. Davis, *Springboard to the White House* (New York: Crowell, 1967).

4. The classic history of the Commission and its aftermath is Byron E. Shafer, *Quiet Revolution: The Struggle for the Democratic Party and the Shaping of Post-Reform Politics* (New York: Russell Sage, 1983).

5. For a more detailed discussion of the caucus process, see William G. Mayer, "Caucuses: How They Work, What Difference They Make," in *In Pursuit of the White House: How We Choose Our Presidential Nominees,* ed. William G. Mayer (Chatham, NJ: Chatham House, 1996), pp. 105–157.

6. Then–senate majority leader Howard Baker, as quoted in Jack W. Germond and Jules Witcover, *Blue Smoke and Mirrors: How Reagan Won and Why Carter Lost the Election of 1980* (New York: Viking, 1981), p. 96.

7. Federal Election Commission, www.fec.gov/press/press2009/20090608Pres/1_OverviewPresFin-Activity1996-2008.pdf, accessed June 15, 2010, and Obama campaign FEC reports.

8. For announcement dates for all presidential candidates between 1952 and 1996, see Michael G. Hagen and William G. Mayer, "The Modern Politics of Presidential Selection: How Changing the Rules Really Did Change the Game," in *In Pursuit of the White House 2000,* pp. 22–25.

9. Emmett H. Buell, Jr., "The Invisible Primary," in *In Pursuit of the White House,* pp. 1–43.

10. For further details, see William G. Mayer, "The Basic Dynamics of the Contemporary Nomination Process," in *The Making of the Presidential Candidates 2004,* ed. William G. Mayer (Lanham, MD: Rowman & Littlefield, 2004), pp. 83–132.

11. Lamar Alexander, "Off with the Limits," *Campaigns & Elections* (October–November 1996): 33.

12. For data on the dominance of these two states, see William G. Mayer and Andrew E. Busch, *The Front-Loading Problem in Presidential Nominations* (Washington: Brookings Institution, 2004), pp. 24–30.

13. For an extended account of front-loading and its effects, see Mayer and Busch, *The Front-Loading Problem.*

14. Not so long ago, one could say that the use of primary elections to select candidates for national leadership positions was a distinctively American institution. In recent years, however, a number of other countries have also started to use primaries for this purpose. See James A. McCann, "The Emerging International Trend toward Open Presidential Primaries: The American Presidential Nomination Process in Comparative Perspective," in *The Making of the Presidential Candidates 2004,* pp. 265–293.

15. E. E. Schattschneider, *Party Government* (New York: Holt, Rinehart and Winston, 1942).

16. "Presidential Campaigns Shifting into Overdrive," *Grand Rapids Press* (Michigan) (March 6, 2008): A6; "Uncertainty Reigns, Hurdles Line Path for Dem., GOP Candidates," *San Diego Union-Tribune* (March 6, 2008): B6; Jill Lawrence and Kathy Kiely, "Back on Attack, Candidates Hit the Airwaves," *USA Today* (March 6, 2008): 4A.

17. Thomas Patterson, *Out of Order* (New York: Vintage, 1994), p. 74.

18. "Voting Participation: Members Maintain High Voting Rate," *2007 CQ Almanac* B15–B25.

19. See William G. Mayer, "A Brief History of Vice Presidential Selection," in *In Pursuit of the White House 2000,* pp. 313–374.

20. During the last two months of the presidential campaigns of 1976–1988, about 40 percent of the lead stories on the CBS evening news were about the election, as were 20 percent of all the stories reported. See Stephen J. Rosenstone and John Mark Hansen, *Mobilization, Participation, and Democracy in America* (New York: Macmillan, 1993), p. 178, n. 26.

21. Jake Tapper, "Obama to Break Promise, Opt Out of Public Financing for General Election," ABC News, June 19, 2008, http://blogs.abcnews.com/politicalpunch/2008/06/obama-to-break.html, accessed June 15, 2010.

22. Ibid.

23. "Party Financial Activity Summarized for the 2008 Election Cycle: Party Support for Candidates Increases," Federal Election Commission press release, May 28, 2009, www.fec.gov/press/press2009/05282009Party/20090528Party.shtml, accessed June 15, 2010.

24. See, generally, *Buckley v. Valeo,* 424 U.S. 1 (1976).

25. *Citizens United v. Federal Election Commission* No. 08-205 (2010).

26. "Advocacy Group Spending," www .opensecrets.org/527s/index.php, accessed June 15, 2010.

27. Thomas Patterson and Robert McClure, *The Unseeing Eye: The Myth of Television Power in National Elections* (New York: Putnam, 1976); and Stephen Ansolabehere and Shanto Iyengar, *Going Negative: How Attack Ads Shrink and Polarize the Electorate* (New York: Free Press, 1995).

28. Darrel West, *Air Wars: Television Advertising in Election Campaigns, 1952–1992* (Washington, DC: Congressional Quarterly, 1993).

29. Edwin Diamond and Stephen Bates, *The Spot,* 3rd ed. (Cambridge, MA: MIT Press, 1992).

30. William G. Mayer, "In Defense of Negative Campaigning," *Political Science Quarterly* 111 (1996): 437–455.

31. Craig Brians and Martin Wattenberg, "Campaign Issue Knowledge and Salience: Comparing Reception from TV Commercials, TV News, and Newspapers," *American Journal of Political Science* 40 (1996): 172–193.

32. Ibid. Not all scholars agree that negative ads are more effective than positive ones or that negative ads depress turnout. For a thorough airing of the issues, see the Forum in the December 1999 issue of the *American Political Science Review.*

33. "2008 Presidential Expenditures," www.opensecrets.org/pres08/expenditures.php ?cycle=2008, accessed June 15, 2010.

34. Brian J. Gaines, "Popular Myths About Popular Vote-Electoral College Splits," *PS: Political Science and Politics* 34 (March 2001): 71–75.

35. Pre-2008 figures come from the American National Election Studies, conducted by the Center for Political Studies at the University of Michigan; 2008 figure comes from the 2008 Presidential Election Exit Poll, http://abcnews.go.com/PollingUnit/ ExitPolls/, accessed June 15, 2010.

36. Although the general notion of "partisanship" has been around for centuries, the social-psychological concept of party ID was advanced in the pioneering work of Angus Campbell, Philip Converse, Warren Miller, and Donald Stokes, *The American Voter* (New York: Wiley, 1960), chaps. 6–7.

37. This is the wording used in the American National Election Studies. The Gallup Poll, which actually invented the question, employs a slightly different wording.

38. Morris Fiorina, *Retrospective Voting in American National Elections* (New Haven, CT: Yale University Press, 1981); and Michael MacKuen, Robert Erikson, and James Stimson, "Macropartisanship," *American Political Science Review* 83 (1989): 1125–1142.

39. The classic demonstration appears in Chapter 8 of Campbell et al., *The American Voter,* although it is generally agreed that the picture presented there is overstated. For balanced treatments of policy issues in recent campaigns, see the series of *Change and Continuity* volumes by Paul Abramson, John Aldrich, and David Rohde, published by CQ Press.

40. Benjamin Page and Richard Brody, "Policy Voting and the Electoral Process: The Vietnam War Issue," *American Political Science Review* 66 (1972): 979–995.

41. Edward Carmines and James Stimson, "The Two Faces of Issue Voting," *American Political Science Review* 74 (1980): 78–91.

42. Ibid. Also see R. Douglas Arnold, *The Logic of Congressional Action* (New Haven, CT: Yale University Press, 1990), chap. 2.

43. Richard Trilling, *Party Image and Electoral Behavior* (New York: Wiley, 1976).

44. Fiorina, *Retrospective Voting.*

45. Scott Teeter, "Public Opinion in 1984," and Gerald Pomper, "The Presidential Election," both in Gerald Pomper et al., *The Election of 1984* (Chatham, NJ: Chatham House, 1985).

46. This figure is derived from a regression analysis, in which the dependent variable is the two-party popular vote percentage and the independent variable is the real growth rate of the U.S. gross domestic product during the first six months of the election year.

47. Samuel Popkin, *The Reasoning Voter* (Chicago: University of Chicago Press, 1991), pp. 60–67.

48. Donald Stokes, "Some Dynamic Elements of Contests for the Presidency," *American Political Science Review* 60 (1966): 19–28.

49. Stokes, "Some Dynamic Elements," p. 222.

50. Indeed, by some calculations, Kennedy ran worse than a "generic" Democrat for that time. See Angus Campbell, Philip Converse, Warren Miller, and Donald Stokes, "Stability and Change in 1960: A Reinstating Election," in *Elections and the Political Order* (New York: Wiley, 1966), pp. 78–95.

51. Fiorina, Abrams, and Pope, "The 2000 US Presidential Election," p. 180.

52. Frank Newport, Jeffrey Jones, and Lydia Saad, "Ronald Reagan from the People's Perspective: A Gallup Poll Review," The Gallup Organization, June 15, 2004.

53. Paul F. Lazarsfeld, Bernard Berelson, and Hazel Gaudet, *The People's Choice,* 2nd ed. (New York: Columbia University Press, 1948).

54. For a discussion, see Marjorie Hershey, "The Campaign and the Media," in Gerald Pomper et al., *The Election of 1988* (Chatham, NJ: Chatham House, 1989), chap. 3.

55. James E. Campbell, *The American Campaign: U.S. Presidential Campaigns and the National Vote,* 2nd ed. (College Station, TX: Texas A&M University Press, 2008), chap. 8.

56. Aaron Smith, "The Internet's Role in Campaign 2008," Pew Internet and American Life Project, April 2009.

57. Donald Kinder and Lynn Sanders, *Divided by Color* (Chicago: University of Chicago Press, 1996).

58. Paul Sniderman and Thomas Piazza, *The Scar of Race* (Cambridge, MA: Harvard University Press, 1993).

59. Paul Abramson, John Aldrich, and David Rohde, *Change and Continuity in the 1992 Elections* (Washington, DC: Congressional Quarterly, 1994); and Herbert Weisberg and David Kimball, "Attitudinal Correlates of the 1992 Presidential Vote: Party Identification and Beyond," in *Democracy's Feast: Elections in America,* ed. Herbert Weisberg (Chatham, NJ: Chatham House, 1995), pp. 72–111.

60. Everett Ladd, "The Public's Views of National Performance," *The Public Perspective,* October/November 1996: 17–20.

61. Robert Merry, "A Rule for Presidents: Go Centrist or Perish," *Congressional Quarterly Weekly Report* (October 26, 1996): 3106.

62. Jane Mansbridge, "Myth and Reality: The ERA and the Gender Gap in the 1980 Election," *Public Opinion Quarterly* 49 (1985): 164–178.

63. Emily Stoper, "The Gender Gap Concealed and Revealed," *Journal of Political Science* 17 (1989): 50–62; and Tom Smith, "The Polls: Gender and Attitudes Toward Violence," *Public Opinion Quarterly* 48 (1984): 384–396.

64. Rhodes Cook, "Race of Muted Differences Has the Nation Yawning," *Congressional Quarterly Weekly Report* (October 19, 1996): 2950.

65. Fiorina, Abrams, and Pope, "The 2000 U.S. Presidential Election."

66. Michael Kinsley, as quoted by Howard Kurtz, "The Premature Post-Mortems Are Starting," *Washington Post,* online extras (October 31, 2000).

67. D. Sunshine Hillygus and Todd G. Shields, "Moral Issues and Voter Decision Making in the 2004 Presidential Election," *PS: Political Science and Politics* 38:2 (April 2005): 201–209.

CHAPTER 11

1. For analysis of the Massachusetts polls see Charles Franklin's posts on Pollster.com. www.pollster.com/blogs/charles-franklin/.

2. For running commentary on the Massachusetts race, see the January posts on the blog of Middlebury Professor Matt Dickinson. http://blogs.middlebury.edu/presidentialpower/.

3. Dan Balz and Jon Cohen, "Poll Frustration with D.C. Fueled GOP in Mass." www.msnbc.msn.com/id/35019673/ns/politics-washington_post/.

4. "Federalist 52," The Federalist Papers, ed. Clinton Rossiter (New York: Mentor, 1961), p. 327.

5. Max Farrand, ed., The Records of the Federal Convention of 1787 (New Haven, CT: Yale University Press, 1966), vol. 1, p. 151.

6. Morris Fiorina, David Rohde, and Peter Wissel, "Historical Change in House Turnover," in Congress in Change, ed. Norman Ornstein (New York: Praeger, 1975), pp. 24–57; and Nelson Polsby, "The Institutionalization of the U.S. House of Representatives," American Political Science Review 62 (1968): 144–168.

7. James Young, The Washington Community, 1800–1828 (New York: Harcourt, 1966), chap. 2.

8. The South was primarily agricultural and had fewer high-status career opportunities outside of politics. From the very beginning, southern members of Congress stayed longer than northerners. Fiorina, Rohde, and Wissel, "Historical Change in House Turnover," pp. 34–38.

9. Robert Struble, Jr., "House Turnover and the Principle of Rotation," Political Science Quarterly 94 (1979–1980): 660.

10. Douglas Price, "The Congressional Career—Then and Now," in Congressional Behavior, ed. Nelson Polsby (New York: Random House, 1971), pp. 14–27.

11. Rhodes Cook, "The Rhodes Cook Letter," May 2001, 14.

12. A good overview of the variety of rules governing congressional primaries is contained in Kristin Kanthak and Rebecca Morton, "The Effects of Electoral Rules on Congressional Primaries," in Congressional Primaries and the Politics of Representation, ed. Peter Galderisi, Marni Ezra, and Michael Lyons (Lanham, MD: Rowman and Littlefield, 2000).

13. For a list of 2006 Congressional filing and primary dates, see www.fec.gov/pubrec/fe2006/2006pdates.pdf.

14. Norman Ornstein, Thomas Mann, and Michael Malbin, Vital Statistics on Congress, 1999–2000 (Washington, DC: American Enterprise Institute, 2000), pp. 70–71.

15. Robert Erikson, "Malapportionment, Gerrymandering and Party Fortunes in Congressional Elections," American Political Science Review 66 (1972): 1234–1245; and Gary King and Andrew Gelman, "Systemic Consequences of Incumbency Advantage in U.S. House Elections," American Journal of Political Science 35 (1991): 110–138.

16. Burdett Loomis, "The Congressional Office as a Small Business: New Members Set Up Shop," Publius 9 (1979): 35–55.

17. Ornstein, Mann, and Malbin, Vital Statistics, p. 133.

18. Glenn Parker, Homeward Bound (Pittsburgh, PA: University of Pittsburgh Press, 1986).

19. Juliet Eilperin, "The House Member as Perpetual Commuter," Washington Post Weekly Edition (September 10–16, 2001): 29.

20. Diana Owen, Richard Davis, and Vincent James Strickler, "Congress and the Internet," Harvard International Journal of Press/Politics 4 (1999): 10–29.

21. Ibid.

22. Morris Fiorina, Congress—Keystone of the Washington Establishment, 2nd ed. (New Haven, CT: Yale University Press, 1989).

23. Ibid., chap. 10. See also Bruce Cain, John Ferejohn, and Morris Fiorina, The Personal Vote (Cambridge, MA: Harvard University Press, 1987), chap. 2.

24. The first to make this observation was Gary Jacobson, "Practical Consequences of Campaign Finance Reform: An Incumbent Protection Act?" Public Policy 42 (1976): 1–32.

25. Gary C. Jacobson, Money in Congressional Elections (New Haven, CT: Yale University Press, 1980).

26. Gary C. Jacobson, The Politics of Congressional Elections, 6th ed. (New York: Pearson Longman, 2004), chap. 3.

27. Kenneth Bickers and Robert Stein, "The Electoral Dynamics of the Federal Pork Barrel," American Journal of Political Science 40 (1996): 1300–1326.

28. David Magleby and Kelly Patterson, "The Polls—Poll Trends: Congressional Reform," Public Opinion Quarterly 58 (1994): 420–421.

29. Sarah Oates, Diana Owen, and Rachel Gibson, The Internet and Politics: Citizens, Voters and Activists (New York: Routledge, 2006).

30. Amihi Glazer and Bernard Grofman, "Two Plus Two Equals Six: Tenure in Office of Senators and Representatives, 1953–1983," Legislative Studies Quarterly 12 (1987): 555–564.

31. Alan Abramowitz and Jeffrey Segal, Senate Elections (Ann Arbor, MI: University of Michigan Press, 1992), pp. 34–35.

32. Morris Fiorina, Representatives, Roll Calls, and Constituencies (Lexington, MA: D.C. Heath, 1974), pp. 90–100.

33. Joe Foote and David Weber, "Network Evening News Visibility of Congressmen and Senators," paper presented to the Association for Education in Journalism and Mass Communication, August 1984.

34. Glenn Parker, "Interpreting Candidate Awareness in U.S. Congressional Elections," Legislative Studies Quarterly 6 (1981): 219–233.

35. Abramowitz and Segal, Senate Elections, pp. 228–231; and Jonathan Krasno, Challengers, Competition, and Reelection: Comparing Senate and House Elections (New Haven, CT: Yale University Press, 1995).

36. Joseph Schlesinger, Ambition in Politics (Chicago: Rand McNally, 1966).

37. For example, this charge was leveled at Democratic Senator Dick Clark of Iowa in his losing 1978 race. Clark had involved himself in U.S. policy toward Africa, which evidently was not much appreciated by his Iowa constituents.

38. David Brady and Morris Fiorina, "Ruptured Legacy: Presidential Congressional Relations in Historical Perspective," in Looking Back on the Reagan Presidency, ed. Larry Berman (Baltimore, MD: Johns Hopkins University Press, 1989), pp. 268–287.

39. Paul R. Abramson, John H. Aldrich, and David W. Rohde, Change and Continuity in the 2004 Elections (Washington, DC: CQ Press, 2006), chap. 10.

40. David Rohde, Parties and Leaders in the Postreform House (Chicago: University of Chicago Press, 1991); Gary Cox and Mathew McCubbins, Setting the Agenda (New York: Cambridge University Press, 2005).

41. Associated Press, "New Congress to Look More Like Real America," November 5, 2004.

42. Carol Swain, Black Faces, Black Interests: The Representation of African Americans in Congress (Cambridge, MA: Harvard University Press, 1993).

43. For a thoughtful treatment of these and related issues, see Jane Mansbridge, "In Defense of Descriptive Representation," working paper, Harvard University, 1997.

44. Library of Congress—Election Archive.

45. "Americans Rate Their Society and Chart Its Values," The Public Perspective (February/March 1997): 25.

46. See Charles Cameron, David Epstein, and Sharyn O'Halloran, "Do Majority-Minority Districts Maximize Substantive Black Representation in Congress?" American Political Science Review 90 (1996): 794–812.

47. David Lublin and D. Stephen Voss, "The Missing Middle," *Journal of Politics* 65 (February 2003): 227–237; Lublin and Voss, "Racial Redistricting and Realignment in Southern State Legislatures," *American Journal of Political Science* 44 (October 2000): 792–810; and Lublin and Voss, "Boll-Weevil Blues," *American Review of Politics* 22 (Fall/Winter 2000).

48. Juliana Gurenwald, "Incumbents Survive Redistricting," *Congressional Quarterly Weekly Report* (November 9, 1996): 3229; D. Stephen Voss and David Lublin, "Black Incumbents, White Districts: An Appraisal of the 1996 Congressional Elections," *American Politics Research* 29 (March 2001): 141–182.

49. Lee Sigelman and Susan Welch, *Black Americans' Views of Racial Inequality* (Cambridge, UK: Cambridge University Press, 1991).

50. Donald Kinder and Lynn Sanders, *Divided by Color* (Chicago: University of Chicago Press, 1996).

51. Former Representative Mike Espy (D-MS), who harbored gubernatorial or senatorial ambitions, openly espoused such beliefs. More recently, the relatively moderate record of Representative Harold Ford (D-TN) was usually explained by reference to his interest in being Tennessee's first black governor or senator. Indeed, Ford ran for the Senate in 2006 and though losing, waged a very competitive race. Nancy Zuckerbrod, "Tennessee Democrat Has His Sights Set High," *USA Today* (March 27, 2000): 29A.

CHAPTER 12

1. Kate O'Beirne, "Introducing Pork-Barrel Homeland Security: A Little Here, a Lot There," *National Review* (August 11, 2003).

2. Sue Stott, "Homeland Security Spending Increased for 2009, Remains Fastest-Growing Government Function." www.hstoday.us/content/view/1984/174/.

3. Veronique de Rugy, "Homeland Security Pork," *Washington Times* (August 1, 2005).

4. These and other examples appear in Rich Lowry, "Homeland Pork," *National Review Online* (July 19, 2005); JoAnn Wypijewski, "Homeland Security on the Range," *MotherJones.com* (March/April 2000; and Veronique de Rugy and Nick Gillespie, "America's Fleecing in the Name of Security," *SFGate.com* (February 19, 2006).

5. O'Beirne, "Introducing Pork-Barrel Homeland Security."

6. Speaker Thomas Reed, as quoted in Neil McNeil, *Forge of Democracy* (New York: McKay, 1963).

7. David Mayhew, *Congress: The Electoral Connection* (New Haven, CT: Yale University Press, 1974), pp. 81–82; and John Aldrich, *Why Parties?* (Chicago: University of Chicago Press, 1995).

8. Richard Fenno, *The United States Senate: A Bicameral Perspective* (Washington, DC: American Enterprise Institute, 1982).

9. http://innovation.cqpolitics.com/media/votestudy2009/.

10. Nelson Polsby, Miriam Gallagher, and Barry Rundquist, "The Growth of the Seniority System in the U.S. House of Representatives," *American Political Science Review* 63 (1969): 787–807. For a partial dissent, see Keith Krehbiel and Alan Wiseman, "Joseph Cannon: Majoritarian from Illinois," *Legislative Studies Quarterly* 26 (2001): 357–389.

11. Barbara Sinclair, *Majority Leadership in the U.S. House* (Baltimore, MD: Johns Hopkins University Press, 1983).

12. For a full discussion, see Steven S. Smith and Marcus Flathman, "Managing the Senate Floor: Complex Unanimous Consent Agreements Since the 1950s," *Legislative Studies Quarterly* 14 (1989): 349–374.

13. Keith Krehbiel, "Where's the Party?" *British Journal of Political Science* 23 (1993): 235–266; and James Snyder and Tim Groseclose, "Estimating Party Influence in Congressional Roll-Call Voting," *American Journal of Political Science* 44 (2000): 193–211.

14. David Rohde, *Parties and Leaders in the Postreform House* (Chicago: University of Chicago Press, 1991).

15. Barbara Sinclair, *Legislators, Leaders, and Lawmaking: The U.S. House of Representatives in the Postreform Era* (Baltimore, MD: Johns Hopkins University Press, 1995).

16. Gary Cox and Mathew McCubbins, *Legislative Leviathan* (Berkeley, CA: University of California Press, 1993); see especially chap. 2.

17. Morris P. Fiorina, with Samuel J. Abrams, *Disconnect: The Breakdown of Representation in American Politics* (Norman, OK: Oklahoma University Press, 2009), chaps. 5–6.

18. Ibid., chap. 5.

19. Jim Drinkard, "Confident Candidates Share Campaign Wealth," *USA Today* (April 19, 2000): 10A.

20. Royce Carroll and Henry A. Kim, "Party Government and the 'Cohesive Power of Public Plunder,'" *American Journal of Political Science* 54 (2010): 34–44.

21. Gerald Gamm and Kenneth Shepsle, "Emergence of Legislative Institutions: Standing Committees in the House and Senate, 1810–1825," *Legislative Studies Quarterly* 14 (1989): 39–66; and Joseph Cooper, *The Origins of the Standing Committees and the Development of the Modern House* (Houston, TX: Rice University Studies, 1970).

22. Richard Fenno, *Congressmen in Committees* (Boston: Little, Brown, 1973), p. 172.

23. Karen Foerstel, "Gingrich Flexes His Power in Picking Panel Chiefs," *Congressional Quarterly Weekly Report* (November 19, 1994): 3326.

24. Barry Weingast and William Marshall, "The Industrial Organization of Congress," *Journal of Political Economy* 91 (1988): 132–163.

25. John Ferejohn, *Pork Barrel Politics* (Stanford, CA: Stanford University Press, 1974); and R. Douglas Arnold, *Congress and the Bureaucracy* (New Haven, CT: Yale University Press, 1979).

26. Keith Krehbiel, *Information and Legislative Organization* (Ann Arbor: University of Michigan Press, 1991).

27. Gary W. Cox and Mathew D. McCubbins, *Setting the Agenda: Responsible Party Government in the U.S. House of Representatives* (New York: Cambridge University Press, 2005).

28. Norman Ornstein, Thomas Mann, and Michael Malbin, *Vital Statistics on Congress: 1999–2000* (Washington, DC: American Enterprise Institution Press, 2001); see especially chap. 4.

29. David King, *Turf Wars: How Congressional Committees Claim Jurisdiction* (Chicago: University of Chicago Press, 1997).

30. http://thatsmycongress.com/index.php/2009/03/10/list-of-websites-for-house-caucuses-in-the-111th-congress/.

31. Andrea Fuller, "For 435 Lawmakers, 250 Groups to Align with," http://www.nytimes.com/2009/07/12/us/politics/12interests.html, accessed March 22, 2010.

32. The most comprehensive study to date is Susan Webb Hammond, *Congressional Caucuses in National Policy Making* (Baltimore, MD: Johns Hopkins University Press, 2001).

33. Barbara Sinclair, *Unorthodox Lawmaking: New Legislative Processes in the U.S. Congress,* 3rd ed. (Washington, DC: CQ Press, 2007).

34. Jeffrey Talbert, Bryan Jones, and Frank Baumgartner, "Nonlegislative Hearings and Policy Change in Congress," *American Journal of Political Science* 39 (1995): 391–392.

35. For a detailed study of how and why individual members participate at these various stages of the legislative process, see Richard Hall, *Participation in Congress* (New Haven, CT: Yale University Press, 1996).

36. On the conference committee in recent years, see Stephen Van Beek, *Post-Passage Politics: Bicameral Relations in Congress*

(Pittsburgh, PA: University of Pittsburgh Press, 1995).

37. Richard Munson, *The Cardinals of Capitol Hill* (New York: Grove Press, 1993).

38. Quoted in Stephen Skowronek, *The Politics Presidents Make* (Cambridge, MA: Harvard University Press, 1993), p. 389.

39. Diana Evans, "Policy and Pork: The Use of Pork Barrel Projects to Build Policy Coalitions in the House of Representatives," *American Journal of Political Science* 38 (1994): 894–917.

40. Harrison Donnelly, "Reagan Opposition Threatens EDA Development Program," *Congressional Quarterly Weekly Report* 40 (1982): 2295–2296.

41. Chuck Henning, *The Wit and Wisdom of Politics* (Golden, CO: Fulcrum, 1992), p. 39.

42. For institutional comparisons, see John Hibbing and Elizabeth Theiss-Morse, *Congress as Public Enemy* (New York: Cambridge University Press, 1995), chap. 2.

43. Kelly Patterson and David Magleby, "Trends: Public Support for Congress," *Public Opinion Quarterly* 56 (1992): 539–551.

44. Glenn Parker and Roger Davidson, "Why Do Americans Love Their Congressmen So Much More Than Their Congress?" *Legislative Studies Quarterly* 4 (1979): 52–61.

45. Richard Fenno, "If, As Ralph Nader Says, Congress is the 'Broken Branch,' How Come We Love Our Congressmen So Much?" in *Congress in Change,* ed. Norman Ornstein (New York: Praeger, 1975), pp. 277–287.

CHAPTER 13

1. Barack Obama, "Remarks by the President in Address to the Nation on the Way Forward in Afghanistan and Pakistan," December 1, 2009, available at www.white-house.gov/the-press-office/remarks-president-address-nation-way-forward-afghanistan-and-pakistan, accessed January 5, 2010.

2. Barack Obama, "Remarks by the President at the Acceptance of the Nobel Peace Prize," December 10, 2009, available at www.whitehouse.gov/the-press-office/remarks-president-acceptance-nobel-peace-prize, accessed January 5, 2010.

3. Charles Babington and Jennifer Loven, "Obama Raced Clock, Chaos, Comedy for Climate Deal," Associated Press, December 19, 2009.

4. Carrie Johnson, Karen DeYoung, and Anne E. Kornblut, "Obama Vows to Repair Intelligence Gaps Behind Detroit Airplane Incident," *The Washington Post* (December 30, 2009): A1.

5. Mike Allen, "Dick Cheney: Barack Obama 'Trying to Pretend,'" *Politico,* December 30, 2009, available at www.politico.com/news/stories/1209/31054.html, accessed January 5, 2010.

6. Dana Perino, quoted in Michael D. Shear, "In West Wing: Grueling Schedules, Bleary Eyes," *Washington Post* (July 13, 2009).

7. John F. Harris, "Both Sides Frustrated as Budget Wars End," *Washington Post* (November 15, 1999): A1.

8. George W. Bush, State of the Union Address, January 28, 2003, Washington, DC: White House Office of the Press Secretary, www.whitehouse.gov/news/releases/2003/01/20030128-19.html, accessed January 8, 2004.

9. Jonathan Weisman, "Thomas Questions Dividend Tax Cuts," *Washington Post* (January 28, 2003): A4.

10. Terry Moe, "The Politicized Presidency," in *The New Direction in American Politics,* ed. John Chubb and Paul E. Peterson (Washington, DC: The Brookings Institution, 1985).

11. Mark Peterson, *Legislating Together: The White House and Capitol Hill from Eisenhower to Reagan* (Cambridge, MA: Harvard University Press, 1990), chap. 6; Jon R. Bond and Richard Fleisher, *The President in the Legislative Arena* (Chicago: University of Chicago Press, 1990), chap. 4; and Steven A. Shull and Thomas C. Shaw, "Determinants of Presidents' Legislative Support in the House, 1949–1995," *Social Science Journal,* 39 (3) 2002: 381–398.

12. Jim Malone, "Republicans Looking Ahead to 2010," Voice of America News, December 16, 2009.

13. Haynes Johnson and David Broder, *The System: The American Way of Politics at the Breaking Point* (Boston: Little, Brown, 1996).

14. Peterson, *Legislating Together,* p. 157.

15. Charles O. Jones, "Campaigning to Govern: The Clinton Style," in *The Clinton Presidency: First Appraisals,* ed. Colin Campbell and Bert A. Rockman (Chatham, NJ: Chatham House, 1996), p. 16. Also see Michael L. Mezey, *Congress, the President and Public Policy* (Boulder, CO: Westview, 1989).

16. As quoted in Chuck Henning, *The Wit and Wisdom of Politics: Expanded Edition* (Golden, CO: Fulcrum Publishing, 1992), p. 240.

17. Jack Nelson, "Angry Clinton Rebukes His Whitewater Critics," *Los Angeles Times* (December 21, 1995): A1.

18. Richard E. Neustadt, *Presidential Power and the Modern Presidents* (New York: Free Press, 1990), p. 29.

19. Benjamin Ginsberg and Martin Shefter, *Politics by Other Means: The Declining Importance of Elections in America* (New York: Basic Books, 1990).

20. Daniel Stid, *The Statesmanship of Woodrow Wilson: Responsible Government Under the Constitution* (Lawrence: University Press of Kansas, 1998), chap. 6.

21. Thomas Bailey, *The American Pageant* (Boston: D.C. Heath, 1956), p. 669.

22. Samuel Kernell, *Going Public: New Strategies of Presidential Leadership,* 4th ed. (Washington, DC: CQ Press, 2007).

23. Kernell, *Going Public,* p. 95.

24. Neustadt, *Presidential Power,* p. 274.

25. Henning, *Wit and Wisdom of Politics,* p. 240.

26. Norman C. Thomas, Joseph A. Pika, and Richard A. Watson, *The Politics of the Presidency,* 3rd ed. (Washington, DC: CQ Press, 1993), p. 204.

27. United States Senate, "Summary of Bills Vetoed, 1789-present," www.senate.gov/reference/Legislation/Vetoes/vetoCounts.htm, accessed January 16, 2010.

28. Nick Anderson, "Deal on Media Could Bring Passage of Spending Bill," *Los Angeles Times* (November 25, 2003): 23; and Bill Miller, "Senators Take Up Homeland Security; Bush Strengthens Veto Threat," *Washington Post* (September 5, 2002): A29.

29. Carl Hulse, "Obama's First Veto Stands," The Caucus: The Politics and Government Blog of the Times, http://thecaucus.blogs.nytimes.com/2010/01/13/obamas-first-veto-stands/, accessed January 16, 2010.

30. "Bush Signs Patriot Act Extension, Military Bill," *Los Angeles Times* (December 31, 2005): A20.

31. "Senators Seek Line-Item Veto for Obama," Politico.com, www.politico.com/news/stories/0309/19589.html, accessed January 16, 2010.

32. As quoted in James P. Pfiffner, *The Modern Presidency* (New York: St. Martin's, 1994), p. 114.

33. John Hart, *The Presidential Branch: From Washington to Clinton,* 2nd ed. (Chatham, NJ: Chatham House, 1995), pp. 26–30.

34. See Matthew Dickinson, *Bitter Harvest: FDR, Presidential Power, and the Growth of the Presidential Branch* (New York: Cambridge University Press, 1997).

35. Harold W. Stanley and Richard Niemi, *Vital Statistics on American Politics 1999–2000* (Washington, DC: CQ Press, 1999), pp. 250–251; and Office of Personnel Management, *Federal Civilian Workforce Statistics: Employment and Trends.*

36. Paul Quirk, "Presidential Compe-tence," in *The Presidency and the Political System,* 4th ed., ed. Michael Nelson (Washington, DC: CQ Press, 1994), pp. 171–221; and John P. Burke, *The Institutional Presidency* (Baltimore,

MD: Johns Hopkins University Press, 1992), pp. 40–42.

37. Colin Campbell, "Management in a Sandbox," in Colin Campbell and Bert A. Rockman, *The Clinton Presidency: First Appraisals* (Chatham, NJ: Chatham House, 1996), p. 60.

38. Charles O. Jones, "Campaigning to Govern: The Clinton Style," in Campbell and Rockman, *The Clinton Presidency,* p. 16.

39. Terry Moe, "The Politicized Presidency"; and Andrew Rudalevige, "The President's Program and the Politicized Presidency," paper presented at the Annual Meeting of the American Political Science Association, Atlanta, GA, September 2–5, 1999.

40. Bruce E. Altshuler, *LBJ and the Polls* (Gainesville, FL: University of Florida Press, 1990); and Lawrence R. Jacobs, "The Recoil Effect: Public Opinion in the U.S. and Britain," *Comparative Politics* 24 (1992): 199–217.

41. *Wall Street Journal* (December 22, 1993): A4.

42. Peter Baker, "Senior White House Staff May Be Wearing Down," *Washington Post* (March 13, 2006): A4.

43. John W. Kingdon, *Agendas, Alternatives and Public Policies* (Boston: Little, Brown, 1981).

44. Tulis, *Rhetorical Presidency,* chap. 3.

45. Ibid.

46. Harry McPherson, *A Political Education* (Boston: Little, Brown, 1972), p. 268, as quoted in Paul C. Light, *The President's Agenda: Domestic Policy Choice from Kennedy to Reagan* (Baltimore, MD: Johns Hopkins University Press, 1991), p. 13.

47. Stephen Hess, *Organizing the Presidency* (Washington, DC: The Brookings Institution, 1988), pp. 11–18.

48. Richard Brody, *Assessing the President: The Media, Elite Opinion and Public Support* (Stanford, CA: Stanford University Press, 1991), p. 40.

49. Thomas Oliphant, "Overdue Realism," *Boston Globe* (May 9, 1993): A7.

50. Alexander Hamilton, James Madison, and John Jay, "Federalist No. 70," *The Federalist Papers* (New York: Bantam Books, 1982), p. 356.

51. William Howell and Jon Pevehouse, *While Dangers Gather: Congressional Checks on Presidential War Powers* (Princeton, NJ: Princeton University Press, 2007).

52. Walter Bagehot, *The English Constitution* (London: Fantana, 1993).

53. Gerald F. Seis, "Soul on High: Clinton Strikes Deeper Chords," *Wall Street Journal* (December 15, 1993).

54. Elisabeth Bumiller with David E. Sanger, "A Day of Terror: The President," *New York Times* (September 12, 2001): A1.

55. Lou Cannon, *President Reagan: The Role of a Lifetime* (New York: Simon & Schuster, 1991), p. 25.

56. Doris Kearns Goodwin, *No Ordinary Time: Franklin and Eleanor Roosevelt: The Home Front in World War II* (New York: Simon & Schuster, 1994).

57. Henning, *Wit and Wisdom of Politics,* p. 261.

58. Paul C. Light, *Vice Presidential Power* (Baltimore, MD: Johns Hopkins University Press, 1984), p. 258.

59. Sidney Milkis, *The President and the Parties: The Transformation of the American Party System Since the New Deal* (New York: Oxford University Press, 1993), p. 81.

60. Theodore Sorensen, as quoted in M. Miller, *Lyndon: An Oral Biography* (New York: Putnam, 1980), p. 254.

61. Stephen Skowronek, *The Politics Presidents Make: Leadership from John Adams to George Bush* (Cambridge, MA: Harvard University Press, 1993), p. 250.

62. As quoted in James L. Sundquist, *The Decline and Resurgence of Congress* (Washington, DC: The Brookings Institution, 1981), p. 31.

63. *United States v. Belmont,* 301 U.S. 324 (1936); Harold Bruff and Peter Shane, *The Law of Presidential Powers: Cases and Materials* (Durham, NC: Carolina Academic Press, 1988), p. 88; and Joseph Paige, *The Law Nobody Knows: Enlargement of the Constitution—Treaties and Executive Orders* (New York: Vantage Press, 1977), p. 63.

64. William Howell, "The President's Powers of Unilateral Action: The Strategic Advantages of Acting Alone" (Ph.D. diss., Stanford University, 1999).

65. Executive Order 13492 (Guantanamo Bay) and Executive Order 13505 (stem cells). See "Barack Obama Executive Orders Disposition Tables," The National Archives, www.archives.gov/federal-register/executive-orders/obama.html, accessed January 16, 2010.

66. Louis Fisher, *Constitutional Conflicts Between Congress and the President,* 3rd ed., rev. (Lawrence: University of Kansas, 1991), p. 154.

67. *United States v. Nixon,* 418 U.S. 683, 709 (1974).

68. Michael Doyle, "U.S. Sues U.S. Over Cheney Files," *Chicago Sun-Times* (February 24, 2001): 21.

69. Sam Youngman, "Social Secretary Not Testifying on State Dinner Crashers," *The Hill* (December 2, 2009), http://thehill.com/homenews/administration/70247-social-secretary-not-testifying-on-state-dinner-crashers, accessed January 16, 2010.

70. The man who cast the decisive vote provided subject matter for John F. Kennedy's

Profiles in Courage (New York: Harper & Row, 1964).

71. *Washington Post*/ABC News Poll, January 28–30, 1999.

72. Robert J. Spitzer, "Clinton's Impeachment Will Have Few Consequences for the Presidency," *PS: Political Science and Politics* 32:3 (September 1999): 541–545.

73. Harvey Mansfield, Jr., *Taming the Prince: The Ambivalence of Modern Executive Power* (New York: Free Press, 1989); and James McPherson, *The Battle Cry of Freedom: The Civil War Era* (New York: Oxford University Press, 1988), pp. 264–275, 505.

74. *Wall Street Journal* (December 22, 1993): A1.

75. Neustadt, *Presidential Power,* chap. 4.

76. Henning, *Wit and Wisdom of Politics,* p. 219.

77. Ibid., p. 222.

78. The effect of time on presidential support is stressed by Paul Brace and Barbara Hinckley, "The Structure of Presidential Approval: Constraints Within and Across Presidencies," *Journal of Politics* 53 (November 1991): 993–1017; and John Mueller, "Presidential Popularity from Truman to Johnson," *American Political Science Review* (March 1970): 18–24. For contrasting views, which stress events rather than time, see Brody, *Assessing the President;* and Samuel Kernell, "Explaining Presidential Popularity," *American Political Science Review* (June 1978): 506–522. Also see Michael MacKuen, "Political Drama, Economic Conditions, and the Dynamic of Public Popularity," *American Journal of Political Science* (May 1983): 165–192; Charles Ostrom and Dennis Simon, "Promise and Performance: A Dynamic Model of Presidential Popularity," *American Political Science Review* (June 1985): 334–358; and James Stimson, "Public Support for American Presidents," *Public Opinion Quarterly* (1976): 401–421.

79. Paul Brace and Barbara Hinckley, *Follow the Leader: Opinion Polls and the Modern Presidents* (New York: Basic Books, 1992), p. 33, Figure 2.3.

80. Samuel Kernell, *Going Public,* 2nd ed. (Washington, DC: CQ Press, 1993), chap. 5.

81. Anthony Stephen King, *Running Scared: Why America's Politicians Campaign Too Much and Govern Too Little* (New York: Free Press, 1997).

82. "Los Angeles Times Interview: Clinton Sees 'A Lot of Insecurity in This Country,'" *Los Angeles Times* (December 5, 1993): A38.

83. Joseph Williams, "Obama Parries and Critics Pounce," *Boston Globe* (July 24, 2009).

84. George C. Edwards III, *At the Margins: Presidential Leadership of Congress* (New Haven, CT: Yale University Press, 1989) pp. 120–124; Calvin Mouw and Michael MacKuen, "The Strategic Configuration, Political Influence, and Presidential Power in Congress" (paper prepared for the annual meeting of the Midwest Political Science Association, Chicago, 1989); and Terry Sullivan, "Headcounts, Expectations and Presidential Coalitions in Congress," *American Journal of Political Science* 32 (1988): 567–589.

85. "Barack Obama: But Could He Deliver?" *TheEconomist.com,* February 14, 2008, www.economist.com/opinion/displaystory.cfm?story_id=10689547, accessed February 17, 2008.

86. James Barber, *The Presidential Character: Predicting Performance in the White House* (Englewood Cliffs, NJ: Prentice-Hall, 1972).

87. Stephen Skowronek, *The Politics Presidents Make.*

88. Henning, *Wit and Wisdom of Politics,* p. 92.

CHAPTER 14

1. Douglas Martin, "George Weissman, Leader at Philip Morris and in the Arts in New York, Dies at 90," *New York Times* (July 28, 2009): A23.

2. "Wayne McClaren, 51, Rodeo Rider and Model," *New York Times* (July 25, 1992): A11; "Deaths," *Washington Post* (October 21, 1995): C6.

3. "The Reports of the Surgeon General: The 1964 Report on Smoking and Health," U.S. National Library of Medicine, National Institutes of Health, available at http://profiles.nlm.nih.gov/NN/Views/Exhibit/narrative/smoking.html, accessed January 27, 2010.

4. Eileen Shanahan, "Health Warning in Cigarette Ads Proposed by FTC," *New York Times* (January 18, 1964): 1.

5. The Federal Cigarette Labeling and Advertising Act of 1965, PL 89–92.

6. Robin Mayes, "Smoking Ban Leaves Bar Owners Fuming," *Business First-Columbus* (December 11, 1998): 29.

7. Martha Derthick, "Federalism and the Politics of Tobacco," in Derthick, *Keeping the Compound Republic* (Washington, DC: Brookings Institution Press, 2001), pp. 86–101.

8. "Candy and Fruit Flavored Cigarettes Now Illegal in United States; Step Is First Under New Tobacco Law," U.S. Food and Drug Administration press release, September 22, 2009, available at www.fda.gov/NewsEvents/Newsroom/PressAnnouncements/ucm183211.htm, accessed January 27, 2010.

9. Ibid.

10. U.S. Centers for Disease Control and Prevention, "Trends in Current Cigarette Smoking Among High School Students and Adults, United States, 1965-2007," www.cdc.gov/tobacco/data_statistics/tables/trends/cig_smoking/index.htm, accessed January 27, 2010.

11. Committee on Government Reform and Oversight, U.S. House of Representatives, *U.S. Government Policy and Supporting Positions ("Plum Book")* (Washington, DC: U.S. Government Printing Office, 2008).

12. Because the dividing line between independent agencies and government corporations is sometimes difficult to pinpoint, these numbers are necessarily inexact. General Accounting Office, *Government Corporations: Profiles of Existing Government Corporations* (GAO/GGD-96-14) (Washington, DC: General Accounting Office, 1995).

13. Martha Derthick, *Agency Under Stress: The Social Security Administration in American Government* (Washington, DC: The Brookings Institution, 1990).

14. Max Weber, *Essays in Sociology* (New York: Oxford University Press, 1958); and Max Weber, *Economy and Society* (Berkeley: University of California Press, 1978).

15. James Q. Wilson, "The Bureaucracy Problem," *The Public Interest* (Winter 1967): 3–9.

16. Michael Lipsky, *Street-Level Bureaucracy: Dilemmas of the Individual in Public Services* (New York: Russell Sage, 1980).

17. Ibid.

18. Lyndsey Layton, "Reversing Itself, FDA Expresses Concerns over Health Risks from BPA," *Washington Post* (January 16, 2010): A1.

19. William A. Niskanen, *Bureaucracy and Representative Government* (Chicago: Aldine-Atherton, 1971), chaps. 2–4.

20. Aaron Wildavsky, *The New Politics of the Budgetary Process* (Boston: Little, Brown, 1988), pp. 84–85.

21. Graham Allison, *Essence of Decision: Explaining the Cuban Missile Crisis* (Boston: Little, Brown, 1971), chap. 3.

22. Tom McGinty and Dan Fagin, "One Tangled Web; Experts Agree: Nation's Electric System Aging, Byzantine," *Newsday* (November 17, 2003): A6.

23. David Talbot, "Lifeline for Renewable Power," *Technology Review* 112:1 (January/February 2009): 40.

24. Laurence J. Peter, as quoted in Chuck Henning, *The Wit and Wisdom of Politics: Expanded Edition* (Golden, CO: Fulcrum Publishing, 1992), p. 16.

25. Thomas Carlyle, *The Works of Thomas Carlyle: (Complete)* (New York: P.F. Collier, 1897), p. 340.

26. Kaufman, *Red Tape,* p. 434.

27. This description of the repair process is drawn from the Minnesota Department of Transportation, http:// projects.dot.state.mn.us/35wbridge/index.html, accessed February 24, 2008.

28. Ron Scherer, "Obama Moves to Cut Big Banks Down to Size," *Christian Science Monitor,* January 21, 2010, www.csmonitor.com/USA/2010/0121/Obama-moves-to-cut-big-banks-down-to-size, accessed January 31, 2010.

29. Lucius Wilmerding as quoted in Herman Finer, "Better Government Personnel," *Political Science Quarterly* 50, 4 (1936): 577.

30. Stanley Elkins and Eric McKitrick, *The Age of Federalism* (New York: Oxford University Press, 1993), p. 170.

31. James Young, *The Washington Community 1800–1828* (New York: Harcourt, 1966), pp. 49, 23.

32. Robert V. Remini, *The Life of Andrew Jackson* (New York: Harper & Row, 1988), p. 185.

33. John Bartlett, *Familiar Quotations: Revised and Enlarged,* 15th ed. (Boston: Little, Brown, 1980), p. 455.

34. Seymour J. Mandelbaum, *Boss Tweed's New York* (New York: Wiley, 1965).

35. As quoted in Henning, *Wit and Wisdom of Politics,* p. 11.

36. A. James Reichley, *The Life of the Parties* (New York: Free Press, 1992), pp. 157–158.

37. William L. Riordon, *Plunkitt of Tammany Hall: A Series of Plain Talks on Very Practical Politics* (New York: E. P. Dutton, 1963), p. 3.

38. Eugene Kennedy, *Hurrah! The Life and Times of Mayor Richard J. Daley* (New York: Viking, 1978), pp. 255, 274.

39. Robert Dahl, *Who Governs?* (New Haven, CT: Yale University Press, 1961); Raymond E. Wolfinger, *The Politics of Progress* (Englewood Cliffs, NJ: Prentice-Hall, 1974), chap. 4; Edward Banfield and James Q. Wilson, *City Politics* (New York: Random House, 1963); and Robert K. Merton, *Social Theory and Social Structure* (Glencoe, IL: Free Press, 1957), pp. 71–81.

40. Paul E. Peterson, *The Politics of School Reform, 1870–1940* (Chicago: University of Chicago Press, 1985), pp. 86–87.

41. Rufus P. Browning, Dale Rogers Marshall, and David H. Tabb, *Protest Is Not Enough: The Struggle of Blacks and Hispanics for Equality in Urban Politics* (Berkeley: University of California Press, 1984), chap. 5.

42. Alben W. Barkley, vice president of the United States from 1949 to 1953, as quoted in Henning, *Wit and Wisdom of Politics,* p. 17.

43. 2004 National Election Study, University of Michigan, www.umich.edu/~nes/nesguide/toptable/tab5a_3.htm, accessed March 29, 2006.

44. Rasmussen Reports poll, December 13–14, 2009, www.rasmussenreports.com/public_content/business/econ_survey_toplines/december_2009/toplines_government_workers_i_december_13_14_2009, accessed January 31, 2010.

45. Paul Light, *Thickening Government* (Washington, DC: The Brookings Institution, 1995), p. 9, Table 1–2; Paul Light, "Fact Sheet on the Continuing Thickening of Government," July 24, 2004, Washington, DC: Brookings Institution, http://www.brookings.edu/papers/2004/0723governance_light.aspx, accessed January 31, 2010.

46. David E. Lewis, "Testing Pendleton's Promise: Do Political Appointees Make Worse Bureaucrats?" *Journal of Politics* 69: 4 (November 2007), 1073–1088.

47. B. Dan Wood and Miner P. Marchbanks III, "What Determines How Long Political Appointees Serve?" *Journal of Public Administration Research and Theory* 18: 3 (2008): 375–396.

48. United States Office of Personnel Management, *Federal Human Capital Survey, 2006,* available at www.fhcs2006.opm.gov/, accessed February 24, 2008, p. 46.

49. "Urgent Business for America: Revitalizing the Federal Government for the 21st Century," Report of the National Commission on the Public Service (the "Volcker Commission"), January 2003, p. 1.

50. As quoted in G. Calvin MacKenzie, *The In-and-Outers: Presidential Appointees and Transient Government in Washington* (Baltimore, MD: Johns Hopkins University Press, 1987).

51. Council for Excellence in Government survey, March 2004, reprinted in Partnership for Public Service, "Poll Watch: Public Opinion on Public Service," PPS-05-03, May 2, 2005, www.ourpublicservice.org/usr_doc/PPS-05-03.pdf, accessed March 29, 2006.

52. Lyn Ragsdale, "Studying the Presidency: Why Presidents Need Political Scientists," in *The Presidency and the Political System,* 5th ed., ed. Michael Nelson (Washington, DC: CQ Press, 1998), p. 50.

53. Thomas E. Cronin, *The State of the Presidency,* 2nd ed. (Boston: Little, Brown, 1980).

54. Jefferson Cohen, *The Politics of the U.S. Cabinet* (Pittsburgh, PA: University of Pittsburgh Press, 1988).

55. "With Tougher Stance, Obama Takes on Banks," *New York Times* "Dealbook" blog, January 22, 2010, http://dealbook.blogs.nytimes.com/2010/01/22/with-populist-stance-obama-takes-on-banks/, accessed February 7, 2010.

56. Kermit Gordon, *Reflections on Spending* (Washington, DC: The Brookings Institution, 1967), p. 15.

57. Marver H. Bernstein, *Regulating Business by Independent Commission* (Princeton, NJ: Princeton University Press, 1955); Harold Seidman, *Politics, Position and Power: The Dynamics of Federal Organization,* 2nd ed. (New York: Oxford University Press, 1975); George J. Stigler, "The Theory of Economic Regulation," *Bell Journal of Economics and Management Science* 2 (Spring 1971): 3–21; Terry Moe, "Regulatory Performance and Presidential Administration," *American Journal of Political Science* 16 (May 1982): 197–224; B. R. Weingast and M. J. Moran, "Bureaucratic Discretion or Congressional Control? Regulatory Policymaking by the Federal Trade Commission," *Journal of Political Economy* 91: 5 (1983): 765–800; and B. R. Weingast, "The Congressional-Bureaucratic System: A Principal–Agent Perspective (with Application to the SEC)," *Public Choice* 44: 1 (1984): 147–191.

58. Stephen Labaton, "Exemption Won in '97 Set Stage for Enron Woes," *New York Times* (January 23, 2002): A1.

59. Herbert Kaufman, *The Administrative Behavior of Federal Bureau Chiefs,* p. 183, n. 8.

60. Hugh Heclo, "OMB and the Presidency—the Problem of 'Neutral Competence,'" *Public Interest* 38 (Winter 1975): 80–98; and Karen Hult, "Advising the President," in George C. Edwards, John H. Kessel, and Bert A. Rockman, *Researching the Presidency: Vital Questions, New Approaches* (Pittsburgh, PA: University of Pittsburgh Press, 1992), p. 126.

61. Richard W. Stevenson, "Bush's Budget Director Girds for a Tough Year," *New York Times* (December 31, 2001): A8 and Esther Schrader and Janet Hook, "Bush's $87 Billion Request Detailed; Most of the Funding Sought by the White House Would Go to Iraq Military Operations," *Los Angeles Times* (September 18, 2003): A10.

62. Elizabeth Jensen, "Public Broadcasters Prepare to Fight Federal Budget Cuts," *New York Times* (February 8, 2008): E1.

63. Ibid., p. 397.

64. Derthick, *Agency Under Stress,* p. 200.

65. Michael Shear, "Richardson Withdraws as Commerce Secretary-Designee," WashingtonPost.com, January 4, 2009, http://voices.washingtonpost.com/44/2009/01/04/richardson_withdraws_as_commer.html, accessed February 7, 2010.

66. *Staffing a New Presidential Administration: A Guide to Personnel Appointments in a Presidential Transition* (Washington, DC: The Presidential Appointee Initiative, a project of the Brookings Institution funded by the Pew Charitable Trusts, November 2000).

67. Frederic Ogg and P. Orman Ray, *Introduction to American Government,* 10th ed. (New York: Appleton-Century-Crofts, 1951), p. 405.

68. Noam N. Levey, "Obama Plans Recess Appointment of Medicare-Medicaid Chief," *Los Angeles Times,* July 7, 2010, http://www.latimes.com/news/nationworld/nation/la-na-obama-recess-appointment-20100707,0,7588388.story, accessed July 11, 2010.

69. David King, "The Nature of Congressional Committee Jurisdictions," *American Political Science Review* 88 (March 1995): 48–62.

70. See *New York Times* (September 5, 1993): Sec. I, 39.

71. James Q. Wilson, *Bureaucracy: What Government Agencies Do and Why They Do It* (New York: Basic Books, 1989), pp. 295–314; and Ezra N. Suleiman, *Politics, Power and Bureaucracy in France: The Administrative Elite* (Princeton, NJ: Princeton University Press, 1974).

72. T. J. Pempel, "The Bureaucratization of Policymaking in Postwar Japan," *American Journal of Political Science* 18 (November 1974): 64. See also, Michio Muramatsu and Ellis S. Krauss, "Bureaucrats and Politicians in Policymaking: The Case of Japan," *American Political Science Review* 78, 1 (March 1984): 126–146.

73. R. Shep Melnick, *Regulation and the Courts: The Case of the Clean Air Act* (Washington, DC: The Brookings Institution, 1983).

74. David Epstein and Sharyn O'Halloran, *Delegating Powers: A Transaction Cost Politics Approach to Policy Making under Separate Powers* (New York: Cambridge University Press, 1999), Figure 5.9, p. 116.

75. Dick Kirschten, "Slicing the Turf," *Government Executive* (April 1999).

76. Robert L. Park, director of the Washington office of the American Physical Society, as quoted in Graeme Browing, "Fiscal Fission," *National Journal* (June 8, 1996): 1259.

77. Jared Allen, "Lawmakers Pushing for Earmark Reform Think Obama Boosted Their Chances," The Hill, January 30, 2010, http://thehill.com/homenews/house/78869-lawmakers-think-obama-boosted-earmark-reform-, accessed February 7, 2010.

78. Joel Aberbach, *Keeping a Watchful Eye* (Washington, DC: The Brookings Institution, 1990), p. 38; Policy Agendas Project, University of Washington, www.policyagendas.org, hearings data.

79. Policy Agendas Project.

80. Matthew McCubbins and Thomas Schwartz, "Congressional Oversight Overlooked: Police Patrols vs. Fire Alarms," *American Journal of Political Science* 28: 1 (February 1984): 165–179.

81. Joel Aberbach and Bert Rockman, *In the Web of Politics: Three Decades of the U.S. Federal Executive* (Washington, DC: The Brookings Institution, 2000), p. 121.

82. Grant McConnell, *Private Power and American Democracy* (New York: Knopf, 1966); Theodore Lowi, *The End of Liberalism,* 2nd ed. (New York: Norton, 1979); and Mark P. Petracca, ed., *The Politics of Interests: Interest Groups Transformed* (Boulder, CO: Westview, 1992).

83. Joel Aberbach, *Keeping a Watchful Eye,* pp. 162–166.

84. Hugh Heclo, "Issue Networks and the Executive Establishment," in *The New American Political System,* ed. Anthony King (Washington, DC: American Enterprise Institute, 1978), pp. 87–124.

85. John E. Chubb, *Interest Groups and the Bureaucracy* (Stanford, CA: Stanford University Press, 1983); John Chubb "U.S. Energy Policy: A Problem of Delegation," in *Can the Government Govern?* ed. John Chubb and Paul E. Peterson (Washington, DC: The Brookings Institution, 1989); Seong-Ho Lim, "Changing Jurisdictional Boundaries in Congressional Oversight of Nuclear Energy Regulation: Impact of Public Salience," paper presented before the annual meeting of the American Political Science Association, 1992; and Frank R. Baumgartner and Bryan D. Jones, "Agenda Dynamics and Policy Subsystems," *Journal of Politics* 53 (November 1991): 1044–1074.

86. Paul E. Peterson, Barry G. Rabe, and Kenneth K. Wong, *When Federalism Works* (Washington, DC: The Brookings Institution, 1986), chap. 8; John J. Harrigan, *Political Change in the Metropolis,* 2nd ed. (Boston: Little, Brown, 1981), pp. 267–268, 350–351; and Rochelle L. Stanfield, "Communities Reborn," *National Journal* (June 22, 1966): 1371.

87. John Dilulio, *No Escape: The Future of American Corrections* (New York: Basic Books, 1991), pp. 19–26.

88. James A. Morone, *Democratic Wish: Popular Participation and the Limits of American Government* (New York: Basic Books, 1990).

89. Francis Rourke, "Executive Secrecy: Change and Continuity," in Rourke, *Bureaucratic Power in National Policy Making,* pp. 536–537.

90. John M. Donnelly, "Lawmakers Battle Pentagon Over War Information," *CQ Weekly Online* (May 21, 2007): 1496–1497, http://library.cqpress.com/cqweekly/weeklyreport110-000002515616, accessed March 2, 2008.

91. Michael B. Farrell, "Terror Probe: Why Is the Threat Level Still Yellow?" *Christian Science Monitor* (September 23, 2009): 2.

92. Lake Research Partners Poll, February 1, 2009.

93. Martin Halstuk, "New Privacy Policy Hinders Public's Right to Know," *Los Angeles Times* (November 19, 2001): part 2, 11.

94. Jeffrey Birnbaum, Eileen Gunn, et al., "Unbelievable! The Mess at the IRS *Is* Worse Than You Think," *Fortune* (April 13, 1998).

95. Ibid.

96. Ibid.

97. Albert B. Crenshaw, "IRS Overhaul Set for Passage; Measure Gives Taxpayers New Rights, Includes Capital Gains Break," *Washington Post* (June 25, 1998): A1.

98. Jonathan Weisman, "GAO Finds Increases in Tax Evasion; Report Says IRS Needs More Resources," *Washington Post* (December 19, 2003): E1.

99. Matthew McCubbins and Thomas Schwartz, "Congressional Oversight Overlooked: Police Patrols vs. Fire Alarms," *American Journal of Political Science* 28: 1 (February 1984): 165–179.

100. Martha Derthick, *Agency Under Stress,* p. 87.

101. Christopher Lee, "Federal Workforce Is Largest Since 1990," *Washington Post* (September 5, 2003): A19.

102. Christopher Lee, "Federal Case; Government Workers Protest Outsourcing," *Washington Post* (May 21, 2003): A31; and Christopher Lee, "Outsourcing Shield Weakened; Appeals Rights Stripped as Worker Raises Are Approved," *Washington Post* (November 26, 2003): A23.

103. Blaine Harden, "Cuts Sap Morale of Parks Employees; Many Fear Losing Jobs to Outsourcing," *Washington Post* (June 10, 2003): A19.

104. Paul Light, "To Restore and Renew: Now Is the Time to Rebuild the Federal Public Service," *Government Executive* (November 2001): 32–47.

105. Richard Rubin, "Push to Bar Tax Collection Outsourcing Gets OK From House Ways and Means," *CQ Weekly Online* (July 23, 2007): 2204–2204, http://library.cqpress.com/cqweekly/weeklyreport110-000002555856, accessed March 3, 2008; and Rob Margetta, "Homeland Security For Hire," *CQ Weekly Online* (November 12, 2007): 3392–3399, http://library.cqpress.com/cqweekly/

weeklyreport110-000002625610, accessed March 3, 2008.

106. David Johnston and John M. Broder, "FBI Says Guards Killed 14 Iraqis 'Without Cause,'" *New York Times* (November 14, 2007): A1.

107. Former Bureau of the Budget director Kermit Gordon, as quoted in Kaufman, *Administrative Behavior,* p. 443.

108. Paul J. Quirk, "Food and Drug Administration," in James Q. Wilson, *The Politics of Regulation* (New York: Basic Books, 1980), p. 199.

109. Terry Moe, "The Politics of Bureaucratic Structure," in John E. Chubb and Paul E. Peterson, *Can the Government Govern?* (Washington, DC: The Brookings Institution, 1988).

110. Brian Hassel, "Charter Schools: Designed to Fail?" (Ph.D. diss., John F. Kennedy School of Government, Harvard University, 1997); Carolyn M. Hoxby and Jonah Rockoff, "Findings from the City of Big Shoulders," *Education Next,* Fall 2005, www.educationnext.org/20054/52.html, accessed April 29, 2006 and Robert Bifulco and Helen F. Ladd, "Results from the Tar Heel State," *Education Next,* Fall 2005, www.educationnext.org/20054/60.html, accessed April 29, 2006.

111. Data from The American Customer Satisfaction Index, www.theacsi.org, accessed February 7, 2010.

112. John Clayton Thomas and Gloria Streib, "The New Face of Government: Citizen-Initiated Contacts in the Era of E-Government," *Journal of Public Administration Research and Theory,* 13: 1 (January 2003): 92.

113. James H. Boren, quoted in Antony Jay, *The Oxford Dictionary of Political Quotations* (New York: Oxford University Press, 2001), p. 48.

114. Charles Lindblom, "The Science of 'Muddling Through,'" *Public Administration Review* XIX (Spring 1959): 79–88.

115. Herbert Kaufman, *The Forest Ranger: A Study in Administrative Behavior* (Baltimore, MD: Johns Hopkins University Press, 1960). For recent confirmations of this analysis, see Warren Wolfe, "A Milestone for the BWCA: 25 Years of Nature and Fighting," *Minneapolis Star Tribune* (October 11, 2003): 1A; Charles Seabrook, "Forest Use Rules May Relax; Logging Expected to Increase," *Atlanta Journal-Constitution* (November 28, 2002): 3A; Glen Martin, "Cattlemen Prod Forest Service; Federal Land Use Policies to Come Under Review, Again," *San Francisco Chronicle* (July 5, 2002): A3; Staci Matlock, "Off-Road Enthusiasts Push for Rule Enforcement," *Santa Fe New Mexican* (November 17, 2009): A5, and Rusty Garrett, "Proposed Land-Use

Restrictions Draw Ire," *Fort Smith (AR) Times Record* (February 21, 2010).

CHAPTER 15

1. "McCain, Obama go head to head in last debate," www.cnn.com/2008/POLITICS/10/15/debate.transcript/, October 15, 2008, accessed February 21, 2010.

2. *Marbury v. Madison,* 5 U.S. 137 (1803).

3. Jeff Sessions (R-AL) quoted in Neil A. Lewis, "Senate Republicans Play Down Chances of Fight on Court Nominee," *New York Times* (May 18, 2009): A10.

4. Warren Richey, "Sotomayor Opponents in Weak Field Position So Far," *Christian Science Monitor* (May 27, 2009).

5. Richey.

6. Christina Bellatoni and Ralph Z. Hallow, "Gingrich Ignites Fight over 'Racism,' Sotomayor," *The Washington Times* (May 28, 2009): A1.

7. "Full Text: Judge Sonia Sotomayor's Speech," Time.com, May 26, 2009, www.time.com/time/politics/article/0,8599,1900940,00.html, accessed February 21, 2010.

8. Calculated by authors from Richard Y. Schlauffer, Robert C. LaFountain, Neal B. Kauder, and Shauna M. Strickland, *Examining the Work of State Courts, 2004: A National Perspective from the Court Statistics Project* (Williamsburg, VA: National Center for State Courts, 2005), p. 14; and Judicial Conference of the United States, "Judicial Facts and Figures," www.uscourts.gov/judicialfactsfigures/contents.html, accessed April 22, 2006, Table 4.1. Most recent data available are from 2003. Total state cases: 100.1 million; total federal court cases: 323,604.

9. Commission to Promote Public Confidence in Judicial Elections, *Final Report to the Chief Judge of the State of New York* (New York: Fordham University School of Law, February 6, 2006), pp. 6–7.

10. *2005 Annual Report: Georgia Courts* (Atlanta, GA: Judicial Council of Georgia, Administrative Office of the Courts, 2005).

11. "The Texas Judicial System," Texas Judiciary Online, www.courts.state.tx.us, accessed April 22, 2006, 15.

12. Melinda Gann Hall, "Justices as Representatives: Elections and Judicial Politics in the American States," *American Politics Quarterly* 23 (October 1995): 485–503.

13. Henry R. Glick, "Courts: Politics and the Judicial Process," in Virginia Gray and Russell L. Hanson, eds., *Politics in the American States: A Comparative Analysis,* 8th ed. (Washington, DC: CQ Press, 2004), p. 240.

14. "Candidate Fund-Raising in Supreme Court Races by Rank, 2000–2008," Justice At Stake, www.justiceatstake.org/media/cms/JAS_20002008 CourtCampaignExpenditur_63951A4654869.pdf, accessed February 21, 2010.

15. Professor Anthony Champagne, quoted in Jerry Crimmins, "Experts: Negative Ads Erode Confidence in Judges," *Chicago Daily Law Bulletin* (November 9, 2001): 1.

16. Chuck Henning, *Wit and Wisdom* (Golden, CO: Fulcrum Publishing, 1992), p. 108.

17. Los Angeles County District Attorney's Office, http://da.co.la.ca.us/oview.htm, accessed February 21, 2010.

18. Robert A. Carp, Ronald Stidham, and Kenneth L. Manning, *Judicial Process in America,* 7th ed. (Washington, DC: CQ Press, 2007), p. 100.

19. Matt Dees, "Legal Bills Climbing for Durham," *The News Observer* (North Carolina), June 7, 2008, www.newsobserver.com/news/story/1099609.html, accessed June 17, 2008.

20. Alexander Hamilton, James Madison, and John Jay, *The Federalist Papers* (New York: Bantam Books, 1982 [1787]), "Federalist 78," p. 393.

21. Federal Judicial Center, www.fjc.gov/history/home.nsf/page/topics_ji_bdy, accessed February 21, 2010.

22. Ibid.

23. Chief Justice John Roberts, "2006 Year-End Report on the Federal Judiciary," United States Supreme Court, www.supremecourtus.gov/publicinfo/year-end/2006year-endreport.pdf, accessed March 6, 2008.

24. Richard A. Posner, *The Federal Courts: Challenge and Reform* (Cambridge, MA: Harvard University Press, 1996), pp. 29–33.

25. Henning, *The Wit and Wisdom of Politics: Expanded Edition,* p. 250.

26. Robert G. McCloskey, *The American Supreme Court, Third Edition* (Chicago: University of Chicago Press, 2000), p. 8.

27. U.S. Constitution, Article III, Section 2.

28. *Beauharnais v. Illinois,* 343 U.S. 250 (1952).

29. William J. Brennan, Jr., "The Constitution of the United States: Contemporary Ratification," in David O'Brien, ed., *Judges on Judging: Views from the Bench* (Chatham, NJ: Chatham House, 1997), p. 204.

30. Ibid.

31. Justice Stephen Breyer, "Our Democratic Constitution," Harvard University Tanner Lectures on Human Values, November 17, 18, and 19, 2004, www.supremecourtus.gov/publicinfo/speeches/sp_11-17-04.html, accessed May 13, 2008.

32. Mark Morris, "Scalia Criticizes 'Living Constitution,'" *Kansas City Star* (March 5, 2008): 1B; Nina Totenberg, "Justice Scalia, the Great Dissenter, Opens Up," National Public Radio Morning Edition, April 28, 2008, www.npr.org/templates/story/story.php?storyId=89986017&ft=1&f=2101289, accessed June 17, 2008.

33. *Dred Scott v. Sandford,* 19. How. 393 (1857).

34. See, for example, Abraham Lincoln's comments in Robert W. Johannsen, ed., *The Lincoln-Douglas Debates* (New York: Oxford University Press, 1965), pp. 14–21.

35. *Lochner v. New York,* 198 U.S. 45 (1905). Ellipses deleted from excerpt.

36. John Agresto, *The Supreme Court and Constitutional Democracy* (Ithaca, NY: Cornell University Press, 1984), p. 163.

37. Congressional Research Service, Library of Congress, *The Constitution of the United States of America: Analysis and Interpretation, 2008 Supplement* (Washington, DC: Government Printing Office, 2009).

38. Excerpted with ellipses deleted. Robert A. Dahl, "Decision-Making in a Democracy: The Supreme Court as a National Policy-Maker," *Journal of Public Law* 6 (Fall 1957): 293–294. See also Richard Y. Funston, "The Supreme Court and Critical Elections," *American Political Science Review* 69 (1975): 795–811.

39. James A. Stimson, Michael B. Mackuen, and Robert S. Erikson, "Dynamic Representation," *American Political Science Review* 89 (September 1995): 555. Also see William Mishler and Reginald S. Sheehan, "The Supreme Court as a Counter-Majoritarian Institution? The Impact of Public Opinion on Supreme Court Decisions," *American Political Science Review* 87 (1993): 87–101; and Helmut Norpoth and Jeffery Segal, "Popular Influence on Supreme Court Decisions," *American Political Science Review* 88 (September 1994): 711–724.

40. Keith E. Whittington, "'Interpose Your Friendly Hand': Political Supports for the Exercise of Judicial Review by the United States Supreme Court," *American Political Science Review* 99: 4 (November 2005): 583–596.

41. Finley Peter Dunne, *Mr. Dooley's Opinions* (New York: R. H. Russell, 1901), p. 26.

42. *Massachusetts v. Environmental Protection Agency* 549 U.S. 497 (2007).

43. David O'Brien, "Background Paper," in Twentieth Century Fund, *Judicial Roulette* (New York: Priority Press, 1988), p. 37; and Sheldon Goldman, "Unpicking Pickering in 2002: Some Thoughts on the Politics of Lower Federal Court Selection and Confirmation,"

U.C. Davis Law Review, 36: 695 (February 2003): 707.

44. Lyle Denniston, "Court Nominee Withdraws in Senate Battle, Democrats Prevail by Way of Filibuster," *Boston Globe* (September 5, 2003): A2.

45. Robert A. Carp and Ronald Stidham, *The Federal Courts,* 2nd ed. (Washington, DC: CQ Press, 1991), p. 116; and *U.S. News & World Report* (May 26, 1997): 24.

46. Richard A. Serrano, "Alito's Sole Trial Before a Jury was a Gamble That Paid Off," *Los Angeles Times* (November 14, 2005): A11.

47. *Martin v. Hunter's Lessee,* 14 U.S. (1 Wheat.) 304 (1816).

48. Congressional Research Service, Library of Congress, *The Constitution of the United States of America: Analysis and Interpretation, 2008 Supplement* (Washington, DC: U.S. Government Printing Office, 2009).

49. Pritchett, *The American Constitution* (New York: McGraw-Hill, 1959), p. 134.

50. Henning, *Wit and Wisdom,* p. 187.

51. *In re Chapman,* 16 U.S. 661 (1897).

52. Akin Gump Strauss Hauer and Feld LLP and ScotusBlog, "End of Term Statistical Analysis, October Term 2008," June 30, 2009, www.scotusblog.com/wp-content/uploads/2009/07/summary-memo-final.pdf, accessed February 21, 2010.

53. This figure refers to cases in which the Court held oral arguments. www.scotusblog.com, accessed July 8, 2010.

54. As quoted in Henning, *Wit and Wisdom,* p. 107.

55. The term *stealth nominee* was coined by Alabama Senator Howell Heflin during nomination hearings for Justice Souter. See Ruth Marcus and Michael Isikoff, "Souter Declines Comment on Abortion," *Washington Post* (September 14, 1990): A1.

56. Elena Kagan, "Confirmation Messes, Old and New," *University of Chicago Law Review,* Spring 1995, 62 U. Chi. L. Rev. 919.

57. Devin Dwyer and Ariane de Vogue, "Kagan Spars with Senate Republicans in Marathon Day of Questioning," http://abcnews.go.com/ Politics/Supreme_Court/elena-kagan-grilled-repbulicans-military-harvard/story?id=11041423, accessed July 8, 2010.

58. Twentieth Century Fund, *Judicial Roulette* (New York: Priority Press, 1988), pp. 10–11.

59. *Parts and Electric Motors v. Sterling Electric,* 866 F 2d 288 (1988).

60. Hart Pomerantz, as quoted in Henning, *Wit and Wisdom,* p. 250.

61. H. W. Perry, Jr., *Deciding to Decide: Agenda Setting in the United States Supreme Court* (Cambridge, MA: Harvard University Press, 1991), p. 27.

62. See "Judicial Business of the United States Courts, 2008," Washington, DC: Administrative Office of the U.S. Courts, 2009, Table A-1.

63. Ibid., p. 99.

64. Address of Chief Justice Vinson before the American Bar Association, September 7, 1949, as quoted in Perry, *Deciding to Decide,* p. 36.

65. *Zelman v. Simmons-Harris,* No. 00-1751 (2002).

66. Jeffries, *Justice Lewis R. Powell, Jr.,* p. 248.

67. Bernard Schwartz, *A History of the Supreme Court* (New York: Oxford University Press, 1993), chap. 13.

68. Linda Cohen and Matthew Spitzer, "The Government Litigant Advantage: Implications for the Law," *Florida State University Law Review* 28 (Fall 2000): 391.

69. Scigliano, *Supreme Court and the Presidency,* p. 162.

70. Jeffrey A. Segal, "*Amicus Curiae* Briefs by the Solicitor General During the Warren and Burger Courts: A Research Note," *Western Political Quarterly* 41 (March 1988): 135–144.

71. Joan Biskupic and Elder Witt, *Guide to the U.S. Supreme Court,* 3rd ed., vol. II, (Washington, DC: Congressional Quarterly Press, 1997), p. 832.

72. Perry, *Deciding to Decide,* p. 71.

73. Perry, *Deciding to Decide;* and Schwartz, *History of the Supreme Court,* chap. 16.

74. Biskupic and Witt, *Guide to the U.S. Supreme Court,* p. 828.

75. As quoted in Henning, *Wit and Wisdom,* p. 106.

76. Jeffries, *Justice Lewis F. Powell, Jr.,* p. 247.

77. Ibid., pp. 245–247.

78. *Harris v. Forklift,* 508 U.S. 938 (1993).

79. Lawrence Sirovich, "A Pattern Analysis of the Second Rehnquist U.S. Supreme Court," *Proceedings of the National Academy of Sciences,* 100 (13) 7432–7437 (at p. 7435).

80. Jeffrey Rosen, "Robert's Rules," *The Atlantic Monthly,* January/February 2007, www.theatlantic.com/doc/200701/john-roberts, accessed May 13, 2008.

81. Kermit Roosevelt, *The Myth of Judicial Activism: Making Sense of Supreme Court Decisions* (New Haven, CT: Yale University Press, 2006), p. 3.

82. David G. Savage, "High Court Sends a Stern Message," *Los Angeles Times* (April 30, 2008): A9.

83. Jeffrey A. Segal and Albert D. Cover, "Ideological Values and the Votes of U.S. Supreme Court Justices," *American Political Science Review* 83 (June 1989): 557–565; and Jeffrey Allen Segal, Harold J. Spaeth, and Sara Catherine Benesh, *The Supreme Court in the American Legal System* (New York: Cambridge University Press, 2005), pp. 319–321.

84. Henning, *Wit and Wisdom,* p. 250.

85. As quoted by Austin Ranney, "Peltason Created a New Way to Look at What Judges Do," *Public Affairs Report, Institute of Governmental Studies* 36: 6 (November 1995): 7.

86. Excerpted with ellipses deleted. "Federalist 2," edited and with introduction by Jacob E. Cooke (Middletown, CT: Wesleyan University Press, 1961), pp. 522–523.

87. Pritchett, *American Constitution,* p. 99.

88. Robert H. Birkby, "The Supreme Court and the Bible Belt: Tennessee Reaction to the 'Shempp Decision,'" *Midwest Journal of Political Science* 10 (August 1966), as reprinted in *The Impact of Supreme Court Decisions,* eds. Theodore L. Becker and Malcolm M. Feeley (New York: Oxford University Press, 1973), p. 114.

89. James Sterngold, "Overhaul of Prison Health System Delayed," *San Francisco Chronicle* (November 3, 2005): B1.

90. Abram Chayes, "The Role of the Judge in Public Law Litigation," *Harvard Law Review* 89 (May 1976): 1281–1316.

91. Alexis de Tocqueville, *Democracy in America,* ed. J. P. Mayer (New York: Harper, 1988), p. 270.

92. R. Shep Melnick, *Between the Lines* (Washington, DC: The Brookings Institution, 1994), p. 149.

93. Jerry Hirsch and Stuart Pfeifer, "Toyota Faces Massive Legal Liability," *Los Angeles Times,* February 12, 2010, http://articles.latimes.com/2010/feb/12/business/la-fi-toyota-liability12-2010feb12, accessed February 22, 2010.

94. Dirk Johnson, "City of Deep Pockets," *Newsweek,* December 15, 2003, 45.

CHAPTER 16

1. Kevin Whitelaw and Chitra Ragavan, "A Good Spy Is Hard to Find," *U.S. News & World Report* (November 22, 2004): 59.

2. Patrick Radden Keefe, "Can Network Theory Thwart Terrorists?" *New York Times Magazine* (March 12, 2006): 16.

3. James Bamford, *Body of Secrets: Anatomy of the Ultra-Secret National Security Agency* (New York: Random House, 2001), pp. 428–429.

4. James Risen and Eric Lichtblau, "Bush Lets U.S. Spy on Callers Without Courts," *New*

York Times (December 16, 2005): 1; and Brian Ross, "NSA Whistleblower Alleges Illegal Spying," ABCNews.com, January 10, 2006, http://abcnews.go.com/WNT/Investigation/story?id=1491889, accessed May 13, 2006.

5. Eric Lichtblau and Adam Liptak, "Bush and His Senior Aides Press On in Legal Defense for Wiretapping Program," New York Times (January 28, 2006): 13.

6. Leslie Cauley, "NSA Has Massive Database of Americans' Phone Calls; 3 Telecoms Help Government Collect Billions of Domestic Records," USA Today (May 11, 2006): 1A.

7. Jewel v. NSA, District Court for the Northern District of California, Case No. 08-cv-4373-VRW.

8. Richard A. Posner, "Our Intelligence Quotient," Wall Street Journal (May 15, 2006): A14.

9. Richard A. Falkenrath, "The Right Call on Phone Records," Washington Post (May 13, 2006): A17.

10. Greg Miller, "New Furor over NSA Phone Logs," Los Angeles Times (May 12, 2006): A1.

11. Paul Taylor, "Qwest Snubbed 'Illegal' Call for Details of Phone Records," Financial Times (May 13, 2006): 1.

12. Brian Ross, Vic Walter, and Anna Schechter, "Exclusive: Inside Account of Eavesdropping on Americans," http://abcnews.go.com/Blotter/story?id=5987804&page=1, accessed March 23, 2010.

13. CNN Poll, May 16–17, 2006 (54% approve); CBS News Poll, May 16–17, 2006 (51% approve); FOX News Poll, May 16–18, 2006 (52% approve).

14. Richard Sisk, "They Know Who We're Calling," New York Daily News (May 12, 2006): 7.

15. Henry Steele Commager, ed., Documents of American History, 6th ed. (New York: Appleton-Century-Crofts, 1958), pp. 125–126. Also see Willi Paul Adams, The First American Constitutions: Republican Ideology and the Making of the State Constitutions in the Revolutionary Era (Chapel Hill: University of North Carolina Press, 1980).

16. Charles R. Ritcheson, "'Loyalist Influence' on British Policy Toward the United States After the American Revolution," Eighteenth Century Studies 7:1 (Autumn 1973): 1–17. See also Paul A. Smith, "The American Loyalists: Notes on Their Organization and Numerical Strength," William and Mary Quarterly, 25:2 (April 1968): 259–277.

17. Arthur M. Schlesinger, Prelude to Independence: The Newspaper War on Britain, 1764–1776 (New York: Alfred Knopf, 1958), pp. 297–298.

18. Ibid., p. 299.

19. Michael W. McConnell, "Establishment and Disestablishment at the Founding, Part I, Establishment of Religion," 44 William and Mary Law Review 2105 (April 2003): 2157–2159.

20. Barron v. Mayor and City Council of Baltimore, 32 U.S. 243 (1833), as quoted in C. Herman Pritchett, Constitutional Civil Liberties (Englewood Cliffs, NJ: Prentice-Hall, 1984), p. 6.

21. Robert G. McCloskey, revised by Sanford Levinson, The American Supreme Court, 3rd ed. (Chicago: University of Chicago Press, 2000), p. 80.

22. District of Columbia et al. v. Heller No. 07-290 (2008).

23. McDonald v. Chicago, 561 U.S. ___ (2010).

24. Alexander Hamilton, James Madison, and John Jay, "Federalist 10," The Federalist Papers (New York: Bantam Books, 1982 [1787–1788]), pp. 45–46.

25. On overconfidence in homogenous groups, see James N. Druckman, "Political Preference Formation: Competition, Deliberation, and the (Ir)relevance of Framing Effects," American Political Science Review 98:4 (November 2004): 671–686.

26. John Emerich Edward Dalberg-Acton, The History of Freedom and Other Essays, eds. John Neville Figgis and Reginald Vere Laurence (Freeport, NY: Books for Libraries Press, 1967), p. 97.

27. John Stuart Mill, On Liberty (New York: Norton, 1859/1975), p. 36.

28. David M. Rabban, Free Speech in Its Forgotten Years (New York: Cambridge University Press, 1997), p. 193.

29. Robert G. McCloskey, The American Supreme Court (Chicago: University of Chicago Press, 1960), p. 224.

30. Mitchell Zuckoff, "A New Word on Speech Codes; One School That Led Way Is Rethinking Its Rules," Boston Globe (October 21, 1998): A1.

31. Tom Mashberg, "Debates Rage on Campus Over Free-Speech Rules," Boston Herald (October 31, 1999): 1.

32. Schenck v. United States, 249 U.S. 47 (1919).

33. Abrams v. United States, 250 U.S. 616 (1919).

34. Stromberg v. California, 283 U.S. 359 (1931).

35. Goldstein, Political Repression, p. 262.

36. Chaplinsky v. New Hampshire, 315 U.S. 568 (1942).

37. As quoted in C. Herman Pritchett, The American Constitution, 3rd ed. (New York: McGraw-Hill, 1969), p. 375.

38. John Mueller, "Trends in Political Tolerance," Public Opinion Quarterly 52:1 (Spring 1988): 1–25; and National Opinion Research Center, General Social Survey 1975, 2004.

39. United States v. Carolene Products Co., 304 U.S. 144 (1938).

40. George Anastaplo, as quoted in Goldstein, Political Repression, p. 532.

41. Papish v. Board of Curators of the University of Missouri, 410 U.S. 667 (1973).

42. Texas v. Johnson, 491 U.S. 397 (1989).

43. R. A. V. v. City of St. Paul, Minnesota, 112 S Ct. 2541 (1992).

44. Schlesinger, Prelude to Independence, pp. 64–65.

45. Near v. Minnesota, 283 U.S. 697 (1931).

46. Frank Ahrens, "The Price for On-Air Indecency Goes Up," Washington Post (June 8, 2006): D1.

47. NAACP v. Alabama, 357 U.S. 449 (1958).

48. Boy Scouts of America v. Dale, 530 U.S. 640 (2000).

49. Rumsfeld v. Forum for Academic and Institutional Rights, 547 U.S. 47 (2006).

50. Morse v. Frederick, 127 S. Ct. 2618 (2007).

51. Miller v. California, 413 U.S. 15 (1973).

52. Linda Greenhouse, "Court, 9–0, Upholds State Laws Prohibiting Assisted Suicide, Protects Speech on Internet," New York Times (June 27, 1997): A1.

53. David G. Savage, "Supreme Court Lets Internet Porn Law Die," Los Angeles Times, January 22, 2009, http://articles.latimes.com/2009/jan/22/nation/na-supreme-court-porno22, accessed March 23, 2010.

54. Anthony Lewis, Make No Law: The Sullivan Case and the First Amendment (New York: Random House, 1992).

55. Diane Ravitch, The Great School Wars: New York City, 1805–1973 (New York: Basic Books, 1974); and Paul E. Peterson, The Politics of School Reform, 1870–1940 (Chicago: University of Chicago Press, 1985).

56. Thomas Jefferson, Letter to Danbury Baptist Association, January 1, 1802, www.loc.gov/loc/lcib/9806/danpre.html, accessed May 18, 2008.

57. Meek v. Pittenger, 421 U.S. 349 (1975).

58. Michael W. McConnell, "Stuck with a Lemon: A New Test for Establishment Clause Cases Would Help Ease Current Confusion," ABA Journal 83 (February 1997): 46–47.

59. Engel v. Vitale, 370 U.S. 421 (1962); School District of Abington Township, Pennsylvania v. Schempp, 374 U.S. 273 (1963); and Wallace v. Jaffree, 472 U.S. 38 (1985).

60. *Board of Education of Westside Community Schools v. Mergens,* 496 U.S. 226 (1990); see also *Good News Club v. Milford Central School,* (99–2036) 533 U.S. 98 (2001).

61. *Mitchell v. Helms,* (98–1648) 530 U.S. 793 (2000).

62. *Agostini v. Felton,* 96–552 (1997).

63. *Meyer v. Nebraska,* 262 U.S. 399 (1923). See also *Pierce v. Society of Sisters,* 268 U.S. 510 (1925).

64. *Wisconsin v. Yoder,* 406 U.S. 205 (1972).

65. *Church of the Lukumi Bablu Aye v. City of Hialeah,* 508 U.S. 520 (1993).

66. *Employment Division, Oregon Department of Human Resources v. Smith,* 494 U.S. 872 (1990).

67. Paul E. Peterson, "The New Politics of Choice," in *Learning from the Past,* eds. Diane Ravitch and Maris Vinovskis (Baltimore, MD: Johns Hopkins University Press, 1995).

68. "Abolitionist William Lloyd Garrison Admits of No Compromise with the Evil of Slavery," *Lend Me Your Ears: Great Speeches in American History,* ed. by William Safire (New York: W.W. Norton, 1997), p. 629.

69. Belief in God: Harris Poll, February 26, 2003; president's beliefs: Pew Research Center Poll, August 18, 2007.

70. Pew Center Poll, August 18, 2007. On the complexity of public opinion on religion and politics, see Ted G. Jelen and Clyde Wilcox, *Public Attitudes toward Church and State* (New York: M.E. Sharpe, 1995).

71. Publius Syrus, as quoted in John Bartlett, *Familiar Quotations,* p. 111.

72. *Olmstead v. United States,* 277 U.S. 438 (1927).

73. *Criminal Victimization in the United States, 2007,* U.S. Department of Justice, Bureau of Justice Statistics, February 2010, Table 1, available at http://bjs.ojp.usdoj.gov/content/pub/pdf/cvus07.pdf, accessed March 24, 2010.

74. Senator Joe Biden, as quoted in Chuck Henning, *The Wit and Wisdom of Politics: Expanded Edition* (Golden, CO: Fulcrum Publishing, 1992), p. 47.

75. Justice Potter Stewart, as quoted in Bernard Schwartz, *A History of the Supreme Court* (New York: Oxford, 1993), p. 264.

76. Bernard Schwartz, *A History of the Supreme Court* (New York: Oxford, 1993), p. 263.

77. *Chimel v. California,* 395 U.S. 752 (1969).

78. *Mapp v. Ohio,* 167 U.S. 643 (1961).

79. Ibid.

80. *United States v. Leon,* 468 U.S. 897 (1984).

81. Joan Biskupic, "Police May Stop, Frisk Those Who Flee at Sight of Officer,"

Washington Post (January 13, 2000): A10.

82. *Herring v. United States,* No. 07-513 (2009).

83. Anne E. Kornblut, "Obama Administration Looks into Modifying *Miranda* Law in the Age of Terrorism," *Washington Post,* May 10, 2010, www.washingtonpost.com/wp-dyn/content/article/2010/05/09/AR2010050902062.html, accessed May 22, 2010.

84. Pritchett, *Constitutional Civil Liberties,* p. 78.

85. *Sheppard v. Maxwell,* 384 U.S. 333 (1966).

86. *Nebraska Press Association v. Stuart,* 427 U.S. 539 (1976).

87. Lisa J. McIntyre, *The Public Defender: The Practice of Law in the Shadows of Repute* (Chicago: University of Chicago Press, 1987), p. 162.

88. Robert B. Spangenberg, Marea L. Beeman, and James Downing, "State and County Expenditures for Indigent Defense Services in Fiscal Year 2002" (West Newton, MA: Report prepared for the American Bar Association, September 2003).

89. *Hamdi v. Rumsfeld,* 03-6696 (2004); *Rumsfeld v. Padilla,* 03-1027 (2004); and *Rasul v. Bush,* 03-334 (2004).

90. *Boumediene v. Bush,* No. 06-1195 (2008).

91. *Wong Wing v. U.S.* 163 U.S. 228 (1896).

92. Casper, *American Criminal Justice;* and Jerome Skolnick, *Justice Without Trial* (New York: Wiley, 1966).

93. *Santobello v. New York* 404 U.S. 257 (1971), as quoted in Lawrence M. Friedman, *Crime and Punishment in American History* (New York: Basic Books, 1993), p. 392.

94. Robert H. Bork, "Neutral Principles and Some First Amendment Problems," *Indiana Law Journal* 47 (1971): 8.

95. *Griswold v. Connecticut,* 381 U.S. 479 (1965).

96. Ibid.

97. *Lawrence v. Texas,* (02-102) 539 U.S. 558 (2003).

98. The Gallup Poll: "Social and Economic Indicators—Homosexual Relations," www.gallup.com/poll/topics/homosexual.asp, accessed February 18, 2002.

99. *Planned Parenthood of Southeastern Pennsylvania v. Casey,* 112 S Ct 291 (1992).

100. *Planned Parenthood of Southeastern Pennsylvania v. Casey,* 505 U.S. 833 (1992).

101. *Gonzales v. Carhart* 550 U.S. 124 (2007).

102. David Streitfeld and Charles Pillar, "Big Brother Finds Ally in Once-Wary High-Tech," *Los Angeles Times* (January 19, 2002): A1.

103. Ibid.

104. Ibid.

105. Harris Poll, February 7–14, 2006.

106. Ibid.; Pew Research Center Poll, December 12, 2006–January 9, 2007.

107. Sonia Arrison, "New Anti-Terrorism Law Goes Too Far," *San Diego Union Tribune* (October 31, 2001): B9.

108. *Kyllo v. United States,* (99–8508) 533 U.S. 27 (2001).

CHAPTER 17

1. Transcript of January 21 Democratic Presidential Debate, Sponsored by CNN and the Congressional Black Caucus Institute, www.cnn.com/2008/POLITICS/01/21/debate.transcript/index.html, accessed May 20, 2008.

2. Matt Stearns and Margaret Talev, "Race, Gender not Driving Clinton and Obama," *Houston Chronicle* (October 14, 2007): A3.

3. Michael Paul Williams, "Ferraro May Cleave Democrats," *Richmond Times Dispatch* (March 14, 2008): B1.

4. Jim VandeHei and Josh Kraushaar, "GOP Fails to Recruit Minorities," The Politico, May 19, 2008, www.politico.com/news/stories/0508/10464.html.

5. Juliet Lapidos, "The AIDS Conspiracy Handbook," Slate.com, March 19, 2008, www.slate.com/id/2186860/.

6. Barack Obama, "A More Perfect Union," transcript of speech as prepared for delivery, March 18, 2008, www.msnbc.msn.com/id/23690567/, accessed June 29, 2008.

7. Ruth Bader Ginsburg, "Employment of the Constitution to Advance the Equal Status of Men and Women," in *The Constitutional Bases of Political and Social Change in the United States,* ed. Shlomo Slonim (New York: Praeger, 1990), p. 188.

8. Martin Luther King, Jr., "Civil Right No. 1: The Right to Vote," in *A Testament of Hope: The Essential Writings and Speeches of Martin Luther King, Jr.,* ed. James M. Washington (New York: HarperCollins, 1986), p. 188.

9. John Agresto, *The Supreme Court and Constitutional Democracy* (Ithaca, NY: Cornell University Press, 1984), p. 27. Ellipses deleted.

10. Philip Converse, "The Nature of Belief Systems in Mass Publics," in David E. Apter, *Ideology and Discontent* (New York: Free Press, 1964), pp. 206–261.

11. John D. Hicks, *The American Nation* (Cambridge, MA: Riverside Press, 1949), p. 21.

12. Eric Foner, *A Short History of Reconstruction* (New York: Harper, 1990).

13. Eric Foner, *Reconstruction, 1863–1877* (New York: Harper & Row, 1988), pp. 425–444.

14. Ibid, p. 428.

15. Richard M.Valelly, "National Parties and Racial Disfranchisement," in *Classifying by Race,* ed. Paul E. Peterson (Princeton, NJ: Princeton University Press, 1995), pp. 188–216.

16. U.S. Commission on Civil Rights, *Report of the Commission on Civil Rights* (Washington, DC: Government Printing Office, 1959), p. 32. Ellipses deleted.

17. V. O. Key, Jr., *Southern Politics* (New York: Random House, 1949).

18. J. Morgan Kousser, *The Shaping of Southern Politics: Suffrage Restriction and the Establishment of the One-Party South, 1880–1910* (New Haven, CT:Yale University Press, 1974), p. 61.

19. Leon F. Litwack, *Trouble in Mind: Black Southerners in the Age of Jim Crow* (New York: Knopf, 1998), p. 229.

20. *Civil Rights Cases,* 109 U.S. 3 (1883).

21. The majority opinion in the Civil Rights Cases suggested that states could ban discrimination in public accommodations, however, and many did so in the 1880s, especially in the North. See Donald G. Nieman, *Promises to Keep: African Americans and the Constitutional Order, 1776 to the Present* (New York: Oxford University Press, 1991), pp. 103–104.

22. *Plessy v. Ferguson,* 163 U.S. 537 (1896).

23. Ibid.

24. Nieman, *Promises to Keep,* p. 110.

25. Edward Banfield and James Q. Wilson, *City Politics* (New York:Vintage Books, 1963); and James Q. Wilson, *Negro Politics* (New York: Free Press, 1960). For caveats, see Steven P. Erie, *Rainbow's End: Irish-Americans and the Dilemmas of Urban Machine Politics, 1840–1985* (Berkeley: University of California Press, 1990).

26. Richard A. Keiser, *Subordination or Empowerment? African American Leadership and the Struggle for Urban Political Power* (New York: Oxford University Press, 1997), p. 27.

27. Harold Gosnell, *Negro Politicians* [1935] (Chicago: University of Chicago Press, 1967); Thomas M. Guterbock, *Machine Politics in Transition* (Chicago: University of Chicago Press, 1980); and Ira Katznelson, *Black Men,White Cities* (Chicago: University of Chicago Press, 1976).

28. David McCullough, *Truman* (New York: Simon & Schuster, 1992), pp. 586–590; and Patricia Gurin, Shirley Hatchett, and James S. Jackson, *Hope and Independence: Blacks' Response to Electoral and Party Politics* (New York: Russell Sage, 1989), pp. 36–38.

29. Gerald N. Rosenberg, *The Hollow Hope: Can Courts Bring About Social Change?* (Chicago: University of Chicago Press, 1991), p. 61.

30. Nieman, *Promises to Keep,* pp. 139–40.

31. Hugo Black (1937), Felix Frankfurter (1939),William Douglas (1939), Frank Murphy (1940), and Wiley Rutledge (1943). See Nieman, *Promises to Keep,* p. 142.

32. *Smith v. Allwright,* 321 U.S. 649 (1944).

33. *Shelley v. Kraemer,* 334 U.S. 1 (1948).

34. *Missouri ex rel. Gaines v. Canada,* 305 U.S. 337 (1938).

35. *Sweatt v. Painter,* 339 U.S. 629 (1950).

36. *Brown v. Board of Education,* 347 U.S. 483 (1954).

37. Ibid., note 11. The citation of six psychological and sociological studies in this note led Herbert Garfinkel to charge that the Court was making decisions on the basis of sociology, not law. "Social Science Evidence and the School Segregation Cases," *Journal of Politics* 21 (February 1959): 37–59; and Kenneth B. Clar, "Effect of Prejudice and Discrimination on Personality Development" (Midcentury White House Conference on Children and Youth 1950, as cited in note 11 to *Brown*).

38. *San Antonio Independent School District v. Rodriguez,* 411 U.S. 1 (1973). Similar reasoning can be found in *Cooper v. Aaron,* 358 U.S. 1 (1958).

39. A. Leon Higgenbotham, Jr., *Shades of Freedom: Racial Politics and Presumptions of the American Legal Process* (New York: Oxford University Press, 1996).

40. A. D. Morris, *Origins of the Civil Rights Movement: Black Communities Organizing for Change* (New York: Free Press, 1984).

41. Martin Luther King, Jr., "Walk for Freedom," in *A Testament of Hope: The Essential Writings and Speeches of Martin Luther King, Jr.,* ed. James M.Washington (New York: HarperCollins, 1986), p. 83.

42. Michael Lipsky, "Protest as a Political Resource," *American Political Science Review* LXII (December 1968): 1144–1158.

43. University of Georgia, CarlVinson Institute of Government, "Historical Documents Related to Georgia," www.cviog.uga.edu/ Projects/gainfo/gahisdoc.htm, accessed April 6, 2000.

44. Rosenberg, *The Hollow Hope,* p. 50.

45. Taylor Branch, *Parting the Waters: America in the King Years 1954–63* (New York: Simon & Schuster, 1988), p. 375.

46. Martin Luther King, Jr., "I Have a Dream," in *A Testament of Hope: The Essential Writings and Speeches of Martin Luther King, Jr.,* ed. James M.Washington (New York: HarperCollins, 1986), p. 219.

47. Gerald D. Jaynes and Robin M. Williams, Jr., eds., *A Common Destiny: Blacks and American Society* (Washington, DC: National Academy Press, 1989), p. 224.

48. Gerald N. Rosenberg, *The Hollow Hope: Can Courts Bring About Social Change?* (Chicago: University of Chicago Press, 1991), Table 2.1, p. 50.

49. Patricia Gurin, Shirley Hatchett, and James S. Jackson, *Hope and Independence: Blacks' Response to Electoral and Party Politics* (New York: Russell Sage, 1989), pp. 42–49.

50. Jaynes and Williams, *A Common Destiny,* p. 233.

51. Joint Center for Political and Economic Studies, *Focus* (Washington, DC: Joint Center for Political and Economic Studies, 1993); and Ralph Everett, "Number of Black Elected Officials Increases, But Not By Much," Joint Center for Political and Economic Studies, October 16, 2007, http://jointcenterjournal.squarespace.com/ journal/2007/10/16/number-of-black-elected-officials-increases-but-not-by-much.html, accessed May 21, 2008.

52. Mark Hugo Lopez, "Dissecting the 2008 Electorate: Most Diverse in U.S. History," Pew Research Center report, April 30, 2009, http://pewresearch.org/pubs/1209/racial-ethnic-voters-presidential-election, accessed May 1, 2010.

53. William J. Grimshaw, *Bitter Fruit: Black Politics and the Chicago Machine, 1931–1991* (Chicago: University of Chicago Press, 1992).

54. Gary Orfield, *The Reconstruction of Southern Education: The Schools and the 1964 Civil Rights Act* (New York:Wiley, 1969); Gary Orfield, *Must We Bus?* (Washington, DC: The Brookings Institution, 1978); and Jennifer Hochschild, *The New American Dilemma* (New Haven, CT:Yale University Press, 1984).

55. Taylor Branch, *Pillar of Fire: America in the King Years 1963–65* (New York: Simon & Schuster, 1998), p. 549.

56. Katherine Tate, *From Protest to Politics* (Cambridge, MA: Harvard University Press, 1993), chap. 8; see also Edward G. Carmines and James A. Stimson, *Issue Evolution: Race and the Transformation of American Politics* (Princeton, NJ: Princeton University Press, 1989).

57. *Milliken v. Bradley,* I 418 U.S. 717 (1974); II 433 U.S. 267 (1977).

58. *Regents of the University of California v. Bakke,* 438 U.S. 265 (1978).

59. *Grutter v. Bollinger,* (02-241) 539 U.S. 306 (2003).

60. Ibid.

61. *Gratz v. Bollinger,* (02-516) 539 U.S. 244 (2003).

62. *Grutter v. Bollinger,* (02-241) 539 U.S. 306 (2003).

63. U.S. Bureau of the Census, Current Population Survey, 2009 Annual Social and Economic Supplement, available at www .census.gov/hhes/www/cpstables/032009/ pov/toc.htm, accessed May 1, 2010.

64. U.S. Department of Commerce, Bureau of Labor Statistics, "Unemployed Persons by Reason for Unemployment Race, and Hispanic or Latino Ethnicity" (data for March 2010), www.bls.gov/web/empsit.supp.toc.htm, accessed May 1, 2010.

65. U.S. Bureau of the Census, *Statistical Abstract of the United States, 2006,* Tables 81 and 104.

66. U.S. Bureau of the Census, *Statistical Abstract of the United States, 2010,* Table 337.

67. Jennifer L. Hochschild, *Facing Up to the American Dream: Race, Class, and the Soul of the Nation* (Princeton, NJ: Princeton University Press, 1995).

68. Jaynes and Williams, *A Common Destiny,* p. 313.

69. U.S. Bureau of the Census, *Statistical Abstract of the United States, 2010,* Table 224.

70. U.S. Department of Education, National Center for Education Statistics, *Digest of Education Statistics, 2009,* http://nces.ed.gov/programs/digest/d09/, accessed May 1, 2010, Table 134. See also: Steven Rivkin and Finis Welch, "Has School Desegregation Improved Academic and Economic Outcomes for Blacks?" *Handbook of the Economics of Education,* Vol. 2 (Amsterdam, Holland: North Holland, 2006), Chapter 17.

71. United States Bureau of the Census, *Statistical Abstract of the United States, 2010,* Table 695.

72. U.S. Census Bureau, "The Hispanic Population in the United States: 2008, Detailed Tables," Table 1, www.census.gov/population/www/socdemo/hispanic/cps2008.html, accessed May 1, 2010.

73. Tony Affigne, "Latino Politics in the United States: An Introduction," *PS: Political Science and Politics,* 33:3 (September 2000): 523–527, Table 3.

74. Pew Research Center, "Fewer Voters Identify as Republicans," http://pewresearch.org/pubs/773/fewer-voters-identify-as-republicans, March 20, 2008, accessed May 1, 2010, for blacks; for Latinos, Pew Hispanic Center, "2008 National Survey of Latinos: Hispanic Voter Attitudes," http://pewhispanic.org/reports/report.php?ReportID=90, accessed May 1, 2010.

75. Tyche Hendricks, "Parade, Enthusiastic Crowd Celebrate Cesar Chavez Day," *San Francisco Chronicle* (April 1, 2001): A18.

76. *Lau v. Nichols,* 414 U.S. 563 (1974).

77. Bernard Grofman, Lisa Handley, and Richard G. Niemi, *Minority Representation and the Quest for Voting Equality* (New York: Cambridge University Press, 1992), pp. 16–25; also see Thomas Weyr, *Hispanic U.S.A.: Breaking the Melting Pot* (New York: Harper, 1959); and

Peter Skerry, *Mexican Americans: The Ambivalent Minority* (New York: Free Press, 1993).

78. Daron Shaw, Rodolfo O. de la Garza, and Jongho Lee, "Examining Latino Turnout in 1996: A Three State, Validated Survey Approach," *American Journal of Political Science* 44:2 (April 2000): 332–340.

79. U.S. Census Bureau 2007 Population Estimates, www.census.gov/Press-Release/www/releases/archives/population/011910.html, accessed May 23, 2008; U.S. Bureau of the Census, *Statistical Abstract of the United States, 2006,* Table 43.

80. Stanley Karnow and Nancy Yoshihara, *Asian Americans in Transition* (New York: Asia Society, 1992).

81. Don Nakanishi, "Beyond Electoral Politics: Renewing a Search for a Paradigm of Asian Pacific American Politics," in *Asian Americans and Politics: Perspectives, Experiences, Prospects,* ed. Gordon H. Chang (Washington, DC: Woodrow Wilson Center Press, 2001), pp. 102–129; and William Schneider, "Asian Americans Will Matter More," *National Journal* (August 14, 1999): 2398.

82. Amit R. Paley, "A Date with Tradition: Chinese New Year Ushers in Quest for Official Holiday Recognition," *Washington Post* (January 29, 2006): C1; and Errol Louis, "Strength in Numbers: John Liu Galvanizes the City's Asian Community to Quash Bias," *New York Daily News* (May 16, 2006): 31.

83. UCLA Asian American Studies Center, "UCLA's New National APA Almanac Lists over 2,000 Asian Pacific American Elected and Appointed Officials Nationwide," www.aasc.ucla.edu/archives/pa_07_08.asp, accessed May 1, 2010.

84. Robert Goldstein, *Political Repression in Modern America: 1870 to the Present* (New York: Schenkman, 1978), pp. 266–267.

85. *Korematsu v. United States,* 323 U.S. 244 (1944).

86. Nakanishi, Beyond Electoral Politics," p. 121.

87. Angelo Ancheta, *Race, Rights, and the Asian-American Experience* (New Brunswick, NJ: Rutgers University Press, 1997).

88. Kenneth D. Wald, James W. Button, and Barbara A. Rienzo, "The Politics of Gay Rights In American Communities: Explaining Anti-Discrimination Ordinances and Policies," *American Journal of Political Science* 40(4) (November 1996): 1152–1178.

89. Timothy Cook, "The Empirical Study of Lesbian, Gay, and Bisexual Politics: Assessing the First Wave of Research," *American Political Science Review* 93(3) (September 1999): 679.

90. Donald P. Haider-Markel, "Creating Change—Holding the Line: Agenda Setting

on Lesbian and Gay Issues at the National Level," in *Gays and Lesbians in the Democratic Process: Public Policy, Public Opinion, and Political Representation,* eds. Ellen D. B. Riggle and Barry Tadlock (New York: Columbia University Press, 1999), pp. 242–268.

91. Data from the Gay and Lesbian Victory Fund, www.glli.org/out_officials, accessed May 1, 2010.

92. Deb Price, "Gays Need Democrats to Win 2000 Elections," *Detroit News* (November 1, 1999): A7; and Human Rights Campaign, www.hrc.org, accessed May 23, 2008.

93. Elisabeth Bumiller, "Top Defense Officials Seek to End 'Don't Ask, Don't Tell,'" *New York Times,* February 2, 2010, www.nytimes.com/2010/02/03/us/politics/03military.html, accessed May 10, 2010.

94. CBS/*New York Times* Poll, April 5–12, 2010: 39 percent approve of "legal marriage" for gays and lesbians; *Newsweek* Poll, December 3–4, 2008: majority approval of gays serving in military, of hospital visitation rights, and job opportunities.

95. Human Rights Campaign, www.hrc.org, accessed May 1, 2010.

96. Vine Deloria, Jr., "The Distinctive Status of Indian Rights," in *The Plains Indians of the Twentieth Century,* ed. Peter Iverson (Norman: University of Oklahoma Press, 1985), p. 241.

97. Ibid., pp. 237–248.

98. U.S. Census, *Poverty in the United States: 2000,* Current Population Reports P60-214 (September 2001), p. 7, Table B.

99. www.opensecrets.org, accessed May 1, 2010.

100. Toby Harnden, "Choctaws Take Their Slice of the American Pie," *London Daily Telegraph* (September 2, 2000): 15.

101. Deloria, "The Distinctive Status of Indian Rights," p. 237.

102. Agresto, *The Supreme Court and Constitutional Democracy,* pp. 148–149.

103. Theda Skocpol, *Protecting Soldiers and Mothers: The Political Origins of Social Policy in the United States* (Cambridge, MA: Harvard University Press, 1992); and Sara Evans, *Personal Politics: The Roots of Women's Liberation in the Civil Rights Movement and the New Left* (New York: Knopf, 1979).

104. As late as 1975 Gallup polls showed 74 percent favored "a constitutional amendment which would give women equal rights and equal responsibilities." (Gallup Poll, October 18–21, 1975).

105. Nancy McGlen and Karen O'Conner, *Women's Rights: The Struggle for Equality in the Nineteenth and Twentieth Centuries* (New York: Praeger, 1983), chap. 9.

106. Jane J. Mansbridge, *Why We Lost the ERA* (Chicago: University of Chicago Press, 1986).

107. Ruth B. Mandel, "The Political Woman," in *American Women in the Nineties: Today's Critical Issues,* ed. Sherri Matteo (Boston: Northeastern University Press, 1993), pp. 34–65.

108. See http://womenincongress.house.gov/ for historical and current data on women in the House and Senate.

109. *Hoyt v. Florida,* 368 U.S. 57 (1961).

110. *Craig v. Boren,* 429 U.S. 190 (1976).

111. Ginsburg, *Employment of the Constitution,* p. 191.

112. *Rostker v. Goldberg,* 453 U.S. 65 (1981).

113. Mansbridge, *Why We Lost the ERA,* chap. 7; Gallup Poll cited in Leonard, "Should Women Be in Combat?"

114. See *Dothard v. Rawlinson* 433 U.S. 321 (1977).

115. *Watson v. Fort Worth Bank & Trust,* 487 U.S. 997–999; *New York City Transit Authority v. Beazer,* 440 U.S. at 587, no. 31; and *Griggs v. Duke Power,* 401 U.S. at 432.

116. *Wards Cove Packing Co. v. Antonio,* 490 U.S. 642 (1989).

117. *Meritor Savings Bank v. Vinson,* 477 U.S. 57 (1986).

118. *Harris v. Forklift Systems,* 510 U.S. 77 (1993).

119. Equal Employment Opportunity Commission, Sexual Harassment Charges, www.eeoc.gov/eeoc/statistics/enforcement/sexual_harassment.cfm, accessed May 1, 2010.

120. "Hillary's Class," *Frontline* (PBS television broadcast, No. 15, 1994), as cited in Karla Cooper-Boggs, "The Link Between Private and Public Single-Sex Colleges: Will Wellesley Stand or Fall with the Citadel?" *Indiana Law Review* 29 (1995): 137.

121. *United States v. Virginia,* 116 S Ct. 2264 (1966).

122. National Committee on Pay Equity, "The Wage Gap Over Time," www.pay-equity.org/info-time.html, accessed May 23, 2008; for a review, see Astrid Kunze, "Gender Wage Gap Studies: Consistency and Decomposition," *Empirical Economics* 35:1 (2007), pp. 63–76.

123. United States General Accounting Office, *Women in Management: Analysis of Selected Data from the Current Population Survey,* GAO-02-156 (September 2001).

124. U.S. Census Bureau, "Americans with Disabilities Act: July 26," press release, May 29, 2007, www.census.gov/Press-Release/www/releases/archives/facts_for_features_special_editions/010102.html, accessed May 1, 2010.

125. Office of Management and Budget, *Budget of the United States Government, Fiscal Year 2011,* Historical Tables, Table 13.1, www.gpoaccess.gov/usbudget/fy11/hist.html, accessed May 1, 2010.

126. Robert A. Katzman, *Institutional Disability: The Saga of Transportation Policy for the Disabled* (Washington, DC: The Brookings Institution, 1986).

127. Frederick J. Weintraub, ed., *Public Policy and the Education of Exceptional Children* (Washington, DC: Council for Exceptional Children, 1976).

128. Paul E. Peterson, "Background Paper," in Twentieth Century Fund, *Making the Grade: Report of the Twentieth Century Fund Task Force on Federal Elementary and Secondary Education Policy* (New York: Twentieth Century Fund, 1983), chap. 5.

129. Linda Greenhouse, "Justices Hear an Argument for Not Hiring the Disabled," *New York Times* (February 28, 2002): A22.

130. *Board of Trustees of the University of Alabama v. Garrett,* 99–1240 (2001).

131. *Toyota Motor Manufacturing, Kentucky, Inc. v. Williams,* 00-1089 (2002).

132. Rufus Browning, Dale Rogers Marshall, and David H. Tabb, *Protest Is Not Enough: The Struggle of Blacks and Hispanics for Equality in Urban Politics* (Berkeley: University of California Press, 1984).

CHAPTER 18

1. Transcription by authors from C-SPAN Video Library recording of "Senator Grassley Town Hall Meeting," August 12, 2009, www.c-spanvideo.org/program/288345-1, accessed May 3, 2010.

2. Centers for Disease Control and Prevention, "Lack of Health Insurance and Type of Coverage," June 2009, Table 1.2b, www.cdc.gov/nchs/data/nhis/earlyrelease/200906_01.pdf, accessed May 9, 2010.

3. Chris L. Peterson and Rachel Burton, "U.S. Health Care Spending: Comparison with Other OECD Countries," CRS Report for Congress No. RL34175, September 17, 2007, http://assets.opencrs.com/rpts/RL34175_20070917.pdf, accessed May 9, 2010; Centers for Disease Control and Prevention, "Lack of Health Insurance and Type of Coverage," June 2009, Table 1.1a, www.cdc.gov/nchs/data/nhis/early-release/200906_01.pdf, accessed May 9, 2010.

4. Rebecca Adams, "Health Care Overhaul Still in 'Happy Talk' Stage," *CQ Weekly* (January 19, 2009): 114.

5. David Herszenhorn and Robert Pear, "Health Bill Passes Key Test in the Senate," *New York Times,* December 21, 2010, www.nytimes.com/2009/12/21/us/21vote.html, accessed May 5, 2010.

6. Consolidated polling data plotted at Pollster.com, www.pollster.com/polls/us/healthplan.php, accessed May 5, 2010.

7. Barack Obama, "Remarks by the President and Vice President at Signing of the Health Insurance Reform Bill," The White House, March 23, 2010, www.whitehouse.gov/the-press-office/remarks-president-and-vice-president-signing-health-insurance-reform-bill, accessed May 5, 2010.

8. David Herszenhorn and Robert Pear, "Final Votes in Congress Cap Battle on Health Care Bill," *New York Times,* March 25, 2010, www.nytimes.com/2010/03/26/health/policy/26health.html, accessed May 5, 2010.

9. Robert Pear and David Herszenhorn, "Lawmakers Recess and Prepare to Defend Health Votes," *New York Times,* March 26, 2010, www.nytimes.com/2010/03/27/health/policy/27health.html, accessed May 5, 2010.

10. John Kingdon, *Agendas, Alternatives, and Public Policies* (Boston: Little, Brown, 1984).

11. Kingdon, *Agendas, Alternatives and Public Policies;* and Paul Light, *The President's Agenda* (Baltimore, MD: Johns Hopkins University Press, 1991).

12. Arthur Maass, *Congress and the Common Good* (New York: Basic Books, 1983).

13. Eugene Bardach, *The Implementation Game,* 4th ed. (Cambridge, MA: M.I.T. Press, 1982); and Jeffrey L. Pressman and Aaron Wildavsky, *Implementation,* 3rd ed. (Berkeley: University of California Press, 1984).

14. Thomas R. Dye, *Politics, Economics and the Public: Policy Outcomes in the American States* (Chicago: Rand McNally, 1966).

15. United Nations Children's Fund (UNICEF), "Child Poverty in Rich Countries 2007," *Innocenti Report Card No. 7,* UNICEF Innocenti Research Centre, Florence, Italy, 2007.

16. Daniel R. Meyer and Geoffrey L. Wallace, "Poverty Levels and Trends in Comparative Perspective," University of Wisconsin-Madison, Institute for Research on Poverty, 2009, www.irp.wisc.edu/publications/focus/pdfs/foc262b.pdf, accessed May 9, 2010.

17. CIA World Factbook 2009, www.cia.gov/cia/publications/factbook/index.html, accessed May 9, 2010. Infant mortality data are from 2009; GDP data from 2007; see also Denise Grady, "Premature Births Are Fueling Higher Rates of Infant Mortality in U.S., Report Says," *New York Times,* November 3, 2009, www.nytimes.com/2009/11/04/health/04infant.html, accessed May 9, 2010.

18. Neil Howe and Richard Jackson, *Entitlements and the Aging of America* (Washington, DC: National Taxpayers Union Foundation, 2001), Chart 4-27, comment.

19. Julia B. Isaacs, Tracy Vericker, Jennifer Macomber, and Adam Kent, *Kids' Share: An Analysis of Federal Expenditures on Children through 2008* (Washington, DC: The Urban Institute and The Brookings Institution, 2009), Figure 6.

20. Thomas A. Bailey, *The American Pageant: A History of the Republic* (Boston: D.C. Heath, 1956), p. 840. See also Daniel J.B. Mitchell, "Townsend and Roosevelt: Lessons from the Struggle for Elderly Income Support," *Labor History,* 42(3) (August 2001): 255–276. The figure is in 2005 dollars—the amount was $200 in 1934 dollars.

21. Martha Derthick, *Policymaking for Social Security* (Washington, DC: The Brookings Institution, 1979); and Theda Skocpol, *Protecting Soldiers and Mothers: The Politics of Social Provision in the United States* (Cambridge, MA: Harvard University Press, 1993).

22. "Life Expectancy for Social Security," Social Security Administration, www.ssa.gov/history/lifeexpect.html, accessed May 26, 2006; and U.S. Department of Health and Human Services, National Center for Health Statistics, *Health, United States, 2007, with Chartbook on Trends in the Health of Americans,* National Center for Health Statistics, 2007, Table 27.

23. R. Kent Weaver, *Automatic Government: The Politics of Indexation* (Washington, DC: The Brookings Institution, 1988).

24. Orlo Nichols, Michael Clingman, and Alice Wade, *Internal Real Rates of Return Under the OASDI Program for Hypothetical Workers,* Social Security Administration, Office of the Chief Actuary (Baltimore, MD: March 2009), Table 1.

25. *Boston Globe* (December 27, 1994): 70.

26. As quoted in Chuck Henning, *Wit and Wisdom of Politics,* expanded ed. (Golden, CO: Fulcrum, 1992), p. 252.

27. *Strengthening Social Security and Creating Personal Wealth for All Americans,* Report of the President's Commission on Social Security, December 21, 2001, p. 8.

28. As quoted in Henning, *Wit and Wisdom of Politics,* p. 95.

29. Larry Lipman, "Social Security Overhaul Fizzles," *Atlanta Journal-Constitution* (January 15, 2006): 1B.

30. *Budget of the United States Government, Fiscal Year 2011, Historical Tables* (Washington, DC: Office of Management and Budget, 2010), Table 16.1 (figures are reported in constant 2010 dollars and do not include premium payments).

31. Richard S. Foster, "Estimated Financial Effects of the 'Patient Protection and Affordable Care Act of 2009,' as Proposed by the Senate Majority Leader on November 18, 2009," Department of Health and Human Services, Center for Medicare and Medicaid Services, December 10, 2009, http://src.senate.gov/files/OACTMemorandumonFinancialImpactofPPAA(HR3590)(12-10-09).pdf, accessed May 9, 2010.

32. U.S. Bureau of the Census, Voting and Registration: Historical Time Series Tables, Table A-1, www.census.gov/hhes/www/socdemo/voting/publications/historical/index.html, accessed May 9, 2010.

33. U.S. Bureau of the Census, Voting and Registration: Historical Time Series Tables, Table A-1, www.census.gov/hhes/www/socdemo/voting/publications/historical/index.html, accessed May 9, 2010.

34. Susan A. MacManus, with Patricia A. Turner, *Young v. Old: Generational Combat in the 21st Century* (Boulder, CO: Westview, 1996), pp. 60, 141.

35. *AARP Annual Report,* 2008.

36. Employment figures: "AARP: Making the Most of Life After 50," www.aarp.org/leadership/Articles/a2003-01-13-aarphistory.html, accessed March 30, 2004; expenditure and volunteer figures: AARP Annual Report, 2008.

37. Robert Rector, *Welfare Reform* (Washington, DC: Heritage Foundation, 1996).

38. Michael Lipsky, *Street Level Bureaucracy* (New York: Russell Sage Foundation, 1980); and Theda Skocpol, "Targeting within Universalism: Politically Viable Policies to Combat Poverty in the United States," in *The Urban Underclass,* ed. Christopher Jencks and Paul E. Peterson (Washington, DC: The Brookings Institution, 1991), pp. 411–436.

39. United States Department of Agriculture, Food and Nutrition Service, Supplemental Nutrition Assistance Program, "Program Data," www.fns.usda.gov/pd/snapmain.htm, accessed May 9, 2010.

40. Internal Revenue Service, "2009 Form 1040 General Instructions," 2007 Earned Income Credit (EIC) Table.

41. Social Security Administration, Office of Policy, "Monthly Statistical Snapshot," March 2010, Table 3, www.ssa.gov/policy/docs/quickfacts/stat_snapshot/, accessed May 9, 2010.

42. This program is now known as the Housing Choice Voucher Program; see www.hud.gov.

43. Office of Management and Budget, "Budget for Fiscal Year 2011, Historical Tables," Table 16.1 (both figures in 2010 dollars).

44. Peter Grier, "Health Care Reform Bill 101: Who Gets Subsidized Insurance?" *Christian Science Monitor,* March 20, 2010, www.csmonitor.com/USA/Politics/2010/0320/Health-care-reform-bill-101-Who-gets-subsidized-insurance, accessed May 9, 2010.

45. Center for Medicare and Medicaid Services, FY CHIP Ever Enrolled in Year Graph," www4.cms.gov/NationalCHIPPolicy/downloads/CHIPEverEnrolledYearGraph.pdf, accessed May 9, 2010.

46. Paul E. Peterson, "An Immodest Proposal," *Daedalus* 121 (Fall 1992): 151–174.

47. U.S. House of Representatives, Committee on Ways and Means, *Overview of Entitlement Programs: Background Material and Data on Programs Within the Jurisdiction of the Committee on Ways and Means* (otherwise known as the 2008 Green Book) (Washington, DC: U.S. Government Printing Office, 2008), Table I-4. All subsequent references to this document in this chapter will be simply to the Green Book. They refer to the 2008 edition.

48. Green Book, Table I-4.

49. Change is in real (inflation adjusted) terms. Authors' calculation, from: Department of Health and Human Services, Administration for Children and Families, Office of Family Assistance, *TANF: First Annual Report to Congress,* August 1998, Introduction; and Department of Health and Human Services, Administration for Children and Families, Office of Family Assistance, "Characteristics and Financial Circumstances of TANF Recipients, Fiscal Year 2008," Table 41, www.acf.hhs.gov/programs/ofa/character/FY2008/indexfy08.htm, accessed May 9, 2010.

50. Joe Garofoli, "Food Stamp Hurdles; For Many, the Hassle Outweighs the Benefits," *San Francisco Chronicle* (February 8, 2002): A21.

51. U.S. Department of Health and Human Services, Office of Family Assistance, *Temporary Assistance for Needy Families (TANF), Eighth Annual Report to Congress,* June 2009, Table 12:7 www.acf.hhs.gov/programs/ofa/data-reports/annualreport8/chapter12/chap12.htm, accessed May 9, 2010.

52. Gene Falk, "Temporary Assistance for Needy Families (TANF): Its Role in Response to the Effects of Hurricane Katrina," CRS Report for Congress, September 16, 2005.

53. Paul E. Peterson and Mark Rom, *Welfare Magnets: A New Case for a National Standard* (Washington, DC: The Brookings Institution, 1990).

54. Rules vary widely by state. See U.S. Department of Health and Human Services, Office of Family Assistance, *Temporary Assistance to Needy Families, Eighth Annual Report to Congress,* June 2009, Table 12:6 www.acf.hhs.gov/programs/ofa/data-reports/annualreport8/chapter12/chap12.htm, accessed May 9, 2010.

55. Ibid., Table 12:5, pp. XII-9, XII-10, and XII-11.

56. Testimony of Mark H. Greenberg, senior staff attorney, Center for Law and Social Policy, Human Resources Subcommittee, House Committee on Ways and Means, March 7, 2002.

57. "Social Security Penalty on Earnings Is Repealed," *Los Angeles Times* (April 8, 2000): A14.

58. Skocpol, *Protecting Soldiers and Mothers.*

59. Mary Jo Bane and Lawrence M. Mead, *Lifting Up the Poor: A Dialogue on Religion, Poverty, and Welfare Reform* (Washington, DC: Brookings Institution Press, 2003), p. 67.

60. *Statistical Abstract of the United States, 2006,* Table 53; and *Statistical Abstract of the United States, 2010,* Table 65.

61. Poverty rate for married couple households: 5.4 percent; for female-headed households: 28 percent. *Statistical Abstract of the United States, 2006,* Table 699.

62. *Statistical Abstract of the United States, 2006,* Table 1319.

63. William J. Wilson, *The Truly Disadvantaged: The Inner City, the Underclass, and Public Policy* (Chicago: University of Chicago Press, 1987).

64. Median incomes used for calculation. U.S. Bureau of the Census, *Current Population Survey,* "Educational Attainment in the United States: 2006, Detailed Tables," www.census.gov/population/www/socdemo/education/cps2006.html, accessed May 26, 2008, Table 8.

65. 2005 IRS Form 990, available via www.guidestar.org, accessed May 26, 2008.

66. Associations Unlimited, 2002.

67. Henry J. Kaiser Family Survey, October 2005; NBS News/*Wall Street Journal* Poll, April 28, 1995.

68. "About FRC" www.frc.org/get.cfm? c=HISTORY_ABOUT, accessed June 8, 2006.

69. Jeff Shear, "The Credit Card," *National Journal* 27(32) (August 12, 1995): 2056–2058; and Marilyn W. Serafini, "Turning Up the Heat," *National Journal* 27(32) (August 12, 1995): 2051–2055.

70. U.S. Department of Education, "The Federal Role In Education," www2.ed.gov/about/overview/fed/role.html, accessed May 9, 2010.

71. U.S. Department of Education, National Center for Education Statistics, *Digest of Education Statistics: 2007,* Table 162.

72. "Land Ordinance of 1785," in *Documents of American History,* 6th ed., ed. Henry S. Commager (New York: Appleton-Century-Crofts, 1958), p. 124.

73. Current expenditures (rather than total expenditures) used. Authors' calculation, based on U.S. Department of Education, National Center for Education Statistics, *Digest of Education Statistics: 2007,* Table 171.

74. Eric A Hanushek, "School Resources and Student Performance," in *Does Money Matter? The Effect of School Resources on Student Achievement and Adult Success,* ed. Gary Burtless (Washington, DC: The Brookings Institution, 1996), pp. 43–73.

75. The Gallup Organization, Roper Center for Public Opinion Research Database, Question ID Numbers USGALLUP. 870.Q005A; Gallup Poll, June 14–17, 2009.

76. David K. Kirkpatrick, *Choice in Schooling: A Case for Tuition Vouchers* (Chicago: Loyola University Press, 1990); and Terry Moe, ed., *Private Vouchers* (Stanford, CA: Hoover Institution Press, 1995).

77. William H. Clune and John F. Witte, eds., *Choice and Control in American Education,* vols. I and II (New York: Falmer Pres, 1990); and Jeffrey Henig, *Rethinking School Choice: Limits of the Market Metaphor* (Princeton, NJ: Princeton University Press, 1994).

78. Diane Ravitch, *National Standards in American Education: A Citizen's Guide* (Washington, DC: The Brookings Institution, 1995).

79. U.S. Department of Education, "Race to the Top Program; Executive Summary," November 2009, www2.ed.gov/programs/racetothetop/executive-summary.pdf, accessed May 9, 2010.

80. Sandra Blakeslee, "Expert Warned That Mad Cow Was Imminent," *New York Times* (December 25, 2003): A1.

81. Joe Ruff, "Mad Cow's Rarity Could Cut Testing," *Omaha World-Herald* (April 29, 2006): 1A.

82. Denise Grady, "U.S. Issues Safety Rules to Protect Food From Mad Cow Disease," *New York Times* (December 31, 2003): A1.

83. Craig Petersen, *Business and Government,* 2nd ed. (New York: Harper & Row, 1985), p. 173.

84. *Heart of Atlanta Motel v. United States,* 322 U.S. 533 (1964); and *United States v. South-Eastern Underwriters Association,* 322 U.S. 533 (1944).

85. Jonathan Krim, "Judge Accepts Settlement in Microsoft Case," *Washington Post* (November 2, 2002): A1; and Jim Puzzanghera, "Keeping Software Giant on Watch," *Los Angeles Times* (May 13, 2006): C1.

86. Norman J. Vig and Michael Kraft, *Environmental Policy: New Directions for the Twenty-First Century,* 6th ed., (Washington, DC: CQ Press, 2006), p. 21.

87. Murray Weidenbaum, "Government Power and Business Performance," in *The United States in the 1980s,* eds. Peter Duignan and Alvin Rabushka (Stanford, CA: Hoover Institution Press, 1990), pp. 197–220.

88. Federal Communications Commission, "FCC Consumer Facts: Regulation of Cable TV Rates," www.fcc.gov/cgb/consumerfacts/cablerates.html, accessed May 27, 2008.

89. Douglas Jehl, "National Parks Will Ban Recreation Snowmobiling; A Further Curb on the Use of Public Lands," *New York Times* (April 27, 2000): A14.

90. T. R. Reid, "For Snowmobiles, An Uncertain Fate," *Washington Post* (March 15, 2004): A23.

91. National Park Service, "The Future of Winter Use in Yellowstone National Park," www.nps.gov/yell/planyourvisit/winteruse.htm, accessed May 9, 2010.

92. U.S. Department of Agriculture, Food and Drug Administration, "Dear Manufacturer Letter Regarding Sugar Free Claims," www.cfsan.fda.gov/~dms/lclmguid.html, accessed May 27, 2008; 21 CFR 101.76.

93. Clair Wilcox, *Public Policies Toward Business,* 4th ed. (Homewood, IL: Irwin, 1971), p. 589.

94. Marc K. Landy, Marc J. Roberts, and Stephen R. Thomas, *The Environmental Protection Agency: Asking the Wrong Questions from Nixon to Clinton,* expanded ed. (New York: Oxford University Press, 1994).

95. Ibid.

96. Ibid., p. 290.

97. Kenneth Meier, *Regulation: Politics, Bureaucracy, and Economics* (New York: St. Martin's, 1985).

98. Charles Seabrook, "Eagle Delisting a Bit Premature?" *Atlanta Journal-Constitution* (February 26, 2006): 7MS.

99. Martha Derthick and Paul Quirk, *The Politics of Deregulation* (Washington, DC: The Brookings Institution, 1985); and Mark C. Rom, *Public Spirit in the Thrift Tragedy* (Pittsburgh, PA: University of Pittsburgh Press, 1996).

100. Hardaway, "Transportation Deregulation," p. 143. Another view is given by Paul Dempsey, "The State of the Airline, Airport and Aviation Industries," *Transportation Law Journal* 129 (1992): 130–200.

101. David Monk, "The Lessons of Airline Regulation and Deregulation: Will We Make the Same Mistakes in Space?" *Journal of Air Law and Commerce* 57(3) (Spring 1992): 715–753.

102. See, for example, Dennis Carlton and William Landes, "Benefits and Costs of Airline Mergers: A Case Study," *Bell Journal of Economics and Management Science* 65(11)(1982): 65–83.

103. Kelly Yamanouchi, "Deregulator Eyes Airlines' Evolution," *Denver Post* (February 18, 2006): C1.

CHAPTER 19

1. This account is drawn from Michael Lafleur, "Subprime Mortgage Toll: A Family's Shattered Dream," *The Lowell Sun* (April 8, 2007).

2. Joe Nocera, "As Credit Crisis Spiraled, Alarm Led to Action," *New York Times*, October 2, 2008, www.nytimes.com, accessed October 5, 2008.

3. Adam Smith, *An Inquiry Into the Nature and Causes of the Wealth of Nations,* Volume 1 (Chicago: University of Chicago Press, 1976 [1776]), p. 18.

4. Authors' calculations based on the Standard & Poor's 500 composite index value as of June 28, 2010. For historical data on this index, see U.S. Census Bureau, *Statistical Abstract of the United States: 1999,* Table 1436, p. 883.

5. "U.S. Theatrical Market: 2005 Statistics," Motion Picture Association Worldwide Market Research, 2006, p. 25.

6. John Mueller, *Wars, Presidents, and Public Opinion* (New York: Wiley, 1973); and Douglas Hibbs, *The American Political Economy* (Cambridge, MA: Harvard University Press, 1987), chap. 5.

7. For a summary of the relevant literature, see Fiorina, "Elections and Economics in the 1980s."

8. Office of Management and Budget, *Budget of the United States Government, Fiscal Year 2011,* Historical Tables, Table 1.1 and Table 1.2 (Washington, DC: Office of Management and Budget, 2010) .

9. Office of Management and Budget, *Budget of the United States Government, Fiscal Year 2009,* Historical Tables (Washington, DC: Office of Management and Budget, 2008), Tables 8.1, 8.3, and 8.5.

10. Paul Peretz, *The Political Economy of Inflation in the United States* (Chicago: University of Chicago Press, 1983), p. 42.

11. Ibid.

12. Office of Management and Budget, *Budget of the United States Government, Fiscal Year 2009,* Historical Tables, Table 1.1, p. 22.

13. Louis Uchitelle, "Ideas and Trends: The Bondholders Are Winning: Why America Won't Boom," *New York Times* (June 12, 1994): D4.

14. Joseph H. Carter, *Never Met a Man I Didn't Like: The Life and Writings of Will Rogers* (New York: Avon Books, 1991), p. 250.

15. "The Credit Crisis," *The Economist,* August 22, 2008, www.economist.com/finance/displaystory.cfm?story_id=11990589, accessed October 7, 2008.

16. Federal Reserve System 2010 Annual Report: Budget Review, www.federalreserve.gov/boarddocs/rptcongress/budgetrev10/default.htm, accessed June 2, 2010.

17. *88th Annual Report* (Washington, DC: Board of Governors of the Federal Reserve System, 2001), p. 383.

18. William Greider, *Secrets of the Temple: How the Federal Reserve Runs the Country* (New York: Simon & Schuster, 1987).

19. Michael Schrage, "It's Time to Put a Transaction Tax on Credit Card Purchases," *Washington Post* (October 17, 1990): F3.

20. John Wooley, *Monetary Politics: The Federal Reserve and the Politics of Monetary Policy* (New York: Cambridge University Press, 1984).

21. Alberto Alesina, "Macroeconomics and Politics," in *NBER Macroeconomics Annual, 1988,* ed. Stanley Fischer (Cambridge, MA: MIT Press, 1988), pp. 13–52.

22. Douglas Hibbs, "The Dynamics of Political Support for American Presidents Among Occupational and Partisan Groups," *American Journal of Political Science* 26 (1982): 312–332.

23. Douglas Hibbs, "The Partisan Model of Macroeconomic Cycles: More Theory and Evidence for the United States," *Economics and Politics* 6 (1994): 1–23.

24. Edward Tufte, *Political Control of the Economy* (Princeton, NJ: Princeton University Press, 1978), chap. 2.

25. GDP grew slightly more than 3 percent in nonelection years, and slightly more than 4 percent in presidential election years from 1960 to 2001. Analysis by authors of data from U.S. Department of Commerce, Bureau of Economic Analysis, National Accounts Data.

26. Donald F. Kettl, *Leadership at the Fed* (New Haven, CT: Yale University Press, 1986).

27. "Steady Greenspan; Clinton Plays It Safe on Choice of Fed Chief," *San Diego Union-Tribune* (February 26, 1996): B4.

28. International Labor Organization, LABORSTA Internet database, http://laborsta.ilo.org/, accessed May 30, 2008.

29. "Judgement Day," *The Economist* (February 18, 1995): 49–51.

30. U.S. Bureau of Labor Statistics, Division of International Labor Comparisons, www.bls.gov/fls/intl_unemployment_rates_monthly.htm#Rtable1. Last updated June 3, 2010 (updated monthly).

31. Study by the McKinsey Global Institute summarized in "How Regulation Kills New Jobs," *The Economist* (November 19, 1994): 78; "Economy Producing Mostly Bad Jobs? Not So Fast," Annenberg Political Fact Check, Annenberg Public Policy Center, University of Pennsylvania, July 9, 2004, www.factcheck.org, accessed August 25, 2004.

32. *Statistical Abstract of the United States, 2008,* Table 602; and *Statistical Abstract of the United States, 2006,* Table 608.

33. *Statistical Abstract of the United States, 2006,* Table 608; and *Statistical Abstract of the United States, 2008,* Table 602.

34. *Statistical Abstract of the United States, 1999,* Tables 1432 and 1442. Arthur S. Alderson, Jason Beckfield, and Francois Nielson, "Exactly How Has Income Inequality Changed? Patterns of Distributional Change in Core Societies," Luxembourg Income Study, Working Paper No. 422, May 2005; and United States Bureau of the Census, Historical Income Tables—Income Inequality, www.census.gov/hhes/income/histinc/ie6.html, accessed June 13, 2006. For a critical survey, see Krugman, *Peddling Prosperity,* chap. 5.

35. U.S. Department of Commerce, Bureau of Labor Statistics, "Overview of 2008-2018 Projections," www.bls.gov/oco/oco2003.htm, accessed August 12, 2010.

36. World Economic Forum, "The Global Information Technology Report, 2009-2010," www.weforum.org/documents/GITR10/index.html, accessed August 12, 2010, Figure 3.02.

37. Arthur S. Alderson, Jason Beckfield, and Francois Nielson, "Exactly How Has Income Inequality Changed? Patterns of Distributional Change in Core Societies," Luxembourg Income Study, Working Paper No. 422, May 2005; and United States Bureau of the Census, Historical Income Tables—Income Inequality, www.census.gov/hhes/income/histinc/ie6.html, accessed June 13, 2006.

38. For a critical survey, see Krugman, *Peddling Prosperity,* chap. 5.

CHAPTER 20

1. James M. Lindsay, quoted in John Donnelly, "Campaign 2000: The Issues; Foreign Policy Is Pushed onto Center Stage," *Boston Globe* (October 7, 2000): A6.

2. Joseph Cirincione, quoted in Steve Goldstein, "Campaigns Drop Foreign Policy Issues; Bush, Gore Put Focus on Topics at Home," *Milwaukee Journal-Sentinel* (October 8, 2000): 23A.

3. Goldstein, "Campaigns Drop Foreign Policy Issues," p. 23A.

4. Ivo H. Daalder and James M. Lindsay, *America Unbound: The Bush Revolution in Foreign Policy* (Washington, DC: Brookings Institution Press, 2003).

5. Aaron Wildavsky, "The Two Presidencies," in Steven A. Shull, *The Two Presidencies: A Quarter Century Assessment* (Chicago: Nelson Hall, 1991 [1965]), pp. 11–25.

6. Alexander Hamilton, *The Federalist Papers, No. 70* (Baltimore, MD: Johns Hopkins University Press, 1981), p. 199.

7. Chuck Henning, *The Wit and Wisdom of Politics: Expanded Edition* (Golden, CO: Fulcrum, 1992), p. 56.

8. Wildavksy, "The Two Presidencies," p. 15.

9. John E. Mueller, *War, Presidents and Public Opinion* (New York: Wiley, 1973); and Gary King and Lyn Ragsdale, *The Elusive Executive: Discovering Statistical Patterns in the Presidency* (Washington, DC: CQ Press, 1988).

10. Mueller, *War, Presidents and Public Opinion.*

11. Steven Lee Myers, "Using the President, But Carefully Only Going So Far," *New York Times* (May 28, 2008): A16.

12. Richard Stevenson, "White House Says Prisoner Policy Set Humane Tone," *New York Times* (June 23, 2004): A1.

13. Wildavksy, "The Two Presidencies," p. 16.

14. James Baker, III, with Thomas M. DeFrank, *The Politics of Diplomacy: Revolution, War, and Peace, 1989–1992* (New York: Putnam, 1995), p. 116.

15. Wildavksy, "The Two Presidencies," p. 17.

16. Barry M. Blechman, *The Politics of National Security: Congress and U.S. Defense Policy* (New York: Oxford University Press, 1990); Duane M. Oldfield and Aaron Wildavsky, "Reconsidering the Two Presidencies," in *The Two Presidencies: A Quarter Century Assessment,* ed. Steve A. Shull (Chicago: Nelson-Hall, 1991), pp. 181–190; Thomas Franck and Edward Weisband, *Foreign Policy by Congress* (New York: Oxford University Press, 1979); Thomas E. Mann, ed., *A Question of Balance: The President, the Congress and Foreign Policy* (Washington, DC: The Brookings Institution, 1990); and Stephen R. Weissman, *A Culture of Deference: Congress's Failure of Leadership in Foreign Policy* (New York: Basic Books, 1955).

17. Hamilton, "Federalist 2," ellipses deleted.

18. Speech before the House of Representatives, March 7, 1800, as quoted in *Marbury v. Madison*, 5 U.S. (1 Cranch) 137 (1803).

19. As quoted in Henning, *The Wit and Wisdom of Politics*, p. 240.

20. *United States v. Curtiss-Wright Export Corporation*, 299 U.S. 304 (1936).

21. *Youngstown Sheet & Tube Co. v. Sawyer*, 343 U.S. 579 (1952).

22. Harold Hongju Koh, *The National Security Constitution: Sharing Power After the Iran-Contra Affair* (New Haven, CT: Yale University Press, 1990); Gordon Silverstein, "Judicial Expansion of Presidential Power," in Paul E. Peterson, ed., *The President, Congress, and the Making of Foreign Policy* (Norman, OK: University of Oklahoma Press, 1994), pp. 23–48; and Gordon Silverstein, *The Imbalance of Powers: Constitutional Interpretation and the Making of American Foreign Policy* (New York: Oxford University Press, 1996).

23. Joint Resolution of Congress, H.J. RES 1145, August 7, 1964.

24. Louis Fisher and David Gray Adler, "The War Powers Resolution: Time to Say Goodbye," *Political Science Quarterly* 113(3) (Fall 1998): 1–20.

25. "A joint resolution to authorize the use of United States Armed Forces against those responsible for the recent attacks launched against the United States," Public Law 107-40, September 18, 2001.

26. "A joint resolution to authorize the use of United States Armed Forces against Iraq," Public Law 107-243, October 16, 2002.

27. Mary Beth Sheridan, "New Nuclear Policy Shows Limits," *Washington Post* (April 7, 2010): A6.

28. United States Senate, "Treaties," www.senate.gov/artandhistory/history/common/briefing/Treaties.htm, accessed June 20, 2006.

29. *United States v. Belmont*, 301 U.S. 324 (1937).

30. Jack Goldsmith and Lawrence Lessig, "Obama's Go It Alone Mistake; A Trade Agreement Raises Constitutional Concerns," *Washington Post* (March 26, 2010): A23.

31. NSC-68, "United States Objectives and Programs for National Security," National Security Council, April 14, 1950.

32. Ibid.

33. George F. Kennan, "The Sources of Soviet Conduct," *Foreign Affairs* 25 (July 1947): 566–582.

34. Gallup Poll, November 1950.

35. White House National Security Council, "The National Security Strategy of the United States of America," September 2002.

36. National Commission on Terrorist Attacks Against the United States, "Staff Statement 17: Improvising a Homeland Defense" (Washington, DC: June 17, 2004), p. 28.

37. George Marshall, secretary of state under Harry Truman, as quoted in Alexander De Conde, "George C. Marshall," in *An Uncertain Tradition: American Secretaries of State in the Twentieth Century,* ed. Norman A. Graebner (New York: McGraw Hill, 1961), p. 252.

38. Ibid., p. 68.

39. Norman A. Graebner, "Dean G. Acheson," in *An Uncertain Tradition: American Secretaries of State in the Twentieth Century*, ed. Norman A. Graebner (New York: McGraw Hill, 1961), p. 13.

40. Michael Beckel, "Big Donors and Bundlers Among Obama's Ambassador Picks," May 28, 2009, www.opensecrets.org, accessed May 25, 2010.

41. Barry Rubin, *Secrets of State: The State Department and the Struggle over U.S. Foreign Policy* (New York: Oxford University Press, 1985), p. 64.

42. Stephen Holmes, "What Russia Teaches Us Now: How Weak States Threaten Freedom," *The American Prospect* (July-August 1997): 30.

43. General Omar Bradley, Chair of Joint Chiefs, Testimony to the Committee on Armed Services, House of Representatives, October 19, 1949, as quoted in John Bartlett, *Familiar Quotations* (Boston: Little, Brown, 1980), p. 824.

44. See www.centcom.mil.

45. These points are taken from an insightful analysis of the way in which the Bush administration changed U. S. counterterrorism policy. See Abraham D. Sofaer, "The 'War' on Terrorism: Doctrinal Foundations," Hoover Institution, March 2002.

46. James R. Locher III, "Taking Stock of Goldwater-Nichols," *Joint Force Quarterly* (Autumn 1996): 10-16.

47. Department of the Army, "FM 3-24: Counterinsurgency" (The U.S. Army and Marine Corps official Counterinsurgency field manual), December 2006, http://usacac.army.mil/cac2/coin/repository/FM_3-24.pdf, accessed May 26, 2010.

48. Steve Bowman and Catherine Dale, "War in Afghanistan: Strategy, Military Operations, and Issues for Congress," Congressional Research Service Report no. 7-5700, December 3, 2009.

49. Loch K. Johnson, *America's Secret Power: The CIA in a Democratic Society* (New York: Oxford University Press, 1989), pp. 12, 43.

50. Ibid., chap. 2.

51. Dan Eggen, "FBI Agents Still Lacking Arabic Skills," *Washington Post* (October 11, 2006): A1.

52. Jane Mayer, *The Dark Side: The Inside Story of How the War on Terror Turned into a War on American Ideals* (New York: Doubleday, 2008).

53. Leon Panetta, "Congress and the CIA: Time to Move On," *Washington Post*, August 2, 2009, www.washingtonpost.com/wp-dyn/content/article/2009/07/31/AR2009073102607 .html, accessed May 25, 2010.

54. Ibid.

55. Eileen Sullivan, "Intelligence Director Blair to Resign," Time.com, May 20, 2010,

www.time.com/time/politics/article/ 0,8599,1990941,00.html, accessed May 25, 2010.

56. Rubin, *Secrets of State*, p. 50.

57. Speech at the Constitutional Convention, as quoted in Hans J. Morgenthau, *Politics Among Nations*, 4th ed. (New York: Knopf, 1966), p. 12.

58. Speech in Philadelphia, February 22, 1861, as quoted in Morgenthau, *Politics Among Nations*, p. 35.

59. George W. Bush, "Remarks by the President on Iraq and the War on Terror," United States Army War College, Carlisle, PA, May 24, 2004.

60. Al Gore, "Our Founders and the Unbalance of Power," Remarks to the American Constitution Society for Law and Policy, June 24, 2004.

61. Barack Obama, "Remarks by the President at the Acceptance of the Nobel Peace Prize," December 10, 2009, www .whitehouse.gov/the-press-office/remarks-president-acceptance-nobel-peace-prize, accessed May 25, 2010.

62. Robert Keohane, *After Hegemony: Cooperation and Discord in the World Political Economy* (Princeton, NJ: Princeton University Press, 1984).

63. Morgenthau, *Politics Among Nations;* Kenneth N. Waltz, *Theory of International Politics* (New York: McGraw Hill, 1979); John J. Mearscheimer, "Back to the Future: Instability in Europe After the Cold War," *International Security* 15:1 (Summer 1990): 5–56; and Samuel Huntington, *The Clash of Civilizations* (New York: Simon & Schuster, 1996).

64. Joel R. Paul, "The Geopolitical Constitution: Executive Expediency and Executive Agreements," *California Law Review* 86:671 (July 1998): 749–752.

Photo Credits

Name Index

Subject Index

Note f = figure; t = table